RUNNING
Microsoft®
Office 2000

Michael Halvorson
and Michael Young

PUBLISHED BY
Microsoft Press
A Division of Microsoft Corporation
One Microsoft Way
Redmond,Washington 98052-6399

Library of Congress Cataloging-in-Publication Data.
Halvorson, Michael.
    Running Microsoft Office 2000 Professional / Michael Halvorson and
    Michael Young.
        p. cm.
    Includes index.
    ISBN 1-57231-936-4
    1. Microsoft Office professional.   2. Microsoft Word.
3. Microsoft Excel for Windows. 4. Microsoft PowerPoint (Computer
file) 5. Microsoft Access. 6. Microsoft Outlook. 7. Microsoft
Publisher. 8. Business--Computer programs. 9. Word processing.
10. Electronic spreadsheets.   11. Business presentations--Graphic
methods--Computer programs.   12. Time management--Computer programs.
13. Personal information management--Computer programs.   14. Desktop
publishing. I. Young, Michael J. II. Title.
HF5548.4.M525H356   1999
005.369--dc21   98-48655
                                                                    CIP

Printed and bound in the United States of America.

1 2 3 4 5 6 7 8 9 WCWC   4 3 2 1 0 9

Distributed in Canada by ITP Nelson, a division of Thomson Canada Limited.

A CIP catalogue record for this book is available from the British Library.

Microsoft Press books are available through booksellers and distributors worldwide. For further information about
international editions, contact your local Microsoft Corporation office or contact Microsoft Press International directly at
fax (425) 936-7329. Visit our Web site at mspress.microsoft.com.

Acquisitions Editor: Christey Bahn
Project Editor: Saul Candib
Manuscript and Technical Editing: Labrecque Publishing

Chapters at a Glance

Table of Contents

Acknowledgments

The really interesting thing about writing computer books is that the whole process begins well before the software is actually finished. Authors meet with computer book publishers, learn about new software features, develop a writing plan, and begin testing their ideas with beta versions of the product. This iterative process produces important insights and continues (with mounting fervor) until the software is complete and the final books are shipped to the printer—whew!

Microsoft Press is an awesome place to write a computer book. At each stage in the publishing process, talented team members work together to cultivate valuable technical contacts and resources, build visionary product deployment strategies, and explore the hidden benefits of emerging technologies. *Running Microsoft Office 2000*, now in its third edition, has benefited handsomely from this dynamic and innovative publishing environment.

In particular, the authors would like to thank Kim Fryer, Casey Doyle, Lucinda Rowley, and Christey Bahn, for their generous support in product planning and book development; Project Editor Saul Candib, at Microsoft Press, who personally handled all of our problems and requests—you saved us, Saul; tireless Project Manager Lisa Labrecque (in lovely San Francisco) and her team of truly dedicated professionals at Labrecque Publishing Services, Inc.; Terrence O'Donnell, our jack-of-all-trades (technical editor, copyeditor, product tester, and all-around Office 2000 guru)—you're amazing, Terry; and Chrisa Hotchkiss, Curtis Philips, Lisa Bravo, and Andrea Fox, who collectively helped us edit and produce three separate editions of this book—roughly 4,500 pages!

The authors warmly acknowledge the writing contributions of Kathie Werner, who revised the PowerPoint Part and wrote four chapters in the Publisher Part. Kathie has an incredible work ethic and writes like a seasoned professional. Thanks for sharing your many talents with us, Kathie!

Introduction

The book you now hold is an insider's guide to Microsoft Office 2000, an exciting collection of application programs and accessories that every business and home can use. We have designed this guidebook with the practical goal of making you an expert in Office 2000 commands, procedures, and techniques. When you're finished, you'll have all the skills necessary to create a wide range of professional and personal documents, and you'll know a few tricks that have been practiced only in the enigmatic halls of Microsoft. The most innovative refinements in Office 2000 are related to the Internet, so if you're looking to leverage your work with Web publishing or online collaboration, just power up your modem, sit back, and relax: We'll show you all the Web tricks right here.

Office 2000 Professional contains Microsoft Word, Microsoft Excel, Microsoft PowerPoint, Microsoft Access, Microsoft Outlook, Microsoft Publisher, and several small business tools. This book shows you how to get the most from these best-selling applications and describes ways that you can use them together to create professional-looking reports, presentations, financial models, and Web pages. We have designed this book to help get you up and running quickly, learn the basics of the Office applications, and then build on your new skills by exploring advanced concepts. If you follow the tips, tutorials, and examples in this book, you'll be creating and printing documents the very first day you use the Office software. As you gain experience with Office, you can also use the book as a reference to the advanced features and capabilities of your applications. A comprehensive index, the table of contents, and our cross-referencing system will guide you instantly to the solutions you need.

How This Book Is Organized

Because Microsoft designed the applications in the Office suite to be used together, you'll be pleased to find that many of the skills you learn in one application will be useful in another. Rather than simply listing the features of each Office application, this book shows you how to accomplish useful work with the Office tools. When it's advantageous to do so, we show you how to use your Office applications in concert to build a special document or create a report. To structure the presentation, we've divided the book into nine major parts.

Part 1 of the book shows you how to master essential skills using the Office software. You'll learn how to start and use each Office application, how to manage programs by using the Windows taskbar, and how to perform essential skills such as navigating windows, completing dialog boxes, naming and saving files, and printing documents. You'll also learn how to open, share, and search Office documents on the Internet World Wide Web (a mouthful we'll simply abbreviate as *the Web*). If you're new to Office applications or the Internet, this is the place you can learn the fundamental skills used in all Office documents.

Part 2 of the book covers Microsoft Word, the word processing application that you can use to create memos, newsletters, reports, and other desktop publishing projects. The first few chapters in this part introduce Word and its newest features; the remaining chapters teach Word's intermediate and advanced features, including document formatting, using styles and templates, designing columns and pages, creating mailing lists, customizing Word, and working in workgroups. If you're an avid user of Word, this could be the only product documentation you ever need.

Part 3 of the book presents Microsoft Excel, the electronic spreadsheet that you can use to create ledgers, invoices, charts, and powerful financial models. If you're new to spreadsheets, you can learn the basics in Chapter 15, "Building a Worksheet." After this foundation chapter, Part 3 introduces you to the depth and breadth of Excel. You'll learn how to use workbooks to organize information, build sophisticated formulas and functions, create presentation-quality charts, manage database information by using lists, customize Excel to suit your needs, analyze business data by creating "what-if?" scenarios, and increase your productivity by using Microsoft Visual Basic macros. Check out Chapter 23, "Analyzing Business Data," if you've never used Excel's Solver feature, and learn how easily you can apply it to help you make complex quantity and pricing decisions.

Part 4 of the book deals with Microsoft PowerPoint, the essential presentation tool for slide shows, overhead presentations, automated demonstrations, and multimedia expositions. If you're like most PowerPoint users, you're an expert in your own field but have little formal experience with desktop presentation software—so you want to create and finish your presentation quickly and get on to more important things. In Part 4, we teach the basic PowerPoint skills in short, concise chapters to get you up and running as quickly as possible. Then, for those who have more time, we move on to advanced topics such as creating special effects and adding variations to the show. Whether you want to learn the PowerPoint basics or explore the newest features in electronic presentation, this part of the book is for you.

Part 5 of the book covers Microsoft Access, the database application that you can use to create and manage customer lists, data-entry forms, product inventories, and other collections of organized information. For those who are new to databases, a quick introduction explains how to design and build a database effectively. (This is easier than ever, because of a collection of stellar database wizards.) If you're already an Access user, you'll find techniques to improve your skill as you work with forms, design queries, and reports.

Part 6 of the book covers Microsoft Outlook, an information management program that allows you to send and receive electronic mail, manage your schedule, make appointments, and track daily tasks. Outlook has gained in popularity significantly over the last year, so we've enlarged and enhanced this part of the book considerably, to provide the most comprehensive coverage available.

Part 7 presents Microsoft Publisher, a new addition to the Office software suite. Publisher is a desktop publishing software package, designed specifically for the newsletters, flyers, brochures, and posters created in small businesses. In this section, we show you how to work with Publisher commands and layout tools, walk you through several desktop publishing wizards, and share our favorite secrets for distributing publications on the Web. If you've never used Publisher before, consider this your introduction.

Part 8 explores four small business tools that are being distributed with Office 2000 Professional for the first time: Microsoft Small Business Financial Manager, Microsoft Direct Mail Manager, Microsoft Small Business Customer Manager, and Microsoft Business Planner. These tools work in conjunction with Excel to help you manage typical transactions in a small business (the sort of tasks you probably handled in the past with ad-hoc ledgers or general-purpose spreadsheet programs). If you need to track invoices, payments, paychecks, or business mailings, give these small business tools a try.

Part 9 of the book focuses on using the Office applications together to prepare reports, presentations, and other projects that benefit from integrated use of the Office tools. In this part of the book, you'll learn how to share data among Office applications, and how to use the Office Binder to store several files in one convenient location.

Who This Book Is For

Running Microsoft Office 2000 Professional is for active business professionals who create or use electronic documents as part of their job. We designed the book to teach fundamental skills to beginners and to provide ongoing, essential information for experienced users of the Office software. Most Office users are familiar with one or two applications, but are less familiar with the remaining programs. To cover all the possibilities, we start from the beginning in each section, and then we move quickly to intermediate and advanced topics that will be helpful to readers who have a variety of skills.

The book contains step-by-step instructions and examples that cover the breadth of each Office product so that you can use this book as either a tutorial or a reference. After you learn the skills you need, we hope that you'll keep the book by your computer to consult when you have a question about your software or want the challenge of using advanced options to make your work product even more professional and attractive. To give you many entry points to the material, we've included sidebars, tips, notes, warnings, and cross-referencing information to help you get the most from your purchase. By the time you finish using this book, your colleagues might think of you as some sort of "Office guru."

Conventions Used in This Book

This book contains concise descriptions of the commands and features in Office, plus step-by-step instructions (often beside a picture of an actual application window) that you can follow to complete a task or solve a problem. Most of the instructions rely on mouse actions, so you'll see the directives *click*, *double-click*, *right-click*, and *drag* a good deal. If you're not familiar with the mouse or with running commands in Windows 98, we recommend that you read *Running Microsoft Windows 98* (Craig Stinson, 1998), a tutorial and reference published by Microsoft Press, or a similar guidebook about working with the Windows operating system.

Occasionally, we give you shortcut key combinations for running commands in Office applications. For example, Ctrl+S means that you hold down one of the Ctrl keys on your keyboard and press the letter *S*. If we have important information or a helpful tip to show you, we'll include it in a shaded box that has a *Tip* icon. Finally, wherever you encounter the *See Also* icon, you find references to other sections in the chapter or the book that provide additional, related information.

Visiting Our Web Site

Microsoft Press has created a Web site especially for this book, and we invite you to use it extensively as you read *Running Office 2000*. On the Web site, you'll find the book's sample projects and exercises, frequently asked questions about the book and the Office 2000 software, contact information, and useful Office links and resources. We believe this is the best way to keep you informed about Office 2000 and the dynamic nature of our subject, so please keep in touch!

To connect to the book's Web site, browse to the following address using Microsoft Internet Explorer or another Web browser:

http://mspress.microsoft.com/mspress/products/2051/

After you are connected to the site, click the Reader's Corner icon for a list of interactive options.

Using the Book's Sample Files

The sample files on the Running Office 2000 Web site are designed to give you hands-on experience working with Office application files. You can use them to experiment with the techniques shown in the book, as templates for your own projects, or as starting points for your own exploration of Office. You can download the files by individual application from the book's Web site, or as a group. To download the sample files, follow these steps:

1 Connect to the Running Office 2000 Web site as described above, and then click the Reader's Corner icon.

2 Click the Sample Files link on the Reader's Corner page to display the list of sample files available. To see a list of the sample files, click the File List link.

3 Download the sample files you want by clicking one or more links. We've listed the sample files by category, so that you can download just the collections you need.

Alternatively, you can download all of the sample files by clicking Download All Files. The sample files are stored in a compressed format to reduce download time, and the files are self-extracting. (A program runs automatically to place the uncompressed files on your system.) Detailed instructions for using the individual files are located in the book.

 NOTE

> If you choose to download all of the sample files, the compressed data file will take up about 1.4MB on your system. The files are compressed in the WinZip format.

Office 2000 and the Y2K Problem

As our computers and electronic devices count down (or, more precisely, up) to the year 2000, computer experts, industry analysts, and social commentators have concerned themselves with a threat known as the *year 2000 problem* (also called *Y2K* or the *millennium bug*). In this section, we'll briefly investigate the year 2000 problem, which can briefly be described as a family of related software defects that collectively have the potential to hinder or completely disable software systems that cannot properly process dates in the twenty-first century.

As you learn about the year 2000 problem, and prepare for its consequences, there are a number of points we'd like you to consider. First, despite dire predictions, there is probably no good reason to prepare for the new millennium by holing yourself up in a mine shaft with sizable stocks of water, grain, barter goods, and ammunition. The year 2000 will not disable most computer systems, and if your personal computer was manufactured after 1996, it's likely that your hardware and systems software will require little updating or customizing.

Second, the year 2000 problem is probably best seen in the context of our general use of computers. Although the year 2000 represents something unusual and threatening to many computers, virtually all of our electronic systems encounter significant problems from time to time, and managing these glitches is simply part and parcel to working with computers, and especially to developing sophisticated application software.

The year 2000 problem is not our only technical speed bump on the road to computing paradise. Remember that not too long ago rogue computer viruses were receiving the same banner headlines that Y2K is now receiving. Before that we had the threat of computer-managed stock transactions on Wall Street, grave concerns about the potential inaccuracy of spreadsheet calculations, and of course infamous concerns about glitches in the world's bank of automated defense systems.

Our point is not that Y2K is a negligible threat to our information infrastructure—in fact, it is a serious threat—but that basically by definition computer engineering (like other scientific pursuits) will predictably bring with the wonderful gains a short list of potential problems that need a watchful eye. Accordingly, it's probably best to think about your computer as a faithful friend who, though devoted to your success and happiness, can occasionally drop the ball big-time. In our opinion, the best strategy with these devices is to remain vigilant about backing up important data files, contact lists, electronic mail, and other information *in anticipation* of a problem like Y2K. In addition, you should plan broadly when a problem like Y2K has been announced, by learning about the threat, analyzing your systems, and finding the necessary technical resources.

The Nature of the Y2K Problem

The year 2000 problem boils down to some pretty trivial mathematics. By custom, most consumers don't bother writing the current century in business or personal transactions, and so checks and casual notations typically feature an abbreviation for the date, such as 1/1/99 for January 1, 1999. Computer programmers have also used this shorthand method in their code over the years, especially when designing financial software packages that processed thousands of dated entries. This shortened date format seemed intuitive enough at the time for programmers, and also saved them significant memory resources. In addition, some earlier computer languages, like IBM OS/VS COBOL, didn't even have date formats that supported a fulsome four-digit year, so planning for the future millennium wasn't really an option.

One legacy of this problem for personal computers is that most PCs use this shorthand date format in their internal system clocks, so when the year changes from 1999 to 2000, some computers will fail to update the *century* portion of the date and will interpret January 1, 2000 as January 1, 1900. (In other words, the *year* portion of the date will increment but the *century* portion—which the BIOS stores in another memory location—will remain the same.) If this happens, the day of the week will also be wrong because January 1, 1900 was a Monday, but January 1, 2000 is a Saturday.

Under MS-DOS and early versions of Microsoft Windows, the operating system will likely view the year 1900 as an error, and will reset the system date to 1980—an important clue that your system needs a BIOS adjustment. However, there is some variation in the behavior of older personal computers to the year 2000 problem. Different "clone" manufacturers have used different BIOS configurations and operating systems over the years, so it is impossible to know exactly how all personal computers will respond to the year 2000 when it comes. (However, more recent computers have been fixed so that this will not be a problem—the concern is mostly older systems that won't know what to do with dates in the new millennium.)

The concern among industry analysts is that with so many systems recording the wrong internal date in the year 2000, financial calculations could be thrown out of sync. A mortgage payment made promptly on 4/1/2000, for example, could suddenly seem 100 years late if an accounting package responsible for recording the payment incorrectly identifies it as due on 4/1/1900, or a banking system could conceivably issue checks on the wrong day of the week if it incorrectly sees January 1, 2000 (a Saturday) as January 1, 1900 (a Monday).

Planning for the Year 2000

The good news is that most personal computers produced since 1996 are compliant with year 2000 standards, and older computers that have problems can be updated with relative ease using software tools from a variety of locations on the Internet (see below). In addition, Microsoft Windows 98 and Microsoft NT 4.0 automatically update most BIOS routines with the proper date information, so if you're running one of these systems, your computer will automatically display the correct date and time when the year 2000 comes.

Even so, dates in the year 2000 will cause problems with some older application programs, and you may need to abandon some of these older applications for newer versions. (Alternatively, you may be able to set your clock back several years and stop it from encountering dates in the twenty-first century, but this isn't a very elegant or practical solution.) One major (albeit older) program that won't work well in the year 2000 is Microsoft Word 5.0 for MS-DOS, which has trouble opening documents that have dates in the twenty-first century, and displays incorrect summary information when you examine the files. Microsoft has identified these and other problems with older software on a Web site dedicated to the year 2000 problem, and other software vendors have created similar lists on their own corporate Web sites. The jury is still out on how large corporations with older, more complex systems will respond to the crisis, but in most cases the direct impact on customers should be manageable. (However, we do expect a few fantastic stories of computer crashes from businesses that planned poorly for the problem.)

Resources for the Y2K Problem

Microsoft Office 2000 is fully compliant with the Microsoft Year 2000 Specification, and includes date formats specifically designed to address the year 2000 problem. In this book you'll see detailed information about preparing for the year 2000 problem. However, most of the work has been done for you in these applications. By thoroughly testing a variety of dates and twentieth-century formats, Microsoft has been able to verify that Office 2000 is fully compatible with the new millennium.

In addition to a thorough exploration of the features in Office 2000, we recommend the following resources to you as you ponder the implications of computing in the twenty-first century:

- **Microsoft Year 2000 Resource Center**
  (*http://www.microsoft.com/technet/year2k/*): A detailed Web site with Microsoft's statement on compliance to year 2000 standards, common questions, useful add-in programs, and a list of Microsoft's older applications and their potential problems.

- **Frequently Asked Questions**
  (*ftp://www.year2000.com/pub/year2000/y2kfaq.txt*): An independent, non-Microsoft Web site that answers frequently asked questions about the year 2000 problem and explores in considerable depth the difficult issues that face solution providers, businesses, and software developers.

- **Year 2000 Tools for PC Users**
  (*http://www.microsoft.com/technet/year2k/tools/tools.htm*): A Microsoft Web page that serves as a gateway to tools and solutions provided by third-party computer manufacturers and software developers. Check here for utilities that will upgrade the BIOS of older personal computers with date problems, and for utilities that can automatically scan your Office documents for potential problems.

- **Government Y2K Standards Index**
  (*http://www.y2k.gov/*): A Web site provided by the United States government that discusses general issues associated with the year 2000 problem.

Office 2000 Support

For support information regarding Microsoft Office, you can connect to Microsoft Technical Support on the Web at:

http://www.microsoft.com/support/

In the United States, you can also call Microsoft Office technical support at (425) 635-7056; in Canada, (905) 568-2294, weekdays between 6 AM and 6 PM Pacific time.

Contacting the Authors

Every effort has been made to ensure the accuracy of the book and the contents of the Web site and sample files. If you would like to post a comment or concern about the book, please use one of the following e-mail addresses.

■ For questions about Word, Access, Binder, or Outlook, contact author Michael Young using the following e-mail address:

mjy@compuserve.com

■ For questions about Excel, Publisher, PowerPoint, the small business tools, or Visual Basic, contact author Michael Halvorson using the following e-mail address:

mikehal@u.washington.edu

■ To contact the Microsoft Press editorial staff with suggestions, corrections, or general comments, use the following e-mail address:

MspInput@Microsoft.com

You can also send your comments via postal mail to:

Microsoft Press
Attn: Running Series Editor
One Microsoft Way
Redmond, WA 98052-6399

Please note that product support isn't offered through the above addresses.

Let's start Running Office!

PART I

Getting Started with Microsoft Office

CHAPTER 1

A Quick Tour of Microsoft Office

Microsoft Office 2000 Professional is a state-of-the-art application suite containing seven application programs for Microsoft Windows and six powerful utilities that will improve your productivity both at home and at the office. In this chapter, you'll learn what to do with the applications included in Microsoft Office and how to launch them using the Start button. You'll also learn how to switch between Office applications using the Windows taskbar and how to use the Office Help system when you have a question or need a little guidance. After you get the lay of the land, you'll be ready to explore a few essential skills that are useful in all Office applications.

Introducing Microsoft Office

Welcome to Microsoft Office 2000 for Windows, Microsoft's best-selling application suite containing the latest versions of Microsoft's most popular business software products. If you're like most users, you have probably had some experience using one or more of the applications in Office. For this release, each program has been enhanced with new features and fine-tuned to publish information on the Web. If you have the Professional edition of Office 2000 (the software described in this book), you have the following application programs:

- Microsoft Word 2000

- Microsoft Excel 2000

- Microsoft PowerPoint 2000

- Microsoft Access 2000

- Microsoft Outlook 2000

- Microsoft Publisher 2000

- Microsoft business tools, including Small Business Bookshelf, Small Business Financial Manager, Direct Mail Manager, and Customer Management Application

> **NOTE**
>
> If you have the Small Business edition of Microsoft Office, you won't have Access, FrontPage, PhotoDraw, or PowerPoint. If you have the Premium edition of Microsoft Office, you'll see Microsoft FrontPage, a useful Web publishing application, and PhotoDraw, a graphics application.

What are the benefits of Microsoft Office 2000, in a nutshell? By combining Microsoft's flagship programs into one unified application suite, Microsoft has created a general-purpose tool that can handle virtually all the data processing, forecasting, communication, and Web publishing activities of a modern business or organization. Each Office application shares common commands, dialog boxes, and procedures, so once you learn how to use one application, you'll be able to apply what you've learned to all the rest.

In addition, the Office applications have been designed to work together, enabling you to combine text from Word, a chart from Excel, and database information from Access into one compelling presentation. Office applications also support a variety of file formats (including HTML), present similar formatting tools and macro languages, and provide full support for electronic mail and workgroup activities, so you don't have to reinvent the wheel each time you start a new project. In short, Microsoft Office 2000 is designed to adapt itself to the way you work.

What's New in the Software?

 If you've used a previous version of the Office software, you'll notice that Office 2000 has a number of new features and improvements:

- A desktop publishing program called Microsoft Publisher, a graphic arts program called PhotoDraw, better Web integration, improved international language support, and hundreds of new commands and options will make your workday more productive and enjoyable.

- Essential toolbars, menus, and Web publishing tools have been standardized across applications, making Office programs even more accessible and easy to use.

- Finally, each application in the Office software suite has been redesigned to save files in HTML format for better integration with the Internet and corporate intranets. When you're ready to share your documents with a colleague down the hall or with a friend on the other side of the world, Office 2000 will make it as simple as clicking a button.

Microsoft Office 2000

The following features are common to all Office programs:

Year 2000 Compliance

Office 2000 has been carefully tested for adherence to the Microsoft Year 2000 Compliance Standard and for handling date issues in general.

Microsoft Publisher

Office now includes Publisher, a popular desktop publishing software program that creates newsletters, brochures, and Web pages.

HTML File Format

Each application in the Office 2000 software suite can now save files in HTML, or *Web page*, format, so you can immediately deploy them on the Internet or corporate intranets. The traditional application file formats are also still available.

Better Web Publishing

Office applications now have a standard Save As Web Page command that lets you seamlessly save your document as a Web page and set useful Internet publication options. A new Web Page Preview command also allows you to view your HTML document immediately in Microsoft Internet Explorer or another browser.

Better Hyperlinks

Enhanced Hyperlink commands allow you to link to electronic mail addresses, new Internet resources, and hot-spots in documents.

Clipboard Toolbar

You can now save several blocks of cut or copied text to the Clipboard (up to 12), and then paste any of these blocks into an Office document. A Clipboard toolbar facilitates the pasting process.

Multilingual Support

Most Office 2000 applications can now automatically detect foreign language text rather than requiring you to mark all blocks of foreign text using language formatting. The proofing tools will then use the appropriate dictionary for correcting text in each language.

Online Collaboration

In creating documents, you can work together with other people on the Internet or on a company intranet using the commands on the Online Collaboration submenu of the Tools menu in most Office 2000 applications.

Total Cost of Ownership Features

Office 2000 is now easier for system administrators to customize and install, and it adapts to your work style by using install-on-demand features, self-configuring menus and toolbars, and improved IntelliSense (natural-language processing) technology.

Microsoft Word

Word now includes the following new features:

Additional Support for Web Pages

The Web page features are now tightly integrated into Word. You can save any Word document in HTML format—that is, as a Web page. You can view the page in Web browsers, and you can later reopen it in Word without losing any features. Word also provides a large collection of templates and wizards for creating documents designed specifically as Web pages, or for building entire Web sites.

Web Tools Toolbar

Word now features a Web Tools toolbar, which allows you to add scripts, forms, movie clips, background sounds, and scrolling text to Web pages.

Click and Type

The new Click and Type feature lets you add text to an empty place in a document by just double-clicking that place and then typing the text. Word adds all necessary space characters and formatting to position the text where you double-click.

More Table Features

Word tables have acquired new features derived from Web-page tables. For example, you can create nested tables and tables that are automatically resized to accommodate the text they contain or the size of the window, and you can have text flow around tables.

Visual Themes

You can now quickly modify the overall appearance of a document by applying a visual theme. The theme will apply a consistent look to elements throughout the document. You can choose from a list of more than 25 themes provided with Office.

Microsoft Excel

The following new features make Excel an even more dynamic program:

Interactive Web Publishing

The new Save As Web Page command creates HTML documents that you can use interactively on the Web via Internet Explorer. Interactive features are provided in Internet Explorer by ActiveX controls called Microsoft Office Web Components.

Pivot Charts

Excel 2000 can now create pivot charts from pivot tables, so you can graphically manipulate the rows and columns in a database list.

New Date Formats

You can now set date entries using two new formats that help combat the year 2000 problem.

Euro Currency Symbol

You can now use the new Euro currency symbol and accounting format to manage European financial transactions.

Microsoft PowerPoint

PowerPoint includes a lot of new features, too:

New Presentation Views

PowerPoint now includes an enhanced Normal view—which combines Outline view and Slide view—for easier editing and slide organization.

Improved Tables

Tables are easier to create and format in presentations, and PowerPoint now handles them internally, which makes them faster.

Web Publishing

The Save As Web Page command creates HTML documents smoothly and efficiently, and offers the same user interface and publication options as Word and Excel.

More Printing Options

The Print dialog box has new Grayscale, Handouts, and Print Hidden Slides options.

Online Presentation Broadcasting

You can now broadcast your presentation, complete with video and audio, over the Internet or your corporate intranet.

Microsoft Access

Access includes the following new features:

New Database Window

The Database window now includes a customizable Shortcut Bar like the one used in Outlook, it provides different ways to list objects, and it contains icons for quickly creating new database objects.

Data Access Pages

A new database object, the data access page, is similar to a form but allows users to manipulate a database in a Web browser as well as in Access.

Subdatasheets

Datasheets can now include subdatasheets, which allow users to view related information from other tables.

Access Projects

You can now use Access to create front-end interfaces, known as projects, for other databases such as SQL Server.

Microsoft Outlook

And finally, here's what's new in Outlook:

Web Views

You can now assign a Web page to any Outlook folder, and you can display that page when the folder is opened.

Favorites Menu

You can browse Web locations stored in your Favorites folder using the new Favorites menu. You can now open Web pages directly in the Outlook program.

Personal Distribution Lists

You can now create personal distribution lists in your Contacts folder so that you can e-mail a message to a group of people by inserting a single entry in the message form's To field.

Mail Merge

You can take advantage of Word's mail merge feature to print form letters, envelopes, or labels using selected items from your Contacts folder.

Choosing an Office Application

The following table shows you the purpose of each Office application and the type of document you might create with it. The tasks performed by the Office applications fall into several general categories, such as word processing and database management, though in many cases you'll find that you can best solve a particular problem by using more than one program. You'll learn considerably more about each of these programs as you work through the chapters in this book.

Office Application	Purpose
Word	General-purpose word processor and desktop publishing tool. Create memos, reports, newsletters, mailings, and customized Web pages.
Excel	Electronic spreadsheet that has high-end data analysis, charting, and analytical functions. Build invoices, order tracking worksheets, general accounting ledgers, database lists, pivot tables, and colorful 3-D charts.
PowerPoint	Presentation graphics software for slide, overhead projector, and multimedia presentations. Create slides for a sales presentation, speaker notes, multimedia demos, kiosk displays, and live conference presentations for the Web.
Access	Relational database management system that has query, reporting, and mailing list management features. Manage inventory and tax records, customer and contact lists, music collections, and corporate databases.
Outlook	Information management software for electronic mail, document management, calendar scheduling, meeting planning, and resource management. Send and receive Internet mail containing attachments, schedule your daily appointments, and plan meetings.
Publisher	Desktop publishing software for newsletters, brochures, Web sites, flyers, postcards, letterhead, and more. Design publications for online use, printing, or deployment on the Web by using wizards, templates, and predesigned artwork.

Office Application	Purpose
FrontPage	General-purpose Web page editor. Design and deploy Web pages for the Internet without learning HTML formatting codes or following elaborate formatting steps. Integrate hyperlinks, Web utilities, and helpful user interface tools.
PhotoDraw	A graphics program for creating, editing, and customizing electronic photos, illustrations, and graphics. Crop and resize digital photographs and scanned images; apply graphics effects and filters to illustrations; and touch up photographs and illustrations with freehand embellishments, color adjustments, and special effects.

Running Office Applications

You can *launch* (start) Microsoft Office applications that display a new document in any of four ways:

- By clicking the Start button and then clicking the program's name on the Programs menu or on a custom group folder's menu

- By clicking the program's icon on the Office Shortcut Bar

- By opening a document template

- By double-clicking a document's filename in Microsoft Outlook or Windows Explorer

We'll discuss each technique in this section.

Clicking the Start Button

The most straightforward way to start an Office application is to click the Windows Start button, point to the Programs folder containing the Office 2000 programs, and then click the Office application you want to start. The Start button is on the taskbar, and using it is the recommended method for starting all programs in the Windows 95, Windows 98, and Windows NT operating systems. (You can also place shortcut icons on the Windows desktop to launch your programs.)

For example, to start Microsoft Word using the Start button, follow these steps:

1 Click the Start button on the taskbar. (The Start button is typically in the lower left corner of the screen.)

2 Point to the Programs folder, and then locate the Microsoft Word program. The programs appear in alphabetical order. If your Start button's menus have been customized to group the Office applications in another location, open that menu to locate the Microsoft Word program.

3 Click the Microsoft Word program. The Microsoft Word application starts in a window, as shown in Figure 1-1.

FIGURE 1-1.
Microsoft Word launched using the Start button.

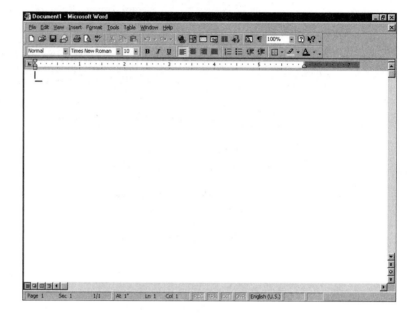

Clicking a Program Icon on the Office Shortcut Bar

Alternatively, you can start applications by clicking a program icon on the Office Shortcut Bar, an optional toolbar that contains customizable buttons and that appears along the top, bottom, side edge of, or floats anywhere over the Windows desktop when you open it (See Figure 1-2). The Office Shortcut Bar is not installed by default in a typical Office 2000 installation, but you can load this useful tool by running the Office 2000 setup program again and choosing the Microsoft Office Shortcut Bar option under the Office Tools category. Setup places the Shortcut Bar in the Start menu's Office Tools folder, and you can start it by clicking the Start button, pointing to the Programs folder, selecting the Office Tools folder, and clicking the Microsoft Office Shortcut Bar icon.

FIGURE 1-2.
The Office Shortcut Bar gives you one-click access to your Office 2000 applications.

You can use the Office Shortcut Bar to start Office applications, open templates, customize the Office software, or start other applications and utilities on your system (such as Windows Explorer). The Shortcut Bar works a lot like the toolbars do in each of the individual Office applications—you simply click the button on the Shortcut Bar corresponding to the program you want to run or the folder you want to open. If you're unsure what a particular button does, hold the mouse pointer over it and you'll see a ScreenTip describing the feature. The list of buttons is fully customizable, so you can add, delete, or rearrange the applications represented by buttons on the Shortcut Bar as you see fit.

Creating Files Using a Document Template

If you need to create a specific business document, but you're not sure what Office application to use, you can click the New Office Document command on the Start menu or the New Office Document button on the Office Shortcut Bar to browse through a variety of predesigned document types, or *templates,* and open exactly the document you need. Templates let you focus on the information you want to present in your document, eliminating time-consuming design and formatting. Each Office application includes a number of useful document templates, and you can open all of them directly using the New dialog box.

Start an Office application using a document template this way:

> **SEE ALSO**
> You'll learn essential skills for working with Office applications in Chapter 2, "Learning the Basics: Windows, Toolbars, and Printing," and Chapter 3, "Managing Documents: From Your Hard Disk to the Internet."

1 Click the Start button, and then click New Office Document (or click the New Office Document button on the Office Shortcut Bar).

The New Office Document dialog box appears. It contains several tabs, each corresponding to a different type of document template. The dialog box also contains a preview window, which displays a small picture of the template currently highlighted in that dialog box, if one is available.

2 Click the tab corresponding to the type of document you want to create. For example, to see a list of the fax templates available, click the Letters & Faxes tab. Figure 1-3, on the following page, shows a typical list of templates. You can see the template file

FIGURE 1-3.
The New Office Document button lets you start Office applications using document templates. Each tab contains a different group of templates. (You might also see filename extensions, depending on how you have set up Windows on your system.)

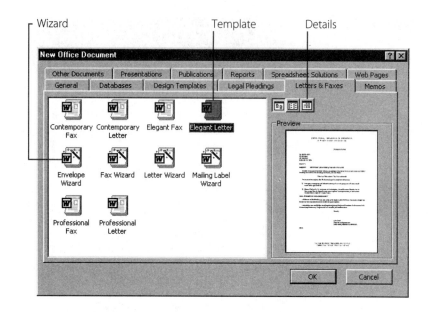

size, type of file (including the associated application), and date the file was last modified if you click the Details button in the dialog box.

Installing on Demand

Your New Office Document dialog box might contain one or more document templates that aren't fully installed on your system (a space-saving measure known as *install on demand*). If this is the case, you'll see the message "Template not yet installed. Click OK to install it now." in the Preview window. If you choose to install new templates, be sure to have your Office setup disc handy.

3 Double-click the template you want to open, and Windows will start the application associated with it and load the template so you can use it. For example, to create a memo based on the Elegant Letter template, double-click the Elegant Letter icon on the Letters & Faxes tab of the New Office Document dialog box. When the template you specify opens as a new untitled document, add your information to the document, and save the information under a new filename to protect the original template. (You'll want to use it again later.) Most templates include basic instructions that tell you how to create the document, as shown in Figure 1-4.

FIGURE 1-4.
Templates are predesigned business forms with instructions. Simply enter your information and print.

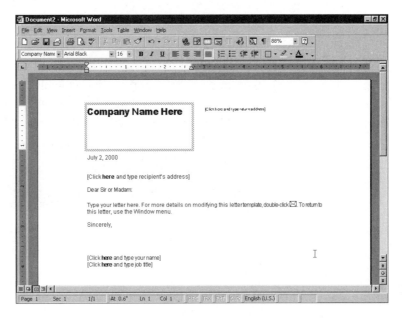

Using a Wizard: A Special Type of Template

Did you notice the icon named Letter Wizard in Figure 1-3? A *wizard* is a special, automated utility that guides you through the process of creating a business document, one step at a time. Wizards provide a handy alternative to templates because they let you change the style or format of a document as you create it. (Templates, by definition, always contain the same format.) For example, the Letter Wizard lets you create customized name, address, and phone number fields (locations) in your letter and add several types of artwork to your document. You'll find useful wizards on many of the tabs in the New Office Document dialog box.

To use a wizard to create a customized Office document, follow these steps:

1   Click the Start button, and then click New Office Document. A dialog box that contains document template tabs appears.

2   Click the tab corresponding to the type of document you want to create. For example, to use a wizard to create a letter, click the Letters & Faxes tab.

3   Double-click the wizard you want to use. For example, to create a letter using a wizard, double-click the Letter Wizard icon on the Letters & Faxes tab of the dialog box.

Windows opens the wizard you select and runs it in the associated Office application. Figure 1-5 shows the opening screen of the Letter Wizard.

4 To complete a wizard procedure, merely answer the questions that the Office Assistant asks by choosing option buttons, entering information, or clicking the wizard control buttons.

FIGURE 1-5.
Wizards are special utilities that automatically create a new document based on your preferences.

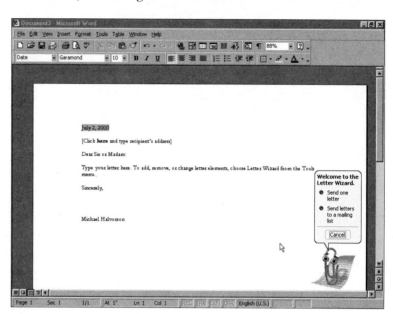

2000 Opening Documents Using Microsoft Outlook

In Office 2000, you can also open documents using the information management program named Microsoft Outlook. Outlook was designed for those people who are constantly dealing with information that originates from a variety of sources. Accordingly, Outlook allows you to manage your Internet and network electronic mail, appointment calendar, project "To-Do" list, business contacts, and important documents—all from one application! Part 6 shows you how to get the most out of Outlook in your daily activities. (You can turn to these chapters at any time—none of the other chapters are prerequisites.) In this section, however, we describe an essential technique that you can use to open existing Office documents from project folders in the Outlook 2000 application.

To open your Office documents in Microsoft Outlook, open Outlook, if necessary, and then follow the steps shown in Figure 1-6.

FIGURE 1-6.
Microsoft Outlook lists
documents by name
so you can open them
while working on
electronic mail or
other tasks.

1 Click the Outlook Bar command on the View menu.

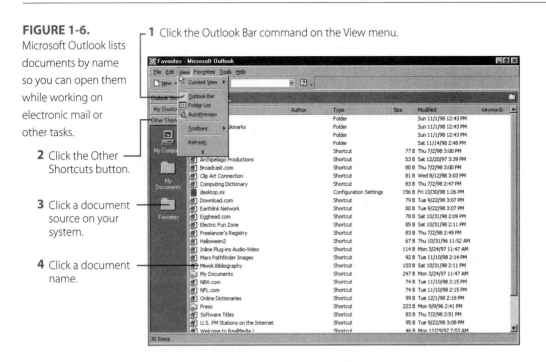

2 Click the Other
Shortcuts button.

3 Click a document
source on your
system.

4 Click a document
name.

Switching Between Office Applications

Microsoft specifically designed Windows and Windows NT to be *multi-tasking* operating systems, capable of running several large applications at once. In plain English, this means you can run two or more Office programs at once and quickly switch between them as your work requires. For example, you can run Outlook, Excel, and Word all at the same time, using the programs jointly to build a report, or individually to create stand-alone documents. As you learned earlier, you start Office applications by using the Start button. To switch between open applications, you use the taskbar, located at the bottom of the screen.

Figure 1-7 shows a typical taskbar, containing a button identifying each application that is running (currently three applications—Word, Outlook, and Excel). The current, or *active,* application (Word) is highlighted on the taskbar, and, if you look, you'll see that the active application's title bar is also highlighted on the screen. (Often the title

FIGURE 1-7.
The taskbar shows
three programs at
work. The active
application appears
pressed in.

Foreground
application

Background
applications

bar appears in a different color and contains a document name.) While all the programs running under Windows can perform useful work, the active, or *foreground,* application is the program that is currently ready to receive your input. If this application contains an insertion point, it will probably be blinking now—a sign that the program is ready for work. In a multitasking environment, you should know the difference between a foreground application (the highlighted application) and the remaining *background* applications (the programs running behind the scenes) so that you can keep track of your programs and know which one is receiving input. The visual clues provided on the taskbar make this easy. To move from one task to the next, simply click the appropriate button on the taskbar.

One Button per Document

In Office 97, each application had one button on the taskbar—no matter how many documents were open in that application. However, Office 2000 displays a new button on the taskbar for each Office document that you open, even if all the documents belong to one Office application. Technically, this change is a move from MDI (Multiple Document Interface) to SDI (Single Document Interface) standards. As a result, you can quickly display Office documents by clicking the corresponding button on the taskbar. When you close a document, only the document closes—the application keeps running until you close the last document.

Using the Taskbar

To switch from the active Windows application to a program that's running in the background, just click the button on the taskbar associated with the program you want to use. For example, to switch from an Outlook message to an Excel worksheet, click the worksheet button on the taskbar. This will move the selected document in front of any others and (typically) will hide the other documents from view. The selected document becomes the new foreground task, standing ready to receive your input.

Increase the Taskbar's Size

If you have more than three or four programs running under Windows, you can make more room for taskbar buttons by increasing the height of the taskbar. To do this, move the mouse pointer toward the top edge of the taskbar until it changes into the sizing pointer (a double-headed arrow), and then drag the top edge up until the taskbar doubles in height.

The number of programs you can run under Windows is limited by the amount of random access memory (RAM) and hard disk space you have, so use some discretion when loading full-sized applications into memory. (The specific limit depends on both the hardware you have and the size of your programs.) If you get a warning message from Windows about low memory or resources, you'll know it's time to exit a few programs.

Using the Help System

If you have used computer software for any length of time, you've probably had plenty of experience using an online (actually, on-screen) Help system. Office 2000 makes online Help easier to use by providing several convenient methods for getting online instruction. You'll find the following tools in each Office application:

- Microsoft Help (F1)—If the Office Assistant's display is turned off, or if the Assistant's Respond To F1 Key is deselected, the F1 key displays a window that lets you type and search for a topic, pick one from a list, or type a question to display a smaller list of topics that are relevant to what you want to do. Otherwise, the F1 key displays the Assistant's balloon in which you can enter a topic to search for.

- Office Assistant—A friendly and animated guide to each application in Office. The Office Assistant appears with its balloon, in which you can type a topic or question about what you're looking for, and then click a Search button to see a list of topics (see Figure 1-8).

FIGURE 1-8.
The Office Assistant.

Behind the Office Assistant's kindly exterior is a powerful, natural-language database containing answers to thousands of the most vexing questions about Office applications. When you select one of the topics that the Office Assistant presents in answer to your question, the Microsoft Help window for the active application appears to show you the detailed information on the topic you selected.

- What's This?—A context-sensitive Help pointer with which you can click an application feature to learn more about it.

- Office On The Web—A convenient connection to the Microsoft Office Web site, which provides several useful online resources for Office users.

Word contains useful online information for users familiar with WordPerfect, and Excel contains useful online information for users familiar with Lotus 1-2-3. Check the Word and Excel online Help menus for information if you're making the transition from one of these products.

The About Command

The final command on the Help menu (About) contains copyright and version information for the program you're using. The About dialog box also includes a System Info button, which you can click to display information about your computer's hardware and software configuration, plus a Tech Support button, which you can use to contact Microsoft Product Support.

The Microsoft Help Command

At the top of each Office application's Help menu there is a Help command that includes the name of the application (for example, "Microsoft Word Help"). If the Office Assistant is turned on—you'll learn how to turn this feature on and off later in this chapter—it will appear with its balloon somewhere within the application's window. If the Office Assistant is turned off, this command displays the Microsoft Help window (like the command, the window's title includes the name of the application). As you can see in this illustration of the Microsoft Word Help window, the window contains a toolbar that has five buttons:

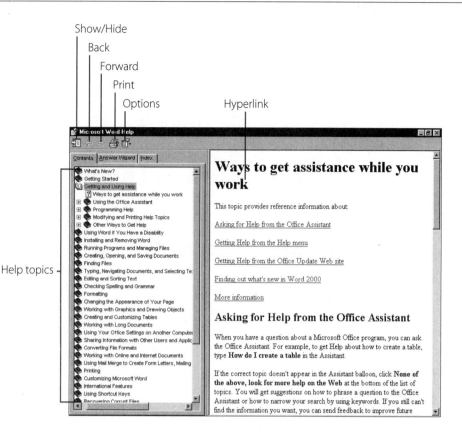

Show/Hide
Back
Forward
Print
Options
Hyperlink
Help topics

The Show/Hide button toggles the display of the pane on the left side of the window. This pane contains three tabs. The Contents tab contains a list of help topics in a familiar hierarchical structure. Scroll through the list to select a main topic, and click the box containing the plus sign to display a list of subtopics. When you find the subtopic you want, click it to display its information in the right pane. The Answer Wizard tab provides a text box into which you can type a question. Then click the Search button. Microsoft Help looks for and retrieves topics relevant to the question that you type. Select one of the topics that Help finds to display the information in the right pane.

The Index tab contains three numbered sections, and each helps you to pin down the information you're after. Section 1 provides a text box into which you can type a keyword; this text box operates similarly to the Answer Wizard tab. As soon as you type the first few characters, the list of keywords in section 2 scrolls to the first keyword that begins with those characters, if there is one. You also have the option of bypassing the text box in section 1 and selecting a keyword in the section 2 list. When you select a desired keyword, click the Search button to display a list of relevant topics in section 3. Then choose one of these topics to display information in the right pane.

While you have the Help window open, you can use the Back and Forward buttons to return to information you have viewed previously. The Print button is available to print the information displayed currently in the right pane. The Options button displays a menu from which you can select commands to toggle the display of the tabs, navigate to other pages or select other options, or open the Print dialog box to change printer settings.

The Office Assistant Feature

Closely linked to the Help system is the Office Assistant, a friendly search tool that uses animation, humor, and a database containing thousands of tips, techniques, and solutions to help you learn how the Office software works. (See Figure 1-8, on page 19.) The Office Assistant acts as an on-demand genie that pops up when you need it to solve your problem or give you some advice. If you don't want the Office Assistant, fine—send her (or him? or it?) away until you need her again. (She won't bug you or get in your way.) Best of all, you can customize the Office Assistant to appear just the way you like, particularly if you don't care for the default character, Clippit.

You start the Office Assistant by choosing Microsoft Help from the Help menu (if the Office Assistant is turned on) or by clicking the Office Assistant button on your application's toolbar. As with the other Help features, the information provided by the Office Assistant is specific to the active application. For example, if you open the Office Assistant in Outlook, all the solutions provided will be related to Outlook. On the other hand, if you're in Word, the same question results in solutions specific to Word.

As you work in your application, the Office Assistant will periodically offer tips to streamline the commands you're using. The Office Assistant doesn't just blurt out its advice (how rude!), but instead advertises its services by discreetly motioning to get your attention or displaying a helpful balloon. For example, if the Office Assistant notices that you're starting to write a letter in Word, it will ask whether you want help. If you accept its offer, the Office Assistant will start the Letter Wizard and help you fill out the options in the Letter Wizard dialog box.

When you're finished using the Office Assistant, right-click it (use the right mouse button), and choose Hide, or choose Hide The Office Assistant on the Help menu, to give Office Assistant the afternoon off.

Customizing the Office Assistant

If you get bored with the default character, you can choose another electronic helper by right-clicking the Office Assistant and then selecting Choose Assistant from the shortcut menu that pops up. When you make this selection, the Office Assistant dialog box appears and displays the Gallery tab, as shown in Figure 1-9.

FIGURE 1-9.
Pick a new Office Assistant with this dialog box.

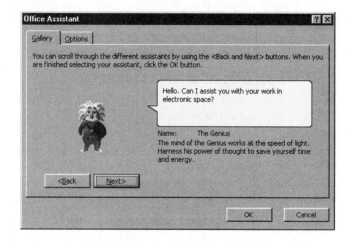

Each time you click the Next button in this dialog box, a new Office Assistant appears, ready to do your bidding.

Finally, you can customize the capabilities of the Office Assistant by clicking the Options tab in the Office Assistant dialog box. The Options tab contains a collection of check boxes that enable and disable features in the Office Assistant. (See Figure 1-10 on the next page.) Simply adjust the settings and, presto, the Office Assistant has a new personality! (Wouldn't it be great to be able to do this with people at work?) A few of the options we like are Only Show High Priority Tips, which stops the Office Assistant from recommending nonessential shortcuts, and Move When In The Way, which forces the Office Assistant to relocate on the screen if it's blocking a dialog box or important data. When you're done customizing the Office Assistant, click OK to close the Office Assistant dialog box.

FIGURE 1-10.
Control your Assistant's manners using this dialog box.

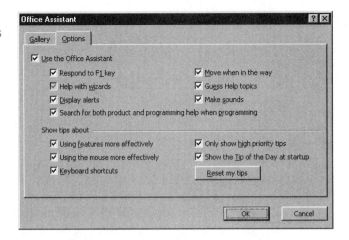

The What's This? Feature

Another useful Help feature in Office applications is an object called the *Help pointer*. The Help pointer appears when you choose What's This? from the Help menu or when you click the Help button that appears in the upper right corner of dialog boxes next to the Close button, which changes the mouse pointer to a question mark. After the transformation, your mouse works just like an alchemist's magic wand—when you move the Help pointer and click a menu item, toolbar button, or window element, the Help pointer displays a Help window showing you exactly what the object does. It's a Help feature designed for tactile people who want to poke and prod while they learn.

Call for Keyboard Help

You can also use the Help pointer to get assistance using keyboard combinations. To try this useful feature, click the Help pointer on the toolbar, and then press the key or keys you want to learn about. For example, click the Help pointer and press Ctrl+B, the keyboard shortcut for bold formatting in Word. The Help system will display a Help article related to the keys you press.

Fixing Problems Using Detect And Repair

Finally, you should note the presence of a special command on the Help menu named Detect And Repair that can identify and fix problems in the Office 2000 software as they arise. Use this command if you experience application crashes when you use a particular program or see error messages that describe missing files or other worrisome conditions.

When you choose Detect And Repair, Office 2000 analyzes the files in your Office application to verify that they are the proper size and contain the necessary binary information. Detect And Repair can also fix corrupt or missing keys in the Windows Registry by reverting to internal application defaults that keep the program you are using from stopping unexpectedly. If Office 2000 locates a missing or corrupt file, it replaces the file from your installation source (typically the corporate network or your setup CD).

Figure 1-11 shows the dialog box that appears when you first choose Detect And Repair from the Help menu in an Office 2000 application. Select the optional Shortcuts check box if you want Office to rebuild any shortcuts you have in folders or on the Windows desktop, and then click the Start button to run the utility. Note that you might need to supply a setup disc or installation path during this process.

 TIP

If All Else Fails

If the Detect And Repair command doesn't fix your problem, you have two additional recourses. First, try reinstalling the application you're having problems with by using the original Office 2000 CD-ROM or network setup. Second—and this is a good general tip—connect to the Microsoft Office Update Web site to see whether other users have had the same problems or whether Microsoft distributes periodic service updates or patches for your application. The URL for this service is *http://www.microsoft.com/office*.

FIGURE 1-11.
The Detect And Repair dialog box works to fix your applications automatically.

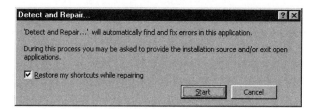

Exiting Office Applications

Whenever you're finished working with an Office application, you should close your documents or spreadsheets and exit the program before you shut down Windows and turn off your computer. If you don't exit applications properly, rest assured that you won't damage your system, though you might leave a few temporary files on your hard disk that will waste disk space. You could also lose the edits you made in your document since you last saved your document by using the Save command. Fortunately, however, all Office applications ask you to save your changes whenever you try to exit a program with an unsaved file open. (You'll learn more about saving documents in the next chapter.)

To exit an Office application, do one of the following:

- From the application's File menu, choose Exit.

- Press Alt+F4.

- Right-click the application name on the taskbar, and then choose Close from the shortcut menu. (This will quit the application if no other documents belonging to the application are open.)

If you have any unsaved changes in your document, you'll be prompted to save them. (If the Office Assistant is running, you'll see a balloon similar to the one shown in Figure 1-12.) If you click Yes when prompted to save, your changes will be stored under the current filename. (If you haven't established a filename, you'll be given a chance to enter one.) If you click No, all the changes you made since your last save will be discarded. If you click Cancel, the dialog box will close without any changes being made, and you'll return to your application.

FIGURE 1-12.
The Office Assistant balloon containing Save options appears if you try to exit an application with unsaved changes.

CHAPTER 2

Learning the Basics: Windows, Toolbars, and Printing

W hen you work with the screens, dialog boxes, menus, and commands in a Windows application, you're using the program's user *interface*. In the Microsoft Office application suite, all programs share the same basic user interface. The information displayed by each application appears in one or more standard windows that can be scrolled, resized, or in some cases, split into two views. Programs present commands on standard menu bars, dialog boxes, and toolbars that share many common features. In addition, each Office application contains uniform printing commands that you can use to configure your printer, preview a document, and create a printout. In this chapter, you'll learn how to use each of these common application features. As you work with Office programs in the future, you'll find that you make use of these basic skills every time you create, modify, or print a document.

Working with Application Windows

When you start an Office application, the program appears in one of three states—minimized (as a button on the taskbar), maximized (to fill the entire screen), or in a Normal window (which appears to float on your screen). Maximizing your application provides the most work-space. Minimizing your application moves it out of the way while leaving it instantly available. Working with your application in a Normal window gives you the ability to change the window size so that you can work with more than one application on the screen at a time (as shown in Figure 2-1).

When you work with a Normal window, you can change the size and shape of the window or move it to another location on your desktop. To change the size of a Normal window, position the mouse pointer over the window edge you want to stretch or shrink, and drag the edge to the new location using the sizing pointer. To move a window, drag the title bar from one location to another. Note that you can't change

FIGURE 2-1.

By sizing and moving application windows, you can position more than one Office application on the screen.

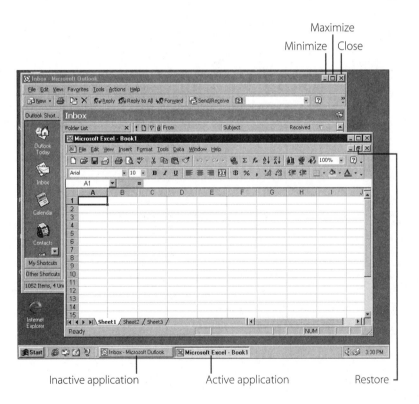

Getting Started

the size or the position of a window that has been minimized to a button on the taskbar nor of one that is maximized to fill the entire screen.

When you have minimized an application to a button on the taskbar, you can either click it to restore it to a window, or right-click it to display a shortcut menu that offers choices for restoring it to a window or maximizing it to fill the entire screen. When an application is within a Normal window or appears maximized, you can use the control buttons on the right side of the application's title bar to minimize the window to a button on the taskbar, maximize the window to fill the entire screen, restore the application to a Normal window, or close the window.

 TIP

Shortcuts Are a Mouse Click Away

Many times you can find the next action you want to perform on the special shortcut menu that appears when you click the right (or secondary) mouse button. The menu changes depending upon the context of your actions, so check it often for possible shortcuts to accomplish your tasks more quickly.

Understanding the Workplace

The user interface elements you see when you run an Office application—the menu bars, toolbars, status bars, and windows—are known as the *workplace* of the program. Each Office application uses a different metaphor for its workplace; Microsoft Word documents resemble typewritten pages, Microsoft Excel documents resemble accounting spreadsheets, Microsoft PowerPoint documents resemble slide presentations, Microsoft Access documents resemble data entry forms, and so on. The trick to learning how to use an Office application is understanding how to create documents that are in sync with the metaphor that application uses.

Figure 2-2, on the next page, shows the workplace of Excel, a typical Office application. Along the top of the application window is the *title bar*, a rectangle containing the program name, the document name, and the *control buttons* used to size and close the window. Below the title bar is the *menu bar*, containing commands that you click to perform the work of the program. Further down are one or more collections of buttons called *toolbars*. Toolbar buttons are typically shortcuts to commands on the menu bar (hence their synonym *command buttons*); to run a command on the toolbar, you simply click the button. (You might see a different arrangement of toolbars in your application workplace.)

FIGURE 2-2.
The user interface
elements shared by
all Microsoft Office
applications.
(See Table 2-1 for
a description of
what they do.)

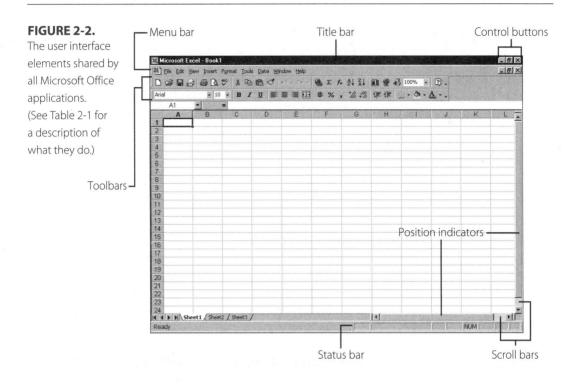

Menu bar

Title bar

Control buttons

Toolbars

Position indicators

Status bar

Scroll bars

TABLE 2-1.   Workplace Elements and What They Do

Workplace Element	Description
Title bar	Rectangular bar at the top of the application window containing the Office application name, the document name, and the control buttons.
Control buttons	Minimize, Maximize, Restore, and Close buttons for the application window and each document window.
Menu bar	Area under the title bar containing the menu names. Each menu opens to provide access to a group of application-specific commands.
Toolbars	One or more rows of drop-down list boxes and command buttons beneath the menu bar.
Scroll bars	Horizontal and vertical bars at the bottom and right edge of the window, used to view parts of a document not currently displayed in the window.
Position indicators	Boxes inside application scroll bars that show the relative distance traveled in a document.
Status bar	Indicators for the Num Lock and Insert toggle keys, plus any application-specific data (such as page numbers or cell contents).

? SEE ALSO

Naturally, each Office application will also have its own unique elements, many of which play an important role in the workplace. For more information, read the application-specific sections in this book.

Below the toolbar is the document area unique to each Office application. In Microsoft Excel, documents are called *worksheets*: ledgers divided into rows and columns to hold text, numbers, and charts. Each Office application uses a slightly different type of document. For example, the Word workplace contains word processing documents, while the PowerPoint workplace contains the slides of a presentation, though all Office workplaces contain a set of common elements that you can use to complete work in your program. Finally, each Office application includes horizontal and vertical *scroll bars* to navigate each document window, plus a *status bar* (located at the bottom of the window) containing information about the toggle keys in use (Num Lock and Insert) and other details specific to each application.

Navigating Document Windows

If a document is too large to be displayed completely in a document window, Office adds vertical and horizontal scroll bars to the window to give you access to the entire file. Figure 2-2 shows the scroll bars on a typical Excel worksheet. Scroll bars let you move through your document at your own pace; you can move:

- up or down one line or row by clicking the top or bottom arrow on the vertical scroll bar.

- right or left a small amount (one column in an Excel worksheet) by clicking the right or left arrow on the horizontal scroll bar.

- in larger increments (approximately one page at a time) by clicking the horizontal or vertical scroll bar itself.

- to a specific location in the document by dragging the vertical or horizontal position indicator on the scroll bars. The position indicator gives you a visual clue of your place in the document.

> NOTE

You can also scroll through a document window by pressing and holding the Up, Down, Right, or Left arrow keys or the Page Up and Page Down keys.

Working with Several Document Windows

Word, Excel, and PowerPoint let you open more than one document window at a time so that you can compare related documents, exchange information between files, and work on a multidocument report or presentation. When you work with documents in separate windows, each open document window has its own title bar, control buttons, menu bar, toolbars, rulers, scroll bars, and status bar, as shown in Figure 2-3. (The Arrange All command on the Window menu created this effect, as you'll see below.)

Excel further organizes document windows by grouping worksheets into collections called *workbooks*. You can scroll through the worksheets in a workbook by clicking the tabs at the bottom of each document window.

FIGURE 2-3.
Two open Microsoft
Word documents.

Renaissance
Autobiography
document (active)

Clandestine Book
Trade document

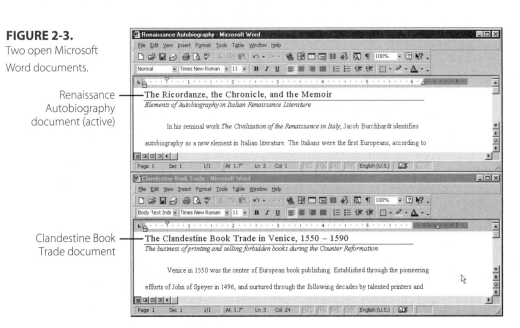

To control how document windows are activated and displayed, Word, Excel, PowerPoint, and Access include a Window menu on their menu bars. Figure 2-4 shows Word's Window menu when two documents are open. At the bottom of each menu in Word, Excel, and PowerPoint are the names of the open documents in the application. (Access only allows you to open one database at a time.) A check mark appears next to the active or highlighted document. To switch between open documents, click the name on the Window menu corresponding to the document you want to display, or type its number.

FIGURE 2-4.
Click the Window
menu to display a list
of your open files.

At the top of the Window menu are the commands you can use to open new windows and to arrange existing windows. In Word, Excel, and PowerPoint, clicking the New Window command opens a new document window and displays the active document in it. This lets you display the same document in more than one window. Each of the windows showing the same document is identified by a number following the document's name on the title bar, as shown here:

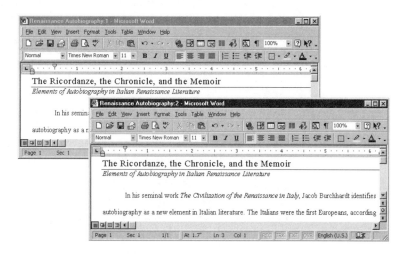

In Word, below the New Window command on the Window menu is the Arrange All command, which divides the workplace evenly between all the open document windows. (Figure 2-3 shows the results of choosing the Arrange All command.) Use Arrange All if you want to compare the documents you currently have open. If part of a document is no longer visible on the screen after you choose Arrange All, then use the scroll bars to bring it into view. Arranging documents using the Arrange All command is often called *tiling*, because you fit them together one on top of the other like floor tiles.

The Split command, available in only Word and Excel, is similar to the New Window command, but rather than creating a new window, it simply splits the screen to give you different views of the active document. In Word, when you choose the command, a shaded split line appears, which lets you specify how you want the window divided up. Click the document in the place where you want the border to appear (the middle of the document usually works best), and then scroll each window until you see the information you want to compare. (You can fine-tune the split by dragging the middle window border using the mouse.)

You'll find the Split command most useful when you want to edit different parts of a document at once within a single window, or when you want to read the instructions in one part of a document while you work on the other. For example, you might want to read the template instructions at the top of a document while filling in the blanks below. Note that the Split command keeps track of the edits you make so that changes in one window are automatically reflected in the second window. When you're finished using the Split command, choose Remove Split from the Window menu.

Resizing and Closing Document Windows

Just like application windows, individual document windows can be moved, resized, minimized, maximized, and closed. The commands you use to manage document windows are located on the document Control menu, which appears when you click the Control-menu icon on the left side of an active document's title bar. Figure 2-5 shows the Control menu for a document in Microsoft Word.

You can also minimize, maximize, restore, or close a document window by clicking the buttons on the right side of a document's title bar, which control the window orientation you're using. These buttons work just like the ones on an application's title bar, and you'll usually find that using them is the quickest way to resize or close a document window. To restore a minimized document to its normal size, just click its taskbar button.

FIGURE 2-5.
Each document window contains a Control menu, which you can display by clicking the tiny Control-menu icon.

Control-menu icon —

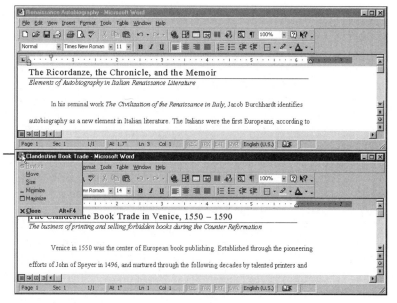

If you work with multiple document windows often, you might also find the keyboard shortcuts given in Table 2-2 useful.

TABLE 2-2.   Useful Keyboard Shortcuts for Document Windows

Keyboard Shortcut	Purpose
Ctrl+F4 *or* Ctrl+W	Close the active document window.
Ctrl+F5	Restore a maximized window to its previous size.
Ctrl+F6	Switch between open documents.
Ctrl+F7	Move the active document window.
Ctrl+F8	Resize the active document window.
Ctrl+F10	Maximize the active document window.
Alt+hyphen (-)	Open the active document's Control menu.

Using Menus and Dialog Boxes

As you have already learned, you can run commands in Office applications either by clicking a command name on the menu bar or by clicking a toolbar button. If the program needs additional information before it can run the command, it displays a *dialog box* in which you "talk" to the program by filling in the blanks or choosing from a list of preset options. This section describes some of the typical options you'll find on Office menus and in dialog boxes. Because Office applications share many of the same features, you'll be able to apply what you learn here to all the menus and dialog boxes in Office.

Menu Conventions

As you learned in the last section, several Office applications maintain Window menus that have nearly identical commands. In addition, all Office applications have File, Edit, and Help menus that have many of the same commands—so once you learn how to use these menus in one Office application, you'll be able to use them in all Office applications. What's more, each program follows a series of conventions for the presentation of commands, buttons, and information on menus and in dialog boxes. Table 2-3 lists the most important menu bar conventions. (You'll learn about dialog boxes in the next section.)

TABLE 2-3. **Important Menu Bar Conventions**

Menu Item	Convention	Example
Dimmed command	The menu command isn't currently available.	Comments
Ellipsis (…)	Choosing the menu item will display a dialog box.	Save As...
Checked command	A command indicating an option that's currently active. (These commands control options or features that can be either on or off.) Clicking a checked command removes the check and turns the option off; clicking an unchecked command turns it on.	✓ Ruler
Cascading menu (or submenu)	Pointing to this menu item will display more menu choices.	Toolbars ▶
Keyboard shortcut	A keyboard alternative for executing the menu command.	Save Ctrl+S
Underlined letter	Pressing the underlined letter (often a mnemonic, as in F for Footnotes) will run the command.	Footnotes
Toolbar shortcut	A toolbar alternative for executing the menu command.	Open... Ctrl+O

Dialog Box Options

Figure 2-6 shows a typical dialog box from an Office application. (This dialog box appears when you choose Print from Word's File menu.) Dialog boxes present you with one or more command options by using list boxes, buttons, and other components. To complete a dialog box, indicate your preferences, and then click the OK button. To move from one item to the next in a dialog box, click the item, or use the Tab key until the item is highlighted. Many dialog boxes don't require you to fill every blank.

If you have second thoughts about using the command after you see the dialog box, you can cancel the command by clicking the Cancel button or by clicking the Close button on the dialog box's title bar. You

FIGURE 2-6.
Dialog boxes have several mechanisms for accepting user input.

Drop-down list boxes contain a default selection.

To change the selection in a drop-down list box, click the down arrow and pick a new item.

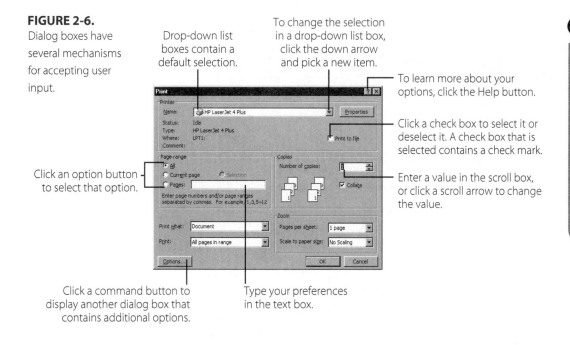

To learn more about your options, click the Help button.

Click a check box to select it or deselect it. A check box that is selected contains a check mark.

Click an option button to select that option.

Enter a value in the scroll box, or click a scroll arrow to change the value.

Click a command button to display another dialog box that contains additional options.

Type your preferences in the text box.

can also get help by clicking the Help button on the title bar and then clicking the item you want to learn more about. Finally, if you need to see document information displayed beneath a dialog box, move the dialog box out of the way by dragging its title bar.

Speed Up Your Dialog Box Selections

The mouse is the most intuitive tool to use when making dialog box selections, but you can often speed up your dialog box commands by using keyboard shortcuts. For example, to move from one item to the next in a dialog box, press the Tab key. (You can also move to the previous item by pressing Shift+Tab.) To move quickly through a list box, press the letter on your keyboard that corresponds to the first letter of the list item you want to select. You can also move through a list box by pressing the Up and Down arrow keys. (Press Enter to lock in your choice.)

You'll also see small panes called *tabs* along the top edge of some Office dialog boxes. These tabs let you display other command settings to further customize your workplace. Figure 2-7, on the following page, shows an example of a dialog box that has four tabs related to printing.

FIGURE 2-7.

Dialog box tabs give you quick access to related options and property settings.

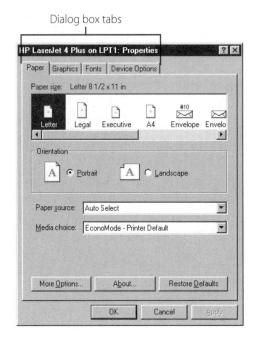

Using the Right Mouse Button

If you have used the Windows operating system for a while, you know that before Windows 95, few applications provided complete support for the right mouse button. Although most pointing devices have two or even three mouse buttons, the left button has traditionally been the only button you could click in a Windows-based application. In Windows 95 and Windows 98, however, the right mouse button has finally been put to use. The following list shows a few important uses for the right mouse button in Office applications:

■ To resize or close an Office application, right-click the application's title bar, and then click the window command you want on the shortcut menu that pops up.

■ To edit or format selected text in a document, right-click the text, and then click the formatting command you want on the shortcut menu.

■ To add, remove, or customize an Office application toolbar, right-click the toolbar, and then click the toolbar you want to view or hide, or click Customize to edit a toolbar.

■ To close an application from the taskbar, right-click the application's taskbar button, and then click the Close command.

Using Toolbars

A *toolbar* is a customizable set of buttons and drop-down list boxes, located below the menu bar of an Office application. Toolbars will likely become your favorite screen elements in Office, for they provide rapid access to the most common commands and procedures of an application. The buttons on Office toolbars typically have command equivalents on the menus of the applications, but are easier to remember than command names because they contain *icons*—graphic representations of the tasks they accomplish. Toolbar buttons are also easier to use because they require only one click to get them started. (Menu commands require a minimum of two clicks.)

Figure 2-8 shows a typical toolbar configuration in the Microsoft Word workplace. The Standard toolbar, the toolbar that has the most useful Word commands, appears directly below the menu bar in the default (preset) Word configuration. Below the Standard toolbar is the Formatting toolbar, a popular toolbar that contains drop-down list boxes and buttons you can use to format text. (A research team at Microsoft has studied how people use Office applications and has placed the most common commands on the Standard and Formatting toolbars.) Word includes a total of 13 toolbars, and you can display none of them or all of them, or you can customize your own toolbars—it's completely up to you.

FIGURE 2-8.
Memorize these essential toolbar buttons.

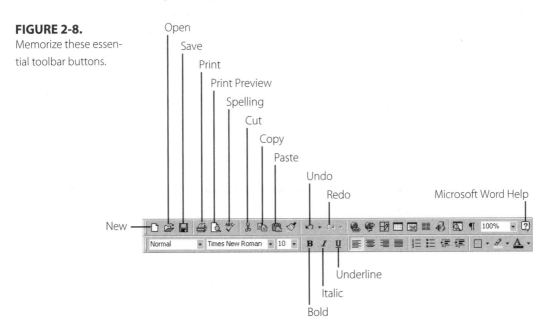

Open
Save
Print
Print Preview
Spelling
Cut
Copy
Paste
Undo
Redo
Microsoft Word Help
New
Underline
Italic
Bold

The labels in Figure 2-8 highlight the most popular Office toolbar buttons. (You'll find them, perhaps arranged in slightly different order, in virtually all Office applications.) If you're not sure what a toolbar button does, hold the mouse pointer over the button for a moment to see the button's name. This Help feature is called a ScreenTip. You can also click What's This? on the Help menu, and then click a toolbar button to learn how to use it.

Get to Know Your Buttons

You'll save lots of work time if you memorize the functions of the toolbar buttons described in Figure 2-8. If Office were a car, these would be the familiar knobs and buttons on your dashboard, and for your ease of driving and safety, you'd want to know what they do.

What If I See Something Different?

In some installations of Office 2000, you might see a different arrangement of the Standard and Formatting toolbars, or different toolbars altogether. For example, the toolbar configuration shown for PowerPoint in Figure 2-9 has the Standard and Formatting toolbars connected together on the same line below the menu bar. This arrangement will give you more space for presentations in the workplace, but hides some of the buttons on the toolbars. (In some Office installations, this view might be the default view.)

You can identify the presence of hidden buttons by tiny double arrows called chevrons (>>) at the end of a toolbar, as shown in Figure 2-9. To see the buttons that are hidden, click the chevrons, and the hidden buttons will appear in a pop-up window. Alternatively, you can move one of the toolbars to a new location to see the entire set of buttons at a glance. (For more information about this technique, see the next section.)

FIGURE 2-9.
Tiny double arrows (chevrons) on a toolbar identify the presence of hidden buttons, which you can display by clicking the chevrons.

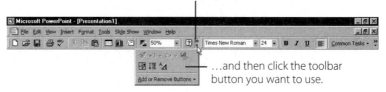

Click the double arrows to display any hidden buttons…

…and then click the toolbar button you want to use.

In this book, we'll usually show the Standard and Formatting toolbars on their own lines with all the default buttons visible so that you can see the entire set of command options available. If you have specific preferences for how Office displays toolbars and menu commands, you can specify them by choosing Customize on the Tools menu and clicking the Options tab, shown in the following illustration.

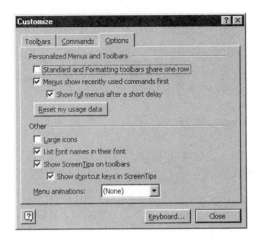

- If you want to save space by merging the Standard and Formatting toolbars, select the Standard And Formatting Toolbars Share One Row check box.

- If you want Office to place the commands you use most often at the top of your menus, select Menus Show Recently Used Commands First.

- If you want to see all the commands on a menu after a few moments (not just the most recently used), select Show Full Menus After A Short Delay.

- If you want to return the menus and toolbars in your application to the way they were when you installed Office, click the Reset My Usage Data button.

Moving Toolbars

If you'd like to customize the look of your application workplace, you can move one or more toolbars to a different location on the screen. Most Office toolbars can be placed at the top of the application window (the default position for most toolbars), or at the bottom, or on either side—or even in a floating palette anywhere in the application window.

To move an Office toolbar, simply click an empty place on the toolbar (the left edge works best), and then drag the toolbar to a new location. As you drag the toolbar, a shaded rectangle moves with your mouse pointer to help you place the buttons. If you move toolbars on top of each other, they will snap into place, or *dock*, in a position that can partially obscure buttons on one or more of the toolbars. (Chevrons at the end of the toolbar will help you identify this useful state.) When you're ready to restore the toolbar, just drag it back to its original position.

> **NOTE**

In Office 2000, you can move the menu bar around the workplace just like the toolbars. Try this special customization option if you want to fine-tune your user interface!

Figure 2-10 shows the Word workplace after the Formatting toolbar has been moved to the bottom of the upper document window and the Standard toolbar has been floated in the upper right corner of the document window. Note that floating toolbars always remain above the

FIGURE 2-10.
Office applications let you move toolbars from one place to the next to match your preferences.

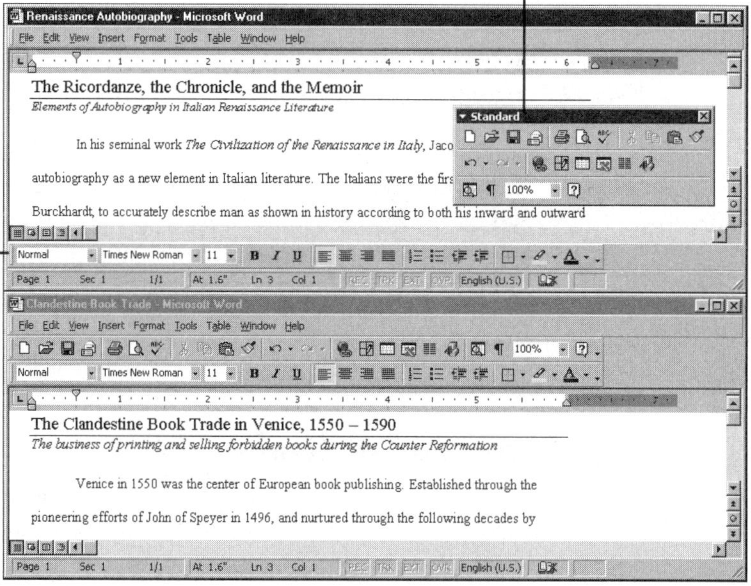

Standard toolbar positioned as a floating toolbar

Formatting toolbar docked at the bottom of the window

document so that you can use them. After a toolbar has been positioned as a floating toolbar, you can also move it (drag its title bar) or resize it using the mouse (drag any of its edges to shrink or expand it).

If you decide to use a floating toolbar, we recommend that you place it in the upper right corner of your screen. It's less likely to get in the way there when you type.

Adding and Removing Toolbars

When Microsoft designed the applications in Office, it conducted usability tests to determine which commands and procedures users ran most often. From the results of these tests, Microsoft created a collection of toolbars for each Office application that provide access to the commands and procedures that users found most helpful for a particular task. The most popular buttons were placed on the Standard toolbar, the buttons related to document formatting were placed on the Formatting toolbar, and so on. Microsoft also designed and created several application-specific toolbars to help you achieve the most effective use of the unique features and capabilities of each Office application. In this section, you'll learn how to organize your workplace by adding and removing these toolbars.

When you first start an Office application, you'll see one or two toolbars at the top of the application window. For example, Word and Excel display the Standard toolbar and the Formatting toolbar when you first start them. To see a list of the common toolbars supported by an application, simply right-click one of the toolbars. (You can click anywhere on the toolbar.) When you do, a list of the available toolbars appears in a pop-up window, as shown in Figure 2-11.

FIGURE 2-11.
To see a list of the available toolbars in an application, click a toolbar using the right mouse button.

The active toolbars in the list (the toolbars currently displayed) have a check mark next to them. Below the toolbar names is a special command named Customize that allows you to change the content and style of the toolbars in the list. You can also use Customize to add new toolbars or reset toolbars you have changed back to their default configurations.

To add a toolbar to your workplace, on the toolbar shortcut menu, merely click the name of the toolbar you want to add. To remove an active toolbar, click the toolbar name you want to hide; the check mark next to its name on the menu will disappear from the application workplace and so will the toolbar itself. Your Office application will immediately configure the workplace based on your request.

Adding extra toolbars to your screen can be fun, but don't get too carried away or you won't have any room left for your documents! We recommend that you limit your workspace to three toolbars or fewer.

Customizing Toolbars

Office gives you complete control over the toolbars displayed in your workplace. You can add buttons to a toolbar, remove buttons, rearrange buttons, and edit the picture that appears on the button face. This section describes how you can customize the toolbars in Word, Excel, PowerPoint, Access, and Microsoft Outlook, which all share similar customization features.

The doorway to customizing toolbars is the Customize command on the Toolbars submenu of the View menu. When you choose Customize, the dialog box shown in Figure 2-12 opens. By default, most Office applications display the menu bar and the Standard and Formatting toolbars, but several additional specialty toolbars are typically also available. The Customize dialog box shown here is for Excel, the Office application we'll be demonstrating in this section.

Adding Buttons to a Toolbar

You can add buttons to a toolbar from the Commands tab of the Customize dialog box. This tab contains the Categories list box, which displays the types of commands you can use. When you select a category in the list box, the associated commands appear in the Commands list

FIGURE 2-12.
The Customize dialog box gives you access to an application's predesigned toolbars.

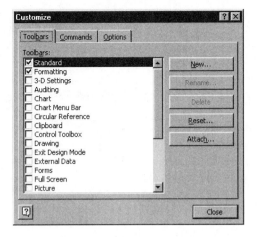

box to the right. (For example, in Excel the File category contains 27 commands in the list box.) Many of the commands featured in the functional categories are not included on the default toolbars, so take a few minutes to review your options and pick your favorites.

Many of the command names also have buttons associated with them, and these tend to make the most efficient toolbar buttons. (If a command doesn't have a button next to it, you can still use it, but Office will place the full command name on the toolbar.) If you want to learn more about what a particular button does, click the button, and then click the Description button near the bottom of the dialog box.

To add a button to a toolbar, follow these steps:

1 Display the toolbar you want to modify.

2 Choose Toolbars from the View menu, choose Customize from the submenu, and then click the Commands tab.

3 Click the group in the Categories list box containing the command you want to select. For example, to add the Strikethrough button (a button that formats text by drawing a line through it), click the Format category.

4 Drag the button you want to insert from the dialog box to the target toolbar, as shown in Figure 2-13, on the next page. (As you drag, the mouse pointer changes to a toolbar pointer.) Place the button exactly where you want it on the toolbar, and then release

? SEE ALSO

You can also use the Commands tab of the Customize dialog box to add commands to the menus in Office applications. For more information, see "Customizing Menus," page 50.

X CAUTION

Adding buttons to a full toolbar might cause some to be hidden from view. See the next page to learn how to remove infrequently used buttons.

FIGURE 2-13.
Adding a button to a toolbar.

Drag the selected button to its new location.

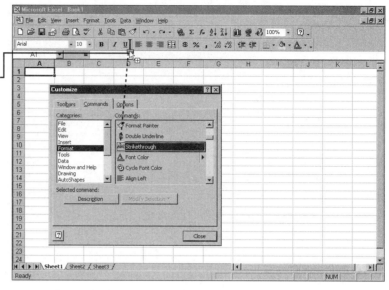

the mouse button. Office will shift existing buttons to the right to make room.

5 Repeat steps 3 and 4 to add additional toolbar buttons, if necessary. When you're finished, click Close.

Removing Unwanted Buttons

If you have added buttons to your toolbars and notice a gray chevron (>>) at the right edge of a toolbar, it indicates that not all the toolbar's buttons are currently visible. In this case, you might want to remove your least-used buttons until the remaining buttons are all visible. To remove one or more buttons, follow these steps:

1 Choose Toolbars from the View menu, and then choose Customize from the submenu.

Opening the Customize dialog box enables you to remove buttons from the toolbars and also causes any toolbars with hidden buttons to automatically resize themselves to show all their buttons.

2 Pick a toolbar button you want to remove. Choose one you don't use often, one that you won't miss. (You might also want to make sure you know how to run the equivalent command by using the menus.)

3 Click and drag the toolbar button (the one on the toolbar, not the one in the dialog box) away from the toolbar until an *X* appears in the mouse pointer, as shown in Figure 12-14. You can now release the mouse button and the toolbar button will be removed from your toolbar. The remaining buttons will shift to the left.

FIGURE 2-14.
Removing a button
from a toolbar.

Drag unwanted
buttons off your
toolbars.

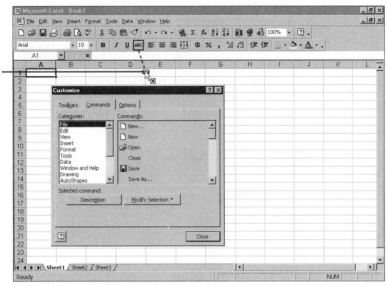

4 Continue to remove as many buttons as you want. When each toolbar fits on one line, you will no longer have any hidden buttons. (Sometimes you can squeeze an extra button onto a toolbar that contains a Zoom, Font, or other text box that Office can automatically resize to accommodate an extra button or two.)

5 When you're finished, or if you want to check whether your application will be able to fit all your buttons onto the screen, Click the Close button in the Customize dialog box.

⭐ TIP

Restore Buttons or Toolbars
When you remove a toolbar button, you don't actually delete it from your system. You can always insert it again by selecting the category it came from on the Commands tab and then dragging it back to a toolbar. You can also restore all the default buttons to an entire toolbar by clicking Reset on the Toolbars tab of the Customize dialog box.

Rearranging Toolbar Buttons

You can also change the order of toolbar buttons, or copy buttons from one toolbar to another, while the Customize dialog box is open. Like adding and removing toolbar buttons, rearranging toolbar buttons is a matter of dragging the buttons from one location to the next.

To rearrange toolbar buttons, follow these steps:

1 Display the toolbar you want to rearrange. If you want to move buttons from one toolbar to another, display both toolbars.

If the toolbars you need aren't visible, choose Toolbars from the View menu, and select the missing toolbars.

2 From the View menu, choose Toolbars, and then choose Customize from the submenu to open the Customize dialog box.

3 Drag toolbar buttons from one location to the next, using as your guide for placement the gray bar that appears above the mouse pointer. When you release the mouse button, the button you're dragging is relocated.

4 When you're finished, click the Close button in the Customize dialog box.

Copy a Toolbar Button Quickly

To copy, rather than just move, a button from one toolbar to another, hold down the Ctrl key while you drag the button. When you release the mouse button, the toolbar button will appear on both toolbars.

Editing the Picture in Toolbar Buttons

Toolbar buttons are displayed as *bitmap* images composed of rows and columns of dots. If you're not content with the picture displayed in a toolbar button, you can edit it in Office's Button Editor dialog box. You can rearrange the dots, or *pixels*, in an existing toolbar button or even create a completely new image. The following example shows you how to change the background lettering in Excel's Spelling button from ABC to XYZ. The change is subtle, but if your friends notice, they're sure to ask how you did it!

To edit the picture in a toolbar button, follow these steps:

1   Choose Toolbars from the View menu, and then choose Customize from the submenu.

2   On the toolbar, right-click the toolbar button you want to edit.
    A menu appears that contains a list of commands. (In our example, we edited the Spelling button on Excel's Standard toolbar.)

3   Click Edit Button Image. The Button Editor dialog box opens, as shown in the following illustration:

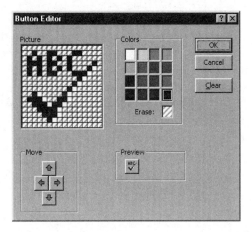

Your toolbar button now appears as a bitmap image divided into rows and columns of dots. To the right of the bitmap is a color palette that offers 16 color options.

4   To change the color of a dot, highlight the color you want to use in the color palette, and then on the toolbar button, click the dots you want to change.
    The area you can draw in is slightly smaller than the button itself. That's to allow for the button's border. Notice how your changes are reflected in the Preview window in the lower right corner of the dialog box.

5   If you want to erase a few dots, click the Erase box in the palette before clicking. You can also click a dot twice to erase it.

You'll find it takes a little time to create artwork using these crude squares, but you can actually create some impressive effects if you keep at it. The following screen shows how we modified the Spelling button:

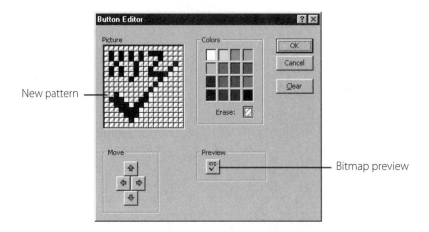

New pattern

Bitmap preview

6 When you're finished editing the button, click OK to close the Button Editor dialog box, and then click Close to close the Customize dialog box and add the button to the toolbar. The results are shown below.

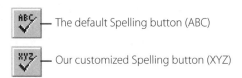

The default Spelling button (ABC)

Our customized Spelling button (XYZ)

What to Do If You Don't Like Your New Button

Should you decide you don't like your new design, open the Customize dialog box again, and right-click the button you want to restore. This time, choose Reset Button Image from the shortcut menu to return to the original design, or choose Change Button Image to choose from a menu of alternate button images. Then close the Customize dialog box.

Customizing Menus

Here's something cool: Office allows you to customize menus and commands in your Office applications in the same way that you customized toolbars. Using the familiar Customize dialog box, you can

Getting Started

rearrange the order of menus, add commands, and remove commands quickly and efficiently. Follow these steps to customize your menus in Word, Excel, PowerPoint, Access, or Outlook:

1 Open the Office application that you want to customize.

2 From the View menu, choose Toolbars. Then choose Customize from the submenu, and click the Commands tab.

3 (optional) If you want to rearrange menus or menu commands, drag them from place to place on the menu bar at this time. (As long as the Customize dialog box is open, you can drag menus and commands back and forth as you did toolbars.)

4 (optional) If you want to add a menu command, select a menu group in the Categories list box, and then pick a command in the Commands list box and drag it onto the menu bar in the location you want to use it.

Figure 2-15 shows the Excel Currency Style command being added to the Format menu.

5 (optional) If you want to remove a menu command, drag the command you no longer want off the menu bar.

6 When you're finished customizing your menus, click the Close button in the Customize dialog box.

FIGURE 2-15.
The Customize dialog box also allows you to rearrange, add, and remove menu commands.

Drag commands to a new menu location using the mouse.

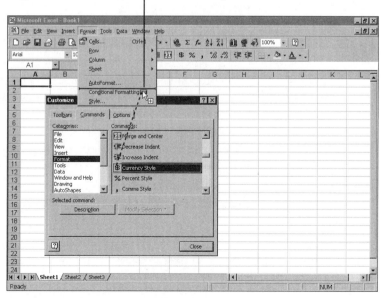

Printing Documents

 **SEE ALSO**

To learn how to distribute documents in a networked workgroup or over the Internet, see Chapter 3, "Managing Documents: From Your Hard Disk to the Internet."

Although you might choose to distribute Office documents electronically from time to time—as files sent over the Internet or by electronic mail (e-mail)—you'll probably wind up printing a hard copy of most of your work. Fortunately, printing a document is straightforward and you do it nearly the same way in each of the Office applications. In this section, you'll learn how to preview a document, print all or part of a document, and control the unique printing options of your printer.

Using Print Preview

 **SEE ALSO**

For more information on Print Preview in Word, see "Previewing and Printing Documents," page 337.

As you work on a document—an essay in Word, for example—you might not be interested in how wide the margins are, how long the essay runs, or where the page breaks occur. But when it comes time to print the document, each of these items becomes important. You might be printing on letterhead paper where specific margins need to be set, or you might need to hold the finished document to a certain number of pages. Fortunately, each Office application gives you the opportunity to see your completed document in electronic form before you print so that you can make any necessary adjustments. In Word, Excel, Access, and Outlook, the command you use to view your document in its final state is called Print Preview.

 **NOTE**

PowerPoint and Publisher don't have specific Print Preview commands.

Print Preview

To open the Print Preview window in Word, Excel, Access, or Outlook, choose Print Preview from the File menu, or click the Print Preview button. Figure 2-16 shows the window that appears in Word when a 15-page report is the active document. (The Print Preview windows in Excel, Access, and Outlook will look slightly different.) Print Preview allows you to zoom in on parts of your document, and you can adjust the margins and other page setup options before printing. The Multiple Pages button controls the number of pages that are displayed in the Print Preview window. (Two pages are shown in Figure 2-16.)

Using the Print Command

After you have examined your document using Print Preview and have made any last-minute adjustments, you're ready to print your work using the Print command. Each Office application has a Print command that sends output to an attached printer by means of special connectors called *ports* on the back of your computer. Your printer might be

FIGURE 2-16.
Print Preview lets you examine your document before printing.

Multiple Pages button

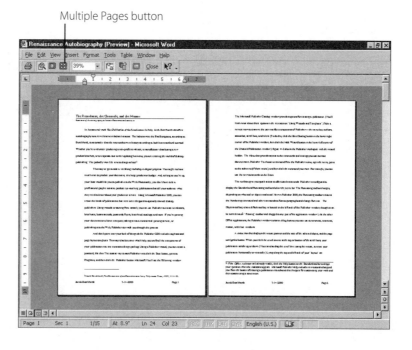

SEE ALSO
For more information about installing printer drivers and setting the unique features of your printer, see the Microsoft Windows documentation or your printer's manual.

Print

attached to your computer by a short parallel or serial cable, or through a long (and perhaps mysterious) series of network routers, cables, and connectors. In either case, your printer needs to be online and ready to go before you print. In addition, you need to have the correct printer driver installed in the Windows Printers folder to take full advantage of the features of your printer.

To start printing, choose Print from the File menu. Figure 2-17, on the next page, shows the dialog box that appears when you choose Word's Print command. (You can also click the Print button on the Standard toolbar, but that will print the document without displaying a dialog box.) Inside the Print dialog box, a Name drop-down list box contains the set of installed printers and devices to which you can send your printer output. The name currently showing in the list box is the *default printer*: the printer that will receive your output unless you select a different printer.

If you're on a network, you might have the ability to send documents to printers that your workgroup set up for different purposes. For example, you might be able to send memos and letters to a printer that prints on letterhead paper and official documents to a printer that has legal-sized paper in it. To find out about your options, ask a co-worker or the system administrator in charge of your network, and then do some experimenting.

FIGURE 2-17.
The Print command
lets you specify
printing options.

Name list box

Printer Properties

Page range options

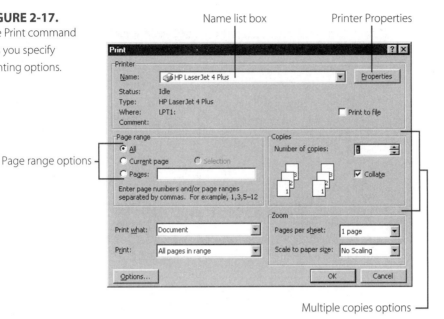

Multiple copies options

Fax Directly from Office

If you have a fax modem in (or attached to) your computer, you can also fax Office documents (with or without a cover page) by selecting the Microsoft Fax device in the Printer Name list box. As long as Microsoft Fax is the default printer, your documents will be sent out over the phone lines. (You'll be prompted each time for the name and fax number of the recipient.)

Setting Printer-Specific Options

The Properties button in the Print dialog box allows you to control the unique features of your printer, such as font resolution, paper type, and double-sided (duplex) printing. Figure 2-18 shows the dialog box that appears when you click the Properties button and a Hewlett-Packard LaserJet 4 Plus is the selected printer.

The LaserJet 4 Plus Properties dialog box has four tabs of information related to the unique features of this particular laser printer. The Paper tab lets you identify the kind of paper that is currently installed in the printer and select the orientation (or direction) you want text to appear on the page. The Graphics tab (shown in the figure) lets you select the font resolution and toner intensity, while the Fonts tab lets you choose the type of fonts you want to use.

FIGURE 2-18.
The Properties dialog box lets you control the unique characteristics of your printer.

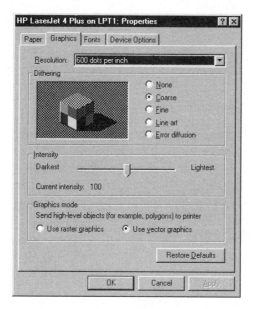

The Device Options tab allows you to control unique characteristics of your printer, including print quality and how your printer's memory is used. The contents of the tabs in your Properties dialog box will vary depending on the type of printer you have. If you don't understand how to use a particular feature, be sure to use the Help pointer. In many cases, the Properties dialog box was designed specifically for you by the manufacturer of your printer and is automatically added to your Office programs when you install the printer.

TIP

To get the best performance out of your printer, learn to use its control panel (if it has one) in addition to the printing options in your application. Sometimes you can get better performance by using the buttons on the printer's control panel to handle the fonts, paper size, and copies printed.

Setting the Page Range and Number of Copies Options

Finally, you might want to set the page range or the number of copies options before you send your document to the printer. The page range setting will vary depending on the application you're using. For example, in Word and Excel you can specify the number of pages you want printed, but in PowerPoint you specify the quantity in slides. In either case, the general procedure is the same—click the buttons next to the options you want, and enter a page or slide range if necessary. When you're finished, click the OK button to send your document to the printer. (For example, to print pages 3 through 5 and page 7 in Word, select the Pages option button in the Print dialog box, and then type *3-5, 7* in the text box.)

To print more than one copy of a document, specify the number of copies by using the Number Of Copies scroll box. If you do print more than one copy, be sure the Collate check box is marked if you want the copies printed in contiguous sets. Otherwise, your application will print all the copies of the first page, all the copies of the second page, and so forth.

Setting Zoom Options

The Print dialog box for Word, shown in Figure 2-17, page 54, contains a new settings group that allows you to print drafts of your work and conserve paper at the same time. You can also scale your final output to fit the dimensions of various sizes of paper, including letter, legal, and several envelope sizes.

The Pages Per Sheet option prints the pages of your multipage document as thumbnails in multiples of 2, 4, 6, 8, or 16 pages per sheet of paper. The default setting is 1, which prints the usual one page per sheet of paper at full-scale size. This option is useful for checking the overall appearance of a long document's pages to ensure that the layout transitions smoothly from page to page and that the positioning of text and other elements, such as graphics, are appealing to the reader.

Use the Scale To Paper Size option to select a different size sheet to which you can scale the content of your documents' pages. Like the reduce/enlarge feature found on most photocopy machines, this option essentially reduces or enlarges the font size and graphics during a single print operation to accommodate the selected page size option. In addition to the No Scaling (default), Letter (8½ × 11), and Legal (8½ × 14) size options, there are three other alternative page sizes and five envelope sizes.

Printing the Document and Watching the Print Queue

When you're finished setting printing options, click OK in the Print dialog box to send your document to the printer. After a moment, you'll see a message box indicating that your document has been submitted. (If you have turned on the Background Printing option in Word, you won't see this message box.) To help manage printing problems (such as out-of-paper error messages) and to get you back to your document as fast as possible, Windows stores all printing jobs in a printing list or *queue* until they've been entirely transferred to your printer's memory or stored in the Windows printing queue.

If you ever need to look at your system's printing queue—for example, if you need to cancel or pause a printing job—just double-click the printer icon that appears on the right side of the taskbar when the printing queue is active. The window that appears will show you all the pending printing jobs, and if you select a document in the list, you can use the commands on the Document menu to pause or cancel the printing job. You shouldn't need to monitor the printing queue often, but if you have to do some troubleshooting, it's nice to know how.

Troubleshooting Your Printer

Because the printing process involves so many variables—printer drivers, ports, cables, paper, toner, and the mechanical process of transferring an electronic image to paper—you'll likely experience a few minor printing problems from time to time. If you're working on a network, you should be especially conscious of what can go wrong when you send documents to a shared printer. Because your files are sent to a remote network printing queue rather than to your own system's print queue, you probably won't see an error message if something goes wrong. To give you a hand, here's a list of solutions you can try if you run into trouble. For more information, check your printer documentation or talk to your system administrator.

- If Windows displays an error message when you try to print, read the message carefully and try to resolve the problem. The most common errors are printers whose power is off, printers that are out of paper or missing a tray, or printers that are off line. Check your printer first to be sure that it's on, has the correct type of paper, and has no paper jam, and then verify that your printer cables are properly connected. An error message typically looks something like this:

- If your printer control panel (if it has one) displays an error message, check your printer documentation for the specific meaning. The most common message is "paper jam," meaning one or more pieces of paper have wedged themselves into the printing mechanism. Turn off your printer, unplug the power cord, and then open the printer and address the problem. If you're using a laser printer or ink-jet printer, you'll also need to clean it periodically to remove loose bits of toner or ink. If you can't fix the problem, call your printer's manufacturer for technical support, or call an authorized dealer for advice or service.

- If you're printing on a network, you might not receive an error message when something goes wrong. Occasionally, the network server that controls your workgroup printer might fail and will need to be restarted by the system administrator. However, the most common problem with printers used by a workgroup is that there is no paper in the tray, or the wrong type of paper is loaded. (For example, a close friend of ours—you know who you are!—loves to put a special letterhead in the tray and leave it for others to discover that it's decorating their documents.)

- If your document doesn't look the same on the page as it did on the screen, you need to verify that you have the correct printer driver installed. Check the Name list box in the Print dialog box. Also be careful about printing from a computer other than the one you created your document on. Although different versions of Office applications are compatible, newer computers might have a different collection of fonts or page settings. In addition, each printer model produces slightly different results.

CHAPTER 3

Managing Documents: From Your Hard Disk to the Internet

A *file* is an electronic storage container on disk used to hold valuable information permanently. Files let you retain important data between computing sessions so that you can work on a report one day and then pick up where you left off the next day. In the Microsoft Windows operating system, files are stored in folders, and each file has its own unique *pathname*. The pathname is the list of folders that describes the path taken from the first level of folders on the drive down to the current folder.

When you save information in a Microsoft Office application, you create a file, or *document*, on disk that you can use again later or share with others. In this chapter, you'll learn how to open documents, save them, and close them in Office applications. You'll also learn how to search for documents on your hard disk, share them over the Internet, and use properties to add tracking information to a document. Although each Office application creates documents in a slightly different format, the process of working with documents is the same, so we can teach it to you in one chapter. After you read this chapter, you'll be prepared to work through the application-specific sections in this book.

Opening an Existing Document

You can use four techniques to open Office documents on your system. If an Office application isn't running, the fastest method is to click Open Office Document on the Start menu, or to click the Open Office Document button on the Office Shortcut Bar. If you're working in an Office application, your best bet is to choose Open from the File menu, or to click the Open button on the Standard toolbar. Figure 3-1 shows the dialog box that appears when you open a document in Microsoft Word. (A similar dialog box appears in each Office application.)

Open

The Open dialog box displays the files and folders in the last folder you used in your application. (The last folder is often called the *current* folder, because that's the place Office puts your files by default.) The name of the current folder is displayed in the Look In box at the top of the dialog box, and the files and folders located in the current folder are displayed below in a list box. Office documents are identified by a tiny application icon next to the filename, and folders are identified by a folder icon. To open a document file displayed in the list box, just

FIGURE 3-1.
The Open dialog box contains several features you can use to find and open Office documents.

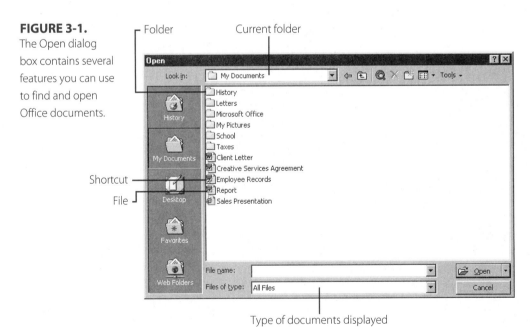

double-click the filename, and it will appear ready for work in your Office application.

Because a typical computer hard disk holds dozens of folders and thousands of files, the Open dialog box includes several features that you can use to locate and open a particular document. For example, you can control the type of files that the dialog box displays by choosing an entry in the Files Of Type drop-down list box. Figure 3-1 shows a typical Open dialog box in Word, in which the All Word Documents option is selected in the Files Of Type list box. This particular setting means that only files identified as being created by Word will appear in the list.

Other files probably exist in this particular folder, such as programs and data files, but the criterion of displaying only files identified as Word

---

Opening Your Most Recently Used Files

In addition to using the Open command, you can open the last few files you have modified by clicking the file's name at the bottom of the File menu or typing the underlined number. This technique is quicker than using the Open command, because you bypass searching for the file using the Open dialog box. (You can adjust the number of files listed by choosing Options on the Tools menu, clicking the General tab, and changing the number in the Recently Used File List text box.)

The following illustration shows four recently used Word files at the bottom of the Word File menu. The file in the first position is the last document you used in the active application, the file in the second position is the second to last document you used, and so on. Each time you open a new file, the new name is added to the top of the list, and the file at the bottom is dropped off. The filename also includes a pathname to the file, unless the file is located in the current folder. The pathname lists the subfolders containing the file (space permitting), which can help you locate the file later if you need to.

<u>1</u> Local-National Govt
<u>2</u> C:\My Documents\Client Letter
<u>3</u> C:\...\Creative Services Agreement
<u>4</u> C:\My Documents\Published Work

Another way to open a recently used file is to click the Start button on the taskbar, point to Documents, and then click the filename you want to open. The Documents shortcut menu that pops up shows recently used files from Office applications as well as from many other programs. Clicking the filename will open the newest version of the associated application if the program isn't already running.

Documents prevents them from appearing. (An exception to this rule is that most Office 2000 applications will also display HTML documents in the Open dialog box, because the HTML format can be edited by most Office applications.) Narrowing the display criteria using the Files Of Type drop-down list box is especially helpful if you have many files in a folder. If you have dozens of unrelated files and utilities in a folder, it will take you longer to find the file you want to open.

 TIP

> **Use All Files to See Everything**
>
> The options in the Files Of Type drop-down list box change from application to application. If you want to see all the files in a particular folder, select the All Files criterion.

Browsing Through Folders

You can locate files in different folders by browsing through your computer's drive and folder structure using the controls in the Open dialog box. Each computer has its own set of disk drives that are used to store and retrieve files located on different types of storage media. Typical computers have a floppy disk drive, a hard disk drive, a CD-ROM drive, perhaps a tape-backup drive, an Internet connection, and, in many cases, a connection to one or more network drives (or file servers). You can look for files on different drives by clicking the Look In drop-down list box and then clicking the disk drive you want to examine. Figure 3-2 shows the available disk drives for one of the computers we used to write this book.

After you select a disk drive in the Look In list box, the list of folders and files in the dialog box is updated to match those on the disk you selected. You can examine the files and subfolders contained in a folder by double-clicking the folder in the list box. Each time you open

FIGURE 3-2.
To look for a file on a different drive, click the Look In drop-down list box, and click the drive.

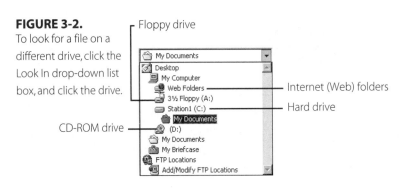

Up One
Level

a new folder, its contents are displayed in the list box. (Some users call this process *drilling down* into the directory structure of a disk.) To move back up to the folder on the previous level, simply click the Up One Level button in the dialog box. Remember that at any time you can open a file you find by double-clicking the filename in the dialog box, or by highlighting the file and clicking the Open button.

 TIP

> **Hook Up to the Internet**
>
> If you'd like to create a link to an FTP (File Transfer Protocol) site for transferring files over the Internet via the Open dialog box, click the Add/Modify FTP Locations entry in the Look In drop-down list box. Office will display a dialog box asking you for the name of the FTP site you want to use for uploading or downloading, plus the password required to connect. After you establish the Internet connection once, your site will appear in the Open dialog box under the FTP Locations entry, and you can jump to the FTP site with one mouse click!
>
> You can also click the Search The Web button in the Open dialog box to open the Search page of your Internet browser.

Search
The Web

Previewing Files Using the Open Dialog Box

As you browse through files and folders in the Open dialog box, you might see a document you'd like to look at more closely. Fortunately, the Open dialog box contains several options that you can use to learn more about a file's size, type, and contents before you open it. Using these preview features, you can avoid wasting time by opening the wrong file. (See Figure 3-3, on the following page, for a description of the commands.)

Figure 3-3 shows the Open dialog box after the Preview command has been selected. Notice that an extra window appears in the dialog box to display the contents of the document highlighted in the list box. (You can use the scroll bars to move through it.) The Preview button is quite useful—it gives you a quick look at a document (though in abbreviated form) so that you can decide whether you want to open it. (Sometimes the filename alone doesn't give you enough information.)

 TIP

> To quickly preview all the documents in a folder, choose Preview, and then use the Down arrow key in the File list box to select each file in the folder one at a time. In this case, the Down arrow key works faster than clicking with the mouse.

FIGURE 3-3.
A Views menu in the Open dialog box lets you display different information about files before you open them.

Click Properties to display useful information about how the file was created and by whom.

Click Details to display the file size, document type, and time the file was last used.

Click List to display files as a simple list (the default view).

Click Preview to display a preview image of the file or a text excerpt.

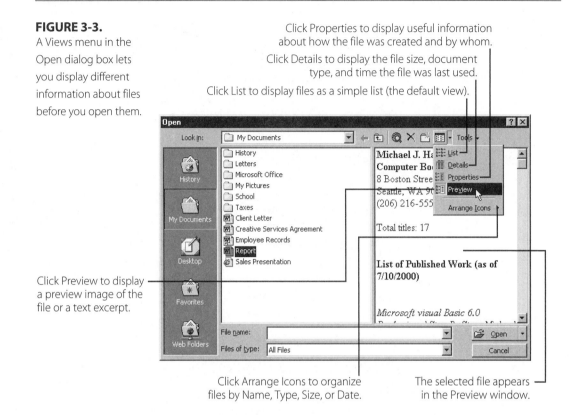

Click Arrange Icons to organize files by Name, Type, Size, or Date.

The selected file appears in the Preview window.

Performing an Automated Search for a File

The Open dialog box gives you a few advanced methods for searching for files and performing routine hard disk management chores such as renaming and deleting files. These commands are located on the Tools menu in the Open dialog box. The most important command, Find, lets you use one or more of the following characteristics when you look for a file:

- Part or all of a file's name

- The document type of the file (that is, Word, Excel, or Access)

- One or more words (called a text string) in the text of the file or in the file's property sheet

- The amount of time elapsed since the file was last modified

- The folder and subfolders to search

> **Use the Nifty Windows Find Utility**
>
> In addition to searching for files in Office applications using the Open dialog box, you can also use a separate utility program called Find that's included with Windows. To run the Find utility to search for files, click the Windows Start button, point to Find, and click the Files Or Folders command. You can even choose Using Microsoft Outlook from the Find shortcut menu to search for words or phrases in your electronic mail messages or in Office documents.

Searching for a Filename

SEE ALSO
In the section "Searching Subfolders," page 67, you'll learn how to extend this search to multiple folders on your hard disk.

If you don't know where a particular file is located on disk, but you do remember part of its name, you can swiftly track it down using the File Name box in the Open dialog box. For example, to list all the files in the current folder that have the word *Work* in their name, type *Work* in the File Name box, and press Enter. (Or you could type the partial word *wor* because case doesn't matter and part of a file's name can be used to search the folder.) Figure 3-4 shows the results of such a search in the My Documents folder. To open the Published Work document that appears, you would double-click the filename in the list box.

Searching for a Document Type

As you learned earlier, you can also search for a particular class of document by using the Files Of Type drop-down list box. By default, each Office application sets the file type in this box to the type of document it creates. For example, Word sets the Files Of Type list box to All Word

FIGURE 3-4.
The File Name text box lets you search for a file using part or all of its name.

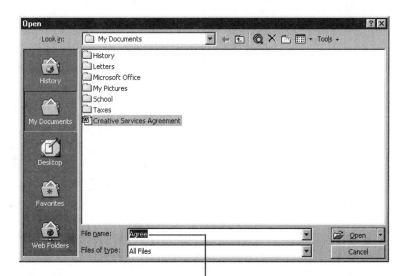

Type a partial filename to display one or more
matching documents in the current folder.

Documents. But at times you'll want to change this value. For example, to view all the text files in a folder, you would select Text Files in the Files Of Type list box. (Word can open and edit text files, which are unformatted documents with the .txt filename extension.)

Opening Files as Read-Only Documents

The Open dialog box also allows you to open files as protected, or *read-only*, documents, meaning that users can open and examine the files but not change them. To open a file in this way, select the file you want to open in the Open dialog box, and then click the drop-down list arrow on the right side of the Open button to display a pop-up menu of editing choices. To open the file as a read-only file, click Open Read-Only. You might also choose Open As Copy, which creates a separate copy of the file on disk for editing, or Open In Browser, which loads the selected file into the default Internet browser on your system (typically Microsoft Internet Explorer or Netscape Navigator).

Using the Find Command

You can run more advanced document searches in the Open dialog box by using the Find command on the Tools menu, as shown in the following illustration.

Click Find to search for elusive documents.

When you click the Find command, you'll see a dialog box similar to the one shown in Figure 3-5. We've added several search criteria to the dialog box to show you how this interesting feature works: a contents search that looks for documents containing the words *book of the year*, a date search that looks for documents created in the last month, and a number of words search that looks for documents containing at least 500 words. (By default, the Find command also added a fourth criterion entitled File Of Type Is All Word Documents to the list, because we built the search in Word. This criteria was an optional setting that we accepted.) When you click the Find Now button, only the documents that satisfy each of the search criteria will appear in the Open dialog box. (The search might take a few minutes to run.)

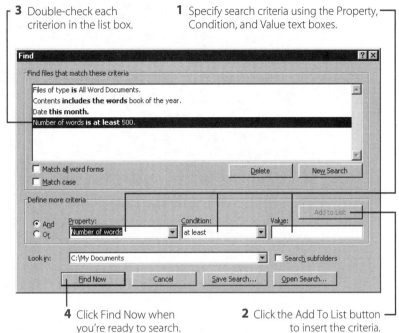

FIGURE 3-5.
The Find dialog box allows you to compose simple or complex searches by using document properties and unique conditions and values.

3 Double-check each criterion in the list box.

1 Specify search criteria using the Property, Condition, and Value text boxes.

4 Click Find Now when you're ready to search.

2 Click the Add To List button to insert the criteria.

Getting Started

 NOTE

The criteria you select in the Find dialog box remain active until you change or clear them. If you want to compose a search without the Find search criteria, clean the slate by clicking the New Search button.

 TIP

If you have a particularly complex combination of search criteria in the Find dialog box, you can save the search for later use by clicking the Save Search button and entering a search name (say, Bestsellers). When you're ready to use the search criteria again later, click the Open Search button and in the Open Search dialog box, click the search you want to run, and then click the Open button.

Searching Subfolders

In our opinion, the most important feature of the Find command is the Search Subfolders check box at the bottom right of the dialog box, which forces Office to search all the subfolders of the current folder for the search criteria you have created. (See Figure 3-6, on the next page.) This simple feature lets you search dozens of folders automatically for the file you want to open. Best of all, you can specify the starting point for the search by clicking the drive or folder name in the Look In drop-down

FIGURE 3-6.

Select the Search Subfolders check box to perform multiple folder searches.

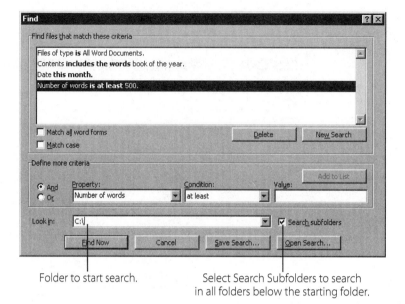

Folder to start search.　　　Select Search Subfolders to search
in all folders below the starting folder.

list box before you start the search. Using the Search Subfolders check box, you can plow through hundreds of files in seconds.

Deleting Files, Renaming Files, and Creating New Folders

An extremely useful feature of the Open dialog box is that it lets you delete and rename files in the current folder and create new folders on your system. This functionality lets you do some on-the-fly hard disk management as you work in Office applications, obviating the need to run Windows Explorer every time you need to delete or rename a file.

The simplest procedure is deleting a file. To remove a file from the current directory, highlight the file, press the Delete key, and then click Yes when you're asked to confirm your deletion. You can also click the Delete button on the Open dialog box toolbar to delete the selected file.

Delete

To rename a file, highlight the file you want to rename using the keyboard or mouse, and then click the filename. (Take care not to double-click the file, or you'll open it. If you're using the mouse, pause a moment between clicks.) When you rename a file, Office places a rectangle around the filename and highlights it, as shown in Figure 3-7. You can then start typing to delete the current filename, or you can press the Right or Left arrow key to move the mouse pointer to a particular location in

FIGURE 3-7.
The Open dialog box also lets you delete files, rename files, and create folders.

Click this button to delete the selected file.

Click this button to create a new folder.

To rename a file, select the file in the list box, wait a moment, and then click the file again to highlight the filename in a selection rectangle.

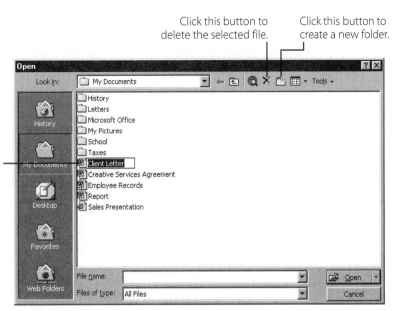

the name to correct it or add to it. When you're finished making your changes, press Enter to write the new name to disk.

Alternatively, you can select a file in the Open dialog box and click Rename on the Tools menu to change the file's name. When you click Rename, Office highlights the file inside a rectangle, and you can use the arrow keys and editing keys (such as Delete, Home, and End) to change or retype the filename.

New Folder

The Open dialog box also allows you to create new folders on your system. To try this technique, click the New Folder button in the Open dialog box, and specify a folder name in the dialog box that appears. Office creates new folders in the current directory by default, so if you want to create folders in other folders, you should browse to them first using the Look In drop-down list box. New folders are especially useful when you know you'll be creating several new or revised files in the current editing session.

Saving Documents and Web Pages

After you open a file in an Office application, you can add to it or revise it based on your needs and interests. When you're ready to save a version of your document to disk permanently, you must save the file. Saving a file is an important step because the changes you make to your document are stored only in temporary memory (RAM) until you transfer them to disk. If you should accidentally pull the power plug on your computer, or if your power fails in a thunderstorm, the changes you made since your last save will be lost. (This thorny problem is the dark side of personal computing, but you'll learn how to plan for this rather unlikely event later in the chapter.) In this section, you'll learn how to save Office documents using the Save and Save As commands, and you'll learn how to create Web pages (HTML documents) using the Save As Web Page command.

Using the Save Command

Save

If your file already has a name, you can update it on disk by choosing Save from the File menu. The Save command copies the Office document you're working on from computer memory to disk, preserving it in a transferable form and safeguarding it from loss if your application closes suddenly because of power failure or other problems. It's a good idea to save your editing changes to disk every 10 minutes or so, either by choosing Save or by clicking the Save button on the toolbar. The Save command doesn't display a dialog box unless your file needs a name. In that case, Office displays the Save As dialog box, which we'll discuss in the next section.

 TIP

> The keyboard shortcut for the Save command is Ctrl+S. If your document doesn't have a filename yet, you'll be prompted for one.

Using the Save As Command

To assign a filename to your Office document, choose Save As from the File menu. The Save As command lets you specify the filename, disk location (such as A: for the attached floppy disk drive), and folder location of the file, and also lets you set a variety of application-specific options, including the document format of the file. Figure 3-8 shows the dialog box that appears when you use the Save As command in Word. (Word has suggested the filename *Summer Picnic*, because those are the first words in the document.) If you worked through the section covering the Open dialog box earlier in this chapter, you'll recognize several of the remaining dialog box options.

The Save In drop-down list box lets you specify the disk and folder location for your file. Office places your file in the current folder (the folder

Managing Documents: From Your Hard Disk to the Internet **CHAPTER 3** **71**

FIGURE 3-8.
The Save As dialog box lets you assign a name to your document and save it to disk.

Current folder   Up One Level   Create New Folder

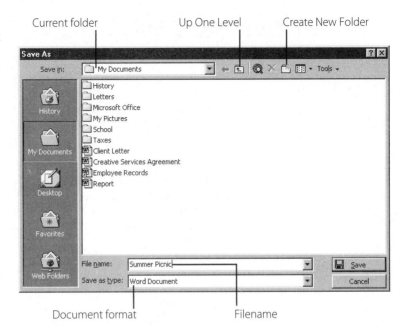

Document format   Filename

displayed in the list box) unless you specify a different location. You can open a subfolder (a folder below the current folder) by double-clicking the folder icon you want to open. (This moves you down a level in the folder hierarchy, or "tree.") If you want to move up a level in the folder hierarchy, click the Up One Level button. As you browse through the folders on your system, feel free to use the commands on the Views menu at the top of the dialog box (List, Details, Properties, and Preview) to get more information about the files you see.

After you set the disk and folder location for your document, you can assign a name to it using the File Name text box. Each file must have its own unique name in the folder so that you can differentiate it from other files and reference it by name. A temporary name will automatically appear highlighted in the File Name text box when you open the Save As dialog box. (In Word, the temporary name comes from the first line in your document.) To place your own filename in the File Name text box, type in the new name. (Be sure to pick a descriptive phrase that reflects the file's contents.) Because your Office applications were written specifically for Windows, you can type up to 255 characters for your filename, with a few typographic caveats. (See the "What Name Do I Choose?" sidebar.) When you're ready to save the file to disk, click the Save button or press Enter.

What Name Do I Choose?

Naming a file isn't as challenging as naming a baby, though you do need to follow some important rules to get it right. Give your file a name related to its contents that you can easily remember later. In other words, don't type the first thought that comes into your head, but choose a few words that will easily distinguish the file from the other documents on your system. (We think it's a good idea to include names and dates in filenames so that later you can tell similar files apart.) Fortunately, filenames in the Windows environment are no longer limited to the eight-character restriction imposed by MS-DOS, so you can type up to 255 characters and include spaces, uppercase letters, and lowercase letters. (Although you can type up to 255 characters in the File Name box, the 255-character total also includes the characters that make up the path to the file, including the names of folders and subfolders.) We recommend that you make filenames two to four words long using 10 to 30 characters so that each filename fits well in dialog boxes. Valid filenames can include letters, numbers, and all but the following symbols:

/ \ < > * ? | : ;

For example, the following filenames are appropriate for typical Office documents:

Current Status Memo (2-1999)

Fall Comdex 2000 Slide Presentation

2nd Quarter '01 Report

Fortune 500 Customers

new hires [probationary] @10-15-99

Saving in a Different Document Format

SEE ALSO
To learn how to save Office documents in Web page (HTML) format, see "Saving Documents as Web Pages," page 75.

After you specify your file's name and folder location, you might want to change the format you're using to save the document. Each Office application uses its own unique document format to translate the words and pictures on the screen into a document that you can print on paper and store on disk. Accordingly, you can't move documents from one word processor to another until you pick a format that both applications can read. Fortunately, Office applications allow you to save documents in a variety of different formats so that you can open your work in many other applications.

To specify a different document format, click the Save As Type drop-down list box in the Save As dialog box, and then click the format you want to use. Each Office application supports a different list of document formats, so you'll have to experiment a little to see which applications you can use. (You can also use the Web Page format, which will prepare your document for viewing in a Web browser and editing in other applications.) With some experimenting, you can learn to use the Save As Type feature to exchange files between many different programs; for example, you might share an important Excel worksheet from your office with Lotus 1-2-3 users at another office. Figure 3-9 shows the Save As Type drop-down list box in Word.

FIGURE 3-9.
The Save As Type drop-down list box lets you save your file in other formats.

Saving Files Automatically in Word

The most useful hidden feature in Word's Save As dialog box is the Save AutoRecover option, which directs Office to automatically save a recoverable copy of your document at a time interval you specify. Save AutoRecover helps you avoid losing unsaved changes in your document because of a system crash (where you lose unsaved data), a power outage, or some other electronic disaster that terminates your application before you save your document using the Save As command.

To enable Word's Save AutoRecover feature, Open the Save As dialog box, click the Tools menu, click General Options, and then select the Save AutoRecover Info Every: check box, shown in Figure 3-10, on the next page. Office will save a copy of your document to the temporary directory on your hard disk at the specified time interval. By default, Office updates this temporary file with your changes every 10 minutes,

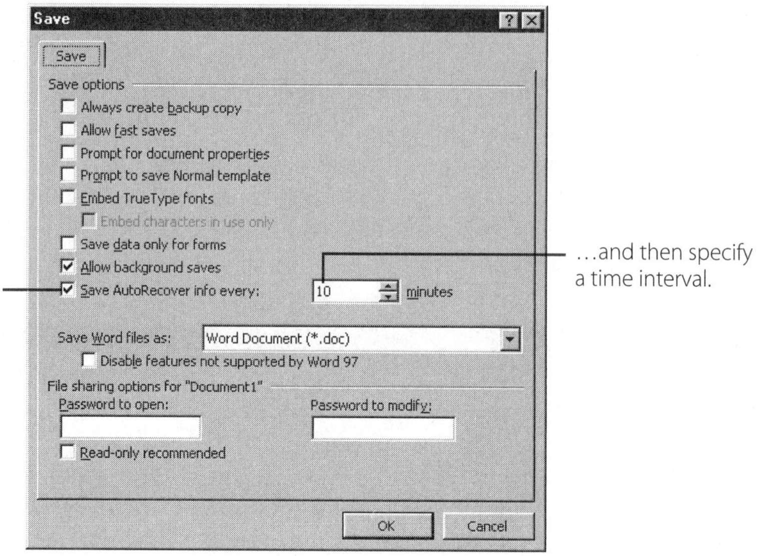

FIGURE 3-10.
Word's Auto Recover feature prevents inadvertent data loss.

Click this option to save a copy of your file automatically...

...and then specify a time interval.

though you can adjust this interval using the scroll box in the Save dialog box. Note, however, that automatic saves don't affect the document you create using the Save command—this file is always separate and contains only the information you specifically save.

Recovering from a Crash

If you do encounter a power loss, a system freeze, a program failure, or another problem that causes you to crash, restart Word, and Office will recover the files that were active when your program crashed. (You'll have one file for each open document.) If the recovered files look correct, save them to disk formally using the Save As or Save command and you'll be back in business. Of course, this works only if you actually enabled the AutoRecover feature before Word bombed. Even then, you'll probably lose the data you entered since your last automatic save. But if you're a little lazy about saving on your own, this airbag feature might save you hours of frustration down the road. (Aren't your files worth it?)

Saving Files Automatically in Excel

Excel doesn't have a Save AutoRecover check box in the Save As dialog box, but you can still configure it to save files automatically for you. Choose Add-Ins from the Excel Tools menu, and then select the Autosave Add-in in the list box and click OK. This action places the AutoSave command on the Tools menu; you can use this command to save your files automatically at set intervals. When you click AutoSave, you can specify how often the file is saved, and whether Excel should save just the current (active) workbook or all the open workbooks.

The AutoSave feature isn't available in Microsoft PowerPoint, Microsoft Outlook, or Microsoft Publisher. However, Access saves database information as you enter it, so you have some measure of automatic protection in that application.

Saving Documents as Web Pages

In Office 2000, you now have the option of saving files in a special Web page format known as HTML (hypertext markup language). This feature allows you to create documents that you can distribute widely by means of Web pages and intranets, and that others can view in Internet browsers such as Internet Explorer and Netscape Navigator. Office applications also allow you to view your Web pages as they will appear on the Web by using the new Web Page Preview command.

To save, or *publish*, an Office document as a Web page, follow these steps:

1 Open the document you plan to save as a Web page.

2 From the File menu, choose Save As Web Page. You'll see a dialog box similar to the one shown in Figure 3-11, on the next page.

The Save As Web Page dialog box is similar to the Save As dialog box. However, the Save As Type list box is set to Web Page, which will save your file using the .htm extension. In addition, the Page Title option lets you control the title text that will appear at the top of your Web page when it's loaded in the Web browser.

3 Click Save to save your document as a Web page.

Office will create an HTML document in the folder you speci-fied. In some cases, Office will also create a folder bearing the

FIGURE 3-11.

The Save As Web Page command includes options that control how your Office document will be converted into a Web page.

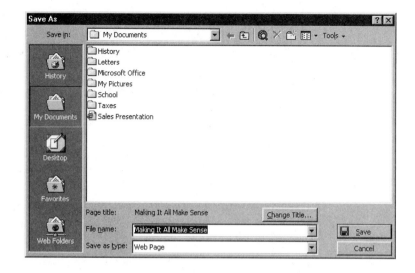

file's name that contains a few extra files that are necessary to view the Web page. (The complete list varies from application to application.) You can now distribute this file as a completed Web page on the Internet or your corporate intranet—you can view it in either Internet Explorer or Netscape Navigator.

 NOTE

Excel, PowerPoint, and Access have a few additional Web page features that you can control using the Save As Web Page command. For more information about these features, see the individual application sections in this book.

Using Web Page Preview

If you'd like to see what your Web page will look like in an Internet browser, use the Web Page Preview command to check out all the details. We recommend this step especially if you plan to distribute the document on the Internet or to a number of people on your corporate intranet. Follow these steps:

1 Choose Web Page Preview from the File menu.

Office converts the active document to Web page format and displays it in your system's default browser (typically Internet Explorer).

2 Use the browser to verify the content, layout, and functionality of the Web page.

3 When you're finished examining the Web page, close the browser and return to your Office application.

TIP

Is Web Page Preview Necessary?

Do you really need to check out the content and layout of your completed Web page? In a word, yes. Although Office applications can convert most document features to HTML seamlessly, the nature of HTML means that a few of the items might appear on your Web page in a different place than they did in your Office application. For this reason, it always makes sense to spend a little quality time verifying the content and layout of your Web page after you create it in Office. In other words, it's a little more important than using Print Preview before you generate hard copy.

Creating a New Document

SEE ALSO

Creating a new database in Access is a different endeavor, and you'll need to follow slightly different steps. For more information, see Chapter 34, "Databasics."

When Office applications start, they typically present you with a new, empty document to work in. (You can set Outlook—depending on the version—to display your personal planning calendar, your e-mail Inbox, or the Outlook Today page.) Often you'll start working with this blank document, customizing it to match your preferences, or you'll open an existing file and start adding to it. However, at other times you'll want to create additional blank documents to work in. Perhaps you'll want to split one document into two, or, after working on one project, you'll remember that you need to start another. If this happens, you can quickly open a new file in your Office application. The following section shows you how.

To open a new document in Word, Excel, PowerPoint, or Publisher, choose New from the File menu. When you choose New in Word, for example, you'll see the dialog box shown in Figure 3-12, on the next page.

The New dialog box presents a series of tabs that contain standard document *templates* (preformatted documents) from which you can choose. Highlight the template you want the new document to be based on, and then click OK. If you want to create a new, blank document based on the default template (without first seeing the New dialog box), click the New button located on the left side of the Standard toolbar.

New

TIP

You can also open a new document by choosing New Office Document from the Start menu or by clicking the New Office Document button on the Office Shortcut Bar. The New Office Document dialog box that appears presents templates for all the Office applications organized on separate tabs.

FIGURE 3-12.
The New dialog
box in Word.

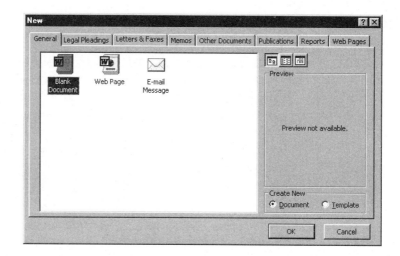

Closing a Document

When you're finished working with a document, you can close it by choosing the Close command on the File menu or by clicking the document's Close button. If you have any unsaved changes in the document, you'll see the dialog box shown in Figure 3-13, prompting you to save your changes. (If the Office Assistant is running, you'll see the same options in its balloon.) If you click Yes, your changes will be saved to disk under the current filename, and Office will close the document.

If the document doesn't have a filename yet, the Save As dialog box appears prompting you to save the document. If you click No, your changes will be discarded and your document will close. If you click Cancel, the Close command will be canceled, the dialog box will close, and you'll be returned to your document.

Take care not to click the No button in the Save As dialog box by mistake, or you will permanently loose the information in your document. As a safeguard, always use the Save command before you use the Close command.

FIGURE 3-13.
Office warns you if you
try to close a file that
contains unsaved
changes.

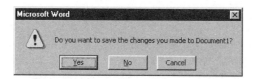

The Close command is most useful when you have several documents open and you want to close one to get it out of the way. (In addition to removing the clutter, closing unneeded files can help you save system resources, or memory.) The Close command operates only on the active, or *current*, document, so it closes only the file in the highlighted window. Alternatively, if you're ready to exit your application, choose Exit from the File menu to close any open documents and exit the application in one step. Like Close, the Exit command also prompts you to retain unsaved changes (if you have any).

Working with Property Sheets

If you have used Windows Explorer to look at the files on your hard disk, or if you have clicked Details on the Views menu in the Open or Save As dialog box, you know that Windows stores information about the size, document type, and modification date for each file on the system. These useful facts will probably give you enough information to open your files and keep them organized, though at times you might require additional information to determine a file's origins or make the best use of its contents. Office addresses this need by attaching a unique set of *properties* to each file as it's created. A property sheet contains information about the content, revision history, author, and attributes of a document, as well as other information unique to the originating application. Some of the fields in the property sheet, such as the file size, application name, and revision dates, are created automatically by the Office application, while others are added independently by you, the user.

To display a property sheet in an Office application, choose Properties from the File menu. (In Access, the command is called Database Properties.) Figure 3-14, on the following page, shows the property sheet for a Word document.

This particular sheet has five tabs of information, which you can access by clicking the tab names at the top of the dialog box. Most of the information on the Summary tab pertains to the content and author of the document, and is typically entered by the author. If you take the time to complete these fields, the members of your workgroup (if you have one) will better understand your goals for creating the document. Summary information could be especially helpful a few years down the road, say when the author of the documents has moved on.

FIGURE 3-14.
Clicking the Properties command displays useful summary information about the active document.

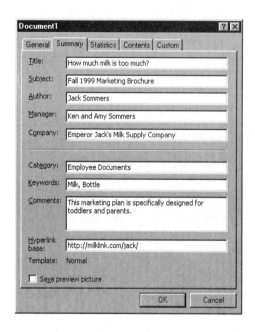

 TIP

> Take care to use standard, memorable words in your property sheets so that you can search for them later using the Find command in the Open dialog box. And watch your spelling, because a search can find only exact word matches. (For example, if you type *Grey* in the subject box, a search won't find *Gray*.)

The most useful Property tab for people who work with text a lot (such as writers, editors, and desktop publishing specialists) is the Statistics tab, shown in Figure 3-15. The data on the Statistics tab is created entirely by your Office application; it features the file's creation date, modification date, author name, revision number, and the total editing time elapsed in the document. The tab lists other important statistics related to the file, including the number of pages, paragraphs, words, and characters in the file. If you're writing an essay or article that needs to be a certain length, the Statistics tab will probably be quite helpful to you.

 TIP

> If you write articles for a living, use the Statistics tab to track how many words you write and how much time you spend doing it.

FIGURE 3-15.
The Statistics tab displays useful information about the file's origin, editing history, and length.

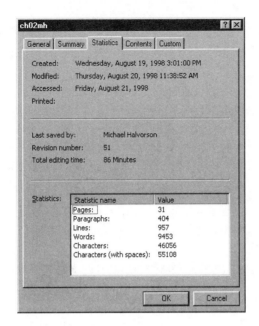

The information in a property sheet is stored in the same file as the document it describes, but the data doesn't appear on the screen when you work with the document or on paper when you print. However, it's always available by means of the Properties command to everyone who uses your file, so be aware that when you give your file to others, those users will have access to all the information presented in the property sheet. (For example, it might be embarrassing to charge a magazine client for a business article of 10,000 words, when the client can see from your summary sheet that you wrote only 8,780.)

Be sure to use this feature to your own advantage, too. If you have a question about the origin of an Office document you're looking at—a file on the Internet, for example, or a document on a disk you just received—open the file and use the Properties command to learn everything you can about the document. Property sheets are excellent sources of information, especially in workgroups.

⭐ TIP

To print the information contained in a Word document's property sheet, choose Print from the File menu, select the Document Properties option in the Print What drop-down list box, and then click OK.

Sharing Documents in a Workgroup

As you create documents on your computer, you should do your best to organize them intuitively in folders and copy them regularly to backup disks for safekeeping. If you work in a *workgroup*—a networked collection of computers sharing files, printers, and other resources—you should also make some of your documents available electronically to your colleagues. You might share floppy disks from time to time, but if your co-workers are using Windows, the Office 2000 applications, and networking software, you can distribute your documents quickly and effectively right from your desktop. The following section describes a few ways you can accomplish this on local area networks (LANs) and larger corporate intranets.

Saving and Retrieving Files on a Network

Let's say you just completed a new marketing plan and want to send it out electronically to your co-workers, both down the hall and across town, so that they can comment on it and revise it. One option is to place the marketing document on a shared network drive to which everyone in your workgroup has access. Network drives are typically maintained by the workgroup system administrator, who monitors the free space on the drive, manages the network hardware, and provides support and training. Ask a co-worker or your system administrator what network drives are available to you and how you can establish a connection. A useful tool for browsing the network and moving files back and forth is Windows Explorer, shown in Figure 3-16.

To use Windows Explorer to copy a file to the network, follow these steps:

1 Close your Office document (you can't copy open files), and then start Windows Explorer by clicking the Start button, pointing to Programs, and then clicking Windows Explorer. Locate the Office document you want to copy to the network by browsing through the Folders list box, and then right-click the file to display the shortcut menu.

2 Choose Copy from the shortcut menu to copy the file to the Clipboard.

3 Scroll to the top of the Folders list box on the left side, and then click the network drive you want to use. (The name of this drive

FIGURE 3-16.
You can copy your
workgroup documents
to the network using
Windows Explorer.

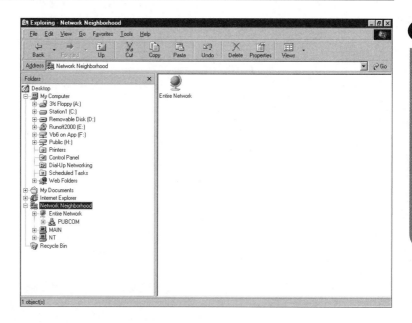

will vary from system to system.) Browse through the folders on the network drive until you find the folder in which you want to place the file. (Be sure to place your file into a folder to which everyone in your workgroup has access.)

4 From the Explorer Edit menu, choose Paste. A copy of the file appears on the network drive (at the bottom of the file list), ready for review.

Contact Your Co-Workers

Notify your workgroup that the file has been posted (by electronic mail or another method), and tell them how you want them to work with the file. To copy the revised document back to your hard disk at a later time, just reverse these steps. (You might also want to give the revised file a new name to differentiate it from the original file.)

Routing Files Using Microsoft Exchange

If you want to route your document to a specific list of users in your workgroup, you can use the Routing Recipient command to send the document along a specific path. This command lets you set up a review chain that leverages the skills of each person in the workgroup. This feature uses Microsoft Exchange to send your file from user to user over the network, complete with routing instructions. To route a document:

1 Choose Send To from the File menu, and then choose Routing Recipient from the submenu. You'll see a dialog box that lets you specify which users should receive the document and the order in which they should receive it.

2 To add users, click the Address button in the dialog box, select the names of users from your Personal Address Book, and then click OK.

  Figure 3-17 shows a sample routing slip created in Word. You can include a brief message with the routing slip and adjust several routing options, including the distribution order, routing status, and return method.

FIGURE 3-17.
You can route a document to users in a particular order using the Routing Recipient command.

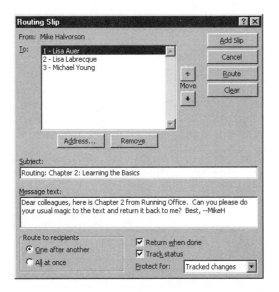

3 When you're ready to route your document, click the Route button, and Office will send your file to the first recipient by means of Microsoft Exchange. If you select the Return When Done option, your document will return to you automatically after everyone reviews it.

Sending Files by Electronic Mail

The slickest way to distribute Office documents over the workgroup network is to embed them in electronic mail messages. This approach has the advantage of sending files immediately to a set list of users in your workgroup, and allows you to type a longer, more stylized message than you can by using the Routing Recipient command. To send a file by electronic mail, simply create your document, and then point to Send To on the File menu and click Mail Recipient (As Attachment) on the submenu. The Mail Recipient command starts your mail editor and displays a dialog box you can use to compose your electronic mail message. Office places an icon in your message to represent the file you have included, and when your co-workers receive the message, they can double-click the icon to review the document and edit it on their own system.

Figure 3-18 shows a sample message created using the Mail Recipient (As Attachment) command in Word.

Notice how users in the workgroup are identified by their real names in the To and Cc (for *carbon copies*, now thoroughly antiquated) text boxes, and how the Word document (ch02mh.doc) appears as an icon in the body of the message. The composition window includes scroll bars so that you can type a long message and then format it using toolbar buttons or commands from the Format menu. When you're finished composing the message (be sure to include review instructions), click the Send button on the toolbar to distribute it. If you decide to cancel the message, click the Close button on the title bar, click No to discard your changes, and the message will be canceled. Note that the Mail Recipient command doesn't route one document and return a copy to you; rather, it simply sends a copy to everyone on the list. It's a less formal, but more storage-intensive, way to distribute documents in a workgroup environment.

FIGURE 3-18

You can send copies of your document by electronic mail using the Mail Recipient command.

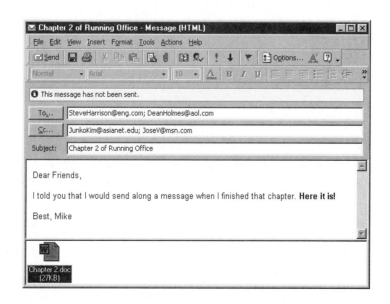

🔵 **Using Online Collaboration**

If you have access to a shared Web site on the Internet, you can use a new workgroup feature in Office 2000 called online collaboration to work collectively with your colleagues on Office documents. This feature is not a routing command, which allows users to edit a document sequentially (one after another), but an interactive feature that permits joint document editing and discussion over the Internet or a corporate intranet. In plain English, online collaboration means that your workgroup can edit a Word, Excel, or PowerPoint document as if you were all gathered together around the same computer. In reality, however, you'll each be using your own computer and discussing a single document that's located in a shared Web folder on the Internet.

Word, Excel, and PowerPoint support online collaboration by means of the Online Collaboration submenu, located on the Tools menu of each application. (See Figure 3-19 for a description of the three online collaboration commands.) To use this menu, you'll need two supporting Microsoft technologies: Microsoft NetMeeting and a Web server configured with the Microsoft Web Server Extensions. NetMeeting is a network scheduling program that is installed when you install Internet Explorer 5. Because Internet Explorer 5 is installed by default when you run the Office 2000 setup program, you probably have NetMeeting on your system now, unless you or your system administrator chose not to install it during setup.

FIGURE 3-19.
The Online Collaboration submenu allows you to discuss a document using the Web.

Start an online meeting using Microsoft NetMeeting.

Schedule an online meeting in your Outlook Calendar folder.

Connect to a Web discussion.

The Microsoft Office Web Server Extensions allow you to save, open, and manage documents on a Web site directly from Office 2000 programs. On the server side, this technology consists of ASP (Active Server Page) applications, a collection of Web Server Extensions, and a workgroup database server that acts as a repository for ASP applications. From the user's point of view, however, using all this Web server technology is easy—in an Office application you merely save files to a shared Web folder using the Save As command, and then use the Online Collaboration submenu to arrange for a joint meeting about the file.

NOTE

The Office Web Server Extensions aren't rocket science, but they are a rather new server technology, so we recommend that you send your system administrator a courteous e-mail message asking whether they have installed this enhancement on your Web server before you try using it. You might ask specifically whether you can manipulate Web folders directly from Office 2000 applications (like you've read about in *Running Office 2000*) and whether you can use the three online collaboration commands.

Scheduling a Collaboration Session

When you're ready to try online collaboration with your workgroup, follow these steps:

1 Open the document you want to discuss online in Word, Excel, or PowerPoint, and then choose Save As Web Page from the File menu.

2 In the File Name text box, type an Internet address and pathname that identifies the Web server you want to use, the shared folder you have access to, and the filename you're assigning, and then press Enter. For example, the pathname *http://officetest.microsoft.com/users/budget.htm* specifies the Web server *http://officetest.microsoft.com*, the folder */users*, and the filename *budget.htm*. If you are not already online, a dialog box appears so that you can connect to the server. Once you are connected, click the Save button to close the Save As dialog box.

NOTE

You'll need to ask your system administrator (or Web Master) for the Internet address of the Web server and the folder name you are authorized to use. In addition, you might need a special username and password to log on to the Web server.

SEE ALSO
You have several additional features available to you in Outlook, including the ability to check your workgroup's schedule online. To learn more about these features, see "Scheduling Meetings," page 1042.

3 Click the Online Collaboration submenu on the Tools menu, and then click Schedule Meeting.

The Schedule Meeting command starts Outlook (if it isn't already open) and displays the Meeting dialog box. This form gathers the necessary information to schedule an online discussion, or *chat session*, and uses the Outlook scheduling software to check the schedule of each participant.

4 Enter the necessary contact and scheduling information. A typical dialog box will look like Figure 3-20.

FIGURE 3-20.

The Schedule Meeting command uses Outlook to arrange a meeting time for the Web discussion.

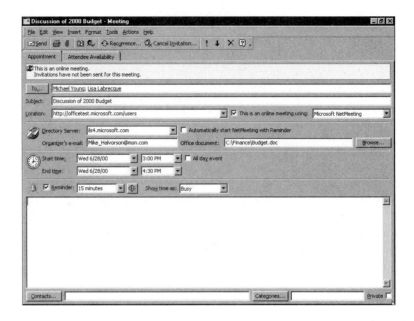

5 Click the Send button to send your meeting request to all attendees. Outlook will mail the meeting invitations and return the appropriate confirmation notices (or regrets) when each attendee has examined the message and agreed to the meeting.

Meeting Online

When the time comes for your online collaboration meeting, you can begin the conversation by choosing Meet Now to connect to the shared Web server and begin the chat. (This feature is available in Word, Excel, and PowerPoint only.) Follow these steps:

1 Click the Tools menu, choose the Online Collaboration submenu, and click Meet Now. Office starts the NetMeeting program to manage your meeting on the Web server.

2 If this is the first time you've used NetMeeting, you'll see a dialog box asking for your personal connection details. Specify your name, e-mail address, and a short comment that you'd like others to read about you, and then click OK.

3 In the Place A Call dialog box, type or click the user or meeting you want to connect to, and then click OK to begin the conversation.

After a moment, a discussion window appears and you can collaborate with your workgroup online.

Web Discussions

Alternatively, you can discuss a particular document online using the Web Discussions command on the Online Collaboration submenu. When you use this feature, comments about the document are stored separately from the document on the Web server, but are transparently merged into the document when you view it in Word, Excel, or PowerPoint. Web Discussions is especially good for users who can't all meet at once but still want to participate in a round-table discussion. Each person in the workgroup can connect to the document as they need to, and then post their comments electronically. Office 2000 can also send you e-mail when the document you're interested in has been updated since you last viewed it.

To run the Web Discussion feature, follow these steps:

1 Choose Web Discussions from the Online Collaboration submenu, and then choose a discussion server and open the document you want to discuss.

2 To insert a comment that will be passed on to the members of your workgroup, click the Insert In The Document button on the Discussion toolbar (located at the bottom of your screen when Web Discussions is active), type a comment in the Enter Discussion Text dialog box, and then press Enter.

Insert In The
Document

3 To track changes other people made to the document, click the Subscribe button on the Discussions toolbar.

Browsing Documents on the Web

Another exciting document management feature of Office 2000 is the ability it gives you to access Internet links quickly and seamlessly while you work. In this section, you'll learn how to connect to the Web in your Office applications, and you'll learn how to navigate a series of hypertext links using the new Web toolbar. You'll also learn how to use Internet Explorer 5 to view Office documents.

Linking Up with the World Wide Web

Connecting to the Web in Office applications is simple—so simple, in fact, that you might be wondering what all the fuss is about. You just select a word or cell in your document that you want to act as the doorway, or *hyperlink*, to the Web, and then you format it by choosing Hyperlink from the Insert menu of most Office applications or by clicking the Insert Hyperlink button. Hyperlink prompts you for the location of your file, which can be a document on your hard disk, a specific location in your document, or an Internet address, such as the home page for your business. (For example, the address for the Microsoft Press Home Page is *http://mspress.microsoft.com.*)

Insert
Hyperlink

Hyperlinks appear as underlined words in a special color, and you activate them by clicking the word in your document. By default, the hyperlink first appears in blue and then when you activate it, it changes color. When you activate a Web hyperlink, Office starts your Internet browser and makes the connection using an attached modem, fax modem, ISDN line, or other communication device. Once the connection is established, the Web toolbar (described below) appears to let you switch back and forth between your open connections.

Creating a Link to the Web from a Document

Create a link to the Web from your Office documents by following these steps:

1 Select the word or cell in your document that you want to associate the hyperlink with. It usually works best if that word or phrase describes the purpose of the link so that users can see what they're connecting to (for example, "Microsoft Press Home Page" or "Volcanoes on the Internet").

2 From the Insert menu, choose Hyperlink or click the Insert Hyperlink button. The Insert Hyperlink dialog box appears, prompting you for the text to display for the link and the pathname of the document or Internet address. If you want, you can specify a particular location in the file that should appear on the screen or an e-mail address as the filename.

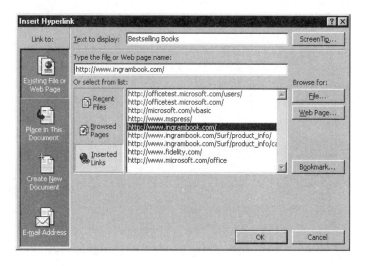

? SEE ALSO

For more information about creating hyperlinks in Word, see "Inserting and Navigating Using Hyperlinks," page 155. For details on creating Internet hyperlinks in Excel worksheets, see "Inserting Hyperlinks," page 433. For the same topic in Power-Point, see "Creating an Internet Hyperlink," page 761.

3 Click OK to add the hyperlink to your document. When the Insert Hyperlink dialog box closes, the highlighted text appears in underlined type and a different color.

4 When you activate a hyperlink in a document, Office starts the application associated with the document, displays the Web toolbar, and loads the linked document. If the hyperlink contains an Internet address, Office will start the default Internet browser on your system and ask you for a username and password, if necessary.

Using the Web Toolbar

After you create or activate a hyperlink in Office, a special Web toolbar appears in your application, which lets you switch back and forth between open hyperlinks, establish additional Internet connections, or run special network-related commands. You don't have to use the Web toolbar when switching between hyperlinks (you can use your browser or the Window menu instead), but in many cases you'll benefit from doing so. Figure 3-21, on the next page, shows the Web toolbar and identifies the purpose of its buttons.

⭐ TIP

To close the Web toolbar, click the Close button on the toolbar's title bar or click the Web Toolbar button on the Standard toolbar.

FIGURE 3-21.
The Web toolbar acts like a remote control for your Internet connections. Browse back and forth between open documents just by clicking a button.

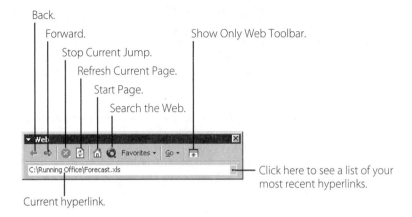

Back.
Forward.
Stop Current Jump.
Refresh Current Page.
Start Page.
Search the Web.
Show Only Web Toolbar.

Click here to see a list of your most recent hyperlinks.

Current hyperlink.

Browsing Your Connections

The most basic features of the Web toolbar are the hyperlink navigation buttons.

- To display the last open document or Web page, click the Back button.

- To display the next open document or Web page, click the Forward button.

- If you want to add the open hyperlink to your favorites collection, click the Favorites button, and then click Add To Favorites. (You can recall favorite hyperlinks at any time by clicking the Favorites button and then clicking Open Favorites.)

- If you want to stop the current hyperlink connection (useful when a number of graphics files are opening and you want to halt the process), click the Stop Current Jump button.

- If you ever want to download the most current version of a document or Web page, click the Refresh Current Page button. (We often use the Refresh Current Page button in tandem with the Stop Current Jump button.)

TIP

You can also use the down arrow next to the Address list box to display your most recent Internet connections. To reestablish one of the connections listed, just click the address.

Using Internet Explorer 5

When you click a Web hyperlink in your Office document, you'll see the Web page in the default Internet browser for your system, typically Internet Explorer or Netscape Navigator. Both of these browsers allow you to view and interact with Web pages written in a formatting code known as HTML (hypertext markup language). In addition to this basic functionality, Internet Explorer and Netscape Navigator allow you to run Web applications and other tools designed specifically for the Internet, and to switch quickly from one Web site to the next.

The default browser supplied with Office 2000 is Internet Explorer 5. As a result, you'll probably see Internet Explorer when you access the Web from Office applications, unless you specifically install the Netscape browser or another program. Figure 3-22 shows how a Web page we like to view looks in Internet Explorer. Notice that the address for the Web page is shown on the Address toolbar and that a collection of useful navigation buttons (Back, Forward, and so on) are presented on the Standard toolbar. At the bottom of the window, the status bar shows information

FIGURE 3-22.
Internet Explorer 5 lets you easily view Web pages on the Internet.

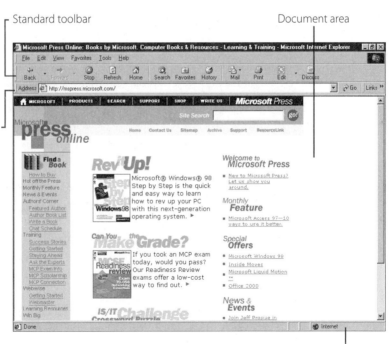

Standard toolbar

Document area

Address toolbar

Status bar

Getting Started

about the current Internet connection, and the contents of the Web page are shown in the large Document area in the center of the window. To view a part of the Web page that you can't see now, click the vertical scroll bar next to the Document area. You can also click hyperlinks in the Web page to view other parts of the Web site.

Opening a New Web Page

To go to a new Web page, find the Internet address, or *URL*, of the Web page you want to view, and follow these steps:

1 Click the Address toolbar text box to highlight the current Web page address.

2 Type the address of the new Web page you want to view. For example, to view the Microsoft Press Web site, type

Http://mspress.microsoft.com/

3 Press Enter. After a moment, Internet Explorer will load the Web page you specified and you can examine it closely in the Document window.

Viewing Office Documents

Internet Explorer also allows you to view Office documents in their own native format or in the new Office 2000 Web page (HTML) format. This feature allows you to open Office documents located on the Internet, your corporate intranet, or your local hard disk, without resorting to Windows Explorer or another tool.

To open and edit an Office document in Internet Explorer, follow these steps:

1 Click Open on the Internet Explorer File menu.

2 In the Open dialog box, click the Browse button. A new, larger Open dialog box appears, allowing you to locate a specific file on your computer, corporate intranet, or the Internet.

3 In the Files Of Type drop-down list box, click the type of file you're looking for. If you want to open an Office document that has been saved as an HTML file, leave the current setting as it is. If you're looking for an Office document stored in native format (the format that's unique to a particular application), click All Files. Your screen will look like this:

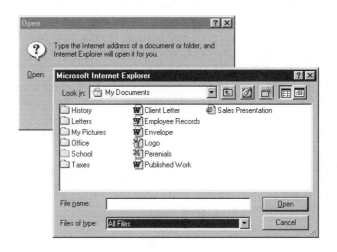

4 Locate the file you want to open in the list box, click it, and then click the Open button.

5 Click OK in the first Open dialog box to open the file for editing.
   At this point, Internet Explorer does something interesting: it opens the document you requested in Internet Explorer, but also adds Office application commands to the Internet Explorer menu bar. This interesting feature is known as *in-place editing*, and it allows you to work on your document in Internet Explorer using the exact same features you're used to in the original Office application. To accomplish this feat, Internet Explorer started the original Office application and is running it in the background. As a result, you might see an icon for it on the taskbar while you work.

6 When you're finished editing your Office document, save your changes, and choose Close from the Internet Explorer File menu or click the Back button on the Standard toolbar. The last Web page you were viewing in Internet Explorer will appear in the Document area.

PART II

Microsoft Word

Getting Started Using Word

Welcome to Microsoft Word, a general-purpose word processing program that provides an unprecedented number and variety of features. The tasks you can perform using Word range from writing simple documents, such as memos and letters, to producing the camera-ready materials for professional-looking publications, such as newsletters and books. You can also use Word to create striking and dynamic pages for the World Wide Web or your company intranet.

Yet Word is relatively easy to use. First, its visual tools—that is, its menus, toolbars, and mouse interface—eliminate the need to memorize an extensive set of keyboard commands. Also, Word provides many predefined templates, styles, and visual themes that can assist you in producing attractive and effective documents or Web pages. Finally, Word fully automates many important tasks, such as creating new documents, formatting paragraphs, and correcting text.

You can compare Word to a sophisticated modern camera, which provides automatic settings for taking quick snapshots as well as manually adjustable settings for achieving precise visual effects. With Word, not only can you choose "automatic" or "manual" methods to control virtually any feature of the documents you create, but you can also customize the Word tools themselves—that is, the menus, toolbars, and shortcut keys—and the way you view and work with documents.

Touring the Word Workplace

⑦ SEE ALSO
The section "Running Office Applications," page 11, describes several other ways to start an Office application.

To run Word and take a short tour of its most basic features, click the Start button on the Windows taskbar, point to the Programs folder, and then choose the Microsoft Word command.

When Word first begins running, it automatically opens a new empty document. Figure 4-1 shows the Word program window displaying a typical set of components.

Because Word is so highly customizable, your window could be quite different. If you are missing any of the components shown in Figure 4-1, you can display them as follows: To display the ruler, choose Ruler from

FIGURE 4-1.
The Word window.

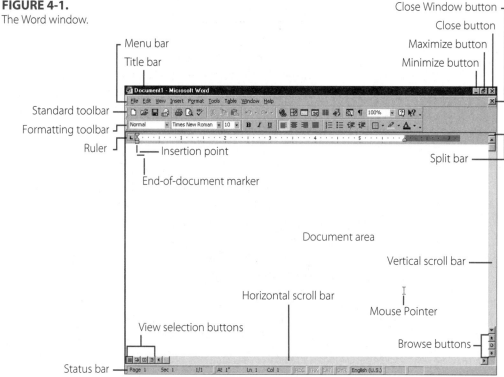

the View menu. (You can also display the ruler temporarily by simply placing the mouse pointer over the horizontal gray bar at the top of the document area of the window.) To show either the Standard or the Formatting toolbar, point to Toolbars on the View menu—or place the mouse pointer over the menu bar or over a toolbar and click with the right mouse button (right-click)—and then choose the Standard or Formatting option from the submenu that appears:

A check mark next to an option on this submenu means that the corresponding toolbar is currently displayed.

Click here to display the Formatting toolbar.

 TIP

Shortcuts Are a Click Away

Many times you can find the next action you want to perform on the *pop-up menu* (also known as a *shortcut menu*) that appears when you click the right (or secondary) mouse button. The commands on a pop-up menu change according to the location of the mouse pointer when you click. (Word provides commands that are appropriate to the context of your actions.) So check the pop-up menu often for possible shortcuts to accomplish your tasks more quickly.

To show the horizontal or vertical scroll bar or the status bar, choose Options from the Tools menu, open the View tab in the Options dialog box, and turn on the corresponding option. (See Figure 4-2, on the following page.)

FIGURE 4-2.
Displaying the
horizontal or vertical
scroll bar or the status
bar using the Options
dialog box.

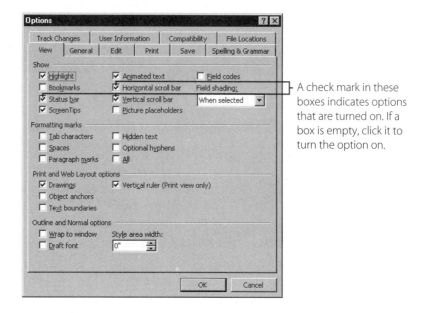

A check mark in these
boxes indicates options
that are turned on. If a
box is empty, click it to
turn the option on.

The Word window shown in Figure 4-1 is in *Normal view*. (Refer to Figure 4-1, page 100, throughout the remainder of this section.) A view is a way of displaying and working with a document; the different Word views will be explained near the end of the chapter. If the interior of your Word window doesn't appear as shown in the figure, a different view might be active. To switch to Normal view, choose Normal from the View menu.

SEE ALSO
For general informa-
tion about working
with toolbars, see
"Using Toolbars,"
page 39.

The Standard toolbar in Word lets you perform a variety of tasks, such as opening and saving documents, printing, copying text or formats, and obtaining help. The Formatting toolbar is typical of a special-purpose Word toolbar; it is used for modifying the *format* (that is, the appearance) of characters and paragraphs. In the following chapters, you'll learn how to use the buttons on these toolbars as well as how to display, use, and even customize or create other specialized Word toolbars to suit your style of working.

The ruler at the top of the document area allows you to use the mouse to change the document margins and also to set the indents and tab stops for individual paragraphs. The vertical and horizontal scroll bars permit you to use the mouse to scroll through a document that is too large to fit within the window. You can drag the split bar down from the top of the vertical scroll bar to divide the Word window into two panes; you can then view a different portion of the same document within each pane. The view selection buttons (the four buttons at the left end of the horizontal scroll bar) permit you to change the document view, as explained later in this chapter in the section "Changing the Way Documents Are Displayed," page 114. The browse buttons (the three buttons at the bottom of the vertical scroll bar) let you browse through the document; they are discussed in "Using the Browse Buttons," page 154.

To learn the purpose of any of these buttons, simply move the mouse pointer over the button *without* clicking a mouse button. Word will display a brief description of the button's action, known as a *ScreenTip*, next to the button.

If ScreenTips don't appear, you can enable them by choosing Customize from the Tools menu, clicking the Options tab in the Customize dialog box, and selecting the Show ScreenTips On Toolbars option. (If you want the ScreenTips to display the key combination for executing each command, also select the Show Shortcut Keys In ScreenTips option.)

 SEE ALSO

For more information about working with Office application windows, see "Working with Application Windows," page 28 in Chapter 2.

The Word *status bar* provides information about the operation of the program. The first six items indicate the current position of the *insertion point* within the document; the insertion point is the flashing vertical line that is displayed at the position where the characters you type appear in the document. The next four items indicate the status of various program modes; if any of these items is displayed in dark print, the corresponding mode is active (for example, Word is recording a macro or typing replaces existing text). Word uses the area to the right of the mode indicators to display appropriate icons when the program is engaged in various operations, such as saving a document, printing a document, or as-you-type spelling or grammar checking. The status bar items are labeled in Figure 4-3, on the next page; the significance of each item will become clear when the related Word feature is discussed later in the book.

TIP

Use the Status Bar to Issue Commands

You can double-click various parts of the status bar to quickly issue certain Word commands. For example, double-clicking the left half of the status bar activates the Go To command (discussed in Chapter 5), and double-clicking one of the program mode indicators toggles (switches on and off) the selected mode. If you have enabled ScreenTips, placing the mouse pointer over one of these parts of the status bar will display a ScreenTip indicating the effect of double-clicking that part.

FIGURE 4-3.
The Word status bar.

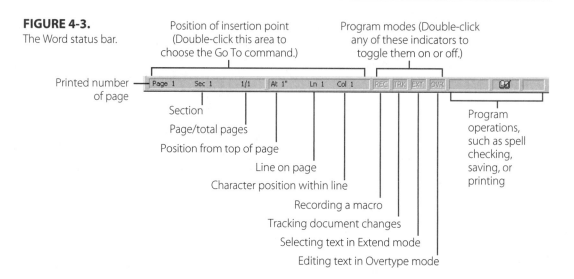

Printed number of page

Position of insertion point (Double-click this area to choose the Go To command.)

Program modes (Double-click any of these indicators to toggle them on or off.)

Section

Page/total pages

Position from top of page

Line on page

Character position within line

Recording a macro

Tracking document changes

Selecting text in Extend mode

Editing text in Overtype mode

Program operations, such as spell checking, saving, or printing

Although Figure 4-1, page 100, shows only a single open document, you can simultaneously open several documents in Word, each one appearing in a separate Word window. You can switch to the document you want to work on by clicking the document's button on the Windows taskbar, by pressing Ctrl+F6 (repeatedly, if necessary), or by choosing the document's name from the Window menu in Word:

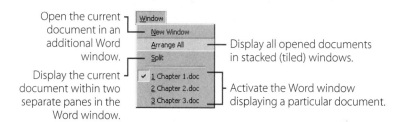

Open the current document in an additional Word window.

Display the current document within two separate panes in the Word window.

Display all opened documents in stacked (tiled) windows.

Activate the Word window displaying a particular document.

If Word terminates abnormally or begins to behave erratically, you might try the new *detect and repair* feature, which attempts to find problems in the Word program files and to fix the errors. To use this feature, choose Detect And Repair from the Help menu.

Creating and Printing a Document from Start to Finish

In this section, you'll open, edit, format, print, and save a simple Word document. All the techniques touched on here—as well as many others—are explained in detail in the following chapters.

> **NOTE**
>
> When you start Word, the program automatically opens a new empty document based on the Normal template, which is called Document1 until you save it and specify a filename. You can immediately begin typing in this document, or you can open another new document using the procedures described in this section.

SEE ALSO

For more information about starting and exiting Office applications, see Chapter 1, "A Quick Tour of Microsoft Office."

The first step in creating a new document is to choose New from the File menu. Word will display the New dialog box, which allows you to choose a template or a wizard for generating the kind of document that you want to compose. Figure 4-4 shows how to use the New dialog box to create a standard, general-purpose document. Word will base the new document on a template named Normal and will open it in a new empty Word window. (You can close the document that was automatically created when you first started Word, or you can simply ignore it.)

FIGURE 4-4.
Creating a new document based on the Normal template.

1 Click here if the General tab is not already displayed.

2 Click the Blank Document icon if it is not already selected.

3 Click OK.

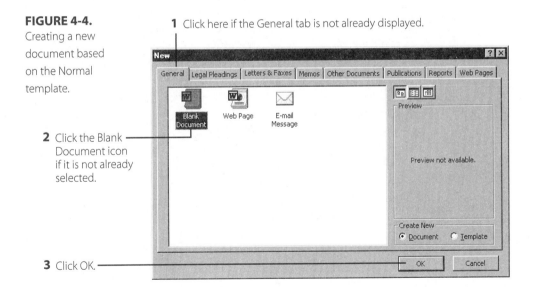

Microsoft Word

New

As a shortcut, you can create a new document based on the Normal template by simply clicking the New button on the Standard toolbar or by pressing Ctrl+N. (If you want to use a wizard or a template other than Normal, you must choose New from the File menu, as previously described.)

Using Templates and Wizards

Word templates and wizards can give you a head start in creating your documents. The New dialog box allows you to choose from a large variety of professionally designed templates and wizards, each of which is tailored to fit a particular type of document.

A *template* serves as a blueprint for a document. It stores formatting styles and sometimes also document text and graphics (as well as several other features). When you create a new document based on a template, your document acquires a copy of the template's contents. You can then modify your document as necessary and add your own text and graphics.

For example, if you want to write a memo, you could choose the Contemporary Memo template (on the Memos tab in the New dialog box). Your new document would then contain the basic text and layout for a memo; you would need only to fill in some details and add your message.

If none of the special-purpose templates is suitable for the document you want to create, you can choose the most general template, Normal, which is labeled Blank Document on the General tab of the New dialog box. The Normal template stores a basic set of styles with *no* document text or graphics. (Recall that you can also create a document that uses the Normal template by clicking the New button on the Standard toolbar or by pressing Ctrl+N.) *Templates are discussed in detail in Chapter 7, "Customizing Styles and Templates."*

Some of the items in the New dialog box are *wizards*. The name of a wizard generally contains the word *Wizard*, and the icon includes an image of a magic wand. When you create a new document based on a wizard, Word automatically guides you through a series of steps in which you choose the document features you want and enter some or all of the document text. After Word generates and opens the new document, you can manually make any necessary modifications. For example, if you want to produce a memo using a wizard, you can choose the Memo Wizard (also on the Memos tab in the New dialog box) and follow the instructions.

TIP

Create a Word Document Using the Office Shortcut Bar or the Windows Start Menu

You can also create a new Word document by clicking the New Office Document button on the Office Shortcut Bar or by choosing New Office Document from the Windows Start menu. The resulting New Office Document dialog box will display templates for creating documents using various Office programs. If you choose a Word template or wizard (identified by a *W* on the icon), Word will start (if it isn't already running), and it will open the new document.

SEE ALSO

For information about using the Office Shortcut Bar to create and open documents, see "Running Office Applications," page 11, and "Clicking a Program Icon on the Office Shortcut Bar," page 12.

After you have opened the new document, the next step is to enter the text. Your document will consist of a heading followed by two paragraphs of body text. Begin by typing your heading at the top of the document window (for example, *My Summer Vacation*). If you reach the end of the line while you're still typing the heading, do *not* press the Enter key (as you would on a typewriter); rather, just keep typing. Word will automatically move the insertion point (along with any characters in the current word) down to the beginning of the next line, and the new characters will appear on the new line. This is known as automatic *word wrapping*. Also, don't end the heading with a period. (If a line ends with a period, the Word automatic formatting feature won't recognize it as a heading.)

ON THE WEB

The Before.doc and After.doc document files, used for the examples in this section, are on the Running Office 2000 Reader's Corner page. For information about connecting to this Web site, read the Introduction.

If you make a mistake or want to make a change, you can use the following simple editing techniques:

1 Use the arrow keys to move the insertion point to the position in your text where you want to make the change.

2 To delete text, press the Backspace key to remove the character to the left of the insertion point, or press the Delete key to remove the character to the right of the insertion point. You can hold down either key to erase more than one character.

3 To add text, simply type it. Word will move any existing characters to the right of the insertion point to make room for the new characters you type. (You must be in the Insert editing mode. If the OVR indicator on the status bar is darkened, double-click it to switch from Overtype mode to Insert mode.)

When you have finished typing the heading, press the Enter key. The insertion point will move to the beginning of the following line, and the next characters you type will belong to a new *paragraph*. A Word document consists of a series of paragraphs; you start each paragraph (except the first one) by pressing Enter. (In chapters 5 through 8, you'll learn about the properties of Word paragraphs.) Type several lines of text into the new paragraph. Again, when you reach the end of a line, simply let Word automatically wrap the text to the next line rather than pressing Enter.

When you have finished typing the paragraph, press Enter to create another new paragraph. As you're typing this paragraph, you'll change the format of some of the characters. First, enter some **boldface** characters by clicking the Bold button on the Formatting toolbar.

Bold

Type the characters, and then click the Bold button again to turn off the bold format.

Similarly, you can *italicize* text by clicking the Italic button on the Formatting toolbar, typing the characters, and then clicking the Italic button again.

Italic

Your document will now consist of three paragraphs: a heading and two paragraphs of body text. (An example is shown in Figure 4-5.) Notice that if you insert or erase characters, Word moves all the following words within the same paragraph—if necessary—so that the text fits within the paragraph margins; this is one of the important properties of paragraphs.

FIGURE 4-5.

An example Word document, before formatting.

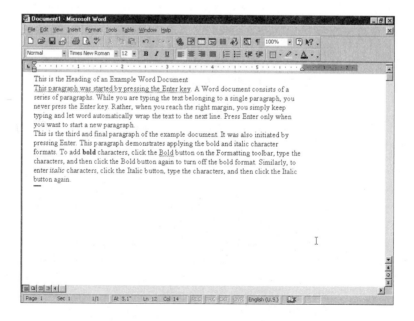

(You might want to experiment with this property using the editing techniques given above.)

As you can see in Figure 4-5, the document is not especially attractive or even readable; it's difficult to distinguish both the heading from the body text, and one paragraph from the next. To improve this situation, the next step is to format the document—that is, to adjust the appearance of the document's characters and paragraphs. To do this, choose AutoFormat from the Format menu. In the AutoFormat dialog box, make sure the AutoFormat Now and General Document options are selected, and click the OK button. Word will automatically format the entire document. Figure 4-6 shows the result of formatting the document shown in Figure 4-5.

Word formatted the document by applying an appropriate *style* to each paragraph. A style contains a set of formatting attributes that is suitable for a particular type of text. The style that Word applied to the first paragraph (named "Heading 1") assigned the characters a large, bold Arial font and added extra space above and below the paragraph. The style that Word assigned to the two paragraphs in the document body (named "Body Text") added space below the paragraphs to separate them. Styles are one of the most useful Word features. As you'll learn later in the book, you can manually apply styles to individual paragraphs or to blocks of characters, and you can even modify styles or create new ones. As you'll also learn, you can apply various individual formats (such as centered text) to a paragraph that override the formats defined by the style.

II

Microsoft Word

FIGURE 4-6.
The example Word document of Figure 4-5 after automatic formatting.

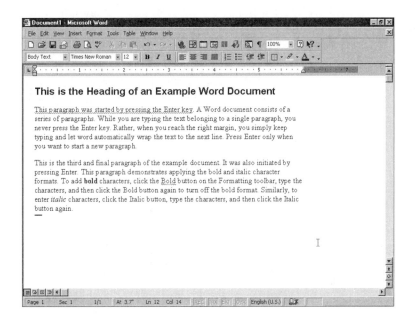

SEE ALSO

For detailed information about different ways to check your spelling or grammar, see Chapter 9, "Using Word's Proofing Tools."

You should now proofread your document. Word helps you do this by marking possible spelling and grammatical errors. Spelling errors are marked with a wavy red underline and grammatical errors with a wavy green underline. (The Check Spelling As You Type and Check Grammar As You Type options must be selected for you to see these wavy lines. Also, the Hide Spelling Errors In This Document and Hide Grammatical Errors In This Documents options must be deselected. You access these options by choosing Options from the Tools menu and clicking the Spelling & Grammar tab.) If you right-click the underlined text, Word will display a pop-up menu listing one or more suggested replacements (if it can derive any). Choose a replacement to have Word correct your text.

This is the Heading of an Example Word Docu

This paragraph was started by pressing the Enter key. A Word document series of paragraphs. Whi | Pressing the Enter key started this paragraph |e 1 never press the Enter key.

Ignore

typing and let Word autor

you want to start a new p

Grammar...

This is the third and final

About this Sentence

pressing Enter. This paragraph demonstrates applying the bold and italic

Just before printing the document, you should check the appearance of the full printed page (or pages) by choosing Print Preview from the File menu, or by clicking the Print Preview button on the Standard toolbar.

Print Preview

Figure 4-7 shows the example document (reduced to fit in the document window) as it is displayed by the Print Preview command. To print the document using the default printer and print settings, simply click the Print button on the Print Preview toolbar displayed in Print Preview. You can close Print Preview by clicking the Close button or by pressing Escape. (When Print Preview isn't active, you can print the document using default settings by clicking the Print button on the Standard toolbar.)

Print

Finally, save your document by choosing Save from the File menu or by clicking the Save button on the Standard toolbar.

Save

The first time you save a new document, Word will display the Save As dialog box, which lets you choose the name and location of the file where the document is to be stored. When working on a longer document, you should save it frequently rather than waiting until you have printed it. Remember this: If the power goes out or your computer fails, you'll lose all the work you have done since the last time you saved!

FIGURE 4-7.
The example document of Figure 4-6 as displayed in Print Preview.

Click here to print the document using default print settings.

Click here to return to the previously active view of the document.

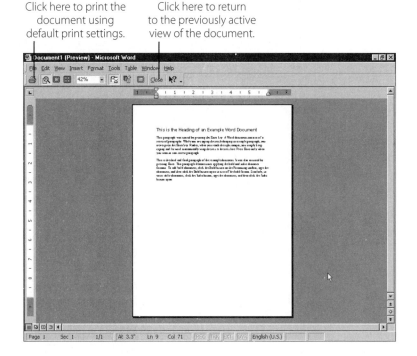

Protect Your Documents by Using AutoRecover

You can have Word automatically save, at regular intervals, information about any changes made to your document. If Word inadvertently terminates, it will use this information to restore the document the next time you run the program. To set this feature, choose Options from the Tools menu, click the Save tab, select the Save AutoRecover Info Every option, and enter the desired number of minutes between saves in the adjacent text box. Specifying a short time will lessen the amount of your work that's subject to loss.

? SEE ALSO

For more information about creating, opening, saving, and closing documents from within an Office application, see Chapter 3, "Managing Documents: From Your Hard Disk to the Internet."

You can now close your document by choosing Close from the File menu. You can later reopen the document by choosing Open from the File menu in Word, by choosing Open Office Document from the Windows Start menu, or by using the Office Shortcut Bar. If you have worked with the file recently, you can also reopen it by choosing the filename from the list at the bottom of the File menu in Word.

Microsoft Word

Creating Web Pages

You can use Word to create a page for the World Wide Web or for your company intranet by saving a document in HTML format (as an HTM file) rather than in native Word format (as a DOC file). HTML (HyperText Markup Language) is the standard format used for Web pages. Once you have generated one or more HTML files, you can copy them (as well as any graphics or other files they display) to your Web server. Your Internet service provider or your company's intranet administrator should be able to provide instructions for doing this.

You can easily convert an existing Word document to a Web page. To do this, open the document, choose Save As Web Page from the File menu, and specify a name and location for the file in the Save As dialog box. (Leave "Web Page (*.htm, *.html)" selected in the Save As Type list box, and make sure that the file is saved with the HTM or HTML extension.)

You can also use a Word template to create a new document that's designed specifically as a Web page. To do this, choose New from the File menu. In the New dialog box, select the Web Page template on the General tab to start with a blank Web page. Or, pick one of the templates on the Web Pages tab to create a new Web page containing an initial layout of text and graphics that's suitable for a particular type of Web page, such as a personal Web page or a table of contents. (Note that the Web-page templates appear with an icon that represents your system's default browser instead of the icon that appears with templates that create regular Word documents.) You can then modify the page and add your own content. When you save the document, it will be stored in HTML format by default.

If you want to create an entire set of linked Web pages (that is, a Web *site*), you can select the Web Page Wizard item on the Web Pages tab. The Web Page Wizard will let you add pages to the site (you can choose a template for each one), and will allow you to specify the folder where the pages are stored, the organization of the hyperlinks that connect the pages, and the visual theme of the pages. *(Hyperlinks are discussed in "Inserting and Navigating Using Hyperlinks," page 155, and themes in "Applying a Theme," page 168.)* After the wizard generates the Web site, you can open, modify, and add content to any of the individual pages.

Finally, you can use Word as a general-purpose Web-page editor to open and modify existing Web pages obtained from Web sites or created in other Web-page editors.

It's best to create a Web-page document using the Web Layout view, which displays the document in much the same way that popular browsers would display it. For a more accurate preview, you can open the document in your browser by choosing Web Page Preview from the File menu.

You can also customize the features of the Web pages that Word generates by choosing Options from the Tools menu, clicking the General tab in the

Creating Web Pages   *continued*

Options dialog box, clicking the Web Options button, and entering your selections into the tabs of the Web Options dialog box.

You can add any Word feature (document element or format) *either* to a regular Word document saved in native Word format *or* to a Web-page document saved in HTML format. However, popular Web browsers such as Internet Explorer 5 don't display certain Word features—for example, double-strikethrough characters or animated text. (Although browsers might not display some Word features, they will all be stored in the HTML file and will be present whenever you edit the document in Word. This is in contrast to Word 97, which removed many Word features when it stored a document in HTML format.)

To avoid inadvertently adding features that aren't supported by a particular browser, you can have Word disable those features when you work on a Web-page document. To do this, select the Disable Features Not Supported By option on the General tab of the Web Options dialog box (described above), and then select a particular browser in the adjoining list box. (If this option is selected, and if you add nonsupported features to a regular Word document and then save it as a Web page, Word will list the nonsupported features and then remove them or convert them to similar supported features.)

Conversely, Word provides some features that are intended primarily for Web pages—for example, movie clips, scrolling text, background sounds, and background colors or images. You can, however, add these features to any type of Word document to enhance viewing the document online in Word. (But note that background colors or images are visible only in Word's Web Layout view or when a Web page document is viewed in a browser.)

 SEE ALSO

For more information on these features, see the section "Adding Movie Clips, Scrolling Text, and Backgrounds," page 335.

NOTE

If only one Word document is open, Word displays a Close Window button at the right end of the menu bar (see Figure 4-1, page 100). Clicking this button or choosing Close from the File menu closes the document but leaves the Word window displayed. If more than one document is open, Word *doesn't* display a Close Window button; and choosing Close or clicking the Close button in the far upper-right corner of the window closes both the document and the Word window in which it's displayed.

To exit Word, you can choose Exit from the File menu, which will close all open Word windows. If only a single document is open, you can also exit Word by clicking the Close button in the far upper-right corner of the Word window. (If more than one document is open, clicking this button closes only the current Word window.)

Microsoft Word

Changing the Way Documents Are Displayed

Word provides many options that affect the way it displays documents and how you work with them. First, you can change the basic document *view*. Table 4-1 lists the different document views, briefly describes each, and identifies the chapters where you can find fuller discussions on each one.

To switch to any view except Print Preview, choose the appropriate option from the View menu:

To switch to Print Preview, choose Print Preview from the File menu, or click the Print Preview button on the Standard toolbar. Also, you can switch to Normal, Web Layout, Print Layout, or Outline view by clicking a button at the left end of the horizontal scroll bar:

Outline view

Print Layout view

Web Layout view (the currently selected view)

Normal view

In addition to changing the basic view, you can also set a variety of options that affect the way a document is displayed within the current view. (Some of these options affect only certain views.)

Type a zoom percentage into this box…

…or select a percentage from the list.

TABLE 4-1.   Document Views

View	Description	Chapter
Normal	Shows document in a general-purpose format, for efficient editing and formatting. Does not display margins, headers, or footers.	4
Web Layout	Displays document in a format that is easy to read on the screen. Ideal for previewing Web pages or for reading regular Word documents online. The text is shown without page breaks and with only minimal margins. Lines of text extend across the whole window, and any background color or image assigned to the document is visible.	4
Print Layout	Displays text and graphics exactly as they will appear on the printed page, showing all margins, headers, and footers. All editing and formatting commands are available, but Word runs somewhat more slowly than in Normal view, and scrolling is not as smooth.	10
Outline	Shows the organization of the document. Lets you view various levels of detail and rapidly rearrange document text.	12
Print Preview	Displays an image of one (or more) entire printed page and lets you adjust the page setup.	10

II

Microsoft Word

? SEE ALSO

For information about other ways to customize Office applications, see "Customizing Toolbars," page 44 and "Customizing Menus," page 50.

First, you can change the size of the characters and graphics on the screen by using the Zoom list box on the Standard toolbar or by choosing Zoom from the View menu. With either method, you specify the character size you want as a percentage of the normal size. Zooming is available in all views. Rest assured that zooming does *not* change the actual size of the text or graphics that are printed and stored in the document; rather, it affects only the level of magnification at which you view the document in the window.

Second, you can expand the Word workspace to fill the entire screen and hide all menus, toolbars, and other tools by choosing Full Screen from the View menu. (The menu bar will appear, however, if you move the mouse pointer to the top of the screen.) This command also affects all views. To restore the normal Word window, press the Escape key or click the Close Full Screen button that Word displays on its own toolbar:

Finally, you can customize many features of the Normal, Web Layout, Print Layout, and Outline views by choosing Options from the Tools menu and clicking the View tab, shown in Figure 4-8. Notice that some of these options affect only certain views.

While you have the Options dialog box open, you might explore some of the other tabs, where you can modify a wide variety of Word features.

Prevent Eyestrain by Using the Blue Background, White Text Option
You can have Word display document text in white characters on a blue background by clicking the General tab in the Options dialog box and selecting the Blue Background, White Text item. This option affects all views except Print Preview and can help prevent eyestrain. (Some Windows users find looking at a white screen similar to trying to read the wattage on a burning light bulb!)

FIGURE 4-8.
Setting view options using the Options command on the Tools menu.

For an explanation of a particular view option, click this Help button, and then click the option.

These options affect the Normal, Web Layout, Print Layout, and Outline views.

These three options affect the Web Layout and Print Layout views.

These three options affect the Normal and Outline views.

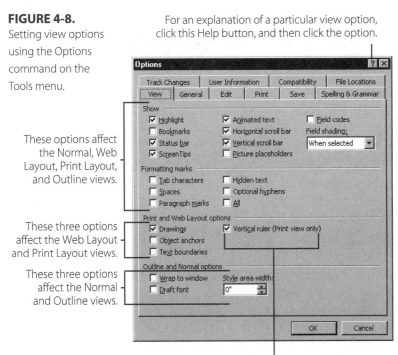

This option affects the Print Layout view.

CHAPTER 5

Entering and Editing Text in a Word Document

Now that you know the basics of running Word, this chapter focuses on the *content* of a Word document—that is, the characters, words, sentences, and paragraphs that compose a document. You'll learn about the many ways to add, edit, find, and navigate through document text. The next chapter focuses on the *format* of a Word document—that is, the appearance of the characters and paragraphs. These two topics are treated separately to make your learning task easier, not to imply that you must finish editing the entire document before you begin formatting it. Typically, you'll use formatting techniques as you are entering and editing the text.

Entering Text

 SEE ALSO

The methods you can use for moving the insertion point are discussed in the "Moving the Insertion Point" section of this chapter, page 130.

As you learned in Chapter 4, to enter text you simply move the insertion point to the location you want in the document and type the text.

Word provides two editing modes: *Insert* and *Overtype*. In Insert mode (the most common mode), any existing characters beyond the insertion point are moved ahead in the document as you type. In Overtype mode, the new characters you type replace any existing characters. When Overtype mode is active, the OVR indicator on the status bar is darkened. To switch between the two modes, double-click the OVR indicator. You can also use the Insert key to do this, if the Use The INS Key For Paste option in the Options dialog box (Edit tab) is not selected.

 TIP

> **Create a New Line Within a Paragraph by Pressing Shift+Enter**
>
> To create a new line within a paragraph, press Shift+Enter. "Why not just press Enter and create a new paragraph?" you might ask. Some paragraph formatting affects only the first or last line of the paragraph, such as an initial indent or additional space above or below the paragraph. By pressing Shift+Enter, you can create a new line without introducing this formatting. In the section "Formatting Text Boxes, Pictures, and Drawing Objects" on page 331, you'll learn how to add a *text wrapping* line break, which causes the following line to be moved below an adjoining text box, picture, or drawing object.

As you also learned in Chapter 4, you press Enter to create a new paragraph. Word marks the end of each paragraph by inserting a *paragraph mark*. A paragraph mark (¶) is one of the nonprinting characters that might be contained in a Word document. Nonprinting characters never appear on the final printed copy of the document. Normally, they are also invisible on the screen. You can, however, make them visible on the screen by clicking the Show/Hide ¶ button on the Standard toolbar.

Show/Hide ¶

The following is an example of some document text on the screen after nonprinting characters have been made visible:

Avoid deleting a paragraph mark unintentionally. (It can be deleted whether it is visible or not.) Doing so will merge the paragraphs on either side of the mark, and any paragraph formatting assigned to the second paragraph will be lost. (Paragraph formatting will be discussed in the next chapter.)

? **SEE ALSO**

To learn how to rapidly insert text at any position on the page, having Word automatically add the required space and formatting, see "Using Click and Type," page 171.

You can also display or hide specific nonprinting characters by choosing Options from the Tools menu, clicking the View tab, and selecting the appropriate options in the Formatting Marks area.

Inserting Special Characters

You can choose Symbol from the Insert menu to insert into your text a variety of symbols and foreign characters that you won't find on your keyboard. For example, if you want to add a copyright symbol (©), choose Symbol from the Insert menu, and use the Symbol dialog box as shown in Figure 5-1. The symbol will appear in your document at the position of the insertion point, just as if you had typed it. You can leave the Symbol dialog box open while you work in your document. After you have inserted the symbols you need, click the Close button to close the dialog box.

The Symbol dialog box displays all the characters belonging to the font selected in the Font list box at the top of the Symbols tab. If you don't immediately see the symbol you want, you might be able to find it by selecting various fonts. Note that selecting the (normal text) item at the beginning of the list of fonts displays the set of characters belonging to the font at the current position of the insertion point in your document. Also, if you click the Special Characters tab in the Symbol dialog box, Word will display some additional characters that you can insert.

Many of the symbols have default shortcut keys assigned to them. Word displays the available shortcut keys in the Symbol dialog box on the

FIGURE 5-1.
Inserting the copyright symbol using the Symbol command on the Insert menu.

2 Select Symbol font if it's not already selected.

1 Click the Symbols tab if it's not already selected.

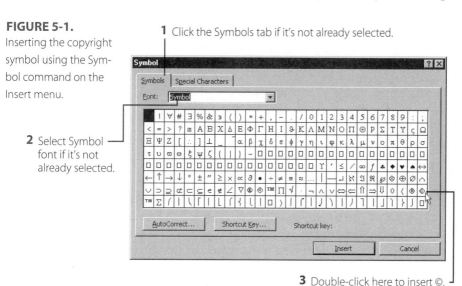

3 Double-click here to insert ©.

Microsoft Word

Special Characters tab, and at the bottom of the Symbols tab if you choose the (normal text) font. You can press the shortcut keys to quickly insert a symbol without opening the Symbol dialog box. For example, you can insert the copyright symbol by pressing Alt+Ctrl+C, and you can insert the foreign character á by pressing Alt+0225. (You must type the 0225 on your numeric keypad with Num Lock on.)

Set up Shortcut Keys for Symbols You Frequently Use

You can define your own shortcut key for a symbol by opening the Symbol dialog box, clicking the symbol, and then clicking the Shortcut Key button.

You can also define a character or group of characters—such as "(ae)"—that Word will automatically replace with a specified symbol such as æ. To do this, select the symbol in the Symbol dialog box and click the AutoCorrect button. *The AutoCorrect feature will be discussed later in the chapter (in the section "Using the AutoCorrect Feature," page 127).*

In addition, you can insert the current date, the current time, or both into your document by choosing Date And Time from the Insert menu, and in the Date And Time dialog box selecting the desired format. (See Figure 5-2.)

FIGURE 5-2.

Inserting the current date or time using the Date And Time command on the Insert menu.

Click the format you want.

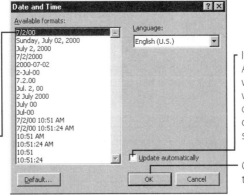

If you select the Update Automatically option, Word will update the date or time whenever you print the document; otherwise, the date or time will remain the same as when you inserted it.

Click OK to insert the date or time into your document.

Automatic Writing

This section is not about a spiritualist activity, but rather discusses several ways that you can have Word automatically insert text into your document.

Using the Repeat Command

If you have just typed some text, you can have Word place that same text at any location in a document as follows:

1 Type the original text.

2 Move the insertion point to the location where you want to repeat the text (in the same or in a different document).

3 Choose Repeat Typing from the Edit menu, or press Ctrl+Y or the F4 key. Word will automatically insert the text that you originally typed. You can do this repeatedly to insert multiple copies of this text.

If you don't like the result, you can reverse it by immediately choosing Undo Typing from the Edit menu, by pressing Ctrl+Z, or by clicking the Undo button on the Standard toolbar. (The Undo command will be described later in the chapter.)

 NOTE

> Repeat Typing is only one example of the Repeat command. The Repeat command repeats any editing or formatting action, not simply text that you have typed. Word indicates the action that will be repeated in the caption for the Repeat command on the Edit menu. For example, if you have deleted a word (by pressing Ctrl+Del), the menu caption will read Repeat Delete Word, and choosing the command will delete another word. As explained later in the chapter, this command will also redo an action that you have just reversed by using the Undo command.

Using the AutoText Feature

A second way to automate the insertion of text is to use the AutoText feature, which allows you to save commonly used blocks of text (or graphics) as *AutoText entries* and lets you quickly insert one of these blocks wherever you need it.

To create an AutoText entry, do the following:

1 Type into a document the block of text that you want to save. (Typing the text into a paragraph that has the same style as the paragraphs in which you'll later use the text can make it easier to insert the entry from the AutoText submenu, as you'll see later.)

2 *Select* (that is, highlight) the block of text. One way to select text is to hold down the Shift key while pressing the appropriate arrow key. Selection methods are discussed later in the chapter.

3 Point to AutoText on the Insert menu, and choose New from the submenu that appears. Alternatively, you can press Alt+F3. Word will display the Create AutoText dialog box.

4 Type a name for your AutoText entry into the text box, and click OK. (Word proposes a name based on the selected text, but you'll probably want to invent a name of your own.) Make the name short because you'll need to type it (or at least part of it) every time you insert the entry. Note that if you type the name of an existing entry, Word will ask whether you want to redefine that entry; click Yes to replace the original text for the entry or No to choose a new name.

Figure 5-3 shows an example.

FIGURE 5-3.
Storing a standard letter closing as an AutoText entry named close.

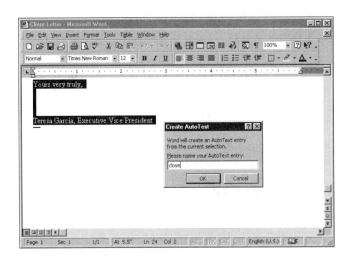

After you create an AutoText entry, it will be stored permanently. You can insert an AutoText entry into a document as follows:

1 Place the insertion point at the position in your document where you want to insert the text.

2 Type the name of the AutoText entry as a separate word. This means that you must type the name at the beginning of a line or following a space, tab, or punctuation symbol. The case of the

letters you type doesn't matter. And you might not need to type the complete name—you need type only a sufficient number of characters to distinguish the name from the names of all other AutoText entries.

3 Press F3 or Ctrl+Alt+V. Word will immediately replace the entry name with the entry text. For example, if you had defined the AutoText entry shown in Figure 5-3, at the end of a letter you could simply press Enter, type the word *close*, and then press F3 or Ctrl+Alt+V:

I'm looking forward to hearing from you soon.

close|

— |
       Press F3 or Ctrl+Alt+V here.

Word would replace the word *close* with your standard letter closing:

I'm looking forward to hearing from you soon.

Yours very truly,

Teresa García, Executive Vice President|

TIP

A Shortcut for Inserting AutoText Entries and Dates

If the Show AutoComplete Tip For AutoText And Dates option is enabled, as you begin typing an AutoText entry name into a document, Word will display the entry text (or part of the text) in a box near the insertion point. The box will appear as soon as you have typed enough of the name to identify the entry. You can then insert the entry text by simply pressing Enter (or the usual F3 or Ctrl+Alt+V key combination), without typing the complete entry name. When this option is selected, you can also have Word complete partially typed dates, using the same method. To select or deselect the option, point to AutoText on the Insert menu and choose AutoText from the submenu that appears. (Word will display the AutoText tab, which is discussed in the following section.)

As an alternative to steps 2 and 3, you can insert an AutoText entry by choosing it from the AutoText submenu on the Insert menu.

II

Microsoft Word

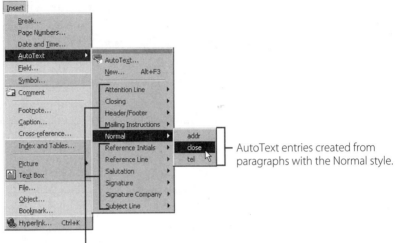

AutoText entries created from paragraphs with the Normal style.

Submenus that contain AutoText entries supplied by Word.

The AutoText submenu lists all AutoText entries you have defined. Each entry is placed on a submenu labeled according to the style of the paragraph from which the entry was originally obtained; for example, if you created an entry by selecting text in a paragraph with the Normal style, the entry will be placed on a submenu labeled Normal. (This arrangement helps you locate entries that are relevant to the type of paragraph you're currently working on.) The AutoText submenu also displays a large collection of entries defined by Word, grouped on submenus according to their functions.

Note, however, that if the insertion point is currently in a paragraph with a style other than Normal, and if you created one or more AutoText entries from paragraphs having that style, the AutoText submenu will list *only* entries created from paragraphs with the same style. In this case, if you want to see *all* AutoText entries, hold down the Shift key when you open the AutoText submenu.

 TIP

Change an AutoText Entry

To modify the contents of an AutoText entry (without having to delete it and reenter it), insert the entry text into the document (using one of the methods just described), make the changes you want, and then use the procedure given at the beginning of this section to save the text again as an AutoText entry, using its original name. You must answer *yes* when Word asks whether you want to redefine the entry.

Using the AutoText Tab of the AutoCorrect Dialog Box

You can use the AutoText tab of the AutoCorrect dialog box to create AutoText entries, to view their contents, or to delete them. You can select this tab using either of the following methods:

- Point to AutoText on the Insert menu and choose AutoText from the submenu.

- Choose AutoCorrect from the Tools menu and click the AutoText tab in the AutoCorrect dialog box. (The other tabs in the AutoCorrect dialog box will be discussed later in the book.)

To create an AutoText entry using the AutoText tab, do the following:

1 Select the document text you want to save.

2 Display the AutoText tab using one of the methods given above.

3 Type a name for the AutoText entry into the Enter AutoText Entries Here box. Note that if you type the same name as an existing entry, the existing entry will be overwritten.

4 In the Look In list box, select the template in which you want to store the AutoText entry. If you select All Active Templates or Normal.dot (Global Template), the Normal template will store the entry and *all* Word documents will have access to it. If the current document is attached to a template other than Normal, and if you select the name of that template in the Look In list box, then the attached template will store the entry and it will be available *only* to documents attached to this same template.

   Chapter 7 explains how templates are attached to documents and shows how to copy AutoText entries from one template to another as well as how to rename them. Note that your selection in this list will also affect the location where AutoText entries are subsequently stored when you create entries using the New command on the AutoText submenu, as described in the previous section.

5 Click the Add button.

Figure 5-4, on the next page, shows the completed AutoText tab just before clicking the Add button.

To view the contents of an AutoText entry or to delete an entry, do the following:

1 Display the AutoText tab using one of the methods given above.

II

Microsoft Word

FIGURE 5-4.
Creating an AutoText
entry using the
AutoText tab of
the AutoCorrect
dialog box.

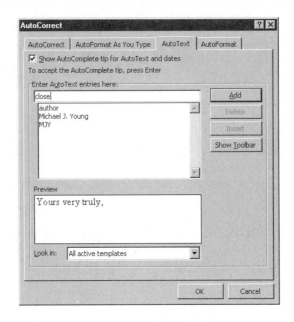

2   Select a template in the Look In list box. Word will list only the
    AutoText entries that are stored in the template you select. Note that
    if you choose All Active Templates, Word will list all entries stored
    in the Normal template, in the template attached to the document
    (if other than Normal), and in any other loaded templates.

    Your selection in the Look In list box will also affect the
    AutoText entries that are subsequently displayed on the AutoText
    submenu of the Insert menu, as well as those that are displayed
    by the AutoText toolbar that is described in the next section.

3   Select the name of an AutoText entry in the Enter AutoText
    Entries Here list. You can now do one of the following:

    • You can view the current contents of the entry in the Pre-
      view area.

    • You can delete the entry by clicking the Delete button.

    • You can insert the entry into your document by clicking the
      Insert button. (This is a useful feature because it allows
      you to preview the contents of any entry immediately before
      inserting it.)

Displaying the AutoText Toolbar

If you use AutoText frequently, you can save time by displaying the
AutoText toolbar, which is shown in Figure 5-5. To display it, point to
Toolbars on the View menu or right-click the menu bar or a toolbar,

FIGURE 5-5.
Using the AutoText
toolbar.

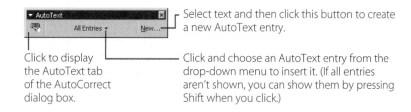

Select text and then click this button to create a new AutoText entry.

Click to display the AutoText tab of the AutoCorrect dialog box.

Click and choose an AutoText entry from the drop-down menu to insert it. (If all entries aren't shown, you can show them by pressing Shift when you click.)

and then choose the AutoText option from the submenu that pops up. You can also display the toolbar by clicking the Show Toolbar button on the AutoText tab.

 NOTE

> If the insertion point is currently in a paragraph with a style other than Normal, and if you created one or more AutoText entries from paragraphs having that style, the middle button on the AutoText toolbar will be labeled with the name of the paragraph style rather than All Entries, and it will list *only* entries created from paragraphs with the same style. If you want to see *all* AutoText entries, hold down the Shift key while clicking the button.

Using the AutoCorrect Feature

A final way to automate text insertion is to use the AutoCorrect feature, which is similar to the AutoText feature. The primary difference between the two is that after you've typed the name of an AutoCorrect entry followed by a space or a punctuation symbol, Word automatically replaces the name with the entry text; you don't need to press a special key or issue a command. Thus, you might want to use AutoCorrect rather than AutoText for text that you insert frequently. Also, you can have AutoCorrect perform certain general text replacements; for example, you can have it automatically capitalize the first letter of a sentence if you fail to do so.

The following are the steps for enabling AutoCorrect text replacements and for defining one or more AutoCorrect entries:

1 If the text you want to save in the AutoCorrect entry has already been entered in a document, select it. (This step is optional because you can type the text later.)

2 Choose AutoCorrect from the Tools menu to open the AutoCorrect dialog box, and then click the AutoCorrect tab if it isn't already displayed.

3 Make sure the Replace Text As You Type option is selected to activate the AutoCorrect entries.

4 In the Replace text box, type a name for the AutoCorrect entry you want to define

 NOTE

Make sure that the name you choose for an AutoCorrect entry is not a word that you might need to type into a document; for example, if you assigned the name *a*, each time you tried to enter *a* into a document, Word would insert the associated AutoCorrect entry.

5 If you selected text prior to opening the AutoCorrect dialog box, that text will already be contained in the With text box. If you didn't select text, type the text for the entry into the With box.

6 Click the Add button to define the new entry and add it to the list. Figure 5-6 shows the AutoCorrect dialog box after you have defined a new entry.

To define an additional entry, repeat steps 4 through 6. When you're finished adding AutoCorrect entries, click the OK button to save your entries and close the dialog box.

 TIP

Creating an AutoCorrect Entry for a Symbol
As mentioned previously in "Inserting Special Characters," page 119, in the Symbol dialog box (which you can open by choosing Symbol from the Insert menu), you can select a symbol and then click the AutoCorrect button to quickly create an AutoCorrect entry for that symbol.

After you have performed these steps, Word will immediately replace the name of an AutoCorrect entry with the entry text whenever you type the name followed by a space, tab, punctuation character, or line break (inserted by pressing Enter or Shift+Enter). Note that you must type the entry name as a separate word; that is, the word must immediately follow a space, tab, or punctuation character, or be typed at the beginning of a line. For example, if you had defined the entry shown in Figure 5-6, typing *mw* followed by a space would cause Word to erase the *mw* and insert *Microsoft Word* in its place.

Notice also that you can have Word perform several kinds of general text replacements by selecting one or more of the four options at the top of the AutoCorrect dialog box. For example, if you select the first option (Correct TWo INitial CApitals), whenever you type a word beginning with two capital letters (and the rest of the characters are lowercase), Word will automatically correct the error by converting the second letter to lowercase. If you select the second option (Capitalize

FIGURE 5-6.

The AutoCorrect tab after adding a new entry named *mw*.

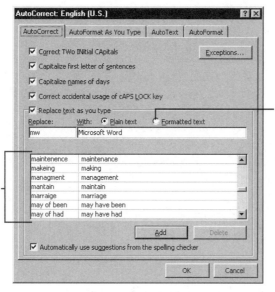

This list displays the AutoCorrect entries that are already defined. Notice that Word provides a collection of useful entries, which are designed for inserting symbols and correcting common typing errors.

If you selected text prior to opening the dialog box, you can select the Formatted Text option to have Word save the text's formatting as part of the entry.

First Letter Of Sentences), Word will automatically capitalize the first letter of a sentence if you fail to do so.

To add or delete exceptions to corrections made by the Capitalize First Letter Of Sentences or Correct TWo INitial CApitals options, or to add or delete specific words you don't want AutoCorrect to alter, click the Exceptions button in the AutoCorrect dialog box. Word will display the dialog box shown here:

On this tab, you can add or delete exceptions to corrections made by the Correct TWo INitial CApitals option.

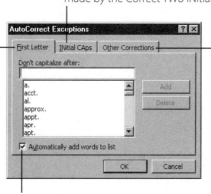

On this tab, you can add or delete exceptions to corrections made by the Capitalize First Letter Of Sentences option.

On this tab, you can add or delete specific words that you don't want AutoCorrect to correct.

If you select this option, whenever you press Backspace and type over an AutoCorrect correction, Word will add the word to the appropriate exceptions list so that it won't be corrected automatically anymore.

Microsoft Word

TIP

Using AutoCorrect to Correct Your Spelling

The collection of AutoCorrect entries defined by Word includes many that correct common misspellings (such as *accomodate, acheive,* and *embarass*). Additionally, when you use the Spelling And Grammar command to check your spelling, whenever Word finds a spelling error, you can quickly create an AutoCorrect entry that will automatically correct that error in the future.

If you select the Automatically Use Suggestions From The Spelling Checker option on the AutoCorrect tab (see Figure 5-6), whenever you misspell a word, Word will immediately replace it with a word from the spelling checker's suggestion list rather than simply marking the misspelling with a wavy red underline. This feature works, however, only if there is a *single* word on the suggestion list.

For information on the spelling checker and using its suggestions for AutoCorrect, see "Checking Your Spelling," page 273.

Moving the Insertion Point

 SEE ALSO

For advanced methods to navigate through a document, see "Navigating Through a Document Using Other Methods," page 148.

After you have created a document, the first step in editing it is to move the insertion point to the position where you want to make the change. Word provides many ways to move quickly through your documents. This section describes some of the basic ones.

The easiest way to move the insertion point to a document position that is currently visible in the window is to simply click the position using the left (primary) mouse button:

Clicking the left mouse button will place the insertion point here.

Move the I-beam mouse pointer to the desired position of the insertion point and click.

 TIP

Scroll Without Losing Your Place

To temporarily view another part of your document, use the vertical scroll bar to move to that location. Provided you don't click anywhere at the new location, you can instantly return to your original position by simply pressing an arrow key. Word will automatically scroll back to the position of the insertion point (which is not moved when you use a scroll bar).

You can use the keys or key combinations in Table 5-1 to move the insertion point to any position in a document:

TABLE 5-1.   Shortcut Key Combinations for Moving the Insertion Point

Use This Key or Key Combination	To Move
←	To previous character
→	To next character
↑	One line up
↓	One line down
Ctrl+←	Backward through the document one word at a time
Ctrl+→	Forward through the document one word at a time
Ctrl+↑	Backward through the document one paragraph at a time
Ctrl+↓	Forward through the document one paragraph at a time
Home	To beginning of line
End	To end of line
Ctrl+Home	To beginning of document
Ctrl+End	To end of document
Page Up	One window up (that is, up a distance equal to the height of the window)
Page Down	One window down

II

Microsoft Word

? SEE ALSO

For information about searching for text, see "Finding and Replacing Text," page 143.

You can also use the horizontal and vertical scroll bars to bring text into view in a document window, as shown in Figure 5-7, on the following page. If either scroll bar is not currently displayed, you can make it visible by choosing Options from the Tools menu, clicking the View tab, and selecting the Horizontal Scroll Bar or the Vertical Scroll Bar option. Note that when you view text using a scroll bar, the insertion point is not moved; in fact, after scrolling, the insertion point will often not even be visible in the window. To move the insertion point, scroll and then click the position where you want the insertion point to appear.

FIGURE 5-7.

The effects of clicking various scroll bar positions to scroll through a document (drag rather than click, where indicated). In this figure, *scroll one window* means to scroll a distance equal to the current size of the document window, in the direction you choose.

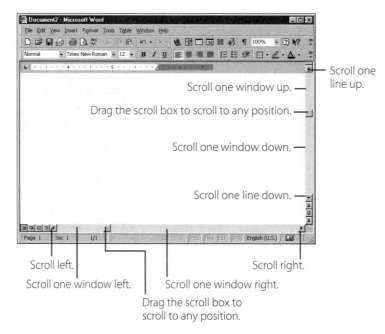

Scroll one line up.

Scroll one window up.

Drag the scroll box to scroll to any position.

Scroll one window down.

Scroll one line down.

Scroll left.

Scroll one window left.

Scroll right.

Scroll one window right.

Drag the scroll box to scroll to any position.

Editing Text

Once you have moved the insertion point to the position in your document where you want to make a change, the next step is to apply a Word editing command. Word gives you an assortment of editing commands for deleting, replacing, copying, moving, or capitalizing text.

To begin, you can delete a limited number of characters by simply positioning the insertion point and pressing one of the following keys or key combinations:

Press These Keys	To Delete
Delete	The character after the insertion point
Ctrl+Delete	Through the end of the word containing (or following) the insertion point
Backspace	The character before the insertion point
Ctrl+Backspace	Through the beginning of the word containing (or preceding) the insertion point

You can hold down any of these keys or key combinations to delete several characters or words. Remember that you can choose Undo from

SEE ALSO

For more information on using the Undo button, see the sidebar "Undoing and Redoing Editing and Formatting Actions," page 136.

the Edit menu, click the Undo button, or press Ctrl+Z to restore text that you've deleted by mistake. If you held down the Backspace key to delete a group of characters, the Undo command will restore all of them. If you used any of the other deleting keys or key combinations, Undo will restore only the most recently deleted character or word. (You can then repeat the Undo command to restore additional characters or words.)

Selecting Text

Most of the Word editing techniques—as well as the formatting techniques that will be discussed in the next chapter—require that you first *select* or *highlight* a block of text (which is known as a *selection*), and then issue a command that affects that block of text. Selecting lets you precisely control the part of your document that's affected by a Word command—from a single character or graphic to the entire document.

This text is selected. In Word, you first select text and then act on the selection.

For example, you could first select a block of text, and then press the Delete key. Notice that having a selection changes the usual effect of the Delete command—it erases an entire block of characters rather than erasing a single space or character. Selecting text removes the normal insertion point; that is, at a given time a document has either a selection or an insertion point, never both. You can select text using either the keyboard or the mouse.

Selecting by Using the Keyboard

The basic method for using the keyboard to select text is to hold down the Shift key, and then press any of the keys or key combinations for moving the insertion point that were discussed in the section "Moving the Insertion Point," page 130. With the Shift key pressed, the keyboard command will select text rather than merely move the insertion point. For example, you can hold down Shift and an arrow key to extend the selection character-by-character or line-by-line in the direction you want.

Table 5-2, on the next page, summarizes the key combinations for selecting text. Keep in mind that these are based on familiar commands; they simply combine the Shift key with the insertion point–moving keys or key combinations you already saw in Table 5-1, page 131.

Microsoft Word

TABLE 5-2.   Shortcut Keys for Extending a Selection

Press This Key or Key Combination	To Extend the Selection
Shift+←	Through the previous character
Shift+→	Through the next character
Shift+↑	One line up
Shift+↓	One line down
Shift+Ctrl+←	Through the beginning of the current word (or previous word if already at the beginning of a word)
Shift+Ctrl+→	Through the beginning of the next word
Shift+Ctrl+↑	Through the beginning of the current paragraph (or previous paragraph if already at the beginning of a paragraph)
Shift+Ctrl+↓	Through the end of the current paragraph
Shift+Home	Through the beginning of the line
Shift+End	Through the end of the line
Shift+Ctrl+Home	Through the beginning of the document
Shift+Ctrl+End	Through the end of the document
Shift+Page Up	One window up (that is, extend up a distance equal to the height of the window)
Shift+Page Down	One window down

An alternative way to use the keyboard to select text is to press the F8 key or double-click the EXT indicator on the status bar to activate the *Extend mode*. (When the Extend mode is active, the EXT indicator is displayed in darker characters.) While working in the Extend mode, you can make selections by pressing any of the keys or key combinations from Table 5-2 without the Shift key. For example, you can select all characters through the end of the line by pressing F8 and then pressing End. To cancel the Extend mode, either press the Escape key or double-click the EXT status bar indicator. (This will not remove the selection, but will merely end the Extend mode.) Also, the Extend mode will be canceled automatically if you perform any editing or formatting action on the selected text.

Other Ways to Use F8 to Select Parts of a Document

You can press F8 repeatedly to select increasingly larger portions of your document. The first press activates the Extend mode, the second press selects the current word, the third press selects the current sentence, the fourth press selects the current paragraph, and the fifth press selects the entire document.

Also, you can extend the selection through the next occurrence of a letter by pressing F8 and then typing the letter.

Finally you can select the entire document by choosing Select All from the Edit menu or by pressing Ctrl+A.

To cancel a selection—and display the insertion point—simply click at any position in the document or press an arrow key. (If you are in Extend mode, you must first press Escape or double-click the EXT indicator on the status bar.)

Selecting by Using the Mouse

The basic technique for using the mouse to select text or graphics is to move the pointer to the beginning of the desired selection, press the left button, and then drag over the text or graphics that you want to select. If you reach a window border while dragging, Word scrolls the document so that you can keep extending the selection.

If the When Selecting, Automatically Select Entire Word option is selected, dragging will select text word-by-word rather than character-by-character. That is, as the selection is extended, entire words will be added to the selection rather than individual characters. If you prefer to select text character-by-character, clear this option. You can find the option on the Edit tab of the Options dialog box, which you display by choosing Options from the Tools menu.

You can also select any amount of text as follows:

1 Click the position where you want to start the selection.

2 Hold down the Shift key while you click the position where you want to end the selection.

Undoing and Redoing Editing and Formatting Actions

You can reverse the effect of your most recent editing or formatting action by choosing Undo from the Edit menu or by pressing Ctrl+Z. Clicking the Undo button on the Standard toolbar

has the same effect. If you repeat the Undo command, Word will undo your next most recent action. Suppose, for example, that you type a word, format a paragraph, and then delete a character. If you subsequently issue the Undo command three times, Word will replace the character, restore the paragraph to its original format, and then erase the word.

Also, as a shortcut for undoing multiple actions, you can click the down arrow next to the Undo button, drag the pointer down to highlight all the actions you want to undo, and then release the button:

1 Click here to display a list of actions.

2 Select action(s) to undo.

(The actions are listed in order from the most recent to the least recent, and you can undo them only in this order.)

As you learned in the section "Using the Repeat Command," page 121, you can issue the Repeat command (by choosing Repeat from the Edit menu or by pressing Ctrl+Y or F4) to perform again your most recent editing or formatting operation. If, however, your most recent operation was to undo an action using any of the methods just described, the Repeat command will redo the action. (And in this case, the command on the Edit menu will be labeled Redo rather than Repeat.) For example, if you delete a word and then press Ctrl+Z, the word will be restored; if you then press Ctrl+Y, the word will again be removed.

You can also redo an action by clicking the Redo button on the Standard toolbar:

Undoing and Redoing Editing and Formatting Actions *continued*

Like the Undo button, the Redo button has an adjoining down arrow you can click to select the exact actions you want to redo. (Note that unlike the Ctrl+Y and F4 shortcut keys and the Repeat [Redo] Edit menu command, the Redo button can be used only to redo an action; it cannot be used to repeat an action.)

Table 5-3 lists some mouse shortcuts you can use to select various amounts of text. The *selection bar* is the area within the document window to the immediate left of the text. It's easy to tell when the mouse pointer is within the selection bar because the pointer changes to an arrow pointing up and to the right:

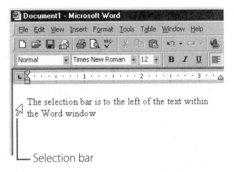

Selection bar

Microsoft Word

TABLE 5-3.   Mouse Shortcuts for Selecting Text

To Select	Do This
A word	Double-click the word.
A sentence	Hold down the Ctrl key while clicking within the sentence.
A line	Click in the selection bar next to the line. (See explanation following this table.)
Several lines	Drag down or up in the selection bar.
A paragraph	Double-click in the selection bar next to the paragraph, or triple-click within the paragraph.
Several paragraphs	Double-click in the selection bar, and then drag down or up.
The entire document	Triple-click in the selection bar or hold down the Ctrl key while clicking in the selection bar.

You can select a column of text by holding down the Alt key and dragging over the area you want to select:

```
To select a column of text, hold
down the Alt key while
dragging over the desired block
of text.
```

Drag while pressing the Alt key to select a column of text.

Pressing the Delete key with the selection shown above would erase the first character of each line.

To cancel the selection, either click at any position in the document or press an arrow key.

Editing the Selection

Once you have selected a block of text, you're ready to apply an editing or formatting command. This section describes the basic editing commands that you can apply to selections. As you begin using these techniques, keep in mind that you can reverse your editing action by issuing the Undo command, as described previously, even if the amount of text deleted or altered is large.

If the Typing Replaces Selection option is active, you can replace the selection by simply typing the new text. When you type the first letter, the entire selection is automatically deleted, and the new text you type is inserted in its place. (If Typing Replaces Selection is not active, the selected text is left in place, the selection is canceled, and the new text is inserted in front of the former selection.) To turn Typing Replaces Selection on or off, choose Options from the Tools menu, and click the Edit tab in the Options dialog box.

To erase the selected text, press the Backspace key or the Delete key, or choose Clear from the Edit menu.

To change the case of the letters in the selection (to lowercase, UPPERCASE, Sentence case, or Title Case), or to toggle all letters between uppercase and lowercase, you can choose Change Case from the Format menu and click the desired capitalization option in the Change Case dialog box. (See Figure 5-8.) Alternatively, you can press Shift+F3—repeatedly if necessary—to switch among various capitalization styles.

FIGURE 5-8.
The Change Case
dialog box.

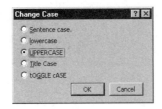

Moving and Copying Text Using the Mouse

You can use the mouse to quickly move or copy text, as follows:

1 Select the text.

2 Place the mouse pointer over the selection (the pointer will change from an I-beam to an arrow), and hold down the left mouse button:

Other text. This text will be moved or copied. Other text.

SEE ALSO

For information about moving blocks of text in Outline view, see "Using Outline View," page 362.

3 To move the text, simply drag it to its new location. To copy the text, hold down the Ctrl key while dragging. If the target location isn't visible, just drag the text to the edge of the window, and the document will automatically be scrolled in the corresponding direction. The target location can be within the same Word document, within a different Word document, or even within a document in another Office application (such as a Microsoft Excel worksheet). If a target location in a different document isn't currently visible, drag the text to the target document's button on the Windows taskbar, and hold the pointer there for a few seconds. The target document's window will then be activated, and you can complete the drag operation. (Keep the left mouse button pressed the whole time.)

To use this method, the Drag-And-Drop Text Editing option must be enabled. You'll find the option by choosing Options from the Tools menu and clicking the Edit tab.

TIP

Use Shortcut Keys to Move a Paragraph Up or Down
You can select and move an entire paragraph by pressing a single key combination. First place the insertion point anywhere within the paragraph. Then to move the paragraph up (that is, before the previous paragraph), press Shift+Alt+Up arrow. To move it down (that is, after the next paragraph), press Shift+Alt+Down arrow.

II

Microsoft Word

Moving and Copying Text Using the Clipboard

You can also move or copy text using the *Clipboard*, which is a Windows facility that temporarily stores text or graphics. The following is the procedure:

1 Select the text.

2 To move the text, choose Cut from the Edit menu or press Ctrl+X. This will *cut* the text—that is, remove it from the document and place it in the Clipboard.

To copy the text, choose Copy from the Edit menu or press Ctrl+C. This will *copy* the text—that is, leave the text in the document and place a copy of it in the Clipboard.

3 Place the insertion point at the position where you want to insert the text that has been cut or copied to the Clipboard. The target location can be within the original document or within a different document.

4 Choose Paste from the Edit menu or press Ctrl+V. This will *paste* the text—that is, insert it into the document.

Word provides two additional ways to cut, copy, or paste text with the Clipboard. One method is to click the appropriate buttons on the Standard toolbar.

Paste

Copy

Cut

? SEE ALSO

For information on different ways to use the Clipboard to transfer data between Office applications, see Chapter 51, "Sharing Data Among Office Applications."

Another method to cut or copy a block of selected text is to right-click it and then choose Cut or Copy from the shortcut menu that is displayed:

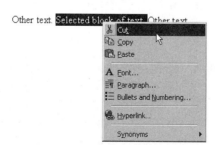

Setting Clipboard Options

Word provides two options that affect moving and copying text with the Clipboard. To set these options, choose Options from the Tools menu and click the Edit tab.

If the Use The INS Key For Paste option is enabled, you can paste by pressing the Insert key rather than by pressing Ctrl+V or by using one of the other methods described earlier. (If this option isn't enabled, pressing the Insert key toggles between the Insert and Overtype editing modes.)

If the Use Smart Cut And Paste option is enabled, Word will remove extraneous spaces that remain after you cut text (or after you delete it using the Clear command on the Edit menu or the Delete or Backspace key). For example, if you cut only the word *expression* from the following text,

    (a parenthetical expression)

Word would automatically remove the space following *parenthetical*.

Likewise, to paste the text, you can right-click the target location, and then choose Paste from the shortcut menu. To remove the shortcut menu without choosing a command, press the Escape key or click anywhere within the document.

An advantage of using the Clipboard is that you can move or copy text or graphics between separate Windows-based programs. (The Clipboard is a shared Windows facility.) Another advantage is that the text is retained in the Clipboard after you paste, allowing you to insert several copies of the text by pasting repeatedly.

However, the text in the Clipboard will normally be lost if you perform another cut or copy operation in Word or in another program. You can preserve the text currently in the Clipboard while moving or copying another block of text by using one of the techniques that don't use the Clipboard, such as dragging (described above) or using the Spike (described later in the chapter). Also, you can make a permanent copy of text that you want to insert repeatedly by using the AutoText or AutoCorrect feature. And finally, you can use the new Clipboard toolbar provided by Office 2000, which is described next.

 Storing Several Blocks of Text in the Clipboard

You can use the Clipboard toolbar to cut or copy several blocks of text (up to twelve) and store them in the Clipboard so that you can insert any of them into an Office document.

The first step is to display the Clipboard toolbar by pointing to Toolbars on the View menu—or by right-clicking the menu bar or a toolbar—and then choosing the Clipboard option. You can then cut or copy up to twelve blocks of text (or graphics) using the instructions given previously. Notice that when you cut or copy each block, an icon representing that block is added to the Clipboard toolbar. (If you cut or copy a thirteenth block, the first stored block will be discarded.)

You can use the Clipboard toolbar to paste one (or all) of these stored blocks, as shown here:

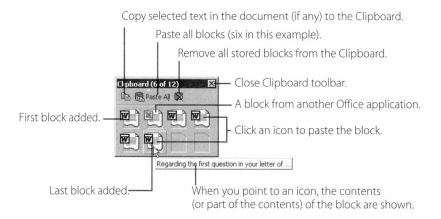

Copy selected text in the document (if any) to the Clipboard.

Paste all blocks (six in this example).

Remove all stored blocks from the Clipboard.

Close Clipboard toolbar.

A block from another Office application.

First block added.

Click an icon to paste the block.

Last block added.

When you point to an icon, the contents (or part of the contents) of the block are shown.

Note that if you use one of the conventional Paste commands discussed in the previous section (for example, Ctrl+V), the last block that was added to the Clipboard will be pasted.

Using the Spike

You can use the *Spike* to remove several blocks of text from a document and then insert all these blocks together at a single document location. The Spike is based on a special-purpose AutoText entry that is assigned the name "Spike." (It derives from the old days when newspaper editors would cut out blocks of lines from typed copy and impale them on a metal spike on their desk for possible later use.) The following is the usual procedure for using the Spike:

1   Select a block of text.

2   Press Ctrl+F3 to remove the block from the document and store it in the Spike.

3   Repeat steps 1 and 2 for each additional block of text you would like to add to the Spike.

4 Place the insertion point at the document position where you want to insert the text, and press Ctrl+Shift+F3. All the blocks of text will appear in the document, and the Spike will be emptied. The blocks will be inserted in the order in which they were stored in the Spike, and a paragraph break will be added after each block.

In the first three steps of the preceding list, Word adds text to the Spike AutoText entry, and in step 4, Word inserts all the entry text into the document and deletes the entry. You can insert the text without deleting the entry by typing *Spike* and then pressing F3. *You can also use any of the other AutoText insertion techniques discussed in "Using the AutoText Feature," page 121.*

Finding and Replacing Text

You can easily search for text, formats, or special items such as paragraph marks and graphics by using the Find command. The following is the basic procedure for using this command to conduct a search in Word:

1 If you want to limit the search to within a specific block of text, select the text.

2 Choose Find from the Edit menu, or press Ctrl+F to display the Find tab of the Find And Replace dialog box. (See Figure 5-9.)

3 If you want to perform a search using the options you set the previous time you used the Find command, proceed to step 4. If, however, you want to set one or more search options, click the More button to display the options—if they aren't already displayed—and select the ones you want. (See Figure 5-10, on the next page.) The search options are summarized in Table 5-4. (If you want Word to search only within the block of text you selected in step 1, you must select Down or Up in the Search list box. If the All option is selected, Word will search the entire document.)

FIGURE 5-9.
The Find tab of the Find And Replace dialog box, without the search options displayed.

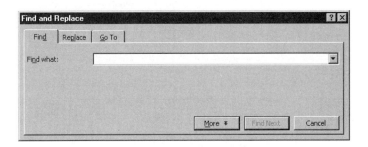

II

Microsoft Word

FIGURE 5-10.

The Find tab of the Find And Replace dialog box, displaying all options.

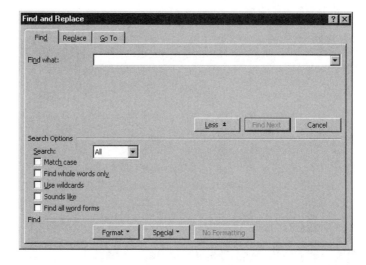

TABLE 5-4.   Search Options on the Find Tab of the Find And Replace Dialog Box

Find Dialog Box Option	Effect
All (in Search list box)	Searches entire document (from insertion point to end of document, and then from beginning of document down to insertion point), including headers, footers, comments, and footnotes.
Down (in Search list box)	Searches from insertion point (or start of selection) to end of document (or selection), excluding headers, footers, comments, and footnotes.
Up (in Search list box)	Searches from insertion point (or end of selection) to beginning of document (or selection), excluding headers, footers, comments, and footnotes.
Match Case	Searches only for text that matches case of each letter in search text.
Find Whole Words Only	Excludes matching text that is part of another word (for example, if searching for *cat*, doesn't find *catatonic*).
Use Wildcards	Allows search text to include general symbols for matching text; for example, ?, which matches any character. To include these symbols in the Find What text box, click the Special button, and select from the pop-up menu. (For more information, look up *wildcards* in the Word online Help.)
Sounds Like	Searches for all text that sounds like the search text. For example, if the search text is *there*, finds *their* as well as *there*.
Find All Word Forms	Finds all forms of the search text. For example, if search text is *go*, finds *go, goes, gone*, and *went*.

4 If you want to search for text (that is, specific words or phrases), enter that text into the Find What box. (You can click the down arrow to select previous search text from a list.) To include a nonprinting character or other special feature in your search text (for example, a paragraph mark or a graphic), click the Special button, and choose the appropriate item. (If the Special button or other button mentioned in these instructions isn't visible, click the More button to reveal it.)

5 If you want to search for a particular format or combination of formats, click the Format button, choose a formatting type, and specify the format in the dialog box that's displayed. Alternatively, if Word provides a key combination for applying a specific format (such as Ctrl+B for bold text or Ctrl+E for centered paragraph alignment), you can specify that format by pressing the key combination when the insertion point is within the Find What text box. *(Formatting and the formatting key combinations are described in Chapter 6.)*

When searching for certain formats (such as bold or superscript text), you can search either for text that has the format, or for text that does not have the format. For example, you can select Bold (to search for text that is bold and meets other criteria) or Not Bold (to search for text that is not bold and meets other criteria), or you can select neither option (to search for text that meets other criteria whether it is bold or not). The formatting that you choose is displayed below the Find What box.

> **NOTE**
>
> If you specify a search format in a dialog box, a check box that has just a check mark means to find text that does have the format, an empty check box means to find text that does not have the format, and a check box that has a gray background and a check mark means the format isn't part of your search criteria. If you specify a search format using a key combination (for example, Ctrl+B for bold text), repeatedly pressing the key toggles between these three states (for example, Bold, Not Bold, and neither Bold nor Not Bold).

You can enter search text into the Find What text box *and* choose formatting. In this case, Word will search for text that matches your search text and has the specified formatting. To remove all your formatting specifications, click the No Formatting button.

Microsoft Word

6 Click the Find Next button to find each occurrence of the search text or formatting. Word will highlight the text it finds. You can edit your document while the Find And Replace dialog box is open; simply click the document when you want to edit it, and then click in the Find And Replace dialog box to continue searching. (If the Find And Replace dialog box is covering the text you want to edit, point to the title bar of the dialog box and drag the box out of the way.)

7 To close the Find And Replace dialog box, click the Cancel button.

After the dialog box is closed, you can continue to search for the same text or formatting using the keyboard. Each time you press Shift+F4, Word will search for the next occurrence of the text or formatting, moving in the direction you specified in the Find And Replace dialog box. Each time you press Ctrl+Page Down, Word will search for the next occurrence moving down in the document, and each time you press Ctrl+Page Up, Word will search for the next occurrence moving up in the document. You can also have Word search for the next occurrence moving either down or up in the document using the browse buttons at the bottom of the vertical scroll bar. *These buttons are described later in the chapter (in the section "Using the Browse Buttons," page 154).*

You can find *and* replace text or formatting using the Replace command. Like the Find command, Replace allows you to search for text, formatting, or a combination of text and formatting. You can replace the text that is found, change its formatting, or both replace the text and change its formatting. The following are the basic steps. (See the previous list of steps in this section for more information on the steps that are common to finding and replacing text.)

1 If you want to replace only within a specific block of text, select the text.

2 Choose Replace from the Edit menu, or press Ctrl+H to display the Replace tab of the Find And Replace dialog box.

3 If you want to perform a replace operation using the options you set the previous time you used the Replace command, proceed to step 4. If, however, you want to set one or more search options, click the More button to display the options—if they aren't already displayed—and select the ones you want. (See Figure 5-11.) These options are the same as those available on the Find

FIGURE 5-11.

The Replace tab of the Find And Replace dialog box, displaying all options.

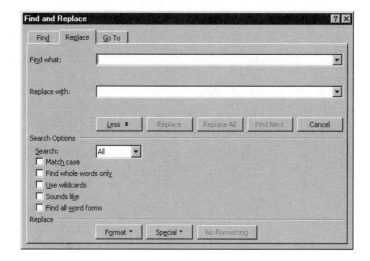

tab and are summarized in Table 5-4, page 144. (If you want Word to search only within the block of text you selected in step 1, you must select Down or Up in the Search list box. If the All option is selected, Word will search the entire document.)

4 If you want to search for particular text, type it in the Find What box. (You can click the down arrow to select previous search text from a list.) To include a nonprinting character or other special feature in your search text (for example, a paragraph mark or a graphic), click the Special button, and choose the appropriate item.

5 If you want to search for a particular format or combination of formats, make sure that the insertion point is within the Find What box. Then click the Format button, choose a formatting type, and specify the format you want in the dialog box that is displayed. Alternatively, if Word provides a key combination for applying a specific format (such as Ctrl+B for bold text), you can specify that format by pressing the key combination when the insertion point is within the Find What text box. (Formatting and the formatting key combinations are described in Chapter 6.)

6 If you want to replace the text that is found, type the replacement text in the Replace With box. To include a special character in the replacement text (such as a paragraph mark), click the Special button. Word will display only those special characters that are appropriate for replacement text.

For information on choosing formatting, see Chapter 6, "Formatting a Word Document."

7 If you want to change the formatting of the text that is found, make sure that the insertion point is within the Replace With box, and choose the formatting you want, as described previously. Word will display the replacement format you have chosen below the Replace With box. Note that if you leave the Replace With box empty and don't choose replacement formatting, each block of text that is found will be deleted.

8 Either click the Replace All button to replace all occurrences of the text or formatting, without confirmation, or click the Find Next button to view and verify the first replacement.

9 If you clicked Find Next, Word will highlight the first matching text. You can now click Replace to replace the text or formatting and find the next occurrence, or you can click Find Next to leave the text unaltered and go on to the next occurrence. You can repeat this step until all text has been replaced, or you can click Close to close the dialog box and stop the process. (The Cancel button is labeled Close after the first replacement, reminding you that you can't cancel replacements that you've already made.) Recall that you can leave the Find And Replace dialog box displayed while you manually edit the document. (You might have to move the dialog box out of the way by dragging its title bar.)

Reversing Your Replacements

If you replaced all occurrences of text in your document by clicking the Replace All button on the Replace tab, issuing the Undo command immediately afterwards will reverse *all* these replacements at once. If you replaced occurrences one at a time by clicking the Replace button, the Undo command will reverse *only* your most recent replacement. (You can then repeat the Undo command to reverse previous replacements.)

Navigating Through a Document Using Other Methods

You have already learned how to move the insertion point within a document by using key combinations as well as the horizontal and vertical scroll bars (in the section "Moving the Insertion Point," page 130). In the following sections, you'll learn some additional ways to move through a document. These techniques are especially useful for larger documents.

Marking and Retrieving Text Using Bookmarks

You can use Word's bookmarks to mark and then quickly return to specific positions in a document.

To mark a position in a document, you need to define a bookmark using the following method:

1 Place the insertion point at the position you want to mark, or select a block of text to mark.

2 Choose Bookmark from the Insert menu, or press Ctrl+Shift+F5, which will open the Bookmark dialog box.

3 Type an identifying name into the Bookmark Name box, and click the Add button. See Figure 5-12.

FIGURE 5-12.
Defining a bookmark named *start* in the Bookmark dialog box.

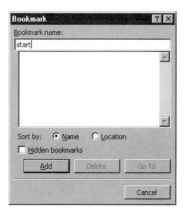

You can use this technique to mark any number of positions in a document. Note that you can make bookmarks visible by choosing Options from the Tools menu, clicking the View tab, and selecting the Bookmarks option (in the Show area); Word will then display an I-beam symbol at the location of each bookmark or, if you marked a block of text, Word will place bracket markers around the bookmark text.

> Bookmarks can be used for a variety of other purposes, some of which will be discussed later in the book—for example, for specifying the target of a hyperlink (discussed in "Inserting and Navigating Using Hyperlinks," page 155), for defining cross-references, and for creating index entries that refer to a range of pages. *(Indexes are discussed in "Creating Indexes and Tables of Contents," page 378.*

II

Microsoft Word

? SEE ALSO

For instructions on writing macros for marking and returning to a document location, see "Macro Examples," page 410.

To move the insertion point to a position marked with a bookmark, open the Bookmark dialog box (choose Bookmark from the Insert menu or press Ctrl+Shift+F5), select the name that you assigned when you defined the bookmark (in step 3 above), and click the Go To button. Word will immediately move the insertion point to the marked position. You can also use the Go To command, discussed in the next section, to move to a particular bookmark.

★ TIP

If you select a block of text prior to defining a bookmark, the bookmark will be assigned to the entire selection. In this case, when you go to the bookmark, Word will select the text.

Using the Go To Command

You can use the Go To command to move the insertion point (or the selection highlight) to a position marked by a bookmark or to one of a variety of other locations in a document. To issue the Go To command, choose Go To from the Edit menu, press Ctrl+G or F5, or double-click anywhere on the left half of the status bar. Word will display the Go To tab of the Find And Replace dialog box (shown in Figure 5-13).

To go to one of the other types of targets, select the appropriate item in the Go To What list, and then enter the number or name for the particular target into the text box, which will be labeled appropriately—for example, Enter Page Number or Enter Bookmark Name. (For certain types of targets, such as bookmarks or comments, you can select the name of the target from a list.) For example, to go to a specific page in

FIGURE 5-13.
Using the Go To command to move the insertion point to the *start* bookmark.

2 Type the name of the bookmark here, or select the bookmark name from the drop-down list.

1 Select Bookmark from the list.

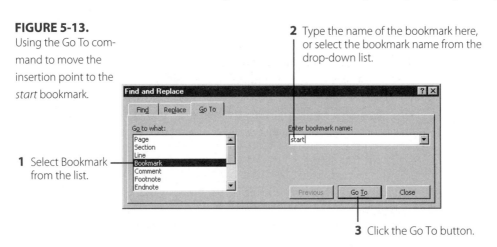

3 Click the Go To button.

your document, select Page in the Go To What list, and then type the page number in the Enter Page Number box.

Likewise, to go to a particular document line, select Line and type the line number in the Enter Line Number box. (Note that for the Go To command, line numbering begins at 1 with the first line in the document and is incremented throughout the rest of the document. In contrast, the line number displayed on the status bar refers to the number of the line within the current page).

For any type of target except a bookmark, if you don't enter a specific target into the text box, the dialog box will display buttons labeled Next and Previous. You can use these buttons to browse through the different instances of the target item. For example, if you select Section in the Go To What list and leave the Enter Section Number text box blank, clicking Next will take you to the beginning of the *next* document section and clicking Previous will take you to the beginning of the *previous* one. *(Document sections are discussed in chapters 8 and 10.)*

Finally, you can enter a plus (+) or minus (-) sign followed by a number in the text box to move forward or back by a certain number of items. For example, if you've selected Page in the Go To What list, you can enter +4 in the Enter Page Number box to move forward by four pages.

You can leave the Find And Replace dialog box open while you work in your document. After you close it, you can press the Shift+F4 key to repeat your last command on the Go To tab (for example, going to a specific bookmark, or going to the next footnote). Unfortunately, however, the Shift+F4 key is also used to repeat the last Find operation. *(This is described in "Finding and Replacing Text," page 143).* Therefore, if you perform a Find, you can no longer use Shift+F4 to return to your last Go To target. (Likewise, if you use the Go To command, you can no longer press Shift+F4 to repeat your last Find.) Note that you can also use the browse buttons, as discussed in the next section, to find the next or previous instance of your most recent Go To or Find target.

NOTE

Another way to move through a document is to press Shift+F5, the Go Back key. Each time you press Shift+F5, Word moves the insertion point back to the location where you most recently added or edited text. You can move to three prior positions, at most; if you press the key a fourth time, the insertion point will cycle back to its original position.

Microsoft Word

Writing Macros for Saving and Restoring Your Place in a Document

This sidebar provides instructions for recording a convenient pair of macros that use bookmarks for saving your place in a document and for rapidly returning to that place. It also provides some suggestions for other macros you might create to automate Word tasks. *For detailed general instructions on recording, writing, and editing macros in Word, see Chapter 14, "Automating Word Using Macros."*

The first macro, named SavePlace, lets you save the insertion point's current position (or the current selection) by pressing Ctrl+Shift+S. The second macro, named ReturnToPlace, lets you later return the insertion point to the saved position (or restore the saved selection) by pressing Ctrl+Shift+R.

You can define the SavePlace macro in the following manner:

1 Begin recording the macro by double-clicking the REC indicator on the status bar and typing the macro name *SavePlace* into the Record Macro dialog box. Make sure that All Documents (Normal.dot) is selected in the Store Macro In list box so that the macro will be saved where it's available to all documents you work on.

2 To define the shortcut key combination, click the Keyboard button in the Record Macro dialog box to open the Customize Keyboard dialog box. Make sure the insertion point is in the Press New Shortcut Key text box, and press the Ctrl+Shift+S key combination. Click Assign, and then click Close. This returns you to your document, ready to record your macro. (By doing this, you will be replacing a shortcut key combination for opening the Style dialog box or activating the Style list box on the Formatting toolbar when this toolbar is visible.)

3 Choose Bookmark from the Insert menu to open the Bookmark dialog box.

4 Type the bookmark name *MarkedLocation* into the Bookmark Name text box, and click the Add button.

5 Stop recording the macro by clicking the Stop Recording button on the Stop Recording toolbar (which is displayed automatically when you start recording a macro).

You can define the ReturnToPlace macro as follows:

1 Begin recording the macro by double-clicking the REC indicator on the status bar and typing the macro name *ReturnToPlace*. Make sure that All Documents (Normal.dot) is selected in the Store Macro In list box.

Writing Macros for Saving and Restoring Your Place in a Document *continued*

2 Define the shortcut key by clicking the Keyboard button and, in the Customize Keyboard dialog box, pressing the Ctrl+Shift+R key combination, clicking Assign, and t hen clicking Close.

3 Choose Bookmark from the Insert menu.

4 Select the bookmark name MarkedLocation in the Bookmark Name box, click the Go To button, and click the Close button.

5 Stop recording the macro by clicking the Stop Recording button on the Stop Recording toolbar.

You can now test these macros as follows: Place the insertion point anywhere in a document (or select a block of text), and then press Ctrl+Shift+S. This will save your position (or selection). Then move the insertion point anywhere else within the same document, and perform any editing or formatting actions you want. When you're ready to go back to your original location in the document, press Ctrl+Shift+R; Word will immediately move the insertion point back to its original position (or restore the original selection).

The following are several additional examples of macros that you might record:

- Record a pair of macros to turn the Wrap To Window option on or off. This option breaks each line at the right edge of the window, rather than at the position where it will be broken on the printed page. You might want to select this option while you're editing in Normal view so that the window contains the maximum amount of text, but then turn it off to view the actual positions of line breaks on the printed copy. To create the first macro, start recording, and then choose Options from the Tools menu, click the View tab, and select the Wrap To Window option (in the Outline And Normal Options area). To record the second macro, perform these same steps but turn off the option.

- Record a pair of macros to switch between the blue window background and the white window background. You might want to enable the blue background to prevent eyestrain, but then switch to the white background to view items that are hard to see with a blue background (for example, dark lines drawn with Word's Drawing toolbar). To create the first macro, start recording, choose Options from the Tools menu, click the General tab, and select the Blue Background, White Text option. To record the second macro, perform these same steps but deselect the option.

Microsoft Word

> **Writing Macros for Saving and Restoring Your Place in a Document** *continued*
>
> ■ Write a macro to prepare a document for printing. Such a macro would be useful if you like to write and edit a document with one set of formatting features, such as single line-spacing and a large monospaced font (such as 12-point Courier New), but you want to print the document using a different set of formatting features, such as double line-spacing and a small proportional font (such as 10-point Times New Roman). In recording the macro, perform all actions that are necessary for printing the document, such as assigning different formatting features to the document's styles. Run the macro just before printing.

Using the Browse Buttons

Word provides a set of browse buttons at the bottom of the vertical scroll bar. These convenient buttons allow you to quickly locate various types of objects within your documents. Figures 5-14 and 5-15 show you how.

FIGURE 5-14.
How to use the browse buttons.

1 Click here to display a pop-up menu of browse objects. (See Figure 6-15.)

2 Click a browse object on the pop-up menu to select that object and to go to the next instance of the object.

3 Click here to go to the previous instance of the selected browse object…

…or, click here to go to the next instance.

Should you use the browse buttons rather than the Go To command? On the negative side, the browse buttons don't provide some of the targets that the Go To command offers (such as Line and Bookmark). Also, you can't specify a particular item number (for example, you can't go directly to page 25); you can only browse forward or back through the objects. On the plus side, the browse buttons are quicker to use. Also, if you've previously used the Find command or the Go To command, you can just click the Next or Previous browse button to instantly go to the next or previous Find or Go To target, without the need to first select a browse object on the pop-up menu.

FIGURE 5-15.
The Pop-up menu of browse objects displayed when you click the middle browse button (Select Browse Object).

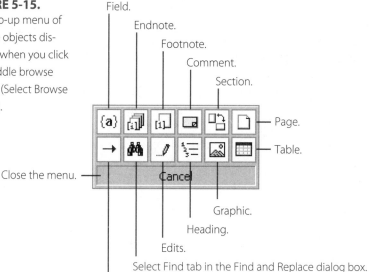

Field.

Endnote.

Footnote.

Comment.

Section.

Page.

Table.

Close the menu.

Cancel

Graphic.

Heading.

Edits.

Select Find tab in the Find and Replace dialog box.

Select Go To tab in the Find and Replace dialog box.

 NOTE

If you select the Edits browse object, clicking the Previous button has the same effect as pressing the Go Back key (Shift+F5) that was described in the prior note. Clicking the Next button moves you through your most recent edits in the opposite order.

Inserting and Navigating Using Hyperlinks

A final navigation tool discussed in this chapter is the *hyperlink*. You can assign a hyperlink to a block of text or to a graphic image in a Word document. The hyperlink connects the block or image to a target location, which can be in the same Word document, or in another document or Web page on a disk, network, or Internet site. Clicking the hyperlink displays the target location. You can click a hyperlink when a document is open in Word, or—for a Web-page document—when it's displayed in a browser. Hyperlinks can be useful in any type of Word document, but they are especially important in Web-page documents (that is, documents you save in HTML format for viewing in Web browsers), where you can use them to tie together the pages in your Web site or to connect to other sites.

II

Microsoft Word

To create a hyperlink, first select the text (or graphic image) to which you want to assign the hyperlink, or simply place the insertion point at the position in your document where you want Word to insert the hyperlink text that you later specify. Then open the Insert Hyperlink dialog box by choosing Hyperlink from the Insert menu (or from the pop-up menu that appears when you right-click anywhere in the document), by clicking the Insert Hyperlink button on the Standard toolbar, or by pressing Ctrl+K. In the Insert Hyperlink dialog box, specify the target location for the hyperlink, as shown in Figure 5-16.

Insert
Hyperlink

To specify a different document or Web page as the target of the hyperlink, select the Existing File Or Web Page item on the Link To bar. (This item is selected in Figure 5-16.) To specify a target location within the current document, select the Place In This Document item, and then select either a heading or a bookmark from the list that's displayed. To

FIGURE 5-16.
Defining a hyperlink
in the Insert Hyperlink
dialog box.

1 Enter or edit hyperlink text here, if necessary. (The text box initially contains selected text in document, if any.)

Click to enter text that will be displayed as a tip when the mouse pointer is over the hyperlink (optional).

Type file path or URL (Internet address) for the target document here...

...or, browse for target document on a local or network disk..

...or, run browser to search for a target document on the Web...

...or, select the target document from the list.

2 In this bar, select the general category of the hyperlink target location that you want. The Existing File Or Web Page category is currently selected.

3 Specify the exact hyperlink target location using the controls in this area.

To define a specific target location within the target document, click this button, and select a bookmark in the target document (optional). If you omit this step, the hyperlink will display the beginning of the document.

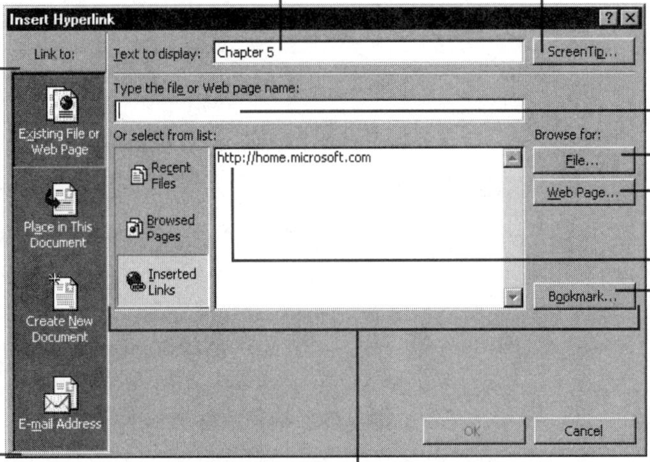

create a new document and make it the target of the hyperlink, select the Create New Document item, and enter a document name and location. And finally, to have the hyperlink send a message to a particular Internet e-mail address (rather than opening a document or page), select the E-Mail Address item on the Link To bar, and then enter the e-mail address and message subject.

When you click the OK button in the Insert Hyperlink dialog box, the hyperlink will be assigned to the block of text or image in your document. By default, hyperlink text will initially be blue and underlined. After you have *followed* the hyperlink (that is, clicked it in Word or in a browser, to open the target), the color will change to violet. You can change the format of an unfollowed or a followed hyperlink by modifying the Hyperlink or FollowedHyperlink built-in Word style. *(For instructions, see "Modifying Styles" on page 198.)* The hyperlink colors will also be modified by applying a theme to the document.

To modify a hyperlink you have already defined, select the text or image again, and then use any of the techniques that were given for opening the Insert Hyperlink dialog box. The dialog box will now be labeled Edit Hyperlink. You can use it to modify the hyperlink, or you can click the Remove Link button in the lower left corner of the dialog box to remove the hyperlink from the text or image in your document.

 SEE ALSO

For information on using the Document Map to rapidly move through a document, see "Browsing Through Outline Headings," page 371.

If you click a hyperlink in Word, and if the target of that hyperlink is a regular Office document (that is, one saved in native format, not HTML), you can use the Web toolbar to navigate back and forth through the document locations you have visited or to open other documents. *(This toolbar is further described in "Using the Web Toolbar," page 91.)* When you first click the hyperlink, the Web toolbar is displayed automatically. (You can display it at any time by pointing to Toolbars on the View menu or by right-clicking a menu or toolbar, and then choosing the Web option.)

Click here to move back through a series of visited locations.

Click here to move forward through a series of visited locations.

Microsoft Word

II

CHAPTER 6

Formatting a Word Document

In this chapter, you'll learn the basic techniques for *formatting* a document—that is, for adjusting the document's appearance. You'll learn how to format individual characters as well as how to format entire paragraphs of text.

This chapter presents formatting techniques beginning with the most automated ones, and then moving on to methods that give you greater levels of formatting control. For many of the documents you create, you might be able to save time by using the more automated methods. For other documents, you might need to use techniques described later in the chapter to modify automatically applied formats or to achieve more exacting formatting results.

The next two chapters—Chapter 7, "Customizing Styles and Templates," and Chapter 8, "Arranging Text in Columns and Lists"—will provide additional information on formatting paragraphs.

In Microsoft Word 2000, you can also adjust the appearance of one or more entire pages. The appearance of a page is generally known as its *setup* rather than its format; this topic will be covered primarily in Chapter 10, "Designing Pages."

As you learn the techniques presented in this chapter, keep in mind that you can reverse the effect of any formatting command by issuing the Undo command, using any of the methods discussed in the sidebar "Undoing and Redoing Editing and Formatting Actions," page 136.

Formatting Documents Automatically

After you have finished entering text into your document, you can use AutoFormat to enhance the appearance of the entire document. AutoFormat will apply a consistent and attractive set of formatting features to the text throughout the document. You can also have AutoFormat make certain replacements in your document text—for example, it can replace straight quotes (" ") with curly quotes (" ") for a professionally typeset appearance. After using AutoFormat, you can quickly adjust the overall look of your document by applying a theme or by using the Word Style Gallery (discussed later in this chapter).

**Modify Automatically Formatted Text
Using Manual Formatting Techniques**

Even if you're going to use AutoFormat, you might want to manually apply character formatting (such as bold or italic) to emphasize individual words or phrases as you enter text into your document. Also, after using AutoFormat, you might need to manually adjust some of the document's formatting. In either case, you can use the manual formatting techniques given later in the chapter.

AutoFormat formats your document by analyzing each paragraph and assigning it an appropriate paragraph *style*, which is a set of formatting attributes identified with a unique name. For instance, if the document begins with a paragraph consisting of a single line of text (that starts with a capital letter and has no ending period), AutoFormat assigns it the Heading 1 paragraph style, which contains formatting features that are appropriate for a document heading. These features typically include a relatively large font, bold characters, and additional space above and below the paragraph. Likewise, if a paragraph is a simple block of text that includes several lines, AutoFormat assigns it the Body Text style, which contains formatting features appropriate for normal paragraphs of text. These features typically include an average-sized font, regular characters, and a small amount of extra space following the paragraph.

NOTE

The actual formatting features belonging to a particular style, such as Body Text, depend on the template that was used to create the document. And the features of a style might be changed when you apply a theme or use the Style Gallery. You can also manually modify a style using the techniques given in Chapter 7.

Before using AutoFormat for the first time, you should specify how you want the command to work. To do this, choose AutoCorrect from the Tools menu, click the AutoFormat tab, and select the particular options you want. (See Figure 6-1 on the next page.) The AutoFormat options are briefly explained in Table 6-1.

TABLE 6-1. AutoFormat Options

AutoFormat Option	Effect If Option Is Selected
Apply	
Headings	Document headings are assigned appropriate styles (Heading 1 through Heading 9, depending on the heading importance).
Lists	Simple or numbered lists are assigned appropriate list styles (List through List 5, depending on the level of indentation).
Automatic Bulleted Lists	Bulleted lists are assigned appropriate bulleted list styles (List Bullet through List Bullet 5, depending on the level of indentation). These styles automatically add bullet symbols such as ●. (Existing bullet characters, such as *, are first removed.)
Other Paragraphs	Document paragraphs other than headings and lists are given appropriate styles (such as Body Text, Inside Address, or Salutation).
Replace	
"Straight Quotes" With "Smart Quotes"	Pairs of straight quotes (" " or ' ') are replaced with pairs of curly quotes (" " or ' '). Also, a straight apostrophe (as in *Joe's*) is replaced with a curly apostrophe (as in *Joe's*).
Ordinals (1st) With Superscript	Plain ordinal expressions (such as 1st, 2nd, and 3rd) are replaced with superscripted expressions (such as 1st, 2nd, and 3rd).
Fractions (1/2) With Fraction Character (½)	The fractional expressions 1/4, 1/2, and 3/4 are replaced with the fraction symbols ¼, ½, and ¾.
Symbol Characters (- -) With Symbols (—)	The symbol expressions (C), (R), (TM), and - - are replaced with the actual symbols ©, ®, ™, and —.

(continued)

II

Microsoft Word

TABLE 6-1. *continued*

AutoFormat Option	Effect If Option Is Selected
Bold And _Italic_ With Real Formatting	Characters enclosed in asterisks are formatted as bold and characters enclosed in underscore characters are formatted as italic. For example, *help* would be converted to **help**. This option is useful for converting text-only e-mail messages (which typically emphasize words by surrounding them with * or _ characters) into formatted document text.
Internet And Network Paths With Hyperlinks	Internet and network paths are converted into actual hyperlinks that can be used to navigate to the sites. See the discussion on hyperlinks in the section "Inserting and Navigating Using Hyperlinks," page 155.
Preserve	
Styles	Only paragraphs that have the Normal or Body Text style are assigned new styles. Paragraphs that have other styles are left unaltered.
Always AutoFormat	
Plain Text WordMail Documents	Automatically applies AutoFormat to plain-text WordMail messages when you open them. (For more information, look up "WordMail" in the Word online Help.)

FIGURE 6-1.
Setting AutoFormat options on the AutoFormat tab of the AutoCorrect dialog box.

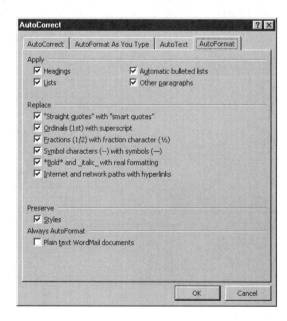

If you want to automatically format only a portion of your document, select that portion before you issue the AutoFormat command. To format the entire document, place the insertion point anywhere within the document. To automatically format your document, perform the following steps:

1 Choose AutoFormat from the Format menu to open the AutoFormat dialog box.

4A Select this option if you want Word to format the entire document or selection without giving you the opportunity to accept or reject each change.

4B Select this option if you want to review and possibly modify each formatting change before accepting it.

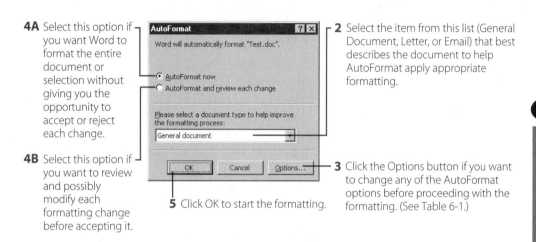

2 Select the item from this list (General Document, Letter, or Email) that best describes the document to help AutoFormat apply appropriate formatting.

3 Click the Options button if you want to change any of the AutoFormat options before proceeding with the formatting. (See Table 6-1.)

5 Click OK to start the formatting.

6 If you selected AutoFormat And Review Each Change, after the formatting is complete Word displays a different dialog box that is also labeled AutoFormat. Note that while this dialog box is displayed, you can scroll through the document to examine the changes.

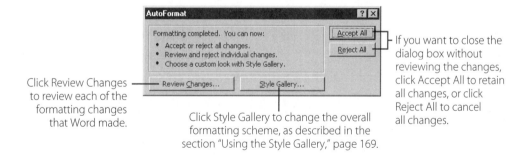

Click Review Changes to review each of the formatting changes that Word made.

Click Style Gallery to change the overall formatting scheme, as described in the section "Using the Style Gallery," page 169.

If you want to close the dialog box without reviewing the changes, click Accept All to retain all changes, or click Reject All to cancel all changes.

7 If you clicked the Review Changes button, Word will mark the changes it made to the document, and it will display the Review

AutoFormat Changes dialog box. Figure 6-2 shows an example document in which one of the formatting changes has been selected.

Word labels the changes by using *revision markings*, which will be described in Chapter 11, "Working with Word in Workgroups." Note that while the Review AutoFormat Changes dialog box is displayed, you can manually scroll through the document and make any editing or formatting changes you want.

8 When you have finished reviewing changes and making modifications, click the Cancel button to close the Review AutoFormat Changes dialog box. You'll return to the AutoFormat dialog box.

9 In the AutoFormat dialog box, click the Accept All button to accept all AutoFormat changes—except those that you rejected—plus any manual changes that you made. Alternatively, if you click Reject All, all AutoFormat changes and all manual changes you made will be canceled, and the document will be restored to its state immediately before you issued the AutoFormat command.

FIGURE 6-2.
Reviewing AutoFormat changes in an example document.

Click Hide Marks to hide the revision marking.

You can undo your previous change by clicking Undo.

Click Reject to cancel the selected change. If you don't click Reject, the change is accepted.

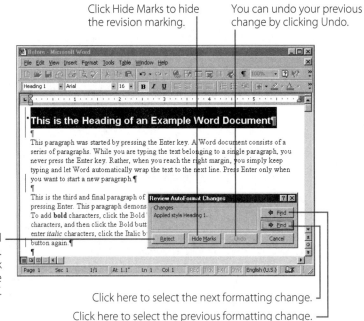

Click here to select the next formatting change.

Click here to select the previous formatting change.

Using the AutoFormat As You Type Feature

You can also have Word automatically make certain formatting changes as you type your documents. To do this, choose AutoCorrect from the Tools menu, and click the AutoFormat As You Type tab. Then select the options for the formatting changes you want Word to make. (See Figure 6-3, on page 167.) Table 6-2 describes the effect of each of the AutoFormat As You Type options.

> **NOTE**
>
> When you first install Word, the AutoFormat As You Type options might already be selected. To disable automatic formatting as you type, you must individually deselect all the AutoFormat As You Type options.

TABLE 6-2.   The AutoFormat As You Type Options and Their Effects

AutoFormat As You Type Option	Effect If Option Is Selected
Apply As You Type	
Headings	If you type a line of text (not terminated with a period) at the beginning of the document or following a blank line, and then press Enter twice, Word will assign it the Heading 1 style. If the line starts after a blank line and with a single tab or a ½-inch indent, Word will assign it the Heading 2 style; if the line starts after a blank line and with two tabs or a 1-inch indent, Word will assign it Heading 3; and so on.
Borders	If you type a line consisting of three hyphens (- - -), underscores (___), equal signs (= = =), asterisks (***), tildes (~~~), or number signs (###), Word will replace the line with a horizontal border appended to the bottom of the preceding paragraph—a thin border for hyphens, a thick border for underscores, a double border for equal signs, a dotted line for asterisks, a wavy line for tildes, or a decorative line for number signs.
Tables	If you type a plus sign (+) followed by a series of hyphens followed by another plus sign, and so on (for example + - - + - - - - + - - +), Word will automatically insert a table. Each plus sign indicates a column border, and the number of hyphens between plus signs indicates the width of each column. For information on tables, see "Using Tables," page 229.

(continued)

TABLE 6-2. *continued*

AutoFormat As You Type Option	Effect If Option Is Selected
Automatic Bulleted Lists	If you begin a paragraph with an asterisk (*), hyphen (-), right angle-bracket (>), or lowercase *o*, followed by a space or tab (or two spaces or tabs after a lowercase *o*), Word will format the paragraph—and each paragraph you subsequently type—as an automatically bulleted list (described in Chapter 8, "Arranging Text in Columns and Lists"). To restore normal paragraph formatting, press Enter twice after a list item.
Automatic Numbered Lists	If you begin a paragraph with a number or letter, followed by a period, hyphen, or closing parenthesis, followed by a space or tab, Word will format the paragraph—and each paragraph you subsequently type—as an automatically numbered list (described in Chapter 8, "Arranging Text in Columns and Lists"). To restore normal paragraph formatting, press Enter twice after a list item.
Replace As You Type	
"Straight Quotes" With "Smart Quotes"	Pairs of straight quotes (" " or ' ') are replaced with pairs of curly quotes (" "or ' '). Also, a straight apostrophe (as in *Joe's*) is replaced with a curly apostrophe (as in *Joe's*).
Ordinals (1st) With Superscript	Plain ordinal expressions (such as 1st, 2nd, and 3rd) are replaced with superscripted expressions (such as 1st, 2nd, and 3rd).
Fractions (1/2) With Fraction Character (½)	The fraction expressions 1/4, 1/2, and 3/4 are replaced with the fraction symbols ¼, ½, and ¾.
Symbol Characters (- -) With Symbols (—)	Two hyphens immediately preceded and followed by text are replaced with an em dash (—). Also, if you type text, a space, one or two hyphens, another space (optional), and then text, the hyphen(s) will be replaced with an en dash (–).
Bold And _Italic_ With Real Formatting	Characters enclosed in asterisks are formatted as bold, and characters enclosed in underscore characters are formatted as italic. For example, *help* would be converted to **help**. This option is useful for converting text-only e-mail messages (which typically emphasize words by surrounding them with * or _ characters) into formatted document text.
Internet And Network Paths With Hyperlinks	Internet addresses (such as *http://mspress.microsoft.com/*) and network paths (such as *\\accounting\c\data\payables.xls*) are converted into hyperlinks that you can click to open the targets. See the discussion on hyperlinks in "Inserting and Navigating Using Hyperlinks," page 155.

(continued)

TABLE 6-2. *continued*

AutoFormat As You Type Option	Effect If Option Is Selected
Automatically As You Type	
Format Beginning Of List Item Like The One Before It	When you insert a new item in a list, Word automatically applies the same character formatting (such as bold) that was applied to the beginning of the previous list item. For information on lists, see "Creating Bulleted and Numbered Lists," page 248.
Define Styles Based On Your Formatting	Word will automatically create new styles based on the paragraph formatting you manually apply to paragraphs so that you can quickly reuse the formatting by applying the new styles to other paragraphs.

? SEE ALSO

For information about bulleted and numbered lists, see "Creating Bulleted and Numbered lists," page 248.

When the AutoFormat feature makes one of the Apply As You Type modifications (the first group of options on the AutoFormat As You Type tab), the Office Assistant (if it's currently visible) might display a tip describing the modification that was made. If a tip appears, you can have the Assistant reverse the modification or show you how to turn off the AutoFormat option that generated the change. You can ignore the Assistant and just keep typing to leave the modification in place. (If you do this several times, the tips stop appearing.)

FIGURE 6-3.
Setting AutoFormat As You Type options.

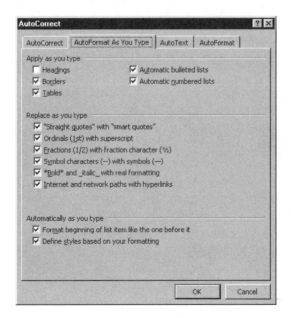

Microsoft Word

Keep in mind that even if an Assistant tip doesn't appear, you can reverse any of the AutoFormat modifications shown in Table 6-2 by using the Undo command. For example, if you type a straight quote (") and AutoFormat converts it to a curly quote ("), you can issue the Undo command to convert it back to a straight quote.

⟨2000⟩ Applying a Theme

After you have automatically formatted your document, you can modify its overall appearance by applying a *theme*: a predesigned visual scheme that applies a consistent look to elements throughout a document. You can choose from a list of more than 25 themes provided with Office.

Applying a theme affects the following document elements:

- The font, size, color, and other features of text throughout the document. (The theme modifies text by changing features of the Normal and heading styles, which are explained later in the chapter.)

- The page background. A theme might apply either a solid background color or a background image to the document. A background color or image is visible only when you view a document in Word's Web Layout view, or when you view a Web-page document in a browser.

- The images used for horizontal dividing lines and for bullets in bulleted lists.

- Hyperlink text colors (for both unfollowed and followed hyperlinks).

- The color of table borders.

To apply a theme, choose Theme from the Format menu, and select the theme and the features you want in the Theme dialog box, as shown in Figure 6-4.

⭐ **TIP**

If you have installed Microsoft FrontPage 4.0 or later, you can use the FrontPage themes as well as the ones supplied with Word. You can also download additional themes from the Web by choosing Office On The Web from the Help menu.

FIGURE 6-4.
Selecting a theme and theme options in the Theme dialog box.

This pane shows the visual effects of applying the selected theme.

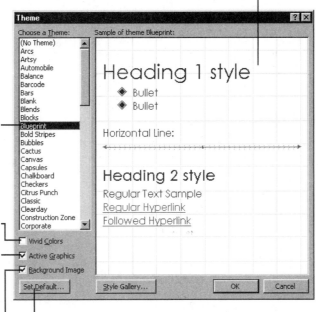

Select a theme from this list to apply the theme to the document. Or, select (No Theme) to remove an existing theme from the document.

Apply brighter colors to text.

Add special effects to bullets and other elements (visible only when a Web-page document is viewed in a browser).

Click this button to use the selected theme for all new documents.

Assign a background image to the document (visible only in Web Layout view, or when a Web-page document is viewed in a browser).

Using the Style Gallery

The Style Gallery is another tool that you can use to modify the overall appearance of a document after you have automatically formatted it. You can open the Style Gallery by clicking the Style Gallery button in the AutoFormat dialog box. (This dialog box is displayed when you perform step 6 of the procedure for automatically formatting a document, given on page 160.) You can also open the Style Gallery by clicking the Style Gallery button in the Theme dialog box, described in the previous section. (See Figure 6-4.) The Style Gallery is shown in Figure 6-5, on the next page.

Microsoft Word

❓ SEE ALSO
For instructions on choosing a template for creating a new document, see "Creating and Printing a Document from Start to Finish," page 105. For information on modifying, creating, and copying styles, see Chapter 7.

How the Style Gallery Works

When you have Word automatically format your document, it assigns each paragraph an appropriate standard style. For instance, a heading might be assigned the Heading 1 style, a paragraph of body text might be assigned the Body Text style, and a paragraph within a list might be assigned the List style. The actual formatting features provided by a given style, however, depend on the particular template you used to create your document (and on whether you have altered the style). When you choose a template in the Style Gallery, Word copies each of the styles from that template into your document, replacing the original document styles. For example, the template's Heading 1 style would replace your document's original Heading 1 style, and the appearance of every paragraph that is assigned Heading 1 would be modified accordingly.

Note that before you use the Style Gallery, you should have Word automatically format your document (or manually apply styles, as discussed in the next section) so that the document paragraphs are assigned appropriate standard Word styles. Otherwise, using the Style Gallery will have little immediate visual effect.

FIGURE 6-5.
Using the Style Gallery.

1 Select a template by clicking it.

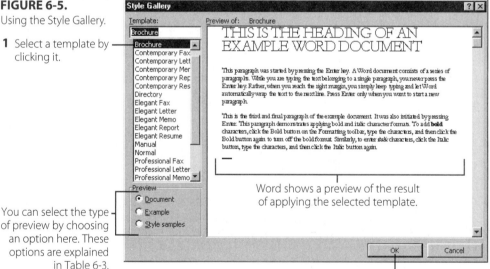

You can select the type of preview by choosing an option here. These options are explained in Table 6-3.

Word shows a preview of the result of applying the selected template.

2 Click OK when you have selected the template you want. Word will then reformat your entire document by replacing styles in the document with styles from the selected template.

TABLE 6-3. Preview Options

Preview Option	Resulting Display
Document	Word will display a reduced image of your document, as it would appear if formatted with the selected template.
Example	Word will show an example document formatted with the selected template. An example might not be available for a particular template.
Style Samples	Word will display the name and appearance of each style provided by the selected template. Samples might not be available for a particular template.

Using Click and Type

Word now provides yet another feature that automatically applies formatting to your document: Click and Type. This feature, available only in Web Layout or Print Layout view, lets you add text to an empty place in a document by double-clicking that place and then typing the text. Figures 6-6 and 6-7 give an example. (In these figures, formatting marks were made visible to clearly show the paragraphs and tabs that Word adds.)

NOTE

To use Click and Type, you must select the Enable Click And Type option. You access this option by choosing Options from the Tools menu and clicking the Edit tab. On this tab, you can also specify the style of any new paragraphs that the Click and Type feature inserts by selecting a style in the Default Paragraph Style list box.

FIGURE 6-6.
Using the Click and Type feature to position text in a document.

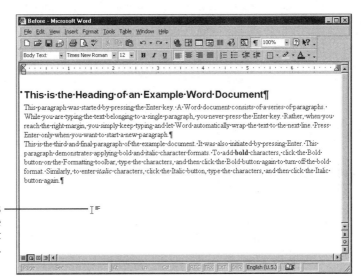

To add text at this position in the document, just double-click here.

Microsoft Word

FIGURE 6-7.
The result of double-clicking and typing at the mouse pointer position shown in Figure 6-6.

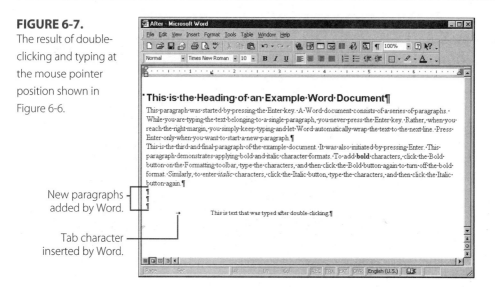

New paragraphs added by Word.

Tab character inserted by Word.

To place the text as close as possible to the double-clicked position, Word automatically applies appropriate paragraph formatting (left, centered, right alignment, or left indentation), and it inserts new paragraphs and tab characters as needed. Note that if the Print Layout view is active, you must double-click within the text area of the page (not within a margin area). When the pointer is at a position where you can use Click and Type, Word displays one of the following four mouse pointers:

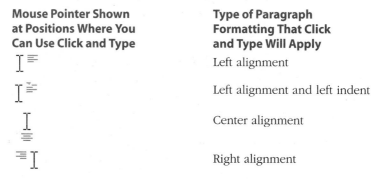

Mouse Pointer Shown at Positions Where You Can Use Click and Type	Type of Paragraph Formatting That Click and Type Will Apply
	Left alignment
	Left alignment and left indent
	Center alignment
	Right alignment

Applying Styles

You'll now learn how to manually apply styles to the text in your document. You might use the techniques given here to modify the formatting applied by the AutoFormat command, by a theme, or by using the Style Gallery. Or, you might use them to format a document yourself from scratch. (In this case, you might apply styles as you're entering the document text). Word provides two types of styles: *paragraph* styles (such as those applied by AutoFormat), and *character* styles (for emphasizing individual blocks of characters).

Applying styles has several advantages over directly assigning character and paragraph formatting (which you'll learn later in the chapter). Applying a style can save you time because it allows you to assign an entire group of formatting features with a single command. Also, using styles promotes consistent formatting—all text that is assigned a given style will look the same. As you'll learn in Chapter 7, you can easily change the format of all text throughout a document that has a given style by merely adjusting the style itself. For example, you could make all top-level headings bold by assigning the bold format to the Heading 1 style, which would be a lot easier than individually reformatting all these headings in the document.

When you create a new document, it obtains a private copy of the styles that are stored in the template that was used to create it. The document's styles are saved within the document file along with the other document content. You saw previously how to use the Style Gallery to replace these styles with the styles stored in a different template. In the following sections, you'll learn how to apply the document's styles to paragraphs or blocks of characters within the document. You can use these techniques to apply both *predefined* styles (that is, those supplied with the Word program) and styles that you define yourself. In the next chapter, you'll learn how to modify the predefined styles and how to define new styles.

Applying Paragraph Styles

A *paragraph style* stores a complete set of paragraph and character formatting features. When you apply the style to a paragraph, all these features are assigned to the paragraph text. Table 6-4, on the next page, summarizes all the formatting features that are stored in a paragraph style, dividing them into six categories. (These categories correspond to the commands that you use to choose the formatting attributes, as described later in this chapter, and in chapters 8 and 9.)

? SEE ALSO

For information on finding and replacing styles, see "Finding and Replacing Text," page 143.

If you haven't used AutoFormat or applied styles to your document, paragraphs will usually have the Normal style. (Paragraphs in documents based on certain templates, however, might be initially assigned a different style, such as Body Text). The Normal style has a set of formats suitable for the bulk of the text in a typical document. In the Normal template supplied with Word, the formatting attributes of the

II

Microsoft Word

Normal style include the Times New Roman font, a font size of 12 points, single line spacing, and flush-left paragraph alignment. (Any of these attributes can be changed.)

To apply a different style to one or more paragraphs, perform the following two steps:

1 To apply a style to a single paragraph, place the insertion point anywhere within the paragraph. To apply a style to several paragraphs, select at least a portion of all the paragraphs. If you have not yet started entering text for a new paragraph, place the insertion point before the paragraph mark for the new paragraph. You can do this whether the paragraph mark is visible or not.

2 Choose Style from the Format menu, and then select the style you want in the Style dialog box, as shown in Figure 6-8.

TABLE 6-4.   Formatting Attributes Stored in a Paragraph Style

Category	Chief Formatting Attributes
Font, Spacing, and Animation	The font name (for example, Times New Roman), as well as the character size, style (bold or italic), underlining, effects (such as strikethrough or superscript), color, intercharacter spacing, and animation effects.
Language	Controls which dictionary (English, French, or German, for example) the Word proofing tools (such as the spelling and grammar checkers) will use to correct the text. Can also be used to exclude the text from proofing. *The proofing tools are discussed in Chapter 9, "Using Word's Proofing Tools."*
Indents, Spacing, and Breaks	Paragraph indentation. Space before or after a paragraph, paragraph line spacing, alignment (left, right, centered, or justified), outline level, and page break control.
Tabs	Position and type of tab stops in effect within a paragraph.
Borders and Shading	Borders around the text and background shading.
Bullets and Numbering	Automatic display of a bullet character or number for a paragraph in a list.

 NOTE

Some of the predefined styles are used for standard Word elements. For example, Word automatically assigns the Comment Text style to comment text (discussed in Chapter 11), and the Header style to page headers. You can, however, assign these styles to any paragraphs in your document.

FIGURE 6-8.
Choosing a style in the Style dialog box. The name of each style suggests its purpose. The descriptions and previews help you find an appropriate style.

Select a style by clicking it. Styles prefaced with a ¶ are paragraph styles. (Styles prefaced with <u>a</u> are character styles, which will be discussed in the next section.)

Shows the appearance of the paragraph as a whole

Shows the appearance of text within the paragraph.

Select All Styles here to list all available styles.

Click here to assign the selected style to the selected document text.

SEE ALSO

For details on defining your own shortcut keys for quickly applying styles, see the section "Modifying Styles," page 198.

If you know the name of the style you want, you don't need to use the Style dialog box. Instead, you can apply the style by selecting it from the Style list on the Formatting toolbar or by typing the style name into the box at the top of the list:

Note that the label for each style on this list is formatted using the style's character formatting attributes and possibly some of its paragraph formatting attributes (such as an indent). The list displays only those styles that are currently used in the document or were previously selected, plus several other common styles (such as Heading 1). To list *all* available styles, press Shift while you click the down arrow. Also,

Word provides the shortcut keys shown in Table 6-5 for applying several of the paragraph styles:

TABLE 6-5.   Shortcut Keys for Styles

Style	Shortcut Key
Normal	Ctrl+Shift+N
List Bullet	Ctrl+Shift+L
Heading 1	Alt+Ctrl+1
Heading 2	Alt+Ctrl+2
Heading 3	Alt+Ctrl+3

Take Advantage of the Predefined Heading Styles

Use the predefined styles Heading 1 through Heading 9 for the headings in your document. Not only do these styles provide appropriate and consistent formatting for various levels of headings, but using them will also allow you to view the organization of your document in Outline view, to quickly navigate through your document with the Document Map, and to easily generate tables of contents.

Additionally, when you drag the scroll box on the vertical scroll bar, Word will display the text of each heading to make it simpler to find the desired location in your document. (*Headings, outlines, the Document Map, and tables of contents will be fully discussed in Chapter 12, "Writing Long Documents."*)

When you press Enter at the end of a paragraph, the new paragraph that is inserted generally has the same style as the previous paragraph. Some styles, however, are defined so that the new paragraph has a different style. For example, if you press Enter while in a paragraph with the Heading 1 style, the new paragraph will typically have the Normal style.

Use the Body Text Style for More Formatting Control

If you use the Body Text style—rather than Normal—for the body text in your document, you'll be able to easily modify the formatting of the body text without altering other text in your document. (Changing Normal alters most other paragraph styles as well, because these styles are based on Normal. In contrast, other styles aren't commonly based on Body Text. *This topic will be fully discussed in Chapter 7.*

Applying Character Styles

You can use a *character style* to apply a set of character formatting attributes to emphasize one or more characters within a paragraph. Character styles differ from paragraph styles in the following ways:

- A character style can store only formatting attributes that belong to the *Font, Spacing, and Animation*, the *Language*, or the *Borders and Shading* categories, described in Table 6-4, page 174. Notice that these are only three of the six categories of formatting that can be assigned to a paragraph style.

- You assign a character style to one or more individual characters, while you assign a paragraph style to one or more entire paragraphs.

- Unlike a paragraph style, a character style doesn't need to fully specify the character format. For example, a particular character style might specify only bold and italic formats. If you assigned this style to a block of text, Word would remove any directly applied character formatting, apply the bold and italic formats to the text, and preserve all the other character formatting that is specified by the paragraph style, such as the character font, size, and effects.

NOTE

If a character style includes formatting that's also part of the paragraph's style, applying the character style can result in turning off the formatting. This will happen with formatting that can be selected or deselected, such as bold, italic, all caps, and strikethrough. For example, if a character style includes italic, applying the character style to text within a paragraph whose style also includes italic will *remove* the italics. This is in accord with common writing practices; for example, a typical way to emphasize a word within an all-italic heading is to remove the italics from that word.

Word provides few predefined character styles. Therefore, the techniques given here will not be truly useful until you learn how to define your own character styles in Chapter 7.

To apply a character style to a group of characters:

1 Select the text, or to apply the style to the text you're about to type, place the insertion point at the position where you want to insert the text. To apply a character style to a single word, place the insertion point anywhere within the word without selecting it.

II

Microsoft Word

SEE ALSO

For instructions on defining your own character styles, see "Creating New Styles," page 209.

2 Choose Style from the Format menu, and in the Style dialog box (see Figure 6-8 on page 175), select a character style from the list. The names of character styles are prefaced with **a**. Notice that Word displays sample text formatted with the selected style. Click the Apply button when you have selected the style you want.

Alternatively, if you know the name of the desired character style, you can simply select it in the Style list on the Formatting toolbar or type the style name into the box at the top of the list. Recall that to list all available styles, you must press Shift while you click the down arrow.

3 If you didn't select characters in step 1, begin typing. The character style will be applied to all characters you type until you move the insertion point or press Ctrl+Spacebar or Ctrl+Shift+Z.

To remove a character style, select the text and either press Ctrl+Spacebar, or Ctrl+Shift+Z, or apply the Default Paragraph Font character style. Choosing this special-purpose character "style" removes any character style or manually applied character formatting previously applied to the text.

Applying Character Formatting Directly

 SEE ALSO

For information about finding and replacing character formatting, see "Finding and Replacing Text," page 143.

Directly applying individual character formatting features gives you the finest level of control over the character formatting in your document.

The paragraph style specifies the predominant character formatting of the paragraph text. Frequently, you'll apply character formatting to one or more characters within the paragraph to emphasize them. For example, you might italicize a word or convert a character to superscript. The character formatting that you directly apply overrides the character formatting that is specified by the paragraph style or by any character style assigned to the text.

The character formatting that you can directly apply belongs to the *Font, Spacing, and Animation*, the *Language*, and the *Borders and Shading* categories listed in Table 6-4, page 174. This chapter covers the attributes belonging to the first category, *Font, Spacing, and Animation*, which are summarized in Table 6-6. *Language* formatting is discussed in the section "Marking the Language," page 270, and

Borders and Shading formatting in "Using Borders and Shading," page 256. (Note that borders and shading can be applied *either* as a character format to one or more characters *or* as a paragraph format to one or more entire paragraphs.)

⭐ **TIP**

> **Don't Overuse Direct Character Formatting**
>
> Avoid directly applying character formatting to entire paragraphs or groups of paragraphs. It's better to assign each paragraph a paragraph style that includes the basic character formatting that you want, and to use direct character formatting only to emphasize smaller blocks of text within paragraphs. This approach will make it easier to modify the basic character formatting and will tend to make your character formatting more consistent throughout the document.

TABLE 6-6.   Font, Spacing, and Animation Character Formatting That You Can Apply Directly

Character Formatting Option	Description
Font	
Font	The general type of the characters: Times New Roman, Arial, Courier New, and so on.
Font Style	The basic look of the characters: Regular, Italic, Bold, or Bold Italic.
Size	The height of the characters, measured in points (1 point = $\frac{1}{72}$ inch).
Underline	Character underlining, which can be single, double, dotted, dashed, words only (which skips spaces), or in one of many other styles.
Underline Color	The color of the underlining, if applied to the text. You can select a standard color, create a custom color, or choose Automatic (which uses the window font color selected in the Display program of the Windows Control Panel).
Color	The color of characters on a monitor or color printer. You can select a standard color, create a custom color, or choose Automatic (which uses the window font color selected on the Display program of the Windows Control Panel).
Effects	Character enhancements: Strikethrough, Double Strikethrough, Superscript, Subscript, Shadow, Outline, Emboss, Engrave, Small Caps, All Caps, and Hidden.

(continued)

II

Microsoft Word

TABLE 6-6. *continued*

Character Formatting Option	Description
Spacing	
Scale	Amount by which characters are increased or decreased in width (expressed as a percent of normal character width).
Spacing	Amount added to or subtracted from intercharacter spacing to produce expanded or condensed text.
Position	Amount by which characters are raised or lowered. (Unlike the Subscript or Superscript effects, character size is not reduced.)
Kerning For Fonts	Moving certain character pairs (for example, *A* and *W*) closer together.
Animation	
Animation	A visual special effect displayed by text, such as blinking, shimmering, sparkling, and so on. Intended for regular Word documents that will be read online. Text animation, of course, won't print. And if it's applied to a Web-page document, it won't be displayed by popular browsers (such as Microsoft Internet Explorer 5).

The following are the general steps for directly applying character formatting:

1 Select the text, or to apply the formatting to the text you're about to type, place the insertion point at the position where you want your new text to appear.

 TIP

> To apply character formatting to a word, you can place the insertion point anywhere within the word rather than selecting the word.

2 Open the Font dialog box by choosing Font from the Format menu, and select the formatting you want. Alternatively, you can apply certain character formatting by pressing a shortcut key or by using the Formatting toolbar. These three methods are discussed individually in the following three sections.

3 If you didn't select characters in step 1, begin typing. The character formatting will be applied to all characters you type until you move the insertion point or press Ctrl+Spacebar or Ctrl+Shift+Z.

A newly inserted character normally acquires the character formatting of the previous character. Or, if the character is typed at the beginning of a new paragraph, it acquires the formatting of the *following* character. This formatting, however, will be modified by any character formatting you select immediately before typing the character.

To *remove* directly applied character formatting and restore the character formatting specified by the paragraph's style, select the text and press Ctrl+Spacebar or Ctrl+Shift+Z. (Also, if you're inserting new text, you can press one of these key combinations to discard any directly applied character formatting acquired from the adjoining text. For example, if you're inserting text following an italicized phrase, you could press Ctrl+Spacebar to begin inserting nonitalicized text—assuming the italics were directly applied and aren't part of the paragraph style.)

To find out what formatting and style (or styles) have been applied to text in your document, choose What's This? from the Help menu or press Shift+F1, and then click anywhere within the text of interest.

Using the Font Dialog Box

The Font dialog box allows you to apply any of the character formatting shown in Table 6-6 on page 179. To open the Font dialog box, choose Font from the Format menu, or right-click the selected text and choose Font from the pop-up menu that appears. You can apply any of the Font formats on the Font tab of the Font dialog box, shown in Figure 6-9, on the following page. You can apply any of the Spacing formats on the Character Spacing tab, shown in Figure 6-10, on the next page. And you can apply Animation formatting on the Text Effects tab, shown in Figure 6-11, on page 183. Selecting the formatting you want is easy because the Preview area of the Font dialog box shows a text example formatted with the selected formatting.

When the Font dialog box is first displayed, it shows the current formatting of the selected text. If a particular formatting attribute varies within the selected text (for example, part of the text is bold and part is not bold), the box indicating the formatting will be left blank. (Or if the formatting is selected by means of clicking a check box, the check box will contain a check mark with a shaded background.) If you select a formatting option, it will be applied to all the text in the selection.

II

Microsoft Word

FIGURE 6-9.
The Font tab of the
Font dialog box.

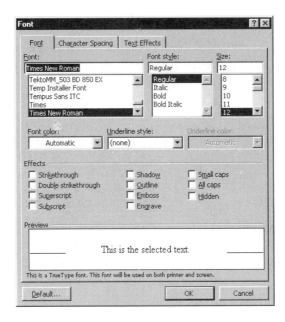

FIGURE 6-10.
The Character Spacing
tab of the Font
dialog box.

Notice that Word displays information on the font that's currently selected in the Font list box (on the Font tab). This information is shown at the bottom of the tab and indicates, for example, whether the font is a *TrueType* font. A TrueType font is a *scalable* font (one that

FIGURE 6-11.
The Text Effects tab of the Font dialog box.

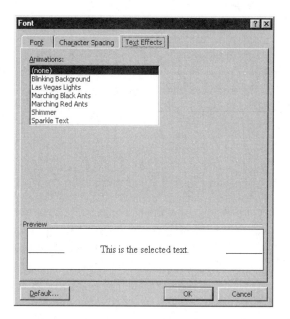

you can make any size) that's installed in Windows. A TrueType font produces high-quality characters on almost any screen or printer, and is a good choice if you want to be able to display the characters in a range of sizes or if you want to be able to print your document on a variety of printers.

Clicking the Superscript or Subscript box (also on the Font tab) raises or lowers the text by a standard amount and reduces the character size. To raise or lower the text by any amount, without changing its size, click the Character Spacing tab and select either Raised or Lowered in the Position list box. (See Figure 6-10.) Then enter in the By box the exact amount that the text should be moved, in points (1 point = $\frac{1}{72}$ inch).

If you select the Hidden effect (on the Font tab), you can make the text invisible on the screen or on a printed copy of the document. To control the visibility of hidden text, choose Options from the Tools menu. Hidden text will be visible on the screen only if the Hidden Text option is enabled on the View tab, and it will be visible on a printed copy of the document only if the Hidden Text option is enabled on the Print tab.

Note that the Small Caps and All Caps effects (Font tab) change only the way the text is displayed and printed; they don't change the actual characters stored in the document. Therefore, if you remove the effect, the original capitalization of the text will reappear.

When you specify a value in the Scale list box (on the Character Spacing tab) other than 100%, you change the actual width of each character. In contrast, when you select Expanded or Condensed in the Spacing list box, you affect the spaces between the characters, but you leave the widths of the characters themselves unchanged:

200% Scale

Expanded Spacing

If you select the Kerning For Fonts option (on the Character Spacing tab), Word will reduce the spacing between certain character pairs— such as *A* and *W*—to give the text a more compact appearance. (In contrast, selecting the Condensed option in the Spacing list box reduces the spacing between all characters in the selected text). Word will perform kerning only on characters that have a size equal to or greater than the size you enter into the Points And Above box. Also, the selected font must be a TrueType (or Adobe Type 1) font.

You can click the Default button in the Font dialog box, which is visible regardless of which tab is displayed, to change the *default* character formatting so that it conforms to the styles that you have selected in the Font, Character Spacing, and Text Effects tabs. Clicking Default (and responding *yes* when prompted) assigns the selected formatting to the Normal style of the document and to the Normal style of the template that was used to create the document. (As you'll learn in Chapter 7, modifying Normal affects many other styles that are based on Normal.) As a result, whenever you create a new document using this template, the document text will display the new formatting. (Clicking Default will not, however, affect other documents that have already been created using the template.)

Using Shortcut Keys to Apply Character Formatting

You can also use the shortcut keys listed in Table 6-7, on page 186, to apply character formatting to the selected text.

The keys that toggle work as follows: If the first character of the selection does not have the formatting, pressing the key applies the format

Entering Measurements into Dialog Boxes

Some of the boxes in Word dialog boxes require you to enter measurements (for example, the By boxes following the Spacing and Position lists in the Font dialog box). Word displays the current value as a number followed by an abbreviation for the units. If you enter a new value, you should generally use the same units.

For example, consider a box in which Word displays the value 3 pt, meaning 3 points. If you typed either *5* or *5 pt* into this box, the value would be changed to 5 points. You can use another unit of measurement, provided that you specify the units. For example, you could enter *.05 in* into this box, and the value would be changed to .05 inches. The next time you opened the dialog box, Word would display this value in points—that is, 3.6 pt. (In some cases, Word will adjust the measurement to match its internal rules. For example, text can be raised or lowered only in half-point increments; therefore, in the By box following the Position list, Word would change .05 in to 3.5 pt.)

Note that you can change the standard units that Word uses for many of the values entered into dialog boxes. To do this, choose Options from the Tools menu, click the General tab, and select the units you want in the Measurement Units list.

The following table will help you work with the different units of measurement that Word recognizes:

Units	Abbre-viation	Points	Picas	Lines	Centi-meters	Milli-meters	Inches
Points	pt	1	1/12	1/12	.035	.35	1/72
Picas	pi	12	1	1	.42	4.2	1/6
Lines	li	12	1	1	.42	4.2	1/6
Centi-meters	cm	28.35	2.36	2.36	1	10	.39
Milli-meters	mm	2.83	.24	.24	.10	1	.04
Inches	in *or* "	72	6	6	2.54	25.4	1

to all characters; if the first character of the selection already has the formatting, pressing the key removes the formatting from all characters. For example, if you select text in which the first character is not bold and press Ctrl+B, all the text will become bold; if you press Ctrl+B again, all the text will not be bold.

TABLE 6-7.   Character Formatting Shortcut Keys

Character Formatting Option	Shortcut Key	Toggles?
Bold	Ctrl+B	Yes
Italic	Ctrl+I	Yes
Underline	Ctrl+U	Yes
Double Underline	Ctrl+Shift+D	Yes
Words Only Underline	Ctrl+Shift+W	Yes
Subscript (P_1)	Ctrl+=	Yes
Superscript (1st)	Ctrl+Shift+=	Yes
Hidden	Ctrl+Shift+H	Yes
SMALL CAPS	Ctrl+Shift+K	Yes
ALL CAPS	Ctrl+Shift+A	Yes
Increase font size to next size in Font Size list	Ctrl+> (that is, Ctrl+Shift+period)	No
Decrease font size to next size in Font Size list	Ctrl+< (that is, Ctrl+Shift+comma)	No
Increase font size by exactly 1 point	Ctrl+]	No
Decrease font size by exactly 1 point	Ctrl+[	No
Assign Symbol font	Ctrl+Shift+Q	No

Using the Formatting Toolbar to Apply Character Formatting

A final way to apply several of the character formats is to use the Formatting toolbar:

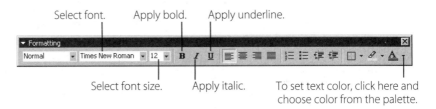

Select font.   Apply bold.   Apply underline.

Select font size.   Apply italic.   To set text color, click here and choose color from the palette.

Like the corresponding key combinations, the Bold, Italic, and Underline buttons toggle the formatting. When the formatting is currently assigned to *all* characters in the selection, the button will be selected (that is, it will appear pressed in).

To make it easier to find fonts, Word lists the recently applied fonts at the top of the Font list. Below these fonts (and separated by a double line), Word lists all available fonts, in alphabetical order.

Applying Paragraph Formatting Directly

Paragraph formatting affects the appearance of entire paragraphs. Generally, you should format your paragraphs by applying appropriate styles. Doing so will make the formatting easier to modify and will enhance its uniformity. (If you don't have a suitable style for a particular type of paragraph, you can modify an existing style or define a new one, as explained in Chapter 7.) However, you might want to directly apply paragraph formatting to make an occasional adjustment to the appearance of a paragraph. For example, you might want to center a specific paragraph or increase its left indent. (If you make the same adjustment often, you should consider defining a new style that you can apply.)

Directly applied paragraph formatting overrides that specified by the paragraph's style. Note that even if you seldom apply paragraph formatting directly, you'll need to understand the techniques and concepts given here when you begin defining your own paragraph styles in Chapter 7.

The paragraph formatting that you can apply directly belongs to the last four formatting categories listed in Table 6-4, page 174—that is, *Indents, Spacing, and Breaks*, *Tabs*, *Borders and Shading*, and *Bullets and Numbering*. In this chapter, you'll learn how to directly apply formatting belonging to the *Indents, Spacing, and Breaks* category of paragraph formatting—that is, the formatting, described in Table 6-8, on the next page, that you can apply by using the Paragraph dialog box. The other three categories are discussed in Chapter 8. (Note that borders and shading can be applied *either* as a character format to one or more characters *or* as a paragraph format to one or more entire paragraphs.)

II

Microsoft Word

TABLE 6-8. **Indents, Spacing, and Breaks**
Paragraph Formatting That You Can Apply Directly

Paragraph Formatting Option	Description
Indents And Spacing	
Alignment	Justification of the paragraph text: Left (text aligned with left indent); Right (aligned with right indent); Centered (centered between left and right indents); Justified (aligned with both indents).
Indentation	Horizontal position of the paragraph text relative to document margins.
Spacing Before	Additional space inserted above the paragraph.
Spacing After	Additional space inserted below the paragraph.
Line Spacing	Height of each line of text in the paragraph—for example, single or double spacing, or an exact line height.
Line And Page Breaks	
Widow/Orphan Control	Prevents printing the last line of the paragraph by itself at the top of a new page (a *widow*), or printing the first line by itself at the bottom of a page (an *orphan*).
Keep Lines Together	All lines in the paragraph will be printed on the same page—that is, Word will not insert a page break within the paragraph.
Keep With Next	Prevents Word from inserting a page break between the paragraph and the next paragraph.
Page Break Before	The paragraph is printed at the top of a new page.
Suppress Line Numbers	If you apply line numbering to the document, the paragraph is excluded from numbering. *(See "Adjusting the Page Layout," page 314.)*
Don't Hyphenate	If you hyphenate the document, the paragraph is excluded from hyphenation. *(See "Hyphenating Your Documents," page 291.)*

The following are the two basic steps for directly applying paragraph formatting:

1 To format a single paragraph, place the insertion point anywhere within the paragraph, or select all or part of the paragraph. To format several adjoining paragraphs, select at least a portion of each of the paragraphs.

2 Open the Paragraph dialog box by choosing Paragraph from the Format menu, and then select the desired formatting. Alternatively,

you can apply certain paragraph formatting by pressing a shortcut key combination or by using the Formatting toolbar or the ruler. These three methods are discussed individually in the following three sections.

? SEE ALSO

For Information on finding and replacing paragraph formatting, see "Finding and Replacing Text," page 143.

To remove directly applied paragraph formatting and restore the paragraph formatting that is specified by the paragraph's style, select the paragraph or paragraphs as described in step 1, and then press Ctrl+Q.

Using the Paragraph Dialog Box

You can apply any of the formatting described in Table 6-9, on page 191, by using the Paragraph dialog box. To open this dialog box, choose Paragraph from the Format menu, or right-click within the selected text, and then choose Paragraph from the pop-up menu that appears. Figure 6-12, shows the Indents And Spacing tab of the Paragraph dialog box, and Figure 6-13, on the next page, shows the Line And Page Breaks tab. As with the Font dialog box, choosing formatting attributes in the Paragraph dialog box is easy because Word displays a text example formatted with the selected attributes.

> NOTE

Outline Level paragraph formatting (which you set on the Indents And Spacing tab of the Paragraph dialog box) is discussed in "Using Outline View," page 362.

FIGURE 6-12.
The Indents And Spacing tab of the Paragraph dialog box.

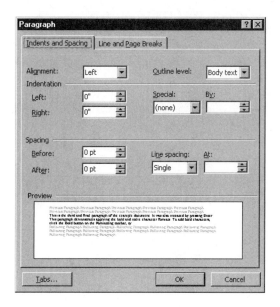

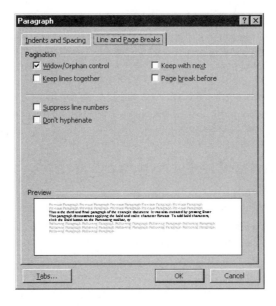

The *left paragraph indent* is the distance that the left edge of the paragraph text is moved in from the left margin area (a positive indent) or out into the left margin area (a negative indent). Likewise, the *right paragraph indent* is the distance the right edge of the text is moved in from the right margin area (a positive indent) or out into the right margin area (a negative indent). The *margins* are the distances between the text and the edges of the page when the indents are set to 0. You set the margins when you adjust the page setup, as described in Chapter 10. The easiest way to learn how to use the various indentation settings is to change the values and observe the effects on the preview text.

SEE ALSO

For instructions on setting the document margins and a description of the difference between margins and indents, see "Adjusting the Page Setup," page 306.

If you select First Line in the Special box (on the Indents And Spacing tab), the first line of the paragraph will be moved to the right of the other paragraph lines (by the amount you enter into the following By box). If you select the Hanging option in the Special box, all lines except the first will be moved to the right (by the amount you enter into the following By box).

The *line spacing* is the total height of each line of text in a paragraph. The options you can select in the Line Spacing list box (Indents And Spacing tab) have the effects shown in Table 6-9.

TABLE 6-9.   Line Spacing Options

Option Selected in Line Spacing List Box	Option Effect
Single	Each line will be made just high enough to accommodate the characters in the line. (If a particular line contains an unusually tall character, that line will be made higher than the others.)
1.5 Lines	Multiplies the Single line spacing by 1.5.
Double	Multiplies the Single line spacing by 2.
At Least	Sets the minimum height of a line. If a character in a line is taller than this value, the height of that line will be increased.
Exactly	Sets the exact height of each line. This option makes all lines evenly spaced. However, if a character in a line is taller than the line height, it will be cut off.
Multiple	Multiplies the Single line spacing by the number you enter into the following At box.

Using Shortcut Keys to Apply Paragraph Formatting

You can use the shortcut keys listed in Table 6-10, on the next page, to quickly apply paragraph formatting to the selected paragraph or paragraphs.

TIP

Use the Tab and Backspace Keys to Adjust Left Indents

If you select the Tabs And Backspace Set Left Indent option (choose Options from the Tools menu, and click the Edit tab), you can use the Tab and Backspace keys to adjust the left indent of a paragraph. To adjust the left indent of all lines uniformly, place the insertion point at the beginning of any line except the first. Then press Tab to increase the left indent to the next tab stop, or press Backspace (or Shift+Tab) to decrease the left indent by one tab stop. If you place the insertion point at the beginning of the first line, pressing Tab the first time will indent only the first line by one tab stop; each additional press will move all lines one tab stop to the right. And the first press of Backspace (or Shift+Tab) will remove the extra indent from the first line, while each subsequent press will move all lines left by one tab stop.

Note that if the insertion point isn't at the beginning of a line, Tab and Backspace will have their usual effects: Tab will insert a tab character and Backspace will delete the previous character. Also, you can't use this technique to create a negative left indent, nor can you use it to indent a new paragraph that doesn't contain text yet.

TABLE 6-10. **Shortcut Keys for Paragraph Formatting**

Paragraph Formatting Action	Shortcut Key	Comment
Increase left paragraph indent	Ctrl+M	Indent is moved to the next tab stop.
Decrease left paragraph indent	Ctrl+Shift+M	Indent is moved to previous tab stop; cannot be used to create a negative left indent.
Increase hanging indent	Ctrl+T	All paragraph lines are indented except the first line. Each time you press the key combination, the hanging indent is moved right to the next tab stop.
Decrease hanging indent	Ctrl+Shift+T	Hanging indent is moved left to the previous tab stop.
Add or remove 12 points of extra space above paragraph	Ctrl+0 (zero at top of keyboard, *not* on numeric keypad)	Toggles on or off.
Create single spacing	Ctrl+1 (1 at top of keyboard, *not* on numeric keypad)	Same as Single option in the Paragraph dialog box.
Create 1.5 spacing	Ctrl+5 (5 at top of keyboard, *not* on numeric keypad)	Same as 1.5 Lines option in the Paragraph dialog box.
Create double spacing	Ctrl+2 (2 at top of keyboard, *not* on numeric keypad)	Same as Double option in the Paragraph dialog box.
Left-align paragraph	Ctrl+L	Text aligned with left indent.
Right-align paragraph	Ctrl+R	Text aligned with right indent.
Center paragraph	Ctrl+E	Text centered between left and right indents.
Justify paragraph	Ctrl+J	Text aligned with both left and right indents. (Word adjusts the character spacing as necessary.)

Using the Formatting Toolbar and Ruler to Apply Paragraph Formatting

You can also use the Formatting toolbar and the ruler to apply paragraph formatting. (If the ruler isn't displayed, choose Ruler from the View menu, or you can display it temporarily by placing the mouse pointer over the gray band at the top of the document area of the window.)

Hold the mouse pointer over this gray
bar to display the ruler temporarily.

You can click the following buttons on the Formatting toolbar to apply paragraph formats:

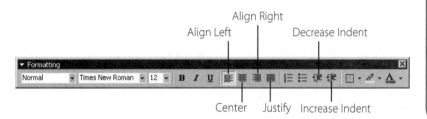

(The Decrease Indent and Increase Indent buttons affect the *left* paragraph indent.)

You can use the ruler to set paragraph indents, as follows:

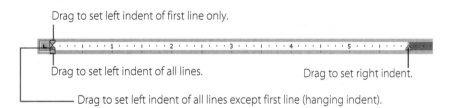

Drag to set left indent of first line only.

Drag to set left indent of all lines.   Drag to set right indent.

Drag to set left indent of all lines except first line (hanging indent).

Copying Formatting

If you have formatted a block of text in a document and want to apply the same formatting to one or more additional blocks of text, you can save time by copying the formatting.

One way to copy formatting is to use the Format Painter tool on the Standard toolbar, as follows:

1 Select the text that has the formatting that you want to copy. To copy character formatting, select one or more characters with the desired format. To copy paragraph formatting, either select an entire paragraph or place the insertion point anywhere within a paragraph without selecting text.

Format Painter

2 Click the Format Painter button on the Standard toolbar. A small paintbrush will appear next to the standard I-beam mouse pointer.

3 To apply copied character formatting, move the I-beam pointer to the text you want to format, and drag the highlight over the text. To apply copied paragraph formatting, either drag the highlight over one or more entire paragraphs, or just click anywhere within a paragraph without dragging.

 TIP

> **Save Time Formatting Several Blocks of Text**
>
> If you want to copy the formatting to several blocks of text, you can save time by double-clicking the Format Painter button in step 2. Then perform step 3 on every block of text that you want to format. When you're done, either click the Format Painter button once or press the Escape key.

You can also copy formatting using the keyboard, as follows:

1 Select the text that has the formatting you want to copy, and press Ctrl+Shift+C. To copy character formatting, select one or more characters with the desired format. To copy paragraph formatting, either select an entire paragraph, or simply place the insertion point anywhere within a paragraph without selecting text.

2 To apply copied character formatting, select the text you want to format, and press Ctrl+Shift+V. To apply copied paragraph formatting, either select one or more entire paragraphs, or just place the insertion point within a paragraph without selecting text, and press Ctrl+Shift+V.

3 If you want to apply the copied formatting to one or more additional blocks of text, repeat step 2 for each block.

 TIP

Copy or Move Text Without Formatting

Normally, when you copy or move text, the text formatting is copied or moved with it (the character formatting, plus the paragraph formatting if the paragraph mark is included). To copy or move text without including its formatting, use the Clipboard technique given in "Moving and Copying Text Using the Clipboard," page 140. However, rather than issuing the Paste command at the target location, choose Paste Special from the Edit menu. In the Paste Special dialog box, select the Paste option, select the Unformatted Text item in the As list box, and click OK. (See Figure 6-14.) When the text is inserted, it will acquire the format of the preceding text—just as if you had typed it!

Finally, you can copy paragraph formatting by using the standard text-copying methods (given in Chapter 5, "Entering and Editing Text in a Word Document") to copy the paragraph mark *from* a paragraph that has the desired formatting *to* the end of the paragraph you want to format. (The paragraph mark doesn't have to be visible to copy it. However, if you want to see it, click the Show/Hide ¶ button on the Standard toolbar.) Conceptually, a paragraph mark stores the paragraph's style as well as any directly applied paragraph formatting. Therefore, when you insert a copy of a paragraph mark at a new document location, the preceding text acquires the same paragraph style and formatting as the paragraph from which you copied the paragraph mark.

FIGURE 6-14.
Inserting unformatted text using the Paste Special command on the Edit menu.

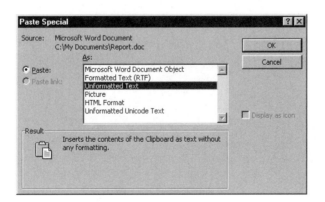

Customizing Styles and Templates

In the previous chapter, you saw how to efficiently format characters or paragraphs by applying the styles available in your document. In this chapter, you'll greatly extend the usefulness of styles by learning how to modify styles, create new styles, and copy styles between documents and templates. You'll also learn how to customize Word templates, which store styles as well as other important document items, such as standard text, AutoText entries, and macros.

Modifying Styles

Each time you open a new document, it obtains a copy of the styles that are stored in the template used by Word to create the document. The particular styles that are provided, as well as the formatting stored in each of these styles, vary according to the template you select. All templates have a basic set of general-purpose styles known as *built-in* styles—for example, Normal, Body Text, and Heading 1 through Heading 9. Some templates provide additional predefined styles for special purposes. For instance, the Professional Report template provides the Company Name, Title Cover, and Subtitle Cover styles for formatting elements on the report's title page. Also, a template or document can contain styles that you define yourself, using the techniques that will be given later in the chapter.

You can modify any of the styles in your document. When you modify a style, all text in your document that is assigned the style acquires the style's new format. This is an important advantage of using styles rather than directly formatting text. Because each document has its own private set of styles, modifying a style affects only the document itself; it does not affect the template or other documents based on the template. (As you'll see later, however, you can easily copy styles between documents and templates.)

 NOTE

> Applying a theme to a document, as described in "Applying a Theme," page 168, modifies the document's Normal style and heading styles (Heading 1 through Heading 9). These styles are given a look that's consistent with the theme.

When you modify or create a paragraph or character style, keep in mind that one style can be based on another style. In the Normal template supplied with Word, the Normal paragraph style is the base style for most other paragraph styles. For example, Body Text is defined as "Normal plus 6 points of space following the paragraph." This definition means that Body Text has all the formatting stored in Normal except the amount of space after the paragraph—Normal has 0 points of space after the paragraph, while Body Text has 6 points of space. (Normal itself isn't based on any other style.) Any formatting specifically assigned to a style supersedes the formatting of the base style.

If you change a style such as Normal, all styles based on it instantly change. For example, if you assigned the Courier New font and "10 points of space following the paragraph" to the Normal style, Body Text would acquire the Courier New font. Body Text would not, however, acquire "10 points of space following the paragraph" because it contains an explicit "space following" value (that is, it does not derive this formatting from Normal).

Use Built-In Styles to Change the Appearance of Standard Document Elements

As mentioned in Chapter 6, Word assigns certain built-in styles to standard elements of your document. For example, it assigns the Comment Text style to comment text, the Footer style to page footers, and the Page Number style to page numbers. You can therefore change the appearance of one of these standard elements by changing the corresponding style. For example, if you change the Header style, you'll modify the appearance of the headers on all pages of your document. (*Assigning headers, footers, and page numbers is discussed in Chapter 10, "Designing Pages." Comments are discussed in Chapter 11, "Working with Word in Workgroups.")*

Basing one style on another promotes formatting consistency. For example, if you assign a new font to the Normal style, all derived styles automatically acquire the new font, and you avoid having dissimilar fonts throughout your document.

In Chapter 6, "Formatting a Word Document," you learned one way to modify the Normal style: When you click the Default button in the Font dialog box, you change the character formatting stored in Normal to the attributes selected in the dialog box. The Normal style is also modified when you click the Default button in the Language dialog box, which is discussed in "Marking the Language," page 270. In the next two sections, you'll learn the two basic ways to modify any property of any style: by using example text and by using the Style dialog box.

View Style Names in the Left Margin

You might find it handy to have Word display the name of each paragraph's style as you're working with your document. Word displays the style name in the left margin of Normal view after you choose Options from the Tools menu, click the View tab, and enter a nonzero measurement in the Style Area Width box. The measurement you enter specifies the width of the area in which Word displays the style name; if the value is 0, Word does not display style names.

Also, you can print a description of the document styles by choosing Print from the File menu and selecting Styles in the Print What list box.

Microsoft Word

Modifying Styles by Example

The easiest way to modify a style is to use example text. You can use this method to modify any style except Normal. The Formatting toolbar must be displayed for you to modify styles by example. The steps are as follows:

1 Select text in your document that is assigned the paragraph or character style you want to modify. (If necessary, apply the style to text somewhere in your document.) The style name will appear in the Style list box on the Formatting toolbar. (If you select text that has been assigned a character style, the name of the character style rather than the name of the paragraph style will appear in the Style list box, and you'll be able to use this method to modify only the character style.)

2 Apply the new formatting directly to the text. You can use any of the methods for directly formatting text that were described in Chapter 6. The best way to modify a character formatting attribute of a paragraph style is to directly apply the attribute to all text in the paragraph.

3 Click in the Style list box on the Formatting toolbar to highlight the style name, and then press Enter:

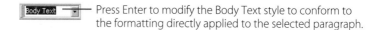 Press Enter to modify the Body Text style to conform to the formatting directly applied to the selected paragraph.

4 Word will display the Modify Style dialog box, which is shown in Figure 7-1.

FIGURE 7-1.
The Modify Style dialog box.

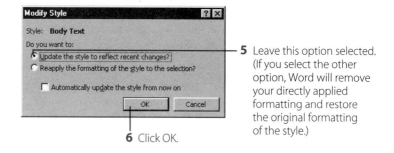

5 Leave this option selected. (If you select the other option, Word will remove your directly applied formatting and restore the original formatting of the style.)

6 Click OK.

NOTE

For a paragraph style, if you select the Automatically Update The Style From Now On option in the Modify Style dialog box, or if you have selected the Automatically Update option when modifying the style using the Style dialog box (as described in the next section), Word will automatically modify the style whenever you directly apply formatting to a paragraph that has been assigned the style. (Word will also instantly apply the new formatting to all other paragraphs in the document that have this style).

In other words, you'll be able to modify a style by performing only steps 1 and 2 in the above procedure. The Automatically Update feature thus ensures that all text throughout the document that has a particular style will have a consistent format. You'll need to use the Modify Style dialog box (the one shown in Figure 7-3, page 203) to deselect this option.

SEE ALSO

For Information on directly formatting text, see "Applying Character Formatting Directly," page 178, and "Applying Paragraph Formatting Directly," page 187.

You can also use the Style list box on the Formatting toolbar to define one or more aliases for a style. A style *alias* is an alternative name for the style. For example, you might want an alias that has a shorter name for a standard style, such as "bod" for "Body Text." To define one or more aliases, type them after the style name in the Style list box, separating each name with a comma, and then press Enter:

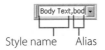

Style name Alias

To apply a style, you can type either its name or any of its aliases into the Style list box, and press Enter. You can also apply the style by clicking the down arrow next to the Style list box and selecting the style name from the drop-down list. Any aliases will be included after the style name separated by commas. You won't see separate list items for each alias.

Modifying Styles Using the Style Dialog Box

Modifying a style by using the Style dialog box is not as fast as modifying the style by example, but it provides the following additional options:

- You can rename the style.

- You can change the style on which the modified style is based.

Microsoft Word

- You can change the style that Word automatically assigns to a paragraph that *follows* a paragraph that's assigned the modified style.

- You can define a shortcut key for quickly applying the style.

- You can copy the modified style to the document's template.

- You can delete the style.

The following is the procedure for modifying a style using the Style dialog box:

1 Choose Style from the Format menu to open the Style dialog box, which is shown in Figure 7-2.

2 Select the name of the style you want to modify in the Styles list box. (Initially, the style of the selected text will be selected.) If you can't find the style, make sure that the All Styles option is selected in the List list box.

3 Click the Modify button. Word will display the Modify Style dialog box, which is shown in Figure 7-3.

4 You can change the name of the style, provided that it isn't a built-in style, by typing a new name into the Name box. (If you attempt to rename a built-in style, Word will add the new name you type as an alias for the style.)

FIGURE 7-2.

The Style dialog box.

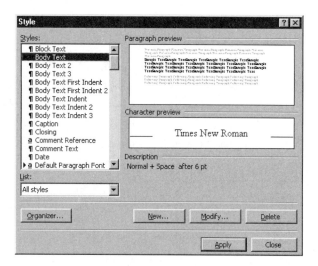

FIGURE 7-3.
The Modify Style dialog box.

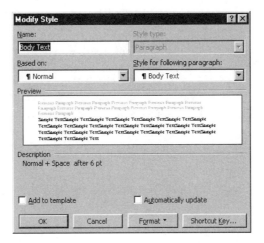

Each style must have a unique name, and style names are case-sensitive—for example, *List* and *list* are considered different styles. Also, for any type of style, you can define one or more aliases by typing them after the style name in the Name box, separating the names with commas.

5 You can change the base style by selecting a style name from the Based On list box. The result of basing one style on another was discussed earlier in the chapter.

For a paragraph style, if you choose the (No Style) option, the style will not be based on another style, and it will contain its own complete set of paragraph and character formatting. (The Normal style can't be based on another style.)

For a character style, if you choose the Default Paragraph Font or (Underlying Properties) option, the style will not be based on another character style. Rather, it will store only the character formatting attributes that are explicitly assigned to the style.

6 For a paragraph style, you can change the style for the *following* paragraph by choosing a style name in the Style For Following Paragraph list box.

For example, if you were modifying the Heading 1 style, you might choose Body Text in the Style For Following Paragraph list box. As a result, if you pressed Enter after typing a paragraph with the Heading 1 style, Word would assign the Body Text style

Microsoft Word

II

to the newly inserted paragraph. (For most styles, you typically choose the same style in the Style For Following Paragraph list box so that the style doesn't change when you press Enter.)

7 Select Add To Template if you want to modify the copy of the style within the template that was used to create the document. If you don't select this option, modifying the style will affect only the copy of the style within the current document.

NOTE

The Automatically Update option in the Modify Style dialog box has the same effect as the Automatically Update The Style From Now On option in the dialog box that's displayed when you modify a style by example. For an explanation, see the note on page 201.

8 To change the formatting stored in the style, click the Format button and, from the menu that appears, choose the category of the formatting you want to change:

When you choose a category, Word will display a dialog box that allows you to modify the individual formatting attributes. Each of these dialog boxes is the same as the dialog box that is displayed when you directly format text in a document. Table 7-1 lists each category and indicates the place in the book where the dialog box is discussed. When you have made the changes you want in each of the dialog boxes, click OK to return to the Modify Style dialog box. Note that for a character format, you can choose only the Font, Border, or Language category.

9 When you have finished making all the changes to the style, click OK in the Modify Style dialog box to return to the Style dialog box and to store your changes.

10 In the Style dialog box, click Apply to return to the document and apply the newly modified style to the selection, or click Close to return to the document without applying the style.

TABLE 7-1. Categories of Formatting You Can Assign to a Style

Style Format Category	Look Here for Discussion of Its Dialog Box
Font	"Applying Character Formatting Directly," page 178.
Paragraph	"Applying Paragraph Formatting Directly," page 187.
Tabs	"Using Tabs," page 224.
Border	"Using Borders and Shading," page 256.
Language	"Marking the Language," page 270.
Frame	"Using Text Boxes to Position Text on the Page," page 316. Here, frame refers to an element for positioning text or graphics on a page, which is similar to a text box. It doesn't refer to one of the panes used to view multiple documents in a Web browser or in Word.
Numbering	"Creating Bulleted and Numbered Lists," page 248.

Assigning a Style to a Shortcut Key

If you want to assign a style to a shortcut key so that you can apply the style by pressing a key combination, choose Style from the Format menu to open the Style dialog box, select the style you want to use, and click the Modify button. In the Modify Style dialog box, click the Shortcut Key button. The Customize Keyboard dialog box will appear, which is shown in Figure 7-4.

FIGURE 7-4.
Defining a shortcut key for applying a style in the Customize Keyboard dialog box.

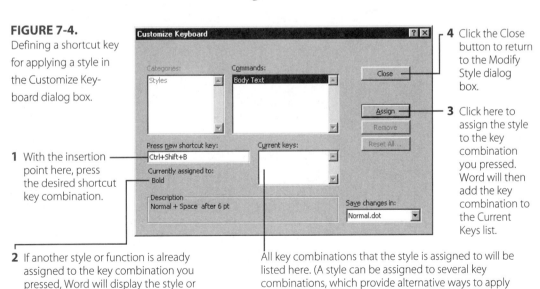

4 Click the Close button to return to the Modify Style dialog box.

3 Click here to assign the style to the key combination you pressed. Word will then add the key combination to the Current Keys list.

1 With the insertion point here, press the desired shortcut key combination.

2 If another style or function is already assigned to the key combination you pressed, Word will display the style or function here. If you proceed, your new assignment will replace the previous one.

All key combinations that the style is assigned to will be listed here. (A style can be assigned to several key combinations, which provide alternative ways to apply the style. However, only one style or function can be assigned to a particular key combination.)

Defining Shortcut Keys

You can define new shortcut keys in Word that will allow you to perform frequently repeated tasks more rapidly. You can also change Word's default key combinations to suit your preferences (perhaps to match the key combinations of another program that you're accustomed to using). Keep in mind, however, that making extensive shortcut key modifications might make it difficult to learn tasks from this book or from the Word manuals and online Help, because these sources refer to the default key combinations. You might therefore wait until you're familiar with the Word skills involved before making extensive customizations.

You can assign a Word command, a macro, a font, an AutoText entry, a style, or a symbol to a shortcut key. Pressing the shortcut key will instantly choose the command, run the macro, apply the font, insert the AutoText entry, assign the style, or insert the symbol.

To assign one of these items to a shortcut key, do the following:

1   Choose Customize from the Tools menu and click the Keyboard button at the bottom of the Customize dialog box (this button is available on all tabs of the Customize dialog box). Word will open the Customize Keyboard dialog box:

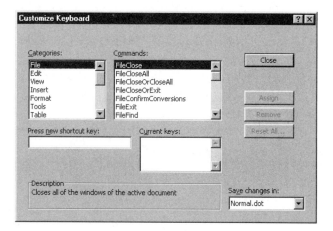

2   Choose an item in the Save Changes In list box. If you choose Normal.dot, the shortcut key will be available when you work on *any* document; if you choose the name of the document template, it will be available only when you work on a document based on this same template; and if you choose the name of the current document, it will be available only when you work on this document.

3   Select a category in the Categories list.

4   In the list to the right of the Categories list, select the specific item that you want to assign to the shortcut key. (This list will be named Commands,

Defining Shortcut Keys   *continued*

Macros, Fonts, AutoText, Styles, or Common Symbols, according to the current selection in the Categories list. To simplify the remainder of the discussion, the term *command* will be used to refer to any item for the selected category.

If you chose the Common Symbols category but don't see the character you want in the Common Symbols list, select Insert from the Categories list and Symbol from the Commands list, click the Symbol button that appears, and choose the character you want in the Symbol dialog box. (*For information on using the Symbol dialog box, see "Inserting Special Characters," page 119.*)

If you selected the Styles category but don't see the style you want in the Styles list, you can assign *any* style to the shortcut key by clicking the Shortcut Key button in the Modify Style dialog box, as explained in "Assigning a Style to a Shortcut Key," page 205.

If the selected command has already been assigned to one or more shortcut keys, these keys will be shown in the Current Keys list. Note that you can assign a command to several shortcut keys; each shortcut key will provide an alternative way to carry out the command.

5   Click in the Press New Shortcut Key box and press the key combination that you want to use to carry out the selected command. A message below the box appears to indicate whether a command has already been assigned to that shortcut key. If a command has already been assigned, your shortcut key will replace the former one. (If you don't want to do this, try another key combination.)

6   Click the Assign button. The key combination will be added to the Current Keys list.

7   Make any other shortcut key assignments that you want. You can assign the current command (the one selected in the Commands list) to additional shortcut keys, or you can assign other commands to shortcut keys.

You can remove a specific shortcut key assignment by selecting the key combination in the Current Keys list and clicking the Remove button. You can remove *all* shortcut key assignments for *all* commands by clicking the Reset All button. (This will remove the assignments only from the template or document currently selected in the Save Changes In list box.)

8   Click the Close button in the Customize Keyboard dialog box and then click Close in the Customize dialog box.

Note that you can print a list of the custom key assignments that are in effect for the current document by choosing Print from the File menu, choosing Key Assignments in the Print What list box, and clicking the OK button.

TIP

Recall from Chapter 6 that Word has already defined shortcut keys for several styles. They are listed in Table 6-5, page 176.

SEE ALSO

For information on copying styles between documents and templates, see "Copying Styles," page 212.

Deleting a Style

To delete a style, choose Style from the Format menu to open the Style dialog box, select the style to delete, and click the Delete button. When you delete a style, Word removes it from any text to which it has been applied. (For a paragraph style, Word then formats the paragraph with the Normal style.)

To delete a group of styles, use the Organizer (explained in "Modifying Templates," page 217).

See the comments on deleting built-in styles in the following sidebar.

Built-In Styles

Some of the predefined styles that Word provides are known as *built-in* styles. A built-in style is one that is always available to any template or document. To see all the built-in styles (not just those currently assigned to text in the document), choose All Styles in the List list box in the lower left corner of the Style dialog box; or, if you're using the Style list box on the Formatting toolbar, press Shift while you click the down arrow. You can't rename a built-in style, although you can assign it an alias.

If you select a built-in style other than Normal or Heading 1 through Heading 9 in the Style dialog box, you can click the Delete button to "delete" the style from the current document, provided that the style has been assigned to text in the document or that it has been modified. Word, however, does not actually delete the style; rather, it does the following:

- Word removes the style from any text to which it has been applied. (If the style is a paragraph style, it then assigns the Normal style to each paragraph.)

- If the style has been modified, Word restores it to its original state. Clicking Delete is thus a convenient way to remove any modifications you have made to a built-in style.

After you click Delete, the built-in style will still be listed in the Style dialog box when the All Styles option is selected.

Creating New Styles

If you find yourself frequently applying the same set of formatting attributes to characters or paragraphs, it's probably time to define a new style. Doing so will save you time and help improve the consistency of your formatting. For example, if you often format figure labels by applying a 14-point Arial font, centered alignment, and extra space above the paragraph, you could define a paragraph style—perhaps named Label— that has all these features. Likewise, if you frequently emphasize words by applying a larger font size and the red color, you could define a character style—say, named Big Red—that has both these features.

Just as when you modify a style, you can create a new style either by example or by using the Style dialog box.

Creating Paragraph Styles by Example

The easiest way to create a paragraph style is by example. (However, you can't use this method to create a character style.) Proceed as follows:

SEE ALSO

For information on directly formatting text, see "Applying Character Formatting Directly," page 178, and "Applying Paragraph Formatting Directly," page 187.

1 Select or place the insertion point within a paragraph in a document. You can save time if you choose a paragraph that already has formatting close to the formatting you want to assign the new style.

2 Directly apply any additional character or paragraph formatting that you want to assign to the style, using the methods given in Chapter 6. The best way to include character formatting in the style is to directly apply the formatting to all text in the paragraph.

3 Type a unique name for the new style into the Style list box on the Formatting toolbar, and press Enter.

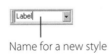

Name for a new style

Word will add the new paragraph style to the styles stored in the document, and it will apply the style to the example paragraph. The new style will be based on the style that was originally assigned to the example paragraph, and it will store all the paragraph and character formatting you directly applied to the example paragraph.

II

Microsoft Word

Creating Styles
Using the Style Dialog Box

Although using the Style dialog box to define a style is a little less convenient than using the Formatting toolbar, it provides the following additional options:

- You can define a character style as well as a paragraph style.

- You can choose the style on which the new style is based.

- You can choose the style that Word automatically assigns to a paragraph that follows a paragraph assigned the new style.

- You can define a shortcut key for quickly applying the new style.

- You can copy the new style to the document's template.

The following is the basic procedure for defining a new style using the Style dialog box. Many of these steps are similar to the steps for modifying a style. The list emphasizes the differences in the procedures; for more detailed explanations of the techniques and concepts, be sure to first read the previous section, "Modifying Styles Using the Style Dialog Box," page 201.

1 To save time, select—or just place the insertion point within—text that has formatting similar to the formatting you want to assign to the new style. (This step is optional.)

2 Choose Style from the Format menu to open the Style dialog box (see Figure 7-2, page 202), and click the New button. Word will display the New Style dialog box, which is shown in Figure 7-5.

3 Word will assign the new style a tentative name, such as Style1. To assign a different name, type it into the Name text box. You can include spaces in the name, and the case of the letters is significant. (For example, *label*, *Label*, and *LABEL* would be considered different styles.) You can also enter aliases into the Name text box by separating them with commas, as described previously.

4 In the Style Type list box, select either Paragraph or Character to specify the type of style you want to define.

5 Word initially sets the base style to the style assigned to the text that is currently selected in the document. To base the new style on a different style—or on no style—choose the appropriate option in the Based On list box.

FIGURE 7-5.
Creating a style in the
New Style dialog box.

6 Word initially makes the style for the next paragraph the same as the new style. To have Word assign a different style to a paragraph that follows a paragraph with the new style, choose a style in the Style For Following Paragraph list box. This option applies to a paragraph style only.

7 If you want to assign a shortcut key that you can use to apply the new style, click the Shortcut Key button in the New Style dialog box, and follow the procedure that was explained previously in the section "Assigning a Style to a Shortcut Key," page 205.

8 Select the Add To Template option if you want to copy the new style to the template that was used to create the document. If you don't select this option, the style will be available only within the current document.

? SEE ALSO

For a more complete explanation on using the Style dialog box, see "Modifying Styles Using the Style Dialog Box," page 201.

9 Select the Automatically Update option to have Word automatically update the style whenever you directly apply formatting to text that is assigned the style (as explained in the note on page 201). This option applies to a paragraph style only.

10 Word initially assigns the new style all the formatting that was directly applied to the current document selection. To change any of this formatting, click the Format button, choose the appropriate formatting category, and enter the desired settings into the dialog box that Word displays. See Table 7-1, page 205, for a list of the categories and where to find information in each of the dialog boxes.

II

Microsoft Word

11 When you've finished making changes to the style, click OK in the New Style dialog box to save your changes as a new style and to return to the Style dialog box.

12 In the Style dialog box, click Apply to return to the document and apply the new style to the selection, or click Close to return to the document without applying the style.

Copying Styles

As you have seen, when you create a new document, it acquires a copy of all the styles that are stored in the template that was used to create it. Each document and each template has its own private set of styles. Therefore, adding or modifying a style in a document doesn't normally affect the template, and adding or modifying a style in a template doesn't normally affect documents that were already created using the template. You can, however, use several Word options and commands to copy styles between documents and templates (or even between two documents). Copying styles allows you to take advantage of any style that is contained in any document or template.

The following two sections describe various ways to copy styles from templates to documents and from documents to templates.

Copying Styles from a Template to a Document

For information on using the Style Gallery, see "Using the Style Gallery," page 169. For information on using the Organizer, see "Modifying Templates," page 217.

To take advantage of a style that is stored in a template, you must copy it into a document. Styles can be copied from a template to a document in a variety of ways. When you create a new document, all styles currently stored in the template on which you base the document are automatically copied into the document.

If you already have a document and want to add the styles from another template to it, you can accomplish this in a number of ways. As explained in Chapter 6, you can use the Style Gallery to copy entire sets of styles from any template into your current document, thereby rapidly changing the overall look of the document. Alternatively, you can use the Organizer. The Organizer lets you copy as many or as few styles as you want from a template to a document. The Organizer is discussed later in this chapter in the section on modifying templates because it is used for copying a variety of template items in addition to styles.

You can have Word automatically copy all styles from the document's template into the document each time you open the document. This option is useful if you periodically update the styles stored in the template and want a particular document to always have the latest style versions. To enable this option for the currently opened document, choose Templates And Add-Ins from the Tools menu to open the Templates And Add-Ins dialog box. See Figure 7-6.

FIGURE 7-6.
Enabling the Automatically Update Document Styles option.

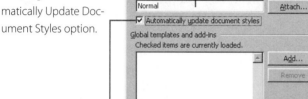

Word displays the name of the document template here (that is, the template that was used to create the document).

1 Select this option by clicking here.

2 Click OK.

Copying Styles from a Document to a Template

When you create or modify a style in a document, you might want to copy the style into a template so that it will be stored there and will be readily available for use in other documents. You can do this several different ways.

- When you modify or create a style in the Modify Style or the New Style dialog box, you can select the Add To Template option. Word will then copy the modified or new style to the document template, as explained earlier in the chapter. (If you want to store a style without changing it, you can open the Modify Style dialog box with the style selected, click the Add To Template option, and click OK without changing any of the formatting settings.)

Microsoft Word

? SEE ALSO

For a description of the Font dialog box, see "Using the Font Dialog Box," page 181. For a description of the Language dialog box, see "Marking the Language," page 270.

- When you select character formatting in the Font or Language dialog boxes, you can click the Default button and respond *yes* when prompted. Word will assign the selected formatting to the document's Normal style, and it will copy the updated Normal style to the document template.

- You can use the Organizer to copy as many or as few styles as you want from a document to a template. When you use the Organizer, you can even copy styles from one document to another. When you use the Organizer is covered in the section "Modifying Templates," page 217.

Style Copying Rules

Whenever Word copies all styles from a template or a document to another template or document—for example, when you use the Style Gallery or choose the Automatically Update Document Styles option—it observes the following rules for each style. (Recall that a style is identified by a unique name in each document or template.)

- If a style exists only in the source template or document, Word adds the style to the target template or document.

- If a style exists only in the target template or document, Word leaves it in place, unaltered.

- If a style exists in both the source and target template or document (that is, both the source and the target have a style with the same name), Word replaces the target style with the source style.

Modifying and Creating Document Templates

A template stores a variety of items that form the basis of a Word document. When you create a new document, some of the items, such as text and styles, are copied into the document from the template that you select. Other items, such as AutoText entries and macros, are kept in the template. The template, however, remains *attached* to the document so that the document can access these items.

> Every Word document is based on a template. If you create a document using the New command on the File menu, the New Office Document command on the Start menu in Windows, or the New Office Document button on the Office Shortcut Bar, you can choose the template. If you create a new document by clicking the New button on the Standard toolbar, the document will be based on the Normal template.
>
> Note that the template that the document is based on is also called the *document template* or the *template attached to the document*. As you'll learn later in the chapter, you can change the document template after you have created the document.

Table 7-2 lists the template items that are copied into a new document. Once you have created a new document, both the document and the template have separate copies of these items. Changing one of these items in the document won't affect the template, and changing an item in the template won't affect the document.

TABLE 7-2. Template Items That Are Copied to a New Document

Template Item	Comments
Text and graphics, together with the formatting assigned to them	Includes headers, footers, footnotes, and comments
Page setup	Margins, paper size and source, page layout, and other features (explained in Chapter 10, "Designing Pages"); also, default tab stops (explained in "Using Tabs," page 224)
Styles	Predefined and custom styles

> Word *will* copy style changes from documents to templates or vice versa if you select Add To Template in the Modify Style dialog box or if you select Automatically Update Document Styles in the Templates And Add-Ins dialog box. See "Modifying Styles Using the Style Dialog Box," page 201, and "Copying Styles from a Template to a Document," page 212.

Microsoft Word

For information on choosing a template when you create a new document, see "Creating and Printing a Document from Start to Finish," page 105.

Table 7-3 lists the items that are kept in the template when a new document is created. A document can access any item stored in the document template. It can also access any item stored in the Normal template. (Of course, if the document is based on Normal, the document template and Normal are the same.) And a document can access any item that is stored in a template that has been explicitly loaded as a *global template*. (*Loading global templates is discussed in "Changing the Template Attached to a Document and Loading Global Templates," page 220.*)

For example, if an AutoText entry named Close is defined in either the document template or the Normal template, you can insert it into your document using any of the methods discussed in "Using the AutoText Feature," page 121. If an AutoText entry named Close is defined in both the document template and the Normal template, Word inserts the text defined in the document template. (That is, an item defined in the document template overrides a similarly named item in the Normal template or other global templates.)

TABLE 7-3.   Template Items Kept Within the Document Template

Template Item	Comments
AutoText entries	An AutoText entry is a frequently used block of text or graphics that can be inserted into a document (as explained in "Using the AutoText Feature," page 121.
Macros	A macro is a script for automating a Word task (as discussed in Chapter 14, "Automating Word with Macros").
Custom toolbar and menu configurations	Modifying toolbars and creating new ones is discussed in "Customizing Toolbars," page 44. Modifying menus is discussed in "Customizing Menus," page 50.
Shortcut key definitions	Defining shortcut keys to run commands, apply styles, or perform other tasks is discussed in the sidebar "Defining Shortcut Keys," page 206.

When you create a macro, a custom toolbar or menu, or a shortcut key definition, you have the option of storing it within the document rather than within a template so that the item will be private to that document.

Modifying Templates

You can modify Word templates in a variety of ways. When you take any of the following common Word actions, you modify the template:

- Creating any of the items listed in Table 7-3—that is, an AutoText entry, a macro, a custom toolbar or menu, or a shortcut key. When you create any of these items, you can save it in the Normal template or in the document template if it's other than Normal. (You also have the option of saving any of these items, except an AutoText entry, within a document.)

- Clicking the Default button in the Font, Language, or Page Setup dialog box and responding *yes* when prompted. Clicking Default saves the character formatting, language, or page setup in the document template. The character formatting and language are stored within the Normal style of the document template.

- Selecting the Add To Template option when modifying or creating a style (in the Modify Style or New Style dialog box) will modify or add a style in the document template.

You can also directly change the contents of one or more templates by using the Organizer. Using the Organizer you can delete, rename, or copy (from one template to another) styles, AutoText entries, custom toolbars, or macros. To open the Organizer dialog box, either choose Style from the Format menu or choose Templates And Add-Ins from the Tools menu, and then click the Organizer button (in the Style or Templates And Add-Ins dialog box). In the Organizer dialog box, first click the tab corresponding to the type of template item that you want to manage, and then follow the guidelines given in Figure 7-7, on the next page.

NOTE You can delete, copy, or rename styles, custom toolbars, or macros stored in either a document or a template. AutoText entries, however, are stored only in templates.

TIP To select a range of items in the Organizer list, press Shift and click the first and then the last item. To select several items that are not adjoining, press Ctrl and click each item.

Microsoft Word

FIGURE 7-7.
Using the Organizer to copy, delete, or rename template items.

Items stored in the file.

To list items stored in a different file, choose an item from this list box.

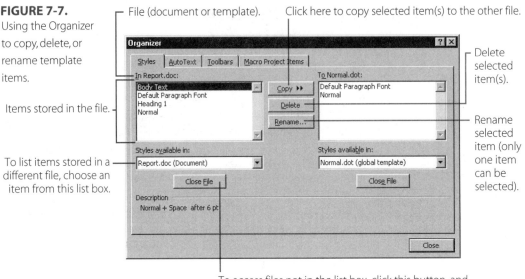

File (document or template).

Click here to copy selected item(s) to the other file.

Delete selected item(s).

Rename selected item (only one item can be selected).

To access files not in the list box, click this button, and then click the Open File button that appears in its place.

> **NOTE**
>
> You might wonder why the Organizer doesn't show all the built-in styles that are available in a template or document. The reason is that a built-in style isn't actually stored in a template or document until it has been modified or applied to text. (Until that time, it's kept only in Word.) The Organizer lists only styles that are actually stored in a template or document. (In contrast, the Style dialog box lists *all* available styles, provided that the All Styles option is selected.)

A final way to modify a template is to open the template file and edit it in the same way you edit a document. The following are the general steps:

1 Choose Open from the File menu, or click the Open button on the Standard toolbar.

2 In the Open dialog box, select Document Templates (*.dot) in the Files Of Type list box, and then select the template file you want to modify. The templates supplied with Word are stored in C:\Windows\Application Data\Microsoft\Templates.

3 Edit and format the template using the same techniques used for documents. You can add or modify any of the template items listed in Table 7-2 (page 215) and Table 7-3 (page 216). For the items listed in Table 7-3, be sure to save your changes in the template itself rather than in the Normal template.

4 Choose Save from the File menu, or click the Save button to save your changes.

Creating New Templates

The procedure for creating a new template is similar to that for creating a new document. The following are the basic steps:

1 Choose New from the File menu.

2 In the New dialog box, select the Template option in the lower right corner, select an existing template to use as the starting point for your new template, and click OK.

3 Enter text and graphics, edit, and format the new template using the same techniques used for documents. You can add any of the items listed in Table 7-2, page 215, and Table 7-3, page 216. For the items listed in Table 7-3, be sure to save your changes in the template itself rather than in the Normal template.

4 Choose Save from the File menu, or click the Save button to save the new template.

The first time you save the template, Word will open the Save As dialog box and will automatically switch to your current Templates folder. If you want the New command to display the template you have created, you must save it in the file folder designated as your Templates folder. If you haven't set up custom user profiles (using the Passwords item in the Windows Control Panel), the default Templates folder is C:\Windows\Application Data\Microsoft\Templates. (For *C:\Windows* substitute the Windows folder on your computer if it's different.) If you have set up custom user profiles, the default User Templates folder will be within your personal profiles folder.

You can save the template directly within your User Templates folder; in this case, the template will be displayed on the General tab of the New dialog box. Alternatively, you can place it within a subfolder of your User Templates folder (an existing subfolder or a new one that you create); in this case, the template will be displayed in the New dialog box on a tab that's labeled with the name of the subfolder.

Choose the Location for Your Templates

You can designate a different folder as your User Templates folder, causing the New dialog box to display the templates stored in the new folder you specify, rather than in the original User Templates folder. To do this, choose Options from the Tools menu, click the File Locations tab, click User Templates in the list, click the Modify button, and enter the new folder path. This change will affect all Office applications that use templates, not just Word.

Notice that on the File Locations tab, you can also designate a Workgroup Templates folder. (Initially, no folder is assigned to this item.) If you do so, the New dialog box will display the templates in the Workgroup Templates folder in addition to those in the User Templates folder. Typically, the Workgroup Templates folder is located on a network and contains a set of templates that you share with co-workers.

Note that in addition to the new and customized templates stored in the User Templates and Workgroup Templates folders, the New dialog box displays the templates that are supplied with Word, such as Contemporary Letter and Professional Memo.

Also, you must name the template file with the .dot extension or omit the extension. (If you omit it, Word will add the .dot.) Note that extensions might not be displayed when you list files, depending on the options you have chosen in Windows.

Base a New Template on an Existing Document

You can get a head start on creating a new template by basing it on an existing document. To do this, open the document and immediately choose Save As from the File menu, select Document Template (*.dot) in the Save As Type list box, specify a name and location for the new template, and click OK. Then make any changes you want and use the Save command to save these changes.

Changing the Template Attached to a Document and Loading Global Templates

You can change the template that is attached to a document. When you do this, all the AutoText entries, macros, custom toolbars and menus, and shortcut keys that are stored in the new template become available to the document (in place of the items stored in the previous template). To change the document template, do the following:

1 Open the document you want to change.

2 Choose Templates And Add-Ins from the Tools menu. Word will display the Templates And Add-Ins dialog box. (See Figure 7-6, page 213.)

3 Click the Attach button.

4 Select the desired template in the Attach Template dialog box. Make sure that Document Templates (*.dot) is selected in the Files Of Type list box. Then click the Open button.

Also, Word allows you to load one or more templates in addition to the document template. An additional template that you have loaded is known as a *global template,* and all the AutoText entries, macros, custom toolbars and menus, and shortcut keys that are stored in these templates also become available to *any* document open in Word. (An item defined in a document template overrides a similarly named item in any of the global templates you load.) To load a global template, choose Templates And Add-Ins from the Tools menu, and do the following:

- If the template is listed within the Global Templates And Add-Ins list, simply select the adjoining check box.

- If the template is not in the list, click the Add button. In the Add Template dialog box, make sure that the Document Templates (*.dot) item is selected in the Files Of Type list box, select the template you want, and click OK. The template will be added to the Global Templates And Add-Ins list and will be checked.

NOTE You can also load a Word add-in, which is a utility program that supplies enhancement features to Word. (You typically obtain such a program from a software vendor.) To do this, use the procedure for opening an additional template, except that in the Add Template dialog box you should choose the Word Add-Ins (*.wll) item in the Files Of Type list box.

A global template or add-in will remain loaded only for the remainder of your current Word session. When you exit and restart Word, you'll need to reload it by checking it in the Global Templates And Add-Ins list. (The template or add-in will still be in the list, although it won't be checked.)

Microsoft Word

CHAPTER 8

Arranging Text in Columns and Lists

This chapter presents a diverse collection of techniques that allow you to arrange, sort, group, and emphasize paragraphs of text in your documents. You'll learn how to arrange text in rows and columns using simple tab characters or sophisticated Microsoft Word tables. You'll learn how to arrange text in snaking newspaper-style columns. You'll learn how to create various kinds of lists, and how to sort the contents of lists as well as of Word tables. Finally, you'll learn how to arrange or emphasize paragraphs of text by adding borders and background shading, and how to separate different parts of your document using horizontal dividing lines.

Many of the features described in this chapter—tabs, bulleted and numbered lists, borders, and shading—are types of paragraph formatting. This chapter thus extends the discussion on basic paragraph formatting that was the focus of Chapter 6, "Formatting a Word Document."

Using Tabs

Pressing the Tab key inserts white space into your document and moves the insertion point so that the next character you type will be aligned on the next tab stop. The Tab key doesn't insert a series of space characters; rather, it inserts a single nonprinting character that you can delete with a single press of the Backspace or Delete key. You can make tab characters visible on the screen—as small arrows—by choosing Options from the Tools menu, clicking the View tab, and selecting the Tab Characters option. (Or you can click the Show/Hide ¶ button on the Standard toolbar to show all nonprinting characters.) See Figure 8-1.

You can use tabs to arrange numbers or small blocks of text into rows and columns. In general, however, Word tables (discussed in the next section) are easier to use and are a more versatile method for arranging text into rows and columns, especially if any of the individual blocks of text you're arranging won't fit on a single line.

FIGURE 8-1.
Tab characters
and tab stops.

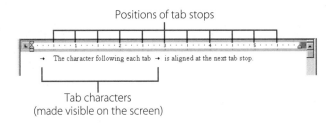

Positions of tab stops

The character following each tab → is aligned at the next tab stop.

Tab characters
(made visible on the screen)

⭐ **TIP**

> **Use Ctrl+Tab to Insert Tabs in Outline View or in Tables**
>
> To insert a tab character within a Word table or to insert a tab when you're in Outline view, press Ctrl+Tab. You must also press Ctrl+Tab to insert a tab at the beginning of a line of text if you have selected the Tabs And Backspace Set Left Indent editing option. This option is described in "Using Shortcut Keys to Apply Paragraph Formatting," page 191.

In Word, you can adjust both the spacing and the type of the tab stops. Word has two basic kinds of tab stops: *default* and *custom*. Default tab stops apply to the entire document; they are not, therefore, strictly paragraph formatting. In documents created from most templates, the default tab stops are set at .5 inch. This means that anywhere in the document (unless you have set custom tab stops), tab stops will be placed at half-inch intervals, starting at the left margin. The default tab stops are marked with small vertical lines at the bottom of the ruler:

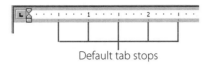

Default tab stops

You can change the default tab stops for the currently opened document, as follows:

1 Choose Tabs from the Format menu. Word will open the Tabs dialog box. (See Figure 8-2.)

2 Enter a new value in the Default Tab Stops box, and click OK.

Changing the default tab stops will affect only the document currently displayed in the Word window. To change the default tab stops for all documents you create based on a particular template, open that template, perform the steps given above, and save the template.

You can also define *custom* tab stops. Unlike default tab stops, custom tab stops are considered paragraph formatting; therefore, they affect only the paragraph or paragraphs to which you have applied them. You can define custom tab stops using either the ruler or the Tabs dialog box.

Because custom tab stop settings are paragraph formatting, you can use the techniques for paragraph formatting discussed in the previous chapters. For example, you can find or replace tab stop formatting, copy the formatting from one paragraph to another, or assign the formatting to a paragraph style.

FIGURE 8-2.
The Tabs dialog box.

Defining Custom Tab Stops Using the Ruler

The easiest way to define custom tab stops is to use the horizontal ruler. (If the ruler isn't shown, choose Ruler from the View menu. You can also temporarily view the ruler by holding the mouse pointer over the gray bar at the top of the window's document area.) The following is the procedure:

1 Select the paragraph or paragraphs for which you want to define custom tab stops. (To modify a single paragraph, you can just place the insertion point anywhere within it.)

> **NOTE**

> If you're in Outline view, you must switch to one of the other views to set tabs.

2 Click the button at the left end of the ruler—repeatedly if necessary—to choose one of the four types of tab stops. Each time you click, the type changes, as indicated by the symbol displayed on the button:

Symbol	Type of Tab Stop
L	Left tab stop.
⊥	Center tab stop.
⌐	Right tab stop.
⊥	Decimal tab stop.
I	Bar. Inserts a vertical bar, not a tab stop.
▽	First Line Indent. Creates a first-line-only indent; doesn't insert a tab stop.
⊔	Hanging Indent. Creates a hanging indent; doesn't insert a tab stop.

The four different types of tab stops control the alignment of the text that you type after pressing Tab, as shown in Figure 8-3.

NOTE

The button for selecting the type of tab isn't visible in Web Layout view. However, you can still select the tab type by clicking the left end of the ruler. The currently selected option will be displayed in a ScreenTip when you place the mouse pointer over the left end of the ruler.

3 Click the position on the ruler where you want to place the tab stop. Word will mark the position of the tab stop using the symbol for the tab stop type (as shown on the buttons in the previous table).

Notice that whenever you position a custom tab stop, Word removes all default tab stops to the left of the custom tab stop. Default tab stops to the right remain in place. The default tab stops work as left tab stops wherever they appear.

TIP

Use the Ruler to Apply Other Formatting

When the Bar option is selected on the button at the left end of the horizontal ruler, you can insert a vertical bar through the selected paragraph by clicking the ruler at the desired bar position. When the First Line Indent option is selected, you can click the ruler to indent only the first line of the paragraph to the position where you click. And when the Hanging Indent option is selected, you can click the ruler to indent all lines of the paragraph except the first line at that position.

FIGURE 8-3.
The four different kinds of tab stops.

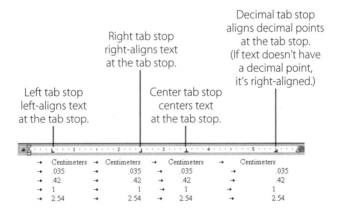

You can change the position of a custom tab stop by dragging it to a new location on the ruler, and you can remove a custom tab stop by dragging it off the ruler.

Defining Custom Tab Stops Using the Tabs Dialog Box

You can also define custom tab stops using the Tabs dialog box, which provides the following additional features:

- You can enter precise measurements for the positions of the tab stops.

- You can fill the space preceding the tab with a leader character.

To use the Tabs dialog box, do the following:

1 Select the paragraph or paragraphs for which you want to define custom tab stops.

2 Open the Tabs dialog box (see Figure 8-2, page 225) by choosing Tabs from the Format menu. Or you can click the Tabs button within the Paragraph dialog box, as described in Chapter 6.

3 To define a new tab stop, enter its position (that is, its distance from the left margin) in the Tab Stop Position box.

4 Choose the type of tab stop you want by selecting one of the options in the Alignment area of the Tabs dialog box. The different types are shown in Figure 8-3. The Bar option adds a vertical line to the paragraph rather than defining a custom tab stop.

5 If you want to fill the blank space before the tab using a leader character, select option 2, 3, or 4 in the Leader area of the Tabs dialog box. For example, the following numbers are aligned with decimal tabs that have been assigned a leader character (option 2):

```
Rent...............→...............$843.00
Advertising.........→.........$640.00
Entertainment......→......$8432.00
```

6 Click the Set button. The tab will be added to the list.

7 Repeat steps 3 through 6 for each additional custom tab stop that you want to define. To remove a custom tab stop, select it in the list in the Tabs dialog box, and click Clear (or click Clear All to remove all custom tab stops and restore the default tab stops).

8 Click OK to accept your custom tab stop or stops and return to the document.

Using Tables

A Word *table* is a highly versatile tool for arranging text in rows and columns. Figure 8-4 shows a Word table as it appears on the screen. Using a table offers many advantages over using tab stops. For example, if a particular text item doesn't fit on a single line, Word creates a new line and increases the height of the row. (The table shown in Figure 8-4 would be difficult to create using tab stops.) Also, when you use tables you can easily rearrange and adjust the size of the rows and columns, and you can emphasize table items by using borders and background shading.

FIGURE 8-4.

A Word table as it appears on the screen.

Paragraph Formatting Action	Shortcut Key	Comment
Increase left paragraph indent	Ctrl+M	Indent is moved to the next tab stop.
Decrease left paragraph indent	Ctrl+Shift+M	Indent is moved to previous tab stop; cannot be used to create a negative left indent.
Increase hanging indent	Ctrl+T	All paragraph lines are indented except the first line. Each time you press the key combination, the hanging indent is moved right to the next tab stop.
Decrease hanging indent	Ctrl+Shift+T	Hanging indent is moved left to the previous tab stop.
Add or remove 12 points of extra space above paragraph	Ctrl+0 (zero at top of keyboard, *not* on numeric keypad)	Toggles feature on or off.

W ON THE WEB

The TableDemo.doc document file, used for the examples in this section, is on the Running Office 2000 Reader's Corner page. For information about connecting to this Web site, read the Introduction.

Inserting a Table

To construct a table at the position of the insertion point, use the Insert Table button on the Standard toolbar, as shown below:

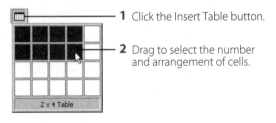

1 Click the Insert Table button.

2 Drag to select the number and arrangement of cells.

2 x 4 Table

? SEE ALSO

For information on applying background shading to tables or adding or modifying borders, see "Using Borders and Shading," page 256.

The new table will consist of rows and columns of empty *cells*. The lines defining these cells are known as *gridlines*. Gridlines can be shown in a variety of different ways. The gridlines in a newly created table are marked with thin, solid *borders*. A border is a line that is visible both on the screen and on the printed copy of the document. (Borders can also be added to paragraphs and other objects.) Later in

Microsoft Word

the chapter, you'll learn how to modify or remove one or more borders from a table. If you remove a border, the gridline will be marked with a light gray line that appears on the screen but is not printed; this line will appear, however, only if you select the Show Gridlines option on the Table menu.

> **Add New Rows to a Table by Pressing Tab**
>
> If you don't know how many rows you'll need when you insert a table, just choose a single row. As you'll see, it's easy to add new rows to the end of the table as you enter the table text by pressing Tab in the last cell. (You should, however, try to choose the actual number of columns, because inserting additional columns is not as easy.)

Entering Text into a Table

To add text to a cell in a table, click in the cell and type the text in the same way that you would in an ordinary paragraph. Notice that if you reach the right border of the cell, Word wraps the text down to the next line and increases the height of the entire row, if necessary, to accommodate the new text. If you press Enter while typing in a cell, Word will insert a new paragraph within the cell. (Each cell contains one or more entire paragraphs.) You can edit and format text within a cell using the standard Word editing and formatting techniques given in the previous chapters.

> You can insert a table within a cell of another table, creating a nested table. To do this, place the insertion point at the position in the cell where you want the nested table, and use any of the methods given in this chapter for inserting a table.

To move the insertion point to another cell, click in the cell or use the arrow keys. To move to the next cell (in row-by-row order) and select any text it contains, press Tab. To move to the previous cell and select any text it contains, press Shift+Tab. When you're in the last cell of the table, pressing Tab adds a new row to the end of the table.

> **Insert Tabs in Tables**
>
> To insert a tab character into a table cell, press Ctrl+Tab. You can set the position of tab stops as described in the previous section. But watch for one oddity—when you set a decimal tab, the text in the cell is moved to that tab stop without your having to put a tab character in front of it.

Inserting and Deleting
Rows, Columns, and Cells

To insert or delete rows, columns, or groups of cells, you must first select the appropriate portion of the table. You can easily select a cell, row, or column as follows:

Click here to select a single cell.

Units	Points	Picas	Centimeters	Inches
Points	1	1/12	.035	1/72
Picas	12	1	.42	1/6
Centimeters	28.35	2.38	1	.39
Inches	72	6	2.54	1

Units	Points	Picas	Centimeters	Inches
Points	1	1/12	.035	1/72
Picas	12	1	.42	1/6
Centimeters	28.35	2.38	1	.39
Inches	72	6	2.54	1

Click here to
select a row.

Click here to select a column.

Units	Points	Picas	Centimeters	Inches
Points	1	1/12	.035	1/72
Picas	12	1	.42	1/6
Centimeters	28.35	2.38	1	.39
Inches	72	6	2.54	1

After you have selected a single cell, row, or column, you can drag to select additional cells, rows, or columns. Alternatively, you can select any block of cells by placing the insertion point within a cell and then pressing an arrow key while holding down Shift. You can select the entire table by placing the insertion point anywhere within it and pressing Alt+5 (the 5 on the numeric keypad with Num Lock off).

The following is a method for adding entire rows or columns to an existing table:

1   To insert rows at a particular position in a table, select existing rows just below that position; select the same number of rows as the number you want to add. For example:

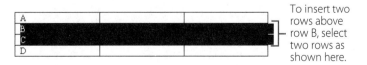

To insert two rows above row B, select two rows as shown here.

II

Microsoft Word

To insert a single row, you can simply place the insertion point anywhere in the row. Likewise, to insert columns, select an equal number of columns to the right of the position where you want to add the new ones.

Insert Rows   Insert Columns

2 If you're inserting rows, click the Insert Rows button on the Standard toolbar. If you're inserting columns, click the Insert Columns button.

> **NOTE** The Standard toolbar actually has only one button for table insertion. When table rows, columns, or cells are selected, the button's ScreenTip reads Insert Rows, Insert Columns, or Insert Cells. When the insertion point or selection is outside a table, the ScreenTip reads Insert Table, and the button inserts a new table. As the selection changes, the image on the button changes to indicate its function.

Alternatively, you can right-click the selection and choose Insert Rows or Insert Columns from the pop-up menu. (The command on the pop-up menu changes depending on whether you have selected rows or columns.)

After clicking the Insert Rows button or choosing Insert Rows from the pop-up menu, the example table shown above (under step 1) looks like this:

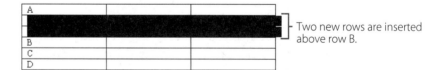
Two new rows are inserted above row B.

Word marks the end of each table cell with an end-of-cell mark and the end of each table row with an end-of-row mark. You can make these marks visible by clicking the Show/Hide ¶ button on the Standard toolbar. In step 1 above, if you want to insert rows, you should include the end-of-row marks in your selection whether they are visible or not. To insert a column at the right end of a table, select the entire column of end-of-row marks before clicking the Insert Columns button. (You can select these marks whether they're visible or not.):

Click here to insert a
new column to the
right of the table.

End-of-cell mark.

End-of-row mark.

As you learned earlier in this chapter, you can insert a row at the end of a table by pressing Tab when the insertion point is in the last cell.

To insert a block of one or more cells without inserting entire rows or columns, do the following:

1 Select a block of existing cells that has the number and arrangement of the cells you want to insert.

2 Click the Insert Cells button on the Standard toolbar. Word will display the Insert Cells dialog box, which you can see in Figure 8-5.

FIGURE 8-5.
The Insert Cells
dialog box.

3 Click Shift Cells Right to have Word move the existing cells to the right when it inserts the new cells, or click Shift Cells Down to have it move the cells down. You can also click Insert Entire Row or Insert Entire Column to insert complete rows or columns even though you didn't select complete rows or columns.

To delete table rows, columns, or cells, simply select them, right-click the selection, and choose Delete Rows, Delete Columns, or Delete Cells from the pop-up menu. (The command will be labeled according to the current selection.) Alternatively, you can point to Delete on the Table menu and choose Delete Rows, Delete Columns, or Delete Cells from the submenu that appears. (You can also choose Table from this submenu to remove the entire table.) If you have selected a block that doesn't include complete rows or columns and you choose Delete Cells, Word will display the Delete Cells dialog box, which lets you choose the way the remaining cells are rearranged after the deletion.

To delete the *contents* of rows, columns, or cells—that is, the text or graphics contained within them—without removing the cells themselves, select the rows, columns, or cells and press the Delete key.

Adjusting the Size of Table Cells

You can adjust the width of a table column by dragging its right vertical gridline:

To change the width
of this column...   ...drag this vertical gridline.

Units	Points	Picas	Centimeters	Inches
Points	1	1/12	.035	1/72
Picas	12	1	.42	1/6
Centimeters	28.35	2.38	1	.39
Inches	72	6	2.54	1

To adjust the width of one or more specific cells in a column (rather than an entire column), select the cells before dragging. The cells in a single column can vary in width.

When adjusting the width of a column, you can modify the way Word changes the widths of the cells to the right of the column, if any exist, by pressing additional keys while dragging. (See Table 8-1.)

Of course, if you drag the rightmost vertical gridline in a table, you'll always change the overall table width. (And pressing Ctrl or Shift will have no effect.) Note that if you drag the leftmost vertical gridline in the table, you'll change the indent of the selected rows (or of the entire table if no rows are selected) from the left document margin.

You can also rapidly adjust the width of one or more cells to accommodate the current contents of the cells. To do this, select the cell or cells and double-click the rightmost vertical gridline of the selection. To adjust one entire column of cells, you can simply double-click the right gridline without selecting cells. Here's an example:

To have Word adjust the
width of this column to
accommodate the
widest cell entry...   ...double-click anywhere on its right vertical gridline.

Units	Points	Picas	Centimeters	Inches
Points	1	1/12	.035	1/72
Picas	12	1	.42	1/6
Centimeters	28.35	2.38	1	.39
Inches	72	6	2.54	1

And here's how the example looks after double-clicking:

Units	Points	Picas	Centimeters	Inches
Points	1	1/12	.035	1/72
Picas	12	1	.42	1/6
Centimeters	28.35	2.38	1	.39
Inches	72	6	2.54	1

(If Word adjusts more than one cell in a particular column, it resizes them equally to accommodate the widest block of text in a cell.) If you later change the contents of a cell, you'll have to readjust the cell or column width.

TABLE 8-1.   Effects of Pressing Keys While Dragging Vertical Table Gridlines

Key	Effect on Cells to Right of Gridline
No key	Word changes the width only of the cells to the immediate right of the gridline, without changing overall table width.
Alt	Has the same effect on table as pressing no key, but Word displays the width of each column within the ruler.
Ctrl	Word changes the width of all cells to the right proportionately, without changing the overall table width. (For example, if the cells to the right have equal widths, they remain equal in width after you drag.)
Shift	Word does not change the width of cells to the right. Instead, it changes the overall table width.

 Alternatively, you can assign the new AutoFit feature to a table to have Word adjust the width of all columns in a table to fit the cell contents or the window width, and to dynamically maintain the adjustment as you change the contents or window width. To do this, right-click anywhere in the table, and on the pop-up menu that appears, point to AutoFit to display the submenu. (Alternatively, you can place the insertion point within the table and point to AutoFit on the Table menu.)

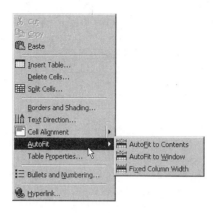

If you choose AutoFit To Contents, Word will adjust the width of each column in the table to accommodate the widest block of text in that column. And as you add or delete text from a column, Word will dynamically adjust the width to maintain the fit.

If you choose AutoFit To Window, the overall width of the table will be adjusted so that the table just fits within the window, and the width will be dynamically adjusted to maintain this fit if the window is resized. AutoFit To Window affects the table only when you view the document in the Web Layout view of Word, or when you view a Web-page document in a browser.

If you choose Fixed Column Width, the column widths will remain constant unless you manually adjust them using one of the techniques described previously in this section.

As you have seen, Word automatically adjusts the height of a table row to accommodate the text contained in the row. You can also manually adjust the height of a row by dragging the horizontal gridline at the bottom of the row. To do this, you must be in Web Layout or Print Layout view. Note that you can't adjust the height of selected cells within a row—you always change the height of all the cells in the row.

You can give two or more rows the same height by selecting them, right-clicking the selection, and choosing Distribute Rows Evenly from the pop-up menu that appears. Likewise, you can give two or more columns the same width by selecting them, right-clicking the selection, and choosing Distribute Columns Evenly from the pop-up menu. (Alternatively, after you make the selection, you can point to AutoFit on the Table menu and choose either of these commands from the submenu that appears.)

TIP

Quickly Move or Resize a Table

In Web Layout or Print Layout view, you can move or resize an entire table by holding the mouse pointer over the table until the Move and Resize handles appear and then dragging a handle, as shown here:

Move handle. Drag to move the table to a new position in the document.

Units	Points	Picas	Centimeters	Inches
Points	1	1/12	.035	1/72
Picas	12	1	.42	1/6
Centimeters	28.35	2.38	1	.39
Inches	72	6	2.54	1

The Move and Resize handles appear when you point to the table.

Resize handle. Drag to change the overall size and proportions of the table.

When you resize a table by dragging the Resize handle, Word changes the sizes of *all* the cells in the table.

Moving and Copying Rows, Columns, and Cells

To *move* entire rows or columns within a table, select them, and then use the mouse to drag them to a new location. The rows or columns will be removed from their current location and inserted into the table at the new location. To *copy* rows or columns, press the Ctrl key while dragging. When you select rows, you must include the end-of-row marks. Otherwise, you'll merely move or copy the contents of the cells.

NOTE

To use the techniques discussed in this section, the Drag-And-Drop Text Editing option must be selected. To locate this option, choose Options from the Tools menu, and click the Edit tab.

To move the contents of table cells, select the cells and drag to a new location in the table. Word will delete the contents of the cells you selected (leaving empty cells behind), and it will insert these contents into the cells at the target location, overwriting the current contents of the target cells. To copy the contents of table cells, press the Ctrl key while dragging. (To move or copy cell contents, you must not select entire columns. You can select entire rows as long as you don't include the end-of-row marks.)

II

Microsoft Word

You can also move or copy text from one cell to another without overwriting the contents of the second cell. To move text, select only the text within the first cell (rather than selecting the entire cell), and then drag it to the new location. (Press Ctrl while you drag to copy.) The moved or copied text will be added to the contents of the second cell.

Changing the Text Orientation and Alignment in a Table Cell

You can modify the orientation of the text in a table cell so that rather than the text reading from left to right, it reads from bottom to top or from top to bottom. You might want to do this to make information fit into a particular table, or to improve the appearance or readability of a table. To change the text orientation within a table, select one or more cells, right-click within the selection, and choose Text Direction from the pop-up menu. (To change a single cell, you can right-click within the cell without selecting it.) Then select the desired orientation in the Text Direction dialog box:

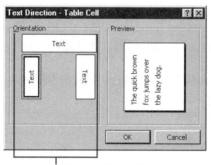

Click one of these three boxes to set the orientation of the text within the selected table cells.

To change the alignment of the text within one or more cells, select them and right-click the selection. (To change a single cell, you can just right-click it.) Then point to Cell Alignment on the pop-up menu and choose an alignment style from the submenu that appears:

Note that Word creates the horizontal component of the alignment by assigning the Left, Center, or Right paragraph formatting attributes to the paragraph(s) in the cell.

Using the Table Menu Commands

The previous sections have focused on working with tables using the Standard toolbar, mouse, and pop-up menus. In general, these interactive methods are the fastest and most convenient. The Table menu provides alternative methods for inserting and modifying tables; it also allows you to perform some additional table operations not possible using the interactive techniques. Table 8-2 summarizes the use of these commands. Keep in mind that for many of these commands, merely placing the insertion point within a table, row, column, or cell is equivalent to selecting the table, row, column, or cell.

Other Ways to Work with Tables

Some of the commands listed in Table 8-2 are also provided on the pop-up menu that appears when you right-click a table or a selection within a table. And keep in mind that the Tables And Borders toolbar, discussed in the next section, provides a variety of tools for working with tables that you have created using any of the available methods.

TABLE 8-2.   Table Menu Commands and Their Effects

Command or Submenu	Description
Draw Table command	Allows you to "draw" a table. This command is discussed in the next section.
Insert submenu	Allows you to insert a new table into a document or into a table cell, to insert columns (to the left or right of the selection), to insert rows (above or below the selection), or to insert cells (specifying the direction in which the existing cells are shifted). The effects of these commands depend on the current selection or position of the insertion point.
Delete submenu	Lets you delete the selected cells, columns, rows, or the entire table.
Select submenu	Lets you select the column(s), row(s), cell(s), or the entire table containing the insertion point or selection.
Merge Cells command	Combines the selected adjacent cells into a single cell.
Split Cells command	Divides the single selected cell (or each cell in a group of selected cells) into two or more cells. You can specify the resulting number of rows and columns of cells.

(continued)

Microsoft Word

TABLE 8-2. *continued*

Command or Submenu	Description
Split Table command	Divides a table into two separate tables, and inserts a regular paragraph (Normal) between the two tables. The division occurs above the selected row.
Table AutoFormat command	Allows you to instantly modify the overall look of the selected table by choosing one of a set of predefined table formats.
AutoFit submenu	Lets you apply the AutoFit feature to the selected table, or to distribute rows or columns evenly. These features were described in "Adjusting the Size of Table Cells," page 234.
Heading Rows Repeat command	Marks the selected row or rows at the top of a table as a heading. If a page break occurs within a table, Word repeats the heading at the top of the next page.
Convert submenu	Lets you convert the selected table to text (removes the table and converts the text it contains to ordinary paragraphs), or convert selected text outside a table to a table (creates a new table and inserts the selected text into the table).
Sort command	Sorts the contents of the selected rows and columns within a table. If the selection is outside a table, the command sorts paragraphs of text. *For information on this command, see "Sorting Lists and Tables," page 253.*
Formula command	Inserts a formula into a table cell. A formula displays the result of a mathematical computation on numbers within table cells. This command lets you create a Word table that functions as a simple spreadsheet.
Show Gridlines command	Causes Word to mark the gridlines around cells in all tables using light gray lines. These lines are visible only on the screen (they don't print) and only where borders haven't been applied. Note that when the option is selected, it's labeled Hide Gridlines, and when it isn't selected, it's labeled Show Gridlines.
Table Properties command	Displays the Table Properties dialog box, which allows you to modify the size, alignment, indent, and text-wrapping style of the selected table; the height and page-breaking style of rows; the height of columns; and the width and vertical text-alignment style (top, center, or bottom) of the selected cell or cells. (By modifying the text-wrapping style, you can have adjoining text wrap around the table rather than staying above and below it.)

Drawing Tables

Another way to insert a table is to interactively draw it, in much the same way that you draw lines or rectangles in a drawing program. To draw a table, choose Draw Table from the Table menu or click the Tables And Borders button on the Standard toolbar.

Tables And
Borders

When you choose Draw Table or click the Tables And Borders button, Word does the following:

- If you're in Normal view, it switches to Print Layout view. (You must be in either Print Layout or Web Layout view to draw a table.)

- It displays the Tables And Borders toolbar, which provides tools for working with tables, borders, and shading. This toolbar is shown in Figure 8-6.

- It selects the Draw Table tool on the Tables And Borders toolbar, which converts the mouse pointer into a pencil.

FIGURE 8-6.
The Tables And
Borders toolbar.

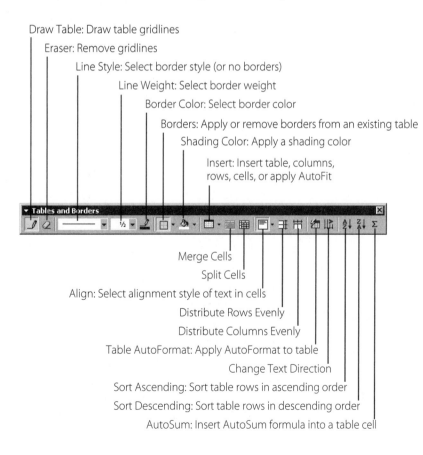

Draw Table: Draw table gridlines
Eraser: Remove gridlines
Line Style: Select border style (or no borders)
Line Weight: Select border weight
Border Color: Select border color
Borders: Apply or remove borders from an existing table
Shading Color: Apply a shading color
Insert: Insert table, columns, rows, cells, or apply AutoFit

Merge Cells
Split Cells
Align: Select alignment style of text in cells
Distribute Rows Evenly
Distribute Columns Evenly
Table AutoFormat: Apply AutoFormat to table
Change Text Direction
Sort Ascending: Sort table rows in ascending order
Sort Descending: Sort table rows in descending order
AutoSum: Insert AutoSum formula into a table cell

Microsoft Word

You can now create a table using the Draw Table tool, as follows:

1 Place the pencil-shaped pointer at one corner of the position in your document where you want to insert the table, press and hold the mouse button, and drag the pointer to the opposite corner. The rectangle you draw defines the outside gridlines of the table, which initially consists of a single cell.

Click here to start drawing the table.

Then drag to draw the outside gridlines of the table.

If you draw the gridlines around an existing paragraph of text, that paragraph will be included within the table cell.

2 You can now divide the table into any number of cells by using the Draw Table tool to draw internal cell gridlines. Drag the pencil-shaped pointer to draw each cell gridline:

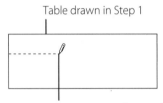

Table drawn in Step 1

Drawing a gridline to divide the table into separate cells

3 To remove a table gridline, click the Eraser button on the Tables And Borders toolbar and drag over the gridline. As you drag, the gridline will be highlighted, and when you release the mouse button, the gridline will be removed. Click the Eraser button again to deselect it when you're finished.

 **TIP**

When the Draw Table tool is selected, you can press the Shift key to temporarily convert it to the Eraser tool for conveniently removing one or more gridlines.

When you draw a table using the Draw Table tool, the way the gridlines are marked depends on the current selections in the Line Style, Line Weight, and Border Color tools on the Tables And Borders toolbar. If you choose No Border in the Line Style list, the gridlines will be marked with light gray lines, provided that the Show Gridlines option on the Table menu is selected. These lines will appear on the screen but won't be printed. If you choose a border style in the Line Style list (such as a single, double, or dotted line), the gridlines will be marked with borders that appear both on the screen and on the printed copy, and the appearance of these borders will be affected by the settings in the Line Weight and Border Color tools.

Note that changing a setting in the Line Style, Line Weight, or Border Color tool affects only the table gridlines that you subsequently draw or redraw with the Draw Table tool; it won't affect table gridlines that you have already drawn. (These tools also affect borders that you subsequently apply using the Borders tool.) Later in the chapter—in the section "Using Borders and Shading," page 256—you'll learn how to add, modify, or remove borders in a table you have already drawn, and also how to apply shading to table cells. Borders and shading are discussed in a separate section because you can apply them to text outside tables, as well as to tables.

As you can see in Figure 8-6, the Tables And Borders toolbar provides a number of buttons that you can use to easily modify existing tables. So you might want to display this toolbar whenever you work with tables, even if you don't use the Draw Table tool.

Creating Newspaper-Style Columns

Unlike the columns created with tables, newspaper-style columns are not divided into rows of side-by-side items. Rather, the text flows from the bottom of one column to the top of the next column, just like it does in the familiar columns of newspapers and magazines. (See Figure 8-7, on the next page.) Newspaper-style columns are intended for regular Word documents that you're going to print or view online in Word. If you're creating a Web-page document, forget about newspaper-style columns—they won't display in a browser. (The text will be displayed in a single column.)

If you want to view newspaper-style columns on the screen, you must switch to Print Layout view or to Print Preview. In the other Word views, text is always displayed in a single column. You can create newspaper-style columns using either the Columns button on the Standard toolbar or the Columns dialog box.

FIGURE 8-7.

A page of a Word document in which the text following the heading is divided into two newspaper-style columns.

 ON THE WEB The ColumnDemo.doc document file, used for the examples in this section, is on the Running Office 2000 Reader's Corner page.

Setting Up Columns Using the Columns Button

To set up equal-width newspaper-style columns throughout your entire document, or in a portion of the document, do the following:

1 To create columns in a part of your document, select that part. To create columns throughout your entire document, place the insertion point anywhere in the document.

2 Click the Columns button and drag to indicate the number of columns you want (from 1 through 6):

Drag to select the number of columns.

Word will divide the selected text, or the entire document, into the specified number of columns. The columns will be equal in width and will be separated by .5 inches.

? SEE ALSO

For more information on sections, as well as on the attributes that can be applied to sections, see Chapter 10, "Designing Pages."

If you selected part of the document in step 1, Word will insert *section breaks* before and after your selection; that is, the selected text will be placed in a separate document section, and newspaper-style columns will be applied to that section. In general, a Word document can be divided into separate sections, and each section can be assigned different page setup attributes, such as margins, headers, footers, and newspaper-style columns. Sections allow you to vary page setup attributes within a document. You can manually divide a document into sections using the Break command on the Insert menu. The steps given in this part of the chapter will work somewhat differently if you have previously divided your document into sections.

Setting up Columns Using the Columns Dialog Box

The Columns dialog box lets you set up newspaper-style columns that have the following additional characteristics:

- You can create columns of unequal width.

- For each column, you can specify the exact column width and the amount of space between that column and the next.

- You can force the columns to remain equal in width, even if you later adjust the column width.

- You can add vertical lines between the columns.

To set up newspaper-style columns with the Columns dialog box, do the following:

1   To create columns in a part of your document, select that part. To create columns from a specific position in the document through the end of the document, place the insertion point at that position. To create columns throughout the entire document, place the insertion point anywhere within the document.

2   Choose Columns from the Format menu to open the Columns dialog box, which is shown in Figure 8-8, on the next page.

3   Choose an option in the Apply To list box to tell Word the portion of your document you want to modify. If you selected text prior to opening the Columns dialog box, choose Selected Text to add columns to the selection only, or choose Whole Document to

FIGURE 8-8.
The Columns
dialog box.

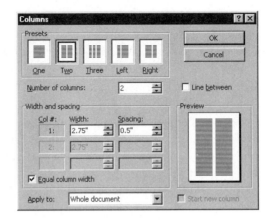

add columns to the entire document. If you didn't select text, choose Whole Document to add columns to the entire document, or choose This Point Forward to add columns from the position of the insertion point through the end of the document.

4 Choose a column arrangement.

- To use a standard column arrangement, choose one of the items in the Presets area.

- To create a custom column arrangement, choose the number of columns you want in the Number Of Columns box. Then for each column, specify its width in the Width box, and enter the space you want between that column and the next column in the Spacing box.

5 To force Word to keep the widths of the columns equal, select Equal Column Width. If this option is enabled, adjusting the column width—using the procedures described in the next section—will affect all columns simultaneously. If this option is not enabled, you can adjust the width of each column individually. Note that if you choose the One, Two, or Three option in the Presets area, Equal Column Width is selected automatically.

6 To add a vertical line between each column, select Line Between. To force Word to move the text following the insertion point to the start of a new column, select Start New Column. (For this option to be available, you must select This Point Forward in the Apply To list box.)

Adjusting Columns

Once you have applied newspaper-style columns, you can change the column width, insert breaks within columns, and adjust other features.

The easiest way to change column width is to activate Print Layout view (choose Print Layout from the View menu) and drag a *column marker* on the horizontal ruler, as shown in Figure 8-9.

FIGURE 8-9.

Adjusting the width of newspaper-style columns using the column markers on the horizontal ruler in Print Layout view.

Drag this column marker to change the left column's width.

Drag this column marker to change the right column's width.

Drag here to change the widths of both columns.

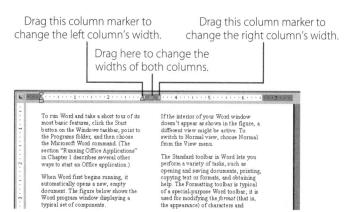

If you selected Equal Column Width in the Columns dialog box, dragging any column marker will adjust the widths of all columns simultaneously, keeping their widths equal. If you didn't select this option, you can change the width of each column independently.

You can force Word to move text into the next column by inserting a *column break* anywhere within a column. (See Figure 8-10, on the following page.) To do this, place the insertion point where you want to break the column. Then choose Break from the Insert menu and click the Column Break option. Or, press Ctrl+Shift+Enter.

You can also prevent Word from inserting a column break within a particular paragraph by selecting that paragraph and applying the Keep Lines Together paragraph formatting option. To locate this formatting option, choose Paragraph from the Format menu and click the Line And Page Breaks tab.

If you want to change any of the other column features, such as the number of columns, just repeat the procedure for setting up columns given in the previous section.

II

Microsoft Word

FIGURE 8-10.
Inserting a column break within a newspaper-style column.

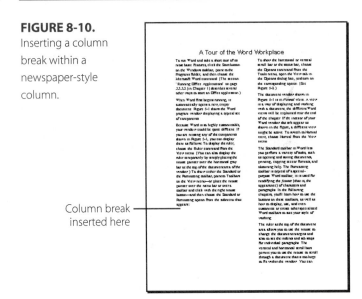

Column break inserted here

Creating Bulleted and Numbered Lists

You can create lists in your document by having Word add bullet characters or numbering, together with hanging indents. Such automatic bullets and numbering are a part of the paragraph formatting. Unlike any bullet characters or numbers you might type in manually, you can't select or perform normal editing on automatic bullets or numbers. Also, if you rearrange the paragraphs in a numbered list, Word renumbers the list for you. Figure 8-11 shows examples of the three kinds of lists you can create by adding automatic bullets or numbers.

FIGURE 8-11.
Examples of bulleted, numbered, and outline-numbered lists.

Bulleted Lists

- Word inserts a bullet character at the beginning of each paragraph.
- You can't select or edit the bullet characters.
- Word indents each paragraph.

Numbered Lists

1. Word inserts a number at the beginning of each paragraph and indents the paragraph.
2. You can't select or edit the numbers.
3. If you add or delete a paragraph from the list, Word automatically updates the numbering.

Outline-Numbered Lists

1) Features
   a) Arrange body text in an outline format.
   b) Word automatically inserts the numbers or letters.
2) Techniques
   a) You create an outline-numbered list using the Outline Numbered tab of the Bullets and Numbering dialog box.
   b) You adjust the level of a paragraph by clicking the Increase Indent or the Decrease Indent button on the Formatting toolbar.

ON THE WEB

The ListDemo.doc document file, used for the example in Figure 8-11, is on the Running Office 2000 Reader's Corner page.

You can apply bullets and numbers using the Formatting toolbar or using the Bullets And Numbering dialog box.

NOTE

> Because bullets and numbering are considered to be paragraph formatting, you can use most of the techniques for paragraph formatting that were discussed in the previous chapters. For example, you can copy the formatting from one paragraph to another, or assign the formatting to a paragraph style.

Adding Bullets and Numbering Using the Formatting Toolbar

The quickest way to have Word apply bullets or numbering to a list is to use the Bullets button or the Numbering button on the Formatting toolbar, as follows:

1 Type the list. Press Enter at the end of each list item so that it's contained in a separate paragraph.

2 Select all the paragraphs in the list.

Bullets   Numbering

3 Click the Bullets button to apply bullets, or click the Numbering button to apply numbering.

If you apply numbering to a series of paragraphs and then delete or rearrange one or more of them, Word will update the numbering. If you place the insertion point at the end of a bulleted or numbered paragraph and press Enter, the new paragraph will also be bulleted or numbered. If, however, you press Enter twice without typing text, the new paragraphs will *not* be bulleted or numbered; this is a convenient way to stop adding bullets or numbering when you reach the end of your list.

SEE ALSO

For information on creating bulleted and numbered lists with the AutoFormat command, see "Formatting Documents Automatically," page 160. For instructions on numbering the lines in a document, see "Adjusting the Page Setup," page 306.

You can remove bullets or numbering by selecting one or more paragraphs and clicking the Bullets button or the Numbering button again. You can also remove the bullet or number from a single paragraph by placing the insertion point immediately following the bullet or number and pressing Backspace.

To control the starting number for a list of automatically numbered paragraphs, you'll need to use the Bullets And Numbering dialog box, described in the next section.

Microsoft Word

TIP

Number Cells in Tables

You can number the cells in a Word table by selecting the cells and clicking the Numbering button. Word will number the cells beginning with the upper left cell and progressing through each row from left to right. If you want to number just the first cell in each row, select the first column before clicking the Numbering button.

Adding Bullets and Numbering Using the Bullets And Numbering Dialog Box

If you apply bullets or numbering using the Bullets And Numbering dialog box rather than using the Formatting toolbar, you have the following additional options:

- You can choose any character or graphic image for the bullets in a bulleted list.

- You can specify the starting number for a numbered list.

- You can modify the appearance and position of the bullet characters or images, or the numbers.

- You can create an outline-numbered list with a custom style. An outline-numbered list displays text in an attractive outline format, without using the Heading styles or Outline view.

The following is the procedure:

1 Select all the paragraphs in the list.

2 Open the Bullets And Numbering dialog box by choosing Bullets And Numbering from the Format menu, or by right-clicking the selection and choosing Bullets And Numbering from the pop-up menu.

3 To apply bullets, click the Bulleted tab of the Bullets And Numbering dialog box (shown at the top of the facing page).

Note that applying a theme to your document will modify the bullets in bulleted lists throughout the document.

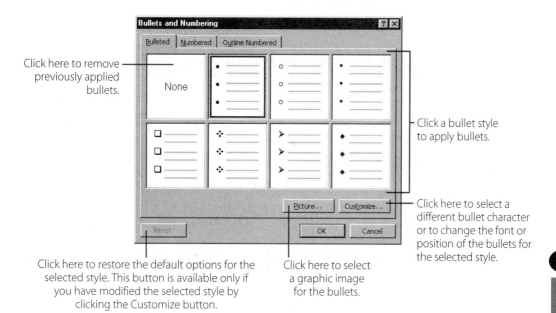

Click here to remove previously applied bullets.

Click a bullet style to apply bullets.

Click here to select a different bullet character or to change the font or position of the bullets for the selected style.

Click here to restore the default options for the selected style. This button is available only if you have modified the selected style by clicking the Customize button.

Click here to select a graphic image for the bullets.

To apply numbering, click the Numbered tab:

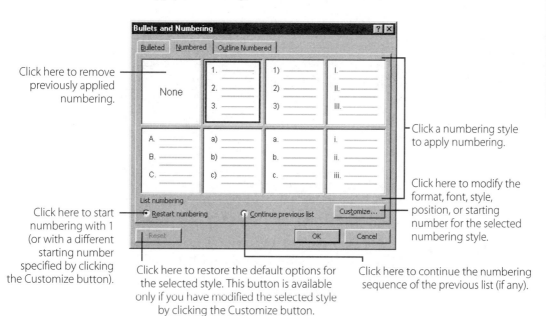

Click here to remove previously applied numbering.

Click a numbering style to apply numbering.

Click here to modify the format, font, style, position, or starting number for the selected numbering style.

Click here to start numbering with 1 (or with a different starting number specified by clicking the Customize button).

Click here to restore the default options for the selected style. This button is available only if you have modified the selected style by clicking the Customize button.

Click here to continue the numbering sequence of the previous list (if any).

Microsoft Word

To apply outline numbering, click the Outline Numbered tab:

Click here to remove previously applied outline numbering from the selected paragraphs.

Click one of these three styles to apply outline numbering to the selected list of paragraphs.

Click here to start numbering with 1 (or with a different starting number or letter specified by clicking the Customize button).

(For an explanation of these four styles, see the following tip.)

Click here to modify the format, font, style, position, or starting number for each level of the selected outline numbering style, or to link each level of numbering to a particular style.

Click here to restore the default options for the selected style. This button is available only if you have modified the selected style by clicking the Customize button.

Click here to continue the numbering sequence of the previous list (if any).

 TIP

Automatically Number Your Document's Headings

You can apply automatic outline numbering to all the headings throughout your document, even though they aren't contained in a list, provided that you have assigned all your heading paragraphs the standard heading styles, Heading 1 through Heading 9. To do this, place the insertion point within any heading in the document, display the Outline Numbered tab of the Bullets And Numbering dialog box, and select one of the four outline-numbering styles in the bottom row, shown earlier. (Notice that the sample on the Outline Numbered tab for each of these styles contains the names of Heading styles.)

? SEE ALSO

For instructions on using Outline view, see "Using Outline View," page 362.

The outline-numbered list feature allows you to arrange text with an outline format. (See the example in Figure 8-11, page 248.) Once you have applied this feature to a series of paragraphs using the procedure above, you can adjust the level of each paragraph as follows:

Increase
Indent

■ To demote a paragraph (that is, convert it to a lower-level list item), place the insertion point in the paragraph and press Alt+Shift+Right arrow or click the Increase Indent button on the Formatting toolbar.

Decrease
Indent

■ To promote a paragraph (that is, convert it to a higher-level list item), place the insertion point in the paragraph and press Alt+Shift+Left arrow or click the Decrease Indent button on the Formatting toolbar.

 TIP

Convert a Simple Bulleted or Numbered List to an Outline

You can convert a simple bulleted or numbered list (created using the Bulleted or Numbered tab or the Bullets or Numbering toolbar button) to an outline-numbered list by demoting some of the paragraphs in the list. When you do this, Word will apply default bullet characters or numbering to the lower outline levels. If you want to choose the style of all levels, you must create or modify the outline-numbered list using the Outline Numbered tab of the Bullets And Numbering dialog box, as explained in this section.

 NOTE

The outline-numbered list feature is convenient for permanently formatting any amount of document text as an attractive outline. In contrast, Outline view allows you to temporarily view an entire document in outline form so that you can quickly organize the text.

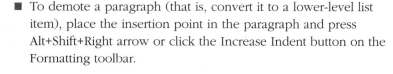

Sorting Lists and Tables

You can have Word sort the items in a list consisting of a series of paragraphs. You can also have it sort rows within a table.

To sort a list of paragraphs, do the following:

1 Select all the paragraphs that make up the list. (Recall that a paragraph consists of any amount of text followed by a paragraph mark.)

2 Choose Sort from the Table menu to open the Sort Text dialog box, shown on the following page.

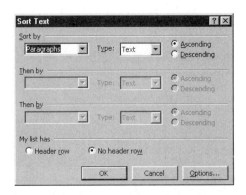

3 In the Sort By list, choose the part of the text that is to be used as the sort criterion. To sort a list of paragraphs, you normally choose Paragraphs to base the sort on all text in each paragraph. If, however, each paragraph is divided into *fields* (entries within the paragraphs separated with tabs, commas, or another character), you can base the sort on a specific field by choosing Field 1, Field 2, and so on. For instance, if you wanted to sort the following list by birthdate,

John, December 18

Sue, April 25

Pete, April 25

Joan, June 10

you would select Field 2. You can also choose a second and a third sort field in the Then By boxes, which Word will use if the previous sort fields are identical. In the example above, if you chose Field 1 in the second Then By box, Word would use the names to sort the paragraphs for Sue and Pete, who have identical birthdays—that is, it would place Pete before Sue.

4 Select an item in the Type list to indicate the way the text should be sorted. You can choose Text to sort alphabetically. If the information you're sorting by consists of numbers, you can choose Number to sort it numerically. If it consists of dates, you can choose Date to sort it chronologically. (In the previous example, you would choose Date for the first sort field and Text for the second.)

5 Select Ascending to sort text from the beginning to the end of the alphabet, numbers from smaller to larger, and dates from earlier to later. Select Descending to sort in the opposite order.

6 Select Header Row to eliminate the first paragraph from the sort, or No Header Row to sort all selected paragraphs. When Header Row is selected, the items in the first row are used to name the fields; in this case, you can select a *name* from the Sort By or Then By list (rather than selecting Field 1, Field 2, and so on).

7 If you want to modify the way Word sorts text, click the Options button to open the Sort Options dialog box. (See the illustration below.) This dialog box lets you specify the character used to separate fields. (The example in step 3 uses commas.) Also, when you select the Case Sensitive option, if two paragraphs are identical except for capitalization, the one that's capitalized will follow the one that's all lowercase (when you sort text in ascending order); if this option is not selected, the case of letters is ignored. You can select a specific language in the Sorting Language list to cause Word to use the sorting rules defined by that language.

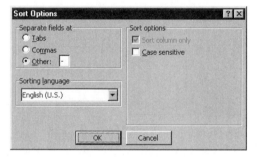

II

Microsoft Word

> **NOTE**

If you sort a list of paragraphs to which you have applied automatic numbering, Word will renumber it properly.

> **SEE ALSO**

For information on using the Undo command, see the sidebar "Undoing and Redoing Editing and Formatting Actions," page 136.

You can also use the steps listed previously to sort rows within a Word table, with the following provisos:

- In step 1, select the rows and columns you want to sort. To sort the entire table, place the insertion point anywhere within the table. Note that Word sorts only in the vertical direction; you can't, for example, select a single row and have Word sort the cells of that row.

- In the Sort By and Then By lists, you choose the table columns that you want to use as sort criteria (assuming that you have selected more than one column in the table).

- In the Sort Options dialog box, you can select the Sort Column Only option to have Word sort only the selected column or columns. Otherwise, Word will sort entire rows even if you haven't selected all the columns.

After you have sorted a list of paragraphs or the contents of a table, you can unsort it by immediately issuing the Undo command.

Using Borders and Shading

You can emphasize, organize, or set apart portions of your document by adding borders or background shading. You can add borders or shading to blocks of characters, to paragraphs, to cells within tables, or to entire tables. (See Figure 8-12.) You can also have Word print borders around entire pages in your document. (See Figure 8-13.)

NOTE As you have learned, if you create a table using the Insert Table menu command or button, it initially has a thin, solid border around all cells; and if you create a table using the Draw Table button on the Tables And Borders toolbar, you can assign it any style of borders (or no borders). In this section, you'll learn how to modify, remove, or add borders to a table that has already been created. Recall also that if you remove a border, Word will mark the cell gridline with a light gray line (which appears on the screen but doesn't print), provided that the Show Gridlines option on the Table menu is selected. Note that applying a theme to your document might modify the color of table borders.

To apply borders and shading to characters, paragraphs, or tables, you can use either the Tables And Borders toolbar or the Borders And Shading dialog box. To apply borders to pages, you must use the Borders And Shading dialog box.

FIGURE 8-12.
Borders and shading applied to a block of characters, a paragraph, and a table.

You can apply borders and shading to blocks of characters.

You can apply borders and shading to entire paragraphs

You can apply borders and shading to tables:

Units	Points	Picas	Centimeters	Inches
Points	1	1/12	.035	1/72
Picas	12	1	.42	1/6
Centimeters	28.35	2.38	1	.39
Inches	72	6	2.54	1

 **ON THE WEB**

The BordersShadingDemo.doc document file, used for the example in Figure 8-12, is on the Running Office 2000 Reader's Corner page.

FIGURE 8-13.

Borders around a document page.

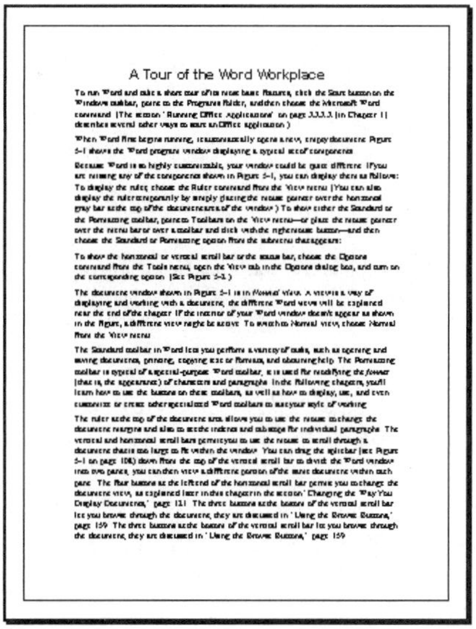

ON THE WEB

The DocBorderDemo.doc document file, used for the example in Figure 8-13, is on the Running Office 2000 Reader's Corner page.

NOTE

Borders or shading applied to paragraphs (not to characters, tables, or pages) are considered to be paragraph formatting. You can therefore use the techniques for paragraph formatting that were discussed in the previous chapters. For example, you can copy the formatting from one paragraph to another, or assign the formatting to a paragraph style.

Adding Borders and Shading Using the Tables And Borders Toolbar

SEE ALSO

For information about automatically adding horizontal borders (to the bottom of paragraphs), see "Using the AutoFormat As You Type Feature," page 165.

You already learned how to use the Tables And Borders toolbar to create and modify tables (in the section "Drawing Tables," page 241). In this section, you'll learn how to use it to apply (or modify) borders or shading around characters, paragraphs, cells within tables, or entire tables. Figure 8-14, on the next page, shows the Tables And Borders toolbar, labeling each of the tools that you use for applying borders and shading. (For a brief description of all the buttons, see Figure 8-6, page 241.) If the toolbar isn't visible, you can display it by pointing to Toolbars on the View menu (or by right-clicking the menu bar or another toolbar) and choosing Tables And Borders.

II

Microsoft Word

FIGURE 8-14.

The Tables And Borders toolbar buttons that are used for applying borders and shading.

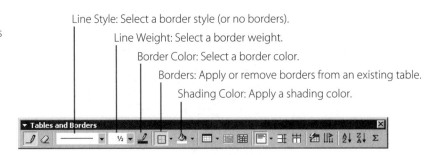

Line Style: Select a border style (or no borders).
Line Weight: Select a border weight.
Border Color: Select a border color.
Borders: Apply or remove borders from an existing table.
Shading Color: Apply a shading color.

The first step to adding borders or shading is to make an appropriate selection in one of the following ways:

- To add borders or shading to a block of characters, select the characters *without* including the paragraph mark at the end of the paragraph.

- To add borders or shading to one or more entire paragraphs, select the paragraphs. To add borders or shading to a single paragraph, include the paragraph mark in your selection, or place the insertion point anywhere within the paragraph without selecting text.

- To add borders or shading to table cells, select one or more entire cells. To add borders or shading to the whole table, you must select all cells in the table. To format a single cell, you can just place the insertion point within the cell without selecting any text. To add borders or shading to part of the text within a table cell without assigning borders or shading to the cell itself, select just that text (selecting *all* of the text in the cell causes the borders or shading to be applied to the cell, not to the text).

To add borders to your selection, do the following:

1 From the Line Style, Line Weight, and Border Color tools on the Tables And Borders toolbar, select the desired style, thickness, and color of the border or borders you want to add. (Note that the Automatic color choice applies the current Window Font color, which is usually black. Window Font color is set by using the Windows Control Panel's Display Properties dialog box.)

2 Click the down arrow next to the Borders button, and on the palette that Word displays, click the button that corresponds to the border or combination of borders that you want to apply:

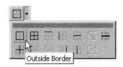

As you position the pointer over each button on the palette, Word displays a ScreenTip describing the border—or combination of borders—that will be applied (Outside Border, Top Border, Left Border, Bottom Border, and so on). Borders labeled Inside are applicable only if you have selected more than one paragraph or table cell. (They will be added between the paragraphs or cells.) Diagonal borders can be applied only to table cells. And clicking the Horizontal Line button inserts a horizontal dividing line, not a border, and will be described in "Inserting Horizontal Dividing Lines" later in the chapter, on page 265.

When you click the button, Word will immediately apply the border or borders to the selection in your document.

TIP

If ScreenTips don't appear, you can enable them by choosing Customize from the Tools menu, clicking the Options tab in the Customize dialog box, and selecting the Show ScreenTips On Toolbars option.

If the Borders tool doesn't have a button for the particular combination of borders you want to add, you can apply the borders one at a time. For example, to apply borders to the left and right of a paragraph, you could first click the Left Border button and then click the Right Border button. If you want the borders to have different properties (for example, different colors), you will have to return to step 1 before applying each border.

NOTE

The Borders button also appears on the Formatting toolbar. On either the Formatting toolbar or the Tables And Borders toolbar, you can click this button (rather than opening and using the palette) to apply the border style you most recently applied.

To remove a border from the selection, you can click the same button on the Borders palette that's used to apply that border. (The button will appear pressed in until you click it.) For you to be able to do this, however, the border's original style, weight, and color must still be

II

Microsoft Word

selected on the toolbar. To remove all borders (regardless of the attributes selected on the toolbar), you can click the No Border button on the Borders palette.

> To modify the properties of a border that has already been applied, select the new properties using the Line Style, Line Weight, and Border Color tools on the Tables And Borders toolbar (step 1 above); and then use the Borders tool to reapply the border (step 2 above).

To apply shading to the selected paragraph or table cells, click the down arrow next to the Shading Color button on the Tables And Borders toolbar, and then select the desired shading color from the palette. To remove shading, select No Fill at the top of the palette.

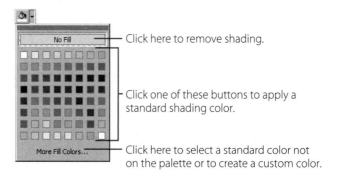

Click here to remove shading.

Click one of these buttons to apply a standard shading color.

Click here to select a standard color not on the palette or to create a custom color.

Adding Borders and Shading Using the Borders And Shading Dialog Box

The Borders And Shading dialog box is not quite as easy to use as the Tables And Borders toolbar, but it provides the following additional options:

- You can create borders that have a shadow or 3-D effect.

- You can specify the distance between the borders and the text.

- You can apply a shading pattern as well as a background shading color. (The Tables And Borders toolbar lets you apply only a background shading color.)

- You can place a border around entire document pages.

To add borders or shading, you must use one of the following methods:

- To add borders or shading to a block of characters, select the characters without including the paragraph mark at the end of the paragraph.

- To add borders or shading to one or more entire paragraphs, select the paragraphs. To add borders or shading to a single paragraph, include the paragraph mark in your selection or place the insertion point anywhere within the paragraph without selecting text.

- To add borders or shading to table cells, select them. To add borders or shading to the entire table, place the insertion point anywhere within the table. To add borders or shading to text in a table cell without assigning borders or shading to the cell itself, select just that text.

To apply one or more borders to your selection, proceed as follows:

1 Open the Borders And Shading dialog box by choosing Borders And Shading from the Format menu.

2 Click the Borders tab:

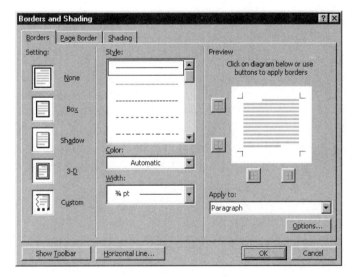

3 From the Style, Color, and Width lists, choose the properties of the border or borders that you want to apply.

4 Click one of the items in the Setting area to specify the basic look and arrangement of the border or borders. Pick the one that's closest to what you want—you can customize it later.

The specific choices in this area depend on what you selected prior to opening the dialog box. (If you begin customizing borders, as explained in the next step, the Custom item will be automatically selected, so you don't need to click it yourself.) If you want to remove all borders, click None, and then click OK to close the dialog box. (In this case, you can skip the remaining steps.)

5 You can add or remove specific borders by clicking appropriate buttons in the Preview area. If you want to modify the properties of a specific border, make the desired selections in the Style, Color, and Width lists just before clicking the button to add the border. (You can thus assign different properties to each border.)

6 If you have selected paragraphs, you can modify the clearance between the borders and the text by clicking the Options button and in the Border And Shading Options dialog box, adjusting the measurements in the From Text area. If you have selected characters, a table, or table cells, you can't adjust the clearance.

 TIP

After you have applied borders to one or more paragraphs, you can adjust the clearance between a border and the text by dragging the border with the mouse.

7 You can choose an item in the Apply To list to modify the portion of your document that receives borders. For example, if you selected several paragraphs, borders would normally be applied to the entire paragraphs (and the Paragraph item would be selected in the list); if you chose the Text item, however, the borders would be placed around each line of characters rather than around the entire paragraphs.

8 When the example borders shown in the Preview area have the look you want, click the OK button.

NOTE

When applying borders or shading, keep in mind that the Automatic color choice applies the current Window Font color, which is usually black. To set Window Font color, use the Windows Control Panel's Display Properties dialog box.

To apply shading to your selection, do the following:

1 Open the Borders And Shading dialog box, and click the Shading tab:

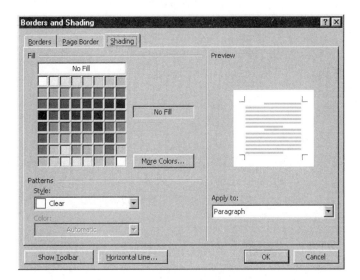

2 Select a background shading color in the Fill area. To pick a standard color, click one of the colors in the palette. To choose a different standard color or to create a custom one, click the More Colors button, and then make your choice in the Colors dialog box. If you don't want a shading color, click No Fill at the top of the palette.

3 Select a shading pattern in the Patterns area. To apply a pattern, choose one of the patterns in the Style list box, and then select the pattern color in the Color list box. If you don't want a pattern, choose Clear in the Style list box.

4 If you want to change the portion of your document that is to be shaded, select an item in the Apply To list box as explained in step 7 of the previous procedure for applying borders.

5 When the example shading shown in the Preview area has the look you want, click the OK button.

II

Microsoft Word

Adding Page Borders

To give your document a polished or decorative look, you can have Word draw borders around entire pages. You can add page borders to the entire document or to part of the document. Borders will be visible in Print Layout view, in Print Preview, and of course on the printed page. If you're creating a Web page, however, page borders aren't for you—they won't be displayed in a browser.

To add page borders, do the following:

1 Choose Borders And Shading from the Format menu to open the Borders And Shading dialog box, and click the Page Border tab:

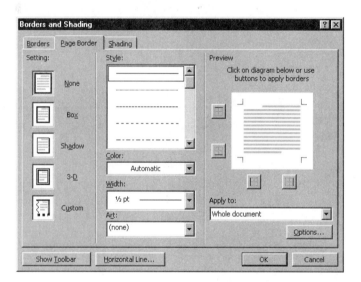

2 Using the techniques described in the previous section for applying borders to characters, paragraphs, and tables, choose options until the example borders shown in the Preview area have the look you want.

3 Rather than applying a page border that consists of lines, you can create a border consisting of artwork. Word provides a lot of different images and patterns. Simply choose the one you want from the Art list (or choose (None) to remove an artwork border).

4 In the Apply To list box, select an option to specify which part of the document is to receive page borders. (You can apply them to the whole document, or—if you have divided the document into sections—to only the current section. Also, you can apply them to all pages, to the first page only, or to all pages except the first page.)

5 You can click the Options button to open the Border And Shading Options dialog box, where you can choose several additional options for applying borders to characters, paragraphs, and tables:

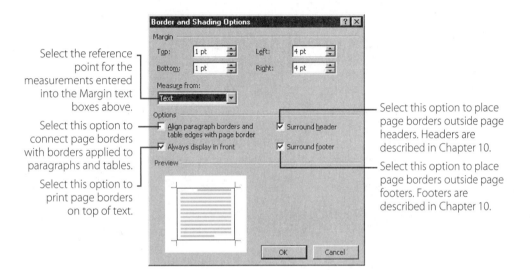

Select the reference point for the measurements entered into the Margin text boxes above.

Select this option to connect page borders with borders applied to paragraphs and tables.

Select this option to print page borders on top of text.

Select this option to place page borders outside page headers. Headers are described in Chapter 10.

Select this option to place page borders outside page footers. Footers are described in Chapter 10.

6 When the example border in the Preview area has the look you want, click the OK button.

Inserting Horizontal Dividing Lines

You can use horizontal dividing lines to separate different parts of your document. Although horizontal dividing lines are typically used in Web pages, you can insert them into any type of Word document to help organize the document's contents. Adding a horizontal dividing line provides an alternative to applying a horizontal border above or below a paragraph. Unlike a border, a horizontal dividing line is a separate document element that you can independently select, move, delete, or format. Also, while a border is drawn using only simple lines, you can use a graphic image for a horizontal dividing line, so it can serve as a decorative element consistent with the overall look of your document. Figure 8-15, on the next page, shows a simple document containing horizontal dividing lines.

To insert a horizontal dividing line, place the insertion point at the position where you want to divide your document. The horizontal

Microsoft Word

FIGURE 8-15.
Horizontal dividing
lines used to separate
parts of a document.

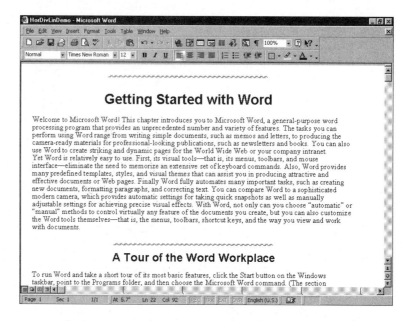

dividing line will be inserted immediately before the insertion point
and will be placed on a separate document line (in its own paragraph).
Then, choose Borders And Shading from the Format menu, and click
the Horizontal Line button at the bottom of the Borders And Shading
dialog box. This will open the Horizontal Line dialog box, where you
can select the horizontal dividing line that you want:

Click here to add more line images
from graphics files on disk.

Click here to download additional
line images from the Web.

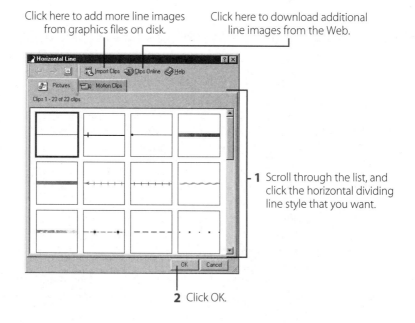

1 Scroll through the list, and
click the horizontal dividing
line style that you want.

2 Click OK.

 The HorDivLinDemo.doc document file, used for the example in Figure 8-15, is on the Running Office 2000 Reader's Corner page.

Once you have used this procedure to select and insert a horizontal dividing line, you can rapidly insert additional dividing lines that have the same style. You do this by clicking the down arrow next to the Borders button on the Formatting toolbar or on the Tables And Borders toolbar and then clicking the Horizontal Line button:

As a further shortcut, once you have clicked the Horizontal Line button on the palette, you can insert additional dividing lines by clicking the Borders button on the Formatting toolbar.

To modify a horizontal dividing line you have inserted into a document, click it to select it. You can then drag it up or down to move it to a new location in the document, or you can press the Delete key to remove it. You can also choose Horizontal Line from the Format menu (or just double-click the dividing line) to open the Format Horizontal Line dialog box, where you can modify the width, height, alignment, or other attributes of the dividing line. Note that applying a theme to the document will modify the horizontal dividing lines throughout the document.

II

Microsoft Word

Using Word's Proofing Tools

Microsoft Word's proofing tools will help you polish your writing and improve the appearance of your documents. Word provides some proofing tools that you can use while you enter the text into a document: namely, the as-you-type spelling and grammar checkers and the thesaurus. It provides other proofing tools—the full-featured spelling and grammar checkers and the hyphenation command—that you generally use after you have finished entering, editing, and formatting the text in your document, but before you preview the printed appearance of the document and make the final adjustments to the page setup (discussed in the next chapter).

Marking the Language

If your document contains text in a foreign language, or text that you want to exclude from proofing, you should perform the steps discussed in this section and in "Using Automatic Language Detection" before using the proofing tools; otherwise, you can safely skip these sections.

In the version of Word sold in the United States, all text is initially marked as English (U.S.), meaning English as written in the United States. If all or some of the text in your document is written in a different language or in non-U.S. English and you want to be able to proof this text, you should mark each block of such text. To do this, select the non-U.S. English text, point to Language on the Tools menu, and then choose Set Language from the submenu to open the Language dialog box. (See Figure 9-1.)

Marking text with a particular language causes the Word proofing tools to search for the appropriate dictionary when you apply those tools to that text. The standard dictionary supplied with the version of Word sold in the United States can be used to proof text marked as any form of English (United States, British, Australian, and so on). (The term *dictionary* here refers to the set of data files used by the proofing tools.)

If you choose a language other than English, you must install the appropriate foreign language dictionary before you can proof that text. For information on obtaining foreign dictionaries, look up the topic "dictionary" in the Word online Help or go to *http://www.alki.com/ win/office 97/*.

FIGURE 9-1.
The Language dialog box.

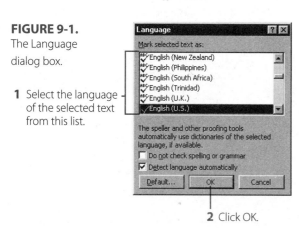

1 Select the language of the selected text from this list.

2 Click OK.

Your document might also contain blocks of text that you want to exclude from proofing. For example, if you're writing a paper on *Beowulf*, you might want to exclude direct quotations that come from the poem so that the spelling checker won't flag all the archaic words and the grammar checker won't try to "improve" the writing style. To do this,

1 Select the text you want to exclude from proofing.

2 Point to Language on the Tools menu and choose Set Language from the submenu.

3 In the Language dialog box, select the Do Not Check Spelling Or Grammar option. (See Figure 9-1.)

TIP

⑦ SEE ALSO
For information on character formatting, see "Applying Character Formatting Directly," page 178. For information on assigning character formatting to a style, see "Modifying Styles," page 198.

> **Use Styles to Assign Language to Text**
> If you frequently mark blocks of text with a particular language or to exclude proofing, you can save time by assigning the language to a style that you can apply to all blocks of text written in that language.

Language is a type of character formatting. If you click the Default button in the Language dialog box, Word will add the selected language format to the Normal style of the document and to the document's template. As a result, the language (or the Do Not Check Spelling Or Grammar option) will be assigned to all text based on the Normal style in the current document as well as in all new documents you subsequently create using the same template.

Using Automatic Language Detection

Rather than marking each block of foreign language text individually, you can have Word automatically detect the language of text in your document and use the appropriate dictionary (if available) for proofing that text. Word will detect only those languages that you explicitly enable for Office applications. Here are the steps:

1 Point to Programs on the Windows Start menu, point to Office Tools on the Programs submenu, and then choose Microsoft Office Language Settings from the Office Tools submenu. This will open the Microsoft Office Language Settings dialog box.

II

Microsoft Word

2 In the Microsoft Office Language Settings dialog box, click the Enabled Languages tab (if it isn't opened), and enable the specific language or languages you want Word to be able to detect in your documents, as follows:

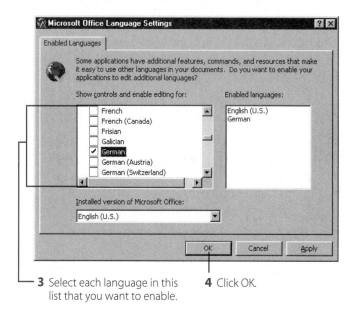

3 Select each language in this list that you want to enable.

4 Click OK.

Note that in the version of Word sold in the United States, English (U.S.) is the language that's enabled by default.

5 If Word is currently running, you'll have to stop it and then restart it for the changes you made in the Microsoft Office Language Settings dialog box to take effect.

6 In Word, point to Language on the Tools menu, and choose Set Language from the submenu.

7 In the Language dialog box, select Detect Language Automatically. (See Figure 9-1.) Word will then begin detecting the language in all open documents and in all documents you subsequently open.

This procedure will cause Word to detect each enabled language and to look for the appropriate proofing dictionary. You still need to install a dictionary for each non-English language, as discussed in the previous section. (If Word doesn't find the dictionary for a detected language, it will omit proofing that text.)

Checking Your Spelling

You can use the Word spelling checker to verify and to help you correct the spelling of the text in your document. You can have Word automatically check your spelling as you type, or you can manually run the spelling checker to check text that you have already entered.

Checking Your Spelling Automatically as You Type

To have Word check your spelling as you type, choose Options from the Tools menu, click the Spelling & Grammar tab (see Figure 9-2), and select Check Spelling As You Type in the Spelling section at the top of the dialog box.

FIGURE 9-2.
The Spelling & Grammar tab of the Options dialog box.

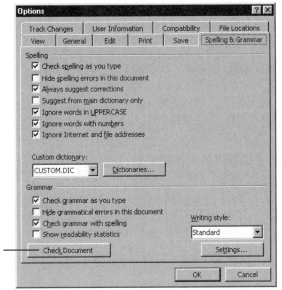

This button is labeled Recheck Document if you have checked spelling or grammar previously in the current document.

Word will then check the spelling of any text that has already been entered into your document, and it will check the spelling of each new word immediately after you type it. If the spelling checker encounters a word that it judges to be misspelled (that is, a word that it doesn't find in its dictionary), it marks the word with a wavy red underline. You can ignore the word, correct it manually, or right-click it to display the pop-up menu shown on the next page.

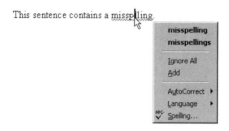

This sentence contains a misspelling.

From the pop-up menu, choose one of the following options:

- Choose one of the suggested spellings at the top of the menu (if any) to correct the word.

- Choose Ignore All to have the spelling checker stop marking the word. (Word will stop marking the word in all documents until you click the Recheck Document button on the Spelling & Grammar tab of the Options dialog box).

- Choose Add to add the word to the custom dictionary so that Word will permanently stop marking the word as misspelled. *(Custom dictionaries will be discussed on page 279.)*

- Point to AutoCorrect, and choose one of the suggested spellings for the word from the submenu that appears:

? SEE ALSO

For information on using AutoCorrect to automatically correct spelling in your document, see "Using the AutoCorrect Feature," page 127; and see the tip "Using AutoCorrect to Correct Your Spelling," page 130.

Word will then correct the word in your document, and it will add the correction to the Replace Text As You Type list of the AutoCorrect feature. From then on, Word will *correct*—not just mark—the misspelling whenever you type it, provided that you have selected the Replace Text As You Type option. To locate this option, choose AutoCorrect from the Tools menu, and click the AutoCorrect tab in the dialog box that appears.

- Use the Language submenu to change the language formatting of the wavy underlined text, as explained in "Marking the Language," page 270.

- Choose Spelling to open the Spelling dialog box, which provides several additional options for correcting spelling and is described in the next section.

If the check-spelling-as-you-type (or check-grammar-as-you-type) feature has marked one or more words in your document, you can locate (and correct) these words by double-clicking the Spelling And Grammar Status icon on the Word status bar. Each time you double-click this icon, Word selects the next marked word and displays the pop-up menu shown above so that you can correct the spelling.

Spelling And
Grammar Status

 TIP

Hide All Spelling Errors

If you don't want to deal with your misspellings until later, you can select the Hide Spelling Errors In This Document option on the Spelling & Grammar tab of the Options dialog box. (See Figure 9-2, page 273.) Word will no longer mark misspellings with red wavy underlines; however, it will still check your spellings and remember which words are misspelled. You can later restore the wavy lines, perhaps during your editing pass through the document, by deselecting this option.

Running the Spelling Checker Manually

Another way to check your spelling is to manually run Word's full-featured spelling checker *after* you've entered a block of text or an entire document. If you're planning to run the spelling checker, you'll probably want to turn off the check-spelling-as-you-type feature so you won't be bothered with the wavy underlines while you write.

 NOTE

After Word checks the spelling of the words in a sentence, it then checks the grammar of the sentence if the Check Grammar With Spelling option is selected. Also, after it has completed its check, it will display readability statistics if the Show Readability Statistics option is selected. You can access these options by choosing Options from the Tools menu and clicking the Spelling & Grammar tab. The instructions in this section assume that both of these options are not selected. Checking grammar and displaying readability statistics are discussed later in the chapter ("Checking Your Grammar," page 282).

To check the spelling of text you have already entered, do the following:

1 If you want to check the spelling of your entire document, place the insertion point anywhere in the document. If you want to check the spelling of a portion of your document, select that portion. (Recall that you can quickly select a single word by double-clicking it.)

II

Microsoft Word

Spelling And
Grammar

2 Begin the spelling check by choosing Spelling And Grammar from the Tools menu, by clicking the Spelling And Grammar button on the Standard toolbar, or by pressing F7.

3 Whenever the spelling checker encounters a word that it can't find in its dictionary, it selects the word in the document and displays the Spelling And Grammar dialog box. (See Figure 9-3.) Within this dialog box, the Not In Dictionary box displays a copy of the sentence containing the questionable word (which is shown in red). And the Suggestions list contains one or more possible correct spellings for the word (provided that the spelling checker can derive any, and that the Always Suggest Corrections option is selected, as discussed later).

To deal with this word, you should do one or more of the following:

■ To change the word and then search for the next misspelling, *either* correct the spelling of the word within the Not In Dictionary box (for your convenience, Word places the insertion point just after the word), *or* simply select the correct spelling—if it's present—in the Suggestions list. Then click the Change button or the Change All button. Clicking Change will replace only the current occurrence of the word. Clicking Change All will replace the current occurrence of the word plus all occurrences that the spelling checker subsequently finds in the document. (It won't change any occurrences that the spelling checker previously encountered and you chose to ignore.)

Note that if you edit the word within the Not In Dictionary box, you can click the Undo Edit button (which replaces the Ignore button) before you click another button, to restore the word. Note also that if you retype the word in the Not In Dictionary box and Word still doesn't recognize the spelling, it will flag the word again.

FIGURE 9-3.
The Spelling And
Grammar dialog box.

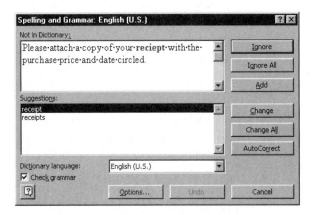

TIP

Use the Spelling Checker to Find Repeated Words
The spelling checker will also stop at any word that repeats the previous word (except for words that are commonly repeated, such as *that* and *had*). If the spelling checker encounters a repeated word, it will replace the Change button with the Delete button. You can click Ignore to leave the repeated word in the document or click Delete to delete the second word.

- To leave the word unchanged and search for the next misspelling, click the Ignore or Ignore All button. If you click the Ignore button, the spelling checker will continue to flag other occurrences of the word that it subsequently finds. If you click the Ignore All button, Word will not flag the word again during the remainder of the spelling check or during any future spelling check in any document until you click the Recheck Document button on the Spelling & Grammar tab (as described in Table 9-1 in the next section).

- To leave the word unchanged and to add it to a custom dictionary so that Word will permanently stop flagging it, click the Add button. (Custom dictionaries are discussed in the next section.)

- To reverse your previous correction, click the Undo button.

- After you have selected the correct spelling in the Suggestions list or have manually corrected the word in the Not In Dictionary box, you can click the AutoCorrect button to have Word define an AutoCorrect entry that will correct the misspelling whenever you type it in the future.

- To check the spelling of the current word using a word list for a different language, choose that language in the Dictionary Language list box (which lists the languages for which dictionaries have been installed). For example, if the current word is *colour* and you choose English (U.K.) in the Dictionary Language list box, the spelling checker would accept the spelling and search for the next misspelling. (However, if the word is *coluor*, it would remain displayed as a misspelling.)

- You can select or deselect the Check Grammar option (near the bottom of the Spelling And Grammar dialog box) to have Word start or stop checking your grammar throughout the remainder of the document. Checking grammar is discussed later in the chapter.

- To change the way Word checks your spelling, click the Options button. (Spelling options are discussed in the next section.)

Edit While You Display the Spelling And Grammar Dialog Box

You can edit your document while the Spelling And Grammar dialog box remains displayed. To edit, click in the document. To resume the grammar check, click the Resume button in the Spelling And Grammar dialog box.

Customizing the Spelling Checker

You can tailor the way Word checks your spelling to your own preferences by clicking the Options button in the Spelling And Grammar dialog box, or by choosing Options from the Tools menu and clicking the Spelling & Grammar tab. Either way, Word will display the Spelling & Grammar tab that was shown in Figure 9-2, page 273. Table 9-1 describes the actions you can perform on this tab that affect the spelling checker. Note that these actions affect both the as-you-type spelling checker and the manual spelling checker unless otherwise noted in the table. The Check Spelling As You Type and Hide Spelling Errors In This Document options were discussed previously, and the options that affect the grammar checker will be discussed later in the chapter (in the section "Checking Your Grammar," page 282).

TABLE 9-1. Options on the Spelling & Grammar Tab

Action	Result
Select the Always Suggest Corrections option.	Whenever the spelling checker finds a misspelled word, the Suggestions list in the Spelling And Grammar dialog box will display, if possible, one or more replacement words. You can then choose an appropriate replacement word to instantly correct your misspelling. This option does not affect the as-you-type spelling checker.
Select the Suggest From Main Dictionary Only option.	The spelling checker will suggest words only from its main dictionary and not from any custom dictionaries. Both dictionaries, however, will be used to check spelling. (Custom dictionaries are discussed in the next section.)
Select the Ignore Words In UPPERCASE option.	The spelling checker will not check the spelling of words that are in all capital letters. This option prevents the spelling checker from flagging acronyms.
Select the Ignore Words With Numbers option.	The spelling checker will not check the spelling of words that contain one or more numbers such as 3-D.

(continued)

TABLE 9-1. *continued*

Action	Result
Select the Ignore Internet And File Addresses option.	The spelling checker will not check the spelling of Internet addresses (such as http://www.microsoft.com) or file paths (such as C:\Book\Chapter1.doc).
Select a dictionary filename in the Custom Dictionary list box.	The spelling checker will add words to this dictionary whenever you click the Add button in the Spelling And Grammar dialog box (or whenever you choose the Add pop-up menu command while correcting a word underlined by the check-spelling-as-you-type feature). This list contains the names of all custom dictionaries that are currently opened (as will be explained later).
Click the Dictionaries button.	Word will display the Custom Dictionaries dialog box, which allows you to create, open, remove, or edit custom dictionaries.
Click the Recheck Document button (labeled Check Document if you haven't checked spelling or grammar in the current document).	The spelling checker will delete its list of ignored words (that is, words for which you chose the Ignore All option), and will begin flagging them again. (Also, the grammar checker will delete its list of grammatical errors for which you chose the "ignore rule" option, explained later.)

Using Custom Dictionaries

Both the manually run spelling checker and the check-spelling-as-you-type feature look up words in the main spelling dictionary *and* in one or more custom dictionaries. When Word is installed, a single custom dictionary file named Custom.dic is created. Initially, this dictionary file is empty. However, every time you click the Add button in the Spelling And Grammar dialog box, and whenever you choose Add from the pop-up menu while you're correcting a word underlined by the check-spelling-as-you-type feature, the current word is added to Custom.dic so that the word will no longer be flagged as misspelled.

If using a single custom dictionary meets your needs, you don't need to do anything except occasionally add a word to it by using the Add command. You might, however, want to create and use one or more special-purpose custom dictionaries. For example, if you write both computer books and science fiction, you might create one dictionary that contains the technical terms you use when writing computer books (perhaps named Computer.dic) and another dictionary that contains the invented words you use when writing science fiction (perhaps named Fiction.dic).

II

Microsoft Word

To create a new custom dictionary, do the following:

1 Choose Options from the Tools menu and click the Spelling & Grammar tab, or click the Options button in the Spelling And Grammar dialog box that appears during a spelling check. The Spelling & Grammar tab that displays is shown in Figure 9-2, page 273.

2 Click the Dictionaries button on the Spelling & Grammar tab to open the Custom Dictionaries dialog box:

3 Click the New button, and in the Create Custom Dictionary dialog box, type a filename for the dictionary in the File Name box:

You can either include the .dic extension in the name you type, or omit the extension. (In this case, Word will add the .dic extension for you.) You can accept the default file location that Word initially selected or you can select a new one. When you click Save, Word will create a new, empty custom dictionary. Also, it will add this dictionary to the list in the Custom Dictionaries dialog box, and it will check the box next to the dictionary name to indicate that the dictionary has been opened. (Opening custom dictionaries is explained later.)

4 If you want to use your new custom dictionary to check text in a specific language, choose that language in the Language list box in the Custom Dictionaries dialog box. The spelling checker will use the dictionary only for text that has been marked for that language. (Marking the language of text was described in the first section of the chapter.) If you select (None) in the Language list, the dictionary will be used for all text, regardless of its language format.

5 Click OK.

To use a custom dictionary that you have created or one that you have purchased or obtained from someone else, do the following:

1 Open the dictionary. (If you created a new dictionary using the steps above, it should already be open and you can skip this step.) To open a dictionary, click the Dictionaries button on the Spelling & Grammar tab (shown in Figure 9-2, page 273), and check the box next to the name of the dictionary in the Custom Dictionaries list:

Check the box next to the name of a custom dictionary to open it.

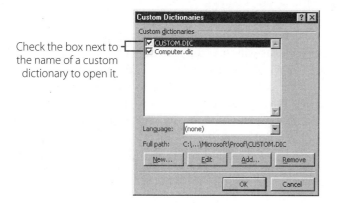

If the dictionary is not in the list, click the Add button and select the dictionary file. When you're done, click OK in the Custom Dictionaries dialog box and on the Spelling & Grammar tab.

The spelling checker will look up words in all custom dictionaries that have been opened. To close a dictionary and not have Word use the words it contains, repeat this step but *clear* the check box next to the dictionary name in the Custom Dictionaries dialog box.

Remove or Edit a Dictionary

While the Custom Dictionaries dialog box is open, you can click the Remove button to remove the selected custom dictionary from the list. (This doesn't delete the dictionary file itself.) Also, if you're not currently running the manual spelling checker, you can click Edit to manually add or remove words from the selected dictionary file. Note that when you edit a custom dictionary, Word turns off the as-you-type spelling checker. After editing, you can turn it back on by reselecting the Check Spelling As You Type option on the Spelling & Grammar tab.

2 To add words to the custom dictionary, select the dictionary name in the Custom Dictionary list box on the Spelling & Grammar tab (which lists all custom dictionaries that are currently open). Subsequently, whenever you click the Add button in the Spelling And Grammar dialog box or choose Add from the pop-up menu of the check-spelling-as-you-type feature, the current word will be added to the selected custom dictionary.

Checking Your Grammar

You can use the Word grammar checker to help polish your writing. The grammar checker will indicate possible errors or weaknesses in grammar, such as a disagreement between subject and verb or the use of passive voice. It will also flag expressions that exhibit poor writing style, such as clichés or misused words. You can have Word automatically check your grammar as you type, or you can manually run the full-featured grammar checker (along with the spelling checker) to check text that you've already entered. When you run the grammar checker manually, you can have it display statistics on the general readability of your document after it has completed its check.

Checking Your Grammar Automatically as You Type

To have Word check your grammar as you type, choose Options from the Tools menu, click the Spelling & Grammar tab (see Figure 9-2, page 273), and select the Check Grammar As You Type option. Word will then check the grammar of any text that has already been entered into your document, and it will begin checking the grammar of each new sentence you enter, immediately after you finish typing it. If the grammar checker encounters a sentence that violates one of its current grammar or style rules (later you'll see how to modify these rules), it marks the offending portions of the sentence with a wavy green underline. (Recall that Word marks a misspelled word with a wavy *red* underline.) You can then ignore the mark, correct the sentence manually, or right-click the underlined portion to display the following pop-up menu:

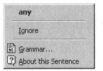

On the pop-up menu, choose one of the following options:

- Choose one of the suggested grammar corrections at the top of the menu (if any) to have Word correct the sentence. Note that rather than displaying actual substitute text that you can choose, the menu might display a tip for manually correcting the sentence. For example, if the checker encounters a sentence fragment, the menu displays *Fragment (consider revising)*.

- Choose Ignore to have the grammar checker ignore the error and to remove the wavy underline from the word or words. (Word will, however, continue to search for violations of the same grammar or style rule.)

- Choose Grammar to open the Grammar dialog box, which is the same as the Spelling And Grammar dialog box displayed when you manually run the grammar checker. It is described in the next section.

■ Choose About This Sentence to display an explanation of the grammatical error that was flagged. (This command is available only if the Office Assistant is currently enabled.)

If the check-grammar-as-you-type (or check-spelling-as-you-type) feature has marked one or more errors in your document, you can locate (and correct) them by double-clicking the Spelling And Grammar Status icon on the Word status bar.

Spelling And
Grammar Status

Each time you double-click this icon, Word moves the insertion point to the next flagged error and displays the pop-up menu shown above so that you can correct the grammar.

If you select Hide Grammatical Errors In This Document on the Spelling & Grammar tab of the Options dialog box (see Figure 9-2, page 273), Word will remove the wavy lines from all grammar errors in the active document. It will, however, continue to check grammar and remember the location of the errors, and you can later restore the wavy lines by turning off this option.

Running the Grammar Checker Manually

You might prefer to use Word's full-featured grammar checker to examine the grammar of a block of text—or an entire document—after you have typed it, rather than having to deal with possible grammatical errors while you write. In this case, you can turn off the check-grammar-as-you-type feature, hide the grammatical errors, or just ignore the wavy underlines. Then when you're ready to check your grammar, you can manually run the grammar checker.

If the grammar checker isn't currently enabled, enable it by choosing Options from the Tools menu, clicking the Spelling & Grammar tab, and selecting Check Grammar With Spelling. If you want to see the readability statistics, also select the Show Readability Statistics option.

Once it has been enabled, the grammar checker will be run whenever you perform a manual spelling check, as described previously (in "Running the Spelling Checker Manually," page 275). The specific steps for checking your grammar are as follows:

1 If you want to check your entire document, place the insertion point anywhere in the document. If you want to check only a portion of your document, select that portion.

Spelling And
Grammar

2 Choose Spelling And Grammar from the Tools menu, click the Spelling And Grammar button on the Standard toolbar, or press F7.

3 For each sentence in the document (or selection), Word first checks the spelling of the words it contains. To handle any word that is flagged as a possible misspelling, follow the instructions that were given in step 3 of the process for checking your spelling, page 276.

4 After checking the spelling of a sentence, Word will check the grammar. If the grammar checker finds a violation of one of its grammar or style rules, it opens the Spelling And Grammar dialog box. (See Figure 9-4.) At the top of this dialog box is a description of the possible grammar or style violation, together with a copy of the sentence showing the offending words in green. Below this, the Suggestions list displays one or more blocks of replacement text (if the grammar checker can generate a replacement).

FIGURE 9-4.

The Spelling And Grammar dialog box.

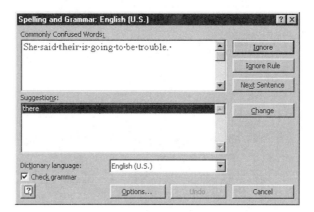

To deal with the possible error, you should do one or more of the following:

- To correct or improve your sentence, *either* directly edit the copy of the sentence displayed at the top of the Spelling And Grammar dialog box *or* select a block of replacement text in the Suggestions list (if one is present). Then click the Change button.

- To ignore the suggestions and move on to the next error, click the Ignore button. The next error might be in the same sentence.

- To ignore the suggestions for the current sentence and to move on to the next sentence, click the Next Sentence button. If the current sentence has additional errors, the grammar checker will skip them.

- To ignore the suggestions and stop Word from flagging violations of the same grammar or style rule, click Ignore Rule. (Violations of the rule won't be flagged again during the remainder of the grammar check, or during any future grammar check in this document, until you click the Recheck Document button on the Spelling & Grammar tab, as described in Table 9-1, page 278.) The checker will then move on to the next error.

- To reverse your previous correction, click the Undo button.

- To check the current error using the rules for a different language, choose that language in the Dictionary Language list box, which lists the languages for which dictionaries have been installed.

- You can turn off the Check Grammar feature to stop Word from checking your grammar. Word will then check only your spelling until you turn the option back on. (As mentioned previously, you can also set this option using the Spelling & Grammar tab.)

- To modify the way the grammar checker works, click the Options button. (Setting options is explained in the next section.)

⭐ TIP

Edit While You Display the Spelling And Grammar Dialog Box
You can edit your document while the Spelling And Grammar dialog box remains displayed. To edit, click in the document. To resume the grammar check, click the Resume button in the Spelling And Grammar dialog box.

If the Show Readability Statistics option is enabled on the Spelling & Grammar tab, Word will display the Readability Statistics dialog box after it has finished the spelling and grammar check. This dialog box shows statistics about the text that was checked, including several standard indicators of the general readability of the text. Figure 9-5 shows the statistics that Word displayed for the original draft of the chapter you're reading.

FIGURE 9-5.
The Readability Statistics dialog box displayed after running a spelling and grammar check on the preliminary draft of this chapter.

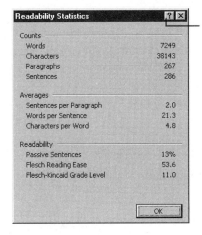

For an explanation of any of the information in this dialog box, click here, and then click the part of the dialog box displaying the information.

 TIP

You can display statistics about the number of pages, words, characters, and so on in your document by choosing Word Count from the Tools menu, or by choosing Properties from the File menu and clicking the Statistics tab.

Customizing the Grammar Checker

You can modify the way the grammar checker works by choosing Options from the Tools menu and clicking the Spelling & Grammar tab in the Options dialog box, which was shown in Figure 9-2, page 273. You can also display this tab by clicking the Options button in the Spelling And Grammar dialog box.

You can select an option in the Writing Style list to specify the general type of writing you want to check—Casual, Standard, Formal, Technical, or Custom. When Word checks your grammar, it will apply a set of rules that is appropriate for the selected type of writing. To have Word apply a general-purpose set of rules, select Standard in the Writing Style list. To apply most of the grammar and style rules, choose Formal; or to omit many of the rules, select Casual. You can select Technical to apply only the rules that are appropriate for technical writing (such as this chapter); for example, with this option the grammar checker doesn't flag passive voice. The Custom option initially applies almost all the rules; it's provided for you to customize.

You can customize any of the writing style options (not just Custom) to specify exactly which rules the grammar checker will apply when that option is selected. To do this, click the Settings button on the Spelling & Grammar tab to open the Grammar Settings dialog box. (See Figure 9-6.)

FIGURE 9-6.
The Grammar Settings dialog box.

1 Select the style option you want to customize from this list box.

To see a description of the rules, click here, and then click the Grammar And Style Options list.

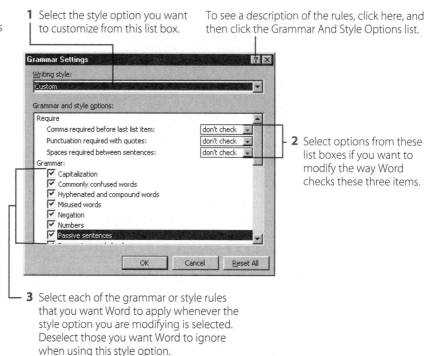

2 Select options from these list boxes if you want to modify the way Word checks these three items.

3 Select each of the grammar or style rules that you want Word to apply whenever the style option you are modifying is selected. Deselect those you want Word to ignore when using this style option.

Using the Thesaurus to Find Synonyms

You can use the Word thesaurus to look up synonyms or antonyms for a word or phrase in your document. You'll probably want to use the thesaurus as you are entering text into your document (in contrast to the other proofing tools, which you often use after you have finished entering text). The following are the basic steps for using the thesaurus:

1 Select the word or phrase. To find synonyms for a single word, you can just place the insertion point anywhere within the word rather than selecting it:

Squire Allworthy was a good person.

2 Point to Language on the Tools menu and choose Thesaurus on the submenu that appears, or press Shift+F7. Word will open the Thesaurus dialog box. Here is the Thesaurus dialog box as it would appear if the word *good* were selected in the document:

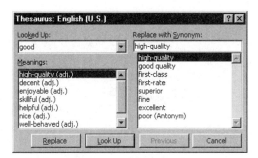

 TIP

> An alternative way to use the thesaurus is to right-click a word or a selected phrase and point to Synonyms on the pop-up menu. Then on the submenu that appears, either choose a synonym or antonym (if any are displayed), or choose the Thesaurus command to open the Thesaurus dialog box discussed in this procedure.

3 In the Meanings list, select the intended meaning of the word. (Note the part of speech following most words: *adj.* for adjective, *adv.* for adverb, *n.* for noun, and so on.) The thesaurus will then list synonyms for this meaning in the Replace With Synonym list.

The Replace With Synonyms list might also display one or more antonyms for the selected meaning of the word. Each antonym will be marked with (Antonym), such as the word *poor* in the Thesaurus dialog box shown above.

The Meanings list will sometimes contain the item Related Words. Selecting this item displays one or more other forms of the word in the Replace With Synonym list. For example, if the word in the Looked Up box is *going*, the Replace With Synonyms list would display *go*.

If the thesaurus doesn't have information on the selected word, it displays an alphabetical list of words with similar spellings. You can select one of these words and click the Look Up button to find synonyms.

II

Microsoft Word

4 Click the best synonym (or the best antonym or related word) in the Replace With Synonym list, and click the Replace button. Here's how the Thesaurus dialog box would appear if you looked up *good* and then chose the meaning *decent* and the synonym *virtuous*:

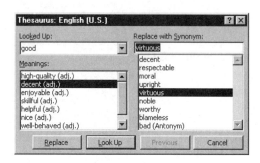

When you click Replace, Word will replace the selected word in the document with the chosen synonym, matching the capitalization of the original word:

Squire Allworthy was a virtuous person.

 TIP

Use the Synonyms Dialog Box to Find More Word Choices

After selecting a synonym in step 4, you can click the Look Up button to find synonyms for the synonym! (You can also do this by simply double-clicking a synonym in the Replace With Synonyms list.) Doing this one or more times might help you find precisely the word you want. Consider this scenario: You look up the word *pretty* and select the synonym *beautiful*, which is better than *pretty* but not perfect. You therefore click the Look Up button and find the perfect synonym, *gorgeous*.

Also, while the Thesaurus dialog box is displayed, you can look up a synonym for any word by typing the word into the Replace With Synonym text box at the top of the list and then clicking Look Up.

To return to the previous looked-up word, click the Previous button.

Hyphenating Your Documents

You can improve the appearance of your document by hyphenating words at the ends of the lines. Once hyphenated, text that is not justified will be less ragged at the margin, and justified text will have more uniform spacing between the characters. You can hyphenate text in one of three ways.

■ You can have Word automatically hyphenate your entire document.

■ You can have Word hyphenate text but allow you to confirm the placement of each hyphen.

■ You can manually insert various types of hyphen characters.

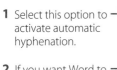

> You should hyphenate your document *after* you finish editing, formatting, and using the other proofing tools, because these operations can change the position of line breaks. Also, if you later change features of the page design that affect line breaks, such as the margins, you might need to hyphenate your document again.

Hyphenating Your Document Automatically

You can let Word hyphenate the document in the active window by pointing to Language on the Tools menu and then choosing Hyphenation to open the Hyphenation dialog box:

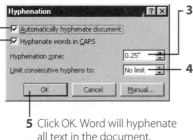

1 Select this option to activate automatic hyphenation.

2 If you want Word to hyphenate words in all capital letters, such as acronyms, select this option.

5 Click OK. Word will hyphenate all text in the document.

3 To adjust the hyphenation zone (described below), enter a new value into this box.

4 To limit the number of consecutive lines Word will hyphenate, enter a number into this box. Limiting consecutive hyphenations prevents unsightly "stacking" of hyphen characters along the right margin.

The *hyphenation zone* controls the number of hyphenations that Word performs. It works as follows: When Word encounters a word that extends beyond the right indent, it must decide whether it can wrap the word (that is, move the entire word down to the next line) or whether it should hyphenate the word. If wrapping the word would leave space at the end of the line that is narrower than the hyphenation zone (.25 inch wide by default), Word wraps it:

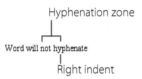

If, however, wrapping the word would leave a space wider than the hyphenation zone, Word hyphenates it:

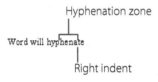

Choosing a wide hyphenation zone reduces the number of hyphenations that Word must perform, but it increases the raggedness of the margin (or makes the intercharacter spacing less uniform in justified text).

> You can assign a paragraph the Don't Hyphenate paragraph formatting to exclude it from automatic hyphenation or hyphenation with confirmation (discussed in the next section). In contrast, applying the Do Not Check Spelling Or Grammar language formatting, mentioned near the beginning of the chapter, blocks *all* proofing (spelling, grammar, and hyphenation).

Hyphenating Your Document Using Confirmation

If you want Word to hyphenate your document but allow you to confirm the placement of each hyphen, do the following:

1 If you want to hyphenate your entire document, place the insertion point anywhere in the document. If you want to hyphenate only a portion of your document, select that portion.

2 Point to Language on the Tools menu, and then choose Hyphenation to open the Hyphenation dialog box:

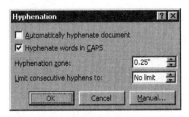

3 In the Hyphenation dialog box, set the hyphenation options you want, but make sure that the Automatically Hyphenate Document option is deselected. These options were explained in the previous section.

4 Click the Manual button. Word activates Print Layout view and begins looking for possible hyphenations. When Word is finished hyphenating, it returns you to your original document view.

5 Whenever Word encounters a word that requires hyphenation, it displays the Manual Hyphenation dialog box, which shows the word and the proposed position of the hyphen, together with all other possible hyphen positions in the word:

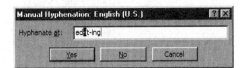

Each possible hyphenation position is marked with a hyphen. The proposed hyphenation position is marked with a blinking highlight in addition to the hyphen. The position of the right indent is marked with a vertical line. Word also carries out the proposed hyphenation in the document and highlights the hyphen character.

You should now do one of the following:

- To hyphenate the word at the proposed position, just click Yes.

- To hyphenate the word at a different position (say, to avoid a hyphen after only the first two letters of a long word, as in the example), use the Left or Right arrow key to move the blinking highlight to that position, and then click Yes.

- To skip hyphenating the word, click No. The word will be wrapped rather than hyphenated.

Inserting Hyphen Characters Manually

When Word hyphenates a word, it inserts a special character known as an *optional hyphen*. If a word containing an optional hyphen is shifted so that it no longer falls at the end of a line, the hyphen is not printed. However, the optional hyphen remains within the word, and it will reappear and allow the word to be broken if the word shifts back to the end of a line.

You can manually insert optional hyphens, as well as several other related special characters, as shown in Table 9-2.

If you click the Show/Hide ¶ button on the Standard toolbar, Word displays on the screen all the characters listed in Table 9-2. To display optional hyphens only, choose Options from the Tools menu, click the View tab, and select Optional Hyphens in the Formatting Marks area.

TABLE 9-2.   Manually Inserted Hyphens and Nonbreaking Spaces

Special Character	Shortcut Key for Inserting It	Properties
Optional hyphen	Ctrl+hyphen (the hyphen key on the top row of the keyboard, *not* on the numeric keypad)	When an optional hyphen falls at the end of a line, it is printed and the word that contains it is broken. When it falls within a line, it doesn't print.
Nonbreaking hyphen	Ctrl+Shift+hyphen (the hyphen key on the top row of the keyboard, *not* on the numeric keypad)	A nonbreaking hyphen is always printed. A word is never broken at the position of a nonbreaking hyphen. It can be used to keep a hyphenated word or expression together on a single line.
Normal hyphen	hyphen (the hyphen key on the top row of the keyboard *or* on the numeric keypad)	A normal hyphen is always printed. Word will break a word at the position of a normal hyphen if it falls at the end of a line.
Nonbreaking space	Ctrl+Shift+Spacebar	A line break can't occur at the position of a nonbreaking space. This character can be used to keep several words together on a single line.

Designing Pages

In the previous chapters on Word, you learned how to control the appearance of individual characters and paragraphs of text in your document. In this chapter, you'll learn how to design entire pages. You'll see how to modify the general appearance of all pages in a document or document section by adding page numbers, headers, or footers, or by adjusting the margins or other page setup features. You'll learn how to enhance the appearance of individual pages by placing blocks of text at specific positions on the page, or by adding graphics. You'll discover how to enhance documents—primarily Web-page documents—by adding movie clips, scrolling text, background sounds, and background colors or images. And finally, you'll learn how to print Microsoft Word documents and how to preview their printed appearance.

This chapter concludes the presentation of the basic steps for creating regular Word documents and Web pages. The following chapters on Word explore techniques for creating longer and more specialized kinds of documents.

Adding Page Numbering

You can use the Page Numbers dialog box to quickly add automatic page numbering to the pages in your document. You can display numbers at the top or at the bottom of each page, and you can choose from a variety of numbering formats. Although you can't see these page numbers in Normal document view, they will appear in Print Layout view and in Print Preview, and of course on the printed copy of the document. If you're creating a Web-page document, don't bother to add page numbering, headers, or footers, because they won't be displayed in a browser.

When you add page numbers using the Page Numbers dialog box, Word creates a simple header or footer consisting of only the page number. In the next section, you'll learn how to create full headers or footers that display any text, graphics, or formatting that you want at the top or bottom of the pages in your document.

To add automatic page numbering to the currently opened document, do the following:

1 Choose Page Numbers from the Insert menu to open the Page Numbers dialog box:

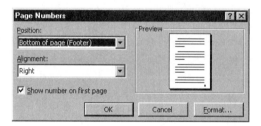

2 In the Position list, select Top Of Page (Header) to place the page numbers at the top of each page (that is, within headers), or Bottom Of Page (Footer) to place the page numbers at the bottom of each page (that is, within footers).

3 In the Alignment list, choose the position of the page numbers within the headers or footers.

Choose Left, Center, or Right to place the page numbers at the left margin, centered between the margins, or at the right margin on each page. Choose Inside to place the page numbers at the right on even numbered pages and at the left on odd numbered pages. Choose Outside to place the page numbers at the left on even numbered pages and at the right on odd numbered pages (as in this book).

SEE ALSO

For an overview of the different document views and how to switch between them, see "Changing the Way Documents Are Displayed," page 114.

4 If you want to eliminate the page number from the first page of the document (or from the first page of the current document section if you have divided your document into sections), deselect the Show Number On First Page option.

If you do this, Word will omit the page number from the first page, though it will count the first page in numbering the pages. For example, if you start numbering at 1, Word won't display a number on the first page, but it will number the second page with 2.

5 If you want to modify the style of the numbering or change the starting number, click the Format button to open the Page Number Format dialog box:

Select this option to add chapter numbers to the page numbering...

...and select options in these two list boxes. You must format all chapter headings using the same Heading style (Heading 1, Heading 2, and so on) and assign them automatic numbering.

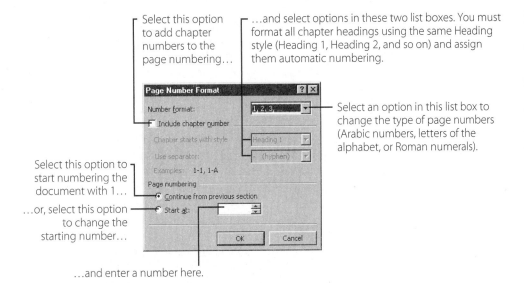

Select an option in this list box to change the type of page numbers (Arabic numbers, letters of the alphabet, or Roman numerals).

Select this option to start numbering the document with 1...

...or, select this option to change the starting number...

...and enter a number here.

To modify the page numbering you have added, you can reopen the Page Numbers or Page Number Format dialog box and change any of the options. You can also edit or delete page numbering by using the Header And Footer command on the View menu, as described in the next section. (Even though you can see page numbers in Print Layout view, you can't edit them unless you choose the Header And Footer command or double-click the header or footer area.)

Microsoft Word

Working with Sections

As mentioned in Chapter 8, "Arranging Text in Columns and Lists," you can divide a document into separate sections and then assign different attributes to each section. The following are the attributes that you can vary from section to section:

- The number of newspaper-style columns (discussed in "Creating Newspaper-Style Columns," page 243).

- Headers and footers, including page numbering (discussed in "Adding Page Numbering," page 296 and in "Adding Headers and Footers," page 299).

- The attributes that the Page Setup dialog box sets, such as the margins and the paper size (discussed later in "Adjusting the Page Setup," page 306).

The page numbering you create using the Page Numbers dialog box is applied to all document sections. You can, however, suppress the first page number (in step 4 under "Adding Page Numbering") or change any of the options set in the Page Number Format dialog box (in step 5) for a specific section. To do this, just place the insertion point in that section before opening the Page Numbers or Page Number Format dialog box and performing the step. Later in the chapter (under "Varying Headers or Footers Within the Document," page 304) you'll learn how to apply completely different headers, footers, or page numbering to different document sections.

To divide your document into separate sections, place the insertion point at the position where you want to insert a section break, choose Break from the Insert menu, and select one of the options in the Section Break Types area:

If you select Continuous, the text in the new section will be placed immediately following the text in the previous section.

If you select Next Page, the text in the new section will start on the next page.

If you select Even Page, the text in the new section will start on the next even page.

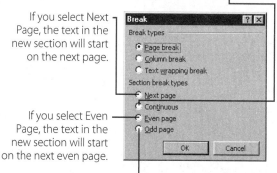

If you select Odd Page, the text in the new section will start on the next odd page.

Working with Sections *continued*

In Normal view, Word marks a section break as follows:

This is the last line of a section.

....Section Break (Next Page)..

This is the first line of a new section.

The text in parentheses will vary according to the type of break you insert. In Web Layout, Print Layout, or Outline view, section breaks are visible only if the Show/Hide ¶ button is pressed on the Standard toolbar. Section breaks aren't displayed in Print Preview.

To remove a section break, select the mark and press the Delete key. The sections before and after the break will be merged into a single section, which will acquire the section attributes (page numbering, margins, and so on) of the section that followed the mark. Any section attributes that you assigned to the section preceding the mark will be lost. Conceptually, a section mark stores the section attributes of the preceding section so if you delete the section mark, you delete these characteristics.

 TIP

Reformat Your Document's Page Numbering Quickly
To change the character formatting of page numbering throughout your document, modify the Page Number character style. Word assigns this style to automatic page numbers. *For information on modifying styles, see "Modifying Styles," page 198.*

Adding Headers and Footers

You'll now learn how to create and modify running headers or footers that Word prints on each page of your document. If you have used the Page Numbers dialog box to create simple headers or footers consisting only of page numbers, you can use the techniques given here to edit or delete these headers or footers. If you're creating a Web-page document, keep in mind that headers and footers won't be displayed in a browser.

To create or edit headers or footers throughout the currently opened document, do the following:

1 Choose Header And Footer from the View menu. Word then:

- Switches to Print Layout view.

Microsoft Word

- Marks the header and footer areas of the page with dotted lines and activates these areas so that you can work within them.

- Dims all text outside the header or footer area. (You won't be able to work on this text.)

- Displays the Header And Footer toolbar, which provides commands for working on the headers and footers.

Figure 10-1 shows the header area in the Word window after the Header And Footer command has been chosen. The footer area at the bottom of the page is similar.

 TIP

If you're in Print Layout view and if the header or footer already contains text, you can work on the headers or footers by simply double-clicking this text rather than choosing the Header And Footer menu command.

2 If necessary, move the insertion point to either the header area or the footer area by pressing the Down or Up arrow key, or by clicking the Switch Between Header And Footer button on the Header And Footer toolbar. (See Figure 10-2.)

 NOTE

Using the arrow keys or other navigation key combinations, you can move to the header or footer area on any page in the document. Usually, it doesn't matter which page you work on because the headers and footers are the same throughout the document. Later, however, you'll learn how to vary the headers or footers within the document (to reflect, for example, different part or chapter names in the document). In this case, you must move to the appropriate page before working on the header or footer.

FIGURE 10-1.
The header area and the Header And Footer toolbar.

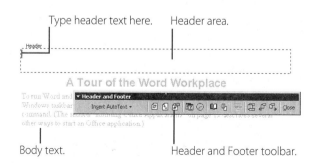

Type header text here. Header area.

Body text. Header and Footer toolbar.

FIGURE 10-2.
The Header And
Footer toolbar.

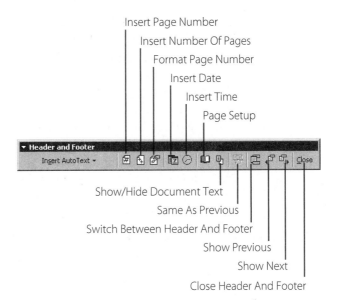

Insert Page Number
Insert Number Of Pages
Format Page Number
Insert Date
Insert Time
Page Setup

Show/Hide Document Text
Same As Previous
Switch Between Header And Footer
Show Previous
Show Next
Close Header And Footer

3 Type the text for the header or footer into the header area or the
footer area. You can enter one or more paragraphs of text into a
header or footer, and you can edit and format the text in the same
way that you edit and format text in the body of a document.

You can press the Tab key to align text on the two predefined
tab stops; the first tab stop aligns text in the center of the header or
footer, and the second tab stop right-aligns text at the right edge of
the header or footer. (Note that the tabs might be set differently in
documents based on certain templates.) To remove headers or footers, just delete all the text in the header or footer area.

TIP

While working on headers or footers, you can completely hide the body text on
the page by clicking the Show/Hide Document Text button. (Normally, when
you work on headers and footers, document text is shown in a dimmed font.)

You can quickly insert the page number, the total number of
pages in the document, the date, or the time into your header or
footer text. To do this, place the insertion point at the position
where you want the information, and click the Insert Page Number,
Insert Number Of Pages, Insert Date, or Insert Time button on the
Header And Footer toolbar, as shown in Figure 10-2. Note that
when you print your document, the number of pages, the date, or
the time that you insert will be updated to reflect the current value.

II

Microsoft Word

The Insert Page Number button adds automatic page numbering to your headers or footers, like that added by the Page Numbers command on the Insert menu described in the previous section. You can modify the format of the numbers or the starting number by clicking the Format Page Number button on the Header And Footer toolbar. This will open the Page Number Format dialog box, also described in the previous section.

You can also insert various types of information by clicking the Insert AutoText button and choosing an item from the submenu. For example, you can choose Filename to insert the name of the document; or you can choose "Author, Page #, Date" to insert your name, the page number, and the date. (The items on this menu are predefined AutoText entries provided with Word.)

4 When you have finished creating or modifying the headers or footers, click the Close button on the Header And Footer toolbar, or choose Header And Footer from the View menu to return to the view you were using previously.

Use Styles to Format Headers, Footers, and Page Numbers

Word assigns the Header paragraph style to header text, the Footer paragraph style to footer text, and the Page Number character style to automatic page numbers within headers or footers. You can therefore uniformly change the formatting of headers, footers, or page numbers throughout your entire document by modifying the corresponding style. Doing this will affect headers or footers in all document sections, even if the headers or footers vary from section to section.

You might, for example, assign to a style borders or shading, distinctive character formatting (such as a font, style, size, color, or enhancement), or other formatting to emphasize your headers or footers and make them stand apart from the text in the body of the document.

Sizing and Moving Headers or Footers

The header or footer text you enter is normally confined within the header area or the footer area at the top or bottom of each page. You can change the size or position of these areas, however, or extend the header or footer text outside the header or footer area, by using one or more of the following techniques:

- You can move the top or bottom boundary of the header or footer area by dragging a marker on the vertical ruler displayed in Print Layout view:

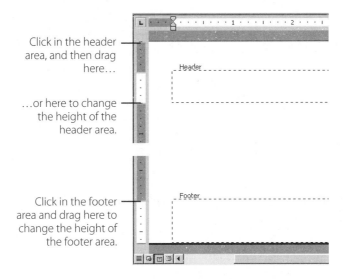

Click in the header area, and then drag here...

...or here to change the height of the header area.

Click in the footer area and drag here to change the height of the footer area.

Header

Footer

If the vertical ruler isn't currently visible, you can display it by choosing Options from the Tools menu, clicking the View tab, and selecting the Vertical Ruler option.

NOTE

If the text or graphics you insert into a header is higher than the current header area, Word will move the bottom boundary of the header area down, so that the header won't overlap the main document text. Likewise, if the text or graphics you insert into a footer is higher than the footer area, Word will move the top boundary of the footer area up.

SEE ALSO

For information on the Margins tab of the Page Setup dialog box, see "Adjusting the Page Setup," page 306. For instructions on creating positive and negative indents, see "Applying Paragraph Formatting Directly," page 187.

- You can also adjust the height of the header or footer area by changing the measurements in the Header box or Footer box on the Margins tab of the Page Setup dialog box, which will be described later in the chapter (in "Adjusting the Page Setup," page 306).

- To move text to the left or to the right of the header or footer area, assign a negative left indent or a negative right indent to one or more paragraphs of header or footer text. To do this, you can use the horizontal ruler or Paragraph dialog box, as explained in Chapter 6, "Formatting a Word Document."

- You can insert some or all of the header or footer text into a Word *text box*, so that you can drag it to any position on the page. To do this, choose Header And Footer from the View menu, and then insert the text box. Text boxes—and the methods for inserting them—are discussed later in the chapter ("Using Text Boxes to Position Text on the Page," page 316). Even though you can place such a text box anywhere on the page, it remains an integral part of the header or footer; therefore, it is displayed on all pages in the section or document, and you can modify it only after you choose the Header And Footer command. Note that a page number inserted by the Page Numbers dialog box is placed within a *frame*, which is an element similar to a text box, so that you can drag it wherever you want.

> **Overlap Headings and Body Text to Create Special Effects**
>
> Normally, if you extend the header or footer area beyond the current top or bottom margin area, Word adjusts the top or bottom margin so that the header or footer text doesn't overlap the text in the body of the document. However, if you enter a minus sign before the Top or Bottom margin setting on the Margins tab of the Page Setup dialog box (discussed in "Adjusting the Margins," page 308), Word will not adjust the margins. This will allow you to extend the header or footer area into the area occupied by the body text and to enter text or graphics into the header or footer that overlaps the body text. You could do this to create a special effect, such as a *watermark* (faint text or graphics that overlaps the body text on each page of the document). You could also create a watermark or similar effect by adding a text box to a header or footer and dragging it over the body text, as discussed above.

Varying Headers or Footers Within the Document

Normally, the same header or footer is printed on every page in the document. There are, however, three ways that you can vary headers and footers within your document.

You can create a different header and footer on the first page of the document, or on the first page of a section if you have divided your document into sections that begin on a new page. (This procedure doesn't work for continuous section breaks.) You might want to do this, for example, to eliminate the header from the title page of a report, or to avoid placing a page number on the first page. The following are the steps:

1 If you have divided your document into sections, place the insertion point within the section for which you want to create a different first page header and footer.

2 Choose Header And Footer from the View menu.

3 Click the Page Setup button on the Header And Footer toolbar (see Figure 10-2, page 301), and click the Layout tab in the Page Setup dialog box.

4 Select the Different First Page option and click OK.

In addition, you can create different headers and footers on odd and even pages. You might do this, for example, if you're writing a book and want the book title at the top of the left page of facing pages (called the *verso* page by book designers), and the chapter title at the top of the right page (called the *recto* page). The following is the technique:

1 Choose Header And Footer from the View menu.

2 Click the Page Setup button on the Header And Footer toolbar, and click the Layout tab in the Page Setup dialog box.

3 Select the Different Odd And Even option, and click OK.

Note that on the Layout tab, you can create a different first page header or footer for the entire document, or for a specific section within a document, by choosing an appropriate option in the Apply To list box. Creating different odd and even page headers or footers, however, always affects the entire document, even if it has been divided into sections and regardless of your choice in the Apply To list box. (*You'll see more about the Apply To list box in "Adjusting the Page Setup," page 306.*)

Finally, if you have divided your document into sections, the headers or footers in separate sections can have different contents. Initially, the headers and footers in every section (except the first) are connected to the headers and footers in the previous section, meaning that they'll be exactly the same as those in the previous section. To create different headers and footers in different sections, do the following:

1 Move the insertion point to any position within the section where you want the headers and footers to be different from the previous section.

2 Choose Header And Footer from the View menu.

3 Click the Same As Previous button on the Header And Footer toolbar to toggle this setting off. This will remove the connection between the current section and the previous one. You can now modify the headers or footers for the current section without changing those of the previous section.

II

Microsoft Word

TIP

> **Modifying Automatic Page Numbering in a Specific Section**
>
> If you have inserted automatic page numbering into your headers or footers, you can modify the format and starting number of the numbering within a particular document section. To do this, place the insertion point in that section, choose Header And Footer from the View menu, click the Format Page Number button on the Header And Footer toolbar that appears, and change the desired options in the Page Number Format dialog box, which was explained in "Adding Page Numbering," page 296. The options you set in this dialog box will apply only to the current document section. Most importantly, you can choose whether to continue the numbering sequence from the previous section, or to start numbering the current section with a specific page number.

If you have varied the headers and footers using any of the three methods just described, then you must, when you choose the Header And Footer command, move to an appropriate document page to enter or modify each of the different headers or footers. For example, if you have created a different first page header, you must move to the first page to enter or modify the first page header or footer; you must then move to any other page to enter or modify the headers or footers for the other pages. When headers and footers differ within a document, each header or footer is labeled appropriately, for example *Header -Section 2-* or *First Page Footer*:

To quickly move to the header or footer on the appropriate page, you can click the Show Previous or Show Next button on the Header And Footer toolbar:

Adjusting the Page Setup

The Page Setup dialog box allows you to adjust a wide variety of options that affect the general appearance of the pages throughout your entire document or in one or more document sections. These options include the document margins, the paper size, the vertical alignment of text on the page, and line numbering.

> If you're creating a Web-page document, keep in mind that none of the settings you make in the Page Setup dialog box will affect the way the page appears in a browser.

To set any of these options, follow these steps:

1 Select the portion of your document that you want to modify by doing one of the following:

- If you want to modify the entire document, place the insertion point anywhere within the document.

- If you want to modify the document from a given position to the end of the document, place the insertion point at that position.

- If you want to modify a portion of the document, select that portion.

- If you have divided the document into sections, place the insertion point in the section you want to modify, or select several sections.

2 Choose Page Setup from the File menu to open the Page Setup dialog box, which has four tabs: Margins, Paper Size, Paper Source, and Layout.

3 In the Apply To list (which appears on all tabs), choose the part of the document you want to modify:

In general, you can modify either the entire document or one or more document sections. The specific choices that appear in the Apply To list depend on the part of your document that you have selected and whether you have divided your document into sections. Note that if you choose the This Point Forward option (which appears if you didn't select text), Word will insert a section break at the position of the insertion point, and if you choose the Selected Text option (which appears if you selected text), Word will insert a section break at the beginning and at the end of the selected text. Choosing one of these options is a convenient way to divide your document into sections without having to manually insert section breaks.

4 If you want to use the options you select as the default settings, click the Default button (which appears on all tabs) and respond *Yes*. Word will assign the current settings on each of the four tabs to the document and to the document template so that the settings will apply to any new documents you create based on this template.

5 Select the page setup options you want. The options displayed on each of the four tabs are discussed in the following four sections. Notice that the Preview area shows the effect of the options that are currently set on all the tabs.

Adjusting the Margins

To set the page margins, do the following:

1 Click the Margins tab of the Page Setup dialog box. (See Figure 10-3.)

2 If you're printing on both sides of the paper and want the margins on facing pages (called a *spread* by book designers) to be symmetrical, select the Mirror Margins option.

 3 If you want to print two half-sized document pages on each piece of paper, select the 2 Pages Per Sheet option.

FIGURE 10-3.
The Margins tab of the Page Setup dialog box.

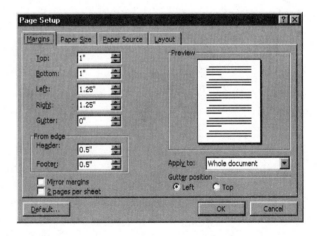

The pages will be printed one above the other if you choose the Portrait orientation, or side by side if you choose Landscape orientation. (Orientation is discussed in the next section.) This option is useful if you're planning to cut the sheets in half, perhaps to make a booklet.

4 Set the page margins in the Top, Bottom, Left, and Right boxes; the corresponding margins are shown in Figure 10-4.

FIGURE 10-4.
The page margins that the Top, Bottom, Left, and Right boxes of the Page Setup dialog box set when you deselect the Mirror Margins and 2 Pages Per Sheet options.

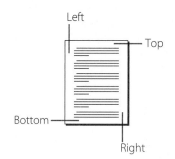

If you selected Mirror Margins, the boxes will be labeled Top, Bottom, Inside, and Outside; the corresponding margins for a two-page spread are shown in Figure 10-5.

FIGURE 10-5.
The page margins that the Top, Bottom, Inside, and Outside boxes of the Page Setup dialog box set when you select the Mirror Margins option.

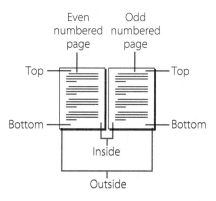

TIP

If you're printing on both sides of the paper, you can also make the headers or footers symmetrical by selecting the Different Odd And Even option on the Layout tab of the Page Setup dialog box and formatting your headers and footers appropriately.

5 You can add extra space to the inside or top margin on each page to make room for the binding. To do this, enter the desired amount of space into the Gutter box, and select either the Left or the Top option in the Gutter Position area to specify the page margin where you want to add the gutter.

If you add a gutter at the left and select Mirror Margins, the gutter space will be added to the right margin on even pages and to the left margin on odd pages, as shown in Figure 10-6. If you add a gutter at the left but don't select Mirror Margins, the gutter space will be added to the left margin on all pages. (If you add a gutter at the top, you can't select Mirror Margins.)

6 To adjust the amount of space between the top of the page and the start of the header text, enter a new measurement into the Header box. Likewise, to adjust the space between the bottom of the page and the start of the footer text, enter a measurement into the Footer box. As you learned previously in the chapter, you can also adjust either of these measurements by choosing Header And Footer from the View menu and dragging markers on the vertical ruler.

SEE ALSO

For information on changing the size or position of headers and footers, see "Sizing and Moving Headers or Footers," page 302.

Alternatively, you can adjust a page margin using a ruler. If you have divided your document into sections, place the insertion point in the section you want to modify, or select several sections to modify all of them. To adjust a margin, switch to Print Layout view (choose Print Layout from the View menu) or to Print Preview (choose Print Preview from the File menu), and drag the appropriate marker on the horizontal or vertical ruler. (If the rulers aren't visible, choose Ruler from the View menu. If the vertical ruler isn't visible in Print Layout view, choose Options from the Tools menu, click the View tab, and select the Vertical Ruler option.) Figure 10-7 shows the markers for adjusting the left, right, and top margins in Page Layout view. (The marker for adjusting the bottom margin is similar to that for adjusting the top margin.)

FIGURE 10-6.
The gutter space added to the left margin, with the Mirror Margins option selected.

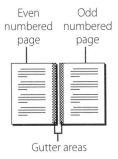

Even numbered page   Odd numbered page

Gutter areas

FIGURE 10-7.
Adjusting the left, right, and top margins using the rulers in Print Layout view.

Drag here to adjust the left margin.

Drag here to adjust the right margin.

Drag here to adjust the top margin.

A Tour of the Word Workplace

To run Word and take a short tour of its most basic features, click the Start button on the Windows taskbar, point to the Programs folder, and then choose the Microsoft Word command. (The section "Running Office Applications" describes several other ways to start an Office application.)

When Word first begins running, it automatically opens a new empty document. Below is the Word program window displaying a typical set of components.

ON THE WEB

The MarginDemo.doc Word document, used in the examples in this section, is on the Running Office 2000 Reader's Corner page. For information about connecting to this Web site, read the Introduction.

When you're adjusting the left or right margin, make sure the pointer has become a double-headed arrow. (Also, if you have ScreenTips enabled, the ScreenTip should read Left Margin or Right Margin.) You could otherwise inadvertently change the indent for the selected paragraph rather than the margin:

Position the pointer between the indent markers.

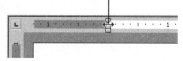

TIP

To see the exact margin measurements, hold down the Alt key while you drag a margin marker on a ruler.

SEE ALSO
For instructions on setting paragraph indents, see "Applying Paragraph Formatting Directly," page 187.

Don't confuse the left and right *margins* with the left and right *indents*. A margin is the normal distance between the text and the edge of the paper, and it applies to an entire document or section. An indent is an adjustment to this distance that applies to one or more individual paragraphs. (It's a paragraph formatting attribute.) If the left or right indent measurement is 0, the paragraph text is aligned with the left or right margin. If the indent measurement is positive, the paragraph text is moved in from the margin, and if it's negative the text is moved out from the margin. See Figure 10-8.

FIGURE 10-8.
Margins and indents.

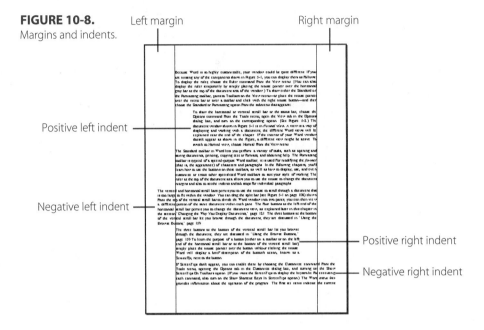

Adjusting the Paper Size and Orientation

Word normally assumes that you're printing on 8½-inch by 11-inch paper. If you're using a different paper size, you must change the paper size setting. You can also change the orientation of the text on the page. To alter either of these settings, do the following:

1 Click the Paper Size tab of the Page Setup dialog box. (See Figure 10-9.)

2 To specify the size of the paper, choose one of the standard paper sizes in the Paper Size list box. (The contents of this list box depend on your current default printer.) If you can't find the correct size in the list, enter the correct size into the Width and Height boxes.

3 In the Orientation area of the dialog box, choose Portrait (the usual setting) to print the lines of text at right angles to the direction of the paper feed, or choose Landscape to print the lines of text in the direction of the paper feed:

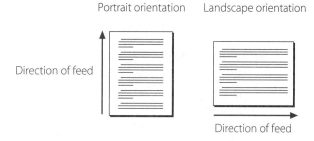

If, for example, your document contains a wide table, you might place the table in its own section and assign the Landscape orientation to that section, leaving the other document sections in Portrait orientation. Word would then print the table sideways so that it would fit on the paper.

NOTE

When you switch paper orientations, Word automatically swaps the current settings of the top and bottom margins for the settings of the left and right margins so that the text occupies the same portion of the page.

FIGURE 10-9.
The Paper Size tab of the Page Setup dialog box.

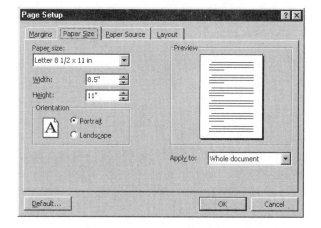

Adjusting the Paper Source

If your printer has more than one paper bin, a manual feed slot, or another paper source, you can print the first page of the document (or of the section) on paper from one source and print all remaining pages on paper from a different source. You could use this technique, for example, to print the first page of a letter on letterhead stock and the remaining pages on blank stock.

Microsoft Word

To set the paper source, click the Paper Source tab of the Page Setup dialog box. (See Figure 10-10.)

FIGURE 10-10.
The Paper Source tab of the Page Setup dialog box. (The contents of these lists depend on your current default printer.)

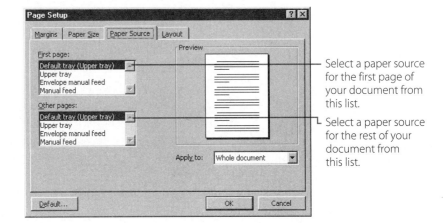

Select a paper source for the first page of your document from this list.

Select a paper source for the rest of your document from this list.

Adjusting the Page Layout

For information on the Headers and Footers options, see "Varying Headers or Footers Within the Document," page 304.

Finally, you can adjust a variety of page setup options by clicking the Layout tab of the Page Setup dialog box. (See Figure 10-11.) To control the location of the text at the beginning of the selected document section or sections, choose an item in the Section Start list.

You can choose an option in the Vertical Alignment list to affect the way Word arranges paragraphs—in the vertical direction—on pages that are not completely filled with text. Figure 10-12 shows the effects of the different options. You might, for example, choose the Center option for the title page of a report.

FIGURE 10-11.
The Layout tab of the Page Setup dialog box.

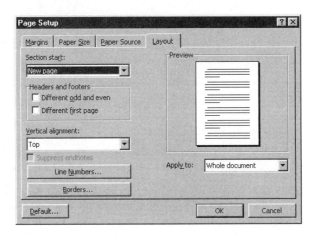

FIGURE 10-12.
The Vertical
Alignment options.

Top   Center   Justified

> To see the effect of whatever Vertical Alignment option you have chosen, you must be in Print Layout view or in Print Preview.

SEE ALSO

For a description of the Paragraph dialog box, see "Applying Paragraph Formatting Directly," page 187.

You can have Word print line numbers in the left margin within one or more document sections by clicking the Line Numbers button. In the Line Numbers dialog box (see Figure 10-13), select the Add Line Numbering option, and select the line numbering options you want. Line numbers are displayed only in Print Layout view and Print Preview and on the printed copy of the document; lawyers and publishers often use line numbering to facilitate discussion of specific lines among several people. Note that you can block line numbering for a specific paragraph by applying the Suppress Line Numbers paragraph formatting option, which you'll find on the Line And Page Breaks tab of the Paragraph dialog box.

FIGURE 10-13.
The Line Numbers
dialog box.

Finally, you can click the Borders button on the Layout tab to open the Borders And Shading dialog box, which lets you apply borders or shading to the selected paragraph or to add a border to all pages in the document or in a document section, as described in "Using Borders and Shading," page 256.

TIP

> You can change the character formatting of line numbers throughout your document by modifying the Line Number character style, using the techniques given in Chapter 7, "Customizing Styles and Templates."

Using Text Boxes to Position Text on the Page

The text in the body of a document is contained in a stream of characters that flows from line to line and from page to page. Generally, you neither know nor care where a particular block of text will fall on a page. In this section, however, you'll learn how to place material at a specific position on the page, outside the normal stream of characters. You can use these techniques to position margin notes, figures, tables, sidebars, and other elements that you want to set apart from the body text.

To place a block of text at a specific position on the page, you insert it into a Word element known as a *text box*, which you can then move to the position you want. Figure 10-14 shows a margin note that was created by placing a text box in the left margin on a page and typing the text for the note into the text box.

To place a text box around existing text in your document, do the following:

1 Select the text you want to include in the text box. You can include one or more characters or paragraphs, or a Word table.

2 Choose Text Box from the Insert menu.

FIGURE 10-14.

A margin note created by inserting text into a text box.

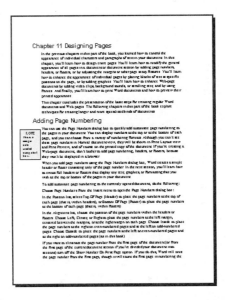

 **ON THE WEB**

The Ch11Demo.doc Word document, used in the examples in Figures 10-14 and 10-18, is on the Running Office 2000 Reader's Corner page.

Word will then create a new text box, and it will move the selected text into the text box. You'll now probably need to adjust the size, position, and format of the text box, as will be described later.

 NOTE

You must be in Print Layout or Web Layout view or in Print Preview to be able to see and work with a text box. If you're not in one of these views when you insert a text box, Word will automatically switch you to Print Layout view.

You can also create an empty text box and then insert text into it, as follows:

1 Without selecting text, choose Text Box from the Insert menu. The insertion point can be anywhere within the document.

2 Drag the mouse pointer to indicate the size and position you want for the text box:

Or, simply click in the document to insert a default-sized text box.

3 You can now insert text into the text box. If the insertion point isn't already in the text box, click within the box (*not* on one of its borders). You can then enter, edit, and format text just as you would for a normal paragraph. A text box can contain one or more paragraphs.

 TIP

If you're creating a Web-page document, don't place a text box in a margin area, because it will probably be partially or completely cut off when the page is viewed in a browser. Recall that neither Web browsers nor Word's Web Layout view display the full document margins.

II

Microsoft Word

As you type text in a text box, Word will wrap the text when you reach the right text box edge. Word won't, however, automatically increase the height of the box when you reach the bottom; you'll have to manually increase the height of the box to make the text at the bottom visible. (Or, as you'll see later, you can link the text box to another text box so that excess text automatically flows into the second text box.)

To change the height or width of a text box, do the following:

1 Click anywhere on the text box to select it. When a text box is selected, Word displays a thick band around it, which contains eight sizing handles:

2 Drag any of the sizing handles to resize the text box as you like. To maintain the original proportions of the text box as you change its size, press Shift while dragging one of the corner sizing handles. To resize the text box symmetrically about its center, hold down the Ctrl key while dragging any sizing handle.

You can move a text box as follows:

1 Place the pointer over one of the edges of the text box (but not over a sizing handle if the text box is selected). Cross-arrows will be displayed at the top of the mouse pointer:

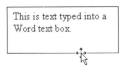

2 Drag the text box to the position you want on the page. If you want to copy the text box rather than move it, hold down Ctrl while you drag.

If you move a text box onto an area of the page occupied by text, you'll notice one of the following two types of behavior:

■ If you selected existing text in the document before inserting the text box (that is, if you used the first method that was given for creating a text box), the document text will move away from the text box; in other words, the document text will *wrap* around the text box.

■ If you didn't select text before inserting the text box (that is, if you used the second method for creating a text box), the text box will *overlap* the document text; in other words, the document text won't wrap around the text box.

The way the text box is positioned with respect to adjoining text in the main part of the document is known as its *wrapping style*. If your text box doesn't currently have the wrapping style you want, don't worry. Later in the chapter (in "Formatting Text Boxes, Pictures, and Drawing Objects," page 331), you'll learn how to modify the wrapping style of a text box, as well as many of its other aspects, using the Format Text Box dialog box or the Picture toolbar.

When a text box is selected, Word will usually display the Text Box toolbar automatically. (If it isn't displayed when a text box is selected, point to Toolbars on the View menu, and choose Text Box from the submenu.)

Create Text Box Link. Click this button, and then click the text box you want to link to, if you want to create a forward link.

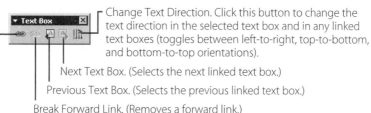

Change Text Direction. Click this button to change the text direction in the selected text box and in any linked text boxes (toggles between left-to-right, top-to-bottom, and bottom-to-top orientations).

Next Text Box. (Selects the next linked text box.)

Previous Text Box. (Selects the previous linked text box.)

Break Forward Link. (Removes a forward link.)

You can use the Text Box toolbar to create a series of two or more linked text boxes. Text will flow from one text box to the next one in the linked series. That is, any text that doesn't fit in a text box will be moved to the next one, in the same way that document text flows from one page to the next.

To remove a text box, plus the text it contains, select it by clicking one of its edges, and then press the Delete key. (If you select the text box by clicking inside an edge, Word will place the insertion point within the text, and pressing Delete will delete only a single character.) If you want to move text from a text box into the main part of the document, be sure to copy the text from the text box and paste it into the document before you delete the box. Note, however, that if a text box is linked to one or more others, deleting the text box won't erase the text, but will merely shift it to the remaining linked text boxes.

Microsoft Word

Adding Graphics

Graphics are another important element you can add to a page. To add graphics, either you can import a picture from a file or from another program, or you can create a drawing using Word's built-in drawing tools.

Importing Pictures

You can import graphics into a document either by inserting the contents of an entire graphics file, or by copying a block of graphics from another program and pasting it into the Word document. After a graphic has been imported into a Word document using one of these techniques, it is known as a *picture*.

> If you have a scanner or digital camera attached to your computer, you can import a picture directly from the device. To do this, point to Picture on the Insert menu, and choose From Scanner Or Camera from the submenu that appears.

To obtain a picture from a graphics file, do the following:

1 Place the insertion point at the approximate position where you want to insert the picture into your document.

2 Point to Picture on the Insert menu, and choose From File from the submenu. This will open the Insert Picture dialog box, which is similar to the Open dialog box you use to open documents.

3 In the Insert Picture dialog box, locate and select the graphics file you want to import. You can import graphics files in a wide variety of different formats (for example, files with the extensions .bmp, .wmf, .gif, and .jpg). Note that if the Preview option is selected in the Insert Picture dialog box, a preview image of the selected graphics file will appear on the right side of the dialog box.

4 Click the Insert button.

> **Use the Clip Gallery to Quickly Insert Graphics**
>
> Another way to add a picture to your document is by inserting clip art from the Microsoft Clip Gallery program. This program, together with a large collection of clip art, is included with Microsoft Office. (And you can use the program to download additional clips from the Web.) To run the Clip Gallery, point to Picture on the Insert menu, and choose Clip Art from the submenu. *Details are given in "Using the Clip Gallery," page 1211.*

You can also insert a picture by copying graphics from another program (such as the Office PhotoDraw program or the Paint program that comes with Windows), as follows:

1   Select the graphics in the other program, and choose Copy from that program's Edit menu.

2   Place the insertion point at the approximate position in the Word document where you want to insert the picture.

3   Choose Paste from Word's Edit menu or press Ctrl+V.

SEE ALSO

See Chapter 51, "Sharing Data Among Office Applications," for detailed information on copying data from one program to another.

Once you have inserted a picture, you can move it to the exact position where you want it. The method depends on the source of the picture and the way you inserted it. If you copied the picture from PhotoDraw (or another program that formats copied graphics the same way), you can move the picture to any position on the page using the following method (which is similar to the method for moving a text box, described previously):

1   Place the pointer over the picture (but not over a sizing handle if the picture is selected). Cross-arrows will appear at the top of the mouse pointer:

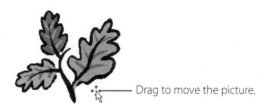

Drag to move the picture.

2   Drag the picture to the position you want on the page.
     If you move the picture over a portion of the page occupied by text, you'll notice that the text wraps around the picture. (It's placed above and below the picture.)

If, however, you copied the picture from Paint (or another program that formats copied graphics the same way), or if you imported the picture from a graphics file, or if you inserted it from the Clip Gallery as described in "Using the Clip Gallery," page 1211, the picture will be placed inline with the text; that is, it will become an integral part of the body text in the document and will be treated as if it were a single text character. It will therefore move automatically as the text moves on the page. To move it to a different position within the text, use the Cut and

Microsoft Word

II

Copy commands or any of the other methods for moving ordinary text that were given in Chapter 5.

The way you move a picture on the page and the way a picture interacts with adjoining text in the main part of the document (for example, whether text wraps around it or it's placed inline with the text) depend on the picture's *wrapping style*. In the section "Formatting Text Boxes, Pictures, and Drawing Objects," page 331, you'll learn how to change the wrapping style of a picture, as well as many of its other features, using the Format Picture dialog box or the Picture toolbar. (Note that the Picture toolbar normally appears when you click a picture to select it. You'll learn how to use it in "Formatting Text Boxes, Pictures, and Drawing Objects.")

You can change the size of a picture the same way you resize a text box. That is, click the picture to select it, and then drag one of the eight sizing handles:

Drag one of the eight
sizing handles to
change the size of
the picture.

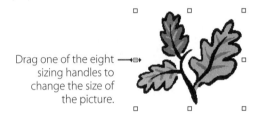

To maintain the original proportions of the picture, drag one of the corner sizing handles. To change the size of the picture without moving the position of its center, press Ctrl while you drag any handle. (This, however, won't have any effect on a picture that's placed inline with the text.) Note that using either of these methods to resize a picture *scales*—that is, compresses or expands—the graphics contained in the picture. In the section "Formatting Text Boxes, Pictures, and Drawing Objects," page 331, you'll learn how to *crop* a picture, which changes the size or proportions of the picture itself without changing the size or proportions of the graphics it contains. Cropping results in either cutting off some of the graphics or adding additional white space around them.

You can also edit the contents of a picture by selecting Edit Picture on the Edit menu. After you've edited a picture's content once, you can double-click the picture to edit it again. The type of editing you can perform depends on the format and origin of the picture. The following are among the ways that Word allows you to edit a picture:

- If the picture is compatible with a Word drawing, Word will open a separate window and allow you to alter each of the picture's component drawing objects. (Drawing objects are discussed in the next section.)

- If the picture isn't compatible with a Word drawing, you might not be able to fully edit the original picture, but only to change its size and add drawing objects to it.

- If you copied the picture from another program, Word might be able to activate the original program so that you can use that program's own tools and commands to edit the picture. *For information about this method of editing a picture, see "Linking Data," page 1197, and "Embedding Data," page 1203.*

To *delete* a picture, click it to select it, and then press Delete.

Finally, note that you can perform several of the operations discussed in this section by right-clicking a picture and choosing a command from the shortcut menu.

Creating Drawings in Word

A final way to add graphics to a document is to use Word's built-in drawing tools to draw them yourself. Each component of a drawing you create in this manner is termed a *drawing object*. You have already seen one type of drawing object, the text box. In this section, you'll learn how to create and modify many additional types of drawing objects, such as lines, cubes, free-form shapes, and special text effects.

The first step in creating or modifying drawing objects is to display the Drawing toolbar by pointing to Toolbars on the View menu and choosing Drawing from the submenu, or by simply clicking the Drawing button on the Standard toolbar. (To hide the toolbar, click the button again.)

Drawing

To view or work with drawing objects, you must be in Print Layout or Web Layout view or in Print Preview. If you aren't already in one of those views when you display the Drawing toolbar, Word will switch the view to Print Layout view either when you select a drawing tool or as soon as you click the Drawing button to display the toolbar. The following is the Drawing toolbar:

The different groups of buttons on this toolbar will be explained in the following sections.

Inserting Drawing Objects

You can use the middle group of buttons on the Drawing toolbar to insert various types of drawing objects:

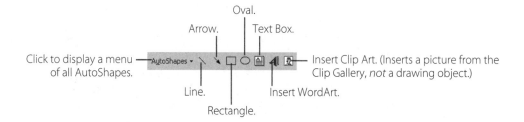

Oval.

Arrow. Text Box.

Click to display a menu of all AutoShapes.

Insert Clip Art. (Inserts a picture from the Clip Gallery, *not* a drawing object.)

Line.

Insert WordArt.

Rectangle.

There are three main categories of drawing objects that you can insert: AutoShapes, WordArt, and text boxes.

An AutoShape is a predefined or free-form figure, such as a line, oval, cube, flowchart symbol, banner, free-form scribble, and so on. You can insert a line, arrow, rectangle, or oval AutoShape object by clicking one of the buttons on the Drawing toolbar labeled above. To insert one of the other types of AutoShapes, click the AutoShapes button, choose a category from the menu, and then click the button for the specific figure you want. For example, you would insert a crescent moon AutoShape figure as follows:

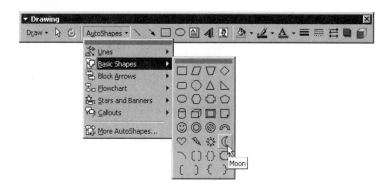

After clicking the button for the AutoShape, simply click at the position on the document page where you want to display the figure, and Word will insert a standard-sized AutoShape object. (You can later change the size, shape, or position.) If you want to give the object a specific initial size and shape, press the mouse button and drag to create the figure:

 TIP

Another Way to Insert AutoShapes

If you want, you can insert AutoShapes by using the compact AutoShapes toolbar rather than the general-purpose Drawing toolbar. To display the AutoShapes toolbar, point to Picture on the Insert menu and choose AutoShapes from the submenu.

A WordArt drawing object allows you to insert text that's formatted in unusual ways—for example, curved, slanted, or three-dimensional text. The following is the method for adding WordArt:

1 Click the Insert WordArt button on the Drawing toolbar or point to Picture on the Insert menu, and choose WordArt from the submenu. The WordArt Gallery dialog box will then be displayed:

2 Select the style of WordArt you want by double-clicking one of the boxes in the WordArt Gallery dialog box (or click the box,

II

Microsoft Word

and then click OK). Word will now open the Edit WordArt Text dialog box:

3 In the Edit WordArt Text dialog box, enter the text, and select the font, character size, and—if you want—bold or italic font style. Click OK when you're done.

Word will then insert into your document a drawing object that contains the specially formatted text, as in the following example:

Finally, you can enter a text box drawing object either by clicking the Text Box button on the Drawing toolbar or by choosing Text Box from the Insert menu. Text boxes were discussed previously in the chapter (in "Using Text Boxes to Position Text on the Page," page 316).

Working with Drawing Objects

Working with a drawing object is similar to working with document text—you first select the object, and then perform an action on it. To select a drawing object, click the Select Objects button near the left end of the Drawing toolbar (unless this button is already enabled—that is,

Select
Objects

pressed in). The pointer will become an arrow slanting up and to the left. Then click the object you want to select. To select several objects so that you can perform some action on them simultaneously, just drag a selection rectangle around all of them, as in this example:

Drag a selection rectangle around two or more drawing objects to select both of them.

Alternatively, you can select several objects by pressing Shift while you click each one; this method allows you to select several objects in a rectangular area without selecting *all* the objects in this area. (To remove the selection from one of the objects, click it again while pressing Shift.) To restore the normal I-beam mouse pointer so that you can work with text, click the Select Objects button again. Note that if you're selecting one (or more) objects by clicking (or Shift+clicking) them, and the objects aren't displayed behind text, you don't need to enable the Select Objects button.

NOTE

If you have selected several objects, you can combine them into a single object so that you can work with them as a unit. To do this, click the Draw button on the Drawing toolbar to open the Draw menu, and then choose the Group command. You can later break apart the group into its constituent objects by selecting the group and choosing Ungroup from this same menu. (You can later choose Regroup to reestablish this same group, without the need to first select the individual objects that belonged to the group.)

To delete the selected object or objects, press the Delete key.

Resizing and Moving Drawing Objects

When you select an object, Word displays rectangular sizing handles around it. You can change the overall dimensions of the object by dragging one of these sizing handles. For some AutoShape objects, Word also displays a special, diamond-shaped sizing handle that's colored yellow; dragging this handle lets you change some aspect of the object's shape, such as the angle of the sides of a trapezoid:

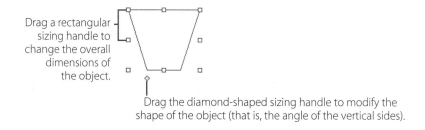

Drag a rectangular sizing handle to change the overall dimensions of the object.

Drag the diamond-shaped sizing handle to modify the shape of the object (that is, the angle of the vertical sides).

(The effect of dragging the diamond-shaped sizing handle varies widely among different types of AutoShape objects.) To maintain the original proportions of the object as you change its size, press Shift while dragging one of the corner sizing handles. To resize the object symmetrically about its center, hold down the Ctrl key while dragging a rectangular sizing handle.

To move a drawing object, place the pointer over the object, and when the pointer displays cross-arrows, drag the object to its new location on the page:

To copy rather than move the object, hold down the Ctrl key while you drag. Alternatively, when an object is selected, you can use the keyboard to move it by pressing the appropriate arrow key: Up, Down, Left, or Right. (You can't copy the object using the keyboard method.)

Notice that if you move a drawing object over the main text on the page, the object overlaps the document text and is displayed on top of it. This is the default wrapping style for a newly inserted drawing object. Later in the chapter (in "Formatting Text Boxes, Pictures, and Drawing Objects," page 331), you'll learn how to modify the wrapping style of a drawing object, as well as many of its other features, using the Format dialog box or the Picture toolbar.

Control What's on Top

If a drawing object overlaps text (as it does when it's first inserted), you can display the object either in front of or behind the text. Also, you can control the overlapping order of different drawing objects that intersect on the page. To make these changes, select the object, click the Draw button on the Drawing toolbar, point to Order on the menu that's displayed, and choose the appropriate command from the submenu:

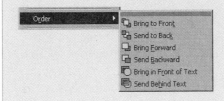

You can also use commands on the Draw drop-down menu (click the Draw button on the Drawing toolbar to display the menu) to move, align, rotate, or flip the selected object or objects:

Adjust the grid used to align objects, or display gridlines on the screen.

Align or evenly space selected objects.

Adjust the shape of a free-form object.

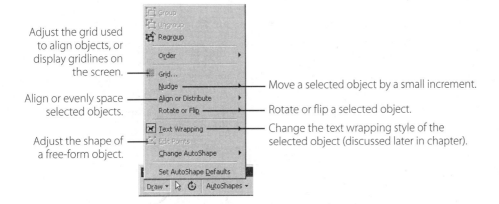

Move a selected object by a small increment.

Rotate or flip a selected object.

Change the text wrapping style of the selected object (discussed later in chapter).

Another way to rotate the selected drawing object is to click the Free Rotate button on the Drawing toolbar and then drag one of the rotation handles that's displayed to rotate the drawing object by any amount.

Free
Rotate

Changing the Colors and Styles of Drawing Objects

You can use the following group of buttons on the Drawing toolbar to change the selected object's fill color or pattern, line color and style, and font color; or to add shadow or three-dimensional effects to the object.

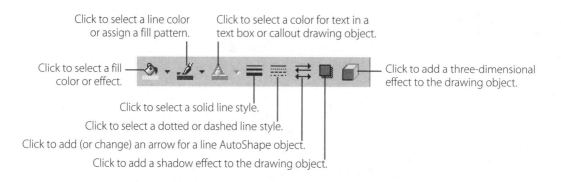

Click to select a line color or assign a fill pattern.

Click to select a color for text in a text box or callout drawing object.

Click to select a fill color or effect.

Click to add a three-dimensional effect to the drawing object.

Click to select a solid line style.

Click to select a dotted or dashed line style.

Click to add (or change) an arrow for a line AutoShape object.

Click to add a shadow effect to the drawing object.

As an example, the following figure shows a rectangle AutoShape object as it appeared when it was first inserted—and then as it appears after adding a fill color and a three-dimensional effect:

 TIP

Convert an AutoShape to the One You Want

If you have spent some time inserting, sizing, and formatting an AutoShape drawing object and then realize that you'd rather be working with a different type of object, you don't need to delete the object and start over. Rather, you can simply convert it to the AutoShape object you want. To do this, select the object, click the Draw button on the Drawing toolbar, point to Change AutoShape on the menu, and then choose the new type of AutoShape object you want from the submenu.

You can experiment freely with these effects. If you don't like the result of applying a particular format or effect, just issue the Undo command to remove it. (*For information on Undo, see the sidebar "Undoing and Redoing Editing and Formatting Actions," page 136.*) If you do like the result of a particular combination of effects, you can make them the default effects that will be applied to all objects that you subsequently draw. To do this, select the object that has the combination of effects you want, and then choose Set AutoShape Defaults from the Draw menu. (Click Draw on the Drawing toolbar to display this menu.)

TIP

Use the Pop-up Menu When Drawing Objects

You can perform several of the operations discussed in this section by right-clicking a drawing object and choosing the command that accomplishes what you want from the pop-up menu that appears. The commands provided on this menu depend on the type of drawing object and the formatting that has been applied to it. Note that if you right-click a closed AutoShape figure such as an oval or star, the shortcut menu provides an interesting command that isn't available elsewhere: Add Text. This command lets you add text to the AutoShape object, so that it functions just like a text box (but one with an interesting shape), as in the following example:

Formatting Text Boxes, Pictures, and Drawing Objects

This section explains how to format the different types of document objects you have learned about in this chapter: text boxes (discussed in "Using Text Boxes to Position Text on the Page," page 316), pictures (described in "Importing Pictures," page 320), and drawing objects (that is, AutoShape and WordArt objects, covered in "Creating Drawings in Word," page 323). You can format these objects by using the Format dialog box or the Picture toolbar.

Using the Format Dialog Box

The Format dialog box provides the largest set of formatting options. To format an object using this dialog box, do the following:

1 Click the object to select it. (To select an object that's behind text, you must first click the Select Objects button on the Drawing toolbar.)

2 From the Format menu, choose the Text Box, Picture, Object, AutoShape, or WordArt command. The command name depends on the type of object you've selected.

   This will open the Format dialog box. The actual title of the dialog box reflects the type of object you have selected—Format

Text Box, Format Picture, Format Object (for some types of pictures), Format AutoShape, or Format WordArt.

3 Select formatting options on the tabs of the Format dialog box, as shown in Figure 10-15.

Selecting the Wrapping Style

The Layout tab of the Format dialog box, shown in Figure 10-15, lets you select the wrapping style of the object. As you have seen, the wrapping style affects the way the object is positioned on the page and its relationship to the text in the body of the document. On the Layout tab, you can choose from five different wrapping styles. To choose from a larger selection of wrapping styles, and to fine-tune the positioning of the object, click the Advanced button on the Layout tab to open the Advanced Layout dialog box.

Other Ways to Set the Wrapping Style

You can also change the wrapping style of an object using the Text Wrapping button on the Picture toolbar (described in the next section). Or, you can click the Draw button on the Drawing toolbar, point to Text Wrapping on the menu that appears, and choose an option from the resulting submenu.

FIGURE 10-15.
The Layout Tab of the Format dialog box. (A picture was selected before the dialog box was opened.)

Select a background fill color; set the color, style, and thickness of the lines around the object; or, for AutoShape lines, add arrows at the ends of the lines (or modify existing arrows).

Resize or rotate an object, or restore its original size.

Select the wrapping style and horizontal alignment.

For a picture only, crop the picture, convert picture colors, and set color brightness and contrast.

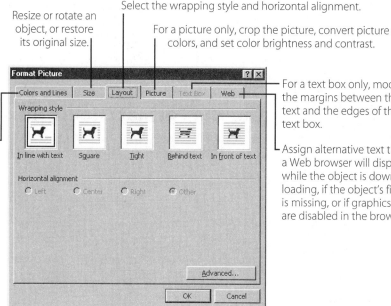

For a text box only, modify the margins between the text and the edges of the text box.

Assign alternative text that a Web browser will display while the object is downloading, if the object's file is missing, or if graphics are disabled in the browser.

When selecting a wrapping style, keep in mind that the styles can be broken down into three basic categories:

- *Inline With Text.* In this style, the object is an integral part of the body text in the document. It's positioned as if it were a single text character, and you can move or copy it using the standard text editing methods given in Chapter 5. This is the default wrapping style for a picture that you insert from a graphics file or the Clip Gallery. You can assign this style only to a picture or WordArt object (not to a text box or AutoShape object).

- *Square, Tight, Through,* and *Top And Bottom.* In these styles, you can place the object anywhere on the page. Document text will wrap around the object in various ways. The default wrapping style for a text box you insert by first selecting text is Square, and for a picture you paste into the document, it's Top And Bottom.

- *In Front Of Text* and *Behind Text.* In these styles, you can also position the object anywhere on the page. However, if the object intersects document text, it will overlap the text and will appear either in front of the text, or behind it. The default wrapping style for a text box you insert without first selecting text, an AutoShape object, or a WordArt object, is In Front Of Text.

2000 TIP

Using a Text Wrapping Break

If an object is assigned the Square, Tight, or Through wrapping style, you can insert a special line break known as a *text wrapping break* into a line of text that's to the right or to the left of the object. The text following this break will be moved down below the object. To insert the break, place the insertion point at the position where you want to break the text, choose Break from the Insert menu, and select the Text Wrapping Break option in the Break dialog box.

Using the Picture Toolbar

Although the Picture toolbar is designed primarily for formatting a picture, you can use at least some of its buttons to format other types of objects. Most notably, you can use the Text Wrapping button to modify any object's wrapping style, and you can use the Format *Object* button (where *Object* is the type of the selected object) to open the Format dialog box to format the object. See Figure 10-16 on the following page.

II

Microsoft Word

FIGURE 10-16.
The Picture toolbar.

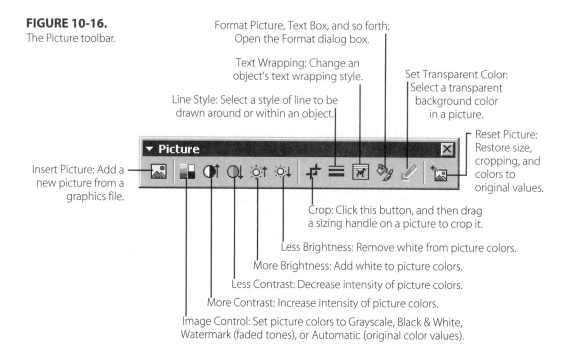

Format Picture, Text Box, and so forth: Open the Format dialog box.

Text Wrapping: Change an object's text wrapping style.

Set Transparent Color: Select a transparent background color in a picture.

Line Style: Select a style of line to be drawn around or within an object.

Reset Picture: Restore size, cropping, and colors to original values.

Insert Picture: Add a new picture from a graphics file.

Crop: Click this button, and then drag a sizing handle on a picture to crop it.

Less Brightness: Remove white from picture colors.

More Brightness: Add white to picture colors.

Less Contrast: Decrease intensity of picture colors.

More Contrast: Increase intensity of picture colors.

Image Control: Set picture colors to Grayscale, Black & White, Watermark (faded tones), or Automatic (original color values).

Cropping a Picture

Changing the size of a picture by dragging a sizing handle or by using the Size tab of the Format Picture dialog box *scales* the picture—that is, it compresses or expands the graphics contained in the picture. Alternatively, you can use the Crop button on the Picture toolbar or the Picture tab in the Format Picture dialog box (see Figure 10-15), to *crop* a picture. Cropping a picture changes the size or proportions of the picture itself without changing the size or proportions of the graphics it contains. Cropping results in either cutting off some of the graphics or adding additional white space around them. Figure 10-17 shows the difference.

To crop using the Crop button on the Picture toolbar, select the picture, click the button, and then drag the appropriate sizing handle on the picture. To use the Picture tab of the Format Picture dialog box, enter the amount that you want to crop each side of the picture—as a positive or negative number—into the Left, Right, Top, or Bottom box.

FIGURE 10-17.
Scaling vs. cropping
a picture.

Original size

Scaled smaller

Scaled larger

Cropped smaller

Cropped larger

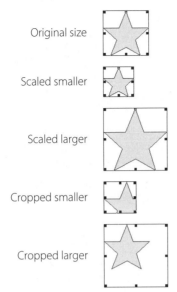

 # Adding Movie Clips, Scrolling Text, and Backgrounds

In this section, you'll learn how to add movie clips, scrolling text, a back-ground sound, or a background color or image to a Word document. Although these elements are designed primarily for Web-page documents, you can add them to any type of Word document. They will function when a document is viewed in Word, as well as when a Web page you create in Word is displayed in a browser. (Note, however, that Word will display a background color or image only in Web Layout view.)

You add a movie clip, scrolling text, or a background sound by using the new Web Tools toolbar:

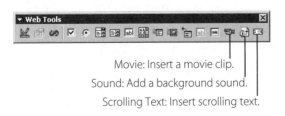

Movie: Insert a movie clip.
Sound: Add a background sound.
Scrolling Text: Insert scrolling text.

(The buttons that aren't labeled here are for creating Web-page forms and scripts, which are beyond the scope of this chapter.)

A movie clip displays a video sequence, with sound, in a rectangular area in your document. You can have the clip played whenever the document opens in Word or a browser, whenever the user points to it with the mouse, or both times. You can also control the number of times the clip plays. To insert a movie clip, click the Movie button on the Web Tools toolbar, and in the Movie Clip dialog box, select the file containing the movie file you want to play, choose the desired playback options, and—if you want—specify an alternate image or text that will be displayed by browsers that don't support movie clips.

A block of scrolling text travels repeatedly across the width of your document. It's also known as a *marquee*, and you can use it to draw attention to a message. To insert scrolling text, click the Scrolling Text button on the Web Tools toolbar, and enter the text and display options that you want into the Scrolling Text dialog box.

A background sound is played when your document opens in Word or in a browser. To assign a background sound to the document, click the Sound button on the Web Tools toolbar, and in the Background Sound dialog box, select the sound file containing the sound you want to play, and specify the number of times the sound should be repeated when the document opens. (You can choose the Infinite option to have the sound repeated continuously as long as the document is open.)

You can assign the document a background color or image by pointing to Background on the Format menu and choosing an option on the submenu that appears. You can choose a background color directly from the submenu, you can choose More Colors to select from a larger set of colors or to create a custom color, or you can choose Fill Effects to select a background image. (You can choose from a large collection of standard background images or you can select a graphics file to use for the background image.)

TIP

Use Frames to View Several Documents at Once

Frames are another new Word feature designed primarily for Web-page documents. You can show several documents simultaneously in the Word or Web-browser window by displaying each document within a separate *frame*, which is an adjustable pane within the window. (Note that the term *frame* also refers to a seldom-used Word element for positioning text on a page, which is similar to a text box.)

The easiest way to create a set of Web pages that are displayed in frames is to use the Web Page Wizard. (*For instructions, see the sidebar "Creating Web Pages," page 112.*) You can also use the Frames submenu on the Format menu to create a document that displays frames (known as a *frames document* or *frames page*), or to add individual frames to such a document. And you can use the Frames toolbar to add or remove frames, or to modify the properties of the frames document or of one or more frames. Note that you can use either the submenu or the toolbar to add a frame containing a table of contents for choosing the document or document section that's displayed in another frame.

For detailed information on using frames in Word, see the Word online help topic "Create Frames and Framesets."

II

Microsoft Word

Previewing and Printing Documents

? **SEE ALSO**

For basic information about previewing and printing documents, see "Printing Documents," page 52.

When you have finally finished entering text and graphics into your document, as well as editing, formatting, proofing, and adjusting the page design, you're ready to print the document. Before doing so, however, you might want to preview the printed appearance of the document on the screen and possibly make a few last-minute adjustments.

As you have already learned, Word provides two document views that display the document exactly as it will be printed: Print Layout and Print Preview. These two views have many features in common; in general, however, Print Layout view is best for editing the document and working with text boxes and graphics, while Print Preview is best for viewing the overall appearance of the document pages immediately before printing.

Print
Preview

To switch to Print Preview, choose Print Preview from the File menu or click the Print Preview button on the Standard toolbar. The Print

Preview screen appears as shown in Figure 10-18. To edit your document while in Print Preview, click the Magnifier button on the toolbar to disable the Magnifier. Click the Close button to close Print Preview and return to the view you were working in earlier.

When you're ready to print your document, choose Print from the File menu or press Ctrl+P. Word will display the Print dialog box, which is shown in Figure 10-20, page 340. Before clicking the OK button to start printing, you can choose the printer, change printer settings, and select printing options.

Print Other Document Elements

Rather than printing the document itself, you can print various document elements by choosing an item other than Document in the Print What list box of the Print dialog box. You can print the document properties (that is, the information displayed and set by the Properties command on the File menu), the comments in the document, a description of the document styles, the contents of the document's AutoText entries, or a list of the document's current shortcut key assignments.

FIGURE 10-18.
Print Preview shows
how your document
will appear when
printed.

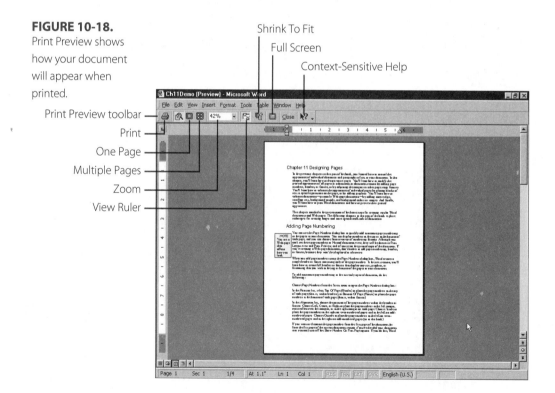

Pagination

Before printing your document, you might want to view and adjust the positions of the page breaks. You should do this after editing, formatting, and proofing your document because these actions can change the positions of page breaks.

In Print Layout view or in Print Preview, you can readily see the positions of page breaks because each page is displayed exactly as it will print. In Normal view, Word marks the position of each page break with a dotted horizontal line if you have selected the Background Repagination option. (To select this option, choose Options from the Tools menu and click the General tab.)

As you saw in Chapter 6, "Formatting a Word Document," the following paragraph formatting features can affect the positions of page breaks: Widow/Orphan Control, Keep Lines Together, Keep With Next, and Page Break Before. See Table 6-8, page 188, for an explanation of each of these features.

Also, the positions of page breaks can be affected by the current setting of the print options that tell Word what to include in the printed copy of the document. These options are contained in the Include With Document area of the Options dialog box's Print tab, shown in Figure 10-19, on the next page. To view this tab, choose Options from the Tools menu and click the Print tab, or click the Options button in the Print dialog box (to be described shortly).

A page break that Word automatically generates when the text reaches the bottom of a page is known as a *soft page break*. You can also force a page break at any position in a document by inserting a *hard page break*. The position of a hard page break is fixed, and it always causes a page break regardless of its location on the page. To insert a hard page break at the insertion point, press Ctrl+Enter, or choose Break from the Insert menu and select the Page Break option. In Normal view, Word marks the position of a hard page break with a horizontal dotted line labeled Page Break. (In contrast, the horizontal line marking the position of a soft page break is not labeled.)

Soft page break mark ....

Hard page break mark .... Page Break ....

In Print Layout view, the text following a hard page break is forced to a new page, but the mark itself appears only if all nonprinting characters are displayed. (To display all nonprinting characters, select All under Nonprinting Characters on the View tab of the Options dialog box, or click the Show/Hide ¶ button.)

To remove a hard page break, just select the mark and press Delete.

FIGURE 10-19.
The Print tab of the Options dialog box.

FIGURE 10-20.
The Print dialog box.

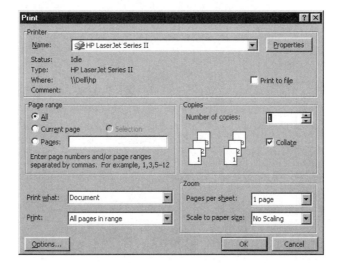

Print

Alternatively, you can quickly print your document using the current default printer and the default print settings by simply clicking the Print button on the Standard toolbar or on the Print Preview toolbar (which is displayed when you switch to Print Preview).

Working with Word in Workgroups

This chapter presents Microsoft Word features and techniques that can make it easier for you to work with other people to produce a document. You might, for example, collaborate with other authors, editors, reviewers, proofreaders, or indexers. The members of your workgroup might work on a single copy of a document, which is shared on a network or is routed from one person to another using Microsoft Exchange Server on a network or simply using a floppy disk. Alternatively, you might distribute a separate document copy to each member using a network, electronic mail, or floppy disks. This chapter focuses on the Word-specific techniques for preparing and working with shared documents. *The mechanics of sharing documents using networks, electronic mail, and Microsoft Exchange Server are discussed in "Sharing Documents in a Workgroup," page 82.*

Adding Comments to Your Documents

You can add comments to a Word document without modifying the main document text. You view and edit comments within a separate pane at the bottom of the document window. They don't appear on the printed document copy (although you can print them separately). Comments are useful for adding notes, explanations, suggestions, and other types of information to specific parts of your document. You might add comments to save information for your own use, or to communicate with other members of your workgroup. Figure 11-1 shows a document that includes several comments.

Save Time Using the Reviewing Toolbar

You can use the five buttons at the left end of the Reviewing toolbar for working with comments. To display the toolbar, point to Toolbars on the View menu, and choose the Reviewing option from the submenu that appears. The Reviewing toolbar is shown in Figure 11-1 and the buttons for working with comments are labeled in Figure 11-2.

FIGURE 11-1.
Viewing comments in a Word document.

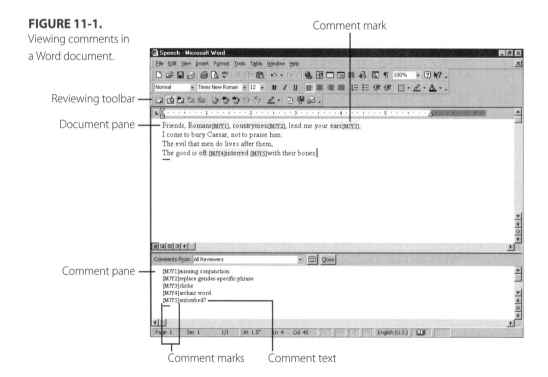

FIGURE 11-2.
The buttons on the
Reviewing toolbar
for working with
comments.

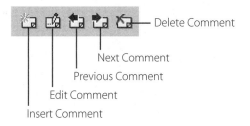

Delete Comment

Next Comment

Previous Comment

Edit Comment

Insert Comment

The Speech.doc and SpeechRc.doc Word documents, used in the examples in the chapter, are on the Running Office 2000 Reader's Corner page. For information about connecting to this Web site, read the Introduction.

To insert a comment into a document, do the following:

1 Select the text to which you want to attach the comment. To attach a comment to a single word, you can just place the insertion point anywhere within the word.

2 Choose Comment from the Insert menu, or click the Insert Comment button on the Reviewing toolbar, or press Ctrl+Alt+M. Word then does the following:

- Highlights in yellow the selected text in your document (or the word before the insertion point). The comment will be attached to this text. (To see the yellow highlighting, you must turn ScreenTips on. To turn on ScreenTips, choose Options from the Tools menu, click the View tab, and select ScreenTips under Show.)

- Places a comment mark at the end of the selected text.

- Opens a separate pane in which you enter and later view the comment text.

- Inserts a matching comment mark in the comment pane and places the insertion point following the mark.

3 Type the text for the comment following the mark in the comment pane. You can use the basic Word editing and formatting techniques on comments in the same way you would for any other Word text.

If you want, you can leave the comment pane open while you resume editing the document. To move the insertion point from one pane to the other, press F6 or click in the pane in which you want to work. If you want more room on the screen for your main document, you can close

II

Microsoft Word

the comment pane by clicking the Close button at the top of the pane, or by clicking the Edit Comment button on the Reviewing toolbar.

Notice that the comment mark consists of your initial or initials, followed by the number of the comment. The initials included in comment marks let you distinguish the comments added by different members of your workgroup. Note that the comment marks in the document pane are formatted as hidden text; accordingly, they're not visible on the screen unless the comment pane is open, the Show/Hide ¶ button on the Standard toolbar is pressed in, or the Hidden Text viewing option is selected. (To locate this option, choose Options from the Tools menu, and click the View tab.)

To view the text of the comment that is attached to a particular block of text in your document, you can place the mouse pointer anywhere over the highlighted text (whether comment marks are visible or not). Word will display the name of the comment author as well as the comment text. (Note, however, that the ScreenTips option must be selected. You set this option by choosing Options from the Tools menu and clicking the View tab.)

Michael Young:
archaic word

The good is oft [MY4] interred [MY5] with their bones.

NOTE

You can change the initials that Word adds to the comments you insert, as well as the author name that appears when you place the pointer over a comment. To do this, choose Options from the Tools menu, click the User Information tab, and enter new initials into the Initials box or a new name into the Name box.

You can browse through the comments in a document by clicking the Previous Comment or the Next Comment button on the Reviewing toolbar. Word will place the insertion point in front of the previous or next comment and will display the comment's text in a ScreenTip.

You can also view comment text within the comment pane. If the comment pane isn't open, either choose Comments from the View menu or click the Edit Comment button on the Reviewing toolbar. Initially, Word displays the comments made by all authors. If you want to view only the comments entered by a specific individual, choose the author's name (rather than All Reviewers) in the Comments From list box at the top of the comment pane. Then scroll through the comment pane—if neces-sary—to view the comment text. (The name used for each author is the name that was contained in the Name box on the User Information tab of the Options dialog box at the time the comment was entered.)

 TIP

> If you double-click a comment mark in the document, Word will open the com-ment pane and display the corresponding comment text.

Notice that if you scroll the comment pane, Word automatically scrolls the document pane to reveal the corresponding comment mark. Like-wise, if you scroll the document pane, Word scrolls the comment pane.

TIP

> **Quickly Locate Comments**
>
> To locate comment marks in the document, you can use the Find command, the Go To command, or the browse buttons, which were described in Chapter 5, "Entering and Editing Text in a Word Document." When using the Find com-mand, enter ^a into the Find What box to find any comment (the *a* derives from the former name for a comment, *annotation*). When using the Go To command or browse buttons, select the Comment target. The Go To command lets you search for any comments or for comments entered by a specific author.

You can remove a comment by selecting the comment mark in the doc-ument and pressing Delete, or by placing the insertion point anywhere within the highlighted text in the document and clicking the Delete Comment button on the Reviewing toolbar. Word will remove both the comment mark and the associated comment text.

TIP

> **Quickly Remove All Your Comments**
>
> Perhaps your comments are personal and you want to remove all of them from the copy of a document that you turn over to a co-worker. A fast way to do this is to choose Replace from the Edit menu, and on the Replace tab, enter ^a into the Find What box, leave the Replace With box empty, and click the Replace All button. *See Chapter 5, "Entering and Editing Text in a Word Document," for more information on the Replace command.*

If you have the necessary sound equipment installed on your computer (a sound card and a microphone), you can also add or listen to *voice comments*.

II

Microsoft Word

Click the Insert Sound Object button and use a microphone
to record your message, if you want to add a voice comment.

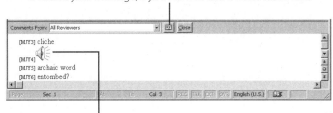

Word will insert this sound icon into the comment text in the
comment pane. To listen to a voice comment (which requires
a sound card), double-click the sound symbol in the comment text.

Printing Comments

You can print the document comments alone, or you can print the comments together with the document.

To print only the comments, choose Print from the File menu, and select Comments in the Print What list box in the Print dialog box.

? SEE ALSO

For a description of hidden text, see "Using the Font Dialog Box," page 181.

To include the comments whenever you print the document, choose Options from the Tools menu, click the Print tab, and select the Comments option (in the Include With Document area). Notice that when you select this option, Word automatically enables the Hidden Text option so that the comment marks (which are formatted as hidden text) will be printed. Whenever you subsequently print the document, the comment text will be printed after the document text, starting on a new page.

Tracking Document Changes

You can have Word track and mark all changes you make to a document, so that you or another author or editor can later review these changes and either accept or reverse them. For each change that is tracked, Word stores the exact modification that was made, as well as the name of the author, the date, and the time of the change; and it displays all this information when you review the revisions. (The name used to indicate the author of a change is the name that was contained in the Name box on the User Information tab of the Options dialog box at the time the revision was made.)

To start tracking changes to a document, point to Track Changes on the Tools menu, and choose Highlight Changes from the submenu that pops up. Then select Track Changes While Editing in the Highlight Changes dialog box, and click OK. Alternatively, you can simply press Ctrl+Shift+E, or double-click the TRK indicator on the Word status bar:

You can also start tracking changes by clicking the Track Changes button on the Reviewing toolbar, which is shown in Figure 11-3. (To display this toolbar, choose Toolbars from the View menu, and choose the Reviewing option from the submenu that pops up.)

 NOTE

> When change tracking is enabled, the TRK indicator on the Word status bar is displayed in dark type.

To stop tracking changes, just repeat any of these procedures (each procedure toggles change tracking on or off). When you turn off change tracking, Word retains a record of all revisions that have already been tracked, but it doesn't track changes that you subsequently make.

When change tracking is enabled, Word stores information on each modification you make to the document, so that any change can later be reviewed, accepted, or reversed. You can also have Word display visible *revision marks* indicating each change that has been tracked. If visible revision marks aren't already enabled, you can enable them by pointing to Track Changes on the Tools menu and choosing Highlight Changes from the submenu that pops up. Then, in the Highlight Changes dialog box, select Highlight Changes On Screen to show

FIGURE 11-3.
The buttons on the Reviewing toolbar used for tracking changes.

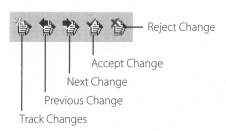

Reject Change
Accept Change
Next Change
Previous Change
Track Changes

Microsoft Word

revision marks on the screen, and select Highlight Changes In Printed Document to include them when the document is printed:

Figure 11-4 shows a document that contains several revision marks. Notice how Word marks inserted text and deleted text. Notice also that it places a vertical line in the margin to flag any line that contains a tracked change. Additionally, when you move the mouse pointer over a revision mark in the window, Word displays the author, date, time, and the type of the change (for example, Inserted or Deleted):

Later in the chapter (in the section "Customizing Revision Marking," page 350), you'll learn how to modify the way Word marks changes.

You can hide revision marking on screen or in the printed document by deselecting the appropriate option in the Highlight Changes dialog box described above. Word, however, will retain a record of all changes that have been tracked, and you can make them visible again by turning revision marking back on. (The only way to permanently remove a revision mark is to accept or reject the tracked change, as described in the next section.)

FIGURE 11-4.
A Word document containing revision marks.

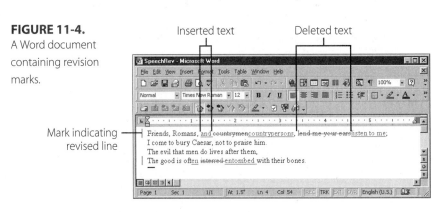

Inserted text   Deleted text

Mark indicating revised line

Reviewing Changes

You can review all changes that have been tracked in your document, and either accept or reject any of them. If you accept a change, the indicated revision is made permanent; if you reject a change, the text is restored to its original state. In either case, Word discards its record of the change and removes the revision mark. To review the changes, point to Track Changes on the Tools menu, and choose Accept Or Reject Changes from the submenu that appears. Word will open the Accept Or Reject Changes dialog box. (See Figure 11-5.) You can accept or reject all tracked changes in the document or review each change separately, as shown in that figure. Note that you can scroll through or edit your document while the Accept Or Reject Changes dialog box is displayed; just click in the document to edit it, and then click in the dialog box to resume reviewing your changes.

 TIP

Choose the Way You View Changes

You can select an option in the View area of the Accept Or Reject Changes dialog box to temporarily change the way Word displays your tracked changes. The Changes With Highlighting option displays revision marks in the document (as shown in Figure 11-4); the Changes Without Highlighting option hides revision marks but displays all changes made to the document; and the Original option hides the marks and shows all document text as it was before you changed it. Note that merely selecting one of these options does not make a permanent change to the document, but only affects the way tracked changes are displayed while the Accept Or Reject Changes dialog box is open.

II

Microsoft Word

FIGURE 11-5.
The Accept Or Reject
Changes dialog box.

Click the Find Previous button to select
the previous change in the document.

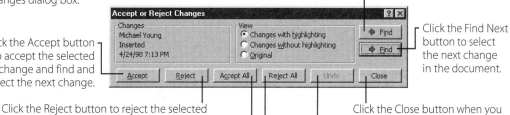

Click the Accept button
to accept the selected
change and find and
select the next change.

Click the Find Next
button to select
the next change
in the document.

Click the Reject button to reject the selected
change and find and select the next change.

Click the Close button when you
have finished reviewing changes.

Click the Accept All button to accept
all changes in the document.

Click the Undo button to reverse your
previous accepting or rejecting action.
Note that you can click Undo repeatedly
to remove a series of prior acceptances
or rejections.

Click the Reject All button to reject
all changes in the document.

Notice that to help you identify the origin of each tracked change, the Accept Or Reject Changes dialog box displays the name of the author, whether the change was a deletion or an insertion, the date, and the time of the selected revision. Also, if several authors have made changes to the document, Word normally marks each author's revisions using a different color. (As you'll see in the next section, however, you can have Word use a single color for all changes.)

Use the Reviewing Toolbar to Quickly Browse Through Your Changes
You can browse through the changes that have been tracked in your document, whether revision marks are visible or not, using the Next Change and Previous Change buttons on the Reviewing toolbar. (See Figure 11-3, page 347.) Clicking the Next Change button selects the next block of revised text in the document, and clicking Previous Change selects the previous block of revised text. You can also accept or reject the selected change, whether revision marks are visible or not, by clicking the Accept Change or Reject Change button on the Reviewing toolbar.

Customizing Revision Marking

You can modify the style as well as the color of the revision marks that Word uses, as follows:

1 Choose Options from the Tools menu, and click the Track Changes tab, or click the Options button in the Highlight Changes dialog box that was described previously (in the section "Tracking Document Changes," page 346). The Track Changes tab is shown in Figure 11-6.

2 For each kind of change that Word tracks (inserted text, deleted text, changed formatting, and changed lines), choose the type of mark that Word will use by selecting an item in the corresponding Mark list box.

3 For each kind of change, choose the color that Word assigns to the revised text by selecting an item in the corresponding Color list box.

For any kind of revision mark except the one used to indicate changed lines, you can select By Author to have Word use a different color for the changes of each author, or you can choose a single color that Word will use for all changes. The Auto item refers to your normal window text color (set in the Display Properties dialog box, which you access in the Windows Control Panel), which is usually black.

FIGURE 11-6.
The Track Changes
tab of the Options
dialog box.

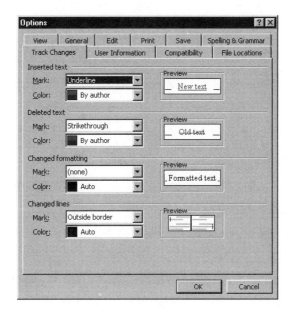

Working with Different Document Versions

In the previous sections, you learned how to use Word's change tracking feature to keep track of the changes you make to a document, and to communicate changes or proposed changes to other members of your workgroup. Word provides two additional features that can help you keep track of the changes you or members of your workgroup have made to a document: the Compare Documents command, which helps you find the differences between two different versions of a document, and the Share Document command, which allows you to easily save and retrieve separate document versions.

Comparing Document Versions

If you have saved a previous version of a document in a separate file, you can compare the previous version to the current version and, if you want, you can restore parts of the current version to the way they were in the previous version. The procedure is as follows:

1 Open the current document version.

2 Point to Track Changes on the Tools menu, and choose Compare Documents from the submenu that pops up.

Word will display the Select File To Compare With Current Document dialog box, which is similar to the standard Open dialog box that's displayed when you open a document.

3 Select the name of the previous document version, and click the Open button.

Word will add revision marks to the current document version to show how it differs from the previous version. These marks will be the same as those that would be created if you opened the previous document version, enabled change tracking and visible revision marks, and edited the document so that it matched the current version. You can review, accept, or reject these changes using the techniques that were explained earlier in this chapter. Note that rejecting a change restores that part of the document to the way it was in the previous version.

Maintaining Separate Document Versions

You can use Word's Versions command to store several separate versions of a document, all within a single document file. Say, for example, that you have written Chapter 1 for your latest novel, and you saved the current version in a file named Chapter1. You now want to revise the chapter, but you also want to keep the original version intact so that you can refer back to it if necessary. Without the Versions command, you would have to save the current version in a separate file (perhaps by making a copy of the document file). Using the Versions command, however, you can save a copy of the current document version right within the Chapter1.doc file, so that you can easily refer back to it later.

To do this, choose Versions from the File menu and in the Versions dialog box, click the Save Now button; Word then prompts you to add a descriptive comment for the version. You can then proceed to revise your chapter and save your work in the usual way when you're done. Now both versions of the document will be stored within the Chapter1.doc file. However, when you open the document you won't see the original version unless you again choose Versions from the File menu and use the Versions dialog box to open the original version in a separate window, as shown here:

Save the current document contents as a separate
version whenever you close the document.

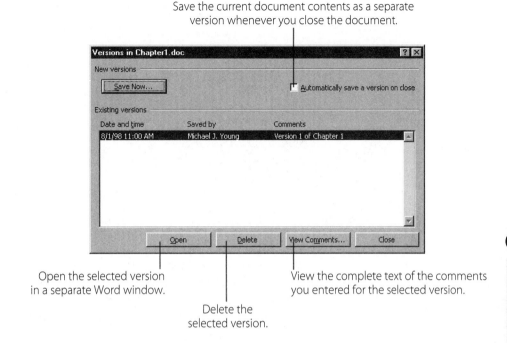

Open the selected version
in a separate Word window.

Delete the
selected version.

View the complete text of the comments
you entered for the selected version.

You can use this same technique to store additional document versions
within the same document file.

Using Other Workgroup Techniques

In the following sections, you'll learn several additional Word techniques that are useful when working in workgroups.

Protecting Documents

You might want to distribute a document—or copies of a document—to other members of your workgroup so that they can review, edit, or make additions to the document. Before you do so, however, you can protect the document to limit the kinds of changes reviewers can make, thereby ensuring the document's integrity. To protect a document, do the following:

1 Make sure the document you want to protect is displayed in the active document window.

2   Choose Protect Document from the Tools menu to open the Protect Document dialog box:

3   Choose one of the three types of protection in the Protect Document For area of the dialog box:

- Select the Tracked Changes option to permanently enable change tracking for the document. When you select this option, change tracking can't be disabled, nor can tracked changes be accepted or rejected. (After you remove the document protection, you'll be able to review, accept, or reject any of the changes that reviewers made.) Note that selecting this option also permits comments to be added to the document.

- Select the Comments option to allow reviewers to add comments to the document, but to prevent them from changing the actual document text.

- If you added a *form* to the document, you can select the Forms option to prevent changes except within form fields, such as check boxes or text boxes. (A form is a collection of check boxes, text boxes, and other fields that you add to a Word document for collecting information. Word forms aren't covered in this book.) Also, if you have divided your document into sections, you can select the Forms option to disallow all changes within one or more specific document sections. Click the Sections button to select the particular section or sections you want to protect.

4   To prevent reviewers from removing the protection, type a password into the Password box. (Word will display only * [asterisk] characters as you type.) You'll be asked to retype the password after you click OK.

Note that the protection you choose will apply to you as well as to other users.

If you have routed a single copy of the document among the members of your workgroup, when you receive the document back, you'll probably want to remove the protection. You can do so by choosing Unprotect Document from the Tools menu. (When the document is protected, Unprotect Document replaces the Protect Document command.) If you entered a password when you protected the document, Word will prompt you for it.

If you have distributed a separate copy of the document to each member of the workgroup, when these documents are returned to you, you can merge the changes they contain into the original document, as explained in "Merging Tracked Changes," page 357.

File-Sharing Protection

You can also protect a document against unauthorized changes by selecting file-sharing options, as follows:

1 Open the document you want to protect.

2 Choose Options from the Tools menu, and click the Save tab, or click the Options button in the Save As dialog box. The Save tab is shown in Figure 11-7.

FIGURE 11-7.
The Save tab of the Options dialog box.

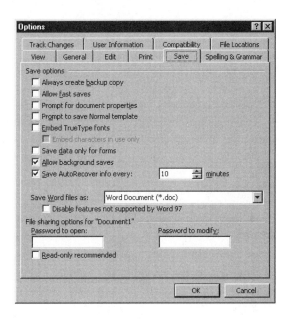

II

Microsoft Word

3 Set one or more of the options in the File Sharing group at the bottom of the Save tab, as follows:

- To prevent unauthorized users from *opening* the document, type a password into the Password To Open box. Word will ask you to retype the password when you click OK. No user will be able to open the document without typing this password.

- To prevent unauthorized users from *changing* the document, type a password into the Password To Modify box. Word will ask you to retype the password when you click OK. Any user will be able to open the document in read-only mode, which doesn't allow the user to save changes to the document. Only users who know the password, however, will be able to open the document in the normal read-write mode, which allows saving changes.

- You can have Word *suggest* that users open the document in read-only mode by selecting the Read-Only Recommended option. Whenever any user opens the document, Word will display a message suggesting that the document be opened in read-only mode. The user, however, can choose whether to open the document in read-only or in normal read-write mode.

You can turn off file-sharing protection (assuming that the document is open in the normal read-write mode) by displaying the Save tab again and then deleting the password or deselecting the Read-Only Recommended option.

Note that you can open any document in the read-only mode—even one that's not protected—by choosing Open from the File menu, clicking the down arrow to the right of the Open button, and choosing the Open Read-Only option on the drop-down menu:

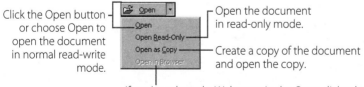

Click the Open button or choose Open to open the document in normal read-write mode.

Open the document in read-only mode.

Create a copy of the document and open the copy.

If you've selected a Web page in the Open dialog box (a file with the HTM or HTML extension), this command opens the page in your browser rather than in Word.

When you open a document in read-only mode, you can freely make changes to its contents. You can't, however, save the modified document under the same name (that is, you can't overwrite the original document version with the changed version), although you can save a copy of the modified document under a different name by choosing Save As from the File menu.

Merging Tracked Changes

If you have distributed a separate copy of a document to each member of a workgroup, when you receive these copies back, you can merge into the original document all the changes that have been tracked within the document copies. After you do this, the original document will contain all the changes made by the other members of your workgroup; you can then review, accept, or reject each change, as described previously (in the section "Reviewing Changes," page 349).

The following is the procedure for merging changes:

1 Open the original document (the one you want to *receive* the merged changes).

2 Choose Merge Documents from the Tools menu to open the Select File To Merge Into Current Document dialog box, which is similar to the standard Open dialog box.

3 In the Select File To Merge Into Current Document dialog box, select the name of a document that contains tracked changes you want to merge into the original document, and click the Open button. Word will then copy all the changes contained in the selected document into the original document that you opened in step 1.

4 Repeat step 3 for any additional documents that contain tracked changes you want to merge into the original document.

II

Microsoft Word

⭐ **TIP**

Ensure That All Changes Are Tracked in Document Copies

To successfully merge modifications from a copy of a document into the original document, the copy must not contain any untracked changes. To ensure that change tracking is enabled when the copy is edited, before you distribute the copy you might open it and select the Tracked Changes option in the Protect Document dialog box, as discussed previously (at the beginning of the section "Protecting Documents," page 353).

Highlighting Text

You can use the Word Highlight tool to permanently mark blocks of text in a document, in much the same way you would use a yellow marker pen to highlight text on a printed page. The text you mark is highlighted both on the screen and on the printed copy of the document.

To highlight a block of text, do the following:

1 Select the text you want to highlight.

Highlight

2 To highlight using the color currently shown on the Highlight button (which is the most recently selected color), just click the Highlight button on the Formatting toolbar or on the Reviewing toolbar. To highlight using a different color, click the down arrow at the right of this button, and then click the color you want on the palette that Word displays:

You can rapidly highlight several blocks of text as follows:

1 Without selecting text beforehand, click the Highlight button or click a color on the palette, as described previously.

2 Using the mouse, drag over each block of text that you want to highlight.

3 When you have finished highlighting text, click the Highlight button again or press the Escape key to return to normal editing mode.

You can remove highlighting by doing the following:

1 Select the text from which you want to remove the highlighting.

2 Click the down arrow at the right of the Highlight button.

3 Click the None item on the color palette:

TIP

> **Hide Highlighting**
> You can temporarily hide all highlighting on the screen by choosing Options from the Tools menu, opening the View tab, and deselecting the Highlight option in the Show area. You can make highlighting reappear by selecting this same option. Also, highlighting will automatically become visible if you add new highlighting to a document.

You can quickly remove highlighting from several blocks of text using the same technique described for highlighting several blocks. In step 1, simply click the None item on the palette.

 TIP

> If you print a document containing highlighting on a monochrome printer, the highlight color will be converted to a shade of gray. For best results on a monochrome printer, choose a light highlighting color (such as yellow).

Sharing Fonts

One problem that you might encounter when you work in a workgroup is that a co-worker might not be able to view or print a particular font that you have assigned to text in a document. To avoid this problem, you should make sure that your document uses only TrueType fonts. A TrueType font can be viewed or printed when you use almost any computer on which the font is installed. The common TrueType fonts (such as Times New Roman, Arial, and Courier New) are installed on virtually every computer that runs Windows.

 SEE ALSO

For a description of TrueType fonts, see "Using the Font Dialog Box," page 181.

If, however, you use one or more TrueType fonts that might not be installed on a co-worker's computer, you can embed TrueType fonts in your document so that your co-worker can view and print them even on a machine that doesn't have them installed. (Doing so, however, will increase the size of the document.)

To embed TrueType fonts, do the following:

1   Open the document in which you want to embed fonts.

2   Choose Options from the Tools menu, and click the Save tab.

3   Select the Embed TrueType Fonts option. To reduce the size of the document, you can also select the Embed Characters In Use Only option, which causes Word to save font information only for those characters that actually appear in the document.

Online Collaboration

To create Word documents, you can work together with other people on the Internet or on a company intranet by using the commands on the Online Collaboration submenu of the Word Tools menu:

Start an online meeting using Microsoft NetMeeting.

Schedule an online meeting in your Outlook Calendar folder.

Connect to a Web discussion.

Choosing the Web Discussions command lets you connect to a Web discussion server, where you can read and post comments about the document that's currently opened in Word. (The document must be stored somewhere where other users can open it—for example, on the Internet or on an intranet.) You could, for example, save a Word document on a Web server (using the new Web Folders feature of Microsoft Office). And then you could open that document in Word and use the Web Discussions command to conduct an online discussion about the document with other people on the Internet. *For a description of Microsoft NetMeeting, Web discussions, and Web Folders, see "Using Online Collaboration," page 86.*

Writing Long Documents

In this chapter, you'll learn how to organize, footnote, index, and add tables of contents to your Microsoft Word documents. Although these techniques are especially useful for developing long or complex documents, such as books, manuals, and academic papers, you can use them when writing any type of document.

Using Outline View

Outline view can be a great help while you're planning or organizing a document, and even while you're entering the bulk of the document text. The following are among the important features and advantages of Outline view:

- The outline headings in the document—and the text that follows them—are indented by various amounts, so that you can immediately see the hierarchical structure of your document.

- You can control the level of detail that is visible in the outline. For example, you can hide all body text and view only the headings.

- You can quickly move an individual paragraph, or an entire heading together with all text and subheadings that follow it.

- You can usually see more text on the screen in Outline view than in other views, because all text is single spaced, regardless of the paragraph formatting.

 NOTE

In Outline view, paragraph formatting isn't displayed and you can't open the Paragraph dialog box to apply paragraph formatting. (You can control whether character formatting is displayed or not, as explained later.) Therefore, to modify the formatting of your paragraphs, you should switch out of Outline view.

Switching to Outline View

Outline View

To switch to Outline view, choose Outline from the View menu, or click the Outline View button on the horizontal scroll bar. Word will display the document as an outline, and it will show the Outlining toolbar, as illustrated in Figure 12-1. In Outline view, the term *heading* refers to any paragraph that has been assigned one of the built-in heading styles: Heading 1 through Heading 9. A heading assigned the Heading 1 style is at the highest level and is not indented. A heading assigned Heading 2 is at a lower level and is indented a small amount when displayed in Outline view. A heading assigned Heading 3 is at an even lower level and is indented more, and so on. The term *body text* refers to all paragraphs visible in Outline view that have not been assigned a heading style.

FIGURE 12-1.
A Word document
in Outline view.

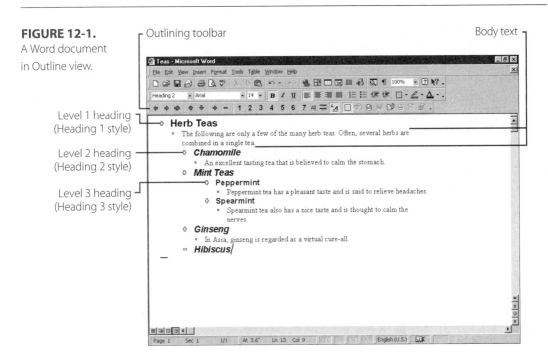

Level 1 heading
(Heading 1 style)

Level 2 heading
(Heading 2 style)

Level 3 heading
(Heading 3 style)

ON THE WEB

The Teas.doc Word document, used in the examples in this section, is on the Running Office 2000 Reader's Corner page. For information about connecting to this Web site, read the Introduction.

NOTE

Switching to Outline view doesn't change your document. It merely displays the document in a different way and allows you to work with it differently.

In Outline view, Word displays one of the following symbols in front of each paragraph. The term *subtext* refers to either subheadings or body text that immediately follows a heading.

Symbol	Type of Paragraph
✚	Heading with subtext
☐	Heading without subtext
▫	Body text

If you have already assigned the Heading 1 through Heading 9 styles to your document headings (as recommended in Chapter 6, "Formatting a Word Document"), Word will indent the headings appropriately in

SEE ALSO
For a general description of styles, see "Applying Styles," page 172. For information about modifying styles, see "Modifying Styles," page 198.

Outline view and the document will look like an outline, as shown in Figure 12-1. If, however, you haven't already assigned the built-in heading styles to your heading paragraphs, the document will consist of a simple list of body text paragraphs, as shown in Figure 12-2, and it won't look much like an outline. Don't worry—by using the buttons on the Outlining toolbar, you can easily apply heading styles and convert the document into outline form.

> **NOTE**
>
> Because each level of heading is assigned a different style, it generally has different formatting. Higher-level headings are typically formatted with larger, bold fonts to convey their relative importance; lower-level headings are typically formatted with smaller, nonbold fonts. To quickly change the appearance of a particular level of heading throughout your document, you can modify the corresponding heading style.

FIGURE 12-2.

A document in Outline view containing headings that haven't been assigned the built-in heading styles.

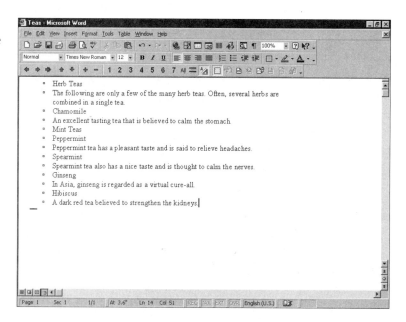

Changing Heading Levels

You can use the first three buttons on the Outlining toolbar to change the level of a heading, to convert a paragraph of body text to a heading, or to convert a heading to a paragraph of body text.

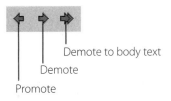

Demote to body text
Demote
Promote

In general, you can perform outlining operations on more than one paragraph (headings or body text) by selecting several paragraphs prior to issuing the command. For simplicity, however, the discussions on outlining use the singular terms *heading* or *paragraph*.

To select a heading together with all its subtext, just click the symbol in front of the heading:

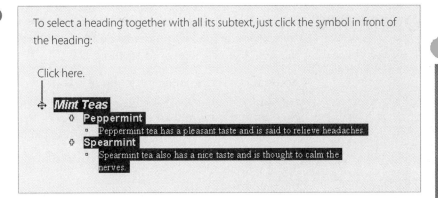

To change the level of a heading, do the following:

1   Place the insertion point in the heading you want to change (or select several headings).

2   To promote the heading to the next higher level, click the Promote button (which points left, to suggest its result of moving the heading further out in the margin for prominence). To demote the heading to the next lower level, click the Demote button.

Alternatively, you can press the Alt+Shift+Left arrow key combination or Shift+Tab to promote the heading, and you can press the Alt+Shift+Right arrow key combination or Tab to demote it.

To enter a tab character while you're in Outline view, press Ctrl+Tab.

Microsoft Word

You can also change the level of a heading as well as any subheadings that follow it by dragging the heading symbol to the left to promote it, or to the right to demote it:

This marker indicates the new level for the top-level heading in the selection. (Releasing the mouse button with the pointer here would promote this heading by one level.)

 SEE ALSO

For information on applying built-in styles, see "Applying Styles," page 172.

When Word changes the level of a heading, it assigns it a new heading style. For example, if you demote a top-level heading, Word changes the style from Heading 1 to Heading 2.

You can convert a paragraph of body text to an outline heading by either promoting it or demoting it, using the methods just described. You can select more than one paragraph of body text, but don't include a heading in the selection. If you promote a paragraph of body text, it's converted into a heading at the same level as the preceding heading, and if you demote it, it's converted into a heading one level lower than the preceding heading.

 TIP

> **Use Styles to Change Outline Levels**
>
> You can also change the level of a heading, convert body text to a heading, or convert a heading to body text by directly assigning the paragraph the appropriate style (Heading 1 through Heading 9 for a heading, or a style such as Normal for body text). Recall from Chapter 6, "Formatting a Word Document," that you can quickly apply the Heading 1, Heading 2, or Heading 3 style by pressing Alt+Ctrl+1, Alt+Ctrl+2, or Alt+Ctrl+3, and you can apply the Normal paragraph style by pressing Ctrl+Shift+N.

To convert a heading to body text, place the insertion point within the heading (or select several headings), and click the Demote To Body Text button, or, if Num Lock is off, press Alt+Shift+5 (5 on the numeric keypad). Word will assign the paragraph the Normal style.

You can also create an outline heading by assigning outline-level formatting to a paragraph that hasn't been assigned a Heading style. To do this, switch out of Outline view, select the paragraph, choose Paragraph from the Format menu, click the Indents And Spacing tab, and choose the desired heading level (Level 1 through Level 9) in the

Outline Level list box. (You can choose the Body Text item in this list to convert an outline heading to outline body text.)

In general, however, it's much better to create outline headings by assigning the Heading 1 through Heading 9 built-in styles, for several reasons:

- In Outline view, you can rapidly and easily assign a Heading style using the Outlining toolbar or the key combinations that were described.

- Assigning a Heading style will apply appropriate formatting for a heading (such as a larger font, bold type, and so on).

- Using the Heading styles will make it easier to maintain consistent formatting of your headings and to quickly modify this formatting throughout the document.

Automatically Number Your Outline Headings

You can apply automatic outline numbering to all the outline headings throughout your document (that is, to all paragraphs assigned the standard heading styles, Heading 1 through Heading 9). To do this, place the insertion point within any heading, choose Bullets And Numbering from the Format menu, click the Outline Numbered tab of the Bullets And Numbering dialog box, select one of the four outline-numbering styles on the bottom row, and click OK. (Notice that the sample on the Outline Numbered tab for each of these styles contains the names of Heading styles.) *For general information on automatic numbering of paragraphs, see "Creating Bulleted and Numbered Lists," page 248.*

Moving Blocks of Text

You can move one or more paragraphs quickly using these two buttons on the Outlining toolbar:

Move Up

Move Down

The paragraphs can be either headings or body text. The following is the procedure:

1 Place the insertion point within the paragraph you want to move (or select several paragraphs).

2 Click the Move Up button to move the paragraph above the previous paragraph, or click the Move Down button to move the paragraph below the following paragraph.

Alternatively, you can press the Alt+Shift+Up arrow key combination to move the paragraph up or press the Alt+Shift+Down arrow key combination to move the paragraph down.

3 Repeat step 2 as necessary to move the paragraph to the desired final position.

You can also quickly move a paragraph by dragging its symbol up or down in the document:

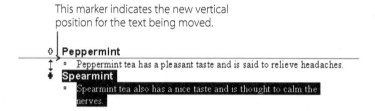

This method always moves a single heading together with all its subtext, because the heading and subtext are selected when you begin dragging the symbol.

Collapsing and Expanding Text

You can use the following buttons on the Outlining toolbar to change the level of detail that is visible in the outline:

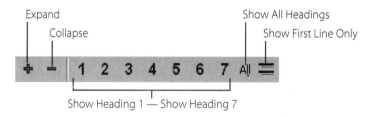

To hide the subtext—subheadings or body text—that follows a heading, perform these steps:

1 Place the insertion point within the heading (or select several headings).

2 Click the Collapse button, or press the minus (–) key on the numeric keypad. Word will hide the lowest level of subtext that is currently visible.

For example, if a level 1 heading is followed by level 2 headings, level 3 headings, and body text, the first time you click the Collapse button, the body text will be hidden. (Body text is considered to be at the lowest level.) The next time you click Collapse, the level 3 headings will be hidden, and the third time you click Collapse, the level 2 headings will be hidden.

3 Repeat step 2 as necessary to hide the desired amount of subtext.

To redisplay collapsed subtext, use this same procedure but in step 2, click the Expand button, or press the plus (+) key on the numeric keypad.

You can also fully collapse a heading (that is, hide all its subtext) by double-clicking its symbol:

Double-click here to hide all subtext.

⊕ *Mint Teas*
   ⊕ **Peppermint**
      ▫ Peppermint tea has a pleasant taste and is said to relieve headaches.
   ⊕ **Spearmint**
      ▫ Spearmint tea also has a nice taste and is thought to calm the nerves.

To fully expand the heading, double-click again. Notice that when a heading contains collapsed subtext, Word marks it with thick underlining:

Double-click here to show all subtext.

⊕ *Mint Teas*

This marker indicates hidden subtext.

You can also change the levels of headings that are displayed throughout the entire document. To display only level 1 headings, click the Show Heading 1 button or press Alt+Shift+1. To display level 1 and level 2 headings, click the Show Heading 2 button or press Alt+Shift+2. In the same way, you can click the Show Heading 3 through Show Heading 7 buttons (or press the Alt+Shift+3 through Alt+Shift+7 key combinations) to include increasingly lower levels of headings. To use the key combinations, you must press the number key on the main part of the keyboard, not on the numeric keypad. Note that all these buttons and key combinations hide body text.

To display all headings, including body text, select the Show All Headings button (click it so it appears pressed), or press Alt+Shift+A or the asterisk (*) on the numeric keypad. To display all headings without body text, deselect the Show All Headings button, or press Alt+Shift+A or the asterisk key again. This will hide body text but leave all headings visible.

You can display only the first line of all paragraphs of body text (together with their headings) by selecting the Show First Line Only button or by pressing the Alt+Shift+L key combination. To show all lines of body text, deselect the Show First Line Only button or press Alt+Shift+L again to disable that option. Word indicates the presence of hidden body text by displaying an ellipsis (…) at the end of the first line of each body text paragraph.

Here are the next two buttons on the Outlining toolbar:

Master Document View

Show Formatting

To display all text in the outline (including headings) using the character formatting currently assigned to the Normal style, click the Show Formatting button to deselect it or press the slash (/) key on the numeric keypad. This doesn't remove character formatting, but merely suppresses its display. To restore the display of all character formatting (fonts, character sizes, font styles, and so on), select the Show Formatting button or press the slash (/) key again.

Selecting the Master Document View button activates Master Document view, which is a special mode of Outline view that allows you to divide a long Word document into separate subdocuments, all of which belong to a single *master document*. The remaining buttons on the Outlining toolbar (those to the right of the Master Document View button) are for working with master documents. (If the Master Document view isn't active, these buttons can be used to divide a document into separate sections.) For information on creating and using master documents, look up the topic "master documents" in the Word online Help.

Browsing Through Outline Headings

Word provides two features that let you quickly scroll to a particular outline heading in a document. These features furnish additional reasons for incorporating outline headings into your documents.

When you drag the scroll box on the vertical scroll bar, Word displays the page number of the current position as well as the text of the preceding outline heading (or at least the first part of the text), as shown in Figure 12-3. (This feature will work only if the Show ScreenTips On Toolbars option is selected. To set this option, choose Customize from the Tools menu, and click the Options tab.)

To locate a particular outline heading, simply drag the scroll box until you see the heading displayed, and then release the mouse button. Note that you don't need to be in Outline view to use this feature.

Document
Map

A second feature that makes it easy to scroll to a particular outline heading is the Document Map, which is displayed in a separate pane in the Word window. (See Figure 12-4.) To display the Document Map, choose Document Map from the View menu or click the Document Map button on the Standard toolbar.

FIGURE 12-3.
The ScreenTip that shows your current document position as you scroll.

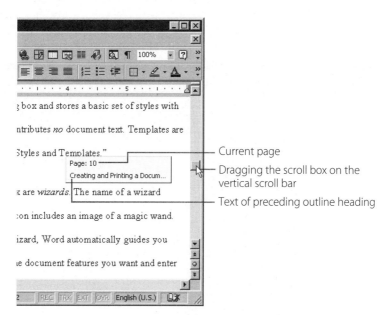

The Document Map lets you see all your outline headings, even if you're not in Outline view. Notice that when you place the mouse pointer over a heading, Word highlights the heading and displays the full heading text:

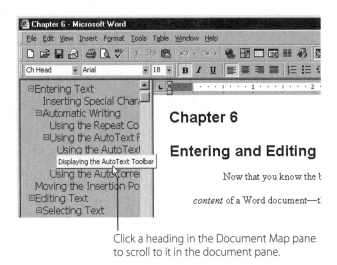

Click a heading in the Document Map pane to scroll to it in the document pane.

To have Word scroll your document to a particular heading, just click that heading within the Document Map. (If not all headings fit in the Document Map, you can use the vertical scroll bar within the Document Map pane to see additional headings.)

FIGURE 12-4.

The Document Map for displaying and scrolling to outline headings in a document.

Document Map scroll bar

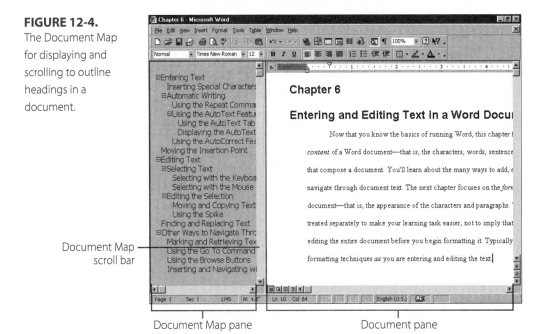

Document Map pane

Document pane

Notice also that if a heading is followed by one or more subheadings, Word displays a square symbol to the left of the heading in the Document Map. You can hide the subheadings in the Document Map by clicking the box:

This symbol means headings are currently visible.

Click here to hide subheadings.

Entering Text
  Inserting Special Chara
  Automatic Writing
    Using the Repeat Cor
    Using the AutoText F
      Using the AutoText
      Displaying the Auto
      Using the AutoCorrec

You can show the subheadings by clicking the box again:

This symbol means subheadings are currently hidden.

Click here to show subheadings.

Entering Text
  Moving the Insertion Po
  Editing Text

If you're in Outline view, hiding or showing headings in the Document Map also hides or shows them in the document pane. In Normal, Web Layout, and Print Layout views, hiding or showing headings in the Document Map doesn't affect the document pane.

? SEE ALSO
To review printing, see "Printing Documents," page 52, and "Previewing and Printing Documents," page 337.

Printing an Outline

When you're in Outline view and print your document, Word prints only the headings and body text that are currently visible. To print the whole document, click the All button on the Outlining toolbar or switch out of Outline view before printing.

★ TIP

Create a Better-Looking Printed Outline

The appearance of a document printed in Outline view is often disappointing. Paragraph formatting doesn't show, lines are always single spaced, and you can't add extra space between paragraphs. Also, the small box symbols that visually separate paragraphs of body text on the screen don't print. To print an attractively formatted outline, consider switching out of Outline view and formatting the text in the document as an outline-numbered list, as explained in "Creating Bulleted and Numbered Lists," page 248.

II

Microsoft Word

Adding Footnotes and Endnotes

Word makes it easy to add footnotes or endnotes to your document. The text for a *footnote* is placed at the bottom of the page that contains the reference mark (or you can choose to place a footnote just beneath the text on the page that contains the reference mark). The text for an *endnote* is placed at the end of the document (or you can choose to place an endnote at the end of the section that contains the reference mark). Figure 12-5 shows a footnote.

FIGURE 12-5.
A footnote in a
Word document.

Footnote reference mark

Common tea is prepared from the leaves of the tea plant[1]. This plant is native to India and grows best in a warm climate with abundant rainfall.

[1] Thea sinensis

Footnote text

To add a footnote or endnote to your document, do the following:

1 Place the insertion point where you want to insert the footnote or endnote reference mark.

2 Choose Footnote from the Insert menu to open the Footnote And Endnote dialog box:

3 Select Footnote to create a footnote, or select Endnote to create an endnote.

4 In the Numbering area, choose the type of reference mark you want to insert, as follows:

- To use an automatically generated number, letter, or other symbol for the reference mark, choose AutoNumber. By default, Word will number footnotes using *1, 2, 3,* and so on; and it will number endnotes using *i, ii, iii,* and so on. (Lowercase roman numerals can be difficult for many readers to comprehend after about *xv,* or 15).

- To use a custom reference mark, choose Custom Mark and type a character, such as * (asterisk), in the Custom Mark box. Rather than typing a custom mark, you can click the Symbol button to select a symbol, such as •, †, ‡, or §. Clicking Symbol opens the Symbol dialog box, which is similar to the Symbol dialog box that you open by choosing Symbol from the Insert menu (as described in "Inserting Special Characters," page 119).

5 To modify the type of numbering the AutoNumber option inserts, or to set other footnote and endnote options, click the Options button to open the Note Options dialog box. (See Figure 12-6.) Note that these options affect all footnotes or endnotes in the document, not just the one you're inserting.

6 Click the OK button in the Footnote And Endnote dialog box.
   Word will insert the reference mark into the body text. Also, in Normal, Web Layout, or Outline view, it will open a separate footnote pane and position the insertion point in this pane, as shown in Figure 12-7, on the following page.

FIGURE 12-6.
The All Footnotes (A) and All Endnotes (B) tabs of the Note Options dialog box.

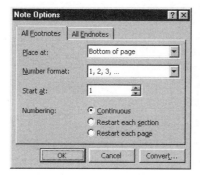
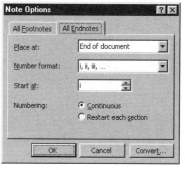

A   B

II

Microsoft Word

FIGURE 12-7.

Entering footnote text
in Normal view.

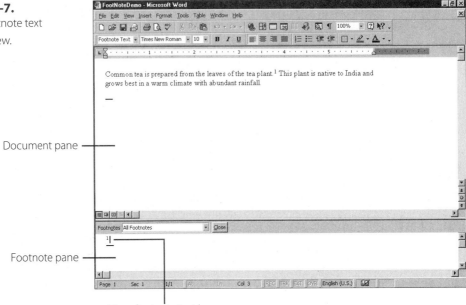

Document pane ——

Footnote pane ——

Type footnote text here.

 **ON THE WEB**

The FootNoteDemo.doc Word document, used in the examples in this section, is on the Running Office 2000 Reader's Corner page.

> In Print Layout view or Print Preview, Word will place the insertion point at the actual position of the footnote or endnote on the page.

7 Type the footnote or endnote text.

8 In Normal, Web Layout, or Outline view, if you want to close the footnote pane when you have finished typing the footnote or endnote text, click the Close button at the top of the pane.

The insertion point will be moved back to the position where you inserted the footnote or endnote reference in the document text. If you want to leave the footnote pane open, you can switch back and forth between that pane and your current position in the document pane by pressing F6.

In Page Layout view or Print Preview, after you finish typing the footnote text, you can move the insertion point back to the position in the document text where you inserted the footnote or endnote reference by pressing Shift+F5 or by using any other navigation method.

TIP

To quickly add a footnote or endnote using the options you previously chose in the Footnote And Endnote dialog box (or using default options if you didn't choose any), place the insertion point where you want the reference mark, and press Alt+Ctrl+F for a footnote or Alt+Ctrl+D for an endnote.

If you later want to view or edit your footnote or endnote text, choose Footnotes from the View menu or simply double-click a footnote or endnote reference mark. In Normal, Web Layout, or Outline view, Word will open the footnote pane. If you have both footnotes and endnotes, in the list box at the top of the footnote pane choose either All Footnotes to view footnotes, or All Endnotes to view endnotes. In Page Layout view or Print Preview, Word will move the insertion point to the footnote or endnote area of the page. You can also view the text of your footnote or endnote by holding the mouse pointer over the reference mark. (This feature works only if the ScreenTips option is turned on. You set this option by choosing Options from the Tools menu and clicking the View tab.)

Thea sinensis

Common tea is prepared from the leaves of the tea plant[1]. This plant is native to India and grows best in a warm climate with abundant rainfall.

After you have added footnotes or endnotes to your document, you can change their position, format, starting number, or other attributes by choosing Footnote from the Insert menu (as if you were going to insert a new footnote or endnote), clicking the Options button in the Footnote And Endnote dialog box, and changing settings in the Note Options dialog box, which was shown in Figure 12-6. Note that you can click the Convert button in this dialog box to convert all footnotes in your document to endnotes, to convert all endnotes to footnotes, or to swap footnotes and endnotes. When you've finished making changes in the Note Options dialog box, click the OK button, and then click the Close button in the Footnote And Endnote dialog box. (Don't click OK here unless you want to insert another footnote or endnote.)

? SEE ALSO

For techniques on moving or copying text, see "Editing The Selection," page 138.

To move or copy a footnote or endnote, move or copy the reference mark to a new document location using any of the editing methods explained in Chapter 5, "Entering and Editing Text in a Word Document." If you chose the AutoNumber option, Word will automatically renumber your reference marks if necessary. If you copy the reference mark, Word will make a copy of the footnote or endnote text.

Microsoft Word

II

> To change the formatting of footnote or endnote reference marks or text throughout your document, you can modify the built-in character styles Footnote Reference or Endnote Reference or the built-in paragraph styles Footnote Text or Endnote Text.

To delete a footnote or endnote, merely select the reference mark and press the Delete key. Word will delete both the reference mark and all the footnote or endnote text.

Creating Indexes and Tables of Contents

You can have Word generate an index or a table of contents for your document. A comprehensive index and an accurate table of contents are important assets for a document, especially a lengthy or technical one.

> **Use a Table of Contents for a Web Page**
> If you're creating a Web-page document, you should use a table of contents rather than an index. The page numbers given in an index are meaningless in a Web page displayed in a browser, because the browser doesn't divide the document into separate pages. However, a table of contents displayed in a browser consists of a list of hyperlinks that the user can click to navigate to different parts of the document, and is therefore quite useful.

> If you have inserted captions using the Caption command on the Insert menu, you can have Word generate a table of figures. Also, you can have it generate a table of authorities for a legal brief. These sorts of tables aren't as common as indexes and tables of contents and aren't discussed in this book. For information, look up the following topics in the Word online Help: "captions," "tables of figures," and "tables of authorities."

Creating an Index

Preparing an index in Word is a two-step process: First, you mark a series of index entries, and then you compile and insert the index based on these entries.

A typical index entry consists of the name of a topic followed by the number of the page on which the topic is discussed:

oolong tea, 1

When you mark an index entry, you specify the topic name, and you tag the location of the topic in the document so that Word can determine the page number when you compile the index. To mark an index entry, do the following:

1   If all or part of the word or phrase that you want to appear in the index entry (such as *oolong tea* in the example above) is contained in the document text to be indexed, select this word or phrase.

> Select the text that you want to appear in the index entry.

> There are three basic types of tea: green, black, and oolong. The leaves for black and oolong teas are first fermented, and are then dried and heated. The leaves for green tea are dried and heated without fermentation.

Otherwise, simply place the insertion point at the beginning of the document text that you want to index.

2   Choose Index And Tables from the Insert menu, and click the Mark Entry button on the Index tab of the Index And Tables dialog box to open the Mark Index Entry dialog box. An alternative way to open this dialog box is to press the Alt+Shift+X key combination.

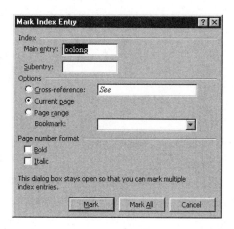

Microsoft Word

3 If you selected text in step 1, it will appear in the Main Entry box; otherwise, the box will be empty. If necessary, edit the contents of this box so that it contains the exact text you want to appear in the index:

4 If you want to create an index subentry, enter the subentry text in the Subentry box.

For example, typing the following into the Main Entry and Subentry boxes

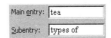

would create the following index entry and subentry:

tea
    types of, 1

5 Make sure the Current Page option is selected on so that the index entry will display the number of the page that contains the indexed topic.

 NOTE

Rather than selecting the Current Page option, you can select the Cross-Reference option or the Page Range option. If you select Cross-Reference, the index entry will display the cross-reference that you type into the box, for example, "*See* herb teas," rather than a page number. If you select Page Range, the index entry will display the range of pages that are marked with the bookmark that you select in the Bookmark list. *Bookmarks are discussed in "Marking and Retrieving Text Using Bookmarks," page 149.*

6 To modify the format of the page number in the index entry, select Bold, Italic, or both.

7 Click the Mark button.

 TIP

If you want to mark as index entries all occurrences of text in your document that exactly match the contents of the Main Entry box, click the Mark All button rather than the Mark button.

8 If you want to mark additional index entries, you can leave the Mark Index Entry dialog box open while you move the insertion point to additional locations in your document. When you have finished marking entries, click Close to remove the dialog box.

NOTE

Word marks an index entry by inserting a block of instructions known as a *field* into the document. The field contains the XE code (for *index entry*), and it is formatted as hidden text. If you can't see it, you can make it appear by clicking the Show/Hide ¶ button on the Standard toolbar.

When you have marked all the index entries, the next step is to compile and insert the index itself. Do this as follows:

1 Place the insertion point at the position in your document where you want to insert the index.

2 Choose Index And Tables from the Insert menu to open the Index And Tables dialog box, and click the Index tab:

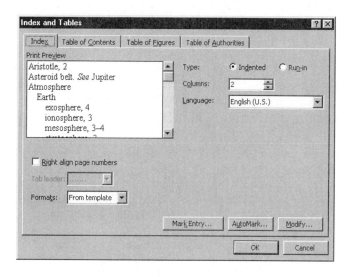

SEE ALSO

For general instructions on changing styles, see "Modifying Styles," page 198. For information on using the Style dialog box, see "Modifying Styles Using the Style Dialog Box," page 201.

3 If you want to modify the appearance of the index, choose options in the dialog box until the model index in the Preview area has the look you want for your index. You can set the type, format, alignment, number of columns, language, and tab leader character for the index.

4 Click the OK button. Word will compile an index and insert it into the document. Word will also add section breaks before and after the index so that it's contained in its own document section.

Microsoft Word

Word creates the index and marks its location by inserting an INDEX field into the document. If you see the field code rather than the actual index, you can make the index appear by placing the insertion point within the field code and pressing Shift+F9. The field code will look something like this:

```
{ INDEX \c "2" \z "1033" }
```

TIP

Customize Your Index Entries

To create custom formatting for your index entries, choose the From Template item in the Formats list. Then click the Modify button to open the Style dialog box, which lets you modify the built-in styles that Word assigns to index entries. (It assigns Index 1 to main entries and Index 2 through Index 9 to subentries.) This dialog box is similar to the Style dialog box that opens when you choose Style from the Format menu, except that it lets you modify only the index entry styles. You can also change the formatting of index headings (that is, the A, B, and C headings, and so on, that precede each index section) by modifying the Index Heading built-in style.

Creating a Table of Contents

You can also use Word to compile and insert a table of contents in your document. A table of contents lists the document headings. When you view a table of contents in any Word view except Web Layout, each entry typically includes the page number of the heading and functions as a hyperlink that you can click to navigate to that heading. When you view a table of contents in Web Layout view or when you view a Web-page document in a browser, each entry consists of only a hyperlink without a page number. (Page numbers would be meaningless in a browser, which doesn't divide a document into separate pages.)

The following is the easiest way to create a table of contents:

1 Make sure that every heading you want to include in the table of contents has been assigned one of the built-in heading styles, Heading 1 through Heading 9. You can assign these styles using Outline view or the methods for applying styles given in "Applying Styles," page 172.

2 Place the insertion point at the position in your document where you want to insert the table of contents.

3 Choose Index And Tables from the Insert menu, and click the Table Of Contents tab:

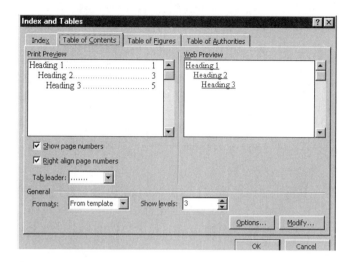

4 If you want to modify the appearance of the table of contents, choose options from the Table Of Contents tab until the model table of contents in the Print Preview or Web Preview area has the look you want.

The Print Preview area shows how the table of contents will appear in any Word view except Web Layout, while the Web Preview area shows how it will look in Web Layout view or when a Web-page document is viewed in a browser. You can choose the table format, alignment of numbers, number of levels, and tab leader character. You can also add or remove page numbers.

★ TIP

Customize Your Table of Contents

To create custom formatting for your table of contents, choose the From Template item in the Formats list box on the Table Of Contents tab. Then click the Modify button to open the Style dialog box, which lets you modify the built-in styles that Word assigns to table of contents entries (TOC 1 through TOC 9). This dialog box is similar to the Style dialog box that opens when you choose Style from the Format menu, except that it lets you modify only the table of contents styles.

II

Microsoft Word

5 Click the OK button.

Word creates a table of contents and marks its location by inserting a TOC field. If you see the field code rather than the table of contents, you can make the table of contents appear by choosing Options from the Tools menu, clicking the View tab, and deselecting the Field Codes option. (If that option was already disabled, you should be able to make the table of contents visible by placing the insertion point within the field code and pressing Shift+F9.) The field code will look something like this:

```
{ TOC \o "1-3" \h \z }
```

CHAPTER 13

Using Word to Automate Mailing

In this chapter, you'll learn two ways that you can use Microsoft Word to automate mailing:

- First, you'll learn how to quickly print a single envelope or mailing label.

- Second, you'll learn how to use Word's mail merge commands to print form letters as well as sets of envelopes or labels.

Printing Individual Envelopes and Labels

 SEE ALSO

For information on using the mail merge facility to print groups of envelopes or labels, see "Printing Sets of Envelopes," page 399, and "Printing Sets of Mailing Labels," page 402.

You can print an individual envelope or label using the Envelopes And Labels command on the Tools menu. This command is especially useful for mailing a letter that you have just finished typing. You can also use the Word mail merge facility, described later in the chapter, to print envelopes or labels for an entire group of delivery addresses.

Printing Individual Envelopes

To print a single envelope, this is what you do:

1 If you have already typed the delivery address into a document (for example, in the heading of a letter), open that document. (This step is optional because you can type the address later.)

2 Choose Envelopes And Labels from the Tools menu, and click the Envelopes tab in the Envelopes And Labels dialog box:

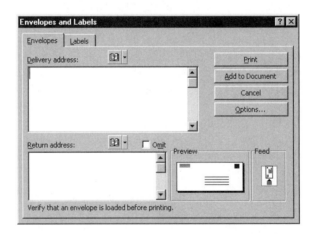

3 Type the delivery address into the Delivery Address box.
   If Word finds an address in the document, this address will already be contained in the Delivery Address box. In this case, you can simply edit the text, if necessary.

4 If you want to print a return address, type it into the Return Address box.
   If you have specified a personal mailing address in Word, this address will automatically appear in the Return Address box. In this case, you can edit the text, if necessary. (To specify a personal mailing address, choose Options from the Tools menu, click the User Information tab, and enter the address into the Mailing Address

box.) Note that if you enter or edit text in the Return Address box of the Envelopes tab, when you click the Print or Add To Document button (in step 6), Word will ask whether you want to save the new address as your default return address. If you click Yes, Word saves the text as your personal mailing address.

If you don't want to print a return address (perhaps you're using preprinted envelopes), you can either delete any text in the Return Address box or just select the Omit option above the box.

⭐ **TIP**

Save Time by Using an Address Book

If you have entered addresses into an address book or your Outlook Contacts folder, you can use the Address Book button at the top of the Delivery Address box or at the top of the Return Address box to select an address from an address book rather than typing one:

 ──── Click here to quickly choose a previously selected address.

Click here to open the Select Name dialog box, where you can select a name and address from an address book.

5   If you need to change any of the envelope printing options, click the Options button on the Envelopes tab to open the Envelope Options dialog box. (See Figure 13-1, on the next page.)

⭐ **TIP**

Vary the Formatting of Your Envelope Text

The Envelope Options tab lets you select the basic formatting of *all* the delivery address or return address text. You can also change the formatting of one or more individual characters within the Delivery Address or Return Address box on the Envelopes tab (overriding the basic formatting). To do this, select the text, and press the shortcut key for applying (or removing) character formatting—for example Ctrl+B, Ctrl+I, or Ctrl+U to apply (or remove) bold, italics, or underlining. You can use any of the first 10 shortcut keys (except Ctrl+Shift+H for hidden text) that are listed in Table 6-7, page 186.

❓ **SEE ALSO**

For information on setting the margins, paper size, and other page setup options for a document section, see "Adjusting the Page Setup," page 306.

6   To complete the envelope, do either of the following:

- To print the envelope immediately, place an envelope in your printer, and click the Print button. You should insert the envelope into the printer so that it has the orientation that is shown in the Feed area in the lower right corner of the Envelopes And Labels dialog box. (You select the orientation on the

II

Microsoft Word

FIGURE 13-1.

The Envelope Options (A) and Printing Options (B) tabs of the Envelope Options dialog box.

Select the envelope size here.

Change the position of the delivery address by entering values here.

Select this option to have Word print a postal bar code on the envelope.

Click this button to change the character formatting for the delivery address.

Click this button to change the character formatting for the return address.

The effects of the options currently selected on this tab are shown here.

Change the position of the return address by entering values here.

Select the envelope feed direction and position here.

Select the paper source here.

If you've changed any settings on this tab, you can click this button to restore Word's default settings.

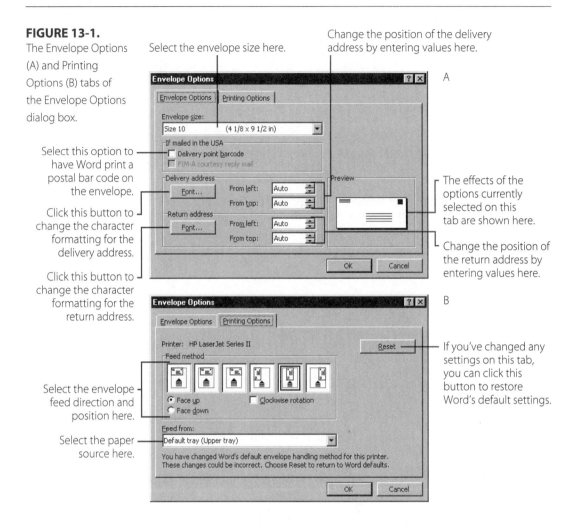

Printing Options tab of the Envelope Options dialog box, as shown in Figure 13-1. You can quickly display this tab by clicking in the Feed area.)

- To add the text for the envelope to the document in the active window, click the Add To Document button. (If you have already added envelope information to the document, this button will be labeled Change Document, and it will replace the former envelope text with the new text.) Word will insert the envelope text into a separate section at the beginning of the document, and it will assign to this section the correct margins, paper size, printing orientation, and paper source for printing the envelope. If necessary, you can edit the envelope text or add text or graphics to it.

Thereafter, the envelope will automatically be printed whenever you print the document. You could use this technique to include the text for both a letter and its envelope within a single document so that you can print both using only one print command.

Printing Individual Labels

You can print a single label, or you can print the same text on every label on a full sheet of labels, by doing the following:

1 If you have already typed the label text into a document (for example, an address in a letter heading), open that document. (This step is optional because you can type the text later.)

2 Choose Envelopes And Labels from the Tools menu, and click the Labels tab in the Envelopes And Labels dialog box:

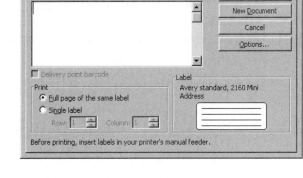
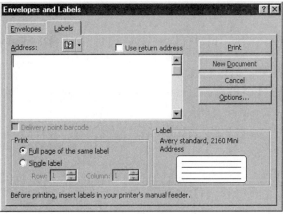

3 Type the label text into the Address box. If Word finds an address in the document, this text will already be contained in the Address box. In this case, you can simply edit the text, if necessary.

Alternatively, you can select the Use Return Address option to have Word copy into the Address box your personal mailing address (the address you set by using the User Information tab of the Options dialog box, as described in the previous section). You could do this to print return address labels for yourself.

Also, if you have entered names into an address book, you can use the Address Book button at the top of the Address box to select an address. For more information, see the tip given under step 4 in the previous section.

Format Your Label Text

You can change the formatting of any block of text in the Address box on the Labels tab. To do this, select the text, and press the shortcut key for applying (or removing) character formatting—for example Ctrl+B, Ctrl+I, or Ctrl+U to apply (or remove) bold, italics, or underlining. You can use any of the first 10 shortcut keys (except Ctrl+Shift+H for hidden text) that are listed in Table 6-7, page 186.

4 To tell Word how many labels to print, do either of the following:

- To print a full page of labels that has the same text on each label, choose the Full Page Of The Same Label option. You might select this option, for example, to prepare a full sheet of return address labels.

- To print a single label, choose Single Label and enter the row and column position on the label sheet of the label you want to print.

5 If you need to change any of the label printing options, click the Options button to open the Label Options dialog box. (See Figure 13-2.)

If your label sheet doesn't match any of the standard labels, you can specify custom label measurements by selecting the closest standard label, clicking the New Label button, and modifying the measurements in the New Custom dialog box. (See Figure 13-3.) You must give your custom label a name, and you can later delete the custom label by selecting its name in the Product Number list of the Label Options dialog box and clicking the Delete button.

FIGURE 13-2.
The Label Options dialog box.

Select the tray or feeder containing the label sheet from this list box.

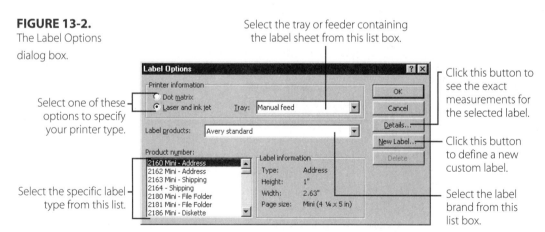

Select one of these options to specify your printer type.

Click this button to see the exact measurements for the selected label.

Click this button to define a new custom label.

Select the specific label type from this list.

Select the label brand from this list box.

FIGURE 13-3.
The dialog box for creating custom label measurements.

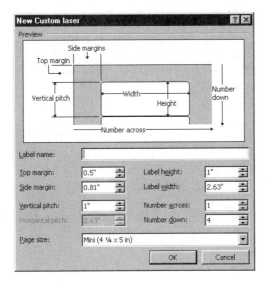

When you click OK in the Label Options dialog box, you'll return to the Labels tab of the Envelopes And Labels dialog box.

> **TIP**
>
> **Insert Postal Bar Codes for Faster Delivery**
> If you have selected a sufficiently large label and if the label text contains a valid postal (ZIP) code, you can select the Delivery Point Barcode option on the Labels tab of the Envelopes And Labels dialog box to have Word print a postal bar code at the top of the label. The bar code is a machine-readable representation of the postal code, and including it might expedite mail delivery.

6 To finish the label, do either of the following:

- To print the label immediately, insert a label sheet into your printer, and click the Print button.

- If you're printing a full page of labels (that is, if you chose the Full Page Of The Same Label option), you can click the New Document button to have Word store the label text in a new document. You can then modify the labels if you want (perhaps adding a graphic logo to each label or applying formatting), and you can print the labels by printing this document. You can save the document so that you can print the same labels again in the future. (In this document, you'll notice that Word has created a table and has inserted each label into a separate table cell.)

Have Word Write Your Letters!

You can have Word automatically insert into a document all the basic elements of a letter (the date line, return and recipient's addresses, salutation, closing, and so on), and format them according to your specifications. To do this, choose Letter Wizard from the Tools menu to open the Letter Wizard dialog box. Then, on the tabs of this dialog box, choose the options you want and supply the required information about the letter sender and recipient. Of course, you will have to type in the text for the body of the letter!

Using Mail Merge for Large Mailings

You'll now learn how to use Word's mail merge feature to print form letters as well as sets of envelopes or mailing labels.

Printing Form Letters

When you print a set of form letters, some text is the same on all the letters (for example, the letterhead, the body of the letter, and the closing), while some text varies from letter to letter (for instance, the recipient's name and address, and the name in the salutation). To print form letters, you create two documents: a *main* document and a *data source* document. The main document contains the text that is the same on all letters as well as instructions for inserting the variable text. The data source document stores the variable text. You then merge these two documents to generate the form letters, as shown in Figure 13-4.

The following are the steps for printing form letters:

1 Open the main document. Either you can create a new document (choose New from the File menu), or you can open a letter that you have already written (choose Open from the File menu).

If you create a new main document, you can get a head start in writing an attractive letter by basing it on one of the letter templates supplied with Word. Choose New from the File menu, and click the Letters & Faxes tab in the New dialog box to view the available templates.

2 Choose Mail Merge from the Tools menu to open the Mail Merge Helper dialog box. (See Figure 13-5.)

FIGURE 13-4.
The mail merge process: merging the data source document with the main document to generate form letters.

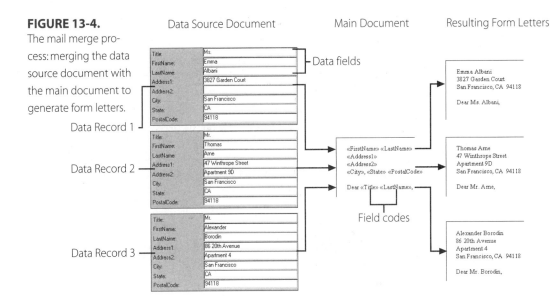

Data Source Document   Main Document   Resulting Form Letters

Data fields

Data Record 1

Data Record 2

Data Record 3

Field codes

FIGURE 13-5.
The Mail Merge Helper dialog box.

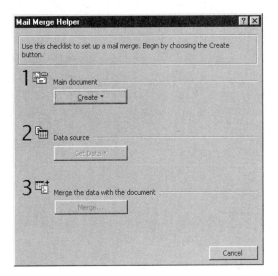

Mail Merge Helper   ? X

Use this checklist to set up a mail merge. Begin by choosing the Create button.

1 Main document
Create ▾

2 Data source
Get Data ▾

3 Merge the data with the document
Merge...

Cancel

3 Click the Create button and from the menu that appears, choose Form Letters:

Create ▾
Form Letters...
Mailing Labels...
Envelopes...
Catalog...
Restore to Normal Word Document...

In the message box that Word next displays, click the Active Window button to use the document you opened in step 1 as the main document. (If you were to click the New Main Document button instead, Word would create another new document, based on the Normal template, to use as the main document.)

Before you enter or edit text in the main document, you need to create the data source document to hold the text that will vary in each document. You'll come back to the main document later.

4 To create the data source document, click the Get Data button and from the menu that appears, choose Create Data Source:

Word will open the Create Data Source dialog box, which allows you to assign a name to each data field of variable data:

Type a name into the Field Name box, and then click the Add Field Name button.

Click to delete the field that is currently selected in the Field Names In Header Row list.

Use these buttons to change the position of the selected field in the list.

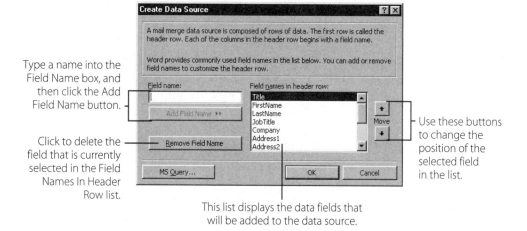

This list displays the data fields that will be added to the data source.

The text in the data source document is divided into *data records*. Each data record contains all the variable text to be used for one form letter (for example, the letter to Emma Albani). Each data record is divided into *data fields*; a data field contains a single item of information (for example, the addressee's last name or the street address). (See Figure 13-4, page 393.) You must assign a name to each data field so that you can reference it in the main document. Initially, the Create Data Source box contains a set of names for the typical data fields you might use in a letter—for example, FirstName for the addressee's first name, Address1 for the first line of the address, and so on.

Note that the instructions in the Create Data Source dialog box refer to a record as a row. That's because in the data source file, each record is stored in a separate row of a Word table. (The first row of this table, called the *header row*, contains the names of the data fields.)

⭐ TIP

Save Time by Using Your Existing Data

Rather than creating a new data source document, you can click the Get Data button, and choose Open Data Source to open a data source document that you created previously. Also, if you have entered names and addresses into an Outlook Address Book, a Personal Address Book, or a Schedule+ Contacts list, you can choose Use Address Book and then select a particular address source to use the data that it stores, rather than manually entering records.

5 Use the Create Data Source dialog box to remove any data fields you don't need and to add any new data fields that you need.

(If you add a new data field, you won't be able to embed space or punctuation characters in the name; for example, you'd have to type *PetsName* rather than *Pet's Name*.) You can also use the Move buttons to change the order of the data fields. The data field order affects the order in which the fields are displayed in the Data Form dialog box (described later); it doesn't affect the order in which they appear on the printed letters.

6 When you're done defining the data field names, click OK in the Create Data Source dialog box, enter a name and specify a location for the data source document in the Save As dialog box, and click the Save button. Word will then display the following message box:

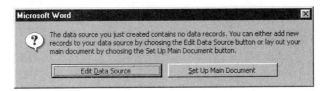

Microsoft Word

7 Click the Edit Data Source button so that you can add the variable text to the data source document. (Clicking Edit Main Document would let you add text and merge information to the main document; you won't do this until later.)

Word will now open the Data Form dialog box:

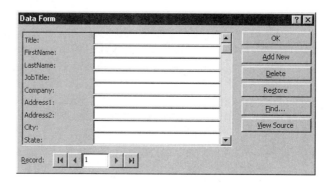

Notice that this dialog box displays a box for each data field that you defined in step 5.

8 Enter text into the data fields for the first data record. When you're done with the first data record, click the Add New button to define the second data record. Repeat this process to define all the data records, one for each person or company to whom you want to write a letter. When you have entered text into the last data record, click the OK button rather than clicking Add New. Word will return you to the main document that you opened in step 1.

 NOTE

If you click the View Source button in the Data Form dialog box, Word will open the data source document, which will contain the data that you have entered using the Data Form dialog box. If you do this, you'll notice that the data source document stores the data in a Word table. The first row of the table, called the *header row*, contains the names of the data fields, and each of the following rows contains the text for a single data record, one data field per cell. If you want, you can add or modify the text directly in this table. (Word will display the Database toolbar, which can help you work with the data source document.) But in general, it's easier to use the Data Form dialog box to enter, modify, or delete data records.

9 Enter the letter text into the main document.

Because this document has been designated as a main mail merge document, when it is open, Word will display the Mail Merge toolbar:

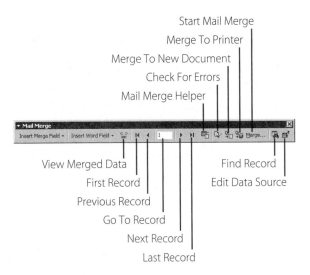

(If the Mail Merge toolbar isn't visible, point to Toolbars on the View menu, and choose Mail Merge on the submenu.) To add a data field from the data source document, click the Insert Merge Field button on this toolbar, and choose the name of the data field from the menu that drops down. For example, to add the addressee's first name to the letter salutation, click Insert Merge Field, and choose FirstName. Word will insert a code for this data field, known as a *merge field*. You can recognize a merge field by the chevrons («, ») that surround it:

«FirstName»

When you print the merge letters, the merge field on each letter will be replaced with the text from the data field in the corresponding merge record of the data source document. Note that the text will be formatted with the same character formatting that is assigned to the merge field. Therefore, to modify the formatting of the merged text, just select the merge field in the main document, and assign the desired character formatting (such as bold or italic). Figure 13-6, on the next page, shows the beginning of a letter containing merge fields as well as ordinary text.

FIGURE 13-6.
The beginning of a
main mail merge
document.

«FirstName» «LastName»
«Address1»
«Address2»
«City», «State» «PostalCode»

Dear «Title» «LastName»,

TIP

Preview Your Form Letters and Check Data Record Text
You can preview each form letter by clicking the View Merged Data button on
the Mail Merge toolbar. (The button should appear pressed in.) Word will
replace each merge code with the actual text from the first data record, just as it
will do when it prints the first form letter. To view the text from another data
record, click the Next Record or Previous Record button, or type a specific record
number into the Go To Record box, and press Enter. You can also click the Find
Record button to display a record that contains specified text. To view the
merge codes again, click the View Merged Data button again.

CAUTION

When you close the
main mail merge doc-
ument, Word will ask
whether you want to
save the data source
document. Be sure to
click the Yes button to
save your data.

10 To generate the form letters, click the Start Mail Merge button on the
Mail Merge toolbar to open the Merge dialog box. (See Figure 13-7.)
Choose the options you want, and then click the Merge button.

If you chose Printer in the Merge To list of the Merge dialog
box, Word will immediately print the merged letters (one letter for
each record that you defined in step 8). If you chose New Document in the Merge To list, Word will insert all the form letters into
a single new document. You can then view or edit the form letters within this document, and you can print the form letters by
printing the document. (It's a good idea to choose New Document before you print a form letter for the first time, to make sure
the results are correct.)

You can use the Merge dialog box to select specific records to
merge, either by entering a range of records or by clicking the
Query Options button and defining query or sort options. For
more information about query options, look up the topic "queries,
mail merge" in the Word online Help.

If you want to merge all data records without changing any
of the merge options, you can click either the Merge To New
Document button or the Merge To Printer button on the Mail
Merge toolbar.

SEE ALSO

For information on
choosing a template
for a new document,
see "Creating and
Printing a Document
from Start to Finish,"
page 105. For a
description of Word
tables, see "Using
Tables," page 229.

If you want to print the same set of form letters later, simply reopen the
main mail merge document, and begin with step 10. If you need to

FIGURE 13-7.
The Merge dialog box.

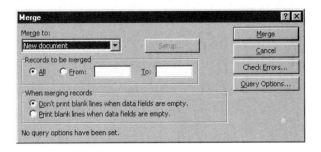

update the merge data before you print the letters, click the Edit Data Source button on the Mail Merge toolbar (shown in step 9, above), and add, delete, or edit records as necessary in the Data Form dialog box. (See steps 7 and 8.)

Printing Sets of Envelopes

You can also use Word's mail merge facility to print a set of envelopes. For example, if you have used mail merge to print form letters, you can also use it to print the envelopes for mailing the letters.

The following are the steps. (Many of these steps are the same as those for creating form letters. For more detail on these steps, see the previous section, "Printing Form Letters.")

1 Open a new document, and choose Mail Merge from the Tools menu to display the Mail Merge Helper dialog box (shown in Figure 13-5, page 393).

2 Click the Create button, and choose Envelopes from the menu that appears.

3 In the message box, click the Active Window button to use the document you opened in step 1 as the main document for the envelopes.

4 In the Mail Merge Helper dialog box, click the Get Data button, and then do one of the following:

   • To use a data source document that you have already created (for example, when you created form letters), choose Open Data Source, select the name of the document in the Open Data Source dialog box, and click the Open button. In the message box, click the Set Up Main Document button. Word will then open the Envelope Options dialog box.

II

Microsoft Word

- To create a new data source document, choose Create Data Source. In the Create Data Source dialog box, define names for the required data fields, and click OK. In the Save As dialog box, enter a name for the data source document, click the Save button, and in the message box that Word displays, click the Edit Data Source button. Enter all the data records into the Data Form dialog box, and click OK. For more information on this procedure, see steps 4 through 8 in the previous section, "Printing Form Letters." Word will return you to the main document you opened in step 1. You should now click the Mail Merge Helper button on the Mail Merge toolbar, and in the Mail Merge Helper dialog box, click the Setup button in the Main Document area. Word will then open the Envelope Options dialog box.

Mail Merge
Helper

- If you have entered names and addresses into an Outlook Address Book, a Personal Address Book, or a Schedule+ Contacts list, you can choose Use Address Book to use the addresses that it contains as your data source. In the Use Address Book dialog box, choose the particular address book you want to use, and click OK. Then, in the message box, click the Set Up Main Document button to have Word open the Envelope Options dialog box.

5 In the Envelope Options dialog box (see Figure 13-1, page 388), make any required adjustments to the envelope or printing options. When you click OK, Word will display the Envelope Address dialog box.

6 Enter the delivery address into the Sample Envelope Address box in the Envelope Address dialog box. To insert a merge field, click the Insert Merge Field button, and choose the name of the merge field from the menu that appears. (For more information on merge fields, see step 9 in the previous section.) In addition to the merge fields, you'll probably need to add spaces, commas, or other characters. Figure 13-8 shows a completed address. When you're done, click OK; Word will return you to the Mail Merge Helper dialog box.

 TIP

You can have Word print a postal bar code on the envelope by clicking the Insert Postal Bar Code button in the Envelope Address dialog box and specifying the data fields that contain the postal (ZIP) code and the street address.

FIGURE 13-8.

The Envelope Address dialog box, after the merge fields and text for an address have been entered.

7 In the Mail Merge Helper dialog box, click the Edit button in the Main Document area, and choose the name of the document you created in step 1 from the menu that appears.

   Word will now display the main document containing the merge fields for your envelope. Notice that Word inserts the merge fields as you arranged them in the Envelope Address dialog box. Also, it inserts your personal mailing address in the return address position (if you have defined one), and it modifies the page setup (the margins, paper size, paper source, and so on) for printing envelopes. (Recall that you define a personal address by choosing Options from the Tools menu, clicking the User Information tab, and entering the address into the Mailing Address box.)

8 If necessary, edit the return or delivery address in the main document. For example, if you're using preprinted envelopes, you'll need to delete the return address. You can use the Mail Merge toolbar as described previously. (See step 9 in "Printing Form Letters," page 396) Figure 13-9, on the next page, shows a completed main mail merge document for printing envelopes.

Start
Mail Merge

9 To generate the envelopes, click the Start Mail Merge button on the Mail Merge toolbar to open the Merge dialog box. (See Figure 13-7, page 399.) Choose the options you want, and then click the Merge button. If you want to merge all data records without changing any of the merge options, you can simply click either the Merge To New Document button or the Merge To Printer button on the Mail Merge toolbar.

FIGURE 13-9.
A main mail merge document for envelopes, ready to print.

Printing Sets of Mailing Labels

Printing sets of labels using Word's mail merge feature is similar to printing sets of envelopes. You can print mailing labels (perhaps to mail a set of form letters you have printed), or you can print other types of labels, such as name tags or disk labels.

> Although you can also use the Envelopes And Labels command (discussed earlier in the chapter in the section "Printing Individual Labels," page 389) to print entire sheets of labels, all labels will be the same. In contrast, when you use the Mail Merge command, each label can be different.

The following are the steps. (Many of these steps are the same as those for creating form letters. For more detail on these steps, see the earlier section "Printing Form Letters," page 392.)

1 Open a new document, and choose Mail Merge from the Tools menu to display the Mail Merge Helper dialog box. (See Figure 13-5, page 393.)

2 Click the Create button, and choose Mailing Labels from the menu that appears.

3 In the message box, click the Active Window button to use the document that you opened in step 1 as the main document for the labels.

4 In the Mail Merge Helper dialog box, click the Get Data button, and then do one of the following:

- To use a data source document that you have already created (for example, when you created form letters), choose Open Data Source, select the name of the document in the Open Data Source dialog box, and click the Open button. In the message box, click the Set Up Main Document button; Word will then open the Label Options dialog box.

- To create a new data source document, choose Create Data Source. In the Create Data Source dialog box, define names for the required data fields, and click OK. In the Save As dialog box, enter a name for the data source document, click the Save button, and in the message box that Word displays, click the Edit Data Source button. Enter all the data records into the Data Form dialog box, and click OK. For more information on this procedure, see steps 4 through 8 in the earlier section "Printing Form Letters," page 392. Word will return you to the main document you opened in step 1. You should now click the Mail Merge Helper button on the Mail Merge toolbar, and in the Mail Merge Helper dialog box, click the Setup button in the Main Document area. Word will then open the Label Options dialog box.

Mail Merge
Helper

- If you have entered names and addresses into an Outlook Address Book, a Personal Address Book, or a Schedule+ Contacts list, you can choose Use Address Book to use the addresses that it contains as your data source. In the Use Address Book dialog box, choose the particular address book you want to use, and click OK. Then, in the message box, click the Set Up Main Document button to have Word open the Label Options dialog box.

5 In the Label Options dialog box (see Figure 13-2, page 390), make any required adjustments to the way that Word prints the labels as described in step 5 of "Printing Individual Labels," page 390. When you click OK, Word will display the Create Labels dialog box.

II

Microsoft Word

6 Enter the delivery address or other label text into the Sample Label box in the Create Labels dialog box. To insert a merge field, click the Insert Merge Field button, and choose the name of the merge field from the menu that appears. (For more information on merge fields, see step 9 in the section "Printing Form Letters," page 396.) In addition to the merge fields, you'll probably need to add spaces, commas, or other characters. When you're done, click OK. Word will return you to the Mail Merge Helper dialog box.

> You can have Word print a postal bar code at the top of the label by clicking the Insert Postal Bar Code button in the Create Labels dialog box and specifying the data fields that contain the postal (ZIP) code and the street address.

7 In the Mail Merge Helper dialog box, generate the labels by clicking the Merge button (in the Merge The Data With The Document area) to open the Merge dialog box. (See Figure 13-7, page 399.) Choose the options you want, and then click the Merge button.

Automating Word Using Macros

You can automate simple or complex Microsoft Word tasks by creating macros. A macro stores a sequence of Word actions and allows you to perform these actions by issuing a single command. By recording macros, you can save time and make Word easier to use. When you create a macro, you essentially add a new command to Word.

You might find yourself frequently performing a Word task that requires a series of steps. For example, you might often need to save the current position of the insertion point so that you can later return to it. Doing so, however, requires that you choose Bookmark from the Insert menu, type a bookmark name, and click the Add button. You can make such a task much easier by recording a macro. When you record a macro, you store a series of Word commands. You can later perform all these commands by simply running the macro. You can run a macro using the Macros dialog box, or, if you make the proper assignment, you can run it by choosing a menu command, clicking a toolbar button, or pressing a shortcut key.

Recording Macros

To record a macro, follow this procedure:

1 Point to Macro on the Tools menu, and then choose Record New Macro from the submenu, or just double-click the REC indicator on the Word status bar:

Double-click here —
to record a macro.

Word will open the Record Macro dialog box, which is shown in Figure 14-1.

FIGURE 14-1.

The Record Macro dialog box.

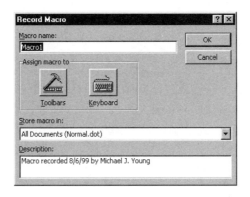

2 You can now perform one or more of the following optional steps:

- Type a name for the macro into the Macro Name box. Word initially assigns it a default name such as Macro1. You might want to enter a descriptive name that indicates the purpose of the macro. (Doing so will make it easier to identify the macro if you need to modify it or perform one of the other operations described in the following sections.)

- Type a description for the macro into the Description box. The default description indicates merely the author of the macro and the date it was recorded. You might want to provide a more detailed description. (The description is displayed when you select the macro in the Macros dialog box, described in the next section; an accurate description will help ensure that you select the correct macro.)

- To assign the macro to a toolbar button or a menu command, click the Toolbars button. To assign the macro to a shortcut key, click the Keyboard button. In either case, follow the instructions in the dialog box that Word displays. *For more information, see the sections "Customizing Toolbars," page 44, and "Customizing Menus," page 50, as well as the sidebar "Defining Shortcut Keys," page 206.* Assigning the macro to one of these elements makes it considerably easier to run the macro. If you don't assign the macro to one of these elements, don't worry; you can still run it using the Macros dialog box, as discussed in the section "Running Macros," page 409, or you can make an assignment later.

- By default, the new macro will be stored in the Normal template so that it will be available when you're working on any document. If the template attached to the current document isn't Normal, you can select the name of the document template in the Store Macro In list; doing so will make the macro available only when you work on a document based on this same template. Or, you can select the name of the current document in the Store Macro In list to make the macro available only when you work on that particular document.

3 Click the OK button to begin recording the macro. While a macro is being recorded, Word does the following:

- It displays a cassette symbol next to the mouse pointer:

- It displays the REC indicator in dark letters.

- It displays the Stop Recording toolbar:

Stop Recording ——————— Pause Recording

For general information on templates, see "Modifying and Creating Document Templates," page 214. For a description of editing methods, see "Editing Text," page 132.

4 Perform all the actions that you want to record in the macro.

Because the macro recorder doesn't record mouse movements within a document window, it won't let you use the mouse to select text or move the insertion point. You'll need to use other editing methods. *For more information, see Chapter 5, "Entering and Editing Text in a Word Document."*

If you want to temporarily stop recording your actions before the macro is finished, click the Pause Recording button on the Stop Recording toolbar. To resume recording, click this button again.

5 When you're finished recording commands, click the Stop Recording button on the Stop Recording toolbar or double-click the REC indicator.

The Stop Recording toolbar will be removed, your macro will be saved, and the REC indicator will again be displayed in faded letters.

Managing Macros

You can change a macro description, delete a macro, or change the contents of a macro by doing the following:

1 Point to Macro on the Tools menu, and then choose Macros from the submenu, or simply press Alt+F8. Word will open the Macros dialog box. (See Figure 14-2.)

2 Select the macro in the Macro Name list.

If the macro doesn't appear in the Macro Name list, make sure that the All Active Templates And Documents option is selected in the Macros In list box. When you select this option, Word lists all macros available to the current document.

FIGURE 14-2.
The Macros dialog box.

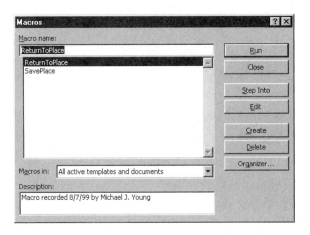

3 Perform one or more of the following actions:

- To modify the macro description, change the text in the Description box.

- To delete the macro, click the Delete button.

- To make changes to the macro itself, click the Edit button. Word will run the Microsoft Visual Basic program, which will display a description of the macro in the Visual Basic for Applications (VBA) programming language. Using the Visual Basic program, you can modify macros that you have recorded, or you can write complex macros that perform tasks that can't be recorded. For information on editing or creating macros using Visual Basic for Applications, use the Help menu in the Visual Basic program. Note that you can also run Visual Basic by pointing to Macro on the Tools menu and choosing Visual Basic Editor from the submenu, or by simply pressing Alt+F11.

⭐ TIP

You can click the Organizer button in the Macros dialog box to open the Organizer dialog box, which allows you to delete, rename, and copy groups of macros known as *macro project items* or *modules. For more information on the Organizer, see "Modifying Templates," page 217.*

Running Macros

If you assign a macro to a toolbar, a menu, or a shortcut key, you can quickly run the macro by clicking the toolbar button, choosing the menu command, or pressing the shortcut key combination. You can assign a macro to one of these elements in one of the following two ways:

- As described earlier in the chapter, when you record the macro you can assign it to a toolbar button or menu command by clicking the Toolbars button, or you can assign it to a shortcut key by clicking the Keyboard button. Both of these buttons are in the Record Macro dialog box, shown in Figure 14-1, page 406.

- You can make an assignment after the macro has been recorded by choosing Customize from the Tools menu.

Both approaches are based on the techniques that are discussed in the sections "Customizing Toolbars," page 44, and Customizing Menus," page 50, as well as the sidebar "Defining Shortcut Keys," page 206.

In addition to running macros you have recorded yourself, you can run macros that other people have recorded or written and that have been stored in a document, template, or Word add-in you've copied or downloaded to your computer. Running a macro that is not obtained from a trusted source, however, or even just opening a document, template, or Word add-in that contains such a macro, can infect your computer with a macro virus. Fortunately, Word offers various levels of protection against macro viruses. For information on this topic, be sure to read "Protecting Yourself Against Rogue Macros," page 658.

You can run any macro—even if you haven't assigned it to a toolbar, menu, or shortcut key—by doing the following:

1 Point to Macro on the Tools menu, and then choose Macros from the submenu to open the Macros dialog box. (See Figure 14-2 on page 408.)

2 In the Macros In list box, choose either the All Active Templates And Documents item or the name of the specific template or document that stores the macro.

3 Select the macro in the Macro Name list. The selected macro's description, if any, will appear in the Description box.

4 Click the Run button.

You can also use the Macros dialog box to run any built-in Word command. For example, you might want to run a command that's not currently assigned to a menu, toolbar button, or shortcut key (such as the useful FileSaveAll command that saves all open documents, macros, and AutoText entries). To do this, choose the Word Commands item in the Macros In list, select the command in the Macro Name list, and click Run.

Macro Examples

This section provides several examples of macros to give you a general idea of the types of Word tasks that you can easily automate.

The first example consists of a pair of macros. One macro, named SavePlace, lets you save the insertion point's current position (or the current selection) by pressing Ctrl+Shift+S. The second macro, named ReturnToPlace, lets you later return the insertion point to the saved position (or restore the saved selection) by pressing Ctrl+Shift+R.

You can define the SavePlace macro this way:

1 Begin recording the macro by double-clicking the REC indicator on the status bar and typing the macro name *SavePlace* into the Record Macro dialog box. (See Figure 14-1 on page 406). To save the macro where it will be available to all documents you work on, make sure that All Documents (Normal.dot) is selected in the Store Macro In list box.

2 To define the shortcut key combination, click the Keyboard button in the Record Macro dialog box to open the Customize Keyboard dialog box. Make sure the insertion point is in the Press New Shortcut Key text box, and press the Ctrl+Shift+S key combination. Click Assign, and then click Close. (By doing this, you will be replacing a default shortcut key combination for opening the Style dialog box or activating the Style list box on the Formatting toolbar.) This returns you to your document, ready to record your macro.

? SEE ALSO

For information about bookmarks, see "Marking and Retrieving Text Using Bookmarks," page 149.

3 Choose Bookmark from the Insert menu to open the Bookmark dialog box.

4 Type the bookmark name *MarkedLocation* into the Bookmark Name text box, and click the Add button.

5 Stop recording the macro by clicking the Stop Recording button on the Stop Recording toolbar (which is displayed automatically when you start recording a macro).

You can define the ReturnToPlace macro as follows:

1 Begin recording the macro by double-clicking the REC indicator on the status bar and typing the macro name *ReturnToPlace*. Make sure that All Documents (Normal.dot) is selected in the Store Macro In list box.

2 To define the shortcut key, click the Keyboard button, and in the Customize Keyboard dialog box, press the Ctrl+Shift+R key combination, click Assign, and then click Close.

3 Choose Bookmark from the Insert menu.

4 Select the bookmark name MarkedLocation in the Bookmark Name box, click the Go To button, and click the Close button.

5 Stop recording the macro by clicking the Stop Recording button on the Stop Recording toolbar.

II

Microsoft Word

You can now test these macros as follows: Place the insertion point anywhere in a document (or select a block of text), and then press Ctrl+Shift+S. This will save your position (or selection). Then move the insertion point anywhere else within the same document, and perform any editing or formatting actions you want. When you're ready to go back to your original location in the document, press Ctrl+Shift+R; Word will immediately move the insertion point back to its original position (or restore the original selection).

The following are several additional examples of macros that you might record:

- Record a pair of macros to turn the Wrap To Window option on or off. This option breaks each line at the right edge of the window, rather than at the position where it will be broken on the printed page. You might want to turn this option on while you're editing in Normal view so that the window contains the maximum amount of text, but then quickly turn it off to view the actual positions of line breaks on the printed copy. To create the first macro, start recording, and then choose Options from the Tools menu, click the View tab, and select the Wrap To Window option (in the Outline And Normal Options area). To record the second macro, perform these same steps but deselect the option.

- Record a pair of macros to switch between the blue window background and the white window background. You might want to enable the blue background to prevent eyestrain, but then switch to the white background to view items that are hard to see with a blue background (for example, dark lines drawn using Word's Drawing toolbar). To create the first macro, start recording, choose Options from the Tools menu, click the General tab, and select the Blue Background, White Text option. To record the second macro, perform these same steps but deselect the option.

- Write a macro to prepare a document for printing. Such a macro would be useful if you like to write and edit a document that has one set of formatting attributes, such as single line spacing and a large monospaced font (such as 12-point Courier New), but want to print the document using a different set of formatting attributes, such as double line spacing and a small proportional font (such as 10-point Times New Roman). In recording the macro, perform all actions that are necessary for printing the document, such as assigning different formatting to the document's styles. Run the macro just before printing.

Building a Worksheet

Microsoft Excel 2000 is a general-purpose electronic spreadsheet used to organize, calculate, and analyze business data. The tasks you can perform with Excel range from preparing a simple invoice for your house-painting services or planning a budget for a family vacation, to creating elaborate 3-D charts or managing a complex accounting ledger for a medium-sized business. This section of the book introduces you to Excel and teaches you how to accomplish a variety of useful tasks with the newest version of Microsoft's flagship spreadsheet application. You'll receive training and support for virtually all your Excel needs, from creating a simple worksheet to forecasting expenses and publishing spreadsheets on the Web. Along the way, you'll learn how to use the newest features of Excel and how to customize Excel to work the way you do. We'll also share our favorite Excel productivity tips with you, including several that come directly from the Excel development team.

This introductory chapter gives you a quick tour of the Excel workplace and shows you how to build a simple worksheet from start to finish. A *worksheet* is an Excel document containing rows and columns of information that can be formatted, sorted, analyzed, and charted. Building a worksheet involves starting Excel, entering information, adding formulas, saving your data, and printing. If you want to get fancy, you can even add hyperlinks to your worksheet to access supporting files on your hard disk or the Internet.

415

Starting Excel and Getting Comfortable

? SEE ALSO

In this chapter, we assume that Excel is installed and ready to go on your computer. If Excel displays an error message or notes a problem when you start it, try evaluating and repairing your software with the new Detect And Repair command. See "Fixing Problems Using Detect And Repair," page 24.

Excel is started like most programs in the Office application suite. To start Excel, click the Start button on the taskbar, point to the Programs folder, and then click the Microsoft Excel program icon.

 Microsoft Excel

When Excel first starts, it displays a new, empty workbook (which will be defined shortly) in the application workplace. Figure 15-1 shows the default opening Excel screen, featuring a standard menu bar, toolbars, formula bar, status bar, and blank workbook. The application window has been maximized to display all the elements of the Excel user interface. If your application window doesn't appear maximized when you start it, you can click the Maximize button on the Excel title bar to give you more space to work with.

★ TIP

> **Want to See More on the Screen?**
> The screen illustrations in this book show Office applications running with a screen resolution of 800 x 600, a popular display size used with 17-inch monitors. You can set your screen size to 800 x 600 by clicking the Start button, pointing to Settings, clicking Control Panel, double-clicking the Display icon, clicking the Settings tab, and dragging the slider control in the Screen Area box to 800 By 600 Pixels. Give it a try!

The *menu bar* gives you access to the complete range of commands and settings in the Excel application. For example, to save a file in Excel you would choose Save from the File menu. The *toolbars* provide access to the most common Excel commands and procedures. During installation, Excel is configured to display the Standard toolbar and the Formatting toolbar below the menu bar. To use one of the toolbars, click the button containing a picture of the task you want to complete. For example, to save a file using the toolbar, you would click the button on the Standard toolbar with the picture of a disk on it. (You'll see many of these command buttons on Excel menus.)

Like most Office applications, the Excel application window also contains *sizing buttons* you can use to minimize, maximize, restore, and close windows, plus a *status bar* that shows the state of various keyboard keys, including Num Lock. A special feature of the Excel status bar is the *AutoCalculate box*, which displays the result of the

FIGURE 15-1.

The Microsoft Excel user interface with important elements labeled.

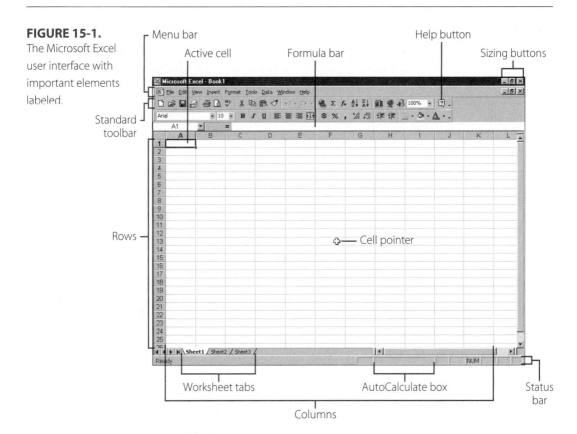

Menu bar

Active cell

Formula bar

Help button

Sizing buttons

Standard toolbar

Rows

Cell pointer

Worksheet tabs

AutoCalculate box

Status bar

Columns

? SEE ALSO

For more information about using menus, dialog boxes, toolbars, and application windows, see Chapter 2, "Learning the Basics: Windows, Toolbars, and Printing." For more details about starting and configuring the Office Assistant, see Chapter 1, "A Quick Tour of Microsoft Office."

selected function (SUM by default) using the highlighted cells in the active worksheet. To get additional help with the Excel interface or with any Excel command, click the Microsoft Excel Help button on the right side of the Standard toolbar. If the animated Office Assistant is not already running, clicking this button will start it.

Excel's application workplace is designed to hold one or more worksheet collections, called *workbooks*. When you first open Excel, the default workbook (Book1) appears on the screen and displays the first worksheet (Sheet1). A worksheet is divided into a grid of rows and columns, as shown in Figure 15-1. (An Excel 2000 worksheet can contain up to 65,536 rows and 256 columns.) A letter is assigned to each column of the worksheet, and a number is assigned to each row. At the intersection of the rows and columns are worksheet *cells*, which are referenced individually by their *cell names*. For example, the cell at the intersection of column A and row 1 is known as cell A1. Cell names are also called *cell addresses*.

III

Microsoft Excel

SEE ALSO

For information about managing the worksheets in a workbook and opening additional workbooks, see Chapter 17, "Organizing Information with Workbooks."

At the bottom of the workbook window are tabs that give you instant access to the remaining worksheets in the workbook. A workbook can contain one or more worksheets, and can also hold chart sheets containing graphic pictures of your worksheet data. Special macros called Visual Basic modules can also be stored in the workbook, but they are not listed among the worksheets. *You'll learn how to create Visual Basic macros, to boost your productivity, in Chapter 25.* Workbooks help you organize your projects and keep related items in one place, and Excel allows you to name your worksheets, add new worksheets, or delete blank or obsolete worksheets. Each workbook window contains scroll bars you can use to move from one worksheet to the next, or from place to place in the active worksheet.

Navigating a Worksheet

In a typical Excel worksheet, information is stored in dozens or even hundreds of cells. To place information in cells that can be used in calculations and that is both visually pleasing and instantly comprehensible, you need to organize your cells carefully. Accordingly, you need to be comfortable with several methods for moving around in, or *navigating*, a worksheet.

To move the active cell from one location to another, you can press the arrow keys (the Up, Down, Left, and Right arrow keys) or click the cell you want to activate with the mouse. This is called *selecting* or *highlighting* a cell. (You can see the name of the selected cell by looking in the Name box.) When you first move the mouse pointer onto the worksheet, it changes its shape to the *cell pointer*, as shown in Figure 15-2. You can use the cell pointer to select individual cells or ranges of cells, as you'll learn later in the chapter.

To view part of a worksheet that isn't currently visible in the workbook window, you can click the vertical or horizontal scroll bars. Each time you click a scroll arrow at the top or bottom of the vertical scroll bar, the active worksheet scrolls vertically one row. Each time you click a scroll arrow at the left or right end of the horizontal scroll bar, the active worksheet scrolls horizontally one column. Note that when you scroll with the scroll bars, you change only your view of the worksheet—scrolling moves the screen but does not change the active cell. Your relative position in the worksheet is identified by the scroll boxes in each scroll bar. (These boxes change size as your worksheet changes

FIGURE 15-2.
Use the cell pointer to select a cell in the worksheet, or use the scroll bars to move to cells not currently visible.

Active cell

Cell pointer

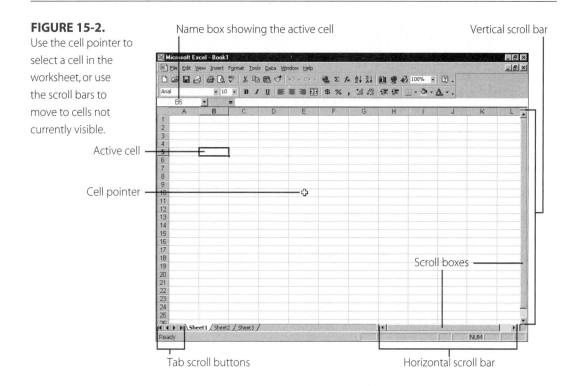

Name box showing the active cell

Vertical scroll bar

Scroll boxes

Tab scroll buttons

Horizontal scroll bar

size, representing the relative portion of the entire worksheet that is currently visible.)

To move among the worksheets in your workbook, you can click the worksheet tabs or use the tab scroll buttons to move among many worksheet tabs.

TIP

To scroll down one page, click the scroll bar below the scroll box. You can also drag the scroll box to move greater distances. As you drag the scroll box, Excel displays the new top row (or leftmost column) in a pop-up window to help you find your place.

Using the Keyboard

Several key combinations let you move quickly throughout your worksheet. Unlike scroll bar movements, these key combinations also highlight a new, active cell. Table 15-1 lists the most useful keyboard navigation keys in a worksheet.

III

Microsoft Excel

Jumping to a Specific Cell with the Go To Command

To highlight a specific cell in the active worksheet by name, you can choose Go To from the Edit menu or press F5. When you choose the Go To command, Excel displays the Go To dialog box, as shown in Figure 15-3. You can jump to a specific cell by typing the name of the cell in the Reference text box and clicking OK. (You can also double-click the name of the cell if it appears in the list box.)

If you would like to highlight a range of cells based on a special attribute, such as all the cells containing formulas or comments, click the Special button and specify the cell contents you're interested in. You can also move to a specific cell by clicking the Name box located to the left of the formula bar, typing the cell name, and pressing Enter.

FIGURE 15-3.
The Go To dialog box lets you jump instantly to a certain cell.

TABLE 15-1. Useful Worksheet Navigation Keys

Use This Key or Key Combination	To Move
↑,↓,→,←	To the next cell in the direction pressed
Ctrl+↑, Ctrl+↓, Ctrl+←, Ctrl+→	To the next cell containing data (the next nonblank cell) in the direction pressed
Enter	One cell down
Tab	One cell to the right
Shift+Enter	One cell up
Shift+Tab	One cell left
Home	To column A of current row
Page Up	Up one screen

(continued)

TABLE 15-1. *continued*

Use This Key or Key Combination	To Move
Page Down	Down one screen
Alt+Page Up	One screen to the left
Alt+Page Down	One screen to the right
Ctrl+Home	To cell A1
Ctrl+End	To the cell in the last row and last column that contains data
Ctrl+Backspace	To reposition the visible portion of the worksheet to display the active cell or selected ranges that have scrolled out of view

Entering Information

ⓧ CAUTION

When you use a slash to create a fraction in a numeric entry, be sure to include a leading zero (0) and a space if the fractional value is less than 1. If you don't, Excel interprets your fraction as a date. For example, Excel interprets the fraction 3/4 as the date March 4 unless you enter the fraction as 0 3/4. You'll learn more about date and time formatting in Chapter 17.

Excel lets you enter the following types of information into a worksheet cell:

- Numeric values, like the numbers 15,000, $29.95, and 33%

- Text values, like the words *Total, 1st Quarter*, and *1820 Warren Avenue*

- Dates and times, like Feb-97, 11/19/63, or 1:00 PM

- Comments to yourself or others, like *This region leads in sales*, or an appropriate recorded sound or voice message

- Formulas, like =B5*1.081 or =SUM(B3:B7)

- Hyperlinks to Internet sites or other documents

- Electronic artwork, like clip art, scanned photographs, maps, and illustrations

Each kind of information has its own formatting characteristics, meaning that Excel stores and displays each entry type differently. The following sections show you how to enter these values into a worksheet step by step.

Entering Numeric Values

To enter a number in a cell, select the cell you want by using the mouse or keyboard, type the number, and press Enter. As you type, the number appears simultaneously in the active cell and on the *formula bar* above the worksheet. The formula bar serves as an editing scratch pad; if you make a mistake entering a long cell entry, you can click the formula bar and move the insertion point to locate the mistake in the entry and correct it, without having to retype the entry (and in so doing possibly making a new error). You can also double-click the active cell, and then move the insertion point within the cell to edit your entry. To the left of the formula bar is a Cancel button, which you can click to discard an unwanted entry on the formula bar (if you haven't already accepted the entry by pressing Enter), and an Enter button, which you can click to accept or *lock in* a revised entry. See Figure 15-4.

A numeric value can be an integer (such as 32), a decimal number (such as 499.95), an integer fraction (such as 10 3/4), or a number in scientific notation (such as 4.09E+13). You can use several mathematical symbols in numbers, including plus (+), minus (–), percent (%), fraction (/), and exponent (E), as well as the dollar sign ($). If you enter a number that is too large to fit into a cell, Excel will automatically widen the cell to accommodate the number or adjust its display of the number by using scientific notation or by showing fewer decimal places. If Excel displays the number in scientific notation or places a row of number signs

FIGURE 15-4.

New values appear both on the formula bar and in the cell when you enter them.

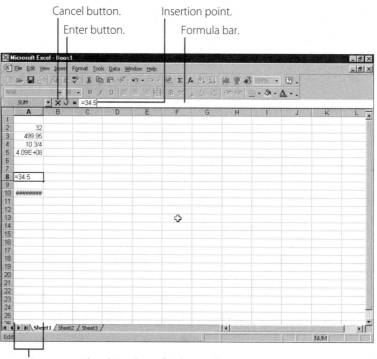

Cancel button.

Enter button.

Insertion point.

Formula bar.

You must widen this column for the numbers to be displayed as you entered them.

(#######) in the cell, you'll need to manually increase the column width to see the number in its entirety. *(See "Changing Column Widths and Row Heights," page 472).* Excel always stores the actual number you typed internally, no matter how it is displayed in the cell, and you can view this *underlying value* on the formula bar whenever the cell is active. By default (the preset arrangement), numeric values are aligned to the right edge of a cell.

Follow these steps to enter numeric values:

1 Select the cell in which you want to store the number. (You can click the cell with the mouse or use the keyboard to achieve this.)

2 Type the numeric value. (Notice how the number appears both in the cell and on the formula bar.)

3 Press Enter or select a new cell to enter the number.

 TIP

> **Use Arrow Keys to Move from Cell to Cell**
>
> If you plan to enter additional numbers, you can use the arrow keys to enter a number and move to a new cell in one step. For instance, if you type a number and press the Down arrow key, the cell pointer moves down one line. The Left, Up, and Right arrow keys move the pointer one cell left, up, or right.

Entering Text Values

SEE ALSO

For details about changing column widths to make room for more information in cells, see "Changing Column Widths and Row Heights," page 472.

To enter a text value into a cell, select the cell, type your text, and press Enter. A text value or *label* can be any combination of alphanumeric characters, including uppercase and lowercase letters, numbers, and symbols. Excel recognizes text values and aligns them to the left margin of each cell. If no information appears in adjacent cells, Excel allows longer text entries to overlap the cells on the right. If the adjacent cells do contain information, the display of the text is cut off, or truncated; however, just as with a truncated value, Excel correctly stores the full text internally, and you can see it on the formula bar when the cell is active.

If you want Excel to store as a text value a value such as a numeric address, date, or part number, precede the value with a single quotation mark. For example, if you enter '55 in a cell, the number 55 will appear left-aligned in the cell without a quotation mark, and a quotation mark will appear on the formula bar to identify the number as a text value. Figure 15-5 shows an example of a cell that has overlapping text, a few cells that have truncated text, and several numeric text entries (that is, numbers stored internally as text).

III

Microsoft Excel

FIGURE 15-5.
Text values are left-aligned and can overlap adjacent cells if they don't contain information.

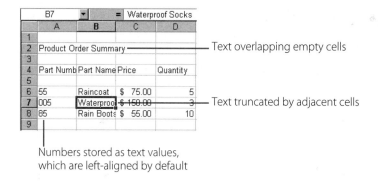

Text overlapping empty cells

Text truncated by adjacent cells

Numbers stored as text values, which are left-aligned by default

Follow these steps to enter text values:

1 Select the cell you want to store the text in. (You can click the cell with the mouse or use the keyboard to achieve this.)

2 Type the text value. (If you're entering a number, date, or time that should be stored as text, enter a single quotation mark before the value.)

3 Press Enter, or select a new cell to enter the text value.

Speed up Your Work with AutoComplete

If Excel recognizes the pattern you're typing when you enter a sequence of characters, it will attempt to complete the pattern using a feature called *AutoComplete*. AutoComplete can be a major time-saver for you if you manage lists in Excel or find that you are entering the same values or functions over and over again. If you activate the AutoComplete feature while entering data, review the characters Excel inserts and, if they make sense to you, press Enter and move on. *For information about turning off AutoComplete, see "Customizing Editing Options," page 534.*

Entering Dates and Times

SEE ALSO
For information about changing the format of date and time values, see "Changing Number Formats," page 462.

If you want to store a date or a time in a worksheet cell, you should use one of Excel's predefined date and time formats to enter the value so that Excel will recognize the number as a chronological entity and you won't need to format it again by using the Cells command on the Format menu. Excel stores identifiable dates and times internally as *serial numbers,* which makes them easier to use in functions and formulas and allows you to change the way they appear in worksheet cells. (If you're interested, a serial number is determined by counting the number of days, starting with 1, between the date you enter in a cell and January 1, 1900. However, these numbers don't appear on your worksheet—they're just internal markers that allow you to perform calculations with dates and times and quickly change how they look.) As you'll learn in Chapter 17, Excel lets you change the format of times and dates with a few simple commands.

⭐ **TIP**

To enter the current date in the active cell, press Ctrl+; (the semicolon key). Excel will use the format *m/d/yy* for the date.

Table 15-2 shows you some of the time and date formats Excel supports. Experienced Excel users will notice two new date formats in the list, each having a four-digit placeholder for the current year (the patterns *m/d/yyyy* and *d-mmm-yyyy*). These date formats have been included to help manage the year 2000 problem, which arises in spreadsheets and accounting ledgers when the century portion of a numeric entry is recorded ambiguously. (For example, the date 3/14/02 could be read as March 14, 1902 or March 14, 2002.) To clarify which century you mean, use one of the new four-digit-year date formats.

TABLE 15-2. Popular Date and Time Formats Supported by Excel

Format	Pattern	Example
Date	*m/d/yy*	10/1/99
Date	*d-mmm-yy*	1-Oct-99
Date	*d-mmm*	1-Oct
Date	*mmm-yy*	Oct-99
Date (four-digit year)	*m/d/yyyy*	10/1/1999
Date (four-digit year)	*d-mmm-yyyy*	1-Oct-2002
Time	*h:mm AM/PM*	10:15 PM
Time	*h:mm:ss AM/PM*	10:15:30 PM
Time	*h:mm*	22:15
Time	*h:mm:ss*	22:15:30
Time	*mm:ss.0*	15:30.3
Combined	*m/d/yy h:mm*	10/1/99 22:15

III

Microsoft Excel

Figure 15-6 shows working examples of the most popular date and time formats and the procedure to enter them. You can change the format of a date or time by choosing Cells from the Format menu, clicking the Number tab, and then modifying the pattern used in the Date or Time categories.

FIGURE 15-6.

Enter time and date values in one of these popular formats.

	A	B	C
C3			10/1/99 22:15

	A	B	C
1			
2	Date Formats	Time Formats	Combined
3	10/1/99	10:15 PM	10/1/99 22:15
4	1-Oct-99	10:15:30 PM	
5	1-Oct	22:15	
6	Oct-97	22:15:30	
7	10/1/1999	15:30:03	
8	1-Oct-2002		

Entering Comments

If you plan to share your Excel worksheets with other users, you might want to annotate a few important cells by using *comments* to provide instructions or highlight critical information. You can add a pop-up comment to a cell by highlighting the cell and choosing Comment from the Insert menu. Choosing the Comment command displays a pop-up window that has a blinking pointer and your name in it, so you can type a short note in the cell. (See Figure 15-7.) When you're finished typing the comment, click another cell to lock in the note.

NOTE

To change the name that appears when you enter a comment, choose Options from the Tools menu, click the General tab, and change the name in the User Name text box.

Active comments are identified by tiny red dots in the upper right corner of a cell. To display a comment in a worksheet, hold the mouse pointer over the annotated cell until a pop-up comment box appears.

FIGURE 15-7.

The Comment command allows you to add a descriptive note to a cell.

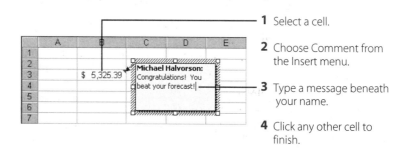

1 Select a cell.

2 Choose Comment from the Insert menu.

3 Type a message beneath your name.

4 Click any other cell to finish.

Managing Your Comments

You can view all the comments in your workbook by enabling the Comments command on the View menu. The Comments command is a toggle that is either off or on; when it is enabled, all the comments in your workbook appear in pop-up windows; when it is disabled, comments only appear when you hold the mouse over the cells in which they reside. The Comments command also activates the Reviewing toolbar, shown in Figure 15-8, which contains a number of useful command buttons. To edit an existing comment, click the Edit Comment button on the toolbar, or right-click the cell containing the comment that needs editing and choose Edit Comment from the shortcut menu.

New/Edit Comment.
Previous Comment.
Next Comment.
Show/Hide Comment.
Show All/Hide All Comments.

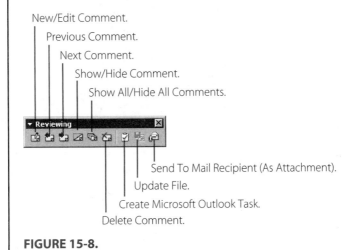

Send To Mail Recipient (As Attachment).
Update File.
Create Microsoft Outlook Task.
Delete Comment.

FIGURE 15-8.
The Reviewing toolbar helps you manage the comments in your workbook.

Remember that because comments are cell annotations, they exist in *addition* to the other entries in cells—they don't *replace* them. To delete an existing comment, select the cell containing the comment in the worksheet, choose Clear from the Edit menu, and click Comments on the Clear submenu.

Entering Formulas

To compute a calculation in a worksheet, you could find your pocket calculator and work the problem. Better yet, enter a formula into an Excel cell and have that formula available instantly, from any cell in your worksheet, for future calculations and modification. A *formula* is an equation that calculates a new value from existing values. For example, a simple formula could calculate the total cost of an item

SEE ALSO
For detailed information about formula syntax, see "Building a Formula," page 538. For detailed information about Excel's collection of built-in functions, see "Using Built-In Functions," page 544.

III

Microsoft Excel

by adding its price, sales tax, and shipping costs. Formulas can contain numbers, mathematical operators, cell references, and built-in equations called *functions*. One of Excel's great strengths is its vast collection of powerful and easy-to-use functions. Entering a formula in a cell is the key to unlocking this potent ally.

All formulas in Excel begin with an equal sign (=). The equal sign signals the beginning of a mathematical operation and tells Excel to store the equation that follows as a formula. For example, the following formula calculates the sum of three numbers:

=10+20+30

Excel stores your formulas internally (you can see them on the formula bar), but it displays the result of each calculation in the cell in which you placed the formula. You can use the standard mathematical operators in a formula—addition (+), subtraction (−), multiplication (*), division (/), and exponentiation (^) as well as a few specialty operators described in Chapter 20. Figure 15-9 lists the steps to follow to enter a simple formula in a worksheet cell.

If your formula results in the message *Error In Formula*, you used an invalid operator or typed the formula incorrectly. Fix the formula in the formula bar, or edit it in the cell by selecting the cell and pressing F2.

> **NOTE**
>
> If you don't begin formulas with an equal sign (=), Excel will interpret the equation as a text value and the formula won't be calculated. If you make this common mistake, press F2 to edit the cell, press the Home key to move the insertion point to the beginning of the formula, type an equal sign (=), and then press Enter.

FIGURE 15-9.
Entering a formula in a cell.

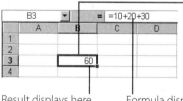

Result displays here.   Formula displays here.

1 Select a cell for entering a formula.

2 Type an equal sign (=) and the equation you want to calculate.

3 Press the Enter key or highlight a new cell to complete the formula and display the result.

Using Cell References in Formulas

Formulas can also contain worksheet *cell references*—cell names such as A1 or B5—so that you can include the contents of cells in formulas and combine them in any way you choose. You can use cell references

❓ SEE ALSO

You can also include groups of cells in formulas. See "Selecting Cells and Ranges," page 442.

along with numbers, mathematical operators, and built-in functions. To specify cell references in formulas, you can type in their names, highlight them individually using the mouse, or highlight them individually using the keyboard. (The procedures follow.) For example, to add the contents of cell B5 to the contents of cell C5, you would create the following formula:

=B5+C5

Figure 15-10 shows the results of such a calculation.

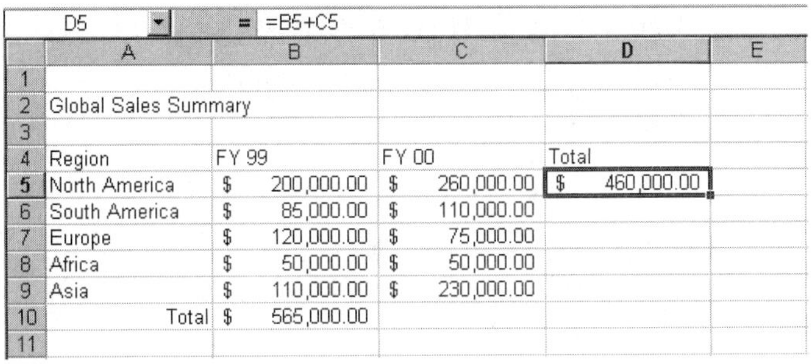

FIGURE 15-10.
To use the contents of cells in a formula, include cell references in the equation.

	A	B	C	D	E
	D5	▼	= =B5+C5		
1					
2	Global Sales Summary				
3					
4	Region	FY 99	FY 00	Total	
5	North America	$ 200,000.00	$ 260,000.00	$ 460,000.00	
6	South America	$ 85,000.00	$ 110,000.00		
7	Europe	$ 120,000.00	$ 75,000.00		
8	Africa	$ 50,000.00	$ 50,000.00		
9	Asia	$ 110,000.00	$ 230,000.00		
10	Total	$ 565,000.00			
11					

Creating Cell References by Typing

Follow these steps to create a formula that includes cell references you type by hand:

1 Select the cell in which you want to place the formula.

2 Type an equal sign (=), and then type the formula you want to create. When it comes time to enter the cell references in your formula, type each cell name in column-first/row-next format. For example, to add cell B5 to cell C5, type *=B5+C5*.

3 Press Enter to store the formula. Excel calculates the result and displays it in the cell.

Creating Cell References by Using the Mouse

Follow these steps to create a formula that includes cell references you highlight with the mouse:

1 Select the cell in which you want to place the formula.

2 Type an equal sign (=) to start the formula. Click the first cell you want to place in the formula, and then type a mathematical operator. For example, click cell B5, and then press the plus (+) key to add B5+ to the formula bar. When you click the cell, a flashing

border surrounds the cell, and its name appears on the formula bar. The border disappears when you type the operator.

3   Click the second cell you want to place in the formula. If the cell you want is not currently visible, use the scroll bars to locate it. If you want to include additional mathematical operators and cell names, you can add them now.

4   Press the Enter key to store the formula. Excel calculates the result and displays it in the cell.

Creating Cell References by Using Arrow Keys

Follow these steps to create a formula that includes cell references you highlight with the arrow keys (Right, Down, Up, Left) on the keyboard:

1   Select the cell in which you want to place the formula.

2   Type an equal sign (=) to start the formula. Use the arrow keys to highlight the first cell you want to include in the formula, and then type a mathematical operator. For example, highlight cell B5, and then press the plus (+) key to add B5+ to the formula bar. As you move the pointer around the worksheet, a flashing border surrounds the currently highlighted cell and its name appears in the formula bar.

3   Highlight the second cell that you want to place in the formula. If the cell you want is not currently visible, use arrow keys to locate it. (If you want to include additional mathematical operators and cell names, you can add them now.)

4   Press the Enter key to store the formula. Excel calculates the result and displays it in the cell.

Adding Artwork

After you enter your worksheet's basic facts and figures into Excel, you might want to spruce things up a bit by adding some electronic artwork such as clip art, scanned photographs, background images, organization charts, or hand-drawn illustrations. The basic mechanism for adding these items to worksheet cells is the same in all Office applications: click a command on the Picture submenu of the Insert menu.

Follow these steps to add a piece of electronic artwork to a worksheet:

1   Select the cell in which you want to place the artwork. (Allow some room in neighboring cells to accommodate the image.)

2 Point to the Picture command on the Insert menu.

3 Choose the artwork type you want to use from the Picture submenu. You'll see the following options:

- **Clip Art** A picture gallery containing thousands of pieces of electronic art for presentations, reports, and brochures.

- **From File** An Open dialog box that lets you locate preexisting artwork on your system.

- **AutoShapes** A toolbar that lets you add arrows, lines, and other shapes.

- **Organization Chart** A utility that helps you build corporate organization charts.

- **WordArt** A wizard and toolbar that helps you build creative banners, headlines, and text elements.

- **From Scanner or Camera** A utility that helps you insert scanned images and photographs into worksheet cells.

4 Move or resize the artwork as desired in the worksheet.

5 If you want to delete the image later, select the artwork object you inserted and press Delete.

 TIP

If you're interested in geographic maps, you can also add a variety of map objects to your worksheet by using the Object command on the Insert menu and selecting the Microsoft Map object type on the Create New tab. You can customize these maps by adding regional information, labels, and data from your worksheet, to create reports that present the facts and figures in visually appealing ways.

Inserting a Background Graphic

If the worksheet you're creating will take center stage in a report or presentation, you might want to embellish it further by adding a subtle piece of artwork to the background. When you add background artwork, Excel places the image you specify behind (below) the current worksheet or chart. (The data in your worksheet cells will appear on top of the image.) If you specify a small pattern rather than a complete image, Excel automatically repeats, or *tiles*, the pattern to fill the entire worksheet or chart.

III

Microsoft Excel

To add a bitmap, metafile, or other electronic image to the background of your worksheet, follow these steps:

1 Display the worksheet you want to customize by adding background artwork.

2 Choose Sheet from the Format menu, and then click Background on the Sheet submenu. The Sheet Background dialog box appears.

3 Browse the folders on your hard disk or network to locate the electronic artwork you want to display as a background graphic. When you find and select it, click the Insert button to insert the graphic. (You'll find several useful images in the Program Files\Microsoft Office\Office\Bitmaps\Styles folder, in the Windows folder, and in your clip art folders.)

Try to use simple, light-colored background images in your worksheets and charts so that the artwork doesn't overpower the text you're using for labels and numbers. Subtle, light gray images often work best.

Figure 15-11 shows what a piece of art named acsndstn.gif looks like as a background graphic in a worksheet. If you decide you don't want this image at some point, choose Delete Background from the Sheet submenu of the Format menu to remove it.

FIGURE 15-11.

The Background command lets you add a background graphic to your worksheet or chart.

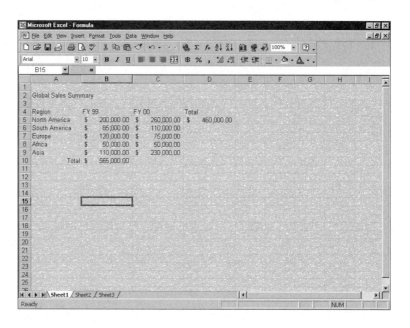

⊙ **Inserting Hyperlinks**

Excel 2000 includes an enhanced feature that allows you to add *hyperlinks* to cells in your workbook, connecting them to other electronic documents on your hard disk, the Internet, or an attached computer network. Hyperlinks in Excel give you a handy way to combine a series of related workbooks or let you provide your users with on-demand access to supporting documents, Web pages, or other reference materials on the Internet. You create a hyperlink using the Hyperlink command on the Insert menu, and the command prompts you for the name of the supporting file or Web page and underlines the text in the worksheet cell that was selected when you ran the command. (The underlined word appears in a special color, and looks similar to linked topics that appear in the Office online Help.) After a hyperlink to another document has been established, you can activate it by clicking the underlined word in your worksheet.

Note that you can specify any supporting document for your hyperlink—provided that you have the application necessary to open the document on your computer. For example, if you have Microsoft Office Professional Edition installed, you can insert a hyperlink in your worksheet to any Office application—Word, Excel, PowerPoint, Access, Publisher, or Outlook—and Excel will open that document when you click the underlined hyperlink cell in your workbook. Similarly, if you have Microsoft Internet Explorer or another Internet browser, you can create a hyperlink to any resource on the Internet for which you have a proper address.

Creating a Hyperlink in Your Worksheet

The following steps show you how to add a hyperlink to your worksheet that opens a document on your hard disk, the Internet, or a network to which you're attached:

1 In your worksheet, select the cell with which you want to associate the hyperlink. You can create a hyperlink in an empty cell, or in a cell containing information, artwork, or a formula.

Insert
Hyperlink

2 From the Insert menu, choose Hyperlink or click the Insert Hyperlink button on the Standard toolbar. The Insert Hyperlink dialog box appears, as shown in Figure 15-12, on the next page. Excel 2000 now asks you two fundamental questions about your selection: what is the type of the hyperlink you are creating, and what content should the hyperlink contain?

III

Microsoft Excel

FIGURE 15-12.

The Insert Hyperlink dialog box in Excel 2000 gives you several options when creating hyperlinks.

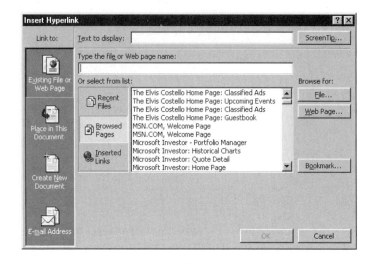

3 Answer the first question by clicking one of the four buttons on the left side of the dialog box. The Existing File Or Web Page Button creates a link in your worksheet to a file on your hard disk or a home page on the Web. On a day-to-day basis, this option will probably cover most of your hyperlink needs, because it is the fastest way to create links to useful files and Internet resources within your worksheet. (See Figure 15-12.)

You also have three additional options. The second button, Place In This Document, creates a link to a different location in the current workbook. Use this option if you want to jump quickly from one location in a spreadsheet to another. (It works like the Go To command.) The third button, Create New Document, allows you to open a new Office document from within your worksheet, which can be another Excel spreadsheet, a Word document, a PowerPoint presentation, and so on. We use this option when we want to give our users a quick way to write notes or jot down estimates while using a worksheet. Finally, E-Mail Address (the fourth button on the left side) allows you to create a link in your worksheet that automatically sends an e-mail message to another user, complete with a custom subject header and a handy screen tip.

4 Fill out the dialog box options corresponding to the type of hyperlink you are creating.

If you are identifying a particular document name or Web page that should be loaded when the user clicks the hyperlink, locate it on your system by using one of the Browse buttons (File or

Web Page), and specify a descriptive label in the cell by typing it in the Text To Display text box. (This text box is available only if the cell is blank or contains a text label.) You can also use three buttons within the dialog box corresponding to frequently used documents: Recent Files, Browsed Pages, and Inserted Links.

TIP

Using a Web Page as a Hyperlink

When you browse for a Web page link, Office 2000 opens your Internet browser and allows you to locate the Web page you want to use. After you locate the page you want to use, return to the Insert Hyperlink dialog box (with your Internet browser still running), select any additional options you want, and click OK. The trick here is to jump back to the Insert Hyperlink dialog box while your browser is still running, or you won't get the right Web page.

5 When you're finished identifying the content of your hyperlink, click OK to add the hyperlink to your worksheet. When the Insert Hyperlink dialog box closes, the text in the highlighted cell appears in underlined type, and the Web toolbar opens. If you specified a descriptive label, it also appears when you hold the mouse pointer over the hyperlink:

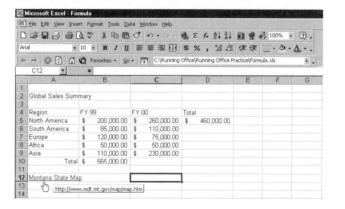

Activating a Hyperlink

To activate a hyperlink in a worksheet, click the underlined cell containing the hyperlink, and Excel will start any necessary applications and load the linked document. If the hyperlink requires an Internet or other network connection, you might be prompted for a member ID (also called a *username*) and password when your browser activates the link.

III

Microsoft Excel

The Web Toolbar

After you activate a hyperlink in Excel, a special Web toolbar appears on the screen, which lets you switch back and forth between open hyperlinks, establish additional Internet connections, or run special network-related commands. If the toolbar doesn't appear, click Toolbars on the View menu and select Web on the submenu. You don't have to use the Web toolbar when switching between hyperlinks (you can also use the Excel Window menu), but in many cases you'll benefit from doing so. To close the Web toolbar, click the Close button on the toolbar's title bar.

The Web toolbar is shown here as a free-standing toolbar, which you can duplicate by dragging the toolbar from its default locked position beneath the Formatting toolbar.

Back.

Forward.

Stop Current Jump.

Refresh Current Page.

Start Page.

Search The Web.

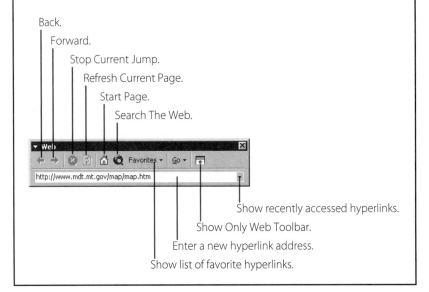

Show recently accessed hyperlinks.

Show Only Web Toolbar.

Enter a new hyperlink address.

Show list of favorite hyperlinks.

If you're not sure whether an underlined word represents a hyperlink, place the mouse pointer directly over the cell and see if the mouse pointer changes shape. The mouse pointer over a cell containing a hyperlink resembles a hand with a pointing finger and often displays a descriptive label.

Hyperlink
pointer

After a hyperlink has been activated, you can jump back and forth between the home document and any supporting hyperlinks by clicking the Back and Forward buttons, respectively, on the Web toolbar. If the hyperlink launched a separate Windows application to load the document—say, the hyperlink started Word or Internet Explorer—you

SEE ALSO

For more information about using Internet documents and the Web toolbar, see "Browsing Documents on the Web," page 89.

can also use the Windows taskbar to move back and forth quickly between the applications. When you're finished viewing a hyperlinked Excel workbook, close it by choosing Close from the Excel File menu. When you're finished using documents associated with other applications, simply exit the application. (If you're using the Internet, this will end your connection.)

Editing and Removing Hyperlinks

To edit or remove a hyperlink from a worksheet cell, follow these steps:

CAUTION

Don't left-click the cell containing the hyperlink or you'll activate it.

1 Right-click the cell containing the hyperlink to display a pop-up menu of commands used to manipulate spreadsheet cells.

2 On the pop-up menu, point to the Hyperlink command to display a submenu of commands used to manipulate the hyperlink you have created. Choose Edit Hyperlink if you want to customize or alter the hyperlink in the cell you clicked. To remove the hyperlink, click Remove Hyperlink.

Saving the Workbook

SEE ALSO

For more information about saving workbooks, see "Saving Documents and Web Pages," page 69. For information about saving summary information in workbooks, see "Working with Property Sheets," page 79.

After you enter information into a new workbook, it's a good idea to save the data to disk—before you make some phone calls and get distracted or go to lunch! This way, you can protect the information and use it again later. Each workbook is stored in its own file on disk and is assigned a filename that is unique to the folder in which it is stored. To assign a new filename to a workbook, use the Save As command on the File menu. To save edits you have made to an existing workbook file, use the Save command on the File menu.

Using the Save As Command

Figure 15-13 shows you the steps to follow to save your workbook to disk. Choose Save As from the File menu. The Save As dialog box appears, prompting you for a filename, as shown in Figure 15-13, on the next page.

TIP

Save Your Favorite Files in a Special Folder

We recommend that you place the files you use most often in the My Documents or the Favorites folder, two special locations on your hard disk set aside for particularly useful files. (If you like, you can also create subfolders in these folders.) You'll see buttons for both of these folders on the left side of Save As and Open dialog boxes when you use Office applications.

III

Microsoft Excel

FIGURE 15-13.
Saving your workbook
to disk using a new
filename.

1 Click a folder icon to choose one of the standard folder options…

…Or, select a folder location in the Save In list…

…Or, use any of these available tools to specify a location.

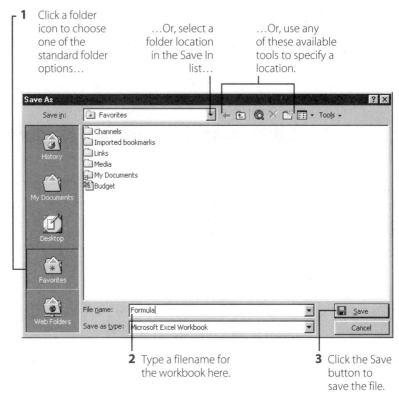

2 Type a filename for the workbook here.

3 Click the Save button to save the file.

Using the Save Command

To save revisions you have made to a workbook that already has a file-name, choose Save from the File menu. That's all there is to it—choosing Save updates your file on disk automatically. If you decide you want to create a new version of the file while preserving the original, choose Save As and specify a new filename.

Save

Quick Saves

You can also save your file by clicking the Save button on the Standard toolbar or by pressing Ctrl+S on your keyboard.

Exiting Excel (A Few Points to Remember)

All right, you've finished building an awesome worksheet and you're ready to get on to other tasks (like the next chapter!). Before you do, read over the following steps that we'd like you to recite quietly to yourself each time you're finished working for the day.

Each time I finish working with Excel, I, [insert name], will do the following:

1 I'll save my workbook to disk with a clear, easy-to-remember file-name. I can do this at any time by choosing Save As from the File menu (for new files) or by choosing Save from the File menu (for existing files).

⭐ TIP

> Please don't wait until you're finished creating your document to save it to disk. We recommend saving your work to disk every 10 minutes or so to avoid losing data in a power outage or system crash.

2 I'll give the spelling of labels and text in my worksheet a once-over by choosing the Spelling command from the Tools menu. Since the spelling checker is smart and only checks the words in my worksheet, I'm not worried that this step will slow me down.

3 (Optional) I'll choose Print from the File menu to print my worksheet. If I want to adjust the margins, headers, or footers in my worksheet before I print, I'll choose Page Setup from the File menu and Print Preview from the File menu.

? SEE ALSO

For more information about issues related to managing files and printing, see Chapter 3, "Managing Documents: From Your Hard Disk to the Internet."

4 When I'm finished working, I'll choose Exit from the File menu to exit Excel. (I won't simply turn off my computer.) If I want to retain the changes in my worksheet, I'll click Yes when prompted by Excel to save my changes.

5 (Optional) After I exit Excel, now and then I'll make a backup copy of my valuable workbook files on a floppy disk by using Windows Explorer. I know that this is the best way to keep my data safe in the sometimes-uncertain world of electromagnetic media.

III

Microsoft Excel

Editing a Worksheet

I f you make a mistake while building a worksheet, you're not expected to live with it. Microsoft Excel features a variety of traditional and innovative electronic editing techniques so that you can fix your typos, reorganize your data, emphasize certain subtotals and totals, fill cells with data, and create room for more information. In this chapter, you'll learn the essential editing techniques you'll need to have at your disposal when managing worksheet data in Excel, and you'll learn how to use innovative features such as AutoFill and the new Clipboard toolbar to replicate and rearrange vital information.

Essential Editing Techniques

? SEE ALSO

For information about tracking and approving edits in a multiuser environment, see "Accepting or Rejecting Revisions," page 507.

Refer to this part of the book regularly when you need to remember how data is moved from cell to cell in Excel. In this section, you'll learn the following editing techniques:

- How to select cells and ranges

- How to clear cells and delete cells

- How to copy data from one cell to another

- How to use the new Clipboard toolbar

- How to move cells by dragging

- How to add new rows and columns to the worksheet

- How to undo and repeat commands

Selecting Cells and Ranges

Several Excel commands work with individual cells or groups of cells called *ranges*. Selecting a cell means making it the active cell; as a result, its name appears in the Name box to the left of the formula bar. To select an individual cell or a range of cells, you can use either the mouse or the keyboard.

? SEE ALSO

To make cell ranges easier to work with, you can assign a name to a cell range, and then use the name in place of the cell reference. See "Using Range Names in Functions," page 554.

If you have used previous versions of Excel, you'll notice that cool blue has replaced black as the default selection color in Excel 2000 when a range is selected.

Excel requires a particular notation when you type out cell ranges. For example, A1:E1 represents a single row of five cells along the top edge of the worksheet, and E5:E8 represents a single column of four cells oriented vertically in the worksheet. Each cell range starts with a beginning cell name, followed by a colon and the ending cell name. You'll use cell ranges in many of the formulas and functions you create in Excel worksheets. In this illustration, a rectangular block of 45 cells (nine rows by five columns) named A1:E9 has been selected:

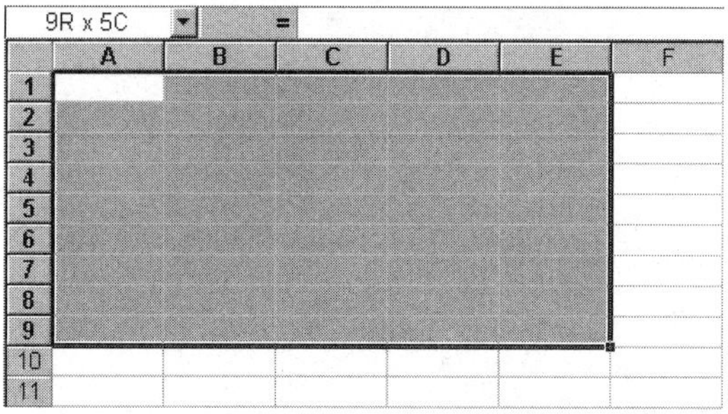

Selecting a Range Using the Mouse

The following steps show you how to select a range of cells using the mouse:

1. Position the cell pointer over the first cell you want to select.
2. Hold down the mouse button, and then drag the mouse over the remaining cells in the selection. Release the mouse button.
3. If you want to select additional, *noncontiguous* cell ranges—ranges of cells that don't touch—hold down the Ctrl key, and then repeat steps 1 and 2 until all the ranges have been selected. When you're finished, release the Ctrl key. Figure 16-1, on the next page, shows a multiple-range selection.

NOTE

In Figure 16-1 two ranges of cells are selected (A5:A9 and C5:C9). Only one of the cells, however, is the active cell—C5—denoted by the Name box and the bar around the cell. Most commands will affect all the selected cells, including the active cell. Entering new information and a few special commands will affect only the active cell and won't change anything in the other selected, or highlighted, cells.

Selecting a Range Using the Keyboard

The following steps show you how to select a range of cells using the keyboard:

1. Use the arrow keys to move to the first cell you want to select.

FIGURE 16-1.
To select noncontiguous ranges, hold down the Ctrl key.

| C5 | ▼ | = | 260000 |

	A	B	C	D
1				
2	Global Sales Summary			
3				
4	Region	FY 99	FY 00	Total
5	North America	$ 200,000.00	$ 260,000.00	$ 460,000.00
6	South America	$ 85,000.00	$ 110,000.00	
7	Europe	$ 120,000.00	$ 75,000.00	
8	Africa	$ 50,000.00	$ 50,000.00	
9	Asia	$ 110,000.00	$ 230,000.00	
10	Total	$ 565,000.00		
11				

2 Hold down the Shift key, and then press the appropriate arrow key to select the remaining cells in the range. Release the Shift key.

3 To select additional, noncontiguous cell ranges, press Shift+F8. The Add indicator appears on the status bar, indicating that you can add a range to the selection. Repeat steps 1 and 2 to add the range.

Clearing Cells and Deleting Cells

Now that you know how to select ranges of cells, you can put your new skill to work and build a worksheet that is of value to you. For instance, if you want to clear the contents from a group of cells, select the cells and press the Delete key. Excel removes the content but keeps the cell formatting so that you can enter new values in the same format. (For example, if you clear cells formatted for dollar values, the next time you place a number in one of these cells it will be formatted for dollars.) To see the complete range of clear options, choose Clear from the Edit menu, and Excel will display a submenu that contains commands for clearing the formatting, the contents, the comments, or all three items together.

 TIP

You can also clear the contents of a cell by right-clicking the cell and then choosing Clear Contents from the pop-up menu.

If you'd rather delete a single cell from the worksheet, moving the rows below it up or shifting columns over to the left, choose the Delete command rather than the Clear command. In many applications, the terms *delete* and *clear* have the same meaning, but in Excel there is a distinct difference between the two commands. Clearing a cell is like using an eraser to remove the contents or the format from a cell, but deleting a cell is like cutting it out with a tiny pocket knife and then moving the remaining cells up or over to fill the gap.

The following steps show you how to use the Delete command to delete cell ranges, entire rows, or entire columns from a worksheet:

1 Place the cell pointer in the cell, row, or column you want to delete from the worksheet. If you want to delete a range of cells, select the range.

2 Choose Delete from the Edit menu. The dialog box shown in Figure 16-2 appears.

3 Click the option button that corresponds to the way you want remaining cells moved after the deletion.

For example, in Figure 16-2 where B3 is the selected cell, to delete cell B3 and move cells over to fill the gap, click Shift Cells Left. To delete cell B3 and move cells up to fill the gap, click Shift Cells Up. You can also click Entire Row or Entire Column to remove all the selected rows or columns. In Figure 16-2 you could, for example, remove row 3 or column B.

4 Click OK to delete the selected cells and move other cells to fill the gap.

Undoing Commands

If you make a mistake when deleting a range of cells or executing another Excel command, you can undo your mistake by immediately

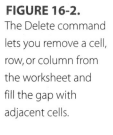

FIGURE 16-2.
The Delete command lets you remove a cell, row, or column from the worksheet and fill the gap with adjacent cells.

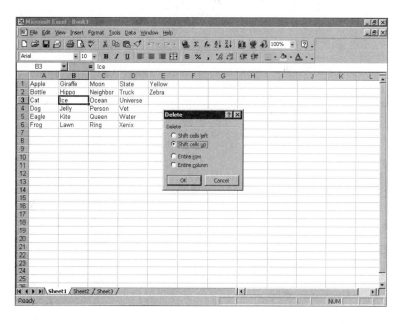

Selecting Rows and Columns Using the Mouse

If you want to quickly select part or all of your worksheet, you can click one of several hot spots on your screen.

To select an entire column with a single mouse click, click the column letter at the top of the column. To select an entire row, click the row number on the left edge of the row. You can also select multiple columns or rows by selecting a row or column head and dragging across the heads of the rows or columns you want to select. Best of all, if you need to select the entire worksheet, you can click the Select All box in the upper left corner of the worksheet. Here you see a worksheet that has two columns selected.

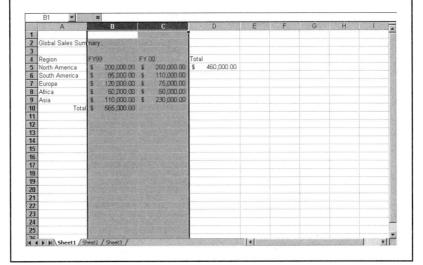

choosing Undo from the Edit menu. For example, if you deleted a range of cells in error, choosing Undo will return the cells to the worksheet as if you had never deleted them.

Undo

You can also click the Undo button on the Standard toolbar, or press Ctrl+Z, to undo a command.

The Undo button on the Standard toolbar also has multiple levels of undo (like Microsoft Word). This lets you "go back in time" to fix editing mistakes you made 3, 4, or 10 commands back. This is an extremely useful feature, because now and then you'll probably think better of a modification you made that took several steps to accomplish. By clicking the small arrow attached to the Undo button, you can scroll through a list of the edits you have made and pick the one you want to reverse. (See Figure 16-3.) Excel will then undo each command, from your most recent action back to and including the one you just picked.

FIGURE 16-3.
Using the Undo button, you can undo one or more editing mistakes in the past.

Undo has a few limitations. For example, you can't undo the actions of adding a new worksheet to your workbook or deleting an existing worksheet. You also can't undo the actions of saving revisions to a file or customizing the Excel interface. If Undo isn't available for a particular command, the Undo command on the Edit menu will be dimmed and will read "Can't Undo."

> Excel is smart about tracking your actions during a given work session. It doesn't create an Undo command when you use the scroll bars, press keyboard navigation keys, run online Help, or look for cell data using the Go To or Find commands. However, your ability to undo ends when you close your workbook or exit from Excel.

Redoing Commands

What happens if you decide to, well, undo an Undo command? For example, what do you do if you delete a range of cells, restore them with Undo, and then, on reflection, decide to remove them after all? One option is to select the cells again and choose Delete. But Excel makes it even easier to be fickle. After you use the Undo command, Excel changes its name to Redo on the Edit menu so that you can run your last command again. This gives you the opportunity to switch back and forth between two different editing commands to see which result you like best. Excel also adds the commands you have reversed to the Redo button on the Standard toolbar, letting you redo several commands at once. (This makes the Redo button the functional opposite of the Undo button, allowing you to restore and remove edits you have made.)

Redo

Repeating Commands

CAUTION
The Redo and Repeat commands are different animals (albeit from the same savanna), so be sure not to confuse them.

Below the Undo command on the Edit menu is the Repeat command, which allows you to repeat the command you just executed but at a different place in the worksheet. Here's how it works: If you just used the Cells command on the Format menu to place a border around cell B3, Excel will display a Repeat Format Cells command on the Edit menu. This allows you to add the same border to a new cell by simply highlighting the new cell and clicking Repeat on the Edit menu. You can make this even faster by pressing F4 or the shortcut key combination Ctrl+Y.

Follow these steps to use the Repeat command:

1 Execute a command you plan to repeat. (The best commands are those that require several steps to complete.) For example, place a border around a cell, select the cell, choose Cells from the Format menu, click the Border tab, click the Outline box, and then click OK.

2 Select the next cell you want to modify with the same command.

3 Choose Repeat Format Cells from the Edit menu.

↻ <u>R</u>epeat Format Cells   Ctrl+Y

Think About Repetitive Actions

The Repeat command is a speed feature, designed to help you work faster in Excel. But most people forget to use it because they don't anticipate repetitive actions. Think about how you work, and you might discover several clever uses for the Repeat command. (We use Repeat most often for formatting labels and changing number formats.)

Using Cut and Paste to Move Data

At times you'll want to move cell entries from one place to another on your worksheet. To accomplish this task, you can use the Cut and the Paste commands on the Edit menu. When you cut a range of cells using the Cut command, Excel places a dotted-line marquee around the cells to indicate which cells will be moved, and then it places the cell contents (including comments and formatting) into a temporary storage location known as the Windows Clipboard. When you select a new location for the data and choose Paste, the cells and their formatting are pasted from the Clipboard into their new location and the original cells are replaced. (If you're pasting a range of cells, they're inserted in a block.) To cancel the move after the marquee appears, press the Escape key.

If you cut and paste more than one cell, they must be in a block. Excel doesn't allow you to move noncontiguous blocks of cells. Also, in contrast to other Windows applications, Excel only lets you paste once after you cut. To paste multiple times, use the Copy command.

Figure 16-4 shows a group of cells after the Cut command was chosen (notice the marquee), while Figure 16-5 shows the same worksheet

FIGURE 16-4.
The Cut command
marks the selected
cells with a marquee.

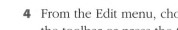

	A	B	C	D	E	F	G
1	Apple	Giraffe	Moon	State	Yellow		
2	Bottle	Hippo	Neighbor	Truck	Zebra		
3	Cat	Ice	Ocean	Universe			
4	Dog	Jelly	Person	Vet			
5	Eagle	Kite	Queen	Water			
6	Frog	Lawn	Ring	Xenix			
7							

FIGURE 16-5.
The Paste command
copies data from the
Clipboard into the
active cell.

	A	B	C	D	E	F	G
1	Apple		Moon	State	Yellow	Giraffe	
2	Bottle		Neighbor	Truck	Zebra	Hippo	
3	Cat		Ocean	Universe		Ice	
4	Dog		Person	Vet		Jelly	
5	Eagle		Queen	Water		Kite	
6	Frog		Ring	Xenix		Lawn	
7							

after the Paste command was chosen. Note that when you use the Paste command, you can also copy over cells containing data that you don't want to delete, so be cautious when moving information. As alternatives to using the Edit menu's Cut and Paste commands, you can use the Cut and Paste buttons on the Standard toolbar or the standard Windows key combinations Ctrl+X and Ctrl+V.

The following steps show you how to move a range of cells using the Cut and Paste commands:

1 Select the group of cells you want to move.

Cut

2 Choose Cut from the Edit menu. (You can also click the Cut button on the toolbar or press the Ctrl+X key combination.)

3 Click the cell to which you want to move the data. (If you're moving a group of cells, highlight the cell in the upper left corner of the area you're copying to.)

Paste

4 From the Edit menu, choose Paste. (Or click the Paste button on the toolbar or press the Ctrl+V key combination.)

Using the New Office Clipboard Toolbar

Once you have cut or copied two pieces of data into the Clipboard, Excel 2000 displays the Office Clipboard toolbar, a special editing tool that retains the last 12 items placed into the Clipboard by *any* Windows application. Figure 16-6, on the next page, shows the Clipboard toolbar in action, which at that moment contained nine data items from my work session (five Excel worksheet ranges, two Word document selections, and two Microsoft Paint images).

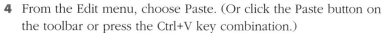

III

Microsoft Excel

FIGURE 16-6.
The Clipboard toolbar stores up to 12 cut or copy operations for future use.

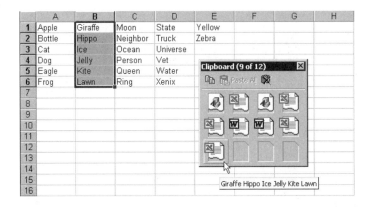

The Office Clipboard is a first-in, first-out *stack* that places the most recent cut or copy operation in the first open slot in the Office Clipboard. The toolbar can hold a total of 12 cut or copy operations—after that point, the toolbar begins discarding the oldest items in the Clipboard. However, we've noted one exception to this rule: the Office Clipboard won't let cut or copy operations in other applications push Excel data out of the Office Clipboard stack. This feature is apparently designed to preserve the Clipboard integrity of the application that is currently being used. (In other words, if you jump out of Excel to edit an e-mail message, you won't come back to discover that the Clipboard toolbar contains only Microsoft Outlook data.)

You can paste any one of the Office Clipboard items into your worksheet. Just select the cell in which you want to place the data, and click the Clipboard toolbar icon corresponding to the data you want to paste. To paste all of the items in the Office Clipboard, click the Paste All button. To empty out the Office Clipboard and start with a clean slate, click the Clear Clipboard button.

Clear
Clipboard

When you're finished using the Office Clipboard toolbar, click the Close button on the toolbar.

Using Copy and Paste to Duplicate Data

If you just want to duplicate a range of cells in the worksheet, not move them, you can use the Copy command on the Edit menu. This command places a copy of the cells you have selected into the Clipboard, and you can transfer these cells any number of times to your worksheet using the Paste command. The Copy command indicates the cells you're duplicating with the dotted-line marquee so that you can see what you're copying as you do it. As when you use the Cut command, you're limited to copying contiguous (touching) blocks of cells when you use the Copy command. If you don't use the Office Clipboard toolbar, only the most recent cut or copy operation is pasted.

To speed up your copy operations, you can use the Copy button on the Standard toolbar or the Ctrl+C key combination.

The following steps show you how to copy a range of cells using the Copy and Paste commands:

1 Select the group of cells you want to copy.

2 Choose Copy from the Edit menu. (You can also click the Copy button on the toolbar or press Ctrl+C.)

Copy

3 Click the cell into which you want to copy the data. (If you're duplicating a group of cells, highlight the cell in the upper left corner of the area you're copying to.)

4 Choose Paste from the Edit menu. (Or click the Paste button on the toolbar or press Ctrl+V.)

Moving Cells by Dragging

The fastest way to move a group of worksheet cells is by dragging. By using the drag-and-drop technique, you can edit a worksheet in an efficient and visibly uncomplicated way—by dragging a group of cells from one location to another. To enable drag-and-drop editing, you need to select cells (usually with the mouse), release the mouse button, and then move the cell pointer toward an outside edge of the selected cells until the cell pointer changes into the arrow pointer. When the pointer changes shape, you can hold down the left mouse button and drag the selection to a new location. As you move the cells, Excel displays both an outline of the range and the current range address, so that you can align the cells properly in your worksheet. (See Figure 16-7, on the next page.)

 WARNING

If you happen to drop cells onto existing data when you drag them, Excel will warn you that you're about to replace the contents of your copy destination. Click OK if you want to replace the old cells, or click Cancel if you want to choose a new place for the data.

 TIP

To copy cells by dragging, hold down the Ctrl key while you drag the selected cells. When you drag with the Ctrl key down, a plus (+) sign is added to the arrow pointer to let you know you're copying data.

III

Microsoft Excel

FIGURE 16-7.
The quickest way to move cells in the worksheet is by using the drag-and-drop mouse technique.

1 Select the range you want to move.

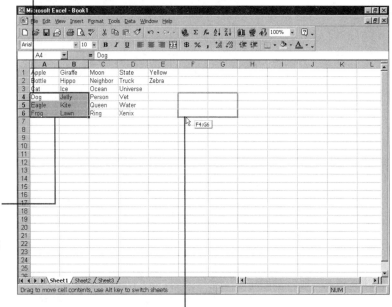

2 Point to a border of the box around the selected cells. The cell pointer changes to an arrow.

3 Drag the selected range to its new location. An outline of the selected range follows the cell pointer. Release the mouse button to complete the move.

Adding Rows and Columns to the Worksheet

Now and then you'll want to add new rows or columns to your worksheet to create space. You might decide to add cells because your existing data is too crowded, or perhaps you're creating a report that has changed in scope and requires a new layout to communicate effectively. You add new rows and columns to your worksheet by using the Rows and Columns commands on the Insert menu. When you add rows or columns to your worksheet, the existing data shifts down to accommodate new rows or shifts to the right to allow for new columns.

The following steps show you how to add a row to your worksheet:

1 Select the row *below* the place you want to enter a new, blank row. (Select the row by clicking the row number.)

2 Choose Rows from the Insert menu.

Inserting Individual Cells

Excel lets you add individual cells to your worksheet's rows or columns by choosing Cells from the Insert menu. Before you use the Cells command, you should select the worksheet cell below or to the right of the new cell you want. For example, if you want to add a new cell to column B between cells B3 and B4, highlight cell B4 before choosing the Cells command. When you choose Cells, the Insert dialog box appears.

Use the Insert dialog box to tell Excel to shift the cells to the right or down. If you're adding a cell to a column, click Shift Cells Down. If you're adding a cell to a row, click Shift Cells Right. You can also insert entire rows and columns by using the Insert Rows and Insert Columns commands.

The following steps show you how to add a column to your worksheet:

1 Select the column to the *right* of the place where you want to enter a new column. (Select the column by clicking the column letter.)

2 Choose Columns from the Insert menu.

Entering a Series of Labels, Numbers, and Dates

? SEE ALSO

For information about replicating formulas in a worksheet, see "Replicating a Formula," page 540.

Excel streamlines the task of entering worksheet data by allowing you to fill a range of cells with one repeating value or a sequence of values, called a *series*. This capability saves you time when you're entering groups of labels, numbers, or dates in a report. For example, you can replicate the same price for many products in a report or create part numbers that increment predictably. To enter a series of values into a range of cells, you use the Fill command on the Insert menu or a mouse technique called *AutoFill*. The following sections show you how you can enter data automatically using these commands.

III

Microsoft Excel

Using AutoFill to Create a Series

The easiest method for entering repeating or incrementing data is to use Excel's AutoFill feature. This feature is activated when you drag a tiny black square called the *fill handle* over new cells. The fill handle is located in the lower right corner of the active cell or a selected range of cells, as shown in Figure 16-8. When you position the cell pointer over the fill handle, the cell pointer changes to a plus sign (+), indicating that the AutoFill feature is enabled. To create a series of labels, numbers, or dates, you drag the pointer over the cells you want to fill with information and then release the mouse button. (Notice that Excel shows the next value in the series in a pop-up box.) Like magic, you have a list of new values!

The AutoFill feature obeys a clear set of rules when it replicates data in cells, as shown in Table 16-1. When you drag the fill handle down or to the right, AutoFill creates values that increase based on the pattern in the range of cells you first select. When you drag the fill handle up or to the left, AutoFill creates values that decrease based on the pattern. If AutoFill doesn't recognize the pattern, it simply duplicates the selected cells.

TABLE 16-1. AutoFill Insertion Patterns

Pattern Type	Series	Example
Label (Text)	No pattern, text is duplicated	Units, Units, Units
Number	Values increase based on pattern	10, 20, 30
Text with number	Series created by changing number based on pattern	Unit 1, Unit 2, Unit 3
Day	Series created to match day format	Mon., Tues., Wed.
Month	Series created to match month format	Jan., Feb., Mar.
Year	Series created to match year format	1998, 1999, 2000
Time	Series created to match time interval	1:30 PM, 2:00 PM, 2:30 PM

 TIP

To suppress the AutoFill feature (and just duplicate the selected cells), hold down the Ctrl key while you drag the fill handle.

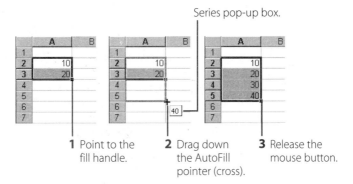

FIGURE 16-8.
Follow these steps to
AutoFill a series of cells.

Series pop-up box.

1 Point to the
fill handle.

2 Drag down
the AutoFill
pointer (cross).

3 Release the
mouse button.

Using the Fill Commands

The mouse-driven AutoFill feature is designed to handle most of the
data copying and replication in a worksheet, but you can also use a
collection of Fill commands on the Edit menu to accomplish simple
copying tasks. You'll find these commands useful if you want to copy
one cell into many adjacent cells, or if you want to fine-tune the way
patterns in an AutoFill series are created.

Filling Up, Down, Right, and Left

When you choose Fill from the Edit menu, a submenu appears that contains several replication commands, including Up, Down, Right, and Left.
These commands let you copy information from one cell to a group of
selected, adjacent cells. Figure 16-9 shows how the Fill Down command
is used to copy the contents of cell A2 to cells A3 through A5. Note that
cell comments are not copied when you use the Fill commands (because
comments are not considered essential to the calculation process).

FIGURE 16-9.
Select the range you
want to fill, and choose
Up, Down, Right, or Left
from the Fill submenu.

The following steps show you how to fill a range using the Fill command:

1 Place the cell pointer over the cell you want to replicate, and then
drag the mouse over the cells you want to fill.

III

Microsoft Excel

2 Choose Fill from the Edit menu, and then choose the command from the Fill submenu corresponding to the direction you want to copy.

 **TIP**

The Excel key combination for the Down command is Ctrl+D. The key combination for the Right command is Ctrl+R.

Using the Fill Series Dialog Box

If you want to specify a custom series, such as a number that increments in fractional portions or a maximum value for the series, select your fill range, and choose the Series command from the Edit menu's Fill submenu. The dialog box shown in Figure 16-10 appears. This dialog box allows you to specify the value type and date type—characteristics that are usually set automatically when you use the AutoFill feature.

FIGURE 16-10.
The Series dialog box lets you create custom fill sequences.

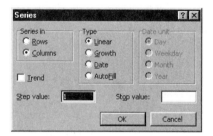

What makes the Series dialog box handy is the Step Value and Stop Value text boxes, which let you control how the specified series increments and specify its final value. For example, if you want to increment a numeric series by 1.5, type *1.5* in the Step Value text box. Similarly, if you want to set 10 as the highest number in the series, type *10* in the Stop Value text box. Figure 16-11 shows the results you get when you start with the number 1 and use both these values in the Series dialog box. Notice that although cells A8, A9, and A10 were selected in the fill range (just as a guess), they were left empty because the stop value in the Series dialog box had been reached.

FIGURE 16-11.
The Series command lets you increment by an amount you specify and stop when a limit you set has been reached.

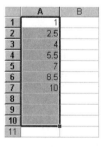

Formatting a Worksheet

After you enter and edit the information in worksheet cells, you can format the data to highlight important facts and make the worksheet easier to read. In this chapter, you'll learn how to format worksheet cells, change column widths and row heights, add and remove page breaks, use formatting styles, and work with predesigned worksheet templates. You'll be surprised at how easily you can improve the appearance of your Excel worksheets by using the powerful techniques discussed in this chapter.

Formatting Cells

? SEE ALSO

For information about creating conditional formatting based on the values stored in worksheet cells, see "Creating Conditional Formatting," page 477.

Effective worksheet formatting is crucial when you present important business information. Formatting the contents of a cell doesn't change how Excel stores the data internally; rather, it changes how the information looks on your screen and how it appears in print. In this section, you'll learn the following techniques for formatting the data in cells:

- How to change the vertical and horizontal alignment of data in a cell

- How to change number formats

- How to change the font, text color, and background color

- How to add decorative borders and patterns to cells

- How to apply combinations of formatting effects using the AutoFormat command

Changing Alignment

The gateway to Excel's formatting commands is the Cells command on the Format menu. When you select a range of cells in the worksheet and choose the Cells command, the Format Cells dialog box appears, as shown in Figure 17-1. The Format Cells dialog box contains six tabs of formatting options that you can use to adjust the appearance of information in worksheet cells. You use the Alignment tab, shown in Figure 17-1, to change the alignment and orientation of information in

FIGURE 17-1.
Alignment tab of the Format Cells dialog box.

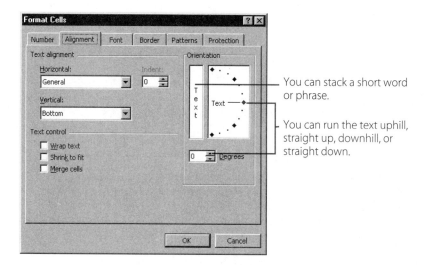

You can stack a short word or phrase.

You can run the text uphill, straight up, downhill, or straight down.

worksheet cells. You can also use the Formatting toolbar to set the most popular alignment options.

 TIP

You can display the Format Cells dialog box by selecting the range of cells you want to format, right-clicking the range, and then choosing Format Cells from the shortcut menu.

Adjusting Horizontal Alignment

To adjust the *horizontal* (side-to-side) alignment of data in a range of cells, select the range you want to align, choose Format Cells, click the Alignment tab, and choose one of the seven alignment options in the Horizontal drop-down list box. General alignment (the default) aligns text to the left edge of the cell and numbers to the right edge. This basic alignment will be suitable for most of your cells' entries. Left, Center, and Right align text to the left, center, and right edges of the cell, respectively. You can also use toolbar buttons to set these common formatting options. (See Figure 17-2.)

The Fill option repeats the data in a cell to fill all the cells selected in the row, although the data is still stored only in the first cell. The Justify option aligns text evenly between the cell borders when longer cell entries wrap within a cell.

The final option in the Horizontal drop-down list box is Center Across Selection, which centers the data in the first cell across a range of selected columns. For example, to center the contents of cell A1 across columns A, B, C, and D, select cells A1 through D1, choose Cells from the Format menu, click the Alignment tab, and select the Center Across Selection option in the Horizontal list box. Alternatively, you can select cells A1 through D1, and then click the Center Across Selection button on the toolbar. (See Table 17-1 on page 463.)

By the way, Center Across Selection won't display text over occupied cells, so for the command to function properly, cells B1 through D1 must

III

Microsoft Excel

FIGURE 17-2.
Use the Formatting toolbar to set the more common cell formats.

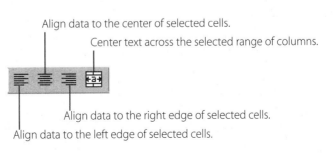

Align data to the center of selected cells.

Center text across the selected range of columns.

Align data to the right edge of selected cells.

Align data to the left edge of selected cells.

be empty. When you choose the command, Excel aligns the data to the center of the selection, but the information is still stored internally in the leftmost cell. By using these seven horizontal alignment options, you can create virtually any tabular formatting effect. Figure 17-3 shows the result of several types of horizontal alignment formatting.

Adjusting Vertical Alignment

The Alignment tab also allows you to adjust the *vertical* (top to bottom) alignment in cells. The default vertical alignment is Bottom, meaning the cell contents are aligned to the bottom of the cell. However, if you change the row height to add additional white space to cells (you'll learn how to do this later in the chapter), you might enhance the appearance of your worksheet by selecting the Top or Center option in the Vertical drop-down list box (see Figure 17-1, page 458). If you have multiple lines of text in a cell, you can also use the Justify alignment option, which spreads complete lines of text evenly between the left and right edges of the cell.

Adjusting Text Orientation

A powerful formatting option on the Alignment tab is the Orientation setting, which changes the text orientation in the selected cells from the default horizontal orientation to an exact angle (measured in degrees)

FIGURE 17-3.
The Horizontal alignment options can create a variety of useful formatting effects.

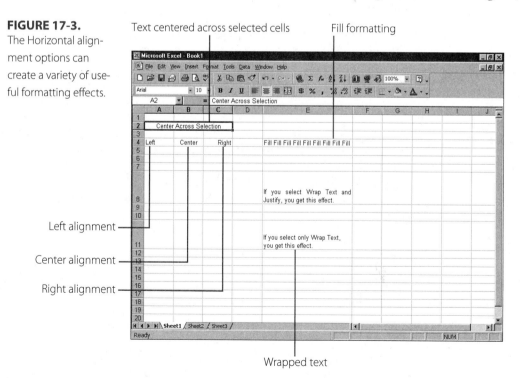

on a 180-degree semicircle. This slick feature lets you create a ledger that includes any of the attractive column labels shown in Figure 17-4. (See step-by-step instructions coming up.)

One nonintuitive option in this Orientation setting is the button you use to "stack" letters vertically in worksheet cells, the effect that's demonstrated in cell B3 in Figure 17-4. To create this neat effect, click the vertical bar on the Alignment tab containing the word *Text*. (See Figure 17-1, page 458.) When this bar is highlighted, Excel will create the stacked-letter effect shown in cell B3, and the text orientation will be set to zero (0) degrees. This is a useful and visually interesting effect for column labels, especially if the text is five or less characters long.

FIGURE 17-4.
The Orientation option on the Alignment tab lets you specify an exact angle for your text—just like using a protractor in art class.

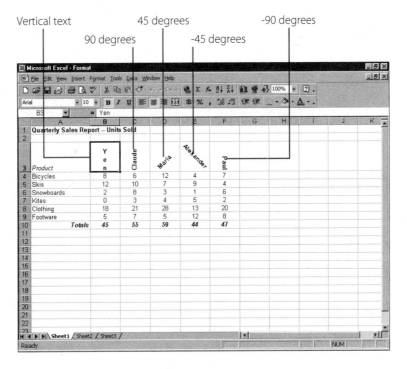

The Format.xls example is on the Running Office 2000 Reader's Corner page. For information about connecting to this Web site, read the Introduction.

To change the text angle for the labels in a group of cells, follow these steps:

1   Select the cells you want to reorient.

2   Choose Cells from the Format menu, and then click the Alignment tab.

ON THE WEB

Microsoft Excel

3 In the Orientation box, click the angle you want to use for the text on the alignment compass. Excel will show you a preview of the orientation you select.

 **TIP**

> Using the Degrees scroll box, you can specify an exact text angle from -90 degrees to +90 degrees.

4 Click OK on the Alignment tab to reorient the selected cells.

Changing Number Formats

Excel allows you to change the appearance of your numeric entries by using several formatting options on the Number tab of the Format Cells dialog box, shown in Figure 17-5. To change the number format for a range of cells, select the cells, choose Cells from the Format menu, click the Number tab, choose a category in the Category list box, and then, if necessary, pick the format you want to use. To help you make your selection, Excel displays formatting examples when more than one option is available to choose from. You can also specify the number of decimal places in most of the formats, and in certain cases, the presence of the currency symbol ($) for dollar amounts and of the comma separator (,) for numbers over 1,000.

The Date category, shown in Figure 17-5, supports two new four-digit year patterns to resolve any confusion over the specified century in the date. The Excel 2000 team added these formats to address the year 2000 problem, which arises when the century is ambiguous in dates used for billing, collection, and other financial transactions.

FIGURE 17-5.
The Number tab lets you change the format of your numeric entries.

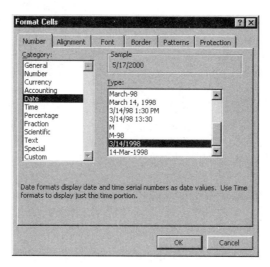

(In other words, you now have the option of printing 3/14/2001 rather than 3/14/01.)

Table 17-1 describes the purpose of each numeric format category on the Number tab, and shows an example of each.

TABLE 17-1. **The Numeric Formats on the Number Tab**

Category	Purpose	Examples
General	The default number format, right-aligned, with no special formatting codes.	15.75 5425
Number	A flexible numeric format that can be enhanced with commas, variable decimal places, and (for negative numbers) colors and parentheses.	3.14159 (1,575.32)
Currency	A general monetary format that can be enhanced with dollar signs, variable decimal places, and (for negative numbers) colors and parentheses. Excel 2000 now supports the Euro format.	$75.35 ($1,234.10)
Accounting	A special currency format designed to align columns of monetary values along the decimal point. (The dollar sign appears along the left side of the cell.)	$ 75.00 $ 500.75
Date	A general-purpose date format that displays calendar dates in several standard styles.	1/15/2000 Jan-15-00
Time	A general-purpose time format that displays chronological values in several standard styles.	3:30 PM 15:30:58
Percentage	A format that multiplies the value in the selected cell by 100 and displays the result using a percentage symbol (%).	175% 15.125%
Fraction	A format that expresses numbers as fractional values. (You specify the number of digits and denominator.)	1/8 2/16
Scientific	An exponential notation for numbers that contain a lot of digits.	1.25E-08 4.58E+12
Text	A format that treats numbers like text. (It aligns them on the left edge of the cell and displays them exactly as they are entered.)	500.35 12345.0
Special	A collection of useful formats that follow an alphanumeric pattern, including Zip Code, Phone Number, and Social Security Number.	98109-1234 535-65-2342
Custom	A list of all standard formats (such as formats for foreign currency) and any custom numeric formats you create. (See next section.)	INV-0075 £150.50

III

Microsoft Excel

In addition to the options on the Number tab, you can use the Formatting toolbar buttons shown in Figure 17-6 to format the numeric entries in selected cells.

FIGURE 17-6.
The buttons controlling numeric formatting on Excel's Formatting toolbar.

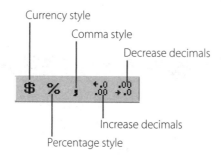

Creating a Custom Number Format

If you routinely enter numeric values in a format that Excel doesn't recognize, you should consider creating a custom number format that you can use to organize nonstandard numeric entries in a consistent and visually appealing manner. For example, you might want to create a custom number format for part numbers or invoice numbers that includes both letters and numbers, or a monetary format that features international currency symbols. To create this type of custom format, choose Cells from the Format menu, click the Number tab, select Custom from the Category list box, and then either:

- modify an existing format by selecting it in the list box and then editing it in the Type box, or

- enter a new format in the Type box using characters and one or more of Excel's special formatting symbols.

Figure 17-7 shows the Custom option on the Number tab after we've created a currency format using the British pound (£) symbol. (You enter the £ symbol by holding down the Alt key and typing 0163 on the numeric keypad. Make sure Num Lock is on.)

To help you organize your custom number format, Excel lets you enter placeholders for digits, special symbols, and other useful characters using the formatting symbols shown in Table 17-2, on page 466. You can also enter characters (such as currency symbols, or useful abbreviations such as *Part* or *INV*) to be included in the format. For example, to create a

Changing Excel's Default Currency Symbol

To change the currency symbol used in Excel and other Windows-based applications, open the Control Panel, double-click the Regional Settings icon, and then select the country you want to use in the drop-down list box on the Regional Settings tab. For example, if you want Excel to display the British pound sign (£) as its default currency symbol, choose English (British) in the drop-down list box, and click OK. Windows will reconfigure your Windows-based applications so that the pound sign (£) is used rather than the dollar sign ($) in all your documents.

If you want to change only particular currency symbols on a worksheet, enter them individually in cells or customize a number format to display them as needed. If standard alphabetical letters or other symbols normally represented on your keyboard are used for the symbol, type them in the appropriate format. For example, the currency symbol for German Marks is DM, and the symbol follows the monetary value, such as 550.57 DM. If a special ANSI code is required for the symbol, make sure Num Lock is turned on, hold down the Alt key, and type the appropriate four-digit code. The following table lists some of the most popular currency symbols and their ANSI codes:

Country	Denomination	Symbol	ANSI Code
United Kingdom	Pound	£	Alt+0163
Japan	Yen	¥	Alt+0165
United States	Cent	¢	Alt+0162

FIGURE 17-7.
To create a custom number format, select the Custom option and modify an existing format or create a new one.

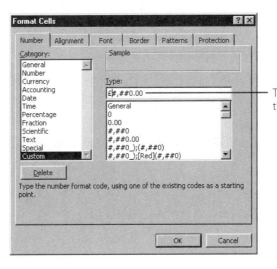

This custom format includes the British pound sign (£).

custom part number format that translates the cell value 25 to the formatted part number *Part AA-025*, enter the code *Part AA-000* in the Type text box. To use the custom format later, click the Number tab, click the Custom Category, and then double-click the custom format in the list box. You can also delete custom formats by highlighting the format and clicking the Delete button. (Excel will not let you delete the default formats.)

TABLE 17-2.   Useful Formatting Characters for Building Custom Number Formats

Character	Purpose	Example	Number Entered	Result
#	Creates a placeholder for significant digits, rounding to fit if necessary.	##.###	50.0048 2.30	50.005 2.3
0	Rounds numbers to fit like the # character, but fills any empty positions with zeros to align numbers and to fill all specified positions	00.00	50.1 5	50.10 05.00
?	Also rounds numbers to fit, but fills any empty positions with spaces rather than extra zeros (if necessary) to align numbers and fill positions.	??.??	5.6 .70 73.27	5.6 .70 73.27
"text"	Adds the characters specified to the value in the cell.	"ID " ##	75 2	ID 75 ID 2
comma (,)	Separates thousands in numbers.	#,###	5600	5,600
$,-,+,:,/,(,), space	Standard formatting characters. Each appears as specified in the custom numeric format.	$#.000	500.5	$500.500
%	Multiplies value by 100 and adds percentage symbol.	##%	.25	25%

Changing Text Font and Text Color

To emphasize headings and distinguish different kinds of information in your worksheet, you can use the Font tab of the Format Cells dialog box, shown in Figure 17-8. The Font tab lets you change the font, style, size, and color of the data in selected cells. It also controls whether data is underlined and allows you to create special formatting effects such as strikethrough, superscript, and subscript. The fonts displayed on the Font tab depend on the type of printer you are connected to and the fonts installed on your system. Fonts preceded by a TrueType

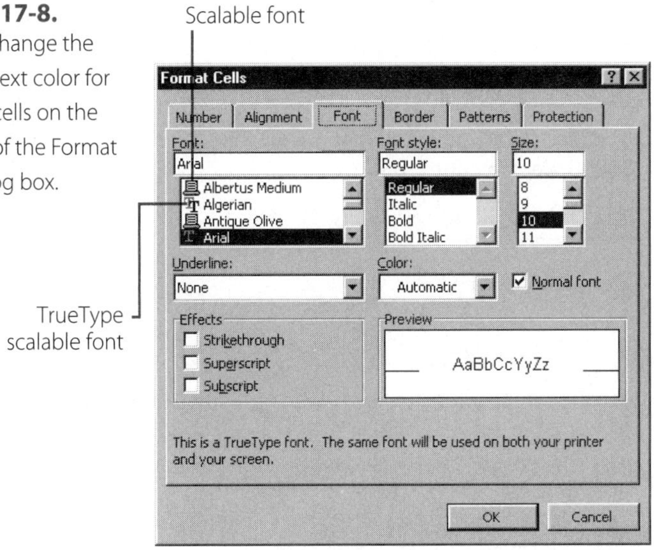

FIGURE 17-8.
You can change the font and text color for selected cells on the Font tab of the Format Cells dialog box.

Scalable font

TrueType scalable font

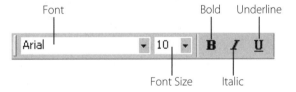

symbol are TrueType fonts, designed to appear in print exactly as they do on the screen. You might also see fonts on the Font tab that have tiny printer icons in front of them; these are scalable fonts, which will look sharp when printed but might not display accurately on the screen. (The size will probably be right but the character shapes might not exactly match.) You can see both typeface symbols in Figure 17-8.

In addition to selecting formatting options on the Font tab, you can also use Excel's Formatting toolbar to change several font and text color options. Figure 17-9 shows the buttons you can use to increase your formatting speed.

FIGURE 17-9.
Selected text cells can be formatted using these Formatting toolbar buttons.

Font   Bold   Underline

| Arial | 10 | **B** | *I* | U |

Font Size   Italic

III

Microsoft Excel

To change the font and text color formatting in one or more cells, follow these steps:

1 Select the cells you want to format. (To format individual characters in a cell, see the sidebar on the next page.)

2 Choose Cells from the Format menu, and then click the Font tab.

3   Use the list boxes and check boxes on the Font tab to adjust the font characteristics you want to change. Use the Preview window to verify that the appearance is what you want.

> If you want to return to the default font setting, select the Normal Font check box on the Font tab.

4   When you're finished, click OK.

Adding Borders to Cells

Another useful technique for highlighting specific information in a worksheet is adding borders to important cells using the Border tab of the Format Cells dialog box, shown in Figure 17-10. The Border tab lets

FIGURE 17-10.
The Border tab lets you underline or box selected cells.

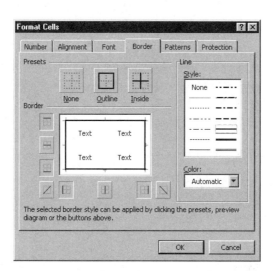

Formatting Individual Characters in a Cell

You can also format individual characters in a cell if the entry contains text. This useful feature lets you emphasize important words in a long entry or create dramatic effects in headings. For example, you can italicize one word in a cell containing many words or change the first letter of a heading to a larger point size. To format individual characters in a cell, double-click the cell and select the characters you want to change. Then choose the Cells command on the Format menu and change the attributes you want, or click the appropriate buttons on the Formatting toolbar. When you press Enter, the formatting will take effect.

you place a solid or dashed line along one or more cell edges, allowing you to create a summary line or boxed effect, or even an interesting combination of squares and rectangles. You can also create diagonal lines in worksheet cells, so that your spreadsheets can contain triangles, "X" patterns, or other intriguing shapes.

To specify borders for the cells you have selected, first click one of the 14 line styles in the Style box (the None style removes existing borders). Then click the lines you want on the preview diagram in the Border box, or click the buttons along the left and bottom of the Border box for the same result. As a shortcut, you can also use one of the three border styles in the Presets box: None (to remove an existing border), Outline (to place a border around the outside edge of the selected cells), or Inside (to draw lines along the inside edges of selected cells). You can also change the color of the border by opening the Color list box.

Figure 17-11 shows an example of the Outline button at work. In the example, we selected cells A3:E9 in the worksheet, chose the Cells command on the Format menu and clicked the Border tab, clicked a heavy border style and the color black, and then clicked the Outline button. The resulting border appears only around the perimeter of the range we selected. If we wanted to outline each of the cells as well as the outer perimeter, we could have selected both the Outline button and the Inside button. Or, to provide a line that runs continuously under the table headings in Figure 17-11, we would select the headings, and then select just the bottom border line in the weight we want.

FIGURE 17-11.
Clicking the Outline button adds a box around the selected text.

	A	B	C	D	E	F
1	*Produce Order Sheet*					
2						
3	**Item**	**Description**	**Price/Lb.**	**Quantity**	**Total**	
4	F-10	*Grapes*	$1.99	10	$19.90	
5	F-22	*Bananas*	$0.79	15	$11.85	
6	F-25	*Apples*	$0.69	12	$8.28	
7	F-18	*Pears*	$1.29	5	$6.45	
8	V-17	*Mushrooms*	$2.49	8	$19.92	
9	V-07	*Green Beans*	$0.89	8	$7.12	
10						
11						

Outline border

The OrderFrm.xls example is on the Running Office 2000 Reader's Corner page.

Microsoft Excel

Making Borders Faster: Using the Borders Toolbar Button

A handy alternative to using the Border tab is clicking the Borders button on Excel's Formatting toolbar. In this case, using the Formatting toolbar is really much faster than using the Format Cells dialog box, and the toolbar also gives you single-step access to some formatting designs that require multiple steps using the Format Cells dialog box. To use the Borders button, select the range of cells you want to highlight, click the Borders button, and then pick from the 12 border options that appear on the Borders toolbar, as shown in the illustration below. The 12 options are actually border formatting shortcuts, and a few of them feature a combination of aesthetically pleasing styles. For example, the bottom left style—useful for creating worksheet tables—places a light border on the top of the cell and a heavier border on the bottom of the cell. Learning to use these border styles will save you considerable time as you format your worksheets.

Adding Shading to Cells

To create effects that complement the borders produced by the Border tab, the Patterns tab of the Format Cells dialog box (see Figure 17-12) lets you add a background color and optional colored pattern to one or more cells in your worksheet. By default, the color you select has no pattern added to it, so you see a solid color in your cells. However, you can also add a background pattern and change its color from the default black to any of the colors displayed in the Pattern drop-down list. To add color and shading to cells, select the cells you want to format, choose Cells from the Format menu, click the Patterns tab, pick a Cell shading color, and then pick a shading pattern in a second color from the Pattern drop-down list box.

Color can make a striking addition to your worksheet, and is ideal—if used in moderation—for documents created to be viewed electronically, such as status reports, departmental ledgers, sales projections, and the like. If you don't have a color printer, your color shading effects will be converted to gray tones when you print. (Not to worry, Excel usually does a good job at this.) To see what this conversion is like, you can view your worksheet using the Print Preview command on the File menu. Figure 17-13 shows a sample worksheet with color and pattern shading.

FIGURE 17-12.
The Patterns tab lets you add color background shading and patterns to your cells.

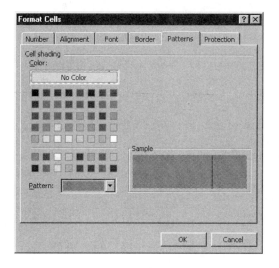

FIGURE 17-13.
Color and pattern shading look nice, even if you don't have a color printer.

	A	B	C	D	E	F
1	*Produce Order Sheet*					
2						
3	Item	Description	Price/Lb.	Quantity	Total	
4	F-10	Grapes	$1.99	10	$19.90	
5	F-22	Bananas	$0.79	15	$11.85	
6	F-25	Apples	$0.69	12	$8.28	
7	F-18	Pears	$1.29	5	$6.45	
8	V-17	Mushrooms	$2.49	8	$19.92	
9	V-07	Green Beans	$0.89	8	$7.12	
10						
11						

Fill Color

You can also use the Fill Color button on the Formatting toolbar to change the background color (but not the pattern) used in worksheet cells. To remove the existing color in worksheet cells, click the No Fill option.

Copying Formatting Using the Format Painter Button

Occasionally, you'll need to copy the formats from one cell to another cell without copying the data in the cell. For example, you might want to copy the cell formats you used to create a 14-point, bold, Times New Roman heading that has a thick border to a second heading you're creating later in the worksheet. Excel allows you to accomplish this task by using the Format Painter button on the Standard toolbar. To copy formatting using the Format Painter button, follow these steps:

Format Painter

1 Select the cell from which you want to copy formats.

2 Click the Format Painter button on the toolbar. A marquee will appear around the selected cell and a paintbrush will be added to the mouse pointer.

3 Select the range of cells you want to change to the new format.

If you decide you don't like the format you copied, remember that you can choose Undo from the Edit menu to remove it. To remove the selection marquee, press Escape.

If you want to copy formats to cells or ranges that are not contiguous, double-click the Format Painter button, and then select the cells you want to format one by one. When you've finished, click the Format Painter button again.

Changing Column Widths and Row Heights

Excel gives you room for about eight digits in a worksheet cell if you use the default 10-point Arial font. In the first versions of Excel, you had to manually adjust the width of a cell whenever you entered a number that exceeded this basic limit. (Excel placed pound characters—#######—in the cell to let you know there wasn't enough room to display the number.) In Excel 97 and Excel 2000, worksheet cells are automatically resized whenever a number doesn't fit.

However, note that if you intentionally reduce a cell so that a number won't fit, Excel will then display the overflow characters. Most of the time this is good—unless you have a specific reason for keeping a column the default width. Fortunately, it's easy to fiddle with your column widths and row heights if you want to format them in a special way. You can resize rows and columns by dragging with the mouse (the fastest method), or by using commands on the Format menu. We'll cover both techniques in this section.

Different columns can be different widths in a worksheet, but each cell in a particular column must be the same width. Likewise, different rows in the worksheet can have different heights, but each cell in a particular row must be the same height.

Adjusting the Height or Width Manually

? SEE ALSO

For an automatic means of fitting spaces to dates, see "Using the AutoFit Command," page 475.

You can widen or narrow a column by dragging the right column edge with the mouse, or by specifying a new width, using the Width command on the Format menu's Column submenu. In addition, you can change the height of a row by dragging the lower edge of the row, or by specifying a new height, using the Height command on the Format menu's Row submenu. Each method is described in the following sections.

Changing Column Width Using the Mouse

Figure 17-14 shows how to change column width using the mouse.

W ON THE WEB

The Formula.xls example is on the Running Office 2000 Reader's Corner page.

FIGURE 17-14.
Follow these steps to change the column width using the mouse.

1 Position the mouse pointer on the right edge of the column heading until it changes into a sizing pointer that has arrows pointing right and left.

2 Drag the sizing pointer to the right or left to change the column width.

The column width display shows the average number of standard-font characters that will fit in the column.

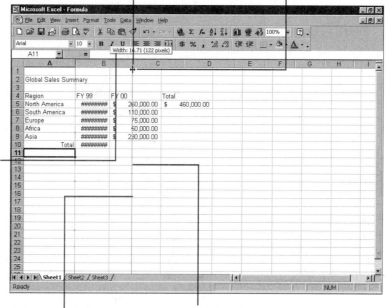

A dotted line indicates the new column width.

3 When the column width is the size you want, release the mouse button.

To change the width of multiple columns with the mouse, select the columns you want to resize, and then drag and adjust one of the columns. When you release the mouse button, each of the columns will be the width of the one you changed.

Changing Column Width Using the Column Width Command

The Width command on the Column submenu is useful if you want to type an exact width for the column you're resizing. The number you specify is the average number of characters that will fit in the cell using the default font (defined as part of the Normal style). To change the column width using the Width command, follow these steps:

1 Select a cell in the column you want to resize. To resize multiple columns, select a cell in each of the columns you want to adjust.

2 Choose Column from the Format menu, and then choose Width from the submenu. The Column Width dialog box appears.

3 Type the new size you want in the Column Width text box.

4 Click OK to resize the column.

> **Set Your Preferred Column Widths Instantly**
>
> To set the default (or standard) width of columns in your worksheet, choose Standard Width from the Column submenu. This command adjusts the width of every column in the worksheet that has not already been resized, or every column you select. To select all the columns of the worksheet, even those you've previously changed, first click the Select All button above row 1 and to the left of column A. This is a good way to customize the cells in your worksheet if you always want them to be a certain shape.

Changing Row Height Using the Mouse

Excel automatically adjusts the row height to fit the font and text orientation you're using, but occasionally you'll want to increase the row height to add white space to your worksheet or to decrease the row height to save room. To change row height using the mouse, follow the steps shown in Figure 17-15.

To change the height of multiple rows using the mouse, first select the rows you want to resize, and then drag and adjust one of the rows. When you release the mouse button, each of the rows will be the same height as the one you adjusted.

FIGURE 17-15.
You can change the row height using the mouse.

The row size is displayed in points.

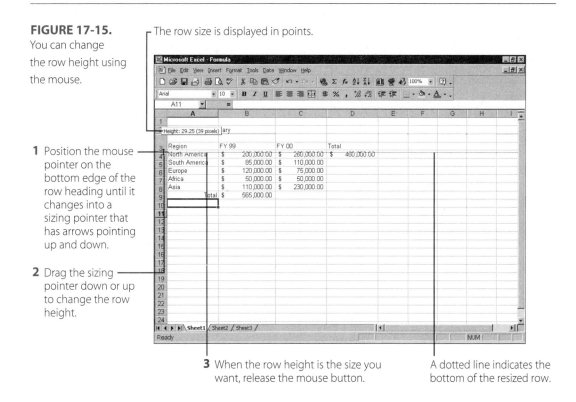

1 Position the mouse pointer on the bottom edge of the row heading until it changes into a sizing pointer that has arrows pointing up and down.

2 Drag the sizing pointer down or up to change the row height.

3 When the row height is the size you want, release the mouse button.

A dotted line indicates the bottom of the resized row.

Changing Row Height Using the Row Height Command

The Height command on the Row submenu is useful if you want to type an exact height for the row you're resizing. The row height is measured in points, and the standard height is based on the size of the default font. To change the row height using the Height command, follow these steps:

1 Highlight a cell in the row you want to resize. If you want to resize multiple rows, select a cell in each of the rows you want to adjust.

2 Choose Row from the Format menu, and then choose Height from the submenu. The Row Height dialog box appears.

3 Type the new size in points that you want the row or rows to be.

4 Click OK to resize the selected rows.

Using the AutoFit Command

If you want Excel to automatically size your rows or columns for you, use the AutoFit commands on the Column and Row submenus. When

III

Microsoft Excel

you select a column and choose AutoFit Selection from the Column submenu, Excel resizes the column to fit the widest entry in the column. This saves you the trouble of manually calculating point sizes or scanning every entry in a column as you drag the mouse. If you select a group of cells in a column, Excel adjusts the width based on the widest cell value in the selection, not the entire column.

Excel automatically resizes rows when you modify the font, so the row AutoFit command is less dramatic. When you select a row and choose AutoFit from the Row submenu, Excel returns the row to the default height for the largest font being used in the row. In short, the main benefit of the AutoFit command on rows is removing white space—it can't be used to compress a row or hide information in a row.

Hide Rows or Columns for Security

If you want to hide a row or column in your worksheet, either to shield the data from unauthorized glances or to keep it out of your way while you work, select the row or column you want to hide, and choose Hide from the Row or Column submenu. When you choose this command, the entire row or column, including the row number or column letter, will seem to disappear from the worksheet (though it hasn't actually been deleted).

To restore the hidden row or column, select the rows or columns on both sides of the hidden entry, and choose Unhide from the Row or Column submenu. The hidden row or column will appear as you last saw it.

Applying a Combination of Effects Using AutoFormat

If you're formatting a block or table of cells, you can apply several formatting effects in one fell swoop by using the AutoFormat command on the Format menu. The AutoFormat command displays a dialog box that features several predesigned table styles in the Table Format list box. Figure 17-16 shows one of the table formats that creates a three-dimensional effect. (As a bonus, Excel 2000 shows each table style in its own preview window.) When you find the style you want, click OK to format the block of cells you selected as a table. You might try several styles on your own data, to get the true visual effect and determine which one offers the most impact.

By default, the AutoFormat command sets the Number, Border, Font, Patterns, Alignment, and Width/Height options to match the table style you select. You can limit the options used in AutoFormat by clicking

FIGURE 17-16.
The 3D Effects 2 style is only one of many AutoFormats requiring just a single click to format your worksheet.

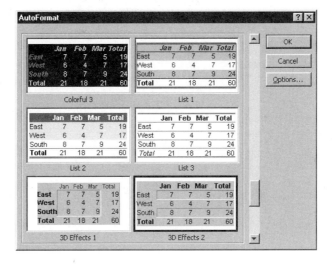

the Options button in the dialog box and deselecting the formats you don't want. For example, if you like a particular table but don't want the border that's included, deselect the Border check box (by clicking it), and click OK to apply other characteristics of the format.

Creating Conditional Formatting

Another slick feature of Excel is the ability it gives you to add *conditional formatting* to your worksheet, formatting that automatically adjusts depending on the contents of worksheet cells. In plain English, this means that you can highlight important trends in your data—such as the rise in a stock price, or a sudden spurt in your college expenses—based on conditions you set in advance using the Conditional Formatting dialog box. Using this feature, an out-of-the-ordinary number will "jump out" at anyone who routinely uses the worksheet.

The following example shows how to add conditional formatting to a sample worksheet that tracks stock prices. If a stock in the Gain/Loss column rises by more than 20 percent, the conditional formatting will display numbers in bold type on a light blue diagonal background. If a stock in the Gain/Loss column falls by more than 20 percent, the number will be displayed in bold type on a solid red background. (Our worksheet is shown in Figure 17-17, on the next page.)

 **ON THE WEB**   The CondForm.xls example is on the Running Office 2000 Reader's Corner page.

III

Microsoft Excel

FIGURE 17-17.

Conditional formatting highlights noteworthy numbers automatically, according to your specifications.

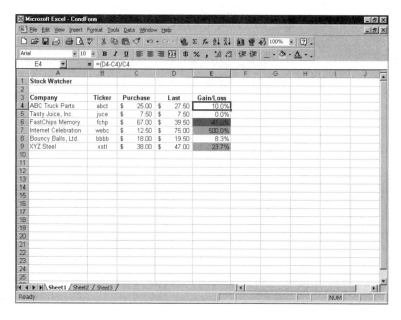

Here's how you would create such a conditional format.

1 Create a worksheet containing one or more cells of numeric information. (The worksheet can be an invoice, a financial document, a sales report, or any other document with useful numeric data.)

2 Select the cell range to which you want to apply the conditional formatting. (Note that each cell can maintain its own, unique conditional formatting, so that you can set up several different conditions.)

3 Choose Conditional Formatting from the Format menu. The Conditional Formatting dialog box appears, containing several drop-down list boxes.

4 In the first list box, indicate whether you want Excel to use the current formula or the current value from the cells that you have selected. (In most cases, you'll want to use the cell value.)

5 In the second list box, indicate the comparison operator you'd like to use in the conditional formatting. For our example, we selected greater than (>), because we're looking for stock returns greater than 20 percent.

6 In the third list box, type the number you want to use in the comparison. We typed 20% or 0.2, because we want to isolate gains over 20 percent.

7 Now click the Format button and specify the formatting you'll use for the cells if the conditional statement you specified in steps 4 through 6 becomes true.

A modified Format Cells dialog box appears that has three formatting tabs. We selected light blue on the Patterns tab, and then clicked OK.

8 If necessary, click the Add button in the Conditional Formatting dialog box to add another condition to the scenario. (We took this opportunity to add a condition that highlighted losses of more than 20 percent in the worksheet.) The dialog box expands to accept an additional condition.

> **NOTE**
> The Add button lets you add up to three conditions. The Delete button removes conditions you no longer want.

9 Specify the operator you want to use in the second drop-down list box, and then type a value in the third list box. We specified less than (<) as the operator, and then typed -20%.

10 If you specified a second condition, click the Format button for Condition 2 and select a unique formatting color or type style. Using the Patterns tab, we specified red shading. Our screen looks like this:

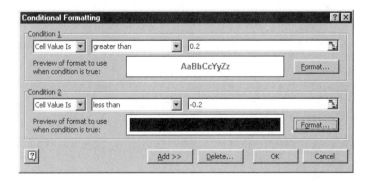

11 Click OK to close the dialog box and see the conditional formatting applied to the selected text. If any numbers fall into the ranges you specified, the formatting you specified will be carried out. Figure 17-17 shows two gains and one loss highlighted by the conditional formatting we entered for this example. Our efforts certainly paid off, especially if we now act on the knowledge of our profits or losses!

III

Microsoft Excel

Using Styles

If you routinely use the same formatting options for cells in your worksheets, you might want to consider creating a formatting *style* (a collection of formatting choices) that you can save with your workbook and use whenever you format information with the same attributes. After you create a new formatting style, or modify an existing one, you can use that style in any worksheet in your workbook, or you can copy the style to other open workbooks. In this section, you'll learn the following techniques:

- How to create your own styles

- How to apply existing styles

- How to copy or *merge* styles from other workbooks

Creating Your Own Styles

Styles are created by using the Style command on the Format menu. When you choose Style, the Style dialog box appears, as shown in Figure 17-18.

If the cell you selected before choosing the Style command has not yet been formatted with a style, the Normal style will be displayed in the Style Name box. Excel predefines several styles in addition to the Normal style, including Comma, Currency, and Percent styles. If you want to modify one of these styles throughout the workbook, you select the style in the Style Name drop-down list box, click the Modify button, update the style using the tabs in the Format Cells dialog box, and click OK to return to the Style dialog box. When you click OK in the Style dialog box, the updated style will be changed throughout your workbook.

The easiest way to create a new style is by selecting a cell that has formatting you want to save, choosing the Style command, and giving the style a new name. This way of creating a style is called *by example*, because you use your own worksheet formatting to define the style.

 TIP

You can also create styles from scratch by using the Add button in the Style dialog box.

FIGURE 17-18.
You can use the Style
dialog box to manage
the formatting styles
in your worksheet.

Style Name drop-down list box
containing currently defined styles.

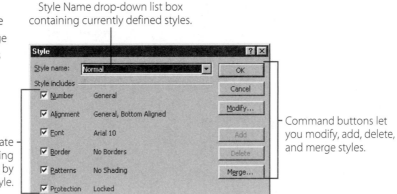

Check boxes indicate
which formatting
options are set by
the current style.

Command buttons let
you modify, add, delete,
and merge styles.

The following steps show you how to create a new style by example.
The style we created is the vertically oriented column heading for
Claude, shown in cell C3 in Figure 17-19. The heading is bold, dark
blue, center-aligned, and rotated up 90 degrees in the cell. We call it
Vertical Head.

FIGURE 17-19.
To create a new style
by example, you select
a cell in your work-
sheet that has the for-
matting you want to
save for the new style.

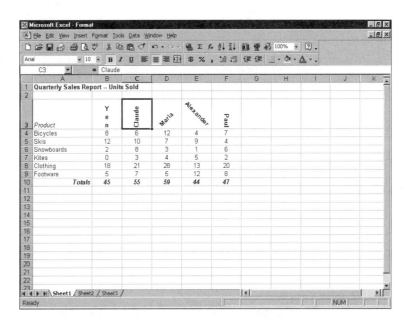

To create the Vertical Head style by example, follow these steps:

1 Format the cell you want to create your style from. For example, you could use the Alignment tab of the Format Cells dialog box to center the text horizontally and change the orientation, and then use the Font tab to change the font style to bold and dark blue.

2 Select the cell you just formatted.

3 Choose Style from the Format menu.

4 Type *Vertical Head* (or another name of your choice) in the Style Name text box.

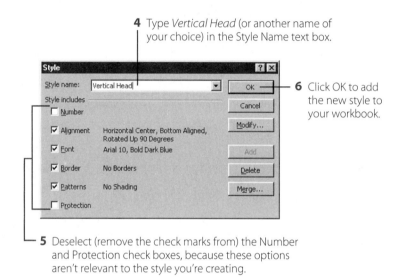

6 Click OK to add the new style to your workbook.

5 Deselect (remove the check marks from) the Number and Protection check boxes, because these options aren't relevant to the style you're creating.

When a style option is deselected (there's no check mark in its check box), it means that any time you apply the associated style, the selected cells will keep their existing formatting for these categories.

To delete a custom style you no longer want, select the style in the Style Name drop-down list box, and click the Delete button.

Applying Existing Styles

To apply an existing style in your workbook, either a predefined style or one that you have created, select the cell or range of cells to which you want to apply the style, and then follow these steps:

1 Choose Style from the Format menu to open the Style dialog box.

2 Click the Style Name drop-down list box to display the styles available in your workbook.

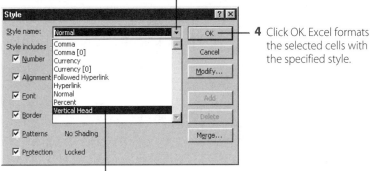

4 Click OK. Excel formats the selected cells with the specified style.

3 Select the style you want. We want the Vertical Head style created above.

CAUTION

Merging is a powerful tool, and you should use it with some caution. If the workbook you merge styles into has matching style names, the new styles can override your existing styles and be applied throughout your workbook.

TIP

Merging Styles from Other Workbooks

When you create a new style, you can use it only in the workbook where you create it—the new style is saved in the current workbook and won't appear in other workbooks. (This way, you won't mix up styles for your stock portfolio with those for your college expense budget.) However, you can copy or merge styles from other workbooks into the current workbook by using the Merge button in the Style dialog box.

> Merging styles is a useful way to give your workbooks a consistent look. You can also use Excel templates (discussed in the next section) to format documents in a standard manner.

To merge styles from other Excel workbooks, follow these steps:

1   Open the *source* workbook (the workbook you want to copy styles from) and the *destination* workbook (the workbook you want to copy the styles to).

2   From the Window menu, click the destination workbook (its name should appear near the bottom of the Window menu) to make it the active window.

3   From the Format menu, choose Style.

Microsoft Excel

III

4 Click the Merge button to display the Merge Styles dialog box shown below:

Other workbooks currently open in Excel

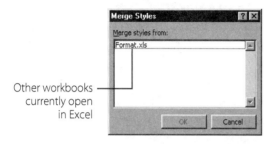

5 Select the name of the workbook you want to copy styles from (the source workbook), and then click OK.

Excel copies all the styles from the source workbook to the destination workbook. If the source workbook contains formatting styles that have the same names as styles in the destination workbook, a warning message will appear asking whether you want to merge the styles anyway. If you click Yes, the styles will be merged and the source styles will be applied throughout the workbook.

⚠ WARNING

> The Undo command does *not* reverse the effects of the Merge Styles dialog box. Be sure you want to copy over *all* the styles from the source workbook before you click the Merge button. (Remember that you can delete unwanted styles before the merge, by using the Delete button in the Style dialog box.)

Creating Templates

? SEE ALSO

You can use Microsoft Office templates and wizards to create many standard documents automatically. For more information, see "Creating Files Using a Document Template," page 13.

Using formatting styles is a good way to organize existing data in a standard format. If you routinely create similar documents from scratch, however—such as monthly reports, purchase orders, or product invoices—consider creating an Excel template. A *template* is a file that serves as a model for worksheets you create in your workbooks. You can use the many preformatted templates that are included with the Office software, or you can create your own templates that you can use whenever you want to create data in a particular format. In this section, you'll learn:

■ How to open and modify an existing template file

■ How to create a new template file

> **Use an Existing Template**
>
> If you just want to use an existing Excel template to create a new worksheet (rather than modify a template to create a new type of worksheet), choose New from the File menu. Select a template from an appropriate tab, and then click OK.

Opening and Modifying an Existing Template File

To open an existing template file—either a template included with Office or one you created on your own—choose Open from the Excel File menu, specify Templates (*.xlt) in the Files Of Type list box, and double-click the template file icon in the files list box. Unless you intend to make changes to the original template, your first step after opening a template should be to save the workbook under a new file-name to protect the original template.

To open an existing template, follow these steps:

Open

1   Choose Open from the File menu or click the Open button on the Standard toolbar. The Open dialog box appears:

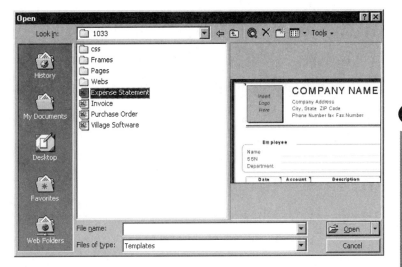

2   In the Files Of Type drop-down list box, select Templates.

> Excel templates have the .xlt file extension on disk.

3 Browse to the folder containing the template you want to open. Office creates a Templates folder in the folder in which you installed Office. (Typically C:\Program Files\Microsoft Office\Templates.) The Templates folder contains several folders of its own for each of the Office applications. You'll find several useful Excel templates in the folder shown above.

> For a description of each of the templates included in Microsoft Excel, search for "Templates" in the Excel online Help.

4 Double-click the template file you want to open. The template appears in a window, such as the one shown here:

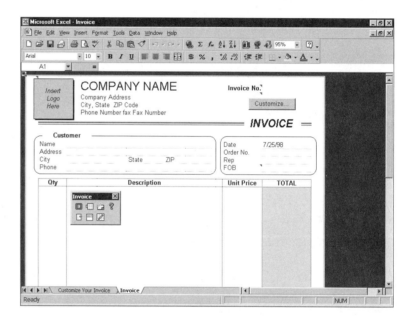

If the template was included with the Office software, it typically contains several worksheet tabs and operating instructions. It may also contain a useful template toolbar that has custom template commands and online Help for the template.

5 Choose Save As from the File menu. When the Save As dialog box appears, give the template a new filename. Also, be sure to specify one of the Office template folders for the location of your template so that the template will appear as an option when you choose New from the Excel File menu. Click Save to save the template file to disk.

6 Your new template is now ready to be customized. When you're finished adding the touches you want, save your changes and close the template. Each time you open this template in the future, it will be ready to use as a boilerplate worksheet.

Creating a New Template File

To make a new template file using one of your own workbooks as a model, complete the following steps. When you're finished, you'll have a template you can use each time you want to create a worksheet that has the formatting you've included.

1 Open the workbook you want to save as a template file.

2 Choose Save As from the File menu. The Save As dialog box appears.

3 Select Template in the Save As Type drop-down list box.

4 Enter a name for the template in the File Name text box, specify a folder location for the template by using the Save In list box, and then click Save.

5 Close the workbook you saved as a template. The next time you want to use the template as a worksheet model, choose New from the File menu, locate the template, and double-click it.

Changing Page Breaks

After you format your worksheet, you might want to adjust where the page breaks fall, particularly for longer worksheets. A *page break* is a formatting code that tells your printer to stop printing information on one page and start printing on the next page. Excel adds a page break to your worksheet when a page is full and identifies the division with a light dashed line. (Excel adds both vertical and horizontal page breaks.) If you don't want to see these breaks as you work, choose Options from the Tools menu, click the View tab, and then deselect the Page Breaks option in the Window Options area.

You can set your own page breaks manually in the worksheet. For example, you might choose to place a page break above a table to keep all the table entries on the same page. To set a manual page break in the worksheet, follow the steps shown in Figure 17-20, on the next page.

The highlighted cell will become the upper left corner of the new page, and the manual page break will appear as a bold dashed line.

III

Microsoft Excel

FIGURE 17-20.
In Normal view, Excel indicates page breaks with bold, dashed lines.

2 Choose Page Break from the Insert menu.

	A	B	C	D	E	F	G
15	Pattern #	Description		Price	Qty	Extended	
16							
17	315	Sonya's Sitting Room		$2.75		$0.00	
18	510	Heartfelt Angel		$2.75		$0.00	
19	515	Country Shores		$2.75		$0.00	
20	510M	Heartfelt Angel Model		$35.00		$0.00	
21	520	Patchwork Santa		$2.75		$0.00	
22	520M	Patchwork Santa Model		$35.00		$0.00	
23	525	Winter Nights		$2.75		$0.00	
24	410C	The Key To Christmas Charms		$4.00		$0.00	
25	415C	Medieval Santa Charms		$4.00		$0.00	
26	530	Keeping Warm		$2.75		$0.00	
27	535	Spring In The Valley		$2.75		$0.00	
28	540	Santa's Favorite Ornaments		$1.93		$0.00	
29							
30							
31				Sub total (A)		$0.00	
32							
33							
34		Please Remit to:		Sub total (A)		$0.00	
35		Sweet Peas, Inc.		Sub total (B)			
36		16541 Redmond Way # 163-C		Shipping		$0.00	
37		Redmond, WA 98052		Total		$0.00	
38		(206) 284-5529		This is your invoice.			
39							

1 Select the cell below and to the right of where you want to insert the page break.

The Invoice.xls example is on the Running Office 2000 Reader's Corner page.

Remove a Manual Page Break

To remove both the bottom and right edges of a page break, click the cell below and to the right of the page break, and choose Remove Page Break from the Insert menu. You can also remove just the bottom of the page break or just the right side by clicking any cell directly below or directly to the right of the page break.

Using Page Break Preview

Excel also provides a special worksheet view called Page Break Preview that quickly identifies the page breaks in your worksheet and allows you to easily manipulate them. Page Break Preview shows you a miniature version of your worksheet (a little like the Print Preview command on the File menu), but marks page breaks with a thick bold line and highlights page numbers with giant labels so that you can quickly find your place. (See Figure 17-21.) To select the page break preview, choose Page Break Preview from the View menu; to deselect it, choose Normal from the View menu.

To view and modify page breaks in Page Break Preview, follow these steps:

1 Choose Page Break Preview from the View menu. Excel starts Page Break Preview mode, as shown in Figure 17-21.

2 If you see a dialog box that displays a welcome message, read the instructions about modifying page breaks, and then click OK. (You can suppress this dialog box by clicking Do Not Show This Dialog Again.)

3 Examine the page breaks in your worksheet by using the vertical and horizontal scroll bars. Individual pages will be marked with large labels, and page breaks will be marked with bold lines.

 TIP

> Page Break Preview is an active editing mode, so you can add information to worksheet cells, select ranges, issue commands, or edit individual entries while you preview your page breaks. However, you'll probably find it easier to read the contents of worksheet cells in Normal view.

FIGURE 17-21.
To change a page break, simply drag a break line to a new location.

Page break line ⎯

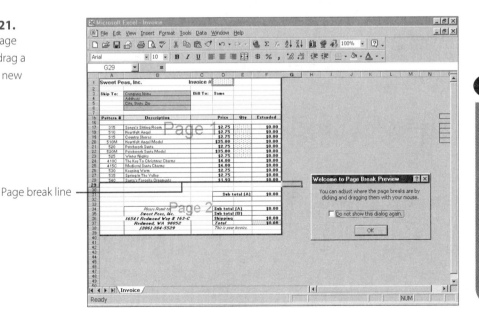

4 To change a page break marked with a bold line, drag the break line with the mouse to a new location in the worksheet. When you release the mouse button, Excel will repaginate the worksheet and display the new page break. (If you want to reverse the change, you can reinstate the old page break by simply clicking the Undo button on the Standard toolbar.)

5 When you're finished working in Page Break Preview, choose Normal from the View menu.

Using Workbooks to Organize Information

I f worksheets are the basic building blocks used to store information in Microsoft Excel, workbooks are the organizational tools you can use to manage data effectively. By default, each Excel workbook contains three worksheets. In this chapter, you'll learn how to switch between worksheets, name worksheets, add worksheets to a workbook, delete unwanted worksheets from a workbook, and rearrange worksheets. You'll also learn how to work with more than one workbook at once, how to link information between worksheets and workbooks, how to create and manage shared workbooks on a network, and how to protect worksheets and workbooks by using password protection. When you're finished, you'll have all the tools you need to manage workbooks effectively.

Managing Worksheets

Workbooks help you organize the reports, ledgers, tables, and forms you use every day. In the first electronic spreadsheets, users typically created a new file for each worksheet they built. This approach worked fine for casual spreadsheet users, but experienced business users, who often worked with literally hundreds of worksheets, were soon swamped with files and folders. (If this sounds like you now, you'll like this section!)

Excel now provides the ability to create default workbooks containing up to 255 worksheets. To smooth out the file management problem, all the worksheets in a workbook are now stored in one file. Although you're not actually required to place more than one worksheet in a workbook, this organizational feature gives you the option of collecting similar worksheets in one place. For example, you could store all the worksheets related to product development costs (research, manufacturing, marketing, packaging, and so on) in one workbook entitled 2001 Development Costs.

In the first part of this chapter, you'll learn the basic skills needed to manage worksheets in workbooks. You'll learn how to:

- Switch between worksheets in a workbook

- Name your worksheets

- Delete worksheets from a workbook

- Add worksheets to a workbook

- Change the order of worksheets in a workbook

Switching Between Worksheets

By default, each new Excel workbook contains three identical worksheets, named Sheet1, Sheet2, and Sheet3. Each worksheet is identified by a *worksheet tab* at the bottom of the worksheet window, as shown in Figure 18-1. To switch between worksheets, you click the worksheet tab you want to display, and it appears as the active worksheet in the workplace. To the left of the worksheet tabs are the *tab scroll buttons*, which you can use to display worksheet tabs not currently visible. Clicking the outside navigation arrows displays the first and last tabs in the workbook, and clicking the inside arrows displays hidden tabs to the left and right. To switch between worksheets in a workbook, follow the steps in Figure 18-1.

FIGURE 18-1.
Switching between
worksheets.

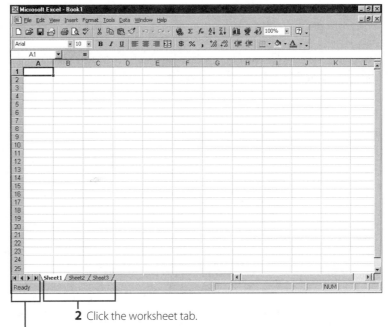

2 Click the worksheet tab.

1 Use the tab scroll buttons to bring into view
any worksheet tabs you can't see.

Naming Worksheets

The default names for worksheets—Sheet1, Sheet2, and so on—are just
placeholders for more useful and intuitive names that you devise. You
can name or rename a worksheet at any time by double-clicking the
worksheet tab to select the title and then typing a new name. Figure
18-2, on the next page, shows the two-step process. (To cancel your
edit, press the Escape key.) You can use up to 31 characters in your
worksheet names (including spaces), but remember that the more
characters you use for the name, the less room you leave for other
worksheet tabs. It's a good idea to strike a balance between meaningful
and brief names.

You can also use a menu command to rename the worksheet that is currently visible: Choose Sheet from the Format menu, choose Rename from
the submenu, and then type the new worksheet name and press Enter.

Deleting Worksheets

While each empty worksheet in a workbook only takes up about 500
bytes of disk space, if you don't plan to use all the worksheets in a
workbook, you can delete the unused worksheets to save space.

III

Microsoft Excel

FIGURE 18-2.
Renaming a
worksheet tab.

1 Double-click the worksheet
tab you want to rename.

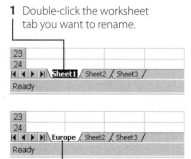

2 Type the new name over the old name, paste
a name from the Clipboard, or edit the old
name using the text pointer, and then press Enter.

(You can always add new worksheets later.) To delete a worksheet, display it in the workplace window, and then choose Delete Sheet from the Edit menu.

⚠️ **WARNING**

> Once you delete a worksheet—even if it contains several rows and columns of data—the worksheet will be permanently erased and you won't be able to undo the command.

To delete a worksheet, follow these steps:

1 In the workplace window, display the worksheet you want to delete by selecting its tab.

2 To select multiple sheets, hold down Ctrl and click additional tabs, or hold down Shift to select a tab and all the tabs in between.

3 Choose Delete Sheet from the Edit menu. Excel displays the following dialog box to confirm the deletion:

4 Click OK to permanently delete the worksheet.

Changing the Default Number of Worksheets

By default, Excel 2000 displays three worksheets in a workbook. However, you can adjust this number by choosing Options from the Tools menu and specifying a new number on the General tab. In the Sheets In New Workbook text box, on the General tab (shown below), specify the number of worksheets you want, either by typing a new number in the text box or by using the text box scroll arrows to increase or decrease the current value. You can specify any number from 1 through 255. This feature is quite useful, especially if you find you're usually adding extra worksheets to your workbooks.

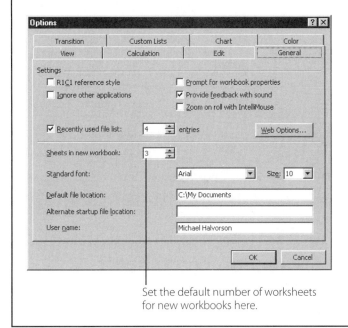

Set the default number of worksheets for new workbooks here.

Inserting Worksheets

Excel lets you add a new, empty worksheet to your workbook at any time by choosing the Worksheet command on the Insert menu. When you insert a new worksheet, Excel places it before the active worksheet and numbers it consecutively; that is, the eleventh worksheet will be given the name Sheet11. Figure 18-3, on the next page, shows how a new sheet will be inserted if your workbook contains three worksheets and if Europe is the active worksheet. After you insert a new worksheet, you can change its name, as described in "Naming Worksheets," page 493.

III

Microsoft Excel

FIGURE 18-3.
Excel inserts a new worksheet before the active worksheet in the workbook.

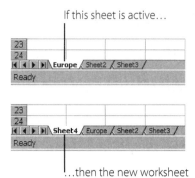

If this sheet is active...

...then the new worksheet is inserted here.

To add a new worksheet to your workbook, follow these steps:

1 Click the worksheet tab that you want shifted to the right to make room for a new worksheet.

2 Choose Worksheet from the Insert menu. A new worksheet appears in the workbook, and it becomes the active worksheet.

 TIP

If you right-click a worksheet tab, a shortcut menu appears that contains commands that let you insert, delete, rename, move, or copy the active worksheet. You can use this technique to speed up many of your workbook management tasks.

Moving Worksheets

If you don't like the placement of the worksheets you have created, you can easily move them within the workbook by using a simple drag-and-drop technique. To relocate a worksheet, click the worksheet tab you want to move, and then drag it between two other worksheet tabs. (A tiny arrow appears to help you place the worksheet.) Figure 18-4 shows how the three-step process works.

 TIP

Make a Duplicate Worksheet with the Ctrl Key

You can duplicate a worksheet in a workbook by holding down the Ctrl key while you drag a tab from one location to another. This procedure creates an extra copy of the worksheet in the workbook, which has identical rows and columns. The name will be copied also, and a "(2)" will be added to show that it's the second worksheet with that name. To remind you that you're duplicating a worksheet, the mouse pointer will include a plus (+) sign during the drag-and-drop operation.

FIGURE 18-4.
To move a worksheet,
drag the worksheet tab
to a new location.

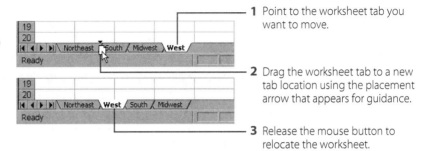

1 Point to the worksheet tab you want to move.

2 Drag the worksheet tab to a new tab location using the placement arrow that appears for guidance.

3 Release the mouse button to relocate the worksheet.

Linking Information Between Worksheets

 SEE ALSO

To learn how to link worksheets together in different workbooks, see "Linking Information Between Workbooks," page 501.

When you create a workbook containing several worksheets, you'll often want to reference the data in one worksheet when you build a formula in another worksheet. Setting up a connection between worksheets is called creating a *link* in Excel terminology. For example, if your workbook contains a separate worksheet for each sales region in the country, you could create a Summary worksheet that includes sales data from each of the supporting worksheets. Linked worksheets also provide an additional advantage: When you change the source worksheet, Excel updates the related information in the linked worksheet.

The following procedure shows you how to create formulas that link worksheets together. The workbook used as an example contains five worksheet tabs, named Summary, Northwest, South, Midwest, and West. The four regional worksheets contain quarterly sales data for each of a company's sales representatives active in the region. (The sales reps are listed individually by name.) The Summary worksheet presents an overview of the sales activity throughout the year and uses several SUM formulas to calculate the quarterly totals from each of the linked worksheets. You might want to use this worksheet structure in your own workbooks.

To create formulas that calculate totals from linked worksheets and place them on a single summary worksheet, follow these steps. Our example uses regional sales data.

1 Create your regional worksheets in a workbook, or use your own data containing a similar pattern of detail-level worksheets that you want to sum up in a summary worksheet.

III

Microsoft Excel

The following screen shows the sample worksheet named Northeast, containing quarterly sales figures for the six sales reps active in the Northeast sales region.

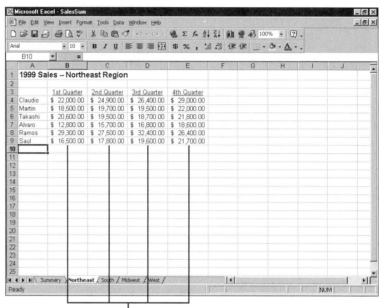

Each column of sales figures will be summed, and those sums will be displayed in the Summary worksheet.

W ON THE WEB

The SalesSum.xls example is on the Running Office 2000 Reader's Corner page. For information about connecting to this Web site, read the Introduction.

2 Add a Summary worksheet to your workbook to display the totals from the other worksheets. (Add the worksheet by choosing Worksheet from the Insert menu, and then change the name to *Summary* or another appropriate name.)

3 Using the SUM function, add formulas to the Summary worksheet that compute totals. Begin each formula by typing *=SUM(*

4 To specify a range for the SUM function, click the worksheet tab you want to include in the formula, and then select the range of cells you want to use within the link. For example, to add the six sales figures from the 1st Quarter column in the Northeast worksheet, click the Northeast worksheet tab, and then select cells B4 through B9. The customized formula appears in the formula bar;

the worksheet name and cell range are separated by an exclamation mark (Northeast!B4:B9).

5 Press the Enter key to complete the formula. Excel will add a closing parenthesis to complete the function.

Excel calculates the result and displays it in cell B4 of the Summary worksheet, as shown in the following illustration. The completed formula also appears in the formula bar.

Formula for cell B4 ——

Sum of 1st Quarter ——
Sales from the
Northeast worksheet

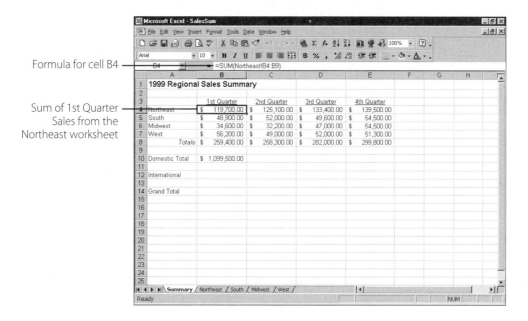

6 Repeat steps 2 through 5 to add linking formulas for the remaining summation cells.

Using More Than One Workbook

As you complete daily tasks with Excel, you'll often find it necessary to open additional workbooks to review sales figures, prepare an invoice, copy data, or complete other work. Excel allows you to load as many workbooks into memory as your system can handle. Each workbook appears in its own window and is given a separate icon on the Windows taskbar. (If you don't see separate icons for multiple open workbooks on your taskbar, choose Options from the Tools menu, click the View tab, and select the Windows In Taskbar option.) You can switch between workbooks by clicking the workbook icons on the taskbar or by choosing the workbook's filename from the Window menu. (Excel lists files on the Window menu in the order that you open them.) The following section shows you how to:

- Switch between workbook windows

- Link information between open workbooks

- Use multiuser workbooks in a network setting

Switching Between Workbooks

You can open additional workbooks in Excel by choosing Open from the File menu, locating the workbook you want to open in the Open dialog box, and then double-clicking it. When multiple workbooks are loaded, you can view them one at a time in maximized windows (the default), or side by side in the workplace. To view workbook windows side by side, choose Arrange from the Window menu.

The Arrange dialog box includes four useful window orientation options that display different parts of the workbook: Tiled, Horizontal, Vertical, and Cascade. Figure 18-5 shows how two open workbooks are arranged if you click the Vertical option button and click OK. To switch between these open workbooks, click the workbook you want to work with. (The active workbook's title bar will be displayed using your system's Active Title Bar color settings.)

FIGURE 18-5.

The Arrange command lets you view more than one workbook at once.

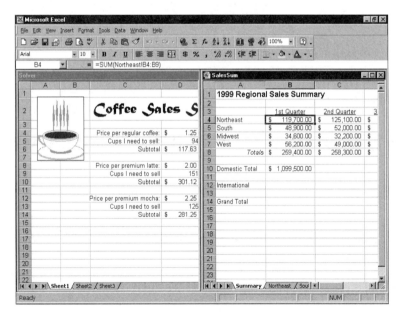

You can also switch between open workbook windows by using a key combination and by choosing filenames from the Window menu.

To switch between windows using the keyboard, follow these steps:

1 Load the workbooks you want to work with by using the Open command.

2 Cycle among workbooks by pressing Ctrl+F6. (To cycle through the workbooks in the opposite direction, press Ctrl+Shift+F6.)

To switch between workbooks using the Window menu, follow these steps:

1 Load the workbooks you want to work with by using the Open command.

2 From the Window menu, choose the workbook you want to display in the active window. The following illustration shows what the Window menu looks like when two workbooks are loaded. The active workbook (SalesSum) is identified by a check mark next to its filename.

Active workbook

Linking Information Between Workbooks

Earlier in this chapter, you learned how to build formulas that reference other worksheets in the workbook. You can also build formulas that reference worksheets in other workbooks. Before you create the linked formula, however, you must open each of the workbooks you plan to use. The following example adds the total revenue from a workbook named SalesLnk (containing international sales data) to the domestic sales total calculated in the SalesSum workbook.

If you want to create formulas that reference other workbooks, follow these steps:

1 Open the workbooks you plan to reference in your formulas.

The following screen shows a sample workbook named SalesLnk, which computes the total revenue received by a company from areas outside the United States:

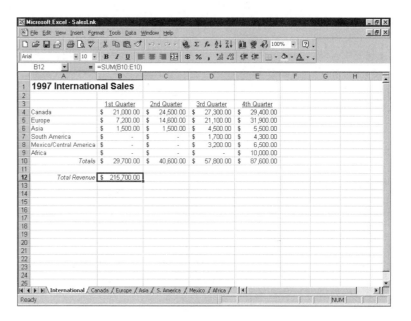

W ON THE WEB   The SalesLnk.xls example is on the Running Office 2000 Reader's Corner page.

2 Add a formula to your worksheet that references cells in other workbooks.

For example, to copy a grand total from the International worksheet in the SalesLnk workbook, start in the cell where you want to copy the data, type an equal sign (=), click the SalesLnk workbook on the Windows taskbar, click the International worksheet tab, click the cell with the total you want to incorporate (B12 in this example), and press Enter. The linking formula appears in the formula bar, composed of the workbook filename enclosed in square brackets, an exclamation mark following the worksheet name, and dollar signs ($) preceding the linked cell's column letter and row number. Your screen will look similar to this one:

Formula showing the linked workbook, worksheet, and cell address

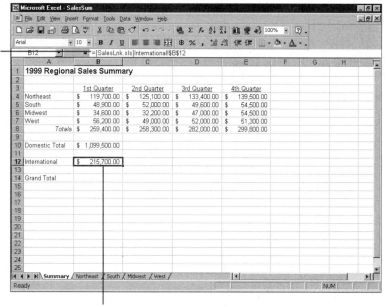

Cell containing data from a different workbook

⭐ TIP

Consolidate Worksheets with Identical Formats

If you want to link together several worksheets that share a common organizational format, you can also use the Consolidate command on the Data menu to assemble workbook information. When you consolidate worksheets, you can use one or more *statistical functions* on the cell ranges you select to obtain useful information about your data. The statistical functions available include Sum, Count, Average, Max, Min, and StdDev. *You'll learn more about using statistical functions in Chapter 20, "Using Formulas and Functions to Crunch Numbers."* For more information about applying the Consolidate command, search for "consolidating data" in the Excel online Help.

III

Microsoft Excel

Saving a Workspace File

If you often use the same collection of workbooks in Excel, consider creating a *workspace file* to save information about which workbooks are open and how they appear on the screen. The next time you want to use the workbooks, simply open the workspace file, and the workbook will appear as it did when you last saved the workspace, including toolbars, cell selections, and other tools in the user interface. The workspace file doesn't include changes you make to your worksheets—you need to save these separately by using the Save or Save As command—but it *does* keep track of your open windows and worksheets, so that you can pick up right where you left off.

To save the arrangement of open workbooks in a workspace file, follow these steps:

1 Open and organize your workbooks as you would like them saved in the workspace file. (Creating a workspace file is a little like taking a picture, so get everything positioned just where you want it.)

2 From the File menu, choose Save Workspace. The Save Workspace dialog box appears. (It works basically like a Save As dialog box.)

3 Type a name for the workspace file in the File Name text box, and specify a folder location if necessary.

4 Click the Save button to save the workspace file. (You might also be prompted to save one or more of the open workbooks.)

When you're ready to open the workspace file later, choose Open from the File menu as you would for any file. Your workbooks and worksheets will appear just as you left them, including any cell selections you made.

Managing Shared Workbooks

 SEE ALSO

If your workbook contains information arranged under uniform headings, you can set it up as an Excel database. See Chapter 22, "Managing Information in Lists."

If you have access to a shared folder on the Internet or on an attached network, you can create shared workbooks that can be opened and used by several people simultaneously. This powerful feature allows you to distribute the responsibility for creating group tasks, such as revolving product inventories, incoming customer orders, or corporate mailing lists. Excel limits the ways in which you can modify a shared workbook. These limitations are detailed in the online Help under "Shared Workbooks, Limitations Of Shared Workbooks." But you can insert and delete rows and columns, modify worksheet cells, and sort entries based on one or more criteria. The following steps show you how to create and maintain a shared workbook.

NOTE

To use a shared workbook, you need access to a shared folder on the Internet or a computer network. If you or your colleagues don't have access to a shared folder, ask your network system administrator how to get one or how to create one on your own computer.

Creating a Shared Workbook

SEE ALSO

To learn how to add comments to worksheet cells, see "Entering Comments," page 426.

To create a shared workbook that can be used by several users simultaneously, follow these steps:

1 Build the workbook you want to share as you would normally. Because the worksheets in your workbook will be accessed by several users, take extra care to format the contents clearly and concisely. You might also want to add cell comments that contain operation instructions and tips.

2 From the Tools menu, choose Share Workbook. When the Share Workbook dialog box appears, click the Editing tab.

3 Select the Allow Changes check box to define the workbook as a shared workbook, and then click OK. A dialog box appears asking you if it's all right to save your workbook (a requirement if the workbook is to be shared).

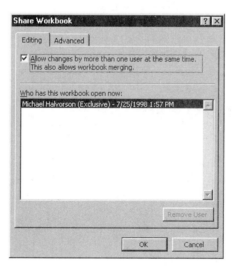

4 Click OK to save the workbook.

After you save the workbook, the word *Shared* appears in the title bar between brackets, indicating that you're now editing a

III

Microsoft Excel

X CAUTION

For the shared workbook to operate properly, your co-workers need to open the same copy of the shared workbook from a shared network folder, *not* separate ones from their own individual hard disks. Users will know the workbook is shared if the word *Shared* appears in the title bar when it's loaded in Excel.

multiuser or shared workbook. As long as the Allow Changes check box is selected on the Editing tab, you won't be able to save formulas in the workbook or modify any cell formatting.

5 Use Windows Explorer to copy the shared workbook to a shared folder on your network or the Internet, and then notify your associates that the file is available for use. From this moment on, each time a user saves changes to the shared workbook, the changes will be copied to the shared list and any changes made by other users will be uploaded into his or her system as well. Excel handles and distributes the revisions automatically!

Monitoring a Shared Workbook

Once a shared workbook is active, you can monitor it by choosing the Share Workbook command to find out who is using it. To see a list of the users working on the file, follow these steps:

1 Choose Share Workbook from the Tools menu. The Share Workbook dialog box appears.

2 A list of the users working on the file appears on the Editing tab, as shown in Figure 18-6. The time displayed next to each user is the moment that user started editing the workbook.

3 If you want to prohibit a user from working on the shared workbook, highlight the user's name and click the Remove User button. The user will be excluded from the editing session and won't be able to modify the shared copy of the file.

FIGURE 18-6.

To see who is working on a shared workbook with you, use the Editing tab of the Share Workbook dialog box.

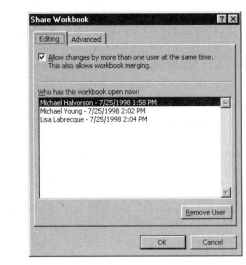

To "turn off" the shared workbook feature and disable multiuser editing in a workbook, choose Share Workbook from the Tools menu, click the Editing tab, and deselect the Allow Changes check box.

⊙ **WARNING**

> Don't disable the Share Worksheet feature until each of your users has finished editing the workbook and has saved changes, or you'll lock them out of the file. Closing a shared workbook discards any revision information in the file and prohibits users from saving their changes to the multiuser copy of the workbook, even if you reopen sharing.

2000 **Accepting or Rejecting Revisions**

If users enter or change data in different cells, each change will be accepted automatically and updated in everyone's workbook as each user saves his or her workbook. The changes to the workbook coming from other users will be highlighted after each save. Moving the cell pointer over each highlight will open a window showing who made the change, as shown in the following illustration:

An interesting problem arises, however, when two or more users change the same cells in different ways. Whose entry for the shared workbook should Excel accept? You have two methods for resolving the conflict.

In the first method, the most recently saved workbook's values replace the values that were entered into the cells on an earlier save. Choose this approach when you feel confident that later changes are always more accurate than earlier changes, such as when entering order numbers or tracking inventory quantities.

The second method enables the user saving the shared workbook to review the conflicting cells and decide whose changes take precedence. The user saving the workbook can accept all his or her own changes, accept all of another's changes, or decide cell by cell. Choose this method if you want to review the accuracy of changes before accepting them, or if you want to give one person's changes precedence over those of another. These choices and other multiuser options are provided on the Advanced tab of the Share Workbook dialog box, shown in Figure 18-7. To customize how your shared workbook handles conflicts in a multiuser environment, use these settings.

When you're ready to examine the list of editing activities in a shared workbook, choose Track Changes from the Tools menu, and choose either Highlight Changes or Accept Or Reject Changes from the submenu. The Highlight Changes command displays a dialog box asking you to specify the editing changes you want Excel to highlight in the workbook, as shown in Figure 18-8. (If your workbook is not currently shared, you can also use the Highlight Changes command to start sharing it as a workbook.)

You can highlight changes that were made at a particular time, by a particular user, or in a particular worksheet range. When you click OK, Excel outlines in blue each modified cell in the workbook that matches your search criteria and places a small triangle in the upper left corner of each affected cell. To see how a highlighted cell was changed, place the mouse pointer over the cell, and Excel will display a comment box containing the user name, date, time, and substance of the edit.

If you want to step through the list of revisions in the workbook and either accept or reject them, use the Accept Or Reject Changes command on the Track Changes submenu. When you choose this command, Excel saves the workbook and then displays a dialog box asking for your search criteria.

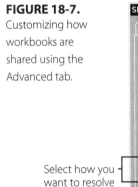

FIGURE 18-7.
Customizing how workbooks are shared using the Advanced tab.

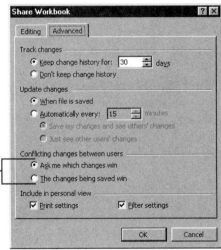

Select how you want to resolve conflicting edits.

FIGURE 18-8.
To have Excel automatically highlight new edits in a shared workbook, use the Highlight Changes command on the Track Changes submenu.

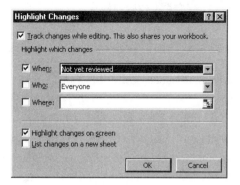

As you do when you choose Highlight Changes, you specify the time, person, and location of the edits you're looking for using the drop-down list boxes in the dialog box. When you click OK, Excel displays the changes one at a time in the Accept Or Reject Changes dialog box. (If more than one user wants to modify a cell, Excel identifies each user and the edits they're requesting.)

To accept an edit and store it in the shared workbook, click the Accept button. To reject the change, click the Reject button. Some cells might have more than one edit, in which case you must click the edit you want to accept. (See Figure 18-9.) After you accept or reject an edit, Excel removes the revision highlighting from that cell.

FIGURE 18-9.
Excel tracks each edit in a shared workbook and lets you accept or reject it. If a change made by another user is inappropriate, you can discard it.

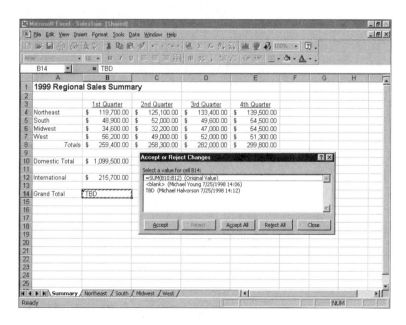

Merging Workbooks

Another method for consolidating changes in a shared workbook is to merge two copies of the workbook together using the Merge Workbooks command on the Tools menu. Merging workbooks is a useful technique when two users are working with slightly different copies of the same file and one user wants to incorporate all the changes the other user has made.

Merging workbooks is a one-step process—you simply choose the Merge Workbooks command and the file you want to merge with the active workbook, and Excel compares the two workbooks and copies any differences to the active file. Unlike the Accept Or Reject Changes command, however, the Merge Workbooks command doesn't give you a chance to compare or sort out the differences between the different copies. Its sole purpose is to update one copy of a workbook with another.

To merge two copies of a shared workbook, follow these steps:

1 Before you make any edits, use the Share Workbook command on the Tools menu to identify the original file as a shared workbook. (The Merge Workbooks command works only on copies of the same file that have been marked as shared.)

2 Use the Save As command on the File menu to create a second copy of the shared workbook. Give this copy of the file a unique name, and then deliver it to the user who will be making the edits by means of a network, the Internet, or a removable disk.

3 When you're ready to consolidate the changes made to the file, open your original copy of the shared workbook in Excel, and then choose Merge Workbooks from the Tools menu to access the updated copy.

4 Click OK to save the file to disk when prompted, and then choose the copy of the workbook in the Select Files To Merge Into Current Workbook dialog box.

> **⊙ NOTE** The file you specify for merging must be a copy of the original file that has a unique filename. It must also be saved as shared.

5 Click OK to merge the files. After a moment, Excel updates the original file by adding the changes from the merge file. (If there are no changes, Excel will notify you in a dialog box.) That's all there is to it!

Remember, the Merge Workbooks command doesn't give you a chance to accept or reject changes, so use it only if you want all revisions merged into your original file.

Protecting Worksheets and Workbooks

You can even require a password from users when they open a workbook. See "Requiring a Password for File Access," page 514.

In Chapter 17, you learned how to hide rows and columns in your worksheet from unauthorized glances. (Turn to the tip "Hide Rows or Columns for Security" on page 476 if you'd like a refresher course.) Excel also lets you protect complete worksheets or an entire workbook from tampering by using a feature called *password protection*. When you guard worksheets or workbooks in this way, users can open the file, but they can't change the parts you have protected. If you want to share your workbooks with others, while protecting them from modification, this is the feature for you.

Protecting Worksheets

To protect a worksheet in the workbook from modification, follow these steps:

1 Click the worksheet tab corresponding to the worksheet you want to protect.

2 From the Tools menu, choose Protection, and then choose Protect Sheet from the submenu. The Protect Sheet dialog box appears, as shown here:

The Protect Sheet dialog box contains a Password text box and three protection check boxes that are enabled by default. When the Contents check box is the only one selected, all the cells in the worksheet are protected, but any objects (such as clip art images) and worksheet scenarios will remain unprotected. To safeguard these items, be sure the Objects and Scenarios check boxes are also selected.

3 Type a short password into the Password text box, and click OK. Note that Excel distinguishes uppercase letters from lowercase letters, so remember any variations you make in your password's capitalization. If you forget this password in the future, you won't be able to unprotect the worksheet.

> **Use a Password (If Any) with Care**
>
> A password isn't required to protect worksheets. If you're afraid you'll forget the password, set worksheet protection without entering a password, and you'll preserve the worksheet from accidental entries and mistakes. (However, a renegade user could easily disable worksheet protection and then modify your document.)

4 When Excel asks you to verify your password, type it in again and then jot it down for future reference. (Try not to put it in an obvious place, however.) If anyone attempts to modify this protected worksheet in the future, Excel will display the following dialog box:

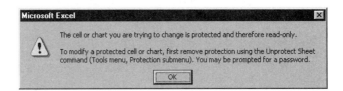

5 To remove worksheet protection at a later time, choose Protection from the Tools menu, and choose the Unprotect Sheet command from the submenu. If you didn't originally use a password, that's all there is to it! If you did, the following dialog box will appear and you must enter the worksheet password:

Lock Specific Cells or Fields

If you want to let users modify some cells in your worksheet but not others, select the cells and clear the Locked option on the Protection tab of the Format Cells dialog box. This technique is useful if you have a field for comments or an area in the worksheet that is typically used for data entry. You must do this *before* you use the Protect Sheet command on the Protection submenu, or the Format Cells command will be unavailable to you. If this happens, turn off Protection, unlock the desired cells or fields, and then turn Protection back on.

Protecting Workbook Structure

To protect the structure of an entire workbook from modification (that is, to guard the names and the order of the worksheets), follow these steps:

1 From the Tools menu, choose Protection, and then choose Protect Workbook from the submenu. The Protect Workbook dialog box appears, as shown in Figure 18-10.

   The Protect Workbook dialog box contains a Password text box and two protection check boxes. When the Structure check box is selected, users can't insert, delete, hide, rename, copy, or move worksheets in the workbook, although they *can* modify data in the worksheets if worksheet protection is not set. When the Windows check box is selected, users can't resize the windows displaying the workbook.

2 Type a password in the Password text box, and click OK. Note any variations you make in your password's capitalization, and take steps to remember the name. You can also click OK without typing a name to set workbook protection without a password.

3 Retype the password when Excel asks for it. From this point on, no user will be able to modify the worksheet's structure without first unprotecting the workbook by choosing the Unprotect Workbook command from the Protection submenu.

FIGURE 18-10.
The Protect Workbook dialog box.

If you work regularly in a multiuser environment, you might also enjoy the protection provided by the Protect And Share Workbook command on the Tools menu's Protection submenu. When you enable this toggle, it prevents users from modifying the revision history of a shared workbook.

Requiring a Password for File Access

If you're using Excel to track confidential information, you might want to limit access to your file by requiring a password to open it. This control goes further than protecting the content and structure of the workbook: it prevents anyone lacking an entry key from viewing your workbook at all.

WARNING

Take care when using password protection. If you forget your password, you'll have no way to open the protected file.

To save a file that has password protection, follow these steps:

1 Create your workbook as you normally would. You don't need to hide or protect confidential parts of the file—your password protection will limit access to every component.

2 From the File menu, choose Save As to display the Save As dialog box. If you haven't already specified a filename, type one now in the File Name text box.

3 Click the Tools drop-down arrow in the upper right corner of the Save As dialog box, and then click the General Options command.

4 The Save Options dialog box appears, as shown in Figure 18-11. It contains two password protection text boxes: Password To Open, which prohibits users from opening the file unless they know the specified password, and Password To Modify, which prohibits users from saving changes to the file without knowing the password.

FIGURE 18-11.
To protect your file from unauthorized access, type a password in the Save Options dialog box.

⭐ **TIP**

If you want to recommend, but not require that users open the file as a read-only document, select the Read-Only Recommended check box.

5 To limit access to your workbook, type a password into the Password To Open text box, and click OK. When Excel asks for it, reenter the password to verify that you spelled it as intended.

6 The next time you (or another user) try to open the file, Excel will prompt for the password in a dialog box. To remove password protection in the future, choose Save As, click the Options button, and remove the password from the Password To Open text box.

III

Microsoft Excel

Customizing Excel to Work the Way You Do

A short time ago, one of the editors of this book moved into a new office. Our first visit to her new digs was a shock; in place of the familiar, delightfully idiosyncratic workspace stood an empty desk, a computer wrapped in packing tape, several boxes of books and supplies, and four white walls bathed in pale, phosphorescent light. However, after several hours of patient adjustment and tinkering, her simple 10' x 10' room again reflected her personality and interests. Books and treasures lined the walls, a soft lamp replaced cold overhead lighting, and the computer displayed a familiar electronic photograph. In a way, this routine relocation reminded us of one of the many aspects we really like about Microsoft Office applications: they're eminently adaptable to your preferences and work style.

? SEE ALSO

You can also change how toolbars and menus are presented in the Excel interface. For more information about these customization options, see "Using Toolbars," page 39.

This chapter provides you with several useful techniques for customizing Microsoft Excel and making it work the way you want it to. You'll learn how to magnify the worksheet and save your favorite views, set your most typical printing options, and configure a time-saving feature called AutoCorrect. You'll also learn how to control recalculation and adjust other hidden settings by using the Options dialog box, and how to install add-in commands and wizards. When you're finished, you'll have all the techniques you need to create your own personalized Excel interface.

Adjusting Views

In Chapter 17, you learned how to increase the point size in worksheet cells to make numbers and headings more readable. You can also change the magnification of the worksheet to zoom in on information you want to see, or back up to view it from a distance. In this section, you'll learn how to use the Zoom command to vary the magnification in your workbook, and you'll discover how to save different views using the Custom Views command.

Using the Zoom Command

The Zoom command on the View menu changes the magnification of the selected worksheets. This command allows you to enlarge the worksheet temporarily to examine a group of cells, or to shrink the worksheet so that you can judge its overall appearance. (It doesn't change any of your data or formatting.) When you choose the Zoom command, the Zoom dialog box appears, as shown in Figure 19-1.

The default worksheet magnification is 100%, or Normal view. To enlarge the worksheet to twice its normal size, select the 200% option button. To shrink the worksheet, select the 75%, 50%, or 25% option

FIGURE 19-1.

The Zoom dialog box lets you enlarge or shrink the selected worksheets without changing cell formatting.

button. Perhaps the most useful option button is Fit Selection, which adjusts the magnification to display only the cells you select before choosing the Zoom command. Finally, the Custom option button lets you specify an exact magnification percentage, from 10% reduction to 400% enlargement.

After you select a magnification percentage and click OK, your worksheet is resized and displayed in the workplace window. Figure 19-2 shows an example of the Fit Selection option button at work. Before we chose the Zoom command, we selected cells A1 through C8 in the Summary worksheet—the only cells that should appear in the workplace window. The enlarged worksheet can be edited just like a normal-sized worksheet (but the enlargement gives your eyes a break), and if you save it to disk, the zoomed view will appear when you reopen the workbook.

FIGURE 19-2.
The Fit Selection option button zooms the worksheet to show only the selected cells.

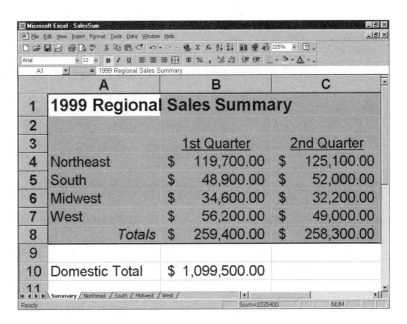

The Zoom control on Excel's Standard toolbar also gives you access to many of the magnification options in the Zoom dialog box. To use the Zoom control, follow these steps:

1 If you plan to magnify your worksheet based on a selection, highlight a range of cells in the worksheet. If you want to magnify several worksheets in the workbook, hold down Shift and click the worksheet tabs you want resized.

Microsoft Excel

2 Click the Zoom control. Your toolbar will look similar to the one shown here.

3 Select the magnification option you want. Excel responds by resizing the selected worksheets.

> Not all the worksheets in a workbook need to be viewed at the same magnification. Occasionally, you might want to vary how your worksheets appear within the workbook.

Saving Views Using the Custom Views Command

If you find you like rotating between two or three different views when you work in your workbook, you can save your views to disk and switch between them freely by using the Custom Views command on the View menu. Custom Views is a replacement for the View Manager add-in available in previous versions of Excel. When you save a view, you give it a name, and Excel records the display options, window settings, printing options, and current selection in your worksheet. You can quickly switch back and forth between these views.

To save a view using the Custom Views command, follow these steps:

1 Set the view and display settings you want to save as a custom view. For example, set the magnification of the worksheet, click a cell to make it the current selection each time you use the view, or resize the workplace window.

2 Choose Custom Views from the View menu. The Custom Views dialog box opens, and any custom views you have previously defined appear in the list box.

3 Click the Add button. You'll get the Add View dialog box:

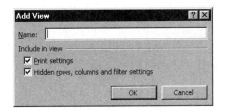

4 Type a descriptive name for your worksheet view, such as *Top Sales Rep*, and then click OK. Excel saves your custom view and stores it in the current worksheet. To display this named view later, click the worksheet tab containing the custom view, and choose Custom Views from the View menu. The Custom Views dialog box appears:

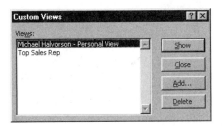

5 Double-click the view you want to show. The dialog box closes and the worksheet adjusts to your custom settings.

Each worksheet in a workbook contains different named views, including the default or personal view associated with each registered user of the product. Before you use the Custom Views command to display a particular view, be sure to select the worksheet the view is stored in. (Clicking a single worksheet is important—if more than one worksheet is selected, the Custom Views command will not be available.) To delete a custom view, highlight the view in the Custom Views dialog box, and click Delete.

Setting Printing Options

Few changes to a workbook are as noticeable as the options you select before printing. Using the Page Setup command on the File menu, you can control the orientation of your page, the width of your margins, the text placed in headers and footers, and the presence of extras like gridlines and cell notes. The Page Setup dialog box contains four tabs that control how printing options are printed. We'll cover each tab in this section.

> You can also display the Page Setup dialog box by choosing Header And Footer from the View menu.

Controlling Page Orientation

To customize your printing options, choose Page Setup from the File menu. The Page tab, shown in Figure 19-3, lets you control orientation and other options related to the physical page you'll be printing on. Orientation governs the direction your worksheet appears on the printed page. Portrait, the default, is a vertical orientation designed for worksheets that are longer than they are wide. If your worksheet is too wide to fit on one page in this orientation, which is often the case, choose the Landscape option to orient your document horizontally.

The Scaling options let you reduce or enlarge your worksheet so that it fits in the specified number of pages. The percentage you type in the Adjust To text box is similar to the percentage you specify when you create custom views using the Custom Views command. *This is discussed in "Saving Views Using the Custom Views Command," page 520.* However, in this case, it affects the printed page, not the view on your screen.

The Paper Size and Print Quality options let you specify a custom paper size and printing resolution. These options are drawn from the

FIGURE 19-3.
The Page tab lets you adjust page orientation and other paper options.

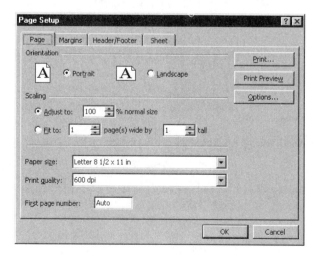

settings of your selected Windows-based printer. To set the unique attributes of your printer, click the Options button in the Page Setup dialog box, and make your changes on the dialog box tabs.

Adjusting the Margins

The Margins tab of the Page Setup dialog box allows you to adjust the margins in your workbook. (See Figure 19-4.) Typical margin settings are 1 inch for the top and bottom, and .75 inch for the left and right. As you change the margins, Excel shows you in the preview window which margin in your document is affected. Customizing the margin settings is especially useful if you're printing on letterhead paper or other sheets that contain graphics or text you don't want to overprint.

If you want to center your worksheet between the margin settings, select the Horizontally check box at the bottom of the Margins tab to center the printout from left to right, or select the Vertically check box to center the printout from top to bottom.

FIGURE 19-4.
The Margins tab gives you control over the placement of your worksheet relative to the edges of the paper you print it on.

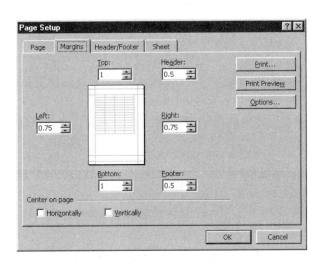

Adding Headers and Footers

The Header/Footer tab of the Page Setup dialog box (see Figure 19-5, on the next page) lets you add a header or a footer to your worksheet when it prints. Headers and footers typically contain reference information about a document, such as the worksheet name, the time or date, or the current page number. Excel permits you to pick headers and footers from a predefined list on the Header/Footer tab, or you can create your own custom entries by clicking the Custom Header or Custom Footer buttons.

FIGURE 19-5.

The Header/Footer tab lets you choose a header or footer from a predefined list or create your own version.

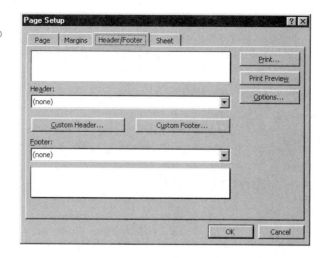

The following steps show you how to choose predefined headers and footers from the Page Setup dialog box:

1 From the File menu, choose Page Setup. (You can also choose Header And Footer from the View menu.) When the Page Setup dialog box opens, click the Header/Footer tab.

2 To pick a new footer, click the Footer drop-down list box, and choose one of the formats listed. The first format—(None)— removes the footer. Note that commas between items separate the header or footer components, which will be aligned to the left, center, and right margins.

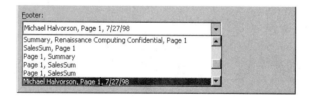

When you select a format (and release the mouse button), the footer is shown in the footer preview window below the closed list box.

3 To pick a new header, click the Header list box, and choose one of the formats listed. Again, the (None) option removes the header from the document.

Commas in the header show how the header will be organized on the page, while the header preview window below shows how it will look. After you set headers and footers, your screen should resemble the following:

Header preview —
Footer preview —

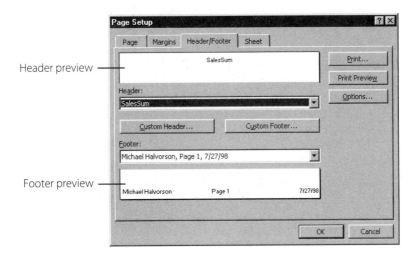

4 When you're finished, click OK. When you print, the specified headers and footers will appear on each page of your document.

 TIP

Delete All Headers and Footers

To remove all headers and footers from a document, select the (None) option in both the Header and Footer drop-down list boxes.

If you don't like the predefined headers and footers, you can create your own by clicking the Custom Header and Custom Footer buttons on the Header/Footer tab. The following steps show you how:

1 From the File menu, choose Page Setup. When the Page Setup dialog box opens, click the Header/Footer tab.

2 To create a custom header, click the Custom Header button. The dialog box shown on the following page appears.

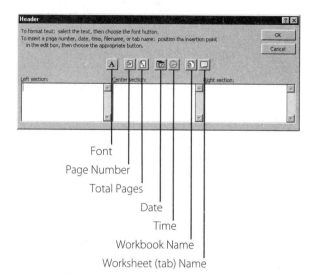

Font
Page Number
Total Pages
Date
Time
Workbook Name
Worksheet (tab) Name

The Header dialog box lets you specify your header in three sections: left, center, and right.

3 Click in one of the sections, and then type the text you want.

You can supplement the text you type by clicking any of seven special buttons to enter codes in your document. For example, if you click the button on the right side of the group (the Worksheet Name icon), the code &[Tab] is placed in the header. This is Excel's special formatting code for inserting the name of the current worksheet of your workbook at this location in the header.

4 To change the formatting of the text, select the portion you want to format, and click the Font button.

5 When you're finished with the header, click OK to view the customized header in the preview window. If you don't like the results, repeat the above steps and make further changes.

6 If you want to create a custom footer, click the Custom Footer button and follow steps 3 through 5 as you did for creating a custom header.

7 When your header and footer are the way you want them, click OK.

⭐ **TIP**

To create multiline headers or footers, press Enter at the end of each line in the section portion of the Header or the Footer dialog box.

Adding Gridlines and Other Options

SEE ALSO

To learn more about using comments in your worksheet, see "Entering Comments," page 426.

The Sheet tab of the Page Setup dialog box (see Figure 19-6) lets you include visual or interpretive aids such as gridlines, comments, and repeating row and column headings in your printout. *Gridlines* are the dividing lines you normally see on your screen that run down each column and across each row, identifying the cells in the worksheet. To print gridlines with your worksheet, simply select the Gridlines check box in the Print category. *Cell comments* are special notes you create by using the Comments command on the Insert menu. You can specify how they're printed by choosing a selection in the Comments list box. The default (None) is not to print any comments the worksheet might contain.

TIP

> To remove gridlines from your screen, choose Options from the Tools menu, click the View tab, and deselect the Gridlines check box.

FIGURE 19-6.

The Sheet tab lets you include extras such as gridlines and cell comments in your printout.

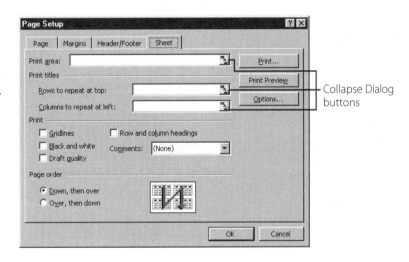

— Collapse Dialog buttons

Two other useful features on the Sheet tab are the Print Area and Print Titles text boxes. Both these features let you select ranges for printing. In the Print Area text box, you specify the worksheet range that will be printed. In the two Print Titles text boxes, you can choose to repeat either row or column headings (or both) on multipage printouts. To use the Print Area feature, follow these steps:

1 From the File menu, choose Page Setup.

2 When the Page Setup dialog box opens, click the Sheet tab.

3 Click the Collapse Dialog button at the right edge of the Print Area text box. The dialog box will temporarily shrink to enable you to see your worksheet. If it still obscures your view, drag its title bar and move it out of the way.

> To delete a print area, click the Sheet tab and delete the cell range in the Print Area text box. (This won't change your original data, only the way it prints.)

4 Select the cells you want to print in the worksheet.

As you select the cells, a marquee appears around the range, a pop-up box shows the number of rows and columns you're selecting, and a description of the cells appears in the Print Area text box, as shown here:

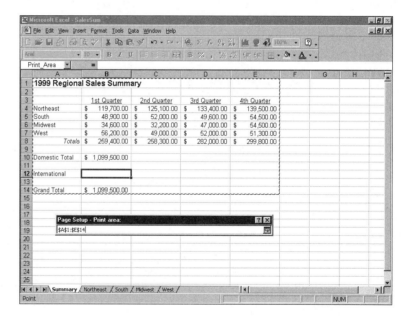

5 When you have selected the cells you want, click the Collapse Dialog button again.

6 After making any other changes, click the Print button, and then click OK in the Print dialog box to print the cells you selected.

> To delete a print area or to choose a different one (without changing your data), click the Sheet tab and delete the cell range in the Print Area text box. Leave it blank or draw a new range on your worksheet.

To repeat row or column headings (or both) on each printed page of a long (or wide) worksheet, follow these steps:

1   Choose Page Setup from the File menu.

2   When the Page Setup dialog box opens, click the Sheet tab.

3   Click one of the Collapse Dialog buttons under the Print Titles heading to select repeating rows or repeating columns.

4   Select the rows or columns you want to have repeated on each page. You can click any cells in the rows or columns you would like to have repeat, or you can select the row or column headings. Excel will highlight the entire rows or columns you select by surrounding them with a marquee.

5   Click the Collapse Dialog button again to complete your selection.

6   You can repeat steps 3–5 if you want to repeat both rows and columns on your printed worksheet.

7   After making any other changes, click OK to close the Page Setup dialog box, or click the Print button, and then click OK in the Print dialog box to print the worksheet.

TIP

You can verify how your print options will look by clicking the Print Preview button in the Page Setup dialog box or by choosing Print Preview from the File menu. This allows you to decide whether to make cosmetic adjustments and to ensure that you have chosen the portion of the worksheet you want.

Setting AutoCorrect Options

Just like Microsoft Word, Excel contains an AutoCorrect feature that automatically fixes mistakes you make in text entries as you enter them in worksheet cells. For example, if you type the word *abscence* (a common misspelling that AutoCorrect recognizes) in a cell and press Spacebar or Enter, Excel changes the word to *absence*, correcting the mistake. You can customize the AutoCorrect feature by adding words you commonly mistype to the Replace list or by selecting or deselecting the five AutoCorrect options. You display the AutoCorrect dialog box, shown in Figure 19-7, on the next page, by choosing AutoCorrect from the Tools menu.

III

Microsoft Excel

FIGURE 19-7.

The AutoCorrect dialog box lets you control how spelling and capitalization mistakes are fixed in your worksheet.

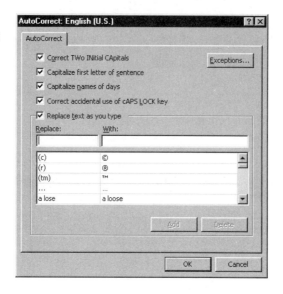

If you don't want Excel to change the capitalization of words that begin with two capital letters, deselect the Correct TWo INitial CApitals check box. Removing the check mark will stop Excel from changing labels like *USmail* to *Usmail*. (Excel will never change a word that starts with three or more capital letters.) Likewise, you can stop Excel from capitalizing days of the week by deselecting the Capitalize Names Of Days check box. When you disable this AutoCorrect feature, *monday* will remain *monday.*

AutoCorrect's word correction feature is controlled by the Replace Text As You Type check box. To disable word replacement, deselect this check box; that is, remove the check mark from this box by clicking it. (Note, however, that capitalization correction is still enabled unless you deselect the two capitalization check boxes.) When the Replace Text As You Type option is active, Excel will use the pairs listed in the Replace and With lists to fix your typing mistakes. You can also use this feature to add abbreviations that you want expanded, saving you time and ensuring accuracy. For example, you can direct Excel to convert the letters *po* into the words *Post Office Box,* or to change *sd* to *San Diego.* To add a correction pair, type the word or phrase you want Excel to replace in the Replace text box, type the correct word or expanded phrase in the With text box, and then click the Add button. To remove a correction pair, highlight the pair, and click the Delete button.

TIP

Create Exceptions for Special Words You Use

In Excel, you can stop the AutoCorrect feature from fixing words that you want to have two initial capitals (like *USmail*) or from assuming that a new sentence is beginning after certain abbreviated words (like *three hrs. per day*). To create a list of special words you don't want Excel to fix, click the Exceptions button in the AutoCorrect dialog box, and then indicate your spelling preferences on the First Letter and INitial CAps tabs.

Customizing Excel Using the Options Dialog Box

To change the way Excel looks and works, experiment with the customization choices in the Options dialog box, shown in Figure 19-8, on the following page. As you do in Word, you display the Options dialog box by choosing Options from the Tools menu. The Options dialog box contains tabs that control virtually every aspect of the Excel interface. Although some tabs customize features that you might be unfamiliar with, such as the settings that help you make a transition from other spreadsheet programs, you can often learn a lot about how Excel works by just browsing through the tabs in this dialog box. In this section, you'll experiment with the following options:

- Formula calculation settings, like manual recalculation and updating remote references

- Worksheet appearance options, like scroll bars and colors

- Adjustable editing options, like drag-and-drop settings and default decimal places

Controlling Calculation

When you enter a formula, Excel automatically computes the result or recalculates. Most of the time, you'll want Excel to recalculate automatically when you modify cells that are included in formulas—it makes sense to keep your numbers up to date. But occasionally you'll want to configure Excel so that it recalculates only when you want it to. For example, you might want to refer to the previous result of a calculation while you enter new values in a worksheet. Or, you might want to disable recalculation temporarily if you're entering several complex formulas in a worksheet, because lengthy calculations can take some time to finish.

III

Microsoft Excel

FIGURE 19-8.
The Options dialog box lets you customize many of Excel's commands and options. The General tab controls basic options such as the standard font.

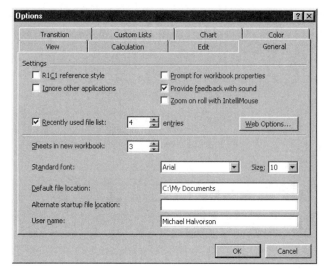

To customize formula calculation in your worksheet, choose Options from the Tools menu, and then click the Calculation tab of the Options dialog box. You'll see the dialog box shown in Figure 19-9. To select manual calculation, click the Manual option button in the Calculation area, and then click OK. From this point on, Excel will only recalculate formulas when you enter or edit them, when you press F9 to calculate manually, or when you click the Calculation tab again and click the Calc Now (F9) button. If you're disabling automatic recalculation, you might also want to disable automatic updating from other applications

FIGURE 19-9.
To control recalculation in a worksheet, click the Calculation tab.

Click here for manual calculation.

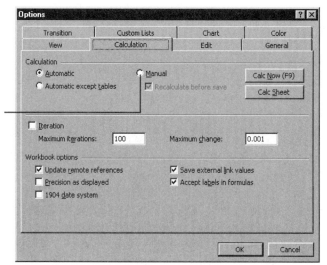

linked to your worksheet. To remove this option, deselect the Update Remote References check box in the Workbook Options portion of the Calculation tab, and Excel won't update links that rely on other programs for data.

WARNING

Remember to select the Automatic option in the Calculation area and to select the Update Remote References check box when you're finished entering data. Otherwise, your workbook might display out-of-date information and present incorrect results.

Customizing Worksheet Appearance

SEE ALSO

For a refresher course on using toolbars and working with document windows, see Chapter 2, "Learning the Basics: Windows, Toolbars, and Printing."

You have already learned how to add toolbars to your workplace and change the layout of workbook windows. Using the View tab in the Options dialog box, you can further adjust your worksheet's appearance. The View tab includes option buttons and check boxes that enable and disable several visual characteristics, as shown in Figure 19-10. You can remove the formula bar and status bar from the screen, giving you more real estate for your worksheet, by deselecting the Formula Bar and Status Bar check boxes. If you don't like the red box that signifies that a comment has been placed in a cell, you can choose None in the Comments category, instead of the Comment Indicator Only or Comments & Indicator options. The red boxes will disappear, but the comments will remain.

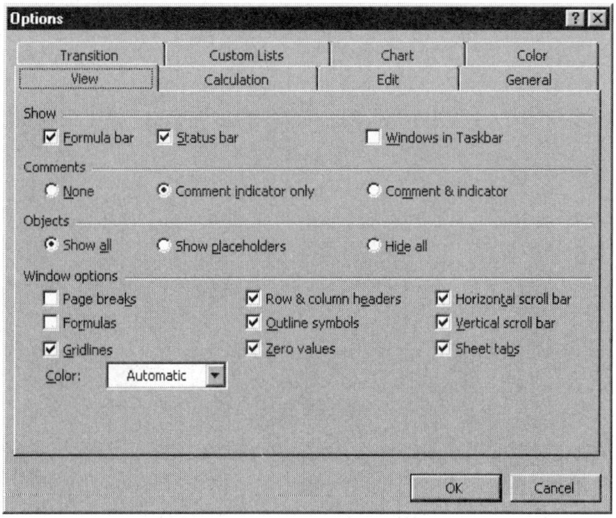

FIGURE 19-10.
The View tab controls how your worksheet appears on the screen.

You might also find it useful to examine the selections in the Window Options category of the View tab. You can use these options to choose whether to view automatic page breaks, gridlines (you can also alter their color), scroll bars, and other visual qualities of your worksheet. When you're finished customizing your worksheet's appearance, click OK to close the Options dialog box.

Customizing Editing Options

If you want to change how Excel responds to your editing instructions, you can modify several special settings, including the way the drag-and-drop technique works, the way Excel updates linked worksheets, and the action the AutoComplete feature takes. Figure 19-11 shows the Options dialog box's Edit tab, which controls these customizations and more.

To disable direct cell editing—the option that lets you move the insertion point into cells when you double-click a cell—deselect the Edit Directly In Cell option. You might want to cancel this option if you often accidentally double-click cells when selecting ranges. When this option is disabled, you must edit the cell's contents in the formula bar.

A related option is Allow Cell Drag And Drop, which enables the drag-and-drop method for copying and moving cells. If you tend to accidentally drag cells, you can disable the option by deselecting the check box. (We recommend that you *never* remove the Alert Before Overwriting Cells safety feature, which protects you from copying one piece of data over another inadvertently.)

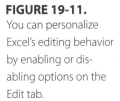

FIGURE 19-11.
You can personalize Excel's editing behavior by enabling or disabling options on the Edit tab.

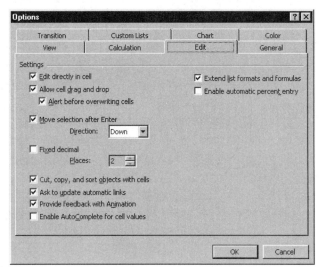

You might consider disabling the AutoComplete feature if you grow weary of Excel automatically entering data for you based on your last entry. While this capability is extremely useful, it can also be tiresome if Excel doesn't guess your intentions correctly. To stop AutoComplete, deselect the Enable AutoComplete For Cell Values check box. When you're finished selecting your editing choices, click OK to close the Options dialog box.

Installing Add-in Commands and Wizards

As you learned in Part 1, the applications in the Office 2000 software suite can customize menus and toolbars on their own to hide seldom-used commands and install specific options *on demand* (or as they are needed). You can also use the Add-Ins command on the Excel Tools menu to install useful tools known as add-in commands and wizards, which further extend the functionality of the Excel application. Typical add-in commands included with Excel 2000 are Solver and Report Manager, which appear on the Tools menu after you install them. A popular wizard included with Excel is the Template Wizard, which creates form templates that have the data tracking option enabled. You can also acquire add-in commands and wizards from third-party software developers.

To install add-in commands and wizards, complete the following steps:

1 Choose Add-Ins from the Tools menu. The Add-Ins dialog box appears, as shown in Figure 19-12.

2 Select the add-in command or wizard that you want to have appear as a menu command. To locate commands that don't appear in this dialog box, click the Browse button and find it on your hard disk.

FIGURE 19-12.
The Add-Ins command on the Tools menu allows you to add and remove add-in commands and wizards.

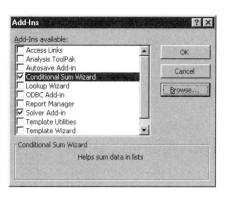

III

Microsoft Excel

> To remove an add-in command or wizard from a menu, deselect the add-in or wizard in the Add-Ins dialog box.

3 Click OK to save your changes and reconfigure the menu. Excel will search for the tool on your system and prompt you for your Office 2000 installation disks, if necessary.

SEE ALSO

To see the Solver add-in at work, see Chapter 23, "Analyzing Business Data."

Most add-in commands appear on the Tools menu after you have installed them, but this isn't a requirement. And occasionally the designer of the utility will opt to locate it someplace else in the menu structure after installation. Excel Wizards are often located on the Wizards submenu of the Tools menu.

CHAPTER 20

20

Using Formulas and Functions to Crunch Numbers

formula is an equation that calculates a new value from existing values. In Chapter 15, you learned how to build simple formulas using numbers and cell references, and in Chapter 18, you expanded your skills by creating formulas that linked to cells from other worksheets and workbooks. In this chapter, you'll discover how to build more sophisticated formulas. You'll learn how to use arithmetic operators and parentheses to control how your formulas are evaluated, you'll explore techniques for replicating formulas, and you'll practice using range names to make your formulas more readable and easier to modify. In addition, you'll learn how to use Microsoft Excel's impressive collection of built-in functions for specialized tasks such as totaling columns, computing averages, and calculating the monthly payments for an auto loan. Using well-organized formulas and functions, you can evaluate business data in new ways, spot important trends, and plan your financial future.

Building a Formula

Figure 20-1 shows two basic Excel formulas. The first calculates a value by multiplying two numbers, and the second calculates a sum by adding three cell references. These formulas have several characteristics in common.

- Each begins with an equal sign (=). The equal sign tells Excel that the following characters are part of a formula that should be calculated and that the result should be displayed in a cell. (If you omit the equal sign, Excel treats the formula as plain text and doesn't compute the result.)

- Each formula uses one or more arithmetic operators. An arithmetic operator is not required when a function is used in a formula, but in all other cases, operators are necessary to tell Excel what to do with the values in an equation. If your formula contains more than one arithmetic operator, you can include parentheses to clarify how the formula is evaluated.

- Each formula includes two or more values that are being combined by using arithmetic operators. When you use Excel formulas, you can combine numbers, cell references, and other values.

The examples in this chapter feature an order-form worksheet that catalogs the merchandise sold in a small pet shop. It's the type of worksheet that pet-shop employees might use to take orders over the phone or that customers might use to purchase mail-order items. As you work through this chapter, you'll see how to use Excel formulas and functions to add information to the order-form worksheet. You can create the worksheet and follow the examples exactly if you want to, or you can customize the worksheet for your own purposes.

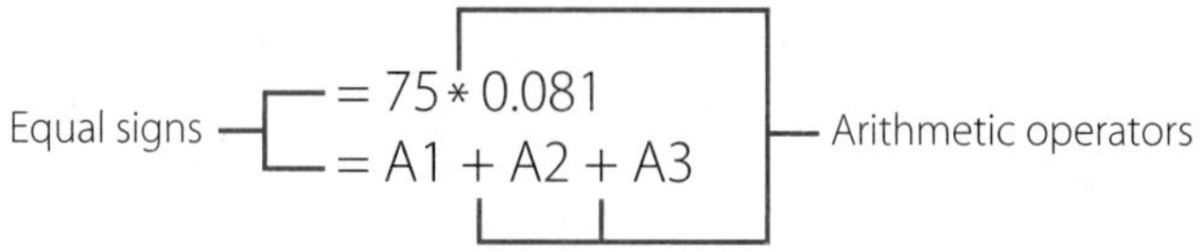

FIGURE 20-1.
The anatomy of two simple Excel formulas.

Equal signs ——⌐ = 75 * 0.081
　　　　　　　└ = A1 + A2 + A3 —— Arithmetic operators

Multiplying Numbers

Formulas that multiply the numbers in two cells are the most basic and the easiest to enter. The following example shows you how to multiply a price cell and a quantity cell to create a subtotal.

1 Create a product order form, price list, or another worksheet containing well-organized Price, Quantity, and Subtotal columns. The order-form worksheet we'll use looks like this:

Click the cell that will contain the formula.

ON THE WEB

The PriceLst example is on the Running Office 2000 Reader's Corner page. For information about connecting to this Web site, read the Introduction.

2 In the Subtotal column, click the cell that will contain the multiplication formula (E4 in our example).

3 Type the equal sign (=) to begin the formula.

An equal sign appears on the formula bar and in the highlighted cell. From this point on, any numbers, cell references, arithmetic operators, or functions that you type will be included in the formula.

SEE ALSO

To learn more about entering simple formulas, referencing cells, and using the formula bar, see "Entering Formulas," page 427.

4 In the Price column, click the cell containing the first number to be multiplied (C4 in this example). A dotted-line marquee appears around the highlighted cell, and the cell reference appears in the formula bar.

5 Type an asterisk (*) to add the multiplication operator to the formula.

6 In the Quantity column, click the cell containing the second number to be multiplied (D4 in this example). The complete formula now appears in the highlighted cell and on the formula bar. Your worksheet should look similar to the one shown on the next page.

III

Microsoft Excel

The formula bar records your formula as you build it.

7 Press Enter to end the formula. Excel calculates the result (79.5 in this example), and displays it in the cell containing the formula. Later you'll add currency formatting to the cell.

Replicating a Formula

? SEE ALSO

For more information about the commands on the Fill submenu, see "Using the Fill Commands," page 455.

Excel makes it easy to copy, or *replicate*, a formula into neighboring cells, using the Fill submenu of the Edit menu. The slick thing about the Fill submenu is that its commands automatically adjust the cell references in your formula to match the rows and columns you're copying to. For example, if you replicate a formula down a column with the Down command, Excel adjusts the row numbers so that the formula includes new references in each cell. (Excel automatically adjusts cell references when you delete cells, too.) The following example shows you how to use the replication feature in the order-form worksheet.

To replicate a formula, follow these steps:

1 Highlight the cell that has the formula and the empty cells you want to fill as one selection. (The Fill command replicates formulas in only one direction; commands on the Fill submenu copy to neighboring, or contiguous, cells only, so be sure that the formula cell is at the top, bottom, left, or right end of the empty cell range.) Our worksheet looks like this:

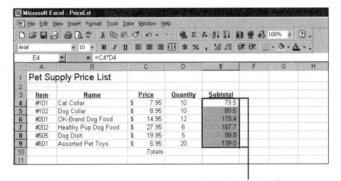

Select the area to fill. The formula should be at the top.

SEE ALSO

To control how Excel calculates formulas, see "Controlling Calculation," page 531.

2 Choose Fill from the Edit menu, and then choose Down from the submenu if your formula is at the top of the selected range, or choose Right, Left, or Up as appropriate. Your formula is replicated within the selected cells, as shown here:

Excel replicates the formula.

3 Select column E in the worksheet, and click the Currency Style button on the Formatting toolbar. The contents of the Subtotal column now appear in currency format.

TIP

You can also replicate a formula by using the AutoFill mouse technique. Simply select the cell you want to replicate, click the tiny box in the lower right corner of the cell, and drag it over the cells you want to fill.

III

Microsoft Excel

Using Arithmetic Operators

As you learned in the previous example, Excel lets you build your formulas by using one or more arithmetic operators to combine numbers and cell references in an equation. Table 20-1 shows a complete list of the arithmetic operators you can use in a formula. When you enter more than one arithmetic operator, Excel follows standard algebraic rules to determine which calculations to accomplish first in the formula. These rules—called Excel's *order of evaluation*—dictate that exponential calculations are performed first, multiplication and division calculations second, and addition and subtraction last. If more than one calculation exists in the same category, Excel evaluates them from left to right. For example, when evaluating the formula =6-5+3*4, Excel computes the answer using these steps:

$$=6\text{-}5\mathbf{+3*4}$$

$$=\mathbf{6\text{-}5}\text{+}12$$

$$=\mathbf{1+12}$$

$$=13$$

TABLE 20-1. **Excel's Arithmetic Operators, in Order of Evaluation**

Operator	Description	Example	Result
( )	Parentheses	(3+6)*3	27
^	Exponential	10^2	100
*	Multiplication	7*5	35
/ or ÷	Division	15÷3	5
+	Addition	5+5	10
-	Subtraction	12-8	4

Parentheses and Order of Evaluation

To change Excel's order of evaluation, you can include one or more pairs of parentheses in a formula. This lets you control how Excel uses operators in a formula, and can also make your equation easier to read and revise later. For example, consider how parentheses create a difference in evaluation between these two formulas:

$$=10+2*0.25$$

$$=(10+2)*0.25$$

Editing Formulas

Excel allows you to edit formulas in the same way that you edit any other cell entry. Simply double-click the cell, locate the mistake using the arrow keys, make your correction, and press Enter. You can also insert new cell references while editing a formula by positioning the mouse pointer on the formula bar and highlighting new cells with the mouse. This handy feature lets you specify replacement cells in your formula if you selected the wrong cells the first time.

The following example shows what a formula in cell E9 looks like when you edit it in a cell. Note that Excel places color outlines around the other cells involved in the formula to make it easy to see their relationships. If you prefer, you can also highlight a cell and click the formula bar to edit the cell's contents there. (To cancel an edit, press Escape.)

Edit formula on the formula bar.

Active cell

The first formula produces a result of 10.5, while the second formula produces a result of 3. By modifying Excel's order of evaluation in the second formula, you create an entirely different answer.

Parentheses can also make a formula easier to read, and you can add any number of parentheses as long as you use them in matching pairs. For example, though the following formulas both produce the answer 15, the first formula is a bit easier to decipher.

=((5*4)/2)+(10/2)

=5*4/2+10/2

NOTE

> If you specify an uneven number of parentheses in a formula, or a pair of parentheses that don't match, Excel displays a message that it found an error in the formula and proposes a correction. Click Yes to accept Excel's proposed correction, or click No so you can correct the mistake on the formula bar or in the cell directly.

Using Built-in Functions

SEE ALSO

For more information on the PMT function, see "Using PMT to Determine Loan Payments," page 549.

To accomplish more sophisticated numerical and text processing operations in your worksheets, Excel allows you to add built-in calculations called functions to your formulas. A *function* is a predefined equation that operates on one or more values and returns a single value. Excel includes a collection of over 200 functions in several useful categories, as shown in Table 20-2. For example, you can use the PMT (payment) function from the Financial category to calculate the periodic payment for a loan based on the interest rate charged, the number of payments desired, and the principal amount.

Each function must be entered with a particular *syntax*, or structure, so that Excel can process the results correctly. For example, the PMT function has a function syntax that looks like this:

$$\text{PMT}(\mathbf{rate},\mathbf{nper},\mathbf{pv},\text{fv},\text{type})$$

TABLE 20-2.   Categories of Excel Functions

Category	Used For
Financial	Loan payments, appreciation, and depreciation
Date & Time	Calculations involving dates and times
Math & Trig	Mathematical and trigonometric calculations like those found on a scientific calculator
Statistical	Average, sum, variance, and standard-deviation calculations
Lookup & Reference	Calculations involving tables of data
Database	Working with lists and external databases
Text	Comparing, converting, and reformatting text in cells
Logical	Calculations that produce the result TRUE or FALSE
Information	Determining whether an error has occurred in a calculation

The abbreviated words shown between the parentheses are called *arguments*. In this function, *rate* is the interest rate, *nper* is the number of payments you'll make, and *pv* is the principal amount. To use this function correctly, you must specify a value for each required argument, and you must separate each argument with a comma. The arguments shown in bold are required, and the others are optional. (In the online Help, the optional arguments are also in bold.) For example, to use the PMT function to calculate the loan payment on a $1,000 loan at 19 percent annual interest over 36 months, you could type the following formula:

=PMT(19%/12,36,1000)

When Excel evaluates this function, it places the answer ($36.66) in the cell containing the function. (The answer is negative, indicated by the parentheses, because it is money you must pay out.) Note that the first argument (the interest rate) was divided by 12 in this example to create a monthly rate for the formula. This demonstrates an important point—you can use other calculations, including other functions, as the arguments for a function. Although it takes a little time to master how these arguments are structured, you'll find that functions produce results that can otherwise take hours to calculate by hand.

The Versatile SUM Function

Perhaps the most useful function in Excel's collection is SUM, which totals the range of cells you select. Because SUM is used so often, the AutoSum button appears on the Standard toolbar to make adding numbers faster. In the following example, we'll use the AutoSum button to sum the Subtotal column in the order-form worksheet.

AutoSum

To total a column of numbers using the SUM function, follow these steps:

1 Click the cell in which you want to place the SUM function. (If you're totaling a column of numbers, select the cell directly below the last number in the column.)

2 Click the AutoSum button.

Excel places the SUM function on the formula bar, and (if possible) automatically selects a range of neighboring cells as an argument for the function. If you selected a cell directly below a column of numbers, your screen will look similar to the one in Figure 20-2, on the following page.

III

Microsoft Excel

FIGURE 20-2.

The AutoSum button inserts the SUM function and automatically suggests the cells to use for the argument.

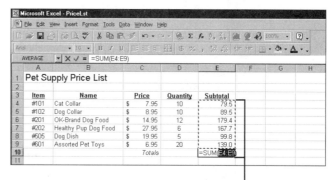

AutoSum automatically selects
a range for the SUM function.

3 If Excel selected the range you want to total, press Enter to complete the function and compute the sum. If Excel didn't guess the range correctly, select a new range now by dragging the mouse over the range and pressing Enter. (You can specify any block of cells in any open workbook to be an argument to the SUM function.) To cancel the AutoSum command, press the Escape key.

 TIP

Use SUM to Add Nonadjacent Ranges

You can use the SUM function to add multiple noncontiguous ranges by separating the cell ranges with commas. For example, =SUM(A3:A8,B3:B8) adds six cells in column A to six cells in column B and displays the total. You might find it easier to use the mouse and select cells by clicking each cell or range of cells while pressing the Ctrl key.

The Insert Function Command

With so many functions to choose from, it might seem daunting to experiment with unfamiliar features on your own. Excel makes it easier by providing a special command named Function on the Insert menu, to help you learn about functions and enter them into formulas. The Paste Function dialog box, shown in Figure 20-3, lets you browse through the nine function categories and pick just the calculation you want.

You can also use Office Assistant to help you learn how each function works and what arguments it requires. (More than 200 functions are carefully documented in the online Help.) When you double-click a function in the Function Name list box, Excel displays a second dialog box prompting you for the required arguments. Give it a try now with a useful statistical function called AVERAGE.

FIGURE 20-3.

The Paste Function dialog box lists function names by category.

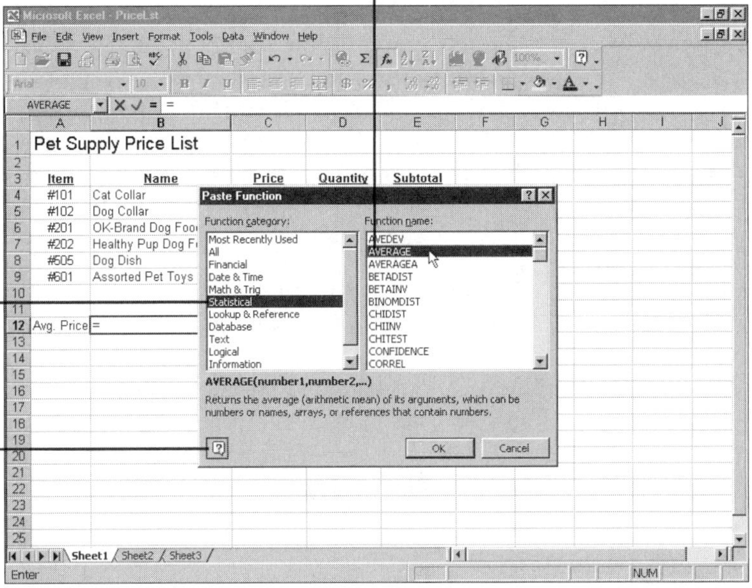

Choose a function name.

Choose a function category.

Click this button to display (or hide) the Office Assistant.

To use AVERAGE to calculate the average of a list of numbers, follow these steps:

1 Click the cell in which you want to place the results of the AVERAGE function. (In the pet-shop example, this is B12. The label Avg. Price has been added in A12.)

2 From the Insert menu, choose Function.

The Paste Function dialog box appears, as shown in Figure 20-3. The nine functional categories appear in the Function Category list box along with the choice for All functions and those Most Recently Used, and the functions in each category are listed alphabetically in the Function Name list box.

TIP

f_x

Paste
Function

> You can save time opening the Paste Function dialog box by clicking the Paste Function button on the Standard toolbar.

3 Click the Statistical category. The mathematical functions in the Statistical category appear in the Function Name list box.

4 Click the AVERAGE function, and then click OK. A second dialog box appears, asking you for the arguments in the function. In the AVERAGE function, you can specify either individual values to

III

Microsoft Excel

compute the average or a cell range. This time, you'll specify a cell range.

5 Click the Collapse Dialog button (small red arrow at the right edge of the Number1 text box shown below), and the dialog box will shrink to show only the text box you're about to fill.

6 Select the cells you want to average. In our example, we selected the numbers in the Price column (cells C4 through C9) to determine the average price of pet supplies in the store.

7 Release the mouse button, and press Enter. The dialog box returns to its normal size, and the cell range you selected appears in the dialog box and in the AVERAGE function on the formula bar. Our dialog box looks like this:

Cell range to average   Collapse Dialog button

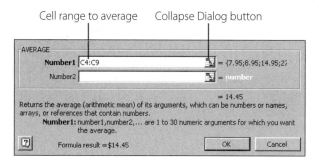

8 Click OK to complete the formula and calculate the result. The average, $14.45, appears in the cell containing the AVERAGE formula.

> You can include one function as an argument in another function if the result is compatible. For example, the formula =SUM(5,SQRT(9)) adds together the number 5 and the square root of 9, and then displays the result (8).

Using Functions to Analyze Finances

Although Excel includes too many functions to discuss exhaustively in this book, we thought you might enjoy seeing a few more examples of functions and formulas to prompt your own exploration. We've decided to highlight three of Excel's most useful financial functions: PMT, FV, and RATE. Using these functions, you can precisely calculate loan payments, the future value of an investment, or the rate of return produced by an investment.

Using PMT to Determine Loan Payments

The PMT function returns the periodic payment required to amortize a loan over a set number of periods. In plain English, this means that you can estimate what your car payments will be if you take out an auto loan or what your mortgage payments will be if you buy a house. Try using the PMT function now to determine what the monthly payments will be for a $10,000 auto loan at 9 percent interest over a 3-year period.

To use the PMT function, follow these steps:

1 Click the worksheet cell in which you want to display the monthly payment.

2 Choose Function from the Insert menu, or click the Paste Function button on the Standard toolbar. The Paste Function dialog box appears.

3 Click the Financial category, and then double-click PMT in the Function Name list box. The arguments dialog box appears. It contains a description of the PMT function and five text boxes ready to accept the function's arguments. You'll enter numeric values for rate (the interest rate), nper (the number of payments), and pv (the present value, or loan principal).

4 Type *9%/12* and press Tab, type *36* and press Tab, and type *10000*. The dialog box should look like this:

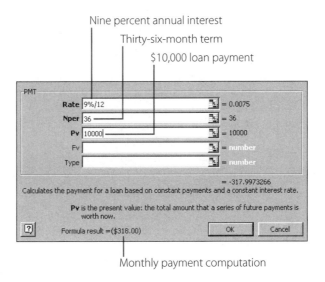

Nine percent annual interest

Thirty-six-month term

$10,000 loan payment

Monthly payment computation

The result of the calculation ($318.00) is displayed near the bottom of the dialog box.

 TIP

> To calculate monthly payments, be sure to type the annual interest using a percent sign and divide it by 12 to create a monthly interest rate. Likewise, be sure to specify the number of payments in months (36), not years (3).

5 Click OK to complete the function and display the result. Your monthly loan payment, less any applicable loan fees, appears in the cell you highlighted. The result, formatted as currency, is ($318.00). The amount appears in red and between parentheses because it represents money that you must pay out.

Using FV to Compute Future Value

Although monthly loan payments are often a fact of life, Excel can help you with more than just debt planning. If you enjoy squirreling away money for the future, you can use the FV (future value) function to determine the future value of an investment. Financial planners use this tool when they help you to determine the future value of an annuity, IRA, or SEP account. The following example shows you how to compute the future value of an IRA in which you deposit $2,000 per year for 30 years at a 10 percent annual interest rate—a possible scenario if you invested $2,000 per year between the ages of 35 and 65.

To use the FV function to calculate the value of your investment at retirement, follow these steps:

1 Click the worksheet cell in which you want to display the investment total.

2 Open the Paste Function dialog box.

3 Click the Financial category, and then double-click FV in the Function Name list box.

    A dialog box appears that contains a description of the FV function and five text boxes for the function's arguments. (The arguments are related to those of the PMT function, but now a Pmt field is added so that you can enter the amount you're contributing each period.)

4 Type *10%* in the Rate text box and press Tab, type *30* in the Nper text box and press Tab, type *-2000* in the Pmt text box and press Tab twice, and then type *1* in the Type text box.

Note that Rate and Nper must be based on the same units of time. In the previous example months were the basis; here, years are the basis for the calculation. Your dialog box should look like the following:

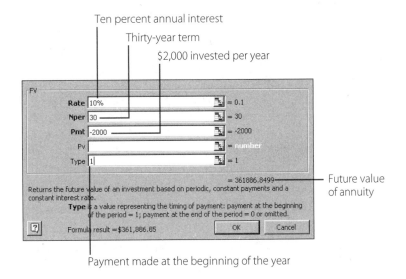

Ten percent annual interest

Thirty-year term

$2,000 invested per year

Future value of annuity

Payment made at the beginning of the year

5 Click OK to display the result.

In our example, the 30-year IRA has a future value of $361,886.85. Not bad for a total investment of $60,000.

> **NOTE**
> By placing a 1 in the Type text box, you direct Excel to start calculating each year's interest at the beginning of the year—a sensible move if you place one lump sum in your IRA at the same time each year. If you omit this argument, Excel will calculate each year's interest at the end of the year, and the total future value will be smaller—about $33,000 less in this example.

Using RATE to Evaluate Rate of Return

You'll often want to evaluate how a current investment is doing or how a new business proposition looks. For example, suppose that a contractor friend suggests you loan him $10,000 for a laundromat/brew pub project, and agrees to pay you $3,200 per year for four years as a minimum return on your investment. So what's the projected rate of return for this investment opportunity? You can figure it out quickly using the RATE function, which allows you to determine the rate of return for any investment that generates a series of periodic payments or a single lump-sum payment.

III

Microsoft Excel

To use the RATE function to determine the rate of return for an investment, follow these steps:

1 Click the worksheet cell in which you want to display the rate of return.

2 Open the Paste Function dialog box.

3 Click the Financial category, scroll down in the Function Name list box, and then double-click RATE.

A dialog box appears that contains a description of the RATE function and six text boxes for the function's arguments. (Scroll down to see the sixth text box, Guess.) The arguments are similar to the ones you have used in previous financial functions, but they appear in a slightly different order.

4 Type *4* in the Nper text box and press Tab, type *3200* in the Pmt text box and press Tab, and type *-10000* in the Pv text box. Your dialog box should look like this:

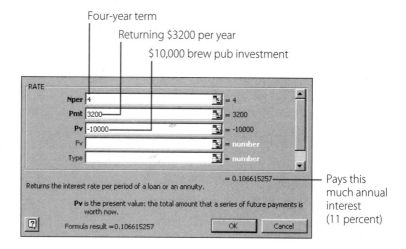

Four-year term

Returning $3200 per year

$10,000 brew pub investment

Pays this much annual interest (11 percent)

5 Click OK to display the result. In this example, your investment of $10,000 today will return 11 percent annually if your friend regularly pays you $3,200 per year for the next four years. With this information in hand, you can decide whether the projected rate of return is enough for you, or whether you'd rather try something less risky—or renegotiate the deal.

In short, Excel functions can't guarantee your financial success, but when used correctly, they can help you make decisions based on the best data available.

Using Function Error Values

The Paste Function dialog box makes entering functions relatively straightforward. If you do make a mistake when typing a function, you might receive a code called an *error value* in one or more cells. Error values begin with a pound (#) symbol and usually end with an exclamation point. For example, the error value #NUM! means that the function arguments you supplied aren't sufficient to calculate the function—one of the arguments might be too big or too small. If you see an error value in a cell, simply click the cell and fix your mistake on the formula bar, or delete the formula and enter it again. (If you're building a function, use the function's online Help to double-check your arguments.) Table 20-3 shows the most common Excel error values and their meanings.

TABLE 20-3.   Common Error Values in Excel Formulas

Error Value	Description
#DIV/0!	You're dividing by zero in this formula. Verify that no cell references refer to blank cells.
#NA	You might have omitted a function argument. No value is available.
#NAME?	You're using a range name in this formula that hasn't been defined in the workbook. (See the next section, "Using Range Names in Functions.")
#NULL!	You attempted to use the intersection of two areas that don't intersect (are not contiguous). You might have an extra space character in one of your range arguments.
#NUM!	Your function arguments might be out of range or otherwise invalid, or an iterative function you're using might not have computed long enough to reach a solution. (Entering a rough answer in the *Guess* argument might reduce the number of iterations Excel needs.)
#REF!	Your formula includes range references that have been deleted.
#VALUE!	Your formula is using a text entry as an argument.
######	Your calculation results were too wide to fit in the cell. Increase the column width.

III

Microsoft Excel

Using Range Names in Functions

To make your functions more readable and easier to type, you can name a range of cells in your worksheet and then use the range name in place of cell references throughout your workbook. For example, you could give the cells E4 through E9 the name Subtotal and then use the SUM function to add the five cells by entering the following formula:

=SUM(Subtotal)

After you assign a name to a cell range, you can use the name in any formula in your workbook.

Creating Range Names

Excel gives you two techniques for naming ranges in a workbook: You can click the Name box and type a range name (the tactile way), or you can use the Create command on the Name submenu (the auto-mated way). If you have a column heading already in place, the auto-mated way is slightly faster.

Range names must begin with a letter and can't include spaces. We recommend that you limit your names to 15 characters or fewer so that they fit easily into the Name box and so that you can type them quickly in formulas.

Creating Range Names: The Tactile Way

To create a range name by selecting, clicking, and typing (the tactile way), follow the steps shown in Figure 20-4. This way is recommended for touchy-feely people.

FIGURE 20-4.
Creating a named range by hand.

1 Select the range of cells you want to name.

2 Click the Name box.

3 Type an unused range name, and press Enter.

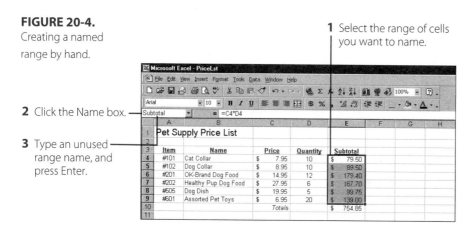

Creating Range Names: The Automatic Way

To create a range name using the Create command, follow these steps:

1   Select the range you want to name, and include a row or column heading in the selection to define the name. For example, the following selection includes the text label Subtotal for the range name:

Quantity	Subtotal
10	$ 79.50
10	$ 89.50
12	$ 179.40
6	$ 167.70
5	$ 99.75
20	$ 139.00
	$ 754.85

2   Choose Name from the Insert menu, and then choose Create from the submenu.

   The Create Names dialog box appears, prompting you for the location of the range name within your selection:

3   Click OK to accept Excel's default selection if you included a row or column label in your range; otherwise, click the option to tell Excel where to find the labels.

   In this example, Excel has detected the text label Subtotal at the top of your selection. You can use this name in computations in any worksheet in the workbook.

Putting Range Names to Work

You can use range names as arguments in functions wherever multiple-cell range references are permitted. For example, you could use the Subtotal range name in the SUM and AVERAGE functions because they accept ranges as arguments, but you couldn't use Subtotal in the PMT function because each of the PMT arguments must be a single number.

To insert a range name into a formula or function, follow these steps:

1 Create the formula or function as you normally would. For example, to determine the average of the cells in the Subtotal range, begin your formula as follows:

=AVERAGE(

2 When it's time to specify a range of cells as an argument, type the named range in the formula:

=AVERAGE(Subtotal)

3 When you have finished entering the formula, press Enter.

> If you can't remember the names you've given the ranges in your workbook, you can choose one from a list by using the Paste Name dialog box. To insert range names in this manner, type your formula, and when it's time to insert a range name, choose Name from the Insert menu, choose Paste from the submenu, and then double-click the range name that you want to include.

Modifying Ranges

Named ranges make your formulas easy to revise because when you modify the range, Excel automatically updates all your formulas. The Define command on the Name submenu lets you modify a range using the Refers To text box. You can add cells to or remove cells from a range, either by typing in the Refers To text box or by highlighting a new range in the worksheet.

To modify the cells included in a named range, follow these steps:

1 From the Insert menu, choose Name, and then choose Define from the submenu.

The Define Name dialog box includes a list of the named ranges in your workbook and a Refers To text box listing the cells in the named range.

2 Click the named range that you want to modify.

3 Change the cell references in the Refers To text box, or select a new range of cells directly in the worksheet. Just click the Collapse Dialog button in the Refers To box to shrink the dialog box. Then select the cells, and press Enter.

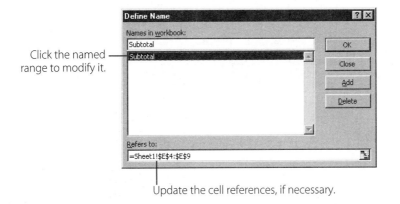

Click the named range to modify it.

Update the cell references, if necessary.

4 Click OK to save your changes.

Deleting Range Names

When you no longer need a range name, you can delete it from your workbook using the Define Name dialog box. Follow these steps to delete a range name:

1 Choose Name from the Insert menu, and then choose the Define command. The Define Name dialog box appears.

2 Click the range name that you want to delete from the workbook.

3 Click the Delete button. The range name is permanently removed from the workbook.

4 Click OK to close the Define Name dialog box.

Range names are an important component of well-documented formulas. When you can use range names well, you'll enjoy using formulas and functions much more.

WARNING

If you delete a range name that a formula is currently using, the error value #NAME? will appear in the cell containing the formula. To fix the problem, you'll need to replace the range name in the formula with an actual cell reference or with a valid range name. Note that you can't undo a range name deletion.

III

Microsoft Excel

Creating Worksheet Charts

When you have worksheet data that you need to present to others, it often makes sense to display some of the facts and figures as a *chart*. Charts are graphical representations of data that transform rows and columns of information into meaningful images. Charts can help you to identify numerical trends that can be difficult to spot in worksheets, and they can add color and flair to an important presentation. In this chapter, you'll learn how to create a Microsoft Excel chart from worksheet data, format your chart's appearance, add special effects, and print your chart. If it's your job to plan for the future or to analyze the past, you'll find Excel's charting tools both useful and addictive.

Planning a Chart

? **SEE ALSO**

If you have your worksheet set up with fields and records like a database, Excel 2000 also allows you to create a new type of interactive chart called a pivot chart. For more information about this powerful charting feature, see "Creating Pivot Tables and Pivot Charts," page 599.

Before you can create a chart, you need to do some general planning. An Excel chart is created from the data in an existing Excel worksheet, so before you build a chart, you need to create a worksheet that contains the necessary facts and figures. Excel can create a chart from data that is distributed throughout a worksheet, but you'll make the process easier if you organize your numbers so that they can be combined and selected easily. For example, Figure 21-1 shows a sales worksheet that contains rows and columns of data that can easily be converted into several types of charts.

You also need to plan for the type of chart that you'll be creating. Excel provides 14 chart types that you can use to present worksheet data, and there are several variations for each chart type. The basic chart types are shown in Table 21-1 along with the typical uses for each. For example, you can use a pie chart to describe the relationship of parts to a whole, or a bar chart to compare different categories of data with each other. If you're gathering information for an annual sales report, you might want to try out both of these chart types.

FIGURE 21-1.

Creating charts is easier when you make neatly organized rows and columns of data.

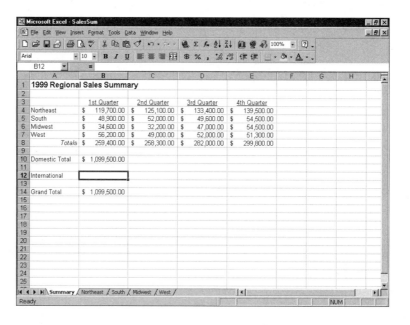

TABLE 21-1.   Excel Chart Types and Typical Uses for Each

Chart Symbol	Chart Type	Typical Use
	Column	Compares categories of data with each other vertically
	Bar	Compares categories of data with each other horizontally
	Line	Shows trends by category over a period of time
	Pie	Describes the relationship of the parts to the whole in a single group
	XY (Scatter)	Depicts the relationship between two kinds of related data
	Area	Emphasizes the relative importance of values over a period of time
	Doughnut	Compares the parts to the whole in one or more data categories; a more flexible pie chart that has a hole in the middle
	Radar	Shows changes in data or data frequency relative to a center point
	Surface	Tracks changes in two variables as a third variable (such as time) changes; a 3-D chart
	Bubble	Highlights clusters of values; similar to a scatter chart
	Stock	Combines column chart and line chart; especially designed to track stock prices
	Cylinder	Uses a unique cylinder shape to present bar or column chart data.
	Cone	Emphasizes the peaks in data; a bar or column chart
	Pyramid	Emphasizes the peaks in bars or columns; similar to the cone chart

> **Measure Twice, Chart Once**
>
> Charting requires some up-front planning to get the best results. Just as a carpenter measures a length of wood twice before cutting it, you're well advised to take your time and think about your goals for a chart before creating it. As you plan your charting strategy, ask yourself the following questions:
>
> - Which worksheet data would I like to highlight in a chart? Can I build my worksheet so that I can copy data directly to the chart?
>
> - How will I present my chart? Do I want to store it as a separate sheet in my workbook, in an existing worksheet, or as part of a Microsoft Word document or a Microsoft PowerPoint presentation?
>
> - Which chart type do I plan to use? Do I want to show one category of data (such as first-quarter sales by geographic region), or several (such as the four most recent quarters of sales by geographic region)?

Creating a Chart

When you have a well-organized worksheet in place, you're ready to create a chart. In the following examples, we'll use the 1999 Sales Summary workbook (SalesSum.xls) shown in Figure 21-1, page 560, to create a pie chart and a column chart. Because charting often involves experimenting with different chart types, feel free to follow your own impulses as you complete the instructions.

 The SalesSum.xls example is on the Running Office 2000 Reader's Corner page. For information about connecting to this Web site, read the Introduction.

To create a pie chart in a new sheet in the workbook, follow these steps:

1 Prepare a worksheet that has rows and columns of information that you can use in the chart. Add row and column labels if you want them included in the chart.

 If you select labels along with the data for your chart before you create the chart, Excel will add the labels automatically.

2 Select the cell range containing the data to be plotted. In this example, we'll be creating a pie chart, so we want to select one category of values (one row or column).

In Excel terminology, a category is called a *data series*. The following screen shows how you would select numbers in the 1st Quarter column for a pie chart, including text that you want to use as chart labels:

	A	B	C
1	1999 Regional Sales Summary		
2			
3		1st Quarter	2nd Quarter
4	Northeast	$ 119,700.00	$ 125,100.00
5	South	$ 48,900.00	$ 52,000.00
6	Midwest	$ 34,600.00	$ 32,200.00
7	West	$ 56,200.00	$ 49,000.00
8	Totals	$ 259,400.00	$ 258,300.00
9			

Chart
Wizard

3 Now create the chart. Choose Chart from the Insert menu, or click the Chart Wizard button on the Standard toolbar. The Chart Wizard starts, and you'll see the following dialog box asking you to select a chart type:

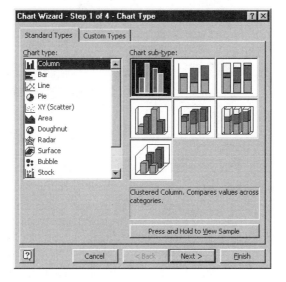

4 If Office Assistant appears, click the Help button to close it so that you'll have a better view of the worksheet.

5 Click the Pie chart type in the Chart Type list box, and then click the Exploded 3-D Pie in the Chart Sub-Type box. (The names of the sub-types appear as you click each one.)

6 Click Next to display the dialog box prompting you for the worksheet cells to include in the chart. The cells you selected in step 2 appear in the Data Range text box (cells A3 through B7).

If you organized your worksheet well, and if you selected the proper data, your chart should now contain the correct information (although the labels might be too small to see). If your chart doesn't look right, use the option buttons and list boxes in this dialog box to change the cells used for the data series, labels, and chart title.

7 Click Next to display the Chart Wizard dialog box that controls the chart's titles, legend, and data labels. Your pie chart appears in a sample window with the default settings, as shown in the following screen:

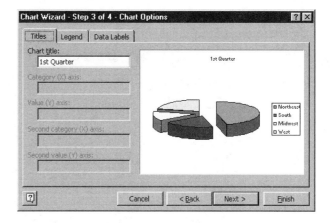

8 Starting from the Titles tab, change the chart title to *1999 Regional Sales Summary*, and then click Next.

The Chart Wizard displays a dialog box asking you for the location of your new chart. You can either create a new workbook tab for the chart, or place it as an object in one of your existing worksheets.

9 Click the As New Sheet button, type *Summary Chart* in the highlighted text box, and then click the Finish button.

Excel completes the pie chart and displays it in a new sheet named Summary Chart in the workbook. Excel adjusts the Zoom control on the Standard toolbar so that the entire chart is visible. The Charting toolbar also appears; we'll cover it in the section "Formatting a Chart," page 569.

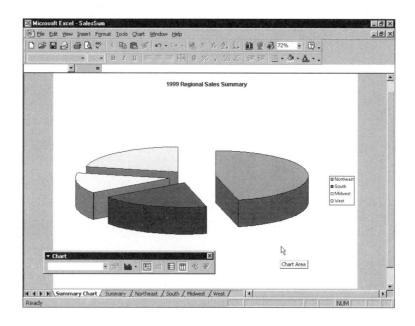

10 Choose Save from the File menu to save your new chart to disk as part of your open workbook. You can now display the pie chart at any time by clicking the Summary Chart tab.

To get a better look at the title, labels, and data in your new chart, click the Zoom control on the Standard toolbar, and select a higher viewing percentage. You'll find that 75% or 100% usually works well for reading the text in your chart and for formatting labels.

Creating an Embedded Chart

Excel also allows you to create an in-place, or *embedded*, chart in an existing worksheet. This technique allows you to closely associate graphical images with the data in your worksheet. For example, you could create an area chart depicting bagel production in a bakery worksheet containing inventory and sales data. In the following example, we'll show you how to add a column sales chart to a sales-summary worksheet.

III

Microsoft Excel

To create an embedded chart in a worksheet, follow these steps:

1 Prepare a worksheet that has rows and columns of data that you can chart. As you create the worksheet, set aside some room for a rectangular column chart.

2 Select the cell range containing the data that you want to plot. In our example, we'll be creating a chart that has groups of columns representing sales regions, so if you want to follow our example, you'll need to select several columns of data. Our selected columns and labels look like this:

	A	B	C	D	E	F
1	1999 Regional Sales Summary					
2						
3		1st Quarter	2nd Quarter	3rd Quarter	4th Quarter	
4	Northeast	$ 119,700.00	$ 125,100.00	$ 133,400.00	$ 139,500.00	
5	South	$ 48,900.00	$ 52,000.00	$ 49,600.00	$ 54,500.00	
6	Midwest	$ 34,600.00	$ 32,200.00	$ 47,000.00	$ 54,500.00	
7	West	$ 56,200.00	$ 49,000.00	$ 52,000.00	$ 51,300.00	
8	Totals	$ 259,400.00	$ 258,300.00	$ 282,000.00	$ 299,800.00	
9						

3 Click the Chart Wizard button on the Standard toolbar. (Creating an embedded chart is exactly like creating a stand-alone chart, except for specifying the chart location in step 10.)

4 In the Chart Type dialog box, specify the chart type you want to use and click Next. (In this example, we'll use the default column chart type.)

5 The Chart Source Data dialog box reflects the data range selected in step 2. Click Next, unless you first want to adjust any of the settings for your data.

6 Customize your chart by choosing from among the options presented in the Chart Options dialog box, or accept Excel's settings. Notice that you have a different set of options for a column chart than you did for a pie chart.

7 When you're finished, click the Next button to display the Chart Location dialog box:

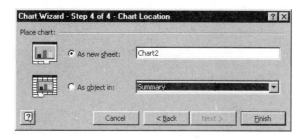

8 Click the As Object In option button, and then specify the worksheet in which you want to place the new chart by using the adjacent drop-down list box. (We placed our chart in the Summary worksheet.)

9 Click the Finish button to complete the chart.

10 The Chart Wizard builds the chart to your specifications and places it in the middle of the worksheet, as shown in the following illustration. (Note that the chart is currently selected and has eight selection handles.)

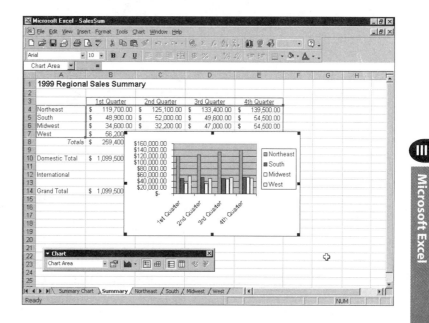

Working with Embedded Charts

When you embed an Excel chart in a worksheet, you create an object that can be resized, formatted, moved, and deleted like clip art or any other object. You can use the following editing techniques on embedded charts:

- To resize an embedded chart, move the mouse pointer to the edge of the chart, and drag one of the selection handles.

- To format an embedded chart, double-click the chart, and the Format Chart Area dialog box appears. Add borders to the chart from the Patterns tab, or choose other commands from the Font or Properties tabs. (See "Formatting a Chart," page 569.)

- To move an embedded chart from one location to another in the worksheet, click within the object, and drag it to a new location. To move the chart to a new worksheet, click the chart, and then choose Location from the Chart menu. To move the chart to another workbook or Microsoft Office application, click the chart, choose Cut from the Edit menu, open or switch to the destination document, and then choose Paste from the Edit menu.

- To delete an embedded chart, select the chart and press the Delete key.

11 Drag the chart to the desired location in the worksheet, and resize it to display the amount of detail you want. (Drag the chart by one of its edges so that you don't inadvertently rearrange the chart components.)

TIP

Excel creates embedded charts small to make them easy to move and format. However, your chart will usually look better if you enlarge it.

12 When you're finished, click outside the chart to remove the selection handles and lock it in place on your worksheet. (Click the chart to reactivate the selection handles in the future.) The final column chart is shown in Figure 21-2.

ON THE WEB

The Charts.xls example is on the Running Office 2000 Reader's Corner page.

FIGURE 21-2.
A completed column
chart embedded in
the worksheet.

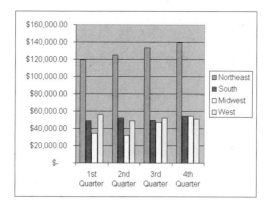

Formatting a Chart

If you're content to use Excel's default formatting for your chart, you're all finished—just tidy up your chart and print it. If you're like most people, however, you probably can't resist adding a label here or changing the point size there. In this section, you'll learn how to format charts by changing the chart type, editing titles and gridlines, adjusting the legend, adding text, and controlling character formatting. What you learn will apply both to embedded charts and to stand-alone chart sheets in the workbook.

Exploring the Chart Menu

When you created the pie chart in the first example in this chapter, you might not have noticed that the Data menu was replaced by a Chart menu on the menu bar, and that several commands on the remaining menus changed. Excel's Chart menu includes commands that are specifically designed for charting, as shown in Figure 21-3. (Note that your Chart menu might be customized differently.)

FIGURE 21-3.
Excel's Chart menu
contains commands
specifically designed
for charting.

Using the Charting Toolbar

The Chart toolbar shown in Figure 21-4 contains several buttons designed to help you format your chart. This toolbar also contains the Chart Objects list box, which you can use to select different components of your chart for editing (such as the chart title, legend, and plot areas). Many of the buttons on the Chart toolbar correspond to commands on the Chart menu, as you'll see in the following sections. Display the Chart toolbar by choosing it from the Toolbars submenu of the View menu.

FIGURE 21-4.

The Chart toolbar appears when a chart is active in the workbook. To remove it, click the Close button.

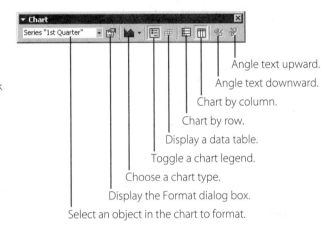

Angle text upward.
Angle text downward.
Chart by column.
Chart by row.
Display a data table.
Toggle a chart legend.
Choose a chart type.
Display the Format dialog box.
Select an object in the chart to format.

Changing the Chart Type

Even after you create a chart, you're not locked in to one particular chart type. If your data supports it, you can reformat your chart to use any of Excel's 14 chart types. (For example, you can change your pie chart into a column chart.) To switch between chart types, click the Chart Type button on the Chart toolbar or choose Chart Type from the Chart menu.

To change the pie chart you created earlier into a column chart by using the Chart toolbar, follow these steps:

1 If the chart is embedded, click it to select it, and click the Chart toolbar. If the chart appears in its own worksheet, simply display the worksheet.

2 Click the arrow on the Chart Type button on the Chart toolbar to display pictures of the various chart types.

3 Click the 3-D Column Chart button. (When you move the pointer over each chart type, its name will appear.)

Your chart will change shape to match the selected chart type. The following screen shows how your pie chart will look when it's changed into a 3-D column chart.

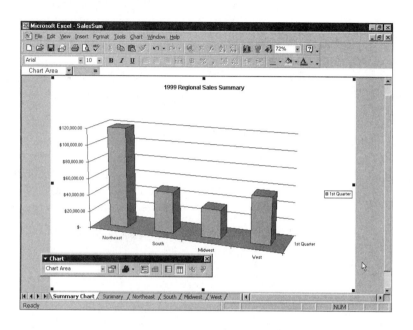

TIP

Choose Additional Chart Sub-Types

For a wider selection of chart types (for example, to change from 3-D view to 2-D view), select the chart, and choose Chart Type from the Chart menu. Here you can pick from over 70 choices in the Chart Sub-Type list boxes for each chart type.

Changing Titles and Labels

You can edit the text in your chart's titles and labels as well as modify the font, alignment, and background pattern. If you select a data label, you can change its numeric formatting.

To edit title or label text, follow these steps:

1 Display the chart that you want to modify. If the chart is embedded in a worksheet, click the chart to activate it and to display Excel's charting commands and tools.

Microsoft Excel

CAUTION
Check that you have
selected the part of
the chart you want to
edit by making sure
the selection handles
indicate the specific
object and not the
entire chart.

2 Use the Zoom control to zoom in on the title or label so that
you can read it, if necessary. The best view for editing text is
usually 100%.

3 Click the title or label in the chart. Selection handles will surround
the text.

4 Click again to insert the text pointer at the spot you want to edit.
You can insert new text and use the Backspace and Delete keys
to delete unwanted text.

 **TIP**

> You can check the spelling of the text in a chart by selecting the text object and
> choosing Spelling from the Tools menu.

5 When you have completed your edits, press the Escape key once
to remove the text insertion marker, and then press Escape a second time to remove the selection handles. (You can also click
outside the chart to remove the selection handles.)

Changing Character Formatting

 SEE ALSO
To learn more about
formatting text, see
Chapter 17, "Format-
ting a Worksheet."

To change a title or label's font, alignment, or pattern, follow these steps:

1 Click the chart title or a label. Selection handles will appear
around the text.

2 From the Format menu, choose Selected Chart Title (for a title) or
Selected Data Labels (for a label). Only one of the commands will
be available. You'll see a dialog box similar to the one shown in
Figure 21-5.

FIGURE 21-5.
You can format chart
titles and labels in the
same way as regular
worksheet text.

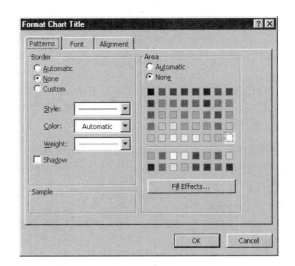

If you're formatting a label, the dialog box will also have a Number tab. We'll discuss this tab in the next example.

3 Use the Patterns, Font, and Alignment tabs to modify the borders or colors, adjust the character formatting in the text, or adjust the text orientation. For example, if you plan to print your chart, you might want to increase the point size of the text using the Font tab.

4 When you have finished formatting the text, click OK.

Adjusting Numeric Formatting in Labels

If you selected a label in your chart, your dialog box includes a Number tab, as shown in Figure 21-6. The following steps show you how to use the Number tab to adjust the numeric formatting in labels:

1 Click one or more labels that contain numeric data such as percentages or dollar amounts. (To select more than one label, hold down the Shift key while clicking.) You can also select numeric values associated with the intersection of the gridlines or the *axis* of the chart.

To add or change data labels, use the Chart Options command on the Chart menu.

2 Choose Selected Data Labels from the Format menu. (If you selected an axis, choose the Selected Axis command.)

FIGURE 21-6.
The Number tab lets you change the number formatting in chart labels.

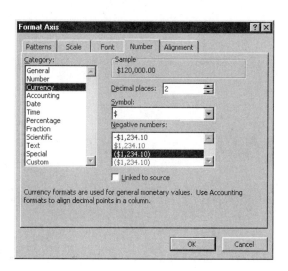

Microsoft Excel

3 Click the Number tab of the Format dialog box. Your screen will look like the one shown in Figure 21-6. (If you're formatting an axis, the dialog box will also have a Scale tab, which you can use to adjust the numbers and tick marks along the x-axis and y-axis.)

4 Click the numeric category that you want to use, and specify a new number of decimal places if necessary. For example, if your labels are in the Currency format, you might want to set the decimal places to zero to remove cents and to make more room on your chart.

5 When you have finished formatting, click OK.

Adjusting Gridlines

If you're creating a column, bar, line, XY (scatter), area, radar, surface, bubble, stock, cylinder, cone, or pyramid chart, you can include gridlines that extend horizontally from the x-axis or vertically from the y-axis. Gridlines help you to associate numbers with the pictures in your chart, and they're especially useful if you need to make exact comparisons between categories of data.

To add gridlines to your chart, follow these steps:

1 Display the chart. If your chart is embedded in a worksheet, click the chart to activate Excel's charting commands and tools.

2 Choose Chart Options from the Chart menu to display the Chart Options dialog box, and then click the Gridlines tab. (See Figure 21-7.)

3 To add gridlines to both axes, select both Major Gridlines check boxes. If you want to create a denser pattern of gridlines, select the Minor Gridlines check boxes also.

4 Click OK to add the gridlines. To remove the gridlines, simply remove all the check marks from the Gridlines check boxes and click OK.

⭐ **TIP**

You can also remove gridlines by clicking the gridlines in your chart and pressing Delete.

FIGURE 21-7.
The check boxes on
the Gridlines tab
determine which
gridlines appear.

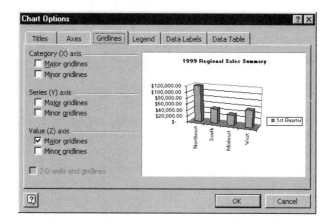

Modifying the Chart Legend

A chart *legend* describes what each color or pattern represents in a chart
so that you can compare the values in a category. Excel lets you change
the font, colors, and location of an existing chart legend by using a special dialog box full of formatting tabs. You can add a legend to a chart
when you first build the chart using the Chart Wizard (step 3), or later by
clicking the Legend button on the Chart toolbar. Because the Legend button is an on or off toggle, you can add or remove a chart legend quickly,
to see whether you like it. If you remove the chart legend, you'll have
more room on your chart for graphing the data.

To modify a chart legend's font, colors, or location, follow these steps:

1 Display the chart and click the legend, which will then be surrounded by selection handles.

2 From the Format menu, choose Selected Legend to display the
Format Legend dialog box, as shown in Figure 21-8, on the following page. The dialog box contains three tabs, which let you
control the border, colors, and patterns used for the legend box;
the font used for the legend text; and the location of the legend
in relation to the chart.

3 Use the Patterns, Font, and Placement tabs to customize the legend. When you have finished, click OK.

TIP

To quickly format the text in a chart legend, you can also use the Font, Font Size,
Bold, Italic, and Underline buttons on the toolbar.

III

Microsoft Excel

FIGURE 21-8.

To customize the chart's legend, use the Selected Legend command.

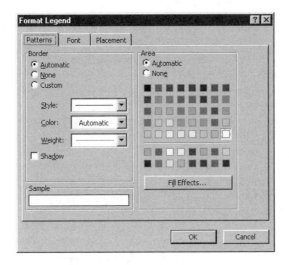

Changing the Viewing Angle in 3-D Charts

Excel offers you three-dimensional chart types in the Area, Bar, Column, Line, Pie, Radar, Surface, Cylinder, Cone, and Pyramid categories. Three-dimensional charts have much in common with two-dimensional charts, but they add a feeling of depth that contributes realism and visual interest to your data. You can change the orientation, or *viewing angle*, of a 3-D chart by selecting the chart and choosing 3-D View from the Chart menu. To tilt the chart up or back, click the large up or down buttons in the 3-D View dialog box above the Elevation text box. To rotate the chart left or right, click the clockwise or counterclockwise buttons beneath the chart preview window. You can also change the perspective or line-of-sight angle by clicking the up or down buttons above the Perspective text box after you type a value. (However, these settings are only available for 3-D charts.)

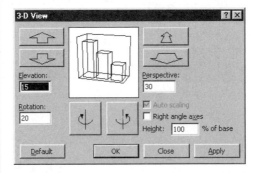

Adding Labels and Arrows

 SEE ALSO

The Drawing toolbar contains several tools to further embellish your charts and worksheets. For more information, see "Adding Graphics," page 320.

Have you ever been lost in a shopping mall, unable to determine your location or find the store you're looking for? When this happens, it's comforting to find the mall map, with its familiar *You Are Here* arrow and message that identify your current location and help you get your bearings. As you design your charts, you can use Excel's charting commands to add similar pointers to your own pictures. If you have important aspects that you want to highlight, this could be the perfect tool.

⭐ **TIP**

> Text and arrows are independent of each other and float freely over the chart where you place them. You can use them individually or together in your charts.

To highlight a chart attribute by adding an arrow, follow these steps:

1   Display the chart that you want to embellish with an arrow. If the chart is embedded in a worksheet, click the chart to activate Excel's charting commands and tools.

Drawing

2   Click the Drawing button on Excel's Standard toolbar. Excel then displays its multipurpose Drawing toolbar, as shown in the following illustration:

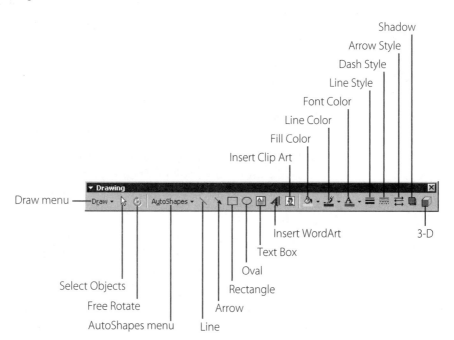

3 Click the Arrow button on the Drawing toolbar. The mouse pointer changes to drawing crosshairs.

4 Draw the line that will be your arrow from the tail to the head of the arrow. When you release the mouse button, a default-style arrow appears.

5 Customize the arrow by adjusting the weight of the line using the Line Style button, selecting a dashed line style using the Dash Style button, or adjusting the tail and head of the arrow using the Arrow Style button.

To add text to the arrow, follow these steps:

1 Click the Text Box button on the Drawing toolbar.

2 Use the drag technique to draw a rectangle to hold your label text. When it's approximately the right size, release the mouse button.

3 Type the label text, and then click near the border of the text box to select it.

4 Use the Formatting toolbar to set the font, size, and style of the text. Use the Drawing toolbar to change the color of the text (click the Font Color button), to set the background color of the text box (click the Fill Color button), to add an outline to the text box (click the Line Style button), and to set the color of the outline (click the Line Color button).

⭐ **TIP**

> You can reposition free-floating text boxes and arrows in your chart by selecting them and dragging them with the mouse. To delete a text box or arrow, select the object and press Delete.

5 Resize the text box using the selection handles, and place the text box where you want it by dragging the border. Then click outside the chart area to remove the selection handles. Our chart now appears like the one on the opposite page.

6 Click the Close button on the Drawing toolbar to remove it from the screen. (If you don't see a Close button, right-click the Drawing toolbar and deselect Drawing to remove it from the screen.)

1999 Regional Sales Summary

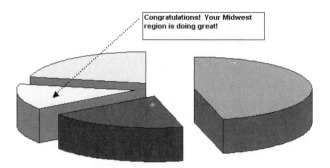

Congratulations! Your Midwest region is doing great!

Printing a Chart

When you have finished creating attractive charts, you'll most certainly want to print them. Printing charts is not much different from printing worksheets, but you have a few extra options available. If you're using a black-and-white printer, you'll want to examine your chart in Print Preview to verify that its colors have been properly converted to grayscale shading. If you're printing an embedded chart, you have the option of printing the chart with or without the worksheet data around it.

To double-check chart colors in Print Preview, follow these steps:

Print
Preview

1 Display the chart that you want to print, and then click the Print Preview button on the Standard toolbar.

2 Verify the chart shading—you should be able to distinguish one shade of gray from another. (If you're using a color printer, of course, you'll see everything in color.)

3 Click Close to exit Print Preview.

4 If you're not happy with the shading, double-click the chart piece you want to change and specify a new color or pattern on the Patterns tab of the Format Data Series dialog box. Excel gives you complete control over the colors and shading patterns used in your charts and legends, so that you can adjust them if necessary.

To print a chart, follow these steps:

1 Display the chart that you want to print, either as a stand-alone chart sheet or as an embedded chart in the worksheet.

III

Microsoft Excel

2 If you want to print an embedded chart only, and not the surrounding worksheet data as well, click the chart first.

3 Choose Print from the File menu to open the Print dialog box.

4 Specify the print options that you want, and then click OK to send your chart to the printer.

Print Your Chart as "What You Get Is What You See"

By default, Excel prints a chart on an entire page. If you want your printed chart to be the same size as the chart in your worksheet, choose Page Setup from the File menu, click the Chart tab, and then select the Custom option before printing. This option tells Excel to render the chart on paper exactly as it appears in your worksheet.

CHAPTER 22

Working with Lists, Databases, and Pivot Tables

I f you routinely track large amounts of information in your business—customer mailing lists, phone lists, product inventories, sales transactions, and so on—you can use Microsoft Excel's extensive list-management capabilities to make your job easier. A *list* is a table of data stored in a worksheet, organized into columns of fields and rows of records. A list is essentially a *database*, but because lists are stored in Excel workbooks and not in formatted files created by database programs such as Microsoft Access or Microsoft FoxPro, Microsoft has chosen to use the word *list* as the preferred term.

In this chapter, you'll learn how to create a list in a workbook, sort the list based on one or more fields, locate important records by using filters, organize entries by using subtotals, and create summary information by using pivot tables and new pivot charts. The lists that you create will be compatible with Access, and, if you're not already familiar with Access, the techniques that you learn here will give you a head start on learning several database commands and terms.

Using a List of Cells as a Database

A list is a collection of rows and columns of consistently formatted data, adhering to somewhat stricter rules than an ordinary worksheet. To build a list that works with all of Excel's list-management commands, you need to follow a few basic guidelines. Figure 22-1 shows a simple sales-history list that has five columns, or *fields,* and a dozen sales transaction *records.* When you create a list, it should contain a fixed number of columns or categories of information, but it should have a variable number of rows, reflecting records that can be added, deleted, or rearranged to keep your list up to date. Each column should contain the same type of information, and no blank rows or columns should appear in the list area. If your list is the only information in the worksheet, Excel will have an easier time recognizing the data as a list.

To create a list in Excel, follow these steps:

1 Open a new workbook or a new sheet in an existing workbook. Using a new worksheet that will contain only your list works best, so that Excel can select your data automatically when you use list-management commands.

2 Create a column heading for each field in the list, adjust the alignment of the headings, and format them in bold type.

3 Format the cells below the column headings for the data that you plan to use. This can include number formats (such as currency or date), alignment, or any other formats.

 ON THE WEB

The Pivot.xls example is on the Running Office 2000 Reader's Corner page. For information about connecting to this Web site, read the Introduction.

SEE ALSO
For information about sharing a list with other users over a network, see "Managing Shared Workbooks," page 504.

4 Add new records (your data) below the column headings, taking care to be consistent in your use of words and titles so that you can organize related records into groups later. Enter as many rows as you need, making sure that there are no empty rows in your list, not even between the column headings and the first record. See Figure 22-1 for a sample list of information.

5 When you have finished, save your workbook. If your list grows to include many records, consider keeping a separate backup copy in a safe place as an extra precaution.

FIGURE 22-1.
A list of information in an Excel worksheet, complete with column headings.

Each column is a field containing one type of information.

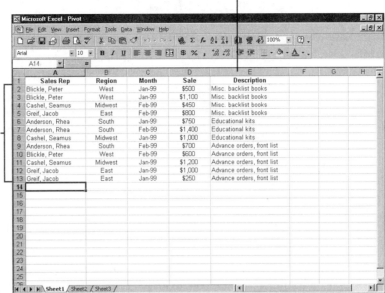

Each row represents a record.

TIP

Let AutoComplete Finish Typing Your Words

Excel's AutoComplete feature will help you to insert repetitive list entries by recognizing the words you type and finishing them for you. To enable this time-saving feature, choose Options from the Tools menu, click the Edit tab, and select the Enable AutoComplete For Cell Values check box. It's important that repeated names and other data (such as *January, Midwest Region,* and so on) be entered identically from record to record, to enable Excel to recognize the data for grouping, sorting, and calculating.

Using a Form for Data Entry

To make it easy to manage the data in your list, Excel lets you add, delete, and search for records by using the Form command on the Data menu. When you choose Form, a customized dialog box appears, showing the fields in your list and several list-management command buttons. (See Figure 22-2 on the following page.) The name of the current worksheet also appears on the dialog box title bar. By default, the first record in the list appears, but you can scroll to other records by

III

Microsoft Excel

FIGURE 22-2.

The Form command gives you another way to enter data into the rows and columns of a list.

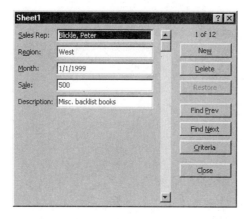

clicking the vertical scroll bar. Excel adds new records to the end of the list; to display a blank record, you can scroll to the bottom of the list or click the New button. Although you'll often add records by typing them directly into the worksheet, using the Form command is a useful alternative (for, say, a less-experienced colleague you've asked to help enter data), and in some cases you'll find that it works faster.

Validating Data as You Enter It

If several people are using your Excel list, you might want to control the type of information they're allowed to enter into worksheet cells to minimize typing mistakes. For example, you might want to require that only January or February dates can be entered into the Month column, or that only dollar values in a particular range (say, $0–$5,000) can be entered into the Sale column. With Excel you can enforce input requirements such as these by using a formatting option called *data validation*. When you use data validation, you protect part or all of your worksheet from erroneous input that might cause formulas or list-management tools to produce incorrect results.

To enforce data validation of a particular range of worksheet cells, follow these steps:

1 Select the cells in the column that you want to protect with data validation. This should include cells already containing data as well as the blank cells below, where you'll be adding new records. (If you're not sure how long your list will be, you may want to select the entire column.)

2 Choose Validation from the Data menu. The Data Validation dialog box opens. Click the Settings tab.

3 In the Allow drop-down list box, specify the input format you want to require for the selected cells. Your options are Any Value (used to remove existing data validation), Whole Number, Decimal, List, Date, Time, Text Length, and Custom (a format you specify by writing your own formula).

When you select a value in the Allow drop-down list box, additional text boxes appear below that let you specify extra input conditions or *restrictions*, such as the smallest number and the largest number Excel will accept.

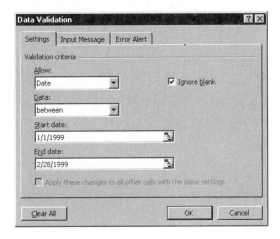

4 Click the Input Message tab, and select Show Input Message When Cell Is Selected to specify a message that will appear when the cell is selected.

5 In the Input Message text box, type the words you want displayed in the pop-up box that appears when a user selects a cell containing the data validation formatting. (This box is optional, but using it will help your users discover the requirements you have established *before* they make a mistake.)

III

Microsoft Excel

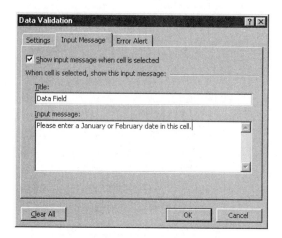

6 Click the Error Alert tab, and select Show Error Alert After Invalid Data Is Entered to specify the type of error message you want Excel to display if a user enters inappropriate information into a cell.

7 In the Style drop-down list box, select one of the following options: Stop (to block the input), Warning (to caution the user but allow the input), or Information (to display a note but allow the input).

8 In the Error Message text box, type the words you want displayed in the error message dialog box that appears if the user enters invalid data. For example, a useful phrase might be *This work-sheet tracks January and February sales only.*

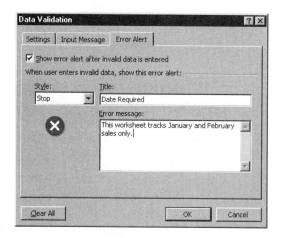

9 Click OK to complete the Data Validation dialog box. If you specified the options shown in step 7, you'll see a gentle error message similar to the following if you enter the wrong type of data in a cell that has active data validation:

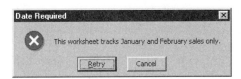

Sorting Rows and Columns

Once your records are organized into a list, you can use several commands on the Data menu to rearrange and analyze the data. The Sort command allows you to arrange the records in a different order based on the values in one or more columns. You can sort records in ascending or descending order or in a custom order, such as by days of the week or months of the year.

To sort a list based on one column, follow these steps:

1 Click the column or field in the list that you want to use as the basis for sorting the list.

2 From the Data menu, choose Sort. Excel selects all the records in your list and displays the following dialog box:

 **ON THE WEB**   The Pivot.xls example is on the Running Office 2000 Reader's Corner page.

3 The Sort By drop-down list box contains the heading for the column you selected. If you like, you can select a different column in the list box now for the sort.

III

Microsoft Excel

4 Click one of the sort order option buttons to specify ascending order (A to Z, lowest to highest, earliest date to most recent) or descending order (Z to A, highest to lowest, most recent date to earliest).

5 Click OK to run the sort. If you sorted the first column in ascending order, your screen will look similar to this:

	A	B	C	D	E
1	**Sales Rep**	**Region**	**Month**	**Sale**	**Description**
2	Anderson, Rhea	South	Jan-99	$750	Educational kits
3	Anderson, Rhea	South	Feb-99	$1,400	Educational kits
4	Anderson, Rhea	South	Feb-99	$700	Advance orders, front list
5	Blickle, Peter	West	Jan-99	$500	Misc. backlist books
6	Blickle, Peter	West	Jan-99	$1,100	Misc. backlist books
7	Blickle, Peter	West	Feb-99	$600	Advance orders, front list
8	Cashel, Seamus	Midwest	Feb-99	$450	Misc. backlist books
9	Cashel, Seamus	Midwest	Jan-99	$1,000	Educational kits
10	Cashel, Seamus	Midwest	Jan-99	$1,200	Advance orders, front list
11	Greif, Jacob	East	Feb-99	$800	Misc. backlist books
12	Greif, Jacob	East	Jan-99	$1,000	Advance orders, front list
13	Greif, Jacob	East	Jan-99	$250	Advance orders, front list
14					

TIP

Sort Ascending

Sort Descending

Click a Cell, Sort a List

To quickly sort a list based on a single column, click a column head or a cell in the column, and then click either the Sort Ascending or Sort Descending button on the Standard toolbar. Excel rearranges the list in the order that you selected.

Sorting on More Than One Column

If you have *ties* in your sort—that is, if some of the records in your list have identical entries in the column you're sorting with—you can specify additional sorting criteria to further organize your list. To sort a list based on two or three columns, follow these steps:

1 Click a cell in the list that you want to sort.

2 From the Data menu, choose Sort. Excel selects the records in your list and displays the Sort dialog box.

3 Select the primary field for the sort in the Sort By drop-down list box. Specify ascending or descending order for that column.

4 Click the first Then By drop-down list box and pick a second column for the sort, to resolve any ties in the first sort. Specify ascending or descending order for the second sort as well.

5   Click the second Then By drop-down list box and pick a third column for the sort, again to resolve any ties remaining after the first two sorts. Once more, specify ascending or descending order. (Your sorts needn't be in the same direction.) A Sort dialog box that has three levels of sorting is shown here:

6   Click OK to run the sort.

The following screen shows how a sort would look based on the options shown above. Note that the columns you specify in the Then By sections are used only to resolve ties in the list—not to control the entire sort. (For this reason, numbers in the Sale column are only in descending order when both the Sales Rep and the Description fields are identical.)

	A	B	C	D	E
1	**Sales Rep**	**Region**	**Month**	**Sale**	**Description**
2	Anderson, Rhea	South	Feb-99	$700	Advance orders, front list
3	Anderson, Rhea	South	Feb-99	$1,400	Educational kits
4	Anderson, Rhea	South	Jan-99	$750	Educational kits
5	Blickle, Peter	West	Feb-99	$600	Advance orders, front list
6	Blickle, Peter	West	Jan-99	$1,100	Misc. backlist books
7	Blickle, Peter	West	Jan-99	$500	Misc. backlist books
8	Cashel, Seamus	Midwest	Jan-99	$1,200	Advance orders, front list
9	Cashel, Seamus	Midwest	Jan-99	$1,000	Educational kits
10	Cashel, Seamus	Midwest	Feb-99	$450	Misc. backlist books
11	Greif, Jacob	East	Jan-99	$1,000	Advance orders, front list
12	Greif, Jacob	East	Jan-99	$250	Advance orders, front list
13	Greif, Jacob	East	Feb-99	$800	Misc. backlist books
14					

These three records demonstrate how ties are resolved in an advanced sort. In this case, the order is by Sales Rep (ascending), Description (ascending), and Sale (descending).

III

Microsoft Excel

Creating Your Own Custom Sort Order

Excel allows you to create custom sort orders so that you can rearrange lists that don't follow predictable alphanumeric or chronologic patterns. For example, you can create a custom sort order for the regions of the country (West, Midwest, East, South) to tell Excel to sort the regions in the way *you* want rather than by strict alphabetic rules. When you define a custom sort order, it appears in the Sort Options dialog box and is available to all the workbooks in your system.

To create a custom sort order, follow these steps:

1 Choose Options from the Tools menu, and then click the Custom Lists tab.

2 Click the line NEW LIST under Custom Lists, and the text pointer will appear in the List Entries list box. This is where you'll type the items in your custom list. (In this example, you'll create the custom order West, Midwest, South, East.)

3 Type *West, Midwest, South, East,* and then click the Add button. You can either separate each value with a comma or type it on a separate line.

The new custom order appears in the Custom Lists list box, as shown in Figure 22-3. You can now use this sorting order to sort your columns, as described in "Using a Custom Sort Order" next.

4 Click OK to close the Options dialog box.

Using a Custom Sort Order

When you want to sort based on an order that isn't alphabetical or numerical—the days of the week, for example, or the months of the year that have been entered as text rather than dates—you can click

FIGURE 22-3.
The Custom Lists tab lets you add, delete, and edit Excel's collection of custom sorting orders.

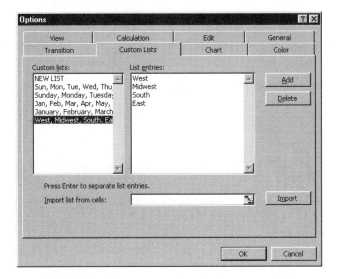

the Options button in the Sort dialog box and specify a custom sort order to use for the comparison. To use a custom sort order, follow these steps.

1 Click any cell in your list.

2 From the Data menu, choose Sort. Excel selects the records in your list and displays the Sort dialog box.

3 Select the primary field for the sort in the Sort By list box. Specify ascending or descending order. (The direction you specify will also apply to the custom sort.) In our example, we selected the Region field, ascending order.

4 Click the Options button to display the Sort Options dialog box.

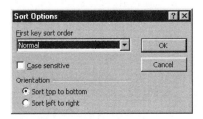

5 Click the First Key Sort Order drop-down list box, and click the custom order that you want to use.

III

Microsoft Excel

NOTE

You can also specify custom sort orders for the second and third sort options if you want to, in which case the title of the sort order drop-down list box will change to match the key that you're defining.

6 Click OK in each dialog box to run the sort. Your list will appear sorted with the custom criteria you specified.

Using AutoFilter to Find Records

When you want to hide all the rows in your list except those that meet certain criteria, you can use the AutoFilter command on the Filter submenu of the Data menu. The AutoFilter command places a drop-down list box at the top of each column in your list. To display a particular group of records, select the criteria that you want in one or more of the drop-down list boxes. For example, to display the sales history for all employees that had $1,000 orders in January, you could select January in the Month column drop-down list box and $1,000 in the Sale drop-down list box.

To use the AutoFilter command to find records, follow these steps:

1 Click any cell in the list.

2 From the Data menu, choose Filter, and then choose AutoFilter from the submenu. Each column head now displays a down arrow.

3 Click the down arrow next to the heading that you want to use for the filter. A list box that contains filter options appears, similar to the one shown in Figure 22-4.

4 If a column in your list contains one or more blank cells, you'll also see (Blanks) and (NonBlanks) options at the bottom of the list. The (Blanks) option displays only the records containing an empty cell (blank fields) in the filter column, so that you can

FIGURE 22-4.

When you choose the AutoFilter command, it places filter arrows at the top of each column in your database.

	A	B	C	D	E
1	Sales Rep ▾	Region ▾	Month ▾	Sale ▾	Description ▾
2	Blickle, Peter	West	(All)	$500	Misc. backlist books
3	Blickle, Peter	West	(Top 10...) (Custom...)	$1,100	Misc. backlist books
4	Cashel, Seamus	Midwest	Jan-99	$450	Misc. backlist books
5	Greif, Jacob	East	Feb-99	$800	Misc. backlist books

Click a filter arrow to display a drop-down list of display options.

locate any missing items quickly. The (NonBlanks) option displays the opposite—all records that have an entry in the filter column. Click the value that you want to use for the filter.

Excel hides the entries that don't match the criterion you specified, and highlights the active filter arrow. Figure 22-5 shows the results of using the January criterion in the Month column.

FIGURE 22-5.
Click the filter arrows to display only the records you want.

	A	B	C	D	E
1	Sales Rep ▼	Region ▼	Month ▼	Sale ▼	Description ▼
2	Blickle, Peter	West	Jan-99	$500	Misc. backlist books
3	Blickle, Peter	West	Jan-99	$1,100	Misc. backlist books
6	Anderson, Rhea	South	Jan-99	$750	Educational kits
8	Cashel, Seamus	Midwest	Jan-99	$1,000	Educational kits
11	Cashel, Seamus	Midwest	Jan-99	$1,200	Advance orders, front list
12	Greif, Jacob	East	Jan-99	$1,000	Advance orders, front list
13	Greif, Jacob	East	Jan-99	$250	Advance orders, front list
14					

This column shows Jan-99 entries only.

You can use more than one filter arrow to display only the records that you want—an extremely useful strategy if your list is many records long. To continue working with AutoFilter but to also redisplay all your records, choose Show All from the Filter submenu of the Data menu. Excel will display all your records again. To remove the AutoFilter drop-down list boxes, disable the AutoFilter command on the Filter submenu.

Creating a Custom AutoFilter

When you want to display a numeric range of data, or customize a column filter in other ways, choose Custom from the AutoFilter drop-down list box to display the Custom AutoFilter dialog box. The dialog box contains two relational list boxes and two value list boxes that you can use to build a custom range for the filter. For example, you could display all sales greater than $1,000 or, as shown in Figure 22-6, all

FIGURE 22-6.
The custom AutoFilter dialog box lets you build your own filter.

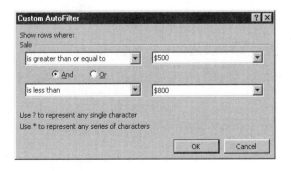

III

Microsoft Excel

sales between $500 and $800. The list boxes are easy to deal with because the most useful values and relationships are already listed in them—all you have to do is point and click. You can further fine-tune your criteria by using the And and Or option buttons as well as the ? and * wildcard characters.

To create a custom AutoFilter, follow these steps:

1 Click any cell in the list.

2 If AutoFilter isn't already enabled, choose Filter from the Data menu, and then choose AutoFilter from the submenu. A drop-down list box appears at the top of each column in the list.

3 Click the arrow next to the heading that you want to use for the customized filter, and select (Custom) from the list of choices. The Custom AutoFilter dialog box opens.

4 Click the first relational operator list box and specify the relation-ship (equals, is greater than, is less than, and so on) that you want to use for the filter, and then click the first value list box and specify the boundary that you want to set. (For example, you could specify all values greater than or equal to $500 with *is greater than or equal to $500.*)

5 If you want to specify a second range, click And to indicate that the records must meet both criteria, or click Or to indicate that the records can match either criterion. Then specify a relationship in the second relational operator list box and a range boundary in the second value list box. Figure 22-6 shows a Custom AutoFilter dialog box with two range criteria specified.

6 Click OK to apply the custom AutoFilter. The records selected by the filter are displayed in your worksheet.

Using the Subtotals Command to Organize a List

The Subtotals command on the Data menu helps you to organize a list by displaying records in groups and adding subtotals, averages, or other summary information. The Subtotals command can also display a grand total at the top or bottom of your list, letting you quickly add up columns of numbers. As a bonus, Subtotals displays your list in Outline view so that you can expand or shrink each section in the list simply by clicking.

To add subtotals to a list, follow these steps:

1   Arrange the list so that the records for each group are located together. An easy way to do this is to sort on the field on which you're basing your groups. For example, you could sort based on employee, region, or store.

2   From the Data menu, choose Subtotals. Excel opens the Subtotal dialog box and selects the list.

3   In the At Each Change In list box, choose a group whose subtotal you want to define. This should be the same column that you sorted the list with. Each time this value changes, Excel will insert a row and compute a subtotal for the numeric fields in this group of records.

4   In the Use Function list box, choose a function to use in the subtotal. SUM is the most popular, but other options are available, as described in Table 22-1, on the next page.

5   In the Add Subtotal To list box, choose the column or columns to use in the subtotal calculation. You can subtotal more than one column by selecting multiple boxes, but be sure to remove any check marks that you don't want. The following screen shows the settings for a typical use of the Subtotals command:

6   Click OK to add the subtotals to the list. You'll see the following screen, complete with subtotals, outlining, and a grand total.

Sales Rep	Region	Month	Sale	Description
Anderson, Rhea	South	Feb-99	$700	Advance orders, front list
Anderson, Rhea	South	Feb-99	$1,400	Educational kits
Anderson, Rhea	South	Jan-99	$750	Educational kits
Anderson, Rhea Total			$2,850	
Blickle, Peter	West	Feb-99	$600	Advance orders, front list
Blickle, Peter	West	Jan-99	$1,100	Misc. backlist books
Blickle, Peter	West	Jan-99	$500	Misc. backlist books
Blickle, Peter Total			$2,200	
Cashel, Seamus	Midwest	Jan-99	$1,200	Advance orders, front list
Cashel, Seamus	Midwest	Jan-99	$1,000	Educational kits
Cashel, Seamus	Midwest	Feb-99	$450	Misc. backlist books
Cashel, Seamus Total			$2,650	
Greif, Jacob	East	Jan-99	$1,000	Advance orders, front list
Greif, Jacob	East	Jan-99	$250	Advance orders, front list
Greif, Jacob	East	Feb-99	$800	Misc. backlist books
Greif, Jacob Total			$2,050	
Grand Total			$9,750	

TABLE 22-1. Summary Functions in the Subtotal Dialog Box

Function	Description
SUM	Add up the numbers in the subtotal group.
COUNT	Count the number of nonblank cells in the group.
AVERAGE	Calculate the average of the numbers in the group.
MAX	Display the largest number in the group.
MIN	Display the smallest number in the group.
PRODUCT	Multiply together all the numbers in the group.
COUNT NUMS	Count the number of cells containing numeric values in the group.
STDDEV	Estimate the standard deviation based on a sample.
STDDEVP	Calculate the standard deviation for an entire population.
VAR	Estimate the variance in the group based on a sample.
VARP	Calculate the variance for an entire population.

 **TIP**

> You can choose the Subtotals command as often as necessary to modify your groupings or calculations. When you have finished using the Subtotals command, click Remove All in the Subtotal dialog box.

Working in Outline View

When you use the Subtotals command in Excel to create outlines, you can examine different parts of a list by clicking buttons in the left margin, as shown in Figure 22-7. (Note that this is similar to the way Outline view functions in Microsoft Word.)

Click the numbers at the top of the left margin to choose how many levels of data you want to see. Click the plus or minus button to expand or collapse specific subgroups of data.

FIGURE 22-7.
The Subtotals command creates an outline view of your list.

These buttons give you three subtotal display options:
1) Grand Total Only, 2) Grand Total and Subtotals, and 3) All Records.

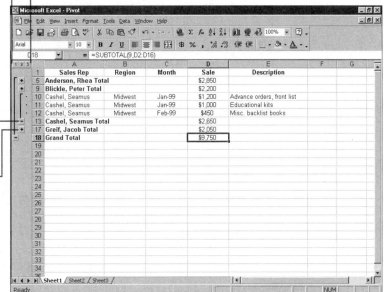

Click the minus button (-) to collapse a subtotal.

Click the plus button (+) to expand a subtotal.

Converting an Excel List into an Access Database

If you have the Professional or Premium Edition of Microsoft Office 2000, you also have Access, Microsoft's relational database management system.

If you have been working with lists in Excel for a while, you might be wondering whether your lists are compatible with Access, and when, if ever, you should move up to a more sophisticated database. What are the real differences between these two products? The short answer is that Excel is perfectly suited to list management as long as your databases don't become too large and you don't need to track unusual data or run especially advanced commands. However, Excel has the following limitations when it's dealing with databases:

- Worksheets are limited to 65,536 rows, meaning that you can't have more than 65,535 records (names in your mailing list, sales transactions, and the like).

- Fields can contain a maximum of 256 characters, limiting you to shorter descriptions or notes in your lists.

- Excel can't store pictures, sounds, and other types of special data in fields.

- Excel lacks advanced data protection or sophisticated backup features.

- You can't create custom data entry forms without using Access.

If you'd like to move your list into Access in the future, be assured that the transition will be relatively painless. To convert your Excel list into an Access database, you start Access 2000, click the More Files entry in the first Access dialog box, and use the Open dialog box to locate and open your Excel workbook. (If Access is already running, you can use the Import command on the Get External Data submenu of the File menu.)

When you open an Excel workbook in Access, Access launches a wizard that saves your list as an Access table. (You need to specify the worksheet that the list is in to complete the conversion.) Figure 22-8 shows the Pivot.xls worksheet used in this chapter organized as an Access database.

After you import and save the table, you'll find many familiar data management and formatting commands on the Access menus. You can learn more about specific Access commands in Part 5 of this book.

FIGURE 22-8.
Excel lists appear as database tables in Microsoft Access. The simple conversion process is handled by an Access wizard.

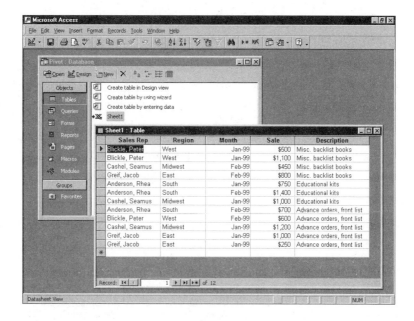

Creating Pivot Tables and Pivot Charts

The most sophisticated data-management feature in Excel is the *pivot table*, an organization and analysis tool that displays the fields and records in your list in new and potentially useful combinations. Pivot tables are made easy in Excel by a powerful wizard on the Data menu, and in Excel 2000 the wizard has been expanded to create colorful *pivot charts*: compelling graphical reports that display pivot table information visually. In this section, you'll learn how to create both pivot tables and pivot charts by using the PivotTable And PivotChart Wizard, and you'll learn how to connect to external data sources to feed this command in powerful new ways.

Using the PivotTable And PivotChart Wizard

The best way to learn about a pivot table is to create one. Fortunately, the PivotTable And PivotChart Wizard gives you complete control over the position of row and column headings in your table, so that you can rearrange all the important variables down the road. To create a pivot table, follow these steps:

1   Click a cell in the list that you want to view as a pivot table.

2 From the Data menu, choose PivotTable And PivotChart Report. The PivotTable And PivotChart Wizard starts and prompts you for the source of data for the table, as shown at the top of the next page.

If the Office Assistant is enabled, you'll have an opportunity now to learn more about pivot tables and the various options you have when creating a database report. Feel free to seek guidance from the Office Assistant as you use the PivotTable And PivotChart Wizard. When you no longer need it, click the Excel Help button in the lower left-hand corner of the wizard dialog box to dismiss the Office Assistant.

3 Verify that the first option, Microsoft Excel List Or Database, is selected, and click Next.

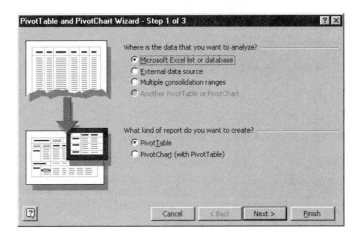

In this example, you'll create a pivot table from a list in your worksheet. However, you can also create pivot tables from external data (such as records received by Microsoft Query), multiple consolidation ranges, or another pivot table or pivot chart. After you select a data source, Excel prompts you for a data range.

4 If you had a list active when you started the wizard, Excel might have already selected it for you. If not, select data from an Excel list now using the mouse. (Be sure to include the column headings.)

Don't worry about the dialog box getting in the way—Excel will minimize it when you start selecting cells, giving you a full-window look at your data. Our example screen looks like this:

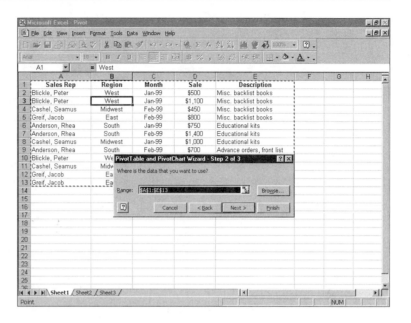

5 Click Next to display the final screen of the PivotTable And PivotChart Wizard. By default, Excel creates pivot tables in new worksheets, though you can also specify an existing worksheet and even an exact location within a worksheet.

Click here to see the old pivot table construction dialog box.

Click Options to customize your pivot table.

In Excel 97, the PivotTable wizard displayed a layout grid at this point to help you build your pivot table, but this feature is now provided directly in the worksheet by means of an enhanced PivotTable toolbar. However, you can use the old pivot table "construction" dialog box if you like by clicking the Layout button in the third wizard screen (Step 3). In addition, you can use the

Options button now or in the future to fine-tune how your pivot table or pivot chart appears.

6   Click Finish to accept the default settings and continue building your pivot table. The PivotTable And PivotChart Wizard opens a new worksheet, creates a blank pivot table, and displays the PivotTable toolbar, as shown in the illustration at the top of the next page.

7   Define the initial layout of your pivot table by dragging fields from the PivotTable toolbar into the Row, Column, Data, and Page Fields areas in the worksheet.

Fields placed in the Row area will become rows in your pivot table, fields placed in the Column area will become columns, and fields placed in the Data area will be added together with the SUM function. You can arrange, or pivot, these values later, so don't worry too much about the final placement of fields now. (The Page area is reserved for fields that you want to take a closer look at.)

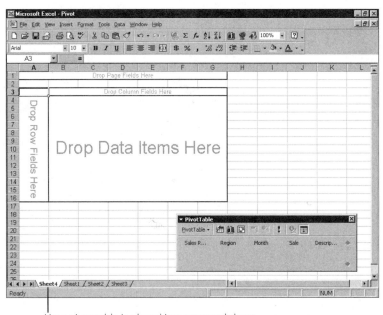

Your pivot table is placed in a new worksheet.

In the following illustration, the Month field has been placed in the Row area, the Sales Rep field has been placed in the Column area, and the Sale field is being selected on the PivotTable toolbar. (We're just starting to drag it to the Data area.)

Sales Rep is placed as a Column field.

Month is placed as a Row field.

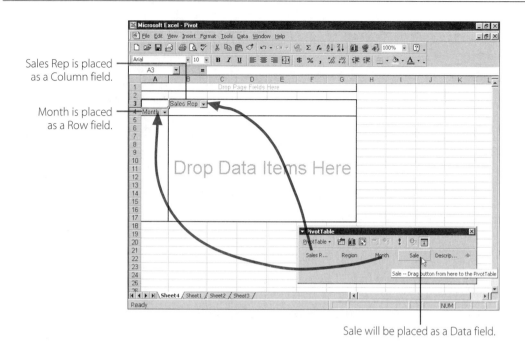

Sale will be placed as a Data field.

After a field has been placed in the Data area, Excel finalizes the pivot table, as shown in Figure 22-9.

FIGURE 22-9.
A pivot table allows you to rearrange the rows and columns in your worksheet, creating new views of your data.

	A	B	C	D	E	F
1			Drop Page Fields Here			
2						
3	Sum of Sale	Sales Rep				
4	Month	Anderson, Rhea	Blickle, Peter	Cashel, Seamus	Greif, Jacob	Grand Total
5	Jan-99	750	1600	2200	1250	5800
6	Feb-99	2100	600	450	800	3950
7	Grand Total	2850	2200	2650	2050	9750
8						

Evaluating a Pivot Table

It might take you a moment to recognize the data in your pivot table, because it presents an entirely new view of your list. It's almost as if you had created new row and column headings, typed all the data again, and used the Subtotals command to summarize the results! However, you didn't have to rearrange your worksheet manually—the PivotTable And PivotChart Wizard did it for you. Best of all, you can easily transpose one or more fields and use new functions to highlight other trends in your list.

III

Microsoft Excel

To help you work with the pivot table and create pivot charts, Excel displays the PivotTable toolbar, shown in Figure 22-10. You'll find this toolbar useful when evaluating and customizing your pivot tables and pivot charts. Take a moment to examine the buttons and commands on the PivotTable toolbar, and then read the summary data in your new pivot table, especially the Grand Total row and column.

FIGURE 22-10.
The PivotTable toolbar contains several unique commands and buttons specifically designed for manipulating pivot tables.

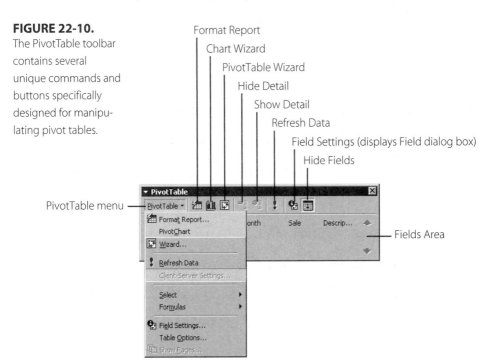

Rearranging Fields in a Pivot Table

To rearrange, or pivot, the data in your pivot table, just click the fields in the table and move them to new locations. You can also remove unwanted fields by dragging them to the PivotTable toolbar and add new fields by dragging field names from the toolbar onto the pivot table.

 TIP

As you edit or rearrange the data in the pivot table, note that your changes don't affect the data in your list (which is in its own worksheet)—your original rows and columns remain the same. However, if you change the cells in your list, you'll need to click the Refresh Data button on the PivotTable toolbar to see the changes.

Changing the Function in a Pivot Table

By default, the PivotTable And PivotChart Wizard uses the SUM function to add up values in the Data area of your pivot table, but you can easily change the function to calculate another value. For example, you could use the AVERAGE function to calculate the average sales in a month, or the COUNT function to total up the number of sales orders written by a particular employee. The list of functions available is identical to the set employed by the Subtotals command, described in Table 22-1 (page 596).

To change the function used in a pivot table, follow these steps:

1 Open the sheet containing your Excel pivot table, if it isn't already open.

2 In the upper left corner of your pivot table (the cell above the Row field and to the left of the Column field), double-click the Data field name. In our example, the cell's location is A3 and contains the title Sum of Sale.

You'll see the PivotTable Field dialog box, as shown in Figure 22-11.

3 In the Summarize By list box, select the new function that you want to use. (For example, select the MAX function to display the largest sales total in the field.)

FIGURE 22-11.
Double-click the cell containing the current function and field to display the PivotTable Field dialog box.

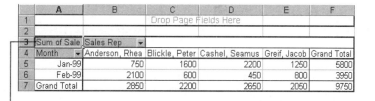

Double-click this cell in the pivot table...

...to display this list of analysis functions.

TIP

You can also use the Field Dialog button on the PivotTable toolbar to display the PivotTable Field dialog box and change the function used to summarize a field in your pivot table. The PivotTable Field dialog box displays different options, depending on the type of entry selected.

Adjusting the Formatting in a Pivot Table

When you use the PivotTable And PivotChart Wizard to modify a pivot table, Excel automatically reformats the table to match the data in your list and to calculate the result of the function that you're using. Avoid making manual changes to the table formatting, because the AutoFormat table feature will overwrite them each time you rearrange the pivot table.

However, you can make lasting changes to the numeric formatting in the Data area by following these steps:

1 Click any numeric data cell in the pivot table (not a row or column heading).

2 Click the Field Settings button on the PivotTable toolbar. The PivotTable Field dialog box opens.

3 Click the Number button. The familiar Format Cells dialog box appears, as shown in Figure 22-12. This dialog box allows you to adjust the formatting of the numbers in the Data area.

FIGURE 22-12.

Use the Number button in the PivotTable Field dialog box to display a list of numeric formatting options for data in your pivot table.

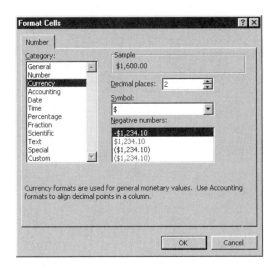

4 Select a type of numeric format in the Category list box, and then select a formatting style. For example, to add currency formatting to numbers, click the Currency category, specify the number of decimal places you want, and specify a style for negative numbers.

5 Click OK to close the Format Cells dialog box, and then click OK to close the PivotTable Field dialog box. Excel will change the numeric formatting in the table, and these changes will persist each time you modify the pivot table.

 TIP

Use AutoFormat for Fast Style Makeovers

To change the heading and line style, highlight a cell in the pivot table, and choose AutoFormat from the Format menu. Excel will display a list of table styles for you to choose from. Select the style you want, and then click OK to reformat and recalculate the pivot table.

Displaying Pivot Charts

If you find pivot tables addictive, you'll want to take advantage of Excel 2000's newest data analysis tool, the pivot chart. A pivot chart is a graphical version of an Excel pivot table. Pivot charts are created from existing pivot tables and are placed in new charting worksheets in the workbook. Like pivot tables, pivot charts have dynamic, customizable fields that you can drag back and forth to the PivotTable toolbar and move around the charting area. You can also modify the functions used to analyze data in a pivot chart.

To analyze an Excel list using a pivot table chart, follow these steps. (If you already have an existing pivot table in your workbook, click a cell in the pivot table, and start with step 4.)

1 Click a cell in the list that you want to view as a pivot chart.

2 From the Data menu, choose PivotTable And PivotChart Report.

 TIP

Although the PivotTable And PivotChart Wizard gives you the option of creating a pivot chart in the first wizard step, you'll still be required to create a pivot table in the third wizard step to base the pivot chart on. For this reason, we recommend that you simply follow the default pivot table options when you create a pivot chart. (You won't lose any time doing so.)

III

Microsoft Excel

3 Answer the questions posed by the PivotTable And PivotChart Wizard, and then create a new pivot table by dragging the appropriate row, column, and data values from the PivotTable toolbar to your new pivot table. *For more information about creating a new pivot table, see "Using the PivotTable And PivotChart Wizard," page 599.*

Chart
Wizard

4 Click the Chart Wizard button on the PivotTable toolbar to open a charting worksheet and build a new pivot chart based on the selected pivot table. You'll see a chart that looks similar to the one in Figure 22-13.

5 You are now free to customize and format the pivot chart as you see fit. See Figure 22-13.

 **TIP**

> In a pivot chart, the legend represents the column field and the charting category represents the row field. To customize either of these values, right-click the associated field button in the chart, and select a command from the pop-up menu that appears.

FIGURE 22-13.
Excel 2000 allows you to analyze your database lists with customizable pivot charts.

Drag fields to and from the chart, using the PivotTable toolbar.

Double-click this field to change the function that is used for charting.

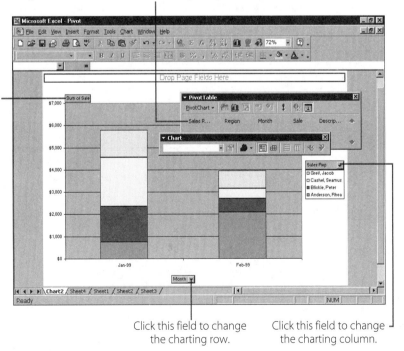

Click this field to change the charting row.

Click this field to change the charting column.

Using External Data Sources in Pivot Tables

When you created your pivot table by using the PivotTable And PivotChart Wizard, you had the option of using external data as the source of your information. One method of extracting external data for your pivot table is by using Microsoft Query, a program shipped with Microsoft Office that you can use to connect to external data sources using a software driver called *ODBC* (Open Database Connectivity). Query acts as a link between Excel and database files that have diverse data formats, such as Access, FoxPro, SQL Server, dBASE, Paradox, and Btrieve. In Excel 2000, you can also use Query to access external data sources for your pivot tables known as *OLAP cubes*. OLAP stands for On-Line Analytical Processing, a format designed to consolidate massive amounts of corporate information using units that are sometimes referred to as *data warehouses*.

Query uses ODBC to translate complex data-filtering questions, or *queries*, into a language called SQL (structured query language). As a result, you can use Query to extract information about compatible database files in sophisticated ways. For example, your query might be, *How many sales reps do we have who sell more than $20,000 in products per year and who work in the South or the Midwest?*

When you want to work with external database files, consider using Query as a stand-alone tool or as a utility to import your data into Excel. Start Query in Excel by clicking the Data menu and picking a command from the Get External Data submenu. To use Query for accessing data in constructing a PivotTable, select External Data Source in Step 1 of the PivotTable And PivotChart Wizard, and then click Get Data in Step 2. (Query is an add-in program, so you'll have to install it using the Office Setup program before it can be accessed.)

For more information about using Query to manage external data sources, search for "Query (Microsoft)" in the Excel Help Index. You can also access a series of helpful cue cards from within the Query Help menu.

III

Microsoft Excel

Analyzing Business Data

R unning a successful business requires many important skills. One of your best management tools is the capacity to build what-if models to help you plan for the future. How many $1.75 coffees do you need to sell to gross $30,000? What will happen to your bottom line if you lower the price of caffè latte but increase advertising expenses? Fortunately, Microsoft Excel provides several useful planning tools to help you map out a robust future. In this chapter, you'll learn how to use the Goal Seek command to find an unknown value that produces a desired result, the Solver add-in to calculate an optimum solution based on several variables and constraints, and the Scenario Manager to create and evaluate a collection of what-if scenarios containing multiple input values.

Using the Goal Seek Command to Forecast

Excel's most basic forecasting command is Goal Seek, located on the Tools menu. The Goal Seek command determines the unknown value that produces a desired result, such as the number of $14 compact discs a company must sell to reach its goal of $1,000,000 in CD sales. Goal Seek is simple because it's streamlined—it can adjust only one variable to complete its iterative calculation. If you need to consider additional variables in your forecasting, such as the effects of advertising or quantity discounts on pricing, use the Solver command (described in the next section).

To use Goal Seek, set up your worksheet to contain the following:

- A formula that calculates your goal

- An empty cell for the missing number that will get you there

- Any other values required in the formula

The empty cell should be referenced in your formula and serves as the variable that Excel changes.

> **NOTE**
>
> When you run the Goal Seek command on the Tools menu, the cell containing the formula is called the Set Cell, for it *sets* the terms that produce a result.

When the Goal Seek command starts to run, it repeatedly tries new values in the variable cell to find a solution to the problem you've set. This process is called *iteration*, and it continues until Excel has run the problem 100 times or has found an answer within .001 of the target value you specified. (You can adjust these iteration settings by choosing Options from the Tools menu and adjusting the Iteration options on the Calculations tab.) Because it calculates so fast, the Goal Seek command can save you significant time and effort over the brute force method of trying one number after another in the formula.

To forecast using the Goal Seek command, follow these steps:

1 Create a worksheet that contains a formula, an empty *variable* cell that will hold your solution, and any data that you need to use in your calculation. For example, Figure 23-1 shows how you might set up a worksheet to determine the number of cups of coffee priced at $1.75 that you would have to sell to gross $30,000.

FIGURE 23-1.
The Goal Seek command requires a formula and a blank variable cell.

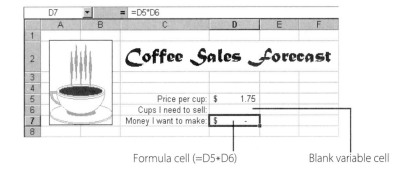

Formula cell (=D5*D6)   Blank variable cell

 **ON THE WEB**

The GoalSeek.xls example is on the Running Office 2000 Reader's Corner page. For information about connecting to this Web site, read the Introduction.

2   In your worksheet, select the cell containing the formula. (In the Goal Seek dialog box, this cell is called the Set Cell.)

3   Choose Goal Seek from the Tools menu. The Goal Seek dialog box opens, as shown here. The cell name you selected appears in the Set Cell text box, and a marquee appears around the cell in your worksheet.

4   Press Tab, and then type the goal that you want to reach in the To Value text box. For example, to reach $30,000 in sales, type *30000* in the To Value text box.

5   Press Tab to select the the By Changing Cell text box, move the Goal Seek dialog box out of the way, if necessary, and then click the cell that is to contain your answer (the variable cell).

   This value is the one that the Goal Seek command will calculate using your goal and the formula in the Set Cell. The cell will be indicated by a selection marquee (cell D6 in this example), as shown on the next page.

III

Microsoft Excel

The Goal Seek command will calculate this unknown number.

6 Click OK to find a solution for your sales goal.

The Goal Seek Status dialog box will display a message when the iteration is complete, and the result of your forecast will appear in the worksheet, as shown in Figure 23-2. This forecast shows that you need to sell 17,143 coffees at $1.75 per cup to reach your sales goal of $30,000.

7 Click OK to close the Goal Seek Status dialog box.

FIGURE 23-2.
The Goal Seek command displays its result in the empty variable cell that you specified in your worksheet.

Variable cell, which contains the number of units necessary to achieve the goal

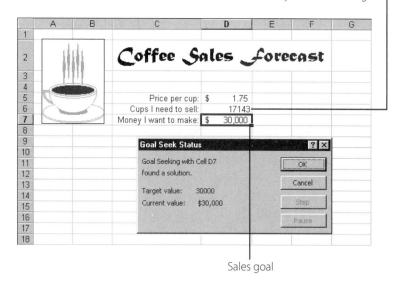

Sales goal

TIP

In a time-consuming calculation, such as a computation that involves several financial functions, you can click the Pause button in the Goal Seek Status dialog box to stop the iteration, or the Step button to view one iteration at a time.

Using the Solver to Set Quantity and Pricing

When your forecasting problem contains more than one variable, you need to use the Solver add-in utility to analyze the scenario. Veterans of business school will happily remember multivariable case studies as part of their finance and operations management training. While a full explanation of multivariable problem solving and optimization is beyond the scope of this book, you don't need a business-school background to use the Solver command to help you decide how much of a product to produce, or how to price goods and services. We'll show you the basics in this section by illustrating how a small coffee shop determines which coffee beverages it should sell, and what its potential revenue will be.

In our example, we're running a coffee shop that currently sells three beverages: regular fresh-brewed coffee, premium caffè latte, and premium caffè mocha. We currently price regular coffee at $1.25, caffè latte at $2.00, and caffè mocha at $2.25, but we're not sure what our revenue potential is and what emphasis we should give to each of the beverages. (Although the premium coffees bring in more money, their ingredients are more expensive, and they're more time-consuming to make than regular coffee.) We can make some basic calculations by hand, but we want to structure our sales data in a worksheet so that we can add to it periodically and analyze it using the Solver.

 NOTE

The Solver is an add-in utility, so you should verify that it's installed on your system before you get started. If the Solver command isn't on your Tools menu, choose Add-Ins from the Tools menu, and select the Solver Add-In option in the Add-Ins dialog box. If Solver isn't in the list, you'll need to install it by running the Office Setup program again and selecting it from the list of Excel add-ins. *For more information, see "Installing Add-In Commands and Wizards," page 535.*

III

Microsoft Excel

Setting Up the Problem

The first step in using the Solver command is to build a worksheet that is Solver-friendly. This involves creating a *target cell* to be the goal of your problem—for example, a formula that calculates total revenue that you want to maximize—and assigning one or more *variable cells* that the Solver can change to reach your goal. Your worksheet can also contain other values and formulas that use the target cell and the variable cells. In fact, each of your variable cells must be *precedents* of the target cell for the Solver to do its job. (In other words, the formula in the target cell must depend on the variable cells for part of its calculation.) If you don't set it up this way, when you run the Solver you'll get the error message, *The Set Target Cell values do not converge.*

Figure 23-3 shows a simple worksheet that can be used to estimate the weekly revenue for our example coffee shop and to determine how many cups of coffee we will need to sell. Cell G4 is the target cell that calculates the total revenue that the three coffee drinks generate. The three lines that converge in cell G4 were drawn by the Trace Precedents command on the Auditing submenu of the Tools menu. They show how the formula in cell G4 depends on three other calculations for its result. (The Auditing submenu contains commands that help track the links between formulas in a worksheet.) The three variable cells in the worksheet are cells D5, D9, and D13—these are the values we want the Solver to determine when it finds an optimum solution to maximizing our weekly revenue.

ON THE WEB   The Solver.xls example is on the Running Office 2000 Reader's Corner page.

FIGURE 23-3.
Before you use the Solver command, you need to build a worksheet that has a target cell and one or more variable cells. The Auditing submenu can help you visualize the relationship between cells.

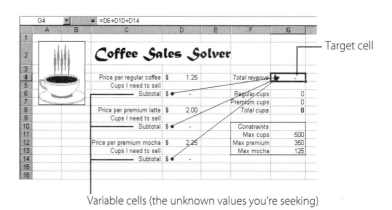

Target cell

Variable cells (the unknown values you're seeking)

In the bottom right corner of our screen is a list of constraints we plan to use in our forecasting. A *constraint* is a limiting rule or guiding principle that dictates how the business is run. For example, because of storage facilities and merchandising constraints, we're currently able to produce only 500 cups of coffee (both regular and premium) per week. In addition, our supply of chocolate restricts the production of caffè mochas to 125 per week, and a milk refrigeration limitation restricts the total production of premium coffee drinks to 350 per week.

These constraints will structure the problem, and we'll enter them in a special dialog box when we run the Solver command. Your worksheet must contain cells that calculate the values used as constraints (in this example, G6 through G8). The limiting values for the constraints are listed in cells G11 through G13. Although listing the constraints isn't necessary, it makes the worksheet easier to follow.

> **Name Key Cells**
>
> If your Solver problem contains several variables and constraints, you'll find it easiest to enter data if you name key cells and ranges in your worksheet by using the Define command on the Name submenu of the Insert menu. Using cell names also makes it easy to read your Solver constraints later. *For more information about naming, see "Using Range Names in Functions," page 554.*

Running the Solver

After you have defined your forecasting problem in the worksheet, you're ready to run the Solver add-in. The steps that follow show you how to use the Solver to determine the maximum weekly revenue for your coffee shop given the following constraints:

- No more than 500 total cups of coffee (both regular and premium)

- No more than 350 cups of premium coffee (both caffè latte and caffè mocha)

- No more than 125 caffè mochas

In addition to the maximum revenue, the Solver will tell you the optimum distribution of coffees in the three coffee groups. Complete these steps:

1   Click the target cell—the one containing the formula that is based on the variable cells you want the Solver to determine—in your worksheet. In Figure 23-3, the target cell is G4.

2   From the Tools menu, choose Solver.

The Solver Parameters dialog box opens, as shown here. Because you clicked the target cell in step 1, the Set Target Cell text box contains the correct reference. The correct Equal To option button (Max) is also selected, because you want to find the maximum value for the cell.

3   Highlight the By Changing Cells text box. Drag the dialog box to the right so that you can see the variable cells in your worksheet. Select each of the variable cells. If the cells adjoin one another, simply select the group by dragging across the cells. If the cells are noncontiguous, hold down the Ctrl key and click each cell. This will place a comma between each cell entry in the text box.

In the following illustration, the three blank cells reserved for the number of coffee drinks in each category have been selected:

Use the Guess Button to Preview the Result

If you click the Guess button, the Solver will try to guess at the variable cells in your forecasting problem. The Solver creates the guess by looking at the cells referenced in the target cell formula. Don't rely on this guess—it will often be incorrect!

4 Constraints aren't required in all Solver problems, but this problem has three. Click the Add button to add the first constraint in the Add Constraint dialog box, which is shown here:

5 The first constraint is that you can sell only 500 cups of coffee in one week. To enter this constraint, click cell G8 (the cell containing the total cups formula), click <= in the operator drop-down list box, and type *Max_cups* in the Constraint text box (using the underline character to link the words). (*Max_cups* is the name of cell G11 in our example.)

> You have the option of typing a value, clicking a cell, or entering a cell name in the Constraint text box. We entered a defined cell name because it makes the constraint easier to read and modify later.

6 Click the Add button to enter the first constraint and begin the second constraint—you can sell only 350 premium coffees in one week. With the insertion point in the Cell Reference text box, click cell G7 (the cell containing the premium cups formula), click <= in the operator drop-down list box, and type *Max_ premium* (the name of cell G12) in the Constraint text box.

7 Click the Add button to enter the second constraint and begin the third constraint—you can sell only 125 caffè mochas in one week. Click cell D13 (the variable cell containing the number of mocha cups), click <= in the operator drop-down list box, and type *Max_mocha* (the name of cell G13) in the Constraint text box.

8 Click OK to add all three constraints to the Solver Parameters dialog box. It should look like the one at the top of the following page.

Microsoft Excel

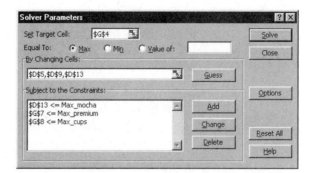

To modify one of the constraints displayed in the Solver Parameters dialog box, select the constraint, and click Change. To customize the iteration and calculation parameters in the Solver utility, click Options and make your adjustments.

9 Your forecasting problem is ready to go, so click Solve to calculate the result.

After a few moments, the Solver displays a dialog box describing how the optimization analysis went. If the Solver ran into a problem, you'll see an error message, and you can click the Help button to learn more about the difficulty. If the Solver finds a solution, you'll see the following dialog box:

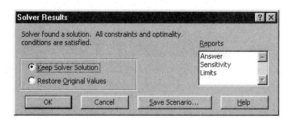

10 To display the new solution in your worksheet, click the Keep Solver Solution option button, and click OK. The Solver places an optimum value in the target cell and fills the variable cells with the best solutions that match the constraints you specified, as shown in Figure 23-4.

In this example, you've learned that if you're limited to selling 500 cups of coffee per week, you can expect a maximum of $918.75 in revenue,

— Optimum revenue

Three variables necessary for optimum revenue

and your optimum drink distribution is 150 cups of regular coffee, 225 cups of caffè latte, and 125 cups of caffè mocha. Although this financial model doesn't consider several realistic business variables, such as the costs associated with running a shop and the benefits of making volume purchases, it does help you to forecast much more easily and quickly than you could using pencil and paper.

Editing Your Solver Forecast

Perhaps the best feature of a Solver forecast is that you can easily edit it to evaluate new goals and contingencies. For example, if you decide that you want to earn exactly $700 per week from coffee drinks, you can use the Solver to tell you what the optimum combination of drinks would be. Setting a target value in the Solver is a little like using the Goal Seek command to determine an unknown variable, though you can use more than one variable.

To edit your Solver forecast to find the variables to reach a specific goal, follow these steps:

1 Choose Solver from the Tools menu. The Solver Parameters dialog box appears, still displaying the variables and constraints of your last Solver problem. You'll adjust these to compute a new forecasting goal.

2 Click the Value Of option button and type *700* in the text box to the right. The Value Of option button sets the target cell to a particular goal so that you can determine the variable mix you need

to reach your milestone. (In this example, the variable cells represent cups of coffee.) Your dialog box should look like this:

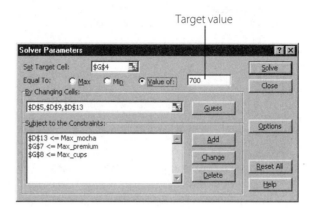

3 Click Solve to find a solution to your forecasting problem. When the Solver has finished, click OK to display the new solution in your worksheet.

Figure 23-5 shows the solution the Solver generates if the variable cells are empty before you run the problem. (You can earn $700 by selling approximately 125 mochas, 151 lattes, and 94 regular coffees. The Solver calculates an exact answer, but because you can't sell partial cups of coffee, the variable cells are formatted to show integer—whole-number—values. Your actual revenue would be $700.75, and the subtotals would be slightly higher.)

What If There Is More Than One Solution to the Problem?

In the previous example, the Solver determined that you could sell 125 mochas, 151 lattes, and 94 regular coffees to reach your sales goal of

FIGURE 23-5.

When you specify a target goal, the Solver computes an optimum product mix that meets your constraints.

$700. But you can also reach the $700 mark using a different product mix; for example, you could sell approximately 125 mochas and 210 lattes to reach $700. (Using this mix, your revenue would actually be $701.25.) So how *did* the Solver decide what the optimum product mix would be? Because you chose not to limit its options with constraints, the Solver simply started with the numbers in the variable cells and incremented them until it found an acceptable solution. For this reason, you can get different results from a nonlinear problem with multiple solutions if you use different starting values.

You can take advantage of the way the Solver reaches its results if there's a particular product mix that you'd like to use. Enter the values that you think might be acceptable in the variable cells before you run the Solver, and Excel will use those as starting values when it computes the solution. If you prefer to find a true optimal solution, you'll need to add extra constraints to the Solver Parameters dialog box before you run the forecast. For example, you might specify that a certain minimum must be met in each category, or that you'd like to minimize the number of products sold to reach your goal. You can have two constraints for each variable cell (an upper bounds and a lower bounds) to structure the computation and reach an optimal solution to your problem.

Using the Scenario Manager to Evaluate What-If Questions

The Goal Seek and Solver commands are extremely useful, though if you run several forecasts you can quickly forget what your original values were. More important, you have no real way to compare the results of the Goal Seek and Solver commands. Each time you change the data, the previous solution is lost. To address this limitation, the Scenario Manager helps you to keep track of multiple what-if models. Using the Scenarios command on the Tools menu, you can create new forecasting scenarios, view existing scenarios, run scenario management commands, and display consolidated scenario reports. We'll show you each technique in this section.

Creating a Scenario

A *scenario* is a named what-if model that includes variable cells linked together by one or more formulas. Before you create a scenario, you must design your worksheet so that it contains at least one formula that's dependent on cells that can be fed different values. For example, you might want to compare a best-case and a worst-case scenario for sales in a coffee shop based on the number of cups of coffee sold in a week. Figure 23-6 shows a worksheet that contains three variable cells and several formulas that can serve as the basis for several scenarios. (This coffee sales worksheet is the same one we used in the Solver example, without the constraints table.) In the following example, we'll use this worksheet to show how to create a Best Case and a Worst Case sales scenario.

W ON THE WEB   The Scenario.xls example is in the Running Office 2000 Reader's Corner page.

To create a scenario, follow these steps:

1 From the Tools menu, choose Scenarios. The Scenario Manager dialog box appears:

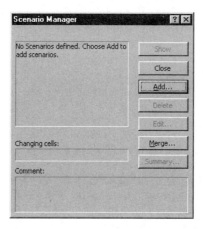

FIGURE 23-6.
Before you create a scenario, you'll need to build a worksheet that has one or more formulas dependent on variable cells.

Variable cells   Dependent scenario formula

2 Click the Add button to create your first scenario. You'll see the Add Scenario dialog box.

3 Type *Best Case* (or another suitable name) in the Scenario Name text box, and press the Tab key.

4 In the Changing Cells text box, specify the variable cells that you want to modify in your scenario. You can type cell names, highlight a cell range, or hold down the Ctrl key and click individual cells to add them to the text box. (If you hold down the Ctrl key, Excel automatically places commas between the cells that you click.) To follow our example, hold down the Ctrl key and click cells D5, D9, and D13. Your screen should look like this:

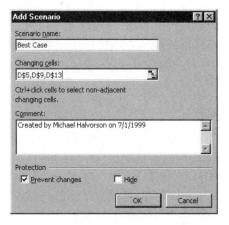

 TIP

You might want to use cell names when you define your variable cells. That way, you'll have an easier time identifying your variables when you create your scenarios and when you type in arguments later.

5 Click OK to add your scenario to the Scenario Manager. You'll see the Scenario Values dialog box, asking you for your model's variables. The default values are the numbers that were already in the cells.

6 Type *150*, press Tab, type *225*, press Tab, and type *125*. These are the values that will produce the revenue in your best-case scenario based on the constraints described in the section "Setting Up the Problem," page 616. Your screen will look like the one shown on the next page.

Microsoft Excel

Scenario Values

Enter values for each of the changing cells.

1:	D5	150
2:	D9	225
3:	D13	125

OK

Cancel

Add

7 Click Add to create a second scenario. Type *Worst Case,* and click OK to display the Scenario Values dialog box.

8 Type *50, 40,* and *30* in the variable cells, and then click OK. (These values represent our guess at the worst case.) The Scenario Manager dialog box appears and lists the Best Case and Worst Case scenarios. Now you're ready to view the results of your forecasting models.

9 Click Close to close the Scenario Manager dialog box.

 TIP

You can save Solver problems as scenarios for future trials by clicking the Save Scenario button in the Solver Results dialog box when the Solver computes a new forecast. The Solver will prompt you for a name, which you can use later to view the scenario in the Scenario Manager.

Viewing a Scenario

Excel keeps track of each of your worksheet scenarios. You can view them by choosing the Scenarios command on the Tools menu whenever your worksheet is open. Before you view a scenario, however, it's a good idea to save your workbook so that you can restore the original values in your worksheet if you want to.

To view a scenario, follow these steps:

1 Choose Scenarios from the Tools menu. You'll see a dialog box similar to the one at the top of the facing page.

2 In the Scenarios list box, select the scenario that you want to view.

3 Click the Show button. Excel substitutes the values in the scenario for the variables in your worksheet and displays the results in your worksheet, as shown in Figure 23-7. (You might need to move the Scenario Manager dialog box to view the results.)

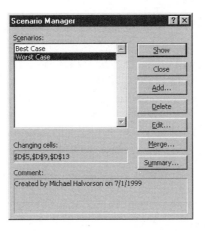

4   Select additional scenarios, and click the Show button to compare and contrast the what-if models in your worksheet. When you've finished, click the Close button. The last active scenario remains in your worksheet.

FIGURE 23-7.
The Show button lets you compare the results of different what-if scenarios in your worksheet.

Worst-case result

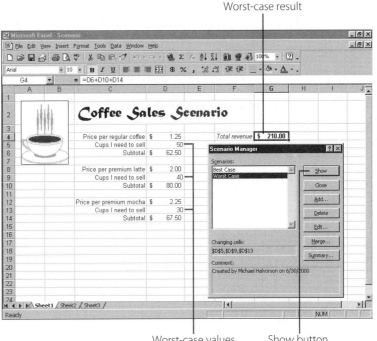

Worst-case values   Show button

III

Microsoft Excel

Creating Scenario Reports

Although you can easily compare different scenarios by switching between them using the Show button in the Scenario Manager dialog box, you might occasionally want to view a report that contains consolidated information about the scenarios in your worksheet. You can accomplish this quickly by clicking the Summary button in the Scenario Manager dialog box. Excel will automatically format the summary report and copy it to a new worksheet in your workbook.

To create a scenario report, follow these steps:

1 From the Tools menu, choose Scenarios. The Scenario Manager dialog box opens.

? SEE ALSO

For more information about viewing pivot table reports, see "Rearranging Fields in a Pivot Table," page 604.

2 Click the Summary button.

The Scenario Summary dialog box opens, prompting you for a result cell to total in the report and also for a report type. A *scenario summary report* is a formatted table displayed in its own worksheet. A pivot table is a special summary table whose rows and columns can be rearranged, or *pivoted*:

3 Select the result cell that you want to total (cell G4 in this example), click the report option button that you want to use (accept the Scenario Summary default if you're not sure), and then click OK.

After a few moments, a new Scenario Summary tab will appear in your workbook, as shown in Figure 23-8. The outlining buttons in the left and top margins of your report will help you to shrink or expand the rows and columns in your scenario summary if you find it necessary to hide or expand values.

 **TIP**

Each time you click the Summary button in the Scenario Manager dialog box, Excel creates a new summary worksheet in your workbook. To delete unwanted summary reports, click the unwanted scenario's summary tab in the workbook, and then choose Delete Sheet from the Edit menu.

FIGURE 23-8.
The Summary button creates a scenario summary report in a new worksheet in your workbook.

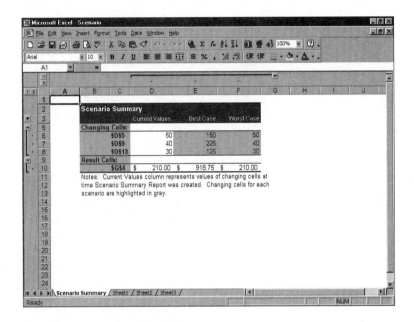

Managing Your Scenarios

Once you have defined a scenario using the Add button, luckily you're not stuck with that scenario forever. You can edit and delete scenarios by clicking the Edit and Delete buttons in the Scenario Manager dialog box. The Edit button lets you change the name of the scenario, remove existing variable cells, add new variable cells, or even choose a completely new group of variables. To remove a particular scenario permanently, simply highlight it in the Scenario Manager dialog box, and click the Delete button. Finally, you can copy scenarios from other open workbooks into your current worksheet by clicking the Merge button in the Scenario Manager dialog box and specifying a source workbook and worksheet in the Merge Scenarios dialog box.

III

Microsoft Excel

CHAPTER 24

Using Excel to Publish to the Web

So far in this book, you've used Microsoft Excel to create reports, invoices, charts, lists, and pivot tables that are ready for use on your own computer or for traditional printing and paper distribution. However, using Excel 2000, you can also save your worksheets in HTML format for electronic circulation on the World Wide Web. This version of Excel introduces several new features to make this process straightforward and useful.

In this chapter, you'll learn how to prepare your worksheet so that it can be saved in HTML—or Web page—format, and you'll learn how to set special publication options that make your workbook more accessible and useful on the Internet. You'll also learn the simple commands that both save and preview completed Web pages, and you'll learn how to use Microsoft Office Web toolbars to issue Excel commands in Microsoft Internet Explorer. When you're finished, you'll have all the skills necessary to create your own Excel Web pages and distribute them on the Internet.

Designing a Web Page

Web pages are documents that contain special formatting codes known as *HTML*, or *HyperText Markup Language*. These formatting codes have been optimized for speedy transmission over the Internet and for displaying information attractively in Web browsers, such as Microsoft Internet Explorer and Netscape Navigator. In the past, only special-purpose application programs such as Microsoft FrontPage allowed you to create HTML documents for the Web, but now you can create Web pages using each of the applications in the Microsoft Office 2000 software suite. The program you choose depends on the features you want to provide and the type of Web site you are constructing.

Naturally, the most effective Excel Web pages will use Excel's rich worksheet formatting, calculation, and data analysis capabilities. We recommend that you build Excel Web pages when you need to distribute the following types of information:

- Electronic invoices and order forms, such as an invoice for a new car or a price sheet for a furniture store

- Database analysis tools, such as summary reporting and pivot tables for a corporate database

- Tables of image collections, such as employee photographs, company clip art, and links to other Web sites

- Statistics and demographic information presented in tables, such as government population statistics, traffic patterns, or water usage

- Testing and survey information presented in worksheets, such as online practice tests, government surveys, or customer satisfaction questionnaires

- Excel charts that present important facts and figures graphically, such as revenue reports and cost comparisons

Creating an Excel Web page is no different than building a regular worksheet from scratch. You enter information in rows and columns, edit the data, and use formulas and formatting commands as you normally would. However, do take care to use fonts and colors in a way that is aesthetically compatible with the other documents on your home page, and use hyperlinks when necessary to connect your Excel Web page to other Internet sites. And be sure to preview your documents carefully, to verify that the HTML file conversion created a Web page that matches your expectations.

In addition, be aware that some of the more advanced features in your Excel worksheet might not be available to your users when the document is published on the Web. Because the Excel application itself will not be available on the Web site (but just the HTML file you create), add-in programs such as the Solver will be unavailable to your users, and some of the more advanced features such as tracking changes, comments, macros, and forms will be disabled. However, if you're planning to view the Excel Web page using Internet Explorer 4.0 or later, you can use Office 2000 Web Components to interactively work with formulas, filters, pivot tables, charts, and worksheet formatting commands. (You'll learn more about these options later in this chapter.)

Static Pages vs. Interactive Pages

? SEE ALSO
You can also share and discuss Excel workbooks with other users on the Web using an Internet connectivity feature known as Online Collaboration. For more information about this feature, see "Sharing Documents in a Workgroup," page 82.

Fundamentally, you have two options when presenting Excel Web pages: you can display a static, noninteractive Excel worksheet (in other words, a snapshot of your worksheet that can't be modified), or you can display a working, interactive worksheet that users can modify directly in Internet Explorer. The option you select will depend on the purpose of your Web site and your particular design goals. Static Web pages are best for showing purchase orders, sales data, and other tabular information that should be viewed but not modified. Interactive Web pages are best for calculation and analysis tools that invite Internet users to experiment with their own facts and figures. (For example, a mortgage calculator that prompts users for their own loan information.)

Setting Web Publication Options

The Save As Web Page command on the Excel File menu saves an existing Excel worksheet or workbook as a Web page and allows you to set a number of useful publication options. Before you use this command, verify that your worksheet contains the proper document style and content for your Web page, and that it presents information in a clear format that includes the necessary operating instructions. And remember: users with no knowledge of you or your worksheet will be opening and running this document on the Internet or an intranet (provided that they have the necessary permissions), so take care to make the user interface for the worksheet simple and intuitive.

III

Microsoft Excel

To save, or publish, an Excel worksheet or workbook as a Web page, follow these steps:

1 Open the worksheet you plan to save as an HTML document. In this example, we'll save the Invoice.xls worksheet (an order form for sewing patterns) as an interactive Web page.

W ON THE WEB

The Invoice.xls example is on the Running Office 2000 Reader's Corner page. For information about connecting to this Web site, read the Introduction.

2 Choose Save As Web Page from the File menu. You'll see a dialog box similar to the one shown in Figure 24-1.

The Save As Web Page dialog box looks similar to the standard Save As dialog box displayed by all Office applications. However, you'll see four new options related to Web publishing: you can specify which part of your workbook you want to publish (the entire workbook or the active worksheet), you can specify whether you want the document to be interactive or not (an option that is valid for worksheets only, not entire workbooks), you can add an HTML document title to the Web page, and you can select advanced options by clicking the Publish button.

FIGURE 24-1.
The Save As Web Page command displays this dialog box, which includes options that control how your Excel worksheet will be converted into an HTML document.

Choose Entire Workbook or Selection: Sheet.

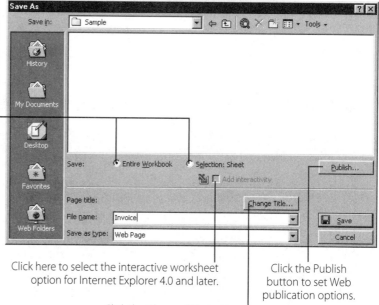

Click here to select the interactive worksheet option for Internet Explorer 4.0 and later.

Click the Publish button to set Web publication options.

Click the Change Title button to enter the HTML document title.

3 Click the Selection: Sheet option button to save the active worksheet as a Web page.

4 If you want to make your worksheet interactive, verify that the Add Interactivity check box has been selected.

5 Click the Change Title button, and modify the HTML page title that will appear above the Web page in your browser. In this example, we typed *Use This Invoice to Calculate Your Order.*

6 Click OK to lock in the page title. The Save As dialog box shows any changes you made.

7 (Optional) Type a new filename in the File Name text box. This isn't a requirement, because Excel can use your existing filename, but you might want to give your Web page a new title now. By default, Excel Web pages have the .htm filename extension.

8 Click the Publish button to display the advanced options in the Publish As Web Page dialog box. You'll see a list of choices that looks similar to Figure 24-2.

The top list box gives you the option of selecting only a portion of your worksheet for the Web page. Although we typically include the whole sheet in our interactive Excel pages to allow the user some maneuvering room, this option is nice if you want to limit what users can see and do on the screen.

FIGURE 24-2.
The Publish As Web Page dialog box lists the entire collection of options available to you.

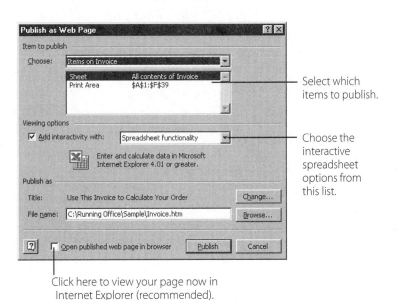

Select which items to publish.

Choose the interactive spreadsheet options from this list.

Click here to view your page now in Internet Explorer (recommended).

III

Microsoft Excel

The Interactivity options control what the user can do with the worksheet when it appears in the browser. To make the Web page static and noninteractive, deselect the Add Interactivity With check box. To specify the type of interactivity you want to use, select the Spreadsheet functionality option in the list box in Figure 24-2. Currently, Excel Web pages support general spreadsheet functionality, pivot table functionality, and charting functionality. (To get the chart functionality option, you need to open a chart in Excel.)

Interestingly, the interactivity features listed here are not provided by the Excel application itself, but by small ActiveX controls called Office Web Components that Excel places in the HTML document when it builds the Web page. When your completed page is viewed in Internet Explorer version 4.0 or later, these components spring to life as toolbars and simulate the capabilities of a real Excel worksheet.

The Publish As Web Page dialog box also lets you change the HTML document title and filename—the same options you saw in the Save As dialog box earlier. And the Open Published Web Page In Browser check box gives you a chance to display the completed Web page in Internet Explorer now. (If you choose this option, Excel starts Internet Explorer 5 when you click the Publish button.) We recommend that you habitually use this preview option whenever you publish Web pages, so that you can see early in the development process how the page will appear to users on the Web.

9 Click the Open Published Web Page In Browser check box, and then click the Publish button. Excel launches Internet Explorer and displays the Web page. Figure 24-3 shows the result for the Invoice worksheet we've been working with. Note that if you have a different browser installed, you'll get different results.

⊛ TIP

Two Ways to Preview

If you don't select the Open Published Web Page In Browser check box while you're saving your Web page, you can preview the document later by choosing Web Page Preview from the Excel File menu. Both actions launch the current Excel Web page in Internet Explorer or the default browser for your system.

FIGURE 24-3.
The Invoice worksheet as it appears in Internet Explorer 5.

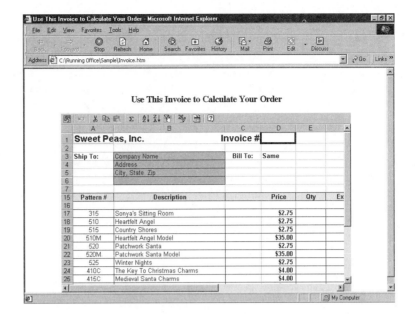

Running Excel Web Pages on the Internet

If you created a static Excel Web page, your options for manipulating the Web page in your Internet browser are rather limited. You can use the scroll bars to view all aspects of the page, and you can copy cell data from the page to the Windows Clipboard by selecting the desired cells, right-clicking the selection, and choosing Copy. However, if you requested an interactive Web page when you saved the Excel worksheet using the Save As Web Page command, you can perform a number of useful editing and calculation activities on your Web page, including filling the worksheet with data, editing and formatting cells, adding new formulas, running filters, modifying charts (if you started with one), and manipulating pivot tables.

⭐ TIP

In Office 2000, only Microsoft Excel and Microsoft Access can create Web pages that are truly interactive. The Web pages produced by Microsoft Word, PowerPoint, Publisher, and Outlook are static, noninteractive HTML documents. (However, note that Word allows you to add useful Web form buttons and input controls to your documents that give you some control over how the documents are used in Internet browsers.)

III

Microsoft Excel

As mentioned earlier, the spreadsheet functionality that Excel Web pages provide comes not from Excel itself, but from a collection of ActiveX controls used in the worksheet called Office Web Components. These components are recognized by Internet Explorer versions 4.0 and later, and offer a subset of Excel's data analysis features to those using Excel worksheets on the Web. You can identify the presence of Office Web Components in Internet Explorer by the special toolbars that appear directly above Excel HTML documents, and by the Office Web icon that appears on the left side of Office Web toolbars. If you click one of these icons in Internet Explorer, you'll see an Office Web Components dialog box similar to the one shown in Figure 24-4.

You can control Office Web components programmatically by using development tools that support COM (Component Object Model) technology. For example, you could load an Excel-interactive Web page into the Microsoft Visual Basic 6.0 Dynamic HTML Page Designer and write event procedures that use the properties, methods, and events exposed by Office Web Component objects. The result would be an interactive Excel Web page customized with features that you designed in Visual Basic and slick new commands that use the power of Office Web Components.

For more information about using Microsoft Visual Basic 6.0 to customize HTML documents, check out Michael Halvorson's self-paced programming tutorial *Microsoft Visual Basic 6.0 Professional Step by Step* (Microsoft Press, 1998, ISBN 1-57231-809-0).

FIGURE 24-4.
The interactive functionality in Excel Web pages is provided not by the Excel application itself, but by Microsoft Office Web Components.

Using Office Web Toolbars

Interactive Excel Web pages allow you to move the cell pointer around the worksheet to enter and edit data. If you enter data into cells that are linked to a formula, a new result is calculated immediately in the worksheet when you press the Enter key. In addition, the Office Web Components toolbars allow you to manipulate your data in meaningful new ways. The following example shows you how to work with an interactive worksheet in Internet Explorer. To follow these steps exactly in a sample document, you can open the Invoice.xls example on the Running Office 2000 home page, save the worksheet as an interactive spreadsheet by choosing the Save As Web Page command, and open the page in Internet Explorer.

To manipulate an Excel Web page using the Office Web spreadsheet toolbar, follow these steps:

1 Open the Excel Web page you want to use in Internet Explorer. (Use the Publish button in the Publish As Web Page dialog box or the Web Page Preview command on the File menu.)

   If your Web page is interactive, it will feature an Office Web toolbar, as shown in the following illustration:

Spreadsheet Functionality toolbar provided by Office Web Components

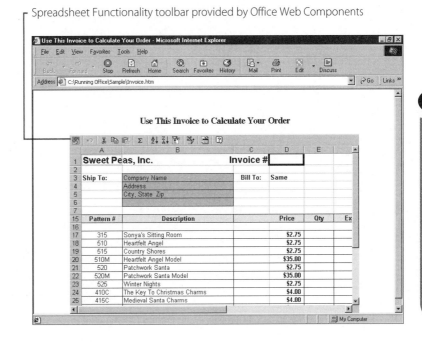

III

Microsoft Excel

2 If the Web page is a worksheet that welcomes data entry, enter some information now by clicking cells on the Web page, typing numbers and labels, and pressing the Enter key.

The following illustration shows what the Invoice Web page looks like when three quantity numbers are entered into the order portion of the interactive worksheet.

You can enter data and calculate formulas in interactive worksheets.

Subtotal is calculated automatically.

3 Scroll to the bottom of the Web page, if necessary, to see the results of any calculations you have entered. (In our example, the page automatically calculated a total of $16.50.)

4 Try entering a formula in the interactive Web page. If you have the Invoice example open, scroll to the Shipping cell near the bottom of the worksheet, click the cell next to it (containing $0.00), press the equal sign (=), press the Up arrow key twice to highlight Subtotal (A), type *0.2, and press Enter. Excel will compute a hypothetical shipping cost for the order (20% of the total, or $3.30) and display it in the highlighted cell:

Subtotal (A)	$16.50
Subtotal (B)	
Shipping	=F34*0.2
Total	$16.50

This is your invoice.

— Entering a new formula here...

Subtotal (A)	$16.50
Subtotal (B)	
Shipping	$3.30
Total	$19.80

This is your invoice.

— ...produces a new result immediately.

5 Now try sorting a group of rows in the worksheet. If you have the Invoice example open, scroll to the product list part of the worksheet, select the twelve product rows and the four supporting columns, click the Sort Ascending button on the Office Web toolbar, and then click the Column 1 field. The worksheet sorts the selected rows alphabetically in ascending order, based on the value of the first column:

Sort
Ascending

Click the Sort Ascending button, and then point to Column 1.

Select the rows and columns you want to sort.

Description	Column 1	Price	Qty	Extended
	Column 3			
Sonya's Sitting Room	Column 4	$2.75	2	$5.50
Heartfelt Angel	Column 5	$2.75	1	$2.75
Country Shores		$2.75	3	$8.25
Heartfelt Angel Model		$35.00		$0.00
Patchwork Santa		$2.75		$0.00
Patchwork Santa Model		$35.00		$0.00
Winter Nights		$2.75		$0.00
The Key To Christmas Charms		$4.00		$0.00
Medieval Santa Charms		$4.00		$0.00
Keeping Warm		$2.75		$0.00
Spring In The Valley		$2.75		$0.00
Santa's Favorite Ornaments		$1.93		$0.00

The worksheet is sorted alphabetically by Column 1.

Description	Price	Qty	Extended
Country Shores	$2.75	3	$8.25
Heartfelt Angel	$2.75	1	$2.75
Heartfelt Angel Model	$35.00		$0.00
Keeping Warm	$2.75		$0.00
Medieval Santa Charms	$4.00		$0.00
Patchwork Santa	$2.75		$0.00
Patchwork Santa Model	$35.00		$0.00
Santa's Favorite Ornaments	$1.93		$0.00
Sonya's Sitting Room	$2.75	2	$5.50
Spring In The Valley	$2.75		$0.00
The Key To Christmas Charms	$4.00		$0.00
Winter Nights	$2.75		$0.00

Property
Toolbox

6 With the sorted rows and columns still selected, click the Property Toolbox button on the Office Web toolbar to modify the formatting in the selected worksheet cells. You'll see a menu bar that has several command categories that are applicable to the active worksheet.

7 Click the Format menu to display the valid formatting commands for the current selection of cells. You'll see the following dialog box.

III

Microsoft Excel

8 Click the Font Color button's list arrow, click the red color, and then click the Font list box and choose Times New Roman from the list of available fonts. The formatting options you pick are immediately updated on the Web page as you select them.

9 Continue to experiment with other formatting options and the remaining Office Web toolbar commands if you want to. When you're finished, close the Spreadsheet Property Toolbox menu, and then exit Internet Explorer.

You're done working with Office Web toolbars for now. If you like, copy the .htm file you created (and any supporting files) up to a server on the Internet and see how it runs live on the Web!

Are Web Pages Read-Only?

After your Web page has closed, you might start wondering what it will look like the next time you open it. After all, you made several changes to the interactive Excel Web page. Will those be part of the HTML document the next time you display it in *your* browser? The answer is no, your Web page will appear exactly as it did when you finished creating it in Excel: the data entry, sorting, and formatting changes are lost as soon as you close the Web page. In this sense, you should think of Excel Web pages as read-only documents. They can be modified by users on the Internet, but each time you reopen the file it will appear as it did the first time. If transmitting a modified document on the Web is what you're looking for, experiment with the commands on Excel's Online Collaboration submenu, which are discussed along with other Office applications in Chapter 3.

Using Macros to Increase Productivity

If you're like most Microsoft Excel users, much of the work that you do in worksheets is repetitive. For example, you might always enter a series of headings in financial reports, or routinely increase the width of the first few columns (ordinarily, the most significant ones) in your workbook. If these actions take up much of your time, consider recording your commands as a macro and then running the macro whenever you need to do the work. A *macro* is a named set of instructions that tells Excel to perform an action for you. In this chapter, you'll learn what macros look like and how they can increase your productivity. You'll also learn how to record, run, and edit macros as well as assign them to buttons on a toolbar.

Carpe Datum:
Knowing When to Build a Macro

Excel's macro recording capabilities are impressive, but before you "seize the data," make sure that Excel doesn't already provide a built-in solution for your repetitive task. For example, if you routinely boldface your column headings and increase their point size, you could record a macro that will automatically format the headings for you. But it would actually be faster for you to use the Style command on the Format menu to apply a heading style that accomplishes the same formatting effect. In other words, don't use a macro unless the commands that you want to record are involved enough to require one.

This word to the wise doesn't mean that you shouldn't use macros to automate your worksheets. Actually, we're arguing just the opposite. But before you get started, it makes sense to take the time to become familiar with most of Excel's features so that you know when Excel offers a built-in solution and when to use macros to their greatest effect. Excel's Visual Basic macro language is sophisticated enough for many advanced tasks, such as communicating with other Windows-based applications or controlling an entire inventory management system. However, the most useful macros are often the ones that automate just four or five simple Excel commands. And although you can create macros from scratch using Visual Basic, the best way to learn about macros is by recording and editing them.

Recording a Macro

Let's start with a simple example. Excel's default cell width is about eight characters wide, but this space is often inadequate for the first few columns, where users typically enter longer strings for customer names, businesses, or geographic regions. In the following example, we'll record a macro that changes the first column in a worksheet to a width of 25 characters, and increases the width of each of the next three columns to 15 characters. We'll use the Record New Macro command on the Macro submenu of the Tools menu to record the macro, and then we'll name the macro in the Record Macro dialog box.

To create a macro that automatically adjusts the column width for you, follow these steps:

1 Display the worksheet in which you want to record the macro.

Your macro will be stored in a separate module in the active workbook, and you'll be able to run the macro in any worksheet as long as the workbook is open.

2 Choose Macro from the Tools menu, and then choose Record New Macro. You'll see the following dialog box:

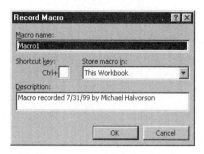

3 Type *Widen4Columns,* or another name if you prefer, in the Macro Name text box, and click OK.

This is the name you'll use to run and edit the macro later. (Macro names can't contain spaces or punctuation marks.) Excel closes the Record Macro dialog box, displays a Macro toolbar containing a Stop Recording button, and starts recording the macro. From this point on, any cell that you highlight or any command that you execute in Excel will be taped by the macro recorder. (When you have finished recording, you'll click the Stop Recording button to end your macro.)

4 Now you'll create your macro. Select the first column by clicking the column A heading; from the Format menu, choose Column, and then choose Width from the submenu. You'll see the following dialog box, prompting you for a new column width:

5 Type *25* in the Column Width text box, and click OK to expand column A to 25 characters.

6 Select columns B, C, and D by dragging over each of the column headings, and then choose the Width command again. Type *15* in the Column Width text box, and click OK.

III

Microsoft Excel

7 Click cell A1 to leave the mouse pointer in a tidy starting place.

As your last step in a macro recording, you should always arrange the screen so that you can start working again with the least amount of effort. The resulting screen is shown in Figure 25-1.

8 Click the Stop Recording button on the Macro toolbar to end your macro recording.

The macro recorder stops, and Excel stores the macro in a special location in your workbook called a *module*.

9 Choose Save from the File menu to save to disk your workbook and your macro. (In this example, we'll use the filename MacroFun.xls.) After all, because you've gone to the trouble of creating the macro, you don't want to lose it.

Ⓦ ON THE WEB

The MacroFun.xls example is on the Running Office 2000 Reader's Corner page. For information about connecting to this Web site, read the Introduction.

FIGURE 25-1.
The Widen4Columns macro has stored the steps to widen the first four columns of your worksheet.

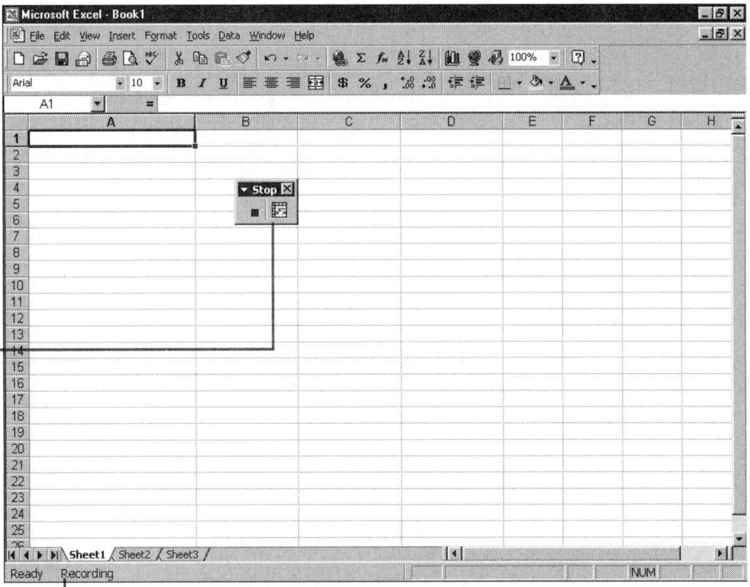

Macro toolbar. ———

The Recording indicator on the status bar shows that commands and edits are being recorded for the macro.

Running a Macro

To give you flexibility in automating your work, Excel provides you with three ways to run your macros. You can:

■ Double-click the macro name in the Macro dialog box.

- Press a macro shortcut key (if you have assigned one).

- Click a custom macro button on a toolbar (if you have created a button for the macro).

We describe the first two automation options in this section, and the last one later in the chapter. We'll use the Widen4Columns macro that we created in the preceding section.

Starting a Macro with the Macro Dialog Box

To run the Widen4Columns macro using the Macro dialog box, follow these steps:

1 Display the worksheet in which you want to run the macro. If you formatted Sheet1 in your workbook when you created the Widen4Columns macro, click the Sheet2 tab in your workbook now to practice in an empty worksheet.

2 From the Tools menu, choose Macro, and then choose Macros from the submenu.

   The Macro dialog box opens, as shown in Figure 25-2. It lists all the macros in your current workbook, plus any macros available in other open workbooks or in your Personal Macro Workbook. (You'll learn more about the Personal Macro Workbook later.)

3 Select the macro you want to run in the Macro Name list box, and click Run.

In the blink of an eye, Excel runs the macro and completes the column formatting you requested. To run the macro again in another worksheet, open the worksheet and repeat steps 2 and 3.

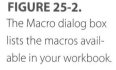

FIGURE 25-2.
The Macro dialog box lists the macros available in your workbook.

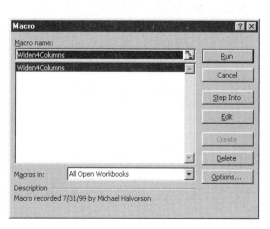

TIP

What's Done Is Done

You can't use the Undo command to reverse the effects of a macro, so be sure that you have the correct worksheet open before you modify it. As a safeguard, you might save your workbook before you run a new or unfamiliar macro. Then, if you don't like the changes made by the macro, you can close the workbook (without saving it), and the changes will be discarded.

Assigning a Shortcut Key to a Macro

You can assign a shortcut key to your macro so that it operates just like any key combination that runs an Excel command. As an example, to assign your Widen4Columns macro the Ctrl+Shift+W shortcut key (*W* for *widen*), follow these steps:

1 From the Tools menu, choose Macro, and then choose Macros from the submenu. You'll see the Macro dialog box.

2 Select the Widen4Columns macro in the list box, and then click the Options button to display a list of customization options for your macro. The Macro Options dialog box opens, as shown in Figure 25-3.

3 Hold down the Shift key, and type the letter *W*. The title of the shortcut key expands to Ctrl+Shift+W, which is the key combination that you'll press to run the macro.

 NOTE

If you type a lowercase letter in the Ctrl+ box, Excel will add Ctrl to the key you specify. If you type an uppercase letter, Excel will add Ctrl+Shift to the key you specify. Because several Excel commands already use Ctrl plus a letter for shortcut keys (for example, Ctrl+W closes the current workbook window), we recommend that you always add Shift to the letter you're using, to avoid conflicts.

4 Click OK to assign the shortcut key, and then click Cancel to close the Macro dialog box.

FIGURE 25-3.
The Macro Options dialog box lets you assign a shortcut key to your macro.

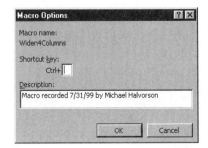

5 Now try using the shortcut key. Click the Sheet3 tab in your workbook to open a new, unformatted worksheet, and press Ctrl+Shift+W. Excel runs the Widen4Columns macro, which immediately increases the width of your first four columns.

Editing a Macro

By default, Excel stores the macros in your workbook in a Visual Basic code module called *Module1*. You can display this module periodically to examine the Visual Basic commands in your macros, add documentation to explain what a macro does, or modify a macro to change its behavior or increase its efficiency. In this section, we'll review the content of the Widen4Columns macro, add a descriptive comment, and edit one of the column width settings.

To edit the Widen4Columns macro in your workbook, follow these steps:

1 Choose Macro from the Macros submenu of the Tools menu. The Macro dialog box opens.

2 Select the Wide4Columns macro, then click the Edit button to open the Widen4Columns macro in the Visual Basic Editor, a special programming tool you can use to create and edit your macros.

(When you create macros in Microsoft Word, Microsoft Power-Point, Microsoft Access, or Microsoft Visual Basic, you'll also use this code editor.) Your screen should look like Figure 25-4, shown on the next page.

Excel macros are stored in individual *subroutines* in the code module; Sub and End Sub statements mark the beginning and the end of the macro. By default, descriptive comments in the macro appear in green type, special Visual Basic keywords appear in blue type, and all other macro commands and values appear in black type.

3 Move the pointer below the line containing the words *Macro recorded*, press the Right arrow key to move the pointer after the single quotation mark, and type the descriptive comment *Purpose: To enlarge columns A through D*. Then press the Down arrow key.

The text appears in green type when you press the Down arrow key, identifying the line you typed as a comment. Descriptive comment lines are for documentation purposes only; you create them by starting a line with a single quotation mark, which excludes them from being used by the macro.

III

Microsoft Excel

FIGURE 25-4.

Excel macros are stored in the Visual Basic language and can be modified using the Visual Basic Editor.

The Sub statement starts the macro.

Macros are stored in code modules.

The End Sub statement concludes the macro.

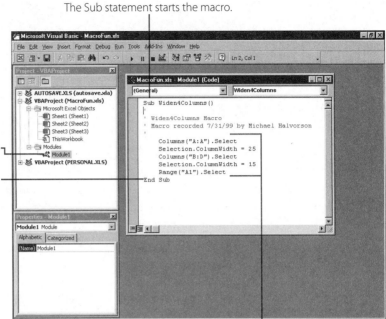

These Visual Basic statements control what the macro does.

4 Move the pointer to the number 25 in the Visual Basic statement

`Selection.ColumnWidth = 25`

This line sets the width of column A to 25 characters when you run the macro. Now we'll edit this statement to use a different column width.

5 Change the column width value from 25 to 30.

Excel updates your macro with the new column size. The next time you run the macro, it will change the width of column A in the active worksheet to 30 characters, not to 25 characters.

6 Click the Save button on the Visual Basic toolbar to save your macro changes in the workbook. (See Figure 25-5.) You're finished editing the macro.

7 Choose Close And Return To Microsoft Excel from the File menu. The Visual Basic Editor closes, and the Excel workplace reappears.

8 Test your revised macro by running it again in Sheet3 or another worksheet. (You can add additional worksheets to your workbook by choosing Worksheet from the Insert menu.)

FIGURE 25-5.
Use the insertion point to move around in your macro and to make additions or corrections.

Click here to save the macro.

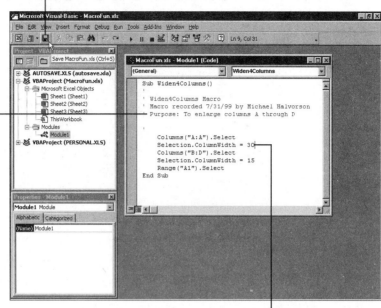

Add a comment.

Change column width from 25 to 30.

The macro should perform exactly as you expect it to. If Excel displays an error message or you get unexpected results, open the macro again in the Visual Basic Editor, and double-check your work against the example shown in Figure 25-5.

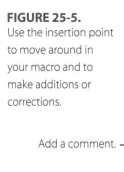

NOTE

To delete a macro from your workbook, choose Macro from the Tools menu, choose Macros from the submenu, select the unwanted macro in the Macro dialog box, and click the Delete button.

TIP

Read More About Macros

To learn more about Visual Basic macros, use the commands on the Help menu in the Visual Basic Editor. If you still want to know more about Visual Basic, we recommend Michael Halvorson's book *Microsoft Visual Basic 6.0 Professional Step by Step* (Microsoft Press, 1998), which describes how to write programs and macros using the Visual Basic 6.0 programming language.

III

Microsoft Excel

Using the Personal Macro Workbook

Now that you have had some practice using macros, let's create one final example that uses the Page Setup command to adjust the headers and footers in your worksheet before printing. You'll record this macro using the techniques you learned earlier in this chapter, though this time you'll store the macro in your Personal Macro Workbook so that you can use it in all your Excel projects. You'll also learn how to create a special button for the macro on the Standard toolbar.

Excel's standard worksheet header and footer are blank, and if you print a lot, you have probably customized this setting many, many times. We'll record a macro that removes the header (blank or otherwise) and creates a custom footer containing your name, the current page number, and today's date. Whenever you want to use these page setup options in a worksheet, simply run the macro.

To create a macro in the Personal Macro Workbook to customize your worksheet headers and footers for printing, follow these steps:

1 Open any workbook or worksheet. (Because this macro will be recorded in the Personal Macro Workbook, which is always open, you can have any worksheet open to record it.)

2 From the Tools menu, choose Macro, and then choose Record New Macro from the submenu. The Record Macro dialog box opens.

3 Type *CustomFooter* or another name of your choice (one that has no spaces or punctuation) in the Macro Name text box. This will be the name of your macro.

4 Click the Store Macro In list box, and then select the Personal Macro Workbook option.

The Personal Macro Workbook

The Personal Macro Workbook is a special hidden workbook that's always open while Excel is running. It's typically used only for macros, but you can put regular worksheets in the Personal Macro Workbook if you want to. The Personal Macro Workbook is stored in the XLStart folder and is loaded when you start Excel. Because you don't need to see it to record macros or run them, it remains hidden from view unless you open it by choosing the Unhide command on the Window menu. (The Personal Macro Workbook doesn't exist until you store a macro in it.)

This option directs Excel to place your new macro in the Personal Macro Workbook so that you can access it from any open workbook. Your dialog box should look like this:

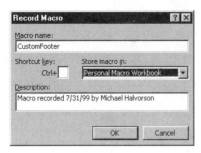

5 Click OK to start recording the macro.

Excel closes the dialog box, displays the Macro toolbar, and starts recording the macro. The commands you issue now will be captured by the macro recorder and stored in your Personal Macro Workbook.

6 Choose Page Setup from the File menu, and then click the Header/Footer tab. You'll see this dialog box, showing the current header and footer.

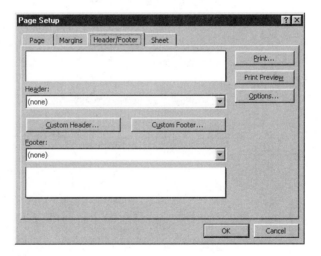

7 Check the Header drop-down list box for the word *none* (signifying no header). If the word *none* isn't there, click the Header drop-down list box, and click None to remove the current header.

8 Click the Footer drop-down list box, scroll the list, and then click the footer entry labeled with your name, Page 1, and the current date. Your macro will add this custom footer to your worksheet. If you prefer a different preset option, select it instead.

9 Click OK to accept the remaining Page Setup options, and click the Stop Recording button to stop recording your macro and to save it in your Personal Macro Workbook.

Now follow these steps to test your new CustomFooter macro:

1 Display the worksheet in which you want to run the macro. Don't use the worksheet that you used to record the macro, because it already contains a custom footer. You might want to close the current workbook and open another to see that the macro is, in fact, not stored in the workbook where it was created, such as the macro practice worksheet you created earlier in this chapter.

2 From the Tools menu, choose Macro, and then choose Macros from the submenu.

The Macro dialog box opens, as shown in Figure 25-6. It lists all the macros in your current workbook, plus any macros available in other open workbooks and in your Personal Macro Workbook. (Because the CustomFooter macro is in your Personal Macro Workbook, it has the filename PERSONAL.XLS in front of it.)

3 Double-click the CustomFooter macro in the Macro dialog box. Your worksheet may flicker briefly as Excel runs the commands in the macro.

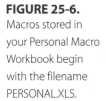

FIGURE 25-6.

Macros stored in your Personal Macro Workbook begin with the filename PERSONAL.XLS.

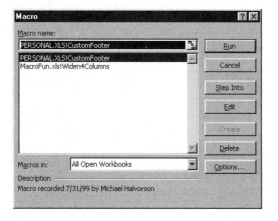

NOTE

Because you opened the Page Setup dialog box as you were recording, Excel reapplies each of the settings that you specified in the dialog box, including the individual header and footer items. If you'd rather not include the peripheral settings such as margin sizes and page orientation in your macro, remove the Visual Basic commands that execute them from the CustomFooter macro in your Personal Macro Workbook.

CAUTION

You can't save this macro using the Save command on the File menu. Instead, when you exit Excel, you'll be prompted to click OK to permanently save your additions to the Personal Macro Workbook.

4 When the macro stops, add one or two entries to the worksheet, if necessary, and click the Print Preview button on the Standard toolbar. (Excel won't preview the worksheet unless you have data in it.) You'll see a preview image of the first page of your worksheet.

5 Using the zoom pointer, click the footer to examine it closely. Your footer should look similar to the one shown in Figure 25-7.

6 When you have finished, click Close to quit Print Preview, and save your worksheet if you want to. Your new CustomFooter macro is now ready for use in all your workbooks.

FIGURE 25-7.
The CustomFooter macro places a stylized footer in your worksheet.

Michael Halvorson	Page 1	7/31/99

Preview: Page 1 of 1   NUM

Adding a Macro to a Toolbar

If you have read each of the chapters in Part 3 of this book (Excel), you deserve one last special effect to make your macros even more accessible and entertaining. In addition to using shortcut keys and the Macro dialog box to run your macros, you can also run macros by creating special macro buttons and adding them to one of your toolbars. To use this technique, record your macro first and give it a name. (If you want your macro button to be on the toolbar at all times, place your macro in the Personal Macro Workbook.) After your macro is finished, use the Customize command on the Toolbars submenu of the View menu to assign the macro to a button.

To add a macro to a toolbar, follow these steps:

1 Record your macro, and assign it a name. If you created the CustomFooter macro in the preceding section, you can use it for this example.

III

Microsoft Excel

? **SEE ALSO**

For more information about customizing Excel toolbars, including adding, removing, copying, and arranging toolbar buttons, see "Using Toolbars," page 39.

2 Choose Toolbars from the View menu, and then choose Customize from the submenu. The Customize dialog box opens.

3 Click the Commands tab in the dialog box.

A list of command categories appears on the left side of the dialog box, and a list of subordinate command buttons appears on the right. When a category in the left list is highlighted, related command buttons appear in the right list.

4 Scroll down the list of categories, and click Macros. In the Commands list, you'll see the Smile custom button, as shown in the following illustration. We'll use this friendly icon for the CustomFooter macro.

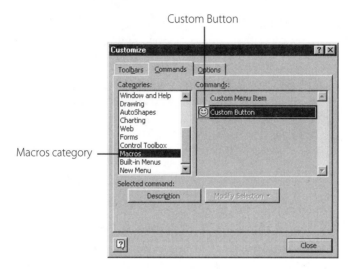

Custom Button

Macros category

5 Click the Smile custom button and drag it to one of your toolbars. As you position it over the toolbar, a vertical bar will appear to guide you in placing it exactly where you want it to appear.

6 After you release the mouse button, the other buttons on the toolbar will shift to the right. If they no longer fit on your screen, you can remove your least-used button from the toolbar by selecting it and dragging it away from the toolbar.

7 With your new Smile button selected on the toolbar, click the Modify Selection button in the Customize dialog box.

> **NOTE**
>
> You can restore a toolbar button by opening the Customize dialog box, clicking the category that contains the missing button, and then dragging the button back onto the toolbar. Or, you can restore all the toolbar's original default settings by clicking the Toolbars tab in the Customize dialog box, selecting the toolbar, and then clicking the Reset button.

8 From the submenu that appears, choose Change Button Image. A collection of custom buttons now appears, from which you can choose the one you like best. (For example, you might want to click the footprints icon to signify footer if you don't care for the smiley face.)

9 If you want to further customize your button selection, choose Edit Button Image from the Modify Selection submenu of the Customize dialog box.

10 When you're done, close the Customize dialog box.

11 Click the new button, and the Assign Macro dialog box will appear, as shown in Figure 25-8.

FIGURE 25-8.
The Assign Macro dialog box lets you attach a macro to a custom toolbar button; it appears when you first click the new button.

Use this dialog box to assign a macro to the button.

New Custom Footer button.

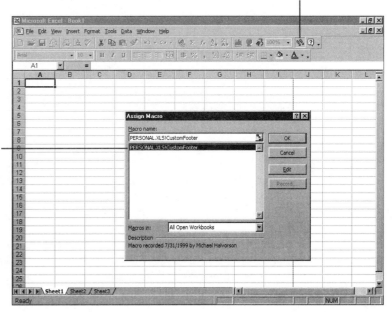

Microsoft Excel

12 Choose the macro for the button, and click OK. The dialog box closes, and Excel enables the new macro button.

13 Verify that the button works by displaying a new worksheet and clicking the button. If you assigned the CustomFooter macro to the button, go to Print Preview and verify that the header and footer were set correctly. Congratulations on your progress!

Protecting Yourself Against Rogue Macros

If you have been using computers for a while, you've probably heard about the potential threat created by the gremlins known as computer viruses. A *virus* is a hidden macro or software program that works behind the scenes to annoy computer users and (in the most heinous circumstances) to destroy important data files and application software. Viruses don't just appear on computers—they are transmitted from one machine to the next via computer networks, the Internet, diskettes, or other media. This transmission or infection process is usually silent and painless (at first): the nasty software developers who create viruses build the little programs so that they attach themselves in hidden ways to files, folders, and application documents.

Because most of the applications in the Microsoft Office software suite have the ability to record and run macros, it is possible that a rogue software developer will try to pass along a hidden macro virus to you in an Office document such as an innocent-looking Excel workbook. Although you shouldn't loose sleep over this potential danger, you should be aware of the threat that viruses pose and practice safe computing by using only documents that come from authorized or known sources. To help simplify this process, Office 2000 provides a special Security command on the Macros submenu that works to detect macros originating from unsafe (or at least unrecognized) sources. If you're feeling obsessive about the threat posed to your data by computer viruses, you might want to use this command to further protect your system.

To use the Excel 2000 Security command to seek protection from unsafe macros, follow these steps:

1 From the Tools menu, choose Macro, and then choose Security from the submenu. The Security dialog box opens and contains two tabs: Security Level and Trusted Sources.

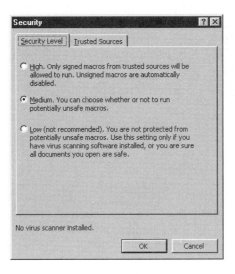

The Security Level tab is pretty self-explanatory. You are given three security options against macro viruses in Excel workbooks: High, Medium, and Low. The High option allows only signed macros to run in Excel worksheets that you open, an indication that the software developer who developed the macro has created a digital signature that features his or her name and other pertinent information. This doesn't stop those macros from doing bad things to your computer, but the thought is that if a developer is fully known and registered, he or she won't mess with other people.

The Medium option asks Excel to display a dialog box each time a workbook is opened that contains macros. You're then given the choice to enable those macros or not. We like this option, because it allows us to run macros that come from our friends, but to disable mystery macros that we download in workbooks from the Internet. When you select the Medium option, a dialog box like the following will appear when you open a workbook containing macros:

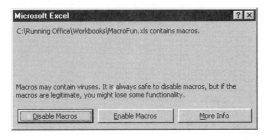

III

Microsoft Excel

Finally, the Low option directs Excel to run all macros in Excel workbooks without warning you in any way (basically, the way it was in previous versions of Excel). This option is fine if you know the workbooks you open are okay. However, be aware that some rogue macros have the ability to start themselves automatically, so don't think that you can safely open any workbook just because you don't run the macros.

2 Click the Security Level option that you feel comfortable with. We recommend you keep the Medium option.

3 Click the Trusted Sources tab to learn more about the macros on your system that are identified by digital signatures. This tab comes with a handy Remove button, so you can remove macros from any vendor you don't trust.

4 When you're finished setting macro security, click the OK button to close the Security dialog box. Excel 2000 will now enforce your security wishes until you update this dialog box in the future.

TIP

Did this final section make macros seem a little scary? If so, that wasn't our intention, really! Most macros are quite helpful and safe, and now that you know computer viruses are only lists of commands like any other macro, perhaps this section has demystified the threat of viruses a bit. Still, it's a good idea to be familiar with Excel's security measures if you ever need them. And it probably wouldn't hurt to read your computer a reassuring bedtime story tonight when you shut it down.

PART IV

Microsoft PowerPoint

CHAPTER 26

Getting Started Using PowerPoint

You're a basement chemist who needs financial backing for a formula that makes even eggs grow hair. You're a teacher who wants students to understand how government works. You're a consultant who needs to help a client cut expenses and reorganize her business. Or perhaps you're an office manager who must show your staff how to use the new features in Microsoft Office 2000.

In these and hundreds of other situations, your objective is simple: clear, attention-getting, persuasive communication. The ways to this goal are many, ranging from white boards to white papers, from slides to slick charts, from memos to printed dissertations. And, of course, there's Microsoft PowerPoint, the audiovisual room in your Office suite. When you need to teach, persuade, or explain, PowerPoint can add punch to your presentation.

Using PowerPoint, you can create and display sets of slides that combine text with drawn objects, clip art, photos, sound, video, and even animated special effects. You can then turn your work into 35mm slides, transparencies, or printed handouts that you can present electronically or interactively on the Web. Furthermore, because PowerPoint is part of a package deal, you can easily blend Microsoft Word outlines, Microsoft Excel worksheets, and Microsoft Clip Art illustrations into your own, original PowerPoint text and graphics.

Thus, using PowerPoint, you can create company information slides, like this:

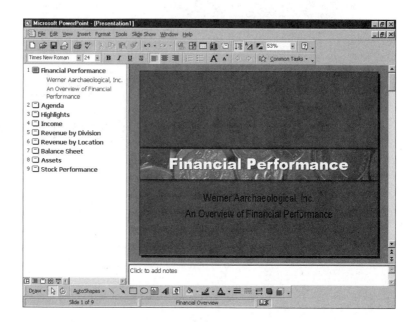

Or a Web page, like this:

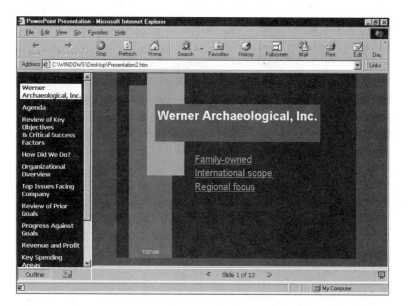

Exploring the PowerPoint Window

You can start PowerPoint, like the other applications in the Office 2000 suite, in any of several ways. The easiest way is to use the Start button. Click the Start button, point to Programs, and select Microsoft PowerPoint from the Programs menu.

The PowerPoint window is shown in Figure 26-1, on the next page. By default, PowerPoint starts by displaying a dialog box that shows your options for creating a new presentation. (You'll learn more about these options later in the chapter.) But for now, take a look at the significant user interface components that PowerPoint shares with the other programs in the Office 2000 software suite.

- A menu bar, the hallmark of virtually every Windows-based application, provides access to the most important commands in the PowerPoint program. To choose a command from a PowerPoint menu, click the menu you want, point to the desired submenu (if applicable), and then click the command you want to run.

> NOTE

In PowerPoint 2000, menu commands automatically configure themselves based on how you use the menu. Unused commands filter down the list; the most popular ones move to the top. If a command doesn't appear listed right away, you can click the bottom of the menu to see more commands.

- The toolbars, as usual, provide quick, one-click access to often-used commands. Because the PowerPoint window includes several toolbars, you might want to walk through the tools, resting the mouse pointer for a second on any that are new to you. Resting the mouse pointer on a tool, you'll recall, displays a ScreenTip that briefly describes the tool's function. The Drawing toolbar at the bottom of the screen now includes the Insert Clip Art button, an AutoShapes menu that has several new shapes, and other commands and tools for drawing. A Tables And Borders toolbar appears automatically when you insert a table on a slide in PowerPoint 2000.

- The Common Tasks toolbar, containing often-used commands such as New Slide and Slide Layout, appears docked on the right end of the Formatting toolbar. You can easily turn it into a floating toolbar by dragging the blue border at the top of the toolbar to any location on your screen.

FIGURE 26-1.

Important parts of the PowerPoint window.

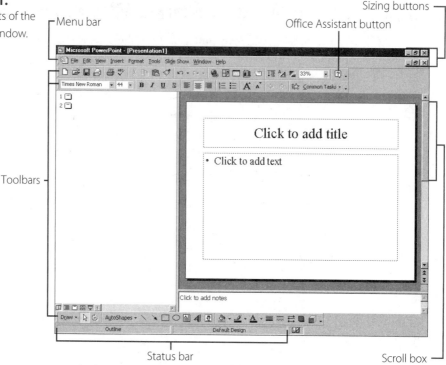

- Menu bar
- Sizing buttons
- Office Assistant button
- Toolbars
- Status bar
- Scroll box

SEE ALSO

For more information about using menus, dialog boxes, toolbars, and application windows, see Chapter 2, "Learning the Basics: Windows, Toolbars, and Printing." For more information about starting and configuring the Office Assistant, see Chapter 1, "A Quick Tour of Microsoft Office."

- Like most Office application windows, the PowerPoint application window also contains sizing buttons that you can use to minimize, maximize, restore, and close windows, plus a status bar at the bottom of the screen that displays the number of the slide you're working on as well as the type of presentation you're creating.

- The scroll box moves you from slide to slide, not up or down through the slide's text (as happens in a Word document, for example). In addition, PowerPoint displays the number and title of each slide as you drag the scroll box. You'll like this feature.

- The two buttons displaying double arrows at the bottom of the vertical scroll bar give you another way to move through slides. Click the button with the upward-pointing arrows to go to the previous slide; click the button with the downward-pointing arrows to move to the next slide.

- The View buttons on the left end of the horizontal scroll bar, although easily overlooked, let you quickly switch to different PowerPoint views. Each view is designed to make some aspect of creating and viewing a slide show as effective as possible. Views are described in more detail in the next section.

- The Office Assistant button on the right side of the Standard toolbar provides access to all the PowerPoint Help documentation and the animated Office Assistant. If the Office Assistant isn't already running, clicking this button will start it.

Understanding PowerPoint Views

To use PowerPoint effectively to create and modify presentations, you need to become comfortable with PowerPoint's *views*. As the name implies, views provide you with different ways of looking at a document. They're somewhat virtual and perhaps more uniquely computer-esque than other aspects of Office applications because they use the power of the machine and the software to display a document in ways that paper and other real objects can't. PowerPoint can display your slides in any of six basic views, all of which are shown in Figure 26-2 on the following page.

- Normal view is the new default view in PowerPoint 2000. It is a combination of slide view and outline view, and includes a pane for adding speaker's notes. In Normal view, you can work not only on text and graphics, but on sound, animation, and other effects as well. You'll probably often choose this new workhorse view: you'll like refining many aspects of your presentation in one view.

- Outline view displays the titles and text on your slides in outline format (like the outlines you used to create in school). Outline view is valuable when you're organizing your thoughts and reordering the points you want to make, although it is also available as part of Normal view.

- Slide view lets you work with individual slides. You can also gain access to the outline and notes panes, but you concentrate on the slide itself in this view. You use Slide view to judge the impact of each slide and the arrangement of text and other elements on it.

- Slide Sorter view arranges all your slides across and down the screen as if they were laid out on your desktop or placed in one of those slide-holder sheets that you insert in an album. You use Slide Sorter view when you want to see your presentation as a whole and when you might want to rearrange the order in which your slides will be shown.

IV

Microsoft PowerPoint

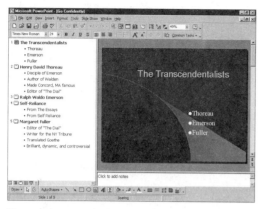

Normal view

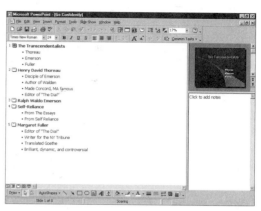

Outline view

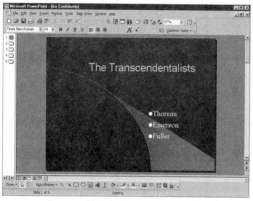

Slide view

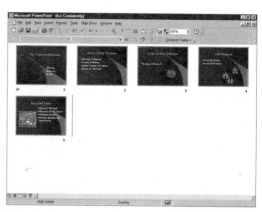

Slide Sorter view

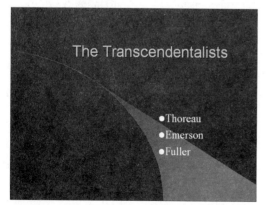

Slide Show view

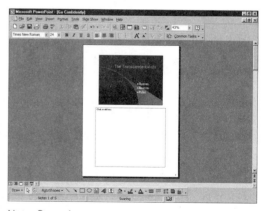

Notes Page view

FIGURE 26-2.
PowerPoint's many points of view.

IV

Microsoft PowerPoint

■ Slide Show view is the most fun. You use it when you want to preview your work and run through your presentation to see how well you did. In Slide Show view, you can also see the results of transitions (how the screen changes when moving between slides) as well as any animation or sound effects you have added to the presentation.

■ Notes Page view allows you to add short messages or "speaker notes" to your slides. In PowerPoint 2000, you arrive at this view by choosing the Notes Page command on the View menu. *For more information, see Chapter 31, "Perfecting Your Presentation."*

Getting Started

Once you're comfortable with the PowerPoint window and its tools and views, the burning question becomes, "How do I create a presentation?" PowerPoint, like most Office 2000 applications, offers you a variety of choices. You see them listed in the dialog box shown below when you first open PowerPoint.

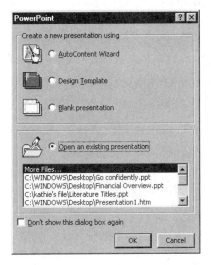

 TIP

After you have experimented with PowerPoint 2000, you might want to select the new check box, Don't Show This Dialog Box Again. PowerPoint will then open immediately and display the New Slide dialog box. You can choose an AutoLayout and begin working right away on a new, blank presentation.

- The AutoContent Wizard—by far the easiest approach to creating a new presentation—asks for information, and then creates a set of slides built around the theme you specify.

- Design Template, which allows you more latitude, lets you apply predesigned outlines, color schemes, and backgrounds to create sets of slides for standard types of presentations, such as progress reports and top-10 lists.

? SEE ALSO

For more information about finding and opening Office documents, and in particular, using the Open dialog box, see Chapter 3, "Managing Documents: From Your Hard Disk to the Internet."

- Blank Presentation gives you a plain canvas on which to create a single slide: this option offers the most flexibility but, as you'd expect, also assumes that you know what you want to do and how to do it.

- The final option, Open An Existing Presentation, lets you choose a PowerPoint presentation that you have already created and saved. In PowerPoint 2000, the four most recent presentations you have worked on are listed here, and you can quickly choose one to modify. You can enhance its look, add some new slides, and save it as a new, different presentation. (If the presentation you're looking for isn't listed in the box, select More Files, and use the Open Dialog box to browse your hard disk for all the PowerPoint presentations you've created.)

Using the AutoContent Wizard

Microsoft wizards provide the friendliest and simplest ways to get work done. Typically, wizards ask you to make some choices and provide some basic information, and then they use what you enter to carry out the task they're designed to do. As already mentioned, the AutoContent Wizard walks you through the initial process of creating a presentation. To start the AutoContent Wizard when the opening PowerPoint dialog box shown previously is displayed, do this:

- Click AutoContent Wizard, and then click OK.

If you have been working in PowerPoint and the dialog box isn't displayed, but you want to begin creating another presentation by using the wizard, do this:

- Choose New from the File menu. In the New Presentation dialog box, click the General tab. Click AutoContent Wizard, and then click OK, or double-click the wizard icon.

However you start it, the wizard opens and displays an introductory dialog box that explains what will happen. Click the Next button to move on, and the wizard swings into action, as shown here.

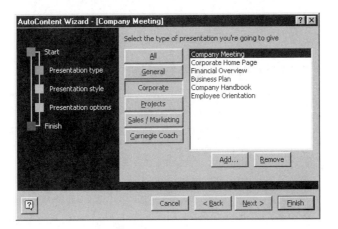

From this point on, the wizard is so friendly that using it is almost a no-brainer. Just remember to click Next to move to the next screen; click Back to return to an earlier screen; and click Cancel to scrap everything you have done. As you work through the wizard, PowerPoint keeps track of your progress, as shown in the bulleted list on the left side of the dialog box. The following list summarizes the steps you go through:

1 The second dialog box (after the introductory one) asks you to select the type of presentation you're going to give by clicking one of the six topics displayed. For example, to see a list of the business presentations, click the Corporate button. (You will see the dialog box illustrated above.)

2 The next dialog box asks you to choose the output type for the presentation you'll be making. PowerPoint comes with a number of built-in templates designed for different situations. You can choose a traditional presentation or one that will run on the Web. The wizard also asks whether you need black-and-white or color overheads, or 35mm slides for your presentation.

3 The next dialog box requests information that will be displayed on the opening, or title, slide. By default, the wizard includes your name. You provide the name of your presentation and the information you want included in the footer on each slide.

That's all there is to it! Click Finish in the last dialog box, and the Auto-Content Wizard creates a basic set of slides built around the choices you made, and ends up by displaying your presentation in Normal view. With the preliminary work done, you're now ready to add text and graphics, modify formatting to add impact to your message, and make the presentation your own, as described in the following chapters.

Using a Template

PowerPoint arrives on your desktop with two types of built-in templates. *Presentation templates* are frameworks for standard types of presentations. They have names such as Business Plan, Company Meeting, Corporate Home Page, and so on. As their names indicate, these templates help you to create a presentation by incorporating suggestions for key points you'll probably want to include as you cover your topic. Figure 26-3 shows some of the slides in the Business Plan template (check the status bar) to help you see what presentation templates—just called *presentations* in PowerPoint 2000—are all about. Naturally, the suggested content is meant to guide; it doesn't replace the business professionals (lawyer, accountant, marketing pro, industry expert, and the like) whom you'd probably want to consult when preparing a business plan to take to a lender for startup capital.

In contrast to presentations, *design templates* help you apply a consistent design and color scheme to an entire set of slides. Design templates have names such as Blue Diagonal, Pulse, Pacific Rim, and

FIGURE 26-3.
Presentations help you organize and build content.

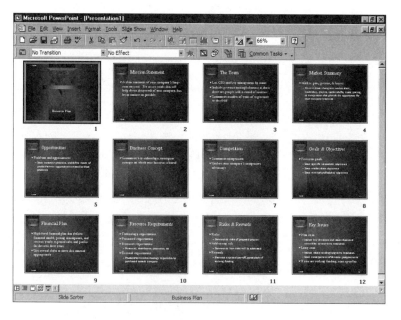

Technology. Put together by professional designers, these templates combine a background color and design with a set of eight complementary colors that PowerPoint uses for elements such as titles, background, slide text, shadow effects, and so on.

The following illustration shows a title page format based on the Notebook design template—suitably whimsical for a new tutoring program, but unsuitable for a stockholders' meeting.

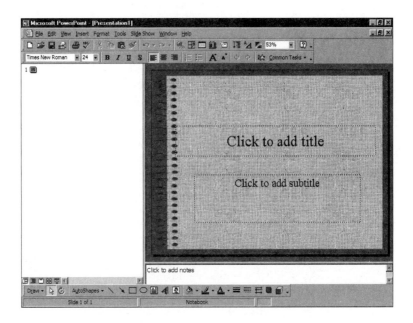

When you work with PowerPoint, you should understand that presentations and design templates are mix-and-match elements of a slide show. You can combine them in any way you choose. Suppose, for example, that you decide to work with the Marketing Plan presentation. By default, PowerPoint uses a design template that has a blue, green, and white color scheme for the Marketing Plan presentation, though you're free to choose any other design from among the many built into PowerPoint—or, when you're more experienced, from any you have created and saved for yourself.

To use templates from within PowerPoint, follow this procedure:

1 If the opening PowerPoint dialog box is displayed, choose Design Template, and click OK. If you have been working on a different presentation, save it (if necessary), and then choose New from the File menu. Either way, the New Presentation dialog box appears, as shown in Figure 26-4, on the following page.

FIGURE 26-4.

The New Presentation dialog box.

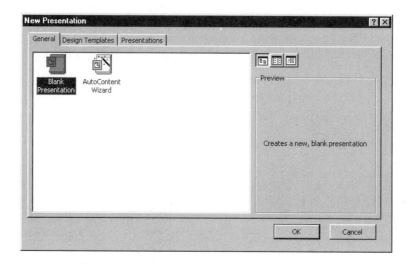

2 Click the Design Templates tab to select a design template, or click the Presentations tab to select a presentation template.

3 Click the icon for the template that has the design you want or the one that most closely matches your topic. If you can't decide on a presentation, choose Generic.

 Remember, you can use the new Save As Web Page command to turn your presentations into ones that are formatted for use in networking settings, such as on your company intranet or on the Internet. Notice that PowerPoint shows you a preview for the template in the Preview area at the right.

4 When you have selected the template, click OK.

- If you selected a presentation template from the Presentations tab, you will now see the opening slide of the new presentation containing the sample text supplied by the template, and you can begin entering the text of your presentation.

- If you selected a design template from the Design Templates tab, choose an AutoLayout in the New Slide dialog box, as shown in Figure 26-5. A slide based on the design template and the *AutoLayout* you chose will appear in the Power-Point window, and you can begin entering the text of your presentation.

FIGURE 26-5.
Selecting an Auto-Layout in the New Slide dialog box.

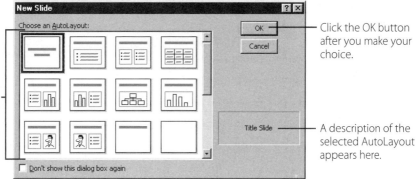

Click the OK button after you make your choice.

Click to select the AutoLayout that includes the elements and arrangement that you want for your slide.

A description of the selected AutoLayout appears here.

 TIP

Create First, Refine Later

If you don't like the design applied to the presentation template you chose, it's easy to improve it. For now, just create the substance of your presentation. *Changing the design is simple and is covered in Chapter 28, "Formatting Text."*

Creating a Blank Presentation

When you want to opt for full creativity instead of relying on the AutoContent Wizard or a template, follow these steps:

1 If the opening PowerPoint dialog box is displayed, choose Blank Presentation, and click OK. If you're already working with PowerPoint, choose New from the File menu. Click to select Blank Presentation on the General tab of the New Presentation dialog box, and then click OK.

2 Complete the New Slide dialog box, as shown in Figure 26-5. A slide that has reserved areas matching the layout you chose appears in the PowerPoint window, as shown in Figure 26-6, on the next page.

Once you have chosen the basic layout for your blank slide, you can enter, edit, and format its contents. PowerPoint uses certain fonts and font sizes by default, though you can easily change them. None of this work is difficult, as you'll see in the next few chapters. First, however, take a look at the easy ways that you can customize your PowerPoint environment to match your needs and preferences. The more you know about your user interface before you start, the more comfortable you'll be when you settle down to work.

IV

Microsoft PowerPoint

FIGURE 26-6.
A blank slide that has space for adding title, text, and a clip art graphic.

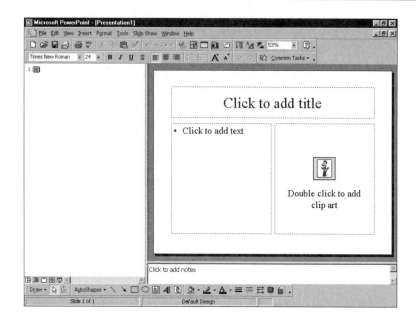

Working with Toolbars

By default, PowerPoint 2000 displays the Standard, Formatting, and Drawing toolbars. The Standard toolbar, as in other Office applications, contains general-purpose tools. In PowerPoint, you use these tools for creating, printing, and enhancing slides. A new Tables And Borders button is included on the Standard toolbar in PowerPoint 2000, as well as an Insert Table button that replaces the old Insert Word Table button. PowerPoint 2000 creates tables right on your slides, allowing you to smoothly add comparative data to your presentations.

The Formatting toolbar, as you'd expect, provides fast access to text and list formatting. You can use the new Numbering button on this toolbar just as you would in Word to make lists in a hierarchy. The Formatting toolbar also contains the Common Tasks toolbar, where you'll find the most popular PowerPoint commands— New Slide, Slide Layout, and Apply Design Template.

The Drawing toolbar helps you insert text, graphics, and special effects on slides. The Drawing toolbar appears at the bottom of the Power-Point window above the status bar (see Figure 26-1, page 666), and is identical to the Drawing toolbar that appears in the Word and Excel applications.

PowerPoint also includes several other toolbars that you'll find useful:

- The Animation Effects toolbar—a delightful one—offers an assortment of tools for adding movement and sound to selected text and graphics on your slides. You can also display it by clicking the Animation Effects button on the Formatting toolbar.

- The Picture toolbar allows you to adjust a number of formatting options for the selected image. For example, you can adjust the contrast, brightness, border line style, and crop marks.

- The Reviewing toolbar lets you add review comments and send electronic mail messages.

- The Visual Basic toolbar helps you create macros that automate tasks in the PowerPoint environment.

- The Web toolbar lets you switch back and forth between open hyperlinks, establish additional Internet connections, or run special network-related commands.

■ The WordArt toolbar gives you the ability to create text entries that have special formatting effects.

■ The new Tables And Borders toolbar appears automatically when you insert a table on your slide and helps you format the table right on your slide.

Try New Techniques on a Practice Slide, and Then Toss It
If you want to experiment with these toolbars—or any other PowerPoint feature, for that matter—start PowerPoint and open a throwaway slide by choosing Blank Presentation in the opening PowerPoint dialog box. Click OK, and when you're asked to choose an AutoLayout, click Blank AutoLayout (the last choice in the lower right corner), and then click OK again. This will give you a blank slide to experiment with. When you're through, exit PowerPoint, and click No when asked whether you want to save the presentation.

It's easy to display and arrange additional toolbars. Remember, however, that each takes valuable screen space, so give yourself plenty of working room by keeping the extras to a minimum. After you've used PowerPoint for a while, you might find it helpful to create a custom toolbar containing the tools you use most, and then hide (or deselect) the toolbars you don't need. (You must be working in Normal, Slide, Outline, Slide Sorter, or Notes Page view to display additional toolbars or to hide those that you don't want to display.)

To change which toolbars are displayed, complete the following steps:

1 Click View, and then point to the Toolbars command, or right-click any toolbar. You'll see this menu:

SEE ALSO

For more information about running commands by clicking toolbar buttons, moving toolbars around the screen, and customizing toolbars and menus, see "Using Toolbars," page 39.

2 Click the name of the toolbar you want to display or hide; this adds or removes a check mark. Toolbars that have a check mark next to their names are displayed.

⭐ **TIP**

Shortcuts Are a Click Away

Many times the action you want to perform can be found on the special shortcut menu that appears when you press the right (or secondary) mouse button. The menu changes depending upon the context of your actions, so check it often for possible shortcuts to accomplish your tasks more quickly.

Using the Options Dialog Box to Customize PowerPoint

To change the way PowerPoint looks and works, experiment with the customization choices in the Options dialog box, shown in Figure 26-7, on the next page. You display the Options dialog box by choosing Options from the Tools menu.

The Options dialog box contains tabs that control virtually every aspect of the PowerPoint interface. Although some tabs customize features that you might not be familiar with, such as the settings that render and export pictures, you can often learn a lot about how PowerPoint works by just browsing through the tabs in the Options dialog box. When you have some spare time, we recommend that you experiment with the settings on the following tabs to personalize your working environment:

- The View tab, which controls the dialog boxes that appear when you start PowerPoint and interface items like the status bar and ruler.

- The General tab, which controls the size of the list of recently used files on the File menu. This tab also allows you to change the user name that appears in comments and e-mail messages, and it contains the new Web Options button, which controls the way your browser displays your slide show.

- The Edit tab, which controls editing features like the drag-and-drop technique and the maximum number of undos available.

- The Save tab, which sets the default file format for PowerPoint presentations and the timing interval (in minutes) of the Auto-Recover backup feature.

 **TIP**

Want Protection Against Unsafe Macros?

Macros speed up your work by automating repetitive tasks using a custom command that you create. However, you won't increase your productivity if you use one that contains a computer virus. Although the Options dialog box no longer contains a macro virus protection check box, you can find an expanded version of this feature in PowerPoint 2000. Click the Tools menu, point to the Macros submenu, and then click Security. You'll probably want to choose the Medium level of security and list your favorite sources by clicking the Trusted Sources tab.

FIGURE 26-7.

The Options dialog box allows you to customize many of Power-Point's commands and features. The View tab controls basic options like the appearance of the workplace and display options in your slide show.

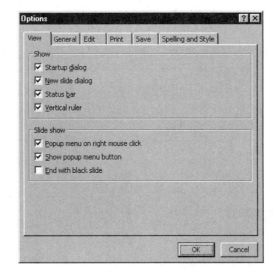

Entering and Editing Text

Although drawings, graphics, charts, colors, and eye-catching background designs help enormously to illustrate your points and keep your audience awake, substance and content still require words. Those words must come from you, but Microsoft PowerPoint can help you add them to your slides in a number of easy and creative ways that focus attention on what you want to say.

This chapter describes ways to build the body of a presentation using elements such as titles, subtitles, and bulleted lists. You'll learn how to manage the text on a slide, expand one slide into many, and add review annotations known as *comments* to slides. So that you won't think of text as simply the gray matter on a slide, you'll also learn how to add some eye appeal by using WordArt objects. Toward the end of the chapter, you'll see how to enlist PowerPoint's advice in making your slides clear and easy to read.

TIP

> This chapter deals with plain text on a slide. PowerPoint also lets you add descriptive text, such as captions and labels, to graphics. That's done differently, however, and is covered in Chapter 29, where you meet the Drawing toolbar.

Entering Text

The way you enter text onto a slide depends on the way you have decided to create your presentation. The basic options are as follows:

- Working with a template, including one designed for you by the AutoContent Wizard

- Working with a blank presentation and applying a built-in AutoLayout

- Working in Normal view

 TIP

> If you'd like the outline to be the bigger picture—the main focus of your view—click Outline View in the lower left corner of your PowerPoint window. The outline pane expands, and you gain a larger space in which to add and order text.

When you start a new presentation by choosing a template, entering text is literally a matter of replacing the suggested topics (the *placeholders*) that PowerPoint provides on each slide. When you start with a blank presentation and choose an AutoLayout format, text entry is much the same as if you had chosen one of PowerPoint's templates. The only difference between the two, which you can see in Figures 27-1 and 27-2, is that the template comes with a colorful presentation design and contains suggestions for content, whereas the AutoLayout offers a plain background and simply reserves portions of the slide for whatever content you want to provide.

Instead of—or in addition to—using templates and built-in layouts, you can organize your thoughts in outline form and then turn your outline into slides. If you're creating a complex presentation, or if you're a person who values structure and likes to see how the parts contribute to the whole, working with an outline is probably a good choice for you.

The following sections describe each of these options in more detail.

FIGURE 27-1.
When you use a template, PowerPoint makes suggestions about the types of information you might want to include on each slide.

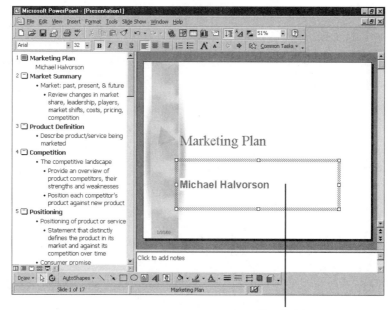

Placeholder

FIGURE 27-2.
When you start with a blank presentation and an AutoLayout, PowerPoint reserves space for text but doesn't offer any suggestions about content.

Placeholders

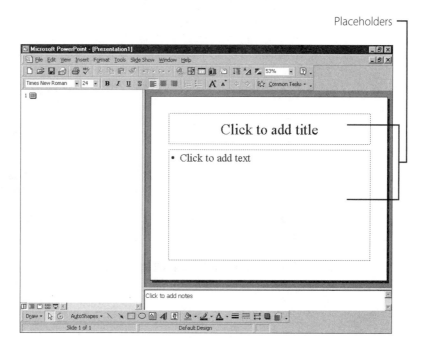

Entering Text into Placeholders

Placeholders, like the ones shown in Figures 27-1 and 27-2, are something like templates within templates. Surrounded by a dotted or shaded border, they're preformatted with a particular font and font size, and they contain text that you replace with your own text. By default, PowerPoint automatically wraps text within the placeholder as you type, so press Enter only when you want to start a new paragraph.

In both templates and AutoLayouts, you do the following:

1 Select the placeholder.

2 Type your own text, as shown in the following illustration.

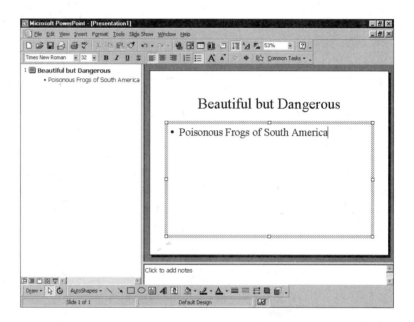

3 When you have finished entering text, click anywhere outside the placeholder to make the border disappear.

Tips for Entering Text

Text entry is simple, but keep these points in mind:

- When you use an AutoLayout, your typing replaces the placeholder text.

- When you use a template, you must select the placeholder text before typing your own text. If you don't, your typing is inserted into the placeholder text.

- When you enter text that isn't found in the Microsoft Office 2000 dictionary or in a custom dictionary, the words are marked with a red wavy underline, indicating a potential misspelling. This as-you-type spell-check feature can be quite useful, but rarely recognizes technical terms or foreign words. To add a word to your custom dictionary, right-click the underlined word and click Add. To correct a misspelling, right-click the underlined word, and pick a correction if one is listed. *(For more information, see "Checking Your Spelling," page 767.)*

- To insert symbols or special characters in a placeholder, choose Symbol from the Insert menu, specify the character set you want to use in the Font drop-down list box, click the symbol you want in the display window, click Insert to add the symbol, and then click Close.

- To add a new, blank text placeholder to a slide, choose Textbox from the Insert menu, drag the mouse on the slide to create the placeholder, and type the text you want.

Tips for Positioning Placeholders

When you're working with placeholders, here are some tips you might want to keep in mind:

- If you're having trouble fitting text onto a slide, try resizing or repositioning another placeholder before enlarging the one in which you want more text. To reposition a placeholder, point to a part of the border other than a sizing handle (the mouse pointer becomes a four-headed arrow), and drag the placeholder up or down on the slide. Moving a title higher, for example, gains you extra space for a bulleted list below it.

- Because PowerPoint automatically wraps text, you can use placeholder resizing as a quick-and-dirty way to realign text. To turn a two-line paragraph into one, for instance, widen the placeholder box. To force text to fill more vertical space, make the box narrower and longer.

- You can resize or realign placeholders to make room for an object, such as a graphic, that isn't provided for on your template or on your AutoLayout slide.

You can choose an *anchor point* for your text. Normally, PowerPoint adds text from the top down. By choosing a different anchor point, you can have PowerPoint add text from the bottom or from the middle of an object instead.

Tips for Positioning Placeholders   *continued*

This feature can help you maintain even spacing above and below text that doesn't completely fill a placeholder. To do this, select the placeholder you want to modify, and then choose Placeholder from the Format menu. Select a new text anchor point in the Format AutoShape dialog box, as shown here:

1 Click the Text Box tab. ——

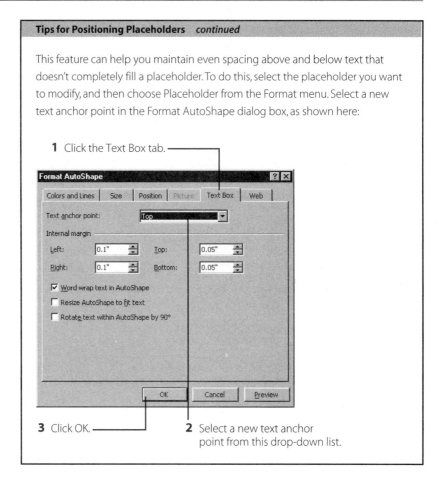

3 Click OK. ——   **2** Select a new text anchor point from this drop-down list.

Selecting Placeholder Text in a Template

When you're working with a template, you have several ways to select placeholder text that you want to replace:

- Double-click to select a single word; triple-click to select a paragraph.

- Position the insertion point at the beginning or the end of a line and drag across the text you want to replace.

- On the keyboard, press Home once, and then press Shift+End to select a line, or press Ctrl+Shift+End to select the entire block of text in the placeholder.

Matching the Placeholder's Size to Your Text

When you type more text than the placeholder can hold, PowerPoint, by default, doesn't expand the placeholder vertically to contain the overflow. Although such a problem is easily corrected, you'll probably want to watch how much you type. PowerPoint will accept your text, but you might end up with a slide that looks like the one in Figure 27-3, on the next page.

If you need to enter more text than a placeholder can hold, one easy solution is to reformat the font size, as described in the next chapter, so that the information requires less space. If you don't need such a signif-icant change, or if one placeholder is too big and another is too small, you can also shrink or enlarge your placeholders.

To change the size of a placeholder, do this:

1 Click the border of the placeholder to display its sizing handles.

2 Place the mouse pointer on one of the handles. When the pointer turns into a two-headed arrow, drag the border in the direction you want to resize the box.

   (You can also drag a corner of the placeholder, like most text boxes in Microsoft Office, to resize it in two directions.) The following illustration shows a placeholder during resizing:

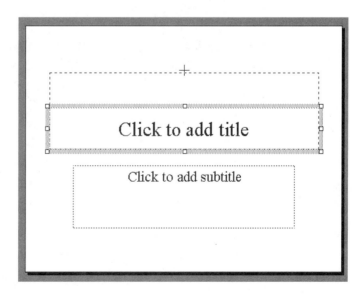

FIGURE 27-3.
You can do this, but your slide won't be very effective.

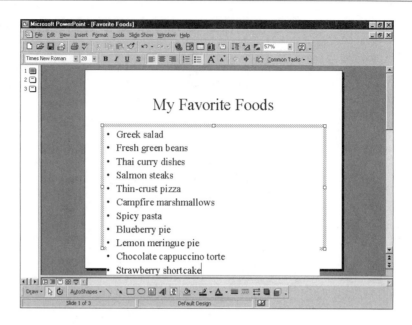

Using Outlines

Outlines in PowerPoint are exactly like the ones that you created in school. Just as in those long-ago outlines, you work with—and present to the world—a series of titles that have subordinate levels and sublevels of headings, as shown in Figure 27-4.

FIGURE 27-4.
Subordinate outline levels in PowerPoint are indented at the left. Templates format them in different font sizes and, sometimes, to have different bullet styles.

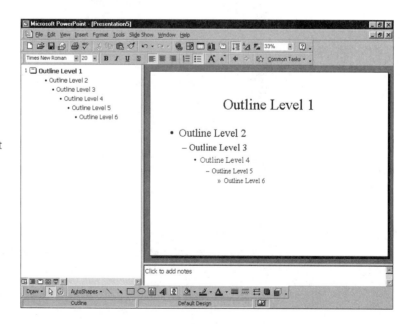

It's easy to see from this illustration that outline indenting can help you organize your thoughts while you're creating slides, and that such indenting can also be highly effective in helping your audience understand the relative importance of the points you make.

Viewing an Outline

To work on an outline in PowerPoint, begin in the outline pane of Normal view, or, to enlarge that perspective, click the Outline View button to the left of the horizontal scroll bar.

If you have opened an existing presentation or if you're using a presentation template, you see the text displayed in outline form, as shown in Figure 27-5. If you're working on a blank presentation, you see a slide number and a slide icon, as shown in Figure 27-6 (next page), but, of course, no text will appear until you type some.

Entering an Outline from Scratch

When you have displayed a blank presentation in Normal or Outline view, generating an outline feels as if you're working on a cross between a Microsoft Word document and a PowerPoint slide. Once you get the hang of it, however, it's simple. The only real trick is to remember the following:

- Depending on the preceding outline level you typed, the key combination Ctrl+Enter toggles between creating a new slide and creating a bulleted item. That is, if the last text you typed was a

FIGURE 27-5.
In this Normal view, two slides and three different heading levels are visible.

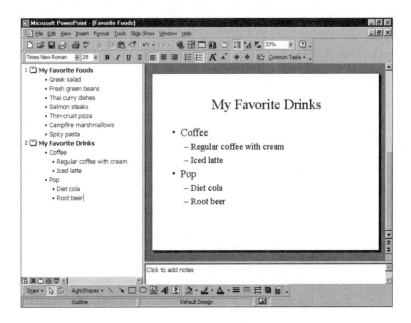

FIGURE 27-6.

A blank presentation in Normal view.

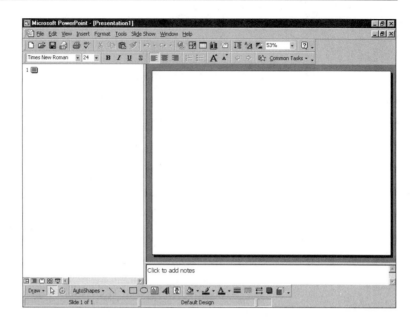

slide title, Ctrl+Enter creates a bulleted item; if the last text you typed was a bulleted item, Ctrl+Enter creates a new slide.

- After you have passed the title/first bullet hurdle, pressing Enter creates a new paragraph exactly like the preceding one. That is, if the last character you typed was a bullet, press Enter to create another bullet; if the last character you typed was a slide title, press Enter to create a new slide.

- If you want to create an outline that has several sublevels (as shown in Figure 27-4, page 688), use the Promote and Demote buttons on the vertical Outlining toolbar:

  - Click the Promote button to raise the importance of a paragraph one heading level—for example, to switch from outline level 3 to outline level 2.

  - Click the Demote button to lower the importance of a paragraph one heading level—say, to switch from outline level 2 to outline level 3. You can also use the Demote button to move the top heading on one slide to the previous slide.

The Outlining toolbar is shown as a floating toolbar in Figure 27-7. By default, this toolbar is displayed docked along the left side of your screen—although, as with all toolbars, you can drag it to another side of the screen or position it as a floating toolbar if you prefer.

FIGURE 27-7.
Tools on the Outlining toolbar.

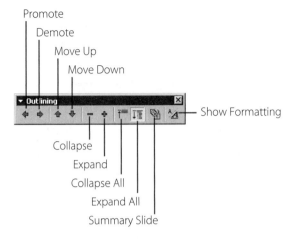

Modifying an Outline

When you're comfortable creating an outline in Normal view, use the following procedures to control and refine either an outline that you have created from scratch or one that you're revising by using the suggestions in a template or the headings in another document:

■ To select a slide title in an outline, drag the mouse pointer over the title.

■ To select a bulleted item and all its subitems, click the bullet (when the pointer becomes a four-headed arrow).

■ To select several consecutive bulleted items, hold down the Shift key as you click. (Although pressing Ctrl while you click lets you select nonconsecutive items in other Office 2000 applications, it doesn't work that way in PowerPoint.)

■ To select an entire slide, click the slide icon.

■ To move a paragraph, select it and either drag it to its new location or use the Move Up and Move Down buttons, shown on the Outlining toolbar in Figure 27-7.

■ Use the buttons shown in Figure 27-7 to change outline levels and to control how much of the outline you see on screen.

As you're working with your slides, you might find that you need to rearrange some of them. You can easily do so by dragging them to new locations in Slide Sorter view, but when you're working on an outline in Normal view, the drag-and-drop technique works just as well. To reorder your slides, follow these steps:

1 Select the slide you want to move. (Be sure to select all of it by clicking the slide icon.)

2 Place the mouse pointer on the slide icon, and drag the slide to a new location. As you drag, watch the horizontal line that shows where you're dragging the slide. To avoid inserting the slide into the body of another slide, don't release the mouse button until the line is completely above or below your target.

To undo a move, either choose Undo Move from the Edit menu or click the Undo button. When you move slides, note that PowerPoint automatically renumbers them for you. A nice touch.

Using Word to Create an Outline

To Microsoft Office, an outline is an outline, whether it's created in PowerPoint or in Word. Thus, you can easily turn a Word outline into a set of slides, and you can just as easily turn a set of slides into a Word document. The only prerequisite (on your part) for this to work smoothly is some familiarity with Word's heading-level styles, because heading levels in a Word document become bulleted items on PowerPoint slides, and vice versa, as shown in Figure 27-8.

If you know Word, importing an outline is simple. If you don't know Word, the process is a little more complex. You'll just have to adjust the outline levels yourself in PowerPoint by using the Promote and Demote buttons.

To use a Word document that contains heading styles as the basis for a presentation, follow this procedure:

1 Click the New button on PowerPoint's Standard toolbar.

2 Choose an AutoLayout, and click OK. The default, which starts with a title slide, is a good choice because PowerPoint is so smart that it leaves the title slide for you to deal with and starts displaying the Word outline on slide 2.

FIGURE 27-8.
These illustrations
show how heading
levels in Word match
outline levels in
PowerPoint.

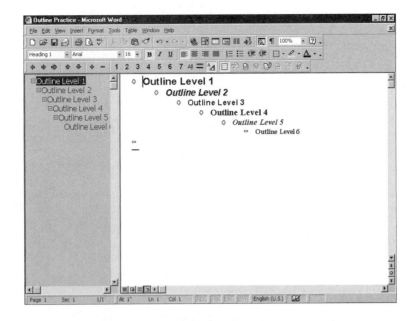

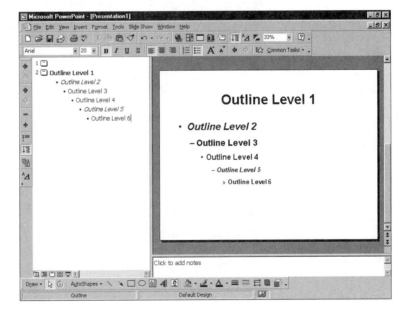

3 From the Insert menu, choose Slides From Outline. The following dialog box appears:

Use the Look In list box and Up One
Level button to find files in other folders.

4 Select the Word document you want to import.

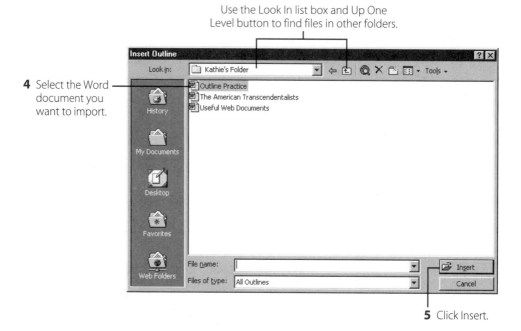

5 Click Insert.

6 After PowerPoint opens the Word document and builds a presentation using the outline, use PowerPoint's Normal view to edit the content of the presentation so that no slide has too much text. (If you used several heading levels, some of your slides might be packed with too much information to fit or to read easily.)

 **TIP**

Another Way to Import a Word Outline

To create a PowerPoint presentation from a Word document that uses heading styles, choose Open from the File menu. In the Open dialog box, select All Outlines in the Files Of Type list box. Then double-click the name of the document you want to open. The imported Word outline will open in PowerPoint in Normal view.

TIP

Each Paragraph in Word Is a Slide

You can turn a Word document that doesn't use heading styles into a Power-Point outline using these same procedures as well, but you must select All Files in the Files Of Type box. Each paragraph in the document will become the title of a new slide. If your Word document contains five paragraphs, for example, PowerPoint will turn those paragraphs into the titles of five slides—a useful technique, if you have nothing else to start with.

SEE ALSO

For more information on applying styles in Word, see Chapter 5, "Formatting a Word Document." For details on using outlines in Word, see Chapter 11, "Writing Long Documents."

To reverse the procedure just described and use a PowerPoint presentation as the basis for a Word document, you have several options. You can copy the presentation as a Word outline, as a set of formatted slides, or as a combination of slides and notes.

To copy a PowerPoint presentation to Word, follow these steps:

1 Create or open the presentation in PowerPoint that you want to export to Word.

2 On the File menu, point to the Send To submenu and click Microsoft Word. The following dialog box opens, prompting you for the presentation components you want to send:

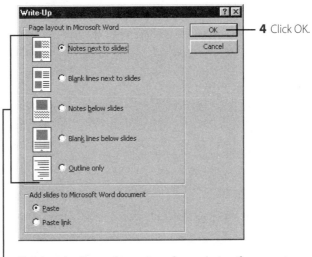

4 Click OK.

3 Select the formatting option of your choice. If you want to send an outline of your presentation and not the clip art and other graphics, select the Outline Only option.

IV

Microsoft PowerPoint

When your presentation opens in a Word window, you can edit and save it as you would any other Word document. If you used heading levels in your PowerPoint presentation, you'll see them in your Word document, and you can proceed to demote and promote the headings as you see fit in Word's Outline view.

Create Links Between Files

If you want your new Word document to be updated automatically whenever you subsequently make a change in the PowerPoint presentation that you exported, click the Paste Link option button in the dialog box that appears when you specify how you want your presentation sent to Word. Using Paste Link creates an electronic pathway between the files that remains active until you break it. (As you might guess, however, this feature is not desirable if you want the files to have their own identity.) *For more information on maintaining links, see Chapter 51, "Sharing Data Among Office Applications."*

Entering Review Comments

If you plan to share your presentations with other users, you might want to annotate a few important slides with comments to provide instructions or highlight critical information. In PowerPoint, you can add a yellow "sticky" note to a slide by displaying the slide in Normal view and choosing Comment from the Insert menu. Choosing Comment displays a yellow comment box that contains a blinking pointer and your name, so that you can add a short comment on the slide. (See the following illustration.) To get a good look at the comment box while you enter your comment, we recommend that you use the Zoom list box on the Standard toolbar to change the slide magnification to 75 percent or larger.

When you finish typing a comment, resize the comment box so that the entire note fits within it, and then click another object on your slide to lock in the comment. It will appear on your slide in each view as long as Comments on the View menu is selected.

Zoom list box   Reviewing toolbar

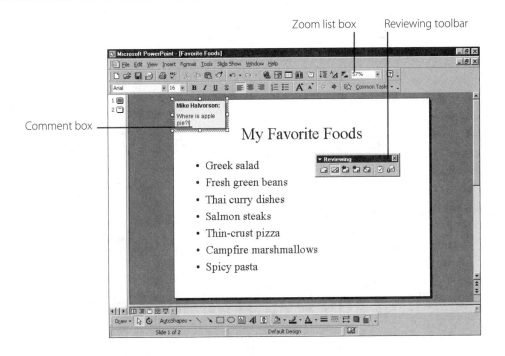

Comment box

(The Comments command is a toggle and is activated when you enter your first comment.) You can also use the Reviewing toolbar to manage your comments; it appears when you create your first yellow note:

Show/Hide Comments

Insert Comment

 TIP

Move It or Lose It

A comment is like any text box object on your slide; you can move a comment by dragging it with the mouse, or you can delete a comment by clicking its placeholder border and pressing Delete. You can also edit a comment by clicking it and then using a combination of arrow keys and text keys to modify the text. Finally, you can change the reviewer name at the top of the comment by choosing Options from the Tools menu, clicking the General tab, and editing the *Name* field.

Here's what a comment looks like in Slide view.

Expanding and Duplicating Slides

Other useful slide management capabilities that PowerPoint 2000 offers you are the ability to expand one slide into several slides and the ability to quickly duplicate a slide.

Using the Outlining toolbar, you can easily turn each text element on a slide—text placeholder, bullet, or paragraph—into a new, separate slide.

To expand one slide into several slides, follow these steps:

1 Display in Normal view the slide you want to expand. (You will be working in the Outline pane of Normal view.)

2 To select a text element (such as a bulleted item in a list), click the element when the pointer becomes a four-headed arrow. To select several consecutive text elements, hold down the Shift key as you click.

3 Click the Promote button on the Outlining toolbar.
   If you selected one text element, it will be expanded into a new slide. If you selected several text elements, each one will be expanded into a new slide.

4 Repeat these steps to expand as many items as you choose into separate slides. If you think better of the expansion and want to remove the new slides, simply choose Undo from the Edit menu.

To create an identical copy of a slide in your presentation, follow these steps:

1 Select the slide in Normal view.

2 Choose Duplicate Slide from the Insert menu. PowerPoint creates a copy of the slide and places it immediately after the selected slide in the presentation.

3 If you want to move the duplicated slide to a new location, you can use the drag-and-drop technique that you learned on page 692 when you modified an outline. Or you can choose Slide Sorter view and drag the slide to a new place.

You'll learn more about Slide Sorter view in Chapter 31, "Perfecting Your Presentation."

Adding Pizzazz by Using WordArt Objects

Lest you mistakenly think that words are better read than viewed, both Word and PowerPoint give you access to an enjoyable utility called WordArt that can add a lot of visual interest to text, as you can see in the following illustration:

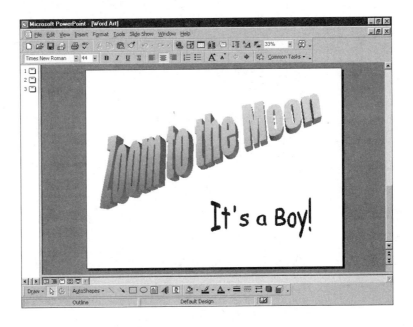

 **ON THE WEB**

The WordArt.ppt file is located on the Running Office 2000 Reader's Corner page. For information about connecting to this Web site, read the Introduction.

If you have a yen to add something of this sort to a slide—a special heading or logo, perhaps—it's easy. You don't even have to worry about positioning at first, because you'll be able to move and size the WordArt object later.

To create special text effects by using the WordArt utility (started from the Drawing toolbar), follow these steps:

Insert WordArt

1 Display the slide you want to modify in Slide view, and then click the Insert WordArt button on the Drawing toolbar. (If the Drawing toolbar isn't visible, choose Toolbars from the View menu and select Drawing.) The following dialog box appears:

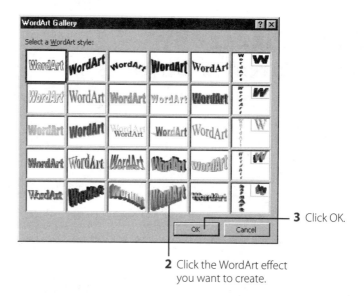

3 Click OK.

2 Click the WordArt effect you want to create.

4 Type whatever text you want in the Edit WordArt Text dialog box, and specify a different font and point size if you like.

5 Click OK to paste the WordArt on your slide. Then drag the WordArt to your preferred location and resize it using the sizing handles as desired.

WordArt is simple enough to use that you should need little more than these steps to become comfortable using it. If you need specifics, however, don't forget the Help menu, which is available at all times in PowerPoint.

Revising Text

? SEE ALSO
Chapters 28 through 30 cover various aspects of enhancing a presentation visually, while Chapter 31 discusses checking spelling and other fine-tuning techniques.

Refining a document—any document—involves several tasks: editing for content and clarity, refining text and layout for effectiveness, and polishing your work by checking for spelling and other errors. The remainder of this section deals with ways to work on content.

Selecting Text to Revise

As already mentioned in this chapter and elsewhere in this book, you can select text by using the mouse or the keyboard.

In addition to dragging the mouse over the text you want to select, you can use the following mouse shortcuts:

- In Normal view, click a slide icon to select the entire slide.

- In Normal view, select any bulleted item by moving the mouse pointer to the left of the item and clicking when the pointer becomes a four-headed arrow.

Using the keyboard, do this:

- To move to the beginning of a line, press Home; to move to the end, press End.

- To select to the beginning or the end of a line, press Shift+End or Shift+Home.

- To select consecutive lines, hold down the Shift key as you press End or Home.

- To select one character at a time, use the Shift+Left (or Right) arrow key.

- To select one word at a time, use the Ctrl+Shift+Left (or Right) arrow key.

Making Changes

Most people do a lot of revising on the fly as they type. You probably do too—backspacing to erase errors and typos, and perhaps selecting text and retyping to replace it. Because PowerPoint slides don't contain as much text as Word or Excel documents, you shouldn't have any trouble revising what you've written. (Because text is so sparse on a slide or transparency, any typos loom embarrassingly large—so be sure to check every word.) You can, however, use a few strategies to make the job go quickly and, as you'll see, you can even ask for PowerPoint's opinion.

Making Text Revisions

The most common type of revision involves changing text, either all or in part. As you probably know, you can replace any amount of text just by selecting it and typing something else. Your new text replaces the old text, even if you replace pages of prose with nothing more than a press of the Spacebar. Because PowerPoint, like other Windows applications, responds to the right mouse button, however, you have other easy ways to revise content:

- To insert new text, position the insertion point and start typing.

- To duplicate text, select it and then do one of the following:

  - Click the Copy button, position the insertion point where you want the duplicate text to appear, and click the Paste button. (Both buttons are on the Standard toolbar.)

  - Right-click the selected text, choose Copy from the shortcut menu that pops up, place the insertion point where you want the duplicate text to appear, right-click, and choose Paste. (This sounds like a lot of work, but it's not. Furthermore, because pop-up menus show only those actions that you can legally apply to an object, they're helpful when you're learning your way around a new application.)

- To move text, select it, and then use one of the following methods:

  - If you're working in Normal view, select the text and drag it to its new location.

  - If you're working in Slide view, use the Cut and Paste buttons on the Standard toolbar.

  - Right-click the selected text, and use the Cut and Paste commands on the shortcut menu.

- To delete text, select it and press the Delete key or use the Clear command on the Edit menu.

- To delete an entire slide, display it (in Slide view) or select it (in Normal view), and choose Delete Slide from the Edit menu.

Searching for Terms and Replacing Them

Sometimes, instead of revising text, you want to replace specific terms—for example, to change *primal scream* to *Tarzan yell*. For these jobs, you use either the Find command, which hunts for the term like a well-trained bloodhound, or the Replace command, which goes Find one better by replacing its quarry with something else.

You can use Find and Replace in any view other than Slide Show. The following describes Find, though it also applies to Replace, which is simply an expansion of Find:

1 Choose Find from the Edit menu. You'll see the following dialog box:

2 Type all or part of the term you want to find in the Find What box. Include capitalization if you need specific instances, such as *Brown* (the name) but not *brown* (the color). If capitalization is important, select the Match Case check box. If you want whole words only—*brown* but not *brownie*—select the Find Whole Words Only check box. (Note, however, that specifying whole words means that Find will locate *Brown* or *brown*, but not *Brown's* or *browns*.)

3 Click Find Next. Find will then search through all slides and high-light the first instance of the term that it locates. Click Find Next again if the term is not the one you seek.

If Find can't match the term you entered, it displays a message telling you: *The search item wasn't found.*

If you want to replace one term with another, you can do so either by clicking the Replace button in the Find dialog box or by using the Replace command on the Edit menu. The Replace dialog box is identical in both cases:

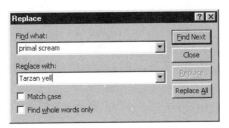

1 Enter the replacement term you want in the Replace With box, again using appropriate capitalization if necessary.

(The Match Case check box applies to the text in the Find What box.) PowerPoint inserts the replacement text exactly as you type it in the Replace With box, including matching the capitalization.

2 If you want to approve each replacement, click Find Next to locate the next instance of the term in the Find What box, and then click Replace. If you want Replace to do the work for you, click Replace All. (Be sure to scan the slides afterward, however, to be sure all replacements are those you wanted.)

> If you click the Replace All button and then decide you made a mistake, you can choose Undo Replace from the Edit menu to undo all replacements. If you use the Replace button, however, choosing Edit Undo Replace undoes only the last replacement. To undo others, use the Undo button for each replacement.

Checking for Visual Clarity

When you're satisfied with the content of your slides, PowerPoint can help you decide whether to make any adjustments to the way you have laid them out.

1 Choose Options from the Tools menu, and then click the Spelling And Style tab, which looks like this:

As you can see, the Spelling And Style tab contains many options that can help you with spelling, style, and punctuation, too. Those aspects are addressed in Chapter 31, "Perfecting Your Presentation," but because checking for clarity can be more helpful when you're constructing a presentation than when you're finalizing it, we cover the Visual Clarity option here.

2 To see what PowerPoint means by *visual clarity*, click the Style Options button on the Spelling and Style tab, and then click the Visual Clarity tab in the Style Options dialog box:

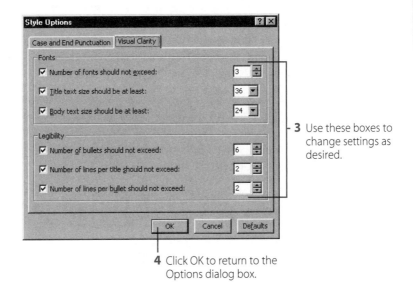

3 Use these boxes to change settings as desired.

4 Click OK to return to the Options dialog box.

Notice that Visual Clarity encompasses not only fonts and font sizes, but—more important when you're constructing slides—legibility. The default settings, such as no more than six bullets per slide, contribute to a clear, well-focused presentation. When PowerPoint checks your slides, it uses these settings as guidelines, notifies you of any slides that don't match the settings, and offers suggestions for addressing the style issue, as shown in the illustration on the following page.

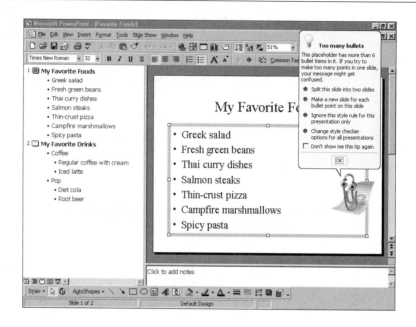

From this point on, it's up to you to decide whether and how you'll follow up on PowerPoint's advice.

CHAPTER 28

Formatting Text

Formatting text means changing its appearance. The look of the words can be as important in conveying your message as the words themselves. This chapter shows you how to change the font, font size, style, and color of your text in Microsoft PowerPoint 2000. You'll see how special effects such as drop shadows and embossing can change the appearance and the feeling of your text. You'll learn that the way you align your text can make it easier for your audience to grasp the information that you're presenting. You can make the text easier to read by increasing the spacing between lines and adjusting the paragraph indentation.

It's easy and fun to experiment with different formatting. Your changes can be subtle or dramatic, depending on the effect that you want to create and the audience that you're targeting. Use restraint, though—using too many design effects at once can detract from your message.

Changing the Appearance of Slide Text

If you know how to pick a new font, change alignment, and use bullets and numbering in Microsoft programs like Word or Excel, then you already have the essential skills to perform these tasks in PowerPoint. *If you don't want a refresher, you can skip this section and start with "Changing the Template," page 718.* If you're new to Microsoft Office, however, you'll want to read this section to learn how to format the text in your presentation.

Changing the Font, Font Size, Style, and Color

The font, font size, style, and color of your text are defined by settings in the current design template assigned to each text object or place-holder. For example, the Azure template uses Times New Roman 44-point font size in turquoise for slide titles and Times New Roman 32-point font size in white for slide text. (You can open the Azure template by choosing New from the File menu and clicking the Design Templates tab.) In both examples, the font style is regular (no bold or italic). When you use PowerPoint, you can easily change the font, font size, style, and color of the title or any other text.

Before you can change the text, you must first select it. To change all the text in a text object, click the text object's border to select both it and all the text it contains. In general, it's best to select the entire text object to ensure that the text maintains a consistent look. Sometimes, however, you might want to change just a portion of the text within a text object. For example, you might see a term that should be italicized or a word that you want to emphasize. To change the formatting of just a portion of the text in a text object, select the text you want to change, and then issue your formatting command. *(Chapter 27 discusses various techniques for selecting text or a placeholder.)*

Figure 28-1 shows sample text formatted by using the Bulleted List AutoLayout and the Azure design template. The text in the title is initially Times New Roman at 44 points, and the bulleted text is Times New Roman at 32 points. In the illustration, we used the mouse to select the first two bullets (Norway and Sweden) individually, and they are ready for formatting.

The interaction of the shapes and colors in your slide determines its overall look. Professional designers use a combination of established graphic principles and their experience to determine how to format the

FIGURE 28-1.
Selecting text is the first step in formatting it. In the Azure template shown here, two items in the bulleted list have been selected.

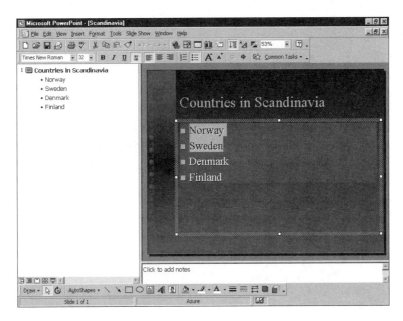

text on their slides, but it's okay to simply try different looks until you find something you like. One of the first changes that you might want to make is to the appearance of the text on the slide.

Settings in the Font dialog box control how the text appears (discussed in the next section), but buttons on the Formatting toolbar (shown in Figure 28-2 on the following page) control many of the most common changes that you might want to make. Here's how to do a little experimenting.

- The term *font* refers to the actual design of the characters used. Your system probably contains a variety of fonts from different sources. The easiest way to discover how each font looks on your slide is by trying it.

- To change the font, select the text, and choose a font from the Font drop-down list on the Formatting toolbar. Try different fonts until you find one that has the look you want.

It's best to use no more than two fonts for all the text in your slide presentation. Too many fonts can spoil the effect and look too busy. If this restriction sounds too severe, remember that you can also use the bold and italic styles of each font to add variety. For example, you might want to use Arial for your title and Times New Roman for text, and then use bold or italic here and there to emphasize certain words.

- To change the font size, select the text, and choose a font size from the Font Size drop-down list box on the Formatting toolbar.

FIGURE 28-2.
The Formatting
toolbar.

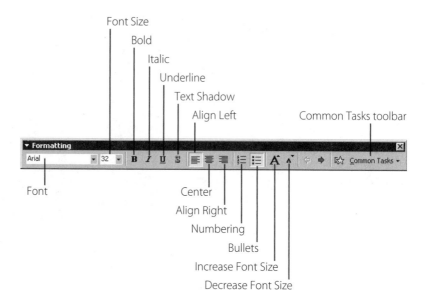

- If you want to enlarge your text but you're not sure what font size you need, click the Increase Font Size button on the Formatting toolbar until you get the size you want. Try increasing the title size to 54 points and the bulleted list size to 36 points.

- The term *font style* refers to variations from the basic look of the font. The most common font styles, bold and italic, are often stored on your system as separate fonts. That's because the design of the characters within the font has been modified to give you the best possible appearance in these styles. Other styles, such as underline, change the formatting of the basic font. For example, when you underline text, PowerPoint draws a line under each character.

- To change the font style, select the text, and click one of the following buttons on the Formatting toolbar:

  - The Bold button makes your text bold.

  - The Italic button italicizes your text.

  - The Underline button underlines your text.

Format
Painter

- To copy text formatting from one placeholder to another, select the first placeholder, click the Format Painter button on the Standard toolbar, and click the second placeholder.

Applying Special Effects

You can use formatting styles alone or in combination to add emphasis to text or titles. As mentioned earlier, use a little restraint, particularly when adding underlines, which can cut off descenders (the tail of a lowercase *g* or *p,* for example). For emphasis in text, it's generally better to use italics and to save the bold formatting for titles. You can also use the following special formatting effects:

Font
Color

- To change the text color, select the text, choose Font from the Format menu, and pick a new color in the Color drop-down list box. (See Figure 28-3.) You can also click the down arrow next to the Font Color button on the Drawing toolbar and choose a color. By adding color to your text, you can emphasize important words or phrases on your slide.

- To add shadow effects, select the text, and click the Text Shadow button on the Formatting toolbar. The Text Shadow button adds a shadow at the bottom and to the right of each character, making the text appear three-dimensional. Shadow effects provide another way to add emphasis and depth to your text.

- To replace one font with another throughout an entire presentation, choose Replace Fonts from the Format menu, specify the font you want to replace in the Replace drop-down list box, specify the new font in the With drop-down list box, and then click Replace.

Embossing Text
Using the Font Dialog Box

If you don't feel like using the Formatting toolbar, or you want to create several formatting effects at once, you can also choose Font from the

FIGURE 28-3.
The Font dialog box gives you complete control over the look of your text.

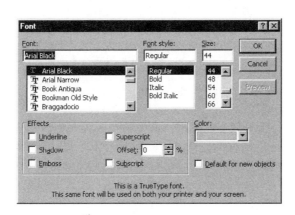

You can use the Colors And Lines command on the Format menu to create special text formatting effects such as rotating text, changing the scale, and customizing the text background color. Since this command also applies to formatting graphic images, we cover it in the next chapter. See "Formatting Text and Graphics: Advanced Techniques," page 739.

Format menu and use the Font dialog box. (See Figure 28-3.) You can use this standard dialog box to make all the formatting changes covered in the previous section. In addition, you can apply a few other special effects, such as embossing and superscript, using the Font command.

If you have used Word or Excel, you'll recognize the placement of most formatting options in the Font dialog box. However, the Superscript and Subscript check boxes are different. Using an offset value, these options in PowerPoint 2000 allow you to control how much a character is raised or lowered on a line. Superscript reduces the font size of characters and then elevates them above the standard line of text. The higher the offset percentage you specify, the higher the characters will go. Conversely, the Subscript option reduces the font size of characters and then lowers them below the standard line of text. As you increase the Subscript offset by a negative percentage, the selected characters will drop lower and lower.

The Emboss check box creates a variation on PowerPoint's shadow text effect. When you select Emboss, PowerPoint surrounds each character with a combination of light and dark outlines so the letters appear to be raised. The exact combination of colors PowerPoint uses depends on the slide's background color. Embossing generally works best with fonts that produce thick characters or with headline-sized text (16-point or larger) that is formatted as bold.

You can format text either to have a shadow or to appear embossed, but not both.

Changing Text Alignment

PowerPoint's templates include default text-alignment settings for placeholders. For example, titles are often centered and text is usually aligned flush left. (The flush-left alignment, with its ragged-right edge, is the easiest alignment for your viewers' eyes to skim.) These alignment settings work for most slides; however, you might want to change the existing alignment or create new text that has a different alignment. You can choose among Align Left, Center, Align Right, and Justify (both margins even) alignment options. Figure 28-4 shows a left-aligned title and right-aligned text.

FIGURE 28-4.
Changing alignment can help you create open spaces for artwork and other objects.

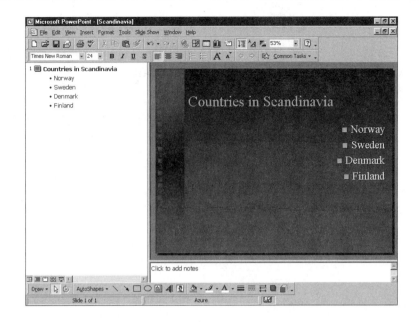

To change text alignment, follow these steps:

1 Select the text you want to align. (Either select individual lines of text using the mouse, or select entire text placeholders.)

2 Click one of the alignment buttons on the Formatting toolbar (Align Left, Center, or Align Right). To apply justified alignment—a formatting option that aligns text to both left and right margins—click the Format menu, point to the Alignment submenu, and then click Justify. (Be careful with Justify, however—it only creates useful effects when you have a lot of text on your slide.)

TIP

Use Borders for Alignment

PowerPoint uses the left and right sides of the text object to determine where it positions your text. You can move these borders to change the position of text on the slide. For example, if you wanted to align your bullets under the word *Scandinavia* in the title, you could position the mouse pointer over the left edge of the text object so that it becomes a two-headed arrow and then drag the border over to the letter *S*. With the left edge of the text object under the *S* and left alignment selected, the bullets would fall in a straight line below the word *Scandinavia*.

Changing Line Spacing

Just as the template defines fonts, color, and other characteristics for a presentation, it also defines line and paragraph spacing for text in a text object. PowerPoint lets you add spacing before or after selected paragraphs, and it allows you to change the amount of line spacing between the lines. For example, you might want to increase the line spacing between each item in a bulleted or numbered list.

Follow these steps to change line spacing or paragraph spacing in a text placeholder:

1 Select the text for which you want to change the line or paragraph spacing. If you're changing the spacing in a bulleted list, select the entire text object so that your choices will affect the entire list.

2 Choose Line Spacing from the Format menu to display the Line Spacing dialog box, as shown here.

3 Click the arrows or enter a number in this box to change the vertical spacing between lines.

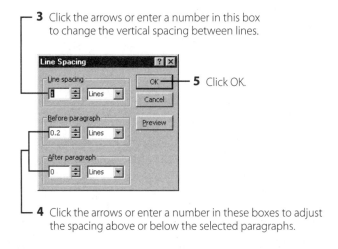

5 Click OK.

4 Click the arrows or enter a number in these boxes to adjust the spacing above or below the selected paragraphs.

If you change the Line Spacing setting (using the first pair of boxes), the space is added proportionately above and below each line within a paragraph. When your paragraphs consist of single lines of text, that's the same as adding the space between each entry. If, however, the text consists of paragraphs containing more than one line of text, space will appear between each pair of lines within each paragraph. For example, enter 2 in this box if you want double-spaced text.

You will often want to add space between the paragraphs on your slide, but not to the lines within the paragraphs. You can use either the Before Paragraph or After Paragraph settings (using the second and third pairs of boxes) to add space before or after the paragraph, without changing the amount of space between the pairs of lines within the paragraph.

⭐ **TIP**

> **Typesetters, Welcome**
>
> When you want even more precise control of your line spacing, you can specify spacing options in printer's points (72 points per inch) rather than in lines. If you use this measurement scale, be sure to specify Points in the appropriate drop-down list box in the Line Spacing dialog box next to the spacing measurement that you're adjusting.

Working with Bullets and Numbering

Bullets are useful when you need to present a list of items that aren't a series of sequential steps. Numbering is helpful when you want to rank the items in a list. When you use a bulleted-list placeholder, Power-Point enters the bullets automatically. You can also insert a bullet in front of any paragraph that you type, including text in the text objects that you create. Simply type a paragraph (usually consisting of a single line of text) on the slide, and then click the Bullets button on the Formatting toolbar. PowerPoint adds a bullet at the beginning of your text. If you change your mind and no longer want the bullet, click anywhere in the paragraph that contains the bullet, and then click the Bullets button again to toggle the bullet off. To insert a numbered list on a slide, follow the same procedure, but instead of clicking the Bullets button, click the new Numbering button on the Formatting toolbar.

When you're feeling creative, you can turn almost any picture or graphic that you want into a bullet. In PowerPoint 2000, you can search your own picture files, import a piece of clip art from the Web, or select one of PowerPoint's pictures to use as a bullet.

To try a different bullet style, follow these steps:

1 Select the bulleted-list object.

2 Choose Bullets And Numbering from the Format menu. Then complete the Bullets And Numbering dialog box, as shown in the following illustration.

3 Select the Bulleted tab, if necessary.

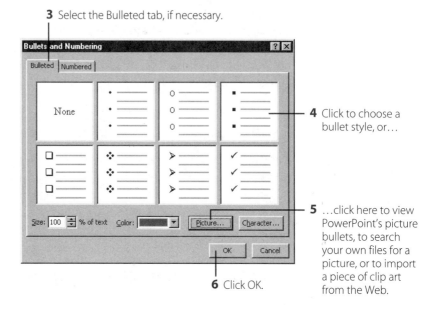

4 Click to choose a bullet style, or…

5 …click here to view PowerPoint's picture bullets, to search your own files for a picture, or to import a piece of clip art from the Web.

6 Click OK.

You can also turn any character into a bullet, as well as change its color and size. For example, as shown in Figure 28-5, you can choose a heart-shaped bullet from the Monotype Sorts font for the bulleted items, make it red, and then increase its size by 125 percent and use it as a decorative element.

To use a PowerPoint character as a bullet, follow these steps:

1 Select the bulleted-list object.

2 Choose Bullets And Numbering from the Format menu.

3 Click the Bulleted tab. Then click the Character button and complete the Bullet dialog box, as shown in the following illustration.

7 Change the bullet color here (optional).

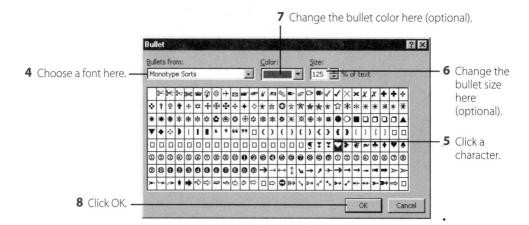

4 Choose a font here.

6 Change the bullet size here (optional).

5 Click a character.

8 Click OK.

If you increase the size of the bullet relative to the font, you might need to add some space before your text to provide enough room for the bullet. (This kerning problem is evident in Figure 28-5.) To correct this problem, you need to adjust the paragraph indentation, as described in the next section.

FIGURE 28-5.
On this slide, the default bullets were changed to red hearts that are 125 percent of default font size.

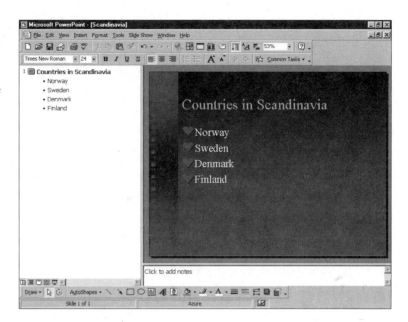

Changing Paragraph Indentations

If you adjust the size of text or bullets, you might also need to adjust the paragraph indentation set up in the template so that enough space exists between the text and bullets and so that the text aligns correctly. To do this, follow these steps:

1 Choose Ruler from the View menu to turn on the horizontal and vertical rulers.

2 Click within the text object you want to modify. The ruler will show the markers for the template's default indentation. Drag the lower triangle-shaped indent marker to change indentation for the text following the bullet and to align any additional lines in the paragraph at the same point. As you drag, you'll see a vertical dotted line, which helps you position the marker.

Drag this marker to increase indentation and
add space between bullet characters and text.

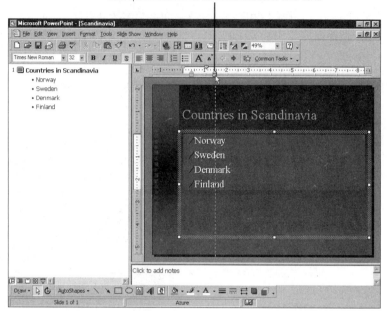

Changing the Template

A design template is a file that contains special graphics elements, colors, font sizes, font styles, slide backgrounds, and diverse special effects. PowerPoint provides dozens of professionally designed templates for you to choose from. The Azure template we've been using in this chapter is one of them.

When you create a new presentation, you can choose a template when you're prompted to do so. You can also choose a template and apply it to your presentation after you have already created your slides; just make sure that your presentation is on screen when you want to change the template.

To change templates, click Apply Design Template on the Common Tasks toolbar. Then complete the following dialog box:

2 This area shows a preview of the selected design. Try different templates until you see the one you like.

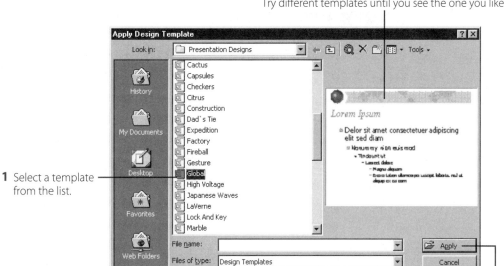

1 Select a template from the list.

3 Click Apply to attach the selected template to the current presentation.

In the following illustration, we changed the Azure template to the Global template. (Notice that our custom heart bullets and the paragraph indentation are still the same, though. PowerPoint doesn't change the formatting elements that you entered on your own, even if they conflict with styles in the new template.)

Changing the Background Color and Shading

If you want to brighten up your presentation or simply give it a different look and feel, you can change the background color and shading for one slide—or for all slides.

> For overhead transparencies, use a light background; for on-screen presentations and 35mm slides, use a dark background.

To change the color scheme, right-click anywhere on the slide itself (not in a placeholder), and then choose Slide Color Scheme from the shortcut menu. (Alternatively, you can choose Slide Color Scheme from the Format menu.) Using either approach, you'll see the following dialog box:

1 Click the Standard tab, if necessary.

2 Click to choose one of the standard color schemes.

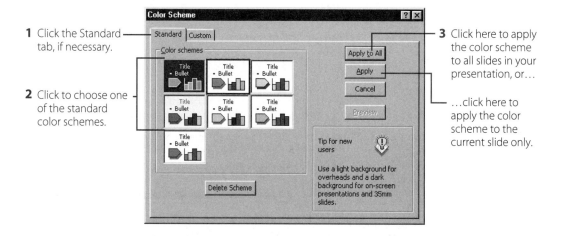

3 Click here to apply the color scheme to all slides in your presentation, or…

…click here to apply the color scheme to the current slide only.

Create a Custom Scheme

If you are artistic, or if you simply enjoy experimenting, you can customize your own color scheme. Click the Custom tab of the Color Scheme dialog box, click the presentation element you want to adjust (the current color is displayed in a box beside the element name), click the Change Color button, and pick a new color. Use this technique to customize each element in your presentation. When you're finished, click the Add As Standard Scheme button, and PowerPoint will save your custom scheme on the Standard tab of the Color Scheme dialog box. Go ahead and try it—it really can be a lot of fun.

Creating a New Background

Using PowerPoint's Background feature, you can create your own background design for all the slides in your presentation. You can start out by making a simple change to the background design by choosing a different color from several color choices. If you want to, you can apply a custom color. If you prefer a fancier background, you can add shading, texture, a pattern, or even a picture (say, your company's graphic logo).

If you really want to impress your audience, you can use a gradient fill, in which the color is darkest on one side of the slide and slowly becomes lighter toward the other side of the slide. For example, you can have a dark blue fill at the top of the slide, medium blue in the middle, and lighter blue toward the bottom of the slide. The direction of the gradient can be horizontal, vertical, or at any angle in between. You can use the Gradient tab (described below) to set your own gradient fill or choose from one of the predesigned gradient fills.

To create a new background design, follow these steps:

1 Choose Background from the Format menu or right-click anywhere (except in a placeholder) on the slide that you want to change, and choose Background from the shortcut menu. Using either approach, you'll see the following dialog box:

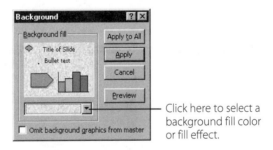

Click here to select a background fill color or fill effect.

2 From the drop-down list for the Background Fill options, choose the background fill color that you want. (If the color you want isn't listed, click More Colors, and choose a custom color.)

3 To create a custom fill effect for your slide background, click the drop-down list box, and click Fill Effects.

You'll see the following dialog box, which presents tabs that control the fill gradient, the wallpaper texture, the fill pattern, and an optional picture.

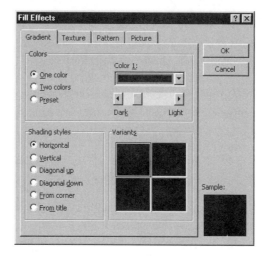

4 Pick the settings for your new background, and then click OK to close the Fill Effects dialog box.

5 Click Apply To All if you want the new background added to each slide in your presentation, or click Apply if you want to modify only the current slide.

The following illustration shows a picture background that we created by loading a bitmap (.bmp) file using the Picture tab of the Fill Effects dialog box. A background design, such as the globe bitmap pictured here, can be used to tie your slide show together by emphasizing particular slides.

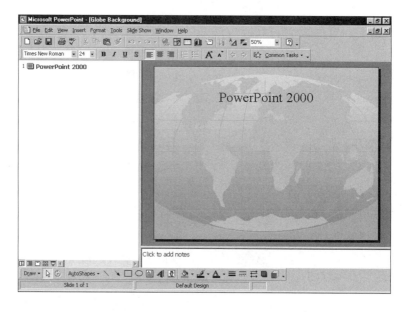

(W) ON THE WEB   The Globe.ppt file is located on the Running Office 2000 Reader's Corner page. For information about connecting to this Web site, read the Introduction.

Editing the Slide Master and the Title Master

After reviewing your presentation, you might decide that you want to change the default formatting for text on your slide. Perhaps you'd like to try a different font or a larger font size for your slide titles. You can make these changes to the *Slide Master* (which controls all the slides in your presentation) or to the *Title Master* (which controls the formatting of title slides).

Formatting the Slide Master

All slides in your presentation are initially formatted based on the Slide Master, which sets the font formatting and text object positions for the slides. Whether the slide contains a bulleted list, a table, text and graphics, or an organization chart, its format is still based on the Slide Master. You can use the placeholders on the Slide Master to control the formatting and position of the title and text on any slide in your presentation.

To customize the Slide Master, complete the following steps:

1 Point to Master on the View menu, and then choose Slide Master from the submenu. The Slide Master appears, as shown on the next page.

  Notice that the Slide Master has several distinct areas. You can format the title for your slides as well as the information that appears in the Date, Footer, and Number regions. The Slide Master also shows several text entries in the main body of the slide.

  Each of these entries corresponds to one level of text on the slide. As we discussed in Chapter 27, you can also view as an outline all the information that you put on a PowerPoint slide. Each of the different levels of entries on the Slide Master formats a different level of text in your outline. You can also change the standard bullet character that each level uses, though a level uses the same text formatting whether the entry displays the bullet or not.

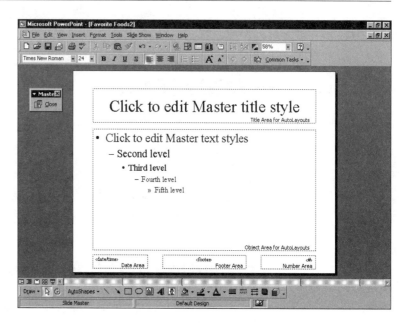

2 Select the placeholder for the area that you want to change, or select the text for the outline level that you want to change.

3 To make any changes that you want, use the Formatting toolbar's controls and the Format menu's commands, or adjust the indentation settings on the ruler.

4 When you're finished, click the Close button on the Master toolbar that floats above the Slide Master to return to Slide view.

Cast New Bullets

To change the bullet style, click in the object area, and then click the bulleted item that you want to change. Choose Bullets And Numbering from the Format menu, and choose a bullet style, picture, or character in the Bullets And Numbering dialog box. Then click OK to confirm your choices. You'll see the new bullet style in the Slide Master's object area.

Formatting the Title Master

Almost all presentations start with a slide that contains the title of the presentation and the subtitle, if any. This slide is called the *title slide* and might also contain information about the presentation (such as when it was created, or for what audience). In addition, you might use title slides within a presentation to separate the major sections.

You can insert a separate Title Master if you want all the title slides to be based on this rather than on the more general Slide Master. You can position and format five areas on the Title Master: Title, Subtitle, Date, Footer, and Number. To create and customize the Title Master, complete the following steps:

1 Point to Master on the View menu, and then choose Title Master from the submenu. The Title Master appears, as shown here:

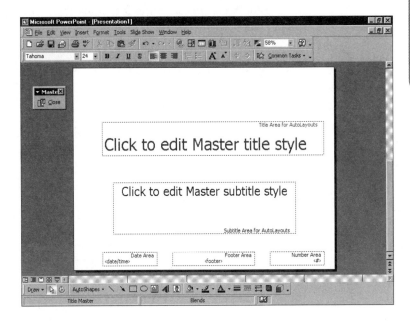

2 Select the text placeholder that you want to change.

3 If you like, apply different formatting effects by using the tools on the Formatting toolbar or the commands on the Format menu. Experiment with the font, font size, style, color, and special effects.

4 When you're finished, click the Close button on the Master toolbar that floats above the Title Master, to return to Slide view.

Any formatting changes that you make to the text objects on the Title Master are then applied to any title slides within your presentation. Only information that is still in the standard format is changed. If you have made manual changes to the formatting of a title slide (using the techniques discussed in the first section of this chapter), that formatting is maintained. You can change the position of objects on your title slides by moving the objects on the Title Master.

If you find the distinction between the Title Master and the Slide Master confusing, an easy solution exists. If you hold down the Shift key while clicking the Slide View button in the lower left corner of your Power-Point window (just above PowerPoint's status bar), you're taken to either the Title Slide or the Master Slide, depending on which one controls the formatting of the current slide. When you use this approach, you're always taken to the proper place for changing the standard formatting. To return to the actual slide in your presentation, click the Slide View button without holding the Shift key.

CHAPTER 29

Inserting Tables, Graphics, and Drawings

E nhancing the text in a bulleted list on a slide isn't the only way to add zip to your presentation. You can use other slide layouts and add graphics to your presentation—a table, a chart, an organization chart, clip art, and even your own drawing. By peppering these graphics throughout your slide show, you can make your point quickly and effectively. Don't get carried away, though. When you use too many visual effects, you can make your presentation look overdesigned and confusing. Keep it as clear and simple as possible.

Microsoft PowerPoint is designed to take advantage of the work that you do in other programs. Because of this, the techniques discussed in this chapter rely on other programs included with Microsoft Office. For example, you can create tables in PowerPoint 2000 just as you do in Microsoft Word, insert worksheets and charts from Microsoft Excel, use Microsoft Organization Chart to create an organization chart, use the Microsoft Clip Gallery as a source for clip art images, or create a drawing using the standard Drawing toolbar that is also featured in Word and Excel.

Inserting a Table

Adding tables to your slide presentation is an excellent way to show important trends and relationships among groups of data. You can use tables to summarize facts and figures—for example, a two-column table containing your competition's product features in one column and your product features in the other. It's a good idea to keep the table nice and simple, having no more than two or three columns and three or four rows, as shown in Figure 29-1. (When you want to illustrate the patterns in more complex data, you can insert a graph instead; see "Inserting a Chart" later in this chapter.)

Don't Table Tables

PowerPoint's table feature is like the one in Word, the formatting king of word processing programs. Yet, in our experience, many Word and PowerPoint users resist using tables because they suspect that learning them will be difficult and that the process will only take valuable time away from their projects. (Rather than use tables, they enter data in columns using the Tab technique, doing their best to line up text using the Tab and Spacebar keys.) However, tables are truly useful organizational structures that will pay handsome formatting dividends if you use them wisely. In addition, tables make adding, editing, and deleting entries much easier than they would be using the brute force Tab method. Take the time to learn this feature in Word and PowerPoint, and you'll save yourself time down the road.

You can create a table that has numbers, words, or both in a PowerPoint slide. Follow these steps to see how it works:

1 Display the slide in which you're going to create the table.

2 Click the Insert Table button on the Standard toolbar or click Table on the Insert menu.

3 In the table grid, drag right and down to select the number of columns and rows that you need. When you release the mouse button, the blank table is inserted into the current slide.

Notice that the Tables And Border toolbar automatically appears, as shown in Figure 29-1. (This will be the case whenever the table is active on your slide.) Feel free to use the formatting commands on this toolbar (as described in the following section) to further customize your table.

3 x 3 Table

4 In your blank table, click in each cell and enter the data. You can also move from cell to cell by using the Tab key or the arrow keys. (When you reach the bottom of the table, pressing Tab adds additional rows to the table.)

5 When you're finished, click the slide background to close the table.

TIP

New
Slide

Slide in a Table

Another way to add a table to your presentation is to add a table slide. Simply click the New Slide button on the Standard toolbar or the New Slide button on the Common Tasks toolbar, and choose the Table AutoLayout. Double-click the table placeholder in the center of your slide, and specify the number of columns and rows that you need in the Insert Table dialog box. Voilà! There's your table.

FIGURE 29-1.
When a table is active on a PowerPoint slide, the Tables And Borders toolbar automatically appears.

Tables And Borders toolbar

Table

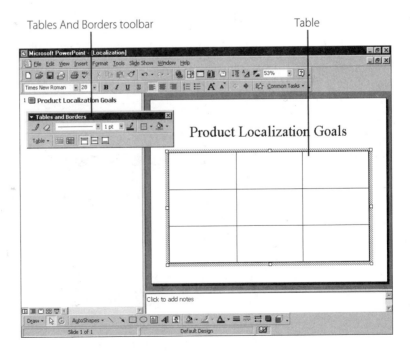

To learn more about
working with tables,
see "Using Tables,"
page 229.

In PowerPoint 2000, tables are handled *natively*, which means that they
open right in PowerPoint, right on your slide. This new feature lets you
quickly perform simple editing tasks on your table by double-clicking
within the table area and making your changes. Use the Tab key or the
arrow keys to move from one cell to another within the table. To correct typos and make simple changes to the data, use the standard editing conventions such as overtype, insert, delete, copy, and move.

If a column is too narrow or too wide, move the mouse pointer to the
column border until the pointer changes to a double vertical bar with
left and right arrows, and then drag the column border to change the
width. You can do the same for a row to make the row shorter or taller.

You can make more involved changes to your table (inserting and deleting rows and columns, changing the format, column width, row height,
and so on) by trying out the formatting options available from the Format
menu and the Tables And Borders toolbar, as described below.

Formatting a Table

Just as formatting the text in your slide presentations makes it easier for
your audience to grasp the information you're presenting, formatting
tables adds clarity to your presentations. You can emphasize the relationships among groups of data by adding shading to a column heading, distinguish groups of cells by giving them their own color scheme, or use a
bold line for the outside border of your table to sharply define it.

When the table is active on your slide, click the Format menu, and then
click Table. The Borders tab of the Format Table dialog box appears, as
shown in Figure 29-2. The Borders tab lets you modify the style, color,
and width of the border around each cell, column, row, or the entire

FIGURE 29-2.

The Borders tab of
the Format Table
dialog box.

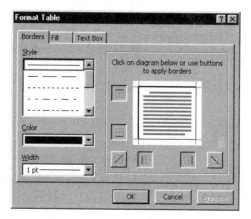

table itself. The Format Table dialog box includes two other tabs as well. The Fill tab lets you select a fill or background color for the table or elements in the table, and the Text Box tab allows you to change the text alignment, adjust the center point, or rotate the text within the cells of your table. (You'll meet a similar dialog box later in this chapter when you explore advanced formatting for text and drawing objects.)

You can also use the Tables And Borders toolbar if you want to fine-tune the appearance of your table. The buttons on this toolbar let you draw your own table, make corrections using the eraser tool, adjust the line size, and insert or delete columns and rows.

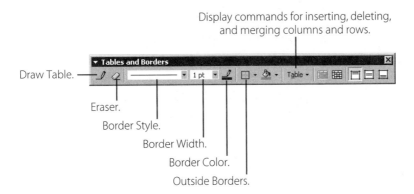

Display commands for inserting, deleting, and merging columns and rows.

Draw Table.

Eraser.

Border Style.

Border Width.

Border Color.

Outside Borders.

Inserting a Chart

Many slide presentations include a set of numbers of some kind—projected sales figures for next year, for example, or comparisons of market trends. Long rows of numbers are excruciatingly boring to look at and—worse—difficult to understand, especially in the short time your audience has to grasp their meaning. A chart can provide quick visual cues to the trends and comparisons that you want your audience to understand, and is a more suitable choice for conveying complex data than a simple table.

To use a chart on a slide, you first need to select a slide layout that has an appropriate placeholder. PowerPoint offers three choices, as shown in Figure 29-3, on the next page. You can insert a new slide and select the slide layout from the New Slide dialog box. You can also convert an existing slide by choosing Slide Layout from the Format menu or by clicking the Slide Layout button on the Common Tasks toolbar and then selecting a layout in the Slide Layout dialog box.

FIGURE 29-3.
Any of these slide layouts let you add a graph to your slide.

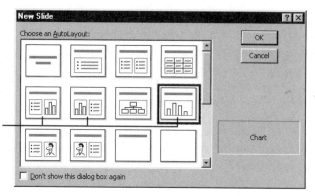

These three slide layouts include a chart.

After you have selected a slide layout containing a chart placeholder, you can add a chart to the slide in two different ways.

Inset Chart

- You can use Excel to create the chart, copy it to the Clipboard, and then paste it onto your slide. The advantage of this technique is that you can use all of Excel's tools for managing your data and creating your graph. In addition, you can use existing charts that have already been created and saved in Excel workbooks.

- You can use Microsoft Graph 2000, a utility program (like Microsoft Organization Chart) that's included in Office 2000. To open Graph, you simply double-click the chart placeholder on your slide or click the Insert Chart button on PowerPoint's Standard toolbar.

When Graph opens in PowerPoint, you'll see a new menu bar, a new toolbar, and a datasheet (like a spreadsheet) that contains *dummy* (placeholder) words and numbers for your chart. Beneath the datasheet will be a column chart, as shown in Figure 29-4.

(?) SEE ALSO

Using Graph and its various tools is also discussed in Chapter 51, "Sharing Data Among Office Applications."

To customize this chart with your own information, modify the dummy chart one cell at a time, or click the Select All button in the upper left corner of the datasheet, press Delete to clear all the dummy information, and rebuild the whole chart. (We recommend that you modify the datasheet one cell at a time until you're comfortable with the placement of the row and column labels.) Like magic, you see the chart change each time you enter new data in a cell.

Using the buttons on Graph's Standard toolbar, you can import data from Excel worksheets to replace the data in the current datasheet,

FIGURE 29-4.
The Graph utility opens a dummy datasheet when you open a chart in PowerPoint.

Graph toolbar
Graph menu bar
Datasheet window
Select All button

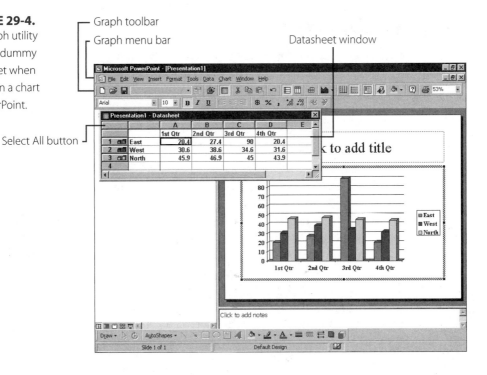

change the chart type from the default vertical-column chart to one of a variety of 2-D or 3-D charts, turn the display of the datasheet window on or off, and modify the chart colors. (For more charting commands, explore the Graph menus.)

Import File   Chart Type

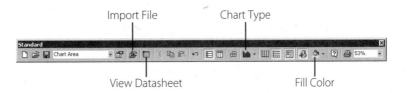

View Datasheet   Fill Color

⭐ TIP

When you want your audience to see at a glance who's who in a company, you can create an organization chart that will display the hierarchy in a readable format. Choose the Organization Chart AutoLayout from the New Slide dialog box, and let the Organization Chart utility do the artwork for you. *For more information on working with the Organization Chart program, see Chapter 51, "Sharing Data Among Office Applications."*

Adding Clip Art

You can add excitement and visual interest to your slide presentation by choosing an evocative piece of clip art. PowerPoint's clip art library contains more than a thousand professionally prepared pictures that will enhance a wide range of topics. Figure 29-5 shows one example, added to new text.

In PowerPoint 2000 you can drag images from the Clip Gallery onto any slide in your presentation, whether or not it contains a clip art place-holder. You can also use two slide AutoLayouts to insert clip art onto a slide. As with other graphics, you can add a new slide (by using the New Slide command on the Insert menu or the New Slide button on either the Standard or Common Tasks toolbar), or you can convert an existing slide (using the Slide Layout command on the Format menu or the Slide Layout button on the Common Tasks toolbar). You can use both these approaches to create a slide that contains a clip art placeholder. You can then double-click the placeholder to start the Clip Gallery.

> **NOTE**
>
> PowerPoint 2000 includes new clip art categories that can add polish to your Web pages. They're listed in the Insert ClipArt dialog box. Experiment with some of these Web graphics the next time you're building a Web page (for example, Web Background, Web Banners, or Web Bullets & Buttons) to guarantee that your site gets noticed.

FIGURE 29-5.
Placing a clip art object next to bulleted text adds visual interest to your presentation.

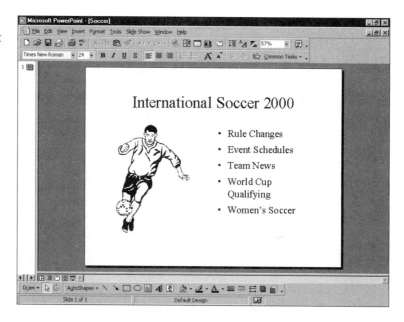

To use the Clip Gallery, follow these steps:

1 Display the slide that contains the clip art placeholder. If necessary, add a new slide using the Insert New Slide button or convert an existing slide using Slide Layout on the Format menu.

2 Double-click the clip art placeholder to display the Microsoft Clip Gallery dialog box, shown below, and then select the category of clips you'd like to view by clicking one of the subject areas.

   Notice that when you point to a clip in that category, you will see a Screen Tip that describes the clip.

3 Click the clip you want to insert. A toolbar appears containing buttons that let you insert the clip, preview it, add it to the Favorites category, or find other, similar clips. Click Insert Clip. Or you can simply drag the clip to your slide without using this toolbar.

? **SEE ALSO**

Working with different types of images is discussed in "Adding Graphics," page 320.

4 The clip art image appears surrounded by handles, and you can move it or resize it to fit your presentation needs. The Picture toolbar also appears when you insert clip art (or when you point to Toolbars on the View menu and then click Picture), and you can use its buttons to refine the color and presentation of the image considerably.

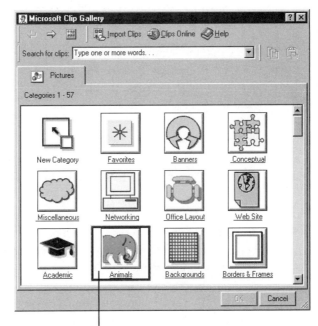

Image category selected

> ### Images Galore!
>
> If you want more images to choose from, you can buy packages of clip art (in black-and-white or color) from software stores and mail-order catalogs. These clip art libraries are packaged by topics such as animals, business, holidays, music, people, and so on. If you want more professional artwork, look for photo collections, which are usually sold on CD-ROMs.

Insert
Clip Art

You can also add a clip art image to your slide by clicking the Insert Clip Art button on the Drawing toolbar, which opens the Insert ClipArt dialog box.

> If you want to, you can add a piece of clip art to your Master Slide so that every slide in your presentation contains the same image.

Drawing a Graphic Object

Despite the huge variety of wonderful clip art that's available, you still might not be able to find that perfect image. Or perhaps you'd just prefer to create your own art. In either case, you don't have to be a talented artist to create vibrant, eye-catching graphics.

By default, the Drawing toolbar appears at the bottom of the PowerPoint window. This toolbar is also available in Word and Excel, so once you learn how to use it in one application, you'll have the skills necessary to use it in all the Office programs. (If the Drawing toolbar isn't visible, display it by pointing to Toolbars on the View menu and then clicking the Drawing toolbar.)

Working with Drawing Objects

We've already covered the Drawing toolbar in Chapter 10, so we won't repeat the detailed information given there about creating Drawing illustrations. *(To review these instructions, see "Creating Drawings in Word," page 323.)* If you have only a few minutes to experiment with creating drawing objects, we recommend that you begin with the AutoShapes menu on the Drawing toolbar. PowerPoint 2000 includes 55 new AutoShapes that you can access by clicking More AutoShapes on this toolbar. Many of these new AutoShapes are suitable for use as Web elements.

Using AutoShapes, you can create a variety of predefined shapes, including flowchart symbols, arrows, banners, and action buttons, and you can also create your own free-form drawings by selecting one of the pen shapes in the Lines category. For example, we created the shapes shown in Figure 29-6 using a few of the more popular tools from the AutoShapes menu. (The figure also shows an example of WordArt, as well as the Line, Rectangle, and Oval tools.)

When you use the Drawing toolbar to create an image on your slide, it becomes an object that you can resize, copy, move, format, and delete. Like other objects on a PowerPoint slide, drawing objects are surrounded by selection handles when they're selected. (In Figure 29-6, a rectangle object has been selected.) Before you can change an attribute of a drawing object, you must select it.

 ON THE WEB

The Draw.ppt file is located on the Running Office 2000 Reader's Corner page. For information about connecting to this Web site, read the Introduction.

After you create your illustration, you can use commands on the Drawing toolbar's Draw menu to format or edit your object. For example, if you created one AutoShape on your slide and you want to exchange it for another, simply select the object, click the Draw menu on the Drawing toolbar, point to Change AutoShape, and choose a new AutoShape from the submenu. Or, if you want to change the orientation of an object (in other words, if you want to spin the object on its axis), select

FIGURE 29-6.
The Drawing toolbar lets you create your own electronic artwork for presentations.

Banner AutoShape

Drawing toolbar

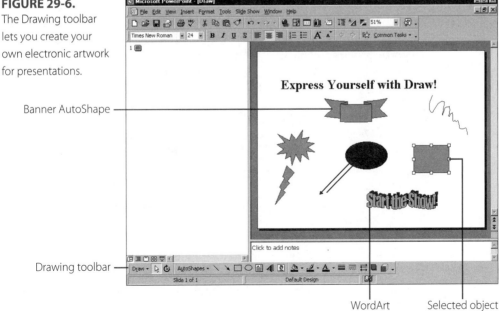

WordArt   Selected object

the object, point to Rotate Or Flip on the Draw menu, and choose one of the rotate or flip commands from the submenu.

Perhaps the most useful set of commands on the Draw menu are those that let you create groups of objects. By creating a group, you can use a single command to change all the objects at once. For example, when you want to perform an action, such as adding a fill color, to more than one object at a time, select the first object and then hold down the Shift key while you select additional objects. Next, choose Group from the Draw menu. The objects are now grouped together into one object. After that, you'll notice that all the objects in the group share a single set of sizing handles.

If you change your mind and no longer want to group a collection of objects, select the object group and choose Ungroup from the Draw menu.

Working with Layers

Like the numerous bands of soil and artifacts that collectively compose an archeological site, each drawing object that is placed on a slide exists on its own layer. This means that some drawing objects (including those closer to the top of the pile) can appear to cover up parts of other objects (those toward the bottom of the pile). If you plan the order in which you create your drawing objects, you can use this feature to create interesting combination effects.

New objects are always drawn at the very front of the slide (on the top of the pile). Because objects toward the front of the slide can cover up those toward the back, it's often necessary to change the order of the objects. Fortunately, some commands on the Drawing toolbar's Draw menu serve just that purpose.

If you want an object to appear behind all the other objects (so that those objects can hide part of the object in the back), select the object, point to Order on the Draw menu, and then choose Send To Back from the submenu. Or, if you want an object to appear at the very front of the slide (so that all of it is visible and it covers up parts of the objects behind it), select the object and then choose Bring To Front from the Order submenu. If you're setting the order for a large number of objects, you can fine-tune the sequence using the Send Backward and Bring Forward commands, which move objects through the pile one step at a time. Because text doesn't look good when it's partially obscured, do your best to create it last so that it always remains on the top of the pile.

Formatting Text and Graphics: Advanced Techniques

In addition to using the commands on the Drawing toolbar, which deal specifically with drawing objects, you can also control the appearance of the text and graphic objects on your slides by using a dialog box that creates interesting formatting effects. You can display this dialog box by choosing either the Colors And Lines command or the last command on the Format menu (labeled AutoShape, Picture, Text Box, and so forth, depending on what's selected). In either case, a dialog box appears that has five formatting tabs. The name of the dialog box and what you can do with it depends on the type of object you selected before selecting the command. In some cases, all the tabs and options are available—in others, only a few. We'll refer to the dialog box generally as the Format AutoShape dialog box.

The following sections describe each of the formatting tabs of the Format AutoShape dialog box.

Using the Colors and Lines Tab

When you choose Colors And Lines from the Format menu, the Colors And Lines tab of the Format AutoShape dialog box appears, as shown in Figure 29-7. The Colors And Lines tab lets you modify the type of line used in the object you have selected and (if applicable) modify the fill color and arrow styles. If a text placeholder is highlighted, you can select a fill color for the interior of the text box and the characteristics of the border around the text box. If a line is highlighted, you can add

FIGURE 29-7.

The Colors And Lines tab of the Format AutoShape dialog box.

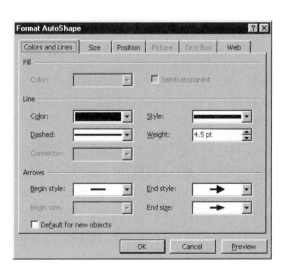

an arrowhead to make it an arrow, change the thickness of the line, or vary the line color.

Using the Size Tab

When a piece of clip art or other electronic artwork is selected, the Size tab of the Format Picture dialog box, shown in Figure 29-8, let's you modify the artwork's size and scale. Because most clip art is resizable, you can often create well-proportioned effects by adjusting the Height and Width options in the Scale area of the dialog box to shrink or expand the image. If the Lock Aspect Ratio check box is selected (the default), all the Height and Width text boxes change in tandem when you modify one of them, preserving the relative dimensions, or *aspect ratio*, of the image.

FIGURE 29-8.
The Size tab of the Format Picture dialog box.

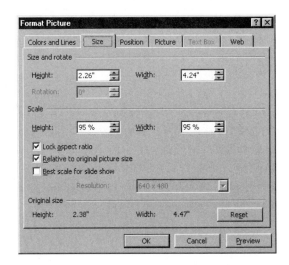

The Rotation option lets you change the orientation of text placeholders or AutoShape graphics, measured in relative degrees around an imagined circle. (The Rotation spin buttons adjust the orientation in 1-degree increments, starting at 0 and moving up to 360.) Using this feature, you can create text boxes that tilt at an angle—a compelling effect if used judiciously.

Using the Position Tab

The Position tab, shown in Figure 29-9, is a relatively straightforward feature that controls the placement of an object on the slide. It allows you to specify horizontal measurement and vertical measurements for the object,

FIGURE 29-9.
The Position tab of
the Format AutoShape
dialog box.

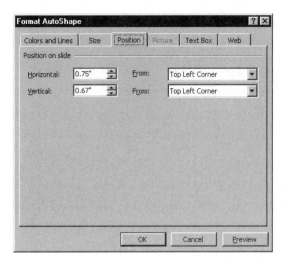

measured from the edge of the slide. To help you fine-tune your alignment, this tab also lets you specify the place in the object from which the alignment measurement is taken. The default setting is the upper left corner, though you can also measure from the center of the object, a useful location when you're trying to center an object on a slide.

Using the Picture Tab

The Picture tab, shown in Figure 29-10 on the following page, is a sophisticated editing tool for clip art, photographs, and other images. To trim or crop the highlighted picture, use the Left, Right, Top, and Bottom text boxes in the Crop From portion of the dialog box. Crop measurements are taken from the edge of the picture; positive measurements trim the image in from the edge, while negative measurements add white space to the picture.

The Image Control portion of the Picture tab lets you control the color, brightness, and contrast of the picture you're including in your presentation. The Color drop-down list box contains four options especially useful for people who want to prepare their images for different types of presentations:

- The Automatic option is the default setting and displays the image in its original representation.

- Grayscale converts a color picture to shades of black-and-white (each color converts to an equivalent grayscale level).

FIGURE 29-10.
The Picture tab of
the Format Picture
dialog box.

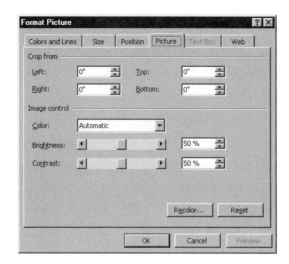

- Black & White converts a picture to true black-and-white, or *line art*, which can be printed by devices that are incapable of grayscale printing.

- Watermark converts a picture to a bright, low-contrast image that looks good when placed behind everything else on a slide. (Some of the PowerPoint templates use Watermark images.)

Using the Text Box Tab

The Text Box tab, shown in Figure 29-11, is an advanced formatting option designed for text placeholders and Draw AutoShapes that can hold text (such as the Banner AutoShapes). The Text Anchor Point drop-down list box lets you adjust the center point for text within a placeholder. PowerPoint also lets you set the anchor point to the top or bottom of the placeholder, and you can further adjust the placement of text by choosing one of the centered anchor points or by using the alignment buttons on PowerPoint's Formatting toolbar.

The Text Box tab allows you to set the internal margins of a text box, which is especially useful for text boxes containing bulleted lists. In addition, you can control how text flows inside an AutoShape object (such as a banner) by using the Word Wrap, Resize AutoShape, and Rotate Text check boxes on the Text Box tab.

FIGURE 29-11.
The Text Box tab of
the Format AutoShape
dialog box.

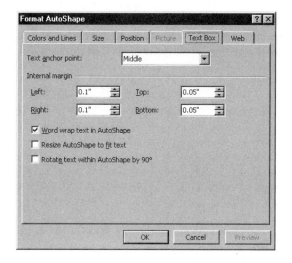

Using the Web Tab

The Web tab, shown in Figure 29-12, is a new formatting option available in PowerPoint 2000. If you are presenting your slide show on the Web, you will want to courteously include a bit of alternative text that will appear if your image doesn't show up right away. In the box, you type the text that you want to accompany your graphic. You can type as much text as you want, but try to keep it short and sweet, because some browsers won't be able to display all the text, and your viewers just need a hint of what's to come or what they've missed.

FIGURE 29-12.
The Web tab of
the Format Picture
dialog box.

Although working with PowerPoint's many text and graphic formatting options takes a little practice, your efforts will pay big dividends in your presentations. PowerPoint slide shows have become popular and recognizable, so a few special effects are likely to impress your audience and bring admiring comments and questions afterwards: "Wow! Good show!" and "How did you do that, anyway?"

Adding Special Effects and Internet Links

Microsoft PowerPoint's basic formatting effects create solid, compelling presentations. But if you really want to grab your audience's attention, you should consider adding one or more multimedia elements to your presentation. In this chapter, we'll explore the most compelling special effects you can create in a PowerPoint presentation. You'll learn how to add animation effects, such as objects that move and flashy slide transitions, and you'll learn how to insert video, sound, and narration clips in your show. In addition, you'll learn how to create action buttons that let you move to a specific slide or to a supporting presentation, or even to a home page on the World Wide Web. By carefully balancing this combination of special effects—video, music, sound, animation, and Web resources—you can make your slide show explode with life and energy.

Adding Animation

PowerPoint enables you to add animation effects to your slides and to use transitions between slides. Both of these make your slides appear more interesting and more energized. By using animation you can have each word fly in from one side of the slide, each paragraph seem to dissolve from the slide background, or any of a variety of other effects. When you use transitions, you can have one slide dissolve into another, make one slide appear to "iris" open like a camera lens, or choose from several other intriguing transition options.

Many of the standard PowerPoint effects are designed to animate text objects (although they can work with clip art or other images as well). You can begin in Normal view: Move to the slide that contains the text object that you want to animate, select the text object, and then click the Animation Effects button on the Formatting toolbar. PowerPoint displays the Animation Effects toolbar, shown in Figure 30-1, which contains 12 buttons and one list box that you can use to control and preview the animation effects on your slide. Table 30-1 summarizes these controls.

Animation
Effects

TABLE 30-1.   Animation Effects Toolbar Controls and Their Effects

Control	Description
Animate Title	Causes a slide's title to appear from the top.
Animate Slide Text	Makes the body of the text appear one step at a time.
Drive-In Effect	Causes an object to fly in from the right and make a car sound.
Flying Effect	Causes an object to fly in from the left and make a whoosh sound.
Camera Effect	Displays an object that makes a camera sound.
Flash Once	Causes an object to blink once when it appears.
Laser Text Effect	Displays text character by character and makes a laser sound.
Typewriter Text Effect	Displays text character by character and makes a typewriter sound.
Reverse Text Order Effect	Displays text (such as a bulleted list) in reverse order.
Drop-In Text Effect	Causes text to appear word by word from the top of the slide.
Animation Order	Displays and sets the order of animations on a slide.
Custom Animation	Displays the Custom Animation dialog box.
Animation Preview	Displays animation in a slide miniature.

FIGURE 30-1.
The Animation Effects toolbar provides access to the most common animation effects.

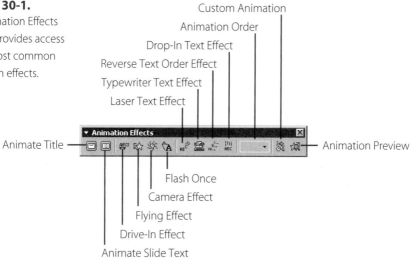

Custom Animation
Animation Order
Drop-In Text Effect
Reverse Text Order Effect
Typewriter Text Effect
Laser Text Effect

Animate Title

Animation Preview

Flash Once
Camera Effect
Flying Effect
Drive-In Effect
Animate Slide Text

The Preset Animation command on the Slide Show menu contains a collection of animation effects similar to (but slightly larger than) what you'll find on the Animation Effects toolbar. The designers of PowerPoint have endeavored to make it easier to animate objects by organizing the animation effects into three different collections that overlap each other significantly. The most basic animation effects are listed on the Animation Effects toolbar, and a larger set of effects is listed on the Preset Animation submenu. The Custom Animation dialog box (which you display by choosing Custom Animation from the Slide Show menu or by clicking the Custom Animation button on the Animation Effects toolbar) gives you the most complete set of effects, as well as the ability to create your own effects by varying the animation timing, sound, and other settings. (You'll learn more about this feature in "Customizing Your Animation," later in the chapter.)

To create a slide that contains animation effects, complete the following steps:

1 Create your slide content first, using text and graphic objects as you normally would. (For example, create a title, a bulleted list, and a piece of clip art on your slide.) You can't create animation effects until your slide content is finished.

2 Select the first object on your slide that you would like to animate.

3 Click the Animation Effects button on the Formatting toolbar. (The Animation Effects toolbar appears.)

4 Click the button on the toolbar corresponding to the effect you want to create. (See Figure 30-1.) If you don't see the effect you want on the Animation Effects toolbar, search the Preset Animation submenu on the Slide Show menu or create a custom effect using the Custom Animation dialog box.

5 Continue selecting objects one at a time on your slide and adding animation effects to them.

6 When you're finished, repeat the process on the remaining slides in your presentation, and then click the Animation Effects button again to close the Animation Effects toolbar.

7 Now click the Slide Show button or choose View Show from the Slide Show menu and preview all your animation effects!

Practice Your Animation

In addition to reviewing an animation full screen in Slide Show view, you can also preview the animation without leaving Normal view by clicking the Animation Preview button on the Animation Effects toolbar. When you click this button, PowerPoint opens a slide miniature in the workspace and runs the slide show using all the sound and animation you have specified. You can click the slide miniature to replay the animation. When you're finished previewing the animations, click the Close button on the slide miniature's title bar to remove it.

Adding Animation in Slide Sorter View

You can also use Slide Sorter view to create animation effects on your slides. While Slide Sorter view doesn't let you animate the individual objects on a slide, it does give you control of both the *transition effects* (the way in which one slide changes to another) and the text animation displayed when bulleted lists appear. You can set these two options using the Slide Transition Effects and Preset Animation drop-down list boxes on the Slide Sorter toolbar, as shown in Figure 30-2.

Selecting Transitions

The purpose of a transition is to add visual interest as you move from one slide to the next.

To create a transition from one slide to the next, follow these steps:

1 Click the Slide Sorter View button at the bottom left of the window to switch to Slide Sorter view, and then select the slide you want the transition to reveal.

FIGURE 30-2.
Slide Sorter view allows you to set slide transition effects and text animation for bulleted lists.

Slide Transition Effects

Preset Animation

Slide Transition

Slide Transition icon

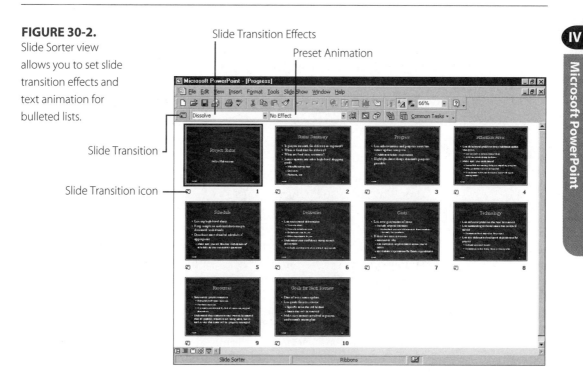

 **TIP**

You can create transitions for multiple slides by first selecting them as a group.
To do so, hold down the Shift key and click each slide in Slide Sorter view.

2 Select a transition from the Slide Transition Effects list box or click the Slide Transition button to open the following dialog box:

4 Click here to apply the transition to all slides in the presentation, or…

…click here to apply the transition to the currently selected slide(s).

3 Choose a slide transition effect from this list.

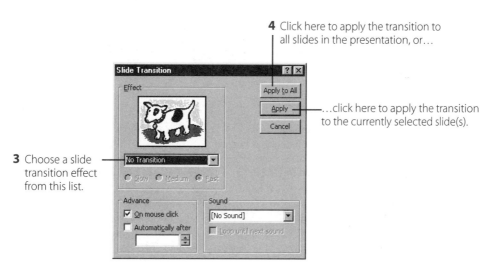

After you specify a transition for a slide, a tiny icon appears below the slide in Slide Sorter view, identifying the slide transition. To preview the transition, click the icon.

Controlling Bulleted List Animation

While you're in Slide Sorter view, you can also control how PowerPoint displays bulleted lists. Bulleted lists are special text elements that often form the cornerstone of a presentation. To draw out your points and give them the proper emphasis, you can use the Preset Animation drop-down list box, which controls how each line of a list appears. If you use this effect properly, your presentation ends up looking like it took several slides to show the bulleted list—not just one. The most popular text animation effects include Appear (where your bullets simply appear on the screen), Fly From Right (where bullets slide in from the right side of the screen), Blinds Horizontal (where horizontal sections of the line materialize in place), and Checkerboard Across (where bullets appear through a checkerboard mesh).

To select a text animation effect for a slide containing a bulleted list, follow these steps:

1 Click the Slide Sorter View button at the bottom left of the window to switch to Slide Sorter view, and then click the slide that contains the bulleted-list placeholder.

2 From the Preset Animation list box, choose the effect that you want.

3 To preview the effect, click the Slide Show button.

 TIP

> **Don't Act Randomly in a Crowded Room**
>
> In most cases, we suggest that you stay away from the Random Effects animation option, which can be distracting, and the No Effect option, which is dull. As mentioned elsewhere, don't use all the effects just because they're there, unless you want a chaotic presentation. Remember, you'll be giving this presentation in front of people you want to impress and persuade, not make seasick.

Customizing Your Animation

To maintain greater control over how the text and objects on a slide behave during an animation sequence, choose the Custom Animation command on the Slide Show menu when the slide is visible in Normal view. You'll see the following dialog box:

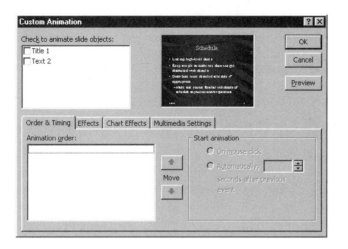

The Order & Timing tab in the Custom Animation dialog box contains an Animation Order list box, which you can use to set the order in which the objects on your slide are animated. (For example, you might want to display the title first to let the viewers know what the subject is, a piece of clip art second to plant a visual image in viewers' minds, and a bulleted list third to flesh out the image with text.) The dialog box also contains a preview window, which you can use to see the object you're working with, plus four tabs that control advanced aspects of the animation sequence you're customizing:

- The Order & Timing tab lets you identify objects on your slide that don't currently have animation effects associated with them, as well as control options that time each animation. (You can move objects when you click the mouse, or after a specific time interval.)

- The Effects tab lets you set the special effect you see when you run the animation and the sound you hear while it happens. You can also use the Effects tab to control both how the textual elements in an animation are grouped together and the order in which they appear.

- The Chart Effects tab is designed specifically to let you animate the charts in your presentation. You can display the chart elements all at once, or one at a time to highlight important trends. You can also specify a particular sound (such as that of a cash register!) to play when important values such as a great bottom-line are displayed.

- The Multimedia Settings tab lets you control how a video object is played during a slide show. You have the option of pausing the slide show while the video rolls or continuing on with your slides as the video runs its course in a window. You can also stop playing the video after a specified number of slides have passed—a useful feature if your video is only relevant to a particular part of the presentation, like an entertainment preview for an upcoming event.

Inserting Video

You can insert one or more video objects into any slide. You might want to play a video quote from your product manager, for example, or run a short documentary movie for a fundraising event. You could even create a video for product tutorials and educational materials. The following illustration shows one frame of a video clip:

When presenting, you can play the video clip or movie—or you can have PowerPoint play it for you.

Before you insert any video objects, make sure that you have the necessary hardware (such as a sound card, speakers, and an enhanced video card) for playing the multimedia items during your presentation. Once you do, adding media objects is the same as adding any other object to your slides, and the special effects are truly exciting.

Check Out a Video

The multitude of videos and movies that come with Microsoft Office are stored on the Office CD. You can also click the Clips Online button in the Insert Movies dialog box to connect to Clip Gallery Live—a Web site where you can preview and download picture, sound, and movie clips. If you still can't find the right video clip, you can find plenty of video software packages in your local software store. Because videos and movies occupy a lot of space on your hard disk, you might want to install only those you intend to use.

To insert a video object into a slide, follow these steps:

1 Move to the slide where you want to place the new video clip or add a new slide by choosing New Slide from the Insert menu or clicking the New Slide button on either the Common Tasks or Standard toolbar.

Don't worry about the slide layout or the placeholders on the slide. Video clips are always inserted directly onto the slide, not into a placeholder.

2 If you want to browse the Clip Gallery for a movie clip, insert your Office CD into the CD-ROM drive, point to Movies And Sounds on the Insert menu, and then choose Movie From Gallery from the submenu. Then, on the Motion Clips tab of the Insert Movie dialog box, double-click the movie you want to add to your slide.

3 Alternatively, if you want to insert a movie from an existing movie file on your hard disk, point to Movies And Sounds on the Insert menu, and then choose Movie From File from the submenu. (Movie clips have an AVI filename extension.) Select the movie file in the dialog box that appears, and then click OK.

4 To customize how your video is presented, select the video object on the slide, choose Custom Animation from the Slide Show menu, and use the options on the Multimedia Settings tab.

> **NOTE**
>
> You can also use the Object command on the Insert menu to insert a video clip, though it's usually more efficient to use the Movies And Sounds submenu. The Object command gives you access to all types of objects on your system (sounds, animation, documents from other programs, and so on) as well as to the tools available for creating new objects (generally the various programs installed on your system). The Movie From File and Insert Movie commands, by contrast, list only video clips that exist on your system. There's no need to define what type of object you're inserting, and PowerPoint assumes that the video clips already exist.

When you insert a video clip, you'll see a sample frame called a *poster*, which is usually the first frame of the clip. Are you ready to play your video? Lights! Action! Camera! Double-click the poster in Slide view or click it in Slide Show view. Make some popcorn, sit back, and enjoy the action. The video will play during your slide show until either the clip ends or you move to the next slide.

> If you have any problems playing your videos, make sure that the video and media player settings are correct. Open the Windows Control Panel and choose Multimedia. Check the sound device, the hardware setup, and the sound setup—and check all cable connections. Also check the volume control by double-clicking the Sound icon on the taskbar.

Inserting Sounds

CAUTION

Before you add sound to your show, make sure that your sound card is Windows-compatible and that sound files are available on your system. Otherwise, PowerPoint can't play or record sounds. To record sound, you'll also need a microphone or another type of input device.

Sound effects, such as music and voice recordings, can add another level of professionalism to your slide presentations. You could play an airplane sound effect to make your animated airplane sequence more amusing or persuasive. You could play a movie theme song as background music for several slides. Or you could play a voice recording that contains advertising slogans or radio jingles.

You can find sound files in several places—the Media folder installed by Windows 95 or Windows 98, the Media folder on the Office 2000 CD, and the folder created by your sound card. There are two primary types of sound files—WAV (often called "wave" files) and MIDI. After you add a sound to a slide, you'll see the following icon:

Here are the steps for adding sound to your slide show:

1 Display the slide to which you want to add sound.

2 If you want to browse the Clip Gallery for a sound file, insert your Office CD into the CD-ROM drive, point to Movies And Sounds on the Insert menu, and then choose Sound From Gallery. Then on the Sounds tab in the Insert Sound dialog box, double-click the sound category to find the one you want to add to your slide.

3 Alternatively, to insert a sound from an existing WAV or MIDI file on your hard disk, point to Movies And Sounds on the Insert menu, and then choose Sound From File. The Insert Sound dialog box appears, as shown in Figure 30-3. Select the sound file that you want, and then click OK.

 NOTE

If you have problems using sound, make sure that the audio and MIDI settings are correct. Open the Windows Control Panel and double-click Multimedia. Check the sound device, the hardware setup, and the sound setup. Also click the Sound icon on the taskbar to check the volume control.

FIGURE 30-3.
PowerPoint lets you add to your presentations a variety of sounds, which you can play by clicking tiny icons.

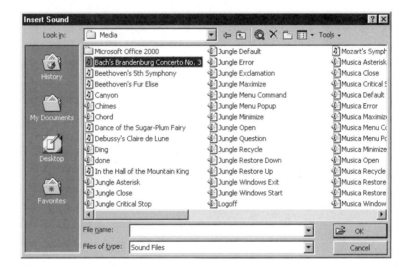

Recording Narration

PowerPoint lets you add voice narration to a slide show so that you can prepare a final presentation in advance, complete with your own voice. If you're building a slide show for presentation in a kiosk or over a network, you'll find this feature especially useful.

 NOTE

To record a voice narration, you'll need a sound card, a microphone, and a set of speakers.

Adding Embedded Documents

PowerPoint lets you add data from another Windows-based application and embed the data as an object that will appear as an icon on a slide. You can double-click the object during the slide show to *drill down* to the information and display the data in its original form. For example, you can embed a Microsoft Word document or a Microsoft Excel spreadsheet as an object in another document. In addition to Word and Excel files, you can embed files created in any Windows-based application that supports OLE in your PowerPoint presentations. (OLE stands for Object Linking and Embedding. You don't have to really understand object technology in depth to appreciate the advantage of Microsoft's invention. OLE technology allows you to put together a document that combines information from a variety of sources, in this case by embedding documents.)

To embed an existing object follow these steps:

1 Choose Object from the Insert menu.

2 Choose the Create From File option in the Insert Object dialog box, and then use the Browse feature to find the file that was created in another application.

3 Select the file, and click OK.

4 When you return to the Insert Object dialog box, choose the Display As Icon option, and click OK.

You'll see an icon on the slide representing the type of object you inserted—generally, the icon that's used to represent documents of that type.

Complete these steps:

1 From the Slide Show menu, choose Record Narration.

You'll see the Record Narration dialog box, showing the amount of free disk space and the number of minutes you can record.

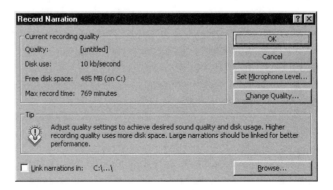

2 To use PowerPoint 2000's new Microphone Setup Wizard, click the Set Microphone Level button.

 The wizard helps you check whether your mike is turned on and set at a pleasing volume level.

3 If you want to customize the recording or playback, click the Change Quality button, and use the options in the Sound Selection dialog box.

4 To begin recording, click OK in the Record Narration dialog box.

5 Record voice content for each slide in your presentation, clicking to move from one slide to the next.

 If you want to stop the narration for any reason, right-click anywhere in the slide, and then click Pause Narration on the shortcut menu. When you're ready to resume, right-click and then click Resume Narration.

6 When you're finished with the recording, click Yes to save it along with the timings you specified. To save only the narration, click No.

 A sound icon appears in the middle of each slide that has narration.

When you run the slide show, the narration will automatically play. To run the slide show without narration, choose Set Up Show from the Slide Show menu, and then select the Show Without Narrations check box.

> **⊗ CAUTION**
>
> Because you can't record and play sounds at the same time, while you're recording you won't hear other sounds you inserted in your slide show.

Creating Action Buttons

By adding action buttons to a slide, you can branch to a specific slide or to a presentation from within another slide show, as well as launch another application or visit a site on the World Wide Web. You click an action button to move around within your show or to temporarily exit your slide show. Using this tool, you can create an interactive training or informational presentation. Within the presentation, the action buttons appear as icons on a slide—and you just click the button to jump to a new location.

Moving to a Slide or File

Perhaps you're showing slides about sales revenue, and at a certain point during the show you want to give yourself the option of moving to a particular slide that contains a pie chart showing sales expenses.

You can create an action button that will let you branch to a specific slide, as shown in Figure 30-4.

 The Soccer.ppt file is located on the Running Office 2000 Reader's Corner page. For information about connecting to this Web site, read the Introduction.

When you create an action button on a slide, you specify the button you want to use, identify the mouse movement you want to trigger the action, and then specify where you want to jump to. When you run the presentation in Slide Show view, the buttons are enabled, and when you click one, PowerPoint immediately jumps to that specific location. Jumping to a slide works the same way as the Go To feature in Word. In Office 2000, however, the jumps are called *hyperlinks*.

To create a jump to a specific slide or file, follow these steps:

1 In Normal view, display the slide on which you want to create the jump.

2 From the Slide Show menu, point to Action Buttons and choose one of the action buttons on the submenu.

PowerPoint supplies several intuitive shapes for the different types of jumps you might want to make. (Different shapes are especially useful when you're adding more than one button to a slide.)

FIGURE 30-4.
This slide's action button lets you jump to another location in your slide show during your presentation.

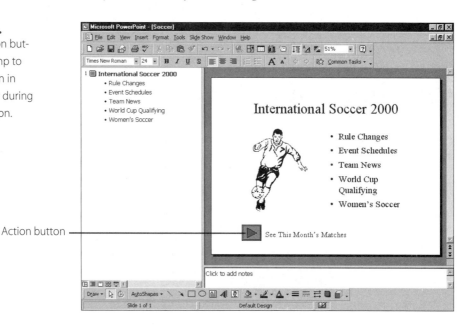

Action button

⭐ **TIP**

To clarify what the button does, add some explanatory text using the Text Box command on the Insert menu or the Text Box button on the Drawing toolbar. For example, you could insert a text box and type *Facts and Figures* or *On the Web* to give yourself a little reminder.

3 Drag the mouse on the slide to create the action button. When you release the mouse button, the Action Settings dialog box appears:

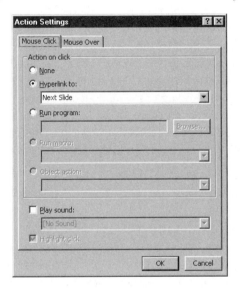

4 If you want to activate the jump by clicking, use the Mouse Click tab. If you'd rather activate the link by simply placing the mouse pointer over the button, click the Mouse Over tab. (Both tabs have identical controls.)

5 In the Hyperlink To drop-down list box, choose the jump option you want to create for your action button. Select the Slide option if you want to jump to another slide in the current presentation, or select the Other PowerPoint Presentation option if you want to open a presentation stored on disk. You can also specify a different type of file by selecting the Other File option, or a valid Internet address by selecting the URL option. In each of these cases, you'll be prompted for the location of the hyperlink you want to establish.

6 If you want to play a sound during the jump, select the Play Sound check box and select a sound in the drop-down list box.

7 When you're finished configuring the action button, click OK.

During your show, you can click the action button or move the mouse pointer over it to move to the specified slide or file location.

Running Another Program

If you want to open a Windows-based application without loading a specific file, you can click the Run Program option in the Action Settings dialog box and use the Browse button to select the name of an application program (.exe file) on your system. You might find this technique useful if you want the ability to respond to audience requests during a presentation, such as demonstrating an application feature during a training session. The "Adding Embedded Documents" sidebar (page 756) explains how to create an embedded application object to run a Windows-based application. You can also use an action button to get the same results. When you use an action button, however, you can control the look of the object that opens the application.

To create a button that starts an application on your system, follow these steps:

1 In Normal view, display the slide on which you want to create a jump to another application.

2 From the Slide Show menu, point to Action Buttons and choose one of the action buttons on the submenu.

3 Drag the mouse on the slide to create the action button. When you release the mouse button, the Action Settings dialog box appears.

4 Click the Mouse Click or Mouse Over tab, depending on how you want to start the application.

5 Click the Run Program option button, and then click the Browse button. Use the navigation buttons in the Select A Program To Run dialog box to highlight the program file you want to run, and then click OK.

6 When you're finished configuring the action button, click OK.

TIP

You'll find handy shortcuts for all the Office 2000 programs in the \Program Files\Microsoft Office\Office\Shortcut Bar\Office folder. You might even want to print these out and post them on your office wall.

When you activate the action button during your show, you'll launch another application. To return to your presentation at the current slide, exit the application as you would any other.

Connecting to the Internet

In the last section, you learned how to create an action button on a slide and use it to open a PowerPoint slide and a Windows-based application, and to display a page on the Internet. If you have the necessary hardware and software installed on your computer, you can also format a text placeholder in PowerPoint so that it will automatically establish an Internet connection. In Office terminology, such formatting is called a *hyperlink*, and the process of creating one is similar to the one you have used throughout this book to create hyperlinks to Web pages and to other documents in your Office applications.

In this section, you'll learn how to connect to the Internet using text hyperlinks, and how to jump back and forth between Web sites using the new Web toolbar.

Creating an Internet Hyperlink

Internet hyperlinks provide a simple way for you to display slides and other useful supporting documents that currently reside on the World Wide Web—rather than having them occupy precious space on your hard drive. You can also use hyperlinks to display a home page on the Web as a resource for the people viewing your presentation.

You create hyperlinks by choosing the Hyperlink command on the Insert menu or by clicking the Insert Hyperlink button on the Standard toolbar. The Insert Hyperlink dialog box then prompts you for the name of the Web page, or the *URL*, of the document you want to open on the Web. You can use the buttons on the right side of the dialog box to help you find the file to link to or you can select from the list of recently opened files, browsed Web pages, and inserted links. The

Browse For buttons on the left also help you narrow down your search for links. Choosing the Hyperlink command will place the text that was selected in the text placeholder on your slide into the Text To Display box, or you can enter text here yourself. (The underlined word appears in a special color and looks similar to linked topics that appear in the Office online Help.) After you have established a hyperlink to another document, you can activate it by clicking the underlined word on your slide when your presentation is running.

> **Hyperlinks Can Be Local, Too**
>
> You can also use the Hyperlink command to open other documents on your system, provided that you have the Windows 95/98-based application necessary to open the document on your computer. For example, if you have Microsoft Office Professional Edition installed, you can create a hyperlink to any Microsoft Word, Excel, PowerPoint, Access, or Outlook document, and PowerPoint will automatically open it when you click the underlined hyperlink in your presentation. Similarly, if you have Microsoft Internet Explorer or another Windows 95/98-based Internet browser, you can create a hyperlink to any resource on the Web.

The following steps show you how to create a hyperlink in your presentation that connects to the Web:

1 Select the text placeholder on your slide with which you want to associate the hyperlink. It usually works best if that word or phrase is a descriptive label that explains the purpose of the link so that users can see what they're connecting to. For example, "The Sage of Concord" or "Check Scores on the Web."

2 Choose Hyperlink from the Insert menu. (You can also click the Insert Hyperlink button on the Standard toolbar.)

Insert
Hyperlink

The Insert Hyperlink dialog box appears, as shown in Figure 30-5, prompting you for the name of the file or Web page that will open when the hyperlink is activated.

3 Type the address of the Web page in the Insert Hyperlink dialog box, select it from the list of recently visited sites, or click the Browse For button to search your hard disk or Internet browser for the address.

Addresses usually are in the format *http://www.xxxx.com*, where *xxxx* is the name of the business or service provider. For example, the address of InfoWord Electric (a free publication) is *http://www.infoworld.com*.

FIGURE 30-5.
The Insert Hyperlink dialog box lets you establish a link between your slide and a document on your hard disk or the Internet.

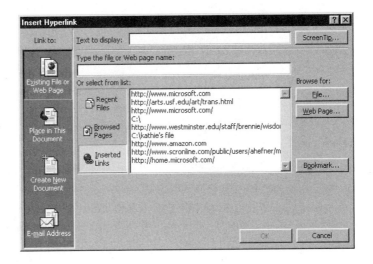

4 Enter the text you would like to associate with the link in the Text To Display box if it's different from the text that the Insert Hyperlink command displays there.

5 Click the ScreenTip button to add a line of text that will appear when the mouse pointer is placed over the hyperlink. This gives your audience a little more information about where the link will take them.

6 Click OK to add the hyperlink to your slide.
   When the Insert Hyperlink dialog box closes, the text in the highlighted cell appears underlined.

When you run your presentation, the hyperlinks will appear underlined, and you can activate them with a click. When you do this, Office starts the application associated with the document and loads the linked document. If the hyperlink contains an Internet address, Office will start the default Internet browser on your system and ask you for a username and password. After you complete the necessary connection details, you'll see the Internet document you requested.

Using the Web Toolbar

SEE ALSO
For more information about using and configuring the Web toolbar, see "Linking Up with the World Wide Web," page 89.

The Web toolbar lets you switch back and forth between open hyperlinks, establish additional Internet connections, or run special Web-related commands. Figure 30-6, on the following page, shows the Web toolbar and the purpose of its buttons. To display the toolbar, point to Toolbars on the View menu and then click Web.

FIGURE 30-6.

The Web toolbar lets you switch back and forth between your open document and Internet connections.

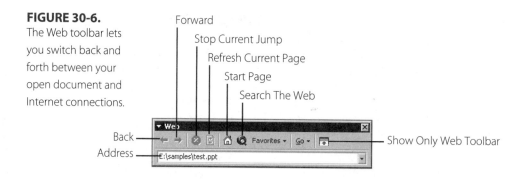

Forward

Stop Current Jump

Refresh Current Page

Start Page

Search The Web

Back

Address

Show Only Web Toolbar

The hyperlink navigation buttons are the essential tools on the Web toolbar. To display the last open document or Web page, click the Back (left-pointing) button. To display the next open document or Web page, click the Forward (right-pointing) button. If you want to open one of your favorite hyperlinks, click the Favorites drop-down list box and select it from the list. To see a list of the recent Internet addresses you've used, click the Address drop-down list box.

Creating action buttons, adding hyperlinks to the Web, and embedding documents from other applications all help widen the scope of your PowerPoint presentations. In Chapter 32, you'll learn how to publish your entire slide show on the Web using PowerPoint 2000's new Save As Web Page command. You'll soon be making persuasive presentations to an international audience!

CHAPTER 31

Perfecting Your Presentation

Perfecting your presentation is an important part of creating a slide show. This chapter discusses how you can fine-tune your presentation before you run your slide show. You'll find that using the notes pane in Microsoft PowerPoint 2000 is an invaluable way to remind yourself of the slide you're talking about and what you're going to say about it. You can run the Spelling feature to eliminate the risk of any humiliating misspellings that would be magnified on a large screen.

You'll probably print audience handouts in grayscale (or black and white) rather than in color. (Remember that your audience will be consulting the handouts while your show is running and your room lighting might not be bright.) To see how objects on your slides will appear when printed in grayscale, you can use the Grayscale Preview option to see a full-size version of your slide in grayscale and an accompanying miniature of the slide in color.

Finally, you can use Slide Sorter view to easily make last-minute changes, such as adding, deleting, or reordering slides. This view shows you miniatures of all slides, displaying several slides on the screen at once. Hiding slides that contain confidential material or skipping over slides that you don't want to show to a particular audience is another last-minute change that you might want to consider. After you learn how to perfect your presentation in this chapter, you can be confident about the quality of your slide show while you're running it.

Adding Notes

Unless you enjoy ad-libbing at a podium in front of an expectant audience, you have probably devised some way of reminding yourself of what you want to say. For example, you might number your slides and then make notes on correspondingly numbered index cards or papers. In PowerPoint 2000's new default view, Normal view, you can easily type notes to yourself for each slide. Figure 31-1 shows a note added to a slide.

> **NOTE**
>
> We recently attended a preview demonstration meeting at Microsoft and heard the PowerPoint 2000 team refer to Normal view as the *Tri-pane view*, which strikes us as quite appropriate: it's such an inclusive view. You can work on many aspects of your presentation without ever leaving it. And while you might make notes on your slide in Notes Page view, staying in the Tri-pane view to make your reminders is certainly more convenient.

FIGURE 31-1.
You add notes to a PowerPoint presentation in the notes pane of Normal view.

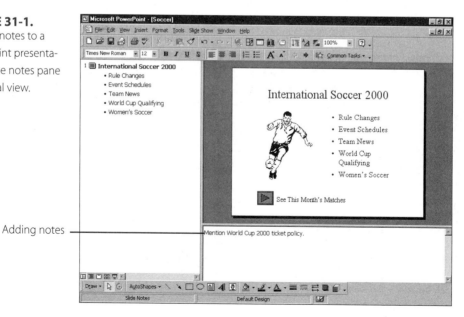

Of course, notes aren't always necessary for every presentation, but it doesn't hurt to have a few cue cards in case you forget your lines or get caught up in the Q&A of the meeting. Another advantage of using the notes pane is that you can make your notes immediately after you create each slide, while the decisions you made when you created it are still fresh in your mind. You can add notes to any slide at any time by following these steps:

1   In Normal view, display the slide to which you want to add notes.

2   Click the notes pane, and type whatever you want.

3   To enlarge the space available to make notes, point to the top border of the notes pane until your pointer becomes a double-headed arrow, and drag the border up.

 NOTE

> When you click in the notes pane in Normal view, PowerPoint 2000 automatically changes the setting in the Zoom box to 100%. You can always see what you're typing in Normal view. If you choose Notes Page view to add notes to your slides, you might want to increase the notes area by changing the setting in the Zoom box to 100%.

4   When you have finished, drag the top border of the notes pane down to make more room for viewing your slide.

You can also add notes to your slides by choosing Notes Page from the View menu. Here you will see your slide at the top of the page and an area to add notes underneath. Whenever you need to revise your notes, all you have to do is display the slide to which you added the notes and then click in the notes pane of Normal view.

Checking Your Spelling

A presentation that contains spelling mistakes reflects poorly on the speaker. Misspellings loom even larger when your slide show is projected onto a big screen. How embarrassing! Before you take center stage, be sure to check the spelling throughout your presentation—perhaps on printouts as well as on screen, to be absolutely sure. PowerPoint's Spelling feature will find and highlight for correction any misspellings in your outlines, notes (less important, because they're not being projected), and text on slides, such as titles and bulleted lists.

? **SEE ALSO**

For more information on using the Spelling feature and custom dictionaries, see Chapter 8, "Using Word's Proofing Tools." To learn more about AutoCorrect, see "Using the AutoCorrect Feature," page 127.

Spelling's first line of defense is to check your spelling as you type. If this feature is active (the default), you'll see the Spelling icon on the right side of the status bar as you begin typing. If you don't see the Spelling icon, you can turn on this feature by choosing Options from the Tools menu. Then click the Spelling And Style tab, select the Check Spelling As You Type option under Spelling, and click OK. As you type, PowerPoint will mark any misspelled words with a wavy red underline. To correct the spelling at that moment, right-click the word and choose an option from the shortcut menu, as shown in Figure 31-2.

You can use the Spelling icon on the status bar to review and correct your spelling. Each time you double-click the icon, PowerPoint will find and highlight the next misspelled word in your presentation and display the shortcut menu. You can also check your entire document by clicking the Spelling button on the Standard toolbar. To check your spelling using this method, do the following:

Spelling

1 Click the Spelling button on the Standard toolbar.

2 When PowerPoint finds a word that it can't match in its dictionary or in the custom dictionary, the Spelling dialog box appears.

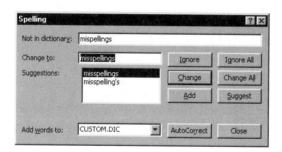

Your options are as follows:

- Click Ignore to skip the word this time.

- Click Ignore All to skip the word throughout this presentation—that is, not to stop on this word again.

- Click Add if the word is correctly spelled and you want to add it to your custom dictionary.

- Select a word from the Suggestions list to replace the selected word, and then click Change to change this occurrence of the word. Click Change All to change all occurrences throughout this presentation.

- If Spelling can't suggest a correct spelling, type the correct word in the Change To box, and then click Change or Change All.

- Click Close to close the spelling checker without making a change.

3 When the spelling check is complete, click OK.

Adding Words to the Custom Dictionary

PowerPoint's dictionary doesn't contain many proper nouns, such as names of people and places. It's a good idea to add your own proper nouns and technical terms to the custom dictionary. This custom dictionary is shared with other Office applications.

FIGURE 31-2.
Right-click a misspelling, marked by a wavy red underline when the Check Spelling As You Type feature is turned on, to display a shortcut menu offering correction options.

Click here to leave the word unchanged and skip all other occurrences.

Click here to add a correctly spelled word to the custom dictionary.

Click here to select a suggested spelling.

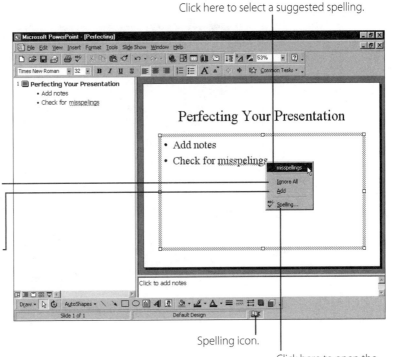

Spelling icon.

Click here to open the Spelling dialog box.

Fixing Mistakes Using AutoCorrect

In an attempt to smooth out your writing and typing shortcomings, Power-Point's AutoCorrect feature catches and corrects common spelling, capitalization, and punctuation mistakes as you type! For example, if you type two initial caps at the beginning of a word, AutoCorrect automatically makes the second letter lowercase. AutoCorrect ensures that no inconsistencies exist in the way you use capitalization; it simply makes the case changes as you type. If you tend to type the names of the days of the week without initial capital letters, PowerPoint can capitalize those for you. If there's a word whose spelling eludes you—for example, each time you type the word *receive*, you ask yourself, "Is it spelled *ie* or *ei?*"—you don't have to guess anymore. AutoCorrect can also replace abbreviations with the entire word—when you type *adv*, AutoCorrect can replace it with *advertising*.

Here's how to have AutoCorrect do the job for you: Choose AutoCorrect from the Tools menu. You'll see the following dialog box:

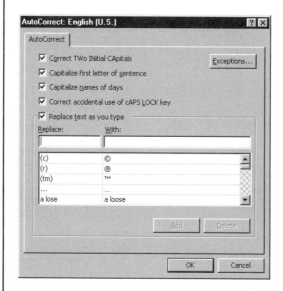

In the Replace box, type an abbreviation or a word that you often misspell, and then type the correct spelling of the word in the With box and click Add. You can leave the other options selected, or you can deselect them. Finally, you can specify individual exceptions to the capitalization rules by clicking the Exceptions button and typing any special cases.

TIP

Don't Like Being Watched?

If you feel that your sixth-grade English teacher is standing behind you while you type, waiting to pounce on you when you make a mistake—or if you're using foreign words or terms that are consistently not in PowerPoint's proofing dictionary—you can disable PowerPoint's Check Spelling As You Type feature by choosing Options from the Tools menu, clicking the Spelling And Style tab, and clearing the Check Spelling As You Type check box. After you disable spell-checking, you'll still be able to review your spelling using the Spelling command, but PowerPoint will no longer underline misspelled words with red as you type.

However, we can't help you with that uncanny feeling that Miss Thistlebottom is still back there, watching.

Viewing Slides in Grayscale

When you want to see how the text and objects on color slides will look in grayscale, display the slide and click the Grayscale Preview button on the Standard toolbar. (See Figure 31-3.) PowerPoint displays the grayscale version on the screen. Then, if you choose Slide Miniature from the View menu, the color version of your slide appears in a tiny preview window so that you can compare the two slides.

FIGURE 31-3.
In Grayscale Preview, color slides are displayed as they will be printed. A slide miniature in color also appears, letting you compare the two versions.

Grayscale Preview button   Color slide miniature

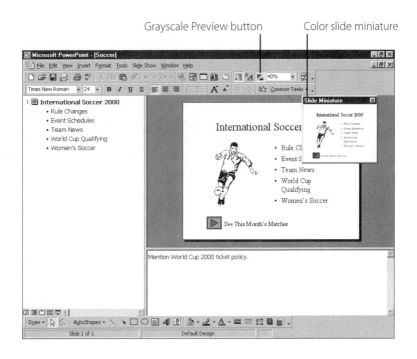

(When you want to see how your slides will look in pure black and white, hold down Shift as you click the Grayscale Preview button.)

Grayscale Preview is useful when you want to see what your audience handouts will look like when printed. (In general, the quality of the slide handout, and the representation of any pictures or graphical items included on it, will be better in grayscale than in black and white. Just remember that grayscale has 256 colors; black and white has two.) The text should be legible, and a strong contrast should be evident between the text and the background of the slide. The clip art and chart objects should print clearly and distinctly and should not blend in with the background color. Figure 31-3 shows a slide in Grayscale Preview (just as it will be printed), with an accompanying slide miniature in color so that you can compare the versions. (Admittedly, some of this distinction is lost in our grayscale screen shot.)

After you display a slide in Grayscale Preview, you can change how PowerPoint displays any of the objects listed in Table 31-1. Just right-click the object, point to Black And White on the shortcut menu, and choose the shading you want from the submenu.

Table 31-1 lists the objects and how they first appear in grayscale and then in pure black and white. Look for the objects you used in your presentation and see whether the default appearances will work for you.

When you're finished using Grayscale Preview, switch back to Color view by clicking the Grayscale Preview button on the Standard toolbar. (This button is a toggle.)

TABLE 31-1.   Objects in Grayscale and Pure Black And White View

Object	Appearance in Grayscale	Appearance in Pure Black And White
Text	Black	Black
Text shadows	Hidden	Hidden
Embossing	Hidden	Hidden
Fills	Grayscale	White
Frame	Black	Black
Pattern fills	Grayscale	White
Lines	Black	Black

(continued)

TABLE 31-1. *continued*

Object	Appearance in Grayscale	Appearance in Pure Black And White
Object shadows	Grayscale	Black
Bitmaps	Grayscale	Grayscale
Slide backgrounds	White	White
Charts	Grayscale	Grayscale

Using Slide Sorter View

Before the age of personal computers, graphics professionals used a *light table* to organize slides for presentations. A light table is a box that has a light inside and a translucent plastic top. When you put slides on the lighted surface, the backlighting illuminates the contents of the slides. Well, the good news is that you don't have to go out and buy a light table or start taping slides in rows on your patio's sliding glass door. You have a much handier solution right in PowerPoint.

The Slide Sorter looks and works just like a light table, as shown in Figure 31-4, on the following page. It displays a miniature version of every slide in your presentation—and in the proper order. The number of slides that you can view at one time depends on your video card, video driver, and monitor, as well as on the zoom percentage used and the size of the presentation window. You can view more slides at a glance if you lower the zoom percentage. If you view your slides at a high zoom percentage, such as 100 percent, you will see very few slides at one time, though you'll see them in greater detail.

To switch to Slide Sorter view, click the Slide Sorter View button at the bottom left of the window. You can also choose Slide Sorter from the View menu. When you use Slide Sorter, you get a thumbnail view (as if holding a slide up to the light at arm's length) of some or all the slides in your presentation. It doesn't matter that the text isn't particularly readable. You really want to look at the slides as a whole, focusing on layout consistency and perhaps contrast from one slide to the next, rather than on the details.

As you can see in Figure 31-4, on the following page, the slide number appears near the bottom right corner of each slide. One slide is currently selected (number 2) and surrounded by a dark border.

? SEE ALSO

To find out about slide transitions and animation effects, see Chapter 30, "Adding Special Effects and Internet Links."

IV

Microsoft PowerPoint

FIGURE 31-4.
Slide Sorter view
showing miniatures
of eight slides.

Selected slide

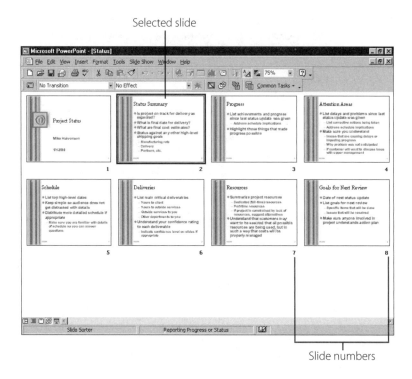

Slide numbers

You can't edit slides in Slide Sorter view; you must make changes to the content of slides in Normal view. However, Slide Sorter view does let you do the following tasks: add and delete slides, rearrange the order of slides, add transitions, hide slides, and rehearse your presentation. The Slide Sorter toolbar makes it a snap for you to perform these tasks.

 TIP

> To get a closer look at a slide, double-click it. PowerPoint shifts to Normal view and displays the slide in the slide pane, enabling you to see the slide in detail. To return to Slide Sorter view, click the Slide Sorter View button.

Adding and Deleting Slides

PowerPoint lets you add slides one at a time or delete one or more slides from your presentation. When working with a single slide, you can work either in Normal view or in Slide Sorter view; the techniques are the same.

To add a slide, click in the space between the slides. A vertical bar appears between the slides to mark the location where the slide will be inserted, as shown in Figure 31-5. Because inserting a new slide is such

FIGURE 31-5.
The vertical bar marks the current location for insertion.

New Slide button

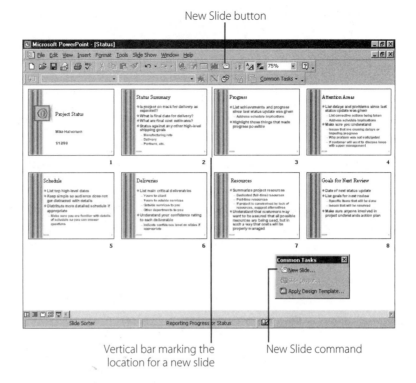

Vertical bar marking the location for a new slide

New Slide command

IV

Microsoft PowerPoint

a routine requirement, PowerPoint offers a number of ways of choosing the command. You can choose New Slide from the Insert menu, press the shortcut key combination (Ctrl+M), click the New Slide button on the Standard toolbar, or click New Slide on the Common Tasks toolbar, which is docked on the Formatting toolbar, but can be dragged to float anywhere in the workspace, as shown in Figure 31-5.

To delete a slide, you must first select the slide and then choose Delete Slide from the Edit menu or press the Delete key. Before you add or delete any slides in Slide Sorter view, you need to know the various ways to select slides in Slide Sorter view.

- Use the arrow keys to highlight a slide, or click the slide that you want to select. A selected slide is surrounded by a bold outline.

- Press Ctrl+Home to select the first slide in a presentation; press Ctrl+End to select the last slide.

- To select a set of adjacent slides, press and hold Shift, click the first slide in the set, and then click the last slide in the set that you want to select.

- To select multiple slides that are not adjacent to each other, press and hold Ctrl, and click each slide that you want to select.

- To select multiple slides using the mouse, hold down the left mouse button and drag the mouse pointer over the slides that you want to select.

- To cancel a selection, click in any blank area of the Slide Sorter view window.

To copy a slide, right-click it to select it and display the shortcut menu. Choose Copy from the shortcut menu, right-click in the space between the slides where you want to copy the slide, and choose Paste from the shortcut menu. Another quick way to duplicate a slide is to select it and choose Duplicate from the Edit menu or press Ctrl+D. The duplicate slide will appear at the right of the original slide. Then you can move the duplicate slide wherever you want. *For more information on moving slides, see the next section, "Rearranging Slides."*

Rearranging Slides

Slide Sorter view gives you a panoramic view of all your slides in the current order. If you want to improve the flow by changing the order of your slides, just select a slide and drag it to a new location. A vertical bar marks the location where the slide will be inserted when you release the mouse button. The slide numbers are changed to accommodate the new arrangement.

You can also move multiple slides within your presentation. For example, if you want to move slides 5 and 6 to the beginning of your presentation, simply select slides 5 and 6 and drag them to the left of the first slide in the presentation. PowerPoint automatically renumbers the reordered slides.

Hiding Slides

In certain cases, some slides might contain material that you'd rather not discuss with a particular audience because of time constraints or the sensitivity of the material. For instance, you might not want to announce in a general company meeting that your controller had vanished with $10 million in cash—but if asked about it you wouldn't want to lie, either. You can prepare a slide and hope that the news hasn't leaked out; if it has, you're covered. More common is the situation where you want to use similar presentations for different audiences. By hiding slides, you can change one presentation to match the needs of more than one group, or speed up your presentation on the spot if time is running short. (You can label a number of slides *Optional* in the notes pane as a reminder that they can be cut.)

PowerPoint lets you create hidden slides to include in your presentation but to show only at your discretion. In Slide Sorter view, a hidden slide appears with its number enclosed in a box that has a line across it.

To hide a slide, make sure that you're in Slide Sorter view. Select the slide that you want to hide, and click the Hide Slide button on the Slide Sorter toolbar. Notice that the slide doesn't disappear from the Slide Sorter. You see the slide, but its number is surrounded by a box that has a diagonal line through it, as shown in Figure 31-6.

(?) SEE ALSO

See "Revealing Hidden Slides," page 800, to learn how to display a hidden slide while presenting your slide show.

> NOTE

The Hide Slide button is available only in Slide Sorter view. In Normal view, you can hide a slide by choosing Hide Slide from the Slide Show menu, though you won't see an indication that the slide is hidden until you switch to Slide Sorter view.

FIGURE 31-6.
Even though you can see slide number 5 in the Slide Sorter view of this presentation, the slide is marked as hidden.

Hide Slide button

A slide marked as hidden

This chapter showed you how to add notes to your slides, check your spelling, preview in grayscale or black and white, look at miniature slides, use the Slide Sorter, and hide slides. These are just a few of the techniques you can use to polish your slide show. The next chapter will teach you how to plan and rehearse the slide show so that it's picture-perfect when you take a deep breath and walk into that crowded room or publish it to the World Wide Web.

CHAPTER 32

Setting Up and Publishing the Slide Show

Once you have created your slide show and perfected it as much as possible, rehearse your presentation so that you become comfortable with the content, flow, and timing of your material. Then decide on the type of media that you'll use to present your slides. If your audience will be a small one, you can go the inexpensive route and print all your slides, speaker's notes, and handouts on paper—and then use your desktop computer to run an electronic slide show. If you're going to use an overhead projector, you can set up your slides as transparencies. For a larger audience, go the extra mile and set up your presentation as 35mm slides. Send the presentation files to a service bureau and have them make professional 35mm slides for you.

If you travel, and you want to run your slide show from your portable computer, just use the Pack And Go Wizard to compress your presentation and copy it to disks. Then you or any other presenter can use PowerPoint Viewer to run the slide show from the portable computer. If you're going to run your show for a potentially vast audience on the Web or for your colleagues over a company intranet, you can use the enhanced Web features of Microsoft PowerPoint 2000 to enter the world of Web publishing with ease. This chapter will help you set up and polish your presentation to meet professional standards.

Picking a Show Type

PowerPoint 2000 includes a number of presentation options to let you customize the type of slide show you're creating. You can set up your show to be presented full screen by an individual (you or a colleague), in a window along with navigation controls, or at an automated kiosk. In addition, you can control which slides are included in the final presentation, how narration and animation are used, and how the slides advance.

To pick the show type, complete the following steps:

1 From the Slide Show menu, choose Set Up Show. You'll see the following dialog box:

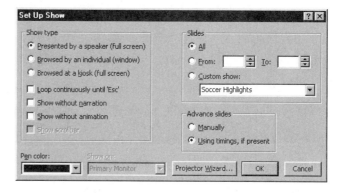

2 Specify the show type; either speaker (full screen), individual (window), or kiosk (full screen).

- If you choose the first option (the most common method), you'll have complete control of the slide show from beginning to end. You can skip slides, stop the presentation, add meeting minutes, and so on.

- The second option is designed for presentations that you want to distribute to co-workers or send out over a network. It runs the slide show in a smaller window, and includes menu commands for navigating the slide show, printing slides, and other useful options.

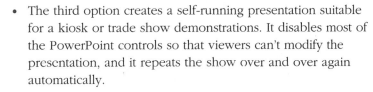

- The third option creates a self-running presentation suitable for a kiosk or trade show demonstrations. It disables most of the PowerPoint controls so that viewers can't modify the presentation, and it repeats the show over and over again automatically.

3 Specify which slides you want included in the show. You can include all the slides (the default), a slide range (in case you have to shorten your show on the spot), or a custom slide show that you have previously defined using the Custom Shows command on the Slide Show menu. *(For more information about custom shows, see the sidebar "Creating a Custom Show," on the next page.)*

4 Under Advance Slides, specify whether you want to advance the slides manually or by using timings if they're present. (You create slide timings by using the Rehearse Timings command on the Slide Show menu, as you'll see in the next section.)

5 When you're finished setting up the show, click OK. To see how your choices have affected the presentation, choose View Show from the Slide Show menu or click the Slide Show button and watch it run!

You're a Quick Study!

If you're going to run the show from your laptop computer using a projector, you might be feeling a little nervous about that procedure. Relax, and let the new Projector Wizard lead you through a few simple steps that will connect your computer to the projector. In the Set Up Show dialog box, click the Projector Wizard button. You'll need to know your projector model and your laptop resolution. (You can find the resolution by double-clicking the My Computer icon on your desktop, opening the Control Panel, opening the Display Properties dialog box, and then clicking the Settings tab. The Wizard suggests that you use a resolution of 800x600.) Follow along as the Wizard sets up the projector, and you won't be rattled by this procedure at showtime.

Rehearsing the Show

When you go to the theater to see a play, you probably don't think about the hours of rehearsal that made everything run smoothly—but rehearsals are the backbone of any professional production, whether it's a Broadway play or a company slide show. Rehearsing your presentation is important so that you know what to say and when to say it, as well as to make sure that you don't run over or under your allotted time. You don't want to have to improvise if you run short or race through your material if you run long. Even worse, at a busy conference, you could be asked to leave the podium if you run over your time limit.

PowerPoint can time your presentation so that it fits precisely into the allotted time. There are two ways to rehearse timings: automatically and manually.

Setting the Timings

Having PowerPoint automatically time your slide show is the best method for rehearsing your timing. That way, you can have PowerPoint determine the length of time to display each slide. PowerPoint will also

Creating a Custom Show

The Custom Shows command on the Slide Show menu lets you create a short list of alternate slide shows based on the slides in your presentation. Although in the past you could create custom shows by hiding slides or by saving different versions of presentations in different files, the new Custom Shows command lets you manage all your slide show's variations in one place. For example, you might want to drop out a few slides for sales reps in your organization who don't need to know your production staff's editorial policies. After you create a custom show, you can then specify it when you're configuring your show's presentation options in the Set Up Show dialog box (described earlier).

When you choose the Custom Shows command, a dialog box appears listing your current collection of custom shows (if any). You can edit, remove, copy, or show one of these presentations by clicking buttons in the dialog box. To define a new custom show, click the New button, give your custom show a name, and then specify the slides you want to include by selecting the slide titles and clicking the Add button. The following illustration shows how you create a custom slide show using the Define Custom Show dialog box:

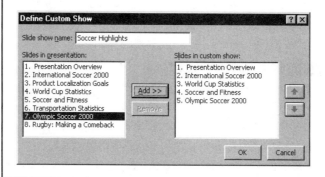

calculate the length of the entire show for you. This feature is a great advantage and one that you should use every time to perfect your timing. (In the next section, you'll learn how to set the timings manually.)

To use the Rehearse Timings feature, follow these steps:

1 Open the presentation that you want to rehearse, and use the Set Up Show command to specify the slides that you want to include. (Or you can just use some practice slides to see how this feature works.)

2 Click the Slide Sorter View button to switch to Slide Sorter view.

Rehearse
Timings

3 Click the Rehearse Timings button on the Slide Sorter toolbar, or choose Rehearse Timings from the Slide Show menu.

4 When the full-screen version of your first slide appears on screen, rehearse exactly what you'll tell your audience about this slide. You'll see the Rehearsal toolbar counting the seconds that the slide remains on screen.

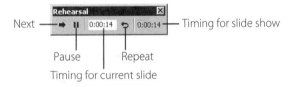

You can perform the following actions using the controls on the Rehearsal toolbar to rehearse timings:

 TIP

Keep It Short

Your audience's attention can wander if you spend too much time on a slide. If you intend to spend more than two or three minutes on the topic covered on one slide, make two or three slides for this subject.

- When you're ready to move to the next element on your slide (bulleted item or graphical element), or to the next slide, click the Next button to advance the slides manually. This resets the counter in the center (which measures the time spent on the current slide).

- To pause a slide and temporarily stop both time counters, click the Pause button. When you want to continue, click the Pause button again. (You might want to pause a slide if you lose your train of thought or if the phone rings.)

- To start over with a slide, click the Repeat button. (You might repeat a slide if you change your mind about what you want to say.)

- To stop rehearsing and return to Slide Sorter view, click the Close button on the Rehearsal toolbar.

5 After you have finished with the last slide, the timing information box appears, giving you the total elapsed time for your presentation and the option to display the new timings in Slide Sorter view.

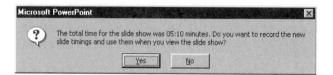

6 If you want to accept the timings, click Yes. If you want to rehearse again to get the timings to fit into an allotted time, click No. If you're prompted to view your slide timings in Slide Sorter view, click Yes. You'll see the timing beneath each slide in Slide Sorter view, as shown in Figure 32-1.

FIGURE 32-1.
The rehearsal timings in Slide Sorter view.

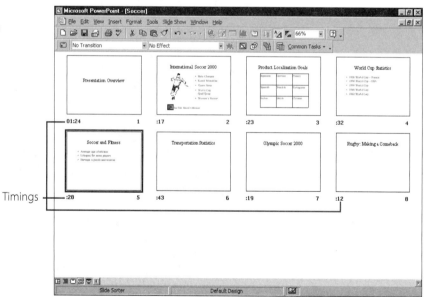

Setting Timings Manually

When you want tight control over the pace of your presentation, the manual method for rehearsing your slide show timings lets you enter the exact amount of time that you want each slide to remain on the screen. For example, you might want your title slide to appear for 45 seconds, the second slide for 2 minutes, the third slide for 1 minute and 30 seconds, and so on. To manually set slide timings:

1 Select the slide in Slide Sorter view.

Slide
Transition

2 Click the Slide Transition button on the Slide Sorter toolbar. You'll see the Slide Transition dialog box. If you had already set a timing for the slide (using the Rehearse Timings command or the Slide Transition dialog box), you'll see a timing in the dialog box, as shown here.

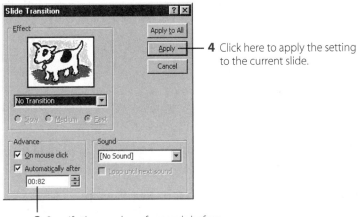

4 Click here to apply the setting to the current slide.

3 Specify the number of seconds before the slide should automatically advance.

5 Repeat the above steps for each slide in your show.

> **NOTE**
>
> If you click the Apply To All button, the timing you specified will be used for all the slides in your presentation. (This feature is useful and powerful—but it might hypnotize your audience if you have many slides each on screen for the same period.)

After you rehearse the timings for your slide show, either you can run the show using the timings, as described in Chapter 33, "Running the Slide Show," or you can remove the slide timings and advance the slides manually. To do the latter, in Slide Sorter view select those slides you want to control manually, click the Slide Transition button on the Slide Sorter toolbar, and select On Mouse Click and clear Automatically After in the Advance section of the Slide Transition dialog box. If both Advance options are selected, the slides will advance automatically after the specified number of seconds have elapsed; if you want to advance the slide sooner, do so manually by clicking the mouse.

Printing Slides, Notes Pages, and Handouts

In many cases, you'll want to print your entire presentation, including your outline, slides, notes, and audience handouts. Even if you're presenting your material electronically, as described in the next chapter, you'll probably want to print your notes and handouts to rehearse with, to pass around to colleagues for a critique, or to fill information gaps. (The handouts contain printed copies of two, three, or six slides per page. These printouts support your presentation and help your audience to follow along with you.)

The process for producing the actual material for your presentation is the same, no matter what type of output you choose.

1 Determine which printer you want to use. (You might be exposing film, for example, for which you wouldn't be using the draft laser printer down the hall.)

2 Open the presentation that you want to print.

3 Set up your slides by choosing the output medium (paper or transparencies, for example) and orientation, such as portrait or landscape.

4 Start producing the material.

For a more professional look, you can print your presentation on inkjet or laser transparencies. If you're giving your presentation at an informal meeting, you can print your material in grayscale on paper.

To print your presentation, follow these steps:

1 Open the presentation that you want to print.

IV

Microsoft PowerPoint

2 Choose Page Setup from the File menu, and select the appropriate size for your medium in the Slides Sized For drop-down list. Click OK.

3 Choose Print from the File menu. The Print dialog box opens, as shown here:

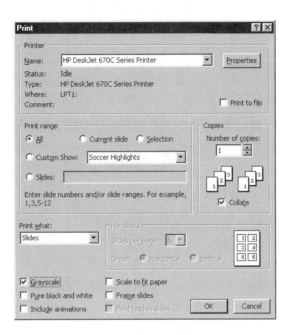

4 Specify the slides that you want to print in the Print Range area. You can print your entire presentation, the current slide, selected slides, a custom show, or a particular slide range. (Just as in Microsoft Word, use commas to separate slides and hyphens to specify ranges.)

5 In the Print What drop-down list, select the material to be printed. Your options are slides, handouts, notes, or an outline of your presentation.

6 To include animations with your printed slides or to print hidden slides, select the appropriate boxes.

7 Click OK to begin printing the selected portion of your presentation.

Print

If you just want to print all your slides quickly, click the Print button on the Standard toolbar. PowerPoint will print your entire presentation immediately, bypassing the Print dialog box.

Using Transparencies

If you have an inkjet or laser printer, you can load the printer's paper tray with transparencies (often called "overheads") made especially for such printers. Some of the transparency products on the market include 3M Inkjet Printer Transparencies (for Hewlett-Packard DeskJets) and 3M Scotch Laser Printer Transparencies. Before you print your slides on overheads, you must change a few options. Choose Page Setup from the File menu to open the Page Setup dialog box, shown here:

Select Overhead before printing to set the dimensions of your slides for overhead transparencies.

By default, slides are set to print in landscape orientation. However, if you print your slides in landscape orientation, you might find that certain overhead projectors will clip off the sides of your transparencies. In that case, consider setting up your slides to print in portrait rather than landscape orientation. To change the orientation, choose Portrait in the Slides area of the Page Setup dialog box. If you change the slide orientation, be sure to review your slides before printing and adjust the placement and sizing of objects on the slides as necessary.

You can print your slides in grayscale, black and white, or color on transparencies, just as if they were paper. When you're ready to print, choose Print from the File menu. To print your color presentation in grayscale or black and white, select the appropriate option in the Print dialog box. This option uses the settings from the Grayscale Preview or pure Black And White view of your slides (described in "Viewing Slides in Grayscale," page 771) to enhance your black-and-white transparencies. To print your color presentation on transparencies using a color printer, choose a color printer from the Name list in the Printer section of the Print dialog box. You'll produce a set of high-quality transparencies that you can project on an overhead projector.

Ordering 35mm Slides

⊗ CAUTION

Give yourself ample lead time if you're going to send your presentation file to a service bureau. If any slides don't develop properly or contain mistakes, you'll have to reshoot them and have them developed again.

The best way to deliver a presentation to a sizable audience is to project 35mm slides onto a large screen. Make sure that the room in which you're going to use a slide projector can be darkened as much as possible. To create 35mm slides, you'll need to copy your presentation to a floppy disk (never send your only original file!) and send the disk to a service bureau. Before you do so, contact the service bureau and ask for the special driver file that you'll need. Your service bureau will provide the file, together with instructions for preparing your files.

In the Page Setup dialog box, select the 35mm Slides option in the Slides Sized For drop-down list so that your slides are the correct dimensions for making 35mm slides. You might need to apply other options as well; your service bureau will tell you what they are.

If you live in North America and you have a modem attached to your computer, you can send your presentation file directly to Genigraphics Corporation. This service bureau will transform your PowerPoint slides into colorful 35mm slides, digital color overheads, large display prints, or posters. Genigraphics gives you a fast turnaround, too. You can use a modem to send your files at any time during the day and you'll get your presentation materials back via overnight delivery.

 NOTE

> If you don't see the Send To Genigraphics command on the File menu, you didn't install the Genigraphics Wizard on your computer. Simply run Setup again to install the option.

To prepare to send your file to Genigraphics, ask yourself the following questions:

- Which file do I want Genigraphics to process?
- What type of presentation output do I want?
- How fast do I want my order processed?
- Do I have my shipping and billing information ready?

Here's how to set up your presentation file for output by Genigraphics:

1 Open the presentation that contains the slides you want to send to Genigraphics.

2 Choose Send To on the File menu, and choose Genigraphics on the Send To submenu.

3 Follow the instructions in the Genigraphics Wizard dialog boxes.

Using Pack And Go

Many presenters run their presentations on a portable computer that they take with them on their travels. Even if you can't install Microsoft Office, including PowerPoint, on your portable computer because of limited hard disk space, you can still use your notebook or laptop computer to deliver your presentation. When you use PowerPoint's Pack And Go feature, you can compress and save your presentation along with all its multimedia files, as well as copy a small portion of PowerPoint called the PowerPoint Viewer onto floppy disks or directly onto your portable computer if it's connected to your desktop system. The PowerPoint Viewer is a mini-application that lets you run your slide show from a computer that has limited hard disk space.

Be prepared. Make sure that you have several formatted floppy disks on hand before you start the Pack And Go Wizard.

To pack up your presentation to go, follow these instructions:

1 Open the presentation that you want to compress and save to floppy disks.

2 Choose Pack And Go from the File menu.

3 Follow the instructions in the Pack And Go Wizard dialog boxes.

To ensure the maximum portability, be sure to select the Include Linked Files and Embed TrueType Fonts options when you're prompted by the Pack And Go Wizard. If you don't select these options, you might need to copy additional files to make your presentation run smoothly.

Publishing the Show to the Web

In this chapter, you've learned how to print material using various output media for your slide show. But what if your show is destined for the Web? How do you take your slides, complete with special effects and Internet links, and publish them to the Web so your family, friends, and business colleagues can view them? PowerPoint 2000 makes giving a presentation on the Web as easy as giving one on your laptop in a conference room down the hall.

After you have put your slide show together, and you're prepared to show it to your immediate audience, you can also make another copy of it in *hypertext markup language* (HTML) to post to the Web. By using the new Save As Web Page command in PowerPoint 2000, you save your slides in a format that can be presented on the Web, including all the animation effects, hyperlinks, and navigation aids that people commonly use for home pages and other Web documents.

To save your slide show in a format suitable for the Web, follow these steps:

1 Open the presentation you want to make ready for the Web.

2 On the File menu, click Save As Web Page.

3 In the Save As dialog box, shown below, enter the filename you want to use for your Web presentation in the File Name box.

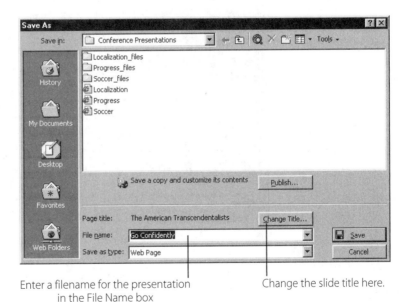

Enter a filename for the presentation in the File Name box

Change the slide title here.

4 Click the Change button to change the page title that will appear when someone views it on the Web.

5 Click Save when you're finished.

That's it! PowerPoint just coded your presentation in HTML and stored it along with all your graphics, animations, and special effects in a folder that you can upload to a Web site.

To see how this slide show will look as a Web presentation, choose Web Page Preview from the File menu. (You can choose this option first, even before you save your PowerPoint presentation as a Web page.)

The slide show opens in your browser, complete with Web navigation controls, as shown in Figure 32-2.

ON THE WEB

The Preview.ppt file is located on the Running Office 2000 Reader's Corner page. For information about connecting to this Web Site, read the Introduciton.

Preview might give you some ideas on how to improve your presentation for a Web audience. To edit your slide show, close the browser window, and you'll be back in PowerPoint. Make any changes you want to your slides before you move them to the big stage of the World Wide Web.

FIGURE 32-2.
A slide previewed as a Web page.

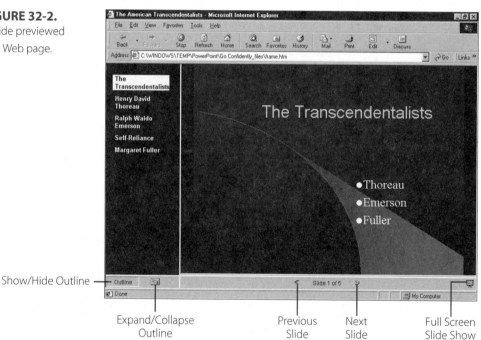

Show/Hide Outline

Expand/Collapse Outline

Previous Slide

Next Slide

Full Screen Slide Show

When you're ready to make your presentation available on the Web, follow this procedure:

1 Click Save As Web Page on the File menu, and check that the filename and page title are correct.

2 Click the Publish button.
   The Publish As Web Page dialog box appears, as shown below.

Select slides to publish to the Web.

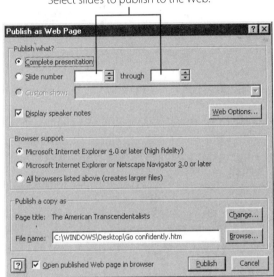

3 Select the options you want for your presentation. You can choose to present a few slides as Web pages, or use your entire presentation.

4 Click Web Options to find more formatting and display options. The Web Options dialog box will appear, as shown below. (You can also open this dialog box by clicking Options on the Tools menu and clicking Web Options.) If you want to include slide transitions and animation effects in your Web presentation, select Show Slide Animation While Browsing.

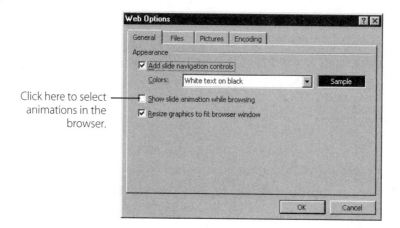

Click here to select animations in the browser.

5 Click the Files tab in the Web Options dialog box. You'll probably want to accept the default settings for managing the files and folder for your Web presentation. If you do, PowerPoint will keep all the necessary related files together to post to the Web. None of your graphic elements or links will be broken.

6 When you're finished selecting Web options for your show, click OK in the Web Options dialog box.

7 To view your presentation as it will look to your Web audience, click Open Published Web Page In Browser in the Publish As Web Page dialog box. Here's the place to thoroughly test your site before you finally publish it: make sure that your links go where you say they will, and that your animations and special effects are displayed properly.

8 Click Publish to complete the procedure.

Your slide show is now in a format ready to be viewed on the Web. When you reopen the presentation you just published as a Web page, you'll notice several files in a folder under the filename you selected. This folder is called a supporting folder, and it contains all the supporting files for your Web page. These files contain all the carefully thought-out graphic elements, bullets, animations, and hyperlinks to other Web sites. When you save your presentation to a Web server, FTP site, or company intranet, you must send this supporting folder with it.

Now that you have mastered the Web, you're ready for the next chapter, which will tell you how to run your show electronically.

Running the Slide Show

You have designed, created, embellished, and planned your presentation down to the last precisely timed second. Now, it's show time! You can deliver your electronic slide show using Slide Show view—one of the best ways to give a presentation. *(Most alternatives involve printing your slides, as discussed in Chapter 32.)* If you created action buttons to branch to other places in your show, this is the time to use them. Microsoft PowerPoint provides many useful features to facilitate your on-screen presentation.

You can use the Slide Navigator tools to quickly locate and move to specific slides during your show. If you're called on to display any hidden slides, you'll learn how to reveal them in Slide Show view. When you use PowerPoint's handy Meeting Minder, you can record action items, take written minutes of the discussion or action points, and even schedule appointments using Microsoft Outlook during the slide show. You can also write and draw (temporarily) on your slides to reinforce a point. Finally, you can broadcast your entire slide show over the Web, including all the rich animation effects, audio and video enhancements, and your own narration for each slide. Because Microsoft PowerPoint 2000 saves and transmits the presentation in HTML, your audience can view your presentation in any browser. When you use PowerPoint 2000, people in a variety of different locations can run your show simultaneously.

Preparing Electronic Presentations

A professional-looking electronic presentation can impress a small or a large audience. A computer slide show fills the screen with your slides, and you can keep the audience interested by using various special effects such as animation, transitions, and timings. For an audience of only three or four viewers, you can use a desktop computer. For a larger audience, you'll need a larger monitor or projection technology such as a projection panel—that is, a transparent color computer display designed to fit on top of an overhead projector.

> **Multiple Monitor Support**
>
> If you have Windows 98 or Windows 2000 installed on your computer, and if you have two adapter cards (one for each monitor), you can run your show on two separate monitors. One projector can present the slide show to your audience, and your own computer monitor can display PowerPoint's Tri-pane view so that you can read your notes and comments as you go.

To make sure that your slide show will be effective and enjoyable, use these guidelines to critique your slides before you set up for your electronic presentation:

■ Transitions and special effects should emphasize your points and not overwhelm your audience.

A sound effect, narration, or some music during a transition will grab your audience's attention. Don't overdo the sound effects, though—they can divert your audience's attention away from the points you want to make. *See Chapter 30, "Adding Special Effects and Internet Links."*

■ Set the timing for your show so that it's neither too fast nor too slow. If you rush through it, you'll exhaust your viewers (and yourself). If you drag it out, you'll put them to sleep! *See the section "Rehearsing the Show," page 781, in the previous chapter.*

■ As you rehearse your timing, study your presentation's visual and informational impact. A good rule to remember is, keep it simple—too many words or pictures on a slide can be confusing and annoying. Your viewer won't know what to look at first and will become too overloaded with information to remember any of it. *See Chapter 27, "Entering and Editing Text," for other guidelines.*

Use the Set Up Show command on the Slide Show menu to finalize the show type and the display attributes of your slide show. (You'll also find the new Projector Wizard in the Set Up Show dialog box.) And use the Page Setup command on the File menu to adjust the size of your slides. That's all you have to do! Now you're ready to run your slide show on a computer.

Using Slide Show View

You have rehearsed and polished your presentation, and now it's time to get on with the show. Any butterflies that you might be feeling will fly away after the first minute or two of your presentation. When you use Slide Show view, you can pull your show off without a hitch. You can move instantly to the next slide or to the previous slide; you can pause a slide to answer questions; you can use the Go feature to go to any slide in the presentation; and you can branch to other slides, documents, or to even a Web page by using the action buttons that you created in Chapter 30. Make sure that you have printed copies of your notes. If stage fright strikes and you can't remember your lines, those notes are your memory on paper. You should also print more audience handouts than you need, just in case some unexpected participants show up.

OK, relax, take a deep breath, and come on stage from any of several wings:

- From Windows Explorer, right-click the PowerPoint presentation file, and choose Show from the shortcut menu. During the presentation, your slides appear in Slide Show view. When you finish the show, you're returned to Windows Explorer.

- Within PowerPoint, you can switch to Normal or Slide view and move to the slide that you want to show first, or you can switch to Slide Sorter view and select the slide that you want to begin with. To start, click the Slide Show button at the bottom left of the window.

- To start your show by using a command, choose View Show from the Slide Show menu, or choose Slide Show from the View menu.

NOTE   To set the amount of time PowerPoint waits before moving through slides, use the Rehearse Timings feature. *(See Chapter 32.)* You set up the timing for each slide and specify how long you want the slide to remain on screen. You can also use the automatic timing method but still advance some slides manually when you need to.

Whichever method you use to start your slide show, the first slide appears on screen. You'll talk about your first slide, and then, if your show is automatically timed, the slide will disappear from the screen, using the transition effect you've specified, and the next slide will appear immediately. If your show doesn't have timings, simply click the slide when you're finished with it and advance to the next slide.

During your show, an icon with an up arrow button appears in the lower left corner of your screen as soon as you move the mouse. When you click this button, you see a pop-up menu. (You can also display this menu by right-clicking a slide.) This menu appears only in Slide Show view, and it's specifically designed to give you fast access to all the commands you'll need while a show is running.

The simplest way to move manually to the next slide in sequence is to click the slide. If you prefer to use the keyboard to move to the next slide, you can press one of the following keys: the letter N, the Space-bar, the Down arrow, the Right arrow, or the Page Down key. To go back to the previous slide, press P, the Backspace key, the Up arrow, the Left arrow, or Page Up. If you prefer to use the pop-up menu, choose Next or Previous from it. To move to a specific slide, type the slide number, and press Enter.

TIP

A fast way to return to your first slide is to hold down both mouse buttons for two seconds.

The mouse pointer arrow appears on the screen when you move the mouse, but you can change its color or remove it by using commands on the Pointer Options submenu. The arrow is useful for pointing to various text and objects on your slides, so you'll probably want to keep it.

If you don't want the mouse arrow pointer or the pop-up menu button to appear on screen, you can hide both of them. You can press Ctrl+H to hide the pointer and button for the entire show. Even when you've hidden the pointer, you can still click your mouse to move to the next slide.

 TIP

Call for "Help!" with F1

If, in the middle of delivering your presentation, you suddenly forget which slide show controls to use—for example, the actions and keys for moving between slides, or for hiding and displaying the arrow pointer, button, or hidden slides—all you have to do is press the F1 key. This key displays a list of controls anytime during your presentation.

Using Slide Navigator

Navigate your way through a slide show with ease by using the handy Slide Navigator. As we indicated in the preceding section, you can click a slide or use keyboard shortcuts to move to slides in sequence or to a specific slide. However, to find a particular slide that you want to discuss with your audience, use Slide Navigator. From Slide Show view's pop-up menu, point to Go, and then choose Slide Navigator from the submenu. You'll see the following dialog box:

Hidden slide ——

Slide Navigator contains a list of all the slides in your show and displays the name of the last slide shown. Notice that the slide number for a hidden slide is enclosed in parentheses. To jump to a slide that's out of sequence, find the slide in the Slide Titles list, and double-click it.

Revealing Hidden Slides

You can place sensitive or confidential information on a hidden slide, but if an audience member presses you for it, you might have to disclose it. PowerPoint gives you several ways to reveal a hidden slide. Right click in the slide that immediately precedes a hidden slide, choose By Title from the Go submenu of the pop-up menu, and then click the hidden slide to show it next. To reveal a hidden slide that appears elsewhere in your presentation, choose it from Slide Navigator's Slide Titles list. Choose Slide Navigator from the Go submenu of Slide Show view's pop-up menu, find the slide whose slide number is in parentheses, and double-click it.

There's a third way to reveal your hidden slides. First jot down a note disclosing where your hidden slide is going to appear in the slide show. To find this out, switch to Slide Sorter view, and look for the slide whose slide number is inside a box that has a diagonal line through it. Then, from the slide that precedes it, just press H to unveil the hidden slide. This is the smoothest way to do it—no menu appears, so your audience won't realize that you're actually displaying a hidden slide.

Closing the Show

At the end of your show, you can display a black slide to indicate that the presentation is over. A black slide is similar to seeing "The End" at the end of a movie (plus, it gives your viewers' eyes a chance to adjust). Before you run the slide show, choose Options from the Tools menu, click the View tab, and select the End With Black Slide option.

As you learned in the last chapter, you can also run your show in a continuous loop, rather than ending it with the last slide. For example, if you're demonstrating a new product at a trade show, you might want to run the show continuously on a computer in your booth. To do so, choose Set Up Show from the Slide Show menu, and select the Loop Continuously Until 'Esc' option in the Set Up Show dialog box. When you decide to stop the slide show, press Escape.

> **NOTE** To stop the slide show at any time, you can press Escape or choose End Show from the Slide Show view pop-up menu.

Using Action Buttons for Branching

After creating those action buttons, you need to know how to use them in your slide show. *See Chapter 30, "Adding Special Effects and*

Internet Links." When you arrive at a slide that contains an action button, just click the button to branch to another slide, to begin another presentation, to start another Microsoft Office 2000 program, or to connect to the Web. If you created an action button on the slide to which you branched, click that button to return to the original slide or to move to a different slide. If you branched to another presentation, PowerPoint automatically returns you to the slide from which you branched in your original presentation at the end of the second presentation. If you launched an application, you can edit the document live for your audience. For example, you can demonstrate the effects of a what-if? scenario in a budget created in an Excel worksheet, and your audience can watch the changes reflected in an Excel chart. When you're ready to move to the next slide, choose Exit from the application's File menu.

Using Meeting Minder

PowerPoint's Meeting Minder is a helpful reminder tool that lets you create action items and record minutes of the meeting—as well as schedule appointments in Outlook—while you're delivering your presentation. During an informal slide show, you might want to create a list of action items based on the feedback you're getting on the slides. For example, at a staff meeting, you might discuss a certain topic that triggers a new idea, task, or question that you need to deal with later.

You can also take minutes during a slide show. Perhaps you're giving a presentation at a quarterly budget meeting, and you're the one responsible for recording the minutes of the meeting. Use Meeting Minder to record the minutes as the meeting progresses, typing up the important points or items to be acted on. After the meeting, transfer your minutes to your note pages or to a new Microsoft Word document. From there, you can print them and distribute copies to all the attendees and to those people who couldn't attend.

Finally, you can start Outlook from the Meeting Minder to update your schedule or handle other administrative tasks. To select this option, you need a working copy of Outlook on your system that has a copy of your schedule.

Follow these steps to work with Meeting Minder:

1 During your show, right-click a slide and choose Meeting Minder from the pop-up menu. You'll see the following dialog box.

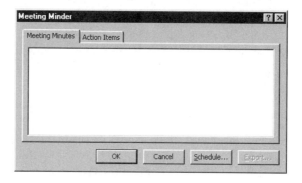

? SEE ALSO

For more information about finalizing and printing presentations, see Chapter 32, "Setting Up and Publishing the Show.

2 Click the appropriate tab that indicates what you'd like to do, or click Schedule to start Outlook.

3 If you're adding an action item or meeting minute, type it in the space provided.

4 To export action items and meeting minutes to a Word document, click Export, and select the Send Meeting Minutes And Action Items To Microsoft Word option. Then click Export Now.

5 When you're finished, click OK.

Action items are added to a new slide at the end of the current presentation. You can refine this information into a finished slide or print it the same way that you print other note pages and slides.

> **Update Your Speaker Notes**
>
> You can also amend your speaker notes during a presentation by choosing Speaker Notes from the Slide Show view's pop-up menu. You might find this command useful if you find a mistake in your notes while you're giving a presentation, or if you think of a new analogy for explaining a tricky point. Your edits will appear in the notes pane of Normal view the next time you need them.

Using the Pen to Mark Slides

Amazingly, you can actually annotate your PowerPoint slides using the Pen feature during an electronic slide show, just as you would use a marking pen on overhead transparencies. You can even choose from a large assortment of pen colors.

To use the Pen feature during a show, right-click a slide, point to Pointer Options on the pop-up menu, and then click Pen on the submenu or press Ctrl+P. This will change the pointer to an on-screen pen. Hold down the mouse button as you write or draw on a slide.

The writing or drawing that you add to a slide during a show is a temporary overlay; it doesn't stay on the slide once you've moved on to another slide in your show.

If you dislike the pen color, you can change it. To do so, right-click a slide, point to Pointer Options, point to the Pen Color submenu, and pick a new color.

To return to the regular mouse pointer, choose Arrow from the pop-up menu, or press Ctrl+A.

Broadcasting Your Presentation

You might have an important presentation for your boss on the opposite coast, for the Mac-based graphics people in the office upstairs, and for the sales team scattered across the country who will view it on their Microsoft Windows laptops. If you want to do the slide show live, and include all the sophisticated effects you have employed, you can use PowerPoint 2000's broadcast capabilities to bring your show dynamically to the Web.

Because PowerPoint 2000 saves your presentation in native HTML format, it will be recognized by your diverse audience, whether they use Macs, Windows-based machines, or a UNIX system, and regardless of which Web browser they favor.

If you're in charge of the broadcast, it could be your responsibility to schedule when it will run, decide whether you will record and save the broadcast, and select which attributes you want to offer your audience. If you have the courage, here's where you can ask for audience feedback!

If you're the presenter, and you want to broadcast your slide show on the Web, follow these steps:

1   In PowerPoint, choose Online Broadcast from the Slide Show menu.

2   Click Set Up And Schedule. Then select the Set Up And Schedule A New Broadcast option. (If you want to use the NetShow Wizard for help in understanding how NetShow contributes to your broadcast, click the Tips For Broadcast button in the Broadcast Schedule dialog box.) Click OK to continue.

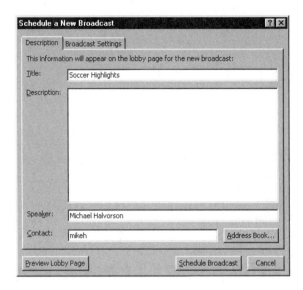

3 In the Schedule A New Broadcast dialog box, click the Description tab, and fill in the information that will identify your presentation. You can also click Preview Lobby Page to see how this information will look in your browser.

4 Click the Schedule Broadcast button in this dialog box, and Microsoft Outlook, or whichever e-mail program you use, will open and you can finish scheduling your meeting.

 TIP

PowerPoint 2000's Online Collaboration

PowerPoint's Online Collaboration feature enables you to share your work with colleagues linked by the Internet or by an intranet, as you can when you use the other Office 2000 applications. You can set up a company-wide meeting by pointing to Online Collaboration on the Tools menu. While you operate the slide show on a single monitor, your audience watches the show on various computers across the network. If you, as the presenter, would like input and editing assistance, you can enable your audience to contribute in this way. *See "Using Online Collaboration," page 86 for more detailed information about how to make the most of online meetings.*

PART V

Microsoft Access

CHAPTER 34

Understanding Data Basics

Just as Microsoft Word is designed to work with documents containing text and images, and Microsoft Excel is designed for use with worksheets containing numbers and charts, Microsoft Access is designed to manage data. *Data* consists of a collection of information; data becomes useful information when it's organized in a meaningful way. Of the Microsoft Office 2000 applications, Access is the tool that you use to provide that organization.

A *database* consists of a collection of *objects*—tables, forms, data access pages, queries, and reports—that you use to manage and present the data. In Access, you manage these database objects using the Database window. The process of creating a database involves these basic steps:

1 Create a database by designing and building tables to hold data.

2 Enter the data.

3 Develop additional database objects for viewing, editing, and printing the information.

The Database Foundation

Before you can begin working with your database, you must establish a vessel to hold your data. In Access, the *table* object holds the data. Each database contains one or more tables, and you can use separate tables to hold related information. For example, one table might hold information about students, and another table might hold information about the classes in which the students are registered. Relationships must be defined between these tables so that they can work together. This combination of all the tables and their relationships makes up the foundation of your database.

Fields and Records

When you look at an Access table like the one shown in Figure 34-1, notice its resemblance to an Excel worksheet. *(Worksheets are covered in Part 3 of this book)*. Both are organized into rows and columns, and individual data items are entered into the cells that are created by the gridlines. What makes an Access table different from an Excel worksheet, however, is that in Access, each column in a table represents a *field,* which is a category of information, while each row in the table consists of a single *record*, which holds all the information for one item in the table.

This distinction is more than just a difference in terms. Unlike a column in Excel, in Access each field can contain only one type of data—text or numbers or dates, and so on. In Access, each record contains the information about a single item (for example, everything you're tracking about one student or everything you're tracking about one class).

When you work with information from the database, you often work with a single record at a time. Specifically, when you use a *form* to view the data in a table, you will generally see only one record at a time; and when you generate a *report*, each line that is printed usually represents a single record. (When you design a form or a report, you determine which fields will be included from the record.)

FIGURE 34-1.

The fields and records in an Access table.

Each column is a field.

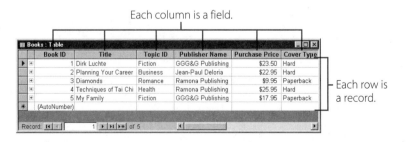

Each row is a record.

Access is quite flexible in the types of data that it lets you define for your fields. You can define a field to store text, numbers, dates, times, amounts of money, or *hyperlinks* (links to Web pages or other documents). In fact, Access includes a special field type, *OLE Object*, which allows you to insert an object from another Windows program, such as a picture, an animation, a sound, or even a movie clip. *(See Chapter 51, "Sharing Data Among Office Applications," for more information on using OLE objects.)* In general, however, you do most database work using the text, number, and date field types that are the focus of the chapters in this part of the book.

The *Relational* in a Relational Database Management System

Database applications can be divided into two basic types: those that create *flat-file* databases, and those that create *relational* databases. Flat-file databases have been around for many years. Among the current programs that create them are Microsoft Works and Microsoft Excel. (In Excel, a database is called a *list*.) In a flat-file database, all related information must fit into a single table. This means that any information that is common to several records will be repeated for each of those records. For example, a table that contains a collection of class-enrollment records, each of which contains duplicate information, is shown in Figure 34-2.

W ON THE WEB

The Sample University.mdb database file, used for the examples in this section, is on the Running Office 2000 Reader's Corner page. For information about connecting to this Web site, read the Introduction.

As computerized databases evolved in recent years into more sophisticated tools, it became obvious that a flat-file database was an inefficient way to store large quantities of data—and thus the idea of a relational

V

Microsoft Access

FIGURE 34-2.

In a flat-file database, duplicate information is common.

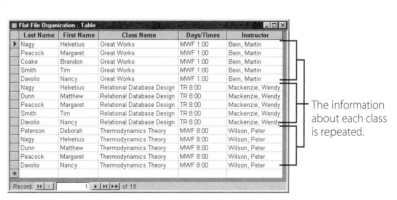

The information about each class is repeated.

database developed. The relational database is the type created in Access. In a relational database, several different tables are used and *relationships* exist between the tables. A relationship lets you enter information into one table and connect that information to a record in another table via an identifier.

Figure 34-3 shows the same information as Figure 34-2, but in Figure 34-3 the information is organized into two related tables, Enrollment and Classes. The Class ID field of the Enrollment table is linked, or *related to*, the Class ID field of the Classes table. Notice that the class information that was repeated in Figure 34-2 needs to appear only once in Figure 34-3, in the second table.

Structuring your data in a relational format has a number of advantages:

- You'll save considerable time by not having to enter the same data again and again across many records.

- Your database will be smaller, often a small fraction of the size of a flat-file database, saving space on your system and making the database more portable if you want to share it with others.

- Data entry errors will be greatly reduced. Imagine entering the same data for a large number of records. How many times can you type *Thermodynamics Theory* into the Class Name field without error? If the repeated data is stored in a related table, you need to enter the correct information just once in the related table; then, in the original table, you enter only the identifier of the information—usually a short numeric or alphanumeric code—each time the repeated data occurs. (You can even set up the field so that the person entering data can just select the identifier from a list, without typing anything!)

- Updating data—such as a new instructor for one of the classes in the example that we just gave—is a one-step process if you have stored the instructor names in a separate Classes table. If instead you had included the instructor names in the Enrollment table for each enrollment, you would have to manually update the name for every enrollment.

Relationships

To see how multiple tables in an Access relational database are related, you can choose Relationships from the Tools menu in Access or, when the Database window is active, you can click the Relationships button on the Database toolbar to see the Relationships window, shown in Figure 34-4. Using the Relationships window is described in detail in the next chapter.

FIGURE 34-3.

In a relational database, repeated information can be entered once in a separate table.

This field is related to this field.

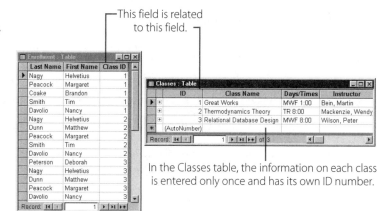

In the Classes table, the information on each class is entered only once and has its own ID number.

FIGURE 34-4.

Access provides an overview of the relationships among your tables.

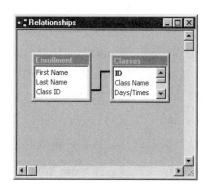

V

Microsoft Access

> **NOTE**
>
> A next step in consolidating the example database shown in Figure 34-3 would be to place the First Name and Last Name fields of the Enrollment table (and any other information you want to store on each student) within a separate related table, because the student information is also repeated in several records. Then, the Enrollment table would need to store only a short identifier for each student who is referenced.

As you can see, relational databases have quite a few advantages. Understanding the theory of relational databases, however, isn't crucial for understanding how Access works. What you do need to understand is that a field is a category of information, an entry is the information that goes into a field for a single record, a record consists of the related entries for an individual item in the database (and fills up a row within a table), and you can set up relationships between separate tables so that you need to enter repeated information only once.

 The Database Window

Access stores all the objects belonging to a single database in one database file. This database file is what you open and work with when you use the Access program. The different objects belonging to a single database can include the tables that contain the actual data; the forms, data access pages, and reports that you use to present the data; queries, which you use to ask questions of the data; and modules and macros, which you use to automate tasks within the database. All the objects within a database are organized by their object type, and are displayed in different sections of the Database window, as shown in Figure 34-5.

 The Book Collection.mdb database file, used for the examples throughout the remainder of the chapter, is on the Running Office 2000 Reader's Corner page.

> **NOTE**
> When you close the Database window, Access also closes all the associated database objects. If you have made changes to the *design* of the database objects but haven't saved the changes, Access asks whether to save those changes. Rest assured that any changes to the *data* stored in the database are automatically saved the moment you make them.

Moving to the Database Window

As you work with the different objects in your database, you might sometimes need to return to the Database window. If the window is currently visible, you can simply click it. Otherwise, you can activate it in one of the following ways:

- Click the Database window button on the Windows taskbar. The button will be labeled with the name of the database that you're working with, followed by a colon and the word *Database*. For example, if you're working with the Book Collection database, the label would be *Book Collection : Database*.

- Choose it from the Window menu. The menu item for opening the Database window is labeled in the same way as the button on the Windows taskbar.

- Click the Database Window button at the right side of the toolbar.

- Press F11.

Database
Window

FIGURE 34-5.
The Database window displaying the Reports section, which lists all reports in the database.

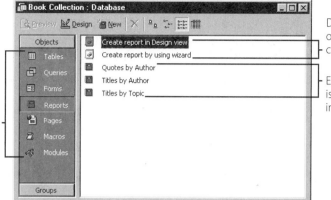

Double-click one of these items to create a new report.

Each of these items is an existing report in the database.

Click one of these items to open the corresponding section of the Database window.

 NOTE

You can use the various commands on the Edit menu to work with database objects themselves. To delete an object, select it in the Database window, and then choose Delete from the Edit menu. To make a copy of an object, select it, choose Copy from the Edit menu, and then choose Paste from the Edit menu. Access prompts you for a name for the copy and might require additional information about exactly what's to be copied. For example, when you work with a table, you can copy the structure, copy both the structure and the data, or append the data to an existing table.

An Alternative — The Switchboard

When you create a database using a Database Wizard (described later in the chapter), in addition to the standard Database window, you also get a Switchboard window like the one shown here:

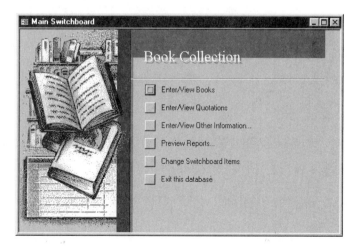

The Switchboard is a simpler and more user-friendly database interface than the Database window, although it provides fewer features. It's intended primarily for people who use the database rather than work on its design, and it lets them easily perform common tasks. It typically contains commands for opening database forms, for previewing and printing reports, for customizing the Switchboard, and for closing the database. You have the option of working with the database by using the Switchboard, by using the Database window, or by using a combination of the two.

If your database has a Switchboard, it will probably appear in place of the Database window when you first open the database, and the Database window will be minimized at the bottom left corner of the Access window. To bypass the Switchboard, click its Minimize or Close button, and click the Restore button in the Database window.

Database Objects

Access provides much more than just a container for a collection of data—it provides the tools you need to present meaningful information. You'll find that the various forms, reports, and queries that make up a database file can be as important as the tables used to hold your actual data.

See What Objects Are in Your Database

You can display a concise list of all the objects that are in your database by choosing Database Properties from the File menu and then opening the Contents tab. You can display the same information by right-clicking the title bar of the Database window and choosing Database Properties from the shortcut menu.

Working with an Access database involves two distinct modes or phases of operation—the *design phase* and the *data-managing phase*.

Before your database can manage your information, you must design it, manually or with the assistance of a wizard. Each and every object within the database—including the tables that hold the data—must be designed. You do this by creating the object and then customizing it to meet your needs. In most cases, you work in Design view, which provides tools for modifying the design. Figure 34-6 shows a table in Design view, and Figure 34-7 shows a form in Design view.

FIGURE 34-6.
Creating or modifying a table in Design view.

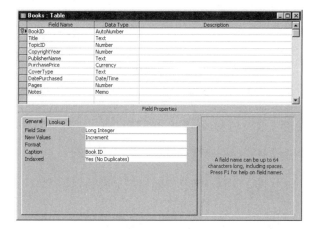

FIGURE 34-7.
Creating or modifying a form in Design view.

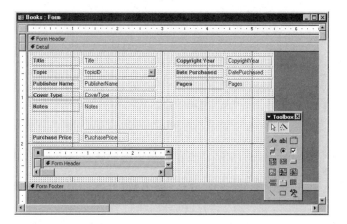

In both cases, the design of the object determines what you see when you work with data using that object. For example, the design of a table controls the type of data that you can enter into the table, and the design of a form determines the particular fields of data that you can access from the form.

After the design phase, you use the various database objects to manage the actual data—that is, to enter information, edit that information, query the database to retrieve the specific data you want, print reports that present your information in the desired format, or work with the data in other ways. When you begin managing the data, you normally switch into Datasheet or Form view, where you can enter, edit, and organize data in various ways, as discussed next.

While it might seem confusing at first, one of the truly helpful features of Access is that as you work with different types of database objects and switch among the different views for designing and using those objects, the menus and toolbars also change to reflect the tasks you need to perform. The commands that become available as you activate different windows are the ones that make sense for you to use in the current window. If you have difficulty locating a command in Access, make sure that the proper object's window is active and that you're in the right view.

Tables

 SEE ALSO

For more information on tables, see Chapter 35, "Creating Tables and Relationships." For details about datasheets, see Chapter 36, "Using Datasheets to Enter and View Data."

As mentioned previously, you define the structure of a table using Design view. Entering and editing the table's data is commonly done using Datasheet view. Datasheet view resembles an Excel worksheet, with the information organized in rows and columns. In Access, recall that each row represents a single record and each column a single field. Figure 34-8 shows how data appears in a table in Datasheet view.

You can sort and filter a table's data using the datasheet, as well as rearrange the layout of the datasheet itself. You can then print the datasheet, and the data will appear on paper exactly as it appears on the screen.

> **NOTE**
>
> As you'll learn later, you can also display an Access form or query in Datasheet view.

FIGURE 34-8.
Datasheet view is useful for displaying several records at a time.

Book ID	Title	Topic ID	Publisher Name	Purchase Price	Cover Type
1	Dirk Luchte	Fiction	GGG&G Publishing	$23.50	Hard
2	Planning Your Career	Business	Jean-Paul Deloria	$22.95	Hard
3	Diamonds	Romance	Ramona Publishing	$9.95	Paperback
4	Techniques of Tai Chi	Health	Ramona Publishing	$25.95	Hard
5	My Family	Fiction	GGG&G Publishing	$17.95	Paperback
(AutoNumber)					

Forms and Data Access Pages

A form is a window that displays a collection of controls—such as labels, text boxes, check boxes, and lists—for viewing, entering, and editing the information in database fields. Rather than directly opening a table in Datasheet view, you can access the data using a form. Keep in mind that a table stores the actual database data, while a form is merely a tool for viewing or modifying the data.

A form typically displays only one record at a time, and provides access to selected fields within one or more tables. A well-designed form arranges the information in a logical and accessible manner. Figure 34-9 shows a typical Access form displayed in Form view. Compare the presentation of data in this form with the Datasheet view of the table that's shown in Figure 34-8.

? SEE ALSO

Forms and data access pages are covered in Chapter 37, "Using Forms to Enter and View Data."

A powerful advantage of using a form object is the ability to pull in data from more than one table. The form in Figure 34-9 displays information from two tables simultaneously. The data at the top of the form comes from a table containing specific information about each book (the Books table). The data at the bottom of the form, labeled Author, comes from a separate table that stores the names of the authors of the books (the BookAuthors table). (This arrangement allows you to enter more than one author for a single book).

A *data access page* is similar to a form, but is stored in a separate file in HTML format so that you can view it in a Web browser and thereby access the database from the Internet or a company intranet. (*HTML*—meaning Hypertext Markup Language—is the standard format for Web pages.)

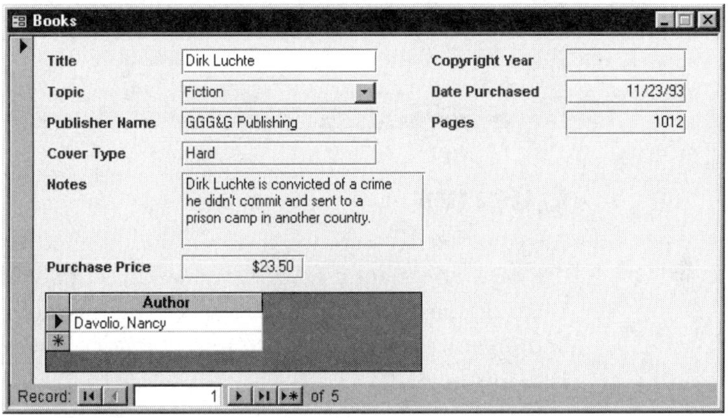

FIGURE 34-9.
A form makes it easy to view and enter data for a single record at a time.

Reports

You use reports for printing information from the database. Designing a report not only lets you print information in an attractive and effective format; it also—like a form—lets you combine data from more than one table and organize data from one table based on the data from other tables, all in the same report. You design a report on screen using Design view, and you have to use your imagination to envision what the final report will look like.

Microsoft Access

SEE ALSO

Creating and using reports is treated in Chapter 39, "Using Wizards to Generate Reports," and modifying both reports and forms is covered in Chapter 40, "Formatting Forms and Reports."

You design the report by adding visual objects known as *controls* to the design grid. Each control displays an item of information. When you define a control, you specify the source of the information within the database, as well as the control's position on the printed report and its printed appearance. When you print your report, the facts and figures from your tables are neatly organized and summarized to create a report like the one shown in Figure 34-10. (This figure shows the report as displayed on screen using the Print Preview command, which allows you to see how the report will look when printed.)

FIGURE 34-10.
Unlike other database objects, reports are primarily intended to be printed rather than viewed on screen.

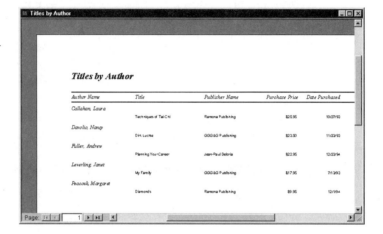

Queries

After you have created your tables and entered your data into them, the most important type of database object might be the query. By using queries, you can gather selected information from your database and organize it either for use in reports or for viewing on screen in Datasheet view or in a form.

You design a query in Design view, using it to ask a question of your database. The answer appears in Datasheet view, which looks exactly like Datasheet view for a table. The primary difference between a datasheet for a table and a datasheet for a query is that the query's datasheet can combine information from multiple tables, based on their related fields.

 TIP

> To include the query results in forms or reports, you must first make sure to save the query design. You then select the query object in place of a table object for your form or report design.

Each query consists of one or more criteria that you use to create a pattern or rule for selecting matching records. For example, if you use the criterion *<20* in your Purchase Price field, the query will match only records for which the value in the Purchase Price field is less than 20. Figure 34-11 shows the design grid in Design view that you use to set up a query.

? SEE ALSO

Queries are described in great detail in Chapter 38, "Using Queries to Get Answers."

The data in each record is compared to the query criteria, and if the information in the record matches the criteria (for example, the price is less than $20), the record is included in the query's datasheet. Each query can contain multiple criteria. The criteria can be organized so that all must be true for a record to be included, or so that any single matching criterion is sufficient for including the record.

In addition to asking questions, you can set up Design view to provide summary information about your data, as well as to group and organize the information in your database. These techniques rely on the use of a total row, which you can add to the query design grid, and they provide an on-screen alternative to generating and printing a report.

FIGURE 34-11.
Use Design view of a query to ask for specific data.

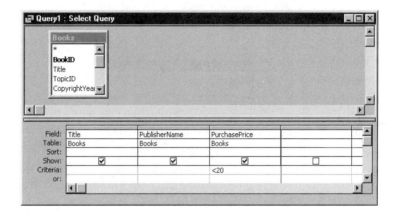

Programming Tools

Access also provides tools similar to those in Word and Excel for creating macros, as well as complete access to the Visual Basic for Applications (VBA) language. Using these tools, you can achieve results that range from automating common database tasks you perform frequently, to creating sophisticated custom database interfaces with entirely new functions and capabilities. These topics, however, fall within the realm of programming and are beyond the scope of this book.

Saving Data and Objects

Because the data is the most important component of your database, Access automatically saves any changes that you make to your tables' contents the moment you make them.

On the other hand, the designs of various database objects (tables, forms, reports, and so on) that you create for your database must be saved individually. For example, if you create a report to summarize the data in several of your tables, you must save that report within the database. When you do, Access asks you to provide a name for the report, and the name then appears within the Database window in the Reports section. In general, you save the objects within the database while designing them, and Access takes care of saving the data while you work with the various objects.

Creating and Opening Databases

The first step in using Access is to create a database. Your starting place is the Microsoft Access dialog box that appears when you start Access:

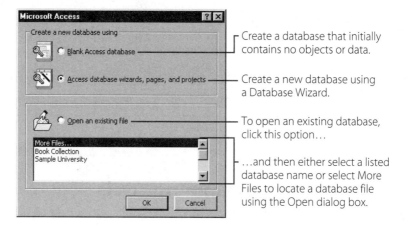

Create a database that initially contains no objects or data.

Create a new database using a Database Wizard.

To open an existing database, click this option…

…and then either select a listed database name or select More Files to locate a database file using the Open dialog box.

If you have already created a database, or if you want to examine a sample database supplied with Access, select the Open An Existing File option, and select a database file at the bottom of the Microsoft Access dialog box.

Creating a Blank Database

A blank database is just that—it contains neither tables, forms, reports, nor any other objects of any kind. You create each and every database object yourself. If you select the Blank Access Database option when you first start the program, Access prompts you for the new database name by displaying the File New Database dialog box, shown in Figure 34-12. Enter the name and location for Access to use when storing the database, and click the Create button. Access will create the new database and open the Database window. You can then begin adding database objects using the techniques described in the following chapters.

If you've already started Access, you can create a blank database by choosing New from the File menu or clicking the New button on the Database toolbar (which is displayed when the Database window is active), clicking the General tab in the New dialog box, and then double-clicking the Blank Database icon. The next section supplies more information on the New command.

Creating a Database Using a Wizard

Another way to create a new database is to use a Database Wizard. If you have just started Access, simply select the Access Database Wizards, Pages, And Projects option in the Microsoft Access dialog box, and click the OK button. Or, if you're already working in Access, you can choose New from the File menu, click the New button on the Database toolbar (which is displayed when the Database window is active), or press Ctrl+N.

New

FIGURE 34-12.
The first step is to name your database, using the File New Database dialog box.

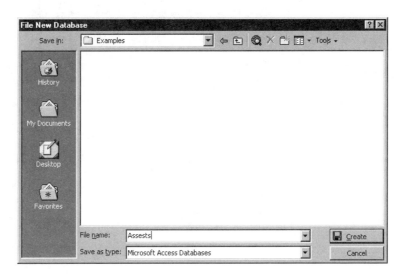

Microsoft Access

Whichever method you employ, Access opens the New dialog box. Click the Databases tab, shown in Figure 34-13.

On the Databases tab, you can select the appropriate Database Wizard to use to build a database for you. (As you saw, the Blank Database icon on the General tab is for creating a blank database, forgoing the assistance of a wizard.)

> You can also get to the various Database Wizards by choosing New Office Document from the Windows Start menu or by clicking the New Office Document button on the Office Shortcut Bar. When the New Office Document dialog box appears, click the Databases tab.

Notice that when you click the icon for a particular Database Wizard, graphic information about the database appears in the Preview area to help you make your selection. Access provides wizards for creating databases that serve a wide variety of purposes, ranging from managing a collection (such as Book Collection, Music Collection, and Wine List) to tracking business accounts (such as Asset Tracking, Ledger, and Time And Billing). Select the wizard that generates the database that meets your needs most closely, and click OK (or simply double-click the wizard). In the remaining chapters in this part of the book, you'll learn how to modify the database to match your needs exactly.

Access will then display the File New Database dialog box (see Figure 34-12, on the preceding page), where you give the new database a name and save the database file on your hard disk. The File New

FIGURE 34-13.
The Databases tab of the New dialog box lists the Database Wizards.

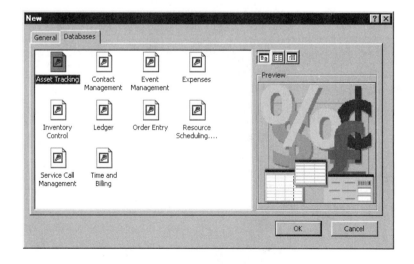

Database dialog box is similar to the Save As dialog box used in other Office programs. *For general instructions on using this dialog box, see "Using the Save As Command," page 70.* When you have specified a name and location for your database, click the Create button to have Access store the database file. The wizard will then open the first Database Wizard dialog box and begin helping you design and create a complete database.

With most Database Wizards, the wizard's opening dialog box lists the different types of information the database will store; it will create a different table for each information type. Figure 34-14 shows an example. When you click the Next button, you can choose the specific fields from these tables that the wizard will add to the database. You make these decisions in a dialog box similar to the one shown in Figure 34-15.

FIGURE 34-14.
The opening dialog box displayed by the Asset Tracking Database Wizard.

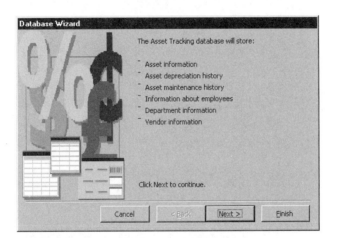

FIGURE 34-15.
The next dialog box that a Database Wizard shows generally lets you specify which fields to include in your new database tables.

These tables will be included in the database.

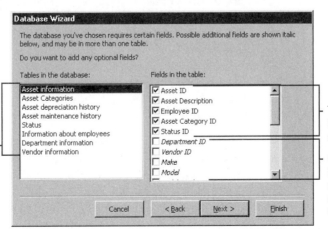

These fields will be included in the selected table.

Optional fields are in italics. Click the check box for each optional field you want to include.

The remaining dialog boxes that the Database Wizard displays allow you to select the style of screen displays and printed reports, the database title, and other attributes. When you have made all your selections, click the Finish button, and Access will create the database, including all the appropriate tables, forms, reports, and queries. Of course, you have the option of adding to these items or modifying them later.

Opening an Existing Database

Once you have created a database, you can open it in several ways from within Access. The first, which becomes available when you start Access, is by using the bottom portion of the Microsoft Access dialog box, shown here:

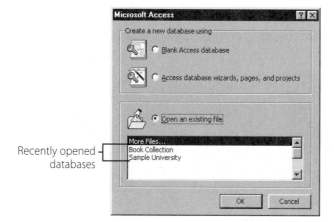

Recently opened databases

The list at the bottom of the dialog box contains your most recently used databases. To open one, double-click its name. If a database that you want to use isn't included in this list, double-click the More Files option at the top of the list to display the Open dialog box, shown in Figure 34-16.

Open

You can also display the Open dialog box by choosing Open Database from the File menu or by clicking the Open button on the Database toolbar (displayed when the Database window is active).

The Open dialog box works the same way in Access as in the other Office applications. In this dialog box, locate the folder that contains your database file, and double-click the database filename to open it. You can use the file search features to help find a specific database. *For instructions on searching for files, as well as general information on using the Open dialog box, see "Opening an Existing Document," page 60.*

FIGURE 34-16.
The Open dialog box displays all the databases on your system, folder by folder.

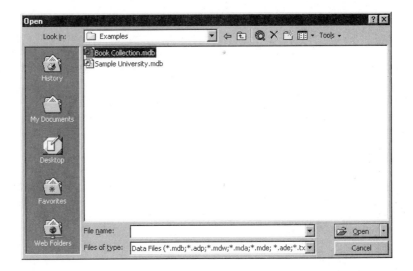

You can also open an Access database by choosing Open Office Document from the Windows Start menu or by clicking the Open Office Document button on the Office Shortcut Bar. In the Files Of Type list at the bottom of the Open dialog box, you can select Databases(*.mdb) so that other types of files won't be displayed.

In the remaining chapters of this part of the book, you'll gain an understanding of how the different database objects work, and you'll acquire the skills for creating a new database from scratch or for modifying a database generated by a Database Wizard.

V

Microsoft Access

CHAPTER 35

Creating Tables and Relationships

The organization of the tables and the relationships among them determine how you'll be able to access the information contained in your database. When you generate a database using one of the Database Wizards, Microsoft Access creates the tables and the relationships for you. If, however, you want to go beyond what Access can do for you, you need to learn how to design, create, and modify your own tables and their relationships.

Designing Your Database Foundation

One of the least understood aspects of creating a database—and what makes it different from using any other type of application—is that you must do much of the work away from the computer, before you start working in Access. Whereas you can sit down at a word processor and start drafting a memo to edit later, or start typing numbers into a spreadsheet, intending to divine your formulas at the last minute, it's less efficient to design your database on the computer than away from it.

Designing your database requires several distinct steps. You might be best served by sitting down with a pad of paper and several sharp pencils with erasers; or, if you prefer, you can use Word for this step, creating and maintaining an electronic version of a design document.

1 **Decide on the content of your fields.** Identify the fields of information you want to include in your database. Try to identify every element that you might ever want to store and access. For example, if you're creating a database about books, you would obviously want to include the book's title, author, and subject. But you might also want to consider including the publication date, the publisher's name, whether the book contains figures, the book's page count, its price (domestic and overseas, if applicable), whether it's paperback or hardcover, and so on.

How Much Data Is Enough?

It's essential to balance the usefulness of having lots of information against the difficulty of managing it. While you might be tempted to design a database that includes every possible fact, you'll quickly tire of filling in all the necessary fields when it's time to enter your data. Therefore, you must include only the information that you really think you'll use. Still, it's better to include too many fields than too few. You'll find it easier to stop filling in some of your less essential fields than to go back later and add fields that require you to update every record manually. Imagine cataloging an extensive music collection and then realizing that you forgot to include a field telling whether each item was on CD, tape, or another medium!

2 **Decide on the type of information for your fields.** Identify the type of information that will go into each field. Your primary choices are text, numbers, and dates, although Access provides several other options. *(The various data types for fields are described later in this chapter in "Working with the Design of a Table," page 835.)*

3   Design your database framework. Decide how to organize the field names and data types within your database. This means deciding which fields should appear within a given table, and in which order. Once you have set up and organized the database properly, you'll be able to arrange the fields in your reports and on screen in almost any conceivable manner.

4   Relate your tables to one another. Another design consideration is whether to relate tables to one another, which is desirable if the information in some fields in a table is repeated in several records. By moving these fields into a separate table and setting up a relationship between the two tables, you can save considerable space and improve the accuracy of your data.

For example, you might have a Books table that lists information on each book in a collection, and many of these books will likely have the same publisher. You might therefore consider placing the information on each publisher (its name, address, and so on) in a separate table, perhaps named Publishers, giving each publisher an identifying ID, and establishing a relationship between the two tables. Then, in your Books table, you would simply type the ID for each publisher rather than having to type the publisher's name and other information each time it occurs.

Organizing and arranging your fields into one or more tables and creating relationships to eliminate duplicated information is called *normalization*. Access provides some assistance with this rather complex process by providing a Table Analyzer Wizard, described in the sidebar "Analyzing an Existing Table," page 850, in the last part of this chapter.

5   Designate your fields as primary keys or indexes. A *primary key* consists of one or more fields that uniquely identify each record in a table. Designating a field as an *index* (that is, *indexing it*) increases the speed of searches or sorts performed with that field. A field designated as a primary key is automatically indexed, but you might want to index additional fields that you'll use frequently for searches or sorts.

You should make primary keys and indexes part of your planning process and define them as you create each table. They're discussed later in the chapter. Identifying relationships between data in separate tables, understanding when it's best to split information into two or more tables, and determining primary keys and indexes are the skills that underlie quality database design.

6 Start building your database on the computer. At this point, you can begin creating your database on the computer. By now you should have formulated the basic definitions for each table and the relationships between the tables. However, you still have planning to do. Consider how you want to enter the data. Will you be importing it from another source that's already computerized, copying it from a list, or entering each item separately? Consider these questions:

- Should you complete certain tables first? Would it be worthwhile, for example, to develop a list of all the publishers, assign them IDs, and have that list available as you enter book information?

- Should you have Access assign default values for some of the fields? This is a particularly common practice in address databases where most of the addresses are within a single city or state.

- Should you include additional fields for asking particular types of questions, or for creating reports? In general, these types of fields consist of information that you can use to group the records. For example, you might decide to include information in your Book Collection database indicating where each book is located.

⭐ **TIP**

Let Access Perform Your Calculations

If need to display values that Access can derive by performing math on other fields in your tables, *don't* include them as part of the table's structure. Instead, in your forms, reports, and queries you can add fields whose values are the result of calculations, without making these fields a part of the table. Adding calculated fields allows Access (rather than the data entry person) to perform the calculation and eliminates storing unnecessary information. For example, if you want to display an inventory of office supplies, your table needs only two fields: Units On Hand (for example, number of boxes of pencils) and Measure Of Unit (for example, the number of pencils in a box). Access can do the multiplication and display on a form or report the total number of each item.

Creating a Table Using the Table Wizard

(?) SEE ALSO

For information on working with datasheets, see Chapter 36, "Using Datasheets to Enter and View Data." For information about defining the table's structure, see "Working with the Design of a Table," page 835. For help in importing a table, see "Importing Data," page 846.

As it does for other database objects, Access provides a wizard to help you create tables. The Table Wizard will walk you through the process of creating a table based on a table in one of the Access Database Wizards. You just choose the table that most closely matches the kind of data you need to track, and then select the specific fields that you want to include.

Before you can use a wizard to help you create a database object, the database file that is to receive the new object must already exist and be open. The database can be a completely empty one (created using the Blank Database template), or it might already contain one or more tables. (The example database, Sales, that you see in the figures in this section already contains two tables, Customers and Products.) *See "Creating and Opening Databases," page 820, for more information about creating a database.*

The following is the procedure for using the Table Wizard to create a new table:

1   Click Tables on the Objects bar in the Database window, and click the New button, as shown in Figure 35-1.

   Access will display the New Table dialog box, which is shown in Figure 35-2, on the next page. This dialog box lets you choose from a variety of ways to create a new table. In this procedure, however, you'll create the table using the Table Wizard.

FIGURE 35-1.
Open the Tables section, and click the New button to start creating a new table.

Click here to create a new table.

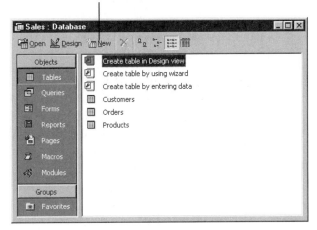

V

Microsoft Access

FIGURE 35-2.
Access offers several
different methods for
creating a new table.

Create an empty table, and
open it in Datasheet view.

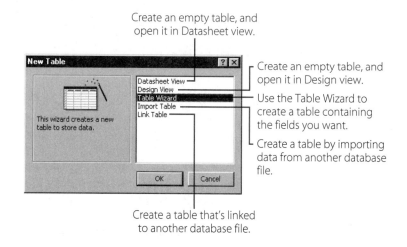

Create an empty table, and
open it in Design view.

Use the Table Wizard to
create a table containing
the fields you want.

Create a table by importing
data from another database
file.

Create a table that's linked
to another database file.

 The Sales.mdb database file, used for the examples in this section, is on the Running Office 2000 Reader's Corner page. For information about connecting to this Web site, read the Introduction.

2 Select Table Wizard from the list in the New Table dialog box, and click OK.

Access will then display the first Table Wizard dialog box, which is shown in Figure 35-3.

 To create a new table using the Table Wizard, you can simply double-click the Create Table By Using Wizard item in the Tables section of the Database window, rather than performing steps 1 and 2

3 Scroll through the Sample Tables list box until you find one that seems similar to what you need, and then select it. (In the example shown in the figures, we selected the Orders table.)

4 Using the four buttons shown in Figure 35-3, copy each of the sample fields that you want from the Sample Fields list into the Fields In My New Table list.

Note that each of these fields is more than just a name: it also has an appropriate data type and other properties for the type of information it stores. For example, the OrderID field is designed to store a unique identifier for each order record, and it is therefore given a numeric data type and is assigned the AutoNumber property (which causes Access to automatically assign the field a unique value for each new record).

FIGURE 35-3.
The first Table Wizard dialog box lets you select the fields for your new table.

First, select the type of sample tables you want listed…

…and then select a particular sample table.

Add the selected field.

Add all sample fields.

Remove all fields from the right-hand list.

Remove the field that's selected in the right-hand list.

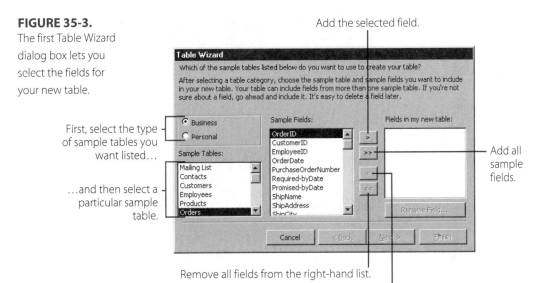

> **NOTE**
>
> If you selected an appropriate sample table, the Sample Fields list should provide all or most of the fields you need for your new table. You can also include fields from more than one sample table in your new table. To do this, merely select different tables from the Sample Tables list as you're compiling your list of fields on the right. If you still need additional fields, you can add them manually after the table has been generated.

5 Once you have added a field, you can rename it. Just select the field name in the Fields In My New Table list box and click the Rename Field button. Access opens a small dialog box in which you type the new name. After you enter the name, click OK.

6 When you have finished selecting fields, click the Next button and the second Table Wizard dialog box will appear. (See Figure 35-4, on the following page.) Here you can change the default name for your table and decide whether to let Access select the primary key for you. If you're not sure how to select a key, let Access do it for you. *(Or see the section "Designating a Primary Key," page 845.)* Click the Next button.

7 If your database contains more than one table, the dialog box shown in Figure 35-5, on the next page, appears and allows you to set relationships between your new table and any of the existing tables in your database.

FIGURE 35-4.
The second Table
Wizard dialog box
lets you specify the
table name and
decide whether to
let the wizard set
the primary key.

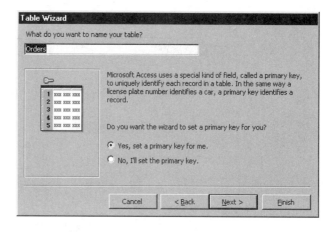

SEE ALSO

For more information
on entering data using
Datasheet view, see
Chapter 36, "Using
Datasheets to Enter
and View Data." For
details about using
forms, see Chapter 37,
"Using Forms to Enter
and View Data."

For each of the existing tables in the database, the wizard displays an item in the list that indicates whether it recommends establishing a relationship with that table. (In the example shown in Figure 35-5, the wizard proposes establishing a relationship between the new table and the existing Customers table but not the existing Products table.) You can change a relationship description by selecting it and clicking the Relationships button. This will open a dialog box that lets you remove or add a relationship. If you add one, you'll be able to select the type of relationship. Click the Next button to continue. *You'll learn more about defining relationships in the section "Relating Your Tables," page 848.*

FIGURE 35-5.
This dialog box
appears only if your
database already con-
tains other tables.

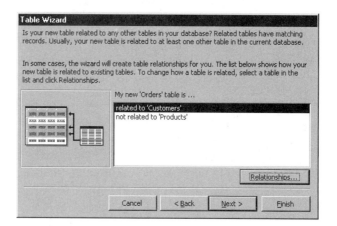

8 The Table Wizard's final dialog box (Figure 35-6) lets you choose what you will do immediately after the wizard creates your table:

- Modify the table design. This takes you directly to Design view, where you can work with the table's structure.

- Enter data directly into the table using Datasheet view.

- Have the wizard create a form for you to use to enter data. If you'll be entering data from the keyboard, consider selecting this option.

  After making a choice, click the Finish button and Access will complete your table.

Let the Wizard Make Your Choices

After you have selected the fields you want in the first Table Wizard dialog box, you can click the Finish button within any of the wizard dialog boxes to have the wizard create the table using any settings you have already made plus the default choices for all the remaining settings. If you accept all the default choices, the wizard gives the table a standard name, defines the primary key, assigns any relationships it considers useful, and opens the new table in Datasheet view for you to begin entering data.

FIGURE 35-6.
The final Table Wizard dialog box lets you choose how to begin working with your new table.

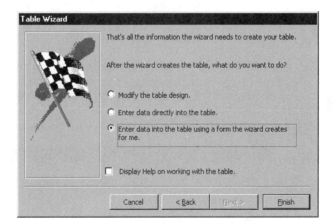

Working with the Design of a Table

To define or modify a table's structure, you use Design view. This view allows you to add, remove, or rearrange fields; define the name, the data type, and other properties of each field; and designate a primary key for the table. You can use Design view to modify an existing table or to create a new one.

The following are several different ways to open a table in Design view. Choose the one that's most appropriate for your current stage of working with the table:

- If you have created a new table using the Table Wizard, refer back to step 8 of the previous section. At this point you can select the Modify The Table Design option to have Access immediately open the newly generated table in Design view.

- To modify the design of a table you have already created, select Tables on the Objects bar in the Database window, select your table, and then click the Design button at the top of the Database window.

View

- If your table is already open in Datasheet view, you can switch to Design view by choosing Design View from the View menu, or by clicking the View button at the left end of the toolbar.

- To create a new table from scratch in Design view, click the New button at the top of the Database window, and in the New Table dialog box, select the Design View option. Or, double-click the Create Table In Design View option in the Tables section of the Database window. (See Figure 35-1, page 831.)

Figure 35-7 shows the Design view of the Books table from the Book Collection sample database. The grid at the top of the Table Design window lists the fields in the table, one per row, and gives the name, data type, and an optional description for each field. (These are three

FIGURE 35-7.
Design view lists all the table's fields and their properties.

The current field.

Properties for the current field are displayed on these tabs.

A property box.

A description of the property that was clicked (here, the Caption property).

A property box.

of the field's *properties*, explained later in this chapter in the section "Setting the Field's Properties"). If you're using Design view to create a new table, this list will initially be empty.

The Book Collection.mdb database file, used for many of the examples throughout this chapter, is on the Running Office 2000 Reader's Corner page.

The tabs in the bottom half of the window show all the other properties for the current field. (The *current field* is the one that was most recently selected or clicked—it's marked with an arrow in the box at the left end of the row.) Each property is displayed in a separate box within the grid. When you click a property box anywhere in the window, the insertion point appears within it, and a description of the property is displayed in the lower right window area.

Adding, Removing, and Rearranging Fields

Using Design view, you can add new fields to a table, remove fields, and move or copy fields from one position in the list of fields to another.

Adding a Field

To add a new field to a table at the end of the list, click in the Field Name column of the first blank row in the grid at the top of the Table Design window, and enter a field name. You can type up to 64 characters for the field name, including spaces. Ideally, however, you should make the name short and descriptive of the contents of the field. You should then proceed to set any of the field properties that you want to change from their default values, following the instructions that will be given later in this chapter (in the section "Setting the Field Properties").

To insert a new field between two existing fields in the list, click the lower of the two fields, and then choose Rows from the Insert menu or click the Insert Rows button on the toolbar. Another way to insert a field is to select the entire row below the desired insertion position by clicking in the box at the left end of the row, and then press the Insert key.

Insert
Rows

Clicking here selects —
an entire row.

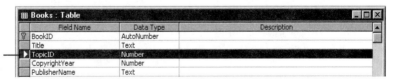

Don't be too concerned about the initial position of your new field—
you can easily move it (as described later in "Moving or Copying a
Field"). Also, keep in mind that the order in which fields are listed in
Design View isn't especially significant. Arranging the fields in a certain
order might be more logical and might make it somewhat easier to
work with the design. Also, the order of the fields in Design view (from
top to bottom) determines their initial order in Datasheet view (from
left to right). However, you can rearrange the fields in Datasheet view
without affecting Design view. And the field order in Design view
doesn't affect the order of the fields on forms, queries, or reports.

 TIP

> **Remember the Pop-Up Menu**
>
> As you work in Access, keep in mind that you can often display a pop-up menu
> of useful commands by right-clicking a field, title bar, column or row heading, or
> other object. The menu will display commands that are appropriate for working
> with the particular object that you clicked. For example, you can insert a new
> field into a table by right-clicking the row below the desired insertion position
> and then choosing Insert Rows from the pop-up menu.

Removing a Field

Delete
Rows

To remove a field from the table, click anywhere in the field's row, and
choose Delete Rows from the Edit menu, or click the Delete Rows button on the toolbar. Another way to delete a field is to select its entire
row by clicking in the box at the left, and then press the Delete key.
You won't be able to delete a field that's used to create a relationship
with another table; you must first remove the relationship.

WARNING

> If your table already contains data, Access will ask for confirmation before actually
> deleting a field. Be aware that deleting a field will delete its data for every record
> of your table.

Moving or Copying a Field

To move a field to a different position in the list, first select its entire
row by clicking in the *row selector* (the box at the left of the row).
Then do either of the following:

- Use the mouse to drag the box up or down to the new position.

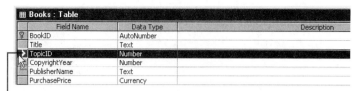

└ Drag the row selector to move the selected field up or down in the list.

■ Choose Cut from the Edit menu (or press Ctrl+X). Then click in the row below the desired new position of the field, and choose Paste from the Edit menu (or press Ctrl+V). Be sure to just click in the row below the desired insert position so that it contains the insertion point; if you select this entire row, it will be deleted when you paste. (Note that this method won't work if the field is currently part of one or more relationships.)

> If you want to make a copy of a field, use the second method for moving a field, but choose the Copy command (or press Ctrl+C) rather than choosing the Cut command (or pressing Ctrl+X). After the field is copied, click the field name and type in a different, unique name. (You won't be able to save your modifications if two fields have the same name.)

Setting the Field Properties

Each of the fields in a table is described by a set of *properties*. The properties of a field determine how the field's data is stored, handled, or displayed. They include the field name, the data type, the description, and other features such as the field size, format, and caption. You can view and set a field's properties within the boxes in the Table Design window (both in the grid at the top of the window and on the tabs in the bottom portion). (See Figure 35-7, page 836.) Note that when the insertion point is within a property box, Access displays information about that property in the lower right corner of the window, and you can get more detailed information by pressing F1.

As you saw in the previous section, when you create a new field in Design view, you must enter a name for it. Initially, each of the other properties of the new field will have a default value. Sometimes the default is no setting at all, and the property box will be blank. You can modify any of these properties, or you can simply accept the default.

Renaming a Field

To change the name property of a field, click in the box containing the name (which is in the Field Name column), and type in the name you want. Changing the field name doesn't affect any of the existing table relationships or change anything within your database.

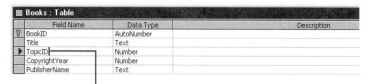

Click in the Field Name property box
to edit or change the name of a field.

Despite what you would expect, changing a field's name might not even change the name that appears at the top of the field's column in Datasheet view. This is because the field name is displayed in Datasheet view only if you haven't entered a different name in the Caption property, one of the field properties you can set in Design view. This property will be described in more detail later.

Setting the Data Type

The data type determines the kind of data that can be entered into a field. As previously mentioned, you must assign a data type to each field in an Access table. Access provides a variety of data types, as described in Table 35-1. The default type is Text.

To enter or change the data type for a field, click in the Data Type column for the field that you want to change, and select a new data type from the drop-down list:

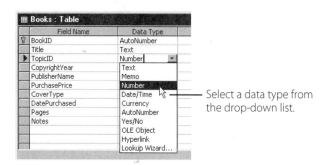

Select a data type from
the drop-down list.

TABLE 35-1. **Data Types Used in Access**

Data Type	Usage
Text (default)	Holds any type of characters, either letters or numbers. The number of characters that can be stored depends on the value (0 to 255) assigned to the Field Size property (described later). Note that even if you set Field Size to 255, Access will use only the amount of memory required by each entry.
Memo	Similar to Text, but holds up to 64,000 characters.
Number	Holds a numeric value that you can use to perform mathematical calculations or comparisons. The size and type of number you can store is determined by the current setting of the Field Size property (described later).
Date/Time	Holds valid calendar dates for the years 100 through 9999 and clock times in either 12- or 24-hour format. This data type lets you sort and calculate data chronologically.
Currency	Accurately stores monetary values for use in financial calculations.
AutoNumber	Stores a unique number that Access assigns as each new record is added. Access either increments the number by one with each new record, or it assigns a unique random number according to the setting of the New Values property. These numbers aren't reused when you delete records, and you can't change their values.
Yes/No	Efficiently stores one of two values: true or false, yes or no, on or off (according to the setting of the Format property). You can set the field using a check box in Datasheet view or on a form.
OLE Object	Holds an OLE object (such as a Microsoft Excel spreadsheet, a Microsoft Word document, or a picture, sound, animation, or video clip) that you insert by using the Object command on the Insert menu. See Chapter 51, "Sharing Data Among Office Applications," for information on OLE objects.
Hyperlink	Holds a hyperlink—that is, the location of another database object, a Microsoft Office document, or a page on the World Wide Web. You insert the hyperlink into the field by using the Hyperlink command on the Insert menu. You can then open the target object, document, or Web page by clicking the hyperlink in the field.
Lookup Wizard	Selecting this item runs the Lookup Wizard, which assists you in adding a lookup column to the field (without changing the field's data type). A lookup column is a list box displayed in the field that contains values from another table or query or a fixed list of values that you specify when you create the lookup column in the Lookup Wizard. To enter a value into the field, you simply select an item from the list box rather than type it in. You can later modify the properties of the lookup column by changing values on the Lookup tab at the bottom of the Table Design window.

V

Microsoft Access

Setting Other Field Properties

If you want, you can assign a description to a field by clicking in the Description property box in the upper portion of the Table Design window and typing the text you want.

You set the remaining field properties using the General and Lookup tabs in the bottom half of the Table Design window. To set additional properties for a field, do the following:

1 Click anywhere within the field's row in the upper part of the Table Design window, or select the row. (It will then become the current field and will be marked with an arrow in the row selector.)

2 Click the General tab in the lower half of the window to set general-purpose properties, or click the Lookup tab to modify a lookup column you have added to the field (as described in the last item in Table 35-1).

3 Click in a box for any property that you want to modify, and enter the new value. Consult the property description displayed in the help area on the right, or press F1 for detailed information about the current property.

The set of additional properties that you can apply to a field depends on the field's data type. In general, these properties control the way data is entered, stored, and displayed in the field, and they also provide a means of enforcing the integrity and consistency of your data. The following sections describe most of the important properties.

Field Size Property

The Field Size property lets you determine how much space is available for a particular field. It's available only for a field that has the Text or Number data type. For a Text field, the Field Size specifies the maximum number of characters that can be stored in the field; you can enter a value between 0 and 255. (The default value is 50.) For a Number field, you choose a value from the drop-down list that determines the size and type of number that can be stored:

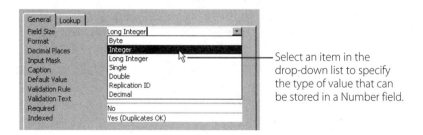

Select an item in the drop-down list to specify the type of value that can be stored in a Number field.

For example, you can choose the default Long Integer value to store whole numbers ranging from approximately -2 billion to +2 billion, or the Double value to store numbers with decimal components (such as 3.14).

Format Property

The Format property determines how the data is displayed on the screen or how it's printed. Choose the format that you want from the drop-down list. For example, for a field that has the Date/Time data type, you could choose to display the date as 30-Jun-99, 6/30/99, and so on.

Decimal Places Property

The Decimal Places property lets you choose the number of decimal places that Access displays for a field that has the Number or Currency data type. (It affects only the way the number is displayed, not the precision of the value that is stored internally.) Choose a specific number of decimal places from the drop-down list, or choose Auto (the default value) to display the number of decimal places specified by the Format property.

Input Mask Property

Most data types also give you the option to define an *input mask*. (By default, there is no input mask.) An input mask assists you in entering valid data into a field. It displays placeholder characters showing you the number of characters you need to enter (usually _ characters, which are replaced by the characters you type); it includes separator characters so you don't have to type them (such as the parentheses and dash in a telephone number); and it prevents you from typing an inappropriate character (for example, a letter when you're entering a phone number). Figure 35-8 shows an input mask for a date field in the Book Collection database.

An input mask is created by using a series of codes as placeholders. For example, the input mask for the date in Figure 35-8 is specified as 99/99/00. The *9* means only a number can be entered, but is not

FIGURE 35-8.

This input mask makes it easier to enter a valid date in the mm/dd/yy format.

	Date Purchased	Pages
⊞	11/23/93	1012
⊞	12/23/94	395
⊞	12/1/94	593
⊞	10/27/93	236
⊞	7/13/93	226
⊞	04/█ /	

Books : Table

required; the *0* means only a number can be entered and is required; and the */* (slash) marks are passed through as constants. For a complete description of the input mask codes, press F1 while the insertion point is in the Input Mask property box.

> NOTE

> Access provides an Input Mask Wizard to guide you in setting up an input mask without entering codes manually. Activate it by clicking the button displaying an ellipsis (…), at the right end of the Input Mask property box.

Caption Property

If you enter text into the box for the Caption property, Access will use this text to label the field in Datasheet view, at the top of the field's column. If you leave the Caption box empty (the default value), Access labels the field using the field name. This property gives you flexibility in how you want your fields to appear for those viewing your database or entering data into it, without your having to change the actual field name.

Default Value Property

If you're creating a database in which a field usually contains the same value—for example, the City field in an address database when most of the addresses are in the same city—you can assign that value to the Default Value property. (By default, this property is blank.) Then, whenever Access creates a new record, it will insert the value into the field for you (for example, *New Orleans*). Of course, you can then change the value if you need to enter another city. Either type the desired initial value into the Default Value property box, or click the button with the ellipsis (…) that appears to the right of the box to get help in building a complex expression.

Required Property

If you select Yes in the Required property box, Access will require that a value be entered into the field when the record is created or modified. If you choose No (the default value), the field can be left empty.

Indexed Property

You can also determine whether a field is indexed. Indexing a field significantly speeds up searching or sorting operations, as well as queries done on the field, but it requires more space for storing the information and can make adding, deleting, or updating records slower. The primary key for a table (discussed in the next section) is automatically indexed. These are the choices available from the drop-down list in the Indexed property box:

- Yes (Duplicates OK)—The field will be indexed, and you'll be able to enter the same value (that is, a *duplicate* value) into more than one record.

- Yes (No Duplicates)—The field will be indexed, and you must enter a unique value into the field for each record so that the index will always be able to retrieve a single record based on only the information in this field. (This is the default for a field that's designated as the primary key, discussed next.)

- No—The field won't be indexed. (This is the default for all fields except the one designated as the primary key.)

Indexes

To see a list of all the indexed fields in a table, or to modify characteristics of the indexing, choose Indexes from the View menu or click the Indexes button on the toolbar.

Designating a Primary Key

While a primary key isn't required, every table should be assigned one. The primary key consists of one or more fields that Access can use to uniquely identify and organize the records contained within the table. When you designate a field (or several fields) as the primary key, the field's Indexed property is automatically set to Yes (No Duplicates), and you won't be able to change this setting. Thus, you can quickly sort or retrieve the records using the primary field key, and you'll be barred from entering duplicate values into this field. Also, when you enter or modify the data in a record, Access doesn't let you leave a primary key field blank.

In most cases, just a single field is used as the primary key, though in situations where the data in a single field can't be unique for each record, two or more fields might be designated. In this case, the data in all the primary key fields combined must be unique for each record. (For example, an inventory table might contain a part number field and a subpart number field, where neither field is unique by itself but when taken together, they form a unique combination.)

Primary Key

If you used the Access Table Wizard to create your table as described earlier in this chapter (in the section "Creating a Table Using the Table Wizard," page 831), you probably had Access create the primary key for you. If not, or if you want to change the primary key that Access selected, you can set it now by clicking the field that you want to use as the primary key and then choosing Primary Key from the Edit menu or clicking the Primary Key button on the toolbar.

To designate multiple fields as the primary key, you must select all the fields before choosing the Primary Key command or clicking the Primary Key button. Recall that to select a field, you click the row selector (the button at the left) for the row containing the field. The entire row will then be highlighted. To select several fields, select the first one, and then select each additional one while holding down the Ctrl key.

Saving the Table Design

Whenever you create or modify a table's definition in Design view, you must save your work before you can enter or edit data. Access will give you the opportunity to save your changes when you close Design view. If you're making extensive changes, however, you should also periodically save your work by choosing Save from the File menu, by clicking the Save button on the toolbar, or by pressing Ctrl+S.

Save

If the table has no data, Access quickly saves the table's structure and allows you to either continue working on the table design or switch to Datasheet view to begin entering data. If data is already stored in the table, however, Access checks to see whether the new structure can hold the old data or whether the changes would cause a conflict.

If your design changes caused a problem, you'll see an error message. You should then write down the design changes you want to make (so that you can implement them later), abandon the changes you made by closing the table without saving the changes, and then open the table in Datasheet view and make any necessary modifications. For example, if you change the Indexed property of a field to Yes (No Duplicates), Access can save this design modification only if the field contains no duplicates. If the field does contain duplicates, Access advises you to go to the table and modify the contents of the field in all records where necessary to eliminate the duplicates. (*An easy way to find the duplicates is to sort the table on that field, as described in the section "Sorting Your Information," in Chapter 36, page 866.*)

Importing Data

You can create a new table in an Access database by importing data from another database file. You can import data from a database file that was created by the current version of Access, by a previous version of Access, or by another program (such as Excel, dBASE, or Paradox).

To create a new table by importing data, follow these steps:

1 Create or open the database that will receive the imported data.

2 Select Tables on the Objects bar in the Database window, and click the New button to display the New Table dialog box.

3 Select the Import Table option, and click OK to start the Import Wizard.

 The Import Wizard will begin by displaying the Import dialog box, shown in Figure 35-9.

FIGURE 35-9.
The first step in importing data is to locate it.

5 Select the file.

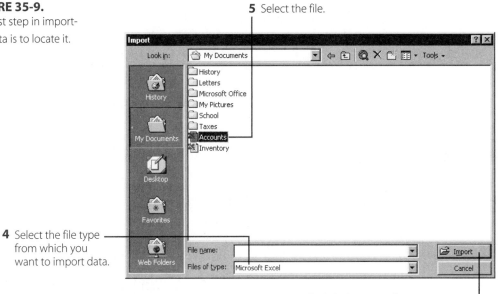

4 Select the file type from which you want to import data.

6 Click the Import button to continue.

7 Make the choices you want in all the dialog boxes that the Import Wizard displays.

 The particular dialog boxes you'll see depend on the type of file from which you're importing the data. If you import from an Access database, you'll be able to select the exact database object and object features to import. If you import from an Excel workbook, you'll be able to select a specific worksheet, choose the columns (fields) to import, and specify the way they're imported.

8 When you're finished, click the Finish button.

 The Wizard will create a new table that will contain the imported data. If some of your records are imported incorrectly, Access will create an Error table listing any problems. If this happens, it's usually best to go back to your original data file, correct the errors, and then import the data again.

Linking Data

When you import data, a copy of the data is brought into the new table, where it becomes an integral part of the database and is indistinguishable from data entered using Access. As an alternative, you can create a new table by linking it to data within another database file. When you link to data, the data is not copied into the new table, but rather remains within the original database file. Access, however, stores a connection to this file so that you can view or modify the data using an Access table. (You can also view or modify the data using the database program that originally created the file.)

To create a new table by linking, follow the same basic procedure as when importing data, except select the Link Table option rather than the Import Table option in the New Table dialog box.

Relating Your Tables

You have already seen the advantages of placing repetitive information in your database in separate, related tables. (*To review these advantages, see the section "The* Relational *in a Relational Database Management System," page 809.*) For instance, in the example database shown in Figure 34-3, page 811, the Enrollment database contains a Class ID field that is related to the ID field in the Classes table. This means that the Class ID field in an enrollment record contains an identifier that matches the identifier stored in the ID field of one of the class records. This links the two records and obviates the need to store a complete class description in the enrollment record.

Although you might be aware of the connection between a field in one table and a field in another table, it's important that this connection be explicitly defined within Access. Such a definition is known as a *relationship*, and each of the fields is said to be *related to* the other field. The tables containing these fields are also said to be related. Once a relationship has been designated, Access can help you maintain the integrity of the related data and can make it easier to access related data. (For example, a lookup column, described near the end of Table 35-1, page 841, can let you choose a value from a related table so that you don't have to remember it and type it in manually.) Relationships also allow you to create queries, forms, and reports that display information from several tables at once (queries, forms, and reports are discussed in the following chapters).

To see the existing relationships among tables in a database, open the database, and choose Relationships from the Tools menu, or, if the Database window is active, click the Relationships button at the right end of the toolbar. Access will open the Relationships window, as shown in Figure 35-10, on the next page, and add the Relationships menu to your menu bar. The lines between the table lists indicate relationships between specific fields. The symbols at the ends of some lines represent the type of relationship and will be explained later in this section.

Relationships

> **NOTE**

If your database doesn't contain any relationships when you issue a command to open the Relationships window (and you haven't previously added tables or queries to the window), Access will first display the Show Table dialog box, which lets you select tables or queries to display in the Relationships window. This dialog box is explained later in this section. When you close it, the Relationships window will be activated.

When working with the Relationships window, be sure to arrange your table lists so that you can see the relationship lines clearly. You can move a table list in the Relationships window by using the mouse to drag its title bar. Do this to untangle the relationship lines and make them easy to see and understand.

When a scroll bar appears at the right side of the table list, it indicates that only some of the field names are visible. (Notice the Books list in Figure 35-10.) To remove the scroll bar and to see all the fields at a glance, you can increase the height of the table list by dragging the top or bottom border of the box containing the list. Likewise, you can increase the width of a table list by dragging a side border so that the complete field names are visible. Figure 35-11, on the next page, displays the same relationships as Figure 35-10, but has the tables arranged more neatly.

> **NOTE**

If you used a Database Wizard to create your database system, Access will create all the necessary relationships among your tables. Also, when you create a new table using the Table Wizard, you can have the wizard create relationships between the new table and existing tables in the database. (See step 7 in the section "Creating a Table Using the Table Wizard," page 831.) At any time you can have the Table Analyzer Wizard (see the sidebar "Analyzing an Existing Table") suggest relationships between tables. In general, it's easier to let Access create relationships for you. You might, however, need to modify or remove a relationship, or add a new one. The instructions given in the remainder of this section will show you how.

FIGURE 35-10.
When the Relation-
ships window is first
displayed, it might be
difficult to see all the
relationships.

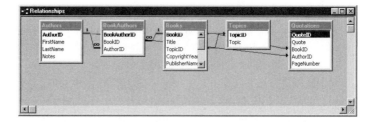

FIGURE 35-11.
The relationship lines
are untangled, and the
Books table list has
been enlarged to show
all its fields.

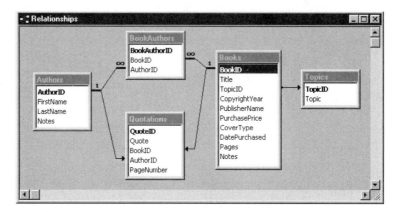

In a typical relationship, the field in one of the two tables has a unique value. That is, Access requires you to enter a different value into the field for each record. Two types of fields store unique values: a primary key field and a field whose Indexed property is set to the value Yes

Analyzing an Existing Table

Say you have a table that was created from a source outside Access, or you realize that a table you've created using Access contains several fields with information that repeats regularly. It's a good idea to let Access analyze such a table, to determine whether it would be best to split it into a series of related tables.

To start this process, point to Analyze on the Tools menu, and then choose Table from the submenu. The Table Analyzer Wizard starts and guides you through its various steps. The first time you use this wizard for a given database, it describes the purpose for analyzing the table and the process of reducing repetitive data. In general, if a table contains one or more fields that contain repeated data, the wizard will give you the option of putting those fields into one or more separate tables that are related to the original.

(No Duplicates). The other table's field in a typical relationship has a nonunique value; that is, its Indexed property is set to No or to Yes (Duplicates OK). The table containing the unique field is commonly known as the *primary* table, and the table containing the nonunique field is commonly known as the *related* table. Because a field in the primary table can match several fields in the related table, the relationship between these fields is called a *one-to-many* relationship.

To illustrate a one-to-many relationship, consider the example tables discussed in Chapter 34 and shown here in Figure 35-12. In the primary table, Classes, each class is listed once; therefore, each class's ID, the primary key, occurs only once, making it a unique field. In the related table, Enrollment, many people enroll in the same class; therefore, the related Class ID field often contains the same value, making it a nonunique field and completing the one-to-many relationship.

 **ON THE WEB**

The Sample University.mdb database file, used for the examples throughout the remainder of this section, is on the Running Office 2000 Reader's Corner page.

FIGURE 35-12.
In a one-to-many relationship, one record in the primary table can match several records in the related table.

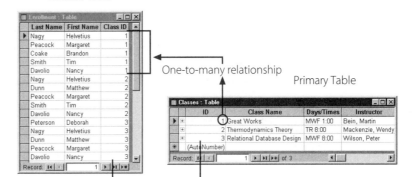

NOTE

Although it rarely occurs, both fields in a relationship can be unique; in this case, the relationship is known as *one-to-one*. It's also possible to indirectly create a *many-to-many* relationship by using a third, related table. These types of relationships are less common than the one-to-many relationship and are not discussed in the book. For more information, look up "relationships" in the Access online Help.

Enforcing Referential Integrity

You can select the Enforce Referential Integrity option when relating two tables to tell Access to make sure that the correspondence between the tables is maintained as you enter data and work with the database. Specifically, it ensures that each record in the related table will properly match a record in the primary table. To select this option, the data types of the related fields must be the same, and the relationship can't be indeterminate. If the option is enabled, Access will control changes you attempt to make to the related fields in the following ways:

- Access won't allow you to enter a value into the related table field that lacks a matching value in the primary table field. You can, however, leave the related table field blank (indicating that it doesn't refer to any record). In the example tables shown in Figure 35-12, on the preceding page, Access would let you enter only *1*, *2*, or *3* into the Class ID field, or leave this field blank.

- Access won't permit you to change the value in the primary table field if matching records are already in the related table field. In Figure 35-12, you wouldn't be able to change the value of the ID field in any of the records in the Classes table because each of the ID values is already used in the Enrollment table. (Actually, in this example you couldn't change this field anyway because it has been assigned the AutoNumber data type.) However, you can select the Cascade Update Related Fields option in the Edit Relationships dialog box, and then Access will let you change the primary table field and will automatically update all the matching values in the related table field so that referential integrity is maintained between the two tables.

- Access won't let you delete a record in the primary table if matching records are in the related table. In Figure 35-12, none of the Classes records could be deleted because each one has matching records in the Enrollment table. However, you can select the Cascade Delete Related Records option in the Edit Relationships dialog box, and then Access will enforce referential integrity by deleting all the matching records in the related table for each record you delete in the primary table.

You'll now learn how to add, modify, or remove individual relationships.

To create a relationship between two tables, follow these steps:

1 Make sure the database is open but that all tables are closed.

2 Open the Relationships window. Check whether all the tables that you want to relate are included in the window.

Show
Table

3 To add one or more tables to the Relationships window, choose Show Table from the Relationships menu or click the Show Table button on the toolbar, and then click the Tables tab.

4 Select a table you want to add, and click the Add button. When you're done adding tables, click the Close button. (The Show Table dialog box appears automatically when you choose the Relationships command if the Relationships window is empty.)

> 🌟 **TIP**
>
> You can remove a table list from the Relationships window by clicking anywhere on it and pressing the Delete key. Doing so won't remove any relationships that are associated with this table, but will merely hide the table and its relationships from view.

5 To create the relationship, just drag one of the fields to the field you want to relate it to. For example, to create the relationship shown in Figure 35-12, do the following:

To create the relationship, drag this field…
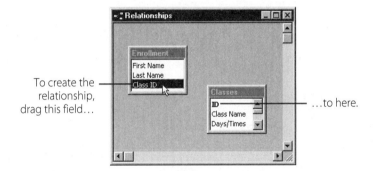
…to here.

In this example, you could also drag the ID field to the Class ID field; the effect would be the same. Access will immediately open the Edit Relationships dialog box, as shown here:

Names of the two fields being related.
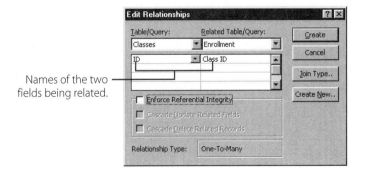

6 The Edit Relationships dialog box lists the names of the fields involved in the relationship and lets you set several options. Access identifies the category of the relationship in the Relationship Type box at the bottom of the dialog box. If neither field is unique, the text box will display Indeterminate. You shouldn't create an indeterminate relationship because it would have limited usefulness. If you select the Enforce Referential Integrity option, Access will make sure that as you enter or modify the data, the correspondence between the related fields is maintained. See the "Enforcing Referential Integrity" sidebar in this chapter.

NOTE

If you click the Join Type button in the Edit Relationships dialog box, you can specify which records will be displayed by default when you create a query that's based on the related tables. Queries are discussed in Chapter 38, "Using Queries to Get Answers."

7 When you have set the options you want in the Edit Relationships dialog box, click the Create button.

Access will return you to the Relationships window, which will now display a line indicating the relationship you just defined, as in the following:

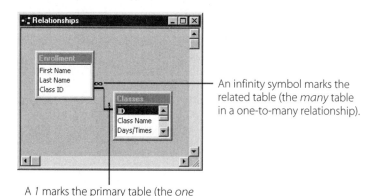

An infinity symbol marks the related table (the *many* table in a one-to-many relationship).

A *1* marks the primary table (the *one* table in a one-to-many relationship).

NOTE

Access will draw a thick line and display the infinity and *1* (numeral one) symbols only if you enabled the Enforce Referential Integrity option. Otherwise, it will draw a thin line without the symbols.

You can modify options for an existing relationship by double-clicking the line representing the relationship to reopen the Relationships dialog box. You can delete a relationship by clicking the line to select it and then pressing the Delete key. You can also perform either of these actions by right-clicking the relationship line and choosing Edit Relationship or Delete from the pop-up menu that appears.

When you have finished working with relationships, close the Relationships window. If you have modified the layout of the window (that is, the tables that are included and their arrangement), Access will ask if you want to save the layout. (Rest assured that the relationships themselves have already been saved.) Be sure to click the Yes button if you want to reuse this same layout.

CHAPTER 36

Using Datasheets to Enter and View Data

In Datasheet view, information is arranged in rows and columns. Datasheet view is the most common way of viewing a table or a query. You can also view a form in Datasheet view, though you almost always work with forms in Form view. *(Tables were discussed in Chapter 35; forms will be discussed in Chapter 37, "Using Forms to Enter and View Data," and queries in Chapter 38, "Using Queries to Get Answers.")*

Figure 36-1, on the next page, shows a table displayed in Datasheet view. In this view, each column represents a single field in your database, and each row represents a record. Even though its organization is simple, a datasheet is quite flexible and you can use it in a lot of ways that you might think would require designing a form or report. You can use a datasheet to do the following:

- View and edit data in a variety of ways.

- Customize the layout of the information by changing the size of rows and columns and by rearranging the order of columns.

- Add, delete, and rename the fields in a table.

 - Access data in related tables or queries using subdatasheets.

FIGURE 36-1.

Datasheets provide an easy way to work with the data stored in your database.

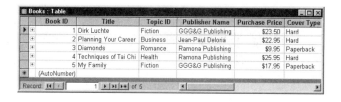

		Book ID	Title	Topic ID	Publisher Name	Purchase Price	Cover Type
▶	+	1	Dirk Luchte	Fiction	GGG&G Publishing	$23.50	Hard
	+	2	Planning Your Career	Business	Jean-Paul Deloria	$22.95	Hard
	+	3	Diamonds	Romance	Ramona Publishing	$9.95	Paperback
	+	4	Techniques of Tai Chi	Health	Ramona Publishing	$25.95	Hard
	+	5	My Family	Fiction	GGG&G Publishing	$17.95	Paperback
*		(AutoNumber)					

- Add, remove, and edit the records in a table quickly and easily.

- Sort your records.

- Find specific field entries.

- Filter the data so that you see only the records you want.

 **ON THE WEB**

The Book Collection.mdb database file, used for the examples in this chapter, is on the Running Office 2000 Reader's Corner page. For information about connecting to this Web site, read the Introduction.

Viewing a Datasheet

When you open a table or query using the Database window, it will be displayed in Datasheet view. (Remember that you open a table from the Database window by selecting Tables on the Objects bar and double-clicking the table object you want to open.) When you open a form using the Database window, however, it is displayed in Form view. Whenever you want to switch to Datasheet view from another view, you can choose Datasheet View from the View menu. You can also click the down arrow on the View button at the left end of the toolbar, and choose Datasheet View from the drop-down menu.

Making Changes in Datasheet View

In this section, you'll learn several ways to modify the design of a datasheet. Some of the changes you can make affect only the layout of Datasheet view and don't alter other views or the underlying structure of the table, query, or form. These changes include adjusting the column width or row height and rearranging the order of the columns. Other changes affect the underlying structure of a table, and will alter the way the table appears in other views such as Design view. These changes include renaming, adding, and deleting fields. (You can make these changes only to a table viewed in Datasheet view, not to a query or form.) Note that many of the techniques for modifying the design of a datasheet resemble techniques used in Microsoft Excel worksheets.

You can change the width of a column in a datasheet by dragging the right border of the column heading, as shown below:

Drag the column heading's right border
to change the column's width.

Original column border.

You can change the height of a row using a similar technique with the row selector (the button to the left of the row):

Original row border.

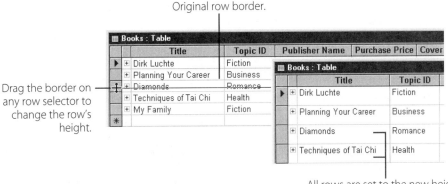

Drag the border on
any row selector to
change the row's
height.

All rows are set to the new height.

TIP

Let Microsoft Access Size Your Columns for You

You can have Access determine the most appropriate width for the column by double-clicking the right border of the column heading. Access will then adjust the column width to the smallest possible size that displays all the information contained within that column (including the caption in the column heading).

You can also change the arrangement of the columns in a datasheet. To move a particular column, select the column by clicking the column heading. Be sure to release the mouse button. Then click again and drag the column heading right or left to the new location. (If you don't release the button after you first click the column heading, dragging will simply select multiple columns.) Note that changing the order of columns in a datasheet doesn't change the underlying order of the fields as displayed in Design view or other views.

In a datasheet, each column heading displays the Caption property of the field displayed in that column, unless the Caption property is blank. In that case, the heading displays the name of the field (the Field Name property). Whichever item is displayed in the heading, you can change the field name by double-clicking the column heading, typing a new name, and pressing Enter. The Caption property will be set to blank (if it wasn't already blank), and the heading will display the field name. (You can't assign a new value to the Caption property in Datasheet view.)

You can also add or delete columns in the Datasheet view of a table. To add a column, select the column to the right of the position where you want the new column by clicking in the column heading, and then choose Column from the Insert menu. Access will create a new column and will assign it an initial name; it will name the first column you add Field1, the second column Field2, and so on. You can then change the field name as described previously.

⚠ **WARNING**

Keep in mind that when you delete a column, you're permanently removing a field—together with all its data—from the table. You can't issue the Undo command to reverse this action. If you delete a column and then realize later that you should have left that information where it was, you'll have to recreate the field and reenter that field's information for every record in the database, perhaps thousands! In short, be careful about deleting a column, and always keep a backup copy of your database.

To delete a column, select it by clicking the column heading, and then choose Delete Column from the Edit menu. You'll have the opportunity to confirm your action.

⭐ TIP

> You can also temporarily hide one or more columns by selecting them and choosing Hide Columns from the Format menu. You can later make one or more hidden columns visible again by choosing Unhide Columns from the Format menu and selecting all the columns that you want to reappear.

Access automatically saves any changes that affect the underlying structure of a table (renaming, adding, or deleting a field, as well as edits to each record). If, however, you adjust the datasheet *layout* (the column width, row height, or column arrangement), you must save your changes by choosing Save from the File menu or clicking the Save button on the toolbar. If you haven't saved your layout changes, you'll be asked whether you want to do so when you close Datasheet view. If the changes aren't necessary, click No and the next time you open the datasheet, it will be displayed in its original layout.

Using Subdatasheets

In Access 2000, a datasheet can contain a *subdatasheet*, which lists the contents of another table. You display a subdatasheet by clicking the plus symbol (+) in the left column of one of the records. The subdatasheet will list one or more records from another table, which are related to the record where you clicked the plus symbol.

For instance, you could add a subdatasheet to the Books table datasheet in the Book Collection example database that would display records from the BookAuthors table. Then, when you click the plus symbol in a particular book record,

Click the plus symbol (+) next to a record to display records from another table that are related to that record.

	Book ID	Title	Topic ID	Publisher Name	Purchase Price
▶ ⊞	1	Dirk Luchte	Fiction	GGG&G Publishing	$23.50
	2	Planning Your Career	Business	Jean-Paul Deloria	$22.95
⊞	3	Diamonds	Romance	Ramona Publishing	$9.95
⊞	4	Techniques of Tai Chi	Health	Ramona Publishing	$25.95
⊞	5	My Family	Fiction	GGG&G Publishing	$17.95
*	(AutoNumber)				

Books : Table

Record: ◄◄ ◄ 1 ► ►► ►* of 5

V

Microsoft Access

the subdatasheet would list all the book's authors:

Click the minus
symbol (-) to hide
the subdatasheet. ──────►
The subdatasheet. ─────────

(In the Book Collection example database, Andrew Fuller is the sole author of *Planning Your Career*. If additional authors existed, they would also be displayed in the subdatasheet.)

The table displayed in the subdatasheet is normally related to the table displayed in the datasheet. Typically, the datasheet table is the primary table and the subdatasheet table is the related table in the relationship. *(To review relationships, see "Relating Your Tables," page 848.)* The subdatasheet displays all records where a match exists in the related fields. In the example shown above, the BookID field in the Books table (the primary table) is related to the BookID field in the BookAuthors table (the related table). The subdatasheet for a particular record in the Books table displays all records in the BookAuthors table that have a matching BookID field.

If the table displayed in the datasheet is the primary table in a single relationship, Access automatically adds a subdatasheet that displays the related table. If, however, the datasheet table is the primary table in more than one relationship, you must explicitly add the subdatasheet and specify the particular relationship you want to use by performing the following steps. (Before beginning this procedure, you might open the Relationships window so that you can see which fields and tables are related.)

1 Open the datasheet where you want to add the subdatasheet.

2 Choose Subdatasheet from the Insert menu.

3 Define the subdatasheet in the Insert Subdatasheet dialog box, as shown in Figure 36-2. Note that you can use a subdatasheet to display a query as well as a table. *(Queries are discussed in Chapter 38.)*

You can use this same procedure to modify an existing subdatasheet.

FIGURE 36-2.
You can add or modify a subdatasheet using the Insert Subdatasheet dialog box.

Select the related table to display in the subdatasheet.

Select the related field in the table displayed in the subdatasheet (the related table).

Select the related field in the table displayed in the datasheet (the primary table).

Entering and Editing Data in a Datasheet

The last row of a datasheet is available for adding new records, and is marked with an asterisk (*) in the row selector at the left end of the row to indicate where the new record goes. You can quickly move to the last row by clicking the New Record button on the toolbar.

New Record

To enter data into a new record, or to modify any record in the table, you can use the mouse to click the field that you want to fill in or modify. If you prefer using the keyboard, you can press the Enter or Tab key to move from left to right through the columns in a record. To move back a column, press Shift+Tab.

You can enter or modify text in a field using the standard editing methods that all Microsoft Office applications provide. For example, you can use the Left or Right arrow key to move the insertion point to the position in the text that you want to edit; you can use the Backspace key to delete the previous character or the Delete key to delete the following character; and you can select text and use the Copy or Cut command and the Paste command on the Edit menu (or the equivalent key combinations) to copy or move blocks of characters.

As soon as you begin entering or changing information in a record, the row selector to the left of the row displays a pencil along with two dots, indicating that the record is being edited, as shown in Figure 36-3, on the next page. When you first enter data into a new record in the last row, Access immediately creates a new blank row below the one that you're editing.

FIGURE 36-3.

As soon as you enter or edit a field in a record, Access automatically stores your changes.

⌐ The Pencil indicator means that the record is being edited.

When you begin entering a new record here...

⊞ Books : Table					
Book ID	**Title**	**Topic ID**	**Publisher Name**	**Purchase Price**	**Cover Type**
1	Dirk Luchte	Fiction	GGG&G Publishing	$23.50	Hard
2	Planning Your Career	Business	Jean-Paul Deloria	$22.95	Hard
3	Diamonds	Romance	Ramona Publishing	$9.95	Paperback
4	Techniques of Tai Chi	Health	Ramona Publishing	$25.95	Hard
5	My Family	Fiction	GGG&G Publishing	$17.95	Paperback
6	A				
(AutoNumber)					

Record: ⏮ ◀ 6 ▶ ⏭ ▶* of 6

└ ...Access inserts a new row here for the next record.

If a field has been assigned a lookup column (explained in Table 35-1, page 841), when the insertion point is in the field, a down arrow appears at the right end. Rather than typing or editing a value in such a field, you should click the down arrow or press Alt+Down arrow to display a drop-down list of valid choices, and then select the choice you want. (The list displays either values from a related table, or a fixed list of values that were defined when the lookup column was created.)

Using Formatted Fields

SEE ALSO

For information on the Format and Input Mask field properties, see "Setting Other Field Properties," page 842.

If you have assigned a specific format to a field's Format property, all you have to do is enter the value that goes into that field, in any convenient form, and press Tab to move to another field. Access will then properly format the entry for you. For example, if a numeric field is formatted for currency, when you type *2.1* and press Tab, Access converts the information in the field to $2.10.

A field that has an input mask, such as a date field, will display a template for you to fill in with the actual values, as shown here:

Date Purchased
11/23/93
12/23/94
12/1/94
10/27/93
7/13/93
/ /

Deleting a Record

Delete
Record

To delete a record, select it by clicking its row selector, and then choose Delete Record from the Edit menu, click the Delete Record button on the toolbar, or press the Delete key.

The record is removed from view and a dialog box appears, telling you exactly what you're deleting. If you realize that you're deleting something by mistake, click the No button to stop the deletion process. To proceed with the deletion, click the Yes button.

WARNING

> Once you delete a record and click the Yes button to confirm your action, you won't be able to restore the record. You can't undo a record deletion by choosing Undo from the Edit menu. If you ever want to restore a deleted record, you'll have to reenter it from scratch.
>
> Keep in mind the distinction between deleting a row (record), which is all the fields of information about a single entry (a customer, for instance), and deleting a column (a field), which is a category of information (the Address field, for instance) for every record in the table. While you don't want to delete either by mistake, and while Access cannot undo either deletion, it's generally easier to reenter a record (all the information about a single customer) than a field (the address for every customer).

You can also select a group of records to delete, if necessary. To select the records, click the row selector of one record and drag the highlight up or down over the other records in the group.

SEE ALSO

For a discussion on referential integrity and cascading deletions, see the sidebar "Enforcing Referential Integrity," page 852.

When you delete a record in a table that's related to another table, Access might need to delete one or more records in the related table (to enforce referential integrity). Before doing so, it will display a message similar to the one shown in Figure 36-4. At this point, you must determine whether you want Access to delete the additional records, which you can't currently see. If you're the least bit uncertain about the information that is about to be deleted, click No to stop Access from making the deletions. Then determine which related information was about to be deleted and decide whether to go back and make the original deletion. You might want to use the Relationships window to help you find the related data.

FIGURE 36-4.
Deleting one record can result in a cascade of deletions in related tables.

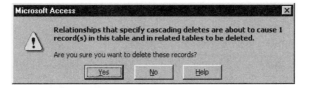

V

Microsoft Access

Sorting Your Information

The easiest way to sort the records in a datasheet is to designate a single column of information to use as the sort key. To begin, select the column by clicking the column heading. Then, to sort the records by the values in that column, point to Sort on the Records menu and choose Ascending from the submenu, or just click the Sort Ascending button on the toolbar. This organizes the records from the smallest to the largest value. For numbers, that means from least to greatest (-3, 0, 1, 2, 10); for date fields, from earliest to most recent (1/19/48, 6/15/94, 3/15/97, and so on); and for text, alphabetical order (A to Z).

Sort
Ascending

Shortcuts Are a Mouse Click Away

Many times you can find the next action you want to perform on the special pop-up menu that appears when you press the right (or secondary) mouse button. The menu changes depending upon the context of your actions, so check it often for possible shortcuts to accomplish your tasks more quickly.

To sort in reverse order, follow the above procedure but choose Descending from the Sort submenu or click the Sort Descending button on the toolbar. Access will reorganize your information based on that field from greatest to least for numeric fields, from most recent to earliest for date fields, and from Z to A for text fields.

Sort
Descending

For greater control over organizing your records, you can create a query and use the sorting instructions that are part of the query design grid, as described in "Sorting," page 909.

Finding Information

At times all you need to do in your database is locate an entry in a field that contains a particular item of information. This information could be text, a number, or a date. The easiest way to locate the item is to choose Find from the Edit menu, click the Find toolbar button, or press Ctrl+F, to display the dialog box shown in Figure 36-5.

Find

FIGURE 36-5.

You can use the Find And Replace dialog box to locate matching entries in your database.

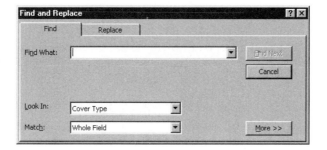

To try out the Find command, follow these steps for searching through a single field of a table:

1 Select any field that you'd like to search by clicking the column heading. For instance, you might select the Cover Type field in the Books table shown in Figure 36-1, page 858.

2 In the Find What text box on the Find tab, type the text you want to locate. Perhaps you might type *Paperback* to see which books are available in that format.

3 Make sure the column label (for example, Cover Type) is selected in the Look In list box, and that Whole Field is selected in the Match list box. (These options will be explained later.)

4 Click the Find Next button. Access will search from the first record of the table and highlight the first match that it finds (or display a message that it found no matches).

5 If a first match was found, click the Find Next button to find each subsequent match. You can also close the Find dialog box and continue the search by pressing Shift+F4 to find the next match.

The following sections discuss how you can customize the search.

Controlling Where Access Searches

If you selected a single column—or just placed the insertion point anywhere within a column—prior to opening the Find And Replace dialog box, you can have Access restrict its search to that field by choosing the column label (such as Book ID or Cover Type) in the Look In list box.

(This option isn't available if the current selection spans more than one column.) If you want Access to search all fields in the table, select the *Name:*Table option, where *Name* is the table name (such as Books).

You can control the direction of the search by selecting an option in the Search list box. If this list box isn't visible, click the More>> button on the Find tab of the Find And Replace dialog box to display all the controls. (After you click the button, it gets relabeled <<Less. See Figure 36-6.) If you select All, Access searches all records. It searches from the selected record down to the end of the table, and then from the beginning of the table down through the record above the selected one. (In these descriptions, the *selected record* refers to the record containing the insertion point or current selection, or if the current selection spans several records, to the first record in the selection.) If you select Down, Access searches from the selected record down to the end of the table and stops. If you select Up, Access searches from the selected record up to the beginning of the table and stops.

FIGURE 36-6.
When you click the More>> button, the Find And Replace dialog box shows all controls for setting options.

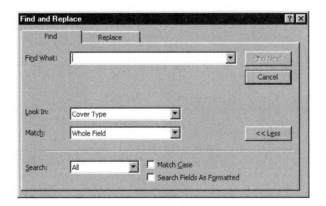

Controlling What Access Matches

The choices in the Match list box determine how Access searches the contents of each field; that is, the criterion for finding a match within a field. The choices are described in Table 36-1.

You can use the other controls in the dialog box to determine how precisely Access matches information. When you select the Match Case option, Access will find only those instances where the text matches the specified capitalization. For example, if the Match Case option is turned off, *Query Grid* matches *query grid, Query grid,* and *Query Grid,* or any other form of capitalization. If the Match Case option is turned on, *Query Grid* will match only *Query Grid.*

TABLE 36-1.   Effects of Changing the Match Settings of the Find Dialog Box

Match Option	Match Criterion	Example	Will Match	Will Not Match
Any Part of Field	Your search text can be contained anywhere within the field.	new	Newton renewal Agnew new	
Whole Field	Your search text must match the field contents exactly.	new	new	Newton renewal Agnew
Start of Field	The field must begin with your search text, but this text can be followed by any additional text.	new	Newton new	renewal Agnew

The Search Fields As Formatted option requires some explanation. Recall from Chapter 35 that fields that have certain data types (such as Date/Time) can be set to appear in different formats. The particular format is controlled by the field's Format property (such as 30-Jun-97 or 6/30/97 for a Date/Time field). If the Search Fields As Formatted option is deselected, you could search for a date such as 30-Jun-97 by entering it in any valid date format (such as 6/30/97; June 30, 1997; or 06/30/1997). (For this type of search to work, however, you must also select the Whole Field option in the Match list box, and select the label of the selected column in the Look In list box.) However, if you select the Search Fields As Formatted option, the only way you could find the entry 30-Jun-97 would be to enter the same text in the Find What box: *30-Jun-97*.

 NOTE

> The options you select in the Find And Replace dialog box can affect the speed at which Access searches your data. Selecting the Search Fields As Formatted option, selecting the *Name*:Table option in the Look In list box, or selecting Any Part Of Field from the Match list box each tend to slow down the search process.

Replacing Data

You can also have Access replace data in a table that matches a text string, number, or date that you specify. Here's the general procedure:

1 If you want to replace data within only a single table field, either select the field's column or place the insertion point anywhere within that column.

V

Microsoft Access

2 Choose Replace from the Edit menu or press Ctrl+H. Access will display the Replace tab of the Find And Replace dialog box, which is shown in Figure 36-7. Notice that the Replace tab is the same as the Find tab, except that it also has a Replace With text box and Replace and Replace All buttons.

3 Enter the data you want to find in the Find What box. (This data is what you'll be replacing.)

4 Enter the replacement data in the Replace With text box.

5 Select all the search options you want. The options are the same as those for the Find command (explained in the previous two sections, "Controlling Where Access Searches," and "Controlling What Access Matches"). If necessary, click the More>> button to show all controls on the Replace tab.

6 Click the Find Next button to begin the search. When Access finds a match, it will highlight the text (or it will display a message indicating that it can't find a match).

7 Click the Replace button to replace the text and have Access look for the next match; or click the Find Next button to look for the next match without replacing the current one.

Replace All—Quick but Permanent

If you're sure your search will match only data that you want to change, you can click the Replace All button on the Replace tab, and Access will make all the replacements without showing them to you or asking for your confirmation. You'll save time, but make sure your search is set up correctly, because you can't undo this operation once you confirm it. The total number of replacements made will be shown on the status bar.

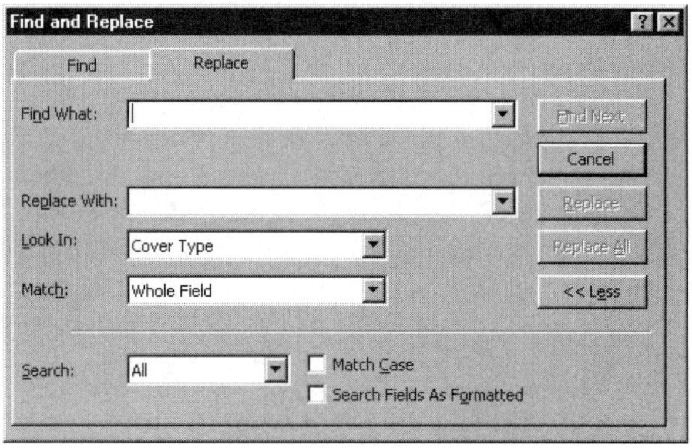

FIGURE 36-7.
The Replace tab is similar to the Find tab. Here it's shown after the More>> button has been clicked to show all controls.

Find and Replace	
Find	Replace

Find What: ▼ Find Next

Cancel

Replace With: ▼ Replace

Look In: Cover Type ▼ Replace All

Match: Whole Field ▼ << Less

Search: All ▼ ☐ Match Case
☐ Search Fields As Formatted

Filtering Records

Although the Find command can be useful for moving from one match to another, at times you might want to display only the records that match your criteria, rather than displaying all the records in the table. Access provides a way to do this using a filter.

Using Filter By Selection

The easiest way to filter records is by finding a field in a record that contains the information you want to use as a filter criterion and then telling Access to list only those records that contain the same entry in that field. For example, in the Book Collection database, you might want to list all the hardcover books in your collection. To do so, you first locate a record containing the entry that you want to use to select your records—in this case, a record that has the entry Hard in the Cover Type field, as shown in Figure 36-8.

Filter By
Selection

Either click anywhere within the field or select the whole entry to tell Access to match the field's entire contents. Then point to Filter on the Records menu, and choose Filter By Selection from the submenu. Or, just click the Filter By Selection button on the toolbar. Access will then show only the records that meet the filter criterion. The datasheet shown in Figure 36-8 would then appear as shown in Figure 36-9, on the following page, where only hardcover books are displayed.

Remove
Filter

To return to viewing all your records, choose Remove Filter/Sort from the Records menu or click the Remove Filter button on the toolbar. You can later reapply your most recently defined filter by simply choosing Apply Filter/Sort on the Records menu or by clicking the Apply Filter button. (When a filter is applied, this button is selected, its ScreenTip label is Remove Filter, and clicking it removes the filter. After the filter has been removed, the button is deselected, its label is Apply Filter, and clicking it reapplies the previous filter.) Access remembers your last filter settings, so you can apply and remove them as often as you like until you define new settings.

FIGURE 36-8.
To start a Filter By Selection, you must first select the information you want to use as the filter criterion.

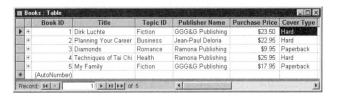

FIGURE 36-9.

When a filter has been applied, only those records that match the filter criterion are displayed.

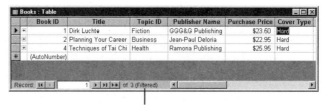

This indicates that a filter has been applied, and therefore not all records are displayed.

If you select a portion of a field entry before issuing the Filter By Selection command, Access will use only that selected text in determining which records to display. For example, in the Books table shown in Figure 36-8, if you select the word *Publishing* in one of the entries in the Publisher Name field and then you apply Filter By Selection, both the books by GGG&G Publishing and those by Ramona Publishing will be included in your list. This process is similar to how the Any Part Of Field option works in the Find dialog box.

You can also filter records using the entries from several fields in a record. In this case, Access will display only records that match all the selected entries. To do this, first be sure that the fields that have the values you want to use are next to each other. (Move columns in the datasheet if necessary.) Then select all the entries to be used for the match, and issue the Filter By Selection command. To select several adjoining field entries in a record, click the left end of one entry to select it (click when the pointer becomes a large plus sign), and drag the highlight left or right over the other entry or entries, as shown below:

Click here to select this entry...

...and then drag through here to highlight (select) both entries.

In the above example, after you issue the Filter By Selection command, only the records for fiction books published by GGG&G Publishing will be listed. (That is, all records except 1 and 5 will be filtered out.)

Finally, you can select entries across adjoining records, rather than fields, and then use the Filter By Selection command. In this case, Access will list records that match any of the selected field values. For instance, if you had dragged a selection from the top of the Fiction entry in the Topic ID column downward across the Business entry below it (as shown on the facing page), Access would display all books categorized as business or fiction. To summarize, if you select horizontally across fields, only items matching all the selected entries are shown; but if you select down through rows, items matching any of the selected entries are shown.

Click here to select this entry...

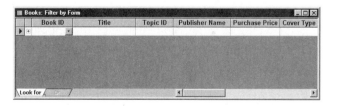

...and then drag through here to highlight (select) both entries.

Using Filter By Form

Filter
By Form

When you want to use more than one value to filter the records, a more versatile approach is to use Filter By Form. To begin, point to Filter on the Records menu, and then choose Filter By Form from the submenu. Or, click the Filter By Form button on the toolbar. Your datasheet will disappear and the Filter By Form window will take its place, as shown in Figure 36-10. (This figure shows the Filter By Form window for the Books table in the Book Collection example database.)

The Filter By Form window displays a single, blank row in the same format as one of your records. (Note, however, that if you previously applied a filter to the table, the fields used in the filter will contain their prior values.) The information in the Filter By Form window is divided into separate tabs: the Look For tab (the one that's displayed initially), plus one or more Or tabs. You display a particular tab by clicking a tab label at the bottom of the window. Next, you'll learn how to use these tabs to enter alternative filter criteria.

Defining the Filter

You begin defining your filter by choosing entries in the fields shown on the Look For tab. When you click in a field, a down arrow appears at the right end. Click this arrow to display a list of the different values that are currently contained in that field within all the records of the table. Select the one you want to use for your filter.

FIGURE 36-10.
The Filter By Form window replaces the Datasheet window when you issue the Filter By Form command.

Book ID	Title	Topic ID	Publisher Name	Purchase Price	Cover Type

Look for

You can select a value in more than one field to reduce the number of records shown. When you apply the filter, Access will display the records that match all the selected entries. For instance, in the Books example table, if you wanted to display all fiction paperbacks, you would select Fiction in the Topic ID field and Paperback in the Cover Type field, as shown here:

After you've selected all the values you want from the Look For tab, you can define alternative filter criteria to expand the number of records shown. You do this by displaying the first Or tab, which will show another row of fields. Select one or more values in these fields the same way you did on the Look For tab. When you apply the filter, Access will display all records that match *either* the values on the Look For tab *or* the values on the Or tab. For instance, in the Books example table, you could list all romance paperbacks as well as all fiction paperbacks by first selecting the values shown above on the Look For tab, and then on the first Or tab, selecting Romance in the Topic ID field and Paperback in the Cover Type field:

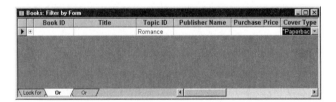

You can expand the number of listed records even further by selecting values from additional Or tabs. Each time you select one or more values from an Or tab, another Or tab becomes available for you to display.

Rather than selecting a value in a field, you can specify a filter criterion by typing an expression containing a comparison operator. The six standard comparison operators are shown in Table 36-2.

TABLE 36-2.   The Standard Comparison Operators

Operator	Definition
>	Greater than
<	Less than
=	Equal to
<=	Less than or equal to
>=	Greater than or equal to
<>	Not equal to

To use a comparison operator, enter the operator, followed by the comparison value, into the field that contains the value to be evaluated. For example, to find all books that cost more than $20, you would enter the greater-than operator and the value 20 (that is, *>20*) into the Purchase Price field. If you don't use an operator and you just select a value in a field, Access assumes that you are searching for exact matches.

> When you use Filter By Form, you can't easily tell Access to look for matches between two values. For example, you can't find books that have prices above $20 but below $40. *For that, you need to use a query as described in Chapter 38, "Using Queries to Get Answers."*

If you select a value in a field or type in a comparison expression and then decide that you don't really want to use it, you can delete the entry, remove the entire tab, or clear the entire filter. To delete a single entry, select it and press the Delete key. To remove a tab that you have created, display it and then choose Delete Tab from the Edit menu. You can clear all the entries in the filter by choosing Clear Grid from the Edit menu or by clicking the Clear Grid button on the toolbar.

Clear
Grid

Applying the Filter

Apply
Filter

Once you have specified all the values for your filter, you can activate the filter by choosing Apply Filter/Sort from the Filter menu or by clicking the Apply Filter button on the toolbar. Access then returns you to the standard datasheet window, showing only those records that match your filter.

V

Microsoft Access

For instance, here's how the example Book table would appear after you choose the filter values from the Look For and Or tabs described in the previous section:

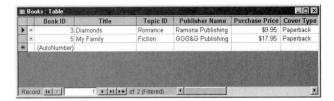

To remove the filter and display all records, choose Remove Filter/Sort from the Records menu, or click the Remove Filter button on the toolbar. You can later reapply your most recently defined filter by simply choosing Apply Filter/Sort on the Records menu or by clicking the Apply Filter button. (When a filter is applied, this button is selected, its ScreenTip label is Remove Filter, and clicking it removes the filter. After the filter has been removed, the button is deselected, its label is Apply Filter, and clicking it reapplies the previous filter.) Access remembers your last filter settings, so you can apply and remove them as often as you like until you define new settings.

Using Advanced Filter and Sort

If you want to filter *and* sort the records in a table, rather than performing the two-step process of first applying a filter and then sorting the records, you can use the Advanced Filter/Sort command on the Filter submenu of the Records menu. This command opens a special query window that's associated with the table you're working with. In this single window, you can define criteria for sorting and filtering the records in the table, using one or more fields. *This window is discussed in "Using The Simplest Grid—Advanced Filter/Sort," page 904.*

CHAPTER 37

Using Forms to Enter and View Data

A form is a tool that makes it easy to enter, modify, and view the information stored in one or more tables in a database. A form consists of a window filled with a collection of *controls*. A control is a visual object used for displaying information, entering or modifying information, performing an action, or decorating a form; examples of controls include labels, text boxes, command buttons, and graphics such as lines and boxes.

Keep in mind that a form doesn't store the information itself; it merely provides a convenient way to access the information that is stored in one or more tables. Each control on a form typically accesses one field within a table (though some controls don't access fields at all). Working with a form, rather than accessing data using the Datasheet view of a table or query, offers several advantages:

- A form allows you to focus on a single record at a time, because typically a form displays all the fields of a single record, unlike a datasheet that displays several records but often requires you to scroll to see all the fields for those records.

- You can arrange the controls on a form in a logical manner that makes it easy to read and access the data.

- The individual form controls provide many features that facilitate entering or modifying specific items of information.

- You can display or run advanced database objects such as pictures, animations, sounds, and video clips in Form view, but not in Datasheet view.

Using a Form

The databases created by the Microsoft Access wizards normally contain forms for entering information or for reviewing the information stored in the database's tables. Once you have opened a database, you can display a particular form by opening the Forms section in the Database window and double-clicking the name of the form.

The techniques for using forms are similar to those for moving through and entering information into standard Office 2000 dialog boxes, with just a few differences. How easy the form is to use depends largely on how well its designer was able to predict your needs.

Figure 37-1 shows an example form named Members, which was designed for entering information about the members of an organization. The figure shows the form ready to accept a new record. In this section, you'll learn how to work with the controls on this typical Access form. You can use these techniques either for defining a new record (as shown in Figure 37-1) or for modifying an existing record. (In the next section, you'll learn how to access existing records.)

 The Membership.mdb database file, used for the examples in this chapter, is on the Running Office 2000 Reader's Corner page. For information about connecting to this Web site, read the Introduction.

To define or modify the information in a particular control, you can simply click the control to activate it and then perform any additional action necessary for the specific type of control, such as typing text into a text box or selecting an item from a list. If you want to enter information into the controls in sequence, activate the first control by clicking it, and then press Tab or Enter to move to each subsequent control. (Press Shift+Tab to move back to a previous control.)

Generally, a form is designed so that pressing Tab or Enter moves you through the controls in a logical order. For example, on the Members

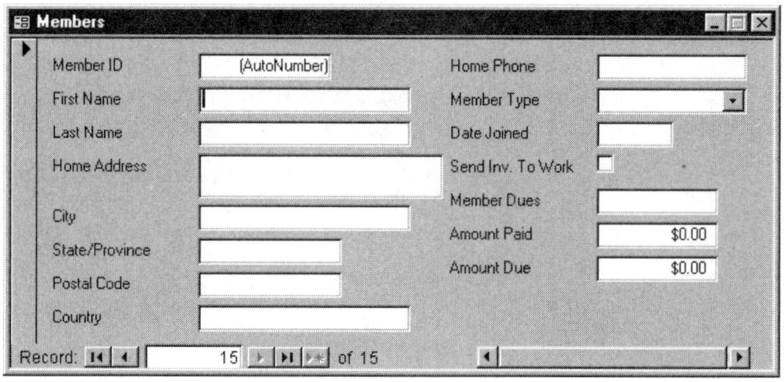

FIGURE 37-1.

An example form named Members, ready to accept a new record.

SEE ALSO

"Setting the Data Type," page 840, discusses the data types of fields in tables. Chapter 40, "Formatting Forms and Reports," discusses setting formatting control properties.

form, pressing the Tab or Enter key moves you down through the controls in the first column and then down through the controls in the second column. (You can't activate the Member ID, Amount Paid, or Amount Due text box, for reasons that will be explained later.) When you get to the last control, pressing Tab or Enter moves you back to the first control. Note that when you press Tab or Enter to move to a text box control, the control's entire contents are selected. You can then replace these contents by just typing the new text. If you need to start a new line in a text box (which would be appropriate for only the Home Address text box), press Ctrl+Enter.

The remainder of this section provides a brief tour of the controls on the Members example form:

- The first control, labeled Member ID, is a text box that has two peculiarities: First, the table field that it accesses has the Auto-Number data type. As a result, the text box initially displays the value (AutoNumber), but as soon as you enter any data into the new record, the value changes to the next incremental record number. Second, the control's Enabled property is set to No. You therefore can neither activate the text box nor change its value.

NOTE

If you delete a record that has an AutoNumber field, that field's number will not be reused. You cannot easily reassign that number to a new record.

- The remaining controls in the first column, as well as the Home Phone control at the top of the second column, are standard text boxes, and each of these controls accesses a field that has the Text data type.

■ The Postal Code and Home Phone text boxes each have an input mask assigned using the Input Mask property, to assist you in entering properly formatted information.

An input mask for entering a telephone number

NOTE

A control inherits certain properties from the field that it accesses, while other properties must be explicitly set for the control. For example, if the Required property of a field in a table is set to Yes, any control that accesses this field will require data input. By contrast, assigning an input mask to a field's Input Mask property doesn't affect controls that access the field; rather, you must assign an input mask to the Input Mask property of the control itself. *For information on setting field properties, see "Setting the Field Properties," page 839.*

■ The Member Type control is a combo box. You normally click the down arrow and select a value from the list that drops down. If the list doesn't contain the value you want, however, you can double-click the text box at the top of the list to open the Member Types form, which lets you enter a new member type into the Member Types table (which stores the list of member types). Once you select a value in the Member Type control, Access enters the appropriate dollar amount into the Member Dues control (different member types pay different dues).

NOTE

When you define a control, you can specify that whenever a particular event occurs within the control (such as the control being double-clicked), Access will perform a specified action (such as opening another form). For example, the Member Type control was defined so that whenever the control is double-clicked, Access opens the Member Types form; and whenever the control is updated, Access inserts a value into the Member Dues control.

■ The Member Dues control is a text box that accesses a field that has the Currency data type. Although this field is automatically filled in when you make an entry in the Member Type control, you can optionally enter a new value directly in the text box (thereby overriding the normal dues owed by that type of member).

- The Date Joined control is a text box that accesses a Date/Time field. Like the Postal Code and Home Phone controls, it has a mask assigned to its Input Mask property, which assists you in entering a properly formatted date.

- The Send Inv. To Work control is a check box that is associated with a field of the Yes/No data type. Checking the box sets the field to Yes, and clearing the box sets the field to No. When you use the Tab or Enter key to move to a check box control, a dotted line is drawn around the control's label to indicate that the control has been activated. You can then press the Spacebar to select or clear the box. If you prefer to use the mouse, you can simply click the box to select or clear it in a single step.

- The Amount Paid and Amount Due text boxes are used only for displaying information. You can't edit the contents of these controls, because the Enabled property of each control is set to No. All the controls on the Members form, except Amount Paid and Amount Due, are directly associated with a field in the Members table, which stores information on each member. (In this example database, both the form and the table it accesses have the same name, but this isn't required.) The Amount Paid field derives the information it displays from the Payments table, which stores all payment records. The Amount Due control subtracts the value in the Amount Paid control from the value in the Member Dues control and displays the result. The Format property of both of these controls is set to Currency so that the results are displayed as monetary values.

Spelling

Did You Spell Your Data Correctly?

You can check the spelling of the text you have entered into a form's controls by choosing Spelling from the Tools menu, clicking the Spelling button on the toolbar, or pressing F7. The Spelling command works the same way it does in other Microsoft Office applications. *For general instructions, see "Checking Your Spelling," page 273.* You can also have Access automatically replace specific text as you type by using the AutoCorrect feature; to set it up, choose AutoCorrect from the Tools menu. *For information on this feature, see "Using the AutoCorrect Feature," page 127.*

Figure 37-2, on the next page, shows the Members form after all the fields have been assigned values. Later in the chapter, you'll learn about other types of controls that you can add to forms.

Microsoft Access

FIGURE 37-2.

The Members form after information has been entered into each of the fields.

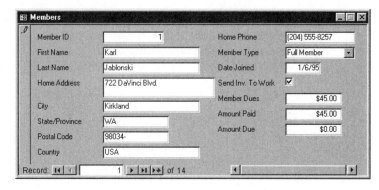

When you finish defining or modifying a record and move on to a new record (using one of the methods that will be described later), Access automatically saves the record's new contents. You can also save the current record's contents at any time by choosing Save Record from the Records menu or by pressing Shift+Enter.

Undo Current Field/Record

You can reverse any changes you made to the value in a control by choosing Undo from the Edit menu or by clicking the Undo button on the toolbar. If you just modified and saved a record (by moving to another record), you can issue the Undo command to reverse all changes you made to that record.

Printing a Form

Although the primary use of forms is to view and work with data on your computer screen, you do have the option of printing a form and its contents. As you do with the other Office programs, you use the Page Setup, Print Preview, and Print commands on the File menu. Of special interest is the Print Data Only option on the Margins tab of the Page Setup dialog box. This option lets you print the data from the on-screen Access form directly onto a preprinted paper form, without printing the labels and lines included on the Access form. This option would be advantageous if, for example, your data tracks employment applicants and you want to print the data on preprinted application forms. To use the option, you must design the Access form to match the paper form and put the paper forms in your printer's paper tray before printing.

Working with Records

A form is always associated with a specific table or query in the database, which is known as the *record source*. Most of the controls on a typical form directly access fields belonging to the record source. (Controls, however, can be used for other purposes.) In a form's window, you can view any of the records belonging to the record source, and you can add new records to the record source or delete records from it. Access provides a small toolbar permanently positioned in the lower left corner of the form window that you can use to navigate through the existing records or to add new records:

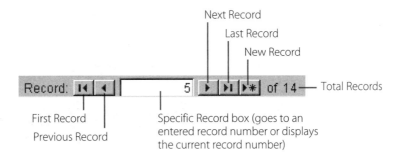

Next Record

Last Record

New Record

Record: ◄◄ ◄   5   ► ►◄ ►* of 14 ── Total Records

First Record

Previous Record

Specific Record box (goes to an entered record number or displays the current record number)

If you prefer to use the keyboard rather than the mouse, press Page Down to move forward a single record or Page Up to move back a single record. To jump to the start of the first record, press Ctrl+Home, and to jump to the end of the last record, press Ctrl+End. (If pressing Ctrl+Home or Ctrl+End moves the insertion point within a field instead of moving between records, press the Tab key once and try again.)

To view a specific record in a table, you can click the Specific Record box, type in the record number, and press Enter. You can also go to a record that contains specific text in one of its fields by choosing Find from the Edit menu, clicking the Find button on the toolbar, or pressing Ctrl+F

Find

Likewise, you can replace the contents of matching fields by choosing Replace from the Edit menu or by pressing Ctrl+H. *For general instructions on using the Find and Replace commands, see "Finding Information," page 866.*

V

Microsoft Access

To create a new record, click the New Record button on the toolbar at the bottom of the form window (shown above), or click the New Record button on the main toolbar. The new record will be added to the end of the record source table and will be displayed in the form window so that you can enter information into it (as shown in Figure 37-1, page 879).

New
Record

Rather than entering mostly repetitive information for a new record, you can copy the data from another, similar record into the new record and then just modify the data as necessary. You can also copy information from one record over another record's data, replacing the original contents of the target record. To copy a record, do the following:

1 Select the record that is the source of the information by displaying that record in the form window and clicking the vertical bar at the left of the form window. (This bar is equivalent to the row selector you see in Datasheet view, and it's highlighted when you click it.)

Click anywhere in this bar to select the entire record.

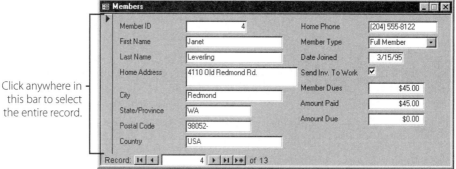

2 Choose Copy from the Edit menu or press Ctrl+C. (If you want to move the source record's contents, choose Cut instead or press Ctrl+X.)

3 Display the target record in the form window. (This record can be an existing one or a newly created one.) Make sure the vertical bar at the left is still highlighted, indicating that the entire record is selected.

4 Choose Paste from the Edit menu or press Ctrl+V. The value of every control in the source record will be copied into the equivalent control in the target record, except for any control that accesses a primary key field or other field that must have a unique value, such as the Member ID field on the example Members form.

Delete
Record

To permanently delete a record, display the record in the form window, and then choose Delete Record from the Edit menu or click the Delete Record button on the toolbar. Access requires that you confirm the deletion before the record can be removed. If the deletion will result in additional cascading deletions in related tables, a dialog box will inform you of that and give you an opportunity to stop. Just as when you delete a record in Datasheet view, once you confirm a deletion the data is permanently lost—it can't be restored using the Undo button, and you'll have to manually reenter it if you want to restore it later.

> You can sort or filter the records you view on a form in the same way that you sort or filter records when you view a table or query in Datasheet view. *For instructions, see "Sorting Your Information," page 866, and "Filtering Records," page 871.*

Note that you can also display a form in Datasheet view. Each row in the Datasheet view of a form displays the controls for a particular record, one per column. Although Datasheet view is generally much less convenient for working with a form than Form view, it has the advantage of allowing you to view multiple records at a time. To switch to Datasheet view, choose Datasheet View from the View menu.

Creating a Form

You can create a form in several ways, but for most purposes the best way to start is to select Forms on the Objects bar of the Database window, and then click the New button. When you click the New button, Access opens the New Form dialog box:

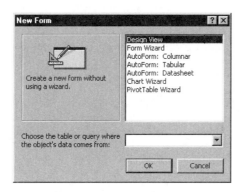

In the list in the New Form dialog box, you can choose from a variety of different ways to create your new form:

- Select the Design View option to create the form yourself by adding controls one at a time in Design view (described in the next section, "Modifying a Form," and in Chapter 40, "Formatting Forms and Reports").

- Select the Form Wizard option to have Access create the form for you, according to your specifications. The Form Wizard option lets you choose the specific fields to include, which might belong to one or more tables or queries.

- Choose one of the three AutoForm options to have the Form Wizard generate the form for you, based on the table or query you select. Rather than asking for your specifications (as the Form Wizard does), it quickly creates and opens a specific type of form—a columnar, tabular, or datasheet form—using the default options. (You can also create any of these three types of forms using the Form Wizard.) A form created by means of an Auto-Form option always includes controls for all the fields of a single table or query.

- Select the Chart Wizard option to take information from a database table or query and create a chart using Microsoft Graph, which is discussed in Chapter 51, "Sharing Data Among Office Applications." The chart is inserted on a new form.

- Select the PivotTable Wizard option to take information from a table and create a pivot table, which is covered, for Microsoft Excel, in "Creating Pivot Tables and Pivot Charts," page 603.

In general, it's easiest to use the Form Wizard or one of the AutoForm options to create at least a rough draft of your form. You can then customize the form, using the techniques described in the next section and in Chapter 40, "Formatting Forms and Reports."

Design View Option

If you selected the Design View option, click OK to open the form in Design view and begin adding controls. (Prior to clicking OK, you can select a table or query from the list box near the bottom of the New Form dialog box to define the record source for the new form. Or, you can leave the list box blank and define the record source later or leave the form without one.)

Using the New Object Button

You can quickly create a simple form that includes controls for all the fields belonging to a single table or query, with all controls placed in a single column. To do this, select Tables or Queries on the Objects bar in the Database window, and select the table or query on which you want to base your form. Then click the down arrow next to the New Object button on the Access toolbar, and choose the AutoForm item from the menu that drops down:

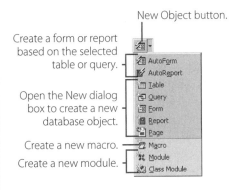

Notice that you can also use the New Object button to quickly create a new report based on the selected table or query or to open the New Table, New Query, New Form, New Report, or New Data Access Page dialog box to create one of these database objects. Finally, you can use it to create a new macro or module.

AutoForm Options

If you selected any of the AutoForm options, you must choose a table or a query from the list box at the bottom of the New Form dialog box and then click the OK button. The wizard will immediately create and open the new form, which will contain a control for each field in the selected table or query.

Form Wizard Option

If you selected the Form Wizard option, choose the table or query that you want to access—that is, the record source—in the list box near the bottom of the New Form dialog box. (This step is optional, however, because you can choose the record source later.) When you click the OK button, the wizard will display a series of dialog boxes.

In the first wizard dialog box, which is shown in Figure 37-3, you select the fields that you want to include on your form. The resulting form will contain a separate control for accessing each of the fields that you pick. To begin, in the Tables/Queries list box, select the table or query that has the fields you want to include. This table or query will become the record source for the table, and all the fields that belong to it will be displayed in the Available Fields list. Then use the buttons labeled in Figure 37-3 as needed to move the name for each of the fields you want from the Available Fields list to the Selected Fields list. When the Selected Fields list has all the fields you want, click the Next button to display the second Form Wizard dialog box.

> **NOTE**
>
> You might get the impression that you're moving fields from a table into your form, but of course the fields and their data remain in the table; you're instead creating a link to those fields by symbolically moving the field name into the Selected Fields list.

The second Form Wizard dialog box, shown in Figure 37-4, lets you choose the basic arrangement of the controls on the form. To make your choice, click each option and observe the way the selected layout will look on your form, as shown in the dialog box. The Columnar layout is the most common and usually enables you to view a complete, single

FIGURE 37-3.
Begin by selecting all the fields you want to access from your new form.

Add the field selected in the Available Fields list.

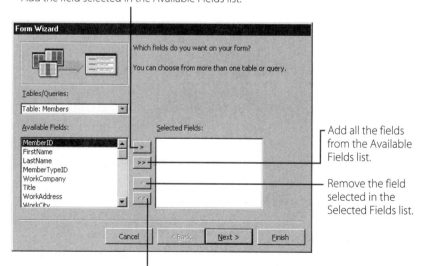

Add all the fields from the Available Fields list.

Remove the field selected in the Selected Fields list.

Remove all fields from the Selected Fields list.

FIGURE 37-4.
Then choose the arrangement of the controls on the form.

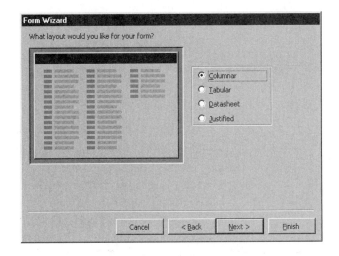

Accessing Several Tables or Queries on a Form

When you define the fields for your form in the first Form Wizard dialog box shown in Figure 37-3, you can add fields from several tables or queries. To add fields from each table or query, select it in the Tables/Queries list box, and then use the buttons to move the fields you want to the Selected Fields list.

If you add fields from several forms or queries, the wizard will show one or more additional dialog boxes that aren't described in this section. These dialog boxes let you designate which table or query will be the record source for the form. The wizard, however, doesn't use the term *record source*. Rather, it asks how you want to view your data and lets you select a specific table. The table you select will become the record source.

The resulting form will display each of the records belonging to the record source, one at a time. That is, using the buttons at the bottom of the form will move through the records of the record source table or query.

Depending on the relationships among the different tables or queries, the additional dialog boxes might also let you set up one or more *subforms*. A subform is an object within a form that displays records from a related table, in either datasheet or tabular format. You might also be able to set up a *linked form*, a separate form displaying related data, which you open by clicking a button on the main form.

A form that accesses data from several tables or queries could be complex to design from scratch or to modify. However, if you create the form using the Form Wizard, almost everything is set up for you.

record at a time in Form view. (The example form in Figure 37-1, page 879, uses this layout.) The Tabular layout lets you view multiple records at the same time in Form view, while the Datasheet layout generates a form that's intended to be displayed in Datasheet view. The Justified layout arranges the form's objects to fill the form window. When you have selected the layout you want, click the Next button.

In the third Form Wizard dialog box, shown in Figure 37-5, you choose the style of your form, which affects the background color or pattern, the fonts, the look of the controls, and other attributes. Again, to help you make your choice, the dialog box shows how the form will look with each style option. (You can later change the style by displaying the form in Design view, clicking the AutoFormat button on the toolbar, and selecting a new style in the AutoFormat dialog box.) When you've made your choice, click the Next button to open the final dialog box, shown in Figure 37-6.

AutoFormat

The final dialog box in the Form Wizard lets you assign a name to the form and choose the way the form is initially opened. If you select the first opening option, the form will be opened in Form view (or Datasheet view if you selected the Datasheet layout) so that you can immediately begin using the form to view or modify data, as discussed at the beginning of this chapter. If you select the second opening option, the form will open in Design view so that you can modify its design, as described next.

FIGURE 37-5.

Choose the style of the form, including a variety of backgrounds.

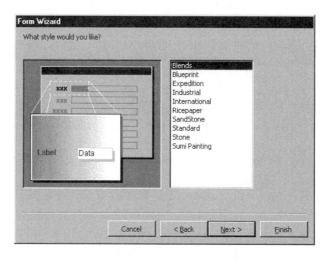

When you have made all your choices, click the Finish button to have Access create the form. (As you can with the other Access wizards, you can click the Finish button within any of the dialog boxes to create the

FIGURE 37-6.
Finally, choose a name
for your form and
the view in which it
will open.

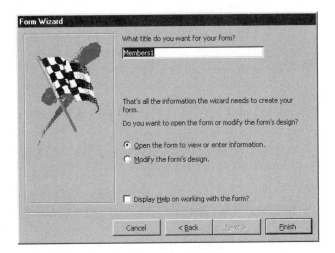

form using the options you have set and the default choices for the
options you haven't set.)

Modifying a Form

You can make changes to a form quite easily by switching to Design
view. As you saw, you have the option of moving directly to Design
view after creating a form using the Form Wizard. If you're already
working with data on a form in Form view, you can switch to Design
view by choosing Design View from the View menu or by clicking the
View button on the left end of the toolbar and choosing Design View
from the drop-down menu, as shown here:

Alternatively, you can open any form in Design view by selecting
Forms on the Objects bar in the Database window and then clicking
the Design button.

Figure 37-7, on the next page, shows the same form shown in Figure
37-1, page 879, but in Design view rather than in the standard Form
view. Design view lets you add, remove, or modify the controls that
make up a form, which you'll recall include text boxes, labels, list
boxes, option buttons, command buttons, lines, and more.

When you open a form in Design view, Access displays the Toolbox toolbar, which provides tools for adding and working with many different types of controls. (If the Toolbox isn't currently displayed, either point to Toolbars on the View menu and choose Toolbox from the submenu, or click the Toolbox button on the toolbar.)

Toolbox

The Toolbox buttons are shown in Figure 37-8, and they are described in Table 37-1. Many of these buttons are the type that toggle between the selected and deselected state each time you click them. A selected button appears pressed in.

FIGURE 37-7.
Design view provides a wide variety of tools for modifying a form's layout and controls.

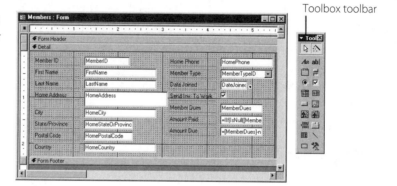

Toolbox toolbar

FIGURE 37-8.
The Toolbox toolbar buttons and their functions.

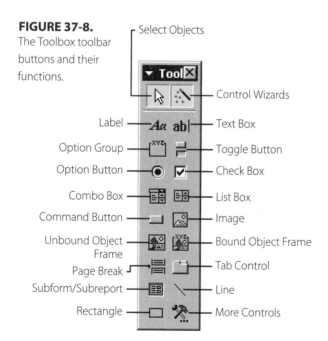

TABLE 37-1.   Toolbox Buttons for Modifying a Form's Design

Button	Name	Description
	Select Objects	Lets you select a single control by clicking it or multiple controls by pressing Shift while clicking each one. When this button is pressed in, you can also select controls by dragging a selection rectangle around them.
	Label	Lets you enter descriptive text to label a control or provide instructions. Labels attach automatically to most controls.
	Option Group	Creates a set of controls that you can select from and that assign a numeric value to a field.
	Option Button	Creates a round button that is usually used in a group of mutually exclusive options (for example, male or female). A selected button contains a black dot.
	Combo Box	Adds a control that consists of a text box that has a list box below it. You can either type text into the text box or select an item from the list.
	Command Button	Adds a rectangular button that can be clicked to perform an action (such as OK or Close).
	Unbound Object Frame	Displays an OLE object, such as an Excel spreadsheet. The object is constant; it doesn't change with each record.
	Page Break	Divides a form into multiple screens (or multiple pages for printing).
	Subform/Subreport	Adds information from an additional table to a form so that you can view or modify its data.
	Rectangle	Draws a rectangle on a form to group or emphasize a set of controls.
	Control Wizards	When selected, guides you through the process of creating a new control—a good idea until you've mastered the intricacies of form design!
	Text Box	Adds a box for displaying, entering, or modifying data.
	Toggle Button	Adds a rectangular push button that can be used to turn an option on or off. It appears pressed in when the option is on.

V

Microsoft Access

(continued)

TABLE 37-1. *continued*

Button	Name	Description
☑	Check Box	Adds a small square box that can be used to turn an option on or off. Contains a check mark when the option is on.
	List Box	Adds a control that displays a list box from which you select an item.
	Image	Adds a constant picture to a form. (It doesn't change when you change records.)
	Bound Object Frame	Displays OLE objects that are stored in the records of a table, such as employee photos. The object will change as you view various records.
	Tab Control	Lets you divide the form into separate tabs, like those you see in tabbed dialog boxes.
	Line	Lets you draw a single straight line on a form to separate or emphasize controls.
	More Controls	Adds from a list of additional controls supplied with Office. These controls are displayed on a menu when you click this tool.

When you're working in Design view, the Standard toolbar near the top of the application window provides commands that are useful for designing a form. In Design view, Access also displays the Formatting toolbar, which is shown below. (If it isn't currently visible, display it by pointing to Toolbars on the View menu and choosing Formatting (Form/Report) on the submenu.) The Formatting toolbar contains a wide variety of commands for modifying the appearance of the form and the controls it contains. It's discussed in detail in Chapter 40, "Formatting Forms and Reports."

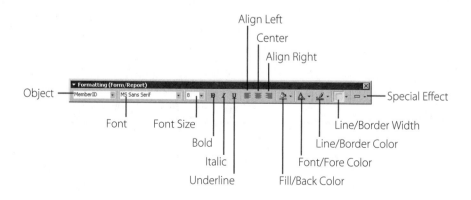

Adding a Bound Control

A *bound* control is one that's associated with a field of the table or query that serves as the form's record source. A bound control lets you view or modify the value of the associated field, and is the most common type of control. (In the next section, you'll learn about controls that aren't bound.) You can quickly add a bound control to your form by using the *field list*, a window that lists all the fields contained in the record source. The following is the field list for the Members form used as an example in this chapter:

To display the field list, choose Field List from the View menu or click the Field List button on the Form Design toolbar. You might need to scroll to see all the fields.

Field
List

To add a control to your form that's bound to a particular field, simply drag the field name from the field list to a point at or near the desired position on the form. Access creates an appropriate control, or pair of controls, based on the data type of the field that you dragged to the form. For example, if you dragged a text field or a numeric field, Access creates a text box together along with a label, as shown here:

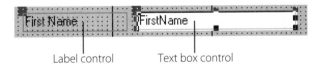

Label control   Text box control

Similarly, if you drag a field that has been assigned a lookup column, Access creates a combo box. (Recall from Table 35-1, page 841, that a field that has a lookup column is one that displays a list of values.)

NOTE

> To delete a control from a form, make sure that the Select Objects button on the Toolbox is selected (that is, it appears pressed in). Then click the control to select it, and press the Delete key.

Adding a Control Using the Toolbox

You can use the Toolbox to change the type of control that Access creates when you drag a control from the field list. For example, if you drag a control that has the Yes/No data type, Access will normally create a text box control together with a label. If you would rather have a check box control, click the Check Box button on the Toolbox immediately before you drag the field from the field list, and Access will create a check box instead. Clicking a button on the Toolbox will have an effect only if the type of control you click is appropriate for the data type of the field that you drag to the form. (For instance, selecting Command Button will have no effect if you drag a text field, because you can't use a command button to access a text field.)

You can also use the Toolbox to directly add a control to your form. To do this, click the Toolbox button for the control you want to add, and then click the form at the approximate location where you want to display the control. Access will add the control, assigning it a default size; you can later adjust its size or position.

If the Control Wizards button on the Toolbox toolbar is selected, and if the field you select is one that requires multiple steps to complete—an option group, a combo box, or a list box, for example—Access starts a wizard to guide you through the steps. During this process, the wizard generally asks you which field you want to associate with the control, and the resulting control will be bound to that field.

If, however, the field you select is a simple one—such as a label, text box, or option button—Access will simply create it directly on the form without running a wizard. In this case, the control won't be bound to a field. You can use a control that isn't bound to a field to display the results of a calculation (such as the Amount Due control on the Members example form), or to display instructions or other information.

Properties

If you do want to bind the control to a field so that it can be used to access the field, you'll need to use the *property sheet*, which is a dialog box containing a set of tabs that let you modify the properties of the currently selected object. To open the property sheet for a particular control, select the control; then choose Properties from the View menu, click the Properties toolbar button, or press Alt+Enter. Alternatively, you can just double-click the control. (If the property sheet is already open, just select the control. You can work in Design view while the property sheet remains displayed.)

Then follow these steps:

1 Click the All tab, which is shown here.

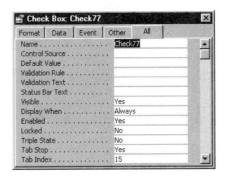

2 To bind the control to a field, click in the Control Source box, click the down arrow that appears at the right of the box, and select the field you want from the drop-down list.

3 You can change the name of the control by typing a new value into the Name property box (though this won't change the label that appears next to it).

4 You can also assign a default value to the control by entering the value into the Default Value property box. *Chapter 40, "Formatting Forms and Reports," provides more information on setting control properties.*

5 You can change any other properties of the control by typing or selecting values in the other property boxes.

Changing a Control

Once you have created a control, you can convert it to another type of appropriate control by pointing to Change To on the Format menu and choosing the new type of control you want from the submenu. Note that you'll be able to choose only a control type that's similar to the original control type (that is, one that would be suitable for accessing the same data types). For example, you can change a text box only to a label, list box, or combo box. Figure 37-9, on the next page, shows the Change To submenu as it appears for several different types of controls.

FIGURE 37-9.

The available choices on the Change To submenu depend on the type of control selected, for example, a text box (A), a combo box (B), or a check box (C).

 A  B  C

The other types of changes you can make to a control include moving the control, changing the control's size or shape, altering the color or style effects of a control, and setting additional control properties. (You already saw how to change several of the properties.) *These topics are discussed in Chapter 40, "Formatting Forms and Reports."*

NOTE

You might be confused sometimes about whether to work with the control itself or with the label next to it. Some controls, such as a toggle button, have a Caption property that you can use to add text directly to the control. In general, however, the label for the control exists as a separate control on the form.

Creating your own forms—and designing them for ease of use—can be a complex process, yet a rewarding one. This chapter has provided a general introduction to get you going. The best way to learn how to

---

Copying a Control

Rather than creating a new control, you can save a bit of effort by making a copy of another control already on the form and then modifying it:

1 Make sure that the Select Objects button on the Toolbox toolbar is selected, and then click the control you want to copy. Access will draw a border along with sizing handles around the selected control.

2 Choose Copy from the Edit menu (or press Ctrl+C), and then choose Paste (or press Ctrl+V). The copy of the control will appear near or perhaps on top of the original control.

3 Move the copy where you want it to be on the form. To move a control, select it by clicking it, if necessary. Then move the pointer near an edge of the control, and when the pointer becomes a small hand, drag the control to its new location.

See Chapter 40, "Formatting Forms and Reports," for more information on moving controls.

create controls is to add bound controls using the field list and then experiment with changing their formats and properties.

Putting Forms on the Web Using Data Access Pages

A data access page, a new feature of Access 2000, is similar to a form. Like a form, it displays a collection of controls, and it allows you to access fields in one or more tables or queries in a database. Unlike a form, however, it's stored in a separate file rather than within the database. Because this file is in HTML format, it can be opened in a Web browser as well as in Access. And when it's opened in a browser, it doesn't merely display static information, but rather allows you to navigate through the records in the source table or query, and to add, modify, or remove information, just as you can in Access. If you place the HTML file for a data access page (plus any files that it displays) on a Web server, other users on the Internet or on a company intranet can work with the database. Figure 37-10 shows a data access page viewed in Access, and Figure 37-11 shows the same page viewed in the Microsoft Internet Explorer 5 Web browser.

FIGURE 37-10.
In Access, a data access page functions like a form.

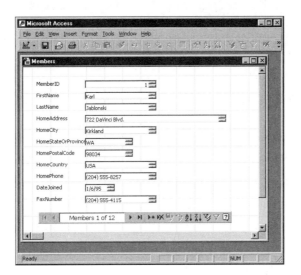

To use a particular data access page in Access, select Pages on the Objects bar in the Database window, and double-click the name of the page.

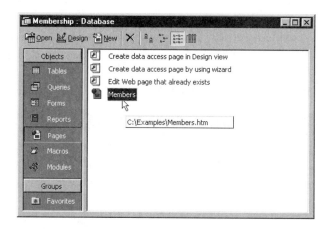

This will open the page in Page view (shown in Figure 37-10), which is analogous to Form view for using a form. To open a data access page in a Web browser, you'll need to run your browser and enter the address (URL) where the page is stored on a Web server, network, or local disk. (If you have already opened a data access page in Access, you can preview its appearance in your browser by choosing Web Page Preview from the File menu.)

FIGURE 37-11.
You can also open a data access page in a Web browser.

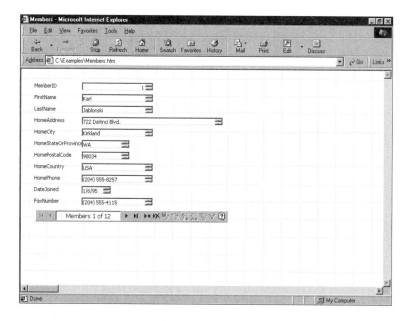

To view and modify records in a data access page, you use the same basic techniques that were described for forms, in the section "Using a

Form," page 878. Notice, however, that a data access page typically contains a more complete toolbar than a form:

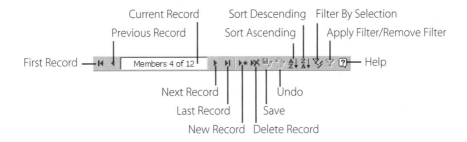

Creating a Data Access Page

The most versatile way to create a new data access page is to select Pages on the Objects bar in the Database window, and click the New button. This will display the New Data Access Page dialog box:

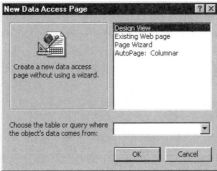

In this dialog box, select an option from the list to specify the way the new page will be created, select the table or query that you want to use as the record source from the list box near the bottom, and click the OK button. The options, listed below, are similar to those you can select in the New Form dialog box when you create a new form.

- The Design View option lets you create the data access page from scratch in Design view.

- The Existing Web Page option lets you create a new data access page based on a Web page you already have.

- The Page Wizard option runs a wizard that creates a new data access page for you, according to your specifications.

- The AutoPage Columnar option quickly generates a new data access page, where the controls are arranged in a single column, using default options.

In general, the easiest way to create a new data access page is to select the Page Wizard option. Using the Page Wizard is simple, yet flexible. It works much like the Form Wizard, which was discussed in "Form Wizard Option," page 887. You might be able to use it to create your final page, or at least a preliminary version of your page that you can then customize, as discussed next.

Modifying a Data Access Page

To modify a data access page, you need to open it in Design view by selecting Pages on the Objects bar in the Database window, selecting the page, and clicking the Design button near the top of the window. Or, if the page is already open in Page view, you can open it in Design view by choosing Design View from the View menu.

Figure 37-12 shows the same form shown in Figures 37-10 and 37-11, opened in Design view. Design view lets you add, remove, resize, or rearrange the controls that make up the page. You can also modify the properties of any of the controls or of the page itself. The techniques for using Design view to modify a data access page are similar to those for customizing a form in Design view, which were described in "Modifying a Form," page 891.

FIGURE 37-12.
Design view provides an extensive set of tools for customizing a data access page.

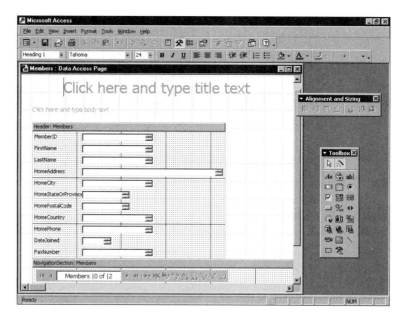

Using Queries to Get Answers

A *query* is the tool you use to get information from your database in response to specific questions. Rather than presenting every record in a table, the results of a query show only those records that are relevant. When you make a query, you set up a condition describing the types of records you want Microsoft Access to include. When you run the query, Access produces a datasheet containing just those matching records.

Queries can be simple—for example, the results of a query can list all records in which the purchase price of a book is more than $50—or complex, involving a series of comparisons among fields and alternative conditions strung together—for example, the results of a query can list all records in which the purchase price of a book is less than 85 percent of the cover price if the book was purchased in a state with no sales tax, or less than 80 percent of the cover price if purchased elsewhere.

All queries are based on the contents of a *design grid,* which provides a row-and-column structure for organizing the fields that are used in the query and for entering the query conditions. In this chapter, you'll learn how to use the Advanced Filter/Sort command, which displays a design grid and offers many of the features of a true query object. You'll then learn how to create a full-fledged query object, which employs a design grid that offers many additional options. Because of the similarities of these two methods, the chapter uses the general term *query* to refer both to an Advanced Filter/Sort operation as well as to a true query.

Using the Simplest Grid—Advanced Filter/Sort

If you're working with a table in either Datasheet or Form view and want to develop a query that creates a list of only a subset of the records in that table, you can use the Advanced Filter/Sort command on the Filter submenu of the Records menu. When you choose this command, a window similar to the one shown in Figure 38-1 appears.

W ON THE WEB

The Book Collection.mdb database file, used for the examples in this chapter, is on the Running Office 2000 Reader's Corner page. For information about connecting to this Web site, read the Introduction.

? SEE ALSO

The results of a query are always displayed in Datasheet view. For more information about rearranging columns, sorting records, and making other changes to datasheets, see Chapter 36.

Take note of several limitations of using the Advanced Filter/Sort command rather than creating a true query:

- Only the fields in the table that is active when you choose the Advanced Filter/Sort command are available for you to use in creating the query.

- Some features of the actual query design grid are not available. *(See "Exploring Features of the Query Design Grid," page 917.)*

Still, the techniques that you learn in working with the Advanced Filter/Sort command are also necessary for creating a true query, so it's a good place to start.

FIGURE 38-1.
The Advanced Filter/Sort command displays a design grid for entering your conditions.

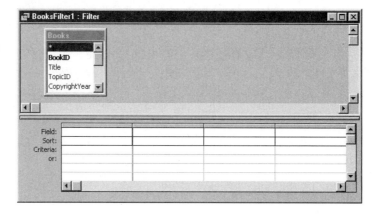

Defining the Conditions

Queries consist of a series of conditions, or *criteria*, that are combined to specify precisely which records are displayed. Each condition consists of three elements:

- The field that will be used for the comparison

- The operator, which describes the type of comparison to be performed

- The value, which specifies exactly what the field will be compared to

For example, if you want to list all records in which the cover price of a book is less than $20, the field would be PurchasePrice, the comparison operator would be the less-than symbol (<), and the value would be 20. See Figure 38-2.

To create the condition, you enter this information in the design grid as follows:

1 Select the name of the field that you will use in the condition. You can select the field name in several ways. One is to click an empty box in the Field row of the filter design grid and then click the down arrow that appears at the right to display a drop-down list of all fields in your table. Scroll through the list, if necessary, and select the field you want to use. Alternatively, you can drag the field name from the field list that appears in the top half of the Advanced Filter/Sort window to a point anywhere on the column you want to use in the grid at the bottom.

FIGURE 38-2.
A condition is entered into the design grid in three parts.

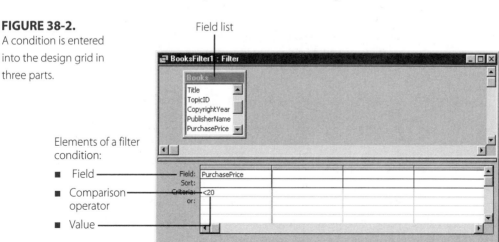

Field list

Elements of a filter condition:

- Field
- Comparison operator
- Value

The asterisk (*) at the top of the field list—and at the top of the drop-down lists in the Field row (following the table name)—represents all fields in the table. You can't specify criteria for this choice. It's useful only for designing a true query object (discussed later in the chapter), when you want to display all fields of the selected records. Note also that the primary key field(s) for each table are formatted in **bold** in the field list.

2 Click the Criteria box in the design-grid column that you're using, and type the operator and the value. If you want to use the Expression Builder, right-click the box and choose Build from the pop-up menu. (The Expression Builder feature lets you select the different components of your condition from a complex dialog box instead of directly typing them in.)

3 Define any additional conditions you want. *The techniques for using multiple conditions will be discussed later, in the section "Combining Conditions."*

You can use the commands on the Edit menu to delete entries from grid rows, to delete entire grid rows or columns, or to clear the grid completely. You can also clear the entire grid by clicking the Clear Grid button on the toolbar.

Clear Grid

Viewing the Results

To see the results of your Advanced Filter/Sort, choose Apply Filter/Sort from the Filter menu or click the Apply Filter button on the toolbar. Access immediately switches back to your original view—Datasheet or Form—and lists only those records that match your conditions. The record indicator at the bottom of the window in Datasheet or Form view will indicate that a filter is currently in place (provided that you didn't use the Advanced Filter/Sort command merely to sort your records, as described later). Datasheet view's record indicator is shown here:

Apply Filter

Indicates that a filter has been applied, so not all records are listed.

Close

To return from the Advanced Filter/Sort window to Datasheet or Form view without applying the filter, simply close the Advanced Filter/Sort window or click the Close button on the toolbar.

After you have applied a filter to a table in Datasheet or Form view, you can remove the filter and view all the records again by choosing Remove Filter/Sort from the Records menu or by clicking the Remove Filter button on the toolbar. (The Apply Filter button will toggle to Remove Filter or back each time you click it.)

Combining Conditions

The advantages of using an Advanced Filter/Sort or a true query, rather than the Filter By Form or Filter By Selection commands (discussed in Chapter 36), include the following:

- You can more easily combine separate filtering conditions.

- You can combine conditions in ways that aren't possible using the simpler filter methods.

- You can sort the records at the same time that you filter them.

You can reduce the number of records shown by entering an additional condition in the same row. For example, you might want to list those books for which the price is less than $20 *and* the type is hardcover. In this case, your query would resemble the one shown here:

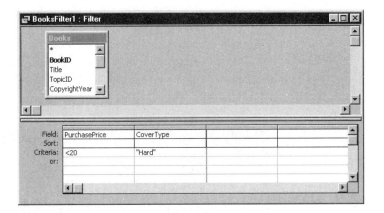

Notice that both criteria are entered into the same row. This tells Access to list only those records that match both requirements.

On the other hand, you can expand the number of records shown by entering an additional condition in a different row. For example, if you want to list those books for which the price is less than $20 *or* the cover is hard, you would put the second condition into the separate Or row, as shown at the top of the next page.

V

Microsoft Access

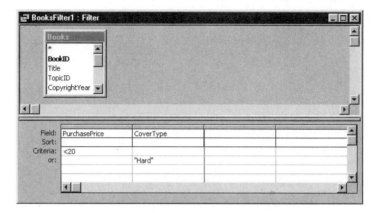

In this case, your query would produce many more matches—all the books costing less than $20 and all the hardcover books would be listed. The only books that wouldn't be included are those that meet neither criterion.

In the previous examples, the additional condition you added used a different field. Sometimes, however, you might want to add a condition that uses the same field as an existing condition. For example, you might want to list all books that have a purchase price between $10 and $50. That is, you want to list all books with a purchase price that is greater than or equal to $10 and is less than or equal to $50. To do this, you would need to combine two conditions for the PurchasePrice field within the same row. One way to combine these conditions is to add the field to the design grid twice—once for each condition, as shown here:

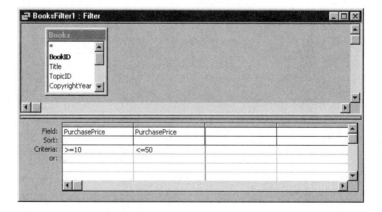

Another way is to enter both conditions into a single Criteria box with the word *and* between them; for example, *>=10 and <=50*. Or, you could use the words *Between* and *And*—for example, *Between 10 And 50*—for equivalent results. In this case, you would need to add the field to only a single column in the design grid.

As another example, in a table that tracks authors, you might want to list the records for authors whose last name is Davolio, Fuller, *or* Leverling. To do this, you would need to add three conditions to separate rows. Because the conditions all involve the same field (LastName), you can place them within the same column:

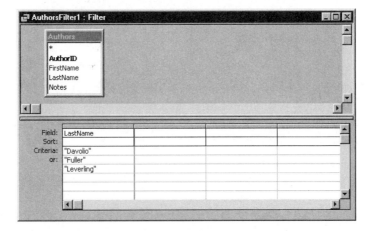

You'll notice in the graphic above that no operator has been used and that quotation marks surround the names entered. When you want an exact match, you can use the equal operator (=), or, if you use nothing, the equal sign is assumed. Access inserts the quotation marks for you when you're specifying conditions using text fields. The quotes imply that the value is to be used literally.

Sorting

You can use the Sort row of the query design grid to organize the information that appears in Datasheet and Form views. When you click a box in the Sort row, a down arrow appears at the right side of the box. Clicking that down arrow reveals a list that offers the choices Ascending, Descending, and (Not Sorted). Select either Ascending or

For more information
on how Access sorts
information, see
"Sorting Your Informa-
tion," page 866.

Descending to have Access sort the records using the values in the field selected in that column. Select (Not Sorted) to have Access ignore that field when it sorts. For instance, to sort the records in the Books table in alphabetical order by title, you would select Title in the Field row and Ascending in the Sort row, as shown here:

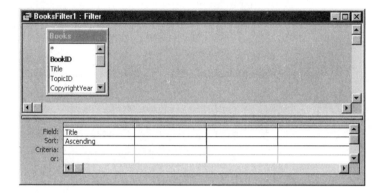

You can also sort information using multiple fields. Access always sorts on the fields from left to right, so your most important sort field should be to the left of any other sort field. When a sort is based on multiple fields, each field to the right of the first one is used for sorting only if records have identical information in the sort fields to its left. For example, you could sort the Authors table so that the authors are arranged by last name, and if several authors have the same last name, their records are further sorted by their first names. The following example shows how you could set up this sort:

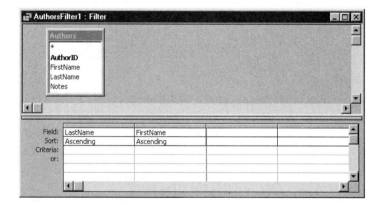

Creating a Simple Query

At times you might find the design of the Advanced Filter/Sort command inadequate to answer the questions you have for your database:

- When you need to ask questions that depend on fields stored in more than one table

- When you want to create a query that displays some, but not all, the fields in a table

In these cases, the solution is to use the formal query features of Access.

You can create a new query in a number of ways. The easiest is to select Queries on the Objects bar in the Database window and click the New button. Alternatively, you could choose Query from the New Object drop-down menu near the right end of the toolbar:

When you use either method, the New Query dialog box appears, which is shown here:

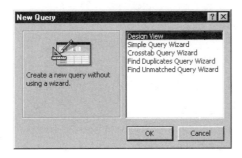

Housecleaning Wizards

No, Access doesn't let you turn your computer into a home maintenance device. Rather, Access includes two wizards designed to help you maintain the integrity of the data in your tables.

The Find Duplicates Query Wizard scans through a selected table or query and lists all records that contain duplicate values for a given field. This wizard can be useful for identifying all customers who live in a particular city or for finding all books in your collection on a particular topic.

The Find Duplicates Query Wizard is also a powerful tool for when you want to create a relationship between two fields. You can use this wizard to determine whether the related field in the primary table has duplicate values. (Recall from Chapter 35 that the field in the primary table in a relationship must have unique values.)

Use the Find Unmatched Query Wizard to compare two tables and locate any records in the first table that lack related records in the second. This wizard can be useful simply for locating special cases within your data (for example, finding students who aren't enrolled in any classes). It can be crucial if you're redesigning your database and want to define a one-to-many relationship between two tables in which referential integrity is to be enforced. (In this case, every record in the related table must have a matching record in the primary table.) *For more information about relationships, refer to Chapter 35.*

To use either query wizard, display the Database window, select Queries, click the New button, and then select the wizard from the New Query dialog box.

This dialog box allows you to select the type of the query and the way it's created:

- Choose the Design View option if you want to create your query from scratch in Design view. *(This topic is described in the section "Doing Without the Simple Query Wizard," page 915).*

- Choose the Simple Query Wizard option to have Access assist you in designing the query. Using this wizard is the easiest way to create a new general-purpose query, and is discussed in this section.

- Choose the Crosstab Query Wizard option to create a special-purpose query, known as a crosstab query, for comparing different subsets of the information in the database. *This topic is covered in "Using the Crosstab Query," page 925.*

■ Choose the Find Duplicates Query Wizard or the Find Unmatched Query Wizard option to run a special-purpose wizard that can help you maintain your data. These two options are discussed in the "Housecleaning Wizards" sidebar.

The following is the procedure for creating a general-purpose query using the Simple Query Wizard. (The figures show the steps for creating a query that lists all the books written by each author, in the Book Collection example database.)

1 Select the Simple Query Wizard from the New Query dialog box, and click the OK button. The Simple Query Wizard will start running.

2 In the first Simple Query Wizard dialog box (see Figure 38-3, on the next page), select all the fields you want to include in your query. To begin, select a table or query in the Tables/Queries list box that has one or more fields you'd like to include. Then move all the fields that you want from the Available Fields list to the Selected Fields list, using the four buttons located between the lists.

You can include fields from additional tables or queries. To add fields from a particular table, select it in the Tables/Queries list box, and then move the fields you want from the Available Fields list to the Selected Fields list. When you finish selecting fields, click the Next button to open the second wizard dialog box.

NOTE

Be sure to include all the fields that you need—for displaying information in the query datasheet, for setting the conditions of the query, or for sorting the results of the query.

3 If you selected one or more numeric fields (in addition to the primary key), the second wizard dialog box, shown in Figure 38-4, on the next page, asks you to choose either a *detail* query or a *summary* query. (If you *didn't* select numeric fields in the first dialog box, the wizard will immediately display the final dialog box, discussed in the next step.) A detail query lists all matching records from the different tables. A summary query displays summary information (such as the total number of records found or the average value of these records) rather than displaying all matching records. *Summary queries are discussed in the section "Summarizing Your Records," page 920.* When you're done, click the Next button.

V

Microsoft Access

FIGURE 38-3.
In the first Simple Query Wizard dialog box, you select all the fields that you need.

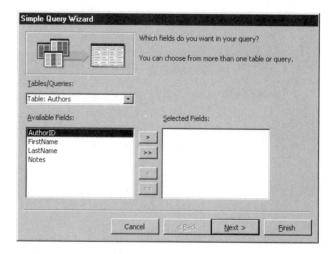

FIGURE 38-4.
If you have selected numeric fields, the second Simple Query Wizard dialog box lets you choose the type of query you want.

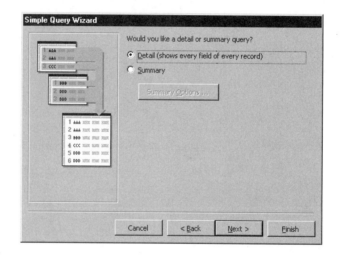

4 In the final Simple Query Wizard dialog box (see Figure 38-5), enter a new title for your query in the text box, or accept the default title. If you're ready to view your query, select the Open The Query To View Information option to immediately open the query in Datasheet view. *(See "Viewing the Results of a Query," page 918.)* Usually, however, you'll want to examine and possibly modify the query design before you view the results. In this case, select the Modify The Query Design option to open the query in Design view, which is discussed next. Click the Finish button to proceed.

FIGURE 38-5.
In the final Simple Query Wizard dialog box, you give the query a name and specify how it's to be opened.

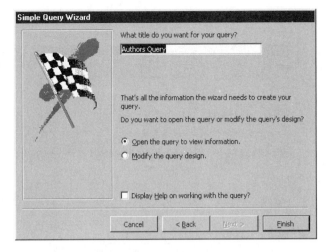

Doing Without the Simple Query Wizard

The main advantages of using the Simple Query Wizard are that it automatically adds to the upper portion of your Design view the required field lists (tables or queries) that you need to use in your query, and that it adds the fields themselves to the grid in the bottom portion of the window, as shown in Figure 38-6, on the next page. (The field lists were rearranged for clarity.)

The Simple Query Wizard adds a field list to the Design view for each table from which you selected fields in the first wizard dialog box (the one shown in Figure 38-2, page 905). It also adds a field list for any table that's needed to establish a relationship between the fields you selected. For example, when the query shown in Figure 38-6 was designed, fields were selected from only the Authors table and the Books table. However, these two tables have no direct relationship; they're related only indirectly because they both are related directly to the BookAuthors table. The wizard, therefore, included a field list for the BookAuthors table. Including the BookAuthors table allows the query to match the appropriate book or books to each author whom it lists.

Instead of using the Simple Query Wizard, if you select the Design View option from the New Query dialog box (opened by clicking the New button in the Database window), Access displays the Show Table dialog box, shown in Figure 38-7, on the following page. In this dialog box, you select the tables or queries that contain the fields you want to include in

FIGURE 38-6.
When you use the Simple Query Wizard, Access adds the field lists and field names to Design view for you.

Field lists added by the wizard

Fields added by the wizard

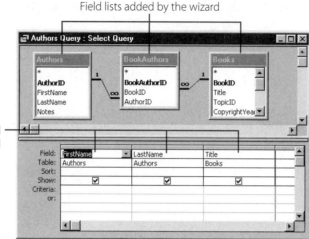

FIGURE 38-7.
Use the Show Table dialog box to add field lists for tables or queries.

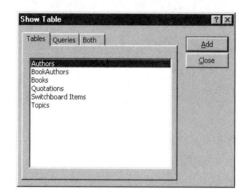

your new query. (You should also select any table needed to establish an indirect relationship between fields, as explained in the previous note.) To select a table or query, just double-click its name, or select it and click the Add button.

When you've finished adding tables or queries, click the Close button to remove the Show Table dialog box. Access will then activate Design view, which will display a field list for each table or query that you selected. (If you later want to add a field list for another table or query, choose Show Table from the Query menu.) You then need to add to the query design grid all fields that you want included in the query. You can add a field either by selecting it from the drop-down list that appears when you click a box in the Field row, or by dragging the field name from a field list at the top of the window to a column in the design grid.

Exploring Features of the Query Design Grid

The following are the most important unique features of the design grid in query Design view. Most of these features aren't provided by the Advanced Filter/Sort command.

■ Perhaps the most useful feature is the Show row, which contains a check box for each field that controls whether that field is displayed in the resulting datasheet. By clearing a check box, you can include a field as part of a condition without displaying the field on the datasheet. For example, the query shown in Figure 38-8 will list the author's first name, the author's last name, and the title for those books that sell for over $20, but won't list the purchase price for the books.

■ As when you use the Advanced Filter/Sort command, you can sort based on any field in the query by selecting either Ascending or Descending in the Sort row. If you select Ascending or Descending for more than one field, Access will apply the fields from left to right. That is, it will use a particular field for sorting only if it finds exact matches in all fields to its left. Unlike when you work with the Advanced Filter/Sort feature, when you're working in Design view, you don't have to display the sort fields in your datasheet.

■ You can add a field list to the Design window at any time by choosing Show Table from the Query menu or by clicking the

V

Microsoft Access

FIGURE 38-8.

When you create a query, you can use fields in your conditions without displaying them in the datatsheet.

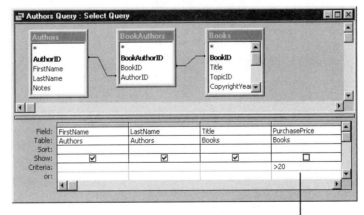

Access will use this field to select records, but won't display it on the query datasheet.

Show Table

Don't add the same field list twice. If you do so, Access will simply add a number after the field list name to indicate that it's a duplicate. While a duplicate field list might not cause problems, it's unnecessary and will make your query design more difficult to comprehend.

Show Table button on the toolbar. The Show Table dialog box is then displayed (described in the previous section and shown in Figure 38-7, page 916). And, of course, you can add fields from any table or query in the database. To remove a field list, click it and then either choose Remove Table from the Query menu, or press the Delete key.

When you add more than one field list to Design view, Access will draw lines to indicate any relationships between fields. These lines are initially the same as those shown in the Relationships window. You can, however, add or alter the relationships shown in the query Design view, using the same basic techniques employed in the Relationships window. These changes will affect that query only; they won't alter the relationships shown in the Relationships window and used elsewhere in the database. Note that if you run a query without valid relationships, the query is unlikely to show the results you expect, or Access might display a message indicating that it can't process the query. *For information on relationships, see "Relating Your Tables," page 848.*

You can show or hide the Table row in the query design grid by selecting or deselecting the Table Names option on the View menu. This row lists the table name for each field included in the grid, and can be helpful when you're creating more complex queries.

Viewing the Results of a Query

Run

When you're designing a query, you often need to switch between Design view and Datasheet view. Fortunately, you have a number of easy ways to do this. From the View menu, you can choose Design View or Datasheet View as appropriate. Also, from Design view, you can click the Run button on the toolbar to view the results of the query in Datasheet view. (Note that switching to Datasheet view automatically *runs* the query—that is, shows the results that correspond to the current query definition.) Additionally, you can switch between various views by clicking the down arrow on the View button at the left of the toolbar and choosing the view you want from the drop-down menu:

Design View
Datasheet View
SQL SQL View

As a shortcut, you can click the View button, without opening the drop-down menu, to switch between Datasheet and Design views.

> **NOTE**
>
> Both the View menu and the View button offer a third option: viewing the SQL (structured query language) information associated with your queries. This view is useful primarily when you use Access to work with data managed by certain other database systems. You needn't worry about this view if all your data is stored within Access itself.

Using Top-Value Queries

Access has one nifty feature that goes a bit beyond sorting and allows you to look at the highest or lowest values for a field when using an actual query. For example, in a query that lists books (such as the example Authors Query shown in the previous figures), you might be interested in looking at only the three least expensive titles. To do this, follow these steps:

1 Display the query in Design view.

2 Sort on the field you want to use to organize your list. In this example, the field would be Purchase Price. To look at the lowest values in the list, sort by selecting Ascending in the Sort row. To look at the highest values in the list, sort by selecting Descending in the Sort row.

3 In the Top Values list box on the toolbar, select the number of top or bottom values that you want to see. If the number you want isn't listed, type your own number into the box at the top of the list, and press Enter. See Figure 38-9, on the next page.

> **TIP**
>
> The Top Values list box also lets you select or type a percentage rather than an absolute actual number of records to be displayed. For example, in a query listing students and their test scores, you could select a Descending sort on the score field and enter 15% into the Top Values list box to retrieve a list of students in the top 15 percent of the class (perhaps the ones who get A's).

4 To view the query results, use any method to switch to Datasheet view. The datasheet at the top of the next page shows the results of the query defined in the example above.

V

Microsoft Access

Authors Query : Select Query

First Name	Last Name	Title	Purchase Price
Margaret	Peacock	Diamonds	$9.95
Janet	Leverling	My Family	$17.95
Andrew	Fuller	Planning Your Career	$22.95

Record: 1 of 3

Summarizing Your Records

Totals

In addition to using queries to provide a list of records that match a set of conditions, you can also use a query to summarize the information contained in those matching records. You accomplish this by using the Total row in the query design grid. To use the Total row, you must be working with a Select query (the standard type of query, as explained later), and the query must be open in Design view. To add the Total row, choose the Totals option on the View menu, or click the Totals button on the toolbar. (To remove the row, deselect the menu option or button.)

Figure 38-10 shows a query design grid to which the Total row has been added. The drop-down list in one of the boxes in this row is open, showing the different summary options that you can apply to the field.

To summarize the values in a particular field, open the drop-down list in the Total box for that field, and select one of the functions listed in Table

FIGURE 38-9.
You can list just the top or bottom values in a sorted query by selecting a number or percentage in the Top Values list box.

Top Values list box (This value will show the first three matching records in the order of the sort.)

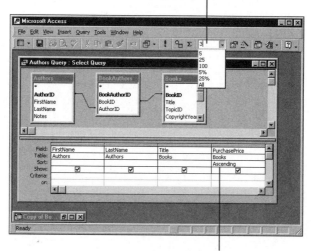

Sorting direction (Ascending starts with the lowest prices.)

FIGURE 38-10.
Adding the Total row creates a summary query.

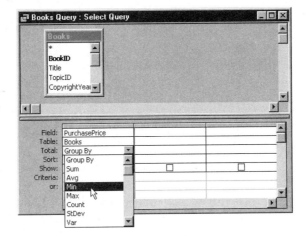

38-1. (The other options in the drop-down list will be discussed later.) For a field that has the Number or Currency data type, you can select any of these functions. For a field that has a non-numeric data type, such as text, you can select only the Count function (which displays the total number of matching records that have any value in that field), or First or Last (which displays the first or the last value encountered).

TABLE 38-1.   The Functions You Can Select in the Total Row

Function	Description
Sum	Adds up all the values within the group
Avg	Finds the average for all the values within the group
Min	Finds the lowest value within the group
Max	Finds the highest value within the group
Count	Determines the number of values within the group
StDev	Determines the standard deviation for the population defined by the group
Var	Determines the variance for the population defined by the group
First	Lists the first value encountered in the group
Last	Lists the last value encountered in the group

If you have only a single field in your design grid, and you select a summary function in the Total box (as shown in Figure 38-10), the resulting datasheet will look similar to the one shown on the next page.

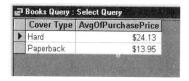

Notice that the datasheet contains only an answer to your query and a column heading identifying the function and field that were used—in this case, MinOfPurchasePrice (the minimum value in the PurchasePrice field).

In addition to using summary functions to provide overall summaries for the datasheet, you can also use these tools to perform calculations on groups of values within the records. To do this, you need to add a field to the grid that will be used to group the records and select the Group By option in its Total box. (This option is the default.) For example, you might want to determine the average price of hardcover books versus paperback books. You would need to have two fields in your design grid: the CoverType field, which is used for grouping the records, and the PurchasePrice field, which is used for the calculation, as shown in Figure 38-11.

When you run this type of query, Access lists each group together with the calculation result for the values within that group, as shown here:

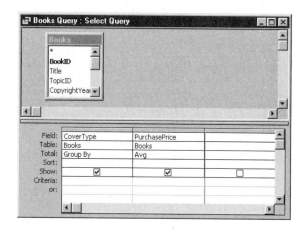

FIGURE 38-11.
Adding a field and selecting Group By in the Total box provides a summary of each group of records.

As you might imagine, you can control the order of the records in the datasheet by using the Sort row to display the records in ascending or descending order.

In addition to selecting the Group By option in the Total row, you can also select the Where option in the Total row drop-down list. Selecting the Where option allows you to add a field to the query design grid that is used only for specifying a condition for selecting records. In this case, the field isn't used to group records, and neither the field nor values derived from it are displayed. It's used simply to determine which records will be included in the group to be summarized. When you use the Where option, you must provide a condition in the Criteria row.

The Expression option in the Total row drop-down list is used to create more complex calculations based not only on the values within fields, but also on the values resulting from operations on fields, such as sum, average, or standard deviation.

Calculating New Values

 SEE ALSO

For information on creating formulas in Excel, see Chapter 20, "Using Formulas and Functions to Crunch Numbers."

Sometimes you might want to display the result of a calculation performed on information within each record, rather than summarizing across records. To do that, the best approach is to create a calculated field. You can create such a field within a query, on a form, or within a report. For example, perhaps you'd like to see the purchase price of books if their prices were all increased by 15 percent. To include this information in a query, you would add a field to the query design grid that would perform this calculation. This new field is called a calculated field because it performs a computation and isn't a regular field from a table.

To create a calculated field, click in the Field row in a blank column in the query design grid, and enter the expression for calculating the value. Rather than typing the name of a field to be used in your calculation, you can click the down arrow to the right of the text box and select the field name from the list; you would then type the remainder of the expression. Formulas for calculating fields are similar to formulas entered into cells in Microsoft Excel spreadsheets—the main difference is that rather than referring to cell addresses, you refer to field names. The formula will be calculated for every record.

Figure 38-12 shows an expression to calculate a 15 percent increase in the purchase price of books (as it would appear immediately after you type it in, before you press Enter or run the query). Because Access doesn't allow you to express values as percentages, the formula multiplies the current price by 1.15—the equivalent of 115 percent.

FIGURE 38-12.
A calculated field contains an expression that computes a value based on other fields.

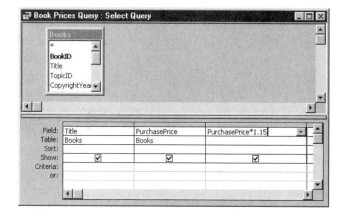

When you run this query, you see the results shown in Figure 38-13. Notice that the field name consists of the letters *Expr* followed by a digit, indicating the sequence in which the calculated field was created, and that the results of the calculation aren't formatted.

FIGURE 38-13.
In a query datasheet, a calculated field displays the result of the computation for each record.

Title	Purchase Price	Expr1
Dirk Luchte	$23.50	27.025
Planning Your Career	$22.95	26.3925
Diamonds	$9.95	11.4425
Techniques of Tai Chi	$25.95	29.8425
My Family	$17.95	20.6425

Record: 1 of 5

Fortunately, you're not stuck with the default format used by Access. It's quite easy to change both the name of the calculated field and its formatting. If you return to Design view, you'll notice that the expression you originally typed into the Field box for the calculated field (in the example, *PurchasePrice*1.15*) has been reformatted to include a field name. In the example, the expression would now appear as follows:

*Expr1: [PurchasePrice]*1.15*

To change the field name, just select (highlight) the text before the colon, and type the new name. For instance, in this example you could replace *Expr1* with *Expected Price*.

To format the calculated field, right-click anywhere in the column for the field in the query design grid, and choose Properties from the pop-up menu that appears. On the General tab, click the Format box, and from the drop-down list that appears, select an appropriate format. For this example, you would choose Currency. Now when you switch to Datasheet view, the information will be much more in keeping with the format of the other material in your database, as shown here:

Title	Purchase Price	Expected Price
Dirk Luchte	$23.50	$27.03
Planning Your Career	$22.95	$26.39
Diamonds	$9.95	$11.44
Techniques of Tai Chi	$25.95	$29.84
My Family	$17.95	$20.64

Record: 1 of 5

Using the Crosstab Query

All the queries discussed so far are known as *Select* queries. A Select query is the routine type of query that displays a list of records or calculates summary values. This section introduces a second category of query, the *Crosstab* query. Sometimes, the information in a database can be organized by two different types of groupings, and you might want to extract information on the various subsets formed by the various groupings.

Imagine, for example, that you have collected test results from a group of students. The students can be grouped based on gender (male or female) as well as age (15, 16, or 17). It might be useful to know the average test score for each of the possible subsets (15-year-old boys, 15-year-old girls, 16-year-old boys, 16-year-old girls, 17-year-old boys, and 17-year-old girls), to consider whether your teaching is equally effective for both genders. You can best accomplish this by using a statistical matrix called a *cross-tabulation*. In Access, you can generate a cross-tabulation by creating a Crosstab query. The results of a Crosstab query for the test score scenario just described are shown on the next page.

V

Microsoft Access

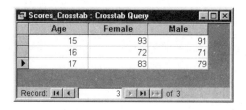

The following is a summary of the steps for creating a Crosstab query using the Crosstab Query Wizard:

1 In the Database window, select Queries, and then click the New button.

2 In the New Query dialog box, select the Crosstab Query Wizard option, which guides you through the steps of designing your Crosstab query.

3 In the first Crosstab Query Wizard dialog box, select the table or query containing the fields you want to include.

   For instance, to create the example Scores_Crosstab query shown above, you would select the name of the table that stores the gender, age, and test score for each student. Here's how such a table might appear in Design view:

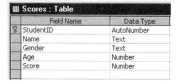

4 In the second dialog box, select from one to three fields to be used for row headings. (For the example query, you would select just the Age field.)

5 In the third dialog box, select a single field to be used for the column headings. (For the example query, you would select the Gender field.)

6 In the fourth dialog box, select the field and the function you want to use to calculate the values displayed in the query for each subset—that is, for each column and row intersection. (For the example query, you would select the Score field and the Avg function to display the average test score for each subset.)

Also, select the Yes Include Row Sums option if you want to include an additional column that summarizes the values displayed in each row—the average of all values if you chose the Avg function, the sum of all values if you chose the Sum function, and so on. For instance, if you selected this option for the example query, the query would include a column that displays the average of the female value and the male value for each age. (To create the example query shown above, you would deselect this option.)

7 In the fifth and final dialog box, enter a name for the query (or accept the default name), and choose whether the new query should be initially opened in Datasheet view or in Design view. When you click the Finish button, the wizard will create the query.

> **From Query to Crosstab**
>
> You can also convert an existing query to a Crosstab query. To do so, open it in Design view, and choose Crosstab Query from the Query menu. This command will add a Crosstab and a Total row to the design grid and will convert the query to a Crosstab query. In the Crosstab row, you designate the field(s) to be used for the row headings and the field to be used for the column headings. In the Total row, you designate the field and function to be used to calculate the result for each subset. The easiest way to learn how to set up a Crosstab query in Design view is to study the design of a Crosstab query generated by the Crosstab Query Wizard.

Understanding Queries that Change Data

You have now learned about two major types of queries: the Select query and the Crosstab query. Four additional types of queries can actually change your data. These last four query types rely on the conditions defined in the query design grid to identify which records should be changed, and they use other information that you provide to determine what sort of changes to make. When you're working with a query in Design view, you can convert the query to one of these types by choosing a query type from the Query menu or by clicking the down arrow on the Query Type toolbar button and choosing from the drop-down menu, as shown on the following page.

V

Microsoft Access

Query Type button

When you convert a query to a different type, the rows in the query design grid change according to the type of information that must be specified. For two of the query types (Make-Table and Append), Access displays a dialog box to obtain more information before returning you to the Design window.

Delete Query

The most dangerous of these four queries is the Delete query, which removes from your tables all records that match your conditions. This query can be useful for housekeeping—for example, you might choose to eliminate from your database all old records with dates prior to January 1, 1997—but it can be tragic if you make a mistake in defining your conditions. Always use the Select query type first, using the conditions you plan to use for deleting records, so that you can first display the records to confirm that you have the right subset of your database. Only then should you go ahead and switch to the Delete query type to remove them permanently.

Make-Table Query

As the name implies, the Make-Table query type creates a new table of all the information your query returns. The Make-Table query type can be particularly useful for backing up your information. For example, in the case above, before you delete all records prior to January 1, 1997, you might want to use the Make-Table query type to make a separate table containing that information. Your first step would be to use the Select query type to specify all records prior to 1997. Then you would use the Make-Table query type to create a new table of just these older records. Finally, you would use the Delete query type to delete the older records from your more recent ones.

Append Query

Like the Make-Table query type, the Append query type copies records from one table (or from a collection of tables) to a new location. The Append query type, however, doesn't create a new table, but rather adds the fields your query retrieves to an existing table. You often use this query to add a new batch of records to update an existing table or database; for instance, you might receive a table or database of new books published in 1999 that you want to integrate with your existing books database.

Update Query

An Update query provides a powerful way to change the value of any fields in your database for those records that match the conditions you specify. When you use an Update query, Access adds an Update To row to the query design grid. You can then use that row to specify a value or an expression that indicates how the value in a field should be changed.

You create expressions using the same general guidelines that you follow when creating calculated fields. *See "Calculating New Values," page 923, for more information.* The example query given in that section included a field that showed the result of increasing the purchase price by 15 percent. This calculated value wasn't part of the database and didn't change any data in the database. But if you decided that you needed to raise the price of books by 15 percent (because of increased overhead, for example), you might use an Update query to actually change the value of the PurchasePrice field in every record in the Books table to 115 percent of its previous value, permanently changing the data in your database.

While using the Select and Crosstab queries can help you view and understand your data, carefully using one of these four query types (Make-Table, Update, Append, and Delete) is a powerful way to update and maintain your data.

V

Microsoft Access

CHAPTER 39

Using Wizards to Generate Reports

R eports are the means that Microsoft Access provides for creating printed copies of the information in your database. You probably won't find it efficient to try to interpret the information presented in a report on your computer screen, for reports are really meant to be printed. (For working on screen with the information in your database, forms are generally preferable. They're discussed in Chapter 37.)

Access includes a number of items under the category of report, in addition to standard printed reports. These include address and other types of labels (Access provides the Label Wizard to assist you) and charts (which you can create using the Chart Wizard). Like the standard type of report, these items take information from the fields in your database tables and then organize and summarize that information in meaningful ways. *The Chart Wizard is shared by the Microsoft Office applications and is discussed in "Using Graph," page 1215.*

In this chapter, you'll create standard reports using the Report Wizard, and you'll learn how to make simple changes to the report design. You'll also learn how to create labels using the Label Wizard.

Creating a Standard Report

Standard reports come in two basic varieties: columnar and tabular. A *columnar report*, as shown in Figure 39-1, resembles the layout of a simple form. Each field is presented in a separate row that has the field name on the left and the contents of the field on the right. Depending on the number of fields in your database, each record might fit on a single sheet of paper or might extend onto several sheets; you might even be able to fit several records on one page.

The Asset Tracking.mdb database file, used for the examples in this chapter, is on the Running Office 2000 Reader's Corner page. For information about connecting to this Web site, read the Introduction.

A *tabular report*, as shown in Figure 39-2, organizes the information so that each field is in its own column and each record is represented as a

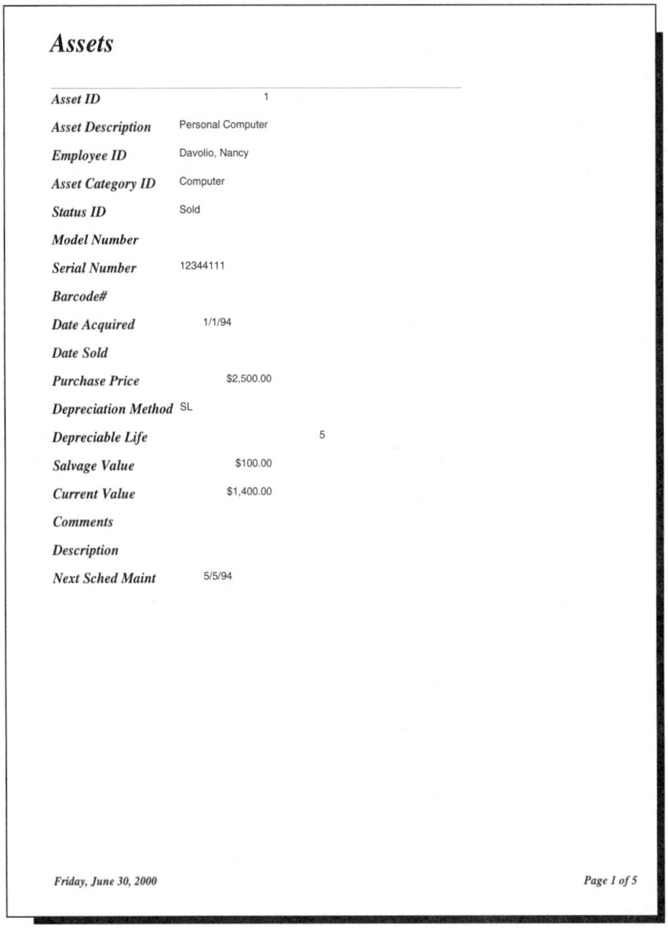

FIGURE 39-1.
A columnar report spreads the information for a single record over many rows arranged in a column.

Assets

Asset ID	1
Asset Description	Personal Computer
Employee ID	Davolio, Nancy
Asset Category ID	Computer
Status ID	Sold
Model Number	
Serial Number	12344111
Barcode#	
Date Acquired	1/1/94
Date Sold	
Purchase Price	$2,500.00
Depreciation Method	SL
Depreciable Life	5
Salvage Value	$100.00
Current Value	$1,400.00
Comments	
Description	
Next Sched Maint	5/5/94

Friday, June 30, 2000   *Page 1 of 5*

FIGURE 39-2.
A tabular report puts the information for each record in a separate row, and it might print best in landscape orientation.

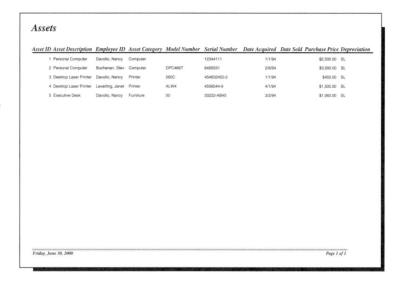

Assets

Asset ID	Asset Description	Employee ID	Asset Category	Model Number	Serial Number	Date Acquired	Date Sold	Purchase Price	Depreciation
1	Personal Computer	Davolio, Nancy	Computer		12344111	1/1/94		$2,500.00	SL
2	Personal Computer	Buchanan, Stev	Computer	DPC466T	6465531	2/6/94		$3,500.00	SL
3	Desktop Laser Printer	Davolio, Nancy	Printer	560C	454632452-2	1/1/94		$450.00	SL
4	Desktop Laser Printer	Leverling, Janet	Printer	ALW4	4556544-9	4/1/94		$1,500.00	SL
5	Executive Desk	Davolio, Nancy	Furniture	50	33222-AB45	3/2/94		$1,060.00	SL

Friday, June 30, 2000   Page 1 of 1

single detail line—this type of report resembles a table displayed in Datasheet view. You can also include summaries (subtotals, averages, and so on) at various levels of the report structure. The tabular report more closely resembles the format typically used for various types of business reports.

The easiest way to begin a new report, like other types of database objects, is to perform these initial steps:

1   Open the database in which you want to include the report.

2   Open the Database window.

3   Select Reports on the Objects bar in the Database window.

4   Click the New button.

The New Report dialog box appears, as shown here:

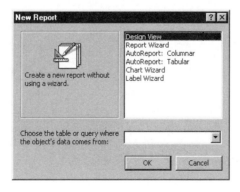

Note that you can also open the New Report dialog box by clicking the arrow on the New Object toolbar button and choosing Report from the drop-down menu:

Here are the different options you can select in the New Report dialog box:

■ Use the Design View option if you want to create a report from scratch using Design view. *Design view is discussed in "Modifying the Report Design," page 944.*

■ Select the Report Wizard option to have Access assist you in designing the report. Instructions for using the Report Wizard are given in the remainder of this section.

■ To use default settings to quickly create a columnar report (as shown in Figure 39-1, page 932) or a tabular report (as shown in Figure 39-2), select the AutoReport Columnar or the AutoReport Tabular option. Either report will include all the fields belonging to the table or query that you select in the list box at the bottom of the New Report dialog box.

■ Select the Chart Wizard option to create a chart using the Microsoft Graph program. *This process is described in the section "Using Graph," page 1215.*

■ Select the Label Wizard option to create mailing or other types of labels. *This procedure is discussed in "Making Labels," page 952.*

Using the Report Wizard is the easiest way to design a report, and yet the wizard is quite flexible. Although selecting one of the AutoReport options is a faster way to create a columnar or tabular report based on the fields in a single table or query, you can use the Report Wizard to create these same types of reports and have much greater flexibility in the choice of fields and in the report design.

TIP

> You can quickly create a simple, plainly formatted report that has a columnar arrangement by selecting a table or a query in the Database window and then choosing AutoReport from the New Object drop-down menu that was shown above.

To run the Report Wizard, select the Report Wizard option in the New Report dialog box, and click the OK button. You don't need to select a table or query in the list at the bottom of the dialog box.

The first Report Wizard dialog box appears and asks you to identify the fields to be included in the report, as shown in Figure 39-3. You have the option of selecting from several tables or queries, as you do when you use other Access wizards. Be sure to include all the fields that have any relevance to your report, whether the field values are to be displayed in each detail line, summarized, or used for grouping the records.

FIGURE 39-3.
In the first Report Wizard dialog box, you select all the fields to be used in the report.

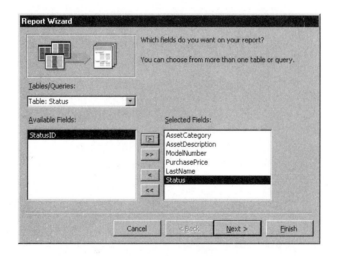

Move the fields you want from the Available Fields list into the Selected Fields list by using the four buttons, as necessary, that are located between the lists. To access fields from different tables or queries, merely select each one in the Tables/Queries list box, and then move the fields you want. This list box includes all the tables and queries defined in your database. When you have finished selecting fields, click the Next button to open the next Report Wizard dialog box.

Microsoft Access

Grouping Records

The dialog box shown in Figure 39-4 appears only if you selected fields from more than one table in the previous step. This dialog box allows you to choose one table for grouping the information in the report.

In the example shown in Figures 39-3 and 39-4, we selected fields in the first dialog box from the Asset Categories, Assets, Employees, and Status tables (all of which are related through one-to-many relationships). In this example, selecting the Asset Categories table in the second dialog box (as shown in Figure 39-4) would group the records in the report by asset category—that is, the report would list all Asset records that match the first asset category (which is Computer), then all records that match the second category (which is Printer), and so on through each of the remaining categories.

> **NOTE**
>
> In the example database, the Asset Categories, Employees, and Status tables are all *primary tables* in one-to-many relationships with the Assets table. Therefore, each record in the Asset Categories, Employees, or Status table can match many records in the Assets table and thus can easily be used for grouping records in the Assets table. This isn't true for the Assets table, however, because it constitutes the *related table* in all the relationships. Accordingly, if you selected the Assets table, the wizard wouldn't attempt to group your records for you. In the next wizard dialog box, however, you would have the opportunity to specify grouping on the basis of individual fields. *For information on relationships and the differences between primary and related tables, see "Relating Your Tables," page 848.*

FIGURE 39-4.
In the second Report Wizard dialog box (which opens only if you selected fields from more than one table), you need to choose a table to be used for grouping the records in the report.

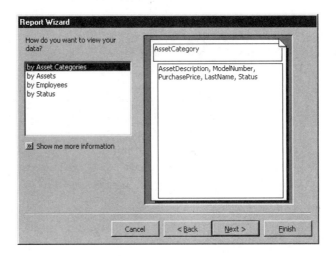

After selecting the grouping table you want, click Next to open the third Report Wizard dialog box, shown in Figure 39-5. In this dialog box, you can add grouping levels to your report by selecting one or more fields to be used to group the records.

In the example shown in Figure 39-5, because we selected the Asset Categories table in the second dialog box, the field from this table, AssetCategory, is already selected as the main grouping field in the third dialog box. (If we had selected the Assets table in the previous dialog box, no grouping field would be defined yet.) You could now add one or more fields to create additional grouping levels.

FIGURE 39-5.
In the third Report Wizard dialog box, you can add grouping levels to your report.

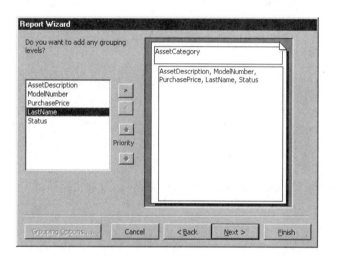

To add a grouping field, select it in the list at the left, and click the > button to move it into the report model at the right. To remove the field that's selected on the right, click the < button to move it back to the left. You can add up to three fields, which—when combined with an initially selected grouping field—would generate up to four grouping levels in your report. You can change the priority level of a grouping field that you have chosen by clicking the field name in the report model and then clicking the up-arrow or down-arrow Priority button.

For instance, if you added the LastName field in the example, records would be grouped by asset category, and then records within each asset category would be grouped by the last name of the holder of the asset. This grouping would be shown in the report model at the right of the dialog box. (See Figure 39-6, on the next page.)

FIGURE 39-6.
The model report in the third Report Wizard dialog box shows all grouping fields that you've selected and lets you change their levels.

Top grouping level added by wizard from previous dialog box choice.

Secondary grouping level added using this dialog box.

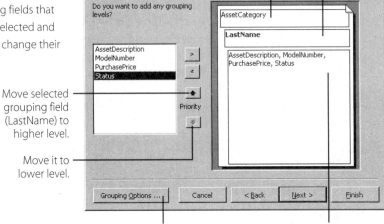

Move selected grouping field (LastName) to higher level.

Move it to lower level.

Click to modify the way records are grouped by each field.

Remaining fields in the report (will be displayed in the detail section).

⭐ **TIP**

Use Grouping Levels to Summarize Information

An important reason for including grouping levels is that they allow you to summarize numeric information within each group. For instance, including the AssetCategory and LastName grouping levels in the example report would allow you to display the total cost of the assets belonging to each asset category as well as the total cost of the assets held by each employee. Instead of the sum, you could display the average, minimum, or maximum asset cost. *Defining summary calculations will be discussed in "Setting Summary Options," page 939.*

When you have finished defining the grouping of your records, click the Next button to move to the fourth Report Wizard dialog box.

Sorting Fields

The fourth Report Wizard dialog box, shown in Figure 39-7, lets you choose the sorting order for the detail section in the report. Note that the report groups are automatically sorted on the fields used for grouping. In this dialog box, however, you can choose one or more fields that will be used for sorting the detail lines falling within each group. Choose the primary sort field by selecting it from the top list box (labeled 1). You can then choose one or more additional sort fields in

FIGURE 39-7.
In the fourth Report Wizard dialog box, you specify how to sort the detail lines in your report.

Click this button to select sort order.

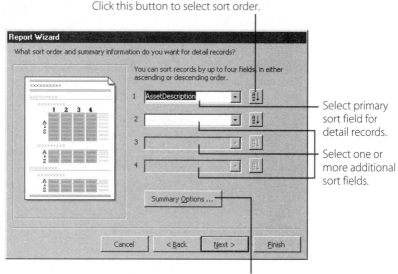

Select primary sort field for detail records.

Select one or more additional sort fields.

Click to add summary information to the report.

the remaining list boxes. (Note that each list box contains the names of only those report fields that are not used for grouping.)

Setting Summary Options

One button in the fourth Report Wizard dialog box is crucial but easy to overlook: the Summary Options button. Click this button to open the Summary Options dialog box, shown in Figure 39-8, on the following page. This dialog box lists each of the numeric or currency fields included in the detail section of your report. In the example shown in Figure 39-8, only the PurchasePrice field (which has the Currency data type) qualifies as a summary field.

You can choose to have Access summarize the values in one or more of these fields for each group in the report. If you want a summary to appear in your report, simply check one of the summary value functions for the field that you want to summarize. Access can calculate the sum, average, minimum, or maximum value.

By selecting one of the Show options, you can specify whether the records within each group will be shown, or only the summary information. In general, the first time you produce a report, you'll probably want to select Detail And Summary so that you can see clearly how Access is organizing the information. Later, you might want to hide the detail information so that your report is more concise and contains

V

Microsoft Access

FIGURE 39-8.
In the Summary
Options dialog box,
you can have Access
summarize numeric
information for
each group.

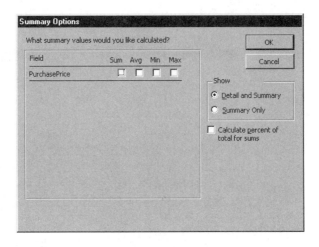

fewer distractions. (You can do this by using Design view, described in "Modifying the Report Design," starting on page 944.)

You can also select the Calculate Percent Of Total For Sums option to have Access calculate the percent of the grand total represented by each group total. In this example, you could determine what percentage of the total cost of assets was spent on computers as compared to printers or furniture, and even break it down further by employee. This option can be useful for seeing how group values contribute to the overall result. When you've finished setting the summary options, click OK to return to the fourth Report Wizard dialog box. Verify that the sorting options are the ones you want, and click Next again to move to the fifth dialog box of the Report Wizard.

Selecting a Layout

The fifth Report Wizard dialog box, shown in Figure 39-9, allows you to select the layout and orientation of your report. Each of the layout options in this dialog box specifies how much of the database information is repeated at each level of the report. When you select an option, the model at the left of the dialog box gives you an idea of how your report will look:

- The Stepped layout (shown in Figure 39-10 on page 942) places each new group header in its own section of the report, putting no other information on the same line.

FIGURE 39-9.
In the fifth Report Wizard dialog box, select the layout and orientation of your report.

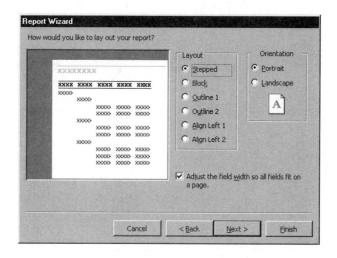

■ The Block layout compresses the information for the group header onto the same line as the information for the first detail listing in that group. This makes for a more vertically compact report, but often it's somewhat difficult to find the information you need.

■ The Outline 1 and Outline 2 layouts overlap the columns used for the grouping values but keep the text for each on a separate line. This is useful when you have a report that's too wide to fit legibly on a single page. Alternatively, you can consider changing the page orientation from the Portrait option to the Landscape option, which gives you a wider page to work with.

■ Finally, the Align Left 1 and Align Left 2 layouts position the grouping fields flush with the left margin and repeat the detail headers at the top of each detail section. These options provide the largest area across your page for your detail records, although they make distinguishing the different groups a bit more difficult. The Aligned Left 1 layout is shown in Figure 39-11, on page 943.

When you're done setting options in the fifth Report Wizard dialog box, click the Next button to go to the sixth dialog box.

Selecting a Style

The sixth dialog box of the Report Wizard, shown in Figure 39-12, page 944, lets you choose a format style for your report. These

FIGURE 39-10.
The Stepped layout
keeps each field in its
own column.

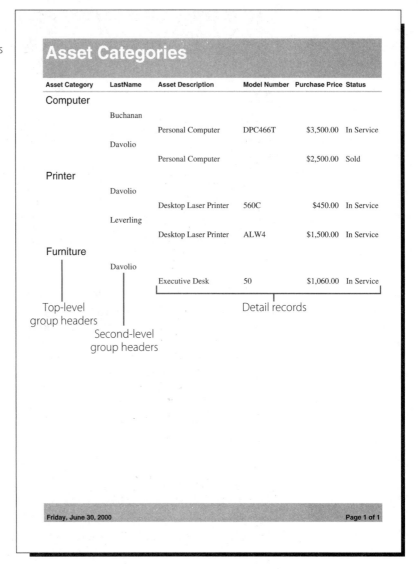

format styles automatically apply fonts, borders, and spacing to your report design. In general, the simpler the design, the better your system's performance in producing the report. Complex designs involving a lot of graphics or shading might take significantly longer to create and, subsequently, to print out. Note that the report shown in Figure 39-10 uses the Soft Gray style, and the report in Figure 39-11 uses the Corporate style.

FIGURE 39-11.
The Aligned Left 1
layout aligns all
grouping fields with
the left margin.

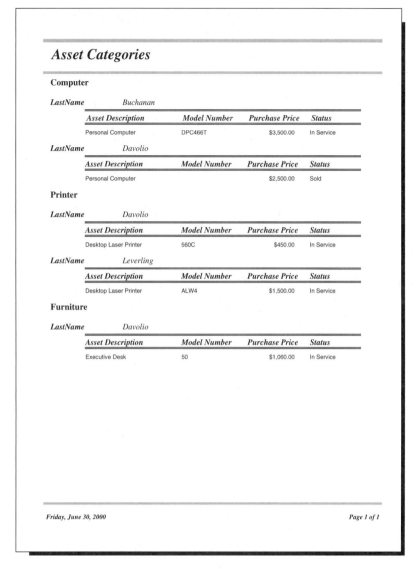

When you're done selecting the style, click the Next button to move on to the seventh dialog box.

Wrapping It Up

In the seventh and final Report Wizard dialog box (see Figure 39-13, on the next page), you can name your report and choose whether to immediately preview the printed appearance of the report or open it in Design view so that you can modify its design, as explained next.

FIGURE 39-12.
In the sixth Report Wizard dialog box, choose the style of the elements in your report.

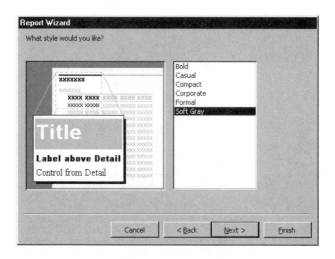

FIGURE 39-13.
In the seventh (the last) Report Wizard dialog box, decide on a report name, and choose how to open the report.

Modifying the Report Design

Once Access has created your report, you might discover that you need to make a number of changes. For example, in a header, Access is often unable to fit an entire field name or caption into the available column width, and so it might cut off letters from the start or the end of the name as necessary. These problems are generally cosmetic and are best solved by changing the font or the font size or by simply editing the text used for the label. *See Chapter 40, "Formatting Forms and Reports," for a discussion of working with the fonts in your reports.*

To work with the design of the report, you must be in Design view. As you saw in the previous section, you can have the Report Wizard open the report in Design view as soon as it has finished generating it. You can also open an existing report in Design view at any time. One of the easiest ways to accomplish this is by opening the Database window, selecting Reports, selecting the report you want to work with, and clicking the Design button. Alternatively, if you're previewing the report, you can choose Design View from the View menu or just click the Close button on the Print Preview toolbar to go directly to Design view.

Close

Figure 39-14 shows a report in Design view.

A report's design consists of a number of controls. These include label controls used for titles, headers, and field labels, and text box controls used for the fields themselves, which represent the data that will be printed. The horizontal bands (labeled Report Header, Page Header, and so on) mark the different sections of the report—namely, the headers, the footers, and the detail section. Rest assured that the bands aren't printed on the actual report.

Figure 39-14 shows the design of the Stepped layout report shown in Figure 39-10, page 942. Notice that all the labels in the design window appear exactly as they do on the actual report, but that the text box for each of the fields in the design window is replaced with the field contents on the report. Furthermore, the text is positioned without

FIGURE 39-14.
To make changes to your report, you must be in Design view.

Labels display exactly as they will print.

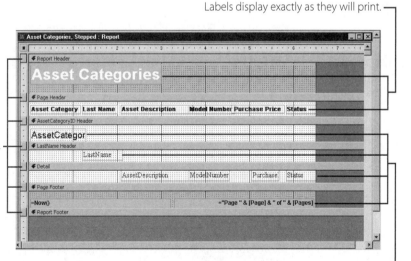

Report sections.
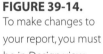

Text boxes will print showing data from the fields, calculations, or other specified information.

gaps, even though in the design window, the controls for the fields are organized into separate sections.

The changes that you most commonly need to make to a report design include changing the positions, sizes, or formats of the labels or text boxes, and perhaps changing the contents of the labels. To change a label's contents, click it to select it; then click the position within the text where you want to make the change (the pointer will be an I-beam), and edit the text. *Techniques for changing the position, size, or format of a control are given in Chapter 40, "Formatting Forms and Reports."*

Figure 39-15 shows the design of the report using the Aligned Left 1 layout given in Figure 39-11, page 943. The primary difference between the report designs shown in Figures 39-14 and 39-15 lies not in which controls appear on the screen, but in how those controls are arranged. The location of the controls in Design view determines the location of the information in the printed report.

Understanding Report Sections

As you can see in Figures 39-14 and 39-15, Design view divides the report into separate sections. The information defined within each section will appear at a specific position on the printed report. The Report Header information appears at the beginning of the first page, and the Report Footer information appears at the end of the last page. The contents of the Page Header section appear at the top of each page, and the contents of the Page Footer section appear at the bottom of each page.

If you chose to group your report using one or more fields (in the second and third Report Wizard dialog boxes), there will also be a header

FIGURE 39-15.
The Aligned Left 1 layout report shown in Design view.

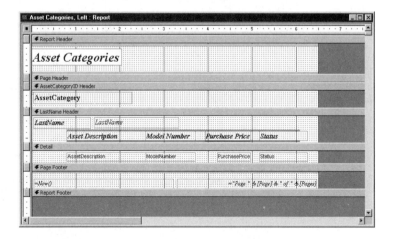

FIGURE 39-16.

A report based on the design shown in Figure 39-17 (next page), showing the location of each of the report sections on the printed report.

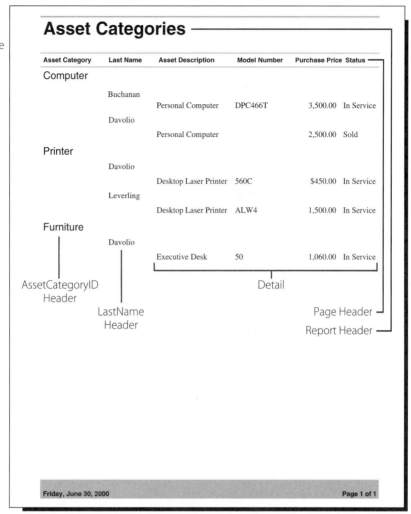

Asset Categories

Asset Category	Last Name	Asset Description	Model Number	Purchase Price	Status
Computer					
	Buchanan				
		Personal Computer	DPC466T	3,500.00	In Service
	Davolio				
		Personal Computer		2,500.00	Sold
Printer					
	Davolio				
		Desktop Laser Printer	560C	$450.00	In Service
	Leverling				
		Desktop Laser Printer	ALW4	1,500.00	In Service
Furniture					
	Davolio				
		Executive Desk	50	1,060.00	In Service

AssetCategoryID Header

Detail

LastName Header

Page Header

Report Header

Friday, June 30, 2000

Page 1 of 1

V

Microsoft Access

section for each of these fields. Also, if you chose to calculate summary values for one or more fields (using the Summary Options button in the fourth Report Wizard dialog box), there will be a footer section corresponding to each of the group header sections. These footer sections are described in the next part of the chapter. *Later in this chapter in "Controlling the Groupings," you'll learn several ways to modify the group headers and footers in your report.*

Finally, the information contained in the Detail section is displayed for each detail record printed on the report. You can study Figure 39-16 to see where the different sections displayed in Design view will appear on a printed report. This figure shows the printed appearance of the report shown in Design view in Figure 39-17, on the next page.

Working with Summary Controls

The footer sections of reports often contain summary information. In a report created with the Report Wizard, summary information can be displayed for each group used in the report, as shown in Figure 39-18. (This report design is the same as the example report design shown in Figure 39-14, page 945, except that we assigned the Sum summary function to the PurchasePrice field, by clicking the Summary Options button in the fourth Report Wizard dialog box.) To eliminate the summary information for one of the groups, simply delete the summary controls from that group's footer, and close up the space. You can adjust or completely close the space within a report section by just dragging—up or down— the top part of the band below that section. (For the Report Footer section, drag the bottom of the white working area.)

Text boxes containing the Sum function ⌐

Each control has its own set of properties that you can use to adjust the way it looks and acts in the report. To access a control's properties, you'll need to open its *property sheet*, which is a dialog box containing a set of tabs for modifying different groups of properties. To open the property sheet, select the control, and then choose Properties from the View menu, click the Properties toolbar button, or press Alt+Enter. Alternatively, you can simply double-click the control. (If the property sheet is already open, just select the control. You can work in Design view while the property sheet remains displayed.)

Properties

Figure 39-19 shows the Data tab of the Properties dialog box for one of the controls used to calculate the sums in the example report. Notice that the Control Source property box on the Data tab contains a mathematical function that operates on the field that is summarized. In this case, the Sum function is used to add all the values contained in the preceding group for the PurchasePrice field. To change the function used, simply highlight the function name, and type a new one. The standard summary functions, Sum, Avg, Min, Max, and Count, are all available. See Table 38-1, page 921, for a description of these and other functions.

FIGURE 39-19.
The Data properties of a control used to sum the PurchasePrice field.

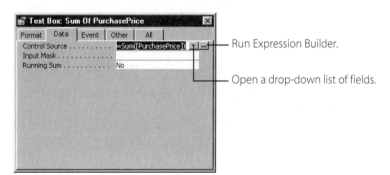

To change the field being summarized, highlight the field name and type a new one, or select a new field from the drop-down list. Alternatively, you can run the Expression Builder to get help in constructing an expression by clicking the button displaying an ellipsis (…) at the right of the Control Source row.

You can use the Format tab of the Properties dialog box to change how the values are formatted. (See Figure 39-20, on the next page.) The controls used to calculate the sums in the example report are assigned the Currency format. Note that the Decimal Places property controls the number of decimal places, unless you assign this property the Auto setting. When you assign the Auto setting, the field is displayed using the default number of decimal places specified by the field's format

FIGURE 39-20.

The Format properties of a control used to sum the Purchase-Price field.

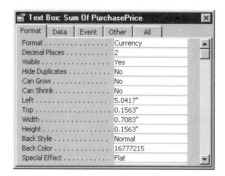

(that is, its Format property setting); for example, if the field has the Currency format, two decimal places will be used. The Decimal Places property represents only the number of decimal places displayed, not the internal accuracy of the data itself (which is controlled by the field's FieldSize property). *See "Setting the Field Properties," page 839, for more information on setting field properties.*

> To display complete information on any property, place the insertion point in the relevant property box in the property sheet and press F1 to access online Help.

Controlling the Groupings

The Sorting And Grouping command on the View menu controls the organization of the groups used for your report and the sorting of the records in the Detail section. Choose this command to open the Sorting And Grouping dialog box, shown here:

Fields used for grouping records.

Records within each group are sorted by this field.

In the example report, we designated the AssetCategoryID and LastName fields as grouping fields in the second and third Report Wizard dialog boxes. (More accurately, because we selected the Asset Categories table in the second dialog box, the wizard designated this table's primary key field, AssetCategoryID, as the grouping field). In the fourth Report Wizard dialog box, we chose the AssetDescription field for sorting detail records within each group.

The display of the Page Header, Page Footer, Report Header, and Report Footer sections is controlled by options on the View menu. To remove both the Page Header and the Page Footer, deselect the Page Header/ Footer option on the View menu. Likewise, to remove both the Report Header and Report Footer, deselect the Report Header/Footer option. Note, however, that removing a header and footer in this way deletes any controls contained in them! (Access will ask for your confirmation first.) If you select one of these menu options again, the corresponding header and footer sections will reappear in Design view, but they will be empty of controls.

By changing properties for the items in the Field/Expression column, you can modify the group headers and footers that appear in the report. You can remove a group header or group footer by selecting the name of the grouping field in the Field/Expression column and changing the Group Header or Group Footer property setting at the bottom of the dialog box to No. You can also specify the sort order for any field by selecting Ascending or Descending in the Sort Order column.

The Group On and Group Interval properties are important options that work together. When the Group On property is set to Each Value (the most common setting), the report creates a new group for every distinct value of the grouping field. In this case, the Group Interval setting has no effect.

To change to a different grouping, select a new setting for the Group On property from the drop-down list. The available settings depend on the grouping field's data type. Then type a number into the Group Interval property box to quantify the Group On setting. For example, if the grouping field is numeric, you could select Interval in the Group On box and type *2* into the Group Interval box. As a result, the report would create a new group for every *other* distinct value, rather than for every distinct value.

As another example, if the grouping field is text, you could select Prefix Characters in the Group On box and then type *1* into the Group Interval box. This would create a group for all records where the grouping field starts with *A*, another group for the *B*'s, a third for the *C*'s, and so on. To group the information in smaller groups (*Aa, Ab, Ac*), you would type *2* into the Group Interval box. Keep in mind that Access doesn't generate a group if no records are contained within that group.

V

Microsoft Access

If you want to ensure that a group—including the header, detail section, and footer—is always printed on the same page if possible, select the Whole Group setting in the Keep Together property box. Note that this setting tends to create blank space at the bottom of pages. By selecting the With First Detail setting, you can save paper and still ensure that the header is always printed together on the same page with at least one of the following detail records. This avoids having a new header appear at the bottom of a page with no data below it. For either of these settings, if there isn't room on a page to fit what's requested (a whole record, or a header plus at least one detail record), Access ignores the setting.

You can obtain detailed information on any group property, like any field property, by placing the insertion point within the property box in the Sorting And Grouping dialog box and pressing F1, the Help key.

Making Labels

Because databases are so often used to store information about a company's customers or physical inventory, it's not surprising that one of the most common uses of database information is to produce labels. Whether these labels are then affixed to envelopes for bulk mailing, used as name tags for a conference, or placed on equipment for inventory control, Access considers these labels a kind of report, and the creation process is similar.

Use Word to Print Labels, Envelopes, or Form Letters

Rather than creating labels directly in Access, you can link an Access table or query to a Microsoft Word mail merge document, which you can then use to print labels, envelopes, or form letters that contain the information from the table or query. To do this, select the table or query in the Access Database window, point to Office Links on the Tools menu, and choose Merge It With MS Word from the submenu. You can link the Access data to an existing main mail merge document or to a new one. *For information on mail merge documents, see "Using Mail Merge for Large Mailings," page 392* .

You can also copy a database object (table, query, form, report, or data access page) to a Word or Microsoft Excel document by choosing Publish It With MS Word or Analyze It With MS Excel from the Office Links submenu. You can then use the Word or Excel tools to edit, format, analyze, or print the information.

Access provides a Label Wizard to help you create labels. To get started, open the New Report dialog box, either by selecting Reports on the

Objects bar in the Database window and clicking the New button, or by clicking the New Object button on the toolbar and choosing Report from the drop-down menu:

1 Select the Label Wizard option in the New Report dialog box, and then in the drop-down list at the bottom, select the table or query that's to be used for generating the labels. For Access to generate labels, all the fields must belong to a single table or query. If you need to combine information from more than one table, you must construct a query combining the fields from the various tables, as described in Chapter 38. When you click the OK button, Access will run the Label Wizard.

2 In the first Label Wizard dialog box, specify the type of labels that you'll be using. (See Figure 39-21.) To use a standard manufactured label, choose the maker of the label in the Filter By Manufacturer list box, specify the unit of measure used for the label (English or Metric) and the type of feed (Sheet Feed or Continuous), and then pick a specific label in the main list near the top of

FIGURE 39-21.
In the first Label Wizard dialog box, specify the type of label you're printing on.

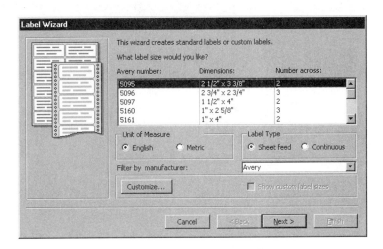

the dialog box. (Note that changing the unit of measure or changing the type of feed changes the list of labels displayed. The wizard provides four separate label lists: English Sheet Feed, English Continuous, Metric Sheet Feed, and Metric Continuous.) In case you don't find a standard label that matches yours, click the Customize button to create a custom label layout. Click the Next button to open the second dialog box.

3 In the second Label Wizard dialog box, select the formatting of the text to be printed on your labels. (See Figure 39-22.) The formatting you select will be applied uniformly to all the text contained in the labels. To move on to the next dialog box, click the Next button.

4 In the third dialog box, specify the fields to be included on the labels. (See Figure 39-23.) The number of characters that will fit in the Prototype Label area is determined by the size of the label you selected in the first dialog box and the size of the font you selected in the second. If you find that you don't have enough lines to organize the information the way you want, use the Back button to change either the size of your labels or the font that you have chosen.

You design your label by working within the Prototype Label area. To define a particular line within the prototype, just click the line and Access will highlight it in light gray. To add a field to the highlighted line in the prototype, select the field name in the Available Fields list, and click the > button between the two boxes; or, simply double-click the field name. If you move a field that you later decide you don't want, select it and press the Delete key. You don't have to use every line; to leave a line blank, simply skip over

FIGURE 39-22.

In the second Label Wizard dialog box, specify the appearance of the text to be printed on your labels.

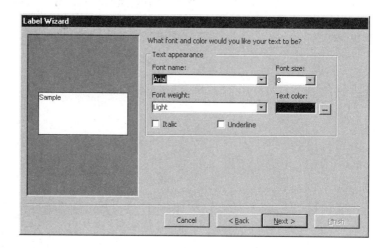

FIGURE 39-23.
In the third Label Wizard dialog box, the Prototype Label area is where you arrange the fields for your label.

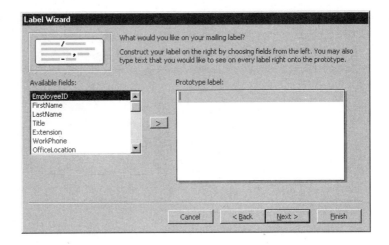

it and add text to the next line. To move to the next line, you can click it, or you can press the Enter or Down arrow key.

Position the various fields as you want them to appear on the label. Type any fixed text (text that should appear on every label, such as *Priority Mail* or *Hello, my name is*) directly into the Prototype Label area. Figure 39-24 shows a sample label for identifying equipment belonging to a particular employee. The words *Title* and *Ext* are examples of fixed text, as are the spaces between fields. When you're done, click Next.

5 In the fourth Label Wizard dialog box, select one or more fields to be used for sorting your labels. (See Figure 39-25, on the following page.) Move each field you want to use for sorting from the Available Fields list to the Sort By list, using the buttons

FIGURE 39-24.
A label is created by using a combination of fields and fixed text.

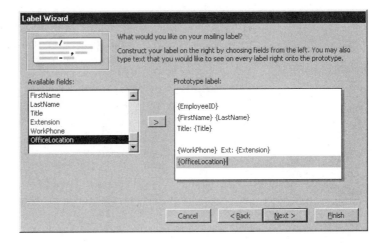

FIGURE 39-25.

In the fourth Label Wizard dialog box, select one or more sorting fields to modify the order in which your labels are printed.

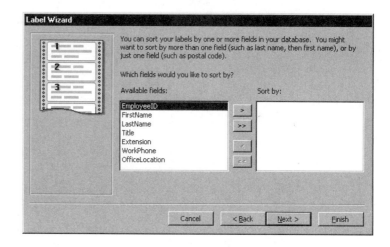

between the lists. Access will sort the labels using the selected fields in the order they appear in the Sort By list. For example, if you added LastName to the list and then FirstName, the labels would be sorted by last name, and those labels with the same last name would be sorted by first name. (To change the order of the labels in the Sort By list, you'll have to remove and add them back in the desired order. You can't directly move them in the list.) Click the Next button.

6 In the fifth and final Label Wizard dialog box, you can modify the report name that the wizard has assigned, and you can choose to either preview the printed appearance of the labels or go to Report Design view to modify the label design. Click the Finish button to generate the labels.

Like other types of reports, your label report will be stored with the other reports in the Database window, and you open the report in either Design view to modify the layout, or in Layout Preview to preview the labels' printed appearance.

If you open the report in Design view, you'll notice that the Label Wizard added several functions to eliminate spaces within fields and to add spaces and text where necessary in the labels. Access also customizes your page setup to ensure that the labels print correctly.

Print

To print the labels, open the label report in any view, or simply select the report name in the Database window. Then choose Print from the File menu or click the Print button on the toolbar.

Formatting Forms and Reports

B oth forms and reports provide ways to display the information contained in your database. Plus, they share another important feature: both use the same techniques and tools to format their controls. (Each control represents an element, such as a field or a block of text, that appears on the forms or reports.) These techniques include methods for moving and aligning the various controls, for changing the font style, and for changing the color, border, and shading effects used for different elements.

To work with the controls on a form or a report, you must be in Design view. If you have an existing form or report to work with, follow these steps:

1 Open the database that contains the form or report you want to modify.

2 Open the Database window.

3 Select Forms on the Objects bar and select a form, or select Reports on the Objects bar and select a report.

4 Click the Design button.

The controls on a Microsoft Access form or report are placed in layers, similar to the graphic objects in Microsoft Word or Microsoft PowerPoint documents. *For a discussion on how these layers can affect your work and how to use the Bring To Front and Send To Back commands on the Format menu, see "Working with Layers," page 738.*

Moving Controls

Often, one of the first enhancements you want to make to a form or report is to reposition the various controls on it. You can do this either by moving individual controls or groups of controls, or by selecting one or more controls and aligning them.

The Membership.mdb database file, used for the examples in this chapter, is on the Running Office 2000 Reader's Corner page. For information about connecting to this Web site, read the Introduction.

To move an individual control, follow these steps:

1 Select the control by clicking it. When selected, the control has eight visible handles around its perimeter:

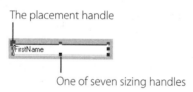

The placement handle

One of seven sizing handles

If the control contains the insertion point, you'll have to select the control by clicking one of its edges. If you click within the control, you'll move only the insertion point.

2 Move the mouse over the border of the control (but not over one of its handles) until the pointer changes to an open hand.

3 Drag the control to its new location.

In many forms and reports, you'll discover that what appear to be two separate controls are actually a linked set—most often, a label control is connected to the control that it's labeling. In this case, when you select one of the controls, the placement handle for the second control also appears, as shown here:

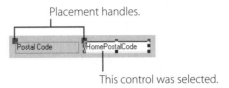

You can use these placement handles to change the relative positions of these two controls. When controls are joined like this, moving one to a new location using the method described above always moves the other. However, when you position the mouse over the placement handle rather than over the control's border, the pointer turns into a hand that has an extended index finger, and dragging the placement handle moves just that one control and not the attached control.

To work with a group of controls, select the group by dragging a rectangle around all the controls. This technique is particularly useful when you're working with the options on the Align submenu of the Format menu. If the controls aren't arranged in such a way that you can draw a rectangle around them, you can still select multiple controls by clicking to select the first one and then holding down the Shift key while you click each of the others.

To reset the form or report so that no controls are selected, click an area of the form that has no controls, such as the form or report background.

> **NOTE**
>
> When a linked control's placement handle is visible, but its seven sizing handles are not, the control is *not* selected. It will move with its attached control, but formatting commands will have no effect on it.

> **NOTE**
>
> Particularly when working with reports, keep in mind that the position of a control might influence how the data within that control is presented. For example, if you move a control from one section of a report to another, you might inadvertently alter the information displayed in the report.

V

Microsoft Access

Aligning Controls

Using the Align commands, you can rearrange a group of controls so that their edges—left, right, top, or bottom—are all aligned along a single axis, making them more readable or attractive in forms or reports. The Align commands won't allow the selected controls to overlap one another, however.

For example, to right-align a group of controls, follow these steps:

1 Select the controls, as shown here:

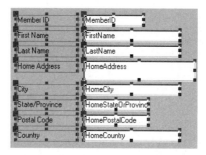

2 Display the Align submenu by pointing to Align on the Format menu, or by right-clicking one of the selected controls and pointing to Align on the pop-up menu.

3 Choose Right from the Align submenu. This command rearranges the various controls, as shown next:

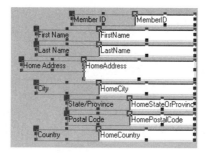

The Right command causes the rightmost controls to align along their rightmost edges, and it moves the other controls as far to the right as possible.

If you have selected a group but want to exclude just one or two controls from the group and format the rest, hold down the Shift key and click each control you want to deselect. Only items that have eight handles showing (seven sizing handles plus one placement handle) will be affected by menu commands.

Using the Grid

In Design view, forms and reports have a handy background grid to help you align controls. You can make the grid visible by selecting the Grid option on the View menu or on the pop-up menu that appears when you right-click the form or report background. You can hide it by deselecting this option. When the grid is visible, it's marked with solid gridlines at 1-inch intervals and dotted gridlines in between. Note that the different ways to use the grid mentioned here will work whether the grid is visible or not.

To make the controls easier to see in this chapter's figures, we hid the grid.

One way to use the grid is to select the Snap To Grid option on the Format menu. When you subsequently move a control, its upper and left borders jump, or *snap*, to the nearest gridline. Likewise, when you resize a control, the border that you adjust will jump to the nearest gridline. When the Snap To Grid option is disabled, you can position a control anywhere you want without regard to the grid.

Another way to use the grid is to realign controls. If you positioned controls while Snap To Grid was disabled, you can later align their upper and left borders on the nearest gridlines by selecting the controls and choosing To Grid from the Align submenu of the Format menu.

Because To Grid doesn't resize controls, the bottom and right borders might not be aligned with gridlines after you choose the command. To align all four borders with gridlines, resizing controls as necessary, you can use the To Grid command on the Size submenu of the Format menu. *(For more information, see the section "Changing a Control's Size," page 963).*

Spacing Controls

Not only can you align controls along one edge, but you can also distribute controls evenly within an area on a form or report, for clarity and appearance. If you select a group of controls that are randomly spaced and choose an option on either the Horizontal Spacing or the Vertical Spacing submenus of the Format menu, Access positions the objects according to your instructions. You can proportionally increase or decrease the distance between selected controls, or you can equalize the space between a selected group of controls.

For example, to make the vertical spacing between a group of controls even, follow these steps:

1 Select all the controls to be positioned, being sure in this case to include their labels, as shown here:

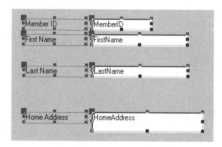

2 Point to Vertical Spacing on the Format menu, and choose Make Equal from the submenu. Here's the result:

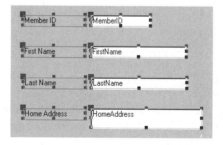

The first and last controls of a group don't move when you use the Make Equal command—only the controls in between are adjusted to even the spacing. However, if you use the Increase or Decrease command, all the controls move proportionally.

Changing a Control's Size

To make room for the information displayed by a control, you can change its size on an Access form or report by following these steps:

1 Click the control to select it and to display the sizing handles. (If the control contains the insertion point, you'll have to select it by clicking one of the *edges* of the control.)

2 Position the mouse over one of the sizing handles (not the placement handle) so that a two-headed arrow—rather than a hand—appears, as shown here:

3 Drag that side of the control to its new location. If you're dragging a corner, the two adjoining sides will be repositioned. (If you hold down the Shift key while dragging a corner, it will move only horizontally or only vertically, whichever direction you first start moving it.)

The Size submenu on the Format menu provides a series of commands for changing the size of the selected control or group of controls:

Only two commands are available if you selected a single control: To Fit and To Grid. All commands are available if you selected several controls:

- To Fit resizes the selected controls so they're just large enough to show the information they contain. Note that you can't use this command to resize controls whose contents will vary; for example, you can't resize a text box that displays a data field, because the amount of data can change from record to record.

- To Grid resizes the selected controls so that all four borders of each control align on the nearest gridlines.

■ To Tallest, To Shortest, To Widest, and To Narrowest resize groups of controls so that each control is the same size as the tallest, shortest, widest, or narrowest control in the selected group. When Access does this kind of sizing, it pays no attention to whether such a change will leave sufficient space to display the contents of a control—so be careful, especially when you adjust to the narrowest width or the shortest height.

Changing a Control's Color and Effects

Each kind of control, including text boxes, has a set of colors assigned to it. One color is assigned to the background of the control, while the other is assigned to the text. In addition, most controls have a border of some sort, which you can display in a separate color.

Fill/Back
Color

To change the background color of a control, just select the control, and click the down arrow to the right of the Fill/Back Color button on the Formatting toolbar. This displays the palette of available colors from which you can choose the color you want. The Transparent button causes the control to acquire the color of the form, report, or any object underneath the control.

To change the background color for an entire section of a form or report, click a blank area within that section (make sure no control is selected), and select the desired color from the Fill/Back Color palette. Each section of a form or a report can have a different background color, placing different emphasis on your various blocks of information. Note that when you're setting the color of the background, the Automatic button on the palette has no effect.

Font/Fore
Color

To change the color of the text associated with a control, select the control, and click the down arrow to the right of the Font/Fore Color button on the Formatting toolbar. From the color palette that appears, select the color you want for the text.

Line/Border
Width

Formatting borders is a bit more complex than simply applying background and text colors, because borders also have widths and special effects. Select the control whose border you want to change, and click the down arrow to the right of the Line/Border Width button on the Formatting toolbar to display the drop-down list of border widths. Then click the width you want. The first width creates a thin hairline border.

The other widths are measured in points, ranging from 1 point through 6 points (72 points = 1 inch). The greater the width of the border, the more noticeable will be the control as well as the color you apply to it.

Line/Border
Color

To change the color of the border, simply select the control, and click the down arrow to the right of the Line/Border Color button on the Formatting toolbar to display a palette of colors. You can then select the color you want for the border. As does the Fill/Back Color button, the Line/Border Color button provides a Transparent option for hiding the border. You could also choose the same color as the control's Fill/Back Color if you want the border to blend with the background of the control.

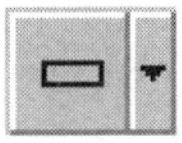

Special
Effect

Finally, you can apply a special effect to a control's border. To do this, select the control you want to change, click the down arrow to the right of the Special Effect button on the Formatting toolbar, and then select the effect you want from the drop-down list that appears. The six styles of borders are illustrated in Figure 40-1.

TIP

Quickly Apply Formatting Options

The most recent formatting option applied by the Fill/Back Color, Font/Fore Color, Line/Border Width, Line/Border Color, and Special Effect buttons appears on each button. To apply one of these options to a different control, you can just select the control and click the relevant button without dropping down the palette.

TIP

Embellish Your Form or Report

You can use the Line, Rectangle, or Image tool on the Toolbox toolbar (shown in Figure 37-8, page 892) to add a straight line, an empty rectangle, or a graphic image to your form or report. These objects are treated as controls, and you can assign them any of the formatting options discussed here except a text color.

FIGURE 40-1.
Applying a special effect to a control affects how its border appears against the background.

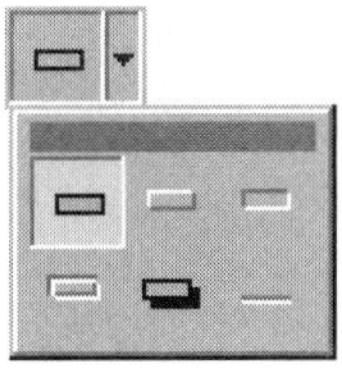

Changing the Look of the Text

Access gives you mastery over the way your forms and reports look by letting you format the text. You can format each control's text independently of another's, but any single control must have all its text formatted the same. To format the text in a control, select the control, and then use any of the controls on the Formatting toolbar that are labeled here:

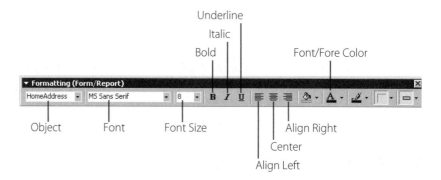

The first list box, Object, shows the name of the currently selected object (control, section, form, or report) and lets you select any control currently on the form, even if that control isn't visible. In general, however, it's easier to select a control by merely clicking it. If you have selected a group of controls, the Object list box will be blank, indicating that you're formatting more than one control simultaneously.

The second list box, Font, allows you to designate the font used in the selected control. This list displays all the fonts installed on your system. The third list box, Font Size, lets you set the size of the characters in points. To change the font or the character size, select a new setting from one of these list boxes, or type a setting into one of the boxes.

You can also set a control's text to bold, italic, underline, or any combination of the three. To do so, select the control you want to change, and then click the Bold, Italic, or Underline buttons as you like.

> **Use Separate Controls to Vary Text Formatting**
>
> Sometimes you might want to have a label that has two different text formats, for example, a label reading "***Full*** Address." You can't have multiple text formats appear in a field containing data, though you can simulate the above effect in a label field by creating two label controls that are lined up to appear as if they were only one. Because each word is in a separate control, you can assign different formats to each.

You can also adjust the alignment of the text within a control. This is especially useful when you're working with labels or text boxes. Use the Align Left, Center, and Align Right buttons to specify where in the control the text will appear. For most controls, you'll want the text to align left or align right. One common layout, shown in Figure 40-2, aligns the labels to the right and their related text box controls to the left. This minimizes the amount of blank space that the eye must track over in moving from the label to the attached information.

Using the Font/Fore Color button and drop-down list to set the text color was discussed in the previous section.

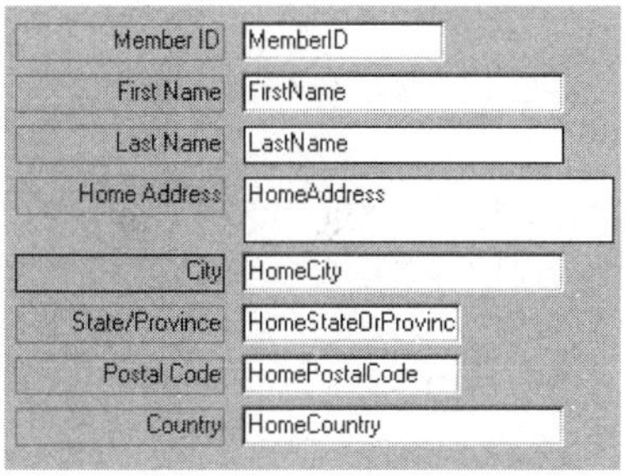

FIGURE 40-2.
Aligning text closer together makes it easier to read.

Member ID	MemberID
First Name	FirstName
Last Name	LastName
Home Address	HomeAddress
City	HomeCity
State/Province	HomeStateOrProvinc
Postal Code	HomePostalCode
Country	HomeCountry

Using Control Properties

All the formatting options in this chapter are also available as property entries in each control's property sheet. To display the property sheet for a control, select the control; then choose Properties from the View menu, click the Properties toolbar button, or press Alt+Enter. Alternatively, you can simply double-click the control. (If the property sheet is

Properties

already open, just select the control. You can work in Design view while the property sheet remains displayed.) Different types of controls have different properties. Most of the options discussed in this chapter affect various settings on the Format tab of the property sheet. Here's an example of the Format tab for a label control:

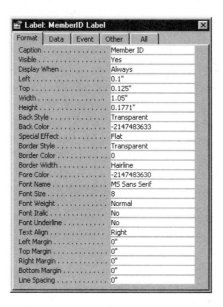

You might notice that the background color (Back Color property) for the label is listed as *-2147483633*—not very informative! Don't worry. When you click in the box for a property that sets a color, a button that has an ellipsis (…) on it appears at the far right. Click this button and you'll open the Color dialog box, in which you can select a standard color or even define a custom color.

A few advanced formatting options, such as setting a custom color, are available only in the property sheet. Here are some more examples. (You can set all these properties on the Format tab of the property sheet.)

- Add scroll bars to a text box control to view text that doesn't fit within the control—such as a three-line address in a one- or two-line address box. To do this, select Vertical in the Scroll Bars property box.

- Have a text box control grow or shrink in the vertical direction automatically, to accommodate the text it displays for each record. The growing or shrinking occurs only when you print or preview a report or form. (It won't have any effect in Form, Datasheet, or Design view.) To do this, assign Yes to the Can Grow property, the Can Shrink property, or both properties.

- Set a control's border line to solid, to transparent, or to one of several dashed or dotted line styles. To do this, select the style you want in the Border Style property box.

Explore Other Properties

To learn how the many properties listed in the property sheet affect different types of controls, select a control, open the property sheet, and click in any property box that you're curious about. Press F1, the Help key, and Access's online Help system will take you directly to a complete explanation of the property. You can also choose What's This? from the Help menu—the pointer will change to an arrow and a question mark—and then click the property box you're interested in.

By using the formatting tools Access provides—and your own creativity—you can design functional, attractive, and highly professional reports and forms.

PART VI

Microsoft Outlook

Getting Started Using Outlook

Microsoft Outlook is a desktop information management program in which you can organize and share many different types of information. When you use Outlook, you can keep track of personal information, share information with other members of your workgroup, and communicate with people in your company or on the Internet. This introductory chapter summarizes what you can do with Outlook, provides some tips and background information to help you set up Outlook, gives you a tour of the different Outlook components, and shows you how to move around in the program and access the different types of information it manages. It also offers a few pointers on using the chapters in this part of the book.

What You Can Do with Outlook

Here are some of the tasks you can perform with Outlook:

■ Send and receive e-mail and fax messages.

■ Maintain a personal calendar of appointments, events, and meetings.

■ Schedule meetings with your co-workers.

■ Store information about your business and personal contacts.

■ Create to-do lists and manage personal or group projects.

■ Keep a journal of messages you send or receive, Microsoft Office documents you access, or other events.

■ Jot down miscellaneous information on electronic "sticky notes."

■ Access and maintain the files on your local or network disks.

■ Explore sites on the Internet.

New Features

Microsoft has added many features to Outlook since the original Office 97 version. Here are some of the new Outlook 98 features:

■ A new "home page" folder called Outlook Today summarizes and lets you access current information from your Calendar, Tasks, and mail folders all in one place, and allows you to perform common tasks.

■ Web-style tools let you quickly find and organize Outlook items.

■ A Preview pane allows you to view your messages without having to open them.

■ A News command on the Go menu lets you run Outlook Express to access Internet newsgroups.

■ Use of the HTML format lets you send and receive e-mail containing formatted text, graphics, background colors and textures, or anything else a Web page can include.

■ Predesigned e-mail stationery gives you a head start in creating attractive e-mail messages.

- Conditional formatting lets you mark certain e-mail messages or other Outlook items; for example, you could color-code all messages from your boss in red.

- User-defined rules automatically move or delete junk e-mail or other messages, or perform other actions.

- Support for standard Internet e-mail protocols lets you send and receive messages using SMTP (Simple Mail Transfer Protocol) for outgoing messages, and either POP3 (Post Office Protocol 3) or IMAP (Internet Message Access Protocol) for incoming messages.

- Use of LDAP (Lightweight Directory Access Protocol) lets you verify e-mail addresses and find information about people.

- Support for additional Internet protocols lets you share information on the Internet: the vCard format for sharing contact information, vCalendar for exchanging appointment requests, and iCalendar for publishing schedules of free/busy times.

NOTE

Receiving messages with the IMAP protocol, checking e-mail addresses using LDAP, and scheduling meetings using the iCalendar format all require the Internet Only installation of Outlook, which is explained in the next section.

And here are a few of the new features debuting in Outlook 2000:

- The *home page* feature lets you associate a Web page or disk file with any Outlook folder and display that page when the folder is opened.

- The Favorites menu allows you to browse Web locations stored in your Favorites folder and to add Web-page addresses to Favorites. Web pages are opened directly in the Outlook program window.

- Distribution lists that you create in your Contacts folder let you send e-mail messages to entire groups of people by adding only a single entry in the To field.

- Access to Microsoft Word's mail merge feature lets you print form letters, envelopes, or labels using selected items from your Contacts folder.

VI

Microsoft Outlook

> **Outlook Express**
>
> Don't confuse Outlook 2000 with Outlook Express. Outlook 2000 is a full-featured personal information manager and messaging client, and it's one of the major members of the Microsoft Office 2000 family of applications. Outlook Express, by contrast, is a specialized e-mail and newsreader program that's included with Microsoft Internet Explorer. Note that choosing News from the Go menu of Outlook 2000 runs the newsreader feature of Outlook Express.

Setting Up Outlook

The first time you start Outlook 2000, it runs the Outlook 2000 Startup Wizard, which displays a series of dialog boxes to help you configure the program. The specific dialog boxes you see depends on your current computer setup and the options you select in the wizard. This section explains some of the significant choices you'll be asked to make and provides important background information to help you understand the different configuration options.

If you're already using an e-mail program when you install Outlook 2000, Outlook might be able to access your existing e-mail messages and use your current address book and e-mail settings with Outlook. Doing so will let you continue to send and receive e-mail using your current e-mail provider without interruption. If Outlook can read and convert the data files of your current e-mail program (Outlook Express, Eudora, Netscape Messenger, and other popular e-mail programs), the Startup Wizard will display the E-mail Upgrade Options dialog box, which will list all the compatible e-mail programs the wizard detects on your computer. In this dialog box, you should either select one of these programs or select None Of The Above to set up Outlook without using your existing e-mail configuration.

 TIP

> After you have set up Outlook, you can import data from an existing e-mail program at any time by running the Import And Export Wizard to import your e-mail messages, addresses, and settings. To run this wizard, choose Import And Export from the File menu in Outlook.

Another important dialog box that the Startup Wizard displays is titled E-mail Service Options. In this dialog box, shown in Figure 41-1, you must choose the basic type of Outlook installation that

FIGURE 41-1.

Selecting the type of Outlook installation you want in the E-mail Service Options dialog box.

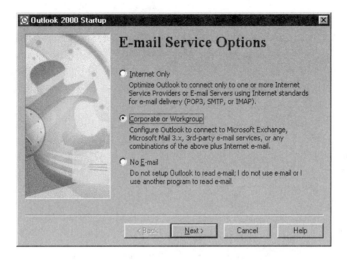

you want. This significant decision greatly affects the Outlook features that will be available. The three options you can choose are described in Table 41-1.

TABLE 41-1.   The Three Installation Types You Can Choose When You Install Outlook

Outlook Installation Type	Select This Installation Type If...
Internet Only	You send and receive e-mail via only an e-mail server that uses standard Internet protocols (namely, SMTP for outgoing messages, and either POP3 or IMAP for incoming messages), and you don't want to use Outlook as a client for Microsoft Exchange Server (discussed in the sidebar "Using Outlook with Microsoft Exchange Server" on page 980).
Corporate Or Workgroup	You want to use Outlook as a client for Microsoft Exchange Server, or you send and receive e-mail using Microsoft Mail 3.x or another e-mail service that doesn't use standard Internet protocols (for example, CompuServe). This installation also allows you to exchange e-mail with a standard SMTP/POP3 Internet e-mail server (using the Internet E-Mail information service, described in Table 41-2 on page 982).
No E-Mail	You don't plan to use Outlook to send and receive e-mail or faxes.

Because the Corporate Or Workgroup installation supports the standard Internet SMTP and POP3 e-mail protocols as well as Microsoft

Exchange Server and nonstandard mail services, it's the most compre-hensive choice. However, the Corporate Or Workgroup installation lacks some of the Internet e-mail and Internet collaboration features provided by the Internet Only installation—for example, support for IMAP e-mail, group scheduling on the Internet using the iCalendar protocol, and the ability to verify e-mail addresses using directory ser-vices. (These features are explained later in the book.) Also, the Internet Only installation was designed to provide better performance for Internet e-mail.

> **NOTE**
>
> A few of the discussions in the Outlook chapters apply only to the Corporate Or Workgroup installation of Outlook (for example, the description of information services and profiles in the following section, and the material on scheduling meetings in Chapter 43). In each of these places, the book includes a note or sidebar that briefly explains how the Internet Only installation differs from the Corporate Or Workgroup installation.

Before you can run the Corporate Or Workgroup installation of Out-look for the first time, you must set up a user profile on your com-puter. User profiles—and the information services they contain—are described next.

> **TIP**
>
> If you choose to have Outlook upgrade an existing e-mail program, the Outlook 2000 Startup Wizard *won't* display the E-mail Service Options dialog box. Rather, it will automatically select either the Internet Only or the Corporate Or Work-group option (whichever is most appropriate for your e-mail settings). However, you can later switch between these two options by choosing Options from the Tools menu in Outlook, clicking the Mail Services tab, and clicking the Reconfig-ure Mail Support button.

Information Services and User Profiles

In Outlook, an *information service* is a facility that either sends and delivers messages or provides a repository for storing and managing information. For example, one information service might allow you to send and receive e-mail messages, another might provide a storage area for holding and organizing your Outlook folders, and a third might store a collection of addresses that you can use for sending messages (known as an *address book*). Examples of specific information services will be given in Table 41-2, page 982.

NOTE

The Internet Only installation of Outlook doesn't use information services or user profiles. Rather, you simply set up an account for each e-mail or fax service that you want to use. If you choose the Internet Only option in the Outlook 2000 Startup Wizard, Outlook runs the Internet Connection Wizard, which prompts you for information and sets up an e-mail account and possibly a fax account, as well as an Internet connection if one isn't already defined. You can later add, remove, or modify accounts by choosing Accounts from the Tools menu, or by opening the Mail item in the Windows Control Panel. *More details are given in the sidebar "Setting Up E-Mail and Faxes in the Internet Only Installation," page 1019.*

A *user profile* is a collection of information services and settings. Each time you run Outlook, it opens a user profile and accesses the information services and uses the settings that it contains. A user profile must therefore be defined on your computer before you can use Outlook.

SEE ALSO

See the sidebar "Using Outlook with Microsoft Exchange Server," page 980, for a description of Microsoft Exchange Server and Microsoft Exchange.

If, before you installed Outlook 2000, you used a previous Outlook version (or Microsoft Exchange), or if you were able to upgrade a prior e-mail program in the Outlook 2000 Startup Wizard, you should already have a user profile defined on your computer. In this case, Outlook can simply use this profile. However, if a user profile isn't currently defined on your computer, the Startup Wizard will start the Inbox Setup Wizard, which lets you define a user profile by adding and setting up the information services that you need.

TIP

Create Additional Profiles

You can define one or more additional user profiles. For example, if more than one person uses a computer, each could have a separate profile. Or, you might define one profile for your business information and one for your personal information. To create a new profile, open the Mail item in your Windows Control Panel folder, click the Show Profiles button on the Services tab, and click the Add button on the General tab of the Mail dialog box that's displayed. This will run the Inbox Setup Wizard to guide you through the steps for defining the profile.

To control which profile Outlook uses, choose Options from the Tools menu, and click the Mail Services tab. If you select the Prompt For A Profile To Be Used option, Outlook will let you choose a profile each time it starts running. If you select Always Use This Profile, Outlook will automatically use the profile you select in the adjoining list box. (You can also set the Outlook profile using the General tab of the Mail dialog box mentioned in the previous paragraph.)

VI

Microsoft Outlook

You can also modify a user profile. That is, you can add, remove, or change the properties of information services; and you can change the way messages are delivered and addressed. To modify the profile that Outlook is currently using, choose Services from the Tools menu of the Outlook program to open the Services dialog box, shown in Figure 41-2. Or, to modify any profile defined on your computer, open the Mail item in the Windows Control Panel.

Whichever method you use to define or modify a user profile, when you add an information service, you can choose from a list of standard services that Outlook provides (briefly described in Table 41-2, page 982). You can also add an information service from a disk or network location. (For example, an e-mail service provider might supply you with a disk containing an information service that you can use to send and receive e-mail with that service.) *The e-mail and fax information services are explained further in the sidebar "Setting Up E-Mail and Faxes in Outlook," page 1017.*

Using Outlook with Microsoft Exchange Server

Microsoft Exchange Server is an application that can be installed on a network server computer running the Microsoft Windows NT Server operating system. It allows the network users to share information, to collaborate on projects, and to exchange messages with other users on the network and on the Internet.

Outlook doesn't require Exchange Server. You can use most of Outlook's features without your computer being attached to an Exchange Server network. However, if your computer is attached to an Exchange Server network, you can use Outlook as a client for Exchange Server—that is, a program that lets you access the messaging and collaborative features provided by Exchange Server on the network. To use Outlook in this capacity, you must include the Microsoft Exchange Server information service in your user profile. The following are some of the unique features and additional capabilities of Outlook when it's used as a client for Exchange Server:

- Your Outlook folders (Inbox, Calendar, Contacts, and so on) will normally be stored in your private mailbox on the Exchange Server computer. (Each Exchange Server user on the network has his or her own private mailbox.) In contrast, if your computer isn't attached to an Exchange Server network, Outlook folders are stored in a .pst file on your computer, which is maintained by a Personal Folders information service.

- You can permit other users to open the Outlook folders in your mailbox, while keeping selected items hidden. These folders are known as *shared private folders*.

> **Using Outlook with Microsoft Exchange Server**   *continued*
>
> ■ You can use public folders on the Exchange Server computer to share Outlook items or files, or to conduct online discussions.
>
> ■ You can exchange e-mail with other people on the Exchange Server network. You can track messages, recall messages that have already been sent, and use messages for voting. (Outlook will tally the results.)
>
> ■ You can schedule meetings with other users on the network. Outlook will let you view each attendee's schedule, it will automatically determine an appropriate meeting time, and it will send invitations.
>
> ■ You can manage group projects by using Outlook to send task assignments to other Exchange Server users and to track these tasks.
>
> Most of these Exchange Server features are discussed later in the book. The book clearly flags all features it discusses that require Exchange Server.
>
> By the way, don't confuse Microsoft Exchange Server with the Microsoft Exchange software—later called Windows Messaging—that's included with Windows. Like Outlook, Microsoft Exchange is a client for various messaging services, although compared to Outlook it's a limited one, supporting only sending and receiving messages. Outlook and Microsoft Exchange both employ the same type of user profiles—that's why if you used Exchange before installing Outlook, you can immediately access your existing e-mail and fax messages as well as your message settings.

FIGURE 41-2.
Modifying the current user profile in Outlook's Services dialog box.

Change the folder where messages are delivered.

Modify Outlook's use of address-book information services.

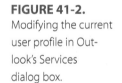

Remove the selected information service from the profile.

Add an information service to the profile.

Change settings of the selected information service.

Copy the selected information service to another profile.

VI

Microsoft Outlook

As you'll learn in the next section, Outlook information is stored in a set of folders (Inbox, Calendar, Contacts, Tasks, and so on). To provide a place to keep your Outlook folders when you use the Corporate Or Workgroup installation of Outlook, you must include the Personal Folders information service (which stores Outlook folders on a local disk) or the Microsoft Exchange Server information service (which stores Outlook folders on the Exchange Server computer and is available only if your computer is attached to an Exchange Server network). See the preceding sidebar for more information on using Outlook with Exchange Server.

TABLE 41-2. Standard Outlook Information Services You Can Add to a User Profile

Information Service	Purpose
Internet E-Mail	Allows you to send and receive e-mail messages through an Internet service provider that uses the standard SMTP and POP3 Internet e-mail protocols.
Microsoft Exchange Server	If your computer is attached to a network on which Microsoft Exchange Server is installed, this information service lets Outlook access the messaging and collaborative Exchange Server features. That is, it lets you use Outlook as a client for Exchange Server. See the sidebar "Using Outlook with Microsoft Exchange Server," page 980.
Microsoft Fax	If you have a fax modem installed on your computer, and if you've installed the Microsoft Fax component of Windows, this service lets Outlook send and receive faxes using the Microsoft Fax software. Note that you should install the Microsoft Fax component before installing Outlook 2000 because the Outlook setup program needs to update the component.
Microsoft Mail	Allows you to use Outlook to exchange e-mail with people who use the Microsoft Mail e-mail application for PC networks.
MS Outlook Support For Lotus cc:Mail	Allows you to send and receive e-mail messages with users of the Lotus cc:Mail messaging application.
Microsoft LDAP Directory	Lets you verify e-mail addresses and find information about people using LDAP (Lightweight Directory Access Protocol).
Outlook Address Book	Lets you look up e-mail and fax addresses and distribution lists that you have stored in your Outlook Contacts folder.

(continued)

TABLE 41-2. *continued*

Information Service	Purpose
Personal Address Book	Allows you to store and retrieve e-mail addresses and to create personal distribution lists. A personal distribution list is used to e-mail a single message to an entire group of people. (A personal address book is kept within a file on your hard disk that has the .pab extension.)
Personal Folders	Stores Outlook folders—Inbox, Calendar, Contacts, and so on—in a file on your hard disk. (This file has the .pst extension.) Outlook folders are described in "Accessing Outlook Folders" on page 985. Note that if your computer is attached to an Exchange Server network, your Outlook folders are normally stored in your mailbox on the server, although you can also use a Personal Folders information service to store additional Outlook folders on a local disk.

Taking an Outlook Tour

You can run Outlook by choosing Microsoft Outlook from the Programs submenu of your Windows Start menu, or by double-clicking the Microsoft Outlook shortcut on your Windows desktop. Alternatively, because Outlook is useful for so many purposes, you might want to have it start automatically whenever you run Windows and leave it running all the time. To do this, you must place a shortcut for the Outlook program within your StartUp folder. For instructions on doing this, choose Help from the Windows Start menu, click the Index tab, and select the topic "shortcuts, adding to the StartUp folder" or "shortcuts, adding to the StartUp menu."

Figure 41-3, on the next page, shows the Outlook program window as it appears the first time you run it. As you can see, the Outlook window is divided into two main panes: the Outlook Bar on the left, and the Information Viewer on the right. In this figure, the Information Viewer contains an additional pane at the bottom, known as the Preview pane; as you'll see later, you can display several different special-purpose panes within the Information Viewer.

VI

Microsoft Outlook

⭐ **TIP**

You can hide the Outlook Bar—or redisplay it after it's been hidden—by choosing Outlook Bar from the View menu. Or, you can hide it by right-clicking on the bar (but not on a shortcut) and choosing Hide Outlook Bar from the pop-up menu.

FIGURE 41-3.

The Outlook program displaying the Inbox folder.

Standard toolbar.

Folder Banner.

Shortcuts to specific folders.

Click one of these buttons to display one of the default groups of Outlook Bar shortcuts.

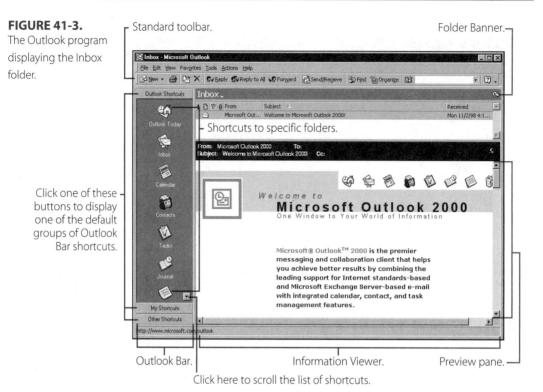

Outlook Bar.

Information Viewer.

Preview pane.

Click here to scroll the list of shortcuts.

The information in Outlook is contained within folders, each of which stores, displays, and manages a specific type of item. Your first step in working with a particular type of information is to open the appropriate folder by clicking its shortcut on the Outlook Bar. A shortcut consists of an icon plus a text label. For example, to manage appointments, you'd open the Calendar folder by clicking the Calendar shortcut on the Outlook Bar. When you open a folder, its contents are displayed in the Information Viewer; also, the Outlook toolbar buttons and menu commands change to provide the commands you need to manage the type of information kept in that folder. Later in the chapter, you'll learn how to modify the way Outlook displays the contents of folders in the Information Viewer.

 **TIP**

You can open a folder in a separate Outlook program window by right-clicking a shortcut on the Outlook Bar and choosing Open In New Window from the pop-up menu.

The shortcuts displayed on the Outlook Bar are divided into three default groups, which are named Outlook Shortcuts, My Shortcuts, and

Other Shortcuts. To display a particular shortcut group, click the corresponding button at the top or bottom of the Outlook Bar.

 NOTE

The Outlook Bar groups described here are the typical defaults that Outlook creates the first time you run the program. The actual groups you see on your computer, however, might differ from these. The initial groups can be affected by your installation choices and—if you upgraded a previous version of Outlook—by the groups you defined in the previous version. *In "Modifying the Outlook Bar," page 1008, you'll learn how to modify both the groups and the shortcuts they contain.*

Accessing Outlook Folders

The Outlook Shortcuts and My Shortcuts groups on the Outlook Bar contain shortcuts to *Outlook folders*. An Outlook folder is one that contains items managed by Outlook, such as messages, calendar appointments, tasks, and journal entries.

The Outlook Shortcuts group contains shortcuts to the general-purpose Outlook folders—Outlook Today, Inbox, Calendar, Contacts, Tasks, Journal, Notes, and Deleted Items. The My Shortcuts group contains shortcuts to folders used specifically for managing *mail items*, which include e-mail messages and faxes. These folders are Drafts, Outbox, and Sent Items. The group may also include a shortcut to update Outlook over the Internet. (The Inbox folder in the Outlook Shortcuts group also stores mail items.) All these Outlook folders are discussed in detail later in the book.

Once you have clicked a shortcut to open an Outlook folder, you can view, organize, print, and search for the items it contains. You can also open an item—such as an e-mail message in the Inbox folder—to read its full contents or to edit it. And you can create new items or delete existing ones. The techniques for performing these tasks are given later.

Accessing File Folders

The Other Shortcuts group on the Outlook Bar contains shortcuts to the file folders on your local or network disks. These shortcuts provide an alternative to using Windows Explorer for working with file folders and files. Initial shortcuts are provided for opening the My Computer, My Documents, and Favorites folders on your computer. (If you're using the Exchange Server information service, the Other Shortcuts group may also include a Public Folders shortcut for opening the root of the

VI

Microsoft Outlook

Public Folders area on the server. *This is explained in the sidebar "Exchange Server Only: Sharing Outlook Information," page 1004.*)

Once you have clicked a shortcut to open a file folder, you can view, organize, manage, and search for the files and file folders it contains. You can also open a subfolder to view its contents, open an Office document or other data file, run a program, or open an Internet shortcut to view a Web page in your browser. If you use the Internet Explorer browser, the Favorites folder will contain the Internet shortcuts that you have saved while browsing. You can use the Favorites shortcut as a quick way to open Web sites in your browser without leaving the Outlook program. (Alternatively, you can open Web pages directly in the Outlook window using the new Favorites menu.) *The techniques for performing all these tasks are explained in "Accessing and Managing Files and Opening Web Sites," page 1067.*

Using the Outlook Today Folder

Outlook Today is a Web-style folder that provides you with an overview of some of your current Outlook information and allows you to access other Outlook folders. It's shown in Figure 41-4.

FIGURE 41-4.
The Outlook Today folder.

Type a name and press Enter to search for a contact in your Contacts folder.

Click to customize your Outlook Today folder.

Folder Banner.

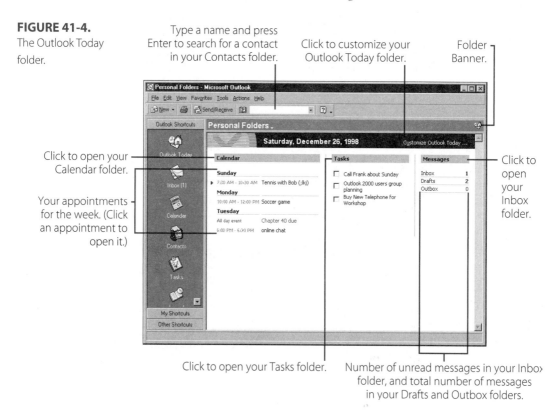

Click to open your Calendar folder.

Your appointments for the week. (Click an appointment to open it.)

Click to open your Inbox folder.

Click to open your Tasks folder.

Number of unread messages in your Inbox folder, and total number of messages in your Drafts and Outbox folders.

Add a Home Page to Any Outlook Folder

You can assign what Outlook calls a *home page* to any Outlook folder. You can then display the home page rather than your ordinary folder view (which shows such items as your Inbox messages or your Calendar appointments). The home page can be a Web page on the Internet, on a corporate intranet, or on your local computer or network. For example, if your organization posts important information about late-breaking meetings and activities on a corporate Web server, you could have that information displayed to you in Outlook by making it a home page for a folder such as your Calendar. Or, a Web page with late-breaking national news or corporate announcements could be made a home page for your Inbox, to be easily checked when you retrieve your personal messages.

To assign a home page to an Outlook folder, right-click the folder's shortcut on the Outlook Bar, choose Properties from the pop-up menu, and click the Home Page tab. Then, in the Address box specify the Internet address or file path of the Web page you want to display (or use the Browse button to find it), and set the other home page options.

When an Outlook folder that has an associated home page is open, you can switch back and forth between displaying the home page and the regular folder view by choosing Show Folder Home Page from the View menu. Each time you select it, the home page will be toggled on or off. You can also return to the regular folder view from the home page view by clicking the folder's shortcut on the Outlook Bar.

You can use Outlook Today as your Outlook "home page." To customize the Outlook Today folder, click Options near the top of the folder to open the Outlook Today Options page. Here, you can select the When Starting Go Directly To Outlook Today option to have Outlook display the Outlook Today folder (rather than Inbox) when you first run the program. You can also choose options to modify the information that Outlook Today displays from your Calendar, Tasks, and mail folders.

Other Ways to Open Folders

You can also open folders by using the hierarchical Folder List. The advantage of using the Folder List rather than the Outlook Bar is that you can readily locate and open any Outlook folder or file folder, not just those for which Outlook Bar shortcuts have been defined. You can open a permanent Folder List by choosing the Folder List option on the View menu or by clicking the Folder List button on the Advanced toolbar. (If this toolbar isn't visible, point to Toolbars on the View menu, and then choose Advanced from the submenu.) Alternatively,

Folder
List

VI

Microsoft Outlook

you can open a temporary Folder List by clicking the left end of the Folder Banner above the Information Viewer.

A permanent Folder List is displayed in a separate pane and remains displayed until you choose the Folder List menu option or click the Folder List button again, or until you click the Close button in the upper right corner of the list. A temporary Folder List overlaps the information in the Information Viewer and disappears as soon as you either use it to open a folder, or click anywhere in Outlook outside the list. You can convert a temporary Folder List to a permanent one by clicking the push-pin button displayed in the upper right corner of the list.

You use the Folder List just like the list in the left pane of Windows Explorer. To expand or contract a branch, click the square button displaying the plus (+) or minus (-) symbol, and to open a folder click the folder name. Figure 41-5 shows the Folder List and indicates how to open and use it. If you have an Outlook folder opened, the Folder List will show all your Outlook folders; but if you have a file folder opened, it will show all your file folders.

FIGURE 41-5.
A permanent Folder List showing the Outlook folders in a Personal Folders file.

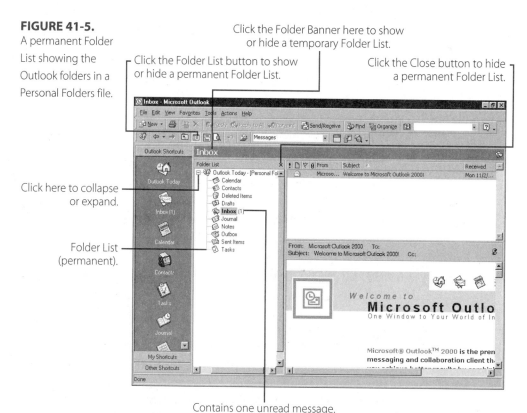

Click the Folder Banner here to show or hide a temporary Folder List.

Click the Folder List button to show or hide a permanent Folder List.

Click the Close button to hide a permanent Folder List.

Click here to collapse or expand.

Folder List (permanent).

Contains one unread message.

If a mail folder or the Deleted Items folder contains one or more unread messages, the folder name is formatted in bold and the number of unread messages is displayed in parentheses. (Note, however, that the number displayed next to the Drafts or Outbox folder indicates the total number of messages contained in the folder, read or unread.)

The following are four additional ways to open either Outlook folders or file folders:

- You can reopen the folder you previously had open by pointing to Go To on the View menu and choosing it, or by clicking the Previous Folder button on the Advanced toolbar. (See the graphic below.) This method is especially useful for returning to the Outlook Today folder after viewing the information in a different folder. You can also click the down arrow adjoining the Previous Folder button and pick a specific previously visited folder from the menu that drops down.

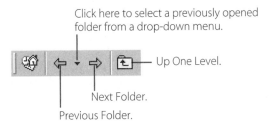

Click here to select a previously opened folder from a drop-down menu.

Up One Level.

Next Folder.

Previous Folder.

- After you've gone back one or more times, you can go forward again by choosing Next Folder from the Go menu or by clicking the Next Folder button on the Advanced toolbar.

- You can open the next folder up in the hierarchy by clicking the Up One Level button on the Advanced toolbar. For example, if the Favorites file folder is open, clicking Up One Level opens the Windows folder—assuming that Favorites is a subfolder of Windows on your computer. (As you can see in Figure 41-5, Outlook folders are also arranged in a hierarchy. Outlook Today is at the top and all other Outlook folders are subfolders of it. As you'll learn in Chapter 42, when you create a new Outlook folder, you can make it a subfolder of any other Outlook folder.)

- You can locate and open a folder by pointing to Go To on the View menu and choosing Folder, or by pressing Ctrl+Y to open the Go To Folder dialog box. In the Look In list box, choose Outlook if you want to open an Outlook folder, or choose File

VI

Microsoft Outlook

System if you want to open a file folder. Next type the name of the folder into the Folder Name box, or select a folder in the Folder Name drop-down list of previously opened folders, or select a folder in the hierarchical list at the bottom of the dialog box. Then click the OK button. This technique is useful primarily if you have added quite a few new folders, some of which might be buried in the hierarchy.

Where to Go from Here

Your next step should be to read through Chapter 42, "Learning Basic Outlook Techniques," to acquire the common skills you'll need for working with any of the types of information managed by Outlook. You can then move on to Chapters 43 and 44, which teach the techniques for working with each of the specific kinds of information (messages in the Inbox folder, appointments in the Calendar folder, contact descriptions in the Contacts folder, and so on). In Chapters 43 and 44, you can focus on just those sections that cover the types of information you want to work with.

Some of the instructions given in Chapter 42 will be more meaningful after you've started reading Chapters 43 and 44 and have begun working with the individual folders. So you might find yourself flipping back and forth between these chapters—don't worry, that's how they were designed to be used.

 NOTE

> Because Outlook is so replete with features and options, the Outlook chapters (41 through 44) can't discuss them all. To assist you in locating additional information, the text includes references to specific *books* within the Outlook online Help system. To access a particular book, you'll first need to turn off the Office Assistant if it's currently enabled. (To do this, click the Assistant, click the Options button in the Assistant's dialog box, and deselect the Use The Office Assistant option.) Then choose Microsoft Outlook Help from Outlook's Help menu, and click the Contents tab within the Microsoft Outlook Help window.

CHAPTER 42

Learning Basic Outlook Techniques

This chapter teaches the important basic techniques that you use for working with almost any of the types of information stored in Microsoft Outlook. First you'll learn how to work with the items stored within an Outlook folder, such as messages in the Inbox folder, appointments in the Calendar folder, and journal entries in the Journal folder. Then you'll discover how to work with Outlook folders themselves. Next you'll find out how to modify the Outlook Bar and the shortcuts it contains. You'll also learn how to search for items in Outlook folders or for files in file folders. Finally, you'll find out how to print the different types of information stored in Outlook.

In the following two chapters, you'll learn the specific techniques for working with each type of information that Outlook manages.

Working with Outlook Items

Once you have opened a particular Outlook folder, such as Inbox, Calendar, or Contacts, you can change the view (the way the information is displayed); you can sort, filter, or group the items contained in the folder; and you can open, edit, create, or delete individual items.

Using Different Views

You can work with an Outlook folder using a variety of different *views*, which vary—often radically—in the way the information is organized and in the amount of detail that is shown in the Information Viewer of the Outlook window. For example, Figure 42-1 shows the Calendar folder in the Day/Week/Month view, which displays all days and appointments in a typical calendar or appointment book format, while Figure 42-2 shows the Calendar folder in the Active Appointments view, which displays a table listing all future appointments.

FIGURE 42-1.
The Calendar folder in the Day/Week/Month view.

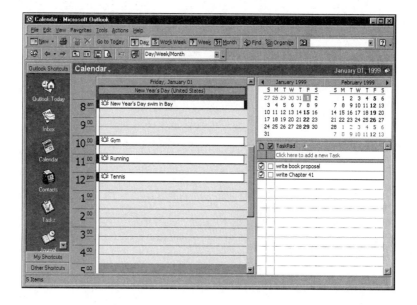

Each folder has available a set of default views that are appropriate for the type of information stored in that folder. To change the view of the opened folder, simply select another item in the Current View list box on the Advanced toolbar:

Available views for the Calendar folder. Change the view by selecting from the list.

Alternatively, you can choose the view from the Current View submenu of the View menu.

For certain views, such as the Day/Week/Month view of the Calendar folder and the Message Timeline view of the Inbox folder, you can control the number of days shown on the screen by choosing the Day, Week, or Month option from the View menu, or by clicking the Day, Week, or Month button on the Standard toolbar. Some views (such as the Day/Week/Month view of the Calendar folder) also have a Work Week option. Notice that the Day/Week/Month view of the Calendar folder shown in Figure 42-1 has the Day option selected.

You can modify any view by pointing to Current View on the View menu and then choosing Customize Current View from the submenu. Choosing this command displays the View Summary dialog box, which contains a

FIGURE 42-2.
The Calendar folder in the Active Appointments view.

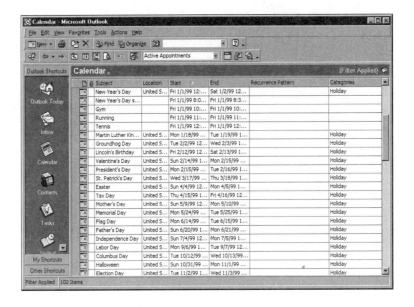

set of buttons you can click to change various features of the current view. Note that in certain views, some of these buttons are disabled because the corresponding features don't apply to that view. For example, if Day/Week/Month is the current view of the Calendar folder, the Group By, Sort, and Automatic Formatting buttons are disabled. Also, the information displayed to the right of each button depends on the particular view that's active and the options that have been selected for that view. This information either gives the current settings or describes the type of settings you can make by clicking the button. Figure 42-3 shows the View Summary dialog box as it appears when the Messages view of the Inbox folder (with default settings) is active.

FIGURE 42-3.
The View Summary dialog box.

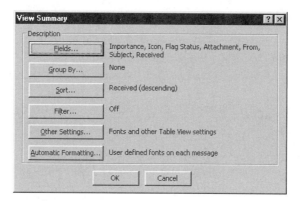

Modifying Columns

In many of the views, the information is arranged in a table consisting of rows and columns (for instance, the Messages view of the Inbox folder shown in Figure 40-3, page 984, and the Active Appointments view of the Calendar folder shown in Figure 42-2). Each column displays the values of a given field of information. A *field* is an individual unit of information within an Outlook item—for example, the subject or date received of a message in the Inbox folder.

In a table view, you can modify the columns in a variety of ways. For example, you can change the width of a column by dragging the right border of the *column heading* (the button-like bar, containing a label, at the top of the column). You can move a column by dragging its heading to a new position in the column heading row. And you can remove a column by dragging the heading anywhere on the screen outside the column heading row. (When the mouse pointer turns into an X, releasing the mouse button will remove the column.)

Modifying Columns   *continued*

You can add, remove, or rearrange columns in a table view by choosing options in the Show Fields dialog box. To open this dialog box, point to Current View on the View menu, choose Customize Current View from the submenu, and then click the Fields button in the View Summary dialog box (shown in Figure 42-3).

You can also modify a column from within a view by right-clicking its heading and choosing commands from the pop-up menu:

The Remove This Column command provides another way to delete a column. The Field Chooser command displays a dialog box that lets you add a new column by simply dragging a field name from the dialog box to the desired position in the heading row. The Alignment submenu lets you apply left (the default), right, or centered alignment to the contents of the column. The Best Fit command makes the column just wide enough to display the column contents. The Format Columns command allows you to change the format, label, width, or alignment of one or more columns in the table. And the Customize Current View command provides an alternative way to display the View Summary dialog box.

For detailed instructions on modifying columns in a table view, see the Outlook online Help book "Customizing Tables."

You can click the Other Settings button of the View Summary dialog box to change the fonts used in the view and to modify other features, which vary according to the current view. In some views, you can click the Automatic Formatting button to apply distinguishing formatting to certain items; for example, in the Messages view of the Inbox folder, you could have the headings for all unread messages displayed in an italic, red font. *(In "Organizing Messages," page 1031, you'll learn how to use the Organize tool to quickly color-code certain messages.)*

VI

Microsoft Outlook

The features set by the Fields button are discussed in the preceding sidebar ("Modifying Columns"), while those set by the Group By, Sort, and Filter buttons are discussed in the next section.

Finally, you can point to Current View on the View menu and choose Define Views from the submenu to modify any of the views available for the current folder, to restore any of these views to its default settings, to rename a view, or to create a new custom view.

For complete information on the views available for each of the Outlook folders and detailed instructions on working with views, see the Outlook online Help book "Changing Views," which is within the "Organizing and Viewing Items in Outlook" book.

Sorting, Filtering, and Grouping Items in Outlook Folders

You can further refine the way information is displayed in a particular view by sorting, filtering, or grouping the items in the folder.

NOTE

> You can sort, filter, or group items in any table view (that is, any view consisting of rows and columns with a row of column headings at the top). You can also perform one or more of these operations in certain other views. For example, in the Address Cards view of the Contacts folder, you can sort or filter items, and in the By Type view of the Journal folder, you can filter or group items. You can tell which operations are possible when a particular view is selected by the buttons enabled in the View Summary dialog box (These buttons are discussed next.)

To sort, filter, or group items, point to Current View on the View menu, and then choose Customize Current View from the submenu to open the View Summary dialog box (shown in Figure 42-3). Alternatively, you can open this dialog box by right-clicking anywhere in the heading row of a table view, or in a blank area of any type of view, and then choosing the Customize Current View command from the pop-up menu.

To sort the items in an Outlook folder, click the Sort button in the View Summary dialog box. This will open the Sort dialog box, which lets you sort the items by the values of one or more fields, in either ascending or descending order. Alternatively, you can sort the items in a table view by the values in one of the columns, by simply clicking the heading above that column. Each click of the heading toggles between an ascending and a descending sort. An arrow is displayed in the heading of a column currently used for sorting—an up arrow for an ascending sort or a down arrow for a descending sort.

When you open a folder, Outlook normally displays all items stored in that folder. However, you can click the Filter button in the View Summary dialog box to open the Filter dialog box, where you can set conditions to determine which items will be displayed. For example, you could display only those messages in the Inbox that contain the word *manuscript* in the message text, or only those messages that are marked as high importance. The criteria you can select are the same as those displayed in the Advanced Find dialog box. *This dialog box is discussed in "Finding Outlook Items or Disk Files," page 1009.*

You can click the Group By button in the View Summary dialog box to open the Group By dialog box, which enables you to group items by the values of one or more fields, rather than displaying the items in a simple list. For example, if you grouped the messages in your Inbox by the Importance field, Outlook would list all high-importance messages in one group, followed by all normal-importance messages in a second group, followed by all low-importance messages in a third group. You can define groups within other groups, creating up to four levels of nested groups. For instance, in the previous example, within each importance group you could group the messages by their sensitivities.

Outlook provides two alternative ways to group items in a table view. First, you can group the items by the values in a column by right-clicking the column's heading and choosing Group By This Field from the pop-up menu. And second, you can choose Group By Box on this same menu (or click the Group By Box button on the Advanced toolbar) to display the Group By box at the top of the Information Viewer. Once this box is displayed, you can drag one or more column headings into the box to group the items by the associated field or fields. You can change the order of the groupings by dragging the field names within the Group By box.

Group
By Box

You can use the Categories command on the Edit menu to assign categories to items in your Outlook folders. For example, you might assign some messages the Business category and others the Personal category. (As you'll learn in the next two chapters, you can also assign a category to an item when you create or edit it in a form.) You can then sort, filter, or group the items based on their categories. You can also locate and display items that belong to a given category using the Advanced Find command, covered in "Using Advanced Find," page 1010.

For complete details on the techniques discussed in this section, see the Outlook online Help books "Sorting Items," "Filtering Items," "Grouping Items," and "Assigning Items to Categories," all within the "Organizing and Viewing Items in Outlook" book.

VI

Microsoft Outlook

Opening, Editing, Creating, and Removing Outlook Items

The amount of information that the Information Viewer of the Outlook window displays for each Outlook item depends on the current view and the view options you have chosen. Some views allow you to enter or edit selected fields of information directly within the Information Viewer. For example, in the Day/Week/Month view of the Calendar folder, you can enter or edit text in the Subject field of an appointment.

To view all the information belonging to an item and be able to edit the contents of any field, however, you need to open the item. The quickest way to open an item is to double-click it. You can also right-click the item and choose Open from the pop-up menu. Or you can click the item to select it and press Ctrl+O. The item will then be shown within a separate window known as a *form*, which displays and lets you modify all the item information. The next two chapters describe the standard forms used for the different types of Outlook items, such as e-mail messages, appointments, and tasks.

You can create a new Outlook item of any type regardless of the folder that's currently opened. To do this, choose the type of item you want to create from the New submenu on the File menu or from the menu that drops down when you click the arrow on the New button. (This is the leftmost button on the Standard toolbar. Its icon and ScreenTip text change to match the open folder, such as "New Mail Message" or "New Contact.")

New button.

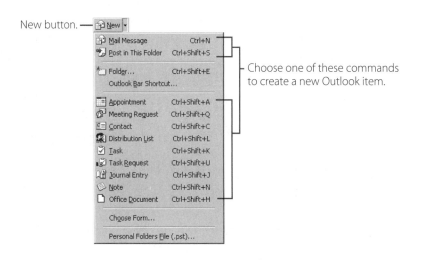

Choose one of these commands to create a new Outlook item.

This graphic shows the New Message button and the menu that's displayed when the Inbox folder (or another folder containing mail items) is open. The contents of the menu vary slightly, depending on which folder is open.

Alternatively, you can create a new item by pressing the appropriate key combination. The key combinations are listed on the menu shown above. Note, however, that the type of item created by clicking the main part of the New button (not the down arrow) or by pressing Ctrl+N depends on the folder that's currently open. For example, if a folder containing mail items (such as Inbox or Outbox) is open, a new message is created; if the Contacts folder is open, a new contact description is created; and if the Journal folder is open, a new journal entry is created. (To create a new message when a mail-item folder isn't currently open, press Ctrl+Shift+M.)

 TIP

Use the Actions Menu

You can also add a new item to the folder that's currently open by choosing an appropriate command from the Actions menu. Typically, the Actions menu provides more choices than the New submenu or New button, but you have to first open the appropriate folder before these choices become available. For example, if your Calendar folder is open, the Actions menu lets you directly create an appointment, an event, a meeting, or a recurring appointment or meeting. *(These Outlook items are discussed in the section "Calendar," page 1034).*

Creating a new item will open a blank form for you to fill in. The blank form is the same as the form you use when you open an existing item of the same type, to view or edit it. When you finish entering the information and close the form, the new item is saved in the appropriate Outlook folder.

When you edit an existing item or create a new one, the commands that the form provides for entering, editing, and formatting text, as well as those for checking your spelling, are similar to commands available in Word and other Office applications. For detailed instructions, see the Outlook online Help book "Formatting Text and Checking Spelling."

You can insert an Outlook item into a field of another item. To do this, choose Item from the Insert menu of the form. Alternatively, you can simply drag an item from another folder to the field. (You can insert an item into a Notes item only by dragging.)

VI

Microsoft Outlook

Quickly Create a New Item from an Existing One

You can use the Outlook AutoCreate feature to rapidly create a new item based on an existing item from a different folder. To do this, simply drag an item from one folder to the Outlook Bar shortcut for a different folder. (You can also drag it to the destination folder's name in a permanently displayed Folder List.) For example, dragging an e-mail message from the Inbox folder to the Contacts shortcut on the Outlook Bar creates a Contact item containing the name and e-mail address of the person who sent you the message. Similarly, dragging an item from the Contacts folder and to the Inbox shortcut creates a new e-mail message addressed to the contact. (You can then fill in the subject and message text.) If the shortcut you want isn't visible, while you drag you can hold the pointer over a group button to open that group, or you can hold it over the top or bottom of a group to scroll through the shortcuts.

Likewise, you can insert or attach a file in some of the fields of an Outlook item by choosing File from the Insert menu of the form, or by dragging the filename from Windows Explorer or a file folder displayed in Outlook to the field where you want to add it. Attaching files is common for e-mail messages, which are explained in Chapter 43. (You can't insert or attach a file in a Notes item.)

Include Hyperlinks in Your Outlook Items

A *hyperlink* is a block of text containing an Internet or e-mail address, which you can click to access the address—that is, to display the Web page in your browser, send an e-mail message, or perform another action, according to the type of the address. You can insert a hyperlink into the large text box of a message form, Contact item, or Calendar item. To do this, simply type the full Internet address (URL), such as *http://www.microsoft.com/* or *mailto:msporder@msn.com*, and Outlook will automatically convert it to a blue, underlined hyperlink. Alternatively, when you create or edit a message, you can insert a hyperlink by choosing Hyperlink from the form's Insert menu. (This command, however, isn't available if you're using the Microsoft Outlook Rich Text or Plain Text e-mail format with the Outlook message editor. *E-mail formats and editors are discussed in Chapter 43.*)

You can save a copy of an Outlook item in a disk file. To do this, select the item in the Information Viewer, or open the item in a form, and choose Save As from the File menu of Outlook or of the form. Before saving the item, select the desired format from the Save As Type list box in the Save As dialog box.

Finally, you can export an entire Outlook folder to a disk file in a choice of formats, and you can import data from a variety of file types (such as an Access database or another Outlook Personal Folders file) to an Outlook folder. To import or export items, run the Import And Export Wizard by choosing Import And Export from the File menu of Outlook.

Removing Items

Delete

You can remove an item from an Outlook folder by selecting it in the Information Viewer of the Outlook window (just click it) and then choosing Delete from the Edit menu, clicking the Delete toolbar button, or pressing Ctrl+D. If you have opened the item in a form, you can remove it by clicking the Delete button on the form's toolbar or pressing Ctrl+D.

⭐ **TIP**

> **Remove Several Items at Once**
> You can quickly remove a group of items by selecting them all in the Information Viewer prior to issuing the Delete command. To select several adjoining items, click the first one, and then click the last one while pressing Shift. To select nonadjoining items, click the first one, and then press Ctrl while clicking each additional one. To select all items in a folder, choose Select All from the Edit menu or press Ctrl+A. (This command isn't available in all folders.)

When you remove an item, it's not permanently deleted right away. Rather, it's initially moved to the Deleted Items folder. If you want to permanently delete the item, remove it from the Deleted Items folder using any of the methods just described.

You can also permanently delete all items in the Deleted Items folder by choosing Empty "Deleted Items" Folder from the Tools menu. Or, you can have Outlook permanently delete all items in the Deleted Items folder each time you exit the program by choosing Options from the Tools menu, clicking the Other tab in the Options dialog box, and selecting Empty The Deleted Items Folder Upon Exiting. To see a message before an item is permanently deleted, click the Advanced Options button on the Other tab, and select Warn Before Permanently Deleting Items.

If you archive your Outlook folders, you can have Outlook permanently delete all items in the Deleted Items folders that are older than a specified age. (See the following tip on archiving.) And if you're using Outlook as an Exchange Server client, the server might delete older items from the Deleted Items folder. (The server administrator sets the length of time items are stored in Deleted Items.)

VI

Microsoft Outlook

TIP

> **Reduce Clutter by Archiving**
>
> You can clean up your Outlook folders by *archiving*. Archiving removes Outlook items either by moving them to an archive file—a separate Personal Folders (PST) file—or by permanently deleting them. You can archive manually, or you can have Outlook do it automatically at specified intervals. For information on archiving, see *the* Outlook online Help book "Archiving Items."

(?) SEE ALSO

The techniques for moving and copying items from one Outlook folder to another are discussed in "Organizing Messages," page 1031.

As long as an item is still contained in the Deleted Items folder, you can restore it to the folder that originally contained it. To do this, just drag the item from the Deleted Items folder to the Outlook Bar shortcut for the original folder. (You can also drag it to the original folder's name in a permanently displayed Folder List.) If the shortcut for the original folder isn't visible, while you drag, you can hold the pointer over a group button to open that group, or you can hold it over the top or bottom of a group to scroll through the shortcuts.

Using the Organize Tool

The Organize tool is a Web-style page that you can display in a separate pane at the top of the Information Viewer and that you can use for working with Outlook items. Although it doesn't let you do anything that you can't do by using the program's conventional commands, it provides fast and easy alternative methods for performing some of the more common tasks. For example, you can

- Move selected items in the folder to another folder. For some folders, you can also have Outlook automatically move items in the future, according to rules that you specify. For example, you could have all future e-mail messages that your boss sends automatically moved to a specific folder.

- Assign categories to items (such as Business or Personal), and create new categories.

- Change the current view.

- Organize messages by color-coding certain messages. Or, automatically color-code, move, or delete junk e-mail or adult-content e-mail. *These features are discussed in "Organizing Messages," page 1031.*

To use the Organize tool, open the folder you want to work with, and choose Organize from the Tools menu or click the Organize button on the Standard toolbar. The Organize page will then be displayed in a separate pane at the top of the Information Viewer. The features that the Organize tool provides vary depending on the current folder. Figure 42-4 shows the Organize tool for the Contacts folder.

You can remove the Organize tool by choosing the Organize command or clicking the Organize button again.

FIGURE 42-4.
Using the Organize tool for the Contacts folder.

Click here to close the Organize pane.

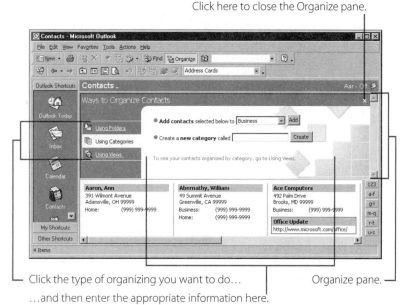

Click the type of organizing you want to do…
…and then enter the appropriate information here.

Organize pane.

Working with Outlook Folders

The Outlook folders described in this book are the default folders created by the Outlook program. You can create additional folders to store specific types of Outlook items. For example, you might create one or more folders for storing saved e-mail messages, rather than keeping them all in your Inbox. Also, you might create a new folder for storing appointments so that you can have one calendar for your personal appointments and another for your business appointments.

Exchange Server Only: Sharing Outlook Information

If your computer is attached to an Exchange Server network, and if you set up Outlook as an Exchange Server client, you can share your Outlook information with other Exchange Server users on the network by using either shared private folders or public folders.

A *shared private folder* is one that has the following features:

■ It's an Outlook folder that's stored in a private mailbox on the server.

■ The folder's owner has allowed other users to access the folder.

On an Exchange Server network, the Outlook folders belonging to each user (Inbox, Calendar, Contacts, and so on) are normally stored within the user's private mailbox on the server. *(See Chapter 41.)* By default, these folders aren't shared; that is, other Exchange Server users on the network can't access them. To share a specific Outlook folder that belongs to you, you must open the folder, point to Folder on the File menu, and choose Properties For "*Folder*" from the submenu (where *Folder* is the folder's name, such as Inbox or Calendar).

Alternatively, you can right-click the folder in a permanently displayed Folder List or right-click the folder's shortcut on the Outlook Bar, and choose Properties on the pop-up menu. Then, on the Permissions tab of the Properties dialog box, you must set the level of permission that you want to grant. You can grant permissions to one or more particular users, or you can grant permissions to all users (by selecting the Default user). For each user (or for all users), you can grant one or more specific types of permission—for example, the permission to read items, to create items, to delete items, or to create subfolders within the folder.

Once you have shared a private folder, a user to whom you have given access can open that folder by pointing to Open on his or her File menu, choosing Other User's Folder from the submenu, and then specifying your name and the name of your shared folder. (Both names can be selected from a list.) Your shared folder will then be opened in a separate Outlook window on the other user's computer.

A user who has access to one or more of your private folders can also display these folders in his or her Folder List and open specific folders in the main Outlook window. To do this, the user must choose Services from the Tools menu, select Microsoft Exchange Server and click the Properties button on the Services tab, and then click the Advanced tab and add your mailbox to the Open These Additional Mailboxes list.

Note that even if you have shared your Calendar, Contacts, Tasks, or Journal folder, you can hide an individual item within that folder by opening the item and selecting the Private option in the form (a check box in the form's lower right corner).

A *public folder* is an Outlook folder that's stored within the Public Folders area on the server. In addition to creating a private mailbox for each user, Exchange

Server maintains a single Public Folders area, where all users on the network can create and access Outlook folders. *You can create a new public folder in the same way you create a new private folder in your mailbox, as explained at the beginning of the section "Working with Outlook Folders," page 1003.* When you select the location for the folder, just place it within the All Public Folders subfolder in the Public Folders area rather than placing it within your private mailbox. (Note that you can't create a new public folder directly within the root of the Public Folders area or within the Favorites subfolder, shown in Figure 42-5.)

A public folder is shared like a private folder in a mailbox, except for the following:

■ *By default*, all users are allowed to view the folder, to read and create items, and to edit or delete the items they create. You can change these default permissions for a public folder that you have created in the same way that you set permissions for a private folder, as described previously in the sidebar.

■ Public folders automatically appear in each user's Folder List, as shown in Figure 42-5. Public folders are thus more readily available to other Exchange users than are shared private folders. Users can open public folders, create shortcuts to them, and read or create items in them in the same way they do with their private folders.

You can create a public folder to store any type of Outlook items, such as mail items, appointment items, or contact items. A public folder that stores mail items is especially valuable because you can use it as a bulletin board for conducting an online discussion as well as for sharing Office documents or other files. In a public mail-item folder used for an online discussion, a user can post a new message by opening the folder, pointing to New on the File menu, and then choosing Post In This Folder from the submenu, or by pressing Ctrl+Shift+S. Other users can then read the message; and they can post a reply to the message by double-clicking it to open it in the Discussion form and then clicking the Post Reply button at the top of the form.

To store an Office document or any other type of file in a public mail-item folder so that other users on the network can access it, you can drag the file from Windows Explorer or from a folder displayed in Outlook or opened on your Windows desktop to the public folder within the Outlook Folder List (or on a shortcut for the public folder on the Outlook Bar if you've created one). Note that Outlook provides a shortcut in the Other Shortcuts group for opening the root of the Public Folders area.

For more information on public folders, see the Outlook online Help book "Using Public Folders," within the book "Using Corporate or Workgroup Features."

VI

Microsoft Outlook

FIGURE 42-5.

A Folder List showing a private mailbox as well as a Public Folders area.

Private mailbox.

Public Folder area.

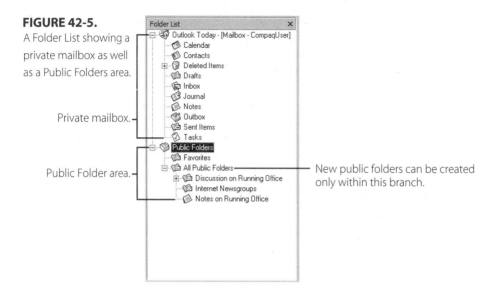

New public folders can be created only within this branch.

To create a new Outlook folder, point to Folder on the File menu and choose New Folder from the submenu, or press Ctrl+Shift+E. (Alternatively, you can point to New on the File menu and choose Folder from the submenu.) Then enter the required information into the dialog box:

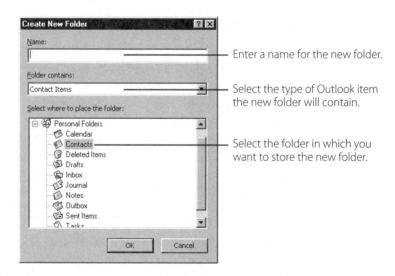

Enter a name for the new folder.

Select the type of Outlook item the new folder will contain.

Select the folder in which you want to store the new folder.

Note that if you choose to place the new folder within an existing folder, the new folder becomes a subfolder and will be displayed under the existing folder in the Folder List.

When you close the dialog box, Outlook will give you the opportunity to add a shortcut for the new folder to the Outlook Bar. If you choose not to do this, you can access the folder using the Folder List; also, you can add a shortcut later using the method described in the next section.

You can also create a new Outlook folder by making a copy of an existing folder and its contents. To do this, open the folder you want to copy, point to Folder on the File menu, and choose Copy "*Folder*" from the submenu (where *Folder* is the name of the opened folder). You'll then have to select the folder where you want to store the copy. Outlook will copy the folder plus any subfolders it contains, together with the contents of these folders, and it will assign the copy a default name. You can later rename it.

You can't move, rename, or remove any of the default Outlook folders (Inbox, Calendar, and so on). However, you can move, rename, or remove an Outlook folder that you've created. To perform one of these operations, open the folder, point to Folder on the File menu, and from the submenu, choose Move "*Folder*", Rename "*Folder*", or Delete "*Folder*" (where *Folder* is the name of the open folder).

? SEE ALSO

Working with file folders (as opposed to Outlook folders) is discussed in "Accessing and Managing Files and Opening Web Sites," page 1067.

As when you remove an item, when you remove an Outlook folder, it isn't permanently deleted at that moment. Rather, it's moved to the Deleted Items folder, where it becomes a subfolder of Deleted Items. You can permanently delete it using the same techniques described for items in "Removing Items," page 1001. And you can restore a folder by moving it back to its original location in the folder hierarchy. Be aware that if you have selected the Empty The Deleted Items Folder Upon Exiting option on the Other tab of the Options dialog box (opened by choosing Options on the Tools menu), the items in your Deleted Items folder will be permanently deleted when you exit Outlook.

★ TIP

Rather than choosing the menu commands discussed in this section from the Folder submenu of the File menu, you can choose them from the pop-up menu that appears when you right-click the Folder Banner above the Information Viewer.

VI

Microsoft Outlook

Use the Folder List to Work with Folders

An alternative way to perform the operations explained in this section is to display a permanent Folder List, right-click an Outlook folder name, and then choose a command from the pop-up menu that appears. Using the Folder List, you can also move an Outlook folder by simply dragging it or copy a folder by pressing Ctrl while you drag. And you can remove an Outlook folder by selecting it and pressing the Delete key.

Modifying the Outlook Bar

You can modify the shortcut groups on the Outlook Bar as well as the shortcuts that appear in each group. (See Figure 41-3, page 984.) If the Outlook Bar isn't currently displayed, choose Outlook Bar from the View menu to make it visible.

To add a new group, right-click anywhere within the Outlook Bar except on a shortcut, and then choose Add New Group from the pop-up menu that appears. To rename a group, right-click the group button (the button displaying the name of the group at the top or bottom of the Outlook Bar), and choose Rename Group from the pop-up menu. To remove a group, right-click the group button and choose Remove Group.

To add a new shortcut to a group, open that group, point to New on the File menu, and choose Shortcut from the submenu, or right-click anywhere within the Outlook Bar except on a shortcut, and choose Outlook Bar Shortcut from the pop-up menu. Then supply the required information in the Add To Outlook Bar dialog box that's displayed:

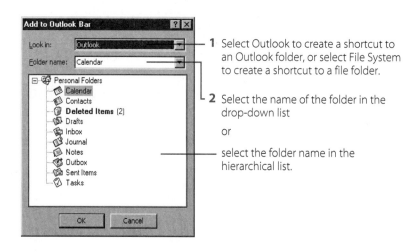

1 Select Outlook to create a shortcut to an Outlook folder, or select File System to create a shortcut to a file folder.

2 Select the name of the folder in the drop-down list

or

select the folder name in the hierarchical list.

If you have a permanent Folder List displayed, an easy way to add a shortcut is to drag the folder name from the Folder List to the Outlook Bar. If the position where you want to place the shortcut isn't visible, while you drag you can hold the pointer over a group button to open that group, or you can hold it over the top or bottom of a group to scroll through the shortcuts.

You can rename a shortcut by right-clicking it, choosing Rename Shortcut from the pop-up menu, and typing a new name. Note that renaming a shortcut doesn't change the folder that's opened by clicking the shortcut, even if you assign the shortcut the name of a different folder.

You can remove a shortcut from the Outlook Bar by right-clicking it and choosing Remove From Outlook Bar from the pop-up menu. Note that removing the shortcut doesn't remove the folder to which it refers. If you have permanently deleted a folder, it's a good idea to remove any shortcut to it on the Outlook Bar, because it won't be removed automatically. (You can leave the shortcut, but clicking it will only display an error message.)

For information on adding an Outlook Bar shortcut that opens a file, see "Accessing and Managing Files and Opening Web Sites," page 1067.

Finally, you can move or copy a shortcut from its current position on the Outlook Bar to another position. To move a shortcut to another position within the same group, simply drag it. To move it to another group, drag it to the button for the other group, hold it over the button—while continuing to press the mouse button—until the other group is opened, and then drag it to its final position in the other group. To copy a shortcut rather than move it, press the Ctrl key while you drag.

You can change the size of the shortcut icons by right-clicking anywhere on the Outlook Bar except on a shortcut and then choosing the Large Icons or Small Icons option from the pop-up menu.

Finding Outlook Items or Disk Files

The easiest way to find specific Outlook items is to use the Find tool, which is a Web-style page that can be displayed in a separate pane at the top of the Information Viewer. To use this tool, first open the Outlook folder containing the items you want to search through. (The Find tool can't be used to search file folders. To search for disk files, you'll have to use Advanced Find, discussed in the next section.) For example, if you want to search for specific e-mail messages, open the Inbox

VI

Microsoft Outlook

or one of the other mail folders; if you want to search for the information on a particular contact, open the Contacts folder. Then choose Find from the Tools menu or click the Find button on the Standard toolbar. Outlook will display the Find tool, which is shown in Figure 42-6 (with the Contacts folder open).

FIGURE 42-6.

Using the Find tool for the Contacts folder.

Click here to close the Find pane.

Click here to open the Advanced Find dialog box.

Type the text you want to search for here…

…and then click here.

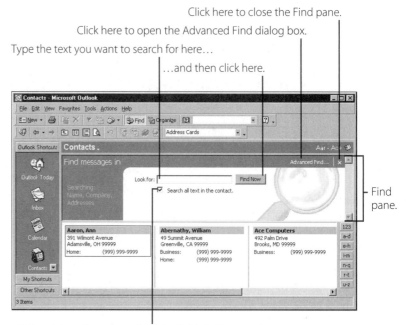

Find pane.

Select this option to search all the fields in Contacts items.

When you click the Find Now button, Outlook will search through the folder for items that match the search text you typed, and it will display any matching items in a table below the Find pane. (If a table view of the folder isn't currently active, Outlook will switch to one.) Also, it will display a Clear Search option that you can click to start a new search, as well as a Go To Advanced Find option that you can click to open the Advanced Find dialog box. See Figure 42-7.

You can close the Find tool by choosing Find from the Tools menu or clicking the Find button again. Outlook will restore the original view (if it switched to a table view to list search results), and it will again display all the folder items.

Using Advanced Find

If you click the Advanced Find button in the upper right corner of the Find pane (or if you click Go To Advanced Find in the Find pane after

FIGURE 42-7.

The Find tool, after searching for contacts

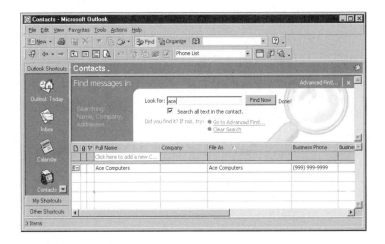

running a search), Outlook will display the Advanced Find dialog box. You can also open this dialog box, even if the Find tool isn't displayed, by choosing Advanced Find from the Tools menu, by pressing Ctrl+Shift+F, or by right-clicking a shortcut on the Outlook bar and choosing Advanced Find from the pop-up menu. (If you're viewing a file folder, the Advanced Find command isn't available on the Tools menu—use one of the other methods.) And you can open the Advanced Find dialog box at any time, even when you aren't running Outlook, by clicking the Start button on the Windows taskbar, pointing to Find on the Start menu, and choosing Using Microsoft Outlook from the submenu:

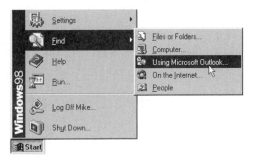

The main advantages of using the Advanced Find dialog box rather than the Find tool are that you can search through multiple folders, you can fine-tune the search criteria, and you can search for files. The Advanced Find dialog box lets you search either for items in Outlook folders or for files in file folders on local or network drives that meet your search criteria.

You can search for items in one or more Outlook folders, and you can search either for items of a particular type (such as messages, contacts, or journal entries) or for items of any type. For example, you could search the Inbox folder for all messages that were sent by a given person. As another example, you could search all your Outlook folders for items of any type that are assigned a particular category, such as Business or Personal.

Likewise, you can search for files in one or more file folders. You can search for files of a certain type (such as Microsoft Word or Microsoft Excel documents), or for files of any type. For example, you could search for all Word document files on your hard disk that contain a specific word or phrase.

Whether you search for Outlook items or disk files, the Find command lets you specify a wide variety of search criteria. Here's how you use the Advanced Find dialog box:

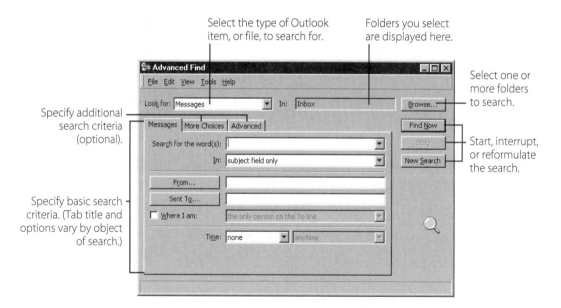

Note that the particular search criteria options that appear on the tabs of this dialog box depend on the type of item or file you're searching for (which you select in the Look For list box).

After you click the Find Now button and the search is completed, Outlook displays all matching items or files in a list that's added to the bottom of the Advanced Find dialog box. You can open an Outlook item or a disk file by double-clicking it within this list. You can also save all of the criteria you have entered into the Advanced Find dialog box by choosing Save Search from the File menu and then specifying the name of the file in which you want to store the search criteria. (The file will be given the .oss extension.) You can later quickly rerun the same search by choosing Open Search from the File menu and selecting this file.

Note that you can leave the Advanced Find dialog box displayed while you work in the main Outlook window. For complete information on using the Find tool and the Advanced Find dialog box, see the book "Finding Items" in the Outlook online Help.

Printing Information Stored in Outlook Folders

Outlook lets you print the information stored in any of your Outlook folders. For example, you can print a message stored in the Inbox folder, a day or a range of days in the Calendar folder, or the information on one or more contacts in the Contacts folder. Outlook provides a variety of methods for printing. The following is a flexible, general procedure that you can use for printing any kind of Outlook information:

1 Open the folder containing the information you want to print.

2 If you want to print one or more specific items—for example, messages in the Inbox folder or days in the Calendar folder—select the item or items. To select an item, click it; to select additional items, press Ctrl while you click each one.

3 Choose Print from the File menu or press Ctrl+P to open the Print dialog box, which is shown in Figure 42-8, on the next page.

4 In the Print Style list in the center of the dialog box, select a printing style to specify the general way the information will be organized on the printed copy and the level of detail to be shown.

5 If you want to modify the selected printing style for the current print job, click the Page Setup button to open the Page Setup dialog box, which lets you modify the fonts, paper size, headers or footers, and other characteristics of the printed pages. If you want to permanently modify one of the default printing styles or create a custom style, click the Define Styles button.

Microsoft Outlook

FIGURE 42-8.

The Print dialog box. (In this example, we opened the Inbox and selected a message prior to opening the dialog box.)

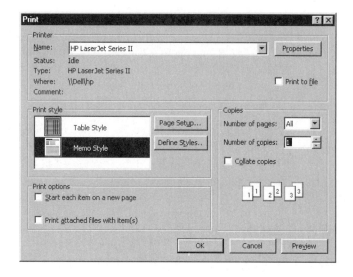

6 Change other print options in the Print dialog box, as necessary. The specific options available depend on the folder you opened and the items you selected prior to opening the dialog box. For example, if you opened the Contacts folder, you can choose whether to print all contacts or only the contact or contacts that you selected.

7 To preview the appearance of the printed output, and to see the effect of all the options you have selected, click the Preview button. When you're done previewing, click the Print button in the Print Preview window to return to the Print dialog box.

8 To begin printing, click the OK button in the Print dialog box.

For more information on printing, see the "Printing" book in the Outlook online Help.

Using Outlook to Manage Messages and Appointments

N ow that you have learned the general methods for using Microsoft Outlook 2000, this chapter begins teaching the techniques for working with each of the specific types of information that you can store in Outlook. *As explained in Chapter 41, "Getting Started Using Outlook," the information in Outlook is contained within folders, each of which stores a specific type of item.* In this chapter, you'll learn how to work with the Inbox and other mail folders, which store messages and other types of items; and how to work with the Calendar folder, which stores appointments, events, and meetings. In the next chapter, you'll learn how to work with all the other default Outlook folders, as well as how to access and manage files and Web sites.

NOTE

> The instructions given in this chapter assume that you have opened the appropriate Outlook folder (using any of the techniques given in Chapter 41). For example, the discussion on creating and editing appointments assumes that you have opened the Calendar folder. Otherwise, some of the menu commands or toolbar buttons referenced might be unavailable.

Inbox and Other Mail Folders

The Inbox, Drafts, Sent Items, and Outbox default Outlook folders are used to store and manage *mail items*. This category of items includes e-mail messages that are sent over your network or across the Internet, faxes you receive using a fax modem installed on your system, discussion postings, and even files such as Microsoft Office documents. (The final two item types are used primarily with public folders, which are discussed in the sidebar "Exchange Server Only: Sharing Outlook Information," page 1004.) Throughout this chapter, the term *message* refers to either an e-mail message or a fax.

All incoming messages are delivered to your Inbox, messages that you have written and saved but haven't yet sent are normally stored in Drafts, copies of all messages that you have sent are usually stored in Sent Items, and the Outbox temporarily stores e-mail messages that you have sent if they can't be delivered immediately.

 NOTE

> The instructions in the following sections for managing your messages assume that you have opened the Inbox folder or other mail folder, such as Drafts, Outbox, or Sent Items.

Reading Messages

If you send and receive e-mail via a network (that is, you're using Outlook as a client for Exchange Server or another e-mail server on your network), your e-mail messages will normally be delivered to your Inbox automatically, and you won't have to issue any commands to retrieve them. Also, if you have set up a fax service, faxes will automatically appear in your Inbox as soon as your fax modem receives them.

Setting Up E-Mail and Faxes in Outlook

As you learned in the section "Setting Up Outlook," page 976, when you install Outlook, you might be able to upgrade from an existing e-mail program. You might also be able to use an existing user profile (perhaps one you defined for a previous Outlook version), together with the e-mail settings it contains. In either case, you can probably just start using Outlook to access your stored messages, and to send and receive messages using your current e-mail provider, without further fuss.

If, however, you weren't able to upgrade an e-mail program and you don't have a user profile already set up for e-mail (or if you want to change your e-mail service), you'll need to add and set up an appropriate e-mail information service in your user profile. *The section "Information Services and User Profiles," page 978, discusses information services, explains how to add them to a user profile, and briefly describes the standard information services that Outlook provides.* This sidebar offers some additional details on the e-mail information services to help you choose one that's appropriate for your e-mail provider.

If you send and receive e-mail via an Internet service provider that uses the standard SMTP and POP3 e-mail protocols, you can probably use the Internet E-Mail information service. For example, if you subscribe to the Microsoft Network (MSN), you can use Internet E-Mail provided that you have version 2.5 or later of the MSN software. If you want to exchange e-mail with users of the Microsoft Mail e-mail program for PC networks, you can use the Microsoft Mail information service. And if you send and receive e-mail via Microsoft Exchange Server on your network, the Microsoft Exchange Server information service will provide all necessary support. And if you need to exchange mail with users of Lotus cc:Mail, you can use the MS Outlook Support For Lotus cc:Mail information service.

All the information services mentioned so far are included with Outlook, and you can add any of them to your profile by simply choosing it from a list. In addition, some Internet service providers furnish proprietary information services that allow you to exchange e-mail with their systems using Outlook as your e-mail program. For example, if you use CompuServe, you can download a free product called CompuServe Mail for Microsoft Exchange. When you install it, it automatically adds to your user profile an information service called CompuServe Mail, which lets you use Outlook—rather than the CompuServe software—to send and receive e-mail via CompuServe.

V

Microsoft Access

Setting Up E-Mail and Faxes in Outlook *continued*

The Information services that some service providers furnish must be manually installed from a disk. To do this, choose Services from the Tools menu, click the Add button on the Services tab, and click the Have Disk button in the Add Service To Profile dialog box.

If you're unsure which information service is appropriate for your e-mail system, contact your network administrator (if you send and receive e-mail over a network), or contact your e-mail service provider (if you exchange e-mail using a dial-up service). Note that if you have more than one e-mail provider, you can add an information service for each one; you can specify which service or services Outlook uses when you send and receive e-mail.

Likewise, if you have a fax modem attached to your computer and you want to send and receive faxes using Outlook, you'll need to include a fax information service in your user profile. Outlook provides a fax information service called Microsoft Fax, which lets you use the Microsoft Fax component of Windows. Note that you should install the Microsoft Fax component before you install Outlook because the Outlook installation program needs to update it.

To install Microsoft Fax in Windows 95, open Add/Remove Programs in your Windows Control Panel, click the Windows Setup tab, and select Microsoft Fax in the Components list. To install it in Windows 98, on the Windows 98 CD, double-click the file \tools\oldwin95\message\us\awfax.exe (for the United States version) or \tools\oldwin95\message\intl\awfax.exe (for the international version).

Recall from Chapter 41 that the Services dialog box in Outlook—opened by choosing Services from the Tools menu—lets you modify the delivery and addressing of messages. (See Figure 41-2, page 981.) The Delivery tab of this dialog box lets you change the folder where your messages are delivered. For example, if you have both an Exchange Server information service and a Personal Folders information service, you can choose whether to have your e-mail delivered to the Inbox in your Exchange Server mailbox or to the Inbox in your Personal Folders. And the Addressing tab lets you modify the way Outlook uses your address books when you send messages.

When you choose the Internet Only installation of Outlook, the Send/Receive button or F5 retrieves e-mail from all accounts for which you have enabled the Include This Account When Doing A Full Send And Receive option. You set this option by choosing Accounts from the Tools menu, selecting an account on the Mail tab of the Internet Accounts dialog box, and then clicking the Properties button. You'll find the option on the General tab of the Properties dialog box.

Setting Up E-Mail and Faxes in the Internet Only Installation

When you select the Internet Only installation, Outlook doesn't use information services and user profiles. Rather, you exchange e-mail and faxes by means of *mail accounts.*

If you weren't able to upgrade an existing e-mail program when you installed Outlook, you'll have to set up a mail account to be able to send and receive messages using your e-mail service. The first time you start Outlook, the Internet Connection Wizard (which runs after the Office 2000 Startup Wizard) will normally prompt you for information and set up a mail account for your e-mail provider. You can also add, remove, or modify mail accounts at any time by choosing Accounts from Outlook's Tools menu and clicking the Mail tab, or by opening the Mail item in the Windows Control Panel.

To send and receive faxes using the Internet Only installation, you use an integrated fax feature named Symantec WinFax Starter Edition. The first time you start Outlook, a wizard will obtain the necessary information and set up a mail account for sending and receiving faxes.

You can modify the way Outlook uses your mail accounts by choosing Options from the Tools menu and clicking the Mail Delivery tab in the Options dialog box. For example, you can specify when Outlook sends and receives e-mail. (Clicking the Accounts button on the Mail Delivery tab provides yet another way to add, remove, or modify accounts.) And you can change fax options by clicking the Fax tab in the Options dialog box. For example, you can control whether your fax line is answered automatically.

Finally, using the Internet Only installation, you can set up *directory service* accounts. A directory service is a database of people's names and e-mail addresses that's maintained by an Internet service provider. It's accessed by means of a protocol know as LDAP (lightweight directory access protocol). A directory service account lets you have Outlook automatically check addresses in your outgoing e-mail messages against that directory service. A directory service account also lets you look up information in that service by pointing to Find on the Windows Start menu and then choosing People from the submenu. When you install Outlook, it sets up a collection of default directory service accounts (such as Bigfoot, InfoSpace, and Yahoo! People Search). You can modify or remove any of these accounts or add new ones by choosing Accounts from the Tools menu and clicking the Directory Service tab.

For more information on managing e-mail and faxes in an Internet Only installation, see the online Help book, "Using Internet Only Features."

V

Microsoft Access

If, however, you send and receive e-mail by means of a dial-up modem connection (for example, from an Internet service provider or an online service), you normally have to explicitly issue a command to connect to your provider and have your e-mail messages downloaded into your Inbox. Outlook provides many ways to do this. The easiest is to click the Send/Receive button on the Standard toolbar or press F5. Outlook will then retrieve all e-mail messages that are waiting for you (and will also send any outgoing e-mail messages stored in your Outbox folder, as described later). It will download your e-mail from all services that are currently enabled for this feature. To enable e-mail services, choose Options from the Tools menu, click the Mail Services tab in the Options dialog box, and in the Check For New Mail On list, select all e-mail services that you want to use.

Use a Specific E-Mail Service

If you have more than one e-mail service in your user profile, you can send and receive e-mail from a particular service (ignoring what's selected on the Mail Services tab) by pointing to Send/Receive on the Tools menu and choosing that service's name from the submenu. (Note that choosing the All Accounts command on this submenu is equivalent to clicking the Send/Receive button or pressing F5.)

NOTE

The Internet Only installation of Outlook differs in several ways from the Corporate Or Workgroup installation in its handling of e-mail messages:

- It gives you more control over when it sends messages or checks for incoming messages. For example, if your e-mail is exchanged over a network, you can choose Options from the Tools menu, click the Mail Delivery tab, and select the Send Messages Immediately option to have Outlook automatically send outgoing e-mail messages immediately, or you can select the Check For New Messages Every option to have Outlook automatically download incoming messages and send outgoing messages from your Outbox at a specified regular interval. If both options are deselected (or if you exchange e-mail via a dial-up connection), e-mail won't be exchanged until you explicitly click the Send/Receive button or choose another appropriate command.

- It doesn't provide a Remote Connection Wizard.

- It includes a set of commands for accessing IMAP folders if you have an IMAP e-mail service.

An alternative way to retrieve your e-mail messages from a dial-up connection is to use the Remote Connection Wizard. This wizard lets you choose specific mail information services if you have more than one. Also, it lets you first download only the headers for your messages, then select specific messages, and finally download the complete message text for only the selected messages. You run the Remote Connection Wizard by pointing to Remote Mail on the Tools menu and choosing Connect from the submenu. For complete information on using the Remote Connection Wizard and other remote mail tools, see the book "Using Remote Mail to Manage Your Messages," within the "Using Corporate or Workgroup Features" book in the Outlook online Help.

 TIP

Automatically Download E-Mail

When you use some dial-up e-mail information services you can have your messages retrieved automatically at regular intervals. For example, with the Internet E-Mail information service you can set this up by choosing Options from the Tools menu and clicking the Internet E-Mail tab. And with the CompuServe Mail for Microsoft Exchange information service, you can set this up by choosing Services from the Tools menu, and on the Services tab, selecting the service and clicking the Properties button. (See Figure 41-2 on page 981.)

When one or more new e-mail messages or faxes arrive in your Inbox, Outlook displays an envelope icon at the right end of the Windows taskbar:

 ── Indicates that Inbox contains a new message

You can also have Outlook notify you of the receipt of a new message by displaying a message box, by playing a sound, or by temporarily changing the mouse pointer. To enable the message box, choose Options from the Tools menu, click the E-Mail Options button on the Preferences tab, and then select Display A Notification Message When New Mail Arrives in the E-Mail Options dialog box. To access the options for enabling the sound or pointer change, click the Advanced E-Mail Options button, also in the E-Mail Options dialog box.

To read your new message or messages, open the Inbox folder in Outlook (you can quickly open it by double-clicking the envelope icon on the Windows taskbar), and you'll see a list of your new messages plus any messages you have already read that are still stored in the Inbox. See Figure 43-1, on the next page.

Microsoft Access

Figure 43-1 shows the Inbox in Messages view, which arranges the messages in a table so that each column displays a different field of information about the messages. These fields are labeled in Figure 43-2.

To read an e-mail message, simply click it to select it, and the message contents will be displayed in the Preview pane. If the Preview pane isn't shown, choose the Preview Pane option from the View menu.

You can also read an e-mail message by double-clicking it to open it in the Message form. In addition to displaying the content of the message, the Message form provides commands for replying to or forwarding the message, printing it, moving it to a different Outlook folder, deleting it, or adding a message flag (a comment such as *Call* or *Follow up* attached to the message). In the Message form, you can also open other messages, create new messages, and perform additional operations, as shown in Figure 43-3. Note that the look and features of the Message form can vary depending on the message format and the format options you have chosen. (See the sidebar "Choosing the Format for New E-Mail Messages," page 1026.)

FIGURE 43-1.

The Inbox displaying both unread and read messages.

E-mail message, read.

Selected e-mail message, shown in Preview pane below.

Columns display message fields, such as source, subject, and date received.

E-mail message, read and replied to.

Fax message, unread.

Number in parentheses indicates the Inbox contains 1 unread message.

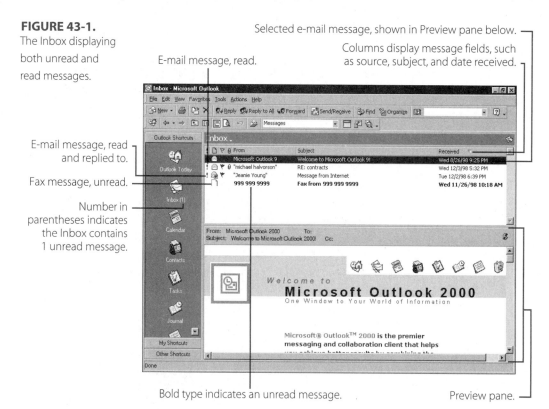

Bold type indicates an unread message.

Preview pane.

FIGURE 43-2.
The default message fields displayed in the Messages view of the Inbox folder.

Importance.
Icon.
Flag status.
Attachment.

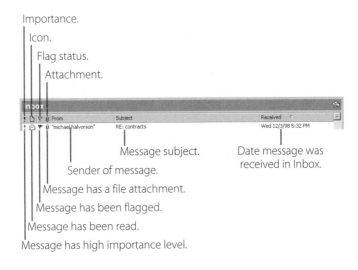

Message subject.

Date message was received in Inbox.

Sender of message.

Message has a file attachment.

Message has been flagged.

Message has been read.

Message has high importance level.

FIGURE 43-3.
Reading a message in the Message form— this message is in HTML format.

Move message to a different folder.
Add a flag to message.   Delete message.
Copy selected text.   View other messages.
Print message.   Change message font size.

Reply to or forward message.

Message header.

Message contents (text and graphics).

To read a fax, double-click it in the Inbox. The fax will be opened in the fax viewer provided by the fax information service. Figure 43-4 shows a fax displayed in the fax viewer supplied by the Microsoft Fax software; this viewer lets you view the fax at various levels of magnification, print it, and manipulate its image in several different ways.

V

Microsoft Access

FIGURE 43-4.
Viewing a fax in the
Fax Viewer window dis-
played by the Microsoft
Fax software.

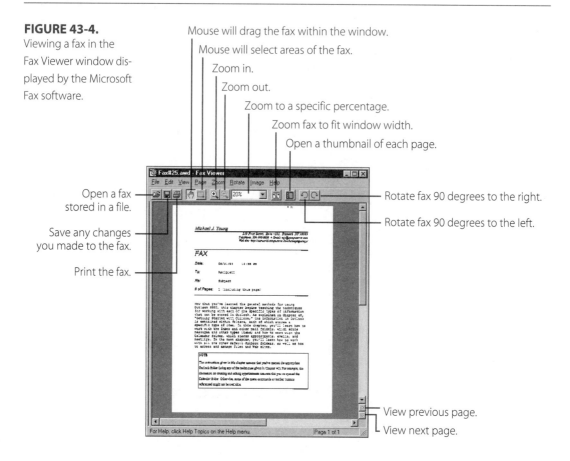

Mouse will drag the fax within the window.

Mouse will select areas of the fax.

Zoom in.

Zoom out.

Zoom to a specific percentage.

Zoom fax to fit window width.

Open a thumbnail of each page.

Open a fax stored in a file.

Save any changes you made to the fax.

Print the fax.

Rotate fax 90 degrees to the right.

Rotate fax 90 degrees to the left.

View previous page.

View next page.

Sending Messages

You can reply to or forward a message you have received, or you can
send a new message. To reply to or forward a message, first select the
message in the Inbox (or another mail folder where you've stored it),
and then click one of the following three buttons on the Standard
toolbar (or choose one of the commands that have the same labels
from the Actions menu):

Reply *Reply to All* *Forward*

If you click Reply, a new message will be sent back to the sender of
the selected message. If you click Reply To All, a message will be sent
to the sender and to all other recipients of the selected message. (As
you'll see, a message can be sent to more than one person.) If you
click Forward, a copy of the selected message will be sent to the recipient or recipients that you specify.

Receiving and Sending Faxes with the Internet Only Installation

When you use Outlook's Internet Only installation, faxes are received and sent using the integrated fax feature (Symantec WinFax Starter Edition), which works somewhat differently from the Microsoft Fax information service used in the Corporate Or Workgroup installation:

- To read a fax, first view it in the Preview pane or open it in the Message form, which will display information about the fax. The actual fax is contained in an attachment to the message. Double-click this attachment to read the fax in the Quick Fax Viewer.

- To send a fax, choose New Fax Message from the Actions menu (*not* New Mail Message). The New Fax Message command will open a Fax form, rather than running the Compose New Fax Wizard as it does in the Corporate Or Workgroup installation. (The Fax form has the same design as the Message form.)

- The Fax form's Tools menu doesn't have a Fax Addressing Wizard command. However, you can type a fax number directly into the To box by entering it in the format *fax@111-1111*, or *fax@9w111-1111* (which dials 9 to reach an outside line and then waits for a dial tone). And of course you can select a fax number by clicking the To button and selecting an address book entry or Contact folder item that has a fax number.

To send a new e-mail message or fax, choose New Mail Message from the Actions menu, or just press Ctrl+N. An alternative way to send a fax is to choose New Fax Message from the Actions menu. (This command is provided by the Microsoft Fax information service.) The New Fax Message command runs the Compose New Fax Wizard, which helps you compose a fax consisting of one or more of the following elements: a cover sheet, a typed note, and the contents of one or more files. The wizard also lets you schedule the fax for later delivery, rather than sending it immediately.

Note that you can also reply to or forward a received e-mail message that you have opened in the Message form—or create a new message—using commands provided by the form. (See Figure 43-3, page 1023.)

When you reply to or forward a message or create a new one, Outlook opens a Message form, which you can use to compose and send your message, as shown in Figure 43-5, on page 1027. (An exception is that choosing New Fax Message from the Actions menu runs the Compose New Fax Wizard rather than opening a form.) Notice that the Message

Choosing the Format and Editor for New E-Mail Messages

Outlook lets you read and write e-mail messages in one of three different formats: HTML (hypertext markup language, the format used for Web pages), Microsoft Outlook Rich Text (which preserves character formatting), and plain text. When you reply to or forward an e-mail message, Outlook matches the format of the received message. When you create a new e-mail message, however, you can select the format.

To select the default format for all new e-mail messages you send, choose Options from the Tools menu, click the Mail Format tab, and select the format from the Send In This Message Format list box.

If you've installed Microsoft Word, you can select the Use Microsoft Word To Edit E-Mail Messages option on the Mail Format tab to use Word as your editor for all new e-mail messages you create, rather than using the built-in Outlook message editor. Word will create the messages in the format you have selected in the Send In This Message Format list box. All received messages will also be opened in Word, unless the message is in HTML format. (HTML messages are always opened in the Outlook editor.)

When you create a new e-mail message, you can select a different format for that specific message, overriding the current selection on the Mail Format tab. To do this, point to New Mail Message Using on the Actions menu, and choose a command from the submenu. If you choose Plain Text, Microsoft Outlook Rich Text, or HTML (No Stationery), the message will be created in the corresponding format using Word (if Word is selected as your default e-mail editor on the Mail Format tab), or using the built-in Outlook message editor (if Word *isn't* selected as your default editor). If you choose Microsoft Word (*format*)—where *format* is the name of the e-mail format currently selected on the Mail Format tab (Plain Text, Rich Text, or HTML)—the message will be created in Word, whether or not Word is your default e-mail editor, and the message will have the indicated format.

You can also create and e-mail an Office document by pointing to New Mail Message Using on the Actions menu, pointing to Microsoft Office on the submenu, and then choosing the type of document you want from the Microsoft Office submenu. You can choose Microsoft Access Data Page, Microsoft Excel Worksheet, Microsoft PowerPoint Slide, or Microsoft Word Document. The corresponding Office application will start, a new document will be opened, and a message header will be displayed above the document. (The header contains fields for the message recipient and subject, and is similar to the one shown in Figure 43-5.) After you have created the document and filled in the header, click the Send button on the header to convert the document to HTML format and send it using Outlook, which will process the document just like an e-mail message created within Outlook.

FIGURE 43-5.

The Message form as it appears when you choose New Mail Message from the Actions menu to send a new message (this message is in HTML format).

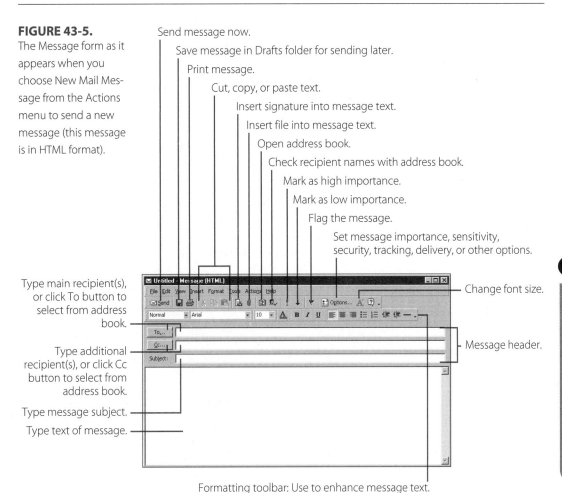

Send message now.

Save message in Drafts folder for sending later.

Print message.

Cut, copy, or paste text.

Insert signature into message text.

Insert file into message text.

Open address book.

Check recipient names with address book.

Mark as high importance.

Mark as low importance.

Flag the message.

Set message importance, sensitivity, security, tracking, delivery, or other options.

Type main recipient(s), or click To button to select from address book.

Type additional recipient(s), or click Cc button to select from address book.

Type message subject.

Type text of message.

Change font size.

Message header.

Microsoft Access

Formatting toolbar: Use to enhance message text.

form shown in Figure 43-5 is quite similar to the Message form displayed when you view a message you have received (shown in Figure 43-3, page 1023). The primary difference is that the Message form for sending a message contains text boxes that allow you to enter or modify the header information (that is, the message recipients and subject). Keep in mind that the look of the Message form and the options it provides can vary depending upon the message format that's being used.

While you're working on your message, Outlook will save a copy of the message every three minutes in the Drafts folder. You can change the folder where unsent messages are saved, as well as the frequency of automatic saves, by choosing Options from the Tools menu, clicking the E-Mail Options button on the Preferences tab, and then clicking the Advanced E-Mail Options button.

NOTE

To send a message that you have created in the Message form as a fax, you can't merely type the fax number into the To text box. Rather, you have to click the To button to select the fax number from an address book in the Select Names dialog box. (When the Select Names dialog box is opened, you can create a new permanent or temporary address-book entry for the fax number if one doesn't already exist.) Alternatively, you can choose Fax Addressing Wizard from the Message form's Tools menu, enter the fax number as prompted, and then click the To button in the message header to add this fax number to the To text box.

Usually, if you create a message by choosing the Reply, Reply To All, or Forward command, the large text box in the Message form initially contains the text of the original message. This provides the recipient with a copy of the message that you're replying to or forwarding. You can then type your reply into the text box (or add your own comments if you're forwarding a message). Note, however, that you can choose whether to include the original message text in a reply or forwarded message, and you can adjust the format of this text, by choosing Options from the Tools menu, clicking the E-Mail Options button on the Preferences tab, and choosing options in the On Replies And Forwards area of the E-Mail Options dialog box.

Figure 43-5 shows the Message form as it appears when the message is being created in the HTML format. (See the sidebar "Choosing the Format and Editor for New E-Mail Messages," page 1026) When you create a message in HTML, the Outlook Message form provides several formatting commands that aren't available with other formats. For

Using HTML Stationery

When you use the HTML e-mail format (see the previous sidebar), you can get a head start in producing attractive e-mail messages by basing them on *HTML stationery* rather than creating them from scratch. HTML stationery adds initial content to a new message, which might include a background color, background graphics, or boilerplate text. After you create a message using stationery, you can customize these elements if you want, and you can add your own text.

Keep in mind, however, that some e-mail recipients can't read messages formatted in HTML. (The recipient's e-mail server and e-mail reading program must support the HTML format, and some of them don't.) Normally, a recipient whose mail system doesn't support HTML will receive a plain-text version of the message. So before expending a lot of creative effort designing beautiful HTML messages, you might send a few text messages to determine whether your recipients can read HTML e-mail.

Insert
Horizontal Line

example, you can choose Horizontal Line from the Insert menu, or you can click the Insert Horizontal Line button on the Formatting toolbar to insert a horizontal dividing line into the message text. You can choose Picture from the Insert menu to insert a graphic image that's displayed within the message text. You can format various elements of your message text by choosing standard styles (such as Heading 1 or Bulleted List) from the Style submenu of the Format menu or from the Style list box on the Formatting toolbar. And you can choose Picture or Color

---

Using HTML Stationery   *continued*

You can select default stationery that'll be used for all new messages you create. To do this, choose Options from the Tools menu, click the Mail Format tab, and make sure that HTML is selected in the Send In This Message Format list box and that the Use Microsoft Word To Edit E-Mail Messages option is deselected. (You can't use Outlook stationery with Word.) Then, on this same tab, select the name of the stationery you want to use in the Use This Stationery By Default list box. (Choose the None option if you want to design your HTML messages from scratch without using stationery.) If you click the Stationery Picker button, you can see a preview image of each type of stationery, edit stationery, remove it, create new custom stationery, or download more stationery from Microsoft's Web site (by clicking the Get More Stationery button).

If you want to use different stationery for a particular message, overriding the default, create the new message by pointing to New Mail Message Using on the Actions menu, and then choosing the stationery you want from the submenu:

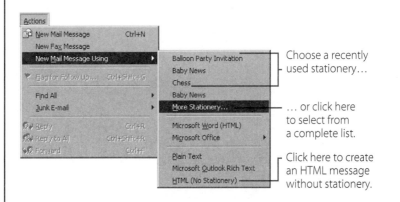

Note that selecting stationery—or the HTML (No Stationery) command—from this submenu lets you create a message in HTML format even if HTML isn't your current default e-mail format; the Outlook message editor or Word will appear, depending on which you've chosen as your default e-mail editor.

E-Mail File Attachments

Attaching a file to an e-mail message is a convenient way to send an Office document, another type of data file, or a program to a colleague or friend. To attach a file to an e-mail message, choose File from the Message form's Insert menu, or click the Insert File button on the form's Standard toolbar. Then, in the Insert File dialog box, select the file and select the Attachment option near the bottom of the dialog box. Alternatively, you can simply drag a file from the Windows Explorer or other file-viewing window to the large text box in the Message form. The attached file will be represented by an icon within the text of your message or in a separate pane at the bottom of the form.

When you receive an e-mail message that contains a file attachment, you can immediately open the file by opening the message and double-clicking the icon for the attachment. Or, if the Preview pane is displayed, you can just select the document in the Information Viewer, click the paperclip icon in the upper right corner of the Preview pane, and choose the name of the attached file from the drop-down menu. Using either method, you must have a program installed that can open the specific type of file.

Alternatively, you can save the attached file in a separate disk file by choosing Save Attachments from the File menu of the Message form, or by just dragging the icon for the attachment to the desired folder in Windows Explorer. Or, you can select the message in the Information Viewer, point to Save Attachments on the File menu, choose the name of the attached file from the submenu, and select a folder to place it in.

When you send an e-mail message across the Internet and attach a *binary* file—that is, an Office document, program, or other file that doesn't consist of plain text—the file data must be *encoded* using a standard Internet format. (The Internet e-mail protocol wasn't designed to transfer binary data. Encoding translates binary data into a sequence of standard characters that can be sent by e-mail.) The most common formats are MIME (Multi-part Internet Mail Extension) and UUE (Unix to Unix Encode).

Normally, your Internet e-mail server will encode outgoing binary file attachments and decode incoming binary attachments, so you don't even have to think about it. However, some servers don't encode outgoing attachments, and some servers don't decode incoming attachments in particular formats. (For example, at the time of this writing, the CompuServe Internet e-mail server doesn't decode incoming binary attachments that are in UUE format, and an attachment appears as a seemingly random sequence of characters.) In these cases, you have to encode or decode your file attachments manually. To do this, you can use a shareware utility such as Transfer Pro (which you can download from many locations on the Internet).

from the Background submenu of the Format menu to assign a graphic image or solid color to the background of the message text.

If you send and receive e-mail over a network, clicking the Send button in the Message form usually sends an e-mail message immediately. Fax messages are also sent immediately, unless you have configured your fax information service to delay sending faxes until a specified time.

However, if you send and receive e-mail by means of a dial-up connection, clicking Send normally just copies an e-mail message to your Outbox folder. The message isn't sent until you choose Send from the Tools menu, which connects to your e-mail service and uploads all outgoing e-mail messages stored in the Outbox. The messages in your Outbox will also be sent if you choose one of the commands for sending and receiving messages—namely, clicking the Send/Receive button on the Standard toolbar, pressing F5, choosing a command from the Send/Receive submenu of the Tools menu, or running the Remote Connection Wizard. *(These commands are described in the section "Reading Messages," page 1016.)* Finally, the Outbox messages might be sent automatically if you have configured an e-mail information service to exchange your e-mail at scheduled times.

Organizing Messages

As you begin to accumulate messages in your Inbox, you might want to do some housekeeping. First, you might want to remove or archive some of your older messages. *For instructions on removing and archiving Outlook items, see "Removing Items," page 1001.*

You might also want to store some of your messages in a different mail folder. For example, you could create a folder named Saved E-Mail, and then move to this folder all the e-mail messages that you want to save. *To create a new folder, follow the instructions given in "Working with Outlook Folders," page 1003.* In the Create New Folder dialog box, be sure to specify that the new folder is to contain Mail Items. *If you want to create a shortcut on the Outlook Bar for a newly created folder, follow the directions given in "Modifying the Outlook Bar," page 1008.*

The following is a way to move one or more messages from the Inbox to another folder. Note that you can use this same general method to move other types of Outlook items stored in any Outlook folder.

1 In the Inbox (or other folder), select the message or messages (or other type of items) that you want to move. To select multiple items, click the first one, and then press Ctrl while clicking each additional one.

2 Click the Move To Folder button on the Standard toolbar, and choose Move To Folder from the drop-down menu that appears:

Folders that you've
recently moved —
items to

Opens Move To —
Folder dialog box

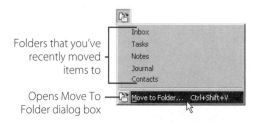

Alternatively, you can choose Move To Folder from the Edit menu or press Ctrl+Shift+V. Outlook will open the Move Items dialog box, shown here:

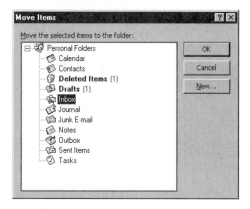

The Move To Folder drop-down menu on the Standard toolbar also lists folders that you have recently moved items to. As a shortcut, you can simply choose one of these folders rather than completing the remaining steps in this procedure.

3 If you haven't yet created the destination folder, you can create one now by clicking the New button.

4 In the list in the Move Items dialog box, select the folder where you want to store the items you're moving, and click OK.

You can copy an item to a different folder by choosing Copy To Folder from the Edit menu, rather than issuing the Move To Folder command in step 2 of the above procedure.

V

Microsoft Access

Streamline Your Copy and Move Operations

You can more quickly move or copy an item by selecting the item in the Outlook window and then doing one of the following:

■ Choose Cut from the Edit menu to move it or Copy to copy it, open the destination folder, and choose Paste from the Edit menu.

■ Press Ctrl+X to move the item or Ctrl+C to copy the item, open the destination folder, and press Ctrl+V to paste the item.

■ To move the item drag it to a shortcut for the destination folder on the Outlook Bar. You can copy the item by pressing Ctrl while you drag. If the destination folder's shortcut isn't currently visible, you can hold the mouse pointer over a group button to open another group, or you can hold it over the bottom or top area of a group to scroll to the shortcut you want.

You can also use the Organize tool to help you do some of your housekeeping. *General instructions for displaying and using the Organize tool are given in "Using the Organize Tool," page 1002.* This tool provides two useful pages of features that are available only for mail folders:

■ On the Using Colors page, you can have Outlook color-code certain messages in the current view. See Figure 43-6, on the next page.

■ On the Junk E-Mail page, you can have Outlook automatically color-code, move, or delete junk e-mail messages, or messages that have adult content, that arrive in your Inbox. (To delete junk or adult-content e-mail, just have it moved to the Deleted Items folder.) See Figure 43-7, on the following page.

Improve Junk E-Mail Filtering by Compiling Lists

Outlook identifies junk e-mail and adult-content e-mail by searching incoming messages for key phrases (such as *order today* or *must be 18*). You can also add e-mail addresses to a junk e-mail list or to an adult-content e-mail list. Any message from an address in one of your lists will be identified as junk e-mail or adult-content e-mail, regardless of its content. These lists are initially empty, until you begin adding addresses. To quickly add the address of a message you have received to one of the lists, right-click the message in a mail folder, point to Junk E-Mail on the pop-up menu, and then choose either Add To Junk Senders List or Add To Adult Content Senders List from the submenu.

FIGURE 43-6.
The Using Colors page of the Organize tool for mail folders.

To color-code messages received from or sent to a particular person, select options in the list boxes, type name of person in the text box, and then click Apply Color.

Click here to modify the conditional formatting you selected, or to define additional conditional formatting rules.

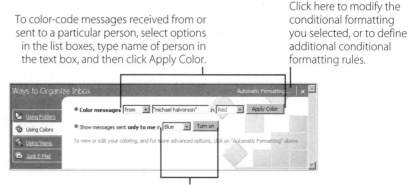

To color-code messages that have no recipients other than you, select a color in the list box and then click Turn On.

FIGURE 43-7.
The Junk E-Mail page of the Organize tool for mail folders.

Color-code or move junk e-mail.

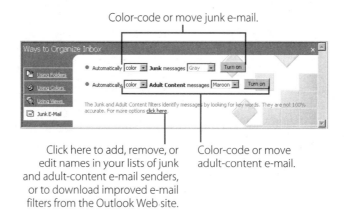

Click here to add, remove, or edit names in your lists of junk and adult-content e-mail senders, or to download improved e-mail filters from the Outlook Web site.

Color-code or move adult-content e-mail.

Calendar

You can use the Calendar folder to schedule appointments, events, or meetings. In Outlook, an *appointment* is an activity that consumes a block of your own time; for example, an interview that you're planning to conduct next Wednesday morning from 9 to 9:30 is an appointment. An *event* is an occurrence that lasts for at least 24 hours but doesn't necessarily fully consume your time; for example, your birthday next May 21 is an event. A *meeting* is similar to an appointment but involves other people and resources *that you schedule using Outlook*; an example is a conference with your team of programmers that takes place in a conference room and uses a computer projector, which you've scheduled using Outlook.

Figure 43-8 shows the Day/Week/Month view of the Calendar folder. The TaskPad area of the window is actually a view of the Tasks folder, not the Calendar folder; it's included in this view of the Calendar folder to help you schedule time for working on your pending tasks. *The Tasks folder is discussed in its own section, titled "Tasks," on page 1055.*

FIGURE 43-8.
The Calendar folder in the Day/Week/Month view, before information has been added.

Date Navigator

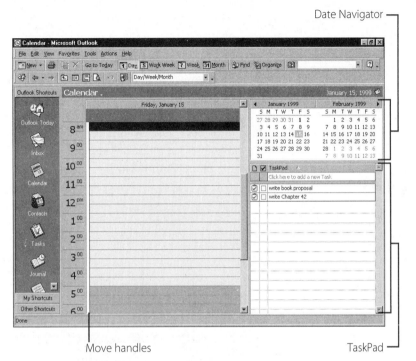

Move handles

TaskPad

To view or modify your schedule for a particular day, click the date in the Date Navigator (the monthly calendar in the upper right pane of the Information Viewer of the Outlook window). To quickly view today's schedule, you can click the Go To Today button on the Standard toolbar. (Notice also that the current day in the Date Navigator has a box drawn around it.) To view several days at once, click the first date in the Date Navigator, and then press Ctrl while clicking each additional date.

Go to Today

You can click the Day, Work Week, Week, or Month button on the Standard toolbar to modify the amount of detail shown in the Calendar:

V

Microsoft Access

(In Figure 43-8, the Day button is selected.) *You can select other views of the Calendar folder by using the techniques discussed in "Using Different Views," page 992.*

Scheduling Appointments

You can schedule either a one-time appointment or a *recurring* appointment. A recurring appointment is one that occurs at regular intervals, such as a basketball game you play every Friday at 4:00 PM.

To schedule either type of appointment, begin by clicking the day and time of the appointment in the Information Viewer of the Outlook window. (This step is optional, because you can set the day and time later.) Then choose New Appointment from the Actions menu or press Ctrl+N, and fill out the Appointment form as shown in Figure 43-9. Consult Table 43-1 for help in completing the form.

FIGURE 43-9.

Defining an appointment in the Appointment form.

Insert a file in the appointment text.

Click to set up a recurring appointment.

Invite attendees to a meeting
(don't click this for an appointment).

Assign high or low importance.

Delete an appointment.

Open other appointments (only if viewing existing appointment).

Print the appointment.

Click here when you've finished defining the appointment.

If you want, you can type a note for the appointment here.

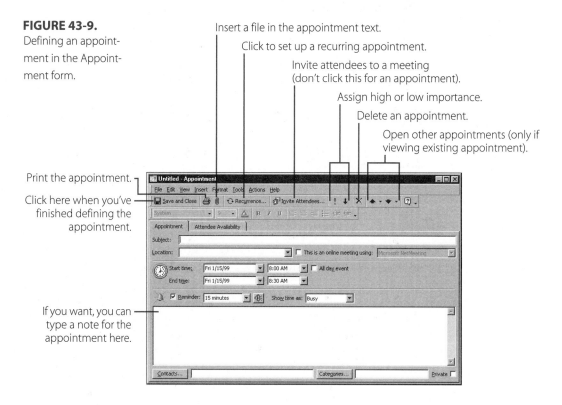

TABLE 43-1.   Controls on the Appointment Form

Appointment Form Control	How to Use the Control
Subject text box	Type the appointment subject, which will be displayed in the Information Viewer.
Location list box	Type or select the room or geographical location for the appointment. (The drop-down list displays previously entered locations.)
This Is An Online Meeting Using check box and list box	Select this check box if your appointment is for an online conference, and in the list box choose the online conferencing program that you will use (for example, Microsoft NetMeeting or Microsoft NetShow). When you select this check box and choose a program, the Appointment form displays any additional controls that are required to supply details on the conference (for example, the directory server address and the organizer's e-mail address for a NetMeeting conference).
Start Time and End Time list boxes	Type or select the starting and ending dates and times for the appointment.
All Day Event check box	Select to convert the appointment to an event. (Don't select this option if you're defining an appointment.)
Reminder check box, list box, and button	Select the Reminder check box to have Outlook display a message reminding you of the appointment. In the list box, type or select the amount of time prior to the appointment that the reminder appears. Click the speaker button to have a sound played when the reminder is displayed.
Show Time As list box	Select an option in the list box (Free, Tentative, Busy, or Out Of Office) to specify the free/busy status of the block of time consumed by the appointment. If your computer is attached to an Exchange Server network, or if you chose the Internet Only installation, your choice will affect the status of the block of time when you or another Outlook user runs the meeting planner to schedule a meeting that includes you. *(See the section "Scheduling Meetings," page 1042.)* In certain views of the Information Viewer, the appointment will be color-coded to indicate its free/busy status. (A description of the colors Outlook uses is given following this table.)
Contacts button and text box	To associate the appointment with one or more contacts, click the Contacts button, and select one or more items from your Contacts folder. The selected contact(s) will be displayed in the adjoining text box. *As you'll learn in "Contacts," page 1048, the Activities tab of the Contact form displays all appointments (and other Outlook items) that are associated with that contact.*

V

Microsoft Access

(continued)

TABLE 43-1. *continued*

Appointment Form Controls	Purpose
Categories button and text box	Click this button to assign one or more categories, such as Business or Personal, to the appointment. The categories you select will appear in the text box to the right of the button.
Private check box	This option is effective only if your computer is attached to an Exchange Server network and you've shared your Calendar folder. Select the check box to prevent other Outlook users from reading the appointment if they open your Calendar folder.
Attendee Availability tab	This tab is useful only if your computer is attached to an Exchange Server network or if you chose the Internet Only installation of Outlook. Use options on this tab to schedule a meeting. (Don't use it for an appointment.) *See the section "Scheduling Meetings," page 1042, for a description of a more straightforward method for setting up a meeting.*

To create a recurring appointment, choose Recurrence from the Appointment form's Actions menu, click the Recurrence button on the form's Standard toolbar, or press Ctrl+G. Outlook will display the Appointment Recurrence dialog box, in which you specify the appointment time and indicate the frequency of the recurrence and how long it is to continue. See Figure 43-10.

When you click OK in the Appointment Recurrence dialog box, Outlook will return you to the Appointment form, which will now be labeled Recurring Appointment and will no longer include the appointment time fields (because, for a recurring appointment, the times are set using the Appointment Recurrence dialog box). You can convert the appointment

FIGURE 43-10.
Setting up a recurring appointment.

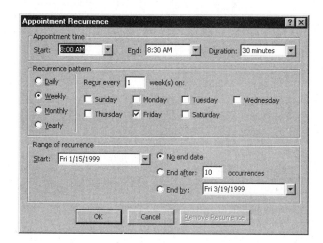

back to a one-time appointment by reopening the Appointment Recurrence dialog box and clicking the Remove Recurrence button.

When you close the Appointment (or Recurring Appointment) form, the newly defined appointment will be displayed within the appropriate box in the Information Viewer of the Outlook window. Here's how an appointment looks in the Day/Week/Month view:

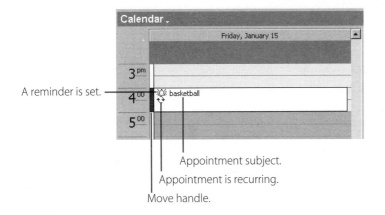

A reminder is set.

Appointment subject.

Appointment is recurring.

Move handle.

When you select the Day or Work Week view option, the color of the move handle—or the color of the entire border around the appointment if it's selected—indicates its free/busy status (the selection you made in the Show Time As list box): Free Time is marked in white, Tentative in light blue, Busy in dark blue, and Out Of Office in dark magenta. You can change the free/busy status of an appointment by right-clicking it and choosing one of the four options on the Show Time As submenu on the pop-up menu.

You can rapidly schedule time for working on a pending task that's stored in your Tasks folder by selecting the time in the Calendar folder and then dragging the task from the TaskPad to any part of the Calendar folder.

To move the appointment to another time, drag the move handle to the desired time slot. To copy the appointment, press Ctrl while you drag. To delete an appointment, select it by clicking its move handle, and press the Delete key (or click anywhere on the appointment, and click the Delete button on the Standard toolbar).

Delete

To open an appointment so that you can view or modify the appointment information, double-click its move handle. For a one-time appointment, Outlook will immediately open the appointment in the

Microsoft Access

Appointment form. For a recurring appointment, however, Outlook will first display the following dialog box.

If you choose Open This Occurrence, you'll be able to change the specific appointment that you selected, without affecting the other

Exchanging Appointment Information on the Internet

You can exchange appointment information on the Internet using the standard vCalendar Internet format. For example, to set up an appointment with a colleague, you could enter all appointment information into your Calendar folder—the time, location, notes on the topics to be discussed, and so on. Then, rather than retyping all this information into an e-mail message or memo, you could simply e-mail the entire Appointment in vCalendar format to your colleague, who could then import the appointment into his or her own Calendar folder in Outlook or into any other calendar program that supports the vCalendar format.

To e-mail an appointment, you can save a copy of it in a file in vCalendar format and then attach this file to an e-mail message addressed to the person you want to receive the appointment. To save an appointment in a vCalendar file, select it in your Calendar folder and choose Save As from the File menu. Then, in the Save As dialog box, select vCalendar Format(*.vcs) in the Save As Type list box, and specify a file name and location. (The file will have the .vcs extension.) Next, address an e-mail message to the appointment recipient, attach the vCalendar file to this message as explained in the sidebar "E-Mail File Attachments" on page 1030, type into the large text box any additional information that you want to send along with the appointment, and click the Send button. The message recipient can then import the vCalendar file attachment into his or her own Outlook Calendar folder (as described next) or into any other personal information manager that can import vCalendar files.

If someone else sends you an e-mail message containing a vCalendar file attachment, the easiest way to add the appointment to your Calendar folder is to open the message in the Message form and then drag the icon for the vCalendar file attachment to the shortcut for your Calendar folder on the Outlook Bar. This will create a new appointment and will open it in the Appointment form. Click the Save And Close button to save the item in your Calendar folder.

appointments in the recurring series. If, however, you select Open The Series, you'll be able to modify the features of the entire recurring series of appointments.

Scheduling Events

To schedule an event, choose New All Day Event from the Actions menu. Outlook will then display the Event form. The Event form is the same as the Appointment form shown in Figure 43-9, page 1036, except for the following:

- *Event* is displayed in the title bar rather than *Appointment*.

- The list boxes for specifying the starting and ending hours are removed, leaving only the list boxes for setting the starting and ending days, because an event is always assigned to one or more whole days.

- The All Day Event check box is initially checked. To define an Event, be sure to leave this box checked; if you remove the check, the form will be converted to an Appointment form.

- The initial value in the Show Time As list box is Free rather than Busy, because the time occupied by an event is normally marked as free. Unlike an appointment, an event generally doesn't fully consume your time. For an explanation of this list box, see the item "Show Time As list box" in Table 43-1, page 1037.

Complete the fields in the Event form following the instructions given in Figure 43-9 (page 1036) and Table 43-1 (page 1037). To create a recurring event, which is analogous to a recurring appointment, choose Recurrence from the form's Actions menu, click the Recurrence button on the Event form's Standard toolbar, or press Ctrl+G, and then fill in the times. For example, you might want to mark a friend's birthday as a recurring yearly event.

When you close the Event form, you'll notice that the event is displayed in a banner at the top of the list of appointments:

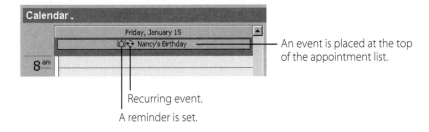

Recurring event.
A reminder is set.

V

Microsoft Access

Don't Miss Any Holidays

You can have Outlook add event items to your Calendar folder for all traditional holidays. To do this, choose Options from the Tools menu, click the Calendar Options button on the Preferences tab of the Options dialog box, click the Add Holidays button in the Calendar Options dialog box, and then select the types of holidays you want to include (United States, Canada, Christian Religious Holidays, and so on).

Scheduling Meetings

If your computer is attached to a network running Microsoft Exchange Server, you can use Outlook's meeting planner to schedule a meeting at a time when all attendees are free and all required resources (for example, a conference room and a computer projector) are available. You can also have Outlook send invitations to all attendees and requests for all resources, and you'll receive the replies to these invitations and requests in your Inbox.

You can use the following method to schedule a meeting using Outlook:

1   Open the Calendar folder, and choose Plan A Meeting from the Actions menu.

  Outlook will open the Plan A Meeting form.

2   In the Plan A Meeting form, enter a list of meeting attendees and required resources, and choose a meeting time when all attendees and resources are available, as shown in Figure 43-11. When you're done, click the Make Meeting button in the Plan A Meeting form.

  Outlook will then open a Meeting form, which is similar to the Appointment form shown in Figure 43-9, page 1036.

By default, for each Outlook user only two months of scheduling information is available to the meeting planner. Therefore, you can't normally plan a meeting that's more than two months in the future. Also by default, scheduling information is updated every 15 minutes. Therefore, the meeting planner won't immediately detect a change in someone's schedule. You can modify either of these default values for your own free/busy schedule by choosing Options from the Tools menu, clicking the Calendar Options button on the Preferences tab, and then clicking the Free/Busy Options button in the Calendar Options dialog box.

FIGURE 43-11.
Planning a meeting time.

Meeting time: Click on a different time slot to change its time; drag an edge to change its duration.

Attendees and resources are listed here.

Light blue indicates attendee or resource availability is tentative.

Dark blue indicates attendee or resource is busy.

Dark magenta indicates attendee is out of the office.

Click icon at left of attendee or resource to disable or enable sending an invitation.

Change hours shown or zoom time display.

Add attendees or resources to All Attendees list.

Find earlier free time.

Change options for finding free time.

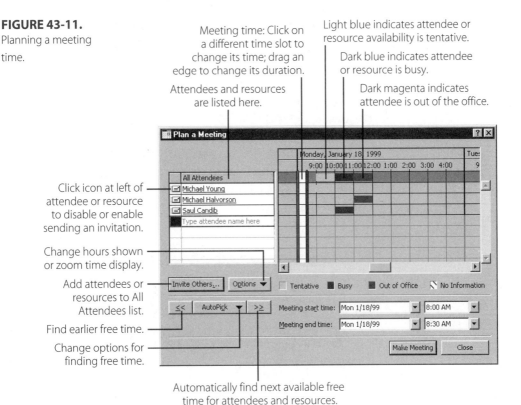

Automatically find next available free time for attendees and resources.

3 In the Meeting form, enter the subject and location for the meeting, and enter or revise other information as necessary. (Refer to Figure 43-9, page 1036, and Table 43-1, page 1037.) To create a recurring meeting, which is analogous to a recurring appointment, choose Recurrence from the Actions menu, click the Recurrence button, or press Ctrl+G, and then enter the times into the Appointment Recurrence dialog box (shown in Figure 43-10, page 1038).

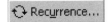

4 Click the Send button in the Meeting form to send an invitation to all meeting attendees and a request for all meeting resources.

The new meeting will be shown in your Calendar folder in the same way as an appointment (except that in some views, a meeting will be marked by an icon that shows the heads of two people, to indicate its group nature), and you can use the techniques described for

Microsoft Access

appointments to open, move, copy, or delete it. Also, for each person you invited or resource you requested, the following occurs:

- An invitation or request message is delivered to the Inbox of the recipient (that is, the Inbox of the attendee or the person managing the requested resource). When the recipient opens the message, it's displayed in the Meeting form (rather than in the standard e-mail form), which makes it easy for him or her to respond. The recipient can reply fast by clicking the Accept, Tentative, or Decline button on the form's Standard toolbar (see Figure 43-12), and can then edit the subject or add a comment if desired before the reply is sent. The reply appears in your Inbox.

FIGURE 43-12.

A meeting request message received by an attendee, opened in the Meeting form.

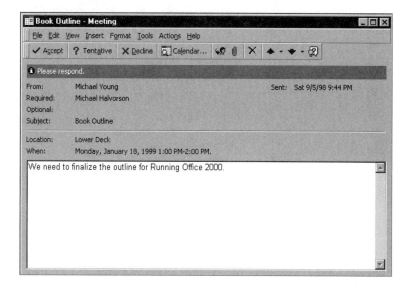

- The meeting is added to the recipient's Calendar folder, and the time is initially marked as tentative.

- When the recipient replies to the message, the meeting is marked in the recipient's Calendar folder as busy if it is accepted, it's left as tentative if it is tentatively accepted, or it's deleted from the Calendar folder if it is declined.

NOTE

An Outlook mailbox account must be set up for each person and each resource that is to be scheduled for a meeting. In previous versions of Outlook, a resource manager had to log on to the resource account and manually reply to meeting requests. In Outlook 2000, however, resource requests can be handled automatically. To set this up, the resource manager needs to log on to the resource account, choose Options from the Tools menu, click the Calendar Options button on the Preferences tab, click the Resource Scheduling button in the Calendar Options dialog box, and then select the desired options and set the required permissions. The manager can then log off. From then on, replies will be sent automatically, without anyone logged on to the resource account.

Scheduling Meetings with the Internet Only Installation

You can also use the Internet Only installation of Outlook—without Exchange Server—to schedule meetings, provided that your attendees have published their schedules of free/busy times on the Internet. Free/busy schedules are published in a standard Internet format known as iCalendar.

An Outlook user can set up automatic publishing of his or her free/busy schedule by choosing Options from the Tools menu, clicking the Calendar Options button on the Preferences tab, clicking the Free/Busy Options button in the Calendar Options dialog box, and entering the required information into the Free/Busy Options dialog box (the number of months of scheduling information to publish, the frequency at which it's published, and the Internet address where it's posted).

For each person you want to invite to your meeting, you need to create a Contacts folder item and enter the Internet address of his or her free/busy information into the Internet Free-Busy Address box on the Details tab of the Contact form. *(Contacts items are discussed in the next chapter.)* You can also specify a default address to be used with attendees for whom you haven't entered a specific free/busy address on the Contact form. You enter the default address in the Search At This URL text box of the Free/Busy Options dialog box, described in the previous paragraph.

In the Plan A Meeting form, you include each attendee by clicking the Invite Others button to select his or her name from your list of Contact items. In this form, you also need to click the Options button and choose Update Free/Busy from the drop-down menu to update the free/busy information for all attendees. You can then use the Plan A Meeting form as described in the adjoining section.

For more information, see the Outlook online Help topic "Sending Internet Meeting Requests," which is within the "Using Internet Only Features" book.

V

Microsoft Access

Using Outlook to Manage Contacts, Tasks, and Other Types of Information

This chapter continues the discussion on the techniques for working with each of the specific types of information that can be stored in Microsoft Outlook. *As explained in Chapter 41, "Getting Started Using Outlook," the information in Outlook is contained within folders, each of which stores a specific type of item.* The previous chapter covered the Inbox and other mail folders, as well as the Calendar folder. In this chapter, you'll learn how to work with the Contacts folder, which stores information on your business and personal contacts; the Tasks folder, which lets you manage personal or group projects; the Journal folder, which you can use to record events; and the Notes folder, which allows you to keep track of miscellaneous bits of free-form information. You'll also learn how to use Outlook to access and manage files on local or network disks, and to open Internet sites.

The instructions given in this chapter assume that you have opened the appropriate Outlook folder (using any of the techniques given in Chapter 41). For example, the discussion on creating and editing contact information assumes that you have opened the Contacts folder. Otherwise, some of the menu commands or toolbar buttons referenced might not be available.

Contacts

You can use the Contacts folder to store names, addresses, phone numbers, and other information for your business or personal contacts. To add a new contact, open the Contacts folder and choose New Contact from the Actions menu, click the New Contact button on the Standard toolbar, or press Ctrl+N. Outlook will open the Contact form. Enter the information for your contact as shown in Figure 44-1. Consult Table 44-1 for descriptions of selected controls on the form.

FIGURE 44-1.
Defining a new contact in the Contact form.

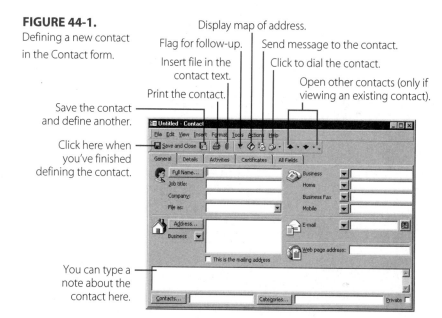

 When you click the Save And Close button on the Contact form to save a new contact, Outlook will notify you if you already have an existing contact with the same name. You can then save the contact as a separate item (Outlook allows you to have Contact items with duplicate names), or you can update the existing contact with the information from the form, rather than creating a new item.

TABLE 44-1.   Controls in the Contact Form

Contact Form Control	How to Use the Control
Full Name text box and button	Type the contact's full name into the text box or click the Full Name button for help in properly formatting the name.
File As list box	Type or select the way the contact should be filed in the Contacts folder (for example, under *Shannon O'Brien* or *O'Brien, Shannon*).
Telephone: down-arrow buttons and text boxes	Enter up to four phone numbers. For each one, first click the down arrow if necessary to change the category (Business, Home, Car, Pager, and so on), and then type the number into the adjoining text box. If you omit the area code, Outlook inserts your current area code (which you can set using the Modems item in the Control Panel and other places in Windows).
Address: down-arrow button, text box, and button	Enter up to three addresses. For each one, first click the down arrow to select a category (Business, Home, or Other). Then type the address into the text box or click the Address button for help in properly formatting the address.
This Is The Mailing Address check box	Select this check box if you want the currently displayed address to be the one printed by mail-merge programs, such as Microsoft Word.
E-Mail: down-arrow button, text box, and address-book button	Enter up to three e-mail addresses. For each one, first click the down arrow to select a category (E-mail, E-mail 2, or E-mail 3), and then type the address into the text box or click the address-book button (to the right of the text box) to obtain the address from an address book.
Web Page Address text box	If the contact has a Web page, type the full URL into the text box, for example, *http://mspress.microsoft.com/*.
Contacts button and text box	To associate the contact with one or more other contacts, click the Contacts button, and select one or more items from your Contacts folder. The selected contact(s) will be displayed in the adjoining text box. The Activities tab of the Contact form (described later in this table) displays all contacts (and other Outlook items) that are associated with the current contact.
Categories button and text box	Click the button to assign one or more categories, such as Business or Personal, to the contact. The categories you select will appear in the text box to the right of the button.

VI

Microsoft Outlook

(continued)

TABLE 44-1. *continued*

Contact Form Control	How To Use The Control
Private check box	This option is effective only if your computer is attached to an Exchange Server network and you've shared your Contacts folder. Select this check box to prevent other Outlook users from reading the contact information if they open your Contacts folder.
Details tab	Enter additional information for the contact (Department, Profession, Birthday, NetMeeting settings, and so on).
Activities tab	View Outlook items that are associated with this contact. A message is associated with the contact if it has been sent to or received from the contact. Other types of Outlook items are associated with the contact if the contact is entered into the item's Contacts field.
Certificates tab	View, modify, or add certificates for the contact. A contact's certificate is a digital ID that Outlook uses to read encrypted e-mail from the contact.
All Fields tab	Access all fields of information on the contact, or create custom fields.

⭐ **TIP**

> **Get a Head Start in Creating Another Contact from the Same Company**
> If you want to enter a new contact that has the same company information as a contact you previously entered, select the previous contact in the Contacts folder, and then choose New Contact From Same Company (rather than New Contact) from the Actions menu. When the Contact form is opened, it will already contain the company information.

Figure 44-2 shows the Contacts folder in the Address Cards view, displaying three cards that have been added. (In this view, a contact item is termed a *card*.) To locate a specific contact, you can scroll through the cards, click a button on the right side to go to a specific alphabetical grouping, or click the Find button on the Standard toolbar to display the Find tool, which you can use to search for the contact. *(For information on using the Find tool, see "Finding Outlook Items or Disk Files," page 1009.)*

To view all the information for a contact—or to edit this information—open the contact's card by double-clicking the card's heading. The contact information will again be displayed in the Contact form shown in Figure 44-1. You can also edit any of the information displayed in the

FIGURE 44-2.

The Contacts folder in the Address Cards view.

Click here to locate a specific contact.

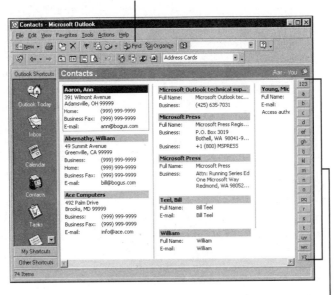

Click to view contacts whose names begin with the corresponding characters or numbers.

Information Viewer of the Outlook window—without opening the contact—by simply clicking the text you want to modify. (You can't, however, edit a heading in the Address Cards view. Also, to edit text in the Information Viewer, you must be sure the Allow In-Cell Editing option is enabled. You can find this option by pointing to Current View on the View menu, choosing Customize Current View from the submenu, and then clicking the Other Settings button in the View Summary dialog box.)

If your computer has a modem that shares a line with a telephone, you can have Outlook dial a phone number by selecting a contact in the Information Viewer, clicking the down arrow to the right of the AutoDialer button on the Standard toolbar, and choosing an appropriate command from the drop-down menu:

Dial phone number for selected contact.

Dial a number you dialed previously.

Dial a number on your list of speed-dial numbers.

Open New Call dialog box to dial a number you enter.

VI

Microsoft Outlook

(You can choose these same commands from the Call Contact submenu on the Actions menu.) To select dialing and modem options, or to define one or more speed-dial numbers, choose New Call from the menu shown above, and then click the Dialing Options button in the New Call dialog box.

Explore
Web Page

If you installed a Web browser on your computer and if you entered a Web page address for a contact (see Figure 44-1 and Table 44-1, pages 1048 and 1049), you can use Outlook to open that Web page. To do this, select the contact in the Information Viewer, and then click the Explore Web Page button on the Advanced toolbar or press Ctrl+Shift+X.

 TIP

> If a contact is open in a form, you can dial the number using commands on the form that are equivalent to those described in the Outlook window. And you can open the Web page by clicking directly on the address in the Web Page Address text box, by choosing Explore Web Page from the Actions menu, or by pressing Ctrl+Shift+X.

Creating Distribution Lists in Your Contacts Folder

In addition to creating a description of an individual contact in your Contacts folder, you can create a *distribution list*, which stores an entire set of contact names together with their e-mail or fax addresses. You can then send a message to all the contacts in the list by simply entering the distribution list into the To field of the Message form, rather than entering each of the individual addresses. For example, you could create a distribution list, named Students, containing the e-mail addresses of all members of a class you teach. To make a general announcement to the class, you could then address an e-mail message to the Students distribution list and it would be sent to all class members.

To create a distribution list, open your Contacts folder, choose New Distribution List from the Actions menu, and fill in the Distribution List form as shown in Figure 44-3, on page 1054.

To address a message to the members of a distribution list, click the To button in the header of the Message form, and select the name of the distribution list from your Contacts folder.

Exchanging Contact Information on the Internet

You can exchange contact information on the Internet using the standard Internet format for electronic business cards, which is known as vCard. For example, you could create an item for yourself in your Contacts folder—containing your name, address, phone numbers, e-mail address, and other information—and then send this item to colleagues on the Internet so that they could add you to their own Contacts folders in Outlook (or to any other personal information manager that can import contact descriptions in vCard format).

You can send contact information to someone on the Internet by opening your Contacts folder, selecting the item you want to send, and choosing Forward As vCard from the Actions menu. This will open the Message form displaying a new e-mail message, which will contain the contact information as a vCard file attachment. (The file will have the .vcf extension.) You can then fill in the To box and enter any other information you want to send along with the contact information, and click the Send button. The message recipient can import the vCard file attachment into his or her own Outlook Contacts folder (as described later in the sidebar) or into any other personal information manager that can import vCard files.

Alternatively, you can save any Contacts item as a vCard file using the Save As command on the File menu and then insert this file into any outgoing e-mail message as a file attachment. Also, if you use the Outlook e-mail editor (not Microsoft Word), you can have a vCard file attachment automatically inserted as a signature at the end of all your outgoing e-mail messages. To do this, choose Options from the Tools menu, click the Mail Format tab, click the Signature Picker button, click the New button, name your vCard and click the Next button, click the New vCard From Contact button, and select the Contacts item (or an item from another address book) that you want to insert at the end of your outgoing e-mail messages. Usually, of course, you would pick an item containing your own name, address, and other personal information.

If someone else sends you an e-mail message containing a vCard file attachment, the easiest way to add the contact information to your Contacts folder is to open the message in the Message form and then drag the icon for the vCard file attachment to the shortcut for your Contacts folder on the Outlook Bar. This will create a new Contacts item and open it in the Contact form—click the Save And Close button to save the item in your Contacts folder.

FIGURE 44-3.
Defining a new distribution list.

Type a name for the distribution list here.

If you want, you can type information on the distribution list on this tab.

Update all members by retrieving their current information from the Contacts folder or another address book.

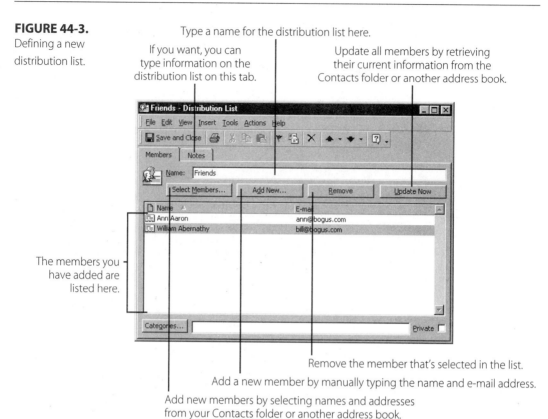

The members you have added are listed here.

Remove the member that's selected in the list.

Add a new member by manually typing the name and e-mail address.

Add new members by selecting names and addresses from your Contacts folder or another address book.

Using Your Contacts Folder to Generate Form Letters

You can have Outlook run Word's mail-merge feature to print form letters, envelopes, or labels, using selected items from your Contacts folder as the data source. You can also e-mail or fax form letters rather than print them. *(To learn about Word's mail-merge feature, see "Using Mail Merge for Large Mailings," page 392.)* Here are the steps:

1 Open your Contacts folder.

2 Select all the contacts that you want to receive the form letter or other item you're sending. (Recall that you can select multiple items by clicking the first one and then clicking each of the others while pressing Ctrl.) If you want to send the item to all contacts in the folder, you don't need to select them.

3 Choose Mail Merge from the Tools menu, and complete the Mail Merge Contacts dialog box as shown in Figure 44-4.

When you click OK in the Mail Merge Contacts dialog box, Word will start running and will open the main mail-merge document.

4 Enter into the document the desired fixed text (the text that is the same on all merge letters) as well as the required merge fields (the text that varies from letter to letter, derived from the Contacts folder). Then complete the merge operation, as explained in "Printing Form Letters," page 392.

FIGURE 44-4.

Selecting mail-merge options in the Mail Merge Contacts dialog box.

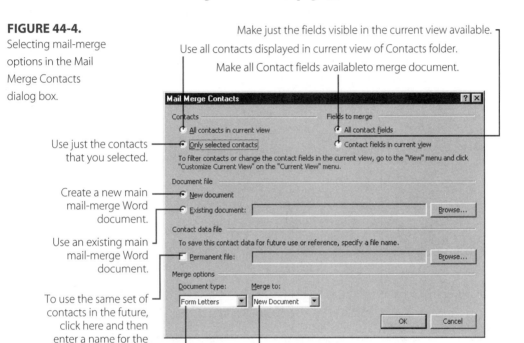

Make just the fields visible in the current view available.

Use all contacts displayed in current view of Contacts folder.

Make all Contact fields available to merge document.

Use just the contacts that you selected.

Create a new main mail-merge Word document.

Use an existing main mail-merge Word document.

To use the same set of contacts in the future, click here and then enter a name for the data set.

Select the desired destination for the merged information.

Select the type of document to be created.

Tasks

You can use the Tasks folder in Outlook to track short jobs that you need to complete or large projects that you're handling. You can manage tasks for yourself, or—if your computer is connected to an Exchange Server network—you can assign tasks to other people in your workgroup and track these tasks.

To start tracking a new task, open the Tasks folder and choose New Task from the Actions menu or press Ctrl+N. Outlook will open the Task form.

You can then enter information for the task as shown in Figures 44-5 and 44-6. Note that you'll need to enter or update some of the information after the task is partially or fully completed (for example, the status and percent complete entered into the Task tab, as well as the completion date and actual work hours entered into the Details tab).

Most fields of the Details tab are self-explanatory. Use the Companies box if you want to enter the names of one or more companies that are associated with the task. If you have been assigned the task and are still the task owner, the Update List box will display the names of all Outlook users who have a copy of the task that is updated whenever you change the task. If you assigned the task to another Outlook user and kept a copy, clicking the Create Unassigned Copy button converts your copy into a task that's owned by you. *(See the section "Assigning and Tracking Tasks," page 1059.)*

FIGURE 44-5.
Defining a task:
the Task tab of the
Task form.

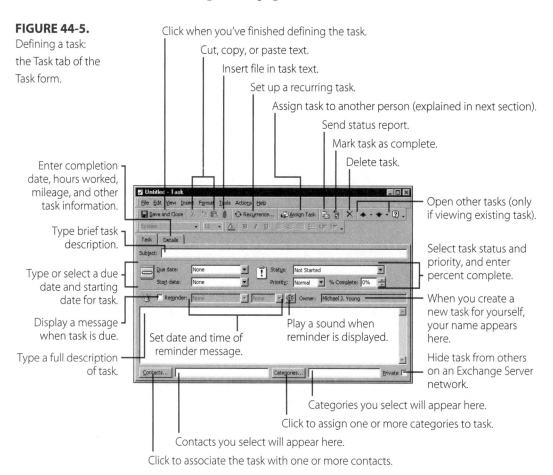

Click when you've finished defining the task.

Cut, copy, or paste text.

Insert file in task text.

Set up a recurring task.

Assign task to another person (explained in next section).

Send status report.

Mark task as complete.

Delete task.

Enter completion date, hours worked, mileage, and other task information.

Open other tasks (only if viewing existing task).

Type brief task description.

Select task status and priority, and enter percent complete.

Type or select a due date and starting date for task.

When you create a new task for yourself, your name appears here.

Display a message when task is due.

Play a sound when reminder is displayed.

Set date and time of reminder message.

Type a full description of task.

Hide task from others on an Exchange Server network.

Categories you select will appear here.

Click to assign one or more categories to task.

Contacts you select will appear here.

Click to associate the task with one or more contacts.

FIGURE 44-6.
Defining a task:
the Details tab
of the Task form.

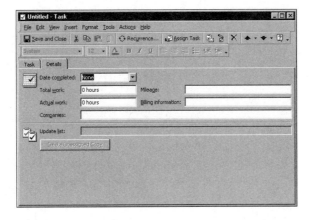

Figure 44-7 shows the Tasks folder, in the Simple List view, after several tasks have been defined. In this view, you can also display the first three lines entered into the large text box of each task (shown in Figure 44-5) by selecting the AutoPreview option on the View menu or the AutoPreview button on the Advanced toolbar. Note that the task list that you see in the Simple List view of the Tasks folders is also

AutoPreview

FIGURE 44-7.
The Tasks folder in the
Simple List view.

Task list

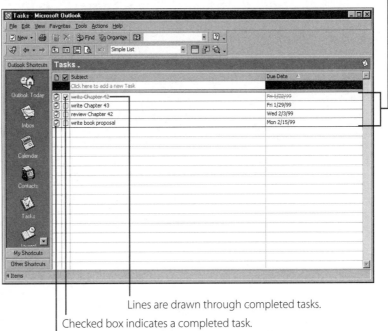

Lines are drawn through completed tasks.

Checked box indicates a completed task.

Task icons: Double-click an icon to open a task in the Task form.

VI

Microsoft Outlook

displayed within the Day/Week/Month view of the Calendar folder (less the Due Date column), as was shown in Figure 43-8, page 1035.

 TIP

Quickly Define a New Task

You can define a task by just clicking the box at the top of the Subject column, which is labeled Click Here To Add A New Task. (This box is present in the Simple List view and in several other views. See Figure 44-7.) Type the task subject into the Subject box, enter the due date (if any) into the Due Date box, and press Enter to add the task to the task list. You can later open the task in the Task form (as explained next) to enter additional information.

To view the complete information on a task, or to update this information, you can open the task in the Task form (shown in Figures 44-5 and 44-6) by double-clicking the task's icon in the task list. You might need to do this, for example, to update the status information on a task.

You can also directly edit any of the information for a task that appears in the task list shown in the Information Viewer, without opening the task. For example, in the Simple List view, you can change the task subject by editing the text in the Subject box, you can mark the task as completed by checking the box to the left of the Subject box, or you can change the due date by clicking the Due Date box, clicking the down arrow that appears, and then choosing a new date from the drop-down calendar:

Click in this box, and then click down arrow to select a new date from the drop-down calendar.

D	✓	Subject	Due Date	∧
		Click here to add a new Task		
✓	✓	write Chapter 42	Fri 1/22/99	
✓	☐	write Chapter 43	Fri 1/29/99	
✓	☐	review Chapter 42	Wed 2/3/99	
✓	⬛	write book proposal	Mon 2/15/1999	

Tasks

◄ February 1999 ►
S M T W T F S
31 1 2 3 4 5 6
7 8 9 10 11 12 13
14 15 16 17 18 19 20
21 22 23 24 25 26 27
28 1 2 3 4 5 6
7 8 9 10 11 12 13
Today   None

Click in this box to edit the task subject.

Check this box to mark the task as completed.

Double-click this icon to open the task in the Task form.

Note that to change information directly within the Information Viewer, you must make sure the Allow In-Cell Editing option is enabled. To find this option, point to Current View on the View menu, choose Customize Current View from the submenu, and then click the Other Settings button in the View Summary dialog box.

Delete

To delete a task, click its icon in the task list and press the Delete key, or click anywhere on the task and click the Delete button on the Standard toolbar. To move a task to a different position in the list, drag the icon. To make a copy, hold down the Ctrl key while you drag. (Note, however, that if a sort is applied, you can copy a task but you can't move it.)

If you want to see your tasks in a timeline arrangement, you can choose the Task Timeline view from the Current View list box on the Advanced toolbar. *(See "Using Different Views," page 992.)* When in this view, you can control the amount of detail that's shown by clicking the Day, Week, or Month button on the Standard toolbar. Figure 44-8 shows the Tasks folder as it appears in the Task Timeline view, with the Week button pressed in. (This figure shows two of the tasks that are listed in Figure 44-7.)

FIGURE 44-8.
The Tasks folder in the Task Timeline view.

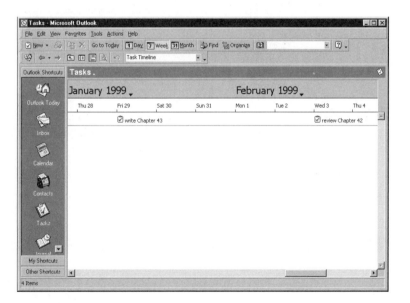

Exchange Server Only: Assigning and Tracking Tasks

If your computer is connected to a Microsoft Exchange Server network, you can use Outlook to assign a task to a co-worker and to keep track of the status of that task. This feature allows you to use Outlook to easily manage group projects as well as personal tasks. A person who accepts a task assignment becomes the task owner. (If you create a task for yourself, as described in the previous section, you're the owner.)

To create a task and assign it to another person, choose New Task Request from the Actions menu, or press Ctrl+Shift+U. Outlook will display the Task form, which you should fill out as shown in Figure 44-9, and then click the Send button. (Refer back to Figures 44-5 and 44-6, on pages 1056 and 1057, for descriptions of parts of the form that aren't explained in Figure 44-9.)

FIGURE 44-9.
Assigning a task to another person in the Task form.

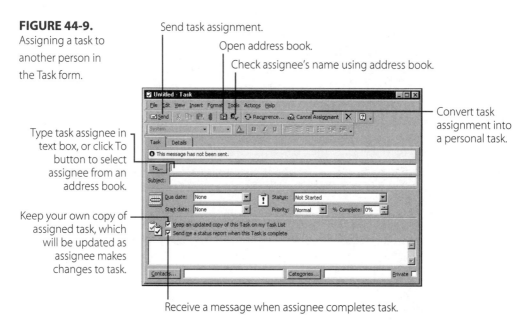

Send task assignment.

Open address book.

Check assignee's name using address book.

Convert task assignment into a personal task.

Type task assignee in text box, or click To button to select assignee from an address book.

Keep your own copy of assigned task, which will be updated as assignee makes changes to task.

Receive a message when assignee completes task.

When you click the Send button in the Task form, the following sequence of events occurs:

1 The *assignee* (the person who is sent the task and becomes its owner) gets a task-assignment message in his or her Inbox, and the task is added to the assignee's Tasks folder.

2 The assignee opens the task-assignment message and clicks either the Accept or the Decline button on the form to take on or to refuse the task. If the assignee clicks Decline, the task is removed from the assignee's Tasks folder.

3 You receive a message in your Inbox, indicating whether the task was accepted or declined.

4 If you selected the Keep An Updated Copy Of This Task On My Task List option when you assigned the task, a copy of the task will be stored in your Tasks folder. Each time the assignee updates the task (for example, changes the task Status or the % Complete), your copy of the task will be updated to match the assignee's copy.

   If you open your copy of the task in the Task form, you'll notice that the assignee is designated as the task owner. You can convert your copy to a task that's owned by you, and stop having it updated whenever the assignee makes a change to the task. To do this, click the Create Unassigned Copy button on the Details tab of the Task form. You can then either remain the owner, or assign the task to someone else.

5 If you selected the Send Me A Status Report When This Task Is Complete option when you assigned the task, you'll receive a message in your Inbox when the assignee sets the status of the task to Completed.

> If a person has been assigned a task, that person can reassign it to someone else by clicking the Assign Task button on the Task form. If the new owner opens the task, the Update List box on the Details tab of the Task form will list the name of each person who has assigned the task to someone else and who has selected the Keep An Updated Copy Of This Task On My Task List option. That is, it lists each person who is storing a copy of the task that will be updated when the new owner modifies the task.

Journal

The Journal folder allows you to keep a record of events and to view these events according to the times they occurred or by other criteria. You can have Outlook automatically create journal entries for certain types of events—for example, receiving an e-mail message from a particular person or opening a document in a specific Microsoft Office application. You can also manually record any type of event—for example, a telephone conversation you had or an interview you conducted.

To have Outlook begin creating journal entries automatically, open the Journal folder. If automatic journal entries aren't currently enabled, Outlook will display a message box that asks if you want to turn the Journal

VI

Microsoft Outlook

on. Click the Yes button to display the Journal Options dialog box, shown in Figure 44-10. (You can also display this dialog box at any time by choosing Options from the Tools menu and clicking the Journal Options button on the Preferences tab of the Options dialog box.)

To have Outlook create journal entries when you send or receive messages, select one or more message types from the list in the upper left corner (Automatically Record These Items), and one or more contacts from the list in the upper right corner (For These Contacts; the contacts listed here are those stored in your Contacts folder, explained previously in the chapter). Outlook will create a journal entry for any message that belongs to one of the selected types and is either from or to one of the selected contacts. For example, if you select the E-Mail Message item and the Ann Aaron contact, Outlook will automatically create a journal entry whenever you send or receive an e-mail message to or from Ann Aaron.

You can view all the journal entries recorded for a particular contact by opening that contact in the Contact form, clicking the Activities tab, and selecting All Journal Entries in the Show list box.

Additionally, if you have installed other Office applications, you can select one or more of them in the list in the lower left corner of the Journal Options dialog box (Also Record Files From). Doing so will cause Outlook to automatically record a journal entry whenever you create, open, close, or save a document using the selected application or applications. Each journal entry will include the date and time you performed the action.

FIGURE 44-10.
Enabling automatic journal entries in the Journal Options dialog box.

Select message types to track in the Journal for the contacts you select.

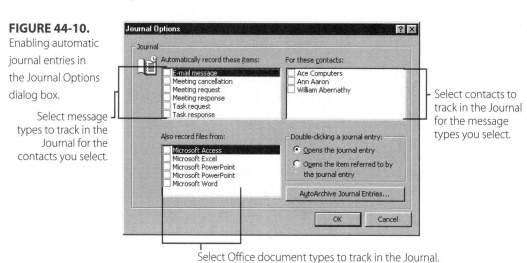

Select contacts to track in the Journal for the message types you select.

Select Office document types to track in the Journal.

You can manually create a journal entry for any type of event. To do this, open the Journal folder, and choose New Journal Entry from the Actions menu or press Ctrl+N. Then complete the Journal Entry form, as shown in Figure 44-11.

FIGURE 44-11.
Manually creating a journal entry in the Journal Entry form.

Click when you've finished defining journal entry.

Print journal entry.

Cut, copy, or paste text.

Open address book.

Check names in Contacts box against address book.

Delete journal entry.

Open other journal entries (only if viewing existing journal entry).

Select the type of the event.

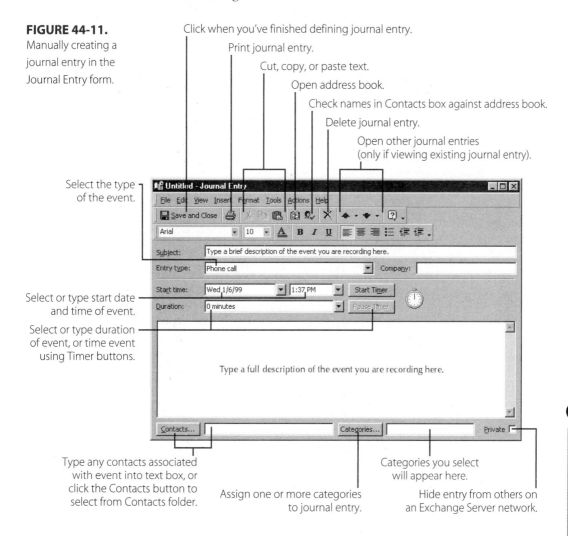

Select or type start date and time of event.

Select or type duration of event, or time event using Timer buttons.

Type any contacts associated with event into text box, or click the Contacts button to select from Contacts folder.

Assign one or more categories to journal entry.

Categories you select will appear here.

Hide entry from others on an Exchange Server network.

The By Type view of the Journal folder shows the journal entries arranged in a timeline (similar to the Task Timeline view of the Tasks folder, discussed previously), and grouped according to the types of the events (phone calls, e-mail messages, and so on). You can select the amount of detail shown in this view by clicking the Day, Week, or Month button on the Standard toolbar. The Journal folder in the By Type view, showing the Weekly level of detail, is shown in Figure 44-12, on the following page.

FIGURE 44-12.
The Journal folder in
the By Type view,
showing the Weekly
level of detail.

Weekly level of detail shown.

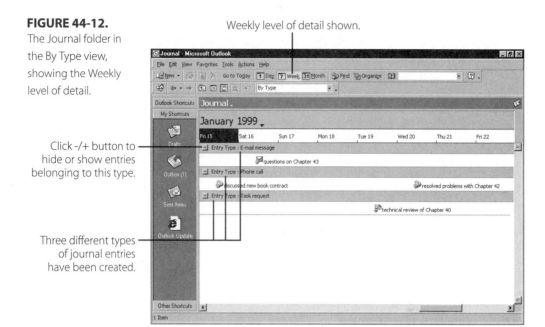

Click -/+ button to
hide or show entries
belonging to this type.

Three different types
of journal entries
have been created.

Quickly View a Particular Date

In the By Type view of the Journal folder or in any other timeline view, you can
go directly to a specific day—without having to scroll through all the intermediate dates—by clicking anywhere in the gray band at the top of the Information
Viewer of the Outlook window where the months are displayed and then clicking the day you want in the calendar that drops down:

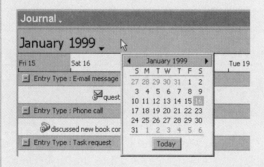

You can display the current day by clicking the Today button in the pop-up calendar, or by clicking the Go To Today button on the Standard toolbar.

To open a journal entry in the Journal Entry form so that you can view or modify any of the entry information, just double-click the entry within the Information Viewer. Note, however, that if the entry was automatically recorded and if the Opens The Item Referred To By The Journal Entry option is selected, double-clicking the item will open the original Outlook item that the entry is based on (for example, an e-mail message or a Word document) rather than opening the journal entry itself. (You set this option in the Journal Options dialog box, shown and described at the beginning of this section.)

Delete

You can delete a journal entry by selecting it and then pressing the Delete key or clicking the Delete button on the Standard toolbar. To move a journal entry to another location in the timeline, you can't simply drag it using the mouse. Rather, you must open the entry and change the start time or duration.

Notes

You can use the Notes folder in Outlook to store and organize miscellaneous bits and pieces of information. You might want to store information that doesn't fit into any of the categories provided by the other Outlook folders (for example, a list of supplies to purchase). You might also want to use the Notes folder to temporarily store information that you'll later enter in the appropriate folder. (For example, you could quickly jot down a name and address that you'll later store in the Contacts folder.)

Once you open the Notes folder, you can create a new note by choosing New Note from the Notes menu, by pressing Ctrl+N, or by merely double-clicking a blank spot within the Information Viewer area of the Outlook window. Outlook will then open a Notes form into which you can type the text for your note, as shown here:

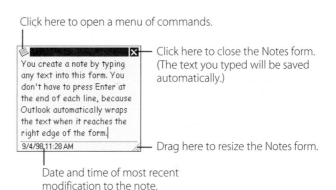

Click here to open a menu of commands.

You create a note by typing any text into this form. You don't have to press Enter at the end of each line, because Outlook automatically wraps the text when it reaches the right edge of the form.

9/4/98, 11:28 AM

Click here to close the Notes form. (The text you typed will be saved automatically.)

Drag here to resize the Notes form.

Date and time of most recent modification to the note.

VI

Microsoft Outlook

You can click the icon in the upper left corner of the Notes form to open a menu of commands for changing the color of the note or performing several other tasks:

When you're done typing the text for your note, you can close the form by clicking the Close box in the upper right corner, or you can simply switch back to the Outlook window and leave the Note form open. In either case, the new note will be added to the Notes folder. In the Icons view of this folder, you can display the notes as large icons, as small icons, or as a list by clicking one of these buttons on the Standard toolbar:

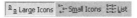

If you choose the By Color view from the Current View list box on the toolbar, your notes will be grouped according to their colors. You already saw how to change the color of a note when it's open in the Note form. You can also change a note's color by right-clicking the note in the Information Viewer of the Outlook window; a menu will appear that allows you to change the color of the note or perform other actions:

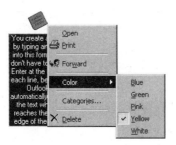

You can open a note in the Notes form so that you can add or modify its text by double-clicking the note in the Information Viewer. To delete a note, select it by clicking it, and then press the Delete key.

Change the Default Features of Notes to Suit Your Preferences

You can modify the default color, size, or font for all new notes that you subsequently create by choosing Options from the Tools menu and then clicking the Note Options button on the Preferences tab of the Options dialog box.

Accessing and Managing Files and Opening Web Sites

You can also use Outlook to access any of the files that are located on your computer or on a network attached to your computer. For example, you can access programs, Office documents, and other types of data files. You can use Outlook to open, copy, move, rename, print, or delete files as well as file folders. You can also create new file folders and Windows shortcuts to files. The Outlook file interface is quite similar to Microsoft Windows Explorer. If you have used Windows Explorer, you'll already be familiar with most of the file access features of Outlook. (If you aren't familiar with Windows Explorer, you can learn the basic skills by reading the Outlook online Help book "Working with Files and Folders.") This section focuses on features unique to the Outlook file interface.

To access files, begin by using the Outlook Bar to open a specific file folder, as follows:

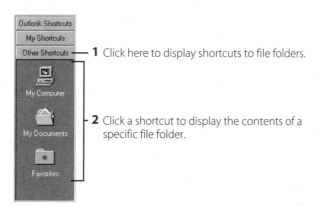

1 Click here to display shortcuts to file folders.

2 Click a shortcut to display the contents of a specific file folder.

Browsing the Web Using the Favorites Folder

You can use the new Favorites menu in Outlook to browse the Web by opening Internet shortcuts you've stored in your Favorites folder. To display a Web page, choose the shortcut for the page from the Favorites menu or from one of its submenus:

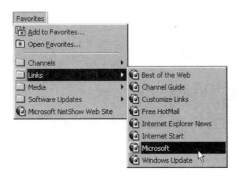

The contents of your Favorites menu will probably differ from this. The submenus and shortcuts displayed on the Favorites menu correspond to the subfolders and shortcuts currently stored in the Favorites folder on your hard disk.

When you open a Web page using the Favorites menu, the page is displayed directly within the Information Viewer area of the Outlook window, and the Web toolbar is displayed to allow you to browse through different pages. (In contrast, when you display the contents of your Favorites folder in the Information Viewer and double-click an Internet shortcut contained in that folder, the page is opened in your browser, *not* in the Outlook window.)

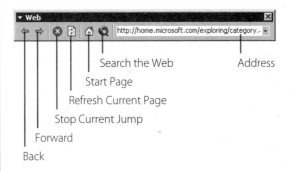

On the Favorites menu, you can also choose Add To Favorites to add a shortcut for the currently displayed Web page to your Favorites folder or to one of its subfolders. And you can choose Open Favorites to open a Web page by selecting a shortcut in your Favorites folder (or in another folder) using the standard Open dialog box.

The My Computer file folder lets you access file folders on any of the disk drives on your computer. The My Documents file folder is generally located on your hard drive and is the default folder for storing your Office documents. If you have installed the Microsoft Internet Explorer Web browser, the Favorites file folder will contain the shortcuts to sites on the Internet that you have saved while browsing; you can double-click an item in this file folder to start your browser and open a Web site. (See the sidebar "Browsing the Web Using the Favorites Folder" to learn about another way to browse Internet sites in Outlook.)

Folder
List

If you click the Folder List button on the Advanced toolbar when a file folder is open, Outlook will list your file folders in a permanently displayed hierarchical list. This list is similar to the one shown in the left pane of Windows Explorer and makes it easier to navigate through your file folders and files. See Figure 44-13. You can also display a temporary Folder List by clicking at the left end of the Folder Banner.

You can use the same techniques that you employ in Windows Explorer to view the contents of file folders; to open files or run programs; to copy, move, rename, or delete files or file folders; or to print files. A few techniques, however, vary slightly from those used in Windows Explorer. For example, to create a Windows shortcut to a program (not an Outlook Bar shortcut), you must drag the program filename to the file folder in

FIGURE 44-13.
The root file folder of drive C: opened in Outlook, with the Folder List displayed.

Folder Banner

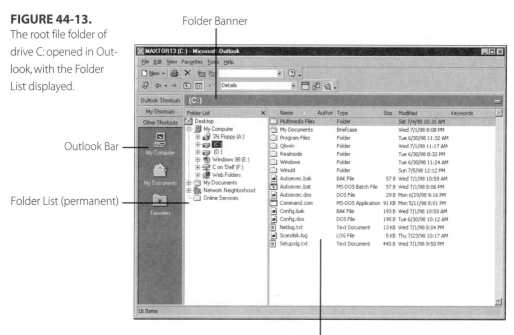

Outlook Bar

Folder List (permanent)

Information Viewer (shows contents of selected folder)

VI

Microsoft Outlook

which you want the shortcut to appear. (In Windows Explorer, you can create a Windows shortcut using the File menu.)

To make it easier to open a file folder you use frequently, you can add a shortcut for this folder to the Outlook Bar. *To do this, follow the instructions given in "Modifying the Outlook Bar," page 1008.*

 You can also add to the Outlook Bar a shortcut to an individual file— an Office document or other data file, a program, or an Internet shortcut. To do this, drag the file from Windows Explorer, from a folder window, or from the Information Viewer, to the Outlook Bar. If the position where you want to place the shortcut isn't visible, while you drag you can hold the pointer over a group button to open that group, or you can hold it over the top or bottom of a group to scroll through the group's shortcuts. When you click an Outlook Bar shortcut to a file, Outlook will open that file. If the file is an Office document or data file, it will be opened in the associated application. If it's a program, it will be launched. And if it's an Internet shortcut, the site it points to will be opened in your browser.

 SEE ALSO

For instructions on using the Outlook Find command to locate specific files, see "Finding Outlook Items or Disk Files," page 1009.

TIP

> ### Run Useful Programs from Outlook
> You can run several programs that are related to Outlook by choosing commands from the Go To submenu of the View menu. You can access Internet newsgroups by choosing the News command, which runs the Outlook Express newsreader program that's installed when you set up Outlook. You can run your Web browser by choosing the Web Browser command. And, if you have installed Microsoft NetMeeting, you can communicate with other NetMeeting users on the Internet by choosing a command from the Internet Call submenu.

PART VII

Microsoft Publisher

Getting Started with Publisher

Whether you're a volunteer producing a nonprofit newsletter, a manufacturer distributing a new product brochure, or an espresso cart owner updating his or her menu, you are entering the world of desktop publishing. You probably won't be sent to design school, or get to take a weeklong workshop in digital prepress. You might not have much time to produce your document or a large production budget. And, as long as you're up, your boss would like you to publish it to the Web!

Fortunately, you don't have to be a professional graphic artist to produce eye-catching publications that tell your audience what they need to know about your product or service. Using Microsoft Publisher 2000, you can create the kinds of publications that were once relegated to specially trained desktop publishers.

Using wizards or starting from scratch, you can use Publisher to create newsletters, brochures, business cards, postcards, flyers, letterhead, catalogs, and more. If you're printing your document on a home computer, taking it to a commercial printing service, or publishing it to the Web, Publisher can walk you through the process. And don't panic over your lack of design skills. Publisher 2000 includes sophisticated page layout templates, which help you unify all the components of your publication into one consistent design package.

Using a Publisher wizard, you can create a postcard, like this:

Or a catalog, like this:

 The Reading.pub file is located on the Running Office 2000 Reader's Corner page. For information about connecting to this Web site, read the Introduction.

Exploring the Publisher Window

The easiest way to start Publisher is to click the Start button, point to Programs, and then click the Microsoft Publisher button. You'll see the window shown in Figure 45-1.

The Microsoft Publisher Catalog window provides options for creating a publication. (You'll learn more about these options in the next section, "Using Wizards and Templates.") Take a minute now to examine the user interface components of Publisher—the menu bar, toolbars, status bar, scroll box, and rulers. To do this, click the Exit Catalog button in the lower right corner of the Publisher window, and then click the Hide Wizard button in the lower left corner of the Unsaved Publication window. (A wizard is a special, automated tool that guides you through the creation of an Office document, in this case, a publication, but you'll look at wizards later in this chapter.) Figure 45-2, on the next page, shows the Publisher workspace with the wizard hidden.

You'll notice that Publisher 2000 shares many of the significant user interface components with the other programs in the Office 2000 suite:

- The menu bar provides access to the commands and settings you use to create documents in Publisher. To choose a command from the Publisher menu, open the menu, point to the submenu (if there is one), and then click the command you want. For

FIGURE 45-1.
The Publisher 2000 opening window displays the Microsoft Publisher Catalog.

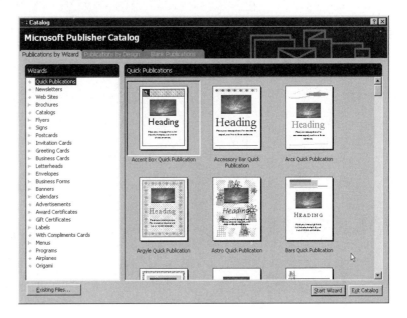

example, you can use the new commands on the Zoom submenu of the View menu—Whole Page and Page Width—to gain perspective on your work.

- The toolbars give you quick access to often-used commands. Publisher is configured to display the Standard and Formatting toolbars below the menu bar. The Formatting toolbar changes, depending on which tool or object is selected. When you are working with text, the Formatting toolbar contains a new Numbering button and other commands to format paragraphs and change font size. The Objects toolbar, also a default toolbar, is located on the left side of the Publisher window, though it can be turned into a floating toolbar when dragged to any part of the application window.

- Like the other Office application windows, the Publisher window contains sizing buttons that you can use to minimize, maximize, restore, and close it, a status bar that displays the mouse position and the size of the selected object, and the Page Navigation button.

FIGURE 45-2.

The Publisher user interface with important components labeled.

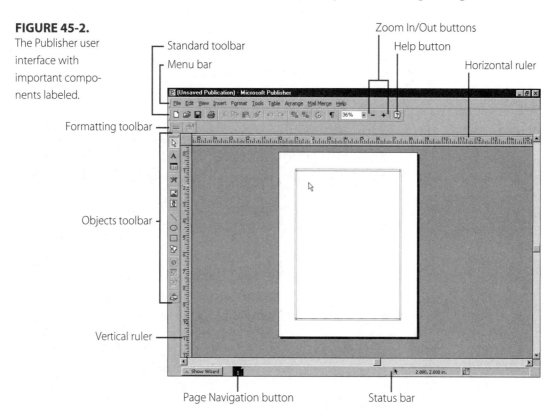

■ When you click the scroll arrows at the top or bottom of the scroll bars, your publication scrolls up or down. (You can also drag the scroll box, using the mouse, to move your publication horizontally or vertically.)

■ Lying along the top and left side of your layout are Publisher's rulers. You use them to measure and align objects and position them in relation to the margins of your publication. (The zero points on the rulers correspond to the upper left edge of your publication page, not to the corner of the window or layout area.)

■ If the Office Assistant isn't already visible, click the Help button on the Standard toolbar and type your question when the Assistant appears. Microsoft Publisher Help includes new tutorials that guide you from the basics of creating a publication into advanced techniques for customizing your work.

The Nature of Desktop Publishing

Publisher 2000 might remind you of Microsoft Word, and that's one reason it's so easy to begin working in Publisher. But it's not a word processing program—it's a desktop publishing program. In Publisher's workplace, you'll create publications that use some word processing tools, but you'll employ these tools in a page layout environment. Because some of the conventions of desktop publishing might be new to you, note a few key elements that distinguish the Publisher workplace from that of a word processing program:

■ Frames: All objects (such as text, graphics and pictures, or WordArt) must be placed inside a frame before you can manipulate them in Publisher.

■ Scratch Area: The area outside the boundaries of the document is where you can drag and store objects while you work on a page. Objects remain in this area when you save a publication.

■ Smart Objects: These special-design components, such as logos or calendars, have wizards associated with them. Wizards help you edit smart objects, or you can ungroup the elements that make them up and edit each element yourself.

■ Synchronization: Publisher changes the formatting of all the smart objects or design elements in a publication, based on a change you make to one component of that object.

■ Print Production: In desktop publishing, you select printing options before you begin document creation because your choices have great impact on the look of your publication.

Using Wizards and Templates

Now that you've walked through your workspace and are familiar with the Publisher window and its tools, you're ready to roll up your sleeves and start designing your publication. Publisher offers you a variety of ways to get started via the Microsoft Publisher Catalog dialog box. (See Figure 45-1, on page 1075.)

- The Publications By Wizard tab allows you to create an entire publication of a particular type, such as a flyer or business card, and also offers you opportunities to customize your work.

- The Publications By Design tab encourages you to work with a consistent design plan by offering suggestions for groups of publications based on design, and here too, the wizard helps you to personalize your design.

- The Blank Publications tab anticipates that you've had some experience in designing a publication. Choosing this option displays several blank publication types, such as Postcard, Web Page, and Book Fold, and asks the questions you need to answer to lay your publication out.

- The Existing Files button in the lower left corner of the Catalog window gives you access to Publisher files you've already created and would like to modify. Clicking this button takes you to the Open dialog box where you can select a Publisher file that you've saved. (A similar dialog box appears in each Office application.)

Using Publications By Wizard

Wizards are Microsoft Office tools that ask you questions pertaining to an objective (in this case, a document you want to create and publish), and lead you through to a successful conclusion based on the information you provide.

NOTE

Before choosing a wizard, you'll want to set your publication up for printing. See the last section in this chapter, "Printing Your Publication," page 1094, for an overview of that procedure.

As already mentioned, Publications By Wizards takes you through the publication process by asking you to choose the kind of publication you want to produce. You'll find a list of 25 types of publications in the opening Microsoft Publisher Catalog dialog box. If you're already working in the program, choose New from the File menu to display this dialog box. Select the Publications By Wizard tab, and then pick the type of publication you want to produce. Publisher 2000 displays Quick Publications as the new default opening type, and has added another new category to the list—Catalogs. Here's how to use a wizard to create a business card:

1 Under the Wizards heading, click Business Cards. Then choose Plain Paper.

2 Select the design style you'd like to use for your card. (The illustration on the following page shows a card based on the Bars design.)

3 Click the Start Wizard button in the lower right side of the Catalog dialog box. The introductory Business Card Wizard dialog box appears.

 NOTE

The first time you employ a Publisher wizard, you'll be asked if you want to tell the wizard about yourself so the wizard can automate the flow of personal information in your publications. Click OK in the Publisher message box and the Personal Information dialog box appears, as shown here:

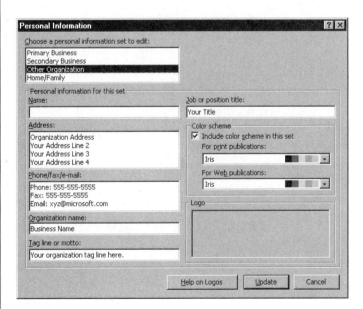

Take a minute to fill it in and you won't have to enter your name, address, company name, and other facts about yourself every time you create a new publication. When you want to edit this information, click the Update button in the Personal Information pane of the Business Card Wizard (or whatever Publisher wizard you are using.)

4 Click the option you want to change from the list on the left, and answer the wizard's questions about that option.

5 When you finish answering the wizard's questions, click the Hide Wizard button to create more workspace. (You can come back to the wizard for help at any time by clicking the Show Wizard button.)

That's all there is to creating a basic business card, which is illustrated here:

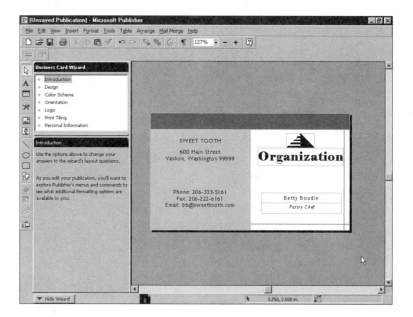

You can continue to embellish your work, adding text and graphics using Publisher's toolbars. Or you can go directly to the File menu to print your publication.

Creating Publications By Design

When Ralph Waldo Emerson wrote, "A foolish consistency is the hobgoblin of little minds," he wasn't thinking of desktop publishing! The hallmark of good publication design is unity—the result of choosing consistent design elements that tie a publication or group of documents into a cohesive whole.

 When you want to create a group of business documents that share the same design scheme, or if you're planning a special event that requires several documents that have a unified theme, select the Publications By

Design tab in the Catalog dialog box. Publisher 2000 contains 10 new Master Design Sets, which provide even more flexibility in creating a cohesive package of publications. Master Design Sets have names such as Arcs, Tilt, Floating Oval, Mobile, and so on. (See Figure 45-3.) Here's how to link publications by design scheme:

1   Click the Master Design Set that you want to use. (Clicking the different Master Sets listed on the left will display a preview in the window to the right).

2   Click the type of publication you want to create.

3   Click the Start Wizard button. Answer the questions the wizard asks. (You can reuse the personal information you supplied in the earlier procedure, "Using Publication By Wizards" or edit the information by clicking the Update button.)

4   Save your publication before you open a new publication from the File menu. Repeat this procedure for other types of publications you want for your set.

You can easily put together a coordinated set of business stationery (letterhead, fax cover sheet, business card, and envelopes) using Publications By Design. You can also create all the documents you need to promote a special event, such as a kick-off party for a new product or a fund-raising initiative, by selecting one of the Special Event Sets or Fund-Raiser Sets.

FIGURE 45-3.
Design Sets create a cohesive group of publications.

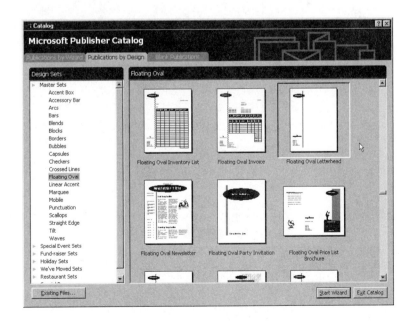

Publisher's publication types and design sets are quite flexible and interchangeable, as you'll see in the next few chapters when you begin complementing the wizard's guidance with clip art, pictures, embedded objects, fill effects, and text from your own files.

Starting with Blank Presentations

If you're feeling creative, and you know just how you want to shape your document, you're ready to begin a publication from scratch. To do that, follow these steps:

1   If the Publisher Catalog dialog box is displayed, click the Blank Publications tab. If you're already working in Publisher, choose New from the File menu to open the Catalog dialog box, and then select the Blank Publications tab.

2   From the examples of blank publications (called *thumbnails* in the design world), click the one that meets your needs. In the following illustration, a postcard thumbnail is selected:

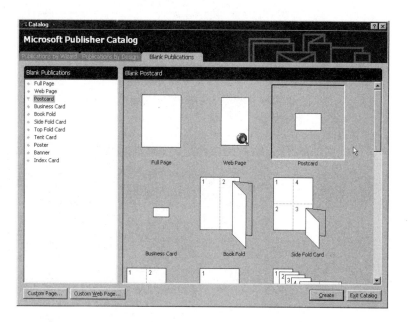

3   Click the Create button to start the selected publication's wizard. Then answer the wizard's questions.

If you want to create a type of publication that isn't represented in the choices for blank publications in the Catalog, click the Custom Page button at the bottom left side of the window. Then choose the options you want in the Page Setup dialog box to lay out your publication. Click OK. This will display a blank publication ready for you to modify in any way that you want.

TIP

Start with a Clean Slate

By default, Publisher opens blank publications by displaying the Quick Publications Wizard. You might want to test-drive your publication without this kind of encouragement. To turn off this setting, click Options on the Tools menu. The Options dialog box appears. Click the User Assistance tab, and clear the check box for Use Quick Publications Wizard For Blank Publications.

Creating Templates

You'll spend a lot of time and creative energy building a publication from scratch. Some of the design elements you choose might resonate for you after you've sent out a postcard, an office announcement, or a new product information flyer. And reusing design elements saves time, cuts costs, and adds a pattern to your work that is unique, personal, and identifiable.

A template is a model publication that you can use as a foundation for building new publications. For example, when you create a postcard, you can have Publisher save the layout, particular graphic objects, and fonts to reuse in all your mailings.

If you're using Publisher 2000 for the first time, you won't find a Templates button. To make a template, follow these easy steps:

1   Create a publication.

2   Change the settings to reflect your own preferences.

3   Click Save As from the File menu.

NOTE

Minute by minute, you're making choices that affect the design of your publication. You'll probably want to keep many of these modifications in your final product. Publisher automatically reminds you to save your work every 15 minutes by default. To change that setting, click Options on the Tools menu. The Options dialog box appears. Click the User Assistance tab, and change the minutes between reminders in the text box if you want more or fewer reminders to save. You can clear the check box for the Remind To Save Publication option, but that's living really dangerously!

4 Type a filename for your template in the File Name box. Choose a standard name, such as Postcard or Card Mailing, so that you won't confuse it with your other Publisher documents.

5 In the Save As Type list box, choose Publisher Template. Your publication will be saved in Publisher's Templates folder.

When you want to access your template to use it as the basis for another publication, you will find a Templates button in the Catalog dialog box, as illustrated here:

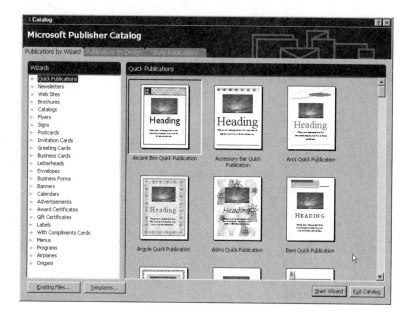

To use a template as the basis for a new publication, simply click the Templates button, select the file you want to use, and begin your new publication. Save it as a Publisher file. The template will remain unchanged in the Templates folder.

Working with Toolbars

 Publisher 2000 displays the Standard, Formatting, and Objects toolbars by default. The Standard toolbar contains often-used Office tools for saving and printing your work, and in Publisher, magnifying your work and moving elements around the page.

The Formatting toolbar changes to reflect what kind of object is selected. If a text frame is active, the Formatting toolbar displays tools for editing text. Publisher 2000 includes more tools on this toolbar: the new Numbering command, Decrease and Increase Indent, and Increase and Decrease Font. If you select a picture frame, the Wrap Text To Frame and Wrap Text To Picture tools are displayed. The Formatting toolbar is shown here when a text frame is selected:

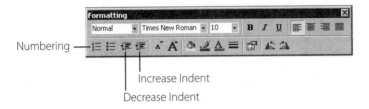

Publisher also includes a small toolbar called Connect Frames, which helps you to format the flow of text in your publication.

The Objects toolbar contains essential tools to work with frames and shapes. Although this toolbar is displayed along the left side of the Publisher window, you might want to undock it and move it to a more convenient place in your workspace by dragging it to another location.

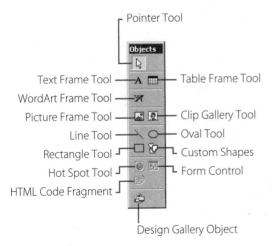

Working with Text Frames

Publisher helps you package your text, graphics, and design scheme into a cohesive format suitable for publication. But first, you must supply the words that shape the message you want to convey to your audience.

All text must be placed inside a frame before you can edit or format it. How you enter text into a frame depends on how you began your publication. If you chose a Publisher wizard to organize your publication, your document contains text boxes filled with sample text, which you will want to replace by following these steps:

1 Select the text frame you want to modify by clicking it. (To enlarge the text frame view so you can see more of your work, press F9.)

2 On the Edit menu, click Highlight Entire Story (or select the text with your mouse).

3 Replace the selected text by simply typing your own text or by pressing Delete to create empty frames for your text.

Text must be selected, as illustrated here in the Newsletter Wizard, before you can enter your own:

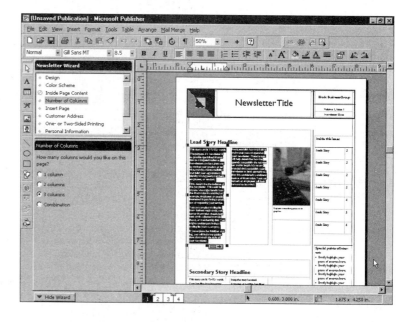

4 If you want to replace the text frames as well as the text, click Select All on the Edit menu.

5 Press Delete.

If you're building a blank publication from scratch, or if you've removed the existing frames, you can create your own text frames and add text to them. Use the Objects toolbar to quickly shape a text frame:

Text Frame
Tool

1 Click the Text Frame Tool on the Objects toolbar.

2 Position the mouse pointer where you want your text frame to begin, and then drag it diagonally to form the frame.

3 Release the mouse button when the frame is the correct shape.

Working in Microsoft Word

You can simply enter text into text frames using Publisher. However, if you're working on a lengthy piece of text, and you want to enlist the powerful capabilities of Microsoft Word in composing or editing your document, follow these steps:

1 Select the text in Publisher that you want to work on in Word.

2 Click Edit Story In Microsoft Word on the Edit menu. Or right-click the selected text, point to Change Text on the pop-up menu, and click Edit Story In Microsoft Word. Word opens a new document with your Publisher text inserted, as shown in Figure 45-4. Continue to work in your favorite word processing program.

3 When you're finished working in Word, click Close & Return To *Filename* (the command will show the name of the Publisher file or "unsaved publication.")

FIGURE 45-4.
Composing text for a
publication in
Microsoft Word.

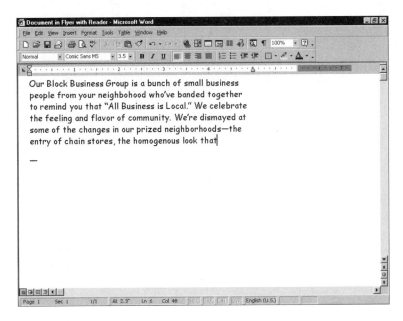

The Character of Fonts

A font is a complete set of characters that have the same typeface (such as Times New Roman), style (such as italic), and weight (such as bold). The fonts you choose will add impact and character to your publications. Fonts are divided into three categories:

- Serif fonts have curved lines or ornaments at the end of the strokes.

- Sans serif fonts (such as Arial) don't have curved lines or ornaments at the ends of strokes.

- Script fonts look like handwriting and are often used for a decorative effect.

Experiment with different fonts to find your favorites, but follow these simple design principles to maximize their effect:

- Body text (the main text of a publication) is often easier to read if you use a serif font.

- Display text (the headings and subheadings in a publication) has a clean, fresh impact if you use sans serif fonts.

- You can create impact without sacrificing unity in your publication if you use only one font in a publication, but you vary its size and weight.

When you click Font on the Format menu, you'll see this dialog box:

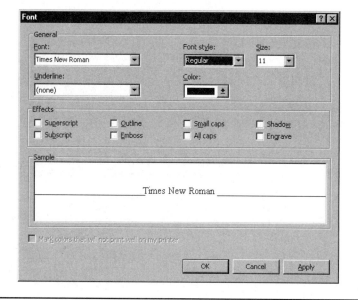

You can also import text from Word documents and insert them into Publisher text frames. Follow these steps to do this:

1 Click Text File on the Insert menu. The Insert Text dialog box appears.

2 Enter the filename you want to insert, and click OK.

The file appears in your publication, and you can use Publisher's formatting tools to position it appropriately.

Formatting a Text Frame

To format text in a frame, first select the text. To change the font, click Font on the Format menu and make your selections in the Font dialog box, or use the Decrease Font or Increase Font button on the Formatting toolbar.

To format the text frame itself, select the frame. Then click Text Frame Properties on the Format menu. In the Text Frame Properties dialog box, shown here, you can make adjustments to margins, columns, text wrapping, and connecting text frames.

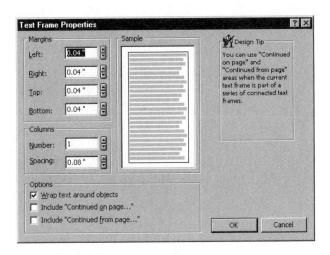

To format paragraphs quickly, use the Decrease Indent and Increase Indent buttons on the Formatting toolbar, or choose Indents And Lists from the Format menu.

Making Text Flow Between Text Frames

When you have entered more text than your text frame can hold, you'll see an overflow symbol at the bottom of the text frame when it is selected. If you rest your mouse pointer over this symbol, a screen tip appears to tell you that you have Text In Overflow, as shown in the following illustration:

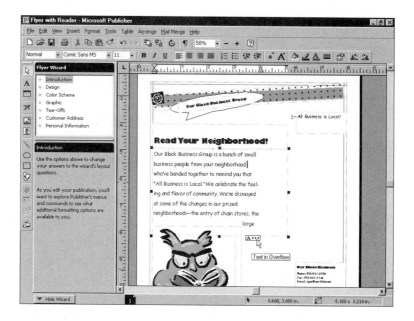

You can create room for the overflow in a variety of ways:

- Enlarge the text frame by pointing to one of its sizing handles and dragging the handle when the mouse pointer becomes the two-headed Resize arrow.

- Create another text frame by using the Text Frame Tool on the Objects toolbar.

- Insert another page by clicking Page on the Insert menu and using the Insert Page dialog box to add a new text frame on each additional page, or to duplicate existing frames on the new page or pages.

- To connect the text frames on your page or several pages, create as many new frames as you want, and select the frame you want to be first in the lineup. The Connect Frame toolbar appears. Click Connect Text Frames. The pointer becomes an upright pitcher when you move it over the page. Place the pointer over an empty text frame, and the pitcher tilts; click the empty frame to connect the two. Any text in the overflow area of the first frame will flow into the newly connected frame.

Using AutoFlow

When you insert a text file that doesn't fit into a Publisher text frame, you can use Publisher's AutoFlow feature to adjust the fit. When Publisher automatically asks if you want to use this feature, click Yes. Publisher will then flow the text throughout your publication and also connect the text frames for you.

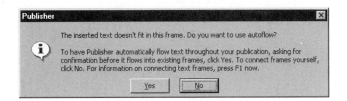

Using Layout Tools

Although Publisher fully supports your work with wizards, you add personality to a publication by creating your own design elements. In honor of good design practice, you wouldn't want to fling random elements at your page. However, if you're comfortable using Publisher's layout tools, you can remain in control of the overall design of your publication.

As you try out some of the tools described in this section, you might want to stand back and take in the big picture of your layout. Or step closer to check how a particular element works in the grand scheme. Use the commands on the View menu to change the magnification and focus of your publication.

Take some time to experiment with Publisher's layout tools; some of the most useful ones are described here.

Using Rulers and Ruler Guides

Rulers lie along the top and left-hand side of the Publisher window. You can turn them off to see more of your publication by right-clicking anywhere in the window (except on a toolbar) and then clicking Rulers. You can move the rulers to measure or align design elements in your publication by placing the mouse pointer on the ruler you want to move, holding down the mouse button, and dragging it to a new location. If you want to move both rulers at once, point to the box where the two rulers meet and drag from there.

Ruler guides are useful when you want to make several ruler marks on a page. To add them to a page, hold down Shift and drag your mouse

FIGURE 45-5.
Rulers are useful when you want to measure or align an object.

Point from which you can move both rulers

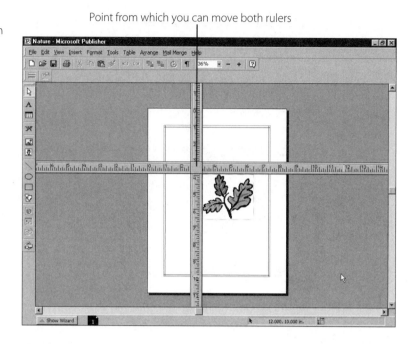

pointer out from the rulers to create a new position for the guide. The ruler guide is displayed as a green dotted line, illustrated here:

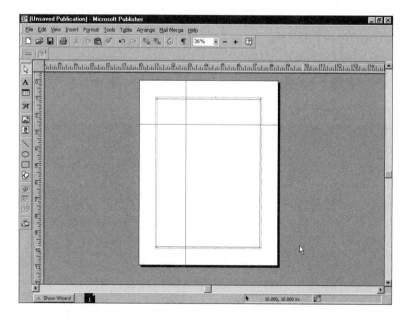

You'll use the ruler guides that you've created on a page-by-page basis. They won't apply to the entire publication.

Using Layout Guides

Publisher's layout guides allow you to make a grid that is repeated on each page of your publication. Repetition contributes to the unified look you want to achieve in your design. To specify how you want objects laid out in your publication, click Layout Guides on the Arrange menu. In the Layout Guides dialog box (shown here), enter the requirements you want for margins, columns, and rows.

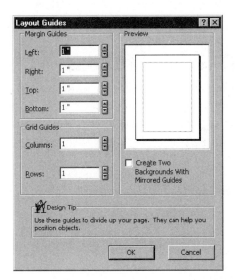

You'll often find it useful to create mirrored layouts for pages that face each other, particularly when you're creating a booklet, newsletter, or catalog. Mirrored-page layout means that objects (such as page numbers, graphics, or headers) are positioned on the background of the left page so that they mirror those on the right background. To create this effect when setting up your grid in the Layout Guides dialog box, select the Create Two Backgrounds With Mirrored Guides check box.

Although working with Publisher's layout tools takes a little practice, your efforts will pay off in sophisticated publication designs that speak clearly to your audience.

Grouping Objects

When you want to edit, format, or rotate several objects at once, you can group them. Press Shift, and click every object you want in the group. A Group Objects button appears under the last object you selected. Click it to group the selected objects, and click it again to ungroup them.

Using Snap To

Publisher's Snap To commands make objects on the page align with the rulers, guides, or other objects. Using this feature, you can position objects exactly where you want them and add a clean, professional look to your publications. On the Tools menu, click the Snap To command you want to use. A check mark indicates that the command is active. If your objects are not snapping to each other, try placing them closer together. If you have selected Snap To Ruler Marks or Snap To Guides, you should clear them to enhance Snap To Objects.

Moving and Copying Objects

You can copy objects in Publisher by applying many of the skills you learned in other Office programs, such as dragging, cutting, and pasting. One of the elements unique to Publisher is the Move icon, which appears when you select an object and place the mouse pointer on it. The mouse pointer will change to the Move icon (a little truck), indicating that you can drag the object to a new location. If you have selected the Snap To command, the object might align with the nearest ruler, guide, or other object.

Printing Your Publication

Watching the pages of your publication emerge from a printer can be pretty exciting. No matter how carefully you've studied your document on the computer screen, it just looks different in print. To ensure that this moment isn't disappointing, plan for printing at the beginning of your project, because the print options you specify will directly impact how your publication looks and the message it conveys.

You have three basic options: you can print a publication on your desktop printer, take a proof from your printer to a copy shop, or send the publication files to a commercial printing service. You'll choose one of these options based on the quality and quantity requirements of your publication.

If you want to print a small number of copies, using standard-sized paper (or a custom size supported by your printer) in low resolution black and white or full color, you'll probably choose to handle the printing process on your home printer. (Table 45-1 defines many of the most frequently used terms in print production.)

TABLE 45-1.   Printing Terms

Term	Definition
Resolution	The quality of detail a printer can produce, measured in dots per inch (dpi); usually the higher the resolution, the better the quality.
Dpi	Dots per inch, a measurement of how many dots per linear inch a printer can produce. Business quality output is 600 dpi.
Color Separation	Commercial printers separate artwork into its component colors (cyan, magenta, yellow, and black) and make film separations for each ink that will be used in your publication.
RGB	Red-green-blue are the kinds of colors seen on a computer screen. They don't translate exactly into print.
CMYK	Cyan-magenta-yellow-black describes the kind of color model a printer uses.
Pantone Matching System	A standardized color specification; you can select from 500 colors contained in a swatch book at your commercial printer.
Spot Color	Printed with premixed inks, each color is printed using a separate plate, and provides a cheaper color option than full color.
Process Color	Separating each block into CYMK components reproduces color; choose process colors from a color-matching system like Pantone Matching System.

Setting Up the Printer

Before you begin to create a publication, check the default printer settings, because Publisher composes your publication based on this printer. To get to the Printers folder, click the Start button on your desktop's taskbar, point to Settings, and then click Printers. In Windows 98, the default printer has a small check in front of it. If you right-click the default printer, a pop-up menu appears. Click Properties and use the Properties dialog box to control the features of your particular printer. Here you can modify specifications relating to paper size, page orientation, printer resolution and other printer options. The settings that you choose in this dialog box will stay in effect for all the publications you print in Publisher until you change them.

Setting Printing Options

To customize your printing options from within Publisher, open the publication you want to print and choose Print Setup from the File menu. The Print Setup dialog box appears, which lets you control the paper size, orientation, and source (whether you will place the paper in the printer's input bin or manually feed it through.) Click the Properties button in the Print Setup dialog box to specify a custom resolution for this print job. To specify how you want graphics to be handled, click the Advanced Button and make your changes in the Advanced Graphics Settings dialog box. The settings you make from within Publisher will remain in effect for this particular publication.

When you are ready to print your publication, click Print on the File menu, and the Print dialog box appears. Here you can specify more advanced print settings that allow you to further refine how your publication will look when it emerges from your home printer. The Print Settings dialog box shown here appeared after we clicked Advanced Print Settings in the first Print dialog box:

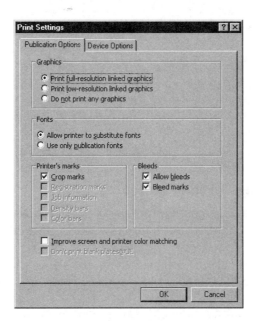

Using Commercial Printing Services

If you want to print on both sides of the paper (and your home printer doesn't support this), select from a wide variety of special papers and sizes of paper, or specify binding or laminating for your publication, you can take it into a copy shop. They can also print more copies of your document in higher quality color than you could at home. It's always a good idea to call the copy shop to find out how they'd like you to set up your publication before you deliver it to them.

PostScript vs. Publisher Files

What is the difference between sending a PostScript file to a commercial printing service and sending a Publisher file to that printing service? And which one should you choose?

A commercial printing service often makes the decision for you. If they use the current version of Publisher in their shop, you can save your publication in its native format (.pub files). Then you can use Publisher's Pack And Go command to prepare your work to hand off to the service.

The advantages to this method are several: Publisher checks that all linked and embedded graphics are present, embeds the TrueType fonts selected, and compresses the file to hand off. The commercial printing service then performs all the necessary prepress tasks—creating color separations, making color corrections, and checking that fonts and linked graphics are available. The disadvantage is that the printing service might not have the TrueType fonts you specified and might substitute ones you don't like. (Call first and ask which fonts they have on hand.) Or they might not use the particular programs you used to create linked or embedded objects and so cannot fix any problems with those images.

If the printing service you selected specializes in high-quality, professional-level printing, they might only accept files in PostScript format. (The Office Assistant offers detailed information about which PostScript printer driver you have or should install.) After verifying that you have the correct printer driver installed, you can format your publication as a PostScript file by clicking Save As on the File menu. In the drop-down list box for Save As Type, click PostScript file (.ps). Publisher then translates all the information needed to print your document into PostScript, a page description language that prints exactly the same on any PostScript printer.

You can't edit a PostScript file. You must edit the source file and then make a new PostScript file for your publication. Therefore, it's a good idea to do your own prepress work quite carefully. Employ Publisher's Design Checker. Make sure that all linked and embedded graphics are present. Print your own color separations. Then compress the file to hand off to the printing service.

If you want your finished product to display high-resolution black-and-white, spot-color, or process-color printing, and you have the appropriate amount of turn-around time at your disposal, you'll want to take your publication to a commercial printing service. You don't even have to really understand what these options mean, because a Publisher 2000 wizard will walk you through the preparation process. (But the more you know about how color looks on your computer screen and on the printed page, the better desktop publisher you'll become.) To set up your publication for a commercial printing service, or to prepare it for a copy shop, follow these steps:

1 Point to Pack And Go on the File menu. Then click Take To A Commercial Printing Service. The Pack And Go Wizard dialog box appears.

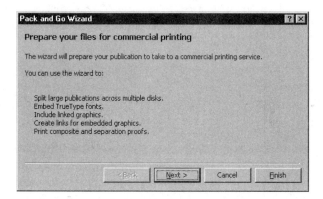

2 The Pack And Go Wizard asks you to choose where you'll save your files. (This could be a floppy disk on drive A, or a folder on your desktop.) Click the drive, or click Browse to search your computer for a location.

3 Specify how you want Publisher to handle fonts, linked graphics, and links for embedded graphics in your publication. Then click Next to continue.

4 Your publication is almost packed and ready to go. Click Finish, and the wizard will compress your publication into a file and store it along with an Unpack.exe file, which the printing service uses to unpack these files.

When you're communicating with your commercial printing service, you'll find that they are probably familiar with Microsoft Publisher. If not, you can tell them that Publisher supports process-color, spot-color, and black-and-white printing; it also supports RGB, HSL, CMYK, and Pantone color models; and finally, it supports automatic and manual color trapping.

Creating Brochures and Newsletters

Publish or perish! You might not be under quite this much pressure, but typically, you won't have as much time as you'd like to produce a publication. For instance, you might decide to publicize an event you've organized by printing a flyer at the last minute. Or you must hurry a newsletter along because your contributors missed their deadlines. Perhaps the two-fold brochure you thought would cover the ground is turning into a three-fold one overnight. How will you pull together an entire publication?

This chapter focuses on three types of publications you can create using Microsoft Publisher wizards: flyers, three-fold brochures, and newsletters. You'll learn how to experiment with decorative fonts, duplicate custom shapes, and add border art to text frames when constructing a simple flyer. If you're the editor of a periodic newsletter, you'll learn to create a consistent, recognizable look for your publication by repeating elements, such as a logo or masthead, on the background of every page. When creating an informational brochure, you can use Publisher's Table tool to create fold lines for your publication. And when your publication is ready to print, you can set up a mass mailing to your targeted audience.

Designing a Flyer

A flyer is an inexpensive, one-page publication designed to announce an event or promotion in an attention-getting format. In a flyer, you can fearlessly try out large font sizes, decorative fonts, and bold colors. Your goal is generally speed and eye-catching appeal when you choose this format. You can print this type of publication on low-grade paper, because you won't need it to last long. The Flyer Wizard can help you produce a quick piece of advertising that whets your readers' appetites for more information about your product, service, or event.

For instance, you can use the Party Announcement Wizard to create an advertising flyer for a small business that looks like this:

FIGURE 46-1.

The Party Announcement Wizard helps you quickly publicize an event.

 The Flyer.pub file, used for the example in Figure 46-1, is located on the Running Office 2000 Reader's Corner page. For information about connecting to this Web site, read the Introduction.

Even a simple Publisher project, like constructing a flyer, will look better if you confirm your printer settings before you select a wizard. Changing printers after you've designed your piece can affect the fonts, paper size, and character formatting you've chosen, as well as the area of the page that will print. For information on setting up your printer for publications, see "Printing Your Publication," page 1094.

Editing Headers and Headlines

When you start a new publication using the Flyer Wizard, text entry is literally a matter of replacing the placeholder text that Publisher provides on the page. If some of this text is grouped with another object or frame, as in Figure 46-2, or layered behind another object, as in Figure 46-3 (shown on the following page), you'll want to use Publisher's tools and techniques to make your page behave.

In Figure 46-2, the Group Objects tool is displayed underneath the frame that includes the date. The header here is actually composed of two sets of grouped frames: a text frame placed on top of a color-filled rectangle.

FIGURE 46-2.
Grouped objects in a header's text frame.

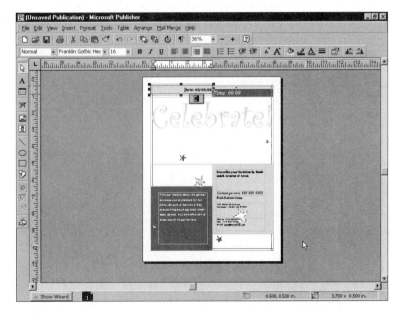

FIGURE 46-3.
A custom shape
obscured by a
filled frame.

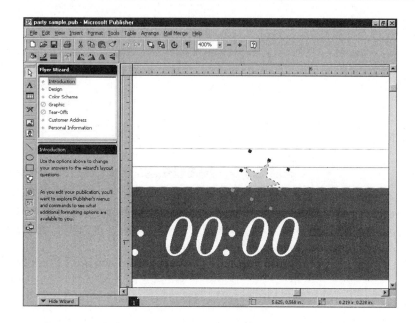

If you create a text frame from scratch and copy it to a color-filled frame or background, you'll notice that the text frame appears glaringly white. To blend the text with the filled background, select the text frame and press Ctrl+T. The text frame becomes transparent like the one shown in Figure 46-3.

As you insert the header information for your particular flyer, you might notice hidden or partially hidden elements in the template. For example, in Figure 46-3, a small graphic is partially obscured by the time frame. To reveal it, select the custom shape's frame in the workspace, point to Zoom on the View menu, and then click Selected Objects. Then click Bring To Front on the Arrange menu to bring the shape into full view.

Font Facts

Decorative fonts, such as Curlz MT, Forte, or Lucida Calligraphy, are fun to use as display type. However, decorative fonts can be hard to read if the font is too small in point size. A *point* is the unit of measurement a printer uses to measure type: there are 72 points to an inch. An old term for metal type gives another unit of measurement its name—the pica—which is also used by typographers. One pica equals 12 points. To create readable headlines, use decorative fonts at 14 points or more. Another rule of thumb used by desktop publishers is to format headlines that are 1.5 times larger in point size than body text.

Duplicating Custom Shapes

You can easily duplicate any of the custom shapes included in your design set by using the copy and paste technique. Right-click the shape you want to duplicate, and click Copy on the pop-up menu that appears. Then right-click again and click Paste. Reposition the new shape by pointing to its border and dragging the frame when the mouse pointer becomes the Move icon. This illustration shows a custom star shape that has been duplicated and selected to move:

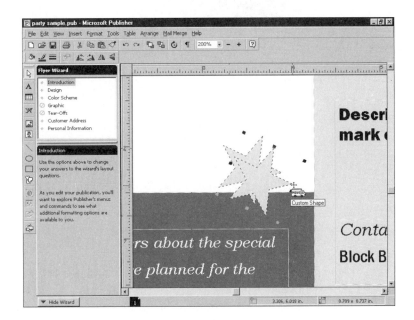

Adding Borders to a Frame

Borders are useful when you want to add emphasis to a text frame and separate it from other text frames on your page. To add a decorative border, select the entire frame you want to format by clicking outside the text that rests in it. Click the Line/Border Style tool on the Formatting toolbar and then click More Styles.

Line/Border Style

The Border Styles dialog box appears. Click the BorderArt tab and select from the list of available borders. To add color to the border, click the arrow in the Color list box. (The color options shown in the illustration are components of the Iris scheme, because it is the default scheme for the Party Announcement Wizard.) Choose a color that complements your color scheme.

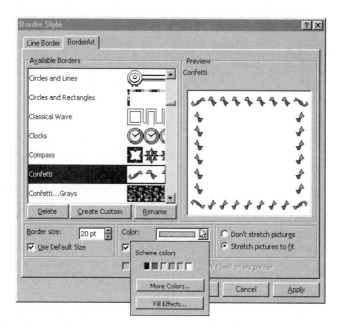

To add a plain border to a frame, select the frame. This time, click the Line Border tab in the Border Style dialog box and choose a point size for the border's thickness.

Using Design Checker

When you're satisfied with the content of your publication, Publisher's Design Checker tool can help guarantee that you don't print it with any embarrassing errors, such as an empty frame, a partially covered graphic element, or text left in the overflow area.

To use the Design Checker, do the following:

1 Choose Design Checker from the Tools menu to display the following dialog box:

Publisher will check the pages you specify and can also check the background pages.

2 Click Options to see which design elements Publisher can check for you:

3 Make your selections, and then click OK in the Options dialog box and OK in the Design Checker dialog box to start the Design Checker.

Publisher will check all the pages of your publication and notify you of its findings by displaying a dialog box like this:

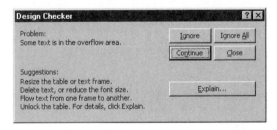

4 Click Explain, and Publisher will provide Help on each problem. It's up to you to decide if you want to follow up on Publisher's advice.

Creating a Three-Fold Brochure

A brochure is a small pamphlet that briefly describes an event, product, or service. It's folded into two, three, or four folds and can include an entry blank or order form and space for a mailing address. One rule of thumb for brochure building: Keep it simple! Short, pithy, and balanced works well in a brochure. It's not the place to provide exhaustive information about your business or service. You'll notice that Publisher's Brochure Wizard offers you lots of *white space*—areas on the page without text or graphic images. This empty space gives the eye a place to rest and adds impact to the rest of your publication.

Using the Brochure Wizard's Frames design (and inserting some clip art, which you'll learn how to do in the next chapter), you can create a brochure promoting a small book that looks like the one shown in Figure 46-4.

FIGURE 46-4.
Publisher's Brochure Wizard creates effective promotional pieces.

 ON THE WEB   The brochure.pub file, used for the example in Figure 46-4, is located on the Running Office 2000 Reader's Corner page.

TIP

What's Inside?

When you begin to create a brochure using a Publisher wizard, you'll notice some valuable design and layout tips on the inside page of the brochure template. You might want to print the template before you customize it, so that you have an actual thumbnail sketch to guide you in creating your publication.

Formatting Text in a Brochure

Large or decorative letters placed at the beginning of a heading or paragraph in a brochure can quickly draw a reader into your publication. Using Publisher, you can format initial capital letters in a variety of distinctive ways, which turn the letter into a graphic element in its own right.

> **NOTE**
>
> Initial caps are first capital letters in text that align with the baseline of the first line of text. Dropped caps are first capital letters that hang, or drop, below the first line of text.

You could manually create ornamental first letters by creating a text frame for them, using the Text Frame Tool button, and then formatting the individual letter. However, Publisher supplies many preformatted drop caps and initial caps for you to choose from. To insert one in your text, follow these steps:

1 Position the insertion point anywhere in the text whose first letter you want to format.

2 On the Format menu, click Drop Cap. The Drop Cap dialog box appears:

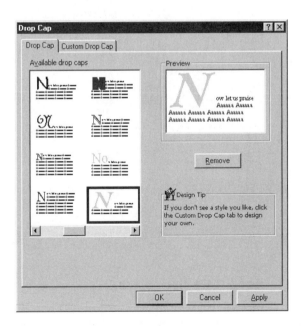

3 Select the Drop Cap tab.

4 Choose the preformatted drop or initial cap that you would like to insert.

5 Click Apply to preview the effect from within the dialog box.

6 Click OK.

If you want to create a custom drop or an initial cap, or if you want to format an entire first word or several letters at once, click the Custom Drop Cap tab. You can customize letter size, position, and font, as well as specify the number of letters you want to enhance.

A three-fold brochure affords limited space in which to type text. To avoid creating long lines of text in a heading, which results in excessive hyphenation, you might want to force line breaks manually. To do this, place the insertion point before the character you want to wrap to the next line, and press Shift+Enter to force a break in the text there.

To add emphasis to text, click Font on the Format menu and experiment with the different effects available. The Font dialog box, shown here, displays the Engrave effect applied to the Century Schoolbook font.

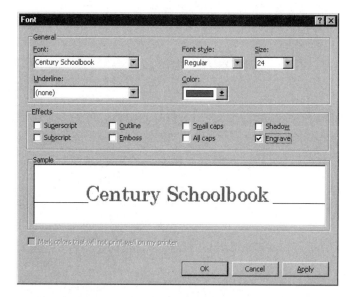

Folding a Brochure

Nothing looks more amateurish than a clumsily folded brochure. To ensure that the finished product looks as professional as its content suggests, you might want to order paper from a specialty paper company, such as PaperDirect, which will be premarked at the folds. Publisher can display some patterned PaperDirect papers when you click Special Papers on the View menu for you to preview. (However, if you select one of these papers, you must order it from the company and take care to fit your brochure design scheme into the paper's scheme.) Or your neighborhood stationery store might carry some papers specially designed for brochures.

You can easily use the Table tool to create a folding grid for yourself on a sample brochure. To make fold marks on a brochure to use as a guide, follow these steps:

Table Frame
Tool

1   Click the Table Frame Tool button on the Objects toolbar.

2   Drag the crosshair pointer over the entire brochure to create a table that is the same size as your layout.

3   In the Create Table dialog box, enter 1 in the Number Of Rows text box and 3 in the Number Of Columns text box. Then click OK.

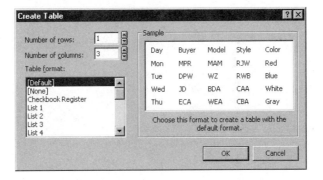

4   Point to Select on the Table menu, and click Columns.

5   When the first column is selected, click the Line/Border Style tool on the Formatting toolbar, and click Hairline.

6   Repeat the procedure in step 5 for the next column.

7   With the table selected, click Send To Back on the Arrange menu.

When you print this sample brochure, the lines will evenly mark the three folds of your brochure, and you can use them as a guide for folding your publication.

Creating a Newsletter

A newsletter can serve as a promotional piece for a business or as a periodical for an organization and is often produced on a monthly or quarterly basis. Publisher provides many newsletter styles that you can modify to speak to your audience. In this section, you'll also learn how to create a newsletter for a mass mailing by using Publisher's mail-merge feature.

Using the Tilt Newsletter Wizard (and inserting some clip art), you can create a small business newsletter that looks like the one shown in Figure 46-5.

 ON THE WEB

The Holiday.pub file, used for the example in Figure 46-5, is located on the Running Office 2000 Reader's Corner page.

When you begin creating a newsletter using a Publisher wizard, you'll notice that the template provides a complete mock-up of a newsletter.

FIGURE 46-5.
A seasonal newsletter created by using the Newsletter Wizard's Tilt design.

It might be useful to print this and review it now. As you examine the layout and read the guidelines, you can begin to plan how and where you'll insert your own information. The guidelines go into great detail, even specifying how many words fit into each column. You can reuse all this information when you let Publisher convert your newsletter into a Web site. *(For more information, see Chapter 48, "Designing A Web Publication.")*

When you've found a newsletter design that works for you, and you've customized it with your company or organization's logo, masthead (the main title of the newsletter), contributors' articles, or other unique design features, you can save it as a template. Reusing design elements is especially important in a periodical publication, because it saves you time during your publication cycle and creates a familiar, recognizable look for your piece.

Editing the Masthead and Headlines

You can replace the generic headline text that the wizard provides by selecting it and entering your own text. If you have created a unique masthead or headline that you would like to repeat on the inside pages of your publication, follow these steps:

1 Select the frame you want to copy. (If the text frame includes a logo or graphic, you might have to group the two objects to copy the whole design element.)

2 Right-click the frame, and click Copy.

3 Use the Page Navigation buttons to move to an inside page.

4 On the View menu, click Go To Background.

5 Right-click in the new page, and click Paste.

6 Then click Go To Foreground on the View menu.

You'll need to resize and position the masthead to suit your design scheme, but it will repeat in the background of every page, giving your periodical a consistent identity.

If you want to replace the entire masthead, click the masthead, and then click Design Gallery Object on the Insert menu. The Microsoft Publisher Design Gallery dialog box appears, as shown on the next page.

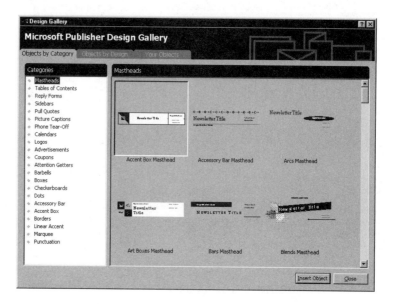

Select a more pleasing masthead, and then click Insert Object. You'll notice that the Design Gallery contains many categories of objects that you can insert to customize your publication.

Using Pull Quotes

Pull quotes are lively quotations that are drawn from the text of your story to provide interest and variety on your page. They're typically placed in the margins of your pages. To add one to the newsletter, follow these steps:

1 Click the Pull Quote placeholder, and press Delete.

2 Revisit the Design Gallery Object on the Insert menu. Select Pull Quotes in the Categories list. The window to the right displays examples of different design styles for pull quotes.

3 Select one that is suitable for your format, and click Insert Object. The selected pull quote appears in its own frame, as shown here, with a button at the bottom that you can click to activate the Pull Quote Wizard:

Selected pull quote frame

Inside Story Headline

"To catch the reader's attention, place an interesting sentence or quote from the story here."

This story can fit 100-150 words.
The subject matter that appears in newsletters is virtually endless. You can include stories that focus on current technologies or innovations in your field.
You may also want to note business or economic trends, or make predictions

Wizard: Click to start. Inside Story Headline

Wizard button

The Pull Quote Creation Wizard, shown here, is a dialog box that contains a list of pull quote designs that you can use to change your design choice:

Inserting a Word Document

The newsletter template tells you the number of words that fit into each story frame. You can create a story in Microsoft Word and place it in your newsletter or import a document that you've already saved. First delete the text in the placeholder. Then click Text File on the Insert menu, and select the file you want to insert into the newsletter. After you click OK to insert, you might find that your story runs over onto the next page of your publication. You can control this overflow by using the Autoflow option. Simply click Yes in the message box that Publisher displays, asking if you want to use this option. You can also manually control overflow by using the Connect Frames toolbar. To do this, follow these steps:

1 Click the text frame that is overflowing.

2 Click Connect Text Frames on the Tools menu. The Connect Frames toolbar appears.

3 Click Connect Text Frames, and move the pointer to the frame that the story will flow into.

4 If your story wraps to another page, right-click the text frame, point to Change Frame, and then click Text Frame Properties. The Text Frame Properties dialog box appears:

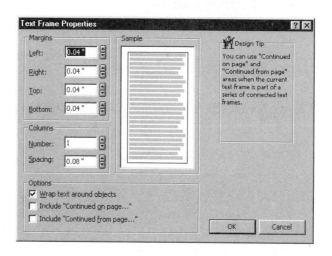

5 Follow the design tip in this dialog box.

You can use the Continued On Page or Continued From Page options to notify your readers that the story flows between pages.

6 Use the Page Navigation buttons on the Publisher window's status bar to move from page to page in your newsletter as you add and edit text.

Creating a Mass Mailing

? SEE ALSO

For a more detailed discussion of mail merge in Microsoft Word, see Chapter 13, "Using Word to Automate Mailing."

Newsletters can be a way of keeping in touch with your readers on a consistent basis as well as extending a service to them in the form of some absorbing content. To automate the mailing process for you, Publisher provides a mail-merge feature. (You might already be familiar with mail merge from your experience with Word.) Mail merge refers to the merging of two documents: in this case, the main document, a newsletter, and the data document, which is your mailing list. To create a mass mailing, you'll first need a mailing list.

1 On the Mail Merge menu, click Create Publisher Address List. The following dialog box appears:

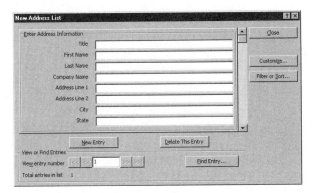

2 Enter the information for the first addressee in the appropriate fields. Click the New Entry button when you're finished with one and ready for the next.

3 Click the Close button when you've entered your entire mailing list.

4 Enter a name for the list in the File Name list box of the Save As dialog box.

Now you're ready to merge the two documents. To do so, follow these steps:

1 Select a field (or line in the address frame) where you want to insert data.

2 Click Open Data Source on the Mail Merge menu. The following dialog box appears:

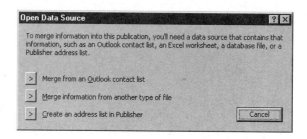

3 Click Merge Information From Another Type Of File.

4 Select the name of the address list file you just created in the next dialog box. Then click Open.

5 In the Insert Fields dialog box, click the first field that you want to insert, and click Insert. The field appears in the box on the right.

6 Continue inserting fields and typing spaces, punctuation, and returns, as necessary, to properly format your fields into an address format. For example, type a comma and a space between the field codes for city and state.

7 Repeat steps 5 and 6 for each field code you want to insert.

8 When your fields are properly arranged in an address format, click Merge on the Mail Merge menu.

When you are ready to send the merged documents (in this case, a newsletter addressed to names from your mailing list) to your printer, you'll notice that the usual Print command on the File menu is replaced by the Print Merge command. Take advantage of the opportunity Print Merge offers to print a test to check that the mail merge is functioning as you anticipated.

Adding Graphics and Special Effects

Now that you can lay out a publication using a wizard and format text in an interesting fashion, you're ready to give your work an even more distinct identity. You'll add a deeper dimension to the message you want to convey by using graphics in your publications.

You don't have to be a professional artist to tap into Microsoft Publisher's graphics arsenal. A visit to the Clip Gallery gives you access to thousands of high-quality clip-art images and hundreds of photos. (You'll also find sound and video clips in the Clip Gallery to use when your publication is destined for the Web.) If all the available art doesn't move you, you can turn to the Drawing toolbar, an old friend from Microsoft Word, Microsoft Excel, and Microsoft PowerPoint, and create your own. Or, using the WordArt tool, you can build dramatically different text effects. Often simply adding a block of color to text or changing the color of an image can subtly affect the message you want to convey.

The Design Gallery contains a wide variety of Publisher-designed objects, which can enhance your publication in an instant. Here you'll find professionally designed logos, headlines, calendars, mastheads, and other design elements that add polish to your work.

You'll learn to add various graphic elements to your publications in this chapter. Continue to experiment with Publisher's tools to position and combine these elements as you create well-designed, original publications.

Inserting Pictures and Clip Art

You can enhance the visual appeal of your publication by choosing graphics that support your message. Depending on which tool you choose to make a frame for an image, Publisher prompts you to search for a photo, a scanned image, a piece of clip art, or a picture from your files. Figure 47-1 shows a picture downloaded from the Web and inserted into an Arcs Quick Publication template.

Inserting Pictures

To insert a picture into a publication, follow these steps:

1 Using the Picture Frame Tool on the Objects toolbar, draw a frame for the object.

FIGURE 47-1.
Graphics personalize your publications.

2 On the Insert menu, point to Picture, and then choose From File. The Insert Picture dialog box appears:

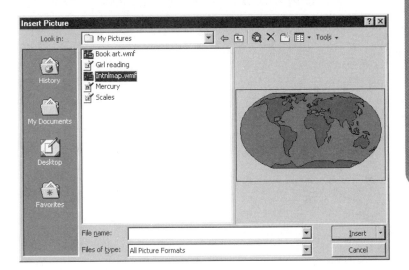

3 In the drop-down list box, select the file location for the picture you want to insert.

4 Click the picture file you want.

   If available, a preview of the picture appears in the window to the right.

5 Click the Insert button in the dialog box, or double-click the image from the list. The image appears in your publication's picture frame.

Choosing Picture Formats

When you find electronic images you'd like to add to your graphics library, you'll notice that each image is stored in a particular file format. The two major file types you'll run into are *bitmap* and *vector* graphics. A bitmapped image consists of a pattern of pixels or dots, such as you see in newspaper photos. If you enlarge a bitmap image to more than 100 percent, you'll loose a great deal in resolution, and the image will appear grainy. A vector graphic consists of separate objects, such as lines or curves, which are defined by mathematical equations. An advantage of this mathematical description is that vector images can be enlarged or reduced—such as when working with logos—and the image remains crisp at any size. Clip art is often stored as a vector image. Table 47-1, on the next page, provides a partial list of graphics file formats that you can import into Publisher.

TABLE 47-1.   Graphics File Formats

File Format	File Name Extension	Type
Windows Bitmap	BMP	Bitmap
Tagged Image Format	TIF	Bitmap
PC Paintbrush	PCX	Bitmap
Kodak Photo CD	PCD	Bitmap
JPEG Picture Format	JPG	Bitmap
Graphics Interchange Format	GIF	Bitmap
Windows Metafile	WMF	Vector
Computer Graphics Metafile	CGM	Vector
Micrografx Designer/Draw	DRW	Vector
Encapsulated PostScript	EPS	Vector
DrawPerfect	WPG	Vector
CorelDRAW! 3.0	CDR	Vector

Resizing Pictures

You can resize or reposition inserted graphics to integrate them more gracefully into your publication. If you want to move a graphic, the easiest way to do so is to point the mouse pointer at a border of the frame and, when the pointer becomes the Move icon, drag the frame to a new location. Or, with the picture frame selected, choose Nudge from the Arrange menu to fine-tune your movements. To resize the graphic, you can use the sizing handles and your mouse. Select the picture frame, and drag a corner sizing handle to resize the frame while maintaining its proportions. (When resizing a custom shape or text frame proportionally, you must hold down Shift as you drag the handle.) To resize the height and width of a picture frame independently while using a corner sizing handle, press the Shift key while dragging.

To bypass the possible imprecision of the mouse moves altogether, explore the commands on the Format menu. For example, clicking Scale Picture (or Scale Object when you are resizing clip art) displays the following dialog box:

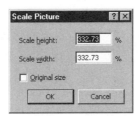

Scale Picture lets you make the image larger or smaller, according to the exact specifications you enter into the text boxes. Clicking Original Size returns the image to height and width values of 100 percent.

You might want to use only part of a picture. If an image contains elements that you want to hide rather than scale down, you can do so by using the Crop Picture tool. With the picture frame selected, click Crop Picture on the Formatting toolbar.

Crop
Picture

Alternately, you can choose Crop Picture from the Format menu. Place the mouse pointer on a sizing handle and, when it becomes the cropping icon, drag the handle inward until just the portion of the graphic you want to see remains. Using the Crop Picture tool doesn't erase parts of the image—it simply hides them from view. You can reveal the cropped area by dragging the handle out from the center of the image.

Working with Picture Frames

You can substitute pictures from your own files for the placeholder graphics in Publisher's templates. To add additional impact to your work, you also might want to change how a picture interacts with surrounding text. Remember that readers enjoy a certain order on the page. To create visual interest and not trigger a migraine in your readers, keep pictures at the end of a text frame or between columns of type or at the bottom of a page when wrapping text around a graphic. To edit a picture frame, select it, and then click the Picture Frame Properties button on the Formatting toolbar.

Picture Frame
Properties

The Picture Frame Properties dialog box appears, as shown on the following page.

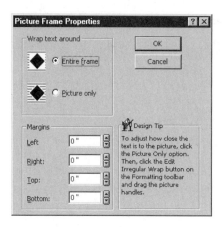

By default, Publisher wraps the text around the entire picture frame. (This dialog box is called Object Frame Properties when a piece of clip art is selected.) If you'd like to drop your picture directly into a text frame and make the text wrap around the picture, click Picture Only. Then enter the margins you want to set around your picture in the Outside Margins text box. To manually create margins around the picture, click the Edit Irregular Wrap button on the Formatting toolbar. (This button is available only after you select Picture Only in the Picture Frame Properties dialog box.) To use this tool to adjust how close the text will come to your picture, follow these steps:

Edit Irregular
Wrap

1 Position the mouse pointer over a sizing handle to change the pointer to an Adjust pointer.

2 Drag the handle to change the outline of the picture.

3 To add another handle, point to the selected border where you want the new handle, press Ctrl, and click the border. You can use this handle in the same way to adjust the irregular wrap around the picture.

Figure 47-2 shows a graphic in a text frame with an irregular wrap.

Controlling What You See

Displaying complex graphics on your computer screen can take up valuable time when you're working under a deadline. Also, you'll often print selected pages of your publication as you edit and proof them. If these pages include graphics, they can take a long time to print or require more memory than your printer can provide. You can use the Picture Display dialog box shown in Figure 47-3 to regulate the degree of detail you'd like Publisher to use to display your graphics. Choose

FIGURE 47-2.
Wrapping text around a graphic integrates the two elements.

Text formatted using the Edit Irregular Wrap button

Clip art inserted in text frame

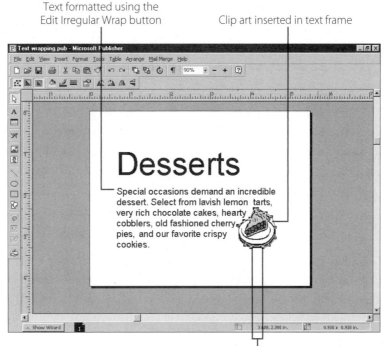

Adjust handles on the text wrapping boundary

FIGURE 47-3.
The Picture Display dialog box gives you three display options for pictures.

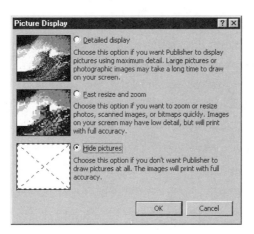

Picture Display from the View menu to display the Picture Display dialog box. If you click the Hide Pictures option, your pages will load quite quickly. If you've selected Hide Pictures in the Picture Display dialog box, when you want to print those pages, Publisher asks if you want your pictures to print or remain hidden. You can proof the text of your publication much faster if you choose to print without pictures.

Inserting Clip Art

Clip Gallery Tool

As you do with other graphics, you insert clip art into a publication by drawing a frame for the object, in this case using the Clip Gallery Tool button on the Objects toolbar.

> You can replace clip art in a placeholder by double-clicking the placeholder to open the Insert Clip Art dialog box.

When you draw the rectangular frame, the Insert Clip Art dialog box appears. To use the Insert Clip Art dialog box, follow these steps:

1 Select the frame that contains the clip art placeholder, if necessary. (Otherwise, use the Clip Gallery Tool to create a new frame. Then the Insert Clip Art dialog box automatically appears. In this case, you can skip step 2.)

2 Double-click the clip art placeholder to display the Insert Clip Art dialog box. (See Figure 47-4.)

FIGURE 47-4.
The Insert Clip Art dialog box contains hundreds of pieces of clip art organized by category and searchable by keywords.

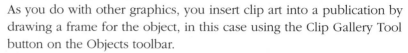

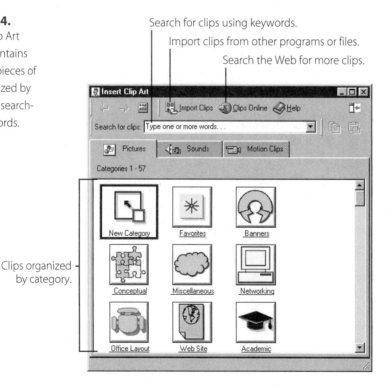

Search for clips using keywords.

Import clips from other programs or files.

Search the Web for more clips.

Clips organized by category.

3 Select a category of clips by clicking a subject area, and then click the image you want to use. (In Publisher 2000 you can drag the clip directly into your publication.)

4 Select the appropriate command that appears in the pop-up menu shown here. You can insert the clip, preview it, add it to your favorites category, or search for similar clips.

— Insert Clip.

— Preview Clip.

— Add Clip To Favorites Or Other Category.

— Find Similar Clips.

When you insert a clip, its art image appears surrounded by handles on your publication's page, and you can move or resize it to fit your needs. The commands on the Formatting toolbar and Format menu help you to refine the color and presentation of the image in a variety of ways.

 NOTE

> Publisher's Drawing toolbar might be familiar to you from your work in other Office programs. *(We cover it in greater detail in the section, "Creating Drawings in Word," page 323.)* In Publisher, you create your own drawing object by creating a picture frame, pointing to Picture on the Insert menu, and then choosing New Drawing. The Drawing toolbar appears, and you can create a drawing object, which you can resize, copy, move, rotate, flip, format, or delete. You'll find the predefined shapes on the AutoShapes menu particularly helpful in making arrows, stars, banners, and other special symbols to enhance your publications.

Creating Color and Fill Effects

If you want to give your publication an elegant touch or create a more unified look, experiment with color and fill effects. Adding color or a texture to a frame emphasizes the content of the frame and can be used to underscore relationships among different frames or content areas in your publication.

When you're selecting color options, remember that the print setup for your publication determines which colors you can choose. If you're printing in black and white or grayscale, you can use black, white, and shades of gray. If you've chosen a spot color, you can use the spot color and tints of it, as well as black, white, and shades of gray. And, if you're printing in full color, you have a rainbow of color and custom color options in Publisher 2000. Figure 47-5 shows a flyer template personalized with background color as well as clip art.

Working with Fill Colors

Of course, the easiest way to alter the color scheme of your entire publication is to revisit the wizard, select the Color Scheme option, and choose a new one. But if you're feeling adventurous, you can start out by making a change to the background color of a frame. If you want to, you can apply a custom color, or you can make a new frame and fill it with a solid color as an accent element. (See Figure 47-6.)

TheBizCard.pub file is located on the Running Office 2000 Reader's Corner page. For information about connecting to this Web site, read the Introduction.

To change the background color of a frame, follow these steps:

1 Select the frame. (Or create a new frame using the appropriate tool on the Objects toolbar.)

Fill
Color

2 Click Fill Color on the Formatting toolbar.

3 Under Basic Colors or Scheme Colors, click a color you want to use.

If you have an artistic bent, you can customize your color scheme. Click More Color Schemes, and then select the Custom tab of the Color

FIGURE 47-5.
The Garage Sale Flyer template customized with background color, clip art, and a new font color.

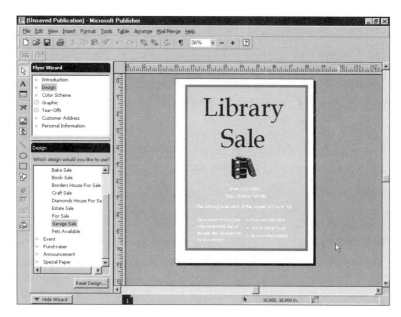

FIGURE 47-6.
Solid blocks of color add emphasis to a business card.

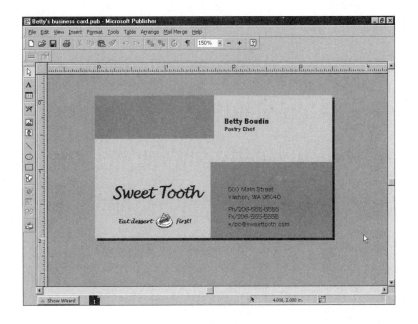

Scheme dialog box and mix your colors. (Or click Color Scheme on the Format menu, or point to Fill Color on that menu, and then choose More Color Schemes.)

 TIP

> **Inspiration at Your Fingertips**
> Graphic artists often create a *swipe file*. A swipe file is a collection of clippings, photos, natural elements like leaves or flower petals, or found objects like coins or bits of metal that have acquired a rich patina, all of which help stimulate the artistic process. You certainly wouldn't want to copy someone else's work, but you can draw inspiration from the great design ideas of the professionals. Just looking at publications with an eye for what works can help you form your own sense of style.

Applying Patterns and Gradients

If you prefer a more emphatic statement, you can add texture, shading, or a pattern to a frame. When you want to add a sense of movement to your work, explore the gradient fill effect. To create a custom fill effect for a frame, follow these steps:

1 Choose Fill Color from the Format menu.

2 Click Fill Effects.

   The dialog box on the following page appears.

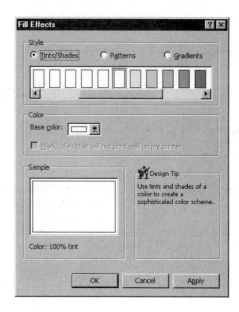

3 Pick the settings you want for the effect you're creating. Style options include effects using tints and shades of a color, different background patterns, and the gradient fill, which provides increasing shading using a tint or shade of one color.

A tint is a color mixed with white. A shade is a color mixed with black. Using different tints of one spot color in a publication can give the impression that you are using a wider swathe of the color spectrum than is actually the case.

If you're taking your publication to a commercial printer, you'll probably want to steer clear of the pattern effects. Patterns will boost your bill at the printer because it takes the service much longer to image this type of file to film.

Using WordArt

To create dramatic special effects using type, turn to Publisher's WordArt utility. This delightful tool might be familiar to you from your work with it in Microsoft Word, Excel, or PowerPoint. WordArt adds a lot of visual interest to text, as you can see in the following illustration:

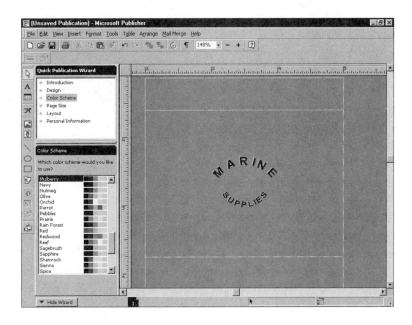

If you'd like to add decorative text to a publication—a special headline or logo, perhaps—it's easy. You don't even have to worry about positioning it at first, because you'll be able to move and size the WordArt frame later. To create special text effects using the WordArt utility, follow these steps:

WordArt
Frame Tool

1 Click the WordArt Frame Tool button on the Objects toolbar.

2 Draw a frame for the WordArt.
   A placeholder for the text appears on the page, and the Enter Your Text Here dialog box appears and is active. The automatic Your Text Here is highlighted. Notice that the Publisher window has been temporarily replaced by the WordArt window.

3 In the Enter Your Text Here dialog box, type the text you want to enhance.

4 If you want to include a symbol in the frame, click the Insert Symbol button. (Notice that the trademark symbol is located in the Insert Symbol dialog box. Trademarks are useful when you're creating a logo.) Click OK after you select the symbol you want to insert.

5 Click the Update Display button to replace the automatic text with the text you typed.

6 Close the Enter Your Text Here dialog box, and you are free to work in the WordArt window where you can specify the font, point size, and special shapes you want for your text. WordArt tools don't display ScreenTips when you rest the mouse pointer over them. Figure 47-7 labels these tools for you.

7 To return to the Publisher window, click outside the gray WordArt frame.

Experimenting with the different formatting capabilities of WordArt is easy and fun. You can add borders, color, shadows, and other effects to WordArt frames. As you try out the various tools in this window, you'll start to develop a sense of what works and what doesn't. Certain shapes are better matched with a particular length of text. For example, the circle shape needs at least four or five words to do it justice. And the more decorative typefaces can create confusion when paired with a WordArt special effect. WordArt can add a nice lively feel to your publication, but the text should always be readable.

FIGURE 47-7.
The WordArt window contains tools for editing text.

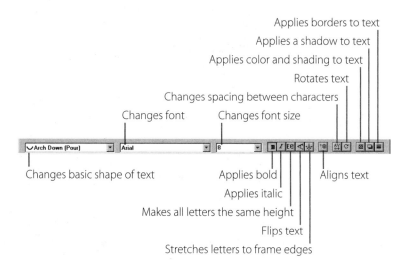

Applies borders to text
Applies a shadow to text
Applies color and shading to text
Rotates text
Changes spacing between characters
Changes font   Changes font size

Arch Down (Pour)   Arial   8

Changes basic shape of text   Applies bold   Aligns text
Applies italic
Makes all letters the same height
Flips text
Stretches letters to frame edges

Using the Design Gallery

Publisher's Design Gallery is full of *smart objects*—preformatted design elements, such as logos, coupons, and mastheads, which have a wizard associated with them. You can use the elements in the Design Gallery to customize your publications. You can even create your own custom designs and store them in the Design Gallery, so you can easily find and reuse them in other publications. To insert a Design Gallery object into a publication, follow these steps:

1 From the Insert menu, choose Design Gallery Object. (You don't have to choose a frame for the insertion. Design Gallery objects are inserted directly into your publication.)

The Microsoft Publisher Design Gallery dialog box appears. (See Figure 47-8.)

2 Select the category of design you want to use from the Objects By Category tab. The available objects are illustrated in the window to the right.

3 If you want to choose an object based on its design style, click the Objects By Design tab, and make your selection from the styles illustrated in that window.

4 When you have made your choice, click the Insert Object button.

FIGURE 47-8.
The Design Gallery dialog box contains an area to store design objects you create.

Click to see design objects organized by design style

Design objects

Design objects organized by category

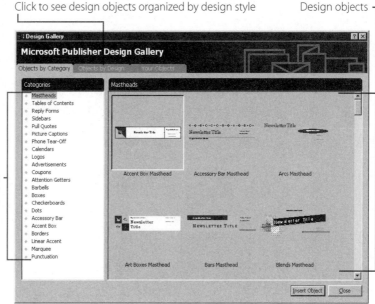

The following illustration shows a sidebar inserted from the Design Gallery into a newsletter:

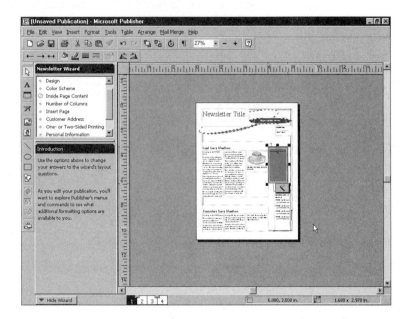

Now you can move, resize, and format this object, using the wizard that's associated with it. If one particular element in a smart object appeals to you, you can separate it from the rest of the objects by selecting the entire object and choosing Ungroup Objects on the Arrange menu. Although you can't use this ungrouped element with a wizard any longer, you can work with it alone or combine it with designs you have created on your own.

CHAPTER 48

Designing a Web Publication

You probably don't think of yourself as an information designer. But that's really the role you're playing when you gather information and supporting graphics and use Microsoft Publisher to shape them into a publication, such as a flyer, newsletter, or brochure.

In this chapter, you'll learn how easy it is to design electronic publications for the World Wide Web, using the same elements that went into your print publications. In addition to text and graphics, you can add multimedia elements to your publication when it's destined for the Web. Publisher 2000 contains photo images, video clips, sounds, and hundreds of small animation files, called GIFs (for Graphic Interchange Format), which add impact to your site. Using Publisher, you can create truly interactive Web pages by allowing visitors to send you e-mail messages. And, because color is free on the Web, you can brighten your pages by applying colorful backgrounds and vibrant graphics without factoring in print costs.

Publisher wizards are available to guide you through every step of the process, so when you want to reach a worldwide audience on the Web or connect with your colleagues on a company intranet, you can do so without having to become a Web master!

Planning for the Web

Publisher provides several options for creating a Web site. You'll learn more about these options later in the chapter. But for now, consider how a Web publication differs from a print publication. When you create a print publication, you generally assume that most people will read it straight through; however, your Web audience won't read in such a linear fashion. They'll enjoy browsing (or *surfing*) through your publication and expect to find lots of interesting jumping off places (or *hyperlinks*) to other pages and sources of information. As you can see in Figure 48-1, a Web page created by a Publisher Web Site Wizard displays the dynamic quality of electronic publishing.

ON THE WEB

The Coffee.pub file is located on the Running Office 2000 Reader's Corner page. For information about connecting to this Web site, read the Introduction.

Although lively hyperlinks are an essential component of Web publishing, they also allow visitors to choose their own path through your Web site. (See Figure 48-2.) While visitors might neatly follow your links to other pages in your site, they might just as easily jump to another site entirely. Therefore, you must create pages that can stand alone, because they could be the only ones a visitor chooses to see.

One of the fun aspects about designing a publication for the Web is that you can make it instantly interactive—you don't have to wait for your customer to receive a document in the mail and send a response

FIGURE 48-1.

A small business home page uses hyperlinks to connect the pages of its Web site.

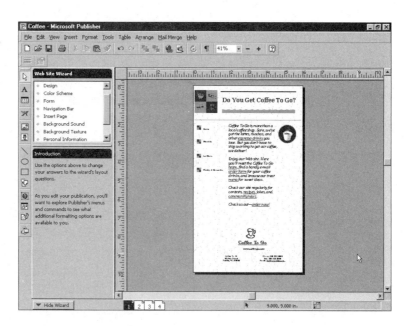

form back to you. Publisher 2000 wizards help you add electronic forms to your Web pages so visitors can communicate with you via e-mail. A business can take orders online and process them quite quickly, as a small espresso shop might do with an e-mail order for several coffee drinks. (See Figure 48-3.)

FIGURE 48-2.
A Web page branded with consistent design elements.

Logo and consistent page design

Link to home page

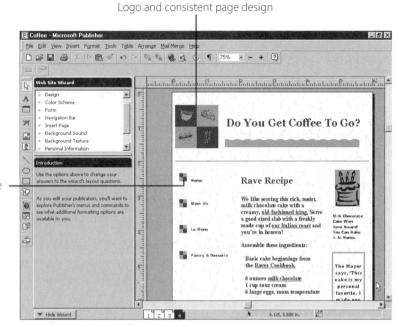

FIGURE 48-3.
Electronic order form created by a Publisher wizard.

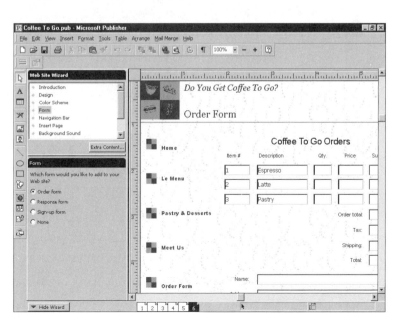

> ## A Web Page Primer
>
> A *Web page* is a single-page publication that is coded in HTML (Hypertext Markup Language) and available for viewing on the Internet. HTML is the language that tells a browser how to display the page. A browser is a software program that allows a user to view HTML documents on the Web and generally permits a user to send and receive e-mail as well. A *Web site* is a collection of Web pages that are connected by hyperlinks. *(You'll find out more about hyperlinks later, in the section "Inserting Hyperlinks," page 1143)* A Web site usually starts with a home page, which introduces the basic concept of the site. Using Publisher 2000, you can create either a single Web page or an entire Web site.

Creating a Web Site

After you have explored some of the differences between print and Web publishing and thought about how you'll edit information that's headed for the Web, you're ready to try your hand at electronic publishing. Publisher 2000 offers a variety of ways to lead you into a Web project.

- The Publisher Web Site Wizard, by far the easiest approach to creating a Web publication, asks for information and then builds a Web site around the answers you supply.

- Create Web Site From Current Publication (a command found on the File menu) begins the process of turning any publication into a Web site, whether you created it using a Publisher wizard or built it from scratch.

- Convert To Web Site (an option available in the Newsletter and Brochure Wizards) allows you to reuse the information in a Publisher-designed publication in a Web site, using a wizard to create the site or asking you to provide your own hyperlinks and layout.

- Creating a Web page using a blank publication provides an opportunity to really try your wings as a Web designer, although this approach assumes that you can handle the design, layout, hyperlinks, and site navigation on your own.

Using the Publisher Web Site Wizard

Microsoft wizards provide the friendliest and simplest way to get work done. If this is the first time you've created a Web site, you might want to use the Web Site Wizard to carry out the task. In Publisher 2000, this wizard gives you access to even more design sets than before to help you apply a consistent design scheme to your Web publication. To start the Web Site Wizard when you're already working in Publisher, choose New from the File menu, or, if the Microsoft Publisher Catalog window is displayed, choose Web Sites from the Publications By Wizard list. (Figure 48-1, page 1134, shows a customized Art Boxes Web site.)

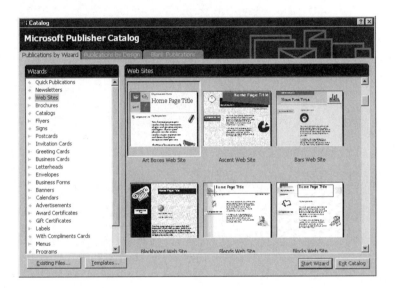

As you work with the sample home page, you'll notice that three tools relating specifically to the Web are now available on the Objects toolbar. (You'll learn more about using them later in the chapter.)

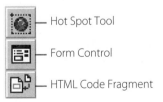 — Hot Spot Tool

— Form Control

— HTML Code Fragment

Just like the Publisher wizards you have used to create other types of publications, the Web Site Wizard gives you an opportunity to change the design and color scheme of your Web site. As you use this wizard-supported layout, you'll find placeholder text and graphics in frames where you can insert your own words and illustrations.

Using Form Controls

If you want to create an interactive form for your Web site, you can select the type of response form you want to include on your Web page. The wizard supplies a form template, which you can customize by experimenting with the Form Control tool on the Objects toolbar. This tool provides a toolbar that supports six different form properties, which you can add to a response form:

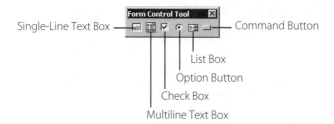

Single-Line Text Box —————— Command Button

List Box

Option Button

Check Box

Multiline Text Box

To adjust the form supplied by the wizard, double-click the control you want to change and make your changes in the appropriate dialog box.

Customizing the Navigation Bar

Visitors move through your site by clicking navigation controls, which form a system of built-in hyperlinks holding the pages of your site together. In addition to answering the Web Site Wizard's questions about this option, you can also select and customize a navigation bar by using the Design Gallery. Figure 48-4 shows a vertical navigation bar in the Capsules Design Set after we added a Design Gallery Web Navigation Bar element.

Inserting Sounds

You'll also find an opportunity to add background sound to a page when you use the Web Site Wizard. When you select Background Sound and click the Select Sound button, the Web Properties dialog box appears. With the Page tab selected, click the Browse button and the following dialog box appears, filled with sound files:

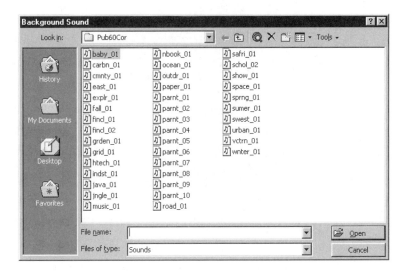

Double-click a sound file to insert it onto your page, and then click OK in the Web Properties dialog box. You won't be able to hear the sound until you preview it in your browser, which you can do by using the Web Page Preview command on the File menu. Test several sounds until you find one that complements your site.

FIGURE 48-4.

You can use a vertical navigation bar to link to other pages on your Web site.

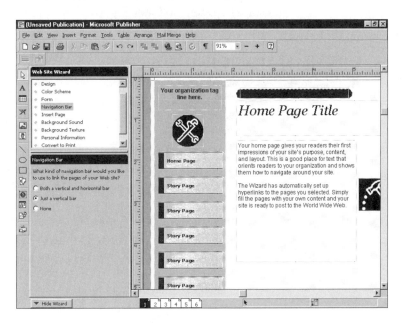

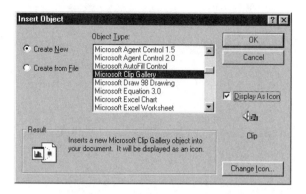

When you want to add a sound file that plays when a visitor selects it (rather than automatically when a page is loaded), visit the Microsoft Clip Gallery. First create a frame for the sound in your publication, using the Clip Gallery Tool button on the Objects toolbar.

When the Microsoft Clip Gallery dialog box appears, select a sound file from those listed in the categories on the Sounds tab. Click the file to display a pop-up menu, and click the Insert Clip button. *This pop-up menu is discussed in the section "Inserting Clip Art," page 1124.* Visitors to your site control this type of sound by clicking the icon if they want to hear a sound and bypassing it if they find the sound annoying. You can preview the sound by double-clicking the frame.

Changing the Background of a Web Page

The Web Site Wizard's Background Texture option allows you to change the background texture of your electronic page. When you click the Select Texture button, the Color And Background Scheme dialog box appears. You can create your own background here or click the Browse button (under Background on the Standard tab) to see Publisher's preformatted backgrounds. When the Web Backgrounds dialog box appears, click a background texture file, and then click the Views button and choose Preview to see what the background looks like. It's possible to pack too much of a punch in your Web page with a busy background, as shown in the illustration that follows. Make sure that you can read your text and hyperlinks against the new background before you choose one. Then click OK to apply it. Used with restraint, a background will harmonize with your content.

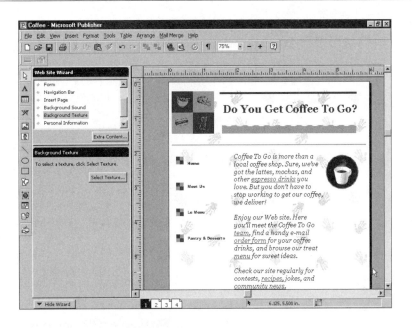

Creating a Web Site from an Existing Publication

When you want to turn any publication into a Web site, whether a Publisher wizard created it or you built it from scratch, open the publication in Publisher, and choose Create Web Site From Current Publication from the File menu. If you are converting a newsletter or brochure, the following dialog box appears and gives you an opportunity to choose how independently you want to work:

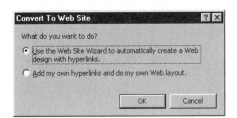

If you select the Web Site Wizard option, you'll be in familiar territory. If you're ready to branch out and add your own hyperlinks, electronic layout, and navigation elements, Publisher provides an opportunity to run the Design Checker, which ensures that your publication will perform correctly on the Web. If you want to convert any other type of publication besides a newsletter or brochure, Publisher provides the

---

Noticing Graphic Regions

When you ask Publisher to run the Design Checker, you'll often be warned that your publication contains text or objects that lie within the graphic region of other objects. What does this mean? When you've inserted a graphic or pattern into a text frame, created some WordArt, or simply placed different frames close together, you'll find that Publisher interprets those frames as one graphic element when it translates them into HTML. Recall that graphics can take a long time to download. Publisher uses the Design Checker to point this out to you and gives you an opportunity to correct your layout if you want to speed up download times. You can move the frames apart, separate graphics from text, or leave them as is if you want to preserve the formatting.

---

opportunity to run the Design Checker directly. You won't have access to the Web Site Wizard.

Converting a Publication into a Web Site

You can effectively reuse information you've compiled for a print publication by posting it to your Web site. If you have created a newsletter or brochure using a Publisher wizard, you'll find the Convert To Web Site option listed among the wizard's layout questions for that publication. When the publication you want to convert is open, click Convert To Web Site, and then click the Create button. Publisher leads you through the conversion process.

Starting a Web Site from Scratch

When you want to apply your design skills to the Web instead of relying on a Web Site Wizard or converting a print publication, follow these steps:

1 If the Microsoft Publisher Catalog window is open, select the Blank Publications tab. (If you've been working in Publisher, choose New from the File menu.)

2 Select Web Page, and click the Create button.

Publisher provides a blank electronic page for you. The tools for Web page construction are available on the Objects toolbar. If you know HTML, you can use the HTML Code Fragment tool to create a frame in which to add the code. When the HTML Code Fragment Properties dialog box appears, you can paste your HTML code over the placeholder text.

When you want to include dynamic graphics on your Web pages, visit the Microsoft Clip Gallery. It contains hundreds of animated GIF files. These compressed image files download quickly and provide movement and variety on your Web pages. You can find the GIF files displayed here in the Clip Gallery's Food & Dining category on the Motion Clips tab:

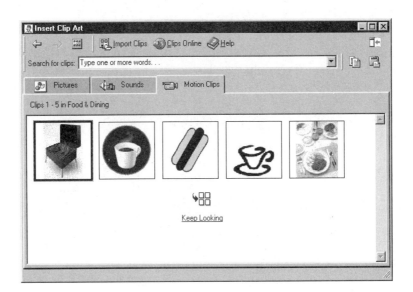

You can import JPEG (Joint Photographic Experts Group) files into the Clip Gallery from your own files or from the Web. JPEGs are most often used for photographs. You can also import video clips to add an interesting dimension to your site, but use them judiciously. Because they take a long time to download and can require users to install special software to play them, video clips are best used when you're sure your audience needs to see them.

Inserting Hyperlinks

? SEE ALSO

For more information about using hyperlinks in other Office programs, see "Inserting Hyperlinks," page 433 and Chapter 30, "Adding Special Effects and Internet Links."

The ability to link content is one of the most exciting features of Web publishing. When you create a hyperlink, you connect text or graphics to either another page on your site, a URL (Internet address) of a different Web site, an e-mail address, or to information you have saved in another Office program, such as a Microsoft Word document, a Microsoft Excel worksheet, or a Microsoft PowerPoint slide.

Hyperlinks add energy and flow to your Web publication, but you'll want to place your links strategically. Too many links placed closely together can create confusion, making your visitor wonder what goes with what.

Your home page is a logical place to start adding hyperlinks, because you'll want this page to lead visitors to other pages on your Web site. To create a hyperlink, select the text you want to turn into a link, and follow these steps:

1 On the Insert menu, click Hyperlink. The Hyperlink dialog box appears:

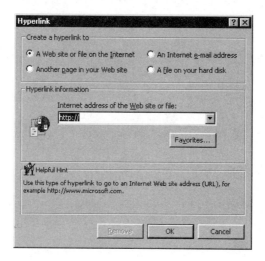

2 Select one of the four options in the Create A Hyperlink To area. The Hyperlink Information area of the dialog box changes for each option. This is where you specify the hyperlink's target location—where your visitors will be led as they navigate your site.

3 Select or enter the location for the hyperlink in the Hyperlink Information area, and then click OK.

You'll notice that the text you selected is now underlined and is displayed in a different color than the surrounding text. When you view these pages in your Web browser, your mouse pointer will change to a little hand when you place it over the hyperlink, and clicking the link will take you (and all the visitors to your site) to the destination you specified.

You can also link an object or graphic to another location. To insert a hyperlink into an object, follow the same steps as you did to insert a hyperlink into text, only this time select the object by clicking it. If you want to delete a hyperlink, it's easy. Right-click the hyperlink, and click Hyperlink on the pop-up menu. When the Hyperlink dialog box appears, just click the Remove button. The text or object remains, but it's not a hyperlink anymore.

When you're finished creating links in your publication, you'll want to check them out by clicking Web Page Preview on the File menu. Publisher turns your publication into Web pages and opens them in your default browser:

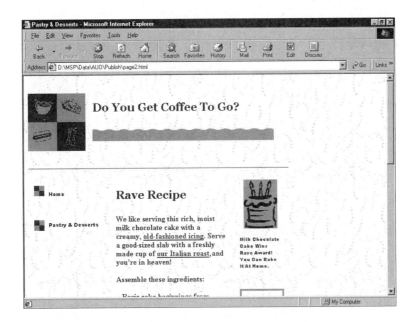

What's a Hot Spot?

A hot spot is the area on an object that is a hyperlink. When you create a hyperlink from an object using the Insert Hyperlink procedure, you're turning that object into one hot spot. In other instances—for example, when you have a large graphic that is segmented into parts, or a company photo of several team members—you might want to create more than one hot spot or hyperlink on that object. To create a hot spot, do this:

1 Click the Hot Spot Tool on the Objects toolbar.

2 Place the crosshair pointer in the upper left corner of the area on the object that you want to be a hyperlink.

3 Drag a rectangle diagonally to create a box around the object area.

When you release the mouse button, the Hyperlink dialog box appears. Enter the appropriate information, and click OK to create the hot spot. Repeat this procedure to create as many hot spots as you want.

Check each hyperlink by clicking it, and make sure that it takes you where you want to go. You can correct the links (editing text or Web addresses, and so forth) when you're back in the Publisher window. To get there, just click the Close button in your browser.

Publishing to the Web

Before you put your site up on the Web, you'll want to check all the details of your Web publication, not just the hyperlinks. Make sure that the text is free of spelling errors and laid out correctly, that the objects are in the right place, that the hyperlinks go where you want them to, that the animations move, and that the sounds make noise. Choosing Web Page Preview from the File menu lets you do this preflight check.

After you have ironed out any onscreen glitches, you might want to save your Web pages in a folder on your computer so you can publish them to the Web or to an intranet later. To do this, click Save As Web Page on the File menu, and type a name for the folder in the list box.

If you're ready to upload the finished product to a Web server to make it available on the Web or on a local area network that serves your company intranet, you can use the Web Publishing Wizard to accomplish this task. This wizard helps you transfer your Web pages, including all the support files containing graphics and other linked content, onto a Web server. To launch the Web Publishing Wizard, click the Windows Start button, point to Programs, point to Accessories, point to Internet Tools, and then click Web Publishing Wizard. The opening window for the Web Publishing Wizard appears:

If you've made an initial connection to the Web, you probably already have an Internet service provider. But, before you can post your files to their Web server, you'll want to call your ISP (Internet service provider) and ask how they want you to organize and name your files. Or contact the person at your company who is in charge of the Web site. He or she will be able to give you the information you need to follow the wizard and successfully post your publication to the Web.

When you learn the properties to assign to each Web page, such as the name of the page or the particular filename extension your Internet service provider uses, you can enter them in the Web Site Properties dialog box. To do this, choose Web Properties from the File menu, and click the Page tab. After entering this information, click the Site tab to provide descriptive words about your site:

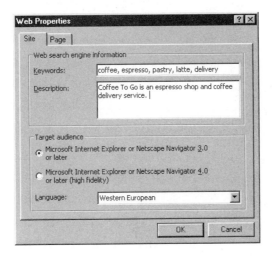

Many people use search engines to find information on the Web. When you include meaningful keywords here, you allow search engines to match your site to searches, which helps bring visitors to your site.

PART VIII

Small Business Tools

CHAPTER 49

Analyzing Business Performance Using Microsoft Small Business Financial Manager

I n this chapter, you'll learn how to use Microsoft Small Business Financial Manager, a powerful business analysis tool that lets you evaluate the cost of loans and leases, spot trends in earnings and cash flow, build periodic reports and performance charts, and analyze information created by third-party accounting software programs. Financial Manager is one of the four popular small business tools included with Microsoft Office 2000. We introduce the capabilities of Financial Manager in this chapter and describe the remaining tools in the next chapter.

Getting Started with Financial Manager

Financial Manager is designed primarily as an information integration tool, which lets you combine third-party accounting data, Microsoft Outlook contacts, cash flow statements, and other information into a central database for financial analysis. Financial Manager accomplishes this by building a comprehensive Microsoft Access database with all your financial material, and then it allows you to create reports and charts based on your company's collective information resources.

Although Financial Manager behaves like a stand-alone program, it is actually an innovative collection of Microsoft Visual Basic macros that run collectively in Microsoft Excel workbooks. Although Financial Manager handles most of the computation and formatting details behind the scenes, it still helps to have some familiarity with Excel before you start using Financial Manager. (Now and then you'll want to move around the information in workbooks, or customize a report or chart.) However, you'll quickly be amazed at how effective the wizards and tools in Financial Manager can be. With just a few keystrokes and clicks, you'll be generating important and valuable information about your small business.

Before you get started with Financial Manager, verify that you have the proper software on your computer by clicking the Windows Start menu, pointing to Programs, and clicking the program named Microsoft Small Business Financial Manager. If this program doesn't appear on your Start Programs menu, add it to your system now (along with the other small business tools) by running the Setup program for the Office 2000 Small Business Tools. (You'll find this Setup program and the necessary program files on one of the supplemental Office 2000 CDs.) Note that you'll also need a copy of Excel 2000 on your system to run Financial Manager, because Financial Manager relies so heavily on Excel to do its work.

When you start the Financial Manager program, Excel starts automatically and displays a customized worksheet containing task buttons and a new Financial Manager menu on the menu bar, as shown in Figure 49-1. To run the commands in Financial Manager, you have two options: you can either click the buttons on the Financial Manager worksheet, or you can click the commands on the Financial Manager menu. (Both options start the same wizards.)

FIGURE 49-1.

Financial Manager runs in Excel 2000 and creates a new menu called Financial Manager.

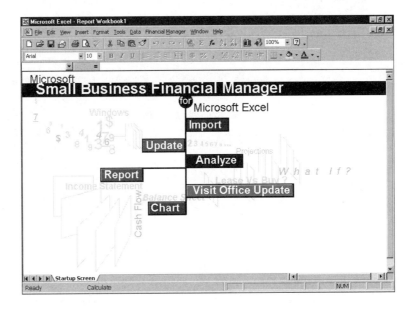

VIII

Small Business Tools

> **TIP**
>
> If Excel displays a warning message about the macros stored in Financial Manager when you first run the program, click the Enable Macros button to accept the Financial Manager macros and allow them to run. These macros are from a trusted source, and are essential to the proper operation of the Financial Manager program.

Comparing Loan and Lease Payments

A simple way to get started using Financial Manager is to compare loan, lease, and cash purchase schemes using the Buy Vs. Lease Wizard, one of the useful financial analysis macros accessible from the Select Analysis Tool command on the Financial Manager menu. Unlike some of the other wizards, however, this wizard doesn't require supporting databases or accounting data, so you can use it with little planning or preparation.

To run the Buy Vs. Lease Wizard, complete these steps:

1 From the Financial Manager menu, choose Select Analysis Tool. (Or click the Analyze button on the Financial Manager worksheet.)

Excel displays a dialog box that contains the complete set of business analysis wizards:

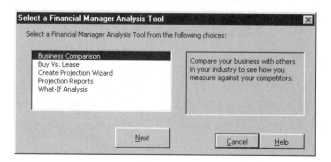

2 Click the Buy Vs. Lease option, and then click the Next button.

Excel starts the Buy Vs. Lease Wizard, which helps you determine whether it's more cost-effective to buy or lease business equipment and personal items. The wizard asks you a series of questions and then builds a worksheet, which provides the quantitative analysis. The first screen (Step 1) of the Buy Vs. Lease Wizard looks like this:

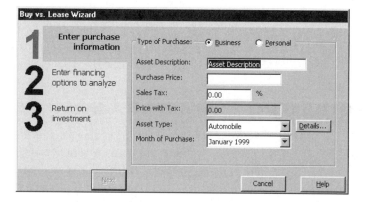

3 Click the type of purchase you want to evaluate (business or personal), type a description of the asset you want to purchase, and type the purchase price.

4 Specify the sales tax rate (if applicable), the asset type, and the month of purchase. When you're finished with Step 1, click Next.

The wizard displays the second screen (Step 2), which lets you specify different financing options that will be compared to the first option (Cash Purchase) that you identified.

The Details button (next to the Asset Type list box) lets you specify a depreciation method for this asset—an important variable for business assets that can be depreciated according to standard accounting principles.

5 Click the Add button to create a new financing option.

   The Buy Vs. Lease Wizard prompts you for a financing type:

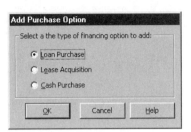

6 Verify that Loan Purchase is selected, and then click OK.

   The wizard displays a dialog box that asks you more about the type of loan you might use to finance the prospective asset.

7 Specify the name of your financial institution, down payment, interest rate, and loan period, and then click OK.

   The wizard adds the loan purchase option to the list.

8 Click the Add button again to add another financing option. Click Lease Acquisition, and then click OK to display the lease dialog box.

VIII

Small Business Tools

Your screen will look like this:

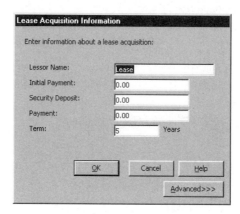

9 Specify the name of the lease company, the initial payment you're required to make, the security deposit, the monthly lease payment, and the term of the lease, and then click OK.

The Buy Vs. Lease Wizard displays your three financing options in a list box. Now you're ready to enter forecasting information about how much money this investment in equipment might return to you (applicable to business purchases only).

If you'd like to change one or more financing variables before you move on, choose the financing option in the wizard list box, and click the Change Financing button. You can also delete financing options from the report by choosing the option and clicking the Remove Financing button.

10 Click the Next button to display the wizard's third screen (Step 3). You'll see the following dialog box:

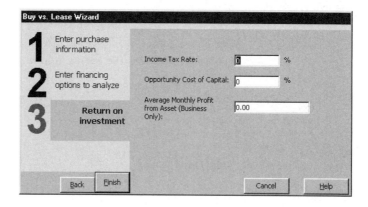

11 Pick a tax rate that applies to your business (you might need to consult your tax table to determine this figure—or ask your accountant). Next specify the opportunity cost of your investment capital (what you could reasonably make if you invested this money elsewhere), and specify the monthly income you expect to realize from this asset when it's fully functional. Click the Finish button after you've entered this forecasting information.

The Buy Vs. Lease Wizard creates a comprehensive comparison report based on the information you specified and then displays it in a new Excel workbook containing several worksheets:

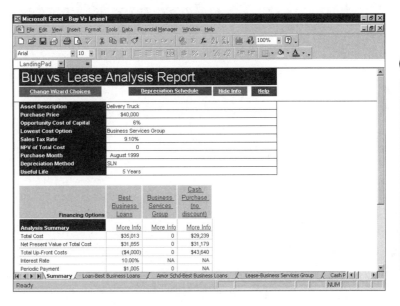

VIII

Small Business Tools

Reading a Comparison Report

To evaluate the comparison report that the Buy Vs. Lease Wizard created, you need to know a little about how Excel builds summary reports and manages worksheets. With the information you specified, the Buy Vs. Lease Wizard created a separate worksheet for each financing option that you considered (an all-out cash purchase, a loan purchase, and a short-term lease acquisition). Spread among the worksheets are tables, charts, and summary figures that present the various merits of your financing options. In addition, the wizard has generated a summary sheet (the first worksheet in the workbook), which displays your financing selections side by side, highlighting the choice that appears the most cost-effective. Other useful details are also listed in this table, including the net present value of the total cost, upfront costs, periodic payments, and so on.

Spend a few minutes evaluating the worksheets that the Buy Vs. Lease Wizard has created, clicking the blue underlined hyperlinks to jump to related information in the workbook. (Remember that you can move from one worksheet to the next by clicking the tabs at the bottom of the Excel window.) When you're finished, save the workbook with a new name using the Save As command so that you can reference this useful information later.

Building a Financial Database: The Import Wizard

Financial Manager has the ability to analyze business information from a variety of sources. To facilitate this analysis, it constructs a database of useful accounting and contact information from existing files on your system, including financial records from third-party programs, business contacts in your Outlook Contacts folder, and other sources. This database is built by the New Database Wizard, a utility that is shared with the Microsoft Customer Management program discussed in the next chapter. The New Database Wizard creates a robust database in Access format that is optimized for use with the Financial Manager reporting and charting tools. In this section, you'll learn how to create a Financial Manager database that contains information from a number of common business data sources. In the next section, you'll use this database to build cash flow reports and charts.

Table 49-1 lists a few of the popular accounting software formats that the New Database Wizard supports. Before you build a financial database, take some time to verify the content and location of your accounting files and contact folders. If you find that your files are in a different format than those listed in the table, or if they aren't listed at all, click the Visit Office Update button on the Financial Manager worksheet to connect to the Microsoft Office home page and check for new filters that will allow you to import your files using the New Database Wizard. The list of supported programs and versions is updated constantly.

TABLE 49-1.   Accounting Software Formats Supported by Financial Manager's New Database Wizard.

Accounting Software	Version	Vendor
ACCPAC Plus Accounting for DOS	6.1a	Computer Associates International, Inc.
BusinessWorks for Windows	9.0	State of the Art, Inc.
DacEasy Accounting for DOS	5.0	DacEasy, Inc.
Great Plains Accounting for DOS	8.0, 8.1, 8.2	Great Plains Software, Inc.
MAS 90 Evolution/2 for DOS	1.51	State of the Art, Inc.
One-Write Plus Accounting	4.03	Automatic Data Processing, Inc.
Peachtree Complete Accounting for DOS	8.0	Peachtree Software, Inc.
Peachtree for Windows	3.0, 3.5, 4.0, 5.0	Peachtree Software, Inc.
Platinum Series for DOS and Windows	4.1, 4.4	Platinum Technology, Inc.
QuickBooks for Windows	3.1, 4.0, Pro 4.0, 5.0	Intuit Inc.
Simply Accounting for Windows	3.0, 4.0, 5.0	Computer Associates International, Inc.

VIII

Small Business Tools

Follow these steps to create a new Financial Manager database:

1 Open an accounting data file on your system using a program listed in Table 49-1, and verify its contents and organization.

   The best files to import contain financial records, cash flow information, general ledger entries, and so forth. If you don't have accounting data files to analyze, you can still create a database with Outlook contact information, but you won't be able to use all of Financial Manager's reporting features.

   The following illustration shows a sample data file in the Intuit QuickBooks version 4.0 accounting program.

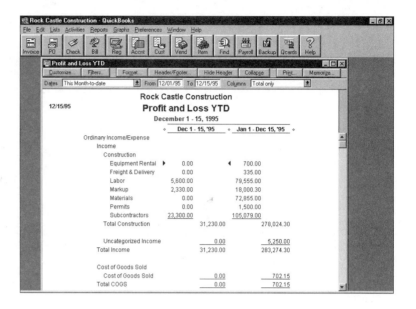

2 After you have verified your accounting data, close your accounting software and use the Windows Start menu to start Financial Manager (if it's not already running).

3 Click the Import button on the Financial Manager worksheet.
   Financial Manager starts the New Database Wizard, and the introductory dialog box looks like this:

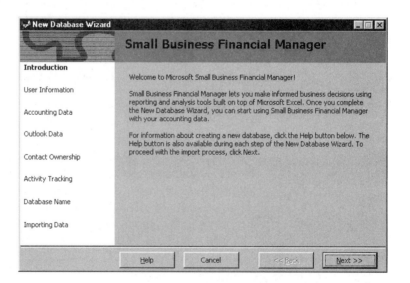

4 Click Next to create a username and password for yourself.

By using a username and password to secure your financial data, you can protect your financial records from wandering eyes.

5 Enter a username (for example, your first name and last initial), a secret password, and a verification of the password, and then click Next.

Financial Manager accepts your entry and begins a search for accounting data files on your system. (If Financial Manager doesn't find any files on your hard disk, click the Browse button and locate them yourself.)

6 Select the accounting data file you want to use in the list box, or click Do Not Import Any Accounting Data to skip existing data files. After you have made your selection, click the Next button. (If you did click Do Not Import Any Accounting Data, click Yes to continue creating a less-comprehensive database for Financial Manager.)

The wizard gives you the opportunity to import customer contact information from Microsoft Outlook, as shown in the following dialog box:

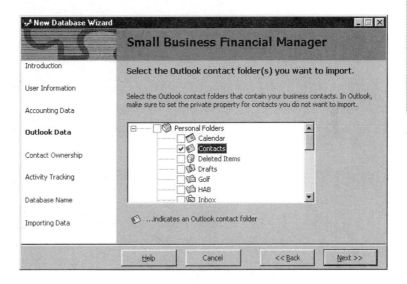

7 Scroll through the list and select one or more Outlook contact folders, identified individually by tiny business card icons. If you don't choose to import Outlook contact information, verify that all check boxes in this list are deselected. After you've made your selections, click Next to continue.

The New Database Wizard asks you if you want to make your Outlook contact information public (available to anyone for editing) or private (viewed by all, but edited only by you).

8 Click Option 1 (public) or Option 2 (private), and then click Next to continue.

The wizard displays a list of activities you can track in Financial Manager and Outlook, such as sending letters and receiving mail.

9 Select the activities for which you'd like to receive automatic notification. By default, two options are selected (Financial Manager events and Outlook events); deselect these boxes if you don't want to be notified when these activities occur. Again, continue by clicking Next.

10 Type the name of your new Financial Manager database, and specify a folder location if you'd like to modify the default.

Your screen will look like this:

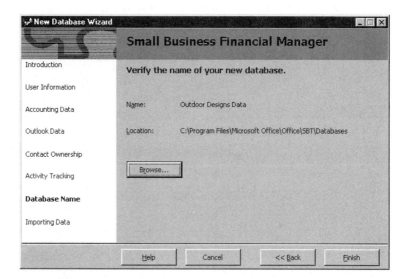

11 Click the Finish button to import your accounting data and Outlook contact information and create the final database.

After a few moments, you'll see a message announcing that the process is finished. Financial Manager has created a new Access database on disk to hold your business information, and you can now use the Financial Manager tools to analyze it.

Creating Financial Reports and Charts

After you create a Financial Manager database using information from your accounting files and Outlook contacts, you can evaluate the data using the Report Wizard and Chart Wizard commands on the Financial Manager menu. (The Report and Chart buttons on the Financial Manager worksheet start the same wizards.) Using the Report Wizard, you can create a balance sheet, cash flow statement, ratios report, and other useful worksheets. Using the Chart Wizard, you can create graphical versions of the most common reports—the perfect embellishment for a shareholder's meeting or annual report.

Using the Report Wizard

The Report Wizard creates a workbook that contains summary information that you can use to assess the financial health of your business at different times. You can create the following reports using Financial Manager:

- **Balance Sheet Report**—Creates a combined statement of your company's general health by listing current assets, liabilities, and stockholder's equity.

- **Cash Flow Report**—Details your company's cash inflow and outflow.

- **Income Statement Report**—Analyzes your company's profit (or loss) performance by summarizing your revenues and expenses for a specific period of time.

- **Ratios Report**—Lists important financial ratios as a test of your company's seaworthiness.

- **Sales Analysis Report**—Builds a pivot table report analyzing sales, expense, gross profit for different parts of your business, or all three.

- **Stockholder's Equity Report**—Evaluates how much of the company your stockholders own and how much is owned by creditors.

- **Trial Balance Report**—Creates a detailed history of the balance and net change for each of your company's accounts.

> The Report Wizard requires a Financial Manager database containing appropriate information from accounting data files on your system. To create such a database, run the New Database Wizard (described earlier).

The following steps show you how to create a Cash Flow Report, a typical financial-analysis tool that many small businesses use to track income and expenses:

1   Choose Report Wizard from the Financial Manager menu.

2   Click Cash Flow in the Financial Reports list box.

3   If the current (selected) database isn't the one that you want to use for your report, click the Browse button and select a new one.

4   Click Next to begin the report. If Financial Manager prompts you for a username and password to access the database, enter them in the Database Login dialog box, and click OK.

5   Click a cash flow report in the Report Types list box, and then click Next.

6   Specify an end date for the cash flow report in the End Date For The Report box. If you selected Rolling 12 Period Trend With Projections, click the number of periods for which you want to project cash flow using the Number Of Periods For Projections box.

7   If you selected a cash flow report with scenarios, click Next, and in the What-If Scenario(s) To Include In The Report list box, click the scenarios that you want to use. You can select more than one scenario by holding down the Ctrl key while clicking.

8   Click Finish to finalize the cash flow report.

Financial Manager creates the report in Excel, which lists the net cash flow for your business from operations, investments, and financing activities over the time period you requested. This type of cash flow report is quite valuable—it quickly points out any hidden cash flow problems in your business and also gives you a solid idea of net income during the given time period. Note that negative values in the report are shown in red, and changes in what-if scenarios are shown in light blue.

> **Recalculating the Report**
>
> If the Date box in your report mentions that your cash flow report is now out of date, choose Recalculate Reports from the Financial Manager menu to update the report with the most recent information in your database.

Using the Chart Wizard

The Chart Wizard gives you the opportunity to see important developments in your business graphically. You can create the following charts using the Financial Manager Chart Wizard:

- **Balance Sheet Composition**—A chart containing data about your company's assets, liabilities, and equity for the month you request.

- **Cash Flow Trend**—A line chart that shows detailed cash flow data from operations, financing, and investing activities.

- **Revenue-Expense Trend**—A line chart that shows trend lines for sales, cost of sales, gross profit, operating expenses, and net income after taxes.

- **Sales Composition**—A pie chart showing how each customer, product, salesperson, or other sales category contributes to total sales, cost of sales, or gross profit.

The following steps show you how to create a Cash Flow Trend chart using the Chart Wizard. You can quickly determine your company's short-term financial health by creating a clear line chart that shows trend lines for important cash flow activities.

> The Chart Wizard requires a Financial Manager database containing appropriate information from accounting data files on your system. To create such a database, run the New Database Wizard (described earlier).

1 Choose Chart Wizard from the Financial Manager menu.

2 Click Cash Flow Trend in the Financial Charts list box.

3 If the current (selected) database isn't the one you want to use for your chart, click the Browse button and select a new one.

VIII

Small Business Tools

4 Click Next to begin the chart. If Financial Manager prompts you for a username and password to access the database, enter them in the Database Login dialog box, and click OK.

The Chart Wizard lists the types of cash flow activities that you can add to your cash flow chart. These include Operations, Investing, Financing, and you can also create a Cumulative chart showing all three trends together.

5 Click the cash flow activities that you want to include, and then click Next. (You can include one or several types.)

6 Specify starting and ending dates, and then click Finish to create the chart.

Excel builds the cash flow chart in the manner you specified and presents a line graph showing cash flow in monthly increments (computed in dollars). You'll find that positive or negative cash flow values are dramatically apparent in this chart, as well as general trends in your cash inflow and outflow. Note that lines moving upward (to the right) indicate positive trends in cash flow, and lines moving downward (to the left) indicate negative trends in cash flow. (Look out for these!)

By using a combination of Financial Manager reports and charts, you can quickly spot trends in your accounting data that might have been difficult to spot otherwise. In addition, the order and polish of these documents makes them quite handy for the materials a small business owner often needs to produce, including quarterly status reports, loan applications, slides for shareholder's meetings, and formal annual reports.

Managing Customers, Direct Mail, and Business Plans

I n the last chapter, you learned how to use Microsoft Small Business Financial Manager to compare loan and lease financing, build an accounting and contact database, and create valuable business reports and charts. In this chapter, you'll explore three additional utilities in the small business tools collection: Microsoft Small Business Customer Manager, Microsoft Direct Mail Manager, and Microsoft Business Planner. Customer Manager and Direct Mail Manager allow you to leverage your contact assets strategically for analysis purposes and targeted mass mailings. Business Planner is a catch-all planning tool—you can use it to design and write business and marketing plans, and to organize and study an extensive collection of business documents.

CHAPTER 50

Using Microsoft Small Business Customer Manager

Microsoft created the Customer Manager application with the idea that small business owners probably had lots of useful customer information on their computers, but rarely used it to its fullest potential. Like Microsoft Small Business Financial Manager, the Customer Manager program helps users create a database of accounting and contact information that they can use to analyze business trends and opportunities. Financial Manager and Customer Manager share the same New Database Wizard, so a financial database created in one program is ready for work in the next.

When you first start the Customer Manager program, you're asked to pick an existing financial database to work with, or create a new one. Financial databases are saved in Microsoft Access format, and contain accounting data from third-party business programs (such as Microsoft Quicken) and, if you desire, contact information from Microsoft Outlook. In Customer Manager, you can use this database information to create useful datasheets or Hot Reports that show your top-selling customers, the order status from an individual account, the electronic mail that you have sent to a particular client, and so forth. In short, Customer Manager lets you analyze your customer and product relationships in detail—an activity that will help you spot important trends and leverage your success.

Starting Customer Manager

The small business tools are included in three versions of Microsoft Office 2000: Small Business, Professional, and Premium. However, you might not have installed these tools when you installed Office, because they're located on supplemental discs that are sometimes excluded to save hard disk space.

Try starting Customer Manager now to verify that it has been installed on your system:

1 Click the Windows Start menu, point to Programs, and click Microsoft Small Business Customer Manager.

Office starts the Customer Manager application and prompts you for the name of a financial database. (See Figure 50-1.)

FIGURE 50-1.
You are asked to specify a database name (or create a new one) when you start Customer Manager.

VIII

Small Business Tools

If you don't see the Microsoft Small Business Customer Manager program, locate your Office 2000 Setup discs and insert the CD that includes Small Business Tools on the label. (If your version of Office is located on a network drive, locate the network folder containing the small business tools.) Run the Office Setup program and install all of the small business tools.

2 If you have a database containing customer information that you'd like to open, select it in the list box, and click OK. (Alternatively, you can use the Adventure Works sample database—adworks.mdb—that comes with Customer Manager to learn the ropes.) Otherwise, click the New Database Wizard option button, and click OK to create a new database on your system with accounting data and information from your Outlook Contacts folder.

3 If you're opening an existing database, type your username and password, and then press Enter to open the database. (Customer Manager requires a username and password to keep your customer database secure.)

After you have specified the required information, Customer Manager opens your database and displays your customer information in a datasheet containing *records* (rows) and *fields* (columns).

Using Hot Reports and Business Rules

To spot important trends in your customer data, you can use two powerful search tools to organize database records: Hot Reports and Business Rules. A Hot Report is a predefined database query that locates a subset of database records and displays them for your review. A Business Rule is a predefined sorting mechanism that displays your records in a particular order. Customer Manager offers you several Hot Reports and Business Rules to choose from on the Go menu. Each query builds a datasheet with information displayed in columns and rows; you can display individual customer records by clicking the records on this datasheet, or you can refine the search further by using predesigned filters (see below).

To run a Hot Report, follow these steps:

1 Click the Go menu, and then click the Hot Report you want to run. For example, to build a list of customers who have the highest sales figures, click Top Customers.

Customer Manager runs the query and displays your top customers in a datasheet.

2 To view the information for a contact or customer, simply double-click the record for the customer, and select the appropriate tab.

To use a Business Rule, follow these steps:

1 Click the Go menu, and then select a Business Rule category. (For example, click the Sales category to search for sales records in the database.)

2 Click the Business Rule that you want to use. (For example, click the Sales By Region rule to sort the database in descending order using regional sales as the criteria.)

Customer Manager displays a datasheet with records organized by your Business Rule.

3 To view the information for a contact or customer, simply double-click the record for the customer, and select the appropriate tab.

⭐ TIP

Customer Manager can display several Hot Reports and Business Rules at once, so feel free to run a number of search queries to locate just the data you want. However, you're limited to having one customer database open at once.

Searching Datasheets Using Filters and the Find Command

If your customer list is extensive, you might find it useful to apply additional search criteria called *filters* to your datasheet. Filters can help you narrow the search for particular database records by helping you specify the unique characteristics of the customers you're looking for. For example, you might create a datasheet using the Top Customers Hot Report (which lists top-selling customers by gross sales), and then refine the search by using a region or product-type filter.

To use a filter to analyze a datasheet, follow these steps:

1   Display the datasheet that you want to filter.

2   Click the Filter list box above the datasheet, and click the filter that you'd like to apply to the Hot Report or Business Rule. Customer Manager filters the list and redisplays the datasheet.

Alternatively, you can search the active datasheet for exactly the text you're looking for by using the Find command on the Edit menu. The Find command scans the datasheet quickly for the first instance of the name or word you're looking for and selects it (if it exists).

To find text, follow these steps:

1   Choose Find from the Edit menu.

2   In the Find box, type the customer name or word you're looking for, and then click OK.

Using Word and Outlook to Contact Customers

The Customer Manager application is fully compatible with Office 2000, so you can select one or more records on a datasheet and send the corresponding customers electronic mail by using Outlook or a letter by using Microsoft Word. The commands used to perform these operations are located on the Actions menu, which automatically starts the required Office 2000 applications.

To create a letter for one or more customers using Word, follow these steps:

1   Run a Hot Report or Business Rule search to display the customer record(s) that you want to use for your mailing.

2 Click each customer record that you want to create a document for. (The current record symbol will appear next to each selected record.)

3 Click Using Current Contact on the Actions menu, and then click New Letter. (If you're sending the letter to more than one customer, click Using Selected Contacts on the Actions menu, and then click New Document To Contacts.)

4 Click the letter template you want to use, and then click OK. Customer Manager starts Word, creates the letter, and (if you chose Using Selected Contacts) prepares for mail merge.

5 Add the finishing touches to the letter in Word, and create an envelope if desired.

6 When you're finished, print the letter and save your changes.

To send an electronic mail message to a customer, follow these steps:

1 Run a Hot Report or Business Rule search to display the customer you want to send mail to.

2 Click the customer record to select it. (The current record symbol will appear next to the selected record.)

3 Click Using Current Contact on the Actions menu, and then click the type of Outlook message that you want to create.
Customer Manager starts Outlook and begins the message for you.

4 Finish the message in Outlook, and click Send to mail it.

Tracking Customer Activities in Your Database

Customer Manager is handy not only for producing database reports and generating correspondence, but also because it can document each personal contact you make with your customers, giving you a detailed record of who you spend your time with and who you don't. For example, when you send an electronic message to a customer in your database using Outlook, Customer Manager records this activity and notes it in the database. When the customer replies to your message, Customer Manager records that also, giving you a complete record of the transaction, including both messages.

⭐ **TIP**

> **Activity Tracking Behind the Scenes**
>
> Customer Manager successfully tracks most activities that occur when you execute commands on the Actions menu (creating Word documents, sending electronic mail, scheduling meetings, and so forth). In addition, activity tracking is a separate feature from the Journal command in Outlook, which records the activities you perform but doesn't link them to a particular customer. However, comprehensive activity tracking requires considerable database activity, so if you find that Outlook runs significantly slower during your day-to-day activities, you might want to turn it off.

Turning On or Turning Off Activity Tracking

To turn the Customer Manager Activity Tracker on or off, follow these steps:

1 Choose Options from the Tools menu, and then click the General tab. In this dialog box, specify whether you want to record Customer Manager events (such as Word mailings), Outlook events (such as Outlook e-mail), or both. You can also turn off Activity Tracker.

2 Select the options that correspond to your activity tracking preferences.

Reviewing Contact Activity

You can review the contact activities associated with any customer record in your database. Follow these steps:

1 Run a Hot Report or Business Rule to display the customer record that you want to review.

2 Click the customer record to select it. (The current record symbol appears next to the record.)

3 Choose Using Current Contact from the Actions menu.

4 Click Show Contact Activity or Show Company Activity.

Removing Old Activity Records

If you find that you don't need the activity tracking records that you've generated, or that you no longer need the older items, you can delete the information you don't want. Cleaning out these records periodically is a good idea, because it frees up disk space and keeps your database as small as possible. An especially nice feature here is the option to delete items older than a specified number of months.

VIII

Small Business Tools

To remove some or all activity tracking records, follow these steps:

1 Click Activity Tracker on the Tools menu, and then click Purge. The Purge Old Audit Trail Entries dialog box appears.

2 Specify the number of months of records that you want to retain in the text box. (All older records will be deleted.) If you want to delete all records, type *0* in the text box.

3 Press Enter to delete your older records. Customer Manager removes the activity tracking data from your database and frees up the corresponding amount of disk space.

Customer Manager is a helpful tool if you have extensive accounting data and Outlook contact information on your system. The activity-tracking feature is especially useful if you need an exact record of the correspondence between customers and business contacts.

Using Microsoft Direct Mail Manager

Microsoft Direct Mail Manager is an Office 2000 application that has a special mission in life: it wants to help you plan and execute great direct mail campaigns for your valued customers and contacts. In business parlance, a *direct mail campaign* is a carefully organized mailing to a target audience of potential customers, supporters, donors, or clients. A typical direct mail campaign consists of a standard form letter and supporting materials, enclosed in a preprinted envelope that satisfies the post office's stringent requirements for bulk mailings.

The actual size of a direct mail campaign can be large or small, but in most cases the source of direct mail names and addresses is a third-party mailing list (provided by a special service bureau) or a customer database on your computer, such as the Microsoft Outlook Contacts folder. Using Direct Mail Manager, you can create well-organized direct mail campaigns in a fraction of the time it would normally take you to assemble the pieces using traditional methods.

Direct Mail Manager is one of the four small business tools in Office 2000. If you haven't installed this program yet, do so now by inserting the Small Business Tools CD into your computer (or locating the proper folder on the network) and running the Office 2000 Setup program.

Planning Your Mailing

Before you create your mailing, it makes sense to do a little upfront planning to assess what your exact mailing goals are. Direct Mail Manager requires a standard list of preformatted names and addresses to do its work, so you should check your system for the proper files now, before you get started. Table 50-1 lists the formats supported by Direct Mail Manager, and you can also use Direct Mail Manager to connect to the Web to locate additional third-party mailing lists online. (The third-party mailing list option is offered to you automatically in Direct Mail Manager's Import phase, although these vendors might charge transaction fees to borrow their lists.)

TABLE 50-1.   List Formats Supported by Direct Mail Manager

Application	File Type (Extension)
Microsoft Access database	.mdb, mdw, .mda
dBASE III or dBASE IV file	.dbf
Microsoft Excel worksheet	.xls
Microsoft Word document	.doc
Paradox 5.x database	.db, .dbf
Text file (delimited)	.txt, csv, tab, asc
Microsoft Outlook Contacts file	N/A
ODBC data source	SQL Server, and so forth

Consider the following questions as you plan your mailing. Direct Mail Manager will ask you about the individual components in your mailing when you run the program.

- What are you mailing? Are they standard envelopes, envelopes with windows, postcards, self-mailing flyers, or packages?

- What is in the mailing? Is it a standard form letter? Do you have response cards or other standard items?

- How many pieces are in your mailing? Depending on the number of addresses you include in your direct mail campaign, you might be eligible for postal discounts and additional services.

■ How are you printing the mailing? Are you using an attached printer? Do you want to use a third-party mailing service located on the Web?

■ How are you sending the mailing? Will you use First-Class mail, Standard mail, or a mailing service?

■ How would you like to pay for the mailing? Will you use regular stamps, a permit, precancelled stamps, or a postage meter?

 NOTE

By the way, Direct Mail Manager can only support up to 3500 pieces in a single mailing—for larger mailings you'll need to upgrade to the enhanced version of Direct Mail Manager, sold by Envelope Manager Software (*http://www.EnvelopeManager.com/*).

Creating Direct Mail Pieces

With your mailing list in hand and some basic planning out of the way, you're ready to create direct mail pieces. Direct Mail Manager handles this process quite seamlessly in four simple compilation steps, or phases:

■ First, Direct Mail Manager imports the necessary mailing lists and creates a database table for the mailing.

■ Second, the program verifies the mailing list by finding postal codes, removing duplicates, checking spelling, and checking other formatting details.

■ Next, Direct Mail Manager prints the components that you have requested, including envelopes, labels, form letters, and so on.

■ Finally, Direct Mail Manager lets you save any changes that you've made back to the original address list—a handy feature if you've corrected spelling or removed duplicate entries.

Follow these steps to use Direct Mail Manager to create your own mailing:

1 Click the Windows Start menu, point to Programs, and click Microsoft Direct Mail Manager.

Office starts the Direct Mail Manager application, as shown in the following dialog box:

Direct Mail Manager operates like a wizard; it constructs your mailing list by asking a series of questions, and you can move back and forth between the query screens by clicking the Back and Next buttons. At any time, you can also learn more about Direct Mail Manager features by clicking the Help button.

2 Click Next to import your direct mail list.

Direct Mail Manager prompts you for the location of your address database. Your options are File (one of the standard database or application file formats listed in Table 50-1, page 1175), Outlook Folder (the address list in your Contacts folder), and Database Via ODBC (a more sophisticated database format such as SQL Server).

TIP

If you want to explore third-party mailing list options on the Internet now, click the Mailing List Providers button near the bottom of the dialog box.

3 Click the option button next to your mailing list choice, specify any additional connection details requested by Direct Mail Manager, and click Next.

Direct Mail Manager opens the file you requested and examines the address fields in your database.

Because different database programs use different internal names for their address fields, Direct Mail Manager is often cautious about assigning fields to mail pieces without asking for additional guidance. If any questions arise about how your address fields compare to direct mail fields, you'll see a dialog box that looks like the one shown on the next page.

VIII

Small Business Tools

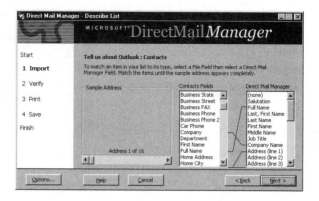

In this particular example, we've asked Direct Mail Manager to import an Outlook Contact list containing 16 addresses for a small, focused mailing. In this dialog box, Direct Mail Manager is asking us to verify that the Company field in the Contacts folder is equivalent to the Company Name field in Direct Mail Manager. In this case, Direct Mail Manager has guessed correctly by visually connecting the fields with solid lines. If a field was not correctly assigned, however, we could select the incorrect field in the left list box and then click the correct field in the right list box, using the scroll bars to display fields that weren't visible.

4 Click Next when your address fields look correct. (If you make a mistake at this point, don't worry—you can click Back at any time to return to this screen and make corrections.)

Direct Mail Manager asks if you want to import the entire list or only part of it.

5 To import a partial list, click the No, Import Only This Part Of The List option button, and then click the Change Filter button to identify the specific addresses that you want to include in the mailing.

6 Click Next to initialize the database and import your addresses. (If Direct Mail Manager mentions that you have one or more entries that are improperly formatted, click OK to continue—you can examine all of your addresses in the next step.)

You now enter the verification phase—the opportunity to see what your addresses will look like when mailed. Your dialog box should look similar to the following:

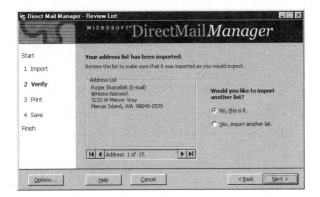

7 Check the format of the first address in the list, and then click the inner right scroll arrow in the mailing list preview window. Review as many addresses as you like. (We heartily recommend a careful review if this is the first time you've used this particular list).

8 If you want to add another mailing list to the one you have visible, click the Yes, Import Another List option button. (Direct Mail Manager allows you to merge multiple mailing lists—a nice feature.)

9 When you're ready to move on, click Next. Direct Mail Manager verifies the postal code format in your list, checks the spelling, and looks for potential formatting problems. In its default setting, Direct Mail Manager will inform you before it begins this process. (It displays a notice you can suppress by clicking the Don't Show This Message Again checkbox.) If you see this dialog box, click OK.

To facilitate the verification process, Direct Mail Manager will automatically connect to the Internet and use a Microsoft Corporation datasheet to verify that each address and postal code conforms to the local and national standards imposed by the post office for direct mail. If an address isn't correct, Direct Mail Manager will use the official list to suggest a correction. (The most common modification is to convert a five-digit postal code to a nine-digit postal code.) When the analysis is finished, you'll see a dialog box that looks similar to the one shown on the next page.

VIII

Small Business Tools

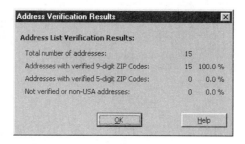

10 Click OK to continue.

Direct Mail Manager displays your entire mailing list in a table that has rows corresponding to each customer name and fields corresponding to the different components of the address.

11 Scroll through the rows and columns of the database, making corrections directly in the table, if necessary. When you're finished, click Next to continue.

Direct Mail Manager now locates duplicate names and street addresses in your list (if any) and gives you the chance to remove them if you want. (This useful feature will help you reduce your postage costs and minimize customer irritation.)

12 To delete duplicate entries, click the Delete button, and then click Next to begin the printing phase.

Direct Mail Manager presents your distribution options in a concise list, as shown in the following dialog box. Note that your options might be different, because mailing list size, sorting requirements, regional factors, and other issues limit your options. (For example, our dialog box doesn't include the Standard Mail option, because our list contains less than 200 names.)

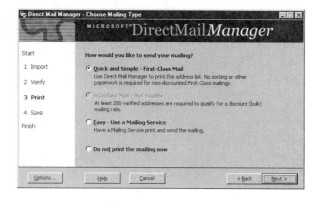

⭐ **TIP**

Choosing Not to Print

If you'd rather not print now, click the Do Not Print the Mailing Now option. Although this won't finalize your list, it gives you the option of moving on (and saving your changes) if you suddenly realize that you don't have the proper envelopes or paper handy.

13 Click Next to continue. Direct Mail Manager prepares your mailing list data and shows you a preview of your envelope or mailing piece. Click the Design button now to change the design of your component. You can also click the Test button to print a hard copy preview to verify that everything is just right.

14 When you're ready to print the entire address list, click Next. If you're asked to specify printer options in a dialog box (such as envelope type, manual feed, and so on) make your selections carefully, and then click OK.

   If you're using an attached printer to create the envelopes or other media, Direct Mail Manager starts Microsoft Word and begins the printing process. Naturally, this will take some time for long lists—be sure you have enough envelopes!

15 After the printing is complete, Direct Mail Manager begins the final phase—saving your work. You'll see a dialog box that looks like this:

Saving changes to a new file is the best choice if the mailing list you created was for a special purpose and featured multiple lists or special formatting or address changes. You definitely want to save your changes in a new file if you want to use it in the future. (Note that Direct Mail Manager uses Access format for the new file, which means that you can view and manipulate it with Access and other Access-compatible programs.)

Updating your contacts is a good idea if you realized that your contact list was out-of-date and in need of revisions and changes. Select the second option if you want to save those changes to their original file (such as the Outlook Contacts folder). Finally, you can ask Direct Mail Manager to discard all changes—a prudent choice if you're sure you don't want the list again (or you don't want to leave a trace of your mailing activities!).

16 Click the option button corresponding to your choice, and then click Next. If you're asked to create a new file, you must specify the location and give it a name.

17 Finally, you're asked if you would like to create a form letter to go along with your envelope or direct mail piece. Skip this step if you already have the contents of your direct mail campaign finished. If you don't, use Microsoft Word or Microsoft Publisher now to create a flyer that has focus and visual appeal for your direct mail customers.

18 Click Word or Publisher options if you want to create a form letter using mail merge, or click No Skip This Step if you're all finished.

If you do select Word or Publisher, you'll be prompted for a file location and given the opportunity to read more about using mail merge in those products. Direct Mail will integrate your form letter and even print it if you like!

19 When you're finished with Direct Mail Manager, click Next until the Finish button appears, and then click Finish to exit the application.

Congratulations! Direct Mail Manager is a highly capable program for handling mailing tasks, especially if you reused existing mailing lists and customer databases. When you use it in concert with other Office applications, Direct Mail Manager can save you considerable time and effort.

Using Microsoft Business Planner

So many documents, so little time. It seems like today, more than ever, the small business owner has little quality time to devote to basic business research and long-range planning. Sure, in larger companies, entire departments probably exist that search out books and articles about important trends and then create fancy new business and marketing plans, but what small business employee has the time to do that?

If you can relate to this common complaint, you're probably in the target audience for Microsoft's newest productivity tool: Microsoft Business Planner. Although Business Planner can't actually *read* the articles for you, it can help you collect the business documents that you need to read, and it offers a wealth of contact information to keep you connected to small business resources in your local community and on the Internet. In addition, Business Planner can help you create business plans and marketing plans by using wizards that are specifically designed for the small business owner and employee. In this section, we'll introduce Business Planner and describe how you can use it to manage one of your most valuable resources: knowledge.

> **NOTE**

Microsoft Business Planner is one of the four small business tools in Office 2000. If you haven't installed this program yet, do so now by inserting the Small Business Tools CD in your computer (or locating the proper folder on the network) and running the Office 2000 Setup program.

Getting Started with Business Planner: The Interview Wizard

When you start the Business Planner application the first time, you're greeted by the Personal Interview Wizard, which asks you a series of questions about your business. The purpose of this interview is to allow Business Planner to assemble a relevant recommended reading list for you and prepare the proper templates and wizards that you'll need. The answers to your questions are completely confidential, and they remain on your computer at all times. You can also skip this interview process if you're just looking around Business Planner—to run it again, click Personal Interviewer on the Go menu.

To run the Personal Interview Wizard, follow these steps. By answering the questions fully, you will tailor Business Planner to your own business interests.

1 Click the Windows Start button, point to the Programs folder, and then click Microsoft Business Planner. Office starts the Business Planner application. If this is the first time you've started Business Planner, the Personal Interview Wizard will start up automatically. If you've already been using Business Planner and would like to run the wizard again, click Personal Interviewer on the Go menu. The opening screen of the Personal Interview Wizard looks like this:

2   Read the brief introductory message, and then use the vertical scroll bar to scroll down the document and answer the interview questions. Specify your business name (if applicable), the type of business you own (sole proprietorship, partnership, Chapter S corporation, Chapter C corporation, or limited liability company).

3   Specify your business address and the name of the owner or CEO. Answer the questions about business ownership, franchises, and where your business is located.

4   Provide the necessary financial details about your business, as applicable, including financing, insurance, licenses, and number of employees.

5   Provide the necessary accounting details, including record keeping, accountant, product pricing, and marketing strategy.

6   If you're interested in learning more about customer relations, click the Yes option button for the last question. When you're finished answering interview questions, simply move on to another task in Business Planner—there is no "Done" button to click. (When you move to the next screen, your answers will be saved and Business Planner will use them to prepare its recommended reading database.)

Picking Commands and Activities

To execute commands in Business Planner, you click commands on the six Business Planner menus (Home, File, Edit, Go, Favorites, Help), or click a button on the toolbar. Although Home is the first menu name on the menu bar, it's actually not a menu but a button that takes you to the Business Planner opening screen or home page, as shown in Figure 50-2. You can click the Home button at any time to display the oversized buttons that show your options graphically.

The home page lists the activities you can perform with the Business Planner application by functional category. You can search for business articles and resources in five specific areas: Planning, Operations, Legal, Finance, and Marketing. When you click one of these buttons, Business Planner displays a recommended reading list of articles that match your areas of interest (as identified by the Personal Interview Wizard).

If you select a research area, you can jump back to the previous page by clicking the Back button on the toolbar. In this regard, the Business Planner toolbar works just like Microsoft Internet Explorer—you can browse backwards or forwards through the Business Planner pages you have visited.

You can also start the Business Plan and Marketing Wizards from the Business Planner home page. We'll discuss these two planning tools later in the chapter.

VIII

Small Business Tools

FIGURE 50-2.
The Business Planner home page shows you graphically what the program can do.

Managing Business Resources

The five functional business categories (Planning, Operations, Legal, Finance, and Marketing) represent the main corpus of business articles prepared for each user by the Business Planner program. These recommended reading lists are customized for each business type, and each contains useful information that is listed thematically, as shown in Figure 50-3. Individual articles often display the source of the information presented (typically in the left-hand column), and you can click these sources for more detailed information from the Web if you're connected to the Internet.

To open a recommended reading list, click the category on the Business Planner home page, or click a topic on the Category submenu of the Go menu. In addition to providing access to the standard reading categories, the Go menu also contains other useful business links and contact lists, as shown in Table 50-2. Many of these links connect to information sources on the Web, but some are also standard lists of agencies and institutions that Business Planner has stored conveniently on your hard disk. Experiment with a few of these resources—you'll be amazed at how detailed some of the lists are!

TABLE 50-2.   Useful Business Resources on the Business Planner Go Menu

Command on Go Menu	Description
Microsoft Sidewalk Yellow Pages	An online search tool for business names and contact information.
Business Profiles Online	A Web page with detailed business information.
Web Links submenu	A submenu with Web connections to the five business categories (Planning, Operations, Legal, Finance, and Marketing).
Reference Directory	An alphabetic listing of useful references, contacts, and organizations for small businesses.
Listing by Business Type	An alphabetic listing of business types and useful contacts.
State and Province Resources	An alphabetic listing of regional business resources (chambers of commerce, education programs, loan programs, and so on).
Federal Resources	Useful resources in the Federal government (regulator agencies, various departments, service bureaus, and so on).

FIGURE 50-3.
Recommended reading is listed by category, and often contains an Internet source for more detailed information.

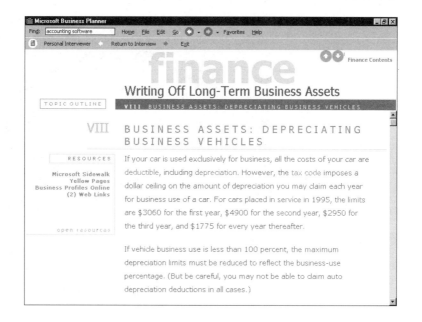

Creating a Business Plan

A solid business plan is the heart of a successful small business. Yes, there are practical applications for business plans—they're often required for business loans, partnership agreements, and other long-term planning activities. But creating a business plan also gives you a chance to roll up your sleeves and do some real research in your industry—a systematic process that's well suited to the information management capabilities of the Business Planner application. When you need to create or review your business plan, let the Business Plan Wizard step you through the process—you'll probably find some data that you didn't know was out there!

To use the Business Plan Wizard to create a business plan, follow these steps:

1 Click Business Plan Wizard on the Go menu.

Business Planner starts the wizard, as shown on the following page.

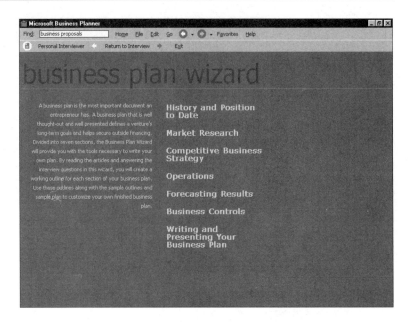

The Business Plan Wizard steps you through seven sections, which are listed one after the other on the right side of the dialog box. Each section gives you the opportunity to answer several questions and read some business literature pertaining to creating business plans and the specific activities of your business. When you're finished with the questions, the wizard completes the report and prepares it for printing.

2 Click the first section, History And Position To Date, which introduces the purpose of a business plan and asks you to read several useful articles about the planning process.

After reading the articles, you're asked a series of interview questions.

3 Complete the first section and the six that follow.

Although the individual answers you give will be unique to your situation, the process will be similar for most businesses and planning documents. When you're finished, you'll have a business plan that you can print and distribute to those who need an inside scoop on your business goals.

Creating a Marketing Plan

A marketing plan is a detailed review of how you plan to sell your product or services and who you think will buy them. A typical marketing plan includes details about the product you're selling, what the target market for your product is, how this particular product fits into your overall corporate sales strategy and product line, and specific details about how you'll bring the product to market and sell it. For the small business owner, a detailed marketing plan is often an afterthought, sometimes because an extremely detailed plan isn't necessary, but other times because the necessary supporting documents and marketing expertise aren't readily available.

The Marketing Plan Wizard is designed to help small business owners create effective marketing plans for their sales and marketing staff and other interested employees and financial institutions. This wizard isn't as detailed as the Business Plan Wizard, but it still follows the same model: it asks simple questions about your business, presents useful reading materials, and helps you create an outline of marketing goals that you can use to build a really effective plan for your company.

To use the Marketing Plan Wizard to create a marketing plan, follow these steps:

1 Click Marketing Plan Wizard on the Go menu.
Business Planner starts the wizard, as shown here:

The Marketing Plan Wizard asks you to complete two sections, each containing several literature review articles and interview questions. When you complete these questions, the wizard will complete your plan and give you the option to print it.

2 Click the first section, Your Marketing Campaign, which provides several conceptual articles for your review and asks you to answer interview questions about your marketing goals.

The wizard uses these answers to create a working outline for your campaign and an action plan.

3 Complete the second section, Marketing And Advertising Materials, and answer the interview questions.

This part of the wizard focuses almost exclusively on advertising methods and ideas, including flyers, direct mail campaigns, radio ads, Web sites, trade shows, and so forth. Using your answers, the Marketing Plan Wizard creates a working outline for the Advertising section of your marketing plan and an action plan that contains points to remember and additional reading resources.

The goal of Microsoft Business Planner is to provide small business owners with the resources that traditionally only larger corporations have had at their fingertips. By managing large amounts of small business data, Business Planner can help business owners make informed decisions faster than ever. In addition, the Business Plan and Marketing Plan Wizards leverage this information in creative ways to provide the essential business documents that every business requires.

PART IX

Integrating Microsoft Office Applications

CHAPTER 51

Sharing Data Among Office Applications

I n the previous parts of the book, you learned how to copy and move data within a single document or among separate documents within a single Microsoft Office program. In this chapter, you'll learn the different ways of exchanging data among separate Office applications. The chapter also describes the Microsoft Office Tools—a set of programs designed for creating and embedding various types of information within Office documents.

Sharing Data in Different Ways

This section provides a general overview of the three basic ways to exchange data among separate Office applications:

- Static copying or moving of data

- Linking of data

- Embedding of data

This discussion will help you choose the most appropriate method. The following sections will discuss the specific techniques for performing each method.

When you use *static copying* or *static moving*, the data that you insert becomes an integral part of the receiving document and retains no link or connection with the document or program from which it was obtained. This type of copying or moving is what you normally perform when you're working within a single document or program, using the techniques discussed in previous chapters. When you statically copy or move data from one application to another, you might or might not be able to edit the data within the receiving document. If the data can be converted to a format that the receiving program understands, you'll be able to edit it—for example, when you copy text from a Microsoft Excel worksheet and paste it into a Microsoft Word document. If, however, the data can't be converted into a format native to the receiving program, the data can be displayed and printed but can't be edited in the receiving program—for example, when you copy bitmapped graphics from some drawing programs into a Word document.

When you use *linking*, the data that you insert retains its connection with the document and the program from which it was obtained. In fact, a complete copy of the data is stored only within the source document; the receiving document stores only the linking information and the information required to display the data. When the data in the source document is edited (by you or someone else), the linked data in the receiving document can be updated automatically or manually to reflect the changes.

When you use *embedding*, the data that's inserted retains its connection with the source program but not with the source document. In fact, there might not even be a source document, because you can create *new* embedded data. The receiving document stores a complete copy of the information, just as it does with statically copied data. However, because of the connection between this data and the source program, you can use the source program's tools to edit the data.

You should use linking rather than embedding when you want to store and maintain data within one document and merely display an up-to-date copy of the data in one or more other documents. Linking is especially useful in the following situations:

- You want to display only part of the source document within the receiving document. For example, you want to display only a totals line from a large Excel worksheet within a Word document. (If you *embed* the data, the entire workbook will be copied into the receiving document.)

- You maintain a single master document that you want to display in several other documents. For example, you have a Word document containing instructions that you want to display within several other Word documents and PowerPoint presentations. By using linking, you need to update the data in only one place—the source Word document—and you ensure that all copies of the information displayed in other documents are identical.

- You want to minimize the size of the receiving document. (In linking, the receiving document stores only the linking information plus the data required to display the item.)

SEE ALSO

For information on using the Binder program to combine entire documents created by Office applications, see Chapter 52, "Using the Office Binder Program."

You should use embedding rather than linking when you want to store an independent block of data as an integral part of the document in which it's displayed. Maintaining documents that contain embedded data is simpler than maintaining documents that contain linked data, because you don't have to keep track of source documents. (To update linked data, the source document must be present in its original location under its original filename.) And you can easily share with other users a document containing only embedded data—without having to provide linked source documents along with it.

In previous parts of the book, you learned how to copy or move data within an Office application using the drag-and-drop technique, as well as by using the Copy or Cut command followed by the Paste command. You can also use any of these techniques to copy or move data among separate Office applications. When you use these general-purpose methods, however, you have little control over how the data is transferred. The data might be copied or moved statically, or it might be embedded in the receiving document, depending on the nature of the data and the specific applications involved. In the following sections, you'll learn how to use the Copy or Cut command followed by the Paste Special command to precisely control the format and the manner in which data is transferred.

IX

Integrating Microsoft
Office Applications

Create Hyperlinks by Dragging or by Pasting As a Hyperlink

Instead of statically copying data from one application or file to another, you can create a *hyperlink* to the data in the source document. To do this, select the data in the source document and drag it to the destination document using the right mouse button. When you release the mouse button, choose Create Hyperlink Here from the pop-up menu that appears. You can also create a hyperlink by first copying the text from the source document and then pasting it into the destination document by choosing Paste As Hyperlink from the Edit menu. Using either method, the text you copy must be from a saved file.

Copying and Moving Data Statically

To copy or move data statically from one Office application to another, as described in the previous section, do the following:

1 Select the data in the source program, and choose Cut or Copy from the program's Edit menu.

2 Switch to the receiving program and place the insertion point at the position in the receiving document where you want to insert the data.

3 Choose Paste Special from the receiving program's Edit menu to open the Paste Special dialog box. Proceed as shown in Figure 51-1.

FIGURE 51-1.
Statically pasting data using the Paste Special dialog box.

5 Select the desired data format from the As list. Choose any format that doesn't contain the word *object*, which would embed the data.

6 Click OK to paste the data.

4 Select the Paste option.

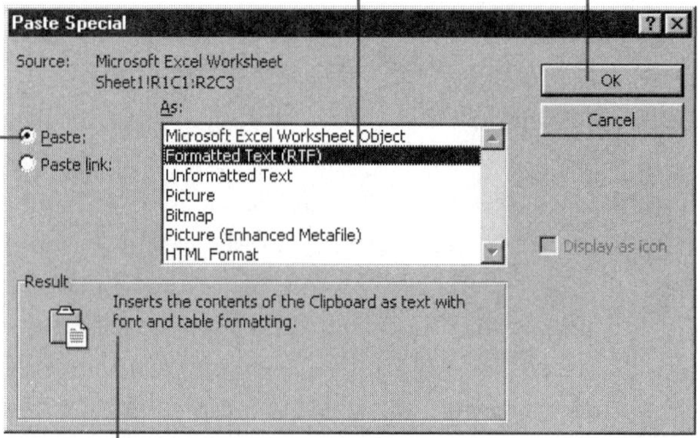

A description of the format selected in the As list appears here.

> The formats listed in the As list in the Paste Special dialog box depend on the source program and the nature of the data.

Linking Data

You can transfer and link many kinds of data among Office applications. The following are some examples:

- You can insert and link part or all of an Excel worksheet or an Excel chart into a Word document or a PowerPoint slide.

- You can insert and link part or all of a Word document into an Excel worksheet or a PowerPoint slide.

- You can insert and link a PowerPoint slide into a Word document or an Excel worksheet.

> You can't link data from the Office Tools programs (such as Microsoft Equation Editor). These programs can be used only for embedding data.

You can transfer and link either a selected part of a document or an entire document. To transfer and link part of a document, do the following:

1 Select the data in the source document, and choose Copy from the source program's Edit menu (don't choose Cut!) to copy the data to the Clipboard.

> To link a PowerPoint slide to another document, you must be in Outline or Slide Sorter view (choose Slide Sorter from the View menu), and you must select a single slide.

2 Place the insertion point at the position in the receiving document where you want to insert the data, and choose Paste Special from the receiving program's Edit menu.

3 In the Paste Special dialog box, select the Paste Link option, and then select the desired data format in the As list.

> If the Paste Link option is not available, this means that the data in the Clipboard— or the selected format—can't be linked or the source program doesn't support linking.

If you want to link an entire document, you can select the whole document in step 1 above, or you can use the following alternative method:

1 Place the insertion point at the position in the receiving document where you want to insert the data.

2 Choose Object from the receiving program's Insert menu, and click the Create From File tab in the Object dialog box. (In PowerPoint and Access, the dialog box is titled Insert Object. Also, Create From File is an option button that you select, rather than a tab.)

3 Select the Link To File option, and in the File Name box, enter the name of the document you want to insert. (In PowerPoint and Access, the option is called Link and the text box is called File.) Click the Browse button if you need help locating the file. See Figure 51-2.

TIP

Display Your Data As an Icon

If you select the Display As Icon option in either the Paste Special or the Object dialog box (the Insert Object dialog box for PowerPoint and Access), the receiving program displays an icon representing the linked data rather than displaying the data itself. Also, when you print the document, only the icon is printed. After you select Display As Icon, you can click the Change Icon button to change the icon and the caption that are displayed in the document. To view the linked data within the source program, use one of the methods for editing linked data, which will be described next. Using icons to display linked data is a convenient way to present various types of information in a compact format within a document that's intended to be viewed on the screen.

You must edit linked data by making the changes within the source document. To do this, you can use one of the following methods:

■ Run the source program and open the source document.

■ Select the block of linked data in the receiving document (or the icon that represents it), or simply place the insertion point anywhere

FIGURE 51-2.
Inserting and linking
an entire document.

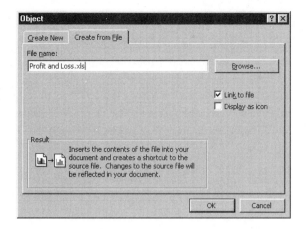

within the data. Then point to Linked *Item* (where *Item* is a description of the selected data, such as Worksheet Object) on the Edit menu, and choose either Open Link or Edit Link from the submenu that appears:

(The commands that appear on this submenu depend on the source program and the nature of the data.) The source document will then be opened in the source program, and you can edit the data.

- For some types of linked data formats (for example, Picture or Bitmap in a Word document), you can open the source document in the source program by simply double-clicking the linked data in the receiving document.

You can modify one or more links within a document by choosing Links from the Edit menu to open the Links dialog box, which lists all the links contained in the active document. The appearance of the dialog box varies among Office applications; Figure 51-3, on the next page, shows how it looks in Word. To modify a link, select it in the list. To simultaneously modify several links, select them by clicking the first one and then pressing the Ctrl key while clicking each additional one.

CAUTION
Although you might be able to edit certain types of linked data directly within the receiving document (for example, Unformatted Text in a Word document), your changes will be overwritten the next time the data is updated! However, formatting changes (such as applying the bold or italic format to text) will generally be preserved when the data is updated.

IX

**Integrating Microsoft
Office Applications**

FIGURE 51-3.
Modifying links in the active document.

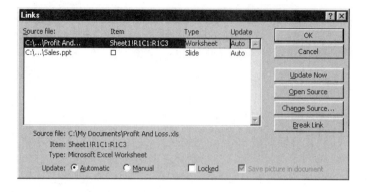

You can now do one or more of the following—but note that not all these actions are available in all Office applications:

■ You can make a link either automatic or manual by selecting the Automatic or Manual option at the bottom of the dialog box. By default, a link is automatic, which means that the data is automatically updated whenever the receiving document is opened and whenever the data is modified in the source document while the receiving document is open. If you make a link manual, it won't be updated until you explicitly issue a command. You might want to make links manual to avoid slowdowns while working with a document that contains many links or linked data whose source is modified frequently.

■ If the selected link is manual, you can update it by clicking the Update Now button.

■ To change the name or location of the source document for the linked data, click the Change Source button to open the Change Source dialog box. (You might also be able to change the description of the data location within the source document—for example, the range of cells in a spreadsheet.) You would need to do this to repair a link after the source document has been moved or renamed.

To specify a new source document, in the Change Source dialog box open the folder that contains that document and enter its filename into the File Name box. To select a new data location *within* the source document, click the Item button and enter a description of the location into the Item dialog box. For a Word document, you would enter a bookmark name. For an Excel workbook, you would enter the name of the worksheet and the row and column range within this worksheet, as in the following example:

Sheet1!R1C1:R2C2

- To open the source document within the source program, click the Open Source button. This has the same effect as using one of the techniques for editing linked data, which were described above.

- To remove the link, click the Break Link button. The data will become an integral part of the receiving document, just as if you had copied it statically. After doing this, you won't be able to restore the link.

- In Word, to prevent the link from being updated, select the Locked option.

TIP

A good way to help ensure that the source document is always available to maintain the link is to place both the source document and the receiving document together within the same folder.

A Linking Example

Imagine that you have created an Excel worksheet containing the daily prices for a commodity—wheat—and you have included a chart illustrating those prices for a past period of 25 days. (See Figure 51-4.) You

FIGURE 51-4.
An Excel worksheet
that includes a chart.

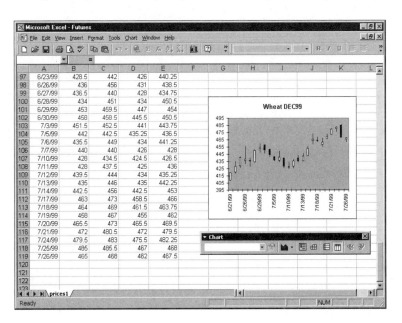

IX

Integrating Microsoft
Office Applications

now want to write an article in Word that describes the price action over that period. To link a copy of the Excel chart to your report, you would perform the following steps:

1 In the Excel worksheet, click the chart to select it, and choose Copy from Excel's Edit menu.

2 In the Word document containing your report, place the insertion point at the position where you want the chart, choose Paste Special from Word's Edit menu, and complete the dialog box as shown in Figure 51-5. The resulting report is shown in Figure 51-6.

FIGURE 51-5.
Linking the Excel chart to a Word document.

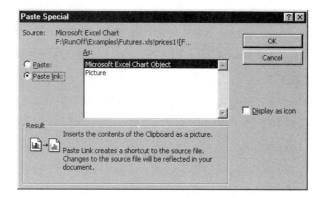

ON THE WEB   The Futures.xls and Futures.doc example files are on the Running Office 2000 Reader's Corner page. For information about connecting to this Web site, read the Introduction.

The following are some advantages of linking this chart rather than embedding it:

■ Only the link and the information required to draw the chart are copied into the receiving document. If you embedded the chart, the entire workbook, including all the price data, would be copied into the receiving document, significantly increasing its size. (Although you would see only the chart, the workbook data is also stored in the document so that you can edit both the data and the chart.)

■ The same chart can be linked to additional Word documents, PowerPoint presentations, or other documents. The chart will then be updated within all receiving documents whenever you change the price data in the Excel worksheet.

FIGURE 51-6.

The Excel chart shown in Figure 51-4 linked to a Word document.

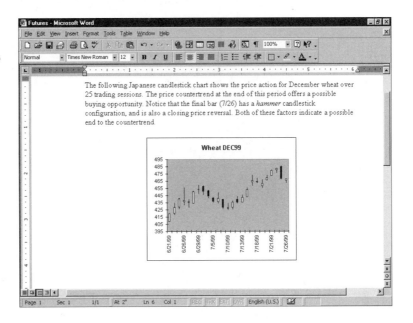

Embedding Data

A block of embedded data is known as an *embedded object*. In an Office document, you can embed data that you have created in another Office application, in an Office Tools program (as described in "Using the Office Tools," page 1209), or in any other Windows-based program that's been designed to be a source of embedded data. You can create an embedded object in three ways, which differ in how you obtain the data for the object. First, you can obtain the data for an embedded object from a portion of an existing document, as follows:

1 Select the data in the source document, and choose Copy or Cut from the source program's Edit menu.

2 Place the insertion point at the position in the receiving document where you want to add the embedded object, and choose Paste Special from the receiving program's Edit menu.

3 In the Paste Special dialog box, choose the Paste option, and in the As list, choose the first format description that contains the word *object*. (See Figure 51-7, on the following page.) Then click OK.

IX

Integrating Microsoft
Office Applications

FIGURE 51-7.
Embedding an Excel
worksheet object.

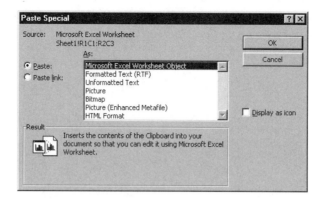

The second way to create an embedded object is to use an entire existing document as the source of the data, as follows:

1   Place the insertion point at the position in the receiving document where you want to embed the object, choose Object from the receiving program's Insert menu, and click the Create From File tab (or option button) in the Object (or Insert Object) dialog box.

2   Make sure that the Link To File (or Link) option is not selected, and either type the name of the source document into the File Name (or File) text box, or click the Browse button to locate the file. (See Figure 51-8.)

FIGURE 51-8.
Embedding an entire
document.

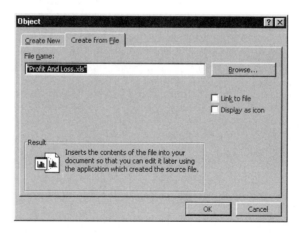

The third way to embed an object is to create *new* data for the object, using the source program's tools, as follows:

1 Place the insertion point at the position in the receiving document where you want to embed the object, choose Object from the receiving program's Insert menu, and click the Create New tab (or option button) in the Object (or Insert Object) dialog box.

2 In the Object Type list, select the type of object that you want to embed. This list contains one or more items for every installed Windows-based program that can be the source for an embedded object. Click OK, and one of two things will then happen:

- The source program's window will open, and will display a blank working area (for example, blank worksheet cells) or other tools (for example, a collection of clip art objects you can insert).

- A blank working area will appear within the receiving document, and the source program's menus and buttons will be displayed within the receiving program's window. The source program's keyboard commands will also be available.

3 In either case, use the source program's commands to enter the data for the embedded object into the working area.

4 When you have finished entering the data, exit the editing mode. If you're working in the source program's window, do this by choosing Exit from the File menu (or using any other method to quit the program) and clicking Yes in the message box if the source program asks whether you want to update the object in the receiving document. If you're working in the receiving program's window, simply click in the receiving document outside the object.

> **NOTE**
>
> With the Office Tools programs (described later), you must use this third method for creating an embedded object, because these programs can't create independent documents.
>
> When you use any of these three methods for embedding an object, you might be able to select the Display As Icon option in the dialog box. For an explanation of this option, be sure to see the tip "Display Your Data As an Icon," page 1198.

To edit an embedded object, simply double-click it. The object will then be opened for editing either within the source program or, more commonly, within the receiving program.

For some types of embedded objects, double-clicking the object does not open it for editing. For example, if you double-click an object containing a sound or video clip, the clip will be played. To edit the object, you must use the alternative method, given next.

Alternatively, you can select the object by clicking it and then point to *Item* Object (where *Item* is a description of the selected object, such as Worksheet) on the receiving program's Edit menu to display a submenu similar to the one shown here:

Choose one of the following commands from this submenu:

- The Edit command, if present, which normally lets you edit the object within the receiving program's window using the source program's menus and toolbars

- The Open command, if present, which normally lets you edit the object within a separate window provided by the source program

The actual commands that appear on the submenu—and their actions—depend on the source program and the nature of the embedded data.

When you have finished editing the object, exit the editing mode. If you're editing in the source program, do this by exiting from the source program and clicking the Yes button in the message box if the source program asks whether you want to update the object in the receiving document. If you're editing in the receiving program, click in the receiving document outside the object.

Convert Objects to the Format You Prefer

If the Object submenu includes a Convert command, you can choose it to change the embedded object to a different object type. The available object types depend on the object you have selected. For example, if you select a PowerPoint Slide object, you can convert it to a PowerPoint Presentation object. This would allow you to add additional slides to the object (a presentation is composed of a group of slides) or to display the presentation in a slide show by double-clicking the object.

An Embedding Example

Imagine that you're preparing a PowerPoint presentation and that you want to include a table of numeric values in a slide. By embedding an Excel Worksheet object, you can use all the features provided by Excel for creating the table. You could do this as follows:

1 Run Excel, open a new document, and enter the data into a worksheet.

2 Select the worksheet cells that you want to display in the PowerPoint slide, as shown in Figure 51-9, and choose Copy from Excel's Edit menu.

3 Open the slide in the PowerPoint presentation in which you want to display the worksheet cells. (You must be in PowerPoint's Normal view; to switch to this view, choose Normal from PowerPoint's View menu.)

4 Choose Paste Special from PowerPoint's Edit menu, and in the Paste Special dialog box, choose the Paste option and select the Microsoft Excel Worksheet Object item in the list, as shown in Figure 51-10, on the next page. Then click OK.

FIGURE 51-9.
Selecting cells in an Excel worksheet.

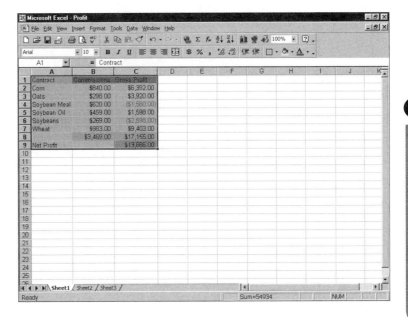

IX

Integrating Microsoft Office Applications

FIGURE 51-10.
Embedding the Excel worksheet cells shown in Figure 51-9 into a PowerPoint slide.

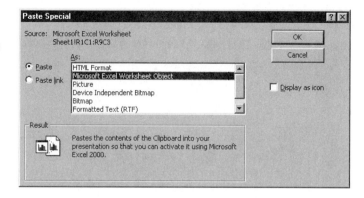

NOTE

After you have pasted the worksheet cells into the slide, you can either save or discard the original Excel document. Note that the embedded object was created by copying cells from an Excel document—rather than choosing Object from PowerPoint's Insert menu to create new data—because the copying method lets you specify the exact number of cells to display in the slide and makes it easier to scale the worksheet within the PowerPoint slide.

The resulting PowerPoint slide is shown in Figure 51-11.

FIGURE 51-11.
Excel worksheet cells embedded in a PowerPoint slide.

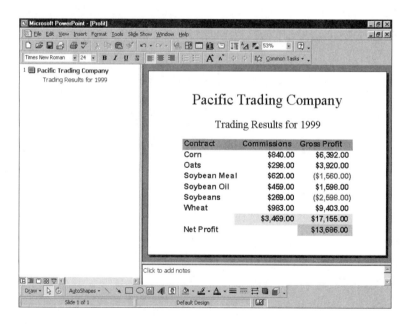

 **ON THE WEB**   The Profit.xls and Profit.ppt example files are on the Running Office 2000 Reader's Corner page.

After embedding the worksheet into the slide, you can edit it within PowerPoint by double-clicking it, as shown in Figure 51-12. Notice that the Excel menu and toolbar are displayed within the PowerPoint window to let you edit the object.

FIGURE 51-12.
Editing Excel worksheet cells embedded in a PowerPoint slide.

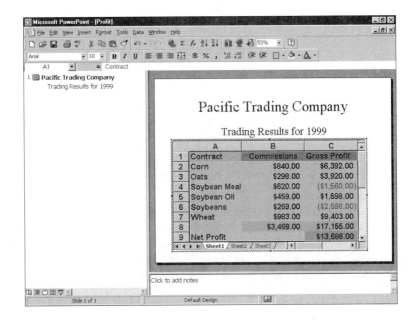

Using the Office Tools

When you install Office, you have the option of installing one or more of a group of Office Tools programs. These programs are designed to generate various types of information that you can embed in your Office documents. The Office Tools programs can't be run independently, nor can they create their own documents. You can run them only from an application, and the data they generate can be stored only as embedded objects. To run an Office Tools program, perform the following general steps:

1   Place the insertion point at the position in the receiving Office document where you want to insert the embedded object.

2   Choose Object from the receiving program's Insert menu, and click the Create New tab (or option button) in the Object (or Insert Object) dialog box.

Integrating Microsoft
Office Applications

3 Select the appropriate object description in the Object Type list, and click OK. Table 51-1 lists each of the standard object descriptions for the Office Tools programs.

4 Use the commands of the Office Tools source program to enter the data for the embedded object into the working area provided. The working area will be either within the receiving program window or within a separate window displayed by the source program. (With the Clip Gallery program, you choose a picture in a list rather than entering your own data.)

5 Exit the editing mode. If you're working in the receiving program's window, exit editing mode by clicking in the program window outside the embedded object. If you're working in the source program's window, exit editing mode by choosing Exit from the source program's File menu or by closing the source program window; to save your work, answer Yes when asked whether you want to update the object.

TABLE 51-1.   The Office Tools Programs

Office Tools Program	Object Description Displayed in the Object Dialog Box	Purpose of Program
Clip Gallery	Microsoft Clip Gallery	Locates and inserts picture, sound, or motion (video) clips into your documents
Equation Editor	Microsoft Equation 3.0	Enters mathematical expressions into your documents
Microsoft Graph	Microsoft Graph 2000 Chart	Creates charts for displaying data
Organization Chart	MS Organization Chart 2.0	Creates organization charts and other types of hierarchical charts

⭐ **TIP**

Try Another Way to Run Office Tools Programs
Some of the Office applications let you quickly run one or more of the Office Tools programs by choosing a command from the Picture submenu of the Insert menu. For example, in Excel you can run the Clip Gallery by choosing Clip Art from this submenu, or you can run the Organization Chart program by choosing Organization Chart. Likewise, in Word you can run the Clip Gallery by choosing Clip Art, or you can run Microsoft Graph by choosing Chart.

To edit an object embedded by an Office Tools program, use any of the methods discussed previously in the chapter under "Embedding Data," starting on page 1203. Note that when you "edit" a Clip Gallery object, you replace the current clip with another one, rather than actually editing the graphic, sound, or video data.

The following sections introduce you to each of the Office Tools programs. Keep in mind that each program provides extensive online Help from which you can learn the details of using the program's commands.

(2000) Using the Clip Gallery

The Clip Gallery program can help you to find and organize picture, sound, and motion clips, and to insert them into your Office documents. When you select the Microsoft Clip Gallery item in the Object dialog box and click OK, the Clip Gallery program is displayed in a separate window. Here are the basic steps for using the program:

1 Click the tab for the type of clip you want to insert: the Pictures tab for inserting a graphic image, the Sounds tab for inserting an audio clip, or the Motion Clips tab for inserting a video sequence. The tab will initially display the different categories of clips. See Figure 51-13.

FIGURE 51-13.
The Pictures tab of the Clip Gallery window, displaying the categories of clips.

Add new clips by importing them from picture, sound, or motion files.

Download new clips from the Web.

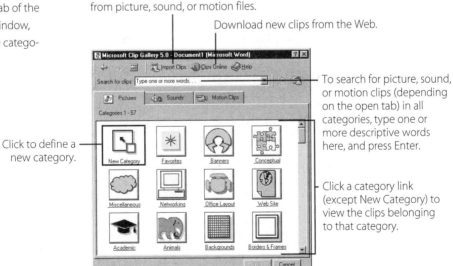

Click to define a new category.

To search for picture, sound, or motion clips (depending on the open tab) in all categories, type one or more descriptive words here, and press Enter.

Click a category link (except New Category) to view the clips belonging to that category.

IX

Integrating Microsoft Office Applications

2 Click the category you want. The tab will now display all the clips belonging to that category.

3 Click the clip you want, and then click one of the buttons on the pop-up toolbar to perform the desired action. See Figure 51-14.

FIGURE 51-14.
Selecting a clip in the Nature category.

Move back or forward through previously selected views.
Return to view of all categories.

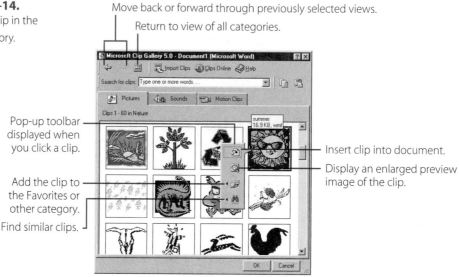

Pop-up toolbar displayed when you click a clip.

Add the clip to the Favorites or other category.
Find similar clips.

Insert clip into document.
Display an enlarged preview image of the clip.

> **NOTE**
>
> The Clip Gallery program comes with a variety of picture, sound, and motion clips. You can add additional clips to the program by importing them from picture, sound, or motion files, or by downloading them from Microsoft's Clip Gallery page on the Web.

Using the Equation Editor

The Equation Editor lets you add mathematical expressions to your documents. When you select the Microsoft Equation 3.0 item in the Object dialog box and click OK, a working area is inserted into the receiving document, and the Equation Editor toolbar and menus are displayed within the receiving program's window. See Figure 51-15.

To create a mathematical expression, do the following:

- To enter numbers or variables, simply type them using the keyboard, such as the y typed to begin the following example equation:

FIGURE 51-15.
Embedding an Equation Editor object in a Word document.

Working area—enter the equation here.

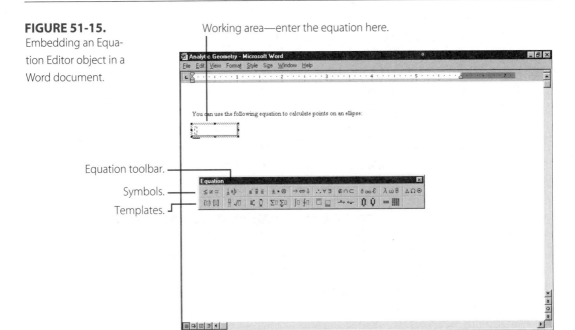

Equation toolbar.
Symbols.
Templates.

■ To enter a mathematical operator that appears on the keyboard, such as the plus sign (+), the minus sign (-), or the equal sign (=), you can simply type it. For instance, you could add an equal sign to the example equation:

■ To enter an operator or symbol that doesn't appear on the keyboard, click the appropriate button on the top row of the Equation toolbar, and then click the desired symbol on the drop-down palette of symbols. For example, you would click the following:

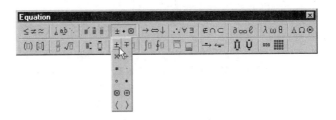

to add a plus or minus symbol (±) to the example equation:

$y = \pm$

- To enter an expression such as a fraction, a square root, an exponent, or an integral, click the appropriate button on the bottom row of the Equation toolbar, and then choose one of the templates on the drop-down palette. For example, you would click the following template:

to add a square-root expression to the example equation:

$y = \pm \sqrt{}$

Then enter the desired numbers and variables into the area marked by dotted lines within the template. For example, you could type the following into the radical expression in the example equation:

$y = \pm \sqrt{1 + a}$

You can insert templates within other templates to create nested operator expressions, such as a fraction within a square-root operator.

The Equation Editor won't let you enter space characters when you're typing an expression because it automatically sets the spacing between the numbers and symbols that you enter (for consistency). You can adjust the spacing or alignment of symbols, however, by selecting symbols from the Spaces And Ellipses palette, as shown below, or by choosing commands from the Format menu.

You can also modify the font, font size, or format (that is, normal, bold, or italic) of characters or symbols by choosing commands from the Style and Size menus.

Using Graph

Using the Graph program, you can insert charts into your Office documents. Graph supports a wide variety of chart types and provides a handy alternative to using Excel charts. The easiest way to create a chart using the Graph program is to use a Word table, as follows:

1 Insert a table into a Word document, enter into this table the data that you want to graph, and then select the entire table. An example is shown in Figure 51-16.

FIGURE 51-16.
Selecting a Word table containing the data that you want to graph.

Contract	Gross Profit
Corn	6,392.00
Oats	3,920.00
Soybean Meal	-1,560.00
Soybean Oil	1,598.00
Soybeans	-2,598.00
Wheat	9,403.00

2 Choose Object from the Insert menu, click the Create New tab, select the Microsoft Graph 2000 Chart object type, and click OK. Alternatively, you can point to Picture on the Insert menu and choose Chart from the submenu.

Graph will immediately embed a chart into the document that depicts the data contained in the Word table. Graph will also display a datasheet containing the chart data. See Figure 51-17, on the following page.

W ON THE WEB

The GraphTab.doc example file is on the Running Office 2000 Reader's Corner page.

3 The datasheet contains a copy of the data from the original Word table that you selected. If you want to change the values plotted on the chart, you must edit the numbers within the datasheet, not

IX

Integrating Microsoft Office Applications

within the original table. (Once the chart is inserted, a copy of the data from the Word table is stored independently within the embedded chart object. Changing the table data won't affect the chart; in fact, you can delete the table if you want to.)

4 If you want, you can now make modifications to the chart using the menu commands and toolbar buttons provided by the Graph program. You can access detailed online information on using the Graph commands by choosing Microsoft Graph Help from the Help menu or by pressing F1.

5 To change the size or the proportions of the chart, drag the sizing handles displayed around the embedded object.

6 When you've finished modifying the chart, click in the Word document outside the chart and the datasheet. The datasheet and the Graph commands on the menu and toolbar will disappear, leaving the chart embedded in your document.

If you later want to modify the chart, simply double-click the embedded chart object. The Graph commands will return, and you can

FIGURE 51-17.
Embedding a Chart object in a Word document. This chart is based on the Word table shown in Figure 51-16.

Table entered into the Word document in step 1

Menu commands and toolbar buttons provided by Microsoft Graph

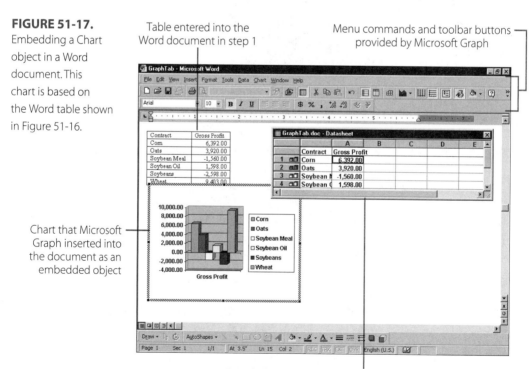

Chart that Microsoft Graph inserted into the document as an embedded object

Datasheet displayed by Microsoft Graph, showing the chart data (which was copied from the table in the document)

change the features of the chart. If the datasheet isn't visible (and you need to change the numbers shown on the chart), you can display it by choosing Datasheet from the View menu or by clicking the View Datasheet button on the Graph toolbar. If you want to display the chart within another Office document (for example, in a PowerPoint presentation), select the Chart object, cut or copy it, and then paste it into the other document.

View
Datasheet

? SEE ALSO

For information on Word tables, see "Using Tables," page 229. For details on creating charts in Excel, see Chapter 21, "Creating Worksheet Charts."

Note that if you embed a new Graph object within a program other than Word (by choosing the Object command from the program's Insert menu), or if you embed a new Graph object in a Word document without first selecting a table containing valid chart data, Graph will create an example chart displaying example data. You'll then need to enter the actual data, as well as the row and column headings, into the Graph datasheet.

Using Organization Chart

You can use the Microsoft Organization Chart program to add organization charts and other types of hierarchical charts to your Office documents. When you select the MS Organization Chart 2.0 object type in the Object dialog box and click OK, the Organization Chart program opens a separate window, which displays a template for a new chart, as shown in Figure 51-18.

FIGURE 51-18.
The Organization Chart program window when you first start the program.

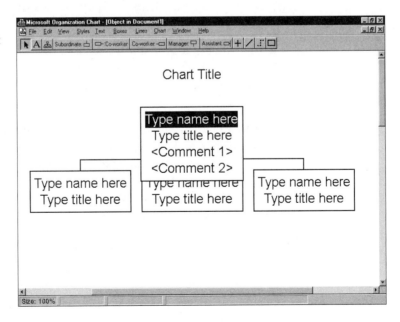

IX

Integrating Microsoft
Office Applications

The following are the basic procedures for creating an organization chart:

- To select a box, click the Select toolbar button if it's not already pressed in, and then click the box.

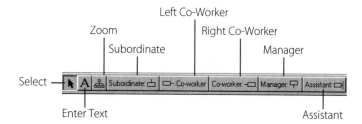

- To add a new box to the chart, click the button for the type of relationship you want to depict: Subordinate, Left Co-Worker, Right Co-Worker, Manager, or Assistant. Then click the existing box to which you want to attach the new box.

- To delete a box, select it and press the Delete key.

- To move a box, click the Select button, and then drag the box onto another box. (Make sure the box isn't selected and doesn't contain the insertion point; otherwise, you won't be able to drag it.) The position where you drop the box determines its relationship to the other box.

- To add or modify text in a box or in the chart title, click the Enter Text button on the toolbar, and then click the text at the position where you want to add or edit characters.

- To modify the format of the chart, first select the part that you want to modify, and then apply a formatting command. To select a box or line, click the Select button, and then click the box or line; to select additional boxes or lines, press Shift while you click each one. To select text, click the Enter Text button, and then highlight the text by dragging over it. Alternatively, you can select various groups of boxes or lines using the Select submenu or the Select Levels command on the Edit menu.

  You can then change the chart type using the Styles menu, the formatting and alignment of text using the Text menu, the appearance of boxes using the Boxes menu, the appearance of lines using the Lines menu, or the chart background color using the Chart menu.

■ You can draw lines and rectangles on the chart using the drawing buttons. To display these buttons, choose Show Draw Tools from the View menu.

Draw a horizontal or vertical line.

Draw a diagonal line.

Draw an auxiliary line.

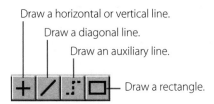

Draw a rectangle.

When you have finished creating the chart, choose Exit And Return To *Document* (where *Document* is the name of your Office document) from the File menu, and answer Yes when asked if you want to update the object in the document. The organization chart will be inserted into your Office document.

Using the Office Binder Program

I n the preceding chapter, you learned how to add blocks of data—derived from other documents and programs— to a Microsoft Office document. In this chapter, you'll learn how to use the Microsoft Office Binder program to combine several entire documents in an Office binder. A binder is like an electronic paper clip—you can use it to store a set of related documents as a collection. Consider, for example, that you have prepared a report that consists of a Microsoft Word document, a Microsoft Excel workbook, and a Microsoft PowerPoint presentation. You can use the Binder program to combine a copy of each of these documents within a single binder. (You can also create new documents within the binder.) All the documents in a binder are stored within a single disk file, and once you have created a binder, you can do the following:

- View, edit, and format all the documents directly within the Binder program window.

- Print the entire set of documents, with consecutive page numbers and uniform headers or footers, by issuing a single print command.

- Take the report on the road or share it electronically with co-workers by copying or sending a single disk file. (You'll never again accidentally omit an essential document.)

You can include Word, Excel, or PowerPoint documents in a binder. You can also add documents created in programs from other software companies that have been designed to support the Binder. *For information on sharing documents electronically over a network, see "Sharing Documents in a Workgroup," page 82.*

Bring in Information from Access and the Office Tools Programs

You can also include data from Access or from the Office Tools programs (discussed in Chapter 51) in a binder by pasting, linking, or embedding the data within a Word, Excel, or PowerPoint document that's contained in the binder.

Throughout this chapter, the term *Binder* (with a capital B) refers to the Microsoft Office Binder program, and the term *binder* (lowercase) refers to a collection of documents created by the Binder program.

Creating a Binder

To run the Binder program, point to Programs on your Windows Start menu, point to Office tools, and choose Microsoft Binder 2000 from the submenu:

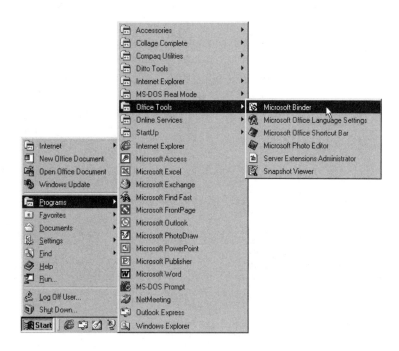

The Binder window is shown in Figure 52-1. Notice that the Binder window is divided into two panes: the *left pane*—also known as the *contents pane*—displays an icon for each document contained in the binder, and the *right pane*—also known as the *document pane*—displays the activated document, allowing you to view and edit it. If the left pane isn't visible, you can open it by clicking the Show/Hide Left Pane button to the left of the File menu. (If neither the left pane nor the button is visible, choose Binder Options from the File menu, and select the Show Left Pane And Left Pane Button option.)

 **TIP**

> **Try Other Ways to Run the Binder Program**
>
> You can also run Binder and create a new, blank binder by choosing New Office Document from the Windows Start menu or by clicking the New Office Document button on the Office Shortcut Bar. Then, in the New Office Document dialog box, click the General tab, and double-click the Blank Binder icon.
>
> You can create a new, blank binder file in a specific folder by opening that folder in Windows Explorer or in a folder window, right-clicking a blank area in the folder, pointing to New on the pop-up menu, and choosing Microsoft Office Binder from the submenu. You can double-click the new file that's created to open it in Binder.

When you run the Binder program, it creates a new, blank binder. The next step is to add documents to this binder. A document that you add to a binder is called a *section*. (Throughout this chapter, the terms *document*

FIGURE 52-1.
The Binder program window, displaying a new, blank binder.

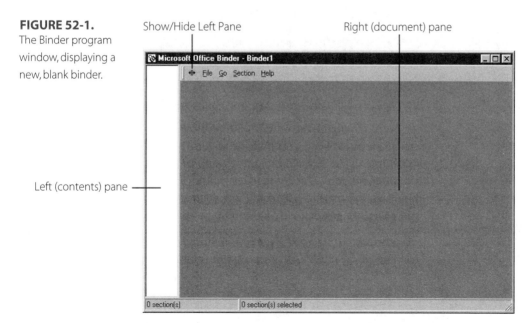

Show/Hide Left Pane

Right (document) pane

Left (contents) pane

and *section* will be used synonymously when referring to a document that has been added to a binder.) You can add a document that you have already created with an Office application (Word, Excel, or PowerPoint), or a new, empty document to which you'll add information.

To add an existing document to a binder, do either of the following:

CAUTION

When you use the drag-and-drop method to add a document to a binder, be sure not to drag the document's icon to the right pane of the Binder window. Doing so would embed the document file within the activated document, rather than adding the document to the binder.

- Choose Add From File from the Section menu in the Binder program, and in the Add From File dialog box (see Figure 52-2), select the document that you want to add and click the Add button. Note that if you select several documents (by holding down the Ctrl key as you click each one), they'll all be added to the binder simultaneously as separate sections. To list all your Office files, be sure that the Office Documents item is selected in the Files Of Type list box at the bottom of the Add From File dialog box.

- Drag a document icon from Windows Explorer or from a folder window to the left pane of the Binder window. If you select and drag several document icons, all the documents will be added to the binder simultaneously.

When you add a document to a binder, the binder stores a copy of the document, leaving the original document file in place. Although the document within the binder has the same name as the source document file, there is no link between the two.

If you drag a binder file (a file with the .obd extension)—rather than an Office document—to the left pane of the Binder program, a copy of

FIGURE 52-2.
The Add From File dialog box.

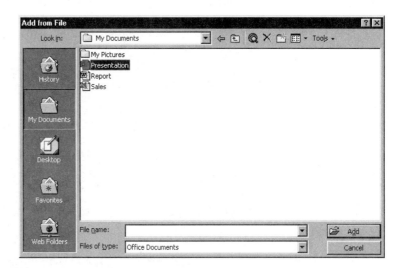

each of the documents contained in the binder file is added to the open binder. You can use this technique to merge the contents of separate binders.

> **Drag a File to a Hidden Binder Window**
>
> If the Binder program is running but its window isn't visible when you begin dragging a document icon from Windows Explorer or a folder window, drag the icon over the Binder's button on the Windows taskbar and hold the pointer over the button without releasing the mouse button. Within a second or so, Windows will activate the Binder window and you can complete the drag operation.

To add a new, empty document to a binder, choose Add from the Section menu to display the Add Section dialog box. (See Figure 52-3.) To create a blank document, select one of the icons on the General tab. (For example, to create a blank Word document, choose the Blank Document icon.) Notice in Figure 52-3 that you can choose to create an Excel worksheet or an Excel chart. In either case, an Excel workbook document is added to the binder. If you choose the Excel worksheet, the workbook will contain a single blank worksheet, whereas if you choose the Excel chart, the workbook will contain an example chart plus a worksheet that contains example data for the chart.

To base the new document on a template, select one of the other tabs in the Add Section dialog box, and select the icon for the template that you want. (For example, to create a business memo, you could click the Memos tab and select the Professional Memo icon.)

FIGURE 52-3.
The Add Section dialog box.

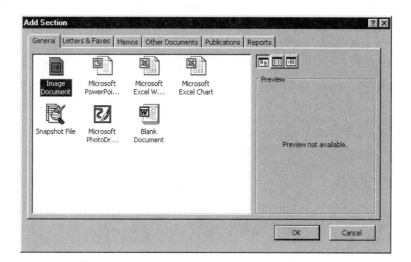

You can create an additional new binder by choosing New Binder from the File menu (or by pressing Ctrl+N), clicking the General tab in the New Binder dialog box (if that tab isn't already displayed), and then double-clicking the Blank Binder icon to create an empty binder. The current binder is left open and the new binder is displayed in a separate Binder program window.

 TIP

Create a New Binder Based on an Existing One

If you have an existing Office binder saved in a file, you can quickly create a new binder that contains a copy of the contents of the existing one. To do this, right-click the existing binder file in Windows Explorer or in a folder window, and choose New from the pop-up menu. The new binder will be displayed in the Binder program window.

Saving a Binder

You can save the entire binder within a single file in either of the following two ways:

? SEE ALSO

For information on saving a copy of an individual document in a binder, see "Managing Binder Sections," page 1231. For a general discussion on Office document properties, see "Working with Property Sheets," page 79.

- To save the binder under its current name, if any, choose Save Binder from the File menu or press Ctrl+S. (If you haven't previously saved the binder, the Save Binder As command will automatically be activated.)

- To save a copy of the binder under a different filename or in a different folder, choose Save Binder As from the File menu and specify the name and location of the file in the Save Binder As dialog box. Be sure that the Binder Files item is selected in the Save As Type list box.

A binder file is normally saved with the .obd file extension. However, you don't need to include this extension in the filename that you enter because the Binder does it for you. (You won't see the file extensions if you have chosen to hide MS-DOS file extensions within Windows.)

TIP

Change Binder or Document Properties to Suit Your Needs

You can set the properties of the binder itself by choosing Binder Properties from the File menu in the Binder program. You can set the properties of an individual document within the binder by activating that document (click its icon in the left pane) and choosing Section Properties from the Section menu.

Closing a Binder

After you have saved a binder, you can close it by choosing Exit from the File menu or by clicking the Close button in the upper right corner of the Binder window. This will close the Binder window as well as the binder. Unlike in most Office applications, it isn't possible to display the Binder window without an open document (that is, an open binder).

Opening a Binder

You can open a binder that you have saved on disk by double-clicking the icon for the binder file within Windows Explorer or within a folder window. A binder filename will include the .obd extension if you've chosen to show MS-DOS file extensions in Windows. You can also recognize a Binder file by its paper clip icon, as shown here.

Also, if you have recently opened the file, you can choose it from the Documents submenu of the Windows Start menu. Alternatively, you can open a binder by using the Open dialog box (titled either Open Office Document or Open Binder). To display the Open dialog box, use any of the following methods:

- Click the Open Office Document button on the Office Shortcut Bar.

- Choose Open Office Document from the Windows Start menu.

- If a Binder program window is currently open, you can choose Open Binder from the File menu or press Ctrl+O.

In the Open dialog box, select the Binders item (or the Binder Files item) in the Files Of Type list box. Then choose the binder file you want to open, and click the Open button. A Binder program window will appear, displaying the binder.

If you open a binder by using the Open Binder command on the File menu of the Binder program, the binder will normally be displayed in a separate Binder program window, and the current binder will remain displayed in the original Binder window. If, however, the current binder is empty and hasn't been saved in a file, it will be discarded and the newly opened binder will be displayed in the same window.

IX

Integrating Microsoft
Office Applications

Editing Binder Sections

You can edit a document within a binder using the commands (that is, the menu commands, toolbar buttons, and shortcut keys) provided by the source program. The *source program* is the application that was used to create the document—typically, Word, Excel, or PowerPoint.

To edit a document, simply click the document's icon in the left pane of the Binder window. If the left pane isn't visible, click the Show/Hide Left Pane button to the left of the File menu. If the document icon isn't visible in the left pane, use the buttons at the top or bottom of the left pane to scroll the icon into view:

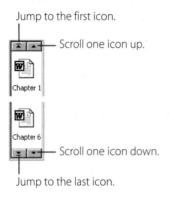

Jump to the first icon.

Scroll one icon up.

Chapter 1

Chapter 6

Scroll one icon down.

Jump to the last icon.

Clicking the document icon *selects* (that is, highlights) the icon. More importantly, clicking the icon *activates* the document. When a document is activated, the following occurs, as shown in Figure 52-4:

- A right-pointing arrow is displayed next to the document's icon in the left pane.

- The document is displayed in the right pane.

- The source program's menus are displayed in addition to the Binder program's menus—that is, the menus of the two programs are merged.

- The source program's toolbars, if any, are displayed.

- The source program's shortcut keys become available.

You can also activate a particular section by choosing Next Section or Previous Section from the Section menu to activate the next or the previous section in the order in which they're listed in the left pane.

FIGURE 52-4.
The Binder program window, displaying a binder that contains several sections. The section containing the Word document "Chapter 5" is currently activated.

Show/Hide Left Pane

Word toolbars

Word menus merged with Binder menus

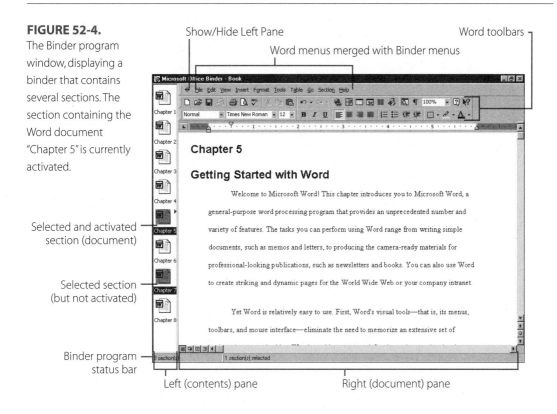

Selected and activated section (document)

Selected section (but not activated)

Binder program status bar

Left (contents) pane

Right (document) pane

<span class="tip">⭐ TIP</span>

Show the Status Bar and Set Other Binder Options
If you don't see the Binder status bar shown in Figure 52-4, you can display it by choosing Binder Options from the File menu and selecting the Show Status Bar option in the Binder Options dialog box. You can also use this dialog box to specify the default location for your binder files and to set other options discussed in this chapter.

You can now use the source program's commands to edit and format the document, following the instructions given in previous chapters. The following, however, are some general ways that editing within the Binder program differs from editing within the source program (that is, within Word, Excel, or PowerPoint):

- In Binder, the commands on the File menu affect the binder as a whole, not just the activated document.

- In Binder, the Section menu provides several of the commands that are normally found on the source program's File menu, and these commands affect only the activated document. Specifically, the Page Setup command on the Section menu is equivalent to the Page Setup command on the source program's File menu, Print Preview is equivalent to Print Preview, Print is equivalent to Print, Save As File is equivalent to Save As, and Section Properties is equivalent to Properties.

- The source program's status bar isn't displayed. It is replaced with Binder's status bar. This makes certain features unavailable, such as the Excel AutoCalculate feature.

- You can run macros while editing any type of Office document (Word, Excel, or PowerPoint) within Binder, but you can't record a macro in a Word document.

TIP

Get Help

While you're working with a document in a binder, the Help menu lets you access online Help both for the program that's the source of the activated document and for the Binder program itself. The source program's help commands are on the main Help menu, while Binder's help commands are on the Binder Help submenu of the Help menu.

While you're editing a document within a binder, you can move data from one binder document to another using the following drag-and-drop technique:

SEE ALSO

For a discussion on Word document templates, see "Modifying and Creating Document Templates," page 214.

1 Select the data in the source document.

2 Drag the data to the icon for the receiving document within the left pane, and without releasing the mouse button, press the Alt key to activate the receiving document.

3 Continue dragging the data to the target location in the receiving document in the right pane.

To copy rather than move the data, hold down the Ctrl key while dragging. If you drag the data to the left pane rather than to the document in the right pane, the selected material will be inserted as a new section.

Remember to Copy Word Templates

As you learned in Chapter 7, "Customizing Styles and Templates," Word macros, AutoText entries, and custom interface configurations are stored within document templates. If a binder contains a Word document and you move the binder to a computer other than the one on which the document was created, macros and other template items might be unavailable when you edit the document. The easiest way to make these items available is to copy the template or templates containing them into the same folder on the destination computer into which you copy the binder file.

Editing Within the Source Program Window

Rather than editing a binder section within the Binder window, you can edit it within a separate window provided by the document's source program (such as Word, Excel, or PowerPoint). You might want to do this so that all the source program's commands are available or so that you can work in the more familiar environment provided by the source program. To edit a binder section within the source program, do the following:

1 Activate the document by clicking its icon in the left pane.

2 Choose View Outside from the Section menu. The source program will open a separate window displaying the document.

3 When you have finished editing, exit the source program. The modified document will appear in the binder.

You might have noticed that this procedure is similar to that for editing an embedded object within the source program, as described in Chapter 51, "Sharing Data Among Office Applications."

Managing Binder Sections

You can use commands on the Binder's Section menu to delete, rename, rearrange, duplicate, hide, and save individual binder sections. You can also use drag-and-drop techniques to perform most of these operations.

IX

Integrating Microsoft
Office Applications

For the majority of the section operations, you first need to select the section that you want to act on. You select a section by clicking its icon in the left pane of the Binder window. Clicking the icon also activates the section—that is, displays the document in the right pane.

For some of the section operations, you can select several sections to operate on simultaneously. Only one of the selected sections will be activated. You can select multiple sections using any of the following methods:

- Click the first section of the group that you want to select, and then click each of the other sections while pressing the Ctrl key.

- To select a group of adjoining sections, click the first one and then click the last one in the range while pressing the Shift key.

- To select all the sections in a binder, choose Select All from the Section menu. To deselect all the sections except the activated one, choose Unselect All from the Section menu.

To deselect a specific section from a group of selected sections, click the section's icon while pressing the Ctrl key. (To deselect the activated section, you must first activate another section within the selected group by clicking its icon.) To delete one or more sections, first select the section or sections, and then choose Delete from the Section menu. If you have selected more than one section, the command will be labeled Delete Selection.

Use the Shortcut Menu

If you right-click in the left pane, you can choose any of the following commands from the shortcut menu that pops up, rather than from the Section menu: Add, Add From File, Delete, Duplicate, Rename, and Section Properties. The Delete, Duplicate, Rename, and Section Properties commands will be available only if you right-click a section icon, and these commands will affect only the clicked section, regardless of which section or sections are selected. (Section Properties is available only if you right-click the activated section.) The Add and Add From File commands will insert a new section below the currently activated section.

To rename the activated section, choose Rename from the Section menu. The insertion point will be placed within the label below the section's icon, and you can type the new name. Alternatively, you can rename any section by clicking its label. (You'll need to click twice if the section isn't selected.)

To rearrange the order of the sections in a binder, choose Rearrange from the Section menu—you don't need to first select a section. In the Rearrange Sections dialog box (see Figure 52-5), highlight a section that you want to move, and click the Move Up or Move Down button. Alternatively, you can move a section by simply selecting it in the left pane and then dragging its icon to a new position within the pane. If you select several icons, you can move the whole group.

FIGURE 52-5.
The Rearrange Sections dialog box.

If the target location isn't visible in the left pane when you perform a drag operation, just hold the pointer over the top or bottom area of the pane—without releasing the mouse button—to scroll up or down through the icons.

To duplicate a section, select it and choose Duplicate from the Section menu. Then, in the Duplicate Section dialog box (see Figure 52-6), select the section after which you want to insert the copy of the section. If you select several sections, you can duplicate them all at once; in this case, the menu command will be labeled Duplicate Selection. Alternatively, you can duplicate a section by dragging its icon to a new location in the left pane while holding down the Ctrl key. If you select several icons, you can copy all of them.

FIGURE 52-6.
The Duplicate Section dialog box.

IX

Integrating Microsoft
Office Applications

TIP

Move or Copy a Section to Another Binder

You can move a section into another binder by dragging its icon to the left pane of the other Binder window. To copy rather than move the section, press the Ctrl key while dragging. If you select several sections, you can move or copy the entire group.

You can also hide one or more sections in a binder. To do this, select one or more sections and choose Hide from the Section menu. A hidden section won't appear in the left pane, it can't be activated, and it won't be printed when you print the binder (as described later). However, it will remain stored within the binder file, and you can display it again later. To redisplay a section, choose Unhide Section from the Section menu, select the section in the Unhide Sections dialog box, and click OK. (To redisplay several hidden sections, you have to repeat these steps for each one.)

Earlier in the chapter, you learned how to save the entire binder within a single disk file. You can also save a copy of an individual binder section within a separate disk file. To save the activated section, choose Save As File from the Section menu. Then, in the Save As dialog box, specify a name and location for the file.

Alternatively, you can simply drag a section icon from the Binder program directly to the folder in which you want to save the document. In this case, a copy of the section will be saved under its original filename. If you select several sections, you can drag them all at once. Note that none of these techniques removes the section from the binder.

TIP

Drag an Icon to a Hidden Window

When dragging an icon from a binder to a folder or to another binder, recall that if the target window is open but isn't visible, you can activate it by holding the pointer over the window's icon on the Windows taskbar without releasing the mouse button.

Using Binder Templates

If you frequently create a particular type of binder, you can save time by preparing a Binder *template* that contains all the basic elements of this binder. You could then get a head start in creating a similar new binder by basing it on the template. The new binder would acquire all the elements contained in the template—the sections, as well as the boilerplate text, graphics, or other content in each section. You could then modify the basic content and add additional text or graphics. You can create a new Binder template as follows:

1 Use any of the methods for creating a new binder that were discussed earlier in the chapter under "Creating a Binder," page 1222.

2 Add documents and data to the binder so that it will serve as a good starting point for the type of binders that you want to create.

3 Choose Save Binder As from the File menu to display the Save Binder As dialog box.

4 In the Files Of Type list box, select the Binder Templates item to save your work as a binder template rather than as a binder document. As soon as you make this selection, the Save Binder As dialog box switches to the folder (usually named \Templates) that's currently designated as your User Templates folder.

 SEE ALSO

For more information on the User Templates folder and how to use Word to change its location, see "Creating New Templates," page 219.

5 Specify a name and location for the template, and click the Save button. Be sure to save the template within your current User Templates folder—otherwise, the New dialog box won't display it. You can save the template directly within your User Templates folder; in this case, the template will be displayed on the General tab of the New dialog box. Alternatively, you can place it within a subfolder of your User Templates folder (an existing subfolder or a new one that you create); in this case, the template will be displayed in the New dialog box on a tab that's labeled with the name of the subfolder. (Take note of where you save the file, so you can modify it later if you want.)

NOTE

A Binder template normally has the .obt file extension. You won't see the extensions, however, if you have chosen to hide MS-DOS file extensions in Windows.

To create a new binder based on a template you have created, first open the New dialog box using either of these methods:

- If Binder is running, choose New Binder from the File menu or press Ctrl+N. In this case, the dialog box will be titled New Binder and it will show only Binder templates.

- Choose New Office Document from the Start menu in Windows, or click the New Office Document button on the Office Shortcut Bar. In this case, the dialog box will be titled New Office Document and it will show templates for all Office applications.

IX

**Integrating Microsoft
Office Applications**

Then click the tab that displays your template and double-click the template's icon.

If you want to modify a binder template you've created, you can open the template file by choosing Open Binder from the File menu in the Binder program and selecting the Binder Templates item in the Files Of Type list box. Then navigate to the folder where you saved the template and select the filename.

Printing a Binder

You can print an entire binder, or print one or more individual sections within a binder, using commands provided by the Binder program. You can also print a single binder section using the more specialized commands provided by that section's source program.

Printing an Entire Binder or a Group of Sections Within a Binder

You can use commands on the File menu of the Binder program to define headers or footers for the binder, to preview the printed appearance of the binder, or to print the binder. You can apply these commands to the entire binder or to one or more binder sections.

To create headers or footers, choose Binder Page Setup from the File menu and click the Header/Footer tab in the Binder Page Setup dialog box. As shown in Figure 52-7, you can define a header, a footer, or both; and you can apply the header or footer to all sections in the binder or to one or more sections that you select.

> If you have defined headers or footers in individual Word documents contained in a binder, those headers or footers will be replaced by any headers or footers you apply to the binder using the Binder Page Setup dialog box.

On the Print Settings tab of the Binder Page Setup dialog box, shown in Figure 52-8, you can specify which sections are to be printed, and you can control the page numbering. The options you select on this tab will be used as the default values whenever you subsequently print the binder, until you close the binder file. (The next time you open the binder, the default options will again be in effect: printing all visible sections, with consecutive numbering starting at 1.) When you print, however, you can change these settings by selecting different ones in the Print Binder dialog box, as explained shortly.

FIGURE 52-7.
Defining headers or footers for one or more sections in a binder.

To apply headers or footers to all sections, click here.

To apply headers to one or more specific sections, click here...

...and then select the sections in this list.

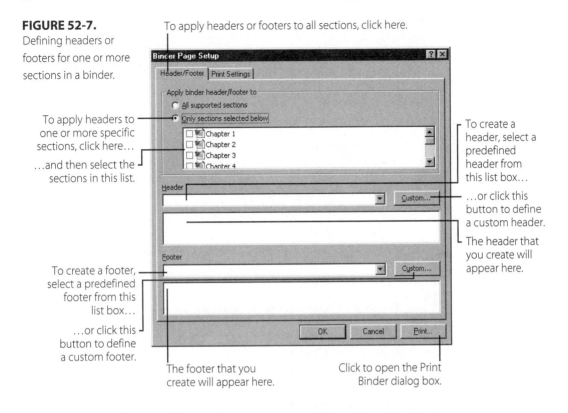

To create a header, select a predefined header from this list box...

...or click this button to define a custom header.

The header that you create will appear here.

To create a footer, select a predefined footer from this list box...

...or click this button to define a custom footer.

The footer that you create will appear here.

Click to open the Print Binder dialog box.

FIGURE 52-8.
Setting default printing options.

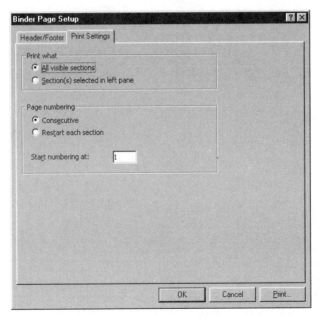

Before you print, you can preview the printed appearance of the binder by choosing Print Preview from the File menu. This will show any options you chose in the Binder Page Setup dialog box. *For more information on previewing documents, see "Previewing and Printing Documents," page 337.*

When you're ready to print, proceed as follows:

1 If you want to print specific sections, rather than the entire binder, select those sections.

2 Choose Print Binder from the File menu or press Ctrl+P. The Print Binder dialog box will be displayed. Proceed as shown in Figure 52-9.

FIGURE 52-9.
Printing an entire binder or selected binder sections.

3 Select this option to print the entire binder (except hidden sections)...

...or select this option to print only those sections selected in step 1.

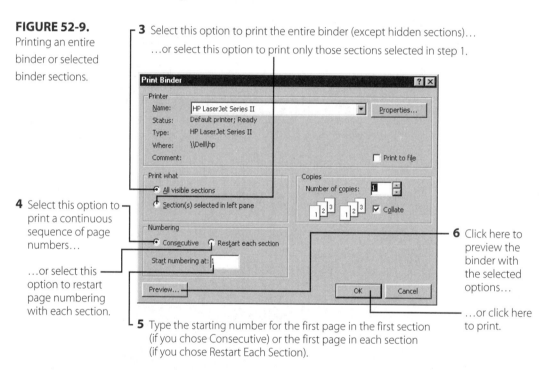

4 Select this option to print a continuous sequence of page numbers...

...or select this option to restart page numbering with each section.

6 Click here to preview the binder with the selected options...

...or click here to print.

5 Type the starting number for the first page in the first section (if you chose Consecutive) or the first page in each section (if you chose Restart Each Section).

TIP

Quick-Print a Binder

You can also print a binder by right-clicking a binder file within a Windows folder or in Windows Explorer and then choosing Print from the pop-up menu. The Binder program will begin running and will immediately print the document. It will print all visible sections, using consecutive page numbering starting at 1. The program will terminate when it's finished printing the binder.

Although you can control page numbering in the Print Binder dialog box, page numbers won't appear on the pages of your binders unless you have defined headers or footers that include page numbers. Note that the numbering sequence you select in the Print Binder dialog box will override any starting page numbers you might have specified for an individual document within the binder.

 TIP

Break Up Large Print Jobs

If you have trouble printing a group of sections, try choosing Binder Options from the File menu and deselecting the Print Binder As A Single Job option. When this option is selected, Binder sends all sections to the printer as a single job, which can tie up the printer for a relatively long time. When the option is deselected, Binder sends the sections to the printer as separate, possibly more manageable, print jobs.

Printing a Single Section

 SEE ALSO

For a general discussion on printing Office documents, see "Printing Documents," page 52. For information on adding page numbers, headers, or footers to a Word document, see "Adding Page Numbering," page 296, and "Adding Headers and Footers," page 299.

The method previously described lets you print a single section by selecting it alone in step 1 and then choosing the Section(s) Selected In Left Pane option in the Print Binder dialog box. Alternatively, you can preview and print a single section using commands on the Section menu. The advantage of this method is that you'll be using the more specialized and feature-rich commands provided by the source program, rather than the general-purpose commands provided by Binder.

For example, if you print a single section using the Print command on the Section menu, the source program's Print dialog box might provide options that aren't available in the Print Binder dialog box. The Word Print dialog box, for instance, provides options for printing the selected text only, for printing a range of pages, for printing only odd-numbered or only even-numbered pages, for printing multiple pages per sheet, and for scaling pages to the paper size.

The first step is to activate the section you want to print. If you want, you can define headers or footers for the section using the commands provided by the source program. For example, to define headers or footers for a Word document, you could use the Header And Footer command on the View menu. If you want to preview the document before you print it, choose Print Preview from the Section menu. (This command isn't available for a PowerPoint document).

When you're ready to print the activated section, choose Print from the Section menu. The section's source program will then display its usual Print dialog box, in which you can select print settings and click OK to begin printing.

Index

About the Authors

Michael Halvorson worked for Microsoft Corporation from 1985 to 1993, where he was employed as a technical editor, an acquisitions editor, and a localization manager. He received a B.A. in computer science from Pacific Lutheran University, and an M.A. in history from the University of Washington. He is currently a doctoral candidate in Renaissance and Reformation History at the University of Washington, and Visiting Assistant Professor of History at Pacific Lutheran University. In 1998, Michael received the Maclyn P. Burg and Günther Findel fellowships for advanced study at the Herzog August Bibliothek in Wolfenbüttel, Germany.

In addition to his historical interests, Michael is also the author or co-author of ten computer books, including *Learn Visual Basic Now, Second Edition, Microsoft Visual Basic 6.0 Professional Step by Step*, and *Microsoft Word 97/Visual Basic Step by Step*, all published by Microsoft Press.

You can send Michael electronic mail at **mikehal@u.washington.edu**

Michael J. Young is an author of books on using and programming computers. He has written more than 20 computer books, including *Visual Basic—Game Programming for Windows* for Microsoft Press, and he has used and written about Microsoft Office applications for more than a decade. He has also written extensively on Windows, C, C++, Java, animation, and graphics programming. Michael graduated from Stanford University and was a member of the ANSI committee on the standardization of the C language.

His Web site is at **http://ourworld.compuserve.com/homepages/mjy/** You can send him e-mail **at mjy@compuserve.com**

Colophon

The manuscript for this book was prepared and submitted to Microsoft Press in electronic form. Text files were prepared using Microsoft Word 97. Pages were composed using Corel Ventura 8 for Windows with text in Garamond and display type in Myriad. Composed pages were sent to the printer as electronic prepress files.

Cover Graphic Design

Tim Girvin Design, Inc.

Layout Artist

Lisa Bravo

Interior Graphic Design

Kim Eggleston
Amy Peppler Adams
designLab

Technical Editor

Terrence O'Donnell

Production Manager

Lisa Labrecque

Copy Editor

Chrisa Hotchkiss

Proofreader

Andrea Fox

Indexer

Katherine Stimson

See clearly—
now!

Here's the remarkable, *visual* way to quickly find answers about the power-fully integrated features of the Microsoft® Office 2000 applications. Microsoft Press AT A GLANCE books let you focus on particular tasks and show you, with clear, numbered steps, the easiest way to get them done right now. Put Office 2000 to work today, with AT A GLANCE learning solutions, made by Microsoft.

- MICROSOFT OFFICE 2000 PROFESSIONAL AT A GLANCE
- MICROSOFT WORD 2000 AT A GLANCE
- MICROSOFT EXCEL 2000 AT A GLANCE
- MICROSOFT POWERPOINT® 2000 AT A GLANCE
- MICROSOFT ACCESS 2000 AT A GLANCE
- MICROSOFT FRONTPAGE® 2000 AT A GLANCE
- MICROSOFT PUBLISHER 2000 AT A GLANCE
- MICROSOFT OFFICE 2000 SMALL BUSINESS AT A GLANCE
- MICROSOFT PHOTODRAW® 2000 AT A GLANCE
- MICROSOFT INTERNET EXPLORER 5 AT A GLANCE
- MICROSOFT OUTLOOK® 2000 AT A GLANCE

mspress.microsoft.com

Microsoft Press offers *comprehensive* learning solutions to help new users, power users, and professionals get the most from *Microsoft technology.*

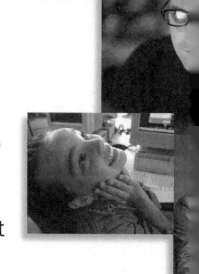

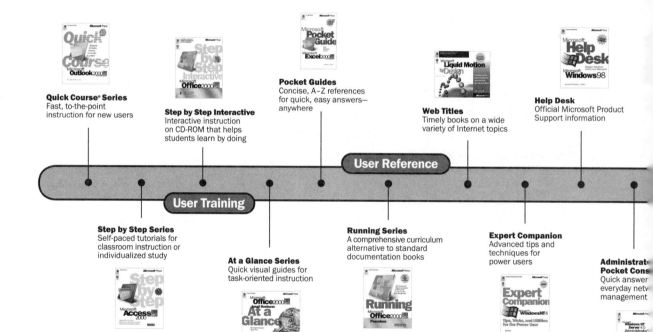

Quick Course® Series
Fast, to-the-point instruction for new users

Step by Step Interactive
Interactive instruction on CD-ROM that helps students learn by doing

Pocket Guides
Concise, A–Z references for quick, easy answers—anywhere

Web Titles
Timely books on a wide variety of Internet topics

Help Desk
Official Microsoft Product Support information

User Reference

User Training

Step by Step Series
Self-paced tutorials for classroom instruction or individualized study

At a Glance Series
Quick visual guides for task-oriented instruction

Running Series
A comprehensive curriculum alternative to standard documentation books

Expert Companion
Advanced tips and techniques for power users

Administrat Pocket Cons
Quick answer everyday netw management

With **over 200** *print,*
multimedia, and online resources—
whatever your information
need or learning style,
we've got a solution to help
you *start faster and go farther.*

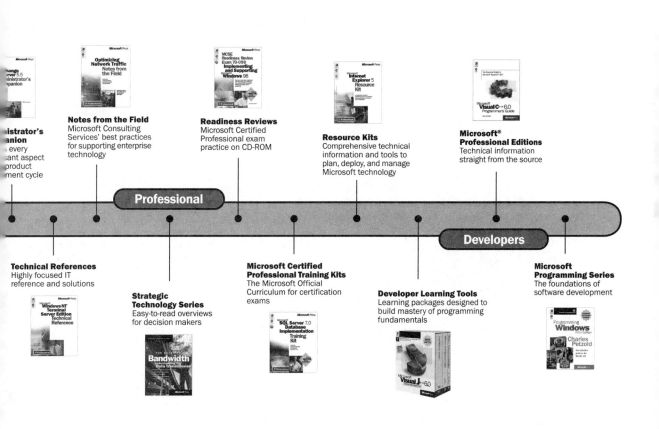

Notes from the Field
Microsoft Consulting
Services' best practices
for supporting enterprise
technology

Readiness Reviews
Microsoft Certified
Professional exam
practice on CD-ROM

Resource Kits
Comprehensive technical
information and tools to
plan, deploy, and manage
Microsoft technology

**Microsoft®
Professional Editions**
Technical information
straight from the source

Professional

**istrator's
anion**
every
ant aspect
product
ment cycle

Technical References
Highly focused IT
reference and solutions

**Strategic
Technology Series**
Easy-to-read overviews
for decision makers

**Microsoft Certified
Professional Training Kits**
The Microsoft Official
Curriculum for certification
exams

Developer Learning Tools
Learning packages designed to
build mastery of programming
fundamentals

Developers

**Microsoft
Programming Series**
The foundations of
software development

*Look for them at your bookstore
or computer store today!*

mspress.microsoft.com

Step up! Step

STEP BY STEP books provide quick and easy self-training—to help you learn to use the powerful word processing, spreadsheet, database, presentation, communication, and Internet components of Microsoft® Office 2000—both individually and together. The easy-to-follow lessons present clear objectives and real-world business examples, with numerous screen shots and illustrations. Put Office 2000 to work today, with STEP BY STEP learning solutions, made by Microsoft.

- MICROSOFT OFFICE PROFESSONAL 8-IN-1 STEP BY STEP
- MICROSOFT WORD 2000 STEP BY STEP
- MICROSOFT EXCEL 2000 STEP BY STEP
- MICROSOFT POWERPOINT® 2000 STEP BY STEP
- MICROSOFT INTERNET EXPLORER 5 STEP BY STEP
- MICROSOFT PUBLISHER 2000 STEP BY STEP
- MICROSOFT ACCESS 2000 STEP BY STEP
- MICROSOFT FRONTPAGE 2000 STEP BY STEP
- MICROSOFT OUTLOOK 2000 STEP BY STEP

mspress.microsoft.com

Register Today!

Return this
Running Microsoft® Office 2000 Professional
registration card today

Microsoft®Press
mspress.microsoft.com

OWNER REGISTRATION CARD   **1-57231-936-4**

Running Microsoft® Office 2000 Professional

_____   _____   _____

FIRST NAME   MIDDLE INITIAL   LAST NAME

_____

INSTITUTION OR COMPANY NAME

_____

ADDRESS

_____

_____   _____   _____

CITY   STATE   ZIP

_____   ( )_____

E-MAIL ADDRESS   PHONE NUMBER

U.S. and Canada addresses only. Fill in information above and mail postage-free.
Please mail only the bottom half of this page.

For information about Microsoft Press®
products, visit our Web site at
mspress.microsoft.com

Microsoft·Press